THE LIFE OF HERBERT HOOVER
The Engineer
1874–1914

THE LIFE OF
HERBERT HOOVER

★

The Engineer

1874–1914

GEORGE H. NASH

W. W. NORTON & COMPANY

New York　　　　　　　　London

Published simultaneously in Canada by George J. McLeod Limited,
Toronto.
Printed in the United States of America.

The text of this book is composed in Janson, with display type set in
Trump. Composition and manufacturing by The Maple-Vail Book
Manufacturing Group.

First Edition

Library of Congress Cataloging in Publication Data

Nash, George H., 1945–
The life of Herbert Hoover.

Bibliography: p. 577 ff.
Includes index.
Contents: The engineer, 1874–1914
1. Hoover, Herbert, 1874–1964. 2. Presidents—
United States—Biography. I. Title.
E802.N37 1983   973.91'6'0924[B]   82-14521

ISBN 0-393-01634-X

W. W. Norton & Company, Inc.
500 Fifth Avenue, New York, N.Y. 10110
W. W. Norton & Company Ltd.
37 Great Russell Street, London WC1B 3NU

1 2 3 4 5 6 7 8 9 0

T O
my mother, father,
and sister

Contents

Preface

I H A V E embarked upon a multivolume biography of one of America's most remarkable public figures. In 1980 a British historian declared that four men dominated political life in the United States between 1901 and 1945: Theodore Roosevelt, Woodrow Wilson, Herbert Hoover, and Franklin Roosevelt. When the longest-lived of these, Herbert Hoover, died at the age of ninety in 1964, he had spent fifty years—a half-century—of his life in one form or another of public service. It was a record that in sheer scope and duration may be without parallel in American history.

Yet of these four men it is fair to say that the least known and least understood, to this day, is Herbert Hoover. In the past decade or so, for reasons unnecessary to relate here, this circumstance has begun to change. Two recent biographies by David Burner and Joan Hoff-Wilson, as well as sundry monographs and interpretive essays by numerous scholars, have begun to fill in the gap and to define more precisely Herbert Hoover's niche in American history. Indeed, there has been a veritable boomlet in Hoover scholarship since the opening of the Herbert Hoover Presidential Library in West Branch, Iowa in 1966. Still—unlike Wilson and the Roosevelts, not to mention other major American leaders—Hoover continues to lack a full-scale biography. For many if not most Americans who remember him or study him, he remains as Henry Pringle described him in 1928: "an enigma easily misunderstood."

My undertaking has a particular genesis. In 1975, a year after the centennial of Herbert Hoover's birth in West Branch, Iowa, I was invited by a nonprofit, educational foundation in Iowa to prepare a comprehensive, independent, scholarly biography of America's only Iowa-born president. The name of this foundation is the Herbert Hoover Presidential Library Association. Some years before, it was responsible for construction of the Herbert Hoover Presidential Library, which is now administered by the federal government through the National Archives and Records Service.

The volume at hand is the first fruit of this enterprise. At least two more volumes will follow. Under the terms of my contract with the Association, all decisions concerning the contents of the biography—including fact and interpretation, proportions and emphasis, inclusions and exclusions—are mine alone. No attempt has been made to control, circumscribe, or alter my research or my findings. The biography that I am writing was explicitly intended to be—and is—a work of free and independent scholarship.

In the fall of 1914, Herbert Hoover shot meteorically upon the world scene. For most people this is where knowledge of him begins: with the outbreak of World War I and the emergence of Hoover as the administrator of food relief to the beleaguered population of occupied Belgium.

Yet when Hoover instituted the humanitarian aid program that gave him an international reputation, he was already forty years old, an extraordinarily successful global mining engineer on the verge of middle age. No full-length study has ever been made of these first, forty formative years: "years of adventure," Hoover called them—a fascinating period worthy of study in its own right. Hoover, in fact, had several successive careers. This volume is the story of the first one: the pre-public career. It is the account of an orphaned son of Iowa pioneers, an engineer and businessman whose interests touched every continent except Antarctica before World War I. It is the story also of his developing social philosophy and his yearnings for a second career, yearnings which found an unanticipated focus when the grim "guns of August" rent western civilization asunder in the summer of 1914.

In studying Herbert Hoover's early years, I have encountered many obscure and hitherto neglected episodes in a phenomenally busy life. To understand them I have been led into some memorable research experiences, including trips to English country houses and to the outback of Western Australia. In the Bibliographical Note following chapter 27, I describe the dimensions of my research in some detail. Here I wish to record something else.

In preparing a book one nearly always writes the preface last. It is fitting to do so, for it gives an author an opportunity to reflect upon those individuals—and they are usually many—who have facilitated his research along the way. While it is not possible to acknowledge separately all the acts of helpfulness from which I have benefited in more than six years of travel and research, it is a particular pleasure to mention a number of people whose interest and cooperation have made this undertaking a deeply rewarding one.

First, I am pleased to thank Thomas Thalken, Robert Wood, and the dedicated staff of the Herbert Hoover Presidential Library, every one of whom has helped to make my research there unfailingly pleasant and profitable. I extend my thanks as well to W. Glenn Campbell, Milorad Drachkovitch, Charles Palm, and their colleagues at the Hoover Institution on War, Revolution and Peace, at Stanford University. Their cooperation and courtesies during my several visits have rendered a stimulating environment even more of an appealing setting for research. At the Stanford University Archives Roxanne Nilan and her staff have answered many queries—sometimes in person, often by mail, and always with good cheer. At the Library of Congress David Wigdor was an accommodating guide to the resources of that marvelous institution. In my home town of South Hadley, Massachusetts, the Mount Holyoke College Library was the pleasant setting for the writing of much of this volume; the library's staff was both helpful and hospitable. In Chicago Richard von Mayrhauser helped me locate a number of dust-laden documents that only a Hoover scholar would ever be likely to need. I am pleased to record also my appreciation for the interest and encouragement shown by two friends and former mentors, Professors Donald Fleming and Frank Freidel.

Among those who facilitated my research in England in 1977 and 1978, I wish especially to thank Mr. A. Chester Beatty, who very kindly arranged for me to examine various papers and letter books of his father, the late Sir A. Chester Beatty, a close associate of Herbert Hoover in several mining ventures before World War I. I am grateful to L. A. Broder and Frances Vale of the London office of Rio Tinto-Zinc Corporation, Ltd. for arranging access to the minute books of the London board of directors of the Zinc Corporation for the years (1905–1916) in which Herbert Hoover was a director. I am grateful also to Mrs. W. R. B. Foster, who made available to me the papers of her late father (and mining associate of Hoover), Leslie Urquhart. At the Bodleian Library, Oxford University, Mr. D. S. Porter was of particular assistance before, during, and after my 1977 visit.

In Australia there are many individuals whose friendship and aid I recall with pleasure. At the J. S. Battye Library in Perth, Margaret Medcalf and her hardworking staff accommodated me efficiently during a busy research trip and then responded helpfully to various queries afterward. The late Hew Roberts extended me several courtesies, and his son Jerry generously helped me obtain access to valuable Hoover documents at the Western Australian Department of Mines. In Kalgoorlie the hospitality of Stanley Brown of the Australian Broadcasting Commission remains a pleasant memory. I am grateful to Frank Strahan of the University of Melbourne Archives for his assistance and to the Australian historians Geoffrey Blainey and K. H. Kennedy for copies of certain Hoover-related materials in their possession. Mr. E. O. Meyers of Poseidon, Ltd. in Adelaide kindly permitted me to examine the early directors' minute books of Lake View and Star, Ltd., which Herbert Hoover was instrumental in founding in 1910.

Undoubtedly my most vivid Australian recollection is of my visit to the abandoned Sons of Gwalia gold mine, in the Western Australian outback, in late 1977. My hosts were Don and Donna Reid, who shared with me their interest in Herbert Hoover (the mine's superintendent in 1898) and described their enthusiastic efforts to preserve this legendary camp as an historic site. It is a special pleasure to acknowledge here their hospitality.

In preparing this book I have had the assistance of several excellent typists. Joanne Duncan and Judy Kaeser coped effectively with my handwritten first draft. Crystal Wahl typed the entire final draft—a considerable assignment cheerfully and efficiently performed. In proofreading the galleys I have had the aid of four skilled and persevering individuals: Jean Nash, Carol Hartland, Molly Snyder, and Miriam Musgrave. At W. W. Norton & Company my editor, Donald Lamm, and his assistant, Nancy Palmquist, have been courteous and helpful guides on the long journey known as the publishing process.

I am grateful to the following individuals and institutions for permission to quote from various documents cited in my footnotes: the Bancroft Library, University of California at Berkeley; Mrs. G. Vernon Givan; the Herbert Hoover Foundation; Allan Hoover; the Herbert Hoover Presidential Library Association; the House of Lords Record Office, London; the Huntington Library, San Marino, California; the Stanford University Archives; and the J. S. Battye Library, Perth, Western Australia. Crown copyright material in the Public Record Office in Great Britain appears by permission of the Controller of Her Majesty's Stationery Office.

I have reserved two special acknowledgments for last. I am pleased to thank the Herbert Hoover Presidential Library Association for its support, encouragement, and appreciation of the requirements of a scholarly biography. Without the Association's continuing commitment, no scholarly undertaking of this magnitude and duration would be feasible in these times.

Finally, there are certain qualities that every biographer needs in order to sustain himself through the long years of preparation before that climactic moment when the book at last appears. Not all of these qualities can be supplied from within. I think now of three individuals above all who know what these other qualities are and who were "always there." To them this book is dedicated.

THE LIFE OF HERBERT HOOVER
The Engineer
1874–1914

1

An Iowa Boyhood

I

H E was a man of remarkable achievements and a succession of careers. A mining engineer and businessman whose far-flung enterprises touched six continents before World War I. A humanitarian whose name came to represent the staff of life to millions of human beings afflicted by famine and by war. An indefatigable traveler who spent more than two years of his adulthood at sea and who circled the globe five times before the advent of aviation. A prodigious worker, a translator of a scientific treatise, an historian and a philanthropist, the author of numerous books and hundreds of articles and speeches. An administrator, a Cabinet secretary, president of the United States. An elder statesman who, by the time he died, had lived nearly half as long as the American Republic. A life that began as a son of pioneers on the American prairie nine years after the Civil War.

On his father's side Herbert Hoover's ancestry derived from a Swiss family named Huber in the High Middle Ages.[1] For several centuries Oberkulm in the Alps was home for the Hubers until, late in the seventeenth century, religious persecution drove some of them north into the German Palatinate. There, in 1723, in the town of Ellerstadt, Andreas Huber was born.

Andreas's father was a successful landholder and winegrower, his grandfather a linen weaver. But for restless, teen-age Andreas, as for his two older brothers, a New World across the ocean beckoned. In the summer of 1738 he sailed to Pennsylvania, joined his brothers in Lancaster County, and settled down. "What then is the American, this new man?" This was the famous question propounded in the eighteenth century by a French settler in America named J. Hector St. John de Crèvecoeur. In the case of Andreas Huber, contact with America eventually brought forth three transformations, as it would for unnumbered immigrants after him. He simplified his name. He decided to follow the frontier. And much of his family adopted a new religious faith.

In 1746 Andreas, now married, left Pennsylvania for Carroll County, Maryland, where he acquired a fifty-acre tract along the Little Pipe Creek. Here he farmed for more than fifteen years. During this period Andrew Hoover (as he now called himself) became the father of thirteen children. Perhaps it was the demands of caring for such a large family that prompted the Hoovers to push south into the mountains of North Carolina in 1762–63, more than a decade before the American Revolution. On the banks of the Uwharrie River in Randolph County, Andrew constructed a grist mill and, again, earned a living from the land.

Sometime before September 1783 Andrew Hoover died and was buried near the wild river. By now the "habit of migration" (as one descendant labeled it) was imbued in the Hoover clan. When, in the late 1790s, destructive floods raced along the Uwharrie, several of Andrew's sons, including John, decided to pull up their roots once more.

By now also, new religious impulses had affected the Hoover family. For although Andrew had been baptized a Lutheran as an infant in Germany, and again as a Separate Baptist in North Carolina, his wife and son John became members of the Society of Friends. The Quakers' objection to slavery was a second compelling motive for the trek that the son now undertook. In 1801 John Hoover, his wife, and children removed to the Western Reserve in Ohio.

For John Hoover, a farmer and a millwright, the village of West Milton in Miami County, Ohio would be home for the remainder of his life. To his son Jesse, however, the continued magnetism of the frontier proved irresistible. By the early 1850s a renewed yearning for land was stirring in the Hoover family. To these Quakers of Ohio, the still sparsely settled prairie beyond the Mississippi River seemed alluring indeed. Already Friends from Ohio and Indiana had moved into eastern Iowa, built homes, and organized meetings. In 1850–51 some had founded West Branch, in Cedar County, between the Iowa and Cedar Rivers. And so, in 1854, with hope in their hearts and their worldly belongings packed in covered wagons, Jesse Hoover, his wife Rebecca, his son Eli, and various other children and grandchildren made their way west to Iowa. Among the participants in this migration was Eli's son Jesse, then about eight years old.

In 1856 the elder Jesse died from the effects of an injury. But life on the frontier did not permit one to tarry over past tragedies, and the widowed

Rebecca, a Quaker preacher, now steeled herself for the future. In her time of bereavement this fifty-five-year-old woman could not know that she would live to be almost ninety-five and would see more than three hundred descendants born. But she could, perhaps, derive some solace from the able and industrious family she was raising. Her son John Y. Hoover became a Quaker minister and evangelist, well known throughout the Midwest. Another son, Eli, was already succeeding in farming a mile outside West Branch. He had a knack for tinkering and experimenting with machinery, as did his young son Jesse. Probably no one in the family was surprised when this son grew up to become one of the village blacksmiths of West Branch.

In 1870 young Jesse Hoover turned twenty-four. In the small Iowa village—perhaps at the solemn Friends meetings on First Days (Sundays)—he had noticed a devout Quaker girl who was herself a child of pioneers. Hulda Randall Minthorn had been born in 1848 in Norwich, Ontario, Canada. Like the Hoovers, the Minthorns had been members of the Society of Friends for several generations, and they, too, had long felt the attraction of the New World. About 1725, ten-year-old William Minthorn had sailed with his family from England to Boston, only to be orphaned when his parents died at sea. After growing up in Massachusetts he acquired a farm in Connecticut, where a son, William, assisted him. About 1802, while the Hoovers of North Carolina were resettling in Ohio, the younger William Minthorn and his family left Connecticut for the province of Ontario. Here, in various locations among fellow Quakers, they remained for half a century.

In the 1850s word of the Quaker settlements west of the Mississippi filtered north into Canada. In 1856 William Minthorn's grandson Theodore traveled south to see for himself and returned with an unquenchable case of "Iowa fever." Finally, in 1859, Theodore, his wife Mary Wasley, and their seven children trekked by wagon to Detroit, boarded a train, and then rode across the plains to Iowa. The Lone Tree Farm between the Quaker settlements of West Branch and Springdale became their new abode.

Life on the land was good, but it could be cruelly capricious. In 1866 Theodore Minthorn died at age forty-nine. On his diminutive widow, a year younger than he, fell now the burden of maintaining her family and her farm. Like Rebecca Hoover, Mary Wasley Minthorn could not foresee that nearly four decades of active life awaited her. For the present she struggled on and inculcated in her children the importance of obtaining an education. She had taught her husband to read and write; she would live to see four of her children become Quaker ministers, and one of these a medical doctor as well. Years later, a granddaughter asked her whether she was related to the founder of Methodism, John Wesley. Her reply epitomized her determination for constructive achievement and became a family motto: "Begone with thee. What matter if we descended from the highest unless we are something ourselves. Get busy."[2]

At the time of Theodore Minthorn's death, his daughter Hulda was eighteen. For a time, between 1865 and 1867, she was a student in the Preparatory Department at the University of Iowa in nearby Iowa City.[3] There followed a period as a schoolteacher near Muscatine, Iowa.[4] On March 12, 1870 came a more fundamental transition: Hulda Randall Minthorn and Jesse Clark Hoover were married.[5]

Early in 1871, the young couple's first child, Theodore (nicknamed "Tad"), was born. That spring, Jesse Hoover purchased a plot of land between the site of his blacksmith shop and the little Wapsinonoc creek to the south. Here Jesse and his father Eli built a three-room cottage facing east on Downey Street. Devoid of ostentation, yet sturdy and functional, it contained a small bedroom, a combined living-dining area, and a "lean-to" room used variously for storage, summer cooking, and occasional guests.[6] The dimensions of the cottage were 14 x 20 feet—"a tiny house," one of Hulda's sisters later recalled, "but always so clean and neat for Hulda was a nice housekeeper, and kept house nice, whether it was small or large. Things were always *finished* with her."[7]

In this home, late on the night of August 10, 1874, Hulda Hoover gave birth to a second son. During the excitement, apparently no one noticed on which side of midnight the baby had arrived. Such a detail was no doubt a minor matter to Jesse, who proudly announced "another General Grant at our house" to a relative the next morning.[8] When Hulda asked her eldest sister Ann to suggest a name for the boy, the sister remembered a didactic children's novel, *Pierre and His Family*, which she had read as a girl. It was a tale of the persecution of the sect known as Waldenses and of their retreat to safety across the Alps. Its hero was a pious and courageous Christian boy named Hubert, devoted to his family and to the faith of the Bible. Apparently Hulda's sister mistakenly recalled that the novel's hero was named Herbert. So Herbert was the name Aunt Ann suggested, and Herbert it would be.[9]

During his first months of life the infant boy almost succumbed to the bane of his Iowa childhood. Like his brother Tad, the baby was afflicted with recurrent attacks of croup. One frigid day a particularly harsh spell seized him; nothing his despairing relatives did could cause his choking to cease. Finally the little boy turned lifeless. Bertie, it seemed, was dead. He had already been "laid out" on a board or table, with a dime placed on each closed eyelid, when one of the relatives noticed a feeble stirring of life. Hulda's brother John Minthorn, a West Branch doctor just back from another call, hastily applied artificial respiration. After an agonizing effort his nephew revived. Said Grandmother Minthorn solemnly to the assembled relatives: "God has a great work for that boy to do; that is why he was brought back to life."[10]

The community into which Herbert Hoover was born was small, self-reliant, and agricultural—not too distant in time from the days of the frontier. Across the gently rolling prairies of eastern Iowa were scattered farms of forty, eighty, occasionally one hundred sixty acres. Although settled by Quakers in 1850–51, West Branch at Hoover's birth still had fewer than 400 residents: 365 early in 1875, the year of its formal incorporation.[11]

Yet the village along the Wapsinonoc was no stagnant rural backwater. Late in 1870 the tracks of the Burlington, Cedar Rapids, and Northern Railroad were laid through West Branch; early the next year a monthly newspaper was founded. In 1875 it became a weekly and the town acquired a bank. While agriculture was the base of the local economy, other callings were represented by storekeepers, mechanics, a dentist, a jeweler, a doctor, a tailor, a harness maker, and, of course, J. C. Hoover the blacksmith. By the end of 1877 West Branch could boast of two hotels and a published business directory.[12] "There is not a saloon in the place," the directory declared, "and the moral influence is such as to recommend it to those seeking a good locality to educate their children. . . ."[13]

Temperance was but one of the humanitarian concerns of the West Branch Quakers. Before the Civil War, antislavery Friends from nearby Springdale gave refuge to John Brown for a time as he plotted what became the raid on Harper's Ferry.[14] After the war some of Hoover's own relatives in West Branch visited the South on missions of good works or went west to help the Indians: another special object of Quaker solicitude.[15] Education was valued in the small community. In the early 1860s both Jesse and Hulda attended a private "select school" near West Branch organized by two noted Quaker missionaries, Joel and Hannah Bean.[16] Politically the town was overwhelmingly Republican. Years later Herbert Hoover recalled, with but slight exaggeration, only one Democrat in the village: a man with too much fondness for liquor.[17]

Sustaining this climate of industrious sobriety was the force of religion. To young Bertie Hoover the precepts and practices of the Friends were a pervasive element of his environment. Every First Day, Jesse and Hulda took their children to the plain white meetinghouse for unprogrammed worship. The building was divided by a low partition. On one side sat the women, dressed in bonnets and modest gray and brown gowns. On the other sat the men, clad in dark suits and broadrimmed hats. For two hours—an excruciatingly long time for active little boys—the meeting gathered in sober silence punctuated only by the prayers and exhortations of those whom the Spirit had called upon to speak. Sometimes—and this was more difficult still—no one would break the endless weighty silence. Through his life Herbert Hoover never forgot the "intense repression" of this mode of worship on a small boy "who might not even count his toes. All this may not have been recreation, but it was strong training in patience."[18]

To the Quakers of Iowa, as to other Christians of that time, religion was no mere Sunday morning formality. In the home of Jesse and Hulda Hoover Bible readings and family prayers were daily duties, and only the most wholesome influences were permitted. Herbert's brother Theodore later remarked:

> Friends did not hold with light reading, and theatres, dancing and card playing were esteemed terribly wicked. My parents did not think even the "Youth's Companion" suitable for the perusal of the young, as, apart from its intrinsic lightness, it contained fiction, which was untruth, and further it incited to adventure, which was bad for energetic little boys. Sunday amusements of any kind were not tolerated.[19]

These prohibitions did not prevent Theodore from acquiring on at least one occasion a copy of the forbidden *Youth's Companion*. But he had to read it "surreptitiously," Herbert recalled, "for mine was a Quaker family unwilling in those days to have youth corrupted with stronger reading than the Bible, the encyclopedia, or those great novels where the hero overcomes the demon rum."[20]

Yet if Herbert Hoover's upbringing was strict, it was only conventionally so for that time and place. If discipline as he remembered it was "stern," it was also "kindly."[21] Nothing could conceal the world of adventure that he set out to explore. One center of it was his father, master of the hammer, the anvil, and the forge. Tall, bearded, with a teasing sense of humor and a "pleasant, sunshiny disposition,"[22] Jesse Hoover was a popular businessman in West Branch. His blacksmith shop, only a few feet from the cottage, was a place of fascination for the Hoover boys. Here they could watch their hero shoe horses and repair plows. Sometimes the workshop could be too attractive, as Tad and Bertie both discovered when they stepped on hot iron with their bare feet, thereby incurring "the brand of Iowa" for life.[23]

Jesse Hoover was an enterprising man, eager to get ahead. Moreover, his family had grown with the birth of a girl, Mary ("May"), in 1876. In 1878 Jesse turned his blacksmith shop over to a man named Hill from nearby Johnson County and proceeded to develop a farm implement business of his own.[24] "Ho, for Kansas!" read one of his many advertisements in the West Branch newspaper. "But if you do not go there go to J. C. HOOVER and buy your Farming Implements. . . . I will not be beat in quality or price."[25]

On May 25, 1878 Jesse and Hulda Hoover formally sold to Hill their cottage, blacksmith shop, and the adjoining property, for one thousand dollars.[26] Where the family lived in the town during the next year is uncertain.[27] In any case, in late May 1879 the Hoover family moved into a new home: a spacious, two-story structure fronted by maple trees at the corner of Downey and Cedar Streets.[28] In this comfortable dwelling, which reflected his father's improved economic status, Herbert Hoover spent much of the next five years.

At his new business Jesse prospered, selling plows, reapers, lightning rods, Crown and Singer sewing machines, buckets, wagons—"in fact anything in my line from a Sewing Machine needle to a Steam Engine."[29] Early in 1880 he and another man applied for a patent for a cattle stile and hog guard.[30]

Later that year his father, Eli, patented an invention of his own: an automatic cattle pump that he manufactured across the street and that Jesse may well have marketed.[31]

Ever alert to the winds of progress, Jesse purchased in 1879 a machine for the manufacture of barbed wire.[32] In order to forestall the rusting of this new product (invented in Illinois only a few years before), he coated each new reel of wire with hot tar. Two days after Christmas this process was the occasion for a near-disaster. "Much smoke and a big scare," the West Branch newspaper reported.

> Saturday afternoon a cauldron of tar which J. C. Hoover was heating for a coating for fence wire took fire and immediately great clouds of fire and smoke were sent up, causing much excitement among our people. Everybody with buckets in hand, rushed pell mell for the scene of the conflagration. . . .

By a "copious application of water" the fire was extinguished before it could spread to Jesse's nearby warehouse.[33]

What the puzzled townspeople did not know was that the fire had been caused by Bertie Hoover. Overcome by curiosity, the five-year-old boy had tossed a burning stick into the kettle of tar. When the smoke promptly billowed the boy recoiled and disappeared in "complete terror." Whether it was a case of fear, prudence, or some combination of both, the boy maintained his silence. He did not confess his role in the episode for thirty years.[34]

There were other sources of adventure for little West Branch boys. The Wapsinonoc creek, not many feet from home. Cook's Hill (at the base of which the Hoovers lived), "a splendid hill for coasting" with sleds during snowy Iowa winters. The homes and barns and fields of numerous relatives just outside town. The banks of the Cedar River, a few miles east, where Jesse and Hulda liked to picnic during the summer.[35]

In many ways it was an idyllic environment in which to grow. But as Herbert remembered decades later, "Sickness was greater and death came sooner."[36] Early in December 1880 Jesse Hoover became ill. "Rheumatism of the heart," the local paper later called it. As his condition deteriorated, May, barely four years old, remained with her mother, but Tad and Bertie were dispatched to Great-uncle Benajah Hoover's home. Here they could play with a cousin while Jesse convalesced. On December 13, 1880, a messenger came to take the two boys home. Their father, aged thirty-four, was dead.[37]

II

SINCE Jesse Hoover died intestate, his wife was appointed administratrix—and, eight months later, guardian of her three children.[38] An inventory of her late husband's property (including his home and business) revealed an estate valued at $1,850.31.[39] The probate court allotted a portion of this property to the widow;[40] presumably she received compensation for the rest when Jesse's Uncle Benajah took over the farm implement business a few weeks later.[41] With these modest assets the fatherless family confronted an uncertain future.[42]

To those who knew her best, Hulda Hoover was a "gifted girl."[43] Sensitive by temperament (she wrote poetry as a teenager), she was beloved by relatives, particularly small children to whom she cheerfully dispensed sweets and read verse. Visits to Aunt Hulda's home, one niece recalled, were "merry and much desired events."[44] An avid gardener, she cultivated flowers in profusion at each of her homes.[45] Hulda was of medium height, with brown hair and gray-green eyes like her son Herbert's. To Theodore her "most prominent" attribute was "an immense self-possession and control at all times."[46] Her sister Agnes remembered that one of her "strongest characteristics" was that "she had a sense of purpose always. As a girl she brought about the things she wanted to do, never in a disagreeable way."[47]

Above all, Hulda Hoover was a deeply religious woman. At the age of eighteen she delivered a prayer at her father's funeral; kneeling by his casket, she publicly dedicated her life to the Lord's service.[48] Before she was married she startled Quaker meetings by singing hymns—a rare and controversial breach of quietist precedent.[49] Once, during the 1870s, her singing is said to have provoked a walkout by disapproving parishioners.[50] Later still, she "created a sensation" by singing at her husband's funeral.[51] Even before Jesse died, the Hoovers held prayer meetings at their home.[52] Active in the Women's Christian Temperance Union, of which she was local secretary,[53] Hulda founded and guided as well the Young People's Prayer Meeting of West Branch.[54] She also taught in the Friends Sunday Schoool and frequently "spoke in meeting" on the theme of Christ's redeeming love.[55]

To raise her three children alone and to provide for their education required all of Hulda's intense faith and inner resources. Recollections differ about the ease with which she responded to the burden. Herbert Hoover, in his *Memoirs*, stated that his mother "took in sewing to add to the family resources."[56] Theodore, however, took comfort from the fact that they "lived without shabbiness and . . . without the labour of her hands."[57] One cannot read her few surviving letters from this period without sensing the cares that she felt and her yearning to provide for her children.

It was not easy. Replying to a letter from her mother and a sister early in 1883, she wrote:

> You will laugh at my poverty if I tell you I could not scratch up enough to pay my postage, but it has been so. I have made poor out collecting this winter so have been kind of short some times. . . . such are life's changes we know not what is before us but as children of the Lord we can trust it *all* to Him who knows what is best.[58]

When another sister invited her to teach one summer in northwest Iowa,[59] Hulda decided against it: "We will raise garden and I will try to do what I can and not neglect the children. I have rented my north room downstairs. . . ."[60] Some months later, after attending a woman's suffrage meeting, she remarked: "This is the next great question that aggitates the public mind of our State and I need only to say let a woman be left a widow and have anything to do with business and she will emphatically be on the side of equal suffrage."[61]

Fortunately there were relatives to assist her. When her brother John visited West Branch early in 1883, he paid her doctor's bill for a year.[62] One summer Hulda took her children to northwest Iowa, where several of her relatives had gone to live. It was an exciting season of fishing and hunting prairie chicken nests for the Hoover boys, and no doubt a period of rest for their mother.[63] More memorable still for Herbert was a lengthy sojourn with other relatives in the Indian Territory south of Kansas. Sometime after Jesse Hoover died, Hulda's sister Agnes, hoping to lift the weight of Hulda's sorrow, took young Bertie by train and buggy to the village of Pawhuska, where her husband, Laban J. Miles, served as government Agent to the Osage and Kaw nations. Here, for several months, the boy attended the agency school, learned "much aboriginal lore," and roamed the Oklahoma hills with his cousins and little Osage braves.[64]

By 1880, the year of his father's death, Hoover was old enough for formal education. In 1879, shortly after his fifth birthday, his parents had enrolled him in the primary department of the West Branch school. From then on, much of each year was devoted to the cycle of schooling.[65] And, when school was not in session, the Hoover boys found much to explore—such as the office of the local dentist, Dr. Walker, whose collection of exotic fossils and minerals fascinated them.[66] In 1883 the youths had new companions: several Indian lads brought from distant reservations to an industrial school established for them in West Branch by Laban Miles's father Benjamin.[67] For one glorious summer Tad and Bert joined them in building "wickyups," shooting small game with bows and arrows, and other prairie adventures.[68]

Meanwhile the boys' mother found joy and consolation in religion. In the two decades since the Civil War, American Quakerism was transformed by waves of evangelical ferment, and the traditional pattern of silent, unprogrammed worship began to dissolve.[69] West Branch itself—rocked by a visiting Quaker evangelist named David Updegraff—succumbed to divisive quarrels and an eventual secession by conservatives. Jesse and Hulda Hoover, however, along with most of the younger generation, accepted the revivalist doctrines and reforms.[70]

As an earnest Christian, Hulda Hoover now felt an increasing call to preach. In the spring of 1883 the Red Cedar Preparative Meeting of Ministers and Elders declared its belief that "a Gift in the Ministry has been conferred" upon Mrs. Hoover and that it was "sufficiently developed to be acknowledged by the Church. . . ."[71] Two months later the Springdale Monthly Meeting formally recorded her as a minister in the Society of Friends.[72]

From time to time Hulda's religious commitments took her from home—occasionally for as long as two or three weeks.[73] In September 1883, for example, she informed those present at the Monthly Meeting of her belief that it was "the will of our Heavenly Father that she attend in the love of Christ, Kansas Yearly Meeting."[74] During this trip to Kansas her children boarded with relatives and friends in West Branch.[75] "I have so much to do all the time," she told her sister, "considering I just keep my self ready first for service for my master, then to work at whatever I can to earn a little to add to our living and then the care of my little ones every day is full and some times the nights."[76]

On January 19, 1884, the Springdale Monthly Meeting of Friends considered the following item of business:

> Our dear Sister, Huldah R. Hoover, expressed before the meeting that she believes the Master calls for her service, in the Evangelistic work during the present year, mostly within the limits of our Yearly Meeting, and perhaps elsewhere as way may open up for it.
>
> This meeting very fully unites in granting her a minute, to attend to such service as the Lord may lead her, She being a minister, of the blessed Gospel of Christ, and in good unity with the church.[77]

A few weeks later, while conducting meetings at Springdale, Hulda Hoover became ill. It appeared to be typhoid fever, the *West Branch Local Record* reported on February 21.[78] Typhoid it was, complicated by pneumonia.[79] On Sunday morning, February 24, 1884, not quite thirty-six, Hulda Hoover died.[80] "The lady of the golden sunshine of little brown house had gone away, and there were left only three small children, adrift on the wreck of their little world."[81]

I I I

A T the request of Hulda's mother Mary and three other relatives, the Probate Court of Cedar County, Iowa appointed Lawrie Tatum guardian of the Hoover children.[82] Tatum, a resident of nearby Springdale, was a Quaker, an early settler of Iowa, a former Indian agent, and author of *Our Red Brothers*. More importantly, he was a man of probity in whose conscientious hands the inheritance of the three orphans now rested.[83]

From the Cedar Rapids Mutual Relief Association Tatum received Hulda Hoover's life insurance policy of one thousand dollars.[84] From the administrator of Hulda Hoover's estate he received a year later a promissory note and cash totaling about another thousand.[85] In addition, the Hoover home and one-acre lot drew a small rental income until April 1886, when Tatum finally succeeded in selling the property for five hundred dollars.[86] With these sums, divided equally among the three children, Tantum prepared to support his wards until adulthood.

Soon after their mother's death the children had gone for a few weeks to Kingsley, in Plymouth County, Iowa, the home of Hulda's mother and several relatives. It was decided that May, not yet eight years old, should remain there with her grandmother.[87] And since Hulda had expressed a wish that Tad should live with Jesse Hoover's brother Davis, this, too, was arranged.[88] In the case of Herbert, his schoolteacher, Mollie Brown, asked for him, but as she was not married, her request was turned down.[89] Laban Miles also offered to take him, but Lawrie Tatum felt that Indian Territory was no environment in which to raise children.[90] It was therefore determined that another uncle, Allen Hoover, would provide him a home. So in early April 1884 the Quaker guardian paid the orphans' great-uncle, the Rev. John Y. Hoover, twenty-five dollars to travel to Kingsley to fetch the boys. After taking Theodore to live with his Uncle Davis in Hardin County, John Y. Hoover returned with Herbert to West Branch.[91] The three Hoover children were now scattered across the state.

For the next year-and-a-half Hoover lived with his Uncle Allen and Aunt Millie on their farm a mile north of town. They were a kindly couple who treated their nephew as considerately as their own son Walter, virtually the same age.[92] Hoover never forgot their solicitude nor his aunt's scrumptious cooking.[93] As the months passed his life settled again into a tolerable pattern. There was school, taught by the woman who had offered to take him in, Mollie Brown.[94] There were schoolmates like Addie Colip, in whose autograph book Bert entered his earliest surviving literary effort—"For Addie[:] Let your days be days of peas / slip along as slick as grease."[95] There were chores to perform, such as cleaning the barn with cousin Walter for two cents apiece or cutting thistles for a nickel a hundred.[96] There were such excitements as the memorable effort to construct a mowing machine out of old junk: when the Hoover boys tied the contraption to a heifer she "gave a frightened bleat and bolted," dragging Bertie in her wake.[97] Since the orphaned boy was too young to earn his keep on the farm, his guardian paid Uncle Allen $1.50 a week for boarding him—a sum supplemented from time to time by expenditures for clothes, school supplies, and croup medicine.[98]

Yes, life was tolerable, but it was not the same. Sometimes during the night the boy would lie awake yearning for his mother who was gone.[99] While his uncle and aunt were decent and understanding, no one could replace his parents. "If thee has nothing good to say, then hold thy peace." So his mother had taught him.[100] So the Quaker discipline prescribed. It was a lesson reinforced by the circumstances of orphanhood. Perhaps unconsciously, Hoover began to develop a certain detachment from his surroundings, a protective reserve that masked the loneliness of one who was, inevitably, an outsider.[101]

In the autumn of 1885 came a message from Hulda Hoover's brother, Henry John Minthorn. An educated man, frontier doctor, and missionary, he had recently become superintendent of a Quaker academy in Newberg, Oregon. Having lost a young son the year before, he requested that his nephew Herbert be dispatched to live with him.[102] Although by 1885 West Branch had grown to a population of 502, the potential educational advantages of the Oregon community seemed compelling to Tatum and the various relatives.[103] And so preparations for the journey were begun. Herbert Hoover's assets, carefully husbanded by Tatum, now slightly exceeded $500;[104] the cost of a train trip to Oregon would be $33.13.[105] Another West Branch family about to depart for the Pacific Northwest would care for the eleven-year-old boy along the way.[106]

It is unlikely that those who saw him leave had any intimation of his future. Years later, when he had become famous, many who knew him as a child remembered him as essentially a youth like any other—more reticent perhaps, industrious certainly, intelligent but with few signs of brilliance.[107] He himself in his laconic way tended to look back with a mellow gaze, preferring, he wrote, "to think of Iowa as I saw it through the eyes of a ten year old boy"—eyes "filled with the wonders of Iowa's streams and woods, of the mystery of growing crops." Days "filled with adventure and great undertakings with participation in good and comforting things."[108]

But for now, as November 10 (the day of departure) approached, the lure of the West mingled with the pain of yet another uprooting. On Thursday, November 12, 1885, the West Branch newspaper reported: "Mr. and Mrs. O. T. Hammell and Bertie Hoover, started on their long journey Tuesday evening."[109]

2

Oregon Years

I

THE journey west was an unforgettable one for an eleven-year-old boy. Across the prairies of Iowa to Council Bluffs, across the Missouri River, the Great Plains, and the Rockies: after several days of travel the train arrived in Portland. Here Bert Hoover was met by his Uncle John, who took him to Newberg, about twenty miles to the southwest in the verdant Chehalem Valley.[1]

At the time of Hoover's arrival, what is now the town of Newberg was little more than a frontier village.[2] Probably fewer than two hundred people lived in the vicinity.[3] Like West Branch, Iowa, it was a Quaker community settled by immigrants from the Middle West. One of the pillars of this young settlement was the man now responsible for Herbert Hoover's upbringing.

Born in 1846 in Ontario, Canada, Henry John Minthorn followed the rest of his family to Iowa in 1859. A restless, intelligent youth, he defied his fellow Quakers in 1864 by enlisting in the Union Army, only to return ill and half-ostracized a few months later. During the next several years he studied, taught school, and decided to become a doctor. After graduating from the State University of Iowa in 1874, he practiced for a time in West Branch. In 1877 he received a degree from Jefferson Medical College in Philadelphia. Never a man to root himself in one locale for long, Dr. Minthorn returned briefly to Iowa and then, in 1879, became a government physician to the Indians of the Ponca Agency in Indian Territory. After assisting in the return of Chief Joseph's tribe of Nez Percé Indians from exile, he again resided in West Branch. In 1883 he was appointed superintendent of an Indian school in Forest Grove, Oregon; a year later he took charge of an Indian school in what is now Oklahoma. During his tenure in the Pacific Northwest, Minthorn became acquainted with the Quaker pioneers of Newberg. As a recorded Quaker minister, doctor, Indian Agent, and missionary, Henry John Minthorn was a versatile man—just the sort of individual, it seemed, to direct a school then being established in Newberg. On September 28, 1885, with the principal building only partly completed, the Friends Pacific Academy opened its doors in Newberg. Dr. Minthorn was selected to be its superintendent.[4]

Minthorn, his wife Laura, and their two daughters, Tennessee (age 11) and Gertrude (age 3), lived in a white, two-story wooden frame house built in 1881.[5] Into this home Herbert Hoover entered in November 1885. When he arrived, his aunt and cousins were making pear butter in a kettle in the yard. Bertie was asked to stir the kettle and was permitted to devour as much of the unfamiliar fruit as he wished. His resulting overindulgence had predictable consequences; it was years before he could bring himself to taste another pear.[6]

In another respect, Hoover's introduction to Oregon was more auspicious. He had carried across the continent a bottle of croup medicine, an unpleasant reminder of the plague of his Iowa boyhood. Upon arriving at his uncle's residence, he placed the bottle on the mantle and announced his hope that he would not need to use it again. He never did.[7]

The Friends Pacific Academy in which Hoover now enrolled had a staff of three: Superintendent Minthorn, his wife Laura, and W. R. Starbuck. The institution was divided into an academy and a grammar school; as principal of the latter, Aunt Laura served as Herbert Hoover's teacher. The first year of the grammar course, which "H. C. Hoover" (as the school catalogue identified him) took in 1885–86, included six subjects: reading, arithmetic, geography and map drawing, writing and drawing, language lessons, and spelling.[8] Each day that school was in session, the young scholars assembled at nine o'clock and dispersed at four.[9] Fifty-nine students attended Friends Pacific Academy during its inaugural year.[10] Bertie Hoover, short and chubby, "an undersized, rosy cheeked boy," was the smallest student in the school.[11]

To the Quaker directors of the academy knowledge alone was not sufficient. Accordingly they took measures to enhance the moral environment necessary for the edification of tender minds. Their first catalogue unequivocally asserted: "Since immoral and sinful practices are incompatible with the highest mental or physical development, no one is desired as a student who is not willing to abstain therefrom, and since some amusements (while they are not considered sinful by some) are calculated to distract the minds of students from their studies, they also are strictly excluded from the pastimes or recreations of pupils while attending the Academy."[12] The daily regimen of the school reinforced this concern. Each day's classes were preceded by prayer and a twenty-minute lecture on "subjects thought to help in character building."[13] But while the atmosphere was strict and designed to be uplifting, Henry John Minthorn evidently did not share his Iowa relatives' objection to children's literature. His academy contained a "well selected library," and his home included books of history, biography, and fiction.[14]

At the heart of this little universe was religion. On Hoover's wall in his room hung two mottoes that his mother had given to him: "Leave me not, neither forsake me, Oh God of my salvation" (Psalms 27:9) and "I will never leave thee nor foresake thee" (Hebrews 13:5).[15] On Sundays the thoughts of the Minthorn household turned entirely to church, with Bert's whole day being devoted to Sabbath school, church attendance, Bible study, and meetings of the Band of Hope, a children's temperance organization.[16] Bert himself was received into membership in the Newberg Monthly Meeting of Friends on January 1, 1887.[17] His Sunday-school teacher, a Quaker named Evangeline Martin, became a devoted friend whom he never forgot and whom he assisted financially in later years.[18]

For young people as well as adults an atmosphere of high seriousness reigned. One Sunday afternoon the Band of Hope held a debate between Hoover and another boy on the question: Which had destroyed more men—war or liquor? It is not known which side Bert took, but he won.[19]

In 1885 the Friends Pacific Academy consisted of but one half-completed building. In the next three years a boarding hall, cottages for students, and other structures were added.[20] As the enrollment of the school increased from nineteen (at its opening) to more than a hundred during 1887–88,[21] the responsibilities of Dr. Minthorn and his staff multiplied. An unfinished school in a tiny and unfinished community required constant toil, dedication, and sacrifice.[22] Everyone was expected to contribute, including a pre-teenage orphan earning his board while living with his relatives.

When schooling and religious exercises were not absorbing his time, Bertie Hoover performed his assigned chores. These included feeding and watering Dr. Minthorn's team of horses, driving the family's cows from the pasture to the barn and milking them nightly, and splitting wood for the fireplace.[23] Years later Hoover could still recall his aunt's firm injunction: "It is time thee gets in the wood," a request which often diverted him from more congenial pursuits.[24]

Even vacations imposed obligations. During the summer of 1887, at the age of thirteen, Bert weeded onions for Ben Cook in the rich beaver dam land near Sherwood, Oregon. His remuneration was fifty cents a day plus board. For as long as eleven or twelve hours a day Hoover and a friend crawled along the rows of onions, wearing knee pads to keep out moisture from the soil. At night they slept on a straw-filled mattress on the floor of the garret of a cabin. Bert long treasured the money he earned from this job.[25] Later that summer he worked in a brickyard in Newberg.[26]

In 1886–87 "Bertie Hoover" (as the catalogue now identified him) took the second year of the two-year grammar school course. Arithmetic (of various levels), United States history, physiology, grammar, and physical geography were his subjects.[27] On May 6, 1887 Hoover graduated from the Grammar School Department. At the school's commencement exercises he delivered a declamation entitled "Keeping His Word."[28] That autumn he ascended to the Academic Department and to such courses as algebra, bookkeeping, and rhetoric.[29] Although one of the youngest members of his class, Bert performed very creditably, particularly in mathematics.[30]

Meanwhile, in September 1887, Hoover's life was enriched by the arrival of his older brother Theodore from Iowa.[31] It was the first time the two boys had seen each other in more than two years. The presence of "Taddie," as Bert sometimes called him, no doubt more than compensated for the recurrent earaches which Bert suffered that winter and for the flea bites that tormented Theodore.[32] For at last Bert had a confidant. During this year the two brothers slept in a room in one of the now-completed academy buildings. Theodore took his meals at the academy's boarding house (administered by Mrs. Minthorn) and later at the home of a schoolmate. Bert earned his board by working for Benjamin Miles, the father of his Aunt Laura.[33]

But life was not exclusively a matter of school, church, and chores. During the school year 1887–88 Hoover's adolescent fancies turned to a new girl at the academy, Daisy Trueblood, who provided the stimulus for his earliest surviving venture in correspondence:

Friend Daisy

(and I hope you are more than my friend, although I do not dare to head it that way yet). You do not know the extent to which I am enthralled, and I am sure that no girl should be allowed such mastery over any person's heart, unless there are such feelings in her own heart. I could not have helped paying my attentions to you, if I had tried and I am sure I did not try very hard. I do not think you care. Do you?

Answer this please.

Bert[34]

I I

FOR nearly three years Hoover lived in the little village in the Chehalem Valley. Newberg, Oregon—said the 1887–88 catalogue of Friends Pacific Academy—"is a temperance town and has a moral and enterprising class of people. There are no saloons nearer than eight miles."[35] It was in such a sturdy and upright environment that Hoover grew into his teens.

Probably the most influential figure during these formative years was his uncle, Henry John Minthorn. Both Herbert and Theodore later remembered him as a "romantic" figure.[36] He was, in Theodore's words, an enterprising man of "great energy and personal magnetism,"[37] with an active, curious mind and a willingness to experiment. He was also reserved, taciturn, even austere. But when he did talk, he was worth listening to attentively.[38] As the only doctor in Newberg, he often made calls to patients in the country. Occasionally on these errands he permitted his nephew to come along and drive the horse and buggy. Bert long remembered the insights that his uncle imparted to him on these journeys.[39]

Minthorn's forceful character was matched by an earnest philosophy. "There are three things essential to happiness," he once declared: "a right relation to God and understanding of his will—Good health—Something worth doing and doing it well."[40] As a Civil War veteran he did not share the pacifism of many Quakers. "Turn your other cheek once," he would say, "but if he smites it, then punch him."[41] Minthorn also believed in the ethic of work, individual responsibility, and self-improvement. The worst thing a man can do, he often declared, is to do nothing.[42]

And yet, for all the advantages that this environment provided, Herbert Hoover's years in Oregon were not years of contentment. According to Theodore, his brother's "sensitive nature" was "jarred" by his strict and rigorous uncle.[43] More than once, it seems, the strong-willed man clashed with the strong-willed boy. Dr. Minthorn himself later acknowledged that uncle and nephew had had their differences:

> . . . I do not think he was very happy. Our home was not like the one he left with his own parents in it (indulgent) and with very little of responsibility and almost no work. I do not think he was ever punished but . . . once . . . but he always seemed to me to resent even being told to do anything by us although he did what he was told to do.[44]

From Bert's point of view his uncle's discipline seemed severe and excessive,[45] and during these "unhappy days" he poured out his feelings of antagonism in letters to his cousin Harriette in Oklahoma.[46]

One theater of disagreement was their attitudes toward horses—the pride and passion of Uncle John, who liked to drive a team at a hectic pace for recreation.[47] Perhaps in consequence, Bert despised horses, as Dr. Minthorn later attested:

> He had no use for horses, his idea of going any place was on a wheel [bicycle]. . . . I sometimes sent him into the country with medicine for people; once when he had to make a trip of this kind and could not use a wheel I wanted him to take a horse but he opposed it and I got the horse out and put him on and gave him the medicine and started him off thinking

he ought to learn to ride a horse but he came home leading the horse. . . . This was when we lived at Newberg and I never tried him with a horse again.[48]

Another anecdote—frequently mentioned in newspapers in later years and probably true—tells of Dr. Minthorn returning home late one night to discover that Bert had forgotten to water the family cow (or horses). After performing the duty himself, the doctor roused his sleepy nephew and sent him to the barn to repeat the chore: the better to learn a lesson in responsibility.[49]

Minthorn, of course, considered his conduct only proper and customary. Years afterward he defended himself against allegations that he had been too harsh. He had been a busy man ("I partly raised 7 orphan children and had four of my own"), and to him Bert, as "the oldest child in the family," seemed "almost like a grown person."

> . . . besides I had many things to look after not the least of which was more than 100 young people that I was responsible for all the time day and night while they were in the school. I thought Bert would see things from my standpoint sometime but . . . I am afraid he has not yet. . . .

Moreover, by the standards of the 1880s, his treatment of his nephew had not been unusual.

> It was . . . before the days of short hours. As I seem to remember, people tried to see how MUCH they could do instead of how little they could get off with. . . . Bert did not have it so hard [as his father] as to injure his health but he had enough [work] to take up all his time and thoughts.[50]

Upright and conscientious, Dr. Minthorn meant well by his nephew. During Hoover's three years in Newberg his uncle boarded, clothed, and educated Bert without charge—evidently making no claim, as others might have done, on Hoover's Iowa inheritance.[51] Some years later Hoover himself told an Oregon friend that his Quaker relatives had been kind to him. Still, inevitably, as an orphan in someone else's home, Hoover felt himself an outsider.[52]

On at least one occasion Bert's unhappiness flared into open defiance. While it is unlikely that he ever literally ran away from home (as some biographers have asserted),[53] for a time he did board with other relatives in Newberg.[54] Evidently this was during late 1887 and early 1888, when he lived with Theodore in the Academy building and worked for his board for Benjamin Miles.[55] One of his tasks, a laborious one, was to grub the stumps of large fir trees.[56] "Every night after school and all day Saturdays I had to bore holes in stumps [prior to burning them]," Hoover reminisced years later, "so I came to look upon a fir tree as a public enemy."[57] In his *Memoirs* he described the difficult process of burning the logs of the fir and added, with revealing understatement, "It was sport the first few times."[58]

It is impossible, of course, to gauge precisely the effects of these tensions on Hoover's developing personality. But it seems quite likely that his smoldering emotions turned inward and that his introversion and self-discipline were accentuated, producing the air of resentful stubbornness which his uncle later remembered. Too young to be independent, Herbert could only nurse his grievances in private and yearn for the day when he would be his own man.

The case of brother Theodore was different. Older and more outspoken, he rebelled forthrightly, dismaying his pious relatives by his "frivolous" associations and his pleasure-minded disregard of their strict Sabbatarianism.[59] If the later recollections of a cousin are correct, Herbert himself once led several young cousins on a clandestine Sunday fishing expedition instead of going to the obligatory Sabbath school, thereby earning a stern and extended remonstrance. According to this cousin, Bert fiercely resented his elders' warnings of the "horrors of hell" as the fate of disobedient youth.[60]

I I I

B y 1888 Henry John Minthorn had new projects on his mind. Part doctor and missionary, part entrepreneur and promoter, he had become interested in Oregon's transition from a wheat-growing to a fruit-growing region.[61] Already by early that year he was vice-president of the Chehalem Valley Board of Immigration, "headquarters for improved and unimproved farming lands." Fruit farms, said the board's stationery, were "a Specialty."[62] In February Minthorn and several associates decided to enter this promising arena in a more ambitious way. They organized a venture called the Oregon Land Company, which was incorporated in Salem, the state capital, about thirty miles from Newberg. The initial capital stock was $20,000.[63] Resigning his superintendency of the Friends Pacific Academy, Minthorn moved his family, including his nephew Bert, to Salem in the summer of 1888. Bert and Tad drove the livestock overland; other belongings were transported by boat down the Willamette River.[64]

When this transition was completed, Theodore, now a husky youth going on eighteen, returned to Newberg and resumed his studies at the academy. That year he boarded with sixty-nine-year-old Benjamin Miles "the best hand I ever met at planning work so that a boy would not have a minute" for diversion.[65] Down in Salem, Herbert and the Minthorns lived temporarily in a barn until their new home at Hazel and Highland Avenues was ready. During the autumn Hoover's sister May and Grandmother Minthorn moved to Salem from Kingsley, Iowa.[66] Through the failed investments of a son-in-law, Mary Minthorn had lost all (or nearly all) of her Iowa property. Now she came to live with her granddaughter in a little cottage next to her son John's home in the Highland Addition of Oregon's capital city.[67]

With that irrepressible faith in the future that characterized developers of the American frontier, Minthorn and his business partners proceeded to actualize their vision. The Willamette Valley transformed from wheat fields to orchards! This was the dream of Minthorn, Ben S. Cook, and other Quaker associates.[68] Operating from offices in the State Insurance Building, the company purchased land in Marion and Polk counties, converted it to prune orchards and other fruits, and then sold it to settlers in tracts of five, ten, or twenty acres.[69] As a "general improvement company," the enterprise was more than a simple vendor of real estate. Dr. Minthorn explained:

> The business grew and covered a variety of enterprises, buying and selling land, setting out and cultivating orchards, building and selling houses; on one tract was built houses, a church, a schoolhouse, and a hotel, also were owned and operated a saw mill and a flour mill. Streets were graded, water systems built, and the Salem Street Railway was owned and operated. Fruit dryers were owned and operated, and other kinds of business.[70]

Through an advertising firm in Chicago the company placed advertisements in newspapers and magazines throughout the United States ("1000 papers," Minthorn later recalled).[71]

The results of all this activity were gratifying to the wide-awake Quaker businessmen. Extensive amounts of land were improved and sold: seven thousand acres, according to one estimate.[72] In 1890 the Oregon Land Company increased its capital stock tenfold, to $200,000.[73] One of its projects during these boom years was the development of the Highland Addition in Salem and the extension through it of the horse-drawn street railway line.[74] Most of its clients seem to have been Quakers from the Middle West. Within a few years the company established fruit-growing settlements of Friends in the area, including Rosedale, Liberty, Scotts Mills, and Prune Ridge.[75]

Still other enterprises absorbed the energies of Dr. Minthorn. Since the Highland Avenue neighborhood possessed no Friends meetinghouse, Minthorn and several other Quakers decided in 1890 to organize a fund-raising drive (to which Herbert Hoover contributed); early in 1891 the Highland Avenue Friends Church was dedicated. Hoover, his sister, and numerous other relatives became charter members.[76] Minthorn and some associates also took the lead in founding the Friends Polytechnic Institute in the Highland Avenue section of Salem. When the school opened in September 1892, Minthorn and his wife were on the faculty, and May Hoover was a student.[77]

Meanwhile Hoover, upon moving to Salem in 1888, had not immediately resumed his schooling. Instead, apparently on his own initiative, he had gone to work for the Oregon Land Company—a decision that his uncle applauded.[78] As an office boy for the firm, Bert was responsible for filing correspondence, serving notices for stockholders' meetings, mailing circulars, handling the advertising, and generally facilitating the flow of business.[79] He also had charge of the stable and often drove potential customers in horse-drawn carriages to lots that the company had for sale.[80] Sometimes he substituted for Salem Street Railway Company drivers.[81] Hoover's uncle was particularly interested in a development known as the Minthorn or "Minthorn Springs" Addition in Portland. On one occasion Bert and some friends transported barrels of water from these springs to Portland's theaters and distributed free samples while the water's "purity and medicinal qualities" were proclaimed on stage.[82]

At first Hoover's salary was twenty dollars a month; by 1890 he was earning thirty-five dollars a month—not a bad salary in those days.[83] By all accounts the teenager had begun to reveal a special aptitude for business and for getting things done. "Bert was the best office boy my firm ever had," said Ben S. Cook. "[He] was always industrious. He was the most systematic boy I ever saw."[84] "If I called for a certain letter, no matter if it had been received a year before, Bert could instantly locate it."[85] Laura Heulat, the company's stenographer, was similarly impressed:

> Herbert Hoover was the quietest, the most efficient and the most industrious boy I ever knew in an office. He even wore quiet shoes and you never knew he was around until you wanted something, and then he was right at your elbow. He knew everything about the office and the rest of us never tried to keep track of things. It was easier and quicker just to ask Bert about it.[86]

During his three years with the land company Hoover learned to type and acquired some knowledge of accounting.[87] And since the company's officers included two prominent Oregon politicians, no doubt he began also to develop a sense of affairs and some experience in the assessment of men, although politics as a possible vocation seems to have held little appeal.[88] For all the vicissitudes of his boyhood and adolescence, one suspects that Bert was happier now.

Dr. Minthorn freely acknowledged his nephew's ability. Bert "was a good worker," he said, who "attended strictly to making the most of his opportunities."[89] One contribution the boy made to the company's prosperity was a scheme to meet travelers arriving at the railroad depot in response to the company's advertising. Instead of allowing the strangers to find their own way to local hotels, Bert met them at the station and transported them directly to private homes where he had already rented rooms. In this way, the strangers were accommodated, good will was generated, and clients were kept away from business rivals. Bert was allowed to retain his profits from the rental of the housing.[90]

In other ways, too, he displayed astuteness. One night a group of creditors entered the Oregon Land Company's offices demanding immediate payment on certain debts. Steadily the atmosphere grew more violent and menacing until—suddenly and mysteriously—the lights went out. Unable to continue their argument effectively, the men, muttering and fumbling through the darkness, went home. It turned out that Bert Hoover, watching the tense and unproductive meeting, had quietly shut off the lights. When the discussion resumed the next day, tempers were cooler and a settlement was reached.[91]

At one point Bert and a young friend organized a business of their own. For twenty dollars they bought a heap of old, broken-down sewing machines and reassembled them into workable ones. Unfortunately, as Hoover later observed, the skeptical women of Salem could not be persuaded to buy the recycled products, and the venture failed.[92]

In all this behavior Hoover was developing traits that tell much about his eventual career. When he came to Oregon at age eleven, he had brought with him a little account book in which he had dutifully recorded all of his assets and expenditures.[93] He was learning prematurely to be self-supporting and to prize the virtues of initiative and self-reliance. He was learning before his time the ways of the world of business: Dr. Minthorn later considered this to be one of the reasons for his nephew's early success.[94]

To many who observed him Hoover seemed unusually reserved—"a modest, reticent boy of few words."[95] Diffident, serious, seemingly unfriendly: even one of his best friends in Salem found him "one of the most difficult boys to meet."[96] "He never said much," said one acquaintance, "but he was a good listener."[97] Laura Heulat later remembered him as "a funny looking little fellow, with a short neck, and a round head which was always surmounted by a funny little round hat."

> It is difficult now to think of anything particularly striking about him except it was his persistent application to his job and his pile of books. It would be much easier to tell a great deal more interesting story about almost any other boy I knew in Salem in those days, for they were always doing things to give people something to talk about while Bert went his silent way and no one thought much about him.[98]

But beneath this unassuming exterior was a person of earnestness, tenacity, and determination.[99] He was "eternally anxious to build himself up," said one who knew him in Salem.[100] He was "always studying when not busy with office work," said another.[101]

Yet Hoover's was not a grim and cheerless youth, all work and no play. Although dancing and the theater were not among his recreations (his relatives did not approve such forms of indulgence),[102] other pleasures were readily available. The Oregon forests and streams provided opportunities for carefree camping and fishing trips in the mountains. In later years Hoover often returned to the Pacific Northwest to pursue his silent hobby of fishing.[103] Hoover excelled at checkers and somewhere learned to play chess.[104]

Another source of amusement was his bicycle. Sometimes, for thrills, he would hitch it by rope to a horse-drawn street railway car and paddle along behind. Often he and another friend set younger children on the handlebars and then scooted through the Salem streets.[105]

Increasingly, though, Bert's thoughts were focusing on education. In the fall of 1889, aided by sixty dollars provided by his Iowa guardian, he attended classes at the Capital Business College in Salem; here he learned more about mathematics.[106] At about this time he became acquainted with a woman whose influence was considerable. At each stage of his young life a teacher had appeared whose memory he subsequently cherished. In West Branch it had been Mollie Brown; in Newberg, Vannie Martin. Now, in Salem, a Miss Jennie Gray inquired at the land company office one day about Bert's educational background. Finding that his reading experiences and tastes were narrow, she took him to a local library and introduced him to *Ivanhoe*. It was a revelation. Soon he read *David Copperfield* and other unsuspected treasures.[107] Hoover also attended Miss Gray's Presbyterian Sunday School class (before the Highland Avenue Friends Church was built) and often visited her for Sunday dinner.[108] Miss Gray, who had a special interest in the education of working boys, helped to inculcate in her young protégé a love of books and an awareness of the unexplored world beyond Salem.

Perhaps almost as importantly, she was able at her dinners and Sunday-school parties to draw the shy youth out of his protective shell. Hoover "worshipped" Miss Gray, said his Salem chum Burt Brown Barker. Anything she asked Hoover to do, he did with alacrity. Invited to join in games with his fellow guests, he joined. But—he never volunteered to take the lead.[109]

Other influences were combining to strengthen his desire for a college education. A few months after the Minthorns' move to Salem separated the two Hoover brothers, Theodore, now almost eighteen, deliberately defied "in a brazen manner" the moral code of his elders by attending a dance in Newberg. The next day, facing expulsion from Friends Pacific Academy, he left the Miles home and went to work on his own as a printer, first in Newberg and eventually in Salem. Theodore chafed at what he considered the unreasonable constraints of his Quaker relatives, who were much offended by his "Sunday excursions" in the country and his visits to the brewery with fellow printers at the Salem newspaper. But when Uncle John Minthorn offered to pay half his expenses if he would attend a Quaker college in Iowa, Theodore gladly accepted. In the summer of 1890, he headed east to William Penn College.[110]

Tad's decision to enter college no doubt encouraged Bert to do the same. So, too, did conversations with an Eastern engineer who chanced to visit the Oregon Land Company. The visitor impressed upon young Hoover the importance of university training as preparation for a profession. The visitor's own field, engineering, prompted Hoover to consider this calling. The excellent economic prospects for mining engineers in particular refined his ambition. He told a friend that mining engineers were "very scarce" and "just about set their own price."[111]

And so Hoover began to study the catalogues of various institutions. Some of his relatives were anxious that he attend a Friends college like Theodore. According to Hoover, they obtained the promise of a scholarship for him from Earlham College in Indiana. But Herbert was determined to make his own selection and to attend a college which offered instruction in engineering (which Earlham did not).[112] According to Uncle John's philosophy of life, two things were especially vital to success: "good opportunities" and readiness "to improve the opportunity."[113] In the summer of 1891 opportunity came. A new, ambitious, modern university devoted to the ethic of usefulness was arising in California—the creation of Senator Leland Stanford in memory of his son. When entrance examinations for the university were scheduled in Portland, Herbert Hoover resolved to take them.[114]

On the day of the examination Hoover performed satisfactorily in the fields he had previously covered. But his studies at the Friends Pacific Academy and at the business college did not constitute a complete high-school level of preparation, and his deficiencies were only too apparent. Judged solely by his examination scores, Hoover was not qualified to enter Stanford.

Yet as he struggled, the examiner—Professor Joseph Swain of Stanford's nascent mathematics department—noticed the "strength of will" of this "quiet and serious" youth who spoke "with monosyllables":

> As Mathematics was my own subject I naturally observed him most when he was working at his Plane Geometry questions. I observed that he put his teeth together with great decision and his whole face and posture showed his determination to pass the examination at any cost. He was evidently summoning every pound of energy he possessed to answer correctly the questions before him. I was naturally interested in him. On inquiry I learned that he had studied only two books of Plane Geometry and was trying to solve an original problem based on the fourth book.

To Swain, Hoover's "method of work" was more revealing than his inadequate preparation. He interviewed the boy and was convinced that he only required an opportunity in order to succeed. Swain decided to admit him.[115] The opposition of Hoover's relatives to his attending a secular university evidently dissolved when Swain, a prominent Quaker, stopped briefly in Salem and informed Dr. Minthorn that his nephew was the kind of student Stanford wanted.[116]

In order to be assured entrance, however, Bert needed to master the geometry he had not yet studied: this Professor Swain required. He also suggested that Hoover come to Stanford early for tutoring before additional entrance examinations and the opening of classes in the autumn.[117] Bert now plunged intently into geometry, poring over books on a table in the upper story of

Dr. Minthorn's barn.[118] One of his friends at this time was Fred Williams, son of a local banker. Mr. Williams offered to compensate Bert if he would tutor Fred in certain subjects. Bert did and thereby added a little to his savings.[119]

During his six years in Oregon Hoover had barely touched his inheritance. Thanks to his own self-sufficiency and to Lawrie Tatum's prudent stewardship of the money (which Tatum loaned out at 8% interest), Hoover's Iowa account increased from $533.99 in August 1885 to $822.67 in August 1891.[120] In that month Tatum reported to the district court of Cedar County that his ward, "an industrious and faithful boy," proposed to enter Stanford University. Tatum recommended that Hoover's wish be granted; the court agreed.[121]

The worst thing a man can do is to do nothing. There is a story, perhaps apocryphal, that as Hoover prepared to depart for California his Grandmother Minthorn prayed he would do a "conscientious work" and that Herbert promised she would someday be proud of him.[122] Certainly he was determined to succeed; as Swain had discerned, he possessed a "superior will."[123] On August 29, 1891, accompanied by his friend Williams, Herbert Hoover left Salem for Stanford University.[124] Less than three weeks earlier he had reached his seventeenth birthday. As he boarded the train he left his boyhood behind.

3

Stanford
University

I

I N 1884 Leland Stanford was a wealthy man. Born on a farm in New York, he migrated to California in the 1850s and became its Republican governor in 1861. As one of the "Big Four" railroad titans of the Golden State, he developed the Central Pacific Railroad and helped to bind the nation with ties of steel. Able, energetic, daring, and farsighted, he personified to his contemporaries the American dream: from humble beginnings to remarkable achievement and spectacular success.

As he grew older Stanford's thoughts centered increasingly on his only son and heir. But in 1884 Leland Stanford, Jr., died of typhoid on a trip to Europe when he was not quite sixteen. Overcome by anguish, his father fell into a fitful slumber and dreamed that he heard his departed son speak: "Father, do not say you have nothing to live for. . . . Live for humanity." The next morning Stanford awoke with words of purpose implanted on his mind and lips: "The children of California shall be my children." He resolved to dedicate his fortune to creating a worthy memorial for his son.

Seven years later, in the summer of 1891, his "monument" was nearly ready. On his ranch of more than eight thousand acres in the Santa Clara Valley, thirty miles south of San Francisco, Stanford, now a senator, had supervised the development of a university. With the acumen that marked his business ventures, he had selected Doctor David Starr Jordan, the youthful president of Indiana University, to transform the still-unfinished assortment of buildings into an institution of learning. Early that summer Jordan took up residence; gradually the faculty filtered in. Scores of laborers hastened to complete the structures before the students—no one knew how many—arrived. Housing was scarce; roads through the campus were dusty, primitive, and few. The nearest villages were Menlo Park and Mayfield; the city of Palo Alto did not yet exist. No wonder skeptics scoffed at the thought of a university located amidst the Senator's stables and vineyards under the hot California sun.[1]

To alleviate the housing shortage workmen quickly built ten wooden-frame cottages for the faculty along what Jordan named Alvarado Row; students soon would label it the "Decalogue." At the invitation of Jordan, two Eastern schoolteachers trekked across the continent to establish a preparatory school for girls near the campus. An unoccupied farmhouse later called Adelante Villa was the only housing Lucy Fletcher and Eleanor Pearson could find, and they promptly converted it into a boardinghouse for early Stanford arrivals.[2] While construction proceeded and the nascent community awaited opening ceremonies, a few faculty members and students sought temporary quarters there. Among them, at the end of August, were "two raw boys from Oregon," Herbert Hoover and Fred Williams.[3]

When Hoover disembarked from the train at Menlo Park and found his way to Adelante Villa, he was seeking more than a place to stay. If he were to be able to seize the opportunity for education that lay almost within his grasp, he must pass the entrance examinations he had failed in Oregon. In the short time before school opened, he was tutored by Misses Fletcher and Pearson.[4] In return for his board and their coaching, he took care of the tutors' horses.[5]

When examination day came, Hoover successfully met the entrance requirements in arithmetic, elementary algebra, plane geometry, geography, and American history. Discovering that he needed to elect another subject in which to be tested, he chose physiology, studied for a night, and passed.[6] The English language test, however, was too formidable; in this subject he was "conditioned." But his objective had been attained: he was permitted to enroll, with the stipulation that he remove this "condition" before graduation.[7]

A few days before opening day Hoover and Fred Williams were assigned to the men's dormitory, Encina Hall—the first Stanford students to occupy rooms in this building.[8] On October 1, 1891 Leland Stanford Junior University formally opened before a large and expectant throng. More than four hundred students registered that day; they greeted the arriving benefactor with a yell:

Wah hoo! Wah hoo!
L. S. J. U.
Stanford![9]

The ethos of the infant university was easily discernible from the addresses delivered at the convocation. To Senator Stanford, a self-made man, education was "training for usefulness in life,"[10] and in his speech he expounded his philosophy:

> You, students are the most important factor in the university. It is for your benefit that it has been established. To you our hearts go out especially, and in each individual student we feel a parental interest. All that we can do for you is to place the opportunities within your reach. Remember that life is, above all, practical; that you are here to fit yourselves for a useful career; also, that learning should not only make you wise in the arts and sciences, but should fully develop your moral and religious natures.[11]

But not education for oneself alone. While the instruction of its own students was the university's immediate goal, Senator Stanford hoped his creation would contribute to "the general welfare of humanity."[12] David Starr Jordan—ebullient and optimistic, Emersonian in his rhetoric—expounded further the uplifting vision. Here, he said, was a university, imbued with grand ideals, "hallowed by no traditions" and "hampered by none." "Its finger posts all point forward." "The Golden Age of California begins when its gold is used for purposes like this."[13] In the audience Herbert Hoover listened and was thrilled.[14]

Five hundred fifty-nine students, mostly freshmen and mostly Californians, enrolled at Stanford University during its formative year, thereby rendering it at once the largest academic institution in California.[15] For a few days the nearly three hundred male students of Encina had to use candles until electricity could be installed. Hot water was not provided until late October. Since the kitchen at Roble Hall, the women's dormitory, was not yet finished, the coeds (or "angels," as they were called) were obliged to take their meals temporarily in the dining hall at Encina. All was excitement and malleability during these first few months. Not without reason did the Class of '95—the first full four-year class—become known as the Pioneers.[16]

As the days passed the students began to organize clubs, athletic teams, and other manifestations of college life.[17] The faculty, meanwhile, instituted Friday evening "at homes" for their students. It was indeed an exciting world, this nascent, still-forming community on Senator Stanford's ranch.

In his first semester at Stanford, Hoover took courses in solid geometry, algebra, trigonometry, linear drawing, freehand drawing, and mechanical engineering (shop). For these he would be graded, as all students were in those days, simply on a pass/fail basis. Perhaps because the head of the geology department had not yet arrived on campus, Hoover initially declared his major as Mechanical Engineering.[18] But when Doctor John Caspar Branner came at the beginning of 1892, Hoover dropped the courses in drawing and enrolled in Branner's course in geology.[19]

Although Stanford University did not charge tuition, board at Encina Hall cost twenty dollars per month, a considerable sum at a time when student workers were paid around fifteen cents an hour.[20] Like many other students Hoover had no cushion of parental wealth to support him—only the $822.67 that Lawrie Tatum guarded back in Iowa. With board, books, clothing, and sundry other expenses now piling up, this reserve would not last very long. It would be necessary for Hoover to work his way through college.

With the help of Professor Swain he secured a temporary job as a clerk in the Registrar's office.[21] For much of the ensuing year he continued to care for the horses at Adelante Villa—performing his chores twice daily, efficiently, wordlessly.[22] During his freshman year he also delivered newspapers on campus and served as agent for a nearby laundry, using as transportation a discarded old bicycle that he had repaired. At first he collected the laundry and distributed the clean clothing himself. Later he sublet the business and kept the accounts. From these two activities he derived a small but steady income.[23] Sometime after Professor Branner reached campus Hoover obtained employment as his office assistant, a position he held for most of his undergraduate career.[24] In the second semester of his freshman year, Hoover's labors were interrupted by a case of measles, the effects of which compelled him to wear glasses during much of his remaining time at college.[25]

During this first year, Hoover, one of the youngest in his class, made relatively little impression on those around him, except for one characteristic repeatedly noticed by acquaintances: his shy, abrupt taciturnity. Years later David Starr Jordan recalled him as "a very quiet and almost retiring youngster."[26] Professor Branner's wife remembered him as "always blunt, almost to the point of utter tactlessness." When students came to the Branners' home for evening receptions, Hoover "usually sat back in the corner and listened. He rarely spoke and always seemed to be a little ill at ease."[27] One of his closest student friends, Lester Hinsdale, who sat with him at meals in Encina in freshman year, recalled that Hoover was "very immature in appearance, probably the youngest looking of us all. He seemed shy to the point of timidity—rarely spoke unless spoken to. It wasn't until later, when we got into politics on the same side and I began to see under his surface, that I realized how much it was possible to like him."[28]

Yet slowly he was emerging from his protective shell. At a meeting of the Geological Club in May 1892 he presented a paper.[29] Sometime in his first year he tried out for the freshman baseball team and briefly served as shortstop. Whether because of an injury to his finger (as his friend Will Irwin later reported) or because of his peers' judgment about his ability (as Hoover himself stated), he soon abandoned his player's uniform for the more congenial role of managing the team's finances and schedule.[30]

By far the most spectacular athletic event of the spring was the first football game between Stanford and the University of California, played in San

Francisco on March 19, 1892. Ten thousand vociferous fans gathered on the Haight Street grounds for the "Big Game" between the team from Berkeley and the Stanford "kidlets," as their opponents derisively called the upstart challengers. At first the game was delayed for an hour by the ludicrous fact that no one had remembered to bring a football. When, to general astonishment, the inexperienced "kidlets" actually won the contest, 14–10, bedlam reigned among the Stanford supporters.[31] Hoover was there.[32]

Later that spring Professor Branner offered Hoover a summer job. One of the most eminent geologists of his day, Branner was still serving as director of the Geological Survey of Arkansas. He arranged for Hoover to work as an assistant on the survey with one of Branner's graduate students, John Fletcher Newsom, at a salary of forty dollars a month. Hoover eagerly accepted; it meant practical experience in the field—and income, too. In the summer of 1892, sometimes alone and sometimes with Newsom, he tramped and rode on horseback through the woods and ravines of northern Arkansas, mapping geological formations on the slopes of the Ozark mountains.[33] Newsom was impressed by Hoover's energy, efficiency, and capacity for work.[34] Hoover's surveying even took him to the vicinity of Pawhuska, Oklahoma, where he located a large limestone deposit.[35] The Ozarks were rugged country, populated by suspicious mountaineers and moonshiners whose cabins were the only available shelter at night. It was also a land of rattlesnakes, which sometimes made life unusually interesting, and of huckleberries, for which, according to local tradition, he developed an inordinate fondness.[36]

I I

WHEN Hoover returned to the university for the fall semester, he changed his major from Mechanical Engineering to Geology.[37] During his sophomore year his studies again focused heavily on science, with courses in mineralogy, paleontology, inorganic chemistry, chemistry laboratory, and geology. He also took (and passed) a year-long course in elementary French, his first venture into the humanities.[38]

Discovering that the cost of room and board at Encina had increased substantially, Hoover and several other friends, including Samuel Collins (class of '95), established a cooperative living arrangement in an off-campus boardinghouse known as Romero Hall. Here Hoover roomed during his second year.[39] It was well that he did so, if he could thereby economize. For despite all his jobs during the preceding school year and summer, he had drawn frequently on Lawrie Tatum's dwindling reserves, which now stood at $418.73, scarcely half the total of the year before.[40]

He told a friend about his plans to go into the "baggage business" when school opened. "Dr. B[ranner] says I can swim it if not he will throw in a cork," Hoover reported. "Am working awful hard. Have considerable buisness worked up & 300000000000 schemes for making more."[41] During this second year he worked for Professor Branner, serving at least part of the time as his assistant in Arkansas Geological Survey work.[42] He also acted as campus agent for a San Jose laundry. In this capacity he met early in the year a tall, lanky, Iowa-born freshman from Riverside, California. Ray Lyman Wilbur (class of '96) instantly took a liking to this quiet, unassuming sophomore who did not condescend toward lowly freshmen. Their acquaintance developed into a lifelong friendship.[43] When Wilbur, anxious to work his way through college, sought Hoover's advice, the experienced sophomore counseled: "Do your work so that they notice it and be on the job all of the time."[44]

Upon termination of classes in the spring of 1893, Hoover helped Dr. Branner complete a massive topographical relief map of Arkansas for display at the Chicago World's Fair.[45] Later that summer he seems to have spent some time in Oregon searching for fossils for Branner. Before going back to college he stopped in Salem to see his brother Theodore, who had left William Penn College and was working once more in the printing trade. To Tad, Bert was no longer "the chubby, small brother" but "a tall, slender sophomore" who "looked very scholarly with glasses."[46] Hoover also visited his old Oregon chum, Burt Brown Barker, and urged him to enroll at Stanford. But Barker, who had been accepted at the University of Chicago, could not be persuaded. Frustrated and annoyed by his friend's intransigence, Hoover climbed into his buggy and said, "Don't go to the University of Chicago. No one goes there except preachers who eat yellow legged chickens." With this parting shot the ardent Stanford loyalist drove off.[47]

III

Hoover received fifteen hours of academic credit—virtually an entire semester's worth—for his modeling and mapmaking work in the Department of Geology that summer. In the fall semester, with the permission of the faculty, he registered for a heavy nineteen hours of course work in paleontology, mineralogy, civil engineering (surveying), chemistry, and philosophy. In the spring he took more courses in mineralogy, surveying, and chemistry, as well as calculus and a course in mining engineering (assaying).[48] During his junior year he roomed again on campus in Encina and became the local agent for the United States Laundry Association of San Francisco.[49] By the start of school in September Lawrie Tatum's fund had sagged to $110.26.[50]

The dramatic events of Hoover's junior year, however, did not occur in the classroom. In 1893 and 1894 the Stanford campus was in ferment, divided between fraternity and nonfraternity students. In its very first year Stanford University had witnessed the introduction of Greek-letter fraternities, whose domination of student affairs increasingly irritated some of the "barbarians" or "barbs," as the nonfraternity students were called. Furthermore, despite the existence of a student constitution and officers, little system or financial accountability prevailed in the management of student activities. Athletic events in particular, involving substantial receipts and the reputation of the Associated Students, were largely unsupervised. As Ray Lyman Wilbur observed, "Student organizations had been rather loosely set up, with no central treasury. They had a football manager and a baseball manager who sold tickets and were accountable for the most part to no one. The Glee Club had developed a habit of going off on trips and leaving debts that were not paid, although contracted in the name of the Associated Students."[51]

To the restless "barbs" the situation was intolerable, and so a reform movement commenced. The first manifestation of the "barbarian" rebellion was the election of E. R. Zion (class of '94) as president of the student body in September of 1893. "Sosh" Zion students called him (for "Socialist") because of his frequent battles against the status quo. During the winter Zion and his executive committee labored to devise a new student constitution to replace the ineffectual document adopted in October 1891.[52]

Among many who later reminisced about these exciting days there was a tendency to attribute to Hoover unique or preeminent leadership of the reformers.[53] Such an allocation of responsibility was exaggerated. It was Zion who chaired the student executive committee that formally drafted and presented the proposed constitution. Hoover was not a member of this committee, nor were such other "barb" leaders as Lester Hinsdale, Sam Collins, and Herbert Hicks.[54] Nevertheless, in the high councils and behind-the-scenes strategy sessions that preceded and accompanied the executive committee's work, Herbert Hoover undoubtedly played his part. One sign of his emerging status appeared on January 23, 1894, when 140 Pioneers held a class meeting. On nomination by Sam Collins (who had first gotten him interested in politics at Romero Hall), Herbert Hoover was unanimously elected treasurer of the junior class.[55]

On February 28 the proposed new constitution was printed in the student newspaper, the *Daily Palo Alto*.[56] The desire to systematize and centralize control of financial and athletic activities was patent. One of the executive committee's principal objectives was to insure that "the treasurer of the Associated Students be such in fact as well as in name, and have charge of all money collected by the various teams. . . ."[57] Accordingly, the draft constitution provided that the treasurer would "collect and have charge of all funds of the association" and would disburse these funds to groups who presented requisitions, which would be audited. The constitution further stipulated that no football, baseball, or track manager could incur debts exceeding five hundred dollars "without the sanction of the president and treasurer of the association."

Early in March an aroused student body gathered to consider the constitution. As originally drafted, the document provided that the athletic managers should receive a percentage of the net profits derived from their team's contests. Many students from Hoover's faction supported this idea. Hoover himself, at one meeting, unsuccessfully moved that each athletic manager be paid 25% of the first $1,000 in profits and 15% of the rest. The idea of a "remunerative clause," however, evoked a storm of opposition, and in the end all forms of it were defeated. As finally adopted, the constitution did not provide for the payment of any officers.[58]

The stage was now ready for the final struggle: the election of the first officers. Elections were to be held in April, with the winners to take office in the fall. As the "barb" leaders pondered slots on the ticket, the name of Herbert Hoover came up as a possible candidate for the key position of treasurer. There was logic in the thought. He was already treasurer of the Pioneer Class and was thoroughly experienced in the laundry agency and other enterprises requiring financial and organizational ability.[59] As a close friend of Collins and Hinsdale, he had been active in the "barb push" and had joined in the debate to adopt the constitution. In the eyes of the "barb" politicians he possessed another asset. Since he was earning his way through college, he might win the voters in the "Camp," four rough barracks originally used to house workmen but now inhabited by impecunious undergraduates who could not afford to live in Encina.[60]

Would Hoover agree to run for treasurer? Years later several of his friends recalled that a matter of principle initially made him hesitant. According to one version, before he accepted he insisted that the new constitution include a clause that the treasurer receive no salary until the second year. He did not want to be accused of supporting a salary for the treasurer and then seeking the position; such a stance would smack of self-interest.[61] Another version asserted that he favored a salary but vowed that he would not take it if elected.[62] In fact, however, when the proposed constitution was first published in late February, it contained a reference only to the athletic managers' compensation.[63] The document's silence about the treasurer's salary may have reflected Hoover's opposition. In any case, when the Associated Students of Leland Stanford Junior University assembled on April 11, 1894 to determine officers for the coming election, Hoover was among those nominated for treasurer; Lester Hinsdale was nominated for president and Herbert Hicks (class of '96) for football manager. The three posts were considered the most prestigious.[64]

For the next few days the fury of a political hurricane gripped the campus. Parades, speeches, demonstrations, midnight caucuses, get-out-the-vote drives, even a campaign slogan:

> Rah! Rah! Rix!
> Hinsdale! Hoover! Hicks!
> Barbs on top
> And the frats in a fix![65]

On election day, April 18, 686 students—a phenomenal 85% of the electorate—cast ballots. The vote was close and, for most of the major offices, inconclusive. For president: Hinsdale, 336; Magee, 330; others, 6. Hinsdale had failed by one vote to gain a majority. For treasurer: Hoover, 253; Grosh, 235; White, 180. For football manager, a similar result. No one had attained a majority; a runoff would be necessary.[66]

Another week of frenzy and calculation followed. Hoover and his colleagues methodically compiled lists of voters and delegated their lieutenants to solicit the support of "queeners," coeds, every constituency, every vote.[67] No resource was overlooked. During the tumult President Jordan was heard to wonder aloud whether he was "presiding over a young Tammany Hall."[68] And when the votes were cast and counted on April 24, the "Three H" ticket won. Hinsdale, 380; Magee, 274. Hoover, 370; Grosh, 282. Hicks, 375; Kessinger, 285.[69] That night the "three H's" celebrated in the barbs' stronghold. So packed was the room in Encina that the victors, carrying boxes of cigars in each hand, had to be lifted and passed overhead to a spot near the window.[70] As the *Daily Palo Alto* reported, cigars and lemonade were "freely dispensed" to the exultant crowd.[71]

There was one election that Hoover did not win that spring. Early in May he was a candidate for business manager of the *Daily Palo Alto* for the coming year. But when the Board of Control of the newspaper met to consider the five applicants, another student was selected.[72]

By now, no doubt, Hoover's attention was turning to the summer. In mid-April the campus newspaper reported that he had been appointed an assistant on the United States Geological Survey for the coming vacation.[73] Probably through Professor Branner, he obtained a summer job with Doctor Waldemar Lindgren, one of the outstanding geologists in the United States. For some reason Hoover's initial assignment to work in southern Oregon fell through, and when summer arrived his job prospects were indefinite.[74] So in early June Hoover, Zion, Collins, and some other friends drove a team of horses from Palo Alto to Yosemite Valley, nearly three hundred miles away. Along the way they painted and posted advertising signs for the *San Francisco Examiner*, thereby paying for the trip. While vacationing in Yosemite, Hoover received a telegram that he could now join Lindgren after all, in the California Sierras instead of Oregon. Despite the attraction of remaining with his comrades, Hoover immediately seized the opportunity. He set out alone on foot for the river boats at Stockton, more than eighty miles away.[75]

On July 1, 1894, having joined Lindgren in the mountains, Hoover officially became an employee of the United States Geological Survey. This was the summer of the great Pullman railroad strike led by Eugene V. Debs, and because of it for three weeks Hoover was unable to begin work. Finally, late in July, Lindgren and his little expedition (consisting of Hoover and the cook) broke camp at Placerville and headed for the High Sierras southwest of Lake Tahoe.[76] Here, in the Pyramid Peak district (thirty by forty miles square), Hoover spent the rest of the summer assisting Lindgren in studying glaciation and in mapping the Pyramid Peak sheet. Echo Lake, Fallen Leaf Lake, Mount Tallac, and other landmarks were their haunts.[77]

It was rugged territory, including "the roughest country that God or man ever saw."[78] And living conditions were not exactly luxurious. At one point Hoover wrote to Professor Branner:

> Kindly pardon this horrible effort, but remember that I sit astride a log and write on one knee with 63 big black ants pasturing on my epidermis and have to listen to the delightful bellow of the calf who likes our barley.
>
> We use five horses, have a *cook*, the most important man in the party, about 5:30 at night. Have Ham and Boston Baked beans and buckwheat cakes instead of sowbelly and cornbread. Sleep on the ground—away ahead of an Arkansas bed. . . .[79]

But he was learning a great deal—"getting a whole jug full of experience"[80]—and pleasing Dr. Lindgren, besides. "Never have I had a more satisfactory assistant," Lindgren declared in later life. The geologist was struck by Hoover's eagerness to learn, his precision in recording his data, and his "keen instinct" for solving problems in the simplest manner.[81] At first Hoover received twenty dollars a month as the geologist's assistant; later Lindgren raised it to thirty for each of the final two months of the expedition.[82]

Because of Lindgren's delays in getting underway in July, his field work had fallen behind schedule. Hoover therefore wrote to Dr. Branner on September 2 of his decision to remain in the Sierras at Lindgren's invitation until October 1. It would mean, however, that he would miss the first three weeks of the fall semester. Since this apparently violated a university rule requiring complete attendance during the senior year, he asked Branner to "fix it somehow."[83] Later in the month Branner thanked Lindgren for giving Hoover an opportunity to serve as his assistant: ". . . I'm confident that he is as faithful and hardworking a man as one can find."[84] Lindgren enthusiastically agreed: ". . . he is as you say a faithful and hardworking man and has done very well indeed this summer; I have been very glad to have had his assistance for I could not have finished this sheet without efficient help."[85]

As it turned out, Hoover did not return to the campus until October 14, more than five weeks late.[86] But he had ample reason to be happy, as he confided to a friend:

> Learnd much and am better morally, physically & financially than 6 months ago. . . . Pleased the cheif some and am in consequence sceduled to return to the U S Geol Survey June 1st 1895. The position to be perminent in all probability. Salary—if perminent—$1200.00 a year to start.[87]

Furthermore, Stanford awarded him eight hours of academic credit for his summer's labors.[88]

I V

STANFORD UNIVERSITY had grown substantially in three years; in
1894–95 its enrollment exceeded one thousand.[89] Self-confident and determined, Hoover, now treasurer of the student community, concentrated on
his new duties. Instituting a voucher system that he had learned while assisting Dr. Lindgren, he strove to establish efficiency where chaos had previously reigned.[90] According to Lawrie Tatum's 1894 report to the court back
in Iowa, he was "frugal, industrious, and energetic."[91] These were precisely
the qualities he now showed.

Hoover soon let it be known that from now on, every expenditure must
be justified; every disbursement must be documented. The story is told that
one day a football player informed Hoover that he needed new football shoes.
"Let's see your shoes," the treasurer replied. After examining the pair Hoover declared, "What you need is a pair of new laces," and authorized them
instead.[92] Such a response was unlikely to win many friends. But Hoover
was not interested in popularity. He wanted order—and influence.

Not everyone on campus was pleased by his relentless insistence on strict
accounting and scrupulous attention to detail.[93] Perhaps this was why in
November 1894 the *Daily Palo Alto*, in response to "numerous inquiries,"
published a lengthy explanation of the new constitution. Among other things,
the newspaper pointed out that the treasurer "receives all incomes from games,
annual dues, etc., directly, and with the advice of the president advances
such sums to managers as exigencies may require." Furthermore, no athletic
manager could contract a debt exceeding five hundred dollars without the
approval of the treasurer and president of the Associated Students.[94]

If any opposition did manifest itself, Hoover seems not to have noticed.
On October 30 he published his first financial report in the student newspaper. It revealed the distressing fact that the student body was more than
$1,200 in debt, including $550 still outstanding from the previous three years.
No wonder, he remarked, that the student body had "an unenviable reputation for careless financiering."[95] Further research disclosed that the old debts
totaled at least six hundred dollars.[96] Throughout the fall and winter months
Hoover arranged to pay off these accumulated liabilities and to rationalize
student finances. Football "absorbs everything—all my time," he wrote to a
friend in November.[97] Frequently he traveled off-campus. He accompanied
the football team on some of its trips, made arrangements for the "Big Game"
against Berkeley at Thanksgiving, and even went to Los Angeles at Christmas for the football contests against the University of Chicago and another
club.[98] Often his balance sheets and reports appeared on the front page of
the *Daily Palo Alto*.[99]

Before Christmas Hoover was able to announce that the Associated Students organization was "a solvent body, the first time since its birth," a statement that earned the student newspaper's encomium for the "business acumen

of the treasurer."[100] When in January Hoover produced an elaborate report for the football season showing a substantial surplus, another student journal editorialized:

> For the first time in the history of Stanford athletics an itemized account of all receipts and expenditures of the football season has been rendered. It was a pleasant surprise to read Treasurer Hoover's report in the *Daily Palo Alto*. His books have been kept in a business-like way and are thrown open to the students, something before unheard of. . . . Treasurer Hoover is to be highly commended for the precedent he has established.[101]

The system that Hoover inaugurated remained virtually unchanged for years.[102]

Since Hoover received no salary as treasurer, it was necessary to scrape up an income from other sources. By the beginning of Hoover's senior year Lawrie Tatum's guardianship fund had diminished to a mere $12.74.[103] During his senior year Hoover undoubtedly earned some money as Professor Branner's assistant. A campus lecture and concert bureau that he and some other friends operated also helped to tide him over.[104]

For all his activism Hoover continued to be somewhat introverted, a kind of "impersonal force" with a "surface repression," as a Stanford friend once put it.[105] Years later many Stanford alumni of those pioneer days still retained an image of him as slightly stooped and diffident, with a tendency to avert his gaze. Some noticed his habit of thrusting his hands in his pockets and jingling his change.[106] When Will Irwin was injured playing football, the student treasurer came to his room to determine the cost of the plaster cast. Although Irwin felt that Hoover was sympathetic, Hoover did not at first utter a word of commiseration; this sort of demonstrativeness did not come easily. Irwin never forgot how, as he left, Hoover "jerked out" the words "I'm sorry."[107]

Yet Hoover was not all aloofness and reticence. His few surviving letters from this period reveal a good-humored, active personality. If not naturally gregarious, he nevertheless impressed many friends. According to Irwin, Hoover participated willingly in his share of the "rushes," practical jokes, and pranks of the high-spirited student community.[108] Behind the mask, in fact, was a clever mind. One night he and some friends decided to race around the oval track in the darkness to determine who was the fastest. When the contest was over Hoover had easily won. His friends were amazed. Back in the dorm he cheerfully divulged the secret of his success. At the start he had deliberately dropped behind, crossed the infield, and placidly waited at the finish line. His comrades gleefully rewarded his "victory" by throwing him in the shower.[109]

Early in his senior year an unexpected influence entered Herbert Hoover's life: a freshman named Lou Henry enrolled in the Geology program at Stanford. It was unusual, if not unprecedented, for a woman to select such a field of study. Hoover became interested in this tall, lithe, athletic young woman who so easily defied the conventions of the time. The more he became acquainted with her in laboratory work, field trips, and social gatherings, the more impressed he became.

It turned out that Lou Henry had been born in Waterloo, Iowa—only seventy miles from West Branch—in March 1874. Ten years later she had migrated to California with her parents and sister Jean because it was feared that her mother had tuberculosis. Since 1890 the family had lived in Monterey, where her father was a successful banker. Lacking a son, Charles Henry had raised his daughter Lou to be an outdoor woman, proficient at horseback riding, camping, fishing, and marksmanship. They had taken strenuous hikes together in the hills.

In 1893 Lou graduated from San Jose Normal School (now San Jose State University) in preparation for a career as a teacher. During the following year she was assistant cashier of her father's bank and then a third-grade schoolteacher in Monterey. But then one of those chance events occurred that change the course of a life. She heard Professor Branner deliver an extension lecture on geology; it inspired her enormously. Swiftly she determined to enter Stanford and study with this gifted teacher. By the second semester of her freshman year, she and the student body treasurer were more than casual friends.[110]

Hoover was a big man on campus now and enjoying himself thoroughly. Honors and influence were coming his way. "I have vertually control of affairs," he wrote a friend in November, "and am making a hard effort to pay of[f] our old indebtedness of $600.00 & conduct the present foot-ball season successfully."[111] He was in the thick of efforts to reform the management of the campus Co-op store.[112] In January 1895 he was elected president of the Geological Club for the second semester. In January also, he left the campus for a few days on a trip to Yuba County to complete some Geological Survey work left undone the summer before.[113] In mid-January he was nominated to be class of '95 treasurer but declined.[114]

At some point early in his senior year (or possibly at the end of his junior year) Herbert Hoover, "barbarian" leader, was even invited to become a member of the Stanford chapter of the Sigma Alpha Epsilon fraternity. Apparently this offer was momentarily tempting, for he "gave it some consideration" and may have accepted briefly. After thinking it over, however, and possibly at the urging of his friends, Hoover decided not to abandon the ranks of his associates and supporters. And so a "barb" he remained.[115]

But now, at mid-year, crisis loomed, the consequence of too much whirl. Not only had Hoover missed the first five weeks of classes; in November he acknowledged that his time-consuming treasurer's work was "a bigger job than I bargained for." Already Professor Branner had warned him that he "must quit at the end of the semester and go to studying." "You may be able to Graduate all right," said Branner, "but we are not turning out A.B.'s but Geologists."[116] When the first term's grades came in, they were a disaster: he had flunked German outright and had been "conditioned" in his two other courses. In short, he received no credit for an entire semester.[117]

To salvage the situation, Hoover, with faculty approval, registered for eighteen hours of courses in the second semester, including nineteenth-century history, personal hygiene, ethics, and three courses in geology.[118] In addition, he strove to eliminate the conditions that he had just incurred. It no doubt took some buckling down, but in the end he passed.[119]

Only one obstacle—the nemesis of his undergraduate career—remained. Despite several attempts he had not yet removed his entrance "condition" in the English language.[120] Professor Anderson of the English department insisted that no student should graduate unless he or she could demonstrate the ability to write accurate English. Unfortunately, Hoover's spelling and punctuation were still noticeably irregular.[121] What had been a nagging requirement was assuming ominous proportions. Finally, just a few days before graduation, Professor J. P. Smith, from whom Hoover had taken courses in mineralogy and paleontology, came to his rescue. He handed Hoover a course paper which Hoover had submitted to him some time before, a paper which, in content, was satisfactory. He instructed Hoover to rewrite it with meticulous attention to spelling, grammar, and punctuation. When Hoover returned, Smith corrected and refined the paper thoroughly, had Hoover recopy it, and then confronted the head of the English department with the finished product. The English professor accepted it as adequate evidence of improvement and Hoover was duly passed in English composition. Without Smith's assistance Hoover probably would not have received his diploma.[122]

Somehow during these waning weeks of college Hoover found time for a final burst of extracurricular activities. With Lou Henry at his side he attended the Junior Hop in April.[123] When he ran short of cash for the Senior Ball, he borrowed $7.50 from Theodore, who had just moved to the Bay Area.[124] Hoover did not miss a single major social event that spring—becoming, in his words, "quite a social swell." And all the while, as student body treasurer, he "ran baseball field athletics and did about as much politics as ever."[125] He helped the "barbs" sweep the campus elections in the spring.[126]

Early in his senior year he privately told a friend that he favored a salary for the treasurer of the Associated Students.[127] Shortly before he graduated, the student body amended the constitution so that the treasurer would henceforth be a postgraduate who would receive a monthly salary. Hoover supported the change. But when he was nominated for another term he declined, probably because he did not plan to be on campus in the coming year. Instead, his friend Lester Hinsdale was elected.[128]

By graduation Hoover had earned a reputation as a student politician, skilled at behind-the-scenes maneuvering and calculation. He found himself humorously memorialized in the class yearbook. Under a picture of Hoover, Zion, and Collins, clad in olive wreaths and togas, appeared these words:

> We are the great triumvirate,
> The awful Trinity of Fate.
> On things scholastic or athletic
> We speak with utterance prophetic.
> This place, we Three, by love inspired,
> Have scientifically wired;
> And so (our motives all the best)
> When an election comes, with zest
> We press the buttons and do the rest.[129]

In four years Stanford University had done much for Herbert Hoover. It had trained him in geology and brought him into rewarding association with several distinguished scientists, particularly John C. Branner and Waldemar Lindgren. Since Stanford used the pass / fail grading system it is impossible to determine precisely Hoover's record in his major. He was certainly a capable, although probably not a brilliant, student. One of his professors, C. D. Marx, later told an interviewer that while Hoover was a good student, he was not preeminent, and was distinguished more for his "first class executive ability" than for intellectual achievement.[130]

But that he was able, resourceful, and ambitious, no one denied. "Do your work so that they notice it and be on the job all the time." It was this quality that had first impressed Dr. Branner about his young office assistant: when he asked Hoover to accomplish something, Hoover did so quickly and quietly, without fuss and bother.[131] "It was characteristic of him," Branner once remarked, "that when a task was set before him he took off his coat, fixed his whole attention on the task in hand, and went at it, and did it."[132] There is a story that one day in the lab Dr. Branner overheard some students grumbling about "Hoover's luck." Branner immediately admonished them, contrasting their behavior with Hoover's ability to get things done. Hoover, he exclaimed, had not enjoyed "luck"; he had received "reward."[133]

Stanford University had done even more for Herbert Hoover. It had inculcated in him an ethos of adventurousness, resourcefulness, and buoyant idealism, an ethos that fit well with his determination to succeed. It had reinforced, in secular terms, the lessons of his Quaker relatives: that one should live productively, that life is meant for accomplishment, that one ought to do a "conscientious work." To the assembled Pioneers of the class of '95 at commencement, President David Starr Jordan invoked such themes. Men and women, he said, "are judged by achievements, not by dreams." "The highest value of tradition lies in the making of it; the noblest wealth is the wealth of promise. . . . In helpfulness alone can wealth or power find consecration."[134] For at least one senior in the audience the message had enduring impact.

Above all, Stanford University had offered the Iowa-born orphan an opportunity—a gift he never forgot. In that self-reliant, pioneering community in the making, created on a ranch by a self-made man and dedicated to the ideal of useful service, Hoover grew and thrived and found warmth. It was an exhilarating environment, and it made an indelible imprint. His alma mater became, in Will Irwin's apt phrase, "a kind of complex" with Hoover.[135] For the rest of his life, wherever he roamed or resided, Stanford University was his home.

The night before he graduated, he and other friends joined in singing "In the Cold, Cold World," a song by his poetical classmate Charles K. Field.[136] But Hoover was not a man to indulge for long in sentimental backward glances. In April Waldemar Lindgren had informed Professor Branner that he thought he could obtain a vacation job for Hoover with one of the U.S. Geological Survey's field parties.[137] On May 29, 1895 Hoover received his A.B. degree in Geology from Stanford University. After visiting a few days with a friend, he prepared to spend another summer with Lindgren in the Sierras.[138]

4

A California
Apprenticeship

I

O n August 10, 1895 Herbert Hoover turned twenty-one and ceased to be the ward of Lawrie Tatum.[1] During the summer Hoover assisted Lindgren in studying and mapping part of the Gold Belt of California for a massive publication by the U.S. Geological Survey. It was rugged outdoor work which took them from icy Sierra peaks to the scorching deserts of western Nevada. By the end of the season they completed a "reconnaisance" of two hundred square miles of the Sierraville sheet and five hundred square miles of the Carson and Markleville sheets.[2] Parts of the Reno, Truckee, and Colfax sheets, along with several mines, were examined as well.[3] In mid-summer Hoover received an increase in salary; his earnings, combined with Theodore's in Oakland, now totaled $175 per month.[4]

In such surroundings Stanford University seemed far, far away. Early in July Hoover mused to a friend: "From quiet Palo Alto with its live oak spotted meadows and its best of people to the jagged grandeur of the High Sierra with its dregs of humanity. But this is life—the other was happiness."[5] He told his sister May that the resort village of Tallac on the shore of Lake Tahoe was "a much bragged about place," but that "the best I can say for it is that its surrounding atmosphere would energize an Egyptian mummy and give him an appetite like a Florida Alligator. . . ." Unfortunately, the hotel's menu was quite inadequate for a hungry geologist: "Pattée-fois-de grás avèc un morcéau du pain au parté was built for the swell cashiers wives who stop here and walk to the wharf when they get anxious to do some mountaineering."[6] As for the landscape between Carson City and Mono Lake, "Camping on the Nevada desert is not what its said to be for if the Good Lord made a few Trial Hades before the completion of the final resort he must have had his Experiment Stations N of Mono Lake."[7]

On another occasion, when one of the teamsters in the party quit his job, Hoover "had to drive four gov. mules to a buckboard over the worst road ever made, slept at Donner Lake one night (Place where the Donner party gave up the ghost) it froze ¾ inch ice, had neuralgia in one jaw and a general bad humor that kept those 4 mules pretty well on the jump."[8]

And yet, in truth, Hoover was happy that summer. His work, for all its hardships, was satisfying and the environment "almost intoxicating." Nothing could compare with the splendor of the Sierras. At one point he climbed an 11,000-foot mountain peak simply "to drink in the view of my old friend Lake Tahoe . . . the most beautiful lake on earth." The scene evoked in him a cascade of youthful prose. "Giant peaks" rising beyond the lake resembled "buttresses and turrets from a great wall, ther sides splashed with snow." "Giant palisades" with "sharp Gothic pinnacles" made his nerves "tingle with awe." He watched a mountain snowstorm: "great whorls" of snow and mist attacked the rocky "battlements spreading their fleeces over turret and crest. . . ."[9] It was exhilarating, unforgettable, and sublime.

What arduous work in stunning mountain scenery did not provide in the way of excitement for a young scientist, frontier revelry and horses did. One night at a dance in a mining camp, Hoover reported, two men "were shot in royal mining style and the dancers . . . danced on and on as if nothing had happened the blood smeared over the floor became slippery then sticky and finally brown again. I did not dance. I am timid about arguments on a six shooter basis."[10] Ornery horses—including a "diabolically wicked bronco" named Napoleon von Sandow[11]—added to Hoover's discomforts as he hiked on horseback through the mountains. Eventually he concluded that "a horse was one of the original mistakes of creation."[12]

As if rambunctious equines were not trouble enough, one morning Lindgren's Geological Survey party discovered that one of its pack mules was dead. Inspection revealed that the animal had been scratching its head with its hind foot and had caught the calk of its hind shoe in the halter rope around its neck. Jerking back, the mule had broken its neck. As disbursing officer for the party, Hoover dutifully prepared a required affidavit to explain this loss of valuable government property. Eventually a distressing message came back from Washington: Hoover's account had been rejected, and one month's salary had been deducted from his pay. The government did not believe that mules could scratch their heads with their hind feet. Lindgren thereupon reimbursed Hoover for the loss and vowed to collect it from "some d——— bureaucrat" in Washington the next winter. He never did; the incident was proof, he later said, of "the dumbness of bureaucracy."[13]

Life as a government geologist, then, was rarely uninteresting. "Don't worry about anything happening to me," Hoover told his sister with characteristically dry humor, "for we always leave definitely with hotel clerks the route we expect to travel during the day with explicit directions as to what use is to be made of the corpse."[14]

As the summer of 1895 wore on, Hoover faced an increasingly pressing question: what would he do when autumn came and work in the Sierras ended for the season? His prospects a year before for a permanent position with the Survey after graduation were now uncertain. Summer work with Lindgren would end on October 1, he told his sister May during the summer, although, he added, "I have some good chances then I think."[15] When a friend informed him of some kind of opening at the University of Oregon, he acknowledged that he would "very much like to have it," but doubted that he could obtain the job without political influence in Oregon.[16]

Instead, in early September, he disclosed his plans to a correspondent:

I shall not return to Stanford. I am going to work at the mines in Nevada City [California] at the expiration of this work and hope to get a fellowship in Geology at Columbia or John[s] Hopkins the year following. I am trying to make a specialty of mining geology for it offers the widest field.[17]

Because of a cut in federal appropriations, Hoover's hope for continued work with the Survey was lost.[18]

Passing through the Nevada City region in mid-September while still working with Lindgren, Hoover met an unemployed Stanford classmate and fellow fledgling geologist, E. B. Kimball. The two headed north to Forest City and American Hill, where for six days Kimball assisted Hoover in resurveying the local topography and correcting the mistakes of their predecessors. Lindgren was pleased that Hoover had been able to save him the trouble of calling in a professional topographer. No longer was his assistant the "pale and slender" student he had first met a year before. In Lindgren's appreciative eyes, Hoover had become a "full size" geologist capable of doing independent work.[19]

As it turned out, Hoover remained with Lindgren until October 15. On that day he made a final entry in his field notebook, took leave of the U.S. Geological Survey, and headed for Nevada City, fifty miles northeast of Sacramento: forty-niner country, gold-mining country, in the foothills of the High Sierras.[20]

I I

I N the 1890s Nevada County was the principal gold-mining county of California. The auriferous Grass Valley belt near Nevada City—home of the

North Star, Empire, and other famous mines—was particularly rich.[21] It was a logical place for a young geologist seeking experience (and cash) to hunt for a job.[22]

For a short time Hoover stayed at Nevada City's National Hotel.[23] At first he sought a white-collar staff position commensurate with his college education.[24] His efforts failed, and Hoover learned, as he later put it, "the bitter despair that comes to men from ceaseless hunting for a job only to be turned away time after time."[25] Too many men, too few jobs.[26] Moreover, the practical mining men of the Grass Valley district were skeptical about the value of a person with a college diploma.[27] He would have to lower his sights.

Finally opportunity smiled wanly through the shadows. Hoover obtained a job pushing an ore car on the night shift in the lower levels of the Reward mine in Grass Valley.[28] After his experienced mate loaded a cart, Hoover shoved it along the damp, dark tunnel to the vertical mine shaft, there to be lifted to the surface. It was grimy, monotonous labor: ten hours a night, seven days a week, for a daily wage of two dollars, he later recollected.[29] A man could not start any lower on the ladder.

After a few weeks, Hoover obtained employment at another well-known mine, the Mayflower, in the Nevada City district.[30] Nevada County in those days was a center for immigrants from the mining county of Cornwall, England.[31] Among these "Cousin Jacks," as they were called, Hoover mingled and worked, and from them he learned the rudiments of mining. Cornish "hard-rock men" like Ed Gassaway (his partner at the Reward) and Tommy Ninnis (his shift foreman at the Mayflower) taught him the difference between a "gad" and a "moil," the use of a drill, and such useful tricks as "how to warm up the bottom of an iron wheel barrow with three stub candles so that it would be more comfortable sleeping during midnight lunch hour."[32] Ninnis later declared that he "learned Bert Hoover everything he knew about mining."[33]

Perhaps it was during his sojourn in Nevada County that Hoover heard the tale of a merchant in the village of Michigan Bluffs who gave away an expensive stock of provisions to an injured prospector living alone in a shack in the hills. The incident had occurred during the Gold Rush days of the early 1850s; Hoover made it the subject of a short story that appeared in a Stanford University magazine in January 1896. This literary effort was his first publication; he entitled it "And their Deeds are Remembered After Them." The philanthropic storekeeper, Hoover revealed, was Leland Stanford.[34]

Hoover worked in the Grass Valley district for about two months, rooming with his Stanford classmate Kimball in a home on Pioneer Hill in Nevada City.[35] From here he tramped regularly through the mud to the mines.[36] Around Christmas 1895, or perhaps a little later, Hoover began to grow restless. In his *Memoirs* he later recorded that he had saved some money and that the holiday season seemed like a good time to move on.[37] Elsewhere he wrote that he had worked in the mines for the experience and that by February 1896 he "had had enough experience on this line."[38] Whatever his primary motivation, a desire to escape the dead-end drudgery of underground labor probably entered into his calculations. He later told a friend that he felt his education had prepared him for something better in life than competing with a mule.[39] Experience was fine, and income a necessity, but Hoover had never intended to become a miner.[40]

At the suggestion of a mining engineer named George Hoffmann, Hoover decided to try for a position with Louis Janin.[41] Waldemar Lindgren had once introduced him to this man,[42] and Hoover undoubtedly knew his reputation. Louisiana-born, educated at the prestigious mining academy in Freiburg, Germany, and experienced from the Rockies to Japan, Louis Janin was one of the most eminent mining engineers in the American West.[43] Furthermore, he was known for helping younger, less-experienced men to establish themselves in their profession.[44] To obtain employment with Janin was to open a path to future success. Hoover did not hesitate for long in Nevada City. Late in 1895 or early in 1896, after two to four months (at most) in the California goldfields, he boarded a train for San Francisco and a meeting with Janin.

III

Louis Janin's office was at 202 Sansome Street, over the Anglo-California bank.[45] A portly, sophisticated man now nearly sixty years old, with something of a reputation as a bon vivant,[46] Janin invited his young job seeker to a sumptuous lunch at his club. Here (according to Hoover's later version of the story) he explained that he had no vacancies for professional staff, either in San Francisco or at any of the mines with which he was affiliated. Perhaps to drive the point home, he remarked that the only opening of any kind was that of a copyist in his office. Immediately Hoover seized the opportunity, disclosed that he knew how to type, and requested the appointment. As Hoover later recounted the story, "Mr. Janin seemed startled, but he laughed and I was hired."[47] His initial salary was meager, perhaps nothing. According to one of his later recollections, he proposed to Janin that he enter the office "without payment,"[48] so anxious was he to gain an entrée. His friend Lester Hinsdale later described the job as essentially that of an office boy.[49] But at least his foot was in the door.

Hoover soon had a dramatic opportunity to demonstrate his usefulness. Early in 1896 Janin was retained as an expert witness for the defendant in a notable lawsuit between two mines in Grass Valley.[50] At issue were complex questions of apex law, the source of endless litigation in the mining West. In such cases the scientific testimony of authoritative witnesses was crucial, and Janin's advice was frequently sought by contesting parties.[51] In the case at hand, Janin's new office assistant was able to contribute significantly. Hoover was no doubt familiar with Waldemar Lindgren's specialized field examination of the geology of these very mines in 1894, the results of which were just then being prepared for publication. He was therefore well equipped to assist Janin in preparing elaborate geologic maps, demonstration slides, and other technical data essential to the case of the defendant, the North Star Mining Company.[52]

A little over two weeks before the circuit court delivered its verdict, Hoover had the satisfaction of publishing a relevant technical article on "crossings" at the North Star Mine in the *Mining and Scientific Press*. It was his first professional publication.[53] In the article Hoover took issue with one of the opposition's geological claims in the still-unsettled lawsuit. Coincidentally or not, on March 16, 1896, the court held for North Star, Janin's client. As a reward for his services Hoover received his first "engineering fee."[54]

His position with Janin was now secure. The day after the court's verdict was announced, Stanford University's student newspaper reported that Hoover had been "promoted to membership" in Janin's firm "in recognition of his recent services in experting some mining properties."[55] By early April the young engineer was earning the satisfying sum of seven dollars a day plus expenses.[56] During the next few months the older man sent his young assistant on numerous forays throughout the Southwest to evaluate mines and prospects. Hoover's talents as a "mine scout" were exceptional. Janin told his son that he never met a man who could survey a mine as quickly as Hoover.[57]

In the spring of 1896 Janin dispatched his aide to New Mexico to serve as assistant to the manager of the newly formed Steeple Rock Development Company, controlled by a British corporate client of Janin's. The firm operated the Carlisle Mine in western Grant County, a few miles from the Arizona border.[58] If the Sierra Nevadas had sometimes seemed to Hoover like the "wild West," New Mexico was rougher still. The hot, arid, dusty desert specked with sage brush was challenging enough. The human environment—Mexican miners, roaring saloons, gambling dens, brawling men in search of gold—added ample spice to anyone's life. When the mine manager had to enforce the law, he used an abandoned mine shaft for a jail.[59] Hoover himself may have carried a revolver and a rifle, but if he did, there is no evidence that he ever used them, except, perhaps, to shoot rattlesnakes.[60]

Hoover's principal responsibility in the Steeple Rock district was to survey, inspect, and sample his company's properties.[61] But each day was unpredictable. On a trip to the Mogollon Mountains thirty miles north of Steeple Rock to study some mining prospects, Hoover and a companion suddenly encountered a little camp of grizzled prospectors. One, stretched out on a blanket, was dying. Lacking medicine, Hoover could do little except honor the dying man's request to write to his girl friend back East. And when the body was lowered into a makeshift grave, the grieving men drafted Hoover to lead an improvised funeral service, right there in the forlorn and empty hills.[62]

One day while in New Mexico Hoover received a letter that abruptly forced him to make a fundamental decision about his career. Lindgren was at last able to offer him a permanent appointment with the United States Geological Survey.[63] It was a tempting offer. A year-and-a-half earlier Hoover had hoped for such a position.[64] The previous September he had indicated his desire to pursue graduate studies in geology at Columbia or Johns Hopkins. For a man who had aspired to be a geologist, what better entry into the field could there be than as a protégé of Dr. Lindgren?

And yet, here he was at Steeple Rock, already an assistant manager of a mining company, already ascending to responsibility as a protégé of Louis Janin. On the other hand, he had neither formal schooling nor a degree in mining engineering as such. Would this not be an obstacle to future advancement? Which course should he choose: pure science or applied science? The profession of geologist or the profession of mining engineer?

Perplexed and hesitant, Hoover sought advice from his old patron, Dr. Branner.[65] In late April the professor sent his reply:

> I am glad to see openings of any kind for you, but I don't like to see you crowded too much just now. When one becomes connected with large interests of any kind nowadays, he has to live on the jump as it were, for such interests, if they are successful, are well organized and run like big machines. The man who looks after his employer's interests in such an organization is often promoted rapidly, while the one who doesn't enter into the spirit of the work is soon dropped out. The fact that you have been given places of responsibility shows that you are quite up to the work, and that your continued promotion is assured. And promotion under such circumstances, and in the employ of such financiers may lead to as good a position as there is in the mining engineering line.
>
> You see which way my advice is leaning. One of the troubles with a U.S.G.S. place is that you can never know when it will end. . . . it is a considerable risk for one who *must* have bread and butter. We usually content ourselves also with taking "glory" as part of our pay, for the cash salary is always small. . . .

Branner did not think Hoover should abandon "scientific geology" completely. He urged him to publish scholarly articles and thereby maintain a reputation "as a geologist as well as a mining engineer." Branner also sought to allay Hoover's apparent doubts about his ability to succeed in his new field: "As for the engineering problems, look as far ahead as you can and remember that they are mainly mathematical problems in their scientific features, and problems of experience in their practical bearings. If you anticipate any hitches on any subjects just write me as long ahead as you can." If Branner could not help Hoover, he would consult his faculty colleagues at Stanford for advice. In short, despite his own commitment to a life of scholarship, Branner counseled Hoover to "stay where you are, and Dr. Jordan thinks as I do about it."[66]

Hoover accepted Branner's advice and remained with Louis Janin. It was a turning point in his career.[67]

Hoover had ample reason in the months ahead to confirm Branner's remarks about the life style of an employee of "large interests." He was indeed living "on the jump"—all over the Southwest. One of the results of his sampling work in New Mexico was to establish that "some curious business" had occurred in the sale of the Carlisle Mine.[68] With fraud uncovered and some of the properties proved worthless, Hoover returned to San Francisco.[69] But not for long. Late in the spring of 1896 Janin sent Hoover and another assistant to Colorado to examine some placer mines for a British syndicate.[70] It was probably during this visit that he studied "a proposed hydraulic installation in connection with working some gravel mines in Routt County" in the extreme northwestern part of the state. "This scheme," he recounted afterward, "involved laying out a large ditch system, some 40 miles in length, and the determination of the value of the gravels themselves. The business having been demonstrated infeasible, I again returned to California."[71] During the next several months Hoover spent much of his time at Janin's office in San Francisco, although his schedule was still punctuated by inspection trips to places like Calaveras County, California.[72] During his nearly fifteen months with Janin Hoover also visited Arizona, Nevada, and Wyoming.[73]

Branner's observations about Hoover's chances for speedy advancement were proving to be accurate. By August 1896, after fewer than nine months with Janin, he was earning two thousand dollars a year.[74] Nor did Hoover forget Branner's advice about professional publications. In the ensuing months he placed at least half a dozen essays in the *Mining and Scientific Press* and *Engineering and Mining Journal* on such subjects as the mining geology of Cripple Creek, the mapping of California's Mother Lode, the Four-Mile Placer Mining District in Routt County, Colorado, and the controversial question of debris created by hydraulic mining near the Sacramento River. Several papers were published under his own name; others, anonymously.[75]

Life was yielding other satisfactions, too. In 1896 and early 1897, for the first time in years, the three Hoover children were reunited. Theodore was a linotype operator for the *Oakland Tribune;* May, having come from Oregon, was a student at Berkeley High School. Hoover's cousin Harriette Miles eventually joined them while she attended the state university.[76] At first the Hoovers lived in Oakland; here Herbert registered to vote on his twenty-second birthday, August 10, 1896. His affidavit recorded that he was 5' 9" tall and that his occupation was "mining engineer." A few months later the Hoovers and cousin Harriette took up residence in Berkeley.[77]

These were happy months for the orphaned family; Theodore remembered this period as "the best of my youth." There were parties with Stanford classmates like Collins and Hinsdale, and Sunday excursions to Golden

Gate Park, the Cliff House, and other Bay Area sites.[78] From time to time
Hoover traveled down the peninsula to visit Lou Henry at Stanford; on such
occasions he often slept on the couch in Will Irwin's room in Encina Hall.[79]
He began to find time also for more varied reading to compensate for the
utilitarian emphasis of his college education.[80]

In the winter of 1896–97 there occurred another of those unforeseen events
that helped to establish the frenetic pace and pattern of Hoover's early career.
On December 1 Janin had a conversation with William H. Shockley, an
American mining engineer representing the British firm of Bewick, Moreing
and Company. Later that day Shockley notified his London principals that
they could rely on any recommendations from Louis Janin, whom Shockley
described as a very judicious and capable judge of men.[81]

Bewick, Moreing had extensive interests in the gold-mining interior of
Western Australia near the raw new towns of Coolgardie and Kalgoorlie,
which had sprung up less than five years before. Possibly in response to
Shockley's certification of Janin's credentials, the London firm contacted the
San Francisco mining expert during the winter. It asked him to recommend
for its West Australian staff an American engineer who could undertake mine
examination and exploration work in the "outback." The salary (so the press
reported) would be $5,000 a year.[82]

There was, however, apparently one stipulation: the nominee should be at
least thirty-five years old.[83] Herbert Hoover was not yet twenty-three. But
Janin decided to take a chance and recommended him anyway. When his
surprised assistant expressed doubts about his youth and relative inexperi-
ence, Janin encouraged him and promised to "fix that."[84] Hoover, for his
part, prudently began to grow a mustache and beard. He realized he had
better *look* mature before he reached Australia.[85]

In early March 1897 Janin and Hoover solicited letters of recommendation
that could be forwarded to London. To the distinguished mining engineer
R. A. F. Penrose, Hoover wrote:

> I have been offered, through Mr. Janin, a situation with a strong English
> company in Western Australia. My duties will be the periodic inspection
> of their different mines and reporting on their various conditions and pros-
> pects, and the examination of new properties with view to purchase. . . .
> The fact that you have offered me charge of one of your properties I take
> as evidence of your confidence. . . . The position is a very excellent one,
> commands a good salary with a good chance of progress.[86]

The results of this effort must have been gratifying to Hoover and reassuring
to Janin. Waldemar Lindgren declared that Hoover's work with the Geological Survey was "extremely satisfactory" and that he concurred with Janin's
estimate of Hoover's "industry, integrity and ability."[87] The manager of the
Steeple Rock Development Company in New Mexico judged him a "very

reliable, and trustworthy, and a perfectly competent, and first class Geologist, and Mining Engineer."[88] From Ben S. Cook in Oregon came a testimonial to Hoover's record with the Oregon Land Company.[89]

As the assembled letters made their way to London, Hoover's desire for the Australian job intensified. When Penrose wrote back offering to marshal some "eastern influence" in Hoover's behalf, the young engineer was grateful; "my success," he declared, "depends on my outside (outside of Janin) backing largely."

> The position pays $6000.00 per year and some fees which make it worth $10,000. a year with expenses. But better than that it is a strong company in a confidential position and in a new country. I am therefore anxious to secure it.[90]

By March 20 Hoover's appointment in Australia was settled,[91] and there now followed a few hectic days filled with last-minute preparations: property to sell, a wardrobe to buy, a life insurance policy to arrange.[92] Hoover was acutely conscious of the success that now awaited him and took steps for the handling of his finances. He promised Theodore that he would cable from Australia if he thought he could handle the job. If so, Theodore was to enter Stanford University with Bert's financial backing.[93] On March 24 Hoover signed a formal power of attorney entrusting to his college friend Lester Hinsdale, now a fledgling attorney in San Francisco, such sums as Hoover would send from Australia. This money was to be used either in "the discharge of my debts or in the support and maintenance of my brother Theodore J. Hoover, my sister May Hoover and my cousin Harriet Miles" and also for such investments as Hinsdale thought wise.[94]

That same day the "inspecting engineer" left San Francisco for London, en route to Australia.[95] During his train trip across the United States he stopped briefly in West Branch, Iowa, to visit his relatives and childhood friends.[96] On March 31, 1897 Hoover sailed from New York for Europe on the White Star liner *Brittanic*. The ship's register listed his age as thirty-six.[97]

5

Australia

I

THE journey to London and then to Australia was an immensely stimulating one for a young man of twenty-two. Years later, reflecting on this voyage, Hoover remarked significantly, "History became a reality and America a contrast."[1] It was his first exposure to the world outside the United States, and the impressions lingered long.

Hoover arrived in Liverpool on April 9 and hurried on to London, where he was interviewed by one of the British firm's senior partners, Charles Algernon Moreing.[2] Hoover stayed at Moreing's home and, for a few unforgettable days, was able to explore the capital of the British empire in the year of Queen Victoria's Diamond Jubilee.[3] He reported to Lester Hinsdale that his employers "like my head very much and they were pleased I was no older"—an apparent reference to his lengthening mustache and beard.[4] According to one story, Hoover's British superior, eyeing the supposedly thirty-five-year-old man before him, marveled at how Americans were able to preserve their youth.[5]

Hoover's first encounter with British propriety was disconcerting. He confessed to Hinsdale that he was "a tenderfoot here—get done up at every turn." Everyone seemed to wear silk hats and dress in formal suits after six o'clock, even in hotel lobbies and theaters. "I'm getting to be quite a swell," he remarked.[6] He felt unnerved when a man-servant assigned to him at Moreing's home attended him while he dressed and silently scorned Hoover's meager wardrobe.[7]

During his brief stay in London Hoover applied for membership in the Institution of Mining and Metallurgy and recorded on the application form that he was over twenty-five years old.[8] From England he sent Hinsdale an initial five hundred dollars for the discharge of certain debts and for assistance to his brother and his cousin Harriette. Hoover urged Hinsdale to be especially careful in handling his large life insurance premiums: ninety-three dollars every three months for the next twenty years. For he was going to "a very bad country"; every one of Bewick, Moreing and Company's thirty-six engineers in Australia had contracted typhoid fever. Six of the fifty-three men sent there, in fact, had died of the disease. He told Hinsdale not to mention this "unhealthfulness" to his insurance agent lest he "cancel my permit to travel."[9]

On April 15, 1897 Hoover boarded a vessel at Dover, crossed the English Channel, and traveled by train to Italy, stopping briefly at Paris, Lucerne, and Rome along the way.[10] The trip was "abominable," he reported, but the Alps were magnificent.[11] At Brindisi, in southern Italy, Hoover boarded the R.M.S. *Victoria*.[12] For the next three weeks the ship slowly made its way through the Mediterranean, Suez Canal, Red Sea, and Indian Ocean, with calls at Port Said and Ceylon.[13] Finally, on May 13, Hoover's vessel reached Albany, the port of entry for Western Australia. But because the ship had stopped at Aden, where smallpox had broken out, the passengers were quarantined on an island in the harbor for five tedious days.[14]

Of all the places on earth where men have dug for gold, Western Australia in 1897 must have been the most remote. When Hoover disembarked at Albany he proceeded first to Perth, the small capital city of the colony, and thence by rail 350 miles east to the town of Coolgardie, deep in the inhospitable "outback."[15] In 1896 the empty vastness of Western Australia contained a population of only 138,000, and by century's end, 180,000.[16] Minuscule figures indeed for a political entity of 1,000,000 square miles: one-third of a continent and equal in size to all of the United States east of the Mississippi River. Along the coast rainfall was adequate, but eastward in the interior lay an arid, desolate, seemingly endless, unbelievably level plateau, surprisingly dotted with large open forests of mulga and gum. When the state geologist of Colorado visited the region, he found the landscape "wearisome beyond words": from horizon to horizon, "one dark unbroken sea of trackless bush."[17] It was, as the saying went, "the land of sin, sand, sweat, sorrow, sore eyes, and Sir John Forrest,"[18] Western Australia's strong-willed premier and a man increasingly unpopular on the goldfields.

Since rainfall in the outback was extremely light (Coolgardie received 5.4 inches in all of 1897),[19] the scarcity of water was acute—and sometimes fatal for prospectors. Such water as could be found in salt-lake beds, soaks, wells, and underground in the mines was usually brackish and had to be condensed. It was an expensive process, costing $63.25 per thousand gallons, Hoover informed a friend.[20] In these circumstances, however torrid the heat, one did not often indulge in showers or baths.[21] Hundreds of condensers were set up in the rapidly growing goldfields districts in the 1890s. This equipment was indispensable to survival until the completion of the great water pipeline from the coast in 1903.

What drew men by the thousands to such a harsh and unforgiving land? One thing and one thing only: the addictive lure of gold. While in the late 1880s Western Australia had witnessed a succession of significant rushes, the truly transforming breakthroughs were still to be made. In the Australian winter of 1892 two prospectors named Bayley and Ford discovered rich deposits about 125 miles east of the town of Southern Cross. Near the site of their success a community known as Coolgardie mushroomed into existence. Nine months later, in June 1893, three Irish immigrants—Hannan, Flanagan, and Shea—found alluvial gold twenty-five miles farther northeast. When Paddy Hannan returned alone to Coolgardie to apply for a reward claim, another stampede was on. Within one week two thousand men raced to the scene, "specking" for telltale glitter in the red and dusty soil. Soon a camp called Hannan's or Hannan's Find appeared on the map; in 1895 it officially became the city of Kalgoorlie. Western Australia's fabulous boom years, the "Roaring Nineties," were fully underway.

Despite the deterrent powers of climate and geography, by 1897 the goldfields east of Perth boasted perhaps a third of the entire population of Western Australia. And for all the discomforts of frontier living, the refinements of civilization were penetrating the outback. To overcome the isolation from the coast, the government of the colony constructed railroads that reached both Coolgardie and Kalgoorlie in 1896. Telegraph communication was also established. To satisfy their communities' insatiable appetite for news, a flourishing and outspoken press sprang up, including the *Kalgoorlie Miner*, *Coolgardie Miner*, and *Coolgardie Pioneer*. By 1896 Coolgardie, with a population of about 8,000, had two morning newspapers, one evening newspaper, and four weeklies. Even the tiny settlements to the north produced their own publications.

Gradually dwellings made of burlap bags and corrugated iron gave way to more permanent structures. In 1898 Coolgardie had twenty-six hotels, fourteen churches, several dozen stores, and numerous other businesses. To the east the twin cities of Kalgoorlie and Boulder were also thriving and soon displaced Coolgardie as the metropolis of the goldfields. By the beginning of 1898 they had attained a combined population of approximately 20,000. In 1897 an impressive stone edifice known as the Palace Hotel was erected at Kalgoorlie. Kalgoorlie became known for its remarkably wide streets—wide, it is said, because camels will not back up and must have ample space in which to make a U-turn.

The goldfields communities of Western Australia were overwhelmingly a man's world. At the turn of the century no more than a third of their inhabitants were women; in some of the smaller settlements, scarcely one in ten.

It was a world of races and other athletic events, copiously reported in the press; a world of stock exchanges, clubs, banquets, processions, and mass meetings to protest the policies of the despised government in Perth. Alcohol consumption was heavy, yet violence was rare. Most of the inhabitants of Coolgardie, Kalgoorlie, and the districts around them were Australians: either "t'othersiders" from the eastern colonies or native West Australians derisively nicknamed "sandgropers." But mingling among them were promoters from Great Britain, mining engineers from America, camel drivers from Afghanistan, prospectors from all over Europe, and even prostitutes from Japan. It was in its way a cosmopolitan little world. Golden Westralia! Not even heat, dust storms, or typhoid fever could stifle the pervasive optimism and the dreams of striking it rich.[22]

I I

THIS was the society that Hoover quietly entered in May 1897 when he reported to Bewick, Moreing's headquarters in Coolgardie. Two local newspapers took notice of his arrival by printing identical stories, possibly a press release issued by Hoover's employer or Hoover himself:

> Mr. H. C. Hoover takes the position as manager in Coolgardie for Bewick, Moreing, and Co., lately vacated by H. P. Woodward. Mr. Hoover was for two years geologist on United States geological survey in mining districts in Colorado and California. He afterwards had the management of various mines in California, Arizona, and New Mexico. Latterly he has been assistant to Louis Janin in San Francisco, who ranks among the leading consulting engineers in the United States. Mr. Hoover has had considerable experience in the occurrence and handling of tellurides in Colorado.[23]

A few weeks later a newspaper in Kalgoorlie, where complex tellurides of gold had been discovered, observed that Hoover's "wide knowledge obtained in the treatment of such ores in Colorado, should render him of great service to the mining industry generally. . . ." Hoover, the paper said, had left "a highly responsible position on the staff of Louis Janin and Co., who are deservedly placed in the front rank of mining men of the United States, being engineers of world-wide reputation. . . ." Moreover, he had "conducted with highly satisfactory results" various "mining undertakings" in three states, including "the development of the 'London Exploration' Company's mines" in the Steeple Rock district of New Mexico.[24]

These accounts of Hoover's American experience were somewhat inaccurate. His work with the U.S. Geological Survey lasted essentially for two summers, not two years, and was confined to California and western Nevada. While he did assist the superintendent of the Steeple Rock Development

Company and was offered a managerial position by R. A. F. Penrose, he had
not served as the sole manager of any American property. Nor is he known
to have had any direct acquaintance at this point with tellurides; his work in
Colorado involved only a dredging effort in the Four-Mile Placer district. On
the other hand, in 1896 he published in the *Mining and Scientific Press* a synopsis of a report by two other men on the "mining geology" of Cripple Creek;
this article did refer to tellurides.[25] And by coincidence one of Hoover's
fellow passengers from Brindisi to Western Australia was an eminent European mining engineer and expert on tellurides, Modest Maryanski, from whom
Hoover may have learned something about tellurides.[26] If Hoover himself
was not a specialist on the subject, he was at least familiar with the challenge
the baffling compound posed for the mining companies at Kalgoorlie.

It is not known whether the press, Hoover's company, or the American
engineer himself was the source of these inaccuracies. Perhaps Hoover, anxious to establish his authority in a tough, demanding environment, overstated his qualifications. Certainly he was sensitive about his age.[27] But his
actual background and ability were impressive enough, and it was not long
before he made his mark on the goldfields.

There was ample need for men of Hoover's training and temperament in
Western Australia by 1897. The discoveries of the early 1890s had unleashed
a sensational speculative boom financed increasingly by British capital.
Between 1894 and 1897 several hundred companies were registered and floated
in London to provide money for exploitation of Westralian mines. By one
count, 780 such companies had been formed by December 1896.[28] While the
nominal capital was huge (perhaps £70,000,000 by mid-1897), only a fraction
ever reached the mines; the rest evidently disappeared into the pockets of
promoters, vendors, and speculators.[29] Mark Twain is supposed to have
defined a mine as "a hole in the ground with a liar on top." The goldfields in
the mid-Nineties were swarming with boomers, unblinking optimists, glad-
handing "Champagne Charlies," glib and not always honest promoters, and
men who thought they were mining experts—or pretended to be.

But optimism alone could not suffice. At the end of 1897 a leading mining
journal analyzed the sobering statistics: of 503 London-based Westralian gold-
mining companies in existence, only thirty-three had paid any dividends
whatsoever. If one excluded the thirteen exploration and promotion companies among them, only twenty bona fide mines in Western Australia had
actually distributed dividends, and three-quarters of these payments emanated from just three mines. Not without reason, the journal complained
about "enormous overcapitalization."[30] By 1901, 82 percent of the London-
registered West Australian companies established by the end of 1896 had
disappeared.[31]

Still, gold production in the colony was rising steadily: from 281,265 ounces
in 1896 to nearly 675,000 ounces in 1897 and more than a million ounces a
year later. Moreover, nearly half of it was coming from Kalgoorlie.[32] What

was happening? The initial stimulus to development of the eastern goldfields had been the presence of alluvial gold on or near the surface: "poor man's gold" that individual prospectors could easily extract, using simple techniques of crushing and dry-blowing. Throughout most of the 1890s alluvial mining flourished, reaching a climax of importance in 1898.

It was becoming evident, however, that the future of the fields lay in a very different form of mining. In the mid-Nineties, about three miles southeast of Paddy Hannan's original claim, auriferous lode formations extending deep into the earth were discovered. When, in 1896, tellurides of gold were identified in these lodes, the extraordinary character of Kalgoorlie was confirmed. The low ridges between Kalgoorlie and Boulder were to be immortalized as the Golden Mile.[33]

The discovery of gold at depth transformed Westralian mining. The successful development of such rich but refractory ore deposits necessitated systematic planning, elaborate machinery, and metallurgical expertise. These in turn required large-scale organization and a steady supply of capital, primarily from London, the financial center of the world. The day of reckless boom was dying; the age of consolidation, rationalization, and efficiency was dawning. One of the new era's principal architects was to be Herbert Hoover.

The American engineer's initial salary befitted his company's expectations. Writing to Penrose from London en route to Australia, Hoover revealed that his salary as an "inspector" for Bewick, Moreing would be $5,000 a year plus some additional fees.[34] Two days later he told Lester Hinsdale that his annual salary would be $6,000 plus "all expenses and possibly some fees."[35] Whatever his exact remuneration, it was big money in 1897 for a man not yet twenty-three.[36]

At first Hoover was "number four" on Bewick, Moreing's staff[37]—"subordinate," he later put it, "to a resident partner of the firm."[38] This was presumably Edward Hooper, a British mining engineer who directed the company's business in Western Australia. Hoover resided at Coolgardie in a company-owned bungalow, complete with cook and valet.[39]

Some of Hoover's early duties were performed in the vicinity of Coolgardie. But since Bewick, Moreing managed the Hannan's Brownhill mine in nearby Kalgoorlie, Hoover spent a portion of his time at this location as well.[40] One of his earliest reports, written in June 1897, analyzed proposals for an adequate pumping plant at this mine.[41] At one point, when the manager of the Brownhill took a vacation, Hoover temporarily replaced him.[42]

Although Coolgardie was Hoover's base in Australia for nearly a year, his principal theater of operations lay elsewhere. For Hoover was an "inspecting engineer."[43] He had been hired not to do office work at headquarters but to take "charge of exploration and mine examination work in connection with the firm's management of the London and West Australian Exploration Company."[44] This was an enterprise controlled by one of Bewick, Moreing's senior partners, C. Algernon Moreing. As consulting engineers to London and

W.A. Exploration, the Australian staff of Bewick, Moreing—notably Hoover—was frequently requested to evaluate mines and prospects for possible purchase, and to assess the condition of mines already in the company's orbit. Hoover was therefore obliged to travel often into the bush, inspect properties, and file reports. It was challenging work that called for a combination of geological expertise, knowledge of every phase of practical mining, and astute calculation of mine valuation and finance. A "hole in the ground," no matter how alluring, was of little value unless it could be turned into a dividend-paying proposition.

And so for the next few months H. C. Hoover made repeated forays into the rugged outback of Western Australia. Usually his trips were to the north to examine mines and prospects in places like Menzies, Cue, Lawlers, Mt. Margaret, Mt. Sir Samuel, and Lake Darlot.[45] The East Murchison goldfields were one of his frequent destinations. Early in July, while on one such inspection trip, he wrote to his friend Hinsdale that he was now 280 miles from railroads and telegraph. Already on this single expedition he had covered seven hundred miles by team.[46] In late July he headed from Lawlers for Lake Way, 210 miles northeast of the town of Cue, which was itself far from Coolgardie: all for the sake of examining two leases.[47] In September he found himself 300 miles northeast of Coolgardie on yet another journey into the dry, dusty, lonely, almost trackless bush.[48]

On these inspection and reconnaissance trips Hoover subjected mining properties to rigorous scrutiny. He did not hesitate to render blunt, negative judgments. During one such tour he "condemned" certain mines and approved others.

> All of these belong to our companies, so you see I am at bad work, but I care not. The bad must go and the good stay on sufferance. They have been bought during boom times, when no regard was paid to the intrinsic value of the mine,—simply the statement that it was in W.A. was enough to sell it. Now the boom has broken. Good engineers are called in as physicians to mend the lame ducks. This we do by killing the bad ones immediately. At least, that's what I do.[49]

Many of Hoover's elaborate reports therefore recommended the abandonment of various mines or the avoidance of dubious propositions that could not meet the criteria of "conservative mining."[50] Hoover was ever alert to crucial cost factors. In one lengthy document he severely criticized the management of the East Murchison United mine for improper development work, inefficient mining methods, employment of excess labor, erection of "lavish buildings," and other wasteful practices resulting in an unnecessary expenditure of £13,200.[51]

It was hard, grueling, unremitting labor. "I am head over heels in work," he informed Hinsdale in July. "Nearly worked to death," he reported in

September. "Buried in work" in October.[52] Many times he drove himself until two or three in the morning. At least once he worked through the entire night.[53] During September and October alone he made eighteen trips to Kalgoorlie and back—twenty-five miles each way.[54]

And the obstacles seemed endless, protean. For one thing, the ores of Western Australia were "erratic in occurrence and value." For another, the tellurides at Kalgoorlie presented complex metallurgical problems that were not yet resolved. No one knew what the cost of treating them might prove to be.[55] Moreover, Hoover remarked candidly, mines that appeared attractive near the surface often failed to contain payable ore at depth. It was "a misfortune inseparable from Gold Mining ventures, and one that the keenest engineering wisdom cannot forestall."[56]

The "human factor" was the source of other difficulties. In September 1897 Hoover undertook an intensive ten-day reconnaissance trip in which he examined four dozen claims north of Mt. Margaret. Hoover hoped that the waning of the boom in the goldfields might induce prospectors to sell out their titles on terms advantageous to Hoover's employers. But while a few promising mines were discovered, the prospectors, he found, entertained "absurd" notions about prices. He therefore recommended that Moreing's exploration company cease development work in the area until the "changed condition of the Industry" and "the depletion of their purses" rendered the prospectors "amenable to reason."[57]

Stubborn and unrealistic prospectors were a minor nuisance compared to the incompetence and inefficiency that Hoover perceived around him. Early in July he felt obliged to discharge eight men from his staff. Several more, he wrote to a friend back home, were "in the noose." After all, he argued, he could not make his branch of the firm a success without the "best men."[58] A few weeks later he expressed pleasure at his "splendid" staff—a result obtained after numerous firings and the General Manager's permission for Hoover to choose whichever replacements he wanted from the rest of the "office corps."[59] But by September he had fired two more of his assistants and was "doing the work myself. They are such damned noddle heads."[60] Once someone even attempted to offer him an $8,000 bribe. "I never dreamed," Hoover commented afterward, that "such a set of scoundrels could exist as some I have had to deal with."[61]

In these circumstances Hoover rapidly developed definite convictions about the caliber of personnel and mining practices on the West Australian frontier. "Australians," he asserted to Hinsdale, "are far behind Californians in mining methods knowledge and general shrewdness so that we have a decided advantage."[62] When Burt Brown Barker inquired about taking a position in Western Australia, Hoover quickly dissuaded his boyhood chum from Oregon. Said Hoover, "Yankees are not well received" on the goldfields. "They only have us because they have to they dont know how to make their mines pay dividends we do."[63] He told Penrose that "no country in the World has

witnessed such rank swindling and charlatan engineering" as Western Australia.[64] He came to the conclusion that laborers in Western Australian mines
"accomplish about two-thirds the amount of work of a Californian miner,
and only about 40 percent more than the Kaffirs of the Rand." Particularly
noticeable to him was the rarity of modern single-hand drilling, except in
mines managed by Americans.[65]

Not surprisingly, Hoover soon sought to import American mining engineers—especially his old Stanford friends—into his Australian enterprises.
Initially he was hesitant about placing friends in necessarily subordinate
positions. As a manager Hoover enjoyed a house and servants, perquisites
that he would be unable to share. Such situations could evoke jealousy.
Nevertheless, as early as July Hoover began efforts to obtain employment
for several of his college friends.[66] One of the first to arrive was Deane P.
Mitchell (class of '96) in September.[67]

On one occasion Hoover's zeal for efficiency produced a poignant problem. One day at Cue he dismissed a seventy-two-year-old accountant who
was no longer able to perform the strenuous tasks required of him. When
Hoover told him he must go, the old man "broke down" and wept, mentioning his wife down in Perth who received his salary for support. Hoover was
distressed. He confided to his cousin that he would have been "too tender-
hearted" to fire the old man had he worked for Hoover alone. Yet the American engineer had a responsibility to "get things in shape for the company,"
and this had to take priority. To cushion the shock of "a very unhappy duty,"
Hoover and three friends voluntarily presented the elderly man a generous
gift of three hundred dollars and tried to arrange a new job for him in Perth.[68]

A more serious difficulty arose when Hoover reorganized the East Murchison United mine, whose wasteful administration he had criticized sharply
in August. On November 1 he installed Mitchell as the new manager. Hoover and Mitchell promised to attempt substantial improvements. But conditions at the site were poor, they warned in early November. "The labour
conditions surrounding an isolated Mine render any sudden change impossible." Furthermore, the outgoing management had manipulated accounts
and attempted to "place the successor in an unenviable light by comparison."[69]

Early in 1898 Hoover reported on the first two months of the new regime.
His figures disclosed a dramatic reduction of working costs and a likely future
profit of £3,500 per month for some time to come. Hoover was pleased: "We
have . . . vindicated our promise to work the mine" for less than thirty-five
shillings per ton. But success at the East Murchison United had not come
easily:

> We have had much difficulty with our laborers. We have initiated four
> reforms which have resulted in decreasing our cost of mining 53% per ton,
> yet such was only accomplished by a struggle, and twice by strikes.

These reforms have been the substitution of 48 hours work per week for 44 hours formerly in vogue, the introduction of singlehand drilling, of changing shifts underground, and of most importance,—the importation of more skilled miners.[70]

Because of the mine's "labor difficulties," Hoover reported, the management's "General Expenses" had considerably increased.[71] The rebellious miners did not appreciate the replacement of the old "double jack," which required two men to operate, by the single-jack hammer, which needed only one. Time and again they refused to use the new tools, threw them into the stamp mill, or buried them in mullock heaps underground.[72] When the work force struck over the issue, Mitchell, undaunted, filled key positions with Italian laborers (evidently the "more skilled miners" mentioned by Hoover in his report). Some of the men struck a second time, only to discover that Mitchell could achieve the same output with a smaller work force.[73]

Like Hoover, Mitchell was appalled at Australian attitudes toward work and productivity. Two months on the goldfields had cured him, he said, of any sympathy for socialism. "Everything here is run by the Government," he complained. "The people have no independence, depending upon the government for everything," and they were "almost useless as laborers."

Every man sticks very closely to his trade. A carpenter will not do a joiner's work and a blacksmith would starve before he would do a job of fitting or machine work.

Almost every other day is a holiday of some sort and everyone must stop work and waste his time, or worse. They all hate Yankees, with their energy and push, and the Yankees are rapidly getting control of every important position in the mining industry.[74]

These were Hoover's sentiments as well.

Metallurgical mysteries, incompetence and inefficiency, resistance to technological reform. To all these headaches was added one more: the burden of daily living in a distant, foreign land. "It's a country of red dust black flies and white heat," Hoover told his friend Barker. "I could not portray the misery of any one of them on paper. The country is an endless desert, no water no nothing but mines."[75] The landscape was so monotonous that one could paint it on a gun barrel.[76] During the Australian summer the temperature sometimes did not drop below 100° F., even at night, while in the daytime it might reach 115° in the shade and 150° or higher in the sun.[77] He wryly remarked to a friend that local chickens were being fed cracked ice "to prevent them from laying hard-boiled eggs."[78]

The discomfort induced by the "dry broil" (as Hoover described it)[79] was intensified by occasional dust storms and swarms of pestiferous flies. "The Australian fly is much inferior, more vicious, and less energetic than the

American fly," Hoover stated. "He always makes for one's eyes, so we always wear nets. . . ."[80] Despite this precaution, despite washing his hands in olive oil to avoid being poisoned by the flies, Hoover contracted "a mild form of blood poisoning" known as barcoo rot, which compelled him to spend a week in bed.[81]

But at least he did not succumb to typhoid fever, although three people a day were dying from it in Coolgardie that October.[82] The country was known as a "white man's grave," he told Hinsdale.[83] (Indeed, today in the Coolgardie cemetery over a thousand men lie buried who never reached the age of twenty-six.)[84]

In his trips into the bush Hoover often lumbered along on the backs of camels, whose tolerance for the desert was a great advantage. More often he used relay teams of horse-drawn buggies: their greater "speed and comfort" somewhat compensated for their expense.[85] But when he did, he took care to pack a bicycle, a popular vehicle on the "tracks." For if calamity should ever befall his horses, he might be fifty miles from water. Then his bicycle would be his "only salvation."[86]

On one such unforgettable trip by camel, he came to a fork in the "track," far from his destination. Hoover wished to turn east; his camel stubbornly refused. No tactic Hoover tried, not even a whip, could make the beast obey. It was late in the day; there was not a drop of water within miles. Finally, in desperation, he took off his shirt and blindfolded the camel. For a short time he permitted it to follow its own course, but slowly he was able to guide it toward the east and safety. After that, Hoover had a leather blindfold made for such emergencies.[87] And he formed a jaundiced opinion of camels similar to his view of horses.[88]

In so many ways, it was a land to make one think of home. Writing to his cousin in August 1897, Hoover declared: "Am on my way back to Coolgardie. Am glad to get back within the borders of civilization. Coolgardie is three yards inside of it; Perth is about a mile, and of course San Francisco is the center. Anybody who envies me my salary can just take my next trip with me, and he will then be contented to be a bank clerk at $3 a week the rest of his life, just to live in the United States. Stanford is the best place in the world."[89]

With sentiments like these, and with his unabashed preference for American men and methods, Hoover soon acquired a nickname in Western Australia. H. C. Hoover. His friends said "H. C." stood for "Hail Columbia."[90]

Yet for all his frustrations, Hoover was succeeding on the Australian goldfields. He had not been there two months when he informed Hinsdale that "by two fortunate strokes" he had "won the entire confidence of my superiors" and had "now full swing to make or kill myself professionally." Moreover, Bewick, Moreing's managing director in Australia had already granted him a 10% share in the profits of his branch (Coolgardie) and had given him direction of a second branch (Lawlers) besides. As a result of this promotion,

Hoover now found himself, in early July, "next to the head in Western Australia."[91] In September he confidentially told Hinsdale that his annual income had been raised to approximately $8,000.[92] In addition, his living expenses ($250 or more per month) were being paid by his employer.[93] He was doing very well indeed.

There were other, more intangible advantages and prospective rewards. "It's a hell of a country," he confided to Hinsdale, "but the chances of getting on are exceptional—especially with the inside position I now hold."[94] He was also acquiring an extraordinary education in cultural anthropology—from the intriguing customs of the aborigines to the idiosyncrasies of his fellow men on the goldfields. Of Englishmen, for instance: "They are very particular about such things as dignity of position, social names ect. ect. They are very distant and friendliness approaching familiarity is greatly abhorred. . . ."[95]

It had not taken long for Hoover to establish himself with Bewick, Moreing. When responsibility for the branch at Lawlers became his in July 1897, it was a reward for services rendered the company in less than three months. Neither he nor his superiors could know that this step was the prelude to immense profits, broader recognition for Hoover, and a secure niche for the American engineer in Australian mining history.

I I I

A B O U T 150 miles north of Kalgoorlie lies a hill called Mount Leonora, which rises perhaps a couple of hundred feet above the flat surrounding countryside. Near its base, in mid-1896, three prospectors discovered gold and staked a claim. Financed by certain Welsh storekeepers in Coolgardie, they registered their lease as the "Sons of Gwalia," in honor of their original sponsors, a Welsh syndicate of the same name. ("Gwalia" is the Welsh term for Wales.)[96]

The miners had scarcely begun to work the lease when they were visited by a veteran mining man who happened to be passing through the remote and little-known district. A Welshman himself, George W. Hall was intrigued by the name of the mine and decided to satisfy his curiosity. Although the claim itself was in a state of what he later called "incipient babyhood,"[97] his experienced eyes soon noticed the "resemblance which the ground exposed bore to that around Hannan's" (Kalgoorlie).[98] Furthermore, the ore samples Hall took showed excellent results. As a partner of a well-known Member of Parliament, William Pritchard Morgan, Hall was scouting for promising mines in behalf of Pritchard Morgan and his associates. He therefore raced to Coolgardie, dickered with the storekeeper owners, and finally bought the Sons of Gwalia mine for his principals: the London and Westralian Mines and Finance Agency and two allied syndicates. The price was £5,000. Hall thereupon cabled his backers that he had acquired what seemed likely to become, in his words, "one of the biggest properties in the whole of Western Australia."[99]

During the next few months Hall eagerly developed his find. In September 1896 the first men were put on the lease. Early in 1897 Hall purchased an old ten-stamp battery in Coolgardie and had it transported more than 150 miles through the bush for installation at the site.[100] When the machinery began to crush ore at the Sons of Gwalia for the first time at the end of May, Hall's enthusiasm was vindicated. By early July just over 750 tons of ore had already been crushed, yielding 2,110 ounces of gold—an excellent showing.[101] Seventy men were employed at the mine on round-the-clock shifts.[102] Although its scale of operations was still small, the Sons of Gwalia was now a working mine.

At this point Herbert Hoover entered the scene. On June 16, 1897 he set out from Coolgardie on an inspection trip north to Lawlers and beyond.[103] It was while on this journey, in a letter dated July 16, that he made his earliest known reference to the Sons of Gwalia, citing it as one of fourteen mines he had already examined.[104] Hoover visited Mount Leonora on June 21.[105] Years later, in his *Memoirs*, he recalled camping near the Sons of Gwalia lease for a night and visiting the miners. Convinced, upon being shown around, that this was a mine of importance, he quickly notified his superiors that it should be scrutinized carefully, provided that an option to buy could be obtained.[106] Hoover urged securing such an option.[107]

During the next few weeks Moreing in London arranged for an option to purchase the mine.[108] On August 17 Hoover returned to Coolgardie.[109] The next day the London headquarters of Bewick, Moreing cabled a terse directive to its Coolgardie office: either Edward Hooper or H. C. Hoover was to examine the Sons of Gwalia and certain other properties and to file reports on their value as quickly as possible. Said the cable: "Do you advise purchase in order to get control of see Hall at once with regard to act promptly."[110]

Neither Hooper nor Hoover could leave for the north for at least eight days, the Coolgardie office replied. Could not another man take the assignment?[111] No, came the immediate response; it must be Hooper or Hoover. London would wait ten days.[112] No one else, it seemed, was considered satisfactory for the task.

On August 24, therefore, just one week after his return, Hoover again left Coolgardie for the north.[113] On September 11 the first results of his inspection of the Sons of Gwalia mine were communicated in a lengthy cable to London. Hoover, the message read, "has made a most careful examination." After summarizing the nature of the ore body, amount of development work, results of assaying, and other subjects, the cable concluded: "I consider it a most valuable property from the peculiar formation of offer(s) very great possibilities."[114] Six days later Hoover informed his cousin: "I have finished the Sons of Gwalia and have recommended it."[115]

On October 6, back in Coolgardie, Hoover completed and signed an elaborate, thirteen-page typewritten report amplifying his earlier recommendation. He, too, noticed that the Sons of Gwalia's ore deposit had "the same origin and nature as those of Kalgoorlie," words that no doubt quickened the pulse of his principals in London. To be sure, the mine in its current state of development had substantial handicaps, notably a very inferior ten-stamp battery and a lack of concentrating machinery for treating low-grade ore. Hoover was convinced, however, that the mining and milling of low-grade ore on a large scale with modern equipment could be accomplished at low cost and a substantial profit. This was the key to the future. In short, said Hoover, the mine was "a most valuable one," with "enormous potential," and "well worth securing control of."[116]

Satisfied by Hoover's reports, Moreing's London and Western Australian Exploration Company swung into high gear. The next several weeks were a hectic period of negotiation and maneuver. Already, on October 9, the *Menzies Miner* had predicted that the Sons of Gwalia mine "is going to live and uphold Leonora as second to none in W.A. as a gold producing centre."[117] As news of the hitherto obscure mine's excellent early crushing results appeared in the press, rival syndicates began to evince an unwelcome curiosity about it.[118] Hoover himself resorted to what a goldfields newspaper called "ingenious ruses" in an effort to mislead the unduly inquisitive. Once, while on his way to the mine, he noticed that he was being watched. He promptly took a casual but pointless detour into the bush.[119]

Finally, on November 17, 1897, Moreing's exploration company formally purchased the Sons of Gwalia mine from the Pritchard Morgan interests that controlled it.[120] A few days later the *Australian Mail* reported that Bewick, Moreing's "American experts," just back from an inspection tour around Mount Leonora, regarded the Sons of Gwalia as "fully equal to the best Kalgoorlie mines."[121] Apparently for flotation purposes a further report from the field was deemed necessary.[122] Accordingly, in mid-November Hoover revisited the Sons of Gwalia for a methodical, five-day examination. He returned to Coolgardie on November 25.[123] The next day Bewick, Moreing's Coolgardie office dispatched a cable to London once again describing the ore chutes, assay values, and expected working costs, and once again affirming its confidence in the mine's rich promise.[124]

On November 30 Hoover completed and signed a meticulous, comprehensive, twenty-four-page report based on his inspection of the Sons of Gwalia. He emphasized the importance of efficient mining and milling of low-grade ore, a task for which a modern 50-stamp mill, cyanide plant, and other improvements would be imperative. With proper equipment and reforms the current working costs could be substantially reduced and gold of low grade profitably extracted, down to the level of ten pennyweights (half an ounce) per ton of ore crushed. Indeed, at an estimated future expense of £1.10.0 per ton of ore processed (a figure he cited as attainable), Hoover declared that the ore already in sight would produce a profit of more than £5 per ton—nearly five times the total cost of production. Put another way, the ore presently in sight was worth a profit of £98,000, or nearly half a million dollars.[125]

The young American engineer had one reservation, however, about his optimistic calculations. On November 26 he cabled Bewick, Moreing in London:

> H. C. Hoover we have telegraphed . . . today Sons of Gwalia report cannot undertake the responsibility with respect to success according to our estimate as to the value of unless entire management designing machinery and plant in our hand.[126]

London's reply was concise and reassuring: "You will have entire management."[127]

The next step was the promotion of the property on the London stock market, a task undertaken with zest by Moreing's exploration company. During late November and December the Australian and British press announced exciting news from the goldfields: a "new Westralian 'sensation,' " "another Hannan's," had been found.[128] Bewick, Moreing's cabled report of November 26 from Coolgardie was printed in entirety in some journals, while many editors noted the property's geological similarity to the mines of the Golden Mile.[129] Meanwhile at the mine itself development continued steadily. By the end of 1897 it had produced 5,667 ounces of gold and had become, in the estimation of the local mining warden, a "splendid property."[130]

At last, early in January 1898, the "Sons of Gwalia, Ltd." was officially registered in London "for the purpose of acquiring and developing" the Australian mine of that name.[131] Stock was issued in the form of 300,000 £1 shares. In return for transferring the mine to the new company, and for agreeing to provide it with a working capital of £50,000, the vendor/ promoter—London and W.A. Exploration—received 250,000 free shares and 50,000 more in exchange for the working capital. Every share in the new company, in other words, was distributed to the vendor / promoter before the stock issue was placed on the market. Moreing's promotional campaign was a tremendous success. On the first day of public trading on the London stock exchange, Sons of Gwalia shares soared to an astonishing £2.2.6, more than double their nominal value.[132] The vendor / promoters, had they wished, could have sold their shares at once at an enormous profit.[133]

All this no doubt delighted C. Algernon Moreing, whose exploration company now leaped to preeminence on the goldfields.[134] The transaction was a boost, too, for the firm of Bewick, Moreing, which according to one journalist was "rapidly acquiring a reputation for astuteness and business capabilities hitherto not met with in connection with mining."[135]

Herbert Hoover's role in these events was crucial. At the heart of the Sons of Gwalia's published prospectus was a verbatim transcript of the résumé and conclusions of Hoover's report of November 30.[136] In a London interview in December Moreing cheerfully acknowledged that his "local agents" in Australia, by their "splendid" service, had enabled him to take "decisive steps" and thereby outmaneuver his competitors.[137] Edward Hooper, the firm's chief of operations in Western Australia, publicly praised Hoover as "one of the most able mining engineers that ever came to this country." Said Hooper flatly: "It was on Mr. Hoover's report that the Sons of Gwalia was purchased by the London and Western Australian Exploration Company."[138]

Hoover's contribution was also remarked upon in the press. The *Coolgardie Miner* acclaimed him as "the man who was responsible for finding the property and pushing on the transaction. . . . It was Mr. H. C. Hoover . . . who recognized the value and similarity of the Sons of Gwalia to the Kalgoorlie district. It was, in fact, on his representations that the new locality was designated 'another Hannans'. . . ."[139]

Hoover did not, of course, discover the Sons of Gwalia; it was already an active, operating mine when he examined it. Nor was he the first man to discern its resemblance to the valuable lode formations at Kalgoorlie. But in another sense he did indeed—as the *Coolgardie Miner* said—"find" the mine. At the time of his first visit, the Sons of Gwalia was a remote, little-known enterprise. Some, like Hall, might proclaim its value. It was Hoover, the expert "inspecting engineer," who proved it. In several examinations he carefully established that this was no mere surface "show" but a mine of magnificent promise. Others, no doubt, would in time have come after him. But it was Hoover who got there first. Once again, he had discovered opportunity and seized it.

It is a measure of Hoover's ability that Moreing was willing to risk £100,000 in cash commitments on the basis of Hoover's judgment. Now, in early 1898, Moreing stood to profit handsomely from his confidence.

Probably as a reward for these services, in November 1897—just after Moreing's company secured the Sons of Gwalia mine—Hoover was promoted to junior partner in Bewick, Moreing's West Australian branches. This position entitled him to a share in the annual profits. He calculated that his total income would now amount to more than $10,000 a year.[140]

And with reward came rising recognition. "Hail Columbia" Hoover was now a public figure on the goldfields, a man whose opinions were eagerly sought by the press.[141] He was also an active member of the executive committee of the powerful Coolgardie Chamber of Mines, serving with distinction as a representative of the London and Western Australian Exploration Company.[142]

To some who met and observed him in Australia, Hoover was "far from being a prepossessing personality." Reserved and serious, he was, in one journalist's words, "a slight figure, of medium height," with a "pallid complexion," a "dull, toneless voice," and no sense of humor. Nor did he participate much in the convivial social life of Coolgardie and Kalgoorlie in the

Roaring Nineties. "His job was work, and his joy was in discussing it—if his
harsh staccato 'yep' and 'nop' could be elevated to the level of discussion."[143]
Furthermore, he had a peculiar habit of looking down and away from people
with whom he was talking and of doodling at his desk with a pencil while
listening.[144] Not the traits that legends are made of.

Yet some who got beyond the mask and the mannerisms detected an intriguing personality. A newspaper correspondent traveling with Hoover on a
trip to the Sons of Gwalia found that while he spoke little he was amiable
and well-informed, and "inspires one with confidence in his ability and experience by reason of his modesty."[145] Another traveler found Hoover "very
reserved" in manner, "yet you felt that a big intellect lay somewhere behind
it."[146] J. W. Kirwan, the influential editor of the *Kalgoorlie Miner*, observed
that the young American was a most attentive listener, with a phenomenal
memory and capacity for work. And Kirwan discerned the "indomitable
energy and ambition," the drive for success, beneath Hoover's laconic exterior. Sometimes, late at night among close friends, Hoover would open up
and become positively garrulous. "He was full of projects for the future,"
Kirwan later recalled. One dream above all attracted him: "the amalgamation
of all the mines of the Golden Mile. . . . In these fancies he was himself
always controlling engineer, organiser, and administrator of the amalgamated group."[147] Another Australian acquaintance became convinced that
Hoover was a man of "Napoleonic" proportions, "one of those rare persons
who can not only conceive a great project, but can execute it."[148]

On one subject, though, Hoover did not open up, even late at night: the
subject of his age. Many people, in fact, believed him to be much older than
he was. He did not correct them.[149] No, Hoover didn't say much. He didn't
gladhand with the boys in the saloons. But he could *think*. He was always
thinking.[150]

Meanwhile the pace of life continued unrelentingly. By the end of 1897,
after less than eight months, Hoover had journeyed 4,886 miles within Western Australia, mostly by camel and by teams of horses.[151] In January 1898,
at his request, another close Stanford friend, George B. Wilson (class of '96),
arrived in Australia to serve as an assistant.[152] In the next four months, sometimes with Wilson at his side, Hoover crisscrossed much of Western Australia—trips duly noted in the newspapers.[153] It seemed that he was constantly
on the go. On February 2 he returned to Coolgardie from a 300-mile trek;
three days later he was off for Menzies and Lawlers.[154] On the twenty-fifth
he was back at Coolgardie, only to leave within a few days for the north, in
heat well above 100° F.[155] At least twice in March he traveled 700 miles
round-trip to Perth, with a visit to Cue sandwiched in between.[156] No wonder an awed newspaper correspondent who joined him on one of these whirlwind journeys remarked:

Mr. Hoover is a rapid traveller. No one I have ever met on the fields gets
over the ground so quickly and finishes what business he has so quietly

and expeditiously. An early riser and tremendous worker, he flies from field to field with amazing rapidity. . . . he is certainly the most ubiquitous man on these fields.[157]

Even bouts of influenza and fever in March and April did not slow him down for very long.[158]

Several times between January and April Hoover visited the Sons of Gwalia mine, which already was employing over one hundred men (a figure soon to be doubled).[159] Although by arrangement the Sons of Gwalia, Ltd. would not take formal control of the property until May 1, Bewick, Moreing began to serve as its general managers and consulting engineers on February 17.[160] It was probably in the capacity of consulting engineer that Hoover visited the mine.

Back in November 1897 Moreing had promised Hoover the superintendency of the mine once the legal transfer was consummated. As this day approached, Hoover found another reason to undertake the new responsibility. At the beginning of 1898 Bewick, Moreing's head man in Western Australia, Edward Hooper, left for London to become a senior partner in the firm.[161] His replacement on the goldfields was Ernest Williams, a Welshman who had several years of experience in South Africa.[162] Hoover soon clashed with his new superior. In late March, as Hoover prepared to change jobs and take over the Sons of Gwalia, he told Hinsdale, "I have been raising hell about some things with the managing director and we are agreed not to agree."[163] Hoover's brusqueness offended Williams, himself a feisty character.[164] For his part, Hoover complained to Hinsdale that Williams "does not wish me to get the credit" for financial successes worth £400,000 to him and "therefore keeps me in the back ground as much as possible." But there were compensations: Hoover's new position at the Gwalia would pay £2,000 (about $10,000) a year plus a share of some profits—an increase over his current salary.[165]

As Hoover prepared to move to the vicinity of Mount Leonora, he could look back on a year of achievement. "Things are going swimmingly," he told an old friend in March. "I have been very successful in getting through one deal that yielded the firm a profit of $1,500,000.00 out of which I haven't been forgotten. . . . Nothing succeeds like success."[166] Moreover, he had been generous with his earnings, a trait which impressed Kirwan and others.[167] Even before he arrived in Australia he had arranged for £50 of his salary (approximately $250) to be sent each month to Hinsdale for discreet distribution to certain relatives and friends.[168] During the ensuing months these payments flowed regularly to San Francisco, so that, as Hoover put it at one point, "my various dependents may not wholly starve."[169] Theodore Hoover, now a student at Stanford University, received eighty dollars a month (later raised to one hundred); cousin Harriette Miles also received substantial monthly assistance.[170] Several intimate Stanford friends, including Ray Lyman Wilbur, Samuel Collins, and Myron Folsom, obtained needed funds through Hinsdale at various times.[171] As Hoover told Hinsdale, "I want to give any of my old pards who are struggling along a lift now that I am making something and should my account with you permit you may let them have according to ther needs without intrest of course."[172]

Evidently Hoover regarded his benefactions not as gifts but as loans.[173] (Whether they were repaid is unknown.) But there was no gainsaying the fact that he was regularly allotting a hefty portion of his income ($3,000 or more a year) for the aid of those he held dear.[174] Characteristically, however, he concealed his acts of generosity. He instructed Hinsdale to be a "sphinx about matters of mine."[175] He did not wish his brother to know that he was supporting his cousin.[176] Not even his beneficiaries always realized the source of their good fortune. Ray Lyman Wilbur, one of his closest friends, did not discover until years later that Hoover had sent money from Australia to help finance Wilbur's way through medical school. And then he only learned this fact from Hinsdale; Hoover himself never mentioned it.[177] "Doing good deeds by stealth," one friend called it.[178] It was a trait that was to find repeated expression in the decades ahead.

Hoover was acutely sensitive to the needs of those who, like himself, had been obliged to scrape and scramble to "make it." He told Hinsdale he hoped that all the "boys who are still in the struggle stages will not hesitate to draw on my account to its utmost limit."[179] But whether from conscious conviction or some deep-seated quirk of personality, he habitually operated indirectly. Direct displays of emotion upset him. Verbal expressions of compassion he tended to avoid.

At the end of April 1898, to the plaudits of the goldfields press, Hoover traveled to the Sons of Gwalia mine to assume personal responsibility as superintendent.[180] His eventual basic annual remuneration would indeed be £2,000: £1,500 as superintendent at the Sons of Gwalia and £500 as Bewick, Moreing's representative in the region around Mount Leonora.[181] In the latter capacity he was to serve (both for Bewick, Moreing and for Moreing's exploration company) as a consulting engineer to several other mines: the East Murchison United, Gwalia South, Mertzy's Reward (at Mount Sir Samuel), Kinambla (Wealth of Nations), and Warronga.[182] It was only fitting that as "one of the first to recognize the value of the Sons of Gwalia mine"[183] and as the principal catalyst of a remarkable stock flotation, he should now take direct charge. His mandate was clear enough: to transform a small but exceedingly promising mine into a great one.

As for his ability, the *Coolgardie Miner* declared, "He has played an important part in the history of the mine, . . . and a more competent manager could not be found."[184]

6

The Sons of Gwalia

I

F o r the first few days the new superintendent of the Sons of Gwalia was assailed by feelings of self-doubt. Not yet twenty-four years old, Hoover was now in sole command of 250 men in one of the most desolate regions on earth. Privately he worried that his "time had really come" and that he "wouldn't be able to make it go."[1] Soon, however, Hoover's nervousness subsided; he told Hinsdale he had concluded that "its simply a matter of self confidence."[2] With this comforting thought in mind, with a mustache to convey an appearance of maturity, and with an air of mastery to match, he settled down to the business at hand.[3]

Within a week he faced his first challenge. Earlier in the year a newspaper correspondent traveling with Hoover had reported that the American engineer was "particularly bitter" on the labor question. He was "by no means yet accustomed to the saucy independence and loafing proclivities of many of the Australian miners."[4] Meanwhile in the mid-1890s a vigorous trade union movement had emerged on the Western Australian goldfields.[5] In late April, shortly before Hoover became superintendent, a union representative addressed two mass meetings of workers at the Sons of Gwalia mine. In response to his appeal, more than one hundred men joined the union.[6]

It was not surprising that a confrontation quickly developed between the efficiency-minded, young Yankee manager and his newly unionized work force. During his first days at the mine Hoover swiftly implemented changes along the lines of those initiated earlier at the East Murchison United mine. On May 9 he reported the results to Bewick, Moreings' head office in Coolgardie:

> We have changed the working hours of the men on the mines from 44 hours to 48 hours per week and after some trouble things have quietened down and work is proceeding smoothly.
>
> We had previously introduced single-hand work and some other reforms, the results of which, from other experience on the Fields, will secure us 20% more work for the same outlay.
>
> We are introducing several Italians, who are in every way superior workers to the men formerly employed; as an instance formerly 26 men were required to stope ore for the 10 stamps while we are now doing it with 15 and expect this to be improved upon.[7]

The next day Hoover notified headquarters, "We have accomplished most of our reforms without any united revolt, chiefly I fancy because the possible ring leaders had been previously dispensed with."[8] Probably to strengthen his hand further, Hoover asked an Italian padrone in the town of Bardoc to supply "three good Italian miners" for work at "the usual wages." Hoover assured the padrone that if these recruits "prove satisfactory it will open the way to the employment of many more."[9]

Hoover's confidence was no doubt reinforced by the results of a meeting of the men a few days before. Despite their displeasure the miners had decided to accept the increase in hours.[10] But when Hoover now proceeded to make further changes in work rules, more trouble ensued, as he reported to his head office on May 23:

> During the week I have had two strikes. In the first instance I asked the men to change shifts at point of employment instead of on the surface— each man by this means cut 20 minutes per diem from his time underground. The men met and determined to strike and I therefore promptly posted a notice that we would not grant the usual hour off on the Saturday shift, but the men would have to work the full 48 hours, and intimated we were prepared for any strikes by importing Italians. The men sent a deputation then asking for a Meeting, at which I agreed to compromise allowing them the Saturday hour as before, if they would change at point of employment.
>
> Again the Truckers in the lower Level struck for a rise in pay owing to

the wet ground. We discharged the entire crew at that level, and replaced them with men at the old rate.

Again it had been formerly the custom to pay double pay for Sunday work, which we stopped, and six men working on Sunday refused to proceed. We discharged them and replaced them with new men.

I have a bunch of Italians coming up this week and will put them in the Mine on contract work. If they are satisfactory I will secure enough of them to hold the property in case of a general strike, and with your permission will reduce wages. We now pay 5/-[five shillings] per day more than any Mine on the Fields.[11]

It is not known how Bewick, Moreing's Coolgardie office responded to Hoover's proposal to lower the wages of his men. While the Sons of Gwalia's wage rates may not have been the highest of any mine in Western Australia, miners' wages on the fields were good ones for the time: generally £3–£4 ($15–$20) a week.[12] In fact, wages in the goldfields in the late 1890s were sufficiently high for miners to mail half their income to their wives and dependents living elsewhere in Australia. The aggregate sum thus transferred was enormous.[13]

Hoover was the first superintendent to introduce Italian workers at the Sons of Gwalia. In doing so, he was apparently following a general policy recently established at other Bewick, Moreing mines in Western Australia.[14] During the next few weeks Hoover hired more Italian laborers and urged the Italian agent with whom he dealt to advertise his services.[15] When Bewick, Moreing's London headquarters learned about the new practice, it cautioned the Coolgardie office to be prudent lest it provoke strikes and turmoil.[16] At least at the Sons of Gwalia, no further difficulties occurred during Hoover's tenure.

Having won his battles with the labor force, Hoover now concentrated on reorganizing the mine. Six months before, he had recommended the erection of a modern 50-stamp battery and metallurgical plant at the Gwalia.[17] But before he could inaugurate all his contemplated improvements, three crucial questions must be answered. First, what was the nature of the ore deep in the earth below the level of surface oxidation? The answer to this question would determine the nature of the giant stamp mill to be designed and constructed. Second, what kind of a water supply would turn up in the mine at depth? This would dictate the form of treatment of the gold slimes that could not be extracted from the tailings by ordinary milling techniques. Third, what would the "lateral extent" of the principal ore body prove to be? The answer here would influence the location of the new main shaft, winding engine, and machinery for the reduction of the ore. Since the Sons of Gwalia leases contained 168 acres, this was not a trivial question. Each problem would necessitate a vast amount of exploratory underground digging, quite apart from the regular ongoing removal of ore already known to be worth milling.

During Hoover's first three months at the mine, answering these questions was his primary objective.[18] Early in May he informed his head office that he hoped to ascertain the proper location of the main shaft in four months.[19] It would be a longer time still before the new shaft and other equipment were in operation.

Meanwhile he would have to get along as best he could with the machinery and resources bequeathed to him by the former management. Hoover was outspoken about the state of affairs he inherited. The assay office, he told his superiors in Coolgardie, was "absolutely useless."[20] The existing surveys of the mine were so inaccurate as to be "valueless." A new survey would be needed.[21] Above all, Hoover took issue with the fundamental development policy of his predecessors. Heretofore the management at the mine had striven to obtain the greatest possible profit in the quickest and easiest manner by exploiting only the richest ore chutes.[22] It was a policy Hoover condemned as "picking the eyes" out of the mine.[23] With the backing of his superiors, Hoover resolved to alter this approach. The Sons of Gwalia, he contended, had "suffered" from the former management's shortsightedness. Instead of trying "to make a profit on the working," its energies "should have gone into development."[24]

Hoover lost no time in tackling the problems before him. During May he directed a "radical" revamping of the inferior 10-stamp battery still in use at the mine. By dint of numerous alterations, he "entirely revolutionized" it and increased substantially the percentage of gold recovered from the crushing apparatus.[25] On another front he introduced the American, or short, ton (2,000 pounds) as the unit of measurement in place of the long ton (2,240 pounds).[26] He assembled a staff of eight men—including an underground manager, chief engineer, surveyor, assayer, and accountant—that he considered "unequalled in the Colony."[27] His underground manager, John Agnew, remained an intimate associate for many years and a loyal friend for life.[28]

Since the Sons of Gwalia mine was about two miles south of the small town of Leonora, a distance too great for easy commuting, many miners camped near the mine in the usual goldfields shelters: tents of burlap bags and little huts of corrugated iron. In response to a suggestion from the local board of health, Hoover in early June designated the blocks adjoining the mine as residence areas for his employees. In this way all the camps were concentrated in one area, facilitating what the local newspaper called "a proper system of sanitation."[29] As for Hoover, at least until mid-August he and his senior staff lived in tents—lodging "neither comfortable nor profitable" in a land of red soil, black flies, and white heat.[30] Consequently Hoover very early decided to have constructed a number of office buildings and cottages for staff, all to be made of brick and built on a rock foundation.[31]

In adopting this course Hoover appeared to reverse a position he had taken the previous August when he had roundly condemned the "general tendency towards lavish buildings" at the East Murchison United—an unwarranted expenditure, he had declared, "considering the age of the Mine." The erection of trimmed stone buildings at that mine "could well have waited," he had then asserted, "until the Mine was paying dividends."[32] Now, however, at the Sons of Gwalia, although no dividends were yet distributed and none would be for two years more, Hoover declared himself "greatly opposed to temporary structures."[33] Soon the manufacture of bricks for the assay office, main office, officers' dining hall, and other proposed buildings was underway.[34] Perhaps to mollify his cost-conscious superiors, Hoover repeatedly stressed the plainness of the buildings and the economic advantages of brick over stone and scarce wood. He also rejected corrugated iron as "out of the question in such a hot place as this."[35] In a way his housing policy reflected faith in the long-range viability of the mine. At any rate, the Coolgardie office did not object and duly informed the London directors of the new plan.[36]

Restive workers, deficient machinery, erroneous assay plans, daily life in tents on a parched and dusty desert: it was not easy to be a mine manager. It was also proving difficult to get along with Ernest Williams, the head of Bewick, Moreing's operations in Western Australia. In his first months at the Sons of Gwalia, Hoover clashed repeatedly with Williams and the Coolgardie office. Hoover did not regard the Coolgardie staff as a paragon of efficiency, and he did not conceal his irritation. When Coolgardie requested certain documents, Hoover replied that he had "long since forwarded" copies and added, ". . . I do not doubt a little research in your files will discover the same."[37] (Coolgardie responded that the man who knew the location of these documents was away.)[38] When in mid-June Hoover called for some urgently needed forms, Coolgardie took twelve days to answer—and then responded negatively without explanation, thereby causing Hoover great inconvenience. He immediately protested this "quite inexplicable . . . refusal to oblige us."[39] When Hoover discovered that the head office was already designing a new stamp mill, he immediately dissociated himself from what he considered a "premature" effort. "My letter book shows a repetition of these points at least six times," he added tartly.[40]

Hoover was quick to challenge anything he construed as a reflection on his competence. When the Coolgardie office at one point told him to "let us have full particulars of everything" in the future, he demanded "to know any instance when I have not done so in the past."[41] On another occasion Williams advised Hoover to install a Cornish pump that Hoover no longer deemed necessary. Williams feared that Bewick, Moreing would be ridiculed if, having already ordered the pump for a specific reason, it now failed to use it.[42] Hoover, in reply, strenuously objected to Williams's comment that "some mistakes are only to be rectified by being persisted in." Hoover denied that any mistake had been made in the first place. He blamed Coolgardie for the delays that now rendered the pump unnecessary. After reciting his arguments, however, Hoover did agree that for reasons of "policy" rather than "technical administration" it might be better to install the pump. For as Williams had observed (and Hoover realized it, too) the "old crowd" they had replaced was looking for opportunities to criticize the Bewick, Moreing management.[43]

A number of Hoover's disagreements with headquarters concerned the East Murchison United mine, managed by his friend Deane P. Mitchell. As a consulting engineer to this and several other mines in the northern districts, Hoover had a measure of administrative responsibility for them. He therefore protested whenever, in his judgment, he was not kept informed or the Coolgardie staff interfered in his domain.[44] How could he "maintain sight of operations" at the East Murchison United, he remarked in May, if all its correspondence did not "pass through my hands"? Coolgardie promised to supply him with copies of this correspondence.[45]

Still another conflict developed when the April milling results at Mitchell's mine turned out poorly because of the use of low-grade ore and the loss of ten days for repairs. To remedy this embarrassing situation, Hoover proposed to prolong the April milling period into mid-May and thus allow time to improve the April returns. A few days later, however, the Coolgardie office instructed him not to do so. Such a course, it said, would "do the Firm more harm than making declaration at the proper time." Instead, it said it must simply disclose the "actual state" of affairs to London and "own up" if certain promises could not be kept.[46]

Hoover was annoyed. He responded stiffly that he had authorized the time extension only after explaining his reasons to Williams and securing Williams's full approval. Furthermore, he *had* kept his promises—all except one, which he attributed to unforeseeable circumstances. Nevertheless, Hoover accepted his new instructions and submitted the original April figures, since (he noted with apparent sarcasm) "it was not considered wise by Mr. Williams to alter tonnage for the Company's good, which certainly was to their interest."[47]

Down in Coolgardie Williams immediately disclaimed responsibility for the abortive time-extension policy. It had been, he contended, Hoover's arrangement, not his. But rather than prolong the dispute, the Coolgardie office decided to drop the subject and hope that London would be ready for the disagreeable news from the East Murchison United.[48]

Despite the handicaps of mediocre equipment and friction between himself and the head office, Hoover was soon able to report encouraging results of his administration at the Sons of Gwalia. His first monthly report, for May, told a story of increasing underground development, alterations in the mill's productivity, improvements in personnel, and other accomplishments, all of which had occurred while his staff had been "overworked in re-organization."[49] During the next few weeks Hoover regularly dispatched to Coolgardie precise reports of progress on all fronts.[50] In accordance with his new development policy, some of the low-grade ore was consigned to a special storage dump for future treatment, while the ore actually used continued to yield the desired ratio of an ounce of gold per ton.

From time to time Hoover drew attention to his steadily decreasing unit costs and other indices of efficient management.[51] At the end of July he cited the "quite unusual" amount of digging done in the various shafts, drives, and crosscuts during that month—mostly by single-hand drilling. One reason for this achievement, he said, was improved labor:

We have some 15 Italians in the Mine and the rivalry between them and the other miners is no small benefit. Although the Italians are fully 20% superior we do not intend placing them throughout the Mine, for when in majority they are somewhat troublesome.[52]

In mid-August Bewick, Moreing and Company compiled its first quarterly report as General Managers of the Sons of Gwalia, Ltd. The firm described how, under its and Hoover's stewardship, the objectives of management had shifted from "maximum monthly profit" to "rapid development" and "early preparation for more extensive equipment." Moreover, instead of exploiting only a few small chutes of high-grade ore (as its predecessors had done), it had consciously sought to "expose all the payable ore," especially the substantial amounts of lower-grade ore nearby. Although such a policy necessarily reduced the "general grade" of the mine, the managers pointed out that the Sons of Gwalia's "life and ultimate profits" had thereby been "greatly increased." Bewick, Moreing reported further that every key technical question about the future had now been answered. It was possible at last to determine exactly what kind of metallurgical plant and other equipment were feasible and to undertake the long-contemplated expansion.

The report also emphasized success in other areas. Thanks to economies of scale, an increase in working hours for labor, a cut in wages "in many instances," and especially "changing the personnel of the Mine employees," the management had substantially reduced its working costs since May 1. In three months under Hoover's management the mine had produced gold worth nearly £12,400 and a surplus of more than £1,638 over all expenditures.[53]

The subject of working costs was of constant concern to Hoover in 1898. Indeed, it was becoming the defining theme of his Australian experience. Early in the year, even before taking on the post of mine superintendent, he contributed an article to an American publication on "The Working Costs of West Australian Mines." In it he reviewed the onerous and expensive conditions facing mining enterprise "down under": the scarcity of water, for instance, and the cost of condensing it; the lack of adequate mining timber and the cost of importing it from Oregon; the expense of transporting materials from the coast to the mines by rail, team, and camel. "One of the most difficult problems," Hoover wrote, "is inefficient labor. This factor is constantly improving with time, but even now the amount of work accomplished per man per day is astoundingly small."[54]

Hoover's emphasis on frugal, efficient management made sense. It was, in fact, the perspective of the future. Gold mining in Western Australia was an expensive business, and many mines were low-grade propositions whose margin between profit and loss was slim.

But more than the logic of the ledger books was on Hoover's mind as he strove for economy at the Gwalia. During July he reorganized the mine's accounting system. One effect of his reform, he told the Coolgardie staff, was that "we wipe off a considerable portion of a rapidly accumulating Capital Account, all of which will come in handy when we go to make a record in Westralian Costs with a large Plant." Hoover rejected one particular bookkeeping change since it would result in an enormously increased figure for working costs per ton and thus "[put] us in a very bad light with former management."[55] Keenly aware of the competition, he was intensely anxious to look good vis-à-vis his predecessors and to create a record of cost effectiveness that would be the envy of Australia.

Young, aggressive, and on the make, Hoover was under constant pressure. After all, in his 1897 reports on the Sons of Gwalia for Moreing's exploration company, he had offered many bold estimates and projections. Now it was up to him to perform. The "old crowd" would be there to criticize if he failed. Moreover, the directors in London were themselves very attentive to expenditures and quick to reprove suspected prodigality. When, for instance, the London board learned about Hoover's satisfaction with his eight-man staff, it pointedly expressed its hope that in making his selections he had given due weight to considerations of economy.[56]

No one could deny, however, that Hoover was earning every farthing of his salary. During his nearly seven months as manager of the Sons of Gwalia, he composed more than six hundred letters and wore his typewriter into disrepair.[57] Early in September he spent about three days inspecting and evaluating mines in the district around Mount Leonora.[58] As consulting engineer to several other mines he had to keep track of developments at those locations as well, all in addition to the unending work at the Sons of Gwalia.

Increasingly the hard-working American was receiving recognition and praise. A local correspondent of the *Financial Times* (London) described the Sons of Gwalia superintendent as "one of the ablest mining engineers in Western Australia," a sentiment echoed by the Melbourne *Leader*.[59] Even Ernest Williams acknowledged his lieutenant's success. After interviewing Williams, just back from a visit to the Sons of Gwalia in early August, a correspondent for the *Australian Mail* described the "extraordinary rapidity" of development at the mine: "The driving and crosscutting work that has been accomplished . . . under Mr. Hoover's energetic management, is unprecedented in Westralian mining. . . ."[60] This was not mere puffery. In the month of August Hoover's miners drove 161 feet and 6 inches on the Main South Drive at the 200-foot level: "the greatest distance," Hoover declared, "yet accomplished in Western Australia."[61]

I I

LIFE on the desert goldfields was not entirely a treadmill of endless work. Nor did Hoover's environment entirely lack amenities. Early in May, he ordered several professional mining and engineering publications for the mine. For the "officers' mess" he entered separate subscriptions to *The Times* (London), *Financial Times*, *Coolgardie Miner*, *Harpers Monthly*, *Punch*, *Scientific American*, and eleven other periodicals.[62] While Hoover himself was not known as a drinker (he may still have been a teetotaler), he did order liquor shipments for the mine staff and bluntly complained when some of the claret proved "undrinkable."[63]

Not surprisingly, liquor consumption in Western Australia during the "Roaring Nineties" was heavy,[64] and drunkenness among miners was a problem with which every manager had to cope. This was especially so at the remote Sons of Gwalia, whose "sodden conditions" Hoover never forgot.[65] On one occasion he berated a mine foreman for habitual drunkenness after every pay day. The foreman replied that "this place" was unbearable unless he could get "good and drunk" from time to time. "How do you know when you are good and drunk?" Hoover asked. "When Mt. Leonora whiskey begins to taste good," the foreman replied.[66]

The Sons of Gwalia, as leasehold property, had no saloons. But since the men were not about to trudge two miles over to Leonora to quench their thirst, Hoover was plagued by the illegal practice of "sly-grogging" (selling liquor on the sly) at the Sons of Gwalia itself. One particularly notorious offender was a woman who had built a house on the lease and was plying her trade while taking care not to be caught red-handed. When Hoover ordered her to vacate the premises, she refused, brazenly asserting that she possessed a miner's right (prospecting permit) and was engaged in the legally permissible search for alluvial gold![67] It then developed that even if it could be proved that she was *not* really prospecting (and thus was in fact trespassing), the law provided no clear means of evicting her. Such were the peculiar frustrations facing a Westralian mine manager in 1898.[68]

Not all of Hoover's problems had such comic overtones. On August 3 falling earth crushed an employee working underground. It was the only fatal accident during Hoover's tenure. The next day a coroner's jury concluded that no one was to blame for this mishap and that the management had taken every safety precaution.[69] Hoover reported to his company's legal manager that the mining inspector and other observers agreed that "no possible precaution had been omitted and that the accident was due to the man's own carelessness." He therefore believed that no lawsuit for damages could succeed, and as far as is known, none occurred.[70]

A separate episode involving a workman's compensation claim was less easily resolved. In February 1898, before Hoover became manager, the Sons of Gwalia, Ltd. purchased an accident insurance policy providing coverage up to £2,000 for any single case. Late in May a man named Swanney caught his forefinger in some machinery; his finger had to be amputated. At first Swanney did not seem inclined to seek damages. But by July, when Hoover notified his company's legal counsel, the situation had changed. At this point Hoover felt that Swanney would accept a compensation of £30. The insurance company hoped he might be persuaded to settle for less; Hoover agreed to try. But evidently Swanney had other ideas, for on August 1 Hoover forwarded certain statements by various individuals at the mine about the case. On the basis of these Hoover thought that Swanney had no real case but that if he went to court he would win most of his claim anyway. A few days later new evidence surfaced that Swanney's foreman had been careless—a fact which made Hoover "not too certain of no liability." Finally, after negotiations with Swanney's lawyer, the claim was settled out of court for £75. But the insurance company's representative warned that Swanney was a troublemaker who ought not to be employed further at the Sons of Gwalia. Hoover agreed and promised not to rehire him.[71]

Just when the Swanney case and the fatal underground accident were vexing Hoover most, he had to appear in court as a defendant in a lawsuit brought by a worker at the mine. In a report to his superiors Hoover explained his version of the genesis of the suit:

> We have this week been summoned in a suit against the Company in the matter of an underground contract. We let a contract for driving the South Drive 200-Ft. Level, and as is our custom 25% of payments is withheld until completion of the work to our satisfaction. These Contractors were to push the work continuously, however they missed one shift and we warned them of the terms of their agreement, they again missed a shift and a second warning was given. The third time they missed a shift we took away their contract and tendered payment less the 25%, which they refused to accept and now bring suit for the entire amount (£26).

Since Hoover relied on a substantial amount of contract labor, he considered it "bad policy" to give in and thereby "vitiate the force of such contracts in the future." It would be better to fight "for the principle sake," even though he felt he might lose given the "general prejudice of local Magistrates in favor of working men against 'Capital.' "[72]

And so on August 4, 1898 the case of *Sullivan v. Hoover* was heard by the Mount Margaret Goldfields mining warden, a man whom Hoover did not admire.[73] Two questions were crucial to the dispute. What were the precise terms of the contract? And why had the miners failed to work continuously on their shifts? In the warden's opinion, the evidence was "weak and conflicting." Hoover testified that he had posted notices calling for tenders on the job. But none of these notices was produced in court and Hoover was uncertain whether they specified that 25% of the contract money would be withheld if the management was dissatisfied. In fact, no written contract was made, and Sullivan claimed that he had not read the posted notice. Instead, the actual letting of the contract was done by verbal agreement between Hoover's underground manager (Agnew) and the contractor (Sullivan), whose recollections of their conversation conflicted sharply. As for the requirement that the men work continuously on shifts, Hoover said this was invariably his policy. Agnew testified he had so informed Sullivan. But the warden could not understand why, if Sullivan and his men knew this, they would leave their shifts and risk forfeiture of 25% of their pay when their job was almost completed.

In the absence of a written contract, the warden awarded Sullivan most of the contract money he sought and advised the defendant to make written contracts in the future.[74] Hoover was disgusted. "We have experienced the bush Magistrates usual ideas of Law," he informed his superiors. According to Hoover, the warden "took a middle course"—an illogical compromise, in Hoover's opinion, since if the plaintiff had "any legal claim" he should have received the full amount he asked for.[75]

Hoover had little time to lament such irksome distractions. The multifarious duties of a mine manager were quite sufficient for any man's energies, particularly now that the outlines of future development were determined. During August, September, and October Hoover pushed ahead on several fronts. With a scorching summer coming on and his staff still living in tents, he was anxious to complete the construction of the new brick office building and staff living quarters. In August cottages for the accountant and underground manager were finished.[76] Early in October the four-room General Office building was completed and occupied.[77] In consultation with the Coolgardie head office Hoover directed much of his attention to the design of the forthcoming mill and metallurgical plant and to the selection of appropriate equipment for the mine.[78] Early in October the construction of a new main shaft—an incline shaft to be set at a 45° angle—was at last begun.[79]

Since the new mill and machinery would not be installed for several months, Hoover continued to direct operations with the resources at hand. At times unexpected obstacles arose. During September a "great flow of water" began to hinder crosscutting at the 300-foot level of the mine. By September 24 over 55,000 gallons were being pumped daily out of the mine.[80] A couple of weeks later the ground at the 300-foot level suddenly became extremely hard. Despite Hoover's use of the most capable men and his offer of bonuses for good results, progress at this level was extremely slow.[81]

Still, Hoover pushed steadily forward. By early August his annual payroll had climbed to £30,000.[82] According to his accounts, working costs at the Sons of Gwalia declined in August to £1.3.9 per ton—"the lowest yet accomplished in the Colony," he reported, "even against Mines with much larger equipment, and consequently greater tonnage to distribute extraneous expenses over."[83] And when in November Hoover submitted his quarterly report for August through October, his results were better still. Working costs for this period averaged only £1.1.4 per ton. During the quarter over 4,600 ounces of gold were mined, yielding a surplus of about £7,620—more than quadruple the profit of the previous quarter.[84]

I I I

Now, however, came another abrupt, unexpected transition in Hoover's engineering career. During the early summer of 1898 C. Algernon Moreing—engineer, promoter, and partner in Bewick, Moreing and Company—made a tour of China. Impressed by its mineral wealth and potential, and particularly by the coal-mining region near Tientsin, Moreing urged the Chinese government to organize a Bureau of Mines and to develop its resources with the aid of European capital and advisers. Upon his return to England he continued negotiations, particularly with Chang Yen-mao, general manager of the vast Kaiping collieries and (from mid-November on) imperial mining administrator for the regions of Chihli and Jehol. Moreing eventually agreed to loan Chang the sum of £200,000 for development of an ice-free port at Chinwangtao near the coal fields. Since Chang was also eager to have British assistance in developing gold mines and other mines in the province of Chihli, it was decided that Moreing would provide a foreign engineer who would serve a dual role: technical adviser to Chang and representative of the foreign bondholders in the construction of the harbor works at Chinwangtao. Before long a cable went out to the Sons of Gwalia.[85]

Hoover later recorded that when Moreing's offer came, he accepted it with alacrity. An increase in pay, the lure of the Orient, the prospect of liberation from the oppressive heat of the outback, above all a chance now to marry and settle down in an environment more hospitable than the bush: all these supplied motivation and enthusiasm.[86] For Moreing, too, the selection must have seemed felicitous. Probably no one in his organization was more proficient at examining gold mines than Herbert Hoover.[87]

If China supplied the opportunity, events in Australia provided the catalyst for Hoover's new assignment. During the latter part of 1898 Hoover's relations with Ernest Williams continued to be strained. Several times the Coolgardie office challenged certain of Hoover's policies and even the accuracy of some entries on his monthly returns. Hoover responded forcefully and often with a hint of asperity. He did not hesitate to point out errors and misunderstandings on the part of the head office.[88] And he was not inclined to muffle his opinions. Some months earlier, in fact, in a mood of irritation, he had written a rather curt letter to Lester Hinsdale. Afterwards, deeply chagrined, Hoover apologized. He urged his old friend to remember that "I deal with such a crowd of damned scoundrels that by habit I say things much stronger than I mean."[89]

And so, to end the friction between his two chief men in Australia, Moreing offered Hoover the job with Chang.[90] By one account the crisis climaxed dramatically. According to Richard Atwater, an American engineer working for Bewick, Moreing in Australia at the time, Hoover became so angry at Williams that he organized an effort to oust him. According to Atwater's story, Hoover, Mitchell, and three other strategically placed American engineers decided to confront Williams together, notify London, and in effect go on strike. They hoped thereby to force London to remove Williams from command. But the Yankee plot collapsed (said Atwater) when Williams learned of it, took countermeasures, and, at the showdown meeting, fired Hoover instead. Outmaneuvered, Hoover appealed to Moreing, who sustained Williams but, in recognition of Hoover's record and ability, decided to send him to China.

This, at least, was Atwater's story,[91] told by a man whom Hoover later removed from his job in Western Australia. Whatever its accuracy (and Atwater was not a friendly source),[92] by November 7, 1898, and probably sooner, Hoover knew that he was leaving the Sons of Gwalia.[93]

For several days Hoover's departure was delayed by negotiations with London about his replacement.[94] He told the Afghan owners of a cartage business in Coolgardie that he was going to "a better land where we're not troubled with camels!"[95] A few weeks later he confided to his cousin that he did not "relish . . . a bit" the prospect of "two years siege" in northern China. Nevertheless, "it can't be any worse than West Australia. . . ."[96]

On November 21, 1898 Hoover formally gave up his reins of authority at the Sons of Gwalia mine.[97] A few days later his successor, Harry James, complimented him highly on his accomplishments as superintendent during his short tenure, despite the obstacles against which he had struggled.[98] The next day, on Ernest Williams's orders, James fired three of Hoover's senior staff.[99]

As Hoover prepared to embark on the long voyage to London, he could reflect on an eventful and productive experience "down under." In eighteen months he had journeyed more than five thousand miles by team and had become probably "the most traveled man" in the Western Australian gold-fields at that time.[100] He had helped to establish single-hand drilling, disciplined management, high standards of efficiency, and other innovations in the aftermath of an extravagant boom.[101] He was one of the first mining engineers in Western Australia to expound the importance of systematically processing vast amounts of low-grade ore through the use of advanced mining techniques.[102]

Above all, Hoover's name became forever associated with the Sons of Gwalia, his first sustained venture in mine administration. One Australian who knew him in this period later credited him with "a complete re-arrangement of the whole organisation" of the mine—in fact, the introduction there of "revolutionary" practices that reduced costs and enabled the business to operate profitably for years.[103] Although Hoover was at this mine less than seven months, he initiated and guided its transformation into a venture that fully justified his confidence. The Sons of Gwalia went on to become a healthy dividend-payer—in fact, the greatest gold producer in Western Australian history outside of Kalgoorlie's Golden Mile.[104] When it finally closed in 1963 after an extraordinarily long life of sixty-six years, it had yielded over 2,580,000 fine ounces of gold from more than 7,000,000 tons of treated ore.[105]

The intense, ambitious, purposeful American engineer had been a "high-pressure man," as one Australian journalist was later to remark.[106] Not everyone liked this hard-driving, self-driven Yankee-in-a-hurry. But at least among the managerial class he had won considerable esteem. When he left the goldfields the Coolgardie correspondent of the *Australian Mail* declared that Hoover's departure was "regretted by a large circle of friends, who recognized in him an eminently capable mining engineer, an indefatigable worker, and an all-round good fellow."[107] Nor did Hoover forget those who were loyal to, or dependent on, him. Early in 1899 he calculated that in the preceding two years he had loaned more than seven thousand dollars to his family and friends.[108]

Early in December Hoover left Albany, Australia, for London, his first stop on the way to China.[109] A few days later the *Engineering and Mining Journal* of New York published a detailed technical article by him on the state of the West Australian gold-mining industry. It was in effect a comprehensive survey of the conditions he had encountered in the preceding year-and-a-half. Hoover carefully analyzed the impact of various metallurgical, environmental, and economic factors on the industry's costs. Labor, for example, was inefficient and Hoover was uncertain how to solve this problem. In some mines," he said, "Italians have been tried and found to accomplish about one-half more work, but they possess certain disqualifications." Hoover did believe that the quality of labor had substantially improved in 1897–98 and that future savings in expense must emanate from "increased efficiency" of labor rather than "reduction of wages."

All in all, Hoover was confident about the future of gold mining in Western Australia. Improved economic conditions, large-scale operations, and better management would lead to lower working costs, an increase of payable ore, and a more broadly based industry. As for specific ways to reduce working costs (a subject crucial to long-range viability) Hoover singled out five: reduced tariffs on food and supplies, lower freight rates, expanded railroads, "removal of restrictions on Asiatic labor," and "decrease in labor requirements to hold title" to mining leases.[110] It is unlikely that the latter two recommendations were popular in Australia.

At the beginning of January 1899, by way of the Suez Canal, Naples, Marseilles, and Paris, Hoover reached London, where he consulted for a few days with his superiors at Bewick, Moreing.[111] Before he left England he was interviewed by the *Australian Mail*. Once again Hoover expressed satisfaction with Western Australia—"one of the leading gold-producing countries of the world." He lavished praise on the cost-cutting success of Deane P. Mitchell at the East Murchison United, "the big mine of the north." Hoover was certain that it had "a splendid career before it." Above all, he spoke with pride about the Sons of Gwalia, whose working costs, he said, were "lower than in any other part of Western Australia."[112]

Hoover believed that working costs would decline in the colony. For one thing, the labor force on the mines was improving in efficiency. With the failure of many "prospecting ventures" and with consequently increasing joblessness, it was now possible for companies to hire only the most competent men from the pool of the unemployed. But, Hoover emphasized, "there must be good management. Bad management has been the curse of the Western Australian goldfields. The only true basis on which to judge the management of a mine is by working costs." This was the correct criterion—not output, not the richness of the ore. The implication of his remarks was unmistakable. By this standard Herbert Hoover was the best mine manager in Western Australia.[113]

It is impossible to say whether this was literally true. Mining was no profession for the diffident. Hoover himself, in his interview with the *Australian Mail*, overstated his accomplishments at the Sons of Gwalia.[114] Other mine superintendents computing their working costs may not have used comparable methods of accounting. Hoover, for instance, did not include expenditures for construction, equipment, and most mine development in the category of working costs. Nevertheless, the boyish-looking Yankee had not acquired a goldfields reputation without reason. Among professional mining men in Western Australia he was recognized as one of the ablest.

The young American did not tarry long in London, London in January with its fog (as he put it) "so thick that the street lamps are lit all day."[115] China and the Orient were on his mind—China and a girl back home. During the three years since his graduation from college Hoover's affection for Lou Henry had not diminished. In mid-1898 she had graduated from Stanford University with a degree, like his, in geology. Now she was living with her parents in Monterey. When Moreing asked Hoover to go to China, the young American made one stipulation: that he be permitted to visit the United States first.[116] Moreing consented. Before leaving Australia Hoover dispatched a cable to Lou in California: would she marry him? By cable she replied that she would.[117]

From London, then, to New York; from New York to Monterey.[118] Hoover arrived at the Henry home on February 1, 1899 and for the next nine days stayed with his fiancée and her parents.[119] A few years before, prior to entering Stanford, Lou had taught school for a time in Monterey and had become a cordial friend of the local Roman Catholic priest, Father Raymond Mestres, in whose parish hall she conducted classes for a time following the destruction of the local school by fire. At the end of the school day she would detain her Catholic pupils until Father Mestres entered to teach catechism. Often she attended parish parties at the church hall. For his part the priest did so much to help the young schoolteacher that she is said to have remarked that if she ever married she would ask Father Mestres to perform the ceremony.

When Lou returned to Monterey after graduating from Stanford, she collaborated with the priest in establishing a baseball park in the town. Now, in February 1899, she and Bert asked Father Mestres to marry them. At first the priest demurred. Since the couple was not Catholic (the Henrys were Episcopalians), Mestres explained that he could not perform the ceremony without a special dispensation from the bishop, which he himself declined to seek. The couple, however, did not give up. Soon afterwards, the bishop of the diocese happened to visit Monterey, and at a reception Bert and Lou forthrightly approached him. Would he grant the requisite permission for Father Mestres to officiate, Hoover asked? The bishop gave his consent.[120]

Accordingly, on Friday morning, February 10, 1899, at eleven o'clock, Herbert Hoover and Lou Henry were married by the priest in the sitting room of the Henry family's home. Bride and groom wore complementary brown traveling suits. Then, at 11:47, they boarded a train for San Francisco, city of the Golden Gate, from which, the very next day, they sailed for China.[121]

Jesse and Hulda Hoover
(Herbert's parents), ca. 1879.

A Hoover family reunion, ca. 1878. Herbert is second to the left from boy in tree.

Theodore, Herbert, and Mary ("May") Hoover, 1888.

Dr. Henry John Minthorn and his wife Laura.

*Herbert Hoover as a Stanford
University sophomore.*

*Herbert Hoover (second from left), his fellow Geology students, and their
professors, ca. 1893 (Dr. John C. Branner, seated, middle).*

Herbert Hoover, 1897 (probably in London, April 1897, on his way to Australia).

Herbert Hoover (seated, left) in Australia, ca. 1897.

OPPOSITE ABOVE. *Miss Lou Henry at the age of seventeen.*

OPPOSITE BELOW. *Lou Henry and Herbert Hoover at the time of their wedding, February 10, 1899 (Lou's parents and younger sister Jean also in picture).*

7

China:
The First Year

I

T H E Hoovers' honeymoon voyage across the Pacific on the steamship *Coptic* took nearly a month, with stops in Honolulu and Yokohama.[1] Long days at sea on a slow boat to China provided time to sort out one's affairs and responsibilities. To his friend and financial agent Lester Hinsdale, Hoover wrote that after loaning seven thousand dollars in the past two years, he could no longer be so unstinting. He had a wife to care for now.[2] Hoover took time also to send a letter of gratitude to the kindly Quaker professor who had been willing to give him a chance eight years before. Without Joseph Swain's support and interest, Hoover would never have gained admission to Stanford University in the autumn of 1891. Now, he told Swain, he was on his way to China "to conduct some negotiations of considerable character" for the firm of Bewick, Moreing. He expected to stay in China for at least two years.[3]

The ocean journey had an interest of its own. On board was a soon-to-be-famous American war correspondent, Frederick Palmer, with whom the Hoovers became quick and lifelong friends.[4] Early in March the *Coptic* reached Shanghai. From there the Hoovers traveled north to the city of Tientsin, on the Peiho River, about sixty miles southeast of Peking in the province of Chihli.[5]

Behind Hoover's arrival in northern China lay a long chain of circumstances. In the closing years of the nineteenth century the once isolated Celestial Empire was reluctantly opening its gates to the West. Conscious of

China's acute weakness and of its need for "self-strengthening," some of her ruling elite perceived the necessity for reform. They hoped to use the for- eigners' superior technology and expertise to develop China's resources, modernize her primitive industry, and restore her self-sufficiency and pride. In the wake of a disastrous and humiliating war with Japan in 1894–95, the vulnerability of China was starkly apparent. When, in November 1897, Ger- man troops seized Kiaochow Bay in the province of Shantung—supposedly to atone for the murder of two German missionaries by Chinese peasants—a new wave of turbulence was unleashed. A few weeks later the Chinese gov- ernment abjectly leased Kiaochow Bay to Germany for ninety-nine years, along with railway and mining rights in Shantung.

With German audacity thus rewarded, rival powers hastened to obtain similar cessions: the Russians at Port Arthur, the French at Kwang Chow Wan, the British at Weihaiwei and the environs of Hong Kong. The partition of China seemed increasingly possible; a furious scramble for concessions had begun.

If territory and spheres of influence were the prizes in this quickening imperial contest, the principal chips were railways and mines. From Britain, France, Belgium, Germany, Italy, and Russia now came a swarm of conces- sion-seekers, supported in varying degrees by their governments: financiers, railway experts, civil and mining engineers—all lured by the vast untapped potential of China and the dream of wealth and power for themselves. Among them, in the spring of 1898, was C. Algernon Moreing.

Moreing's interest in China had been stimulated by his sometime business associate William Pritchard Morgan, M.P., from whose interests Moreing had bought the Sons of Gwalia mine in Australia. In 1896 Pritchard Morgan met Li Hung-chang, viceroy of the province of Chihli and the most respected Chinese statesman of the late nineteenth century. Encouraged by Li, Prit- chard Morgan returned to England, where he entered into collaboration with Moreing. In 1897, accompanied by one of Moreing's best engineers, Prit- chard Morgan conducted a preliminary survey of mining opportunities in northern China and returned to England to urge the British government to guarantee a massive loan to China.[6]

On January 3, 1898 Moreing cabled Li Hung-chang, informing him that he had begun a campaign to influence British public opinion to support the huge British government-guaranteed loan. China's finances were in a precar- ious state; no doubt Moreing hoped that Li would appreciate his services. But, Moreing added candidly, if his effort proved successful he must have his reward: a mining concession in the province of Chihli. As an inducement to win Li's approval, Moreing promised to "reserve" for the viceroy a per- sonal "interest" in such a financial venture.[7]

A few weeks later Moreing published an article in an influential British periodical on the subject of "Great Britain's Opportunity in China." He painted an alluring portrait of China's economic potential and urged the British government to exploit it via the "epoch-making" new loan. Among other things, Moreing urged the British government to use the loan to compel the Chinese to institute a modern "organisation and code of mining regulations."[8]

That spring Moreing and Pritchard Morgan visited China at Li Hung-chang's invitation.[9] Impressed by the immensity of China's undeveloped mineral wealth, Moreing proposed to Li that the Chinese government establish a single Mines Department, or Central Mining Administration, for the entire empire. Such a bureau would have a European mining adviser. It would be complemented by a geological survey and geological museum to be created in each province. Then, he argued, China could undertake properly the "exhaustive expert examination" of her mineral resources antecedent to the development of her mines using "the best European and American methods."[10]

The role Moreing envisaged for himself in this grand design soon became evident. During his tour Moreing inspected the coal-rich Kaiping mines near Tangshan, northeast of Tientsin, and became acquainted with its powerful general manager, Chang Yen-mao. He also met and consulted with Gustav Detring, the Commissioner of Customs at Tientsin since 1877. Detring, a German, was one of the most influential Europeans resident in northern China; he was a friend and confidential adviser to both Li and Chang. To Moreing such a man must have seemed the ideal vehicle for entrance into the competition for China's riches. To Detring, therefore, he offered an alliance: they would work together to establish the Central Mining Administration— Detring to be its "head in China," Moreing's engineering firm "to supply the experts and the financing." The profits would be divided evenly between them.[11] It was a daring, ambitious, almost intoxicating vision: Bewick, Moreing the mining engineers for a government of 300,000,000 people and more than 3,000,000 square miles!

In the end it proved to be too ambitious; Moreing was obliged to scale down his scope of operations to one province only: Chihli. A self-made millionaire who told his friend Pritchard Morgan that only wealth ever impressed anybody, Moreing seriously misjudged Li Hung-chang. According to Pritchard Morgan, the viceroy took offense at Moreing's boasts about his wealth and power and forebade Moreing to enter his residence again. At Li's request, Pritchard Morgan severed his ties with Moreing.[12]

When Moreing returned to England in the early summer of 1898, nothing was yet settled. But while his effort to impress Li had gone sour, his contacts with Chang and Detring had not. The Kaiping mines needed capital for an additional colliery and for harbor facilities at the projected new treaty port of Chinwangtao, as yet only a barren stretch of rocks on the coast. Before departing, Moreing discussed a loan for these purposes with Detring.

Chang, however, was hesitant. For one thing, China's young emperor had just launched an unprecedented reform movement. The mandarin aristocracy was in ferment; who knew what might happen next? Furthermore, the Chinese Engineering and Mining Company, which managed the Kaiping mines, had only recently borrowed heavily for another project from the Deutsch-Asiatische Bank, with the stipulation that any further loans must first be sought from it. Whether this German financial institution would welcome Moreing's appearance on the scene was problematic. Above all, Chang was concerned about the steep 12% interest rate that Moreing wanted and about the trouble that his political enemies might make over it.[13]

Finally, in mid-August, after what Detring termed "endless discussion," Chang signed a letter authorizing Moreing to raise a loan of £200,000 (nearly one million dollars) to finance the new colliery and the construction of a pier at Chinwangtao. "I feel sure," Detring told Moreing, "that you have an opportunity now to get into your hands the lead in mining matters in this country. . . ."[14]

Chang and Detring were motivated by more than a desire for much-needed capital for the Kaiping enterprise. As Detring explained to Moreing, Chang was deliberately seeking to "amalgamate" British, Chinese, and German "interest in the mines of Chihli." In this way he might win "sufficient protection in case of a general debacle or invasion from the north."[15] Too feeble to prevent encroachment by the western powers, China might yet be able to divide them by turning some (such as Britain and Germany) against the designs of others, such as the Russian colossus advancing into Manchuria. Whatever the strategy of the Chinese, C. Algernon Moreing had reason to savor Detring's words: with Chang, Detring, and Cartwright (a retired British customs official working with Moreing) all cooperating, "you will have the best chance of winning the mining race in China."[16]

In September 1898, only 103 days after it began, the young emperor's bold reform movement abruptly terminated. In a swift coup d'etat the monarch was placed under virtual house arrest, and power reverted to his formidable aunt, the Empress Dowager: aging, autocratic, increasingly xenophobic, and determined to control China as she had for nearly forty years. The demise of the "Hundred Day" Reform did not, however, retard Chang Yen-mao's ascent to prominence. On November 19, by imperial edict, he was appointed Director-General of Mines for the province of Chihli and district of Jehol.[17] Three weeks later he was named Assistant Director of the Northern Railways.[18] At some point during the year he was also promoted from general manager to Director-General of the Kaiping coal mines, managed by the Chinese Engineering and Mining Company.[19] One of the wealthiest men in northern China, a "large speculator," and a man apparently adept at palace intrigue, Chang was known to have friends at the imperial court—notably the Empress Dowager's principal eunuch.[20]

Even before the November decree formally granted him control over mining in Chihli, Chang took steps to expand his horizons. Early in the autumn, through Gustav Detring, he asked Moreing to recommend a mining engineer to survey and report on the mines—particularly the gold mines—of Chihli and southeastern Mongolia.[21] Eager to oblige, Moreing cabled Detring on October 10 that he could dispatch a "young energetic gold mining engineer"—a man of "great reputation"—at a salary of £2,500 (about $12,500). And so it was arranged.[22] Five months later Herbert Hoover arrived in Tientsin.

C. Algernon Moreing had not, however, sent the young American engineer all the way to the Orient merely to accommodate Chang Yen-mao. Moreing was not a philanthropist, and in a letter to Hoover in January 1899 he requested the American engineer to oversee the administration of the £200,000 Chinwangtao harbor loan that Moreing was then arranging. Moreing promised to pay Hoover ten percent of his own receipts for this service.[23] According to Hoover's later recollection, this meant another £1,000 per year in income.[24] Hoover, then, was to have two simultaneous responsibilities in China: technical consultant to the Director-General of Mines in Chihli and Jehol, and guardian of the interests of the foreign bondholders at the Kaiping mines.[25]

I I

H o o v e r and his wife entered Tientsin, a sprawling city of half a million people, on March 20, 1899.[26] At once the studious young American engineer began to compile data about the state of mining in Chihli.[27] He also started to assemble a trusted personal staff, beginning with George Wilson, his friend from Stanford days who had worked with him in Australia, and Daniel Francis, his former assistant accountant at the Sons of Gwalia. Both men arrived in China shortly after him.[28] Francis had been fired at the Gwalia soon after Hoover's departure; now he served as Hoover's personal secretary and stenographer. Hoover paid Francis's salary and travel expenses to China himself.[29]

Less than a fortnight after reaching Tientsin, Hoover embarked on a two-month tour of inspection of the gold mines of northern Chihli and Jehol.[30] His bride of but seven weeks stayed behind in the foreign settlement at Tientsin, tending the office with Francis and looking for a house to rent.[31] Accustomed in Australia to traveling fast and traveling light, Hoover was appalled to discover that in China such efficiency was unthinkable. Despite his protests, his hosts insisted on an elaborate expedition commensurate with his status and "face." When Hoo Yah or Hu-hua (as the Chinese called Hoover) finally embarked with Woo Sung (Wilson), the expedition had swollen into a retinue consisting of several Chinese mining officials, six grooms and personal servants, two interpreters, a military escort of up to twenty soldiers, a Chinese cook who knew how to prepare foreign food, about fifty mules and ponies, and an enormous clutter of baggage, mattresses, and provisions.[32] Hoover never forgot his ingenious cook who unflaggingly served five-course meals even when the cuisine was reduced to five varieties of cooked chicken and eggs.[33]

Such a cumbersome procession could not possibly cover more than twenty-five miles a day. Nevertheless, all precautions and proprieties must be observed for the foreign engineer. As one Chinese told Hoover, "Because you are a very expensive man, we can't afford to have you get sick."[34]

The province of Chihli in 1899 was vast, nearly the size of France, and divided in half from east to west by the Great Wall of China.[35] Beyond the wall, to the north, lay a mountainous, mineral-rich region and Mongolia. These were Hoover's objectives during his first journey of exploration for Chang Yen-mao. It was an unforgettable experience. There was the Great Wall itself, fifteen feet thick and thirty feet high in places, coursing over the most steep and rugged terrain. There were the dirt roads, so trammeled and eroded and dug up for soil that in places they sank thirty feet below the level of the surrounding fields. Every available space, even on the mountainsides, was tilled by peasants living precariously off the land. Near the walled-off imperial mining camp at Chin Chang Kou Liang, almost two hundred miles north of Tientsin, bandit gangs of up to a thousand men roamed, necessitating the presence of armed guards and sentries. Prudent payments to the more important bandit leaders earned the company protection from harassment by smaller gangs.[36] When Hoover entered one such mining settlement, hordes of curious Chinese gathered to observe this amazing foreign magician who could peer through the ground and discover gold. Hoover's Chinese servant passed the word that Hoover had this ability because his eyes were green.[37]

Despite two decades of intermittent application of Western methods in northern China, the prevailing level of Chinese mining practice was staggeringly primitive. To his wife in Tientsin (Hoo Loo, the Chinese called her), Hoover wrote from the field that most of the Chinese mine managers and officials he met had never even descended into a mine! Underground work was for coolies, they insisted. Hoover had yet to see a mine shaft or underground tunnel more than three feet two inches high and three feet eight inches wide. Most were a scant two feet by three.[38]

Mining and milling techniques were rudimentary. First, the ore was underhand-stoped, brought to the surface, carried in baskets to the mill (perhaps a mile away), and then hammered by hand into nut-size pieces. Next, this broken ore was spread on a flat stone about five feet in diameter and then ground by a cylindrical rock hitched to and propelled by a mule. Then the powdery ore was washed, and the concentrates panned off, yielding the gold particles at last.[39] Most of the mines Hoover visited were small, but a few, like the mine at Chin Chang Kou Liang, employed a thousand or more men and yielded respectable quantities of gold from extensive workings.[40]

Far more disturbing to Hoover than outmoded mining techniques was something that no Western engineer, however skilled and determined, could easily alter: a social system riddled with managerial incompetence, thievery, and "squeeze." Scarcely a month after he ventured into the field, Hoover reported to Gustav Detring that the "condition of things" in one company he was investigating was "simply rotten and discouraging enough when one contemplates trying to do good technical administration with these people." Already losing 2,000 taels (about $1,400) a month, the company would lose more when its laborers abandoned the mine for their fields during the coming rainy season. Furthermore, its directors were utterly ignorant of mining. And a faction opposed to the current management was even striving to sabotage its policies in hopes of bringing back its predecessor. "The mine is rampant with petty fraud," said Hoover, "to an extent that is simply sickening."[41]

Early in June Hoover returned from his long first journey into the interior. He had gone as far as the town of Jehol, 140 miles northeast of Peking, and to the southern part of Mongolia.[42] He now held extensive interviews with Chang in Peking, where he found himself "treated with the highest consideration and most exceptional honors."[43] Hoover was ablaze with proposals for developing the mines and instituting reforms. In a careful report to Chang he vigorously urged that the unprofitable (but potentially lucrative) gold quartz mine at Chin Chang Kou Liang be closed for a year until proper Western machinery could be imported and installed. He recommended that the company's valuable placer mine at the same location be further developed and reorganized under the "absolute control" of George Wilson (subject only to Hoover's supervision and Chang's approval). Hoover pointed out that laborers thrown out of work at the quartz mine could be reemployed at the placer mine (thereby expanding its production and profits). Wilson, meanwhile, could control the expenditures, reform the muddled accounts, and take measures to prevent the loss of gold.[44] Privately Hoover told Detring that with "a thorough sweeping of useless employees," "good management," and adequate technology, the quartz mine could eventually yield "hansome returns."[45] At various other mines owned by the same company Hoover recommended closures or further development as circumstances warranted.[46]

Hoover also proposed that three existing Chinese companies be consolidated and then floated as a single "Chinese-English Exploration Company" with £50,000 in working capital to be spent opening up and developing mines in the region of Inner Mongolia, beyond the Great Wall. Once these mines were fully equipped, they could be spun off as distinct companies with separate pools of working capital, all under the continuing control of the "parent company." Hoover stressed that for this scheme to be viable the proposed exploration company must obtain "exclusive title to the four counties here abouts." Then, he prophesied, it would become "one of the best ventures yet inaugurated in China." Hoover was certain that Moreing would approve this idea and that the necessary capital for it could be readily obtained.[47]

Throughout the summer of 1899 Hoover devised a variety of other undertakings for consideration by his Chinese employer. As in Australia, he was always thinking. To Detring and then to Chang he proposed that a "foreign mercantile house" be organized as the exclusive supplier to China of certain brands of foreign-made explosives, mining tools, and other goods needed by Chinese concerns. As Hoover described the plan to Chang, the Chinese official himself, along with Detring and the firm of Bewick, Moreing, would be part owners of this company. Its managers (also to be part owners, to give them incentive) would be Hoover's secretary Francis and an American "of unusual ability and experience in such business": Sam Collins, one of Hoover's closest friends in college. Such a business, he argued, could yield very substantial profits.[48]

But as Hoover soon discovered, Western-style innovations were not easily implemented in China. The "foreign mercantile house" proposal seems never to have gotten off the ground. At the large mining camp at Chin Chang Kou Liang in northern Chihli, Hoover eventually succeeded in placing Wilson as a director (the only Westerner on the site), but his efforts at reform were like the labors of Sisyphus. In letter after anguished letter Wilson described an infuriating web of "squeeze," mismanagement, thievery, and inefficiency. For one thing, the scales for weighing gold had been rigged. For another, gold that spilled onto brass pans was given to servants; gold clinging to iron filings was designated for the local director. Placer gold was pilfered. The accounts were a mess; some transactions were not even recorded. The local Chinese cashier loaned money indiscriminately. The payroll, Wilson estimated, was ten times what was necessary.

Despite repeated requests by Hoover, Chang Yen-mao declined to close the quartz mine, dismiss superfluous miners, and inaugurate Western methods. Chang evidently feared the political consequences of a Hooverian assault on squeeze and featherbedding. By April 1900, a full year after Hoover's initial recommendations, the needed Western machinery was not even purchased, the quartz mine was not yet shut down, and 60,000 taels (about $42,000) had been wasted.[49]

Hoover's scheme for an Anglo-Chinese gold-mining company in Mongolia fared no better. The British and Russian governments had recently signed a railway convention dividing their spheres of influence at the Great Wall, and Chang and Detring believed that the Russians would not tolerate a British-financed exploration company in their domain. Hoover thereupon suggested that Moreing establish an exploration company with *American* friends and at least some American capital. While Moreing would actually "technically direct" it, as an ostensibly American enterprise it might circumvent Anglo-Russian rivalry. Hoover's strategem appealed to Chang and to Detring, who hoped that "through Hoover," an American, "it can be managed to preserve the technical direction of the Mongolian Mines in [Moreing's] hands." But Moreing was apparently uninterested, and nothing was accomplished.[50]

Such obstructions no doubt aggravated the youthful American engineer, so accustomed to getting things done. An assertive modernizer in a highly traditional society, Hoover faced daily frustrations. When to the burdens of "squeeze," poor technology, and international intrigue was added what Lou Henry Hoover called "the utter apathy of the Chinese to *everything*, their unconquerable dilatoriness," the result, in her words, was "sometimes near heart-breaking to an energetic Yankee."[51]

During the summer, fall, and winter of 1899, Hoover led frequent forays into the interior of Chihli province and neighboring areas. This was work he excelled at: inspecting, analyzing, and evaluating prospects and mines. At times Hoo Loo joined him, riding on horseback at his side—both ignoring the stately sedan chairs to which their rank, in Chinese eyes, entitled them. Upon arriving at an official residence or mine, the expedition would be acclaimed by natives waving banners and detonating firecrackers. Sometimes Lou went underground into the mines herself—an unprecedented act for a woman in China. When she emerged, and particularly if an injury or fatal accident had occurred, Chinese armed with firecrackers, lanterns, and drums would enter the mine to expel the demons she had supposedly taken down with her.[52]

By early 1900 Hoover and two of his assistants had explored fifty gold-mining districts for Chang in the provinces of Chihli and Shantung alone.[53] His wanderings took him even farther: to Shensi province, to Inner Mongolia, to the Gobi desert and beyond; from Shanghai, on the coast, to Urga, capital of Outer Mongolia, 700 miles northwest of Peking.[54] At Urga (known today as Ulan Bator), Hoover met the Hutuktu or "Living Buddha," the third highest ranking Lama of Tibetan Buddhism. The divine Hutuktu turned out to be a youth tearing about on a bicycle in his courtyard.[55] On another occasion, when offered champagne by the elderly viceroy, Li Hung-chang, Hoover promptly choked on its contents. He learned later that Li had served this same bottle to foreign guests before and had poured the putrid "leavings" back into the bottle after they left. Hoover found the great Li to have a most peculiar sense of humor.[56]

When Hoover arrived in March 1899 his role under Chang Yen-mao was initially limited. In effect he was a consulting engineer only, not an administrator. He was to survey the mines of Chihli and to report on how best to develop them, using foreign methods.[57] The next stage—actual development—was still to come.

But even while Hoover was on his first inspection trip that spring, events were combining to augment his responsibilities. At the end of May, while Hoover was in the interior, Gustav Detring asked Moreing to "think about a man" he could send to China to serve as "technical adviser to Chang in all mining matters coming under his control." Such a man, said Detring, would supervise operations at all the mines in Chihli and Jehol, would investigate causes of mining accidents, and would "practically have to lead and foster the sound and safe development of the Mining Industry and especially Collieries." Detring expected that Chang would soon turn over to Moreing's engineering firm the "General management of the region under Chang's jurisdiction." If this happened, Detring wanted Chang's "technical adviser" to be a man so trusted by Moreing that he could act in China as Moreing's "alter ego."[58]

As usual, however, events moved glacially. It was not until September 1899 that Chang petitioned the Throne for permission to set up a Mining Association under his supervision and initially funded out of his own pocket.[59] In due course Chang received the necessary sanction, and the Mining Bureau for Chihli and Jehol was established. Its Mining Engineer-in-Chief was Hoover.[60]

Hoover now expanded his technical staff. From the United States in November came an old friend, John H. Means (Stanford, M.A. in Geology, 1892).[61] At once Hoover sent him on a seven-week expedition northeast of Peking.[62] From Australia he selected John Agnew and J. Wilfred Newberry, both of whom had worked under him at the Sons of Gwalia.[63] These three men, plus George Wilson and Daniel Francis, comprised Hoover's inner circle in China.

And always there were tasks to perform, plans to implement, schemes to lobby for with Chang and Gustav Detring. Early in 1900 Hoover formulated yet another such idea—this time to stimulate prospecting for metal mines throughout the province of Chihli. Hoover began by observing that soon he would have inspected most of the known metal mines in the region. But what about unknown ore deposits? To conduct a thorough search of "every hill and gully" would entail a gigantic outlay of time and money. Even if some promising prospects were discovered, further exploratory work would be necessary. Such a course of action would be utterly unprofitable, as Western experience demonstrated. In countries other than China, he pointed out, "thousands of men search over a region at their own cost because they own whatever they find." Costs of exploration and initial development they bore themselves. "If the Mine should turn out good they sell it to some company who erect machinery and work it. . . . The only people who make the profits are the Companies; of the original prospectors not one in 10,000 but dies a poor man. Therefore we cannot afford to place ourselves in the position of the prospector. . . ."

Hoover therefore proposed a scheme to harness this drive for the Mining Bureau's own ends. "There are always thousands of people," he asserted, "willing to do the prospecting in the hope of gaining great riches—the same as men investing in a lottery." Let them do exactly that, he advised. Let anyone, foreign or Chinese, organize metal mining companies in Chihli, and let half the shares in these concerns be allocated to the Mining Bureau at no expense to itself. In return for a half-interest, the Bureau would "undertake all official relations," pay all royalties to the Chinese government, and provide consulting engineers.[64] In short, Hoover proposed to let individual prospectors, enticed by the hope of a lucky strike, do the searching for metals. If they succeeded, then the Mining Bureau could step in, furnish technical assistance, pay the taxes—and collect half the profits.

Chang Yen-mao's reaction to this plan in unknown. Hoover himself acknowledged that it might be too partial to the interests of the recently established Mining Bureau.[65] But survey work for Chang, and development of gold and silver mines, were not Hoover's primary reasons for being in the Celestial Empire. He was not just a scout and mining expert for an ambitious Chinese bureaucrat. Nor was he there, by late 1899, solely as mining engineer-in-chief for the nascent Mining Bureau of Chihli. He was also C. Algernon Moreing's alter ego in northern China.[66] And the introduction of Western capital and expertise to develop the mines of Chihli was what Moreing had in mind. As the months passed, Hoover's attention increasingly turned to the most valuable prize of all: the vast Kaiping coal mines operated by the Chinese Engineering and Mining Company.

Founded in 1878 under the patronage of Li Hung-chang, the Kaiping collieries by 1899 had become, in Hoover's words, "the only successful mining venture on a foreign basis inaugurated in China."[67] The mines themselves consisted of operating pits at Tangshan and two other sites and were located in an enormous bituminous coal field stretching for more than twenty miles along the Tientsin-Newchwang Railway northeast of Tientsin.[68] The center of this rich field was nearly ninety miles northeast of Tientsin and seventy-three southwest of Chinwangtao. As the first successful major attempt to apply Western technology to a Chinese industry,[69] the Kaiping enterprise had to struggle against "almost stupendous obstacles" of prejudice and superstition in its first twenty years.[70] Would modern mining, for example, enrage the earth dragon or disturb the imperial tombs?[71] Only gradually did the company overcome native resistance in the early 1880s and build the first railroad in China.[72]

By the end of the century the Chinese Engineering and Mining Company was a thriving business, with approximately 9,000 employees, three collieries, a fleet of six steamers, more than fifty miles of underground workings, a network of wharves and warehouses in several cities, extensive land holdings, and a factory that produced several million bricks a year.[73] (The bricks were used instead of timber to shore up the tunnels underground.)[74] Although foreign engineers provided technical assistance, the administration lay entirely with the Chinese.[75] During the 1890s the annual output of the Kaiping mines tripled; in 1899 it reached nearly 780,000 tons of coal.[76] The Kaiping collieries were not only the largest and most valuable in China; they were now some of the greatest in the world.[77]

But like other mining ventures in the Celestial Empire, the Chinese Engineering and Mining Company was beset by numerous problems, as Hoover learned first hand when he and his wife visited Tangshan early in the summer of 1899.[78] For one thing, Chinese labor was appallingly unskilled and inefficient. The Tangshan colliery alone had 5,000 workers yet produced only three-tenths of a ton of coal per day per man—barely 10% of the average daily output of an American miner.[79] Moreover, the mines were administered under what Hoover bluntly called a "contractor slave labor system." Instead of hiring and controlling the work force itself, the company merely farmed out tasks to contractors, who then hired laborers of uncertain skill to do them. Hoover urged that this loose, primitive, and wasteful mode of industrial organization be abolished. Chinese miners should be "put on individual merit as much as possible," he advised. He was confident that they would respond to monetary incentives.[80]

"Individual merit." Individual initiative. Once again, as in Australia, Hoover was attempting to apply his social values in a less than receptive setting. As usual, his advice was ignored; a generation later the contract labor system still reigned at Tanghsan.[81] Chang Yen-mao later asserted that whenever Hoover returned from inspection trips he was always bursting with "all sorts of schemes for development of mines" that were "not practicable" and "did not conform to Chinese usage."[82] And without Chang's support, there was little that the foreign engineer could do to uproot the customs of an alien, pre-industrial society. For the present Hoover had to content himself with survey work and with preparing for the opening of an ice-free port for Kaiping coal at Chinwangtao.

Although Chang had authorized Moreing to raise a £200,000 loan for Chinwangtao in August 1898, a year later the deal was still not formally consummated. Despite the high interest rate that Moreing had insisted on, he was initially able to obtain takers in Europe for only half of the bonds and was obliged, at first, to underwrite the rest himself.[83] Moreing's difficulties in securing financial backing were not the source of the extreme delay, however. Once again the hindrances were in China. Even before Hoover arrived in Tientsin in March 1899, Moreing had dispatched a civil engineer to China to draw up plans for the proposed new harbor.[84] Hoover himself, arriving on March 20, carried legal papers for Chang to sign, thereby effecting the loan agreement.[85]

But then, as was to become almost a pattern, Chang temporized and declined to sign. English legalese, when translated into Chinese, he found "indigestible."[86] Furthermore, Moreing was demanding a substantial portion of Kaiping's assets as security for the loan. Chang worried about the public reaction if the Kaiping collieries were hypothecated to Moreing without his shareholders' consent, and he feared the political consequences if he turned to Moreing instead of the Chinese money market for funding.[87] Accused by the British ambassador and powerful British commercial interests of pro-Russian sympathies and of machinations to divert Northern Railway funds to his pet project at Chinwangtao, Chang was wary of taking any controversial or precipitate actions.[88]

Meanwhile Moreing, who had hitched his wagon so closely to Chang's

star, was striving to convince the British Foreign Office that Chang was reliable and not pro-Russian. Struggling to keep his post as Assistant Director
of the Northern Railway, Chang was grateful for Moreing's assistance.[89] By
now it was early summer 1899, and Moreing wished to increase the loan to
£270,000 with additional security.[90] And so the negotiations dragged on.

At long last, on September 20, with Hoover and Detring as witnesses,
Chang formally empowered Moreing to raise a fifteen-year loan of £200,000
for the construction of a pier at Chinwangtao and for a new colliery in the
Kaiping coal fields. As security the Chinese Engineering and Mining Company mortgaged its collieries at Tangshan and Linsi as well as numerous
other assets. The new colliery, the Chinwangtao facilities, and all related
expenditures, were to be controlled jointly by Moreing, Detring, or their
deputies. In other words, Herbert Hoover and Detring together would
supervise the project and authorize disbursement of the loan money.[91] Some
weeks later the Chinese government granted Chang permission to proceed.
"Chihli is the foremost province of the Empire," the imperial rescript
observed. It commanded Chang to proceed "gradually" and with care.[92]

No sooner did Chang sign the necessary document in September than
further difficulties ensued. Instead of mailing his letter of authorization and
mortgage bond at once, Chang delayed for nearly four weeks. And when he
did dispatch them, he requested of Moreing substantial changes in the contract he had just assented to. The clever Chinese bureaucrat directed his
courier to obtain Moreing's agreement to these alterations before surrendering the signed documents.[93]

How Moreing reacted to this negotiating tactic is not known. But it was
not until the end of January 1900 that the first installment of the loan was
actually received in China.[94] And it was not until after Moreing himself came
to China that winter that the final hurdles were overcome and the final loan
arrangements hammered out.[95]

Still, for all the maddening obstructions and delays, glimmers of progress
were appearing. During 1899 the Chinese Engineering and Mining Company
bought all the land within a three-mile radius of Chinwangtao (13,500 acres),
and in the final weeks of the year a large jetty was constructed.[96] It was a
grandiose conception. If successful, ice-free Chinwangtao would be the only
year-round open harbor in northern China and the center for the export of
the burgeoning output of Kaiping.[97] Hoover told the American Minister in
Peking that the Kaiping mines could produce 2,500,000 tons of coal a year
and that the new wharves at Chinwangtao would be equipped to handle
automatically shiploads of 2,000 tons or more—triple the current capabilities
of the company.[98]

When Moreing arrived in Tientsin in February 1900, the promise of Chinwangtao must have seemed bright indeed. An English-language newspaper
in China described the project as "the most prodigious and ambitious scheme
that was ever proposed by foreigners in Far Cathay."[99] And Hoover, not yet

twenty-six, would be co-director of disbursements. In the meantime Chang was doing his best to keep the Chinese imperial court interested by seeing to it that the Empress Dowager's entourage was well provided for.[100]

Significant though the Chinwangtao loan was, Moreing, Detring, and Hoover had even greater ambitions. During 1899 various ideas for reorganizing the Kaiping mines under Moreing's "technical direction and management" were discussed.[101] In a long letter to Moreing in June, Detring presented a detailed plan to achieve "the chief aim—the 'exploitation' of the important Kaiping coal basin." Detring proposed that the Chinese Engineering and Mining Company be converted into a joint Anglo-Chinese concern with a share capital of £800,000 and two co-directors, one foreign and one Chinese. Bewick, Moreing and Company would provide the technical staff and control the technical administration; the capital would come from Britain, Germany, and China. With foreign personnel and methods, Detring believed that the Kaiping collieries' "running expenditure" could be cut by as much as one-half. But Detring conceded that political obstacles lay ahead. While Chang would be glad to seek British protection for such an undertaking, his enemies would use this chance to destroy him by inciting Chinese patriotic antagonism against such collusion with the foreigner.[102]

While Detring was developing proposals for a multinational company to develop the Kaiping mines, Hoover was busy offering ideas as well. As early as June 1899, less than three months after his arrival, he boldly suggested to Chang that Moreing form an entirely new company capitalized at £1,000,000 to develop new coal mines and the harbor at Chinwangtao. To this company the Chinese Engineering and Mining Company would transfer all its property and assets in return for half the shares in the new venture.

Once again, however, Hoover's zeal ran into resistance. He soon had to report to Moreing that obstacles, as always, lay in their path. For one thing, the Chinese Engineering and Mining Company, in Hoover's opinion, had an exaggerated notion of the value of its property at Tangshan. This stood in the way of its accepting only £500,000 (or half-interest) for handing its entire undertaking over to Moreing. Furthermore, the fact that the Chinese Engineering and Mining Company was "of a quasi-official character" raised "almost insuperable difficulties in its sale."[103] Hoover undoubtedly realized that under Chinese law all mines theoretically belonged to the Emperor and that administrative control of mines, no matter how much foreign capital was invested in them, must reside with Chinese merchants.[104]

To circumvent these impediments Hoover devised another approach. A new company with £600,000 capital would be formed in which the Chinese Engineering and Mining Company would have a 30% share interest, in return for all its assets *except* Tangshan (thus avoiding the conflict over the Tangshan colliery's proper valuation). Since under this scheme the quasi-official company would continue to exist (instead of selling itself whole), and since it would hold what he later called a "large proprietary interest" in the new concern,[105] Hoover believed that the legal complications would thereby disappear. As he put it, "This places the Chinese Engineering and Mining Company merely in the position of a parent Company and obviates all objections." But there were limits to which Hoover would go in his pursuit of economic opportunity for Moreing, as he explained to his patron:

> The rottenness of Chinese officialdom is of course fully known to you. To obtain support for the most righteous cause influence is an insufficient acceleration. I have said that you would in no way consider any proposition which required bribery to secure it nor will I be mixed in such business.[106]

Hoover's proposal reached Moreing in early August 1899. Moreing cabled back that Hoover's suggestion could be carried out, and he instructed his agent to continue negotiations. Moreing himself planned to sail for China in December and could close the matter after reaching Tientsin.[107]

Even as the two men exchanged correspondence, however, the political climate in China seemed to be cooling toward concession-hunters. At the end of July a revised set of imperial regulations imposed stringent new restraints on foreign exploitation of China's mineral resources. Henceforth the shares of joint foreign-Chinese ventures must be at least half Chinese, and concessions must be confined to specific mines (instead of broad areas). The administration and management must be completely Chinese, with foreigners limited to technical roles. No foreign applications on other terms would be accepted. Moreover, the Chinese government continued to exact 25 percent of the profits as a royalty.[108] To many Westerners, Hoover reported, these regulations were "obstructive tactics."[109] Moreing pronounced them "impossible and unworkable."[110] The way of the Western businessman in China was hard.

During the remaining months of 1899, while waiting for Moreing to arrive, Hoover inspected gold mines, contemplated Chinwangtao operations, and attempted to relieve the tribulations of George Wilson at Chin Chang Kou Liang. During the winter Hoover enlisted Dr. Noah F. Drake, a Stanford-educated geologist and student of Dr. Branner, to undertake a geologic mapping of some coal fields west of Peking. Drake, who was then teaching in the Department of Mining at the Imperial Tientsin University, reported that the deposits were likely to sustain some large mines if the Chinese did not interfere.[111]

Hoover was excited by Drake's discovery. Initially he had retained Drake with the understanding that Drake would be free to publish his findings. But when Hoover learned of the field's enormous potential, he requested Drake to withhold publication for at least a year; premature publicity might interfere with Hoover's plans. Drake, the scholar, reluctantly acceded to the wishes of the businessman.[112] By the spring of 1900 three of Hoover's assistants were busily working in the area, which contained more anthracite coal than all the other known anthracite deposits in the world combined.[113]

Sometime also during these busy months, after his encounter with Li Hung-chang and his bottle of rancid champagne, Hoover undertook an engineering survey of flood control works along the Yellow River at Li's insistence. According to Chinese legend, disastrous floods always presaged the collapse of a dynasty. Hoover found that the condition of the dikes was none too good.[114]

Life was not all business. There was the tall, buoyant woman he had married in Monterey. During Hoover's initial journey into the interior Lou stayed at the Astor House hotel and then at the home of a friend.[115] Soon, however, the young couple rented a spacious, two-story, blue-brick house on Race-course Road at the edge of the foreign settlement.[116] Here they lived for nearly a year, assisted by a staff of fifteen Chinese servants.[117] Nearby, on Taku Road, Hoover's staff resided on the second floor of a house built by the Mining Bureau.[118]

Very popular with the "better class" in the foreign community, Lou Henry Hoover especially participated in the good life of Tientsin.[119] An enthusiastic horsewoman, she took steps soon after her arrival to acquire a trap and driving pony as well as a lively horse for solitary riding.[120] In the ensuing months the Hoovers obtained a pony for the popular local races and five other ponies besides.[121]

During the winter Hoover delivered several lectures on mining at the local university.[122] By winter also, with Drake, Wilson, and Means among their friends, the Hoovers were at the center of a growing "Stanford Colony" in the Orient.[123] In the spring of 1900 the Hoovers even held a banquet at their home; seven Stanford graduates living in China attended and formed an alumni association.[124]

The Hoovers evinced intense curiosity about the exotic old civilization in which they now lived. To Professor Branner at Stanford Mrs. Hoover wrote that she and her husband were fascinated by the history of mining in ancient China. With the aid of a Chinese scholar and translator, they were gathering data that she thought she might publish. Lou confided to Branner that she might write a general-interest book about China as a way to channel her enthusiasm. In the meantime she was devoting two or three hours a day to learning the Chinese language.[125] Hoover himself learned only a few score words—enough, however, to form a basis for communication with his wife on *"sotto voce* occasions" in later years.[126]

Mrs. Hoover's love of Chinese culture soon found a focus in the hobby of collecting antique Chinese porcelains, particularly blue-and-whites of the Ming and early Ching dynasties. Several decades later, by the time she died, her collection contained hundreds of items, some of extraordinary value.[127]

The Hoovers quickly discovered that running a household in China had its peculiarities. In the absence of the telephone, ricksha boys served as messengers.[128] While their servants were dedicated and honest (the Hoovers did not fear petty theft in the least), the pervasive custom of "squeeze" nevertheless produced peculiar results. Western housewives, for example, were not supposed to shop for their own food; this was the province of the cook, whose "squeeze" rights must not be interfered with. And when Mrs. Hoover complained that her household expenses were turning out to be twice that of Hoover's secretary, the chief servant replied that this was because Hoover's salary was twice that of his secretary.[129]

Early in February 1900 Moreing arrived in Tientsin, accompanied by a prominent British civil engineer whose firm was to supervise harbor development at Chinwangtao.[130] Anxious to bring matters to fruition, Moreing drew up a design for the projected new city on the still nearly desolate beach on the Gulf of Chihli.[131] He was also eager to acquire a promising gold mine that Hoover had surveyed for Chang in Shantung. And as the days lengthened into weeks he explored again with Detring ways of funneling foreign capital and expertise into the Kaiping mines.[132]

Hoover, too, was being drawn further into the vortex. On February 4 the Director-General of Mines for Chihli and Jehol issued a directive to his Mining Engineer-in-Chief. Chang authorized Hoover and Detring to raise a foreign loan of £1,000,000 to develop the mines that Hoover and the Mining Bureau had examined in the preceding months. Chang requested that regulations for working these mines and administering the loan be submitted to him for approval as quickly as possible.[133] During the next few weeks Hoover and Detring consulted with Moreing (who agreed to offer the loan) and drafted proposed regulations. Finally, in mid-May, Chang accepted their petition and permitted them to proceed.[134]

Meanwhile Hoover became embroiled for the first time in the internal affairs of the Chinese Engineering and Mining Company. As Engineer-in-Chief for the provincial Mining Bureau, Hoover's general sphere of operations included all the mines in the province. But Chang Yen-mao was also Director-General of Kaiping, which had a separate administrative structure. At its Tangshan headquarters Andrew Burt, a Scotsman, worked as Engineer-in-Chief with his own staff of twenty foreigners.[135] Late in the winter, while Moreing was still in China, the Chinese Engineering and Mining Company appointed Hoover to "take entire charge" of its mines at Tangshan and Linsi. Hoover's mandate was to reorganize these mines and render them more profitable. Burt was instructed to cooperate and to accept Hoover's orders.[136]

Soon, however, Hoover clashed with his nominal subordinate, who refused (according to Hoover) to carry out certain of his commands. Hoover accused Burt of costly mistakes, ineptitude, and an absence of "backbone," "grit," "energy," and "pride." Burt, in turn, accused Hoover of unfair criticism.[137]

Unable either to control Burt or to oust him, Hoover angrily resigned his position in late April. In his letter of withdrawal Hoover asserted that he had been pressured to take the assignment against his will anyway, since the mines had been in a dangerously bad state at the time. Moreover, he had lacked from the start the degree of authority that in other countries was "always considered absolutely necessary for good administration." And his request for even as much authority as he had received had led to an impugning of his motives. And so, lacking the "absolute control" he deemed essential in these poor conditions, Hoover bluntly terminated all connection with and responsibility for the Tangshan and Linsi mines.[138]

Since Burt evidently refused to cooperate fully with his superior, Hoover no doubt had grounds for complaint.[139] The company's Chinese directors, however, may not have shared Hoover's opinion of Burt's abilities. Several months later the Scotsman was still Engineer-in-Chief of the Chinese Engineering and Mining Company. Perhaps it was but one more case of the "unconquerable dilatoriness" of the Chinese. (Eventually Burt was replaced by George Wilson.)[140]

The Burt episode revealed much about Hoover. Back in 1897 he had told Moreing that he could not fulfill his promises for the Sons of Gwalia unless the "entire management" was in his hands. Now, in China, he would not take responsibility for mines that he said were unsafe unless he had "absolute control" over them. On one level Hoover's conduct at Kaiping made excellent sense. Why should he assume responsibility for dangerous mines if he lacked the power to do what needed to be done? But the significance of his behavior in the Burt affair went deeper than that, for it disclosed a pattern that emerged repeatedly in the years ahead. Behind the boyish countenance lay a strong will, combative temperament, and sensitive ego. Not a man to tolerate perceived incompetence, Hoover seemed to work best when "absolute control" was in his hands alone. When he had to deal with independent-minded men (like Ernest Williams and Burt) whom he did not esteem, friction often resulted. And when on occasion Hoover did not obtain what he considered his due, he could withdraw into a shell of offended righteousness.

Hoover and Moreing had more weighty matters on their minds that spring than Andrew Burt. Once more the exasperating difficulty of doing business in China was becoming manifest. At the last minute Moreing's attempt to acquire the gold mine in Shantung and convert it into an English concern fell through. Shantung was in the German sphere of influence.[141] As for Kaiping and other mines in Chihli, Detring continued to push for an international mining company or syndicate that might neutralize Great Power rivalry. Perhaps, he suggested, Belgium could serve as a source of capital. As a small country it might arouse less resentment, and its leading financiers had excellent connections with French, Russian, and German investors.[142] But such arrangements required time to effect.

To further complicate matters, Chang Yen-mao's mother died during the winter. Piety toward his ancestors dictated a hundred days of mourning and abstention from business: still another delay for Moreing and his Yankee representative. While Moreing called on Chang as he kept vigil at his mother's coffin, there was not much more he could do.[143] And as Moreing had learned already in the Chinwangtao loan negotiations, Chang's professed interest in a provincial loan did not necessarily assure a prompt agreement. Chang was not known for promptness.

When Moreing left China for London at the beginning of May 1900, the great project at Chinwangtao was finally underway,[144] but little else had been settled.[145] Moreing was considerably annoyed. Three months' exposure to the Chinese Engineering and Mining Company's management had given him "very bad impressions." If he had known earlier what he knew now, he grumbled, he would never have undertaken to raise the Chinwangtao loan.[146]

It now fell to Hoover and to Moreing's associate Cartwright to conclude the various negotiations. Their labors proceeded against an increasingly menacing backdrop of antiforeign disturbances throughout northern China. In the early months of 1900, armed Chinese zealots were organizing to extirpate the foreign devil and all his works. These militant bands of perfervid patriots took the ominous name of I-ho-ch'uan: "righteous harmonious fists." The foreigners called them Boxers.

All this swirling uncertainty only intensified Chang Yen-mao's well-developed propensity to procrastinate. Although Chang authorized the £1,000,000 provincial loan in mid-May,[147] this scarcely resolved the matter. The Westerners required additional authority in the form of Western-style legal documents written in a Western language.[148] Such documents must of course be signed. And obtaining Chinese signatures, as Hoover and Moreing well knew, was never a routine matter.

On June 10 Hoover described to Moreing how he was using China's growing turmoil to nail down the huge but elusive provincial loan:

> I have been devoting myself to propagating the theory that Changs mining rights are bound to be forfieted by the certain changes in government which are bound to insue and [I] have drawn [up?] a General Loan Agreement on the lines agreed upon when you were here . . . and Chang has promised to sign it at once but still he believes the Govt. may stand and [therefore he] delays. . . .[149]

Hoover reported that he was attempting to render the terms of this agreement favorable to Moreing's interests. Instead of Chang's offering the loan agreement to only one person, for instance, Hoover preferred to have the Chinese official address it to three "concessionaires" representing three foreign nationalities: Detring, Moreing, and Hoover himself. Hoover feared that it would not be "entirely in our hands if drawn in one name" (presumably Detring's). Already, it seemed, Detring was in contact with certain Belgian interests.

As originally drafted, the provincial loan agreement provided for Chang to receive 50% of the profits. But Chang was worried that he would lose this share if a change should occur in the Chinese government. Accordingly, Hoover rewrote the agreement, eliminating all or nearly all explicit provision for Chang's profits. Instead, as Hoover explained to Moreing, Chang would hold onto the provincial loan agreement "until the change came and then [he would] turn it over to us upon terms *to be agreed upon then.*" At that point

Chang could sell the agreement to Detring, Moreing, and Hoover and thereby make his profit. "You can imagine," Hoover added, "the negotiations in that case when it *must* come to us or lose all."[150]

As of June 10, though, nothing was concluded. Hoover was concerned that Chang would delay too long. As China's political unrest worsened, Hoover's anxiety to get results was deepening. "If the govt. changes," he told Moreing, "we must find an opportunity somewhere!"[151]

Meanwhile unexpected trouble was developing over the Chinwangtao loan. Moreing was no novice at the art of negotiation. If Chang wished to maneuver for new advantage, so could he. In response to Chang's demand back in October for alterations in the Chinwangtao loan agreement he had signed, Moreing during his winter visit successfully had demanded a quid pro quo. Moreing would accept a Supplementary Agreement modifying the original terms of the loan; in return, Chang would approve a separate "memorandum of appointments for administration" for the new colliery. Chang, in short, would get his alterations, but Moreing would control the personnel.

Probably because of his mother's death, Chang never actually signed these two documents—or at least the memorandum—before Moreing headed home to England. Now, however, when Hoover approached Detring in order to secure Chang's signature to the memorandum, Detring suddenly refused to cooperate, saying *he* had not agreed to Moreing's memorandum at all. The result was that Hoover now found himself at the center of a bitter row. On the one side Chang clamored for Hoover to turn over the Supplementary Agreement. But Hoover insisted that Moreing's memorandum on administration and personnel "be adopted first."

At this point Detring advised Chang to drop his demand for the Supplementary Agreement since, among other things, Moreing's memorandum was unfavorable to Chang anyway. And there for the moment the matter rested.

This bizarre chain of events—which Hoover later described as "tragic-comic" and "wearysome"—still had not run its course. With or without the Supplementary Agreement and memorandum, the £200,000 Chinwangtao loan was now in effect. Before long a £40,000 installment arrived, by prior arrangement with Moreing. Perceiving an opportunity to advance some designs of his own, Detring (in Hoover's words) used this money "as a lever" to gain Chang's signature to certain documents. In exchange for Chang's assent to these documents Detring promised to release the £40,000 to him.

Detring, however, had failed to reckon with Herbert Hoover. Under the terms of the Chinwangtao loan, Hoover and Detring controlled disbursements *jointly*, and now Hoover refused to co-sign! Hoover believed that Moreing's grant of the £40,000 was conditional on Chang's adopting the still-unsigned memorandum of administration. So now Hoover, in his own words, "refused to deliver [the £40,000] until Chang signed a similar form of administration."

The result was pandemonium. Chang (in Hoover's words) "fought against" signing a memorandum of administration "with every weapon he knew." Detring also was outraged. Having just extracted a signature from Chang, he was unable to fulfill his part of the bargain. Detring accused Hoover of breaking *Detring's* promise to Chang to turn over the money—a promise Hoover had neither known about nor agreed to.

At last Chang capitulated and signed a document containing everything originally in Moreing's memorandum of administration. Said Hoover simply, "He had to have the money." The upshot, in Hoover's opinion, was total victory: "we gained everything and gave nothing." Moreing had now gotten the substance of his memorandum on administration without even having to accept Chang's Supplementary Agreement in exchange. Chang was "a bit wild" over this outcome, Hoover reported, but blamed Detring.[152] The Chinese official and his German adviser had been outmaneuvered by a youth not half their age.

While all this bargaining was going on, Hoover found time to publish articles in two professional journals in the spring of 1900. In one he briefly surveyed the "present situation of the mining industry in China." Hoover had little enthusiasm for Chinese mining regulations and administration. Indeed, he said, the "smallest weakness" of Chinese administration was its "unfamiliarity with the business." Still, the tone of his article was moderate—and noticeably complimentary to his associates in China. Hoover acclaimed Detring above all for bringing about the "progressive measures accomplished so far" in Chinese mining and for farsightedly urging the Chinese government to exploit its mineral resources "upon a basis of broad national polity." And whatever Hoover's private doubts and reservations, he cited Chang Yen-mao's Kaiping coal mines as "the only successful mining venture on a foreign basis inaugurated in China."[153]

In his second article, an account of metal mining in Chihli and Shantung, Hoover summarized the geology, mining techniques, and other features of mines which he had inspected during the previous months. While parts of Chihli clearly had great potential, Hoover cautioned against inferring too much from the incredibly low wage rates for Chinese labor:

> The fact that an unlimited amount of able-bodied labour can be obtained in China for 6*d*. [about twelve cents in 1900] per day is often estimated in too favourable a light. To work, in the sense of Western miners, is an unheard-of exaction, and, even where these men have been employed under foreign direction for a number of years, the ratio of effectiveness is about 5 to 1. However, even at this rate, mining should be very cheap. The men are docile and easily handled, and their tendencies to dishonesty are probably no greater than those of other human beings under the same conditions.[154]

By early June 1900 Hoover had been in China about fourteen months. Now he had a further reason to reflect favorably on his accomplishments.

Among the documents which he sent to Moreing on June 10 were two which catapulted him to a new plateau of responsibility and financial success. The first took the form of a memorandum of agreement between Hoover and the Mining Bureau of Chihli. Under this contract Hoover was appointed Engineer-in-Chief for the next three-and-a-half years at an annual salary of £2,500 plus travel expenses and 600 taels a year for house rent. Hoover was to examine all mines in the province (or elsewhere) controlled now or in the future by the Bureau and was to serve as Engineer-in-Chief of any newly opened mines to which the Bureau might appoint him.[155]

The second document was a simultaneous despatch from Chang Yen-mao appointing Hoover Chief Engineer of the Wu-Sui-Chwang colliery about to be excavated by the Chinese Engineering and Mining Company under the terms of the Chinwangtao loan. For this responsibility Hoover was awarded an additional annual salary of £500 plus the right to recommend a subordinate mining engineer who would actually reside at the site. Chang praised Hoover as a man of experience and expertise, "well-qualified" in "both character and ability," "harmonious with the Chinese," and "straightforward."[156]

Hoover had ample cause to feel exhilarated. His annual salary would total £3,000 (almost $15,000) plus expenses and a rent allowance, not counting anything he might receive from Moreing.[157] On June 8, 1900 Chang Yen-mao formally signed the two contracts.[158]

The timing could not have been worse.

I I I

THROUGHOUT the winter and spring of 1900 portents of upheaval were multiplying across northern China. Emboldened by the Chinese government's hesitations and increasingly benign neglect, the Boxer phenomenon was acquiring ever more menacing dimensions. Sweeping northward from Shantung into the province of Chihli, rampaging Boxers massacred Chinese Christians (sometimes by burning them alive), set fire to missionary churches and Western property, and threatened to kill every foreigner in China. A mixture of superstition, patriotism, and nativist fanaticism, the Boxers practiced magic rituals and asserted their powers to fly, to rise from the dead, and to resist the penetration of Western bullets after a period of training.[159]

The first signs of trouble reached Hoover in May while on a trip to inspect the anthracite deposits in the Western Hills beyond Peking. Summoning his staff from the interior (Wilson on May 1 was at the edge of the Gobi desert in Mongolia),[160] Hoover retreated to the comparative safety of Peking.[161] Here he discovered that his wife, who had been visiting the capital city, was seriously, perhaps dangerously, ill. Catching the first available train, Hoover and Lou returned to Tientsin, where, as he later put it, "there was a better doctor available."[162] Early diagnosis had been alarming: it was feared that she might not pull through. Subsequent examination, however, revealed that her sickness was only a sinus infection.[163]

By late May Mrs. Hoover was well enough to attend a dinner at the Hoover home for seven of the eight Stanford graduates then residing in China.[164] On June 10 Hoover wrote to Moreing that his wife had "nearly recovered."[165] Yet the news was not all good. Hoover himself had been sick in bed for the past two weeks, and Francis, his secretary, had died of pneumonia on May 27.[166]

Daily now, almost hourly, the situation in northern China was deteriorating. In the villages, in the countryside, even in the cities, Boxer mobs were acting with terrifying ferocity against missionary schools, native Christian converts, anyone and anything tainted with the foreigners' intrusion into China. By early June the dead totaled in the hundreds, including a number of foreigners. In Tientsin, on June 5, columns of uniformed Boxers marched near Detring's home on Racecourse Road.[167] That same day the railway link between Tientsin and Peking was severed.[168] On June 9 Boxers set fire to the grandstand at the international racecourse outside Peking. Numerous Chinese Christian captives perished in the flames.[169]

As the crisis escalated several Western nations dispatched warships to the coastal city of Taku, on the Gulf of Chihli. Here on the night of June 9 Admiral Edward Seymour, commander of British naval forces in the area, received a telegram from the British Minister at Peking imploring relief at once. Early the next morning Seymour's forces, augmented shortly by contingents from seven other nations including the United States, rode inland by rail to Tientsin. From here, at mid-morning, the hastily assembled relief column embarked by train for Peking. After reinforcements the next day, the emergency force numbered about 2,500 men. Ahead of them, across a hot flat plain filled with hordes of Boxers as well as Chinese army units, waited the anxious foreign legations at Peking.

Seymour's gallant expedition soon turned into a nightmare. By June 13 it was bogged down scarcely half the distance to Peking. Attacked by fanatical Boxers, increasingly short of rations, and lacking enough materials to repair the torn-up railway lines ahead, the force began on June 15 a slow, harrowing retreat toward Tientsin.[170] The plodding ineptitude of the expedition was to attract the criticism of Hoover and many others.[171]

The exposed foreign settlement at Tientsin, meanwhile, was confronting ever greater perils. The foreign concession itself was a narrow corridor of land only a few hundred yards wide at most, stretching for more than a mile along the banks of the Peiho River. To the north and northwest a mere two miles away across a patch of ditches, burial mounds, and native huts, lay the walled native city. To the west, a level plain. To the south, a fifteen-foot mud wall—inviting cover for snipers. To the east and northeast, the Peiho.[172] The Hoovers, like the Detrings, lived beyond the southern embankment on the road running southwest toward the racecourse.

On June 10, soon after Seymour's expedition set out, Tientsin lost telegraphic contact with Peking.[173] On the fourteenth mobs of Boxers entered the native city without resistance from Chinese authorities. That night and the next, the skies over the old city turned eerily orange as the French cathedral and various missionary structures went up in flames. Boxer incendiaries attempting to infiltrate the foreign concession were repelled.[174]

On June 15 about 1,700 Russian soldiers arrived at Tientsin from the coast with orders to join Seymour's column. Camping that evening at the railroad station across the river from the concession, the Russians intended to head north the next morning. Suddenly, near midnight, charging Chinese assaulted the railway depot, only to be driven off with many casualties.[175] After this incident the Russian commander changed his plans and remained in Tientsin. Without this reinforcement (which more than tripled its meager defense force), the foreign settlement probably would have been annihilated in the days ahead.[176]

During this chaotic period Chinese servants, fearful of Boxer reprisals for consorting with foreign devils, deserted their Western employers in mounting numbers.[177] The Hoovers lost twelve of their fifteen servants in this way.[178] Clearly it was becoming risky to remain on the outskirts of the settlement. For several nights two of Hoover's assistants, Wilson and Newberry, had stood guard over Detring's home a mile-and-a-half south of the foreign concession. When torch-bearing Chinese attacked the railway depot, Wilson and Newberry raced on horseback to the settlement before being cut off. Safely inside the defense perimeter, they at once took part in a second skirmish, during which Western firepower proved its effectiveness. Unable for days thereafter to bury the Chinese dead left behind on the exposed plain, the foreigners had to endure the odor of decaying human flesh.[179]

Then on the night of the sixteenth a new element appeared. Thirty miles downriver, where the Peiho flowed into the sea, stood the strategic Chinese forts at Taku. In response to reports that the Chinese were laying mines in the river, moving reinforcements to Taku, and attempting to interdict the railway to Tientsin, all but one of the Western admirals issued an ultimatum to the Chinese garrison: surrender or face attack. Early the next morning, after a sharp fight, the vital Taku forts fell to the Western allies.[180]

To Hoover and many others it seemed that the admirals who approved the seizure were "insane." At that time, Hoover later told the press, "there were only 2,000 foreign troops in the foreign settlement at Tientsin, there were only 400 in Peking and the Seymour relief column, 2,000 strong, was midway between the two places. With the foreigners thus unprotected and unprepared the allied fleets did the very thing to fire the whole mine and to unite all the factions of the natives in opposition to us."[181] The Hoovers believed that it was "foolhardy" to precipitate official Chinese resistance so dramatically without even first alerting and supplying more protection to the beleaguered foreigners in Peking and Tientsin. Surely a diplomatic request to the Chinese to desist from provocative acts at Taku should have been tried before resorting to an act of war.[182] Defenders of the admirals, however, argued that China was already in a state of insurrection, that the situation was already grave, that Seymour was already trapped, and that further delay in securing communications on the coast would have been disastrous.[183]

On the afternoon of the sixteenth, one of Hoover's assistants spotted a small herd of dairy cows roaming on the plain south of the concession. He promptly rounded them up and brought them to the Hoovers' residence. This prize was to be most welcome in the days just ahead.[184] On Sunday afternoon, June 17, at three o'clock, barely eight hours after the capture of the Taku forts, an artillery shell exploded in the foreign settlement.[185] Hoover and his friends knew instantly what it meant: the Chinese army stationed around Tientsin had gone over to the Boxers.

For the next several days the besieged foreign settlement battled desperately for survival: 400 male civilians, 300 women and children, and about 2,500 foreign soldiers confronted 5,000 trained Chinese troops and more than 25,000 aroused Boxers.[186] The Chinese, moreover, possessed an array of artillery pieces, which, if properly used, could have reduced the concession's defenses to rubble.[187] The situation on June 18 and 19 was especially bleak, as Chinese soldiers attacked at several points and subjected the settlement to a fierce barrage of bullets and shells. In one assault, the Hoovers recorded, reckless Boxers "charged dancing, waving their guns in peculiar circles, giving out their fiendish howl."[188] More coordinated attacks at more locations could have breached the thinly defended line.[189] On the nineteenth, with ammunition running low, the military authorities considered whether they should make a break en masse for Taku.[190]

The mounting hysteria soon focused on several hundred Chinese, including "pro-foreign" Christian refugees and Chang Yen-mao, who for one reason or another were in the foreign concession when the bombardment commenced. Chang and some other Chinese owned flocks of pigeons that carried little whistles under their wings. During the shelling the pigeons flew wildly about, creating an unsettling sound. Swiftly the rumor spread that the Chinese in the settlement were using their birds to communicate with the Boxers and the Chinese army. On June 22 Chang and another prominent Chinese official were arrested by the British naval commander. Hoover was incensed. Years later he denounced the Chinese prisoners' European accusers as "rabble" and "hysterical wharfrats"; the British naval officer, Captain Bayly, he called "bigoted" and "pompous."[191]

For three days the two Chinese languished in confinement in almost unbearable heat. Only by strenuous exertions (including an appeal to the Russian commander) were Hoover, Detring, and several other foreigners able to arrange the prisoners' release and save them from execution as spies. Detring later praised Hoover for acting with "great courage" in this tense drama.[192]

These hundreds of Chinese refugees—numbering a thousand or more—

became one of Hoover's responsibilities as the siege wore on. Each day Hoover visited their quarters and arranged for them to receive supplies of rice and water, thereby earning himself the suspicion and antipathy of many Westerners in the settlement. And when a 750-pound Chinese shell slammed into the home of the American-educated Chinese manager of the Peking-Shanhaikwan Railway, Hoover and John Agnew rushed across the street to assist. They found that the manager's wife and one daughter were dead. While the distraught man dragged his wife's body to the cellar, Hoover carried one of the surviving daughters to his own home. The railway executive, T'ang Shao-yi, later became the first premier of the Republic of China. His daughter became the wife of the Chinese ambassador to the United States.[193]

Around the start of the fighting the Hoovers abandoned their home on the outskirts for the more centrally located residence of Edward Bangs Drew, the American Commissioner of Customs.[194] Every available man was needed now. Besides helping the Chinese refugees find food, Hoover worked daily at fighting fires (a constant hazard) and at building street barricades out of sacks of rice, sugar, and peanuts taken from warehouses.[195] At times he ran errands on his bicycle to obtain ice and other necessities for the makeshift hospitals.[196] At night, under armed British escort, he and his staff slipped beyond the barricades to the city's water plant where they boiled precious water for the settlement.[197] There was no let-up. There was no time for a let-up.

Dominating the foreign settlement was its large City Hall, named after the heroic British general "Chinese" Gordon. Now the symbolism seemed unpleasantly foreboding: fifteen years before, Gordon had died in the massacre at Khartoum. In Gordon Hall's spacious cellar, nearly three hundred women and children huddled for safety from the shells and bullets overhead. Not, however, Lou Henry Hoover—not for her the cloistered passivity of the "weaker" sex. Carrying a Mauser automatic .38 caliber pistol, Lou pitched in with zest—managing her dairy herd, bicycling on errands, and devoting long hours every day as a volunteer nurse in the hospitals. Someone humorously dubbed her the "Captain of the Guard" for her compound, and so every evening she selected the men for that night's watch—and kept her share of vigils, too. But while she was a good shot with her revolver and was ready to use it if the settlement were overrun, she never did fire her weapon.[198]

On June 23 a mixed force of nearly 2,000 men broke through to Tientsin from Taku. Three days later Admiral Seymour's battered expeditionary force, rescued by reinforcements, returned safely to the foreign settlement.[199] Although the risk of imminent death now receded, the battle of Tientsin was by no means won. The relentless showers of bullets and shells were a reminder of that. Despite the steady infusion of foreign detachments from the coast, the disparity of the opposing forces was actually getting wider. Eighty thousand Chinese army troops and 300,000 Boxers were now concentrated in the neighborhood of the concession.[200] The Westerners did not yet know that hostility between the Boxers and the Chinese regulars was preventing effective exploitation of their vast superiority in numbers and heavy guns.

Shortly after the advent of reinforcements on June 23 and the return of Seymour on June 26 came a number of war correspondents from America, including Frederick Palmer, the Hoovers' tablemate on their voyage to China the year before. For the next two weeks or so the Hoovers gave Palmer, Oscar King Davis, and some other journalists the use of their home.[201] Eventually the Hoovers themselves returned to their still-unscathed quarters on Racecourse Road.[202] Palmer was struck by Hoover's behavior, "coursing the streets at the double quick—nervously jingling coins or keys in his pocket and seeming to be chewing nuts without shucking them."[203] On one occasion Palmer watched as Hoover, deep in thought, walked down a street where bullets were falling—apparently unconcerned or (more likely) oblivious to his environment.[204]

If Hoover gradually became accustomed to the excitement, his wife seemed verily to thrive on it. To Hoover's considerable annoyance, and despite his pleas, Lou refused to leave when the first groups of women and children were sent downriver early in July.[205] One of Hoover's staff felt that she enjoyed the battle and did not appreciate the danger she was in.[206] One day a shell burst in the yard of the Hoover home. Instead of prudently seeking shelter at once behind a wall, Lou went to investigate where it had landed. A moment later a second shell crashed on the nearby street. Since the Chinese gunners were known to fire three missiles at a target in a row, another could be expected within seconds. It came—and exploded inside the Hoover house at the foot of the stairs. In a nearby room Palmer discovered Mrs. Hoover amidst the dust calmly playing solitaire.[207]

Finally, Lou agreed to leave—if Bert would do so, also. On Sunday, July 8, they spent much of the day packing and supervising the departure of a hundred of Hoover's Chinese dependents—a job interrupted for a time when another shell slammed into the home upstairs.[208] Hoover was reluctant to depart while his business interests were topsy-turvy and before all his Chinese friends were safely beyond the reach of the military authorities.[209]

The grisly climax of the month-long ordeal now approached. From the inception of the siege (although the Westerners could not know it), relations among the Boxer militants, the disciplined Chinese army, and the native populace had been anything but harmonious. In the first week of the battle several thousand Chinese corpses floated past the foreign settlement on the Peiho River.[210] When around July 1 Boxer looting inside the walled native city of Tientsin became unbearable to the local merchants, General Nieh's Chinese army units expelled the Boxers with bayonets.[211] According to Hoover's later account, some two thousand more Chinese bodies were spotted on the bloody Peiho. Denounced by the Boxers and rebuked by the Chinese government, Nieh committed suicide on July 5 by exposing himself to Western fire.[212]

Now General Ma took over, but he, too, despised the lawless Boxer irregulars. If they really possessed supernatural powers and invulnerability, he said, let them capture the railroad station or face the consequences. On July 11 the Boxers tried with ferocity but failed. When they returned that night to their quarters, General Ma's machine guns mowed them down.[213]

Early on Friday, July 13, a total of 5,650 foreign troops, spearheaded in the center by the Japanese, launched a daring and dangerous assault on the native city. Outnumbered ten to one, they would have to cross a forbidding, flat, two-mile stretch of no-man's-land pockmarked with ponds, huts, and mud. If successful, the Japanese must then attempt to dynamite a hole in the sixteen-foot-thick, twenty-two-foot-high wall that guarded the city.

Two American regiments participated in the day-long action, including the First Marines under Colonel Robert Meade and Major Littleton Waller. At Waller's request Herbert Hoover, on the morning of the thirteenth, joined the Marines on the left flank of the advancing allied force. Since Hoover knew the local terrain as a result of horseback riding with his wife, Waller wanted his services as a guide.[214] Years later Hoover recalled that day:

> We came under sharp fire from the Chinese on [the city] walls. We were out in the open plains with little cover except Chinese graves. I was completely scared, especially when some of the Marines next to me were hit. I was unarmed and I could scarcely make my feet move forward. I asked the officer I was accompanying if I could have a rifle. He produced one from a wounded Marine, and at once I experienced a curious psychological change for I was no longer scared, although I never fired a shot.[215]

By nightfall the situation was inconclusive. But next morning Japanese sappers succeeded in detonating the massive south gate to the native city in a spectacular explosion. Minutes later they opened an inner gate and entered the city to find the Chinese fleeing in disorder. The twenty-eight-day ordeal was over.[216]

Nearly one out of every seven men in the Allied attack force was a casualty in the two-day battle, including six killed and twenty-one wounded in the First Marines, whom Hoover accompanied.[217] In four weeks literally thousands of shells had fallen on the foreign settlement, although precise estimates varied widely: 5,000, said the American consul; 40,000, said Lou Henry Hoover; 60,000, according to Herbert Hoover.[218] For all the bombardment, however, the number of foreign civilian casualties at Tientsin was relatively small.[219]

In the aftermath Allied soldiers, joined by mobs of Chinese, looted what remained of the native city.[220] Hoover remarked that "the natives were as bad as the foreigners in the thievery. They stole from their neighbors, taking everything left by the foreign soldiers." According to Hoover, French and Russian soldiers participated in an orgy of rape and killing of Chinese civilians.[221] Of the Russians, the British consul probably expressed the local consensus. "They have fought most bravely against the enemy," he acknowledged—indeed, only their presence had saved the settlement from a horrible fate—"but have butchered harmless Chinese to an extent which will never be known."[222] In the weeks to come Chinese atrocities were repaid in kind by some of the avenging foreign armies.[223]

As the chaos and tension subsided Hoover and his wife took stock of their losses. Five shells had hit their home in Tientsin; many more had landed in their garden, stable, and dairy paddock.[224] Hoover calculated that damage to the buildings, plus lost furniture, silverware, and bric-a-brac, totaled $1,624. The Hoovers had also lost six ponies and several saddles valued at $500 as well as $600 worth of books, clothing, and other goods stored in warehouses destroyed on the coast.[225]

What, now, of the future? Business in northern China was at a standstill, his mining operations in disarray. At Peking the foreign legations were in desperate straits, and it seemed unlikely that Allied troops would arrive in time to rescue them alive. And if their rescue mission did fail, European revenge would surely be drastic. To foreigners living in Tientsin the partition of China, the end of the Celestial Empire, seemed imminent.[226]

Yet fate was twisting and whirling once again. From the anarchy and torment of the Boxer Rebellion arose a shimmering opportunity and the most controversial episode of Hoover's engineering career.

8

The Kaiping Mines
Are Acquired

I

O N June 23, 1900 Gustav Detring visited Chang Yen-mao in his prison headquarters in the besieged foreign settlement of Tientsin. It was an anxious interview. Arrested the day before as a Chinese "spy," Chang was facing possible execution. Outside, the clatter of gunfire and artillery rent the sultry summer air. All across northern China, anarchy reigned—portending catastrophe for the economic interests of the Director–General of Mines for Chihli and Jehol.

Detring explained to Chang that the largest of these interests—the Chinese Engineering and Mining Company—was in desperate straits. At Taku, on the coast, its property had reportedly been seized and plundered by foreign troops. At Tientsin many of its buildings were either on fire or already destroyed. Moreover, Russian and Japanese soldiers had occupied two of the company's coal yards, and the Russians were helping themselves to the coal. The fate of the collieries around Tangshan was unknown, since communication had been lost for several days, but it was known that Boxers had torn up the rail lines within two or three miles of Tangshan. If the Boxers themselves had not wrecked the mines already (as Hoover surmised), Detring anticipated that the Russian army would soon "liberate" the area—with predictable consequences.

Detring therefore urged Chang to take emergency measures to save the Chinese Engineering and Mining Company from depredation, military seizure, and ruin. To do this he suggested that the company's property be "placed under the protection of a foreign flag," preferably the British. Certainly not the Russian: Detring feared that if the colossus of the north ever got control of the Kaiping mines it would never relinquish them. In order to accomplish his risky plan, however, Detring needed formal authority to proceed. In response, Chang, still in custody, signed a document appointing Detring "the attorney and general agent" of the Chinese Engineering and Mining Company with "full powers" to "deal with" the company's property "as he shall think best in the interest of the shareholders."[1]

Armed with his power of attorney, Detring moved to salvage what he could from the chaos. Among the Chinese Engineering and Mining Company's principal creditors was the Deutsch-Asiatische Bank, from which the company had borrowed heavily about two years before. On June 30 the next installment in the company's repayment would fall due, and the company lacked the funds to pay it. Detring perceived in this imminent default an excellent opportunity. Informing the Deutsch-Asiatische Bank of the company's inability to pay its debt, he invited the bank to foreclose on all the company's property hypothecated to it as security for the loan. The bank obliged and at once requested the local German naval authorities to guard the affected property. In this way the company's fleet of six steamers, as well as wharves at Tientsin and Taku, were rescued from destruction and seizure by less cooperative Powers.[2]

Detring had more in mind than simply gaining temporary protection for the Chinese Engineering and Mining Company. He informed Chang that if foreign protection for the enterprise were to be obtained, they would have to prove that foreigners held "a part of the proprietorship of the property involved."[3] For more than a year Detring had promoted, without decisive result, a grand design for reorganizing the Kaiping mines under joint Chinese and foreign direction. Now, unexpectedly, dire necessity was working to effect his ambition.

Several days after his meeting with Chang, Detring had a conversation in Tientsin with Herbert Hoover. Exhibiting his written authorization from Chang to protect the company's interests, Detring said that he wished to "place the Company" under the control of C. Algernon Moreing with a mandate to reform it completely. He asked Hoover to "undertake a mission" to Europe to persuade Moreing to accept this responsibility.[4]

Hoover's initial response (as he later portrayed it) was not enthusiastic. Anxious to leave China, Hoover told Detring that the idea of reorganizing the Kaiping mines now, amidst violent upheaval, seemed virtually "hopeless."[5] Detring was insistent, however, and within a few days Hoover's reluctance began to dissipate. He told Detring that Chang should be involved directly in any decisions of this magnitude. Detring agreed.[6]

By July 10 Hoover's attitude had altered. On that day, even as the siege of Tientsin continued, he boldly pressed Chang to authorize nothing less than the much-delayed provincial loan for £1,000,000:

Foreign capitalists not fully understanding Chinese methods and customs usually desire as your Excellency knows, agreements written in their own language and stated in exact and legal manner as is their custom. Therefore to facilitate the completion of these negotiations it is very desirable that Y.E. [Your Excellency] should formally sign the inclosed agreement.[7]

Whatever Hoover's reluctance of a few days before, he now sensed the opportunities opening up from the plight of Chang Yen-mao.

Chang, however, was not to be so easily persuaded. That very same day, at the insistence of the foreign military authorities, the Chinese official left Tientsin for the coastal town of Taku—without signing the provincial loan agreement.[8] Hoover and Detring soon followed.[9] Here, in mid-July, they began to ponder in earnest how to achieve Detring's dual objective: the placing of Kaiping "in a secure harbour . . . under the British flag,"[10] and the acquisition of desperately needed foreign capital for the mines' development.

Although the siege of Tientsin was lifted on July 14, the prevailing conditions were anything but auspicious. The foreign diplomatic community at Peking was still encircled, and few expected that it could be reached in time. Should the legations be overrun and annihilated, Detring expected that China would be carved up by the Western Powers and would lapse into further turmoil for years to come.[11] The status of the Chinese Engineering and Mining Company was equally perilous. In the four weeks since foreign engineers had abandoned Tangshan, not a word had come in from the mines.[12] If, as seemed likely, the Boxers had destroyed the underground pumps, the mines would flood, leaving the shaft at Tangshan "irretrievably ruined."[13] Moreover, the value of the company's stock was plummeting. Each of the issued shares had a par value of 100 taels. By mid-summer the shares had tumbled to 60, 40, even 21 taels.[14]

In the comparative calm of Taku, Chang and Detring took stock of their difficulties. Since Chang had signed the letter of attorney of June 23 while he was under arrest, Detring feared that this document lacked legal efficacy. Moreover, Chang had not affixed to it his official seal (an important requisite in China).[15]

To provide a more solid legal footing for their actions, the two men now carefully devised at Taku (or so they later alleged) three documents, which eventually became known as A, B, and C. Since foreign military officials were not apt to accept the validity of any documents issued after the outbreak of the rebellion, Chang and Detring resorted to the simple expedient of antedating the documents.[16] In the first despatch, pre-dated to read May 17, Chang instructed Detring either to "raise a foreign loan" or to "invite the investment of foreign capital in shares of the Company, converting the Kaiping Mining Company of Tangshan into a Chinese and Foreign Mining Company." He requested Detring to "draw up for my approval" appropriate regulations.[17]

In reply Detring submitted a set of "draft rules for the joint administration of the Company by Chinese and foreigners, and for the raising of shares." Detring proposed that the company should be registered "in accordance with British law," should increase its capital "by the addition of foreign shares," and should be "converted into a Company under joint Chinese and foreign management." The company would keep its current name. And "control of all the matters connected with the administration of the Company" and with the land would "continue to be vested in the Director General," Chang Yen-mao. Among other items Detring proposed that the reorganized company should have 1,000,000 shares of £1 each. Of these, 375,000 were to be allotted to the shareholders of the old company in return for their old shares. Nowhere in the document did Detring indicate that the company was to be sold outright.[18]

Detring's regulations (Document B) were undated but apparently prepared in mid-July. In reply Chang issued a despatch (Document C), dated June 24, approving Detring's proposals and authorizing him to take the necessary steps to implement them.[19] The formal documentary groundwork was now in place.

Meanwhile Detring was negotiating simultaneously with Hoover. On July 15, having just arrived on the coast at Taku, Detring wrote to C. Algernon Moreing in London. Detring told his British friend that Hoover was "about contracting for taking over the management of the Chinese Engineering and Mining Company in order to re-organise it and make of it an English Company as soon as peace will be re-established or the mines become accessible." Detring also reported that Chang Yen-mao had already signed an indenture selling the entire Kaiping enterprise to Detring personally, so that he, a German, could register it at the German consulate in case he could not obtain British protection.[20] But for political reasons Detring preferred to go with the British. He never used the alternate form of authority entrusted to him by Chang.[21]

For the next several days Detring conferred with Hoover about the company's future. To alleviate the immediate financial emergency Hoover consented to release for the company's general use the Chinwangtao loan funds deposited in the local bank. Although this violated the mortgage bond's terms (which restricted the loan to certain specified purposes), Hoover felt that the emergency warranted his action.[22]

Hoover was uneasy, however, about how he should proceed. Detring entreated him to go at once to London with a letter turning the Kaiping properties over to Moreing personally for registration and refinance.[23] Hoover, however, knew little about the intricacies of British law and corporate finance. Furthermore, he was not the financial agent of Moreing or his firm; he had no power to bind them to an arrangement about which they knew nothing.[24] Having gone out on a limb with the Chinwangtao loan money, he wanted something more formal than a "mere letter" to show to Moreing.[25]

In order to resolve these and other complexities, Hoover on July 23 brought down to Taku the only British lawyer practicing in Tientsin, J. Bromley

Eames. After a period of consultation among all the parties, Hoover retained Eames as his own attorney.[26]

With Eames's assistance Hoover and Detring hammered out a document providing for the twin goals of securing foreign protection and a massive infusion of foreign investment capital. Secrecy was imperative lest the Germans and Russians discover and torpedo the ambitious scheme.[27]

It was not easy for Eames to reconcile Detring's and Hoover's inconsistent desires. Detring insisted on a binding deed of conveyance made out directly to Moreing. If the deed were not binding but instead merely provisional, foreign protection might not be assured. Moreover, Detring feared that if the deed were made out directly to Hoover instead of Moreing, Hoover might run off and "deal with it in some [other] way."[28]

For his part, Hoover was unwilling to commit Moreing absolutely (which he had no right to do anyway) to such a chancy venture. He therefore requested a document in the form of an option, made out to himself. At the same time he, too, craved ironclad assurances. He wanted to be "absolutely secured against the assets of the Company being dealt with" by Chang or Detring behind his back once he left China.[29] He must, he told Eames, have "something they could not get out of."[30] As Eames afterward observed of Hoover and Detring, "Neither of these men seemed to trust one another very much. . . ."[31]

While Eames labored over the legal phraseology, events reached a climax on another front. On July 25 Chang Yen-mao signed a letter addressed to Detring, Hoover, and Moreing sanctioning at last the much-delayed provincial loan. In sweeping terms Chang empowered the three men to raise a minimum of £1,000,000 over thirty years to "develop the mines of Chihli and Jehol" under their management, "sole direction and control." All the mines and minerals of the province, except those of the Chinese Engineering and Mining Company and certain others, were pledged as security for the loan. No mines could be sold to foreigners or developed by foreign methods without the consent of the three concessionaires. After providing for repayment of the loan and interest, the three were to receive half of the profits from the mines. The other half would be divided equally between the Chinese government and the provincial Mining Bureau (that is, Chang). Chang gave the three concessionaires carte blanche to arrange financing, transfer their privileges, set up companies, and open mines at their discretion. They must, however, implement the agreement within two years or it would be nullified.[32] Chang later claimed that this loan was merely a nominal one that "gave the appearance of these mining interests being protected by foreign shareholders."[33] It was not evident, however, that the three foreigners had the same interpretation.

During July also Hoover was busy settling the accounts of his personal staff, no longer employed by the now moribund Mining Bureau. At the end of June, while the siege of Tientsin still raged, a thoroughly disenchanted

John H. Means took off for Japan at the first opportunity.[34] On July 4 John Agnew and George Wilson signed receipts for their June salaries of £50; on the same day Hoover collected his own combined monthly income of £250.[35] At the end of July Hoover arranged for Means, Wilson, Agnew, and New-berry to receive severance pay from the Mining Bureau in the form of four months' salary plus travel expenses home. At the same time Hoover requested and received his own monthly salary for July.[36]

These were but peripheral details, however, compared to the main drama then unfolding. On July 25 Eames completed a draft indenture agreeable to both Hoover and Detring. Soon afterwards, leaving final arranagements to Detring, Chang departed on a ship for Shanghai. Hoover, Eames, and Detring returned to Tientsin. There Eames prepared the final document, dated July 30, for signature.[37]

On August 1, 1900 Detring and Hoover signed Eames's indenture for-mally conveying the Chinese Engineering and Mining Company in entirety to Hoover.[38] The transfer was subject to certain stipulations. Hoover was to hold the proffered property in trust for a new British company that he and Bewick, Moreing would form. To establish this new company Hoover was empowered to use "such means and agencies as are ordinarily used and usu-ally regarded as proper to be used in the formation of Companies of the kind hereby intended." The new company was to have a capital of £1,000,000 in £1 shares. In return for assuming all the old company's assets and liabilities, it was to allot three-eighths of its shares—375,000—to the old shareholders as full compensation for "all their rights and interests." By February 28, 1901 Bewick, Moreing and Company must also provide the new enterprise £100,000 in working capital (which Detring was extremely anxious to acquire). The deed gave Bewick, Moreing ninety days to ratify or reject the agree-ment. Detring pledged to execute and sign all necessary documents once the new company was established according to the provisions of the indenture. Detring also promised not to dispose of any of the Chinese company's prop-erty before the agreement was submitted to Bewick, Moreing.[39]

The terms of the document reflected Eames's effort to reach a compromise between Hoover and Detring. Hoover secured a document made out to him-self (albeit as agent for Bewick, Moreing) and a ninety-day escape clause for his principals in London. The deal was provisional; Bewick, Moreing could still back out. Moreover, Detring was bound not to sell the property to some-body else in the meantime and also to cooperate later if the deal went through in London. For his part Detring obtained a document unequivocally convey-ing the Kaiping enterprise to a satisfactory foreigner for at least ninety days. Furthermore, this foreigner (Hoover) bound himself to act as a trustee. He could not now disappear and make off with the property.

Eames's search for common ground also resulted in another striking fea-ture of the July 30 deed: in explicit terms Detring *sold* the company to Hoo-ver. On its face this was a remarkable step. As experienced Westerners living in China both Detring and Hoover surely realized that Chinese law prohibited the unconditional sale of Chinese property to foreigners. In fact, just two months earlier, Hoover himself had published a summary of Chinese mining law and had noted its requirements that all companies must be at least one-half Chinese and must be administered solely by Chinese, "foreigners participating only in technical capacities."[40] Now, in July, both men were signing a document in clear contravention of Chinese law.

In addition, nothing in Chang's recent commmunications to Detring appeared to sanction an unequivocal deed of sale. The power of attorney granted on June 23 merely authorized Detring to "deal with" the Kaiping company's affairs, not (at least not overtly) to sell the property off. Yet here was the July 30 deed, asserting in its preamble that Detring as the Chinese company's agent and attorney had "full power to dispose of" its property. Moreover, in the three antedated despatches of late July—A, B, and C—the word "sale" was not mentioned. Instead, the more ambiguous word "conversion" was used. Detring, to be sure, did receive from Chang by July 15 an indenture purportedly selling the Kaiping mines to Detring personally for registry at the German consulate if Detring failed to obtain British protection. But Detring had not used this document, and its legal validity, in any case, was questionable.

What, then, had happened? Long afterwards Eames recalled how the idea of an outright sale to a trustee made its way into the document:

> Mr. Hoover wanted the form to be such that he was absolutely secured against the assets of the Company being dealt with in the absence, and I said the only way to do that is to get an absolute conveyance, Mr. Detring is quite willing to give an absolute conveyance because he wanted foreign protection, and I think he accepted my advice that that would be a good way of transferring to the [new] Company. Mr. Detring asked me in what way it could be done and I told him conveying to Mr. Hoover as agent or trustee. . . . I said that if he took the deed in the form I drafted, conveying it to him in trust for a company to be formed, Mr. Hoover could go home and form a Company, and it would have to be carried out on the lines of the trust, or not at all.[41]

Other motives may have influenced Detring. Perhaps he remembered that there was precedent in China for temporarily placing Chinese property under foreign protection during a crisis.[42] Perhaps he construed Chang's "German" indenture as ample evidence of Chang's intent. Hoover, at least, believed that Chang himself assented to the sale in July—a claim Chang later denied indignantly.[43]

Above all, to Detring the circumstances of July 1900 must have seemed starkly compelling. Civil government in northern China had collapsed; Tientsin itself was under Allied military occupation. To seek formal imperial sanction for the sale under such conditions was impossible. If the mines were to be saved from plunder and ruin, immediate action was imperative, whatever the technical requirements of Chinese law.

The deed of July 30 was also noteworthy for its omissions. Curiously, there was no stipulation that the new company would be a *joint* "Chinese and foreign mining company" such as Chang had supposedly authorized in the A, B, C despatches of less than two weeks before. Nor did the deed allude to such crucial topics as joint management and Chang's function as administrator. Yet both subjects had been explicitly covered in Detring's rules, which Chang (so he later claimed) had just approved. And what about the new enterprise's projected share capital of £1,000,000? Only £375,000 of it was specifically accounted for in the deed. How would the remaining £625,000 be raised—and when? What remuneration would Hoover and Moreing receive for undertaking such a risky venture? Surely they were not going to do it for nothing.

According to Hoover and Eames these fundamental questions were indeed discussed in late July. But for reasons that seemed persuasive at the time, a definitive resolution of them was postponed. Hoover orally agreed that there would be "a joint Chinese control" and that Chang would head the managerial board in China. But—he later testified—he "did not know enough about Company machinery, and Mr. Eames did not, to know how that could be done, and it was agreed to leave it to be arranged in Europe."[44] This, said Eames, was his "maiden effort in company conveyancing," and he was none too sure of his ground.[45]

The terms regarding financing were similarly left open, according to Hoover. How could it be otherwise? China was in upheaval, the Kaiping mines in disarray. Who knew whether it would even be possible to induce European financiers to invest in China under such desperate conditions? To Hoover and Eames the intent of the deed was to give Moreing a free hand both in raising the working capital and in disbursing the uncommitted shares. It was entirely up to Moreing to refinance and reorganize the Chinese Engineering and Mining Company—just how, no one at Taku could predict. And so 625,000 unapportioned shares were placed in Moreing's lap to dispose of as he deemed necessary.[46]

As for profits to be made from promotion of the undertaking, the negotiators agreed—said Hoover and Eames—that Hoover would "have something out of it" and that Bewick, Moreing also would receive a profit.[47] According to Hoover, he and Detring concluded that after Moreing had absorbed all the expenses of reorganization anything left over was to be profit—to be divided, under the old understanding, 50-50 between Moreing and Chang/Detring.[48]

So it was all left up to Moreing: this was Hoover's and Eames's version of the understandings of July. But was it Detring's? Detring's thoughts at this time are harder to pin down. It does seem certain, though, that under the volatile political and economic circumstances then prevailing, he was willing to leave many subjects unformulated, for the moment, in writing. Detring was evidently more distrustful of Hoover than of Moreing.

On the specific subject of promotion profits, however, Hoover and Detring did appear to reach a definite, if informal, understanding. During their discussions Hoover speculated that 200,000 free shares in the new company might be the promoters' total profit, of which 100,000 would be distributed to Chang and Detring themselves.[49] Detring's later recollection was similar:

> There was at the time of the signature of the Agreement of 30th July 1900, between myself and H. C. Hoover an understanding between us that, in the event of the successful flotation of the Company for £1,000,000, an amount of two hundred thousand pounds would be recognized as a legitimate amount to be allotted to cover Expenses, Bankers' Commission Flotation Profits, and all other charges. Of this £200,000 it was understood between us that £50,000 should be sent to China with which to overcome possible opposition to the idea of the novel step of admitting foreign capital into the Chinese Engineering and Mining Company.[50]

In other words, money to bribe Chinese officials who might object. Such was the price of doing business in China.

Whatever the precise figure, substantial flotation profits were anticipated. Two hundred thousand shares at a nominal value of £1 each equalled nearly $1,000,000. And if the share prices went higher. . . .

But beyond this general shared expectation, sharp differences eventually arose. According to Hoover, for instance, at one point in July Chang explicitly wished to know how much *he* would profit by the transaction, while Detring conveyed an impression that he, too, "wanted remuneration" for past services to the company.[51] Chang strenuously denied Hoover's claim, while Detring asserted that *he* always remained "mute" and "neutral" about his personal gain and resisted the entangling "nets" that Hoover was trying to throw over him.[52]

These conflicts of recollection raised a question that was ultimately to have crucial significance: how much did the Chinese official know about what was being done in his name? Chang Yen-mao neither signed, nor was present at the signing of, the final version of the July 30 deed. Hoover and Eames later declared, however, that they explained—and Chang approved—every clause and paragraph of the July 30 deed (in draft form) before Chang sailed for Shanghai. They had done so, they said, for self-protection, lest the wily Chinese businessman later pretend he was uninformed.[53] Chang, on the other hand, later denied that he ever saw the July 30 deed beforehand, or that its terms were explained beforehand, or that he even conferred with Eames at Taku at all.[54] And Detring, by his account, said he did not show Chang the final, signed version of the July 30 deed, portions of which were settled after Chang left in late July for Shanghai.[55] Had Detring, in his anxiety to secure foreign protection, consented to an open-ended sale, thereby exceeding Chang's instructions?

This cloud of confusion was not yet visible at the end of July 1900. Harmony still reigned at Tientsin. On August 4 Hoover and his wife departed for Shanghai and Europe by way of Nagasaki, Japan. Before leaving Tientsin he had a final rendezvous with Gustav Detring. Hoover long remembered the German's parting words. Tell Moreing, said Detring (alluding to the July 30 indenture), that I have given him "plenty of room in which to move around."[56]

On August 11 Hoover cabled to Moreing from the port city of Shanghai: "Have obtained necessary agreement signed placing under offer to you Kaiping. . . . Have obtained necessary agreement signed placing under offer to you Provincial Loan upon better terms than what has been proposed."[57] Three days later, the Allied expeditionary force finally rescued the besieged foreign legations at Peking. Incredibly, the Westerners there were still alive; it seemed a miracle. The Empress Dowager and her court fled into the interior.[58]

On August 15 Moreing cabled to Hoover in Shanghai: "Approve scheme. I shall be able to carry it through. You can come home."[59] The trip itself was long, monotonous, and uncomfortable: six weeks on a German mail boat. "Table is atrocious, service worse," Hoover complained by letter to Detring. The heat of the Red Sea and Gulf of Suez was oppressive.[60]

However dreary the ocean voyage, it gave Hoover time to read, time to pace the deck, time to reflect. That he and his brave wife Lou had survived the Boxer Rebellion. That the Kaiping mines—the greatest industrial enterprise in China—as well as the provincial mines of all Chihli lay now within his grasp.

That, on August 10, he had reached the age of twenty-six.

I I

E ARLY in October 1900 Hoover arrived in London.[61] Moreing was well pleased with what his youthful Yankee negotiator had accomplished. At once he submitted copies of the provincial loan agreement and the July 30 indenture to the British Foreign Office. With thinly concealed satisfaction Moreing pointed out that the provincial loan's terms were "of a very comprehensive character," that "the whole of the mines of this important Province" were "now mortgaged to myself and my friends," and that these same people (himself, Hoover, and Detring) were now entitled to half the profits of every mine in Chihli.[62] As for the other agreement, Moreing declared that "my Firm have entered into a contract to transform" the Chinese Engineering and Mining Company into "an English limited liability Company." He informed the

Foreign Office that he and his firm were now "proceeding with the formation of the English Company."[63]

On October 13, through his solicitors in China, Moreing notified Gustav Detring of his firm's decision to "ratify and confirm" the agreement of July.[64] Moreing's acceptance was unconditional; the contract as it stood was now in force. Moreing immediately turned to the task of creating and financing the new company.

To assist him in his efforts, on October 16 Hoover prepared a document entitled "Memoranda of Procedure, Chinese Engineering and Mining Company" for submission to prospective European financiers. His paper revealed more about the understandings of late July. According to Hoover "a local Advisory Board of the Company" must be established in Tientsin. It would be called "the Chinese Board" and would have three members: Chang as "Director General," Detring, and Hoover himself. In order to "evade friction with the Sovereign rights of China," the "present Chinese Engineering and Mining Company" would continue to exist. Since China did not permit foreigners to own freehold property outside the treaty ports, the Kaiping "mines, coalfields and property" not in these ports "must be leased to the New Company for a term of years." Hoover described how the Deutsch-Asiatische Bank had foreclosed many of the company's assets in June. This property, he said, was "to be re-transferred upon a financial adjustment." Hoover also candidly stated that the mines needed drastic technical reorganization since "squeeze now absorbs fully 50 percent of the income." It would require a "general manager of no ordinary calibre" to administer the giant coal company. Hoover offered to visit the United States and select such a man from one of the major American coal and railway enterprises.[65]

Upon his arrival in London Hoover briefed Moreing on other unwritten aspects of his July agreement. He told Moreing that he had consented to keep the "old arrangement with Chang and Detring" about dividing their profits.[66] In order to improve the company's debt structure the Chinwangtao harbor loan with its high 12% interest rate must somehow be "financed down" to 6%.[67] Both Detring and Chang must be directors of the reorganized company,[68] and Chang must be appointed Director-General for life—a point whose importance Hoover stressed.[69]

Moreing now set out to secure financial support for the conversion of the Chinese Engineering and Mining Company into a British-registered concern. According to Moreing's later recollection, his path was strewn with obstacles. In the wake of the Boxer Rebellion British investors were little disposed to invest in the tottering Celestial Empire. Nor were the company's substantial indebtedness and the novelty of the ambitious scheme reassuring, despite the almost incalculable coal deposits of Kaiping. Furthermore, one of the most influential British banks in London and the Orient opposed Moreing's plan—a result of its antipathy to Chang.[70]

Armed with Hoover's memorandum of October 16, and accompanied by his American engineer, Moreing contacted two London financiers, Edmund Davis and W. F. Turner.[71] Less than a year before, Davis and Turner had formed an entity known as the Oriental Syndicate, with a share capital of £100,000, for the purpose of financing Moreing's contemplated mining ventures in the Far East. This was just prior to his visit in early 1900 to China.[72] With the British money market unavailing, Moreing and his two associates decided to contact powerful Belgian interests headed by Colonel Albert Thys, a leading financial adviser to Belgium's ambitious king, Leopold II.[73] Thys's Compagnie Internationale d'Orient, in fact, had purchased from Moreing nearly half of his Chinwangtao loan bonds of 1899.[74] According to Moreing, Detring himself had urged him to involve Thys and the Belgians in underwriting the Kaiping reorganization.[75] On the surface, then, Moreing's actions seemed consistent with Detring's objective: enmesh enough European powers in a cooperative quest for profit, and they would not then lapse into destructive rivalry among themselves. Detring apparently did not anticipate that they might instead unite against him and exploit the Chinese together.

Sometime between mid-October and early November, Moreing and Davis visited Colonel Thys in Brussels and settled upon a plan. Moreing would hand complete control of the new company to the Oriental Syndicate in exchange for 79,500 (nearly 80%) of the syndicate's shares. Then Moreing would redistribute these shares among the interested parties: the Belgians, Turner, Davis, Moreing himself, Hoover, and various others. As Moreing later explained the arrangement, ". . . I turned over the business to the Oriental Syndicate for them to make as much profit as they could out of it, I sharing with all the others in that result, whatever it might be. I had the most absolute confidence in Mr. Davis and in Colonel Thys, that they . . . would make the best terms that it was possible to make. . . ."[76]

Now, however, unforeseen and disturbing difficulties arose. Under the July 30 contract Hoover was named trustee for the new company. To the European financiers it appeared that this trust provision might legally prevent Hoover or anyone else from making any profit out of floating the new company. To remove this inhibiting ambiguity, the deed of July 30, already ratified by Moreing, must be altered. Otherwise, the Oriental Syndicate wouldn't touch it.[77]

On November 9 Moreing therefore prepared a letter to Detring for Hoover to carry back to China. Much was eventually to hinge on whether this letter was a truly candid statement, a clever deception, or a subtle bribe. Moreing began by explaining that the July 30 deed required "some slight alterations." The trouble, said Moreing, was that the document presented Hoover "both as agent for the old shareholders and trustee for the new shareholders, a position legally tenable, but not permitting profits to anyone, which" —he added—"I deem is not the desire or intention of yourself and Chang." He noted that in order "to avoid criticism over the sale of land outside of Treaty Ports it is advisable that the 'sale' of land and coal rights be altered to 'lease.' "

This change would be "safer" for Chang. Like Hoover and Detring, Moreing knew that Chinese law forbade the sale of Chinese property outside treaty ports to foreigners.

Moreing next described to Detring the financial arrangements that he said had been determined:

> In order to carry through the business on an international footing I have turned it over to the Oriental Syndicate. They have very large cash resources behind them, among other important financial institutions the Compagnie d'Orient and the Russo-Chinese Bank being largely interested.

"I am negotiating with the Oriental Syndicate," Moreing continued, "with a view to you being offered position of Chinese Adviser at £1,000 per year, and you are to receive 5,000 shares in the Oriental Syndicate" (with a par value of $25,000) "in order to identify your interests with them." Moreing emphasized that the Chinese Engineering and Mining Company's "heavy liabilities" and the current European suspicions of "all China ventures" rendered his efforts "very difficult" indeed. It would be necessary to diminish the company's debt burden by refinancing certain loans at 6%. But, he added in a crucial sentence, "In order to raise the money at this low rate it is necessary to give shares of the Chinese Engineering and Mining Company, and when sufficient shares have been given to induce the subscription of an additional £100,000 cash, there is no great margin."

Finally, Moreing reviewed other matters of common interest. He told Detring that two boards, one in London and one in China, were being established to look after the interests of their respective shareholders.

> Upon Hoover's insistence Chang has been made Director General for life of the China Board by special agreement—yourself upon the China Board also. Negotiations are proceeding with a view to obtain for yourself and Chang ample remuneration as members of the China Board. Please discuss with Hoover the question of your remuneration and Chang's. . . .

Moreing said that he himself would not own shares in the new company but would be a shareholder in the Oriental Syndicate instead. Hoover "has also been given some shares" in the syndicate. The syndicate itself would have "a good many shares" in the new company as its reward for refinancing the Chinwangtao loan and for raising the £100,000 in working capital.

In a cheerful conclusion Moreing held out the prospect that the company's shares would double in value within two years, yielding a "very handsome profit" as well as "very great value" for the shares allotted to Chang and Detring. The Chinese shareholders, too, would benefit immensely. Moreing claimed to have "laid the foundation" for Detring's goal of a multinational institution uniting the great banks of England, Belgium, Russia, Germany, and France. The Oriental Syndicate would also satisfy Chang's desire for "no individual national encroachment."[78]

Moreing's letter, taken a sentence at a time, appears to have been an accurate account of his understanding with his friends in Europe—*if* the deal went through. It was also a skillful appeal to Detring's self-interest. Yet Moreing failed to convey one extremely important point: how conditional the entire undertaking had now become for the European financiers. What if Detring refused to accept Moreing's proposed "slight alterations"? The whole deal (vis-à-vis the Oriental Syndicate) would founder, and Moreing would be obliged to seek financial backing elsewhere, with very unpromising prospects. Detring, however, would not know this from Moreing's letter. *He* would know only that he stood to lose the platter of profits spread before him, all because of the obstructive trustee clause. Of course, had Detring realized Moreing's predicament he might have taken advantage of it to extract a better bargain for himself, in exchange for acceding to the deed revisions. Perhaps this explains Moreing's avoidance of the subject.

November 9, 1900 was also a busy day for Herbert Hoover. On that day he formally appointed Moreing his attorney with "absolute and uncontrolled discretion" to sell, transfer, or otherwise deal with any mines, concessions, options, or other property acquired by or belonging to Hoover in China. Evidently anticipating that the trust clause in the July 30 deed would soon be deleted, Hoover authorized Moreing to "sell and transfer the benefit" of Hoover's contract for the purchase of the Chinese Engineering and Mining Company—something the trust clause prohibited his doing.[79]

The next day Hoover and his wife left for China by way of the United States.[80] Besides Moreing's letter to Detring, Hoover carried two other documents of importance: a list of the desired alterations of the July 30 deed and a revised draft of certain articles of association of the still-to-be-registered new company. Late in October Hoover had discovered that the Oriental Syndicate's initial page proof of the articles contained no provision for a China board with Chang Yen-mao as Director-General for life—something Hoover had insisted on. Upset at this omission, Hoover protested. The syndicate thereupon prepared a revised article, and on November 7 Hoover received a draft indicating that Chang would be "Director General for life, that there should be a China Board, and that the China Board should have the supervision and management of the Company in China."[81] This revised text also provided that the local China board would "superintend the transaction of the Company's business in China." Significantly, though, it added that the China board's actual powers were to be conferred by and determined by the directors of the company and that the directors might "revoke, withdraw, alter or vary" these powers. Ultimate control, in other words, would remain in London. This revised draft Hoover now took with him to the Orient.[82]

On November 18, the American engineer and his wife reached New York, where he gave a press interview about his experiences in the Boxer Rebellion.[83] Hoover was anything but sanguine about the prospects for stability in China. "Unless our Government adopts a most forcible policy," he told the *New York Times*, "we will have a calamity in China that has not been equalled in the history of the world." Even now, he declared, the "whole of China" was "preparing to rise." Hoover denounced what he perceived as a policy of weakness by the United States government:

> It is very humiliating for an American to know that although the United States controls 45 percent. of the trade of Northern China, there is not a soldier there to protect it. Our whole policy has been to pat a rattlesnake on the head. Diplomacy with an Asiatic is of no use. If you are going to do business with him you must begin your talk with a gun in your hand, and let him know that you will use it.[84]

Enough, though, of China—at least for the moment. For the first time in nearly two years the couple was on American soil. They hurried across the country to California for a few weeks of well-earned relaxation.

Back in London Moreing was putting the legal machinery into place. On December 13 he formally confirmed to the Oriental Syndicate his agreement to sell *to it* the Chinese Engineering and Mining Company, "which I am about to acquire," as well as the provincial loan agreement of July 25. Moreing admitted that his deal with the syndicate was contingent upon his obtaining satisfactory alterations of the July 30 deed—a task he pledged his "best endeavours to accomplish."[85]

On December 6 Hoover sailed from San Francisco for China accompanied by his wife and her younger sister, Jean Henry.[86] Hoover was at sea when on December 21 the Chinese Engineering and Mining Company, Ltd. was duly registered in London.[87] The company's general intent to conduct extensive coal-mining operations in China was clear enough from the registration documents. But in two respects the manner of this registration was peculiar. According to the company's memorandum of association one of its principal objectives was to implement "the agreement mentioned in Clause 3" of the separate articles of association.[88] Clause 3 of the articles, however, was oddly reticent about what this agreement actually was:

> The Company shall forthwith enter into an agreement in the terms of the draft which, for the purpose of identification, has been initialed by two of the Subscribers to the Memorandum of Association, and the Board shall carry the same into effect, subject to any modifications thereof which the Board may approve.[89]

Curiously, the exact contents of this "draft" were not revealed. Nor were they attached to the registration documents. Nor was the draft ever found in later years. In all likelihood, however, this draft (if it existed) was a document by which Moreing would formally sell the new company to the Oriental Syndicate.[90]

The articles contained another startling anomaly. Whether by accident or design, the final official version omitted the very item that Hoover had just insisted upon and that he was now taking (in draft form) to China: the provision for a China board and for Chang Yen-mao to be Director-General for life. Instead, the relevant clauses (83A and 83B) merely empowered the board of directors in London to establish, if it wished, *local* boards and managing directors with such powers as the London board "deem fit." No mention was made of Chang Yen-mao. And the board of directors retained plenary powers to revoke any such appointments.[91]

Hoover was unaware (he later maintained) that the articles of association as now registered were in error.[92] Why—Hoover having made an issue of the point—had this omission again been made? Was it an oversight? Or was someone in Europe deliberately keeping him in the dark?

Of the immediate purpose of his mission, however, Hoover had no doubt. He knew that his own profits, and everyone else's, depended on his successfully revising the July 30 agreement. If he failed, the Oriental Syndicate would back out. Then Moreing would be stuck, under the agreement, with somehow finding £100,000 in less than two months—and might never make a penny for his pains. Having ratified in haste, he would repent at leisure. Charles Algernon Moreing was in a fix, and it was Herbert Hoover's job to bail him out.

I I I

THE twenty-six-year-old American engineer arrived in Japan near the end of December. Leaving his wife and sister-in-law in Yokohama, he proceeded alone to Shanghai, where he arrived on New Year's Day, 1901.[93] From there, amidst harsh winter conditions, he traveled north, reaching Tientsin around January 10.[94] On that day the local American consul listed Hoover on his register of Americans resident in the district. He recorded Hoover's age as thirty-one, more than four years off the mark.[95] Apparently, as in Australia, Hoover was still concealing his comparative youth.

Much had happened in China during Hoover's absence. Following their capture of Peking in August, foreign soldiers now occupied much of northern China, pending the outcome of negotiations for a peace protocol with the Chinese. At Tientsin a provisional government controlled by Allied military commanders ruled the area.[96] Contrary to Hoover's and Detring's apprehensions of July, the Chinese Engineering and Mining Company's coal mines around Tangshan had survived the Boxer upheaval. The Chinese employees of the old company had actually managed to keep operating the collieries until the end of September, when Russian soldiers "liberated" the area. Fleeing for their lives, the native miners abandoned the pumps. For at least two weeks the Russians refused to permit the company's Western representatives to enter the mines and resume pumping operations. As a result, the lower levels of the Tangshan mine were flooded—at a loss, Detring calculated, of at least £50,000.[97]

Only after strenuous efforts by Detring, and protests by the British government to the Czar's government, were the mines reopened during the autumn and British technicians permitted to reenter the mines.[98] The Russians continued to occupy the property, however, and to abuse the local Chinese. From time to time, under pretext of military necessity, they arbitrarily requisitioned coal, tools, and other supplies for the nearby railway (as well as for private resale by their own officers).[99] They also imposed on the Chinese Engineering and Mining Company a tax of a dollar on each ton of coal extracted.[100] Still, thanks in considerable measure to Detring's determined efforts and his friendship with the Russian general, the company's property was mostly intact when Hoover returned in January.[101]

Hoover wasted little time in seeking Detring's assent to the alterations in their July 30 deed. Producing Moreing's letter of November 9 as well as his list of desired changes, the American explained the necessity for revision. According to Detring, Hoover told him that the July 30 contract as originally written lacked certain clauses "essential for drawing out an effectual deed" and that the proposed alterations "were necessary to make the deed valid."[102] According to Hoover, he explicitly stated to Detring that Moreing wanted to remove his firm's name from the deed (since it was Moreing's personal business only) and that the Oriental Syndicate wanted to "straighten out" the trust clause ("so that there could be no question") before it could "take over the business" from Moreing.[103] Hoover also said he told Detring that the original deed posed problems "as to whether I could receive any profits or not, and it was quite understood that I should have some of the profits."[104]

Hoover later claimed that Detring "raised no objection . . . at all" to the proposed alterations.[105] On January 14, in fact, Hoover informed the British consul in Tientsin that the Kaiping mines already belonged to a British firm "to whom they are conveyed pending the formation of an English Limited Liability Co. to work them." Hoover added that this transfer was not yet registered at the British Consulate-General in China (as, presumably, it should have been). This, he said, was because "the promoters of the Company" wanted the deed to be changed "in one small detail," which, he said, "has been agreed to but not yet executed." Whether or not the deed was altered, it would still be valid—said Hoover—since the "contemplated alteration" would not "affect the validity of the conveyance." It would only "alter the relations of the promoters among themselves."[106]

This same day, January 14, Hoover wrote to his wife and sister-in-law in Japan that he now expected to remain in China for another year.[107] He seemed confident of success.

Detring, however, may have been more hesitant than Hoover thought.

The next day the German confided to J. Bromley Eames that he did not fully understand the reason for these belated alterations. After all, Moreing had already approved the original deed without reservation back in October. Eames, too, was puzzled and "very doubtful" about the legality of altering the ratified deed. Yet Eames was not very experienced in corporate law and was reluctant to take issue with the attorneys in England. During their conversation he said to Detring, "It looks as though we'll never get [foreign] protection unless it [the transfer] goes through."[108] His remark evidently touched a nerve with Detring who, without further hesitation, consented to the desired alterations. Eames advised the German to re-execute the document of July 30 with the revisions included.[109]

As revised the July 30 deed now stated that Hoover was the agent of Moreing personally and not of Moreing's firm. The original deed said that the old Chinese Engineering and Mining Company was to be "transformed into" a British company. Now it was to be "transferred to" the new company, a subtle but portentous shift in vocabulary. All references to Hoover as a trustee were eliminated. In the original version, Hoover's power to form a new company had been confined to the use of methods that were "ordinarily used and usually regarded as proper" in such cases. In the revised version, he was now empowered to use any means he "may deem proper" and on "such terms and conditions" as he "may think expedient"—a far more sweeping grant of power. In the original deed the projected new company was committed to pay 375,000 of its shares to the stockholders of the old company. This clause was reworded to read that Hoover himself was obliged to carry out the exchange. The effect of this was to make Hoover himself (and not the new company) the out-and-out purchaser of the property. Since Hoover had already given Moreing his power of attorney, and since Moreing in turn had already promised on December 13 to sell the deed (if revised) to the Oriental Syndicate, this arrangement freed the syndicate to promote the enterprise however it wished.[110]

It is uncertain whether Detring fully appreciated the extraordinary latitude as to promotional profits and procedures that he had just granted Hoover. Perhaps Hoover himself did not realize all the implications; he afterwards insisted that he never understood the legal requirements involved and never participated in the financial planning for the flotation.[111] He later stoutly contended that the changes *were* "slight alterations," designed to facilitate the enactment of the understanding of July 1900.[112] And slight indeed they were—*if* Hoover's version of the July agreement was correct, namely that the "means and agencies" regarding finance were to be left completely to the discretion of Moreing.

Whether Detring had this same expansive understanding, or whether instead he had just been fraudulently misled by Moreing and Hoover, were to become crucial issues before long. Certainly Detring knew from Moreing's letter that profits for himself and Chang depended on his accepting Hoover's alterations. Whatever Detring's state of mind, he did not inform Chang Yen-mao of the revisions. Nor did he show Chang the amended deed, which he, as Chang's attorney, had just accepted in Chang's behalf.[113]

On January 17, 1901 Hoover and Detring formally assented to the alterations by initialing every amendment after Eames inserted them into the original parchment deed of July.[114] Later that day Hoover cabled the welcome news to Moreing: the "agreement re conversion" was "successfully altered." Although Hoover evidently regarded the initialings alone as sufficient for his purposes, Eames drew up two clean copies of the deed as amended and had Hoover and Detring re-execute them, with the same two witnesses signing as on the thirtieth of July.[115]

At this point a peculiar problem arose: what date should they affix to the new, amended deed? The obvious thing to do was to put down the true date, January 17, 1901. Indeed, Hoover observed, it was "absolutely necessary if we executed a clean copy to give it the present [January] date."[116] But Eames thought it would look odd to have in existence identical documents separately dated (January 17 and July 30).[117] Far worse, from Hoover's and Detring's point of view, was a host of political and legal hazards which a true (January) date would now raise. According to Hoover, Detring had already "assured a good many people" that the deed was operative from July 30, 1900; a new date on the deed might undermine his claim.[118] Furthermore, the Russians had occupied Tangshan after July 30: all the more reason to shore up an antecedent British claim to the area. Otherwise the Russians might try to hang onto the property on the grounds that it was really still Chinese when they seized it.[119] Another complication was that new consular regulations affecting "the transfer of property during hostilities" had been issued since July 30.[120] A new deed dated January 1901 would have to conform to these inconvenient regulations. Furthermore, local diplomats had already been notified of the original date. Hoover wanted to keep them satisfied about "our clear intentions." The result, in Hoover's words, was that he and his colleagues were in "a hopeless mess."[121]

Three weeks later Hoover reported to Moreing how he, Eames, and Detring resolved their dilemma: "In order to escape from as many difficulties as possible we executed a clean copy with the original date [July 30] and had it certified to by the [British] Consulate as a copy." That is, the amended version of January was officially registered and certified as merely a copy of the unamended version of the previous July. By this subterfuge the drawbacks of a January date were avoided and "official status before the Authorities here" was obtained. Such status was "necessary," Hoover said, "before we could get them to interfere on our behalf."[122]

Meanwhile Hoover was discussing with Detring the question of apportionment of their respective financial interests in the new company. According to Hoover, he verbally informed Detring in mid-January that Moreing wanted 50,000 free shares in the new company for his own personal profit—a request not expressed in Moreing's November 9 letter to Detring. Hoover also told Detring that Moreing "proposed" that Chang and Detring receive an equal number of shares.[123] On January 17, 1901 Hoover cabled to Moreing the results of his negotiations:

> Remuneration demanded by Detring and Chang according to your letter of November 9th, 50,000 shares Chinese Engineering and Mining Company. Includes several friends. I have agreed to. No cash.[124]

Detring's understanding of their conversation—or so he later asserted—was somewhat different. Detring claimed that he neither accepted nor rejected Hoover's offer of 50,000 shares *in profits*. Hoover, he said, was adept at dropping hints and ambiguous "*sub rosa* proposals," but Detring contended that he always remained silent and noncommittal. Nevertheless, Detring agreed to take the shares—not as profits for himself, he later asserted, but only for the "whole interests" he represented. If Moreing "required" 50,000 shares "to compensate himself with," then, said Detring, his own "side" should have an equal number. But Detring insisted afterwards that he was "very careful in not individualizing who was to receive this allotment of shares. I left myself free. . . . Mr. Hoover always spoke of His Excellency [Chang] and myself. I always spoke of the interest I represented."[125]

Detring's later distinction between his profit and his "interest" seems strained and unconvincing. But whatever his intent or mental reservations, one fact was clear. The division of shares—50,000 to each side—was settled by January 17, the very day the deed revisions were agreed to. By acquiescing in the changes Detring could now look forward to at least a portion of 50,000 free shares worth a quarter of a million dollars.

The German adviser to Chang was apparently not satisfied, however, with verbal assurances from Hoover. A week later, therefore, Hoover wrote Detring a letter evidently confirming their previous discussion.[126] Like Moreing on November 9, Hoover on January 24 painted an alluring portrait of Chang Yen-mao's future prosperity—if the deal went through.

> Re our conversation regarding H.E. Chang's ultimate profits from business at hand, my understanding is as follows, and will I believe be found correct.
>
> (1) H.E. Chang is the holder I believe of 3,000 of the present shares; he will be entitled to 75,000 new shares of the par value of £75,000;
>
> (2) There will be held for yourself and H.E. 50,000 new shares of a par value of £50,000. If equally divided H.E. will be entitled to 25,000. Inasmuch as Mr. Moreing has had to provide for his friends and influence from his interest it is no more than just that H.E. should meet the expenditure of any shares from this side that might be necessary;
>
> (3) The new Company has accepted the liability to H.E. Chang of 340,000 taels (inc. his banks);

(4) H.E. is to be in the new organisation as Director General in China at a salary and for life which, with prosperity to the Company, will be no bagatelle;

(5) With reorganisation, extension and reasonable success there are great possibilities in other directions such as we have discussed.

Hoover claimed that the Oriental Syndicate would obtain "no great profit" until its own shares doubled in value. Therefore, Hoover advised, the syndicate's "ambitions must be directed to that end." If it were successful, he asserted, Chang's "holdings will in round numbers become worth about 2,000,000 taels [$1,400,000]" instead of their probable "present realisable value" of less than 250,000 taels. Chang, he said, would also share in "the general benefits derived from protection of the property from foreign encroachment, from the fact that only ruin stares them in the face because of their monumental liabilities and from such other benefits as reduction of Chinwangtao loan interest to 6 per cent, &c." Hoover concluded with a reassuring reference to the presumed harmony of interest of the Europeans and the Chinese: "All of our own hopes lie in success; without it none of us will have any reward for past or future effort, and in the working out of our own salvation we work out that of H.E. and other shareholders."[127]

In one respect Hoover's letter was inaccurate: there was no guarantee that Chang would be Director-General in China for life. Hoover later testified that he did not realize at this point that this provision had been omitted from the company's articles of association when they were registered in London a month before.[128] In any case, Hoover did not know that the new company had been registered at all until January 29, five days after he wrote this letter.[129]

Hoover's letter seems to have satisfied Detring; there is no evidence that Chang's adviser ever objected to its contents.[130] And yet the process of acquiring the old company was far from concluded. In order to put into effect the altered contract, Hoover and his associates must now execute a separate, formal, explicit deed of transfer or conveyance. And for this they must secure the direct assent of Chang Yen-mao himself.[131] Perhaps this factor was another reason for Hoover's letter to Detring on January 24 spelling out the huge profits which Chang would presumably make personally— if he cooperated. There were plenty of hurdles still to be surmounted in the quest for the Kaiping mines.

I V

To assist Hoover in consummating the transfer a new figure now appeared in Tientsin. Chevalier Emmanuel de Wouters d'Oplinter was a former Belgian legal adviser to the Chinese Foreign Office as well as an agent in the Far East for Colonel Albert Thys's Compagnie Internationale d'Orient.[132] Early in January 1901, at the request of Thys's company, de Wouters proceeded to Tientsin as the representative of the large Belgian interests in the coming flotation. De Wouters took no part in Hoover's negotiations with Detring over the July 30 contract revisions. Rather, the Belgian's mission was diplomatic: to "exert himself," as Hoover put it, with the local envoys of jealous "Continental Powers."[133]

For just as Hoover and his principals were preparing to grasp their long-coveted prize, formidable European opposition was surfacing. Shortly after Hoover returned to Tientsin around January 10, he discovered that the German government had ordered the Deutsch-Asiatische Bank to "thwart" the transfer. Meanwhile, apparently in response to pressure from other European powers, the Russian army was getting ready to evacuate Tangshan. Hoover was alarmed at this combination of circumstances. Even though the Kaiping company was no longer in default on its debt to the German bank, Hoover feared that when the Russian troops moved out of Tangshan the Germans would move right in.[134]

On January 14 he therefore appealed to the British Consul-General in Tientsin to dispatch British troops to Tangshan to fill the dangerous vacuum just as soon as the Russians left. According to Hoover, the mines already belonged to "an English firm" anyway. And since "Belgian and Russian interests," he said, would have "a subordinate footing" in the new Chinese Engineering and Mining Company, Hoover anticipated no trouble from them.[135] The Germans, however, were less controllable. The Germans must not get their clutches on the mines.

Three days later Hoover's apprehension remained high. He cabled Moreing in London that it was imperative that the transfer of property from the old company to the new be expedited. He urged Moreing to "bring every pressure to bear upon" the Germans and to send Alfred White-Cooper (Moreing's Shanghai attorney) to Tientsin at once.[136]

The next several days were frantic ones as Hoover and de Wouters teamed up for a diplomatic mission to Peking.[137] While Hoover called on the American and British ambassadors, de Wouters contacted the Belgian and the French. All were sympathetic and promised to cooperate in the coming transfer.[138] Hoover also visited Chang in Peking and outlined the current state of the transaction.[139]

The Russians, however, proved far less compliant. Both the local Russian bank manager and the Russian Minister strenuously demurred at the prospect of an overtly British presence at Kaiping and Chinwangtao. Such an economic nexus would not only compete with Russia's port of Talienwan (later known as Dairen), across the Gulf of Chihli; it would also be (in Hoover's words) "an English barricade on their road to Peking." Only after considerable diplomatic maneuvering (including a suggestion that the local Russian bank might become the designated bank of the new Chinese Engineering and Mining Company) did de Wouters win a Russian pledge not to interfere for the time being.[140]

But it was tough sledding for the American engineer and his Belgian colleague. On the one hand, Hoover told Moreing on January 26, the Chinese were "in a blue funk" because the Russians still held the mines. On the other hand, Hoover was agitated that the Russians were about to leave, raising the specter of anarchy or worse. All this made him "extremely anxious to have the important transfers signed at once." Yet, he complained, the Oriental Syndicate had seemingly done nothing to furnish him with a competent attorney. Instead he was being forced to draft legal documents himself, relying on the less than satisfactory expertise of J. Bromley Eames.[141]

Later that day, the Oriental Syndicate finally came through. It cabled Hoover that it had retained a lawyer from Shanghai (who turned out to be White-Cooper) to go to Tientsin. It ordered Hoover to consult with de Wouters in his negotiations and in settling the legal issues.[142] Three days later, January 29, C. Algernon Moreing notified his American agent that the new Chinese Engineering and Mining Company was finally registered. He did not tell Hoover (he later claimed he did not know) that its articles of association contained no explicit reference to Chang Yen-mao and the proposed China board.[143]

All these annoyances and uncertainties were not easy to bear. But at least the protracted struggle was having one useful influence on the twenty-six-year-old Hoover: it was honing his talent for diplomacy, an essential skill in the treacherous game of international power politics and mining finance. The "main difficulty," Hoover told Moreing in late January, had not emanated from Russian diplomats. It had come from Chevalier de Wouters. The Belgian had an unfortunate tendency to "get discouraged" and dispatch gloomy messages to Europe. Hoover confided to Moreing how he handled de Wouters: "I have had to set up the contention that it is all a bluff [by the Russians], thinking to undermine us by frightening the Belgians from our support."[144] Whether or not Hoover really believed that Russian opposition *was* a bluff was irrelevant. His argument was a tactic designed to dispel de Wouters's self-defeating pessimism. Hoover was learning how to use men—men older and more experienced than he—in the pursuit of his objectives.

Not all the maneuvers were originating with agents of Moreing and the Oriental Syndicate. On January 30 Sir Ernest Satow, the British ambassador to China, informed his Foreign Office that the Russo-Chinese Bank was "offering to buy out Moreing" as part of a general Russian drive to expel British influence from northern China. Satow had evidence that Viceroy Li Hung-chang was trying to play off the Russians against the British. Satow was convinced that Moreing's Kaiping contract was a Chinese ploy to get the British to "pull Chinese chestnuts out of the fire."[145]

The developing struggle for Kaiping was even more complicated than that. From correspondence of de Wouters to his superiors in Brussels in early 1901 it is apparent that the Belgian financiers to whom Moreing had turned for capital had an objective of their own: the conversion of the enormous Kaiping enterprise into an exclusively Belgian company. Operating on the scene in behalf of Thys's Compagnie Internationale d'Orient, de Wouters recognized that caution was imperative. Already, in early February, the British government was becoming suspicious. On February 12 Thys's company cabled de Wouters, evidently requesting even further changes in the amended Detring-Hoover contract of July 30. De Wouters, in reply, counseled delay. The main thing, he believed, was for the new Chinese Engineering and Mining Company to gain possession of the Kaiping properties. Once in control, it could sell these properties to another company or convert itself into a Belgian concern—without further intervention by the Chinese.[146] It is unlikely that Moreing or Hoover had any inkling of the Belgians' designs.

Meanwhile, at the end of January, Hoover filed with the American consulate in Tientsin an indemnity claim against the Chinese government for losses he had incurred in the Boxer Rebellion. Of the scores of such claims the United States government received from American citizens and firms, Hoover's, totaling $55,009, was one of the largest. Aside from the loss of personal property valued at about $2,700, Hoover held the Chinese responsible for the "cost of sending family abroad to Europe and America and medical attendance necessitated by the siege": in other words, the journey he and Lou took to London and back to China (by way of San Francisco) in order to arrange the sale of the Kaiping mines. But by far the greatest proportion of his claim arose from what he called a "breach of contract caused by the actions of the Government" of China. Hoover referred to the now-inoperative contracts signed the previous June by Chang Yen-mao. Under them Hoover was to have held official appointments as Engineer-in-Chief for the Mining Bureau and for a colliery in Chihli for a full thirty-six months. Since Hoover had received only one month's salary before the rebellion struck, he now requested compensation for the other thirty-five, amounting to over $51,000. Hoover informed the American consulate that he was attempting to reinstate the Mining Bureau of Chihli "on a new basis." If successful, he considered himself "morally bound" to "withdraw all but such losses as I may actually incur by idleness" in the interim.[147]

Hoover's campaign to acquire the old Chinese Engineering and Mining Company now focused squarely on Chang. Early in February, even before the arrival of the Oriental Syndicate's lawyer from Shanghai, Hoover journeyed up to Peking, where Chang was currently residing. Mindful of Chinese laws on the transfer of property, Hoover carried with him a perpetual lease that he and Eames had prepared for the coal fields and for "all land outside of the Treaty Ports."[148] At this point Detring—reassured, no doubt, by Hoover's letter of January 24 about profits—was fully cooperative. In a letter to Chang on February 1 he implored the Chinese official to ratify and sign Hoover's lease, which he represented as necessary to complete the transfer. As usual, the desire for protection from foreign encroachment was weighing on Detring's mind. Chang's signature, he declared, was needed "to enable us as an English Company to defend its rights and property against the arbitrary acts to which the old Company has been and is still exposed."[149]

Once more, however, as so often in the past, Chang Yen-mao backed off, informing Hoover that he wanted to ponder the question further and to talk with Detring about it first. He would visit Tientsin later, he said. Not for the first time, Hoover returned to his quarters empty-handed.[150]

Early in February 1901 the Russians finally abandoned the mines around Tangshan; British troops speedily and obligingly replaced them.[151] To insure that the British took control before the Germans could interfere, de Wouters supplied the local British commander with a shipment of British flags that were raised over the mine shafts in the first hour of occupation. The tactic worked.[152]

Having by this time reached an accommodation with Detring over profits, Hoover now conferred with him at length over the other critical issue in the deal: the precise nature of the proposed "joint Chinese and foreign management" of the new company. As Hoover afterwards rightly observed, "there was no precedent" in China for the course they were pursuing.[153] And as with the division of their financial "interests," Detring was not inclined to rely on mere oral explanations from the young American. At his request Hoover therefore wrote him a letter on February 9.[154] Like Moreing's letter of November 9, much was later to hinge on whether this letter was a plain, honest statement, an innocent misrepresentation, or a disingenuous blend of flattery and deception.

The subject of Hoover's letter was "the arrangements regarding the administration of the newly reorganized Company as far as it is possible to anticipate them in advance." The "details," he asserted, "can only be settled by experience, and it is impossible to go into detailed plans until such experience is gained; nothing can be done suddenly; it must be a step by step process which will still be in progress ten years from now."

Hoover then laid out the "relations" of Detring and "the Chinese owners" to the "new administration":

The vital principle agreed upon [in July] was that the reorganized company should be incorporated as an English Company. The laws of England are very full on this subject and give absolute necessity to efficient, honest, above-board administration such as you have been endeavoring to introduce for several years.

"In order to facilitate the smooth working of the concern and thus meet the demands of so widely scattered shareholders," Hoover continued, two boards had been organized, "one in London and one in China." Hoover was evidently still unaware that no such provision existed in the articles of association registered in London on December 21.

The London Board is elected by all the shareholders of the Company, each share having one vote. Chinese as well as foreigners can sit on the

London Board if elected. You know what a large number of shares will be in the hands of the Chinese and their friends.

(How could this be? The Chinese would hold only a minority of the 1,000,000 shares. Hoover later testified that he considered "Mr. Moreing and others," as well as the Oriental Syndicate, to be the Chinese shareholders' friends.)[155] "It requires no insistence," said Hoover to Detring, "to show you the preponderating influence that under your able guidance they may have in the appointment of the London directors."

Hoover further explained that the London board "must of all necessity be entrusted with the general financial business of the New Company," including the crucial power of "floating the shares, &c., &c." Since, he added reassuringly, "no important action could be taken" by the London board under British law "without consulting the shareholders I do not need to point out where the final Court of Appeal lies."

With regard to the China board, Hoover declared that Chang Yen-mao was "desired to decide" its organization. "It is suggested," he added, that this board have three members:

1. H.E. Chang, who by agreement is Director General for life and thus furnished a never before heard of guarantee of the interests of one portion of the shareholders.
2. A director chosen by H.E. Chang. It is hoped in London that you will be the one chosen by H.E. to sit on the China Board. If H.E. goes abroad I know that it would meet with their great satisfaction to know that you should assume his functions.
3. The third member of the Board will be an experienced general coal mining manager chosen by the London Board. He will have the usual functions of a mine manager.

"The Board thus constituted," Hoover concluded in a vitally important sentence, "will have in itself the entire management of the Company's property in China, and before it the new manager will have to lay his plans for such change as may be necessary to effect the greatest and most profitable results which are the common aim. I have no doubt some system similar to that you propose—the Maritime Customs—will prove advisable."

Hoover closed with a paean of praise to Detring, the foreign financiers, and the wise Chinese shareholders who were about to surrender sole control over Kaiping.

It must be realized that it was with the very greatest difficulties that we have been able to persuade our friends to invest money in a concern with such a machinery of management. It is the first time that any foreigners have allowed Chinese to cooperate in the management of a large business

in which there is such an exceedingly large amount of money at stake. . . .
The Chinese have every reason to be congratulated on the acceptance of
such a scheme by foreigners. . . . I might add that the thing would never
have been accepted at all were it not for the special confidence that they
have in you and their knowledge of your influence on Chang and the other
Chinese connected with the Old Company.[156]

Hoover did not mention—again, if his later statements are correct, he did
not yet realize it—that the new company's articles of association provided no
guarantee for "entire management" of the property in China by a China board.
There was *no* binding stipulation that Thys, Moreing, and the other Europeans would be as generous toward the Chinese as they now allegedly deigned
to be. Whatever Hoover's understanding, the safeguarding of the Chinese
stake in the new venture would ultimately depend on an identity of interest
between the Chinese shareholders and their European "friends."

On February 18 Alfred White-Cooper arrived in Tientsin.[157] Discarding
as unsatisfactory the perpetual lease drawn up by Hoover and Eames, the
British lawyer from Shanghai instead readied for Chang's signature a deed
of transfer formally conveying the Kaiping properties to the British company
pursuant to the amended contract of July 30, 1900.[158] The new indenture
was dated February 19, 1901, the Chinese New Year.[159] At about this same
time the elusive Chang came down at last from Peking.[160] The showdown
was at hand.

V

I F Hoover and his colleagues believed that the Chinese official would now
routinely seal the vital transfer deed, they were abruptly disillusioned. To
the consternation of the foreigners, Chang Yen-mao refused to execute the
conveyance. What had gone wrong? According to Detring, Chang by mid-
February had become "very suspicious" that Hoover was "not acting straight."
Hoover's "personality" particularly made him apprehensive. Moreover, Chang
hesitated because he still did not know the precise contents of the July 30
contract (a point contradicted by Hoover and Eames, who said they thoroughly briefed Chang about it back in July before it was ever signed).[161] For
his part Hoover later claimed that the Chinese "tone towards the negotiations
seemed to change" in early February once the Russians evacuated the coal
fields around Tangshan.[162] The inference, presumably, was that Chang could
now dare to drive a harder bargain.

Certainly Chang's personal circumstances were less abject than eight months
before. And although political uncertainty still abounded, the Chinese government was again functioning, even if headquartered for the moment in the
interior, far from Peking.

However much Chang may have known back in July, when White-Cooper interviewed him in mid-February he found the Chinese official to be uninformed about the terms of the July 30 deed and the effect of the proposed arrangement. According to White-Cooper, Detring had failed to keep his promise to show the July 30 agreement to Chang and secure Chang's assent. And when Chang now discovered that the Kaiping company was to be turned over in entirety to the new British-registered company, he began to raise obstacles and resist.[163]

Whatever Chang's motives and knowledge, once he examined White-Cooper's proposed deed he flatly declined to sign it. According to his version of the episode, he saw that the proposed indenture neither carried out his "original intention" nor comported with his "original instructions" (the A, B, C documents of the past summer).[164] For White-Cooper's deed was "tantamount to a sale of the Company to the other parties"—something Chang could not and would not authorize: ". . . he could not give away Chinese property. It belonged to Chinese merchants. It was under the supervision of the authorities, and he had no right, nor did he intend to sign away these rights to others." All this Chang told White-Cooper, de Wouters, Hoover, and Detring—or so he later said. Chang also rejected the deed because, as he put it, his government "would object to it altogether."[165] According to Detring's version, Chang told *him* that "we were altogether in the hands of the other side if he signed only this deed of transfer."[166] The "other side" soon suspected that Chang's true reservations were not nearly so high-minded.

And so began what eventually became known as the "four days' row,"[167] during which, as the local British consul expressed it, "Detring, Hoover and everybody else lost their tempers, fell out, fell in again, and generally made their lives miserable. . . ."[168] According to Chang, on the second day the Westerners offered him a separate "Supplementary Agreement" that, they said, would answer all his objections. Still Chang refused. The first document (White-Cooper's deed of transfer) went too far (it amounted to an outright sale). Moreover, he wondered, why were two documents necessary anyway? Why not combine them into one? According to Chang, the Westerners replied that he did not understand that British law required the first document. The second one, though, they promised, would be the one "acted upon." When Chang continued to be adamant, the Westerners (he eventually alleged) threatened to invoke diplomatic pressures to "crush" him and to seize the mines militarily if he would not sign.[169]

The third day, February 23, passed even more acrimoniously.[170] By now the pressure on the foreigners to nail down an agreement was reaching a climax. For under the deed of July 30, 1900, the deadline for completing the transaction at hand was February 28, 1901, now less than a week away.[171] By now also Chang had learned (or so he said) that his wife was very ill in Shanghai; he therefore announced that he would leave for Shanghai on the twenty-fourth. He told de Wouters that he would put off signing the transfer agreement until he returned.[172]

Early on the morning of Sunday, February 24, Gustav Detring went to interview Chang Yen-mao. Ill at the time and cracking under the strain, he insisted that Chang complete the transfer and thereby gain protection for the mines from foreign depredations at last. Attach such terms and conditions as you wish, Detring advised. De Wouters, said the German, was influential with the Chinese authorities and could easily settle "the task of regulating and stretching the thing afterwards" with the Chinese government. When Chang still resisted, Detring stalked out "in a rage."[173] The matter was hopeless, he declared; Chang was dead set against the arrangement.[174]

Until the middle of the fourth day, Hoover remained in the background while White-Cooper and de Wouters attempted to elicit a signature from Chang.[175] Hoover did so, said White-Cooper, for reasons of expediency; evidently Chang had become estranged from his former chief engineer.[176] But at mid-day on February 24, with Chang still recalcitrant, the Belgian diplomat and British lawyer called in Hoover.[177] From them Hoover learned (in his words) "that Chang was raising difficulties, that he was demanding 500,000 taels [about $350,000] for himself and that he generally objected to going on; that he said that he had to go to Shanghai and made other excuses; said that he must wait till the Court came back from . . . the Interior."[178]

Hoover was outraged. His "excitement," the British consul reported, "now became dangerous."[179] Were his long, laborious negotiations to fail on the brink of victory? Hoover wondered whether he had not been the victim of a "trick." Had Chang, he wondered, *ever* meant to come to terms? Or had he merely strung Hoover along and used him?[180]

That afternoon Hoover held a sometimes vehement three-hour interview with Chang. Unwilling to rely on a Chinese interpreter who might tone down his words in translation, Hoover took with him his own interpreter: Dr. C. D. Tenney, the American president of the Imperial University at Tientsin. According to Hoover's version of the encounter, he bluntly told Chang that he was "very much surprised" at the posture Chang had adopted toward the agreements—agreements which Detring had "entered into . . . on his behalf" and which Chang himself (according to Hoover) knew about. Since any remaining legal documents required under the July 30 contract must be executed by the end of February 1901, Chang's departure now for Shanghai without signing would constitute "a violation of the agreements, and I possibly, with some indignation, intimated to him that I thought his going to Shanghai was merely a Chinese excuse." Hoover reviewed for Chang how Moreing had "stood by" Chang, had "enlisted his friends" to reorganize the Chinese Engineering and Mining Company, and had lined up the financing. After all this trouble, after all the arduous diplomatic negotiations, Hoover said he "could not see how, as an honourable man [Chang] could back out." According to Hoover, Chang "then contended that he did not want to back out altogether, but that there were certain things that he required, and we discussed his requirements."

Hoover afterwards acknowledged that their conversation was "very heated."

His Excellency at one time intimated to me that I was causing him to 'lose his face,' which I deemed was a Chinese expression for being insulted, and this especially arose out of the fact that I told him if he did not go on and carry out his obligations in good faith I should be compelled, out of common honesty, to go to the Ministers, whose support we had enlisted, and tell them so.

Such was Hoover's story of the stormy conversation.[181]

But was it the whole story? According to Detring (who was not present), Hoover also threatened to find ways to keep Chang in Tientsin, away from his ailing wife in Shanghai, unless he ratified the transfer. And (said Detring) Hoover promised to "give information" (presumably to the ambassadors) if "this contract should come to nothing."[182] Hoover later denied that he ever attempted to "frighten" Chang, or threatened to "crush" him, or threatened to have foreign soldiers seize the mines. He did, however, admit to warning Chang "that we should certainly complain to the Ministers that he had not kept good faith with us."[183] To Chang this probably sounded like a threat.

In any case, after Chang complained that he had been insulted, Hoover apologized (he said), and (as he later put it) the two men "came to more amicable arrangements."[184] Chang demanded that the new company agree to pay 500,000 taels allegedly due in bonuses to the old company's employees, in previously undivided profits due to the old shareholders, and in repayment of a loan owed to the provincial government of Chihli.[185] To de Wouters and White-Cooper, Chang's request was little more than a blatant attempt at "squeeze." Indeed, the British lawyer believed that Chang's opposition to the transfer stemmed from his realization that he would lose power and "squeeze" under the new regime and might be denounced by his enemies for selling out. Whatever Chang's motive, by the afternoon of the fourth day and probably before, he had (according to White-Cooper) made it clear that he would not approve the transfer unless he received 500,000 taels (roughly £70,000) for bribing his government and for satisfying the Kaiping company's workers.[186]

Squeeze or not, at this point the foreigners had little choice. According to de Wouters, Hoover was certain that no deal was possible without some accommodation of Chang Yen-mao. Furthermore, Hoover believed that it would be in the Westerners' interests to put at Chang's disposal a substantial sum of money for transmittal to the Chinese government.[187] Hoover therefore agreed with Chang that the new company would quickly pay 200,000 taels (£30,000) to the Chinese government—not in a bribe but in repayment of an existing, recognized government loan to the old Chinese Engineering and Mining Company. On the rest of Chang's agenda Hoover took a harder line. As for the large bonuses that Chang asserted were due former employees, Hoover argued that since the new company was pledged to assume all of the old company's liabilities anyway, explicit statements on the subject were unnecessary. The new company would automatically absorb the obligation to pay the bonsues. This same reasoning applied to the question of undistributed dividends to the old shareholders.

According to Hoover, White-Cooper and de Wouters sat in on the latter part of his conversation. When Chang requested a written statement recording "what the Chinese were going to get out of the business," White-Cooper suggested a memorandum. According to Hoover, Chang wanted a document that was not drawn up in unfamiliar and disquieting English legal prose and that Chang could present to Chinese government officials and business associates to reveal "what their interest in the business" was. From then on, said Hoover, the negotiations moved expeditiously toward a conclusion.[188]

If Hoover's account is accurate,[189] why, after more than three days of bitter wrangling, did Chang suddenly become so cooperative? According to Chang, the breakthrough occurred only after Hoover, through his interpreter Tenney, promised that the foreigners "would recognize the second document and . . . were prepared to act on the second document, and that the second document would be the ruling one." Only then did Chang introduce the financial questions of employee bonuses and shareholder dividends. And, claimed Chang, Hoover, urged on by Tenney, assented to his terms. Chang said he was persuaded to sign the indenture only because he "put absolute credit" in Hoover's express "assurance" that the separate memorandum would in fact be the governing document in the transaction.[190]

There is some plausibility in Chang's story. He did, after all, hold out for nearly four days before coming to terms. A second document—a memorandum—was his sine qua non. Yet other factors may also have been at work. Possibly, if the story about his wife's illness was true, he was now more anxious to terminate matters. Possibly also Hoover's sharp words—be they construed as intimidating threats or justified warnings to call in the Western ambassadors—had an effect.

Finally, there was one possibly decisive factor that none of the contending parties ever mentioned later on. On January 26, only two days after the climactic "row," C. W. Campbell, the British consul in Tientsin, informed his ambassador in Peking about the episode. Campbell stated that when Hoover discovered that Chang was seeking 500,000 taels "in hard cash over and above his settled bargain," Hoover wanted the British ambassador to intervene immediately. Instead, Campbell decided to investigate the matter himself. Campbell concluded that Chang was either "bluffing" or trying to get "the customary pressure" (squeeze) "which Chinese think de rigeur." Campbell accordingly permitted White-Cooper to inform Chang that Campbell, as Britain's representative on the scene, would intervene in behalf of the British persons involved unless Chang changed his mind about signing the papers—papers that, in Campbell's words, Chang "was bound by the authority" vested in his agent Detring "to execute." According to Campbell, the Chinese official promptly came to terms "without further humbug."[191]

Events now rushed to completion. Late in the day, at Hoover's residence across the street from Chang's quarters, the final formal documents were prepared.[192] Dropping in, Detring recalled the scene: it was "an infernal laboratory, at the time the people had very big eyes, and were in an awful state," "immensely busy" drawing up the legal papers, "and busy in a way as struck me as suspicious" (or so he later alleged).[193] This time, though, there was no turning back. Detring himself, "under pressure," was acquiescent.[194] That evening, February 24, 1901, after twelve consecutive hours of negotiations, Chang and the others formally signed the fateful documents, which were written both in English and Chinese.[195]

Three separate papers were approved: the indenture or deed of transfer itself, a contemporaneous memorandum, and a supplementary power of attorney from Chang empowering Detring to "execute all further documents that might be required" to give effect to the sale.[196] The "deed of transfer" recited how Chang, the year before, had authorized Detring to organize a company with £1,000,000 capital "to be furnished jointly by Chinese and foreigners [and] to take over the management" of the Chinese Engineering and Mining Company. It then recorded how Hoover and Detring had made an agreement dated July 30, 1900 and how the provisions of this agreement had since been implemented—including the incorporation of the new Chinese Engineering and Mining Company, Ltd. in London. In pursuance of the July contract, the old company along with Chang and Detring (as two of its directors) therefore now vested (with Hoover's consent) various properties in the new company. Chang, as Director-General of Mines in Chihli and Jehol, "confirmed" this conveyance. The indenture listed in detail the various assets of the old company thus assigned "absolutely" to the new. Chang and Detring pledged to sign all documents and perform "all other acts . . . reasonably . . . required for completing the transfer." The new company accepted the bona fide liabilities of the old. Hoover, Chang, and Detring signed this document.[197]

One feature of the indenture was curious, even remarkable: Chang and Detring explicitly conveyed to the new company not only the old company's well-known lands, fleet, and other assets but also "all the lands, mines and coalfields known as the Estate Kaiping coal field." The grant included not only seven particular sites (specified in the indenture) but all mines and seams of coal "geologically connected with" them. The indenture also gave the new company the "exclusive right to search and mine for coal and minerals within the area and coal fields aforesaid."

This sweeping phraseology (which White-Cooper inserted)[198] had no precedent in the contract of July 30, 1900. Indeed, the old Chinese Engineering and Mining Company's coal-mining rights extended no more than three miles beyond its working shafts, as Hoover almost certainly knew.[199] And some of the seven listed sites apparently had never been operated by the old company. Such a wording of the indenture could scarcely have been accidental.

Yet nowhere in the extensive contemporary documents does there appear to be any explanation for this extraordinary enlargement of the new company's jurisdiction. Whether intentionally or not, whether legally or not, Chang and Detring in February 1901 purported to hand Moreing and his associates nothing less than a monopoly over the entire, fabulously rich Kaiping coal basin.[200]

Like the deed of transfer, the "Memorandum Relating to the Reorganization of the Chinese Engineering and Mining Company" opened with a recital of past circumstances: the "disturbances of last summer," the danger of "confiscation" or compulsory surrender of the company's property, the desire for additional capital, the decision to "convert" the old company into "an Anglo-Chinese Company registered under English law and protection." Therefore, the memorandum continued, Detring, on Chang's authority, had made the "necessary arrangements," specifically a "deed of sale" with Hoover permitting Moreing to "take the necessary steps" to raise capital in Europe and to register the company, "[i]t being understood that after conversion the Company should keep its name and be managed according to the Articles of Association covering as well the interest of the Chinese as of the foreign shareholders, making all alike participants in profits and losses, and that a working capital of £100,000 should be raised before the end of February [1901]."

Since these conditions had now been met, the memorandum declared that "it has today been settled and decided that the Company shall in the future be constituted and managed" according to fourteen points. Among these, several were to prove critically important:

(6) The management of the Company shall be conducted by two Boards of Directors, one in China and one in London.
(7) His Excellency Chang Yi [Chang Yen-mao] will be Director General resident in China as before in general charge of affairs, and as such will have power to appoint a Chinese Director who will have equal powers with foreign Directors in China.
(8) The management of the property of the Company in China will be in the China Board.
(9) The London Board will be elected by all the shareholders, Chinese and foreign.
(13) It is understood that the Company will be managed in such a spirit as to make Chinese and Foreign interests harmonize on a fair basis of equality and to open an era of cooperation and protection that will enrich both the Government and the people.

The memorandum was signed by Chang Yen-mao, Detring, Hoover, and de Wouters.[201]

The memorandum was Chang's price for signing the transfer deed. As Alfred White-Cooper acknowledged, this last-minute document was "a condition precedent to the transfer of the Old Company's property."[202] Yet this soon to be famous memorandum teemed with potentially troublesome ambiguities. It stated that the new company would be governed by its articles of association, but no copy of the finished articles had yet arrived in China. It stipulated that the Chinese would receive certain shares but was silent about the disposition of the rest. Clause 7 stated that Chang would remain "in general charge of affairs" but failed to define what this meant. Clause 8 vested "the management" of the new company's property in China in the China board. This was not quite the same as the "entire management" that Hoover had promised to Detring in his letter of February 9, barely two weeks before. And just what powers were subsumed by the word "management"? The memorandum did not say.

If the memorandum's exact meaning was clad in ambiguity, so, it turned out, was its true purpose. De Wouters afterwards asserted that this document (signed without his European principals' knowledge or authorization) was intended to be a face-saving device for Chang in dealing with his potentially skeptical, squeeze-minded government.[203] Certainly there is considerable evidence to support this contention. The memorandum itself referred to a "deed of sale" (clearly the deed of July 30)—thus undercutting Chang's later claim that he initially refused to sign the transfer on the principled ground that he had no power to sell. Indeed, Chang later admitted that he objected to White-Cooper's transfer deed "because the [Chinese] Government would object to it altogether, and they [White-Cooper et al.] said: Well, let us get something which your Government will approve of, and that was the history of their agreeing to [the memorandum]."

This was Chang's own later testimony—in court, under cross-examination.[204] It may well explain his insistence during the row on prompt repayment of the 200,000-tael loan to his government and his sudden solicitude for his employees' bonuses and his shareholders' dividends.[205] He wanted something to pacify his Chinese critics.

Yet Chang's behavior may not be entirely reducible to a desire for self-protection. The row of mid-February did, after all, last for four turbulent days. If all Chang really wanted was a slice of "squeeze" for his associates and a piece of verbal windowdressing that he knew to be meaningless, would the final settlement have been quite so hard to achieve? That principle as well as interest was involved White-Cooper himself asserted many months later, in 1902. At the time of the transfer of February 1901, he recalled, no text of the articles of association was available in China. All Hoover had with him was a draft. Since a mere draft "could not be relied upon," White-Cooper prepared the memorandum "to maintain the rights" of Chang, Detring, and the Chinese shareholders.[206]

White-Cooper's letter of 1902 (when controversy over the transaction was building) did not completely comport with what he wrote to the Oriental Syndicate on February 25, 1901, the day after the climax of the row. In this letter the British lawyer declared that the memorandum was simply an individual interpretation of the overall arrangement by the men who signed the document. Nevertheless, the British lawyer observed that the "spirit"of the memorandum should be adhered to by the new British-registered company.[207]

De Wouters took a somewhat similar position. He told his superiors in Brussels that neither he nor Hoover had the power to sign such a document binding the Oriental Syndicate and that the memorandum had no value without his superiors' approval. But de Wouters said he considered himself and Hoover obliged in good faith to try to obtain their assent. He hoped that the men in Brussels would approve his conduct during those difficult February days—when all might easily have been lost.[208]

It is impossible to know what was in Chang's mind as he signed the papers set before him on the night of February 24. But the A, B, C documents of July 1900 suggest that Chang—initially, at least—did not propose to cede total control to the European financiers. What he clearly intended in 1900 (and the words of the memorandum seem to support this) was a *jointly managed* Anglo-Chinese mining company, a fusion of Chinese and foreign interests over which *he* would retain ultimate control.[209] The Oriental Syndicate had other ideas, as the revised deed of July 30 intimated: the Kaiping mines were not merely to be converted or "transformed" (the original wording) but "transferred" outright to a British-registered company—over which Europeans would have control. In the minds of the European promoters this new company was not to be just nominally headquartered in London.

And so the deed was done. By the documents dated February 19, 1901 the Chinese Engineering and Mining Company headed by Chang sold itself to the foreign-organized company in return for a ⅜ interest (375,000 shares) in the new company and a promise of £100,000 in working capital by the end of the month. Nothing was stipulated in writing as to the allocation of the remaining ⅝ interest. If Chang at the moment of transfer really believed that the memorandum protected him, that it assured him his plenary, pre-Boxer powers, that it guaranteed him a truly substantive "general charge of affairs," he was profoundly mistaken.

9

A Mine Manager
in China

I

THE next day, February 25, 1901, Chang Yen-mao departed for Shang-hai.[1] According to Gustav Detring, Chang had extracted one other conces-sion before signing the transfer agreement: that Herbert Hoover would sever his connection with the company at Tientsin. He had so offended Chang by his "threats" that the Chinese official regarded him as persona non grata. However, when Chevalier de Wouters requested that Hoover remain as his associate, Detring acquiesced. De Wouters, the diplomat, said he needed Hoover's engineering expertise.[2]

Whatever the accuracy of this story (and Detring when he told it was unfriendly to Hoover), the American engineer had no intention of leaving China. Hoover, in fact, moved with alacrity to solidify his position. On the day of the signing of the transfer, he cabled C. Algernon Moreing: "H. C. Hoover must be appointed to be temporary general manager, only he must be authorised to sign cheques." Hoover then told Moreing precisely what to cable to Detring:

Telegraph instructions to G. Detring as follows: Please accept our hearty congratulations. Board have decided to appoint temporarily H. C. Hoover general manager. He must take possession of property on behalf of the Company.[3]

Hoover's European backers promptly complied with his request. A few days later the Oriental Syndicate notified Detring: "Please accept our hearty congratulations, the board have appointed general managers Hoover and de Wouters temporarily; they must take possession in the name of Chinese Engineering and Mining Company."[4] If Detring had anticipated that Hoover would quietly disappear from the scene, he was speedily disillusioned.

In a separate cable on February 28 the syndicate informed Hoover of its message to Detring. It then instructed Hoover and de Wouters what to do: "Take possession of property pending arrival of staff, which will start on 4th March with Francqui. You are authorized sign cheques jointly and make all necessary arrangements provisionally."[5] Emile Francqui, the former Belgian consul in Shanghai, was now the Agent-General of Colonel Albert Thys's Compagnie Internationale d'Orient.[6]

The two designated co-managers promptly swung into action. The next day, March 1, a provisional Tientsin Board of Administration was established. In a letter to certain Chinese officials at Tangshan, Detring explained that this board was one of two "Provisional Boards" and would "control the Company's affairs in China." (The other "provisional" board was situated in London.) It would be comprised of Chang, a Chinese deputy, and "for the time being" Detring, de Wouters, and Hoover. Its secretary was the local British lawyer, J. Bromley Eames.[7] For the next two months Eames served in this capacity until resigning to become a counsel for the new company.[8]

During the first week of March Hoover acted swiftly to take charge of the sprawling business venture. Not a man to sit in his office and issue paper directives, he immediately hastened to the Kaiping coal mines, where he installed his old friend George Wilson as acting general manager.[9] Newberry, his former Australian assistant, he soon placed at Linsi.[10] During this first week Hoover also initiated what he called "certain wideranging reforms in the finances." From now on, he ordered, no money was "to be disbursed, received nor any agreements entered into without the consent of the foreign officer, over whom I shall keep a close supervision."[11] The purpose of all his actions, he wrote to Moreing, was to revamp the company's administration so that the new manager could achieve "complete control immediately on arrival." Repeatedly frustrated for two years by Chinese graft and inertia, Hoover hankered to strike while conditions were propitious:

> The presence of the troops on the mines and the absence of the Chinese Directors gives us an opportunity to introduce sweeping reforms with much less of struggle than will be possible in two months from now when the Chinese get satisfied that all their old perquisites are to be returned.[12]

De Wouters also considered circumstances to be favorable for reform. Thanks to the presence of British troops at the mines, he reported to Brussels, the Chinese workers were living in a state of "salutary fear."[13]

Recognizing that their control was as yet only nominal, Hoover and de Wouters at once endeavored to achieve three paramount objectives. First, "to have the agreements" with Chang Yen-mao "definitively confirmed" in order to "render them unassailable" from challenge. Second, inside the treaty ports, to register the old company's property in the name of the new; outside the treaty ports, "to take possession of the title deeds" of company property under direct Chinese jurisdiction. Third, "to take over from the old Company's officials the actual management inclusive of the transfer of the Cash in the banks."[14]

The obstacles the two men faced were formidable. The old Chinese company had more than 9,000 native employees as well as five hundred Chinese officials not known for their integrity or competence.[15] The company, in Hoover's words, was "full of fraud and corruption from one end to the other"—a mess compounded by the anarchy of the past nine months and "a very lax administration" going back for years.[16] Never before had Westerners exercised any real control over Kaiping. Previous foreign advisers, Hoover noted, had held no power over finances and could not fire "even a common coolie."[17] Squeeze had become institutionalized, said de Wouters.[18] Furthermore, military units from Japan, Germany, France, and Russia still occupied much of the company's property. Somehow it must be weaned from their jealous grasp.

For Hoover and de Wouters the next several months were a period of unremitting struggle. To their surprise the first challenge came from a source they least expected: Gustav Detring. Instead of routinely effecting the transfer under the revised power of attorney which Chang Yen-mao gave him on February 24, the German (in Hoover's and de Wouters's words) "simply refused to execute his engagements"—engagements he had promised in the indenture to carry out. According to the two co-managers, Detring would not inform local banks that the transfer had occurred. He would not hand over the old company's cash assets. He did everything he could "to keep the Chinese control on the management."[19] And he repeatedly made "demands as a quid pro quo for every move to vest the New Company in its property."[20]

According to the American and Belgian co-managers, Detring justified his conduct by two arguments. First, under the July 30, 1900 contract Moreing was obliged to raise £100,000 in working capital by February 28, 1901 and to deposit it at the Tientsin office of the Chartered Bank of India, Australia, and China.[21] Instead, when the money arrived it was placed in the local Russo-Chinese Bank. Detring contended that this violated the terms of the July 30 contract. Secondly, he stressed that the new company had not yet repaid the loan installment of 200,000 taels specifically mentioned in clause 4 of the memorandum.[22]

To Hoover and de Wouters, Detring's stated objections were but pretexts to cover up an unjustified breach of his contractual obligations. As they saw it, the German's actions were rooted in Chang's fears and in Detring's own "personal vanity." The morning after Chang signed the agreements of February 24, he began to worry that he had gone too far. Detring, therefore, decided that as the attorney entrusted by Chang to "complete the details" of the deal, he must act as guardian of Chinese interests. And that, to him, meant retaining "in his hands the whole administration of the Company." According to Hoover and de Wouters, Detring feared that as Chinese mastery of Kaiping waned, so, too, would his personal prestige and "influence."[23]

The co-managers' analysis, of course, was based on their own interpretation of the meaning of the transfer accords. It was precisely this interpretation that came into dispute. To Detring, it appears, the deal called for a coalition government, and as he later put it, he meant "to keep at least a handle in my hands."[24] To Hoover and de Wouters the deal called for an orderly transfer of power to themselves. In the eyes of each side, the other was a treacherous usurper.

Hoover and de Wouters eventually convinced Detring (though "not without the greatest difficulty") that the agreement about delivering the £100,000 in working capital had been satisfactorily implemented.[25] Meanwhile during the first three weeks of March the question of repaying the 200,000 taels in Chinese government loans assumed a threatening hue. Before the four days' row of late February, Li Hung-chang, viceroy of Chihli, had been briefed about the Kaiping negotiations. According to Hoover and de Wouters, Li had given "his verbal approbation to our projects." Indeed, they said, the viceroy had even sent Chang from Peking down to Tientsin in mid-February.[26] How much Li truly understood about Hoover's and de Wouters's "projects" cannot be determined. In any case, the memorandum dated February 19 unequivocally stipulated that 200,000 taels of Chinese government loans must be repaid by the new company "out of the first funds." Li was well aware of the pledge.

In a letter to their superiors Hoover and de Wouters later referred to the 200,000-tael repayment as having been "promised" to Li "under you know which circumstances."[27] The co-managers did not elaborate. Had Chang demanded that the sum be used to pacify Li? Or had Li himself demanded prompt repayment as his price for pressuring Chang to come back to Tientsin? Whatever the case, Li was clamoring for the money now. The Chinese imperial government, which he was representing in post-Boxer Rebellion talks with the Western powers, desperately needed funds, and Li was anxious to send the sum on to the Chinese court. Hoover and his Belgian colleague knew that they must make the payment quickly or risk the viceroy's enmity.[28]

On February 24 Hoover cabled Moreing that he "urgently" needed £30,000—the rough equivalent of 200,000 taels.[29] Day after day, however, no money came from Europe, and the fate of the enterprise became more perilous. Yet Hoover was able to turn adversity to advantage. On March 22 he informed Moreing:

> Chevalier de Wouters has just returned from Peking from an interview with Li, and Li tells him if he has any more trouble with Chang to let him know, and to hurry up with the 200,000 taels. . . . Chang returns tomorrow from Shanghai, and we propose to demand from him all of the title deeds which we now lack (we by main force on my part took possession of most of them) and to demand that all the funds in the bank be handed over to us at once and sundry other things before we pay the 200,000. If he does not attend to these matters promptly he will be in a difficult position of not having 200,000 taels.

In short, Hoover would not release the 200,000 taels to Chang (for transmittal to Li) unless Chang surrendered deeds and money belonging to the new company. By exploiting Chang's vulnerability vis-à-vis Li, Hoover hoped to compel Chang to do what, in Hoover's opinion, he was duty-bound to do already.[30]

At one point Hoover and de Wouters were so fearful that the whole deal might collapse because of failure to pay Li that they arranged for an emergency overdraft, if necessary, on their own responsibility at two local banks. The co-managers were also prepared to sell some of the company's shares in a dock company to cover the overdraft.[31] In the meantime they waited for instructions from Europe.

Li Hung-chang continued to exert "great pressure," and for several more weeks Hoover and de Wouters, by their account, resorted to "the most various pretenses" to fend off his importunings.[32] The financiers in Europe, it seems, were far from eager to turn over the 200,000 taels. Nor was Chang proving any easier to deal with. Badgered by Li for the money, and told by de Wouters that he would get it when he fulfilled all his contractual obligations, Chang retaliated by refusing to give up the title deeds to his home and to the company's offices—property that belonged to the new company.[33] Later in the spring, the embattled managers finally received both money and authorization from Europe.[34] The 200,000-tael debt was paid and the viceroy appeased.[35] In the words of Hoover and de Wouters, "there was nothing more to fear" from Li Hung-chang.[36]

Throughout the spring the American and Belgian also struggled to establish legal control of the Chinese Engineering and Mining Company's far-flung properties. Particularly in the treaty ports their task was complicated by acute diplomatic rivalries. Not only must they register each title deed separately in various consulates; they must overcome the opposition of unfriendly interests like the Deutsch-Asiatische Bank, which held mortgages on certain company property. Nor did possession of the deeds always settle disputes. When the Deutsch-Asiatische Bank surrendered the deed to a Tientsin wharf, it turned out that the wharf fell within Russian jurisdiction.

The British consul refused to recognize this and asked Hoover and de Wouters to register the deed at his consulate. The Russians, however, promised to recognize the new company's title only if the deed were registered at *their* consulate. Hoover and de Wouters yielded to the Russians and then tried to mollify the British. Meanwhile *German* troops actually occupied the wharf and would not budge![37]

In the case of company property outside the treaty ports, Hoover and de Wouters felt able to be more assertive. The two men knew that physical control of property combined with possession of title deeds was "the best title one can have in China"—"legitimate proof of property."[38] Accordingly, immediately after the transfer in late February, Hoover, in his words, seized most of the title deeds "by main force."[39] Hoover and de Wouters later acknowledged to their European superiors that foreigners could not own land outside the treaty ports in China. Consequently, as the two managers put it, they could "only substitute the new Company in the rights of the old one." Fortunately for the pair, the "local mandarins" did not comprehend what was happening: the Chinese believed that the old Kaiping company had merely augmented its capital and made some "modifications in its management." Such an attitude no doubt facilitated the managers' quest. Hoover and de Wouters placed the deeds in a local bank.[40]

Sometime in April or early May Emile Francqui arrived in Tientsin. A brilliant, domineering individual, a former military officer who ten years before had helped King Leopold conquer the Congo, Francqui was on his way to becoming one of the richest men and ablest financiers in Europe. For now, as representative of Colonel Thys's financial "trust," Francqui was in China to oversee its operations and advance Belgium's interests in the Far East.[41]

Francqui's arrival brought no relief for Herbert Hoover. For three grueling months Hoover had been striving to put the Kaiping enterprise in order and to gain control, as he put it, over "9000 thieves."[42] Now, instead of bringing the full technical staff which Hoover had been led to expect, Francqui showed up with a single engineer—a man aptly named Malaise.[43]

Hoover was disgusted. In a letter in mid-May to the new company's board of directors, he angrily complained that the Europeans had "no adequate conception" of the burdens and "volume of business" that he and his associates had borne: "Aside from the undescribable villainy of Chinese administration," the company for a year had been "practically under no administration at all, and the new abuses which had grown up seemed almost insuperable." Beyond that, Hoover reported that he had lacked "anything like the necessary assistance to bring order out of chaos." His foreign staff in Tientsin and at the mines consisted of five men. For the vast company he had only one foreign accountant.

Hoover recorded how "as a first move"

we placed a foreigner in every branch and enacted that no money was to be spent or received but on his approval. We followed this by the introduction of a voucher system, and later by a day book. . . . We soon found that to enforce honesty our reforms had to go much farther, and we have had simply a running fight to hold our own against a solid wall of Chinese opposition.

According to Hoover the bloated Chinese office staff—several hundred strong—had "no desire to see honesty of administration, for it means diminution of their collective income by probably 500,000 taels [$350,000] per annum." To stop unauthorized sale of company supplies, Hoover and his colleagues had revamped the stores departments and eliminated twenty-seven out of thirty-two jobs. But they had "dared not" fire the twenty-seven superfluous officers, lest they precipitate a strike while the Western staff was too sparse to "run the works" itself. In order to stop unauthorized disbursements by the Chinese cashier it had finally become necessary, Hoover reported, to "seize by violence" all the funds and put them under "the manager's key."[44]

A month later Hoover reported some progress against the "united front" of Chinese opposition. Already more than $1,500,000 a year in "squeeze" had been traced. In every department Hoover had had to set up a parallel structure of "our own men." Once his loyalists were entrenched, he then dispensed with the Chinese staff. It had, he said, required "the greatest of diplomacy and even intrigue" to avert a general strike by the Chinese.[45]

Sometime in April Lou Henry Hoover and her sister Jean came over from Yokohama to Tientsin.[46] Once again the house on Racecourse Road was home, a refuge from the "daily difficulties" emanating from Detring and the Chinese. Although angered at Detring's lack of cooperation, Hoover and de Wouters felt too weak as yet to risk an "open fight." Still, although "not yet the masters," the co-managers felt that they were advancing. At one point they entered the company's office and "nearly by main force" grabbed the company's accounts and correspondence files.[47]

All these forcible seizures may explain the story spread many years later by an anti-Hoover Chinese that Hoover himself on one occasion brandished a revolver and threatened to kill a terrified Chinese employee unless he surrendered certain title deeds. The story seems melodramatic and implausible, and there is in fact no specific evidence to corroborate it.

But Hoover did, by his own account, seize certain deeds "by main force"— deeds to which he believed the new company was entitled. During the turmoil of 1900 Chang Yen-mao had sold some of the company's property at Hong Kong and pocketed the profit himself, even though the property was mortgaged to the company's bondholders. In part to forestall acts like this, Hoover was determined to get hold of the title deeds. On one occasion he went with a former Chinese director to the bank where some documents were deposited. According to Hoover, the Chinese "insisted on taking documents which did not belong to him but belonged to the Company, and I resisted it." He did not say how he resisted, but he did thwart the Chinese.[48]

All this was not business as Hoover had known it in America and Australia. It was a war of attrition.

I I

AFTER Viceroy Li Hung-chang received his 200,000 taels, Detring—according to Hoover and de Wouters—shifted his ground. Now the German and his allies demanded that a China board (not merely the current provisional one) be established in pursuance of the February agreements. Late in April Hoover and de Wouters reached what they described as "a vague and verbal understanding" with Detring about the desired board. In return Detring released to the new company a large amount of cash under his control. It was also agreed that henceforth the company's checks would be co-signed by Detring and either Hoover or de Wouters. The local banks were so notified.[49]

Detring soon discovered that matters went right on as before: the company's checks were signed by Hoover and de Wouters only, and Detring was totally ignored. When Detring asked the local bank manager for an explanation the man repeatedly refused to give one. When Detring confronted de Wouters over his breach of promise, de Wouters (according to Detring)

> declared that he was very sorry that he had done it, and at that time I warned him against the doings of Hoover. I said he is the man who induces you in doing these things and I warn you and you ought to be careful that you do not repeat it again, but they did it all the same.[50]

What Detring apparently did not know was that the new company's directors in Europe had explicitly ordered the banks in Tientsin to make checks subject to the signatures of Hoover and de Wouters, and apparently of Hoover and de Wouters only.[51] Once again the German had been outmaneuvered.

By now Detring's relations with the co-managers had deteriorated badly.[52] Still, on June 4, 1901—after extensive consultations involving Chang Yen-mao—Detring, de Wouters, and two Chinese deputies of Chang signed a set of "Regulations for the Provisional Administration of the Chinese Engineering and Mining Company, Limited."[53] The new rules provided that during "the period of organization" the new company's "affairs" would be "managed in China" by a "China Board" of six members, elected by the shareholders and then appointed by the Director-General of the province. Two directors must be Chinese, two (including the general manager) must be foreigners, and two (a shareholders' representative and the chairman of the board) might be either Chinese or foreign. The chairman would exercise "high supervision over all of the Company's departments and employees." The "Foreign Gen-

eral Manager" would "control all the affairs (great and small)" of the company's "different departments and employees."

Among various other provisions of the document, two stood out. First,
although this China board was to "manage" the company and was to "meet
and deliberate on all important affairs," nevertheless the "final decisions"
were to be made by the chairman and the general manager. If the chairman
(like the general manager) were a foreigner, effective control—despite the
memorandum of February—would lie in foreign hands. Secondly, and more
remarkably still, Chang's authority over the company as Director-General of
the province was explicitly defined as comprising "such official control over
the Company" and "such powers in relation to its working" as the government of Great Britain possessed over mines in England. To be sure, the
mines would remain under Chinese sovereignty, and the new company would
abide by Chinese government regulations. But the company itself would
henceforth be "managed under English law," and English law in 1901 scarcely
countenanced unlimited government control over private business. Whether
he realized it or not, Chang had just agreed to a radical curtailment of his
once plenary powers over the Kaiping mines.[54]

As soon as the new regulations were executed, and in clear violation of the
shareholder election provision, Chang at once appointed two deputies as
Chinese directors and Detring as chairman.[55] Hoover and de Wouters also
joined; the sixth seat on the board was left vacant. [56] In view of the limits
thus placed on his powers (not to mention the potential for foreign domination), why did Chang accede to this document at all?[57] One can only speculate. Perhaps he assumed that since board members were supposed to be
elected by the shareholders, he had nothing to fear. He and his friends—so
he may have reasoned—could always control a majority of the shares. Chang
may also have known by this time that he had been selected to join a Chinese
mission to Germany in July to apologize for the murder of the German Minister to Peking during the Boxer Rebellion.[58] Possibly he wished to have
something definite in writing before he left.

Chevalier de Wouters had a different explanation: to him the new regulations were merely an exercise in saving the face of Chang. In a letter to
the new company's directors in July, the Belgian attributed Chang's and
Detring's protracted balkiness to a "desire to assure themselves of the execution" of Moreing's original promise: that the Chinese "would continue to
have . . . rights" in "the direction of the new Company." De Wouters reported
that Hoover himself had told him about Moreing's promise and about the
Oriental Syndicate's concurrence with it. De Wouters therefore did not try
to "contest" this understanding.[59]

A couple of months later Hoover joined de Wouters in ascribing the new
regulations of June to Chang's desire for camouflage:

> The Chinese face was safe and it was the only thing that Chang really
> wanted. He had understood by this time that he had lost all sort of control

on the Company and accepted the situation, but he was anxious to avoid the resentment of the old shareholders and to prevent them from memorialising against him.

So Hoover and de Wouters informed their superiors.[60]

Whether Chang had any such motive is uncertain. What *is* clear is that the provisional regulations of June 4 were quite unpalatable to the foreigners. Hoover, for instance, later said that he opposed the new regulations outright, "had nothing to do with them," and let others draft the document. In his view these regulations "went too far," even beyond the February memorandum. He strongly urged the European board of directors to reject them out of hand.[61] When the rules were signed on June 4, Hoover's name was not on them—partly, it seems, for reasons of principle, and partly because Detring's antipathy toward Hoover was now so deep that he wished to exclude Hoover from the talks.[62] De Wouters reported that when Chang "did not insist" that Hoover sign, de Wouters felt it expedient to say nothing: "the less signatures there were on such a strange document . . . the better."[63]

De Wouters's name, however, *was* on the document, and in an apologetic letter to the European board of directors in mid-July he endeavored to justify his action. De Wouters told how he "together with Mr. Hoover" had been working to "take over the entire control" of the company and "to set aside as much as possible Chinese intervention." He described the memorandum of February—which mandated a China board and management "on a fair basis of equality"—as "absolutely without value." De Wouters pleaded with his directors to understand the circumstances under which he and his foreign colleagues had been obliged to make concessions to the Chinese, lest they provoke strikes and a "veritable tempest" which "envious groups of Europeans" might exploit. Even if the Chinese members of the new provisional board were improperly appointed, said de Wouters, they could not "injure us." So why not "momentarily leave them to their illusions"? A "little diplomacy" could go far to consolidate European control. As for the June 4 document itself,

> in view of the counterweight of your telegram to the banks making cheques subject to Hoover's signature and mine, it does not bind us to anything. It has, on the contrary, permitted us to constitute a board of directors which has no power and whose decision it will always be possible for us to pass over, but which saves the face of Chang and insures for us the local support indispensable in the Celestial Empire.[64]

So, unlike Hoover, de Wouters the diplomat favored acceptance of the June 4 regulations. It was now up to Emile Francqui to resolve the conflicting advice between his co-managers. The trouble, Francqui told the European directors, was that one (de Wouters) was too accommodating to the Chinese point of view, while the other (Hoover) "thinks only of the interests of the

Europeans and only seeks to give satisfaction" to them. Francqui advised the board to avoid the twin "errors" of flat approval and flat disapproval. Instead, the board should merely "acknowledge receipt of the regulation 'submitted for its approval' " (thereby implying that *it* was the supreme authority), pending a later, definitive settlement.

> In the meantime we will continue to act as we are doing now, i.e., that we will take—without the consent of the Chinese—all the necessary measures to assure the even march of the enterprise, confining ourselves to mentioning to Detring only those things which he may know without its being inconvenient. Finally, it is important that during the stay of Chang Yen Mao in Europe, that the subject of the China Board should be avoided, and that each time that he mentions it the conversation should be changed.[65]

Francqui's hardheaded sentiments, of course, were sharply at variance with the terms of the February memorandum. Whatever Chang and Detring thought they were getting out of the June 4 regulations, the Belgians, at least, had no intention of being constrained by its terms. As Hoover and de Wouters jointly reported in September, these "provisional regulations" signed only by de Wouters had "no value."[66]

I I I

M E A N W H I L E, in the boardrooms in Brussels and London, remarkable transactions were taking place in the spring of 1901. Back in December, C. Algernon Moreing had promised to sell the entire Chinese Engineering and Mining Company to the Oriental Syndicate for flotation purposes—if he could obtain the required revisions in the contract of July 30, 1900.[67] Hoover had henceforth done so, and on May 2, 1901, in a series of deft legal maneuvers, Moreing carried out his bargain.

In the first of three agreements, the Oriental Syndicate contracted to give 50,000 free shares in the new company to Moreing in return for Moreing's signing a second agreement the same day. These 50,000 shares were to go to the persons "through whose agency or intervention" Moreing had succeeded in obtaining the July 30 sale contract.[68] As it turned out, these were the same 50,000 shares promised by Hoover and Moreing in the winter to Detring and Chang Yen-mao.[69]

In the second agreement, Moreing sold (or purported to sell) the July 30 contract itself (and the separate July 25 provincial loan contract) to the Oriental Syndicate. In return, Moreing received 79,500 (or nearly $4/5$) of the Oriental Syndicate's own shares.[70]

The third document of May 2 was between the Oriental Syndicate and the new Chinese Engineering and Mining Company registered more than four months earlier in London. In this document the syndicate took the July 30 agreement just acquired from Moreing and proceeded to sell it to the new company—in return for virtually every one of the new company's 1,000,000 shares.[71] No reference was made to the property transfer that had already occurred in Tientsin in February. Thus the Oriental Syndicate purportedly sold to the new company the very assets that Chang Yen-mao had already transferred to the new company three months before! By this device, the Oriental Syndicate acquired total financial control over the new company. Things had come a long way since Moreing told Detring in November 1900 that the Oriental Syndicate would hold "a good many shares" in the new company.[72]

Legal anomalies aside, the company now proceeded to organize itself in Europe. Back in December, seven Englishmen—in reality, mere clerks and agents of the European financial interests involved—had purchased one share apiece and formally registered the Chinese Engineering and Mining Company, Ltd. under British law. In February these men transferred their shares to seven Belgians who now became the sole stockholders in the company. (The remaining 999,993 shares had not yet been issued.) In May 1901 the seven Belgians, quite in conformity with the company's articles of association, proceeded to select the first directors of the new company. The new directors—none of them elected by the shareholders at large,[73] none of them Chinese—now emerged from behind the scenes and set to work.[74]

In late June and again in mid-July, extraordinary general meetings of the shareholders were held in London—at which, among other things, the articles of association were revised to provide fixed salaries for the directors.[75] No prior notice of these meetings seems to have been sent to China. Indeed, at this point the old Chinese shareholders had not even received their shares in the new company. Nor—even at this point—had a set of the governing articles of association (drawn up more than six months previously) reached China. Detring did not receive a copy until autumn.[76]

All this was distant indeed from Hoover's written assurances to Detring on February 9 that the London board of directors would be elected by all the shareholders and that the "preponderating influence" over its composition would rest with "the Chinese and their friends."[77] (Technically, the first directors *were* elected by all the shareholders—all seven of them.) It was distant also from clause 5 of the February memorandum: that Chinese and foreign shareholders would have "equal votes" at all stockholder meetings. The contrast between Hoover's words and the London board's actions—and the interpretation to be placed on it—were to cause him embarrassment before long.

Far more important than these transactions were the tremendous financial decisions that the European directors now speedily made—again, without any apparent prior consultation with the Chinese. On May 25 the new directors issued 375,000 shares to the old company's shareholders, 50,000 to

Moreing (for passing on to Chang and Detring), and 150,000—evidently in promotional profits—to the Oriental Syndicate. So far, nothing had been done to violate the written and verbal understandings of Hoover and Detring: 375,000 shares to the Chinese shareholders, and 200,000 free shares in profits.

This still, however, left 425,000 shares.[78] The European directors now simply allotted them—for no cash at all—to "the nominees of the Oriental Syndicate."[79] A few weeks later W. F. Turner of the Oriental Syndicate informed a London meeting of the company's stockholders of another fait accompli taken by the directors on June 5:[80]

> . . . the requisite funds have been provided for the discharge of all the liabilities of the old company and for working capital by an issue of half-a-million sterling in 6 per cent debentures. . . . The whole of this debenture has been placed privately, without any cost whatever to the company. . . .[81]

Turner did not disclose that, supposedly to induce the subscription of £500,000 in debentures, the directors had *given* away the company's 425,000 remaining shares (worth over $2,000,000) as bonuses to the debenture holders.[82] How this parting with nearly half its nominal share assets was a case of not incurring "any cost whatever to the company," Turner did not explain.

None of the Chinese shareholders was consulted about this step.[83] Nor, perhaps, need they have been—*if* Hoover and Moreing were correct that the financing had all been left up to Moreing by the agreement of July 1900. Nor, indeed, was the board legally obliged to consult the shareholders beforehand. Under the new company's articles of association the board was explicitly permitted to borrow sums amounting to as much as one-half the issued capital of the company "without the sanction of a General Meeting."[84] And this was precisely what the board had just done.

Moreing and others afterwards stoutly defended this mode of finance. The debenture issue was necessary, they alleged, both to clear off the old company's heavy debts and to raise working capital for an ambitious program of reform and expansion. The company's Chinwangtao loan obligations, for example, were drawing 12% interest. To induce the holders of these bonds to give them up for new debentures bearing only 6% interest, a generous stock bonus was required. According to Edmund Davis (one of the key financiers involved), the old company was staggering under a £250,000 debt.[85]

These arguments had some plausibility. The Kaiping mines were in fact undercapitalized. In view of the company's political and financial handicaps, the obtaining of £500,000 in capital at only 6% interest might almost be considered a triumph, as Moreing's lawyer later insisted. Yet the whole remarkable scheme bristled with peculiarities. Why was it necessary to wipe out the old debt all at once? And why raise all the money by debentures instead of

shares? In the course of eliminating £250,000 in old debt the directors sad-
dled the company with £500,000 in new debt that would not be paid off
completely for fifty years.[86] If the difference of £250,000 were desired for
working capital, why, again, raise it by the costly method of debentures?
Why not simply issue shares directly on the stock market?

The European promoters vigorously asserted that necessity dictated their
decision. According to Moreing, Davis, and (later on) Hoover himself, it was
absolutely impossible to go into the open market at that time. The company
was in desperate straits. In the eyes of British investors, post-Boxer China in
1900–1901 was hardly a mecca for venture capital. Even a debenture issue,
they said, had proved hard to arrange. Hence the generous offer of free
shares—to coax capital from skeptical investors. And far better to pay it back
at six percent instead of twelve.[87]

That the company was *in extremis* during mid- and late 1900 was unques-
tionable. But was its financial state so perilous in mid-1901 when the debenture plan was actually enacted? One person, at least, did not think so at the
time: Herbert Hoover, the company's co-manager in China. Only three weeks
after taking command on March 1, 1901, Hoover reported to Moreing that
the old Kaiping company's shares were selling at "more than par for the new
shares." In fact, Hoover "firmly believe[d]" that 50,000 shares could be sold
on the Tientsin or Shanghai stock markets "at par or higher."[88] On May 23
he cabled Moreing that the old company's shares had actually risen to nearly
triple their face value.[89] All through the spring and summer the shares in
China continued well above par, partly in direct response to reports that the
old company had been converted into a British company.[90] Whatever the
situation in the London and Brussels financial markets, in China the company's prospects seemed excellent.

So excellent, in fact, that on May 19 Hoover informed Moreing that in his
first three months as manager the company had already earned a profit of
200,000 taels (about £30,000) and could expect more as conditions improved.
Hoover therefore emphatically denied the rationale of the European financial
program:

> I wish to express the positive opposition to the issue of debentures more
> than are absolutely necessary to secure the £100,000 working capital and
> to re-finance the Ching Wan Tao loan, for we do not need more money,
> and every debenture issued robs the Oriental Syndicate of part of its pos-
> sible profits.

Hoover knew, then, of the debenture / share bonus plan.[91] He went on:

> Mr. Francqui informs me that it is the intention to issue £500,000 in
> debentures, and I do not see the use of it, it seems to me £300,000 will be
> enough. . . . I am fully convinced that in 18 months we can make the [£1

par value] shares of the [new] mining Company worth £2, and in three years £3, and I strongly oppose parting with any of them even at par.[92]

Hoover's opposition, then, was based, in part, on self-interest. As a large shareholder in the Oriental Syndicate he did not want to dilute his own future profits. The more shares in the new company that the syndicate gave away, the fewer that were left for itself (and thus for him).[93]

It is possible that Hoover's objection to the raising of so much capital was ill-founded. He may not have been fully cognizant of the directors' plans and capital requirements. Perhaps also his projections of the company's profits were too optimistic. The new company's shares, for instance, did not rise even to £2. Hoover afterward stated that he had been "entirely misled" about "the position of the property" at this time and "considerably misled" about the company's future profits by a temporary surge in coal sales.[94] As Moreing later observed, "I am more experienced in these matters than Mr. Hoover."[95]

In any case, Hoover apparently did not communicate his foreknowledge of the debenture plan to any of his Chinese colleagues—at least not to Gustav Detring, who only learned about the plan (he said) during the summer from his son-in-law, von Hanneken, to whom Hoover had already offered some debentures and bonus shares. According to Detring, Hoover and de Wouters were constantly pressing von Hanneken to "work upon" his father-in-law to expedite Detring's transfer of various documents. But, said Detring, he refused to succumb to this indirect pressure. Rather, he desired to surrender the documents "very gradually" and "would not be shoved along."[96] Detring thus created the impression (without quite saying so) that Hoover offered the share bonus and debentures to von Hanneken in order to gain Detring's cooperation.

Hoover's May 19 letter of protest against the debenture plan could not have reached London in time for the debenture decision on June 5. (It took about six weeks for mail to travel from China to England.) From Hoover's cable on May 23, however, Moreing, at least, knew that the shares were booming in China. But Moreing was not yet a member of the new company's board of directors,[97] and it is doubtful that knowledge of Hoover's opposition would have affected the directors' decision. The circumstances strongly suggest that something other than sheer desperation or a total lack of alternatives prompted the debenture / bonus plan. Just who took up the debentures and thus gained the bonus shares? Who were the "nominees of the Oriental Syndicate"?

It turned out that £310,000 in debentures (and a corresponding proportion of free shares) went to Colonel Thys's Compagnie Internationale d'Orient and his allies, and £190,000 to various British interests.[98] Reflecting this Belgian predominance, on May 28, 1901 Albert Thys—already chairman of the board of directors of the Oriental Syndicate—became the chairman of the new Chinese Engineering and Mining Company's board as well. In fact, there was a considerable overlap between syndicate directors and the new company's directors. Thys, Davis, and Turner were members of both boards. The directors of the Oriental Syndicate, the directors of the new company, and the controllers of the debentures were therefore essentially an interlocking group of British and Belgian financiers.[99]

Furthermore, both Moreing and the Compagnie Internationale had been major holders of the Chinwangtao loan bonds of 1899, which were now to be turned in for new debentures—with a bonus, of course—as part of the refinancing plan. Thus in quickly winding up this old debt (which defenders of the flotation insisted it was necessary to do), Thys and his associates gained another opportunity to distribute more free bonus shares among themselves.

The financial arrangement thus described offered three advantages to the promoters. First, by avoiding the issue of any shares on the uncontrolled open market, they made it impossible for the Chinese side (with its 375,000 designated shares) to combine with outsiders to capture control of the company. Secondly, if the company prospered its shares would rise in value and the debenture holders would twice prosper—from debenture interest and share earnings. If it failed, the debenture holders would still be protected, for upon dissolution of the company they, as creditors, would be compensated first, before any ordinary shareholders. Either way, the debenture holders couldn't lose.[100] Finally, the share bonus plan provided a quite legal opportunity for the promoters to apportion large extra profits to themselves. Nothing on paper forbade them. Detring had indeed given them "plenty of room in which to move around."

There was no denying one point, however: whether or not the new company actually needed all the money at once (and some later doubted it),[101] the scheme did succeed. The company did obtain half a million pounds in capital. Of course, the company must eventually repay this money at interest and without further unissued share capital to fall back on.

By June 20, 1901 Hoover had received 7,500 free shares in the new Chinese Engineering and Mining Company.[102] Whether these represented a bonus for subscribing to some debentures is not known. Certainly de Wouters took up some debentures and thus acquired a block of bonus shares.[103] So, too, did Moreing, as compensation for exchanging his personal portion of the 12% Chinwangtao debentures for the new 6% debentures (a loss of interest, he said, that justified his receipt of free shares).[104] Aside from the 20,000 company shares he gained in this way (which he portrayed as a sacrifice), Moreing said he also eventually received another 43,500 as his personal profit.[105] There is some evidence that this may have been an understatement, since in late 1902 the company's share register credited Moreing with 62,500 shares and Mrs. Moreing with another 25,100.[106] It is difficult to penetrate the fog, however, since in the murky world of mining finance as practiced in the Edwardian era it seems to have been common to hold in one's own name shares that actually belonged, by private understanding, to somebody else.[107]

Hoover profited from the transaction in another way: he received more than 7,900 free shares in the Oriental Syndicate, or about 10% of Moreing's original allotment.[108] When in 1902 the syndicate dissolved, Hoover's shares in it were converted to more than 12,200 shares in the Chinese Engineering and Mining Company, with a par value of about $60,000.[109]

I V

BACK in China it was now early summer 1901. Chang Yen-mao was about to depart for Germany, and still Hoover and de Wouters had not completely achieved any of their three primary aims at the Kaiping mines: legitimacy, control of the property, and control of the management.

Although the co-managers professed not to need imperial Chinese sanction for the Kaiping mines deal,[110] they both probably realized that the contrary was the case under Chinese law. According to Chinese law, foreigners had no right to acquire any property in China (outside foreign settlements) without obtaining an explicit edict from the emperor. Furthermore, Chinese law decreed that all mining companies must be at least half-Chinese—a state of affairs that scarcely existed in the new company. And under the imperial mining regulations of 1898, the administrative control of all mines must remain in Chinese hands.[111] Such rules, of course, had been promulgated before the Boxer Rebellion. Now the political circumstances were very different: China was weak, partly occupied by foreign armies. Still, from a Chinese perspective the status of the new company was, to say the least, tenuous—unless the February 1901 transfer could gain imperial approval.

Hoover and de Wouters continued to press Chang to seek such approval— a step, they noticed, that Chang was reluctant to take: it meant "very heavy disbursement" to the outstretched palms of the Chinese court.[112] Finally, on July 11, 1901, Chang submitted his memorial—"conjointly," he asserted, with Viceroy Li Hung-chang. Chang related the desperate circumstances of 1900, how he had "invited" foreign capital into the Kaiping enterprise, and how the old business had now become "a Chinese and foreign cooperative limited liability company." As for the new managerial staff, Chang stated that Chinese and foreigners would have "the same rank and power."[113]

Something was very much amiss. Did Chang really believe that his memorial to the Throne accurately represented the past winter's transaction? Not if Hoover and de Wouters were correct: they claimed that Chang knew he was beaten.[114] Was Chang therefore concealing the full truth from his own government? Or was he still not fully cognizant of what he had done? Some time after receiving his memorial the Chinese government issued a cool and guarded rescript: "This has been noted. The said Minister must bear the whole responsibility. Let him zealously and satisfactorily manage the Company in order to protect the sources of profit."[115]

Before Hoover and de Wouters could relax, however, they must eliminate a potential source of opposition: the holders of the old company's shares in China—all still oblivious of what had been perpetrated in their name. Under the provisional regulations of June 4 Chang Yen-mao had the option of calling a meeting of these shareholders and informing them of the old company's transformation.[116] Chang was willing to hold such a meeting and confident that he could sway most of the shareholders. Hoover and de Wouters, however, objected. They did not feel "strong enough" to risk "public exposure of our deal." Nor did they trust the intentions of Chang Yen-mao. Far better, in their view, simply to arrange for the Chinese shareholders to swap old shares for new.[117]

The two foreign co-managers eventually persuaded Chang to go along, and on June 17 the English-language *North China Daily News* carried an advertisement explaining procedures for the exchange.[118] Suddenly, Chang balked— in Hoover's and de Wouter's view, broke his pledge. When Chang momentarily contemplated issuing a second advertisement countermanding the first and stopping the share exchange, the result, in the co-managers' words, was "rather violent." But as they subsequently reported to their superiors in Europe, "we managed to get the best of him" and induced Chang to place an announcement in the Chinese-language press on July 10.

Once again, ingenuously or disingenuously, Chang failed to disclose the true state of affairs—or at least the state of affairs according to the American and the Belgian. To the Chinese shareholders Chang declared:

> The business and the capital of the [new] company are conjointly controlled while the power is equal. Since the registering of the Company in London we have been accustomed to consult with the shareholders in Europe the desire being that all shall have equal rights and that there shall be no encroachments made one upon another.

Chang therefore requested the old shareholders in China to exchange their shares for provisional scrip in the new British-registered company. At Hoover's and de Wouters's "special request" Chang obligingly inserted a clause saying that all future profits would be "divided according to scrip." In other words, if the old shareholders wanted any more dividends, they could only collect them via the new company.[119]

The strategy worked brilliantly. In six weeks the co-managers acquired virtually all of the old company's shares.[120] Objective number one was attained.

On one matter, however, success proved elusive: Chang left for Europe in mid-July without submitting for imperial consent the £1,000,000 provincial loan agreement of July 25, 1900. Chang was no fool. He took with him his official seals as Director-General of Mines for the province, apparently to prevent the viceroy from using them behind his back. As Alfred White-Cooper suggested to Hoover, Chang evidently intended to insure that he, and no one else, would garner such profits as might be got from the proposed provincial loan.[121]

The rest of the summer was a mopping-up operation. Hoover and de Wouters continued to make progress toward solidifying the new company's legal title to its lands, although they repeatedly discovered that securing the deeds was but a first step in a protracted campaign. At Chinwangtao, for instance, mere possession of the deeds did little to deter the Japanese, Germans, and French, who continued to occupy the area. Time and again Hoover and other company representatives protested the hoisting of flags and other harassing tactics by foreign troops, whose acquisitive designs were all too transparent. With the support of British diplomats, Hoover and his colleagues repeatedly asserted their right of ownership. If the rival nations could be made to recognize this in principle, ultimate victory was assured.[122]

The pair made progress, too, in consolidating the management at the mines. "Hoover and myself are doing what we want, informing the China Board only of those things which it may know without danger and going squarely to the front without it when necessary," de Wouters reported in July.[123] Hoover himself had little patience for the China board although he thought it might under controlled circumstances serve a useful purpose:

> If the Chinese Board can be legally constituted as the registered holders of Chinese shares and be elected by them, and its interference in the administration limited to advices and complaints to London, it would be a valuable body. It is a Daly opera now.[124]

Aided by Chang's lengthy absence (along with that of a Chinese member of the provisional board), Hoover and de Wouters forged ahead. Only Detring and a man named Yen Fuh remained to oppose them on the board, and the latter proved complaisant—"clever enough," the managers said, "to feel from what side the wind was blowing."[125] While Hoover and de Wouters did convene "two or three meetings of the 'China Board,' " they only "brought up the matters regarding which the Chinese could be of any use to us, and satisfied with two or three hours of useless discussion they never concern themselves with the details of the administration."[126]

Although the attainment of legal impregnability, the title deeds, and managerial supremacy were, by their own account, Hoover's and de Wouter's primary objectives during their seven months in China, the period was also marked by constructive technical achievement. Hoover revealed not only his talents as a negotiator and battlefield tactician but also ability approaching brilliance as an administrator and organizer. He was in charge of one of the largest industrial enterprises in China, with a workforce of 9,000 men,[127] few of whom could speak his language, many of whom were hostile, and essentially all of whom were separated from him by enormous cultural barriers. It was a tremendous responsibility for a man who was still in his twenties.

The beneficial results of Hoover's management were soon manifest. During the month of March coal production at Tangshan was only 300 tons a day. By June it had more than tripled, and progress in pumping the water out of flooded shafts augured further leaps in productivity.[128] On June 25, thanks in part to a coal shortage, Hoover reported a first-quarter profit of £41,000 and a quarterly cash balance of £86,000.[129] Although some of Hoover's projections of future profits turned out to be overly optimistic (the coal famine did not persist), the new company was off to an auspicious start.[130] By the end of the summer Hoover considered the company to be well on its way toward producing 2,000,000 tons of coal a year.[131]

Hoover also acted quickly, and as forcefully as he dared, to revamp the management, install an honest accounting system, revive transport, ferret out "squeeze," and abolish featherbedding. By the time he departed from China, he had reduced the staff of 500 Chinese officials by more than 60% and had purged the payroll of the time-keeping department at Tangshan of 600 imaginary employees. Despite protests from certain banks and a strike by some of his workers, he and his associates reformed the mode of payment and currency regulations in such a way that "the Company saved some 20% of its pay-roll in exchange alone." And all the while he lacked a single secretary to prepare his correspondence.[132]

In September 1901 the seven-month provisional administration of Hoover and de Wouters ended. No doubt with some relief, they turned over their managerial duties to a newly arrived company appointee, J. H. Dugan, an American who seems to have acted under the general supervision of Francqui.[133] For Hoover the opportunity to leave China was especially welcome. As early as June 28 he had become involved in negotiations to reorganize Bewick, Moreing and Company in London. Edward Hooper, once his boss in Western Australia, was retiring as a partner.[134] By the time Hoover left China in the autumn, the matter was settled: he would become, at age twenty-seven, one of four partners in the prestigious firm.[135]

Many years later in his *Memoirs* (and, indirectly, elsewhere) Hoover stated that his exit from China was far from amicable. According to Hoover, he resigned following a heated quarrel with Emile Francqui over the February 19 memorandum. Francqui, said Hoover, had proclaimed that the memorandum was not binding and that cooperation with the China board would now "cease." Hoover, on the contrary, considered Francqui's view an "immoral repudiation" of the memorandum and insisted with de Wouters that the memorandum *was* both legally and morally binding.[136]

It is impossible to corroborate these crucial assertions. All the contemporary evidence suggests that Hoover's departure was in fact routine, anticipated, and overdue. Hoover's management was temporary and provisional only, and a new job was awaiting him in London. In 1902 he told one of his successors that he had stayed in China as long as he did "much against my will, constantly imploring" the company to dispatch a coal mining specialist to replace him.[137] In 1905 he told a British court, "During the whole of that time [1901] I did not expect to remain in China more than another month. I was constantly expecting someone to come from Europe to relieve me."[138]

It is certainly possible that Hoover quarreled with Francqui before leaving China. Like Hoover, Francqui was a man of definite opinions and far from submissive temperament. He was also a Belgian imperialist and zealous follower of King Leopold II, who was himself trying to carve a sphere of influence in the crumbling Celestial Empire. As Agent-General for the Compagnie Internationale d'Orient, Francqui vigorously advocated the transfer of the Kaiping mines to total Belgian control.[139]

Francqui's ambition was not his alone. For months the Compagnie Internationale had apparently been pressuring de Wouters to transform the new enterprise into an exclusively Belgian company, only to be told that it was still too dangerous to try. We must be patient, de Wouters said in late March. Neither Chang Yen-mao nor Li Hung-chang loves the British, he reported, and will not oppose such a conversion when order is restored.[140] Now, in mid-summer, Francqui evidently decided to help matters along. He informed King Leopold that he was recruiting Belgian personnel for the mines. On September 20, just before Hoover left China, Francqui placed fourteen Belgian engineers and foremen at the Kaiping collieries. He told Leopold that he planned to have about a hundred Belgians on the scene in a few months.[141]

Hoover may well have resented and resisted Francqui's attempt to aggrandize Belgian influence at the expense of the British. The new company—nominally, at least—was a joint Anglo-Belgian enterprise, and Hoover, as Moreing's man on the spot, was more or less representing British interests. Conceivably, too, Hoover differed with Francqui over the ideal function of the China board. In early August Hoover did feel that such a body could have its place: a subordinate and advisory place. Perhaps Francqui did not care to make even this concession to the memorandum. But there is no evidence that Hoover's dispute with the hard-boiled Francqui, if one occurred, was over the fundamental issue of moral principle described in Hoover's *Memoirs* or that such a dispute precipitated Hoover's exodus from China.[142]

In their final report in September, Hoover and de Wouters summarized the results of their labors:

> As always in China time has proved a most powerful ally. The open resistance of the beginning had given way first to a passive opposition, and then to a complete neutrality. Actually except from the Chinese officials on the mines, there is hardly ever an attempt from the Chinese to creep in the Company's management.

Each of the co-managers' three objectives had been realized. The company's "actual form" was "universally recognized." All but a few of its properties were properly registered. As for the management, this, Hoover and de Wouters stated, was "in foreign hands, the Chinese intervention being confined to a consultative Board, who will very likely prove useful and certainly harmless."[143]

For all his frustrations, Hoover could look back on the past seven months with satisfaction. In considerable measure he could take credit for reconstructing the giant enterprise and laying the foundation for its future prosperity. Hoover also had profited personally from his efforts under almost unbelievable conditions. Aside from the 7,500 free shares in the new company that he received by late June, and the 7,900+ free shares in the Oriental Syndicate that Moreing gave him, Hoover's annual salary as general manager of the Kaiping mines during 1901 seems to have been at least £5,000, or about $25,000.[144] By the time he left in September it had climbed to $33,000.[145] Apparently during 1901 he again assumed his position as Engineer-in-Chief of the Mining Bureau of Chihli and Jehol, although what salary he may have drawn is unknown.[146] Three years later, in a letter to his brother, Hoover indicated that his assets upon leaving China amounted to a quarter of a million dollars.[147]

Hoover probably found it easy to rationalize his conduct toward the Chinese during these eventful months. The Western expertise and procedures he implemented were no doubt superior to Chinese methods. The Kaiping mines as he found them were rife with corruption, and in cleaning up the mess he facilitated future economic progress. Many of the Chinese officials he encountered were indeed "less than idealistic"[148] and addicted to squeeze. Moreover, had it not been for Hoover and the capitalists he represented, the Chinese Engineering and Mining Company might well have succumbed to chaos and the imperialistic appetites of Russia, France, Germany, and Japan. In his own mind, therefore, Hoover had reason to consider himself a benefactor. And if his methods were often rough and devious, and contrary to the spirit of harmonious equality mandated by the February memorandum, well—considering the behavior of Chang and Detring—there was not much spirit to violate.

The brusque and decisive American engineer may, however, have omitted one intangible factor from his calculations: the subtle chemistry of Chinese nationalism and Chinese "face." The reorganized Kaiping mines would now prosper, but to whose benefit and under whose control? Be that as it may, Hoover's sojourn in China had taught him something about the Oriental mind and Oriental attitudes toward the industrial West. Three years earlier Hoover had recommended the importation of Asiatic labor into Australia as a way of cutting costs of mining.[149] After his experience in China Hoover never again advocated the use elsewhere of cheap labor from the Far East.

On September 22, 1901 Hoover, his wife, and sister-in-law sailed from Tientsin for London, via Yokohama and the United States.[150] The Kaiping coal mines, however, were not to be left behind.

10

The Celestial Empire Strikes Back

I

E ARLY in November 1901 Hoover arrived in London to take up his partnership in the firm of Bewick, Moreing and Company, "perhaps the most noted mining syndicate in the world."[1] Less than a month later he joined the board of directors of the new Chinese Engineering and Mining Company. Chevalier de Wouters soon followed. To accommodate them the directors convened a special stockholders meeting which promptly amended the company's articles of association, thereby permitting an increase in the size of the board. At the meeting the British financier W. F. Turner explained that it was "most desirable" for the board to include the two men "who had effected the transfer of the old company to the new one."[2]

Hoover was enthusiastic about the new company's prospects. While passing through San Francisco in October, he told an interviewer that China possessed more coal reserves than any nation on earth. Already, he said, the new Chinese Engineering and Mining Company was preparing to export coke to California at only six dollars a ton. "Cheap labor and cheap back freights" would permit this to be done economically.[3] During his brief stopover in the United States Hoover tentatively arranged for the company to export 300,000 tons of coal annually to the American west coast, once the port of Chinwangtao was equipped to load the coal.[4]

Hoover's optimism also found expression in a professional paper on the Kaiping coal fields and mines that he presented in June 1902 at a meeting of the Institution of Mining and Metallurgy in London. It was a careful survey of the history, geology, mining methods, and immense economic potential of the area, as well as a distillation of his experience as a general manager. The recoverable coal from the field, Hoover estimated, amounted to a staggering 400,000,000 tons. Already the new company was gearing up for an annual production of 2,000,000 tons—nearly triple its output in 1899, the last normal year before the Boxer Rebellion.

Hoover made no effort to conceal the obstacles confronting Western mining men in China—obstacles he had inveighed against for more than two years. Matters like the old Kaiping company's accounting records, which, he noted, were "neither available nor designed to elucidate costs." Or the unpublicized aspects of the "very low" Chinese wage rates—10 to 15¢ a day for coolies, 12 to 20¢ a day for miners, 24 to 36¢ for skilled mechanics:

> Much has been written of the cheap labour of China, but those who have experienced its disadvantages have said but little. The simply appalling and universal dishonesty of the working classes, the racial slowness, and the low average of intelligence, gives them an efficiency far below the workmen of England and America.[5]

Hoover warned against equating the average Chinese worker in China with the Chinese immigrant laborer encountered in America after the Civil War. The latter, he said, was not typical. He was a product of "natural selection," a representative of "the best working class." Moreover, in America he was affected by a new environment—"freed from a maze of custom and superstition" in China and "imbued by the spirit of another country." When one took into account Chinese inability to use machines efficiently, the "increased cost of superintendence," the need for "eternal vigilance against fraud," the "innate lack of administrative ability" of Chinese administrators as well as "their more consummate dishonesty," Hoover found the advantage of cheap labor to be much diminished.

Hoover also took note of other conditions peculiar to mining in the Celestial Empire: pervasive superstition and the use of firecrackers to expel demons, the "mulishness of the native miner in his refusal to accept instruction," the "capacity for thieving," the "phenomenal capacity for bribery and 'squeeze.' "

> The disregard for human life permits cheap mining by economy in timber, and the aggrieved relatives are amply compensated by the regular payment of $30 per man lost. Cases have been proved of suicide for the amount, and other cases where six grief-stricken fathers claimed the reward for the same man.

Years later some of Hoover's enemies seized on this passage as "proof" of Hoover's inhumanity as a mining manager. It was far more likely a simple sociological statement of conditions as he found them, not as he wished them to be.

Despite these handicaps Hoover predicted that within two years the new Chinese Engineering and Mining Company, under superior Western management, would "prove the economic value of the cheapest labour in the world, and will be of no mean interest from an industrial standpoint." His paper was printed and reprinted in England, America, and China.[6]

For the next several years Hoover's principal endeavors as a mining engineer lay elsewhere than in China. But events in the Orient were not to leave him alone. For as 1901 passed into 1902 the dispute over the control of the Kaiping mines, a dispute already festering when Hoover left China, burst into an international controversy that threatened to besmirch his growing reputation.

I I

E v e n before Hoover's departure from China in September 1901, the real locus of power in the Chinese Engineering and Mining Company had become increasingly apparent. In part because certain powerful British financial houses opposed the new venture, and in part because of his desire to involve continental interests in a multinational enterprise, C. Algernon Moreing in late 1900 had been obliged to approach Belgian capitalists for funds.[7] The result, as the distribution of debentures and share bonuses in mid-1901 suggested (62% to the Belgians and their friends, 38% to the British), was that effective control of the new company passed to Brussels and to the interests headed by the chairman of the company's board of directors, the formidable Colonel Albert Thys.

Like the company's Far Eastern representative, Emile Francqui, Thys was a military-officer-turned-financier who had intimately assisted King Leopold in establishing and exploiting his African fiefdom known as the Congo Free State.[8] For a time, as a British Foreign Office memorandum later put it, Thys was the "financial right-hand man" of the Belgian monarch.[9] In 1900, at least partly on Leopold's urging, Thys organized the Compagnie Internationale d'Orient—an enterprise widely (if mistakenly) seen as a tool of Leopold's ambitions for empire.[10] Thys was an exceptionally able and forceful man. One of his Socialist political foes in Belgium later described him in unforgettable, if severely partisan, terms:

> With his Emperor's face, his powerful jaw prematurely toothless, his brick-coloured complexion, his reddish hair, his yellow wild-beast eyes, Albert Thys could at once be seen for what he was: another Cecil Rhodes, a sort of capitalist Pizarro or Cortez, a conquistador whose inflexible will knew no obstacles. . . .[11]

And with something of the self-assurance of conquistadors, the Belgians now proceeded to exercise their will over the Kaiping mines. On June 5, 1901 the board of directors appointed a local board in Brussels.[12] Three months later, the Brussels board was authorized to run the company's affairs in China until the general board's next meeting.[13] Early in July Moreing himself was obliged to make a fight to get the seat he felt he deserved on the board of directors.[14] Although by the beginning of 1902 the board was split, six apiece, between Belgian and non-Belgian directors (including Hoover),[15] the Brussels voice remained dominant.

Supporting the Belgians was their imperial-minded ruler, Leopold II. In August 1901 the monarch told Thys that the Kaiping mines must become a Belgian affair at the opportune time. Early in 1902, acting through de Wouters, Leopold purchased 25,000 shares in the new company in a move to bolster Thys's financial group. During the year, through intermediaries, the king steadily increased his holdings.[16]

The result of this shift in control was soon evident in the field. Although Hoover's successor as general manager in China, J. H. Dugan, was a fellow American, the real authority on the scene (according to Detring) was the company's autocratic "Inspector General," Emile Francqui. Dugan soon found himself unable to be effective.[17] In December 1901 the British ambassador informed the Foreign Office that several British employees had been fired and "a crowd of Belgians" installed instead.[18] During the winter reports circulated in London about a Belgian grab for power at Kaiping. Friction between Belgian and British personnel at the mines was said to be rampant.[19] By early the next summer the foreign staff at Tangshan had divided into two warring factions with the British / American group protesting to London against the arrogance and alleged incompetence of the Belgian engineer-in-chief. The quarrel began to seep into the English-language press in China.[20]

Far worse than the feud gripping the foreigners, from the Chinese point of view, was the Westerners' failure to implement joint management under the China board. According to Detring, when Dugan first showed up, Francqui conveniently took off for Shanghai, leaving Dugan to profess that he had no authority from his principals to carry out either the memorandum of February 1901 or the provisional regulations of June.[21] On September 27, 1901, in fact, five days after Hoover left China, the Brussels board informed his successor that the provisional regulations of June 4 establishing the China board were unacceptable to the company. Many of these regulations, it asserted, were contrary to British law and to the new company's articles. Other provisions were "incompatible" with the "unity . . . of direction" needed by any company. It therefore ordered that the manager's "prerogatives" continue "entire at least as regards the daily acts of his management." It asked Francqui to submit a revised set of rules for the local China board.[22]

A few weeks later, however, the European board resolved to pay Detring, as head of the China board, £250 a month as a salary, evidently pursuant to article 5 of the June 4 regulations that it had just repudiated. Was it hoping thereby to purchase Detring's cooperation? Whatever its motive, this action perplexed Francqui. Should he now accept the China board after all, or should he instead formulate a new set of regulations for it? Pending further instructions, Francqui decided to "maintain the status quo": he would, he said, "give Mr. Detring and his group every satisfaction" (so he said) "without however recognizing" the June 4 agreement and "without compromising in any way the interests of the Company."[23]

All this time Chang Yen-mao was absent from China on his government's mission of apology to Germany. During his visit to Europe Chang met Colonel Thys, who, according to Chang, admitted that Dugan was not satisfactorily managing the company and promised to dispatch an agent to investigate. Thys assured Chang (or so Chang later said) that the "supplementary memorandum" (of February 1901) would indeed be carried out.[24]

Early in 1902 Chang returned to China.[25] At about this time an agent of Thys named Leon Trouet also appeared in Tientsin.[26] According to Chang's later recollection, Trouet admitted that "matters had not been managed 'fairly' " in China and pledged that he would so inform Colonel Thys.[27] After several discussions with Detring, Trouet and the German reached an agreement on how to implement the memorandum of February 1901—above all, its clauses relating to management and to Chang's powers. Trouet and Detring agreed that the June 4 regulations would continue on the books (subject to amendment "by mutual agreement") but would "have no application." Instead, Chang would choose a Chinese director (nominated by Detring and acceptable to the Europeans) who would be permitted to exercise "in practice" powers exceeding the explicit sanction of British law and the company's articles of association. These powers would include "the control and inspection of the administration and the right of intervention over and above the ordinary daily acts of carrying on the business." The Chinese director would be entitled to receive copies of important correspondence coming from Europe and would be kept informed of decisions taken by the European board. He would be aided by a Chinese manager and accountant and would have certain other powers. No more, it seemed, would the Chinese simply be ignored.

The Trouet / Detring understanding contained, however, one crucial proviso:

> It is clearly understood that in order to conform with the provisions of the law and English customs in the matter of limited Companies, all the measures taken by the Chinese Director in accordance with the powers conferred on him as above must be sanctioned by the Board of Directors in order to bind the Company.[28]

Ultimate control, in other words, when all was said and done, would remain in Europe.

Although he later tried to deny it, Detring personally found these terms of settlement acceptable. He promised Trouet to submit them to Chang for approval.[29] Trouet thereupon left China in early February to secure the assent of his superiors.[30] A few weeks later Chang—unaware, or so he later asserted, of Detring's deal with Trouet—wrote to Thys. Recounting his dissatisfaction with the old regime of Hoover and de Wouters, Chang expressed confidence that Trouet on returning would "honestly expose matters" to Thys and that Thys would then "do what is necessary to put the Company on the footing for which the Conventions and Appendices of the Articles of Conversion provide. . . ."[31]

On April 30, 1902 the board of directors in Europe unanimously ratified the Detring / Trouet agreement concerning the China board.[32] From Brussels went out a cable notifying Detring of its decision, applauding his "coming collaboration," and informing him of steps to make him a member of the European board of directors.[33] Detring did not dispute this message. Instead he cabled back his thanks but asked, "What instructions have you given to the general manager?"[34] From Brussels came the reply that the general manager had been commanded to "show all deference" and that a formal document embodying the peace settlement would soon be on its way to China for signature and registration, alongside the original memorandum of February 1901.[35]

A few weeks later Moreing wrote Detring that "at last a thoroughly competent general manager" named T. R. Wynne, a British engineer, was about to sail for China to take over the company's affairs.[36] According to Wynne British interests, not Belgian, were now ascendant in the company.[37] With the Trouet / Detring agreement ratified in Europe, with a British engineer on his way to China (presumably to replace the Belgians), it must have seemed, in British circles at least, that peace was finally at hand.

The vision was illusory. On June 28, Chang Yen-mao—through his local board chairman, Detring—suddenly addressed a sharp letter to the London board. Chang asserted that every provision of the February 1901 memorandum and the June 4 regulations had been "disregarded, if not violated" by the London board and its representatives. He therefore "summoned" the London board to implement these provisions by the end of September. He also requested London to submit to him a full account of its financial dealings since the transfer and a copy of its articles of association, a document "never communicated to me or the China Board."[38]

On July 25 (before Wynne's arrival) Detring sent a blistering letter to the new company's legal advisers in China: the firm of Drummond & White-Cooper in Shanghai (the same White-Cooper who had been involved in the transfer eighteen months before). Detring bluntly asserted that the memorandum of February 1901 had been "studiously ignored" and that the articles of association were "expressly at variance" with its terms. Detring accused the Europeans of a "lack of good faith" and of failing to supply any informa-

tion about the company's financing. He pointed out that at the time of the
debenture issue and share bonus of mid-1901 the Chinese shareholders did
not possess the kind of stock certificate necessary to vote at company meetings and thus influence the company's affairs. It was a case, he said, of being
"deliberately excluded" from such an extraordinary decision. Detring
demanded full particulars about the debenture issue—why, for instance, it
was necessary at all when the company had unissued shares in its treasury,
and shares on the open market were worth double their face value at the
time. Furthermore, how much profit had Hoover and his associates made out
of this flotation? Detring flatly rejected the legal validity of the articles of
association, which contravened the ruling deed of transfer and memorandum
of early 1901. White-Cooper's clients, he charged, had behaved like "men
shunning the light of day." Detring demanded now their full adherence to
the memorandum, particularly its stipulation that "the Property of the Company shall be managed in China." Detring warned that "when the time comes,
the final issue will not be on Legal Formulae in London, but on broad principles of justice in China."[39]

What on earth had happened? Why, in view of the company's acceptance
of the Trouet / Detring agreement, was Chang now demanding that the memorandum and June 4 regulations be instituted by September 30? Was he not
aware of Detring's settlement in February with Trouet? If not, why had
Detring not told him? Detring knew that the European board had approved
his agreement with Trouet in early May, for he himself had acknowledged
the board's cable. Why, then, in July, with a new general manager on the
way, was he complaining anew that the memorandum had not been enforced
and that it ought to be implemented? London had agreed three months before
that it *would* be implemented—along lines that Detring himself had agreed
to. And why protest now (as if it were a revelation) that the memorandum
contradicted the articles of association, when Detring had known about the
articles for almost a year[40] and when the Trouet agreement explicitly
acknowledged the difficulties posed by the articles? Were Detring's words
disingenuous? Had Chang overruled him? Had Chang grown tired of European promises?

And why now the sudden indignation about the debentures? Detring, at
least, had been aware of the debenture issue for an entire year.[41] Chang later
claimed that *he* never knew about the debentures until August 1902, when
Wynne arrived. Yet here was Chang's own adviser raising the roof about the
debentures nearly two weeks before Wynne arrived.

These anomalies compel one to wonder whether this sudden shift was
more than a simple expression of outraged innocence. As of mid-1902 Moreing still had not delivered the 50,000 shares which he, through Hoover, had
promised Detring and Chang a year-and-a-half before. Detring was considerably annoyed.[42] Perhaps more importantly, rumors about the company's
management and financing were now circulating openly in northern China.

Signs of the ferment had surfaced in the English-language Chinese press by early summer. Were Chang and Detring now fearful that as the truth about the company's status became known they would be held to account in China for letting the Kaiping mines slip from their control? Had they decided to launch an assault on the Europeans in an effort to save themselves?

That the controversy was assuming ominous proportions by early summer was evident from a letter Hoover wrote in London on June 27 and published in China in early August. In it he boldly defended the new company's mode of finance. This in itself was a noteworthy change of position; a year before, Hoover as general manager had strongly opposed the contemplated debenture issue. Now, as a director on the London board, he unequivocally asserted that the entire arrangement was both necessary and beneficent.

According to Hoover the "merest tyro" could see that any company "overloaded with liabilities" was worth less than one that was debt-free. The new Chinese Engineering and Mining Company at its inception, he said, was burdened with £400,000 in debts "hanging from its neck." To induce the holders of these bonds to part with their hold over the company, they were not only repaid their actual loans in cash but were given "outside compensation"—namely, free shares in the new company. Hoover emphasized that both diplomatically and financially the old company had been in a precarious state in the summer of 1900. Under these conditions it was impossible to raise the requisite capital in the English money market. To overcome the hesitation of investors about the debenture issue, bonus shares were necessary. To induce the armies of five covetous foreign powers to abandon their occupation of Kaiping properties, the company's promoters arranged for citizens of these countries to take an interest in the company. "Upon this basis," Hoover asserted, the company recovered all its property—"at some cost, of course," namely, more disbursement of free shares.

Hoover pointed out that "immediately after the definite transfer had been completed" (apparently a reference to February 1901), the company's value on the Chinese stock market soared nearly tenfold. The "original organizers" of the new company, he asserted, had profited not at all from the refinancing—a scheme considered "absolutely impossible" at the time. Their profit was "so little as to represent no compensation for the effort and risk involved." As for the company's nationality, Hoover asserted that most of the enterprise's key personnel in China were British and that most of the shares were held by British interests. To be sure, continental European interests were represented on the London board and in the company's administration—as they had a right to be. After all, said Hoover, half the debentures had been subscribed on the continent. Hoover appeared anxious to minimize the extent of Belgian influence in the enterprise—a sore point among Englishmen residing in China.

Finally, Hoover expected the new company shortly to declare a handsome dividend, double what the old company's shareholders had ever gotten. And he disclosed that, in contrast to the old company's geographically limited rights to coal, the new company had obtained "the exclusive right to the Kaiping coal basin"—in one stroke, a quintupling of its already huge reserves. Hoover's message to the Chinese was clear: you have no grounds for complaint.[43]

Hoover's argument contained certain omissions and apparent inaccuracies. If the company no longer had £400,000 in old debt "hanging from its neck," now—because of the massive debentures—it bore an even larger one. His statement that half the debentures had been placed on the continent conflicted with Edmund Davis's report that well over half—in fact, 62%—had gone to the Compagnie Internationale d'Orient and its allies. In addition, Hoover's tally of the old debt did not square with that offered by Davis, who claimed that the old debt amounted to £250,000.[44] Nor did Hoover mention that the paid-off old creditors notably included Moreing and Thys, now serving as directors of the new company.

Hoover was probably right that straight finance in the British markets was impossible in 1900 and early 1901. Probably this explains why the initial £100,000 in working capital in February 1901 came not from London but from the Banque d'Outremer in Belgium, to which Moreing turned. And if the company's debt burden was now greater than ever, the infusion of new capital augured increased productivity and enhanced prosperity. Still, since old Kaiping company shares skyrocketed right after the February transfer (and remained well above par for months), why were debentures necessary at all? Hoover also did not explain how the new company had managed to acquire a monopoly over the whole Kaiping coal basin. How could the old Chinese company cede rights it did not have? Above all, he was silent on the second Chinese grievance—the treatment or mistreatment of the China board.

A few days after Hoover's letter appeared in the English-language northern Chinese press, a pseudonymous correspondent issued a lengthy rejoinder. Reviewing in detail the history of the transfer, the correspondent contended that the London board "systematically" continued to ignore the Chinese side's key demands: a clear accounting of the financing; management by a board of directors elected in China according to the company's "charter" (the transfer agreement and memorandum of 1901); and revision of the articles of association, which allegedly violated this charter and "deliberately excluded" the Chinese from effective participation. The letter writer declared that shareholders in China should organize and, if unsuccessful in getting satisfaction from the London directors, should institute legal proceedings against them. This public letter, which very closely resembled much of Detring's private letter of July 25 to Drummond and White-Cooper, may well have been written by Detring himself.[45]

The fat was in the fire, then, when in early August T. R. Wynne arrived in China to take over the management.[46] According to Chang Yen-mao's later testimony, Wynne's visit was a revelation. It was only now, from Wynne, that Chang learned for the first time about the "selling agreement" of July 30, 1900 and the issue of debentures and share bonuses in 1901. Up to this point, Chang claimed he had never even seen the July 30 provisional contract (even though it was mentioned in the memorandum, which he signed). He was aware only that Detring had drawn up some kind of memorandum of terms in July 1900, a document Chang understood to be merely a confirmation of his original A, B, C instructions. When Wynne informed him otherwise, Chang protested that the British company's actions did not comply with the original deal as he understood it and that the Chinese government would not assent to what had actually transpired.[47]

According to Chang, Wynne also admitted that the London board was "not behaving properly." But, said Wynne, it was too late: the company was now a British firm under British law. The situation was "out of Chang's hands."[48]

For the next few weeks Wynne attempted to negotiate a new settlement with Detring. A newcomer to the controversy, Wynne conceded that the British-based company had not, "so far, carried out the stipulations of Clauses 5, 6, 7, and 9" of the February 1901 memorandum. Nor had the Chinese side transferred all its property to the new company. Both sides had violated their pledges. Moreover, the provisional regulations of June 4, 1901 "were actually never acted on." Wynne, however, strongly defended the legality and propriety of the financial promotion and warned against any lawsuit or agitation to challenge it. A transfer of the company's management to China, he declared, would simply cause the withdrawal of European capital and cooperation. Any attempt by the Chinese side to repudiate the entire deal would destroy the company, provoke a lawsuit, and evoke "a most emphatic protest" by European diplomats in China.

Still, Wynne granted the need for "substantial reforms" to quell "the present deplorable agitation." He therefore proposed the creation of a local board in China that would determine mutually and equally with the London board basic questions of management, finance, and policy. No more capital would be raised without the concurrence of both boards. In effect, Wynne was saying: do not try to undo the past. For the future, let us have equality and cooperation.[49]

Wynne's effort at compromise soon collapsed. While Detring found Wynne's proposals regarding the China board "wise and suitable," he demanded a number of important modifications to insure greater Chinese participation and to protect the Chinese interest. Above all, the China board must be irrevocable. It "must not be at the mercy of London. It must have control and the appointment of the staff in China" except for the general manager, who might be chosen jointly. As for the other great issue (finance) Detring was willing to let the European promoters receive a profit. But "no risk" known to him at present could justify the gigantic profits which the promoters (who were the same as the new directors) had taken—a figure

Detring calculated as £375,000. In Detring's view the London directors seemed "ashamed" to reveal the truth. The London board, moreover, having "elected themselves" without Chinese participation as required by clause 9 of the memorandum, was "invalid."[50]

If Detring's response to Wynne's proposals was stern, it did not match the stiff rebuke that the chairman of the London board, Colonel Thys, administered to Wynne in November. In no uncertain terms Thys informed Wynne that there was no "deadlock" (as Wynne had admitted to Detring) threatening the existence of the company.

> The agreements executed are final and have been approved by the Imperial and Provincial authorities. To attempt to go back on what has been done would be nothing less than an attempt at confiscation of the rights of this Company. . . .

Thys asserted that Viceroy Li Hung-chang's receipt for repayment of the 200,000-tael loan in 1901 proved that Li had confirmed the deed of transfer. (In fact, nothing in the receipt proved that Li knew that any such transfer, at least of the kind construed by the Europeans, had occurred.)[51] Thys further asserted that the emperor's edict attached to Chang's July 1901 memorial ratified the transfer. (But this imperial rescript was based on Chang's report that a "Chinese and foreign cooperative limited liability company" had been set up—an ambiguous phrase which scarcely conveyed what Thys claimed.) The Belgian also contended that the "ruling document" (contrary to Wynne) was not the transfer agreement of February 1901 but the amended July 30, 1900 deed (which said nothing whatever about any China board).

As for the famous memorandum, Thys was breathtakingly blunt:

> The memorandum has vis-à-vis our Company no binding force whatever. In fact:
> 1. Messrs. Hoover and de Wouters who signed it had no power to make such an engagement.
> 2. The Board of Directors had no knowledge of it until several months afterwards and has never since ratified it.

Similarly, the June 4, 1901 regulations, signed only by de Wouters without authorization from Europe, were not binding either. Nor were the Chinese untainted, Thys said. Chang and Detring had been "under formal obligation" to hand over the old company's assets and they had not done so. *They* had violated the agreement. They had no right to accuse London of failing to fulfill nonexistent commitments regarding the China board. The London directors had broken no commitments at all.

Still, Thys and the London board agreed to set up a local Chinese board under clause 6 of the memorandum. But the body they had in mind was far indeed from the coordinate one envisaged by Wynne and Detring. Thys offered only a China board of five members, three of whom would be directly controlled by London. Said Thys, "The Local Board can only derive its powers from the Board of Directors who are solely responsible under English Law." Wynne's proposal, he contended—indeed, anything more than what London now offered—was completely untenable under British law. Probably more to the point, Thys said that Wynne's ideas would "weaken our position vis-à-vis the Chinese."

Thys reminded Wynne of one other fact of life:

One point which must never be lost sight of is that more than one half of the share capital and nearly all the debenture capital is held in Europe. . . . Less then 500,000 shares are actually in the hands of China. . . . It is therefore just and necessary that the preponderant influence belongs to those who have the preponderant interest in the business.

Just how the Europeans had acquired this dominant position Thys did not say.[52]

Thys's letter to Wynne was approved by, and sent on behalf of, the London board of directors. Hoover was present at the board meeting, but the record does not indicate how he voted.[53]

The result of the impasse was almost inevitable. In August and October 1902 public indignation meetings of shareholders in China were held in Tientsin and Shanghai.[54] At the latter gathering, a committee was organized to secure "effective control and management" in the hands of a China board, according to the 1901 memorandum.[55] On November 28 Chang Yen-mao himself convened in Tientsin a large meeting of angry shareholders, including many British and other Europeans living in China.[56]

To the assembled stockholders Chang and Detring explained the company's history, its current "unsatisfactory status," and the details of their burgeoning grievances. His voice shaking with emotion, Detring confessed that his effort to "assure the amalgamation of foreign and Chinese interests" had been up to now "a grand failure." In his own speech, Chang appeared to reject an open repudiation of the entire Kaiping transaction. Instead, he declared that he "adhere[d] unconditionally" to the transfer and memorandum of 1901 and wished only to have them properly carried out. The assembly voted overwhelmingly to establish a committee to manage the property itself and to negotiate with London to enforce a "just observance" of the deed and memorandum. The committee that was selected contained five Chinese and six Europeans.[57]

Two weeks later the protestors' solicitors, a British firm in Shanghai, took an even tougher stance. In a letter to the company's solicitors in London, the Shanghai attorneys demanded that the memorandum be adhered to "in spirit." Furthermore, a China board with control over funds and staff appointments must be established; it, not London, must run the mines in China. The European directors and / or promoters must make restitution of £375,000 in cash or shares in compensation for their financial operations "in gross violation of the spirit and intention" of the July 1900 contract. The Shanghai solicitors then issued an ultimatum: settle now, set up the China board and make pecuniary restitution, or face repudiation and reversion to control by the Chinese government.[58]

At this point (December 1902) C. Algernon Moreing turned up in Tientsin. For more than a year Moreing had been jockeying by mail with Detring over the 50,000 shares that Hoover had promised to Detring in January 1901. Despite Detring's continuing entreaties,[59] Moreing had refused to deliver the prize. The 50,000 shares were contingent, he alleged, on Detring's obtaining Chinese ratification of the *other* agreement of July 1900: the still-pending £1,000,000 provincial loan. As long as this was in abeyance, Moreing—so he told Detring—could not turn over the shares. Detring and Chang were not "entitled" to them.[60]

Nevertheless, in his correspondence with Detring in late 1901 and 1902, Moreing seemed chagrined at the course events had taken.[61] He blamed the mess on Thys and the Belgians, who, he told Detring in mid-June, "have played a very underhand and unlovely role throughout."[62] The Belgians, he said, were trying "to obtain complete and entire control of the Company without any reference to China or London or myself or anyone else."[63] Early in August Moreing again acknowledged the troubles caused by the Belgians at Kaiping. He pledged to assist Detring and Chang in "your endeavours for reform." The Oriental Syndicate, he disclosed, had now been dissolved because "the Belgians could not work with the English."[64]

Moreing's embarrassment was understandable. He, after all, had engineered the great Kaiping conversion, only to be pushed aside (it seems) by operators bigger than he. Now the whole venture was threatening to explode, and he was powerless (or so he later asserted) to block the Belgians.[65]

Moreing's version of the feud may not have been the whole story. To the Belgians, it appears, it was Moreing himself who had harmed the company by failing promptly to turn over the 50,000 shares promised to Chang. Trouet told Detring that Moreing was a "brigand" whom the other directors shunned, even refusing to shake his hand. If the account of various Belgians is correct, it was to get rid of Moreing that Thys and his allies forced the dissolution of the Oriental Syndicate in the summer of 1902.[66] Moreing, however, remained a member of the Chinese Engineering and Mining Company's board.

Just before Christmas 1902, Moreing at last met Detring in Tientsin. The German was in no mood to dicker and demanded the 50,000 shares before he would discuss any business with his visitor. Detring declared that there was no chance now for the provincial loan scheme to gain Chinese approval. It was dead. Faced with this information, Moreing tried first to extract some "compensation" for this "loss" before surrendering the 50,000 shares. How about a railroad concession, he asked, or a concession for the coal-rich Western Hills outside Peking? When Detring flatly refused to address such business issues beforehand, Moreing handed over the shares, and Detring signed a receipt.[67]

Having completed this transaction, each man quickly entered his version of it on the record. Moreing informed the British chargé d'affaires in Peking that the delivery of these shares completed all of Moreing's obligations under the 1900–1901 bargain. The 50,000 shares, he said, were Chang's reward for having agreed to the removal of the trustee clause from the original July 1900 contract. Moreing also asserted that the memorandum of February 1901 was not binding but that the London board had agreed anyway to set up a China board with "somewhat less extended powers" than the memorandum had stipulated. And although half of the London directors were Belgian, Moreing assured the British chargé that the company itself was not really Belgian and that the Belgians now had "practically no voice" in the actual management.[68]

Detring, meanwhile, moved to dispel any suspicion that he had just engaged in an act of bribery or extortion. For not only had Detring taken 50,000 shares in the company after publicly berating its mode of finance; he had also just accepted from Moreing 4,875 *additional* shares in the company, shares supposedly due Detring upon dissolution of the Oriental Syndicate, in which Moreing had reserved for him a small interest. To avoid "misrepresentation" Detring filed a statement of explanation at the British consulate. The German acknowledged that the 50,000 shares were part of the £200,000 in flotation profits that he had agreed to with Hoover in July 1900. These shares, he said, were supposed to have been used to "overcome possible opposition" in China to the "novel" idea of bringing foreign investment into the Kaiping company. (In short—though he did not put it this way—to buy off Chinese officialdom.) Detring asserted that for some time he had resolved not to accept these shares should Moreing come to China and offer them as "bait." Detring feared that they might become an "entanglement."

Yet now he had taken the shares, worth at par about a quarter of a million dollars. Why? He had done so, he declared, with the concurrence of an associate in the Chinese protest movement, only in order to get control of as many shares as he could and to provide financial "sinews of war" for his struggle against the London directors.[69] Detring mentioned the 4,875 extra shares that he had just accepted. He did not record, however, that he had also just taken a check from Moreing for nearly £4,000 in interest on the shares, although he later stated that this amount, too, went into a fund used only "to obtain justice."[70]

If Moreing had any hope that his "golden syrup" (as the British chargé called it)[71] would quell the agitation in China, he was wrong. It was too late. By the winter of 1903 disturbing stories were appearing in the London press.[72] In early February, before Moreing returned to London, a pseudonymous letter writer who claimed "intimate knowledge of the facts relating to the transfer" (but no part in the profits) issued a forceful defense of the new company and its promoters in a London newspaper. According to this source, "the charges of breach of faith made by the ringleaders in this agitation have no foundation whatever." Instead, the writer traced the uproar to three unflattering causes: Chinese officials' resentment at their loss of "squeeze" under the new management; Chinese shareholders' sorrow that such a valuable company was controlled by the "foreigner"; and "the chagrin" of "Shanghai speculators." The writer strongly defended the debenture issue, the amount of promotional profits, and other financial aspects of the transaction. While emphasizing the catastrophic circumstances of mid- and late 1900, he neglected to mention the more promising circumstances of mid-1901, when the debentures were actually created. As for the China board, the writer claimed that every effort to establish such a body had failed because of "the dissensions of the members."

Although positive identification of the author of this letter is impossible, there were very few men in London at the time who possessed the "inside" knowledge revealed here, and some of the details could only have emanated from Hoover. It is therefore quite possible that Hoover himself was the author of this piece.[73] If so, he was once again defending the European side.

When Moreing arrived back in London in late February he, too, publicly defended the company's financing. A straight issue of shares on the open market was "out of the question" in 1900, he asserted. But he, too, said nothing about the more auspicious financial conditions of mid-1901. And like the anonymous letter writer before him, Moreing imputed less than honorable motives to the protesting Chinese. Moreing accused Chang of "wilfully" concealing from his own government and associates the existence of the "unassailable" deed of sale of July 1900. The "agitation" was "bogus," he charged—an outgrowth of pressure on Chang by Chinese officials (large numbers of whom the new management had fired) "who had plundered the [old] company for years." Under the circumstances Chang, said Moreing, did not dare to reveal that he had sold the property. Instead, he was "posing as a badly used person" in order to save his own skin.[74]

It is easy to understand Moreing's (and, in all likelihood, Hoover's) viewpoint in early 1903, given their professed understanding of the original deal of July 1900. Granted a free hand (they insisted) as to finance, they had saved the Kaiping mines from depredation and foreign annexation. Then, against enormous odds, they had introduced foreign capital, modernized the enterprise, and liberated it from graft. Now that the venture was prospering to an unprecedented degree, Chang and Detring—who (they claimed) knew all along what the deal was and who had been very amply provided for—were turning ungratefully on *them*.

And not only the Chinese, or so it may have seemed to Herbert Hoover. When the American engineer's technical paper on the Kaiping mines was reprinted in a Chinese newspaper in November 1902, T. R. Wynne, in a letter to the editor, publicly labeled it an inaccurate "fairy tale" and scoffed at its claim that the mines would soon produce 2,000,000 tons of coal per year. Summoning up his considerable capacity for righteous indignation, Hoover dispatched a stinging private rejoinder to Wynne. Hoover declared himself "utterly astounded" that Wynne had not investigated matters properly before publishing what Hoover held to be erroneous and injurious criticisms. Detailing at length the burdens he had borne as general manager in 1901, Hoover asserted that he had been "made a scapegoat," "slanged by every succeeding Manager, charged with all the errors which had accumulated in the administration for over 20 years, and, above all, am now told that I have mis-stated things which I have never entered upon. . . ." Hoover requested a retraction, which Wynne eventually wrote, more than fifteen months later.[75]

This episode illustrated not only Hoover's marked sensitivity to criticism (which appears to have been justifiably aroused in this case) but also the extraordinary lengths to which he would go throughout his life to rebut alleged misrepresentations. For Hoover did not stop at simply soliciting an apology from Wynne. Instead, he pursued the matter for a year-and-a-half. In May 1904, at Hoover's specific request, the Chinese newspaper in question published Wynne's retraction—eighteen months after Wynne's original letter.[76] By then, no doubt, nearly everyone had long forgotten Wynne's remarks. But not Hoover, who now had the documentary vindication he wanted.

By the spring of 1903 there were signs that friction among the European staff at Kaiping was abating—or so some Europeans wanted to believe. Wynne himself informed a British friend in March that he had finally dislodged his Belgian chief engineer and was now in more effective control.[77] An English-language newspaper in China pleaded to let bygones be bygones, lest the "agitation" enable the Chinese to "get rid of foreign ownership altogether." Belgian representation on the mines was declining, it asserted; the present predominantly British management "should be backed up in every way."[78]

Certainly the company itself was prospering under foreign management. Toward the end of 1902 it declared a 7½% dividend of £75,000, far more than ever before.[79]

Yet all was scarcely serene beneath the surface. Privately Wynne complained that Chinese officials were "impossible . . . to deal with." Nor were the Belgians much better; Wynne viewed them with "profound distrust" and distaste. For all the talk about declining Belgian influence in the company, Wynne still received his letters from Brussels written in French.[80] Meanwhile Chang, as Director-General of Mines in the province, was preventing the new company from exploring the coal region that it claimed, and was refusing to authorize the sinking of any new shafts.[81]

Most worrisome of all, the Chinese government was by now aware, apparently for the first time, that the Chinese Engineering and Mining Company was not a cooperative Anglo-Chinese enterprise in any decisive respect at all.[82] During the winter of 1902–3 Chang came under sharp attack from various Chinese, including the provincial viceroy since late 1901, Yüan Shih-k'ai. Yüan contended that Chang had no authority under Chinese law to sell the property outright to Hoover and Moreing without imperial consent. Chang's memorial of July 1901, he said, did not represent the true state of affairs.[83]

In a memorial to the emperor, Chang denied that he *had* sold the mines. His intent throughout, he said, had only been to change the old Kaiping company "into a Chinese and Foreign Company together," in the hope that European troops would not then seize the mines. The problem, he argued, arose from the Westerners' violations of the February 1901 agreements, which he now hoped, through negotiations, to enforce. Declaring that he had been "cheated by bad people," Chang bitterly accused Hoover of plotting to "swindle" and "swallow up" the Chinese company. Unless the memorandum of February 1901 was now observed, Chang told the emperor, the agreement of that date would be "cancelled at once."[84]

As the weeks passed Chang's hope for victory through negotiations went unfulfilled. While apparently willing to make some compromise concerning a local China board, the European board of directors adamantly refused to surrender ultimate control over the company's capital and expenditures.[85] But now, instead of repudiating the contract, as he and his solicitors in Shanghai had threatened several months before, Chang adopted another strategy. On May 7, 1903 attorneys in London filed a lawsuit in behalf of Chang and the old company. The suit named three defendants: Moreing; Bewick, Moreing and Company (in which Hoover was currently a partner); and the Chinese Engineering and Mining Company, Ltd. The British courts were asked to declare the memorandum of February 19, 1901 "binding on all the defendants" and to order it carried into effect. But if the courts should hold the memorandum not to be binding, the plaintiffs requested other redress. The courts should either declare that the transfer itself of February 1901 had been "obtained by the fraudulent representations and fraud of the defendants or their agents" and should therefore set it aside. Or the courts should hold the defendants "not entitled to retain the benefit" of the transfer unless they henceforth fully carried out the provisions of the memorandum. The plaintiffs also requested unspecified damages, court costs, and other relief.[86]

The issue was joined—in a British court.

I I I

FOR the next year-and-a-half the broadening controversy dragged on amidst a tangled skein of delays, legal maneuvers, further negotiations, and an increasingly hostile political climate in northern China.[87] Time and again

Chang's frustrated solicitors in London—six weeks distant by mail from Tientsin—were unable to procure key documents from their own client and to supply copies of these documents to the increasingly impatient defendants. In March 1904 Moreing's solicitors, citing these failures and delays, filed an affidavit with the court urging that the suit be dismissed for want of prosecution.[88]

It soon became apparent that the fundamental source of the delay was Chang himself. At one point his own agent in London was unable to establish contact with him for several months.[89] Why, as the affair mushroomed into a cause célèbre, had Chang become so elusive, so apparently unwilling to press his claim? Was Moreing right—that Chang, deep down, knew that the transfer was legal? Was he afraid that the truth would come out in court?

Chang's behavior arose from his increasingly untenable political position in China during 1903 and 1904. According to the British ambassador, Sir Ernest Satow, Chang realized that if he left his country for a trial in London his domestic enemies would exploit his absence.[90] Furthermore, according to Satow, Chang's memorial to the Throne of July 1901, and the imperial rescript thereto—which Thys said proved the validity of the transfer—proved no such thing at all. The company's title, if based on these documents, was "a bad one." Chang in 1901 had "effected a transfer," which he had no legal sanction from the Chinese government to do. The rescript had approved a *joint* Anglo-Chinese company (as Chang had described it) with foreign capital added, not a flat-out sale to a foreign-controlled concern. Hence in the ambassador's eyes Chang's predicament arose not because the transfer was legal (as Moreing professed to believe) but precisely because it was illegal. Even if Chang achieved victory in the British courts he would still "find it difficult to justify" to the Chinese government "his action in recognizing" the new company's title earlier. Even if he won, he would lose.[91]

Chang's troubles were more excruciating still. He was now opposed by the implacable Viceroy Yüan Shih-k'ai, and what Yüan demanded diverged dramatically from Chang's objectives. Early in 1903, following a complaint by Yüan, the emperor of China ordered Chang to "recover" the Kaiping mines. Toward the end of December, after another denunciation of Chang by Yüan, the emperor formally stripped Chang of all his titles and commanded him to regain control of the property within a time limit set by Yüan, or face more severe punishment. The viceroy promptly gave Chang two months to recover the mines.[92]

But what did "recovery" mean? All along, Chang's professed goal had been not to overthrow the transfer deal but rather to enforce the memorandum and get financial restitution from London. What Yüan desired, however, was nothing less than total repudiation of the transfer itself and a restoration of the pre-Boxer status quo. To British diplomats in China Yüan disclaimed any intent to seize the property by force. He said he merely wished to "frighten" Chang.[93] Nevertheless, "recovery" to the viceroy meant not joint management as interpreted by Chang but elimination of the foreign presence altogether.[94]

Disgraced, accused of "enriching his own pockets," and facing an even worse fate, the hapless Chang negotiated a six-point "compromise" with the company's new general manager, W. S. Nathan, in early 1904. Among other points, the company's "general administration" would henceforth be "discussed and settled" by Chang and the general manager alone.[95] To the viceroy of Chihli this proposal was totally unacceptable. "Complete restoration" of the company to its original Chinese owners, he declared, meant that the London company's registration must be "cancelled and nullified" and all properties returned to Chinese management and control. Chang, he said, had failed to obey the imperial edict.[96]

When Chang abjectly communicated Yüan's veto to Nathan, the new general manager in turn rejected the viceroy's demands. Nathan told Chang that the dispute over the memorandum would be "readily settled" and expressed willingness to set up a local board. But it was obvious that its powers would be only diplomatic and advisory; London would stay supreme. Nathan denounced any forcible cancellation as "impossible" and illegal; seizure of the property by the Chinese would be "disastrous." And why this talk about "recovery"? Nathan asked. "Now who lost anything that requires to be recovered?"[97]

Beneath Yüan Shih-k'ai's veneer of intransigence was a strong streak of practicality. Late in the summer of 1904 Yüan indirectly offered the London company a deal. The lawsuit would be dropped and Chinese opposition ended if, in return, Yüan was appointed president of the company with a seat on the London board, if Yüan could appoint a Chinese government representative on a China board, and if the company quickly paid 200,000 taels in royalties due the Chinese government! In view of the company's "great danger" from all-out Chinese resistance if this deal were rejected, Nathan recommended that the company's board of directors accept it. And, indeed, the board declared its willingness to do so—if the "constitution and powers" of the local board in China proved satisfactory to the London board. For some reason, though, Yüan's proposal fell through.[98]

Meanwhile the unending crisis was taking its toll on Chang, who, according to Yüan, was afflicted with a mild form of insanity.[99]

Viewing the struggle in China from the vantage point of London, Hoover and Moreing exhibited growing impatience at what they construed as Chang's consciously dilatory tactics. Moreing asserted that Chang had instituted the lawsuit "for ulterior purposes" and was deliberately trying to protract it as long as possible "without bringing it on for trial." Chang was merely trying to "make it appear" to his government that he was endeavoring to regain the property.[100] To Moreing the company's new-found prosperity under European management was the real reason for the Chinese government's order to Chang to recover the mines.[101] Either directly by affidavit or indirectly through their solicitors, Hoover and Moreing chastised the plaintiffs' attorneys for failing to produce key documents expeditiously and resisted the plaintiffs' efforts to take testimony by special arrangement in China.[102]

And when the plaintiffs' solicitors asserted in late 1904 that Alfred White-Cooper and Dr. C. D. Tenney should be called as witnesses, since both had been involved in the climactic negotiations of February 1901, Herbert Hoover strenuously objected. White-Cooper, he asserted, had acted "upon my personal instructions" as Moreing's solicitor; Hoover therefore invoked the claim of lawyer-client privilege. Tenney, who was present toward the end of the "four days' row," Hoover dismissed as an unnecessary witness: he had merely been Hoover's personal interpreter and "took no part in any of the negotiations," which were in fact "definitely concluded" before he arrived.[103] Hoover's rejoinder was evidently successful. When the trial occurred, White-Cooper and Tenney were not called as witnesses.

On October 31, 1904 Chang's agent in London revealed in an affidavit that neither Chang nor Detring had yet left for London. The agent added, however, that the two men had promised to attend a trial if set for December or January.[104] The next day Hoover replied. This case, he said bluntly, "involves the most serious allegations against myself personally." For more than a year, he said, he had been attempting either to have it tried promptly or dismissed for failure to prosecute. Some weeks ago, believing that the case would either be tried or dropped by mid-autumn, he had made arrangements to take a business trip to Australia on December 22. Asserting that it was "absolutely necessary" that he keep this commitment, Hoover charged that Chang and Detring did not genuinely intend to attend the trial, whether set in January or not. Hoover therefore urged that the case be held "at once" (presumably before Chang and Detring could arrive) or be dismissed before he left for Australia.[105] The next day (November 2) Hoover added in a separate affidavit that if Chang and Detring were instructed to leave for London immediately they could arrive in time for a trial in mid-December, before Hoover's planned trip to Australia.[106]

Hoover's attempt to expedite the case or quash it failed. Instead, the lawsuit was set for trial in London in early January 1905.[107] In late November Detring and Chang, the latter with formal imperial approval, sailed at last from China.[108]

But why to London, half a world away from the Kaiping mines? And why, if the viceroy of Chihli really sought repudiation, did he and his government not forthrightly do so themselves? Why pin all the responsibility for "recovery" on Chang Yen-mao? The answers to these questions lie principally in the attitude and policy of the British government, under whose jurisdiction the transfer of 1901 was registered. By 1905 the Kaiping affair had become a serious international controversy between Britain and China. The Foreign Office's extensive files on the case reveal much about the interior workings of what was turning into the gravest crisis of Hoover's business career.

On the one hand, British diplomats and Foreign Office personnel evinced marked distaste for the antagonists and their ethics. Many British officials had long distrusted Chang; the British ambassador, Sir Ernest Satow, considered him "notorious."[109] Nor was Detring much admired; one British embassy secretary in Peking called him "a fearsome scallywag and adventurer, but as sharp as they make them."[110] Another embassy official said of Chang, Detring, and Detring's son-in-law that at least two of them should have been shot in the Boxer Rebellion.[111] "Neither Chang Yen Mow nor Mr. Detring are entirely to be trusted," the British chargé d'affaires in Peking, Walter Townley, told London late in 1902.[112] "What makes such as Detring, von Hanneken and Chang Yen Mow wild is that they thought themselves rather smarter than most people, and yet got themselves fairly had by a Yankee man of straw acting for Moreing."[113]

Moreing and the "Anglo-Belgian gang" (as the chargé put it) were no favorites at the Foreign Office, either. On one occasion Moreing so annoyed Lord Curzon, the under-secretary of state for foreign affairs, during an interview that Curzon evicted him from the room.[114] One Foreign Office official expressed the view that the flotation of the company was "very shady on both sides."[115] F. A. Campbell, head of the China desk, considered the affair "a case of rogues falling out."[116] To the British chargé in Peking there seemed "small doubt that Messrs. Moreing and others have made a pretty pile at the expense of the Chinese."[117] To Satow it appeared that all of the principals were dishonest.[118]

And yet, for all their criticism of the participants in the affair, the British diplomats were loathe to permit the Chinese simply to take back the mines. For one thing, many innocent shareholders would be hurt by such confiscation.[119] For another, if the Chinese got away with repudiation, the whole enterprise might eventually land in the paw of the Russian bear, scarcely a palatable outcome. The presence of Belgians, backed by their increasingly notorious monarch, suggested that Russian and French interests lurked behind—a fact that must be taken into account.[120] For reasons of empire, then, the British were not willing simply to wash their hands of the Kaiping controversy.

And so British policy toward the dispute evolved in a curious fashion which bordered at times on schizophrenia. On the one hand, it followed the decision of the Foreign Secretary, Lord Lansdowne: the affair was "a wasp's nest into which we had better not poke our fingers"; the Foreign Office should "keep our fingers out of this financial pie."[121] On the other hand the British government officially asserted the company to be a legally constituted British firm. It therefore considered the company's dispute with the Chinese to be an internal one, which must be resolved within the framework of British law, by recourse to British courts. Thus on direct Foreign Office instructions British diplomats in China repeatedly admonished the Chinese not to try repudiation or to forcibly seize the mines.[122] In late 1903 and 1904, in fact, Satow (with Foreign Office approval) was even prepared to use British troops to repel any Chinese attempt to nationalize what he insisted to Viceroy Yüan was British property.[123] Yet Satow simultaneously and sincerely encouraged the viceroy to pursue the case vigorously in the British courts.[124] The British government genuinely desired justice for the Chinese—but justice as determined by a British tribunal.

And so in early 1905 the Chinese, whatever their real preference, did just that: they took their case to London. It was a dramatic measure of Chinese weakness after the Boxer Rebellion. Up to now the company in London had remained serenely confident, at least in public. The lawsuit was "merely to enforce the terms" of the memorandum, W. F. Turner assured the company's shareholders late in 1903. The memorandum had "no legal effect whatever." There was "nothing in it," he proclaimed; the board of directors was not bothered a bit.[125]

Sir Ernest Satow was not so sure. Back in 1901 the Western powers had imposed upon China a massive indemnity for the Boxer Rebellion. Now, in late 1904, as Chang finally headed for England, Satow reported that the Chinese Engineering and Mining Company had quietly offered Yüan Shih-k'ai and the Chinese government a loan of almost £1,000,000 to wipe out the arrears of the Boxer indemnity—if, in return, Chang's lawsuit were dropped.[126] For whatever reason, the board of directors' last-minute attempt to buy off Yüan Shih-k'ai did not succeed.

The time for deals, threats, and accusations was past. Nearly two years after filing suit, Chang Yen-mao was to have his day in court.

11

Chang Yen-mao
v. Moreing

I

T H E trial in the Chancery division of the High Court of Justice in London opened on January 17, 1905 before Justice Matthew Ingle Joyce.[1] For Chang Yen-mao the stakes were high, and he was not in a conciliatory mood toward his former employee, Herbert Hoover. Shortly before the trial Chang told his British solicitor that Hoover had exploited the Boxer Rebellion "to carry out his designs" on the Kaiping company. Gustav Detring "knew well . . . that I had absolutely no power to sell it," but he "fell into the trap set by Hoover." And Hoover was "perfectly aware," asserted Chang, "of the contents of my letter of instructions [of mid-1900] to Detring, but as he was so anxious to make a fortune, he cast all this aside, and allied himself with Eames to carry out his schemes." Chang charged that the original July 30, 1900 sale contract was "unauthorized" and that Hoover had "suppressed my letter of instructions" in England in late 1900.[2]

All this, of course, Hoover denied. He insisted that Chang Yen-mao did know beforehand the terms of the original July 30 deed, that Hoover, Eames, and Detring carefully explained its terms to him, and that Chang, in fact, approved the deed in draft form before he left for Shanghai. Hoover also emphatically denied that he ever saw—let alone "suppressed"—Chang's "letter of instructions" (evidently document C of the A, B, C set) before 1901.[3]

For Hoover personally, although not named explicitly as a defendant, the stakes were also high, as he himself remarked in his affidavits of early November 1904. His professional reputation was on the line. The importance of the case to the contesting parties was reflected in the stellar array of legal talent assembled, particularly by the defendants. One of the two chief barristers for Moreing and his firm was the outstanding attorney Rufus Isaacs, later an ambassador to the United States and Lord Chief Justice of England. The principal barrister for the Chinese Engineering and Mining Company was Richard Haldane, a noted lawyer and philosopher who was soon to become a leading Cabinet member in two Liberal governments.[4]

Nor surprisingly, the case attracted considerable attention in London, including the avid interest of King Edward VII.[5] It was not every day that a Chinese mandarin sued for justice in a British court. Indeed, except for Moreing and J. Bromley Eames, the principal witnesses were not even British. They included a Chinese, a German, an American, and two Belgians (de Wouters and Trouet)—a tribute to the remarkably multinational character of the case. The sale of the Kaiping mines in 1901 was the largest transfer of property to foreigners in the history of China.[6] In the Far East and in Europe, diplomats and men of affairs were awaiting the outcome.

Chang Yen-mao's principal professed object in the lawsuit was to obtain a ruling that the memorandum of February 1901 was binding and then to have it enforced. Failing that, he sought to have the entire agreement either annulled as a product of fraud and misrepresentation or continued only if the memorandum were adhered to (whether technically binding or not).

The unprecedented case lasted sixteen days and generated a massive transcript.[7] It raised many perplexing legal issues and evoked displays of legal pyrotechnics as well as artful pleadings over dubious technicalities (to the annoyance of the judge). But as always the central issues were two: the management in China and the company's financial flotation. For several years, both publicly and privately, various company directors, including Moreing, had dismissed Chang's memorandum as not legally binding.[8] But at the trial, to the judge's considerable surprise, the defendants shifted ground. They now solemnly asserted that they had sincerely tried to implement the memorandum all along. A China board had, after all, been established, argued Haldane, and the company had repeatedly endeavored to reach an agreement over the board's precise powers. The question, he now contended, was really this: what was the true *meaning* of the memorandum? How should it be construed?[9] Moreing's attorney, for his part, insisted that Hoover and Moreing had "done their utmost" to carry out the memorandum "loyally."[10]

Consider clause 7 of the memorandum:

His Excellency Chang Yi will be Director General resident in China as before in general charge of affairs, and as such will have powers to appoint a Chinese Director who will have equal powers with foreign Directors in China.

What did this really mean? That Chang was merely to reside in China as before, or that he was to have "general charge of affairs" as before? Did the whole convoluted case turn on the placement of a comma?

And what did "general charge of affairs" mean? With the imperial command to "recover" the mines *in toto* probably weighing on his mind, Chang asserted at the trial that the memorandum clearly meant that he was to retain his pre-1901 authority over the company—an authority that was nearly unconditional:

> [Question] 477 [to Chang]. What were his powers in the Old Company when he was director?
> [Answer] Under the old director [sic] he had absolute authority. . . . he had the power to do everything, the power to employ individuals, the arrangements of the capital . . . everything was in fact under his control.
>
> 478. Had the shareholders of the Old Company no control over him?
> ———If there was anything that the old shareholders objected to they could submit their views in a petition to himself, or if they wished to they could petition the Viceroy of Chihli. . . .
>
> 479. Unless the minister interfered the shareholders had no power to control him?
> ———That is so, that is all they could do, to petition his superior officer.
>
> 480. Now . . . is that the position he seeks to have with the New Company?
> ———It is so according to the agreement [the memorandum].[11]

To the defendants and their lawyers, Chang's interpretation of the memorandum's intent was preposterous. It was ludicrous—and contrary to British law—for a Chinese potentate to exercise such absolute powers over shareholders in a British-registered concern, they argued. No European in his right mind would invest in such a venture. No one had dreamed of such a thing.[12] Hoover testified that he had never agreed with Chang or Detring that the memorandum would be carried out in any such manner. Nor had he urged his fellow directors to implement it in these terms. Hoover said that the memorandum did not mean what Chang now said it meant.[13] Moreing labeled it "absurd" to put a British company in such a position that "all the shareholders could do would be to send a petition to a Chinaman out in China."[14]

The defendants' attorneys accused Chang of attempting to use the memorandum as a pretext to nullify the contract, cancel the new company's registration, and seize control of the enterprise in order to comply with the imperial command to recover the mines. Such a course, they argued, was illegal under British company law and utterly unfair to innocent shareholders who had invested in the company. Chang's true aim was recision of the contract, and recision Haldane fought with every resource at his command. It was "impossible"; the arguments against it were "overwhelming."[15] "We have been in possession of this company for four years, and have spent our money on it and have issued debentures . . . and have incurred liabilities[,] and restitution in a case of this kind is out of the question."[16]

As for the memorandum, Haldane pleaded for the judge to construe it in its "natural meaning," its "natural and reasonable construction": that Chang was simply to become an official in a company incorporated under and subject to British company law—under which Chang could not possibly exercise the sweeping powers he claimed. The company was quite willing to appoint Chang Director-General with this understanding and to appoint a China board "subject to the English shareholders in general meeting assembled." *Then* the memorandum was binding—"if it is to do what we contend it is to do," if, that is, it meant what the defendant company said it meant.[17]

His "only contention," Haldane proclaimed at one point, was that "the general meeting should be absolute over the proceedings of all boards whether they are English or whether they are Chinese."[18] In his defense of the principle of stockholder supremacy, however, Haldane failed to mention how his client's European directors and promoters had acquired a majority of the stock in the first place and hence domination over the general meeting, to the effective exclusion of the Chinese.

As the testimony unfolded, the claims of each major witness were challenged. In defiance of considerable evidence to the contrary, Chang Yen-mao denied that he had ever contemplated the conversion of the old Chinese Engineering and Mining Company into a partly foreign concern.[19] He denied that he had any knowledge before August 1902 of the particulars of the July 30, 1900 deed of sale.[20] Yet the memorandum of February 1901, which Chang signed, expressly referred to this deed of sale. If Chang was not aware of, or did not comprehend, the July deed's terms and import, Herbert Hoover could hardly be blamed for inferring otherwise. Whatever Chang intended (or said he intended), the language of the two indentures was there for all to read.

In his testimony Chang also asserted that clause 7 of the memorandum provided him the same autocratic powers "as before." Yet Chang subsequently approved the June 4, 1901 provisional regulations, which explicitly confined his powers to those that the British government exercised over companies in England. Chang strenuously denied that he ever evinced a desire for personal profits. Yet in February 1901 he held out for several hundred thousand taels (for employees' bonuses and shareholders' dividends, he said).[21] Chang was hardly a novice at business dealings in China. During the Boxer troubles he even sold some of the old Kaiping company's property for his personal gain. Yet at the trial he testified that he never discussed splitting profits with Detring and could not understand what Detring was talking about in mid-1901 when, supposedly for the first time, Detring informed him of the 50,000 free shares expected from Moreing.[22]

It is easy to see why Chang advanced these and other dubious claims.

Accused in China of betraying his trust in order to enrich himself, he knew that further punishment, conceivably execution, awaited him if he failed to recover the mines. He therefore had compelling reason to deny that he had even dreamed of selling the Kaiping mines or that the slightest calculation of self-interest had ever crossed his mind. Chang's real audience at the trial was in China. He must avoid compromising admissions at all costs—including the cost of implausibility.

Gustav Detring's credibility also suffered under scrutiny. On February 1, 1901, for instance, he urged Chang in writing to consummate the transfer in pursuance of the contract signed with Hoover on July 30, 1900. (So Chang had to know at least that this document existed.) Yet at the trial Detring tried to maintain that he had not informed Chang about the exact contents of this deed or about its subsequent crucial alterations. If true, it was a remarkable admission for Chang's own adviser to make. When confronted at the trial with the assertion (staunchly made by Hoover and Eames) that Detring *had* explained the July deed's contents to Chang in July 1900, Detring at first denied it and then, under pressure, said that he couldn't remember.[23]

Similarly, Detring testified that he first learned about the issue of £500,000 in debentures in July of 1901. But Chang testified that *he* did not learn about it until August of 1902. Yet Chang had returned from Germany by the previous February. If each man's recollection was accurate, why did Detring not inform Chang about the debentures sooner? And what about Detring's abortive settlement with Leon Trouet in February 1902 concerning the China board, a settlement that made the Chinese director ultimately subordinate to London? At the trial Detring at first swore that he had not agreed to this arrangement. Then he said that he could not remember. Finally he admitted that he did tell Trouet that he would submit the proposal to Chang "for favourable consideration," not (as he first tried to claim) just for "discussion."[24]

Had Detring from the first been willing to make concessions that he suspected Chang would not like? Had his zeal for foreign protection and capital outrun his judgment? Particularly with respect to profits and the 50,000 shares, Detring emerged as a cagey figure. In early 1901 he requested Hoover to put matters in writing. But when it came to specifying his own stake in the transaction, Detring said now that he had tried to remain uncommitted, saying nothing and keeping his options open. When Moreing's letter of November 9, 1900 reached China (via Hoover)—a letter filled with enticing statements about profits for Detring and Chang—Detring did not respond to it, he now testified, even though he actually "did not agree" with it.[25] When confronted at the trial with Hoover's letter to him of January 24, 1901 summarizing "our conversation" concerning Chang's profits, Detring now claimed to have "no clear recollection" that he in fact requested Hoover to write this letter. He could not even recall whether he "accepted it in particular" after receiving it.[26]

Detring's vulnerability was obvious. By his own admission he had agreed with Hoover in July 1900 that £200,000 in profits and related recompense would be a reasonable profit for the promoters. He also knew from Moreing's November 9 letter that Moreing was planning to give away shares in the new company in order to refinance its debts. Detring knew from this same letter that at least some shares would be offered to "induce the subscription" of £100,000 in working capital. He even knew that after Moreing and his financier-friends had done all this there would be (as Moreing put it) "no great margin," that is, not many leftover unissued shares.

Knowing all this from Moreing (but not, he now said, "agreeing" with it), Detring nevertheless signed the July 30 deed revisions that opened the gates to the flood. (Yet did not—so he claimed—inform Chang.) It is very possible that Detring never expected the Oriental Syndicate to dispense with the shares as it did. Yet he was the one who gave Hoover and Moreing legal carte blanche. If Detring now admitted that he had allowed himself to be enticed by the lure of profits for himself, this might have been a more candid statement, but it would hardly have been an uplifting one. Instead, Detring took the course of portraying himself as the innocent victim of someone else's deception.

Hoover, too, was subjected to the rigors of cross-examination. It was hard for the opposing attorney to believe that during the crucial months of January and February 1901 Hoover had been just an unknowing pawn of shady financiers in London and Brussels. Still, late in the trial the plaintiff's barrister, Levett, was willing to concede that there was a reasonable doubt on this point.

Levett's remarks came about in this way. On the thirteenth day of the trial, after all the witnesses had been called, Levett petitioned the court to amend his statement of claim. Moreing's lawyer objected vehemently; the judge took the application under advisement.[27]

Levett's proposed amendments made more explicit the implicit thrust of Chang's case. They advanced two claims. First, that Gustav Detring was "induced to agree" to revise the original July 30, 1900 deed by the "misrepresentations" of Moreing and Hoover. Second, that Chang was "induced" to execute the February 1901 indenture of transfer by the "misrepresentation" of Moreing and Hoover. The attorney said that he would use the phrase "fraudulent misrepresentation" if necessary.[28]

What was the evidence? Moreing's letter of November 9, 1900 and Hoover's letter of February 9, 1901: both written to Detring, both allegedly untrue, both allegedly quite misleading. In the former, Moreing described the coming flotation and Detring's stake in it, noting that the Oriental Syndicate would hold "a good many shares" in the new company. In fact, the syndicate initially controlled them all and controlled 625,000 of them after giving the rest to the Chinese. To Levett, Moreing knew quite well what was being planned and thus wrote a thoroughly and willfully deceitful letter.[29] Hoover's letter of February 9, among other things, declared that the Chinese would have a "preponderating influence" in the new company (with their "friends") and that the "entire management" would rest in a China board. All this was untrue, Levett contended. The articles of association, for instance, did not provide for such a board at all.

But did Hoover *know* it was untrue *when he wrote it?* If it was misrepresentation, was it fraudulent misrepresentation? Hoover testified that he *did not know* on February 9, 1901 about the mysterious omission of a key point from the articles.[30] Nor, he indicated, had he yet heard about the "financial plan" for the new company.[31] In his summation Levett concluded that Hoover probably did not realize that he was uttering untruths. The lawyer was therefore willing to grant that Hoover had been "kept in ignorance" and had engaged in what Levett later called "innocent misrepresentation."[32] Thus on the first issue—the financing—Chang's own lawyer was willing to absolve Hoover (but not his European principals) of culpability.

Certainly Hoover was not an architect of the company's refinance, although he did personally benefit from it and did afterwards publicly defend it. On the second great issue, however—the management in China—it was more difficult for Hoover to vindicate his conduct. For seven months following the transfer of February 1901, Hoover was joint general manager of the company in China. At the trial Hoover insisted repeatedly that he always considered the memorandum to be binding and that he fully, honorably, and fairly carried it out during those seven months. After that, as a member of the company's board of directors in London he advocated on "innumerable" occasions that the memorandum be carried out.[33]

To maintain this stand Hoover had to contend against some seemingly plain evidence to the contrary. What, the plaintiff's barrister asked, about Chevalier de Wouters's letter of July 14, 1901, in which he told the company's directors that the February memorandum was "absolutely without value"? Hoover testified that this was not his own view.[34] What about de Wouters's statement in the same letter that "step by step . . . we have succeeded in becoming the masters"? Hoover testified that he did not know what de Wouters meant.[35] What about de Wouters's statement, again in this letter, that "Mr. Hoover and myself are doing what we want, informing the China Board only of those things which it may know without danger"? Hoover testified that this was not what they were doing at the time.[36] According to Hoover now, he and de Wouters "were doing everything in consultation with the board [in 1901] as far as I know."[37] Hoover pointed out to the court that he did not write this letter; de Wouters was not speaking for him.[38] Yet in a report that he himself did sign about two months later, he and de Wouters jointly stated that they had only convened the China board two or three times—and then had brought before it only topics about which "the Chinese would be of any use to us."[39]

As for Emile Francqui's letter of July 20, 1901, asserting that he and his associates would "take without the consent of the Chinese all the necessary measures to assure the even march of the enterprise" and would only inform Detring of "those things which he may know without its being inconvenient": Hoover agreed with Chang's counsel that this did not comply with the memorandum. In fact, according to Hoover, Francqui "never did carry out" any of the memorandum. "I do not know what these gentlemen were doing," he protested. Hoover insisted that his views and Francqui's did not coincide. He did not want to be linked with Emile Francqui.[40]

What, then, about T. R. Wynne's statement in 1902 that the company had *never* carried out clauses 5, 6, 7, and 9 of the memorandum? Hoover asserted that this was "not a fact"; Wynne was mistaken. He "arrived on the ground a year after I left," said Hoover, "and during the interregnum, Mr. Francqui had had control, and he repudiated it."[41] Only *after* Hoover left China had the memorandum been ignored. This was his contention. Once again, he pointed his finger at Francqui.

Was it, then, solely a plot by unscrupulous Belgians? At the trial Hoover was also confronted by statements that he himself had written as a general manager in 1901. On February 9, 1901, before the transfer was completed, Hoover wrote to Detring that the China board would have "in itself the entire management" of the company in China. Clause 8 of the memorandum, drawn up about two weeks later, stated, "The management of the property of the company in China will be in the China Board." Yet on March 9, 1901, scarcely two weeks after he signed this document, Hoover told Moreing that the company's head office should be moved from Tientsin to Tangshan in part to protect "the future administration" from "any interference from the 'China Board.' "[42]

At the trial Hoover attempted to reconcile this letter with his professed adherence to the memorandum:

The China Board, like all boards of directors, was presumed to be a legislative body which acted through a general manager of the property, and this manager was to get his authorisation from the board. But on the other hand the Provisional Board insisted on taking on itself administrative as well as legislative functions. The members of the Board insisted on interfering in administration, and to get the thing under proper and adequate control it was necessary that the detailed administration should be separated from the board.

[Question] 2605. What do you mean by complete control?
[Answer] Complete control of the staff which was being interfered with by members of the Provisional Board.

2606. Then you did want to prevent the board from interfering?
———We did want to prevent the board from interfering with the detailed

administration; the board had no right to interfere in the detailed administration.

2607. That is your view?
————That is my view.

2608. That the management of the property is to be in the China Board?
————Yes.

2609. And they shall not interfere at all?
————Only through the manager, who is to have his control subject to the Board.

Who had been interfering with the administration—and how—Hoover did not state. He insisted, though, that he had "had no idea of excluding the board" except from "interfering with detailed administrations."[43] Time and again he claimed that he did not ignore the China board; he had only tried to prevent what he regarded as its illegitimate intrusion.

What, then, about his letter of August 7, 1901, in which he called the China board a "Daly opera" whose "interference in the administration" should be "limited to advices and complaints to London"? Was this an implementation of clause 8?

Yes. That is no attempt to break down Clause 8; but I thought the Board would be improved if it was reduced to those functions, but I did not insist that it should be.

Hoover denied that he, de Wouters, and Francqui had worked in concert to render the China board a Daly opera. The board, he testified, had so "reduced itself . . . by the interference of every single member in the administration." (It is hard to know quite what he meant by this, since the board in August 1901 apparently only included himself, de Wouters, one cooperative Chinese, and Detring. Perhaps Hoover meant to refer to the broader technical staff.)

2657. Has a board, then, nothing more to do than to advise, or than to complain? Is that a board which is to have the management of the property in China?
————Well, I thought it would be better for the property if they were confined to those functions.

2658. Do you think that it was what Chang meant when he signed that?
————No. I only offered this as an opinion, as to what I thought would be better for the Company.[44]

But was his letter of August 7, 1901 merely an expression of personal opinion? A few weeks later Hoover and de Wouters signed a joint report on their seven months together. In it they stated that they *had succeeded* in confining "Chinese intervention" to a "harmless" "Consultative Board" and that they now left the management "in foreign hands."[45] How was *this* compatible with clause 8? Chang's attorney wanted to know.

2664. Will you tell me how the management of the Company could be at the same time in the China Board and in foreign hands?

————Because the foreign manager in China was a member of the board.

2665. Did you mean the London people to think that, or did you mean the London people to think you had ousted the China Board altogether?

————No, I did not. The last thing done was to elect the new manager on to the board before I left China.

2666. Did you mean the words "foreign hands" to include the Chinese directors?

————"The management in foreign hands" refers to the detailed administration of the mines.

2667. Did you mean the words "foreign hands" to include the Chinese directors?

————No.

2668. Was the intervention of the Chinese confined to a consultative board?

————Yes.[46]

So it came to this: Hoover unwaveringly asserted that he had carried out the memorandum in good faith—*as he construed it.* And as he contrued it, the management *was* in the China board because it was in the hands of the foreign manager who was also a member of the China board. It was now up to the judge to determine whether this was a reasonable construction of the memorandum's terms.

From a purely administrative point of view Hoover's position had considerable merit. No enterprise of 9000 workers could truly be managed by a committee. Indeed, Chang's own provisional regulations of June 4, 1901 granted very extensive powers to the general manager of the mines. Said Hoover at the trial, ". . . the administration of any concern successfully must be done by one head."[47]

Still, Hoover's management of the mines in 1901, and his rationale for it at the trial, did not comport easily with the words of the memorandum. By his own account Hoover had worked as co-manager to turn the China board into a merely "consultative" (not even "legislative") body—one that had no right, in his opinion, to "interfere" in "detailed administration." The memorandum, however, did not provide for a "consultative" or "legislative" China board. It stipulated that the *management* of the property in China would lie with the China board. And with the *board*, it said, not the general manager. Whether Hoover explained his distinctive interpretation of these terms to Chang Yen-mao ahead of time is doubtful. As Hoover admitted at the trial, a merely advisory board was not what Chang had in mind when he signed the memorandum.

Hoover's partner Moreing was also drawn into what—to the opposing attorney—was implausible testimony. On November 9, 1900 Moreing wrote Detring a letter giving a broad if imprecise outline (deceitfully imprecise, said attorney Levett) of the financial scheme for the new company. Detring should have known from this letter that some shares, perhaps a lot of them, were to be given away to "induce" the raising of capital and refinancing of debts. And if Detring should have known, then Moreing, who wrote the letter, surely knew at least something about the flotation scheme to come. Yet at the trial Moreing insisted that he "had nothing to do" with the Oriental Syndicate's "financial arrangements" after he "turned over the whole of my position" to it in late 1900. The flotation was "entirely managed then" by the syndicate; Moreing said he "trusted them entirely and left it all to them."[48] Even though the idea of offering share bonuses was broached in his letter of November, Moreing claimed that he did not know about the debenture plan in January 1901, two months later. And he claimed not to know until he became a director of the company in July that the article about a China board, which Hoover had insisted be included in the articles of association, was not in fact printed in the articles when registered.[49] For a man whose financial stake in the deal was substantial, for a man of business with worldwide enterprises, Moreing seemed oddly uninterested in the details and progress of the flotation. The men who undoubtedly did know its "whole inner working" (as Chang's attorney put it)—Edmund Davis, W. F. Turner, and Albert Thys— were not called as witnesses. Deliberately not called, the attorney charged.[50]

Like Hoover, Moreing argued that he sought to implement the memorandum from the start. He insisted that he always "dissociated" himself from the board of directors' view that the memorandum had "no legal effect whatever" since the board had neither signed it nor known of it until much later.[51] Well, the opposing attorney asked, did he object at the board meeting of October 28, 1902 to Colonel Thys's letter to Wynne (approved by the board) stating in behalf of the board that the memorandum had "no binding force whatever"? "It was no use my protesting," Moreing replied. "I had no formal approval of it, and it was very little use objecting."[52] He was outnumbered.

Why, then, didn't he resign? Moreing said he thought it "very much better for me to remain on the board and try and do what I could." Did he have any written evidence to corroborate his testimony on this point? "I do not believe it was ever put in writing, I cannot recall that it was ever put in writing, I attended board meeting after board meeting and did my best to carry it out and so did Mr. Hoover."[53]

Chang's attorney did not know that, contrary to his present testimony,

Moreing himself in December 1902 told the British chargé in Peking that the memorandum was *not* binding and could not be held to be binding.[54] Conceivably Moreing felt morally (though not legally) obliged to carry it out anyway, although he had nothing to substantiate such a claim.

And so Justice Joyce confronted essentially three competing theories of the whole turgid affair. On the one hand, he had to weigh the possibility that Chang Yen-mao and Detring, both sophisticated men of business, knew perfectly well the essence of the original deal: that the Europeans would have "absolute discretion"[55] in raising the capital and reorganizing the mines. In return, Chang and Detring would be remembered; they would receive a very tidy share of the profits. And they neither sought nor expected undiluted control over the mines, as the June 4, 1901 regulations and the Detring / Trouet agreement proved. But when the Chinese government finally caught on to what had happened, and Chang found himself under dangerous political pressure, he and Detring were obliged to institute a lawsuit posing, against the evidence, as the deceived, innocent victims of a European plot.

On the other hand, the judge must ponder whether a shrewd cabal of Western capitalists, with Hoover and de Wouters as their instruments, had not perverted Chang's intentions in a well-planned campaign to wrest the mines from his hands. The friction over management, after all, began long before Chinese political agitation burst into the open, long before Chang was forced by domestic enemies to justify his deeds. The mysterious handling of the articles of association (and failure promptly to send them to China) occurred well before there was trouble in Tientsin. Exploiting their legal discretion in ways that Chang and Detring probably never anticipated, the European promoters capitalized on Chang's and Detring's anxieties, credulity, negligence, and venality to take over the mines and make a killing. Like the famous Tammany Hall boss, George Washington Plunkitt, the promoters had "seen their opportunities and they took 'em."

A third possibility was that the parties were victims of linguistic and cultural differences, fatefully compounded by the failure to write all their understandings down. Just what, after all, *had* been agreed to in July 1900 and February 1901? Did Chang and Detring have the same understanding of the terms of the deal as did Hoover, de Wouters, and White-Cooper? Just what did words like "management" mean? One man's "general supervision" was another man's "interference." From ambiguity emerged misunderstanding, and from misunderstanding arose the possibly sincere mutual sense of betrayal.

From an early point in the trial Justice Joyce evinced a noticeable lack of sympathy toward many arguments advanced by the defendants.[56] On March 1, 1905 he rendered his verdict. First, Joyce found as a fact that the terms of the February 1901 memorandum "formed the basis and foundation of the whole arrangement, and were well understood by all parties to be an essential condition" of the transfer. Assurances had been given to Chang that the memorandum would be the "ruling document," that it would be binding and would be carried out. And "upon the faith of and in reliance on these assurances" Chang had been "induced to affix his seal" to the fateful documents. Joyce further found as a fact that the memorandum's terms had not been performed. Indeed, said the judge, right up to the trial the defendant company had "declined to recognize" that the memorandum had "any force or effect" at all and had "declined . . . to abide" by its terms. Noting that Hoover had taken some of the old company's title deeds "by main force" shortly after the transfer, Joyce declared bluntly that it would be "contrary to one of the plainest principles of equity" to allow the defendant company to hold on to the property yet disregard the memorandum on the "pretext" that Hoover and de Wouters were unauthorized to agree to it or that the company could not abide by it without amending its articles of association. If he allowed that, the judge said, he would be sanctioning "such a flagrant breach of faith as in my opinion could not be tolerated by the law of any country."

Joyce therefore ruled that the memorandum of February 1901 was binding against the defendants and that the Chinese Engineering and Mining Company, Ltd. was "not entitled to take or retain possession or control of the property" unless it carried out the memorandum. That is, unless the memorandum was now complied with in a reasonable time, Joyce held that "this Court ought to do what it can to restore to the Plaintiffs the mines and property, . . . and probably by injunction if necessary, to prevent the Defendant Company, its agents and servants from retaining possession." In short, the defendants must implement the memorandum or lose the property.

If Justice Joyce was angered by the defendants' attitude toward the memorandum, he was scarcely less disturbed by the financial flotation of 1901. Indeed, he found "at least plausible grounds for contending" that the defendant company had been "defrauded" by its promoters of nearly 425,000 shares, "to the injury and loss of the Chinese shareholders." Joyce noted that £500,000 in debentures had been issued without the knowledge or consent of the Chinese shareholders. He noted, too, that nearly one-half of this debenture money (£200,000)—supposedly so necessary to raise in 1901—had not yet been expended four years later. All the debentures and bonus shares had gone to the promoters and their friends.

But Joyce held that he could not judge the flotation question within the framework of the current lawsuit. In addition, he did not believe that Moreing and his firm could be held responsible to the Chinese, on the basis of the memorandum, for any losses caused by misfeasance in the flotation by the Oriental Syndicate or the new company's directors. Nevertheless, the judge said that his decision was without prejudice to future litigation that might be brought by the defendant company or against any of the defendants on the issue of the financial promotion. This matter, if fought, would have to be fought elsewhere on another day.

As for the plantiff's lawyer's proposed amendments regarding "fraudulent misrepresentations" allegedly contained in the Moreing and Hoover letters of November 9, 1900 and February 9, 1901, Joyce decided that he "ought not to allow" these amendments. His grounds were essentially technical: for various reasons Joyce considered the amendments irrelevant to the verdict he was rendering now. But Joyce added that his ruling on this point also was without prejudice to future litigation. If the plaintiffs wanted to start another suit on the issue of misrepresentations, they were free to go ahead.

In a further rebuke to the defendants, Joyce ordered the Chinese Engineering and Mining Company, Ltd. to pay the plaintiffs' costs in the lawsuit.

At several points in his judgment Joyce seemed unfriendly to Hoover and Moreing. He observed that Hoover admitted to uttering "threats" against Chang during the "four days' row." He noted, without explaining the context, that Hoover had forcibly seized certain title deeds soon after signing the 1901 transfer agreements. Joyce's finding that the memorandum had not been followed was directed toward the defendant company and its directors. He did not comment explicitly on Hoover's contention that he, at least, had faithfully implemented the memorandum during his seven months as co-manager in 1901. In the context of the judgment, however, it seems doubtful that Joyce agreed. As for Moreing and his firm, Joyce asserted that "their conduct in these proceedings and otherwise" had "seriously increased" the costs of the lawsuit. So, said Joyce in evident annoyance, they could pay their own court costs.

Joyce believed that his judgment would result in complete compliance with the memorandum. If not, he said pointedly, the new Chinese Engineering and Mining Company "will not be allowed to retain the property." But what (as Haldane had kept asking) did the memorandum actually *mean*? Justice Joyce's decision said nothing on this point.

Joyce closed with a sharp, if one-sided, observation:

> . . . it has not been shewn to me that His Excellency Chang has been guilty of any breach of faith or impropriety at all, which is more than I can say for some of the other parties concerned.

It was, perhaps, only in keeping with the turbid character of the controversy that Joyce never specified who these "other parties" were.[57]

I I

So Chang had won. But what had he won? "All important points," said *The Times* of London.[58] But were they the points important to Yüan Shih-k'ai?

Chang tried immediately to create that impression. He telegraphed the viceroy from London that since the memorandum had been upheld, the

Chinese "Director-General" would now have "complete power in the management of the Company's affairs," the same administrative control "as before." The mines were therefore still in Chinese possession. Chinese power was restored to pre-Boxer levels. The Chinese government could now expel the British employees. Thanks to the British court's verdict the British government would "surely" not resist.[59]

Chang's tendentious cable (which contained many inaccuracies) did not please or fool the viceroy. As the situation became clarified, the imperial government of China again commanded Chang to regain the mines.[60] As one prominent British observer in China remarked: "Yüan does not care a fig for the London decision: it is nothing to him whether there is or is not a Board in China." Yüan wanted the mines restored to Chinese control, "and how is Chang to give him that?"[61]

Meanwhile, in London and elsewhere, several newspapers acclaimed Joyce's decision as a vindication of British justice and a politically useful demonstration of British fair play toward the Chinese.[62] Moreing and his co-defendants did not escape criticism. One journal noted the "grasping nature" of the flotation and declared that the defendants had impaired confidence in the enterprise.[63] In some mining quarters it was assumed that the Chinese really would regain control (to the detriment of foreign shareholders and good management).[64] At the British Foreign Office an official reported that the Chinese Engineering and Mining Company was "in very bad odour."[65]

The defendant company, Moreing, and Moreing's firm quickly appealed the verdict.[66] And on March 8, 1905, only one week after Justice Joyce's decision, Chang Yen-mao initiated a second lawsuit in the British courts. This time he explicitly named Hoover as a defendant, along with Moreing, his firm, Davis, Turner, and Thys.[67]

Taking aim at the Chinese Engineering and Mining Company's flotation in 1900–1901, Chang asked the courts to declare Hoover, Moreing, and Moreing's firm guilty of "a breach of trust" for not conveying the property in China to the new British-registered company in accordance with the original, *unamended* deed of July 30, 1900—the version in which Hoover was named a trustee for the property. Chang asked that the three be held "jointly and severally liable to account" to the new company for all sums paid for the Chinese property in excess of £375,000 (the amount in shares allotted to the Chinese shareholders). Chang further asked the courts to declare the revisions and re-execution of the July 30 deed in January 1901 "a breach of trust" by the same three defendants, and to hold these acts void.

Chang's suit then turned to the financing. He asked that all the defendants except Hoover (whose name was omitted) be found guilty of fraudulently inducing the Chinese Engineering and Mining Company to sign the May 2, 1901 agreement with the Oriental Syndicate whereby the company issued to the syndicate and its nominees 624,993 free shares (that is, all but the seven original registration shares and the 375,000 issued to the Chinese side). Chang was asserting, in other words, that the arrangement by which the new company "bought" its property in China from the Oriental Syndicate—instead of receiving it directly from trustee Hoover—was a fraud. The plaintiff demanded £624,993 in damages for these "breaches of trust and fraud" as well as court costs and unspecified "damages for misfeasance" relating to the issue of the free shares.

In short, Hoover was charged with breach of trust for failing to carry out the July 30, 1900 contract as originally written. The other defendants were accused of fraud in the subsequent flotation.[68]

The unresolved legal tangle headed for resolution before the Court of Appeal in London. Early in the fall of 1905 Chang's British solicitor candidly advised Chang that if he won on appeal and if the company did not then instate him with the powers intended by the memorandum, Chang should ask the Chinese government to put him back in charge and to support him with force if necessary. The solicitor, B. F. Hawksley, argued that Chang should do so "on the ground that although the London Company is subject to the English laws those laws cannot be enforced in China by the English Courts."[69]

When Hawksley's frank advice reached the attention of the British ambassador, Satow, it speedily evoked the other side of the British government's policy position and the other side of Satow. The ambassador bluntly told the Foreign Office that Hawksley apparently was ignorant of the treaty law between Britain and China. Under it, if a Chinese had a grievance against a British subject (in this case, the new company), he could only "enforce his rights" against this subject "in the British Court according to British law." Satow was willing to enforce the Appeal judgment if it favored Chang. Indeed, if it then came to a crunch between the company and the Chinese, he suspected that the British company would simply yield if it knew it lacked Foreign Office support. Satow repeated his opinion that Chang's property transfer of 1901 was unauthorized by his government and therefore illegal under Chinese law. Satow therefore believed the company "are in possession of what is not their property." But—and here came the incredible paradox—if the Chinese "desire to recover possession" of their lost property they must take their case to a *British* court, such as the British Consular Court in Tientsin. If the Chinese instead tried to seize the disputed property outright by force, Satow declared that it would be a *casus belli* between Great Britain and China. He was quite prepared to use British military units at his disposal to stop the Chinese from any such act of force.[70]

In the end Sir Ernest Satow did not have to risk a war with China. In January 1906, for six days, the Court of Appeal in London heard exhaustive arguments about the convoluted case in all its arcane legal ramifications. During the hearing the judges indicated that their sympathies lay with Chang, an intimation that evoked a spirited rejoinder from Moreing's chief lawyer, T. R. Hughes. Hughes closed with a paean to Hoover and Moreing, who—

"entirely owing to their courage"—saved the great Kaiping enterprise from "shipwreck" and "enormously increased" its value. Thanks to their exemplary courage, Chang and his fellow shareholders had benefited immensely. Thanks to Hoover and Moreing they had been "extremely fortunate."[71]

On January 24, 1906 the tribunal announced its verdict. Whatever the three judges' sympathies, the legal outcome was not favorable to Chang. The complicated technical issues, involving such questions as the proper legal remedies and the competence of the courts to invoke them, need not detain us here. In short, the Court of Appeal held, as did Justice Joyce, that the 1901 memorandum was binding against all the defendants and had been broken by the defendant company. It therefore ordered an inquiry to determine what damages, if any, had arisen from this breach.

But unlike Joyce, the appeal tribunal now defined what the memorandum meant, and its interpretation could not please Chang Yen-mao. The court declared that the only powers the memorandum conferred, meant to confer, or could validly confer on Chang were simply the powers of a managing director of the company as defined in the company's own articles and memorandum of association. Chang's bid to make himself Director-General "as before" was lost. Chang may have thought that his memorandum was to be the "ruling document" in the 1901 transaction. But the British court held that the memorandum must be construed according to the company's own rules and regulations—which Chang had never seen when he signed the transfer agreements in February 1901.

The Court of Appeal also dismissed Chang's claim for damages against Moreing and his firm for breach of a certain clause of the memorandum. And it stayed any further proceedings "in this action" against Moreing and his firm, who, in other words, were not to be parties to the inquiry over damages for breach of the memorandum. However, the court left open the way for other litigation over the financial promotion of 1901 and the alleged misrepresentations by Hoover and Moreing in their letters of 1900–1901.[72]

For Herbert Hoover the immediate crisis was over. There is no evidence that Chang's second lawsuit (over the deed revisions and the financial promotion) was ever pursued or brought to trial.[73] The Chinese, in any case, were little interested in inquiries and suits about damages.[74] Frustrated in their attempt to recover the mines in the British courts, the Chinese now resorted to a new and more effective tactic. Late in 1906 Yüan Shih-k'ai organized a rival coal company, the Lanchow (or Lan-chou), with the explicit aim of subverting and eventually driving the British company out of existence. Within short order the Chinese company, vigorously backed by its government, became an effective economic competitor. Furthermore, it succeeded in confining the British firm's operations to the areas already under its control before 1901—not to the vast Kaiping coal field it had tried, via the 1901 transfer terms, to claim. In mid-1907 Viceroy Yüan officially granted the Lanchow company rights to mine the entire Kaiping coal field except for the British-based company's narrow sphere of operation around Tangshan and Linsi.[75]

The Chinese Engineering and Mining Company was outraged at these developments and particularly at the Chinese government's infringement on its territorial "rights." Yüan's granting of the sweeping concession to Lanchow, said the London board's spokesman, was "a wanton act of aggression" against the British company.[76] The British Foreign Office was also upset and determined to resist the viceroy's campaign to "dispossess" the company.

The British government's hard-line attitude was tempered, however, by its awareness of China's grievances and its desire to effect a rapprochement. Privately, in fact, various Foreign Office personnel conceded the powerful nature of China's legal claims.[77] The British-based company, for instance, adamantly contended that the property transfer of 1901 was valid because the emperor of China approved Chang's memorial on the subject in July of that year. The British ambassador after 1906, Sir John Jordan, denied this claim. He pointed out that Chang's memorial did not reveal that a British company "independent of Chinese control" had been formed. The imperial rescript of 1901 could not be construed as sanctioning an out-and-out sale.[78] In 1908 the Foreign Office's legal adviser, in a memorandum on the case, remarked that the 1901 transfer was "not altogether free from sharp practice on the British side," since the Chinese thought they had retained "joint control" when "really the entire control had been transferred to London."[79]

As for the new company's finance, Jordan acknowledged in 1909 that this was "the weak part of their case." There was "no concealing the fact," he declared, that 625,000 of the company's 1,000,000 shares had been issued "for a consideration other than cash, and it requires no special knowledge of the financing of industrial Companies to recognize that a transaction of that nature is difficult to explain satisfactorily."[80]

For several more years the bitter controversy festered, culminating in a rate war between the two companies in 1910 and 1911. Negotiations at compromise continued spasmodically; at one point the Chinese nearly arrived at a settlement by which they would buy out the British company and thus at last recover the Kaiping mines.[81] All during this period Hoover remained a director of the London-based company. (In fact, the board of directors remained almost unchanged; Moreing left in 1907).[82] But there is no indication that Hoover played any distinctive role in the later stages of the conflict.

In 1911 the Chinese Revolution overthrew the Manchu empire. Shortly thereafter, the decade-long struggle for Kaiping was resolved. In 1912 the two rival companies agreed to merge their operations (yet remain separate business entities) under a new structure known as the Kailan Mining Administration. By this device the cutthroat competition, political instability, and era of bad feeling drew to a close. The terms of their agreement, although beneficial to both sides, were on balance favorable to the Europeans. Sixty percent of the first £300,000 in profits would go to Chinese Engineering and

Mining Company stockholders, forty percent to the Lanchow Company's stockholders. The Chief Manager of the Kailan Mining Administration's general office would be chosen by the British company for the first ten years. Although a Deliberating Board of three members from each side would be set up, in case of a tie the decisive vote would be cast by the company with the greater number of debentures: in practice, the British-registered enterprise. In 1922 Lanchow would have the right to purchase the property of the British company but only on mutually satisfactory terms.[83]

At the time of this settlement none other than Yüan Shik-k'ai was president of the new Chinese republic. Yüan appointed his son Director-General of Mines, a position of limited powers with a salary paid by the new Kailan Mining Administration.[84] Revolution or no, the ways of the past died hard.

In the summer of 1912 the London-based Chinese Engineering and Mining Company was dissolved and reconstructed as a new company of the same name. At this point, after more than ten years as a director, Herbert Hoover left the company he was so instrumental in creating, never again to take part in its affairs.[85] For nearly thirty more years, until World War II, the Kailan Mining Administration developed and prospered as one of the greatest industrial enterprises in China.[86]

And what of Chang Yen-mao, Hoover's employer-turned-antagonist? Under the terms of the Kailan agreement the British company agreed to pay him the sum of 1,000,000 taels (about $750,000) in satisfaction of all his claims against it.[87] By this time Chang, who had managed to survive all the political wars against him, was an old man. In less than a year he was dead.[88]

12

A Partner in
Bewick, Moreing

I

LET us return to the autumn of 1901. On October 23 Herbert and Lou
Henry Hoover arrived from China, by way of Vancouver, at San Francisco.[1]
San Francisco! City of the Golden Gate. How appealing it must have appeared
after two trying years in China. Upon arrival Hoover gave an interview to a
local newspaper, the *Chronicle*, which disclosed the next day that the twenty-
seven-year-old engineer was "reputed to be the highest salaried man of his
years in the world."[2]

If San Francisco for Hoover was the hub of civilization, still, it was not
quite home. That was thirty miles down the peninsula: Stanford University,
"the best place in the world." Here Bert and Lou spent a cheerful day with
friends on October 25.[3] And then, on to Monterey to see Lou's parents,
Charles and Florence Henry. During this visit (or perhaps a bit later) Hoover
made arrangements to establish a "mooring" in California. He supplied his
father-in-law with money to purchase land and build a cottage in Monterey.
Charles Henry obliged and held the property in his own name but transferred it by unrecorded deed to his daughter Lou. In turn Lou—no doubt
drawing on Bert's income—furnished the money with which her father paid
the taxes on the property. In this indirect way Herbert Hoover became a
landowner in California.[4] The little cottage in Monterey, Hoover later wrote,
was intended to be "our legal and spiritual foothold on American soil," a
"geographical anchor" to which he and his wife could turn when desired.
And so, for several years, it remained.[5]

The young couple could not stay long in their beloved California; business beckoned. Passing through Chicago on their way east, Hoover and his wife sailed from New York for Liverpool and arrived in London early in November.[6] There he entered into final arrangements with his new partners at Bewick, Moreing and Company.

The old partnership of the same name had dissolved on September 30 with the retirement of Thomas B. Bewick and the departure of Edward Hooper, Hoover's boss in Western Australia in 1897.[7] As reconstituted, the firm was to consist of four men: Moreing himself as senior partner, Hoover, A. Stanley Rowe, and Thomas W. Wellsted. Moreing, 46, an Australian by birth, was an experienced civil engineer and early president of the Institution of Mining and Metallurgy in London. An apprentice to and later a partner of the elder (Thomas J.) Bewick, he had contributed in the 1880s and 1890s to notable mining ventures in South Africa and to the creation of the port city of Beira in Mozambique.[8] In addition to his large interests in Australia and China, Moreing had dabbled in American ventures. For a time in the 1880s and 1890s the firm itself had maintained branch offices in San Francisco and Salt Lake City, while in 1899 Moreing became president of the St. Lawrence Power Company, which was constructing facilities at Massena, New York.[9] Rowe, 36, a clerk and accountant, had been an employee of Bewick, Moreing for six years.[10] Wellsted, about 31 and a mechanical engineer, was also being elevated from employee to junior partner.[11]

Of the four partners, then, Hoover, 27, was the youngest. While his business contacts with Moreing dated from 1897, his acquaintance with Wellsted and Rowe could only have been slight. Hoover's visits to London in April 1897 and January 1899 had been brief, while his autumn 1900 sojourn lasted barely a month: not much time to become intimate with his new business associates.

The partnership agreement, dated December 18, 1901, divided the firm's prospective profits thusly: 50% to Moreing, 20% each to Hoover and Rowe, and 10% to Wellsted.[12] In addition, Hoover was obliged to buy out the share of one of the departing partners, Edward Hooper. That is, he must pay to the firm the portion of the goodwill allotted to Hooper. This sum amounted to £8,000, or about $40,000.[13] Although Hoover later informed his brother that when he left China in 1901 he could have come home with a quarter of a million dollars, his liquid assets that December were not sufficient to purchase his partnership. Unable to put up the £8,000, Hoover borrowed the sum from Moreing and thereby entered the firm in debt to his senior partner.[14]

The new partnership had a definite division of responsibilities. As the oldest, wealthiest, and best known of the partners, Moreing concentrated on mining finance: the flotation of loans, negotiation with stockbrokers, wheeling and dealing with syndicates and financial allies like Edmund Davis and W. F. Turner.[15] Among other things, Moreing was managing director and dominating spirit of the London and Western Australian Exploration Company, which had promoted such famous mines as the Sons of Gwalia and the Hannan's Brownhill; his firm served as the exploration company's consulting engineers.[16] In the adulatory words of one of his fellow directors, Moreing was "no amateur, but a great mining expert and a very clever financier."[17] An upwardly mobile Colonial, he also had (or soon acquired) political ambitions; eventually he became a Unionist (Conservative) candidate for Parliament.[18]

The considerable clerical, accounting, and related duties of the firm became the responsibility of Wellsted and Rowe. As a partnership of mining engineers and mine managers, Bewick, Moreing not only supplied resident mine superintendents, engineering staff, and attorneys for various companies' mines in far-off lands, but also contracted (for a fee) to furnish offices, facilities for stock transfers, and clerical staff for mining companies registered in London.[19] Thus from 1901 on (and even before) Bewick, Moreing's own offices in the City (London's financial district) simultaneously served as the offices of some of the greatest mines in Australia and elsewhere. As he had done before becoming a partner, Rowe served as secretary of several of the companies Bewick, Moreing had contracted to manage.[20]

The technical, engineering aspects of the reorganized firm's business thus fell squarely on Herbert Hoover. Years later he observed succinctly, "My job was to operate the mines—both as engineer and administrator."[21] Moreing himself acknowledged in 1902 that "although I am the nominal head of my firm I do not attend to the ordinary engineering part of the business, relying upon other and very competent men to advise me. . . ."[22] Chief among them was Hoover. To develop and administer a profitable mine required an unusual fusion of scientific knowledge, practical engineering know-how, executive ability, and acute business sense. It did little good, for instance, to locate an auriferous ore deposit unless the gold recovered would be worth more than the cost of extracting it. A mine that could not produce "payable" ore was only a hole in the ground—nothing more.

It was precisely in this area that Hoover had so distinguished himself in Western Australia and China. As a "mine scout" of rare ability, as an expert examiner and judge of "prospects" and "propositions," as a tireless, cost-cutting, hard-driving, ever-striving manager of mines and of men, Hoover possessed qualities that fitted him well for the business of extracting precious metals from the earth.

From his position at the apex of the global Bewick, Moreing hierarchy, Hoover, via cables and written correspondence, could to some extent direct the firm's far-flung operations. But there was no substitute for periodic personal inspection of the mines that he and his partners had contracted to manage. Indeed, the firm's prosperity and reputation depended on it. At least one of its contracts in 1902 stipulated that a Bewick, Moreing engineer visit a certain company's mine "in order to exercise an efficient supervision over the resident Manager" and "thoroughly inspect the Mine" every three months.[23] Such work, of course, was done by Bewick, Moreing's branch office managers. Still, someone must supervise the supervisors, and who could do that better than Hoover? When it came to rationalizing operations and eliminating wasteful expense, few, if any, could equal him.

There was a monetary incentive behind the Yankee engineer's relentless zeal for efficiency and lower working costs. Under a typical Bewick, Moreing contract the firm was obligated to manage a mine over a certain period of time for a specified annual fee (perhaps £2,000) and a small percentage of net profits.[24] Naturally the lower the total expenditure of the mine, the greater the profit and the greater Bewick, Moreing's slice of it. A reputation for cost-effectiveness would also yield more contracts from other companies and more profits still.

And so, in December 1901, after scarcely a month in London, Hoover left England on his first journey of inspection as junior partner in Bewick, Moreing. His wife Lou accompanied him. In this, the heyday of the international mining engineer, the firm's enterprises were scattered indeed. During Hoover's first year as a partner his firm maintained offices in London, Johannesburg, Tientsin, Kalgoorlie, Auckland, and Tarkwa in the Gold Coast Colony.[25] A turquoise mine in Egypt, a silver mine in Nevada, a coal mine in the Transvaal, and a tin mine in Cornwall added further diversity to its interests.[26] The real focus of its operations, however, was Australia—above all, the goldfields of the Western Australian outback: Kalgoorlie's Golden Mile and several great mines to the north.

From London to Paris to Marseilles, thence by the P. and O. liner *China* through the Suez Canal and on to Fremantle, Western Australia: Hoover knew the route well.[27] On January 15, 1902 he and Lou arrived at the port of Fremantle. Then inland to Kalgoorlie—smack in the blistering Australian summer, back in the scorched, arid "bush" he once depicted as "a country of red dust, black flies, and white heat."[28]

Yet this time it was different. He was no longer an insecure twenty-three-year-old Yank trying to hide his age behind a beard. "Hail Columbia" Hoover was a general now, not a lieutenant. He came prepared to give orders.

I I

I N the three years since Hoover had left the Sons of Gwalia mine, "Golden Westralia" had lost much of its luster. The fever of the "Roaring Nineties" had subsided, leaving, in Hoover's words, "the bitter headache of the morning after."[29] By the end of 1896, at the peak of the speculative boom, 780 Western Australian mining companies had been registered in London. Five years later only 140 of them remained.[30]

What had gone wrong? In a sense, nothing. The frenetic early days of

insatiable optimism and absurdly extravagant finance, the era of suave promoters and "champagne Charlies," could not last forever. The transition to
sounder, systematic mining—from romance to business—was inevitable.

But how the transition hurt. The collapse of the speculative phase of the
Westralian boom was due to a combination of discouraging factors. For one
thing, the gold-bearing lodes of Kalgoorlie and its environs were proving to
be distressingly erratic. Time and again, as Hoover was to discover, promising surface "shows" "failed in depth," petering out at or below the level of
surface oxidation (200 feet down at most). Even if chutes of unoxidized ore
were discovered farther down, their length and breadth were notoriously
difficult to predict. By 1900 it began to appear that the great mines of Kalgoorlie, in one way or another, "had gone seriously wrong in depth."[31]

Furthermore, the complex unoxidized sulpho-telluride ores, on which Kalgoorlie's future prosperity depended, posed formidable and unprecedented
puzzles for metallurgists. What was the best process for extracting the gold
from such refractory ore? As of 1901, despite much progress by authorities
such as Dr. Ludwig Diehl (an eminent German metallurgist who worked
closely with Bewick, Moreing), a consensus on treating Kalgoorlie's peculiar
ore had not yet emerged.[32]

To the vicissitudes of geology and the harsh burdens of geography were
added problems of human origin. By 1901, the population of Western Australia was about 200,000, one-third of it in the eastern goldfields. In that year
Sir John Forrest finally resigned the premiership of the state for a seat in the
first parliament of the new Commonwealth of Australia. His departure,
though, did not eliminate the vociferous complaints of the goldfields population about discrimination and incompetence on the part of the government
in Perth.

In 1896, for instance, the state parliament had authorized the construction
of a weir and a nearly 350-mile water pipeline from the coastal mountain
ranges to Kalgoorlie. It was an audacious engineering enterprise, entailing
the raising of water almost 1,300 feet from the coast to the interior goldfields
plateau. By 1901, however, the Goldfields Water Supply Scheme was far
from complete, the fields still dependent on condensers to treat brackish water.
Mine owners and their allies also repeatedly denounced the government's
discriminatory rail rates and its high tariffs on mining machinery and imported
timber, which added to the costs of gold mining in an already high-cost region.
The rising power of labor unions, which established a political foothold in
the goldfields in the election of 1901, was another source of concern for the
mining interests.[33]

Quite apart from geological obstacles, high costs, and political problems,
Western Australian gold mining as directed from London reeked with abuses
in 1901. Sometimes it seemed that the "experts" and "promoters" had not
disappeared but had merely congregated in London's financial district. At
the root of many problems was secrecy; it was not yet customary to permit

inspection of mines or to publish development and milling results on a regular basis. Some boards of directors, in fact, did not even inform their own
shareholders—let alone the general public—about disturbing developments
at depth on the Golden Mile.[34]

The practice of secrecy facilitated further abuses. With few except the
board of directors (usually three to five men) in command of accurate knowledge about a mine, it was easy to resort to shameless propaganda in the rather
venal mining and financial press. During this period promoters commonly
bought advertising space (and sometimes bribed editors) in order to boom
new ventures among gullible investors or influence the stock market, where
the big money was to be made.[35] Anyone reading the London mining press
for the years 1895–1905 (and even somewhat later) must wonder which articles and editorials were truly independent contributions and which were simply the effusions of pens for hire.

Secrecy, too, permitted collusion between unscrupulous directors and resident Australian mine managers, some of whom were not above rigging results
and sending misleading cables to London on the eve of shareholder meetings.
And since directors usually knew the latest word from the mines before anyone else, "jobbing" in shares was a widespread practice. If, for example, a
manager cabled a bad report on the mine's condition to the London home
office, the directors could suppress the information for a few days while quietly unloading their own shares on an unsuspecting stock market.[36]

Even Bewick, Moreing and Company had not been immune from temptation, as Hoover soon learned. Upon entering the firm he discovered that
its profits had averaged a paltry £7,000 a year (at most) for the past several
years. The real profits accrued from the partners' "jobbing in the stock market," exploiting Bewick, Moreing's strategic position as managers of various
mines and hence possessors of accurate knowledge about developments in
the field.[37] (Since many companies made Bewick, Moreing's offices their own
legal headquarters, the firm was in a position to know the contents of cables
from the field even before the directors did.)

It was also common for London boards to include a titled aristocrat or
two—derisively called "guinea pigs"[38]—presumably to convince the public
of the prestige and probity of the company. Unfortunately, such nobility
were usually ignorant of mining and hence easily manipulable by the promoters and mining engineers who really controlled the operations. At the
other end, in Australia, many a mine manager, even if ethical, was not necessarily competent. When Hoover arrived in late 1901 he was dismayed by
what he perceived as a reversion, in just three years, to traditional English
and colonial mining practice: away from the use of well-educated engineers
and back to the old custom of promoting foremen up from the ranks. Indeed,
it was this very problem (according to Hoover) that led Moreing to urge him
to become a partner.[39] In the new era of large-scale, high-expenditure mining
and advanced metallurgy, the old ways could no longer suffice.

The *coup de grace* for "Golden Westralia," at least in the eyes of many British investors, occurred in 1900–1901 with the collapse of the empire of the most remarkable company promoter of them all. By the late Nineties Whittaker Wright—brilliant, glib, self-confident, rich—was the dominant figure in Western Australian finance in London. His London and Globe Finance Corporation and other finance companies, thoughtfully adorned with "guinea pig" directors, controlled numerous mines throughout Western Australia and abroad. Some, like the Lake View Consols and Ivanhoe at Kalgoorlie, were solidly successful. But the bulk of Wright's operations rested on stock market manipulation, "frenzied finance," and, as it turned out, dishonest finance as well.

In the end Wright, who lived a life of luxurious ostentation, overreached himself. Betrayed by his own mine manager at the Lake View Consols, who cabled in falsely optimistic reports about the mine's value at depth, Wright gambled heavily on a bull market for shares. When the Lake View's production suddenly plummeted, so, too, did the value of the shares, and Wright was never able to recover. At the end of 1900, the London and Globe and its sisters went bankrupt, leaving in their wake a trail of failed mines and ruined investors.

It took more than three years to clean up the wreckage. Bankruptcy proceedings uncovered a host of irregularities. Finally, in January 1904, after two years of public and Parliamentary agitation, Wright was brought to trial for deliberately falsifying company balance sheets, was convicted, and was given the maximum sentence of seven years. Proud and defiant to the end, he had vowed never to spend a day in prison. Just moments after receiving his sentence, and while standing in a chamber next to the courtroom, Wright committed suicide by swallowing poison.[40]

The sensational Wright scandal, of course, had not reached its tragic denouement at the time of Hoover's 1902 trip "down under." But enough was known for the affair to epitomize the kind of mining practice with which a professional mining engineer must now cope. The exploiting of "insider" knowledge for self-aggrandizement, the use of secret ore reserves to bolster stock market shenanigans, the borrowing of money to pay dividends, the "picking of the eyes" out of a mine for short-term speculative gain, the bribing of newspaper editors, the overcapitalization of companies, not to mention outright fraud—all these deeds Whittaker Wright had done. Wary stockholders might be forgiven for thinking that the only things in short supply in Australian gold mining were a code of ethics and a reliable source of dividends.

Hoover and his firm were to be principal beneficiaries of Wright's debacle. As it happened, on the very same vessel that Hoover took from Marseilles to Fremantle in December 1901 was a prominent London stockbroker with whom he became acquainted on board.[41] Francis Algernon Govett, 43, an honors graduate in law from Oxford, was on his way to Kalgoorlie to inspect the Lake View Consols mine in behalf of shareholders who had recently deposed Wright's dummy directors.[42] Govett, in fact, was the recently elected chairman of the board.[43] Hoover evidently impressed the British financier. A month after reaching Kalgoorlie, Govett removed the local superintendent of the Lake View and turned the company's management over to Bewick, Moreing.[44]

As Hoover remarked long afterwards, Govett's decision marked the start of an "important expansion" in Bewick, Moreing's business.[45] Beyond this, his shipboard meetings with Hoover initiated more than a decade of close personal collaboration. On the one side was Govett the financier: able, polished, outspoken—a spirited, "interesting personality" and "fearless controversialist" to those who liked him, an arrogant eccentric to one of his detractors.[46] On the other side was Hoover the laconic Yankee mining expert, who preferred to work behind the scenes and who often prepared the technical data and speeches that Govett, a layman, delivered with gusto and aplomb at shareholders meetings.[47] In years to come Govett publicly acknowledged his indebtedness to Hoover, to whom "I owe a considerable measure of my education in the matter of the management of mines."[48] For Hoover, too, as an alien and therefore an outsider, the association with a leading City financier was to be a crucial business alliance.

Perhaps, as 1902 began, the situation in Western Australia was not quite as gloomy as it seemed. As Hoover and Govett set foot on the Golden Mile they could take heart from one fact. Notwithstanding the agonizing vicissitudes of many mines in depth, notwithstanding the scandals and the demise of hundreds of companies, total gold production in the state actually increased in 1901 to the highest level yet.[49] Now if only one could eliminate the residue of graft, puffery, incompetence, and waste. . . .

I I I

H OO VER wasted little time in initiating a drastic overhaul of Bewick, Moreing's operations. Apparently unimpressed by the firm's top personnel, he turned swiftly to the United States for replacements. Within short order more than a dozen college-educated American engineers and metallurgists were on their way to Australia.[50]

Many of these recruits were Stanford men, including his friend Deane P. Mitchell (class of '96) and William A. Prichard (class of '98), a friend of Hoover's older brother Theodore.[51] Prichard immediately became manager of the Lake View Consols.[52] Theodore, who had graduated from Stanford in 1901 at the age of thirty, was himself starting up the mining engineering ladder in California, having been given his first job after college by Prichard.[53] Negotiating through Theodore, Herbert invited still another able Californian, W. J. Loring, to become the new superintendent of the Sons of

Gwalia. Loring eventually accepted, at a salary of $9,000 plus expenses, and sailed from San Francisco in early February.[54] Hoover was willing to pay a high price for the man he wanted. If he demanded much, he rewarded well.

Hoover also secured the services of graduates of Columbia, the University of California, and the Colorado School of Mines. From China he recruited John Agnew and J. Wilfred Newberry, who had been with him since Sons of Gwalia days.[55] Before long every Bewick, Moreing mine in Western Australia had a new superintendent.[56]

Why did Hoover institute such a far-reaching shakeup of his staff? Primarily it was because of his conviction that technically-trained university graduates in geology and mining were more capable than the products of the apprentice system that still prevailed in the British empire. Other factors may also have influenced his calculations. The infusion of so many newcomers had implications that Hoover, as a shrewd, effective executive, could hardly have overlooked. The new men all owed their jobs to him. Moreover, most of them were Americans, and many were Californians—two sources of additional "kinship" with their Californian employer in a land where all of them were outsiders. Finally, there was in several cases the further cement of the old school tie and personal friendship dating back nearly a decade. Whether consciously or unconsciously, Hoover had selected lieutenants who were likely to be loyal to their chief.

That loyalty was much on Hoover's mind was the burden of remarks some years later by one man whom Hoover did not keep on at his post: Richard M. Atwater, superintendent of the Sons of Gwalia from 1900 until March 1902. Although he was an American, Atwater found himself "promoted" out of his position to make way for Loring. (Hoover dispatched him to Malaya to examine some tin mines.) Many years later Atwater told an anti-Hoover biographer that Hoover's removal of him in 1902 was an act of vindictiveness. Atwater, it seems, was the American mining man who in 1898 refused to join Hoover's alleged conspiracy to stage a coup against their superior, Ernest Williams. Hoover's attempted strike by the American engineers thereupon failed; Hoover, defeated, ended up on his way to China. According to Atwater, Hoover never forgave him for siding with Williams and failing to support Hoover's plot. Atwater also claimed that W. J. Loring later told him that Hoover took pleasure in 1902 in sacking every remaining employee who had been loyal to Williams in 1898.[57]

Atwater's story received some independent corroboration from Loring himself. To the same anti-Hoover biographer Loring alleged that Hoover in 1902 fired many employees in Australia "who had not properly appreciated him" in 1897–98.[58] The implication was that Hoover's motive in his housecleaning was not managerial efficiency but revenge.

Since Hoover in effect kicked Atwater upstairs (or at least sideways) in 1902, Atwater's later testimony may be only the tale of an ex-employee with a grudge. Loring, too, came to have reasons for disliking Hoover.[59] Whatever

Hoover's motivation, one man he did not need to replace in 1902 was his former boss, Ernest Williams. The "irascible little Welshman" left the Australian goldfields in 1899.[60] He was succeeded by a South African, W. R. Feldtmann, who was still on the scene at the start of 1902.[61] According to Atwater, Hoover fired Feldtmann, too, but the records show that he did not leave his post as Bewick, Moreing's general manager in Western Australia until early 1903. Then—at least officially—he resigned and was replaced by Prichard and Loring as joint general managers.[62]

For two-and-a-half months—from mid-January to early April 1902—Hoover and his wife resided in Western Australia. As always, Hoover was a dynamo, working long hours, driving himself as well as others, constantly investigating, analyzing, and striving for efficiencies. If he rewarded well, he demanded much. Meeting him for the first time in Kalgoorlie, W. J. Loring was struck by Hoover's youthfulness and "unique way of getting at the root of things without preliminaries, avoiding unnecessary detail. . . . He appeared to have the faculty of getting at the essentials by eliminating non-essentials."[63]

Although Bewick, Moreing's regional office was in Kalgoorlie, where several of its principal mines lay, the firm also managed numerous mines in the outlying districts. These included the two greatest mines in the state outside the Golden Mile: the Sons of Gwalia, 150 miles north, and the Great Fingall near Cue, on the Murchison field, well to the northwest of the Gwalia.[64] To these and other outposts in the bush Hoover traveled on his tours of inspection during the first months of 1902. To Leonora, Laverton, Lake Way, Lawlers, Cue—and his wife Lou Henry at his side. The Hoovers afterwards calculated that in just 2½ months they traveled 3,500 miles in Western Australia, at a time when horses-and-buggies and camels were the only mode of transportation in the outback.[65]

Besides supervising and revamping the operations of going concerns, Hoover during his visit sought out new prospects to develop and float. On behalf of Moreing's exploration company he secured an option on the Lancefield mine at Laverton.[66] On behalf of the London and Hamburg Gold Recovery Company (which controlled Australian rights to the Diehl process for gold extraction) he spent several days examining some leases it owned at Pindinnie. His report was a model of incisiveness.[67] Hoover also investigated the feasibility of amalgamating the Hannan's Brownhill and the Hannan's Oroya, two big mines at Kalgoorlie.[68] Back in 1897 and 1898, at age 23, he had dreamed of amalgamating all the mines on the Golden Mile. One giant combination, and himself the head of it! Himself the all-controlling engineer![69] Whether or not such grand ambitions still percolated through his veins, the limited amalgamation scheme he now endorsed after surveying the two companies' properties was a portent of Kalgoorlie's future. The era of consolidation and efficiency was at hand.

Efficiency. The word seemed almost to define Hoover's driving mission on the fields. In London one of his partners told a group of Great Fingall stockholders that Hoover "had gone out to conduct a campaign" against high working costs at the Great Fingall and elsewhere.[70] There was merit in his quest. Gold mining in Western Australia was no longer a matter of skimming surface outcrops and making lucky strikes. It was an industry dealing in increasingly low-grade ore: less than an ounce of gold to the ton. The successful handling of this low-grade ore was the key to the industry. For such mining to be commercially viable, unit costs of extraction must be small indeed. The lower these expenses, the poorer the grade of ore that could be economically processed. The poorer the grade of ore, the greater the number of marginal mines that could be worked and the longer their productive lives. Everyone benefited, then, from efficiency: investors, from higher (and longer-lasting) dividends; the government, from increased revenue; workers, from steady employment and more jobs on the fields. Efficiency was the key to enduring prosperity. It became one of Hoover's lifelong principles.

At the end of February 1902 a highly pleased Moreing relayed his compliments to Hoover in Kalgoorlie. Moreing praised his partner's energy during his two months "down under." He believed that Hoover's zealous efforts would lead to a mighty boost in the firm's business.[71]

Not all the news from Kalgoorlie was encouraging. It is often forgotten that gold mines are not immortal; sooner or later every mine gives out. This hazard was exacerbated in Western Australia by the highly erratic character of its ore bodies. Many times, to the surprise and dismay of engineers and stockholders alike, a promising mine would shrivel in value as the underground reef thinned out or vanished.

One such disappointment was the East Murchison United mine at Lawlers. Three years before, upon leaving Australia, Hoover had touted it as "the big mine of the north," one of the best in the colony. It had "passed through all its troubles," he asserted, and had "a splendid career before it."[72] From 1897 to 1900, in fact, the mine developed steadily and paid several modest dividends.[73] By late 1901, however, the mine was in desperate straits; from November through the following April each month's output was lower than the last.[74] The mine had unexpectedly failed in depth.[75]

For the next several years Hoover and his associates tried to save the company. Borrowing heavily to keep afloat, the East Murchison United purchased additional mines that supplied ore for crushing and hence gold for operating expenses. Meanwhile, skilled Bewick, Moreing engineers, sometimes working under Hoover's personal supervision during his periodic visits, carried out systematic development efforts in hopes of finding payable ore reserves, all within the severe constraints of limited funds and mounting indebtedness.[76] It was a valiant but failing endeavor. The one-shilling-a-share dividend declared in November 1900 was the last the unfortunate shareholders ever received. The company was liquidated in 1905.[77] Like many a mine before it, its total dividends reached only a fraction of its invested share capital[78] As was true of most gold mines, far more money went into the ground than came out of it.

The East Murchison United's tribulations in 1902 probably did not arouse Hoover's personal anxiety as much as conditions at another mine he visited that year: the famous Sons of Gwalia, on whose enormous potential Hoover had rested his reputation in 1897. On February 4, 1902 Hoover and his wife arrived at the mine for an inspection. The former superintendent "must have been pleased," opined the local *Mount Leonora Miner*, to examine the underground workings and see "all his prophecies verified."[79]

The *Mount Leonora Miner* was mistaken. Even as Hoover examined the Sons of Gwalia's drives and stopes, the assay samples were telling a disturbing story. From May 1898 to the end of 1900 the grade of ore crushed and treated at the mine had averaged a respectable 23 dwt. (a little over an ounce) per ton. In 1901 the average yield suddenly plummeted to a distressing 12 dwt. Now, as 1902 began, as mine excavation went deeper, there was still no sign of improvement.[80]

Indeed, the situation seemed, if anything, to be getting worse. The 23-dwt. average had been achieved with ore taken solely from the upper four levels of the mine. Now, however, the shaft was down over one thousand feet, the mine was down to the seventh level (that is, the seventh horizontal passage cut from the shaft), and the ore found in the lower levels was not matching the upper workings in richness. On the whole northern side of the mine, exploratory development at the sixth and seventh levels had failed to find any ore on the main lode whatever.[81] Moreover, and most inopportunely, working costs—the measure of managerial success—were rising.[82]

Was the mine—dread thought—failing in depth? Was liquidation of the much-advertised company inevitable? During much of 1901 Bewick, Moreing's mine managers on the scene had sent several optimistic reports to London forecasting improvements in output. Their confident projections had gone unfulfilled.[83] By January 1902, under pressure from London, the engineers could promise only enough of a monthly surplus to pay off the company's large accumulating debts—and none left over for a dividend. "We can only continue," the Bewick, Moreing managers declared on January 4, "to work the mine at high pressure and at as low a cost as possible, and everything else depends upon the grade of ore obtainable."[84] To the nervous directors half a world away, this was not much reassurance.

At this point Hoover turned his attention to the problem. Ten days after his trip to the Sons of Gwalia he dispatched a lengthy report on the mine to the London board. Fearful, as he later put it, that he and his associates in the field "might condemn the mine unjustifiably," Hoover decided to inform the directors by letter (rather than cable) and "await the arrival of that letter in London before cabling further news."[85] Since his letter, mailed from Kalgoorlie, would not reach London for five weeks,[86] Hoover had deftly given himself that much time to turn the crisis around.

In his letter, dated February 14, Hoover was candid but cautiously optimistic. While acknowledging that the sixth and seventh levels on the north side of the main shaft were "disappointing," he found "every reason to hope that ore will again appear." Still, he conceded that the failure to discover ore at the north end "greatly cripples our anticipated ore reserves, and throws our dependence into the south end of the Mine for milling ore." Fortunately, the south end was showing no signs of abating in richness and reliability. Hoover predicted that working costs would go down once a new pumping plant was installed and a railway line completed, permitting cheaper transport of vast quantities of wood from the coast for timbering the walls of the mine.[87]

Hoover, then, put the best face possible on a discouraging situation. On February 20 and March 4, as his unsettling report about the main lode slowly made its way to London, the Kalgoorlie office of Bewick, Moreing used the telegraph to rush news of a more favorable character. The B lode on the seventh level north was yielding rich, payable ore.[88]

Once again, however, the engineers had jumped the gun. Within a few weeks the B lode turned out to be "very short and unsatisfactory."[89] What was more significant was Kalgoorlie's eagerness to send London good news quickly by cable while Hoover sent bad news by slow surface mail. It was a tactic to buy time. As Hoover told a shareholders meeting a few months later, "There is always a chance in mining that things may improve, and no man who is not sanguine will ever make anything out of a mine."[90]

Privately, however, Hoover was worried. When Loring arrived to take the helm at the Gwalia, Hoover suggested that twenty of the mine's fifty stamps for crushing ore should be taken out of production for awhile so that the mine could be systematically developed: a major retrenchment that Loring was reluctant to make. After inspecting the mine Loring concluded that the plant could be revamped and that the mill could continue operating fully with no decrease in stamps. On April 11, 1902 he took over the mine.[91] The next day the Kalgoorlie office of Bewick, Moreing and Company gloomily declared: "Unless an improvement speedily manifests itself, it may very shortly become necessary to seriously consider the question of reducing the number of stamps running."[92]

On at least one occasion—and possibly with Hoover's approval—Bewick, Moreing engineers deliberately manipulated the output returns in order to come up with the results they desired. Early in March the Kalgoorlie regional office, run by Feldtmann, wrote to the Sons of Gwalia's secretary in London. The letter explained that the Sons of Gwalia's total output for February would probably fall far short of normal. On the other hand, output in March should improve. Kalgoorlie therefore had ordered Richard Atwater, still at this point superintendent of the mine, to augment the February figure by counting in two or three days' output in March. While normally opposed to such a course, the Kalgoorlie office was certain that in this instance the directors in London would approve. Would not such a scheme be preferable to a huge decrease in February followed by an odd upsurge in March? The Kalgoorlie office added that the goal of its statistical juggling was to create a figure that, while acceptable for February, could be surpassed in March, despite the deduction of two or three days' output.[93]

It is not known how London reacted to this proposal from the field. Nor is it known how Hoover reacted; there is no direct evidence that he either knew about or approved it. On the other hand, Feldtmann knew,[94] Atwater knew, and Hoover, their boss, was present in Western Australia at the time. It would have been surprising if Hoover did not know. The idea of "extending" a month in order to jack up returns was not novel to Hoover. He himself had advocated this same measure at the East Murchison United in mid-1898, only to be overridden by his superior, Ernest Williams.[95]

What was the purpose of this unorthodox expedient? It seems most likely that Bewick, Moreing's men in the field were anxious not to disturb the company's shareholders while Hoover and his colleagues were struggling to rescue the mine from its troubles. If the shareholders discovered that the February returns were dismal, they might panic, sell their shares, and depress the Sons of Gwalia market even further. If that occurred, a lot of prominent investors might be harmed, among them Moreing himself, whose London and Western Australian Exploration Company held more than 57,000 Sons of Gwalia shares.[96]

In any case, it now became the duty of Atwater to compile a "correct" set of returns and to fend off the local mining warden. Early in March Atwater was summoned to appear at the warden's court to explain why he had not submitted his February returns on time. Instead of complying, Atwater took off for Kalgoorlie, explaining that company business beckoned and that it was impossible for him to appear at court. How the warden greeted this interesting assertion of priorities is not known. Atwater claimed to the warden that since March 1 had fallen on a Sunday, he was unable to institute a cyanide cleanup under Sunday labor laws until the next day, and that it then required six days to complete the task and obtain the bullion assays.[97] It is far more likely, however, that Atwater simply stalled until he could arrange the desired results for his superiors.

Not all the Sons of Gwalia's difficulties were traceable to erratic ore bodies. Since the company's founding in early 1898, its management in London had pursued a number of controversial policies. Under the terms of the 1897–98 flotation, Moreing's exploration company had agreed to supply the infant enterprise with £50,000 in working capital. Instead, however, of paying up immediately, Moreing's company arranged to fulfill its obligation in installments. More than a year later (May 1899) only a third of the £50,000 had actually been paid.[98] It "had not been wanted," the managing directors alleged.

Meanwhile in the thirteen-month period ending in December 1898 the mine accumulated over £30,000 in profits. Instead, however, of distributing this sum as a dividend, the directors decided to use it for erection of plant and machinery—always an unpopular action among stockholders anxious for dividends, and particularly so when Moreing's promised working capital was lying nearby, untapped. Why not distribute the profits to the stockholders and call up the remaining £33,000 due from Moreing's exploration company?

At the May 1899 meeting the managing director of the Sons of Gwalia stated that both the £33,000 *and* the undistributed profits soon would be required to help pay for the new plant and machinery. But the director's defense of the board's "conservative and prudent policy" was unconvincing to several irate stockholders. According to them, the £33,000 had not been called up because a majority of the directors had in fact been nominated for their jobs by Moreing's exploration company. The obvious inference was that the working capital "had not been wanted" because Moreing had not wanted to give it, and the pliant board, dominated by his own nominees, had obliged him.[99]

Other problems rankled various shareholders. In his 1897 report recommending purchase of the mine, Herbert Hoover had urged the installation of a 50-stamp mill. During his own tenure as superintendent he had had to carry on with an old 10-stamp mill. By May 1899, a year-and-a-half after Hoover's report, no machinery had yet been sent to the mine.[100] It was not until the beginning of 1901, more than two whole years after Hoover's departure from the Gwalia, that the new 50-stamp mill commenced operations.[101] Why the delay? Caution, said Bewick, Moreing. Maladministration, said the critics.[102]

Furthermore, although the mine generated substantial profits from the start, the company did not distribute its first dividend until June 1900 and its second until July 1901.[103] In both cases the directors borrowed money to pay the dividends.[104] Probably they justified this expedient by counting on easy repayments as the mine developed and prospered. (They planned, in fact, eventually to issue 25,000 new shares at £3 each—three times face value—to raise money to straighten out their finances.)[105] But now, in 1902, the mine was not developing as anticipated, and the company was wallowing in debt. The drain was remorseless; the company's liabilities exceeded £50,000.[106] By now, too, Gwalia shares on the market had fallen well below £3, thereby destroying the possibility of a new stock issue.[107]

The Sons of Gwalia's future was distinctly uncertain, then, when in early April Herbert Hoover and his wife sailed from Fremantle for London, by way of Colombo, the Suez Canal, Genoa, and Paris.[108] The fate of the mine that had made Hoover's reputation now depended more than ever on the secrets, a thousand feet down, that awaited grimy men with picks and drills—and on the abilities of Hoover's chosen manager, William Joseph Loring.

I V

BERT and Lou returned to London in early May, with the American engineer looking "remarkably well," according to one of the local mining papers.[109] The next few weeks were busy ones, as they always were with Hoover. One

of his first tasks was to find a place for the summer. Eventually the couple
settled on a small home called the White House at Ashley Drive, Walton-on-
Thames, a few miles southwest of London.[110] During the spring Hoover also
found time to present an impressive paper on the Kaiping mines and coal
fields in China before a meeting in London of the Institution of Mining and
Metallurgy, of which he was an associate member.[111]

Early in June, perhaps in consequence of its increased volume of business,
Bewick, Moreing and Company moved its offices from Broad Street House
to 20 Copthall Avenue in the City.[112] At about the same time, Hoover and
his firm joined many directors of other Western Australian mining companies in forming a trade association called the Council of West Australian
Mine Owners. F. A. Govett was elected president.[113] The Council had much
to agitate about, particularly the partiality of the state government toward
coastal and pastoral interests. In its first blast at the Western Australian government the mine owners' association protested a recent increase in railway
rates.[114] Didn't Perth realize that the future of the gold industry lay in low-
grade mining and that every increase in costs was a blow to the prosperity of
the state?

On June 5 Hoover attended the annual stockholders' meeting of the Sons
of Gwalia, Ltd. in London. It was a dramatic and unhappy gathering.[115]
While insisting that "the position is far from desperate," the chairman of the
board admitted that the mine had been "an excessive disappointment" and
that the company was "now in a state of temporary paralysis." With the
grade of ore having dropped from 23 dwt. to 12, with the seventh level north
having given out, the owners must revise every estimate ever made about the
mine. To be sure, the company's profit-and-loss account showed a huge current surplus of £140,000. The chairman proposed, however, to allocate this
entire amount to depreciation, that is, to "writing down the assets of the
company to a point more nearly representing the prospects of the mine as a
dividend payer in the future." The chairman stated that if the present grade
of ore (now 12½ dwt. per ton) went lower, there would be no choice but "reconstruction or liquidation."[116]

Such medicine was bitter indeed for many shareholders, and at the meeting several demanded that a committee of investigation be appointed. It was
"most extraordinary," said one, that the engineers' reports from the mine
were so "very satisfactory" even as late as January 1902. "There was no doubt
that someone had blundered"; the shareholders should try to change the
management. William Pritchard Morgan echoed the call for investigation—
the same Pritchard Morgan from whose interests Moreing had obtained the
mine in 1897. Once a friend of Moreing, Pritchard Morgan now cast asper-
sions on his firm's competence and integrity.[117]

Moreing fought back fiercely against the variety of charges leveled at his
firm and himself. "All through the fall in the market in Gwalias," he told the
meeting, "I have been a staunch believer in the mine." He was "bitterly

disappointed" and "utterly upset" by the ominous developments in depth—developments he had not "the slightest reason to suspect" in advance. "No one can say that I am a 'bear' in West Australians," he proclaimed. "I am the greatest 'bull' that was ever connected with Western Australia. . . . If there is a blunder anywhere, it is a blunder on the part of the men who made the mine—whoever is responsible for it—who did not put payable ore on the seventh level."[118]

Hoover also emphatically defended his firm's management against the attacks. Hoover reminded the shareholders:

> The fact that we are able to make a profit on 12-dwt. ore is clear proof that we are working at a low cost. No other London company is working in Western Australia so economically.

To the accusation that the machinery and development costs had been excessive, Hoover rejoined:

> There has been no plant constructed at Kalgoorlie within 30 per cent of the cost of the Sons of Gwalia plant, in spite of the fact that we spent £12,000 on cartage to the mine.[119]

In the end the directors and Moreing defeated Pritchard Morgan's motion to reject the accounts and set up a committee of investigation, but only by the narrow margin of 14–12.[120] But if the immediate challenge was beaten back, the mine's future was still in doubt. At the meeting Hoover remarked that he was not as pessimistic about the mine as the chairman; for one thing the southern end of the working looked better than ever.[121] Others were less sanguine. From January 25 to June 7 Sons of Gwalia shares plummeted on the London stock exchange.[122] The reason the mine had "failed to come up to expectations," said the *Economist*'s special mining commissioner that summer, was that it had been "absurdly over-rated" in the first place. "For months," he complained, he "could never take up a paper without seeing some special mention" of it, "and the higher the shares went the louder rose . . . the paeans of praise. When the crash comes we find that in Gwalia, like many hundreds of mines before it, the ore chutes are going wrong in depth. . . ."[123]

Meanwhile Hoover was helping to consummate the major reorganization on the Golden Mile that he had investigated during his recent visit to Kalgoorlie. Appearing before the directors of the Hannan's Brownhill Gold Mining Company, he recommended a merger with the nearby Hannan's Oroya.[124] The proposed amalgamation made sense. Since its founding eight years before, the Hannan's Brownhill had been one of the giants on the fields.[125] By 1902, however, its days of glory were clearly past.[126] The mining commissioner of the *Economist* estimated that the mine probably had one year's supply of rich ore left.[127] Although not hopeless, its situation was clearly "bad": another case of vanishing ore in depth.[128]

While the Brownhill had little ore, the nearby Hannan's Oroya mine was blessed with a considerable quantity of already developed ore and a recently discovered chute of rich sulphide ore: just what the Brownhill's treatment plant could devour economically on a large scale. So with virtually no stock-holder opposition, in mid-July 1902 the two companies agreed to amalgamate under the name of the Oroya Brownhill Company, Ltd.[129] Said the *Economist* approvingly, "The Brownhill-Oroya project differs from the Whittaker Wright and most other proposals of the same kind in the essential particular that it relates to mines of proved value and not to either derelicts or purely speculative 'propositions.' " The *Economist* praised the merger as likely to reduce considerably "the rate of working expenditure," which, around Kal-goorlie, was "notoriously excessive."[130]

Hoover could not claim originality or sole responsibility for this success; amalgamation schemes between the two companies had been pursued actively if sporadically for at least two years.[131] Hoover's original recommendation may also have been more ambitious than the one adopted. Three months before, an abortive proposal had circulated to include a third company in the merger.[132] Nevertheless, it was Hoover who had carefully surveyed the two mines, pushed for a merger, and helped to assure its acceptance. It was the first demonstration of an ability he exercised repeatedly in the years ahead, a talent for the financial reorganization and consolidation of mining ventures. Even his ex-employee Atwater conceded him that.[133] Hoover was not only a good exploration geologist, not only an able boss in the field; he was a budding financier.

With the Hannan's amalgamation scheme ratified in mid-July, Hoover sailed for the United States on July 19, after a stay in England of less than three months.[134] Lou remained behind at the White House in Walton-on-Thames.[135] His six-week trip took Hoover to New York, Denver, San Fran-cisco, and western Canada.[136] Part of the debris left by the collapse of Whit-taker Wright's empire was the Rossland Great Western Mines in British Columbia (near the Montana border), and Hoover had been asked to deter-mine whether Bewick, Moreing could salvage and manage this property. Herbert's brother Theodore, then an assistant manager of a mine in Bodie, California, joined him for the inspection of the mines and smelters in the vicinity of Rossland, Nelson, and Brooklyn, British Columbia. Hoover decided not to accept the offer.[137]

Before heading east Bert and Tad traveled down to Newberg, Oregon, to visit their sister May, now married to a businessman, Van Ness Leavitt.[138] In Denver he met his old friend R. A. F. Penrose, Jr. and looked for men—probably Colorado School of Mines graduates—who might fill slots in Bewick, Moreing's expanding global network.[139] Then, back east to New York and thence to London, where he arrived on September 4. In six weeks he had traveled 16,000 miles.[140]

At some point during the year the Hoovers began renting an apartment at 39 Hyde Park Gate in the Kensington section of London. For the next five years this was their "in town" residence—when they were in town.[141] During 1902 also, they bought their first automobile (still a novelty in those days): a French Panhard, which they used frequently for weekend forays into the English countryside.[142] In 1902 alone Lou traveled 2,000 miles on auto trips through England and Wales.[143] Their pace, in retrospect, seems almost frenetic.

During the rest of 1902, however, the young couple remained in England. Amidst the incessant pressures of business Hoover was able toward the end of the year to write two anonymous articles for the *Financial Times* of London and a piece for the *Engineering and Mining Journal* in New York. The subject of these essays was the mining industry in Western Australia.[144]

Taken together, Hoover's articles had two themes. On the one hand, he extolled the development of "practically a new science" of mining in Western Australia. In the realms of economy in water, reduction of working costs, and treatment of refractory telluride ore, progress in just a few years had been exceptional. In fact, said Hoover, "Kalgoorlie can now claim, without refutation, to have solved the question of treating telluride gold ores."[145] Hoover boldly compared the working costs at Kalgoorlie to those at Cripple Creek, Colorado, the only other gold-mining region in the world where tellurides were found. Wage rates in each district were virtually the same, said Hoover. If one discounted Cripple Creek's advantage in water supply and reduced Kalgoorlie's costs to "a basis of Cripple Creek conditions," the evidence was unambiguous: Kalgoorlie's mines were operating at 35 to 40% less cost than those of Cripple Creek—proof of "the superiority of mine administration in Kalgoorlie."[146] Since one of the principal mine managing concerns on the Golden Mile was Bewick, Moreing, the evidence presented was indirectly complimentary to Hoover himself.

Hoover obliquely called attention to his firm in other ways. One of the sources of reduced costs in Western Australia, he claimed, was "the grouping of the mines for mutual purchase of supplies in large amounts by one of the principal firms,"[147] a reference to Bewick, Moreing's recent decision to centralize supply purchases in Fremantle for the many mines under its control.[148] Hoover also compiled what he said were the administrative expenses in London of fourteen mining companies in Western Australia. Of the seven lowest-cost companies, five were managed by Bewick, Moreing.[149]

Hoover was far less laudatory of the Western Australian government (his second theme). It "has not rendered the assistance to be expected in an enlightened self-governing colony," he charged. Voicing the complaints of many mine owners, Hoover detailed several festering grievances: the onerous and discriminatory rail freight rates, the tariff on imported foodstuffs and mine machinery, a high tax on mining company profits, and the failure to build a direct rail line from the goldfields to the relatively nearby port of Esperance on the south coast. In these ways "the bulk of the burden" fell on the mines—deliberately so, Hoover charged, in order that politicians might gain votes from the majority of the electorate who did not live on the eastern goldfields. To Hoover, writing anonymously, the West Australian government was practicing "a form of statecraft" that was "the most short-sighted of any civilised nation." The "real interest" economically of the mining industry, he argued, lay "not in the discovery of bonanzas, but a decrease in the costs of production." If these costs could be reduced so that lower-grade ore could be profitably worked, "the number of producing mines in the colony could be at least quadrupled." Alas, Western Australian politicians seemed "oblivious" to these basic truths.[150]

Hoover contrasted such indifference to the mining industry's grievances with the government's growing responsiveness to the mine workers. While working costs in the state declined in 1902—thanks to "the agencies of management and enlarged and more economical equipment"—wages did not. Instead, a "forced arbitration at Kalgoorlie" had, "as usual with such commissions, compromised, and thereby increased wages. One beneficial result was, however, the establishment of a uniform scale at Kalgoorlie." It was obvious from Hoover's syntax that he did not approve the raise in wages.[151] Nor, it was clear, did he approve the new workmen's compensation act, which he labeled "more favorable to the workmen and more prejudicial to the owner than [that of] any other mining region in the world."[152] As in 1897 and 1898, so still in 1902: in the squaring off of management against labor, Hoover revealed himself to be staunchly on the side of management.

V

DESPITE various frustrations, Hoover's first year as a partner in Bewick, Moreing was one of gratifying success. On a wide front he had inaugurated reforms and taken constructive initiatives in his principal theater of operations, Western Australia. From Cue to Kalgoorlie, from Gwalia to Laverton, scientifically trained American mining engineers—Hoover's men—were taking charge, and with a mandate for efficiency. The pernicious system of secrecy was slowly weakening as a number of mines (including several run by Bewick, Moreing) began to publish monthly accounts for all to see. At the Lake View Consols F. A. Govett now permitted anyone who wished to inspect the mine's underground workings.[153] At the port of Fremantle, Bewick, Moreing's centralized supply store was in place, managed by the brother of Hoover's partner Wellsted.[154] And on the Golden Mile in Kalgoorlie the merger of the Oroya and Brownhill mines was an accomplished fact.

Already Hoover's campaign to reduce working costs was bearing fruit. The Lake View Consols mine, where William A. Prichard was at the helm, was steadily recovering from the Whittaker Wright era of extravagant mis-management. By October working costs were declining, monthly profits substantially increasing. The company, in Govett's words, was "in first-class financial shape." At the annual shareholders meeting Govett warmly compli-mented Hoover, Feldtmann, and Prichard for their "first-class work." Their "ability and integrity" had won his confidence: ". . . if energy and intelli-gence can pull your mine through," said Govett, "you may surely feel that success is only a question of time."[155]

To the north the Great Fingall was emerging as a superlative producer with years of "big profits" before it.[156] Perhaps most gratifying of all to Hoo-ver were the reports coming from the Sons of Gwalia. In January 1902 the mine employed 873 men and paid over £12,000 in wages. At the end of the year, after nine months under W. J. Loring's vigorous management, it employed only 500 men and paid out about £7,400 in wages. Profits and ore reserves were increasing; working costs during the year declined more than 25 percent. The south lode had substantially improved, holding out the promise of extended prosperity for the mine. By mid-1903 the Sons of Gwa-lia's crisis had passed, and its entire £50,000 in liabilities had been paid off. The company paid its first dividend in two years.[157]

Many factors accounted for this extraordinary reversal, including the fun-damental one that made all else possible: a "partial recovery" of the mine. Payable gold continued to turn up on the south lode. Among "human fac-tors," several were significant: the extension of the government railroad to the nearby town of Leonora, the building of a special tramway for transport-ing firewood from the surrounding bush, and the introduction of a Cornish pumping plant, which permitted a decrease in labor employed. At the June 1903 annual meeting the company's chairman singled out another: the appointment of Loring as manager of the mine. The chairman heaped praise on Loring, whose handling of the "labour question" was the chief reason for celebrating his selection.[158]

And behind Loring, of course, was the man who selected him and the firm whose broad policies were helping to transform West Australian mining. At the end of 1902 Bewick, Moreing and Company controlled fully a dozen important mines in the state.[159] Under Herbert Hoover's engineering direc-tion, the firm was rapidly moving from eminence to preeminence on the fields.

Hoover's personal prosperity was improving as well. Aside from his share of partnership profits, he had begun to invest in the stock market. During the autumn of 1902 Hoover compiled a kind of diary in which he recorded certain of his stockholdings and market transactions of the time.[160] This memorandum may or may not have been exhaustive, and it did not disclose his partnership earnings or net savings. Still, it provides a glimpse of his worldly estate during his first year as a Bewick, Moreing partner.

For September 1, 1902 the document reads:

Balance:

Oriental Synd. Ord.	7,900	
Oriental Synd. Def.	1,250	
Chinese Eng. & M.	17,030	
Geduld Deeps	500	Moreing's name
Chinese Eng. Deb.	£4,800	Lous name

Clearly many, and perhaps most, of Hoover's assets derived from the Chinese Engineering and Mining Company's flotation of 1901. During late 1902 the Oriental Syndicate was in the process of dissolution, and Hoover eventually obtained more than 12,000 additional Chinese Engineering and Mining Company shares in exchange.[161] The Geduld Deeps, held in Moreing's name, was a mine in South Africa. "Lous" probably referred to Hoover's wife Lou (with the apostrophe omitted).

During the autumn Hoover steadily sold off his shares in the Chinese Engineering and Mining Company, until by mid-December he had sold more than 15,000 shares for a total of about £15,400, or approximately $75,000.[162] (This was the autumn of rising public outcry about the Kaiping transaction in China.) It seems likely that most of the shares he disposed of were originally free shares issued in reward for his services in transferring the mines to European control. If so, his sale price was pure profit. During the fall Hoover also bought 1,500 shares in the Great Fingall mine and loaned £2,000 to a friend in trouble on the stock market.[163] The scale of Hoover's operations was not massive, but it must have seemed satisfying indeed to a blacksmith's son from Iowa. Seventy-five thousand dollars was a hefty amount of money for any man of twenty-eight in 1902. Only seven years before, he had graduated from college with scarcely forty dollars to his name.[164]

As Christmas 1902 approached, Hoover could look back on a year well spent. It had been a year of transition in Western Australia—from bonanzas and busts to sober low-grade mining, from the day of self-proclaimed "experts" and guinea-pig directors to the day of control by professional mining engineers, from an era of shameless speculation and scandal to an era of conservatism and efficiency. As much as any other man concerned with Western Australian mining, Hoover could take credit for the change.

And then, without warning, a spectacular new scandal broke—in Bewick, Moreing's own offices.

13

The Case of
A. Stanley Rowe

I

O N December 26, 1902, Boxing Day (a legal holiday in Great Britain), Herbert and Lou Henry Hoover joined Mr. and Mrs. A. Stanley Rowe for dinner and an evening at the theater.[1] Such an entertainment no doubt would have shocked Hoover's Quaker relatives back in Iowa and Oregon. But how far in just a decade he had come from his small-town roots. The Hoovers were living in London now, cosmopolitan capital of a world empire. Young, prosperous, adventurous, and progressive, they were not much inclined to be constrained by tradition.

Following the play, the Hoovers returned home to Hyde Park Gate. The evening had been a somewhat peculiar one. Rowe, one of Hoover's three business partners, had seemed agitated and apprehensive about the future. He had even asked Hoover during the performance whether Mrs. Hoover would raise his children should any misfortune befall him. Talking it over afterwards, the Hoovers decided that Rowe was suffering from that British form of depression known as "the liver."[2]

Monday morning, December 29, Hoover went to his office in the City.[3] Rowe was not there. Instead, at 10:00 A.M. Hoover received a letter that Rowe had written the day before. In it he stated that he was compelled to leave London to attend to some business in the country relating to a transfer of shares. Consequently he might not be back in time to attend an emergency Monday meeting of the board of directors of the Great Fingall Consolidated, of which he was secretary. He then made a vague but ominous revelation: he had gotten into deep trouble and had no alternative but to resign as Great Fingall secretary and as a partner in Bewick, Moreing. Saying he had refrained from disclosing this matter earlier so as to permit Hoover an untroubled Christmas holiday, Rowe promised to explain fully when he returned to London on Tuesday. In the meantime he had cabled to C. Algernon Moreing, then on a business trip in China. Moreing's reply, Rowe intimated mysteriously, would ease the situation substantially.[4]

Puzzled and no doubt a little alarmed, Hoover telephoned Mrs. Rowe, only to find her sobbing and nearly hysterical. Hoover immediately dispatched his wife to his partner's household, but A. Stanley Rowe was not to be found. After shaving off his mustache and saying goodbye to his wife and five children (all under seven), he had disappeared during the night. To his distraught wife Rowe had seemed like a man gone insane. He was totally ruined, he told her; he would let her know his whereabouts eventually. But, he said, there was still hope for Bewick, Moreing and Company. He had just begged Moreing by cable to act. If Moreing agreed to do so, the firm would be saved.[5]

But saved from what? While at the Rowes' home that Monday morning, Lou Henry Hoover found that Mrs. Rowe possessed a second letter written by her husband to Hoover the day before. This letter, however, he had instructed his wife to deliver on Wednesday. It was soon to be obvious why Rowe had not intended Hoover to receive it before then. Obtaining this second letter at once from Rowe's wife, Lou sent it by messenger to Hoover's office, where it arrived around 1:00.[6]

It was a confession. In nine pages of anguished handwritten prose Rowe revealed that he had committed forgeries and frauds of massive dimensions. As secretary of the Great Fingall, with access to its official seal and stationery, he had forged certificates for Great Fingall shares. (The certificates were supposed to have been signed by two directors. Rowe had forged their names.) He had then issued this false scrip as security to three large stockbrokers, from whom he had borrowed (he said) a total of £55,000, or more than a quarter of a million dollars. Fifty-five thousand pounds, that is, obtained on the security of worthless paper.[7]

Why? Since the spring of 1902, it turned out, Rowe had been speculating in the stock market. Thoroughly convinced of the future for Great Fingall shares, he had bought heavily when they stood at more than £9 per share. But then a bear market combination had driven the shares down, causing Rowe to lose more than £70,000. In over his head, and deeply in debt, Rowe resorted to the fatal expedient of borrowing more money on the security of forged shares. He hoped desperately that the Fingalls would rise, enabling him to sell his shares at a profit and repay the large sums he had borrowed on fraudulent grounds. Then no one would be the wiser. Unfortunately for Rowe, the market did not cooperate.[8]

The worried speculator's web of deception began to unravel toward Christmas. Late in November Rowe was again anxious for cash. He therefore borrowed about £15,000 from Messrs. Robinson and Company, stockbrokers, on the security of 5,000 (forged) Great Fingall shares. But when the brokers examined the Great Fingall share register shortly afterward, they found that their newly acquired shares were not recorded. Inquiring of Rowe, Lionel Robinson was informed that the transfer had not yet been entered on the books. The next day, checking again, the brokers found the 5,000 shares duly recorded. But when they looked a third time a day later, the entry had been excised with a knife.

At this point Robinson confronted Rowe, who said it was merely due to a mistake in the numbering. Probably to quell Robinson's suspicions, Rowe immediately offered to repay his £15,000 debt. Unknown to Robinson, Rowe had to borrow from someone else to do this. He turned to the brokerage firm of Ruben & Ladenburg, from whom he quickly got £20,000 on the security of yet another forged transfer for 5,000 Great Fingall shares. To stave off one defrauded creditor, he cheated another.

Rowe's frantic effort to placate Lionel Robinson failed. Although not alleging any forgery, Robinson reported Rowe's irregularities to a committee of the stock exchange and to the chairman of the Great Fingall board, Colonel Nisbet, on December 23. The next day Nisbet, anxious to avoid a public scandal but unaware of the enormous frauds involved, personally requested Rowe to resign his secretaryship of the company. In addition, Nisbet said, Rowe must leave the firm of Bewick, Moreing.

Instead of confiding in Hoover, as he promised Nisbet, Rowe said nothing. It was Christmas Eve; he did not want to spoil his partner Wellsted's holiday (he said). But he would be seeing Hoover on Christmas, he said, and would tell him then. Christmas passed, and Boxing Day, and the weekend. Rowe went to the theater with the Hoovers but remained silent. The Great Fingall chairman called a directors meeting for Monday morning. Sunday night Rowe fled.[9]

One of the curious aspects of this sequence of events was the behavior of Colonel Nisbet and his fellow directors of the Great Fingall Consolidated. By Tuesday, December 23, each one of them had received a letter from Lionel Robinson's solicitors disclosing the mystery of the altered share register.[10] Instead, however, of contacting Bewick, Moreing directly or initiating an immediate scrutiny of the books, the directors apparently did nothing on the twenty-third. In a reply on that day to Robinson's solicitors, Nisbet said merely that he was unaware of the matter but would convene a directors meeting on "as early a day as possible" in order to investigate the case thoroughly.[11]

Robinson's solicitors were angered by Nisbet's seemingly casual response. The next day (December 24) they wrote Nisbet: "We should have thought that instead of calling a Board meeting, which probably cannot take place for several days, you would at once have seen the Auditors of the Company, and with them have made personal examination of the register, transfer registers and other books of the Company." Robinson's solicitors also were surprised that Nisbet was unaware of a stock transaction for 5,000 shares, especially since the certificate bore his signature.[12]

Meanwhile, on the twenty-fourth, Nisbet and the Great Fingall's solicitor confronted Rowe, requested his resignation, and told him to report his irregularities to Hoover.[13] Trusting Rowe to do that, they evidently made no effort to notify Hoover themselves.

The Great Fingall directors' conduct was probably explainable by several facts. Robinson's complaint did not allege forgery, and Rowe had reimbursed him promptly. Moreover, they were anxious to avoid bad publicity and apparently thought that they could count on Rowe to settle quietly.[14] And, of course, Christmas was nearly upon them—not the best of times to call in auditors and schedule directors meetings. Nevertheless, for six days Nisbet and his colleagues had an inkling that something was wrong yet did not, it appears, notify the firm of Bewick, Moreing.

Rowe's confession was a mixture of pathos and practical advice. He begged Hoover's forgiveness and expressed remorse for his desperate deeds. He had led an honest and upright career, he said, had meant well, and had harbored no dishonorable intent. He was a victim of circumstances, of temptation— and more to help his friends than himself. Several times he had taken over Great Fingall shares from friends and then absorbed huge losses as the shares fell. Had he not resorted to his first fraudulent loan, he would not have been able to pay the debts he already owed, and several brokerage firms would have collapsed. He could not bear to see such a fate befall his friends.

Still, he told Hoover, there was a way out. Let Moreing pay back the unsecured £55,000. He could afford it; Rowe had made more than that much for him. Only £20,000 was needed at once; the rest could be paid back later. Ruben & Ladenburg need not even know that anything was amiss. Rowe, meanwhile, would resign. If Moreing would take over Rowe's share of the partnership Rowe would apply all his interest toward repayment of the £55,000. With Moreing's cooperation, public scandal and disgrace could be averted.[15]

In the meantime Rowe had been communicating with Moreing directly. At 10:20 P.M. on Sunday night, the twenty-eighth, he cabled his senior partner in Tientsin. Rowe revealed that his irregularities probably would be exposed and would cause Bewick, Moreing irrevocable harm unless Moreing came speedily to the rescue. While Rowe's own situation was hopeless, it was still possible, he argued, to salvage the firm.[16] Having cabled his plea to Moreing, Rowe vanished into the night.

Reading Rowe's pitiful confession the next day, Herbert Hoover was stunned. Of the four partners, only the two youngest—himself and Wellsted— were in London. Moreing, the senior partner, was in China, at least four weeks' travel away, dickering with Gustav Detring over the promised 50,000

Chinese Engineering and Mining Company shares and endeavoring to cool Chinese anger over the Kaiping mines affair.[17] What on earth to do?

At once Hoover and Wellsted called in auditors, notified the Great Fingall board of Rowe's confession, and communicated to the brokers who held the forged shares.[18] Later that afternoon the two partners convened a meeting of prominent City brokers, including Francis Govett. Reeling under the blow, Hoover and Wellsted felt the need for advice from older, more experienced business leaders. From them Hoover received a fresh unwelcome disclosure. Rowe's forgeries were not the only irregularity he had committed. In contravention of his partnership agreement Rowe had been keeping a large speculative open account in Great Fingall shares.[19]

Like Rowe, Hoover would have preferred—he told the assembled brokers—simply to settle accounts with the holders of forged shares and to avoid any scandal or "public noise."[20] But it was now too late for that. Already, thanks to Lionel Robinson, stories and rumors were circulating on the stock exchange, where Great Fingall shares were falling sharply.[21] By the next morning the affair would be disclosed in the press.

Sure enough, the latest mining sensation exploded on Tuesday, December 30, in the London newspapers. "Great Share Forgery," proclaimed one headline.[22] "The Latest Westralian Scandal," said another.[23] The distasteful term "Westralianism"—a synonym for reckless and sometimes crooked finance—was once again on investors' lips.

The news accounts, however, also contained a remarkable announcement. Said the *Daily Mail:*

> Three of the [Bewick, Moreing] partners seen by our representative last evening, expressed their determination, so far as the firm was in any way nominally involved, however unjustly, to endeavour to make good any losses in which the unfortunate victims might be involved.[24]

Said the *Financial Times:*

> . . . although Messrs. Bewick, Moreing do not admit any legal liability, they propose for the honour of the firm's name to endeavour to come to an amicable arrangement with the lenders of the money on the forged certificates, so that if possible the latter shall not suffer any loss.[25]

The Westminster Gazette:

> Though the firm disclaim any responsibility in connexion with the affair, they have decided, as an act of grace, to make good the loss so that no innocent parties may suffer.[26]

The Pall Mall Gazette:

> Messrs Bewick, Moreing and Co., although repudiating any personal responsibility, propose for the honour of their own name to endeavour to

come to some arrangement with the lenders of the money on the forged
certificates, but of course they have nothing to do with Mr. Rowe's speculative account.[27]

Whence had this news come? Several years later Hoover recalled that the
decision to commit himself and his partners to repay Rowe's losses was his
own: ". . . as the senior partner in London, I decided that there was only
one course to pursue and that was for the firm to undertake to make good all
of these monies."[28]

According to Hoover this daring decision was taken during his conference
with the brokers on the afternoon of the twenty-ninth. When asked what he
would like to do, Hoover replied that he would *like* to pay up the losses and
keep the scandal quiet. But neither he nor Wellsted had the money to do so.
On the other hand, he added, Moreing and the recently retired Bewick were
wealthy men and could well afford to sustain the loss.

According to Hoover, Govett and the other brokers then agreed that if
Hoover and Wellsted were willing to cover the losses, Moreing should be
even more willing. He, after all, had selected Rowe to be a partner; his firm's
prestige was on the line. Hoover turned to Moreing's best friend, J. C. Moreton Thompson, a solicitor, who was present in the room. Did Thompson
think that Moreing personally would supply any cash that the firm could not
locate? Thompson answered affirmatively. And so, Hoover later recalled,
"taking the risk of Moreing's disapproval," and acting without Moreing's
authorization, he issued the assurances that appeared in the press the next
day: the firm of Bewick, Moreing would attempt to make good the losses
caused by a man for whose actions it was not legally responsible.[29]

That evening, December 29, before Hoover's statement of assurance
appeared in the press, he and Wellsted received a cable from Moreing, in
response to Rowe's appeal of the night before. Moreing's message does not
survive among the records of the Rowe affair, and what instructions, if any,
he gave to his junior partners are therefore uncertain. But it appears that
Moreing simply said he was coming home by the earliest possible mail boat
and asked that nothing be done until further notice.[30]

At 8:30 Tuesday morning, with the story now public, Herbert Hoover—
apparently for the first time—cabled to Moreing in China.

Rowe has absconded. We have received confession. Gt. Fingall certificates
have been forged for 15,000 shares; borrowed £55,000 on the security of;
also borrowed £5,000 from Hoover. Rowe's property consists of £12,000
further Gt. Fingall shares being carried over on the market paid to 6⅛.
Some other small amounts besides his interest B., M. & Co. Will be cause
of failure several houses. Great Fingall [down] to £6 [on the stock market].
  Referring to your telegram, if you intend arrange with defrauded parties, do you consider it advisable that you should take over Fingall shares

carried over, with a view to recovering part of loss? Great Fingall mine is
looking better than at any previous time. Shares worth £8.[31]

In two respects Hoover's message was a curious one. Not a word was said
about his assurances—printed in the press that very morning—that Bewick,
Moreing and Company would try to compensate Rowe's victims. Also
noticeable was Hoover's phraseology in the cable's second paragraph: "if you
intend arrange with defrauded parties." *If* you intend. . . . Since Moreing had
evidently not yet made up his mind to do so, Hoover had indeed gone out
on a limb. He had publicly pledged his senior partner to pay out a huge
amount of money—without his senior partner's prior knowledge or consent.

Moreing's reply to Hoover's cable of the thirtieth came in later that same
day from Peking. Yes, Moreing said, if disgrace could be averted he would
pay the losses. However, he would not take over Rowe's Great Fingall shares
that were carried over on the market. He was leaving at once for London.[32]

Moreing's cable was no doubt a relief to his partners. He had sanctioned
their *fait accompli*. They would not be obliged to retract what they had told
the press. Nevertheless, the news in London that day was bad. Although no
duplication in the Great Fingall share register was uncovered, the directors
deemed it prudent to postpone payment of a dividend pending further scrutiny of the books.[33] Meanwhile, it was developing that Rowe's written
confession had failed by far to divulge the true extent of his transgressions.
Not only had he forged certificates for at least 15,000 Great Fingall shares;
he had also forged and confiscated checks and dividend warrants totaling tens
of thousands of pounds sterling. His were no acts of momentary madness
but the clever operations of a skilled embezzler. By nightfall on the thirtieth
estimates of Rowe's frauds had soared to £80,000.[34]

Publicly Hoover and Wellsted tried to maintain a stance of optimistic
silence. "We are engaged in overhauling the Great Fingall papers and
accounts," one of them told the press, "and we must decline to make any
statement at present beyond expressing our belief that the affair will probably prove to be much less serious than has been made out."[35]

Privately, however, the two partners were anything but sanguine. The
scandal was spreading. On Wednesday, December 31, they addressed a new
cable to Moreing:

Position much worse than anticipated. Defalcation covers a period of about
eighteen months. £72,000 has been borrowed on the security of forged
certificates; £45,000 has been appropriated in cash and securities belonging
to Gt. Fingall and Hannan's Oroya. According to the best advice, [Great
Fingall] Company is liable for the certificates; practically certain that we
in turn are liable to Companies. If we go bankrupt should be liable whole
amount in our personal capacity, and entirely ruined for the future and
the firm destroyed. On the other hand, if we settle as act of grace, our

position City would be preeminent. If you can authorize Wellsted to use your Power of Attorney guarantee total and provide immediately £15,000 in cash or £20,000 in securities, most confident should be able to tide over until your return and make terms for gradual payments. Have been advised that all property transferred into respective wives' names within two years will be liable; therefore you and Hoover in any event must pay. Thompson constantly with us. Must reply at once.[36]

In a separate cable Thompson, the solicitor, advised Moreing to accept the Hoover / Wellsted proposal. The two junior partners, he said, had done all they possibly could. They had reached their limit without the assistance they now appealed for.[37] Curiously, neither cable divulged that Hoover and Wellsted had *already* pledged Moreing's credit in the press.

The cables of December 31 underscored the discrepancy between Hoover's public and private postures. For two days he and Wellsted had denied in the press that the firm was in any way liable for Rowe's misdeeds.[38] Now Hoover was asserting to Moreing that massive liability and bankruptcy stared them in the face. Similarly, for two days the newspapers had carried their assurances that Bewick, Moreing would make restitution for Rowe's defalcations. Yet here they were *asking* Moreing to settle "as an act of grace"—as if the whole question of restitution were still open. If they did *not* make this calculated act of generosity, Hoover and Wellsted argued, they would probably be ruined anyway. But if, "voluntarily," they did make the gesture, they might turn it to their advantage and garner the plaudits of the City. Had Hoover and Wellsted perhaps overstated their plight in order to force Moreing's hand? Whatever the case, their plea to Moreing was based not on grounds of ethical obligation but on a frank appeal to self-interest.[39]

It was curious that Hoover and Wellsted needed to cable at all. Moreing had already stated the day before that he would pay the losses if disaster could thereby be deterred, and his cable had already reached London.[40] Perhaps, as calamity threatened, the junior partners craved more formal assurance from their wealthy senior partner. More likely they needed something more substantial than verbal pledges in order to placate importunate creditors. Hence the specific requests for £15,000 immediately and authorization for Wellsted to use Moreing's power of attorney. Matters could not wait until the head of the firm returned home.

On Thursday, January 1, 1903, Moreing cabled his answer from Shanghai. He authorized Wellsted to use his power of attorney to guarantee the total of Rowe's defalcations and to supply £15,000 at once. He instructed his partners to provide plenty of time for gradual payment of the sums due. This was not, he remarked, an easy matter to arrange.[41]

Moreing's message was terse and devoid of sentiment. Was he angry? Did he feel outmaneuvered or trapped by circumstances? It was impossible from his words to be sure. All Hoover knew was that his partner was boarding a steamer for San Francisco, where he would arrive near the end of January en route to London.[42]

I I

ARMED with Moreing's authorization, Hoover and Wellsted worked feverishly to clean up the mess. With each day it seemed that new tremors awaited them. By the end of the first week in January investigators ascertained that Rowe's misappropriations of checks and securities, added to his borrowings on forged stock certificates and transfers, amounted to £100,000 in the case of the Great Fingall alone.[43] Among other things, in January 1900—even before he was a partner—Rowe misappropriated and sold for his own benefit 14,000 Sons of Gwalia shares belonging to the Great Fingall company.[44]

Nor was this all. Rowe also had "applied to his own use" more than £13,000 belonging to his own firm, Bewick, Moreing.[45] Hoover himself personally lost several thousand pounds at the hands of his absconding partner.[46] And in the case of the Oroya Brownhill company, Rowe engaged in an array of complicated frauds and misrepresentations, including outright appropriation of 5,000 shares.[47]

In untangling the maze of Rowe's misdeeds Hoover and Wellsted struggled mightily to contain the scandal. When rumors surfaced that Rowe had forged Sons of Gwalia shares, Wellsted and the Sons of Gwalia board chairman officially denied it. Such rumors, said Wellsted, were "absolutely untrue."[48] This was technically correct. But neither Hoover, Wellsted, nor the chairman publicly revealed that Rowe had actually stolen (not forged) 14,000 Sons of Gwalia shares.[49] Similarly, Wellsted denied that any securities belonging to Bewick, Moreing had been "tampered with."[50] This also was technically correct, if by "tampering" one merely meant forgery. But neither Wellsted nor Hoover publicly disclosed that Rowe had helped himself liberally to Bewick, Moreing monies for his own purposes.

Hoover's and Wellsted's desire to minimize the scandal's dimensions was understandable. One thunderclap (the Great Fingall) was enough. Any new revelations might devastate the Westralian shares market, weaken faith in Moreing's promises, and fatally undermine the reputation of the firm. Not surprisingly, then, the two junior partners perceived the Oroya Brownhill situation to be "by far the most critical one."[51] Here they obtained the cooperation of G. P. Doolette, chairman of the Oroya Brownhill company. Doolette forcefully denied in the press that "Oroyas and Brownhills" were "in some indirect way involved." "You may take it from me," he declared, "that there is nothing in the rumour."[52] On the strength of his assertion the *Financial Times* attacked "irresponsible rumour-mongers" who were allegedly trying "to drag the names of other companies into the trouble."[53] The *Westminster*

Gazette reported the "suspicion" that stock market "bears" were trying to exploit false rumors that the Oroya Brownhill and Sons of Gwalia were involved in the Rowe affair.[54]

While Doolette denied that there was any Oroya Brownhill scandal to contain, Hoover and Wellsted attempted behind the scenes to resolve the dangerous Oroya Brownhill tangle. In addition to taking 5,000 Oroya Brownhill shares and selling them on the market, Rowe had—through a cooperative broker named Aarons—borrowed £10,500 from the Oroya Brownhill company on the security of forged Great Fingall shares. Even worse, he had told Aarons that Bewick, Moreing wished to borrow this sum from the Oroya Brownhill company "without doing so openly." Worse still, Rowe had written letters to Aarons signed by Bewick, Moreing—letters which, Hoover and Wellsted discovered, "implicated us in a most disastrous way."[55] Just how, Hoover and Wellsted did not say. Probably Rowe's letters contained misrepresentations that would prove embarrassing to Hoover and his partners if made public. And Aarons presumably had these letters in his files.

This circumstance no doubt made it more imperative than ever to come to terms with Aarons. Fortunately for Hoover and his partners, the stockbroker had compromised himself in his dealings with Rowe. Instead of turning over to the Oroya Brownhill company £10,500 that he owed to it from a certain transaction, Aarons had improperly handed the sum to Rowe. As security for this loan Aarons had received forged Great Fingall shares from Rowe— shares which now turned out to be no security at all.[56] Aarons's extreme vulnerability vis-à-vis the Oroya Brownhill may have induced him to settle quickly and quietly with Hoover and Wellsted.

And so a bargain was made. First, Hoover and his partner returned Aarons the £10,500, enabling him to repay his debt to the Oroya Brownhill. In this way Hoover was spared an unwanted new scandal. Second, it transpired that Rowe owed Aarons a further £3,600 from his private stock market account and that as security for this debt Rowe had given Aarons more than 7,000 shares of stock he did not even own. Hoover and Wellsted agreed to pay Aarons this £3,600 if he would return the stolen shares. In this way the two partners recovered some pilfered assets. Nevertheless, by the time they got through with Aarons, Rowe's Oroya Brownhill deeds had cost Bewick, Moreing £17,000.[57]

By January 5, 1903 Hoover and Wellsted were able to dispatch encouraging news by cable to Moreing: "We shall be able to pull through with very great credit." But the price was going to be high. They had already sold 25,000 Chinese Engineering and Mining Company shares and 6,000 shares of a mine in southern Africa, presumably to raise funds to cover Rowe's defalcations.[58]

Part of Hoover's strategy was to play for time, to promise that "all will be made good" but that settlement of "details" must await Moreing's return.[59]

In one case Hoover asked a broker who had arranged a £20,000 loan to Rowe on forged security to defer taking action until Moreing arrived back in London. Moreing would have to settle the case personally, Hoover said. He himself was "not in a position" to do so. Hoover indicated, though, that Moreing would come to terms "up to a certain point."[60]

The struggle, however, was far from over. While police searched for Rowe, the firm of Bewick, Moreing confronted assault from a new quarter. On January 2 Lionel Robinson and several other large shareholders in the Great Fingall Consolidated issued a confidential circular, which appeared in the press five days later. Although disclaiming any antagonism toward the Great Fingall board of directors, the signatories called for a meeting of shareholders on January 8 "to consider the present situation" and to "decide upon common action in the interests of the shareholders." Their only motive, they asserted, was a feeling that the board of directors, in the current crisis, should be "strengthened by the infusion of new blood."[61]

Herbert Hoover was not fooled by this pious pronouncement. The Great Fingall Consolidated was controlled by Bewick, Moreing,[62] and Hoover noted that the new "agitation" was emanating from shareholders "inimical to us." Far from seeking a mere "infusion of new blood," the shareholders' movement—in Hoover's and Wellsted's view—was really attempting "an abolition of the Board and the destruction of our position in the Company."[63] The London press echoed Hoover's suspicions. Several papers sharply questioned the good faith of the movement and doubted the wisdom of any major change in the management at this juncture.[64]

Hoover and his allies reacted strenuously to the threat. On the evening before the meeting, the chairman of the Great Fingall board issued a circular of his own. After stating that Rowe's frauds against the company now amounted to £100,000, the chairman reported receipt of a letter from Bewick, Moreing declaring that "whilst not admiting any legal obligation, Mr. Moreing has authorized them to inform the directors that he will recoup to the company all losses it may sustain in consequence of the frauds. Mr. Moreing . . . is returning to England immediately."[65]

In a way this was hardly news. Moreing had cabled his authorization to his partners a week before, and Wellsted was acting on it as early as January 3.[66] Up to then, of course, the press had carried stories that Bewick, Moreing would make good the losses. But it was apparently not until January 7 that Moreing's own formal, unconditional promise to indemnify the company against Rowe's frauds appeared in the press.[67] Perhaps for this reason, its impact was more profound.

For when the meeting was held on January 8, it was clear that the shareholders movement had failed. Instead of acting to overthrow the board, the movement's leaders now joined with it to effect a compromise, and abjured any desire to embarrass Bewick, Moreing in its present "very awkward position." One reason for this change (or so the meeting's chairman, P. A. Horn,

alleged) was Moreing's response to the crisis. Horn admitted that the dissidents' "original intention" had been to appoint a committee "to strengthen
the hands of the board." But now, "in view of the honourable intentions" of
Bewick, Moreing to "make themselves responsible for the defalcations of Mr.
Rowe, the aspect is quite changed."

Horn then unveiled a prearranged compromise, which he had cleared with
Hoover the day before. Two members of the present board of directors would
resign and be replaced by independent directors. For his part, Hoover, representing the incumbent board, informed the meeting that, in response to
many shareholders' wishes, the board would consent to elect two new directors. The meeting then approved two men nominated by Horn and not
rejected by Hoover at his conference with Horn the day before.

Not all the assembled shareholders were content with this outcome. Two
new directors seemed a nice concession on the surface, but they would be a
minority on the five-member board. Why not elect three? Horn's response
revealed nothing—except that a deal had obviously been struck with his
opposition. It had been agreed, said Horn, that "it was best to accept the
nomination of two" directors. Why it was best, Horn conspicuously did not
say. When another shareholder decried the fact that Rowe had been succeeded as secretary by one of his own former partners (Wellsted), Horn
deemed it not "advisable to go into that question to-day." He merely expressed
his conviction that a new secretary would be appointed as soon as the new
directors joined the board.[68] Horn's behavior was that of a man who had
either switched sides or lost the battle.

The attempt to oust Moreing and his associates from control of the Great
Fingall had fizzled. The next day Hoover and Wellsted told Moreing that
they had repelled the dissidents' challenge by "a vast amount of intrigue and
diplomacy, and counter-action" and had "finally narrowed the movement
down" to the election of just two new members of the Great Fingall board.
In this way the "situation" would still be "open" when Moreing returned to
London.[69]

On January 9, 1903 Hoover and Wellsted addressed a nine-page letter on
the scandal to Moreing. Hoover sent it to his brother Theodore for delivery
to Moreing in San Francisco.[70] In this document the two junior partners
sought to explain and justify their conduct during their senior partner's
absence. Evidently unsure and apprehensive still about Moreing's attitude
toward the "moral questions involved of the Firm's responsibility," Hoover
and Wellsted declared that they were leaving this matter "entirely open for
discussion after your return." In fact, they seemed deliberately to play down
the moral dimension of the case. They pointed out that Rowe's "errors" were
fourfold:

1. Embezzlement of corporate securities and moneys, "in which there can
   be no doubt as to the question of moral responsibility";

2. Forging of transfers and stock certificates belonging to various third parties;

3. Debts owed to brokers on Rowe's speculative account;

4. Large personal debts incurred by Rowe.

Only the first two categories, they said, involved any issue of moral obligation. Hoping perhaps to placate Moreing, Hoover and Wellsted indicated that the firm obviously had no responsibility for Rowe's personal (as opposed to his official) dealings.

The affair had been a harrowing experience—"the most horrible events which could possibly have happened to us"—but Hoover and Wellsted took comfort from the solicitude of friends and "the gratification throughout the City consequent upon the policy we have pursued." They emphasized, too, the sympathetic response of the press:

. . . we did the best we could in the Press to give ourselves a creditable turn over it, so that we have had only kindly treatment from the whole of the Press from the very beginning of this matter. . . .

Hoover and Wellsted therefore exuded confidence for the future of the firm:

We think if we can continue the thing on the lines which we have started— and which we believe we have acted in accordance with your wishes—our credit in the City will have been enhanced to a very high standard indeed.[71]

If the reaction of the press was any indicator, Bewick, Moreing had indeed survived its ordeal with an enhanced reputation. Although two newspapers found the decision to fund the losses an act of "quixotism,"[72] sympathy and acclaim for the firm's conduct were "universal."[73] The *Mining World and Engineering Record*, a consistent friend of the Moreing interests, was particularly effusive. The firm's response to the cataclysm, it editorialized, was "courageous"; Moreing himself had acted "most nobly."[74] The *Pall Mall Gazette* said that Moreing's "handsome" act "must be accounted to him for righteousness."[75] Several papers noted that the scandal ironically had befallen the very firm which had been endeavoring so vigorously to rescue Westralian mining from "the quagmire of disrepute."[76]

Beyond these pleasant signs of increased stature, the episode taught Hoover an abiding lesson. Probably for the first time, he came to appreciate the power and strategic value of the press. His firm's magnanimity had not only forestalled creditors but had reaped dividends in the realm of public opinion. With the assistance of a sympathetic press Hoover had converted a financial catastrophe into a public relations triumph.

I I I

O N January 19, 1903 Hoover and Wellsted cabled to Moreing in Honolulu, one of the stops on his long trip home.

> Matters proceeding smoothly. £30,500 defalcations have been settled practically without drawing your funds. £65,000 will settle balance. We are now endeavouring to await arrival of yourself before we do anything further.[77]

Eight days later, after reading his partners' long explanation of January 9, Moreing, now in San Francisco, cabled his thanks and appreciation. He approved everything Hoover and Wellsted had undertaken in the crisis, he said, and now he was departing for New York and London.[78]

On February 14, 1903 Moreing arrived home at last.[79] Despite his message of thanks from California, the firm's senior partner was anything but satisfied by the situation he was in. According to Hoover, Moreing "returned to London in a towering rage," only to find himself "committed beyond redemption." Then, said Hoover, Moreing "made the best face of it, and subsequently for many years afterwards, never failed to claim the credit" for the decision to assume the burden of Rowe's frauds.[80] A decision that Hoover, in fact, had made first.

To be sure, Hoover and Wellsted had asked for and received Moreing's sanction for their acts. But as they had outlined their predicament to him by cable, they really left him no choice. The grim alternative to an "act of grace," they asserted, was bankruptcy and ruin. And so, apparently with reluctance, Moreing acquiesced. It seems likely that Hoover's commitment of Moreing's financial resources on December 29, a commitment carried in the press before Moreing approved it, opened a rift with his senior partner, a rift that widened in the years ahead.

Moreing certainly had reason to feel unhappy. Five days after his return, Wellsted informed the press that Rowe's enormous defalcations amounted to nearly £140,000—nearly seven hundred thousand dollars. Already Moreing had "made good" £75,000–80,000.[81] Moreing proceeded to apportion the burden amongst himself and his two remaining colleagues. Under the 1901 partnership contract Moreing had been entitled to 50% of the firm's profits, Rowe and Hoover to 20% each, and Wellsted to 10%. Moreing now arranged to divide the firm's losses the same way. He himself would take over Rowe's share and thereby assume 70% of the total loss. But Hoover must bear his share (20%) and Wellsted his.[82]

Unfortunately, neither Hoover nor Wellsted possessed the resources at this moment to contribute their portion. Moreing was therefore obliged to advance their share, to be repaid to him out of their percentage of the firm's future profits.[83] A little over a year before, Moreing had also loaned Hoover

£8,000 for "goodwill" so that Hoover could enter the partnership.[84] It is not known when Hoover cleared up this obligation. Now, in early 1903, he found himself again (and more deeply) in debt to his own senior partner.

Moreing and his two associates also took steps to reconstitute their partnership without Rowe, whom they legally expelled at the beginning of January.[85] On June 26, 1903 Moreing, Hoover, and Wellsted signed a new partnership agreement, effective for seven years from the preceding January 1. Rowe's share was divided between Hoover and Wellsted, so that the new ratio of participation in profits (and losses) became: Moreing, one-half; Hoover, one-third; Wellsted, one-sixth. The goodwill of the firm was reckoned at £15,000, of which Hoover's portion was £5,000. Since Hoover apparently lacked the ready cash to put up more than a fraction of this sum, the firm—in reality, Moreing—loaned him more than £4,500 toward his share. Moreing similarly assisted Wellsted. For goodwill, then, as well as for their portion of Rowe's losses, the two junior partners were heavily in debt to Moreing.[86]

Meanwhile Moreing acted swiftly to exploit his newly attained prestige as a businessman of honor. At the informal Great Fingall stockholders meeting in early January, P. A. Horn, the chairman, expressed his confidence that Bewick, Moreing would change secretaries as soon as the independent directors took their seats.[87] But if anyone inferred from this that Bewick, Moreing was prepared to relax its grip on the Great Fingall, he was entirely mistaken. Less than a week after his return to London in mid-February, Moreing was elected to the Great Fingall board of directors—by the directors themselves. In a circular to the shareholders on February 20, the Great Fingall directors also reported that Moreing had "completely confirmed" the "informal undertaking previously given by his partner" (Hoover) to compensate the company for all losses caused by Rowe's defalcations.[88] A few weeks later Moreing was elected chairman of the Great Fingall board.[89]

Moreing's sudden accession to the board without any stockholder vote was controversial, and some of the press endeavored to cast it in an agreeable light. The ever-friendly *Mining World and Engineering Record* said that the directors acted "wisely and well" in choosing Moreing as their leader. As managers and consulting engineers of the Great Fingall mine, Moreing's firm had "reduced costs to a point which can challenge comparison with any property on the Westralian field." Bewick, Moreing's management had produced "brilliant" and "magnificent" results; there was "absolutely no ground of complaint" against it. Furthermore, in reimbursing the Great Fingall for Rowe's defalcations, it had acted in a "noble" and "heroic" manner.[90] The London correspondent of the *Engineering and Mining Journal* portrayed Moreing's new role as almost a duty:

> He recognizes that he must personally help to put the company on a satisfactory footing once more, and has accepted a place on the board of directors.[91]

Since Bewick, Moreing was going to continue to manage the mine, since Moreing had paid off Rowe's losses although not legally obliged to do so, and since he had offered to make his firm legally liable for future misdeeds by its employees, it was "only . . . common sense" that Moreing should become chairman of the board.[92]

Not everyone shared this correspondent's view of common sense. Regardless of the results obtained on the mine, many shareholders questioned the propriety of Moreing's being chairman and dominant influence on the board, while his own firm managed the company.

The controversy erupted acrimoniously in April at a packed annual shareholders meeting of the Great Fingall Consolidated. Moreing, as board chairman, opened the gathering with a glowing account of the mine's success during the past year—a description to which even the opposition did not object. According to Moreing the Great Fingall had only two competitors for low working costs in all of Western Australia: the Sons of Gwalia and the Cosmopolitan, both of them Bewick, Moreing-managed.[93]

The angry anti-Moreing faction, however, led by W. A. Horn, was not interested in discussing the mine's excellent progress. Announcing that he held proxies totaling one-half the company's share capital, Horn launched a vehement attack on the company's structure of management. Horn charged that upon returning to London, and behind the facade of noble generosity, Moreing had exacted from the Great Fingall a quid pro quo:

> Mr. Moreing, instead of proceeding to at once carry out the promises made in his name, proceeds to bargain that if he carries out these promises he should firstly have a seat [on the board], and secondly that the term of his firm's engagement as Managers shall be extended five years.

Furthermore, the directors had abdicated their responsibility to control the mine:

> A firm of mining engineers had been selected to act not only as the mining engineer of the Company, but as practically its Managers and the real control of the Company's affairs placed in their hands. . . . The books and papers of the Company are in the custody of Bewick, Moreing and Co., and before any information can reach the Directors . . . it must come through that firm. The Board of Directors, instead of directing the working of the Company as we expected, . . . in effect subordinate their very responsible position to that of our Engineers.

Horn also criticized Moreing's becoming a director "without any consultation with the Shareholders" and urged him to bow to the nearly "universal feeling on the subject and resign his seat." For Moreing as chairman of the board to give orders to himself as the company's engineer, said Horn, "partakes of comic opera." In addition, it was "preposterous" that the mine manager in Australia should report to Bewick, Moreing and not directly to the Great Fingall's directors. "We must," Horn said, "be independent of any agents of the Company." He therefore requested that both Moreing and the remaining old directors retire, that no director have "an office of profit under the Company" (a thrust at Moreing's alleged conflict of interest), and that from now on the directors have "absolutely dominant power" over the mine management.[94]

F. H. Hamilton, a new director, responded to Horn's sweeping attack. Hamilton asserted that Moreing had become chairman of the board simply because none of the other directors would. Moreing had also promised to resign the chairmanship "at the first opportunity." But why had he been made a director at all? According to Hamilton, Moreing had merely replaced a director who was his own nominee, and it was "our obvious duty" to select the principal over his agent. In addition, Moreing was well qualified and could not vote as a director on matters affecting his firm.

But what about the charge that Moreing had compelled the company to renew his firm's management contract as a condition of his paying off Rowe's debts? Hamilton explained:

When [the other independent and I] joined the Board, we were face to face with the direct loss (apparently) in consequence of Mr. Rowe's defalcations of some £30,000, and an indirect loss which might have amounted to some £70,000. The first thing we had to ascertain was the legal position of Messrs. Bewick, Moreing and Co. towards the Company, and what was the position with regard to us of anybody who had suffered loss?

In the opinion of the Great Fingall's counsel, it was "very doubtful" that Moreing's firm was legally liable for Rowe's crimes.

Well, gentlemen, in those circumstances, the best we could do was to make terms with Mr. Moreing, and I am bound to say that there never was the slightest difficulty in doing so.

Why it was necessary to "make terms" at all—given Moreing's supposedly unconditional pledge on grounds of morality—Hamilton did not explain.

According to Hamilton, Moreing stated that he "would do as he promised" concerning Rowe's transgressions.

Then Mr. Moreing suggested—I do not know whether it is correct to say that he stipulated, but at all events the two things were put together and it was suggested that his firm's agreement should be extended for five years.

Hamilton conceded that the Great Fingall would have to pay Bewick, Moreing £26,000 in fees over those five years. But this sum, he said, was less than the "direct responsibility" that the Great Fingall was avoiding by Moreing's assumption of Rowe's losses. So "merely on the cash basis it was obviously worth our while," argued Hamilton, to "compromise" with Moreing "on the lines suggested." Finally, Hamilton said, the Bewick, Moreing contract was extended for the good reason that the Great Fingall under its stewardship was "one of the best managed mines in Westralia."[95]

So the allegations were correct: Moreing *had* bargained, and bargained hard. From Hamilton's words it was evident that Moreing had retreated from the unconditional offer of restitution that Hoover had first issued in his name, and that Moreing had subsequently authorized. In Hamilton's mind, at least, Moreing might legally refuse to pay for any of Rowe's defalcations unless he got the five-year contract renewal for his firm. Moreing was not *legally* obliged to pay a penny. He had the Great Fingall board over a barrel, and the directors, under the circumstances, came to terms.

The fact that Moreing was "both master and servant" (as one speaker put it) clearly disturbed many shareholders, and at the meeting the opposition revealed that it had the proxies to defeat an incumbent director up for reelection: Moreing's former partner, Thomas Bewick. At the start of the meeting Moreing announced that Bewick had just withdrawn from the contest. The opposition candidate was accordingly elected. But when the fury of the long meeting had subsided, it seemed doubtful that Moreing would be dislodged. While "independents" now comprised a majority on the board, at least one of them (Hamilton) was clearly partial toward Moreing.

The Great Fingall's annual meeting was the subject of considerable comment in the mining press. The *Mining World and Engineering Record* pointed out that the structure of management against which Horn had inveighed was in fact typical of successful mines of the time.[96] The journal roundly defended Bewick, Moreing and Company's record: "They have done more to place the formerly disgraceful management of Westralian mines . . . on a sound basis than any individual or collection of individuals has been able to achieve."[97] The *Mining Journal*, although less than enthusiastic about Moreing's dual role, also acclaimed the firm. Bewick, Moreing was pulling Australian mining out of the "slough" of scandal and disrepute:

> One after another as the mines fell under their management . . . they ceased to be available for the wire-pulling speculator. They have instituted at their mines what is known locally as the "reign of terror," which means that advance information can no longer be purchased from the employés, and the inside pull of the speculator has disappeared. It is not to be supposed that they have done this without making enemies or that there are not people who would like to return to the old days of manipulated outputs and inside information, but the investing public and the mining industry at large have reason to be grateful to Messrs. Moreing, and they deserve a generous and not a grudging support from the shareholders they serve.[98]

Yet if Bewick, Moreing's probity and competence were so exemplary, why was half the Great Fingall company against it? Why the extraordinary animosity displayed toward Moreing at the shareholders meeting—even to the point of forcing a poll to dismiss the auditors for being "closely associated" with Moreing's firm? Was the campaign to discredit Moreing in fact coming from those who resented the efficiencies and reforms he was bringing to Western Australia?[99] The *Mining World* seemed to think so. It portrayed the Great Fingall battle as a struggle between a Stock Exchange "clique" and an eminent firm of engineers. The Rowe affair, it suggested, provided Moreing's jealous enemies, especially "those in whose hands he has refused to be a pliant tool," an excuse to attack him.[100]

Very possibly. But the antipathy toward Moreing may also have derived from more immediate sources. Clearly Moreing himself had capitalized on the Rowe affair to advance his own interests. Perhaps there were other such occasions. Behind their public posture of moral obligation, Moreing and his partners had engaged in some complicated bargaining, private arrangements, and intrigues. The full "inside" story of the Great Fingall scandal will probably never be known. But not every interested party was satisfied by the deals struck. One of the anti-Moreing faction's leaders at the Great Fingall meeting, in fact, nursed a grievance against Herbert Hoover—£6,000 of grievance, as it turned out.

With the conclusion of the Great Fingall meeting, Hoover's immediate ordeal was over. Now must come the long, arduous journey back. Now he must restore his shattered finances, scramble to recover, and start over. If it was any consolation, all the favorable publicity in the press had augmented Bewick, Moreing's prestige and hence its potential prosperity.[101]

He would need it. Hovering over him now was another residue of the Rowe scandal: two lawsuits, which, if lost, would wreck his business career.

I V

IN September 1902 Edgar Storey, a colliery operator in Liverpool, desired to sell 3,000 Great Fingall shares. He contacted A. Stanley Rowe, at this time under no suspicion as a Bewick, Moreing partner and secretary of the Great Fingall Consolidated.[102] Rowe agreed to arrange a sale of Storey's block for £21,000, or £7 per share.[103]

Immediately complications developed. It turned out that Rowe himself was involved in the purchase. Using his prospective shares as security, he borrowed £15,000 to pay Storey but, because of recent stock market losses, found himself unable to deliver the balance. Would Storey mind waiting "until next Account," he asked, for the remaining £6,000? Probably to induce Storey to acquiesce, Rowe stated, "Hoover and I are taking your shares on joint account. . . ."[104]

Rowe's disclosure had its desired effect. Although unhappy about Rowe's inability to make full payment (Storey, too, was losing heavily in the market), Storey was "very pleased to note that you and Mr. Hoover are taking the shares. It is very encouraging to me as a large stockholder to note that you have sufficient confidence in the mine to do so."[105]

Rowe's promises to deliver up the balance due Storey went unfulfilled. Despite Storey's repeated requests the money was not forthcoming. Throughout the autumn the harried Rowe offered various excuses as well as pledges to pay up soon.[106] "Things are so bad," he told the Liverpool investor in November. "I have had most unexpected trouble in arranging my finances . . . such hard knocks that each time I have got the cash ready I have had to pay it out again."[107] Finally, on Christmas Eve, his patience with Rowe's procrastination exhausted, Storey requested return of one-third of his shares. The situation was "not tenable," he told Rowe. ". . . I have no security of any kind. . . ."[108]

Storey was too late. On Monday, December 29, Wellsted informed him by telephone that Rowe had absconded. According to Wellsted, Storey replied, "Why, he owes me £6,000 on some Great Fingall shares he bought of me. I suppose I shall have to lose that."[109] Storey afterwards denied under oath that he made this statement.[110]

Hurrying down to London, Storey met Herbert Hoover on December 30. What transpired in this pivotal conversation soon became a matter of sharp dispute. Two days later Storey asked Wellsted in writing to supply full particulars about the formal transfer of "the 3,000 shares which Mr. Rowe and Mr. Hoover bought from me some time ago."[111] Hoover's reply to Storey's letter was swift: "I should like to call your attention to the fact that I have never purchased any shares from you, in any shape or form."[112]

Clearly, it seemed, some misunderstanding had arisen. On January 3, 1903 Storey wrote to Hoover:

> When I asked Mr. Rowe some time ago whether he could find me a purchaser for 3000 shares he replied that he could, and on my confirming the sale he wrote that you and he were taking them between you. This fact you admitted and confirmed to me personally only last Tuesday [December 30] when I saw you at your office.[113]

The point of this dispute was immediately obvious. If Hoover and Rowe really had bought the 3,000 shares from Storey *on joint account*, Hoover was jointly liable for the unpaid £6,000 debt to Storey. Now that Rowe had skipped town, Storey was anxious to collect his money from the remaining purported debtor. On January 5 Storey's solicitors requested that Hoover pay the £6,000.[114]

Hoover immediately refused:

. . . I have never purchased any Fingall shares from Mr. Edgar Storey, nor had any transactions with him, nor authorised any one to have transactions with him on my behalf, in any connection whatever, either on loan or joint account of Mr. Rowe.[115]

Hoover flatly contradicted Storey's version of their meeting on December 30:

As to your statement that I admitted and confirmed this [taking the shares on joint account] personally to you last Tuesday, I did nothing of the kind. I told you that I had purchased 1500 shares from Mr. Rowe, but your name is unknown to me in the transaction and I am quite sure that the shares concerned are in no way connected with you. I have never had any shares delivered, although I paid my money.[116]

Hoover, then, admitted that he had bought from Rowe 1,500 Great Fingall shares (half of Storey's block of 3,000). But, he insisted, he had bought these shares *from* Rowe, not *with* him. In Hoover's version of the affair, Rowe had purchased 3,000 shares on his own from Storey and then resold half of them to Hoover in an entirely independent transaction. Legally, this made all the difference: it meant that Hoover had no liability toward Storey whatever.

Evidently Storey confronted Hoover again, for on January 9 the American engineer addressed another letter to the Liverpool businessman:

Since thinking over your unkind remarks of yesterday I am led to the conclusion that your action has not been the result of misunderstanding on your part but a deliberate attempt to draw me into entirely wrong position of obligation to you and as such is certainly far from what I expected of a gentleman of your standing.

In sacrificing my entire means to make good claims of only moral character against my good name, and in doing so indirectly benefit yourself as well as others it seems very unkind to be subjected to such actions as the last; and is one which many of the best people here denounce in more strong terms than I have permitted myself.[117]

Through his solicitors Hoover pointed out that he himself was "a heavy loser" because of Rowe's "failure to deliver certain shares for which Mr. Hoover had paid. . . ." He also again denied that he had formed a joint account with Rowe or had authorized Rowe to make such a representation to Storey.[118]

The dispute now took a decisive turn. On January 17 Storey filed suit against Hoover and the absent Rowe to recover the unpaid £6,000.[119]

The trial was held in the High Court of Justice, King's Bench Division, in London on May 18, 1903. At Hoover's request a special jury of businessmen heard the case.[120] Hoover's courtroom attorney was Rufus Isaacs, later the

brilliant prosecutor of the notorious Whittaker Wright. According to the judge
the question was this: was Storey's sale in September 1902 made to Rowe
acting jointly with Hoover, or to Rowe alone, who afterwards sold half of
them independently to Hoover?[121] Or as the defense preferred to phrase it,
was there any evidence that Hoover had authorized Rowe "to pledge his
credit in respect of 3,000 shares"? For Hoover to be liable, Isaacs argued, it
must be proved that he actually authorized Rowe to make a joint purchase
from Storey.[122]

The evidence presented in Storey's behalf was legally tenuous. To be sure,
Rowe had *told* Storey that Hoover was in joint account, and Storey no doubt
believed it. But Rowe's assertion by itself could not prove authority. As Hoover's lawyer remarked, ". . . no man could pledge another man's credit without authority to do it. . . ."[123] Rowe's letters to Storey were not evidence
against Hoover "unless Hoover authorised them."[124] Up to December 29 all
of Storey's correspondence and transactions, in fact, had been with Rowe
alone.[125] And Hoover swore that he never knew about this correspondence.[126]

Storey's case against Hoover boiled down to his version of the crucial
interview of December 30. When Storey asked Hoover in this conversation
about the 3,000 shares, Hoover (according to Storey) replied that Rowe had
come to him about Storey's shares and said, "Will you take them with me?"
At first Hoover had demurred, telling Rowe, "I cannot afford to pay for
them." But Rowe had said, "That does not matter. What can you put up?"
Hoover had replied that he could only supply £5,000. According to Storey,
Hoover admitted to him on December 30:

> He [Rowe] took my £5,000. I have lost that, and all I have got from him
> was a receipt saying he had taken this from me against Great Fingall Shares,
> and that receipt even now has disappeared.[127]

All this Hoover confided to Storey on December 30—according to Storey.
Under cross-examination the Liverpool businessman insisted that Hoover
had mentioned receiving from Rowe a "receipt" he could not now locate—a
"receipt," Storey emphasized, not a "memorandum."[128] The legal significance of Storey's assertion was enormous. If Hoover really had obtained a
receipt from Rowe for a £5,000 contribution toward the purchase of Storey's
shares, this would corroborate Storey's claim that a joint Hoover/Rowe
account existed. Hoover's case would collapse and he would lose £6,000.

Hoover's version of the December 30 interview was radically different:

> I extended my sympathy to Mr. Storey in the matter, and told him that I
> had also lost, personally, a considerable sum, and I am not quite sure but
> I think Mr. Storey asked me how that was and I told him that I bought
> from Mr. Rowe 1,500 Fingall shares, on which I had paid him a sum of

£3,000 or £4,000. Mr. Storey made some inquiries about the time and particulars of this, and I told Mr. Storey that the memorandum which I had of the matter had been mislaid, but that I would be glad to get the details when I could get hold of them if I could. . . . I told him that Mr. Rowe, before he had gone, had destroyed a lot of papers and we were generally at sixes and sevens at that moment. . . . I told Mr. Storey at that time that it was the intention of myself and the partners to make good all those frauds of people who had entrusted us with the management of their business.

Hoover flatly denied telling Storey that he had a "receipt" signed by Rowe: "I never said anything of the kind." What he did mention to Storey, he testified, was an entirely different document: a "memorandum" that he himself had prepared but that was mislaid at the time of Storey's visit.[129]

To substantiate his testimony Hoover produced at the trial what he said was this very memorandum. He testified that the document had turned up a few days after his conversation with Storey.[130] It was a kind of diary of Hoover's personal stock transactions from September to December 1902.[131] The first relevant entry was September 25, one day after Rowe informed Storey that "Hoover and I are taking your shares on joint account":

Sept. 25   Agreed buy from Rowe
                  Fingalls, 1,500
             Price best   pd.   1,500 on a / c.

This entry stated that Hoover purchased 1,500 shares *from* Rowe, not 3,000 shares with him. ("Price best," Hoover explained, meant the highest stock exchange price for the shares that day. It was afterward agreed upon as £7 per share.)[132] The second entry revealed a further transaction with Rowe:

Oct. 15   Agreed pay Rowe £2,500
            a / c Fingalls (1,500) purchased
            at 7 0 0   £10,500.
            Dividend also credited £475.

As it happened, Hoover found (after consulting his checkbook) that he actually had paid £2,000, not £2,500, on October 15.[133] Thus Hoover's memorandum showed that he had handed Rowe a total of £3,500 toward the purchase of 1,500 shares—yet had never, so he told Storey and the court, actually received the shares.[134]

Like Storey's correspondence file with Rowe, Hoover's undated "memorandum" had questionable evidentiary value. "It is like an ordinary entry in a diary, only it is worse, because it is not in a diary at all," the judge remarked.[135] Storey's attorney claimed that the memorandum was worthless, "not evidence at all really": "There is no telling when it was made."[136] The attorney also found it strange that Hoover supposedly purchased the shares from Rowe, and even paid £3,500 toward them, yet never got delivery of the shares. This was "an abominably unbusinesslike method," he argued. He urged the jury to "consider the probabilities of the case."[137] It was obvious that to him the probabilities were that Hoover had never bought any shares *from* Rowe at all—hence no delivery.

Hoover's attorney vigorously rebutted the implication that Hoover was "concocting a story." "It was not even put to him [in cross-examination]," he protested, "and there is no foundation for the suggestion that a gentleman who has been in the city for some years would do anything of the kind."[138] Of Hoover's credibility generally, Isaacs noted that Hoover belonged to a "respectable firm" and had been in business for several years. ". . . I really do not know why you should not believe him; I do not know why suggestions should be made against him. . . ."[139]

As for Hoover's failure to get delivery of his 1,500 shares from Rowe, Hoover conceded on the witness stand that he had been "very" naive to pay Rowe £3,500 without receiving any security in return. But his behavior, he contended, had been quite understandable in context. He had turned over the purchase money to Rowe as a favor because Rowe had asked him. He had trusted Rowe. After all, "Mr. Rowe was my partner and my friend."[140]

Hoover's attorney hit hard at a seeming discrepancy in Storey's account of his December 30 meeting with Hoover. At the trial Storey unequivocally stated that the word used that day was "receipt," not "memorandum." "I did not hear him use the word 'memorandum,' " Storey testified.[141] Yet on January 9, only a few days after the event, Storey's own solicitors used the word "memorandum" to describe the document Hoover allegedly told Storey he had obtained, signed, from Rowe.[142] And in pre-trial interrogations Storey used the word "memorandum" to describe the document Rowe allegedly gave to Hoover stating that Rowe "was holding half of the said 3,000 shares" for Hoover.[143] Under cross-examination Storey professed not to discern "any great importance" in which term had actually been used but repeated that the word Hoover did use was "receipt."[144] To Hoover's attorney, however, it "makes all the difference."[145]

In the end, with two contradictory accounts of the December 30 conversation before the court, it was—legal issues aside—a question of Storey's veracity (or recollection) versus Hoover's. "Which do you believe?" the judge remarked to the jury, adding that the case was "quite open to doubt."[146] After twelve minutes of deliberation the jury found for the plaintiff.[147]

Hoover promptly appealed. Among other grounds, he argued that the verdict was "against the weight of the evidence" and that there was in fact "no evidence" that he had authorized Rowe to make a contract with Storey on his behalf. Hoover also asserted that the judge misdirected the jury in various important ways.[148] Throughout the summer and early autumn of 1903 Hoover waited for the Court of Appeal to render its verdict.

Meanwhile the mess left behind by Rowe had generated yet another lawsuit—and yet another headache for Hoover. Just before the collapse of his stock gambling in December 1902, Rowe borrowed £20,000 through a firm of friendly stockbrokers, Ruben & Ladenburg. As security he presented a certificate for 5,000 shares in the Great Fingall. Unknown to Ruben & Ladenburg, the certificate was forged. The cooperative brokers placed the certificate with Lazard Brothers & Co., bankers, who thereupon furnished the £20,000, which was passed on to Rowe. Two Lazard Brothers representatives became the owners of the transferred shares.

A few days later Rowe absconded, and Lazard Brothers discovered that its representatives were not listed on the register of Great Fingall shares. When Lazard Brothers requested that its representatives be added to the list, the Great Fingall company refused. The certificate for the 5,000 shares, it pointed out, was a forgery. Lazard Brothers then turned to the intermediaries, Ruben & Ladenburg, and demanded either new security for its loan or repayment of the £20,000. Ruben & Ladenburg repaid the loan.

Now it was Ruben & Ladenburg which found itself out of pocket for £20,000, and with no security on which to foreclose. On March 13, 1903 Ruben & Ladenburg filed suit against the Great Fingall for £20,000 (plus interest) in damages for refusing to honor the forged certificate issued by its former secretary. Bewick, Moreing and Company was cited as co-defendant on the grounds that it effectively controlled the defendant company and was bound by the acts of its former partner Rowe, who had been its appointee and agent as secretary of the Great Fingall Consolidated at the time. In its suit Ruben & Ladenburg claimed £20,000 (plus interest) against Bewick, Moreing if it failed to collect from the Great Fingall.[149]

The two unfolding lawsuits posed an immense financial peril for Herbert Hoover. All through 1903 the stark specter of ruin from adverse court judgments hung over his head. Shortly after the initial Storey verdict in mid-May Hoover confided to his brother Theodore:

I have just had a judgement against me for another $35000 on account of Rowe making with the $150000 that I paid voluntarily about everything I possess—also have a further suit on for $100000 more which if I lose will ruin me completely as it means bankrupcy and my retirement from London.

Hoover thought he had a "fair show to win the case" against Ruben & Ladenburg.[150] But the strain was unending.

The second suit was tried in London in late November and early December 1903. Each side had much claim to equity. Everyone admitted that when Ruben & Ladenburg arranged the loan it had ample reason to rely upon the validity of the share certificate produced by Rowe. The certificate contained every appearance of genuineness, including the Great Fingall's official seal. There had been no reason at that time to distrust Rowe, who was in fact an officer of the Great Fingall and a proper individual to deliver the certificate. On the other hand, the certificate Rowe delivered was forged and invalid. Moreover, in forging it Rowe undeniably acted fraudulently, entirely for his personal advantage, and not "on behalf of or for the benefit of" the Great Fingall company. Nor did the Great Fingall directors authorize Rowe to issue the certificate or use the official seal.[151] Nor had the company been accused of being negligent.[152]

Who, then, should bear the burden—£20,000 of burden—for the bankrupt Rowe's misdeeds? The innocent, defrauded firm of stockbrokers? Or the innocent Great Fingall company, whose servant had committed forgery?

While the Ruben & Ladenburg case was wending its way to trial, another event excited London. On September 17, 1903 Rowe was arrested in Toronto, Canada, where he was working under an alias in the office of a stock-broker.[153] In fact, he was about to become a partner when he was traced by a detective and apprehended.[154]

Brought back to London for trial, Rowe appeared in the Central Criminal Court on December 17 and pleaded guilty to three counts of forgery and fraud. Rowe's lawyer gamely pleaded for mercy, arguing that Rowe's fate had resulted from yielding to a "terrible temptation." But at the trial it was revealed that in 1885, at age 20, Rowe had been convicted of embezzlement and sentenced to nine months in prison. Several years later he had robbed another employer, who, however, had not pressed charges. With these revelations, any lingering solicitude for A. Stanley Rowe dissipated. Were it not for Moreing's "exceptional and high standard of honour," the judge declared, many people would have suffered from Rowe's crimes. The judge sentenced Rowe to ten years' imprisonment. Upon hearing his words Rowe fainted in the dock.[155]

If Hoover took any satisfaction from Rowe's severe punishment, the record does not show it. No doubt he was gratified, however, by the judgment of the Supreme Court of Judicature in the Storey case on November 18, 1903. The three-judge appeals court unanimously reversed the jury's original verdict for Storey and entered unequivocal judgment for Hoover. There was no evidence, the court ruled, that Hoover gave any prior authority to Rowe to bargain in his name with Edgar Storey before the 3,000-share sale contract was consummated in mid-September 1902. And this, said the chief judge, was "the whole point in the case." If no prior authority was proven, then no Hoover contract with Storey was proven and therefore no Hoover liability to Storey. Furthermore, the trial judge had misdirected the jury by not adequately stating that the Storey / Rowe letters of 1902, including Rowe's "joint-account-with-Hoover" letter, were "simply nothing in the case at all," were not binding against Hoover, "unless they were based on proof of prior authority given to Rowe." In the words of one judge, the "sole evidence of this supposed contract" between Storey and Hoover was Storey's assertion that Rowe had said to Hoover in September, "Storey wants to sell 3,000

Great Fingalls. . . . Will you take them with me?" The judge indignantly commented: "Was there ever such slippery evidence offered to prove a contract?"[156]

Now it was Storey's turn to appeal—to Great Britain's highest tribunal, the House of Lords. Meanwhile, on February 6, 1904, the judge in the Ruben & Ladenburg case announced his verdict. Prior to his decision the judge had dismissed the defendant Bewick, Moreing from the action for lack of a case against it.[157] But this ruling, although welcome to Hoover, was not as conclusive as it might seem. For what if the judge should hold that the remaining defendant, the Great Fingall company, must pay £20,000 to Ruben & Ladenburg? In that event Bewick, Moreing would still lose £20,000, since it had promised to indemnify the Great Fingall for all losses incurred via Rowe.[158]

The judge decided, reluctantly, for Ruben & Ladenburg. He would, he said, have preferred to side with the defendant company and with the view that a company was not legally liable to pay a third party for losses caused by forgery and fraud committed by its employee without authority and "solely for his own private purposes and ends." Nevertheless, the judge felt obliged to abide by one particular contrary precedent that seemed indistinguishable from the current lawsuit.[159]

The Great Fingall company promptly appealed, and on July 29, 1904 the Court of Appeal unanimously reversed the lower court's ruling. The higher tribunal held that the Great Fingall was not responsible for the fraudulent, unauthorized acts of its servant Rowe acting to promote his own private interests. Ruben & Ladenburg must take their loss.[160] Then this case, too, headed for the House of Lords.

Mid-1904: two lawsuits still undecided, and Hoover's solvency swaying in the balance. A few days before the appeals court decision in the Great Fingall case, Hoover wrote to Theodore:

> . . . with no further bad luck I shall be out of debt and have my share of the "goodwill" of the firm paid for by Jan. 1, 1905, otherwise assetts nil. Nor will I own any share of B.M. Co.'s assetts—they belong to Wellsted & Moreing.[161]

The years 1903, 1904, 1905—tough, hard, driving, striving ones."Worked like a dog," Hoover later put it.[162] In June and December 1903, December 1904, and June and December 1905 he made heavy payments to Moreing toward relieving Rowe's financial burden assumed by the firm.[163]

Finally, on June 30, 1905, the House of Lords delivered its judgment in *Storey v. Hoover*. It was a complete victory for the American engineer. The Lord Chancellor declared that there was "not a particle of evidence" that Rowe had purchased Storey's shares in 1902 on joint account with Hoover. The case should never have gone to the jury. The Court of Appeal's decision for Hoover was sustained and Edgar Storey's appeal dismissed.[164]

It was not until July 19, 1906 that the House of Lords decided the case of *Ruben & Ladenburg v. Great Fingall Consolidated.* Again it sustained the Court of Appeal; the Great Fingall was not liable for £20,000.[165] Ruben & Ladenburg would have to absorb the loss themselves.

Hoover was free.

Why, however, had Bewick, Moreing not reimbursed the brokers Ruben & Ladenburg for the forged stock certificate in the first place? Whatever the Great Fingall company's technical liability (or lack of it) for the £20,000, why did not Bewick, Moreing fulfill its "moral obligation" here also? Why had Ruben & Ladenburg been forced to go to court at all? In his *Memoirs* Hoover, evidently alluding to Ruben & Ladenburg, offered an explanation:

> We found in two cases that the receivers of forged documents were in collusion with Rowe, they having discovered earlier frauds and compounded them. We refused to pay their claims. These crooks brought suit in the courts, but lost.[166]

There is nothing in the written record of the case (including the trial transcript) to corroborate Hoover's allegation. Certainly Ruben & Ladenburg helped Rowe obtain the £20,000 loan from Lazard Brothers, but this in itself was not "collusion" in a pejorative sense. Certainly also Rowe hurriedly procured this loan in order to pay back and perhaps mollify the broker Lionel Robinson. But did Ruben & Ladenburg know that this was Rowe's true intent? Did it know that Rowe already had acted irregularly toward Robinson? Hoover apparently thought so—hence his reference to "crooks" compounding the frauds.

Ruben & Ladenburg, of course, had a different explanation. According to its version, Rowe said he wanted the money in order to buy out the interest of a friend in a joint account.[167] Ruben & Ladenburg thus presented itself as an innocent victim of Rowe's forgery.

The absence of written proof for Hoover's charges is not in itself conclusive. Much went on behind the scenes in the tangled Rowe affair, much that cannot be documented. Perhaps Hoover had good grounds for believing that Ruben & Ladenburg had forfeited any moral claim to Moreing's magnanimity. Curiously, the "friend" whom Rowe mentioned to Ruben & Ladenburg—and whose name he then forged on the 5,000-share transfer form— was Edgar Storey. Rowe, of course, had no authority from Storey to execute any such transfer.[168] When it came to deceiving his friends, Rowe acted with impartiality.

V

How much had it all cost? Estimates varied considerably and an exact figure is impossible to determine. In February 1903 Wellsted publicly placed the total of Rowe's frauds at close to £140,000 (or nearly $700,000).[169] Hoover's attorney in the Storey trial used the same figure.[170] At a bankruptcy hearing in mid-1905 Rowe, then in prison, admitted to forging certificates and transfers for 22,500 shares and then borrowing £180,000 on this false security. As of this hearing Rowe's liabilities exceeded £160,000, of which more than £105,000 was unsecured.[171]

At some point Hoover himself compiled a table showing, in round figures, the "total position" after Rowe's misdeeds. Hoover itemized an array of losses amounting to £157,500. He then added to this another £12,500 for an unexplained entry, "T. Consols" (possibly Tarkwa Consols, a company operating in western Africa), making a total of £170,000. When £20,000 of "law costs" were added to that, his final figure reached £190,000, or well over $900,000.[172] In his *Memoirs* Hoover stated that the "ultimate total" was "about" $1,000,000.[173]

How much of this loss did Hoover and his firm actually absorb or pay back? Of the four categories of Rowe's defalcations listed in the Hoover / Wellsted letter of January 9, 1903, Bewick, Moreing seems to have underwritten completely only the first: the "direct embezzlement of Companies' funds and securities."[174] In the case of the Great Fingall Consolidated, this amounted to at least £31,000.[175] The third and fourth categories, covering Rowe's personal debts and his losses on his speculative account (which was forbidden under his partnership contract), were beyond the scope of the "act of grace." Even Hoover and Wellsted, whose sense of moral obligation seemed more expansive than Moreing's, did not feel responsible for Rowe's purely private acts. "No question" had arisen over these categories, they informed Moreing on January 9. On the other hand, in at least one case (the broker Aarons) they did pay off one of Rowe's private debts in order to attain a satisfactory settlement.[176]

The second category of Rowe's transgressions was more ambiguous: "forging certificates and transfers in the hands of third parties" (stockbrokers).[177] Wellsted told the press in February 1903 that Moreing, just back from China, was handling instances of "forged scrip" on a case-by-case basis "on their merits." He "is inclined to admit moral responsibility in some instances, but is not inclined to extend it to others," said Wellsted.[178] Clearly Moreing must have reimbursed some holders of forged shares. But not all. Ruben & Ladenburg, for instance, in the end had to absorb a loss of £20,000, plus court costs—or more than $100,000. The total *unrecompensed* losses, in fact, may have amounted to £50,000,[179] or roughly a quarter of the grand total.

How much, then, did Bewick, Moreing actually disburse? An undated account sheet in the firm's surviving papers indicates that the firm incurred just over £56,000 (or about $280,000) in "defalcation charges." Whether this included legal fees is unknown. Initially Moreing was obliged to advance all of it, but in the end he absorbed 70% (about £39,000). Hoover (about £11,200) and Wellsted (about £5,600) eventually reimbursed him for the rest: their share of the collective burden.[180]

This financial sheet, however, does not reflect the full financial dimensions of the scandal. At the *Storey v. Hoover* trial in May 1903, Hoover's attorney told the court that Hoover and his firm already had paid £90,000 "in respect of liabilities which were incurred by Mr. Rowe in matters in respect of which they were advised they were under no legal liability. . . ."[181] At Rowe's trial in December, the prosecution declared that Bewick, Moreing had paid out more than £100,000.[182] Several years later the firm stated that its payments in the Rowe case exceeded £120,000.[183] There is little reason to believe that it grossly exaggerated its commitment. More likely the account sheet represented only a partial tabulation of the firm's total expense. Certainly Hoover lost far more than the £11,218.16.3 that the account sheet showed he paid Moreing.

How much more? Hoover's own statements and recollections varied. In mid-1903 he told his brother that he had already "paid voluntarily" $150,000 in the Rowe affair; a year later he put the figure at $240,000.[184] In his *Memoirs* he asserted that he absorbed 25% of Rowe's losses, which he calculated at "about" $1,000,000, thus putting his own share at about $250,000.[185] These figures were probably excessive.

Probably the most reliable figure emerges from the "total position" table Hoover prepared sometime after the event. Of the £190,000 in losses listed, Hoover computed his own liability thus:

HCH Losses

Cash	4500
Shares	4000
Law Costs	1500
Pd. C.A.M. [Moreing]	11200
B M Co.	4200
(Re T. Consols)	
	£25,400

The £4,000 of shares probably referred to what Hoover paid Rowe toward the 1,500 undelivered Great Fingall shares Rowe purchased from Storey. The "C.A.M." entry represented Hoover's 20% contribution to the firm's "defalcation charges" of £56,000. The "T. Consols" entry remains a mystery, unmentioned anywhere in the record.[186]

In all likelihood, then, the total cost of Rowe's transgressions was close to one million dollars, of which Hoover's personal loss was about £25,400, or nearly $125,000. More like an eighth than a quarter, but a staggering load in any case.

It took Hoover at least three years to remove this burden.[187] According to the Bewick, Moreing financial sheet, he paid the last installment of his £11,200 debt to Moreing in December 1905.[188] On his "total position" sheet Hoover noted that it took "all profits" for several years to "pay out even."[189] In a subsequent autobiographical fragment Hoover remarked: "finally July 1st 1907 out of debt and interest in the firm clear."[190]

Yet even the Rowe catastrophe had its silver lining. Bewick, Moreing and Company emerged from the scandal with a "much enhanced" reputation, Hoover afterwards noted, and in consequence its business "grew steadily."[191]

Whatever the exact date that Hoover emerged from debt, W. J. Loring, the firm's general manager in Western Australia, later recalled Hoover's reaction. According to Loring, Hoover was visiting Kalgoorlie when word came in by cable that he was out of debt at last. No doubt jubilant, he opened a bottle of wine.[192]

V I

R o w e's involvement with Hoover's life was not quite over. For several years, while Rowe served his term in prison, Hoover quietly helped to support Rowe's five young children. From time to time Hoover sent checks— £10, £15, £20, £25—to Rowe's unmarried sister who, by 1909, was alone caring for Rowe's sons.[193] (What happened to Rowe's wife is unknown; Hoover later said she divorced her husband after he left prison and then married another man.)[194] For Rowe's sister it was a pitiful struggle, as she strove to save her home for the boys. At one point she begged Hoover outright for help; he immediately responded with a check for £15 and a list of other gentlemen to whom she might appeal.[195] Moreing also sent a small annual sum.[196] In 1909 Hoover even assisted Rowe's sister in an unsuccessful petition, evidently to have Rowe's prison sentence reduced.[197]

In 1911, after serving eight years in prison, Rowe was released. He thereupon wrote to Hoover thanking him for his assistance to his children and asking to meet Hoover personally.[198] Hoover replied:

My wife and myself have done the same for the children that we should have done for any other under similar circumstances and I think your real indebtedness is towards your sister, few people of whose loyalty exist in this world.

I do not think any good could arise from a meeting between us for, when all is said and done, your actions caused me five years of absolutely fruitless work in the best portion of my life; nor do I see that we should have any further relations. I have no vindictive feeling in the matter and I shall be only too glad if by your future career you can re-establish your good name, and above all, give your children a proper position in the world.

If I can be of any fitting service to you, I shall be glad to do so.

He enclosed a check for £20.[199]

Middle-aged, with five youngsters and a criminal record, Rowe endeav-

ored to reestablish himself. He thought he would travel to Canada or the
United States.[200] Evidently, though, he had not quite conquered the speculative virus that had brought him down, for in June 1911 Hoover sent Rowe's
sister an urgent admonition—and an offer:

> I would strongly advise you under no possible circumstances to borrow
> money on your small amount of personal securities; nor have I any confi-
> dence in a shipping business started in Canada.
>
> It seems to me that the only normal thing to do for your brother would
> be to go to the Canadian North West and take a position of some kind
> where he could put himself in possession of an income.
>
> In this matter I shall be prepared to assist to the extent of a second-class
> ticket to Winnipeg. Further than that I do not think I can be of any assist-
> ance.[201]

Whether Rowe ever accepted Hoover's generosity is unlikely. As late as
1913 Hoover sent £10 to Rowe's sister, who told him that her brother was
trying hard (evidently in England) to make it, to come up the ladder again.[202]

And here the record stops. Eleven years after the sensational scandal that
"nearly broke H. C. H." (as his brother Theodore expressed it),[203] A. Stanley Rowe apparently disappeared at last from the life of Herbert Hoover.
Whatever happened afterward to Rowe, his five children, or his sister is not
known.

14

"No Cleverer Engineer in the Two Hemispheres"

I

ON February 19, 1903, in the immediate aftermath of the sensational Rowe scandal, Herbert Hoover published an article in London's *Financial Times*. Using the pseudonym "A Practical Mining Man," Hoover drew attention to an "underlying development" taking place in mining company administration: the rise in London of certain mining firms as "controllers" of mining enterprise. Among these preeminent firms—Hoover cited several names—was Bewick, Moreing and Company.

According to Hoover these ascendant mining firms shared several characteristics. Each consisted of specialized partners, such as "financial men" and "expert engineers," all "devoting their entire energies to the mining business." Most were affiliated with a "central finance company which they manage" and through which mining properties were located for "purchase, development and flotation." The mining firms, using their "financial connection and clientele," would obtain money for these newly floated ventures and then manage them "in detail."

These newly dominant mining firms, Hoover continued, had similar field organizations as well. At the apex of each firm's group of mines, all clustered in the same region, was a "general staff," headed by "the most eminent of engineers." His assistants included metallurgists, accountants, secretaries, and other expert personnel. Under this head office, in the chain of command, were the individual mines, each with its own managerial team, "subordinate to" and "constantly under inspection" by the "general administration." In addition to furnishing superior engineers and administrators, the various leading firms provided their clients office space and staff in London, as well as mine supplies purchased at bulk rates.

According to Hoover, the mining firms he mentioned possessed manifold advantages. No scandal like the Lake View Consols affair in Western Australia had ever besmirched these firms; in fact, their administrative structure in the field rendered such scandals "impossible." Moreover, thanks to central purchasing and other efficiencies, working costs at the firms' mines were "far below" those of "outside companies."

Above all, Hoover lauded the standards of excellence and professional responsibility that Bewick, Moreing and its fellow controlling firms were bringing to the mining industry. They were drawing upon a worldwide network of contacts and pool of talent. They promoted men for proven "efficiency," not because they were "nephews of Directors." They offered employees "permanence of organisation" and broad career opportunities, not jobs tied to a single mine and subject to the "vagaries" of incompetent boards of directors. Anxious to "preserve their credit with their shareholders," the firms endeavored to make their mines yield dividends and were "invaluable" in helping to locate working capital. Their very organization helped to temper the inherently speculative business of mining.

As an example of these firms' acute sense of responsibility toward stockholders, Hoover cited his own firm's conduct only a few weeks before in the Rowe scandal. Such a feeling of obligation, Hoover argued, "is a safeguard for shareholders not to be overlooked." Of all the defalcations which had occurred in London mining businesses, he asserted, "this is the only one that has been made good."

Hoover concluded with an appeal for reform. Each of the rising mining firms, he said, was associated with a number of "every-day working business men" and mining engineers who served as directors of companies in the firm's "group." Such men were dedicated to the "common good of the group and their shareholders." Such a system was superior to the scandal-prone regime of dummy directors and "guinea pigs" still prevailing in "isolated companies." The "obvious reform," Hoover declared, was for shareholders in mining companies to "put themselves under the wing of some group who will look after them, and whose future depends on the business necessity of doing the right thing in order to continue in business." Such protection would not come free, of course; the firms must be "paid for their services." But, claimed Hoover, their fees were "but a bagatelle compared to the benefits which they can confer."[1]

Hoover's article was more than an objective survey of new trends in mining administration, more than a disinterested plea for reform. However accurate his analysis, the American engineer had also written a skillful tribute to his own firm's competence and integrity. In urging shareholders to "put

themselves under the wing" of protective mining firms, he had in effect solicited business for himself. Probably to avoid the appearance of self-advertisement, Hoover discreetly resorted to a pseudonym.

If Hoover hoped to generate new business by cleverly publicizing Bewick,
Moreing's virtues in the press, he could scarcely be blamed for trying as 1903
began. Facing bankruptcy at worst and prolonged indebtedness at best, Hoover was anxious for all the business and prestige he could garner. Besides, he
might have added, what he had written was true, wasn't it? Bewick, Moreing
was steadily "coming to the front" in its principal sphere, Australia, and for
the very reasons Hoover enumerated: well-trained experts, tight administrative control, cost-cutting efficiency, and methodical professionalism. Who
was doing more than he to remove the stigma of "Westralianism" from the
mines of the Golden Mile and the West Australian bush?

Hoover's piece in the *Financial Times* was an excellent sketch of Bewick,
Moreing's administrative structure (and Hoover's self-image) as 1903 began.
At the apex was the "firm": Moreing, Hoover, and Wellsted. Allied with the
firm was Moreing's "central finance company": the London and Western
Australian Exploration Company, with its substantial share interests in
numerous Bewick, Moreing-managed mines.[2] In the field was the chief headquarters at Kalgoorlie, with Hoover's handpicked lieutenants, Loring and
Prichard, dividing responsibility for the firm's operations throughout Western Australia. At the bottom of the pyramid were the mines. Early in 1903
Bewick, Moreing managed twelve large mining companies in Western Australia alone, including such substantial producers as the Lake View Consols,
Oroya Brownhill, and Great Fingall. Twelve mines, 3,000 miners, and one-
quarter of the gold production in the state.[3]

Such a structure could survive even the massive frauds of A. Stanley Rowe.
Bewick, Moreing—said a friendly periodical in January 1903—"has a record
of success in Westralia behind it such as none other approaches."[4] According
to the *Economist*'s mining commissioner, Bewick, Moreing "by the introduction of some of the ablest American mine managers and the sound handling
of the mines under their charge, have helped to raise the industry to a mate-
rially higher plane. . . . Personally, I look on Mr. Hoover as a most valuable
factor in the mining industry to-day."[5]

The structure was intact, as was Hoover's reputation. Now they must win
him a living.

I I

E x c e p t for a trip in March to Genoa, the Riviera, Monte Carlo, and
Paris, Hoover and his wife remained in England for the first eight months of
1903.[6] Lou was expecting their first child in mid-summer, and Bert was
preoccupied with the Storey lawsuit and other debris of the Rowe affair.

Hoover was also busy on other fronts. In January he joined the board of the Oroya Brownhill Company—his second directorate.[7] In the same month he became a director of a small syndicate formed to "carry on a finance and exploration business in the Dutch Indies." The Dutch Indies Exploration Company did not become very active, however, and wound up about 1907.[8] During the spring and summer of 1903 he published several technical articles in professional journals, including a widely discussed essay on working costs in West Australian mines.[9]

On August 4, 1903 the Hoovers' first son, Herbert Charles, was born in London.[10] Five weeks later, on September 7, Lou and the baby left London for Southampton, where they boarded a vessel bound via Gibraltar and the Mediterranean for Australia. On the twelfth Bert departed separately for Genoa, where he joined his wife and son. From there it was on to Western Australia, where they arrived in mid-October and sped inland by train to Kalgoorlie.[11]

As the Bewick, Moreing partner in charge of operations in the field, Hoover had plenty to do during his visit. There were mines and prospects to examine, managers and staff to size up, plants and machinery to evaluate. These were tasks that required an unusual breadth of expertise. Not only must Hoover be familiar with geology and with mining techniques; he must be conversant with chemistry, metallurgy, assaying and sampling, mechanical and electrical engineering, surveying, bookkeeping, and accounting. He must also be an astute judge of men, some of whom probably knew more than he did about their specialties, and a few of whom—one never knew—might not be trustworthy. It was a tough business. And he was only twenty-nine.

While Lou and the baby stayed in Kalgoorlie, Bert inspected Bewick, Moreing mines in Western Australia for more than a month.[12] Hoover brought with him for the purpose an automobile, one of the first ever on the gold-fields, and was able to cover an unprecedented 125 miles a day in the bush. On a lengthy trip to the outlying mines of the north, Hoover covered 452 miles at an average speed of 13 miles per hour, with not a single stop for repairs. To induce Afghan camel drivers on the "tracks" to make way for his horseless carriage, Hoover offered a standard inducement of three bottles of beer. The Afghans moved their beasts aside with zest.[13]

Hoover was pleased by much that he observed. To the Sons of Gwalia directors in London he wrote that his inspection confirmed "in every particular the satisfactory nature" of developments and management at the mine.[14] He filed a similar report about the Great Fingall near Cue.[15] Hoover was also undoubtedly gratified by the completion, early in the year, of the Eastern Goldfields Water Scheme, one of the great engineering feats of its day. From a weir near Perth came a supply of water pumped 350 miles inland to Kalgoorlie's Golden Mile. Five million gallons a day were propelled through the thirty-inch steel pipeline by pumping engines at relay stations along the route.[16] As a result, the price of water and hence the cost of mining declined on the fields.[17]

From Western Australia in mid-November Hoover sailed for the Australian state of Victoria, where his firm had become interested in some alluvial mining properties northwest of Melbourne.[18] Thence to the city of Sydney, and a quick trip up to Brisbane. Then 1,200 miles by sea to New Zealand to inspect the struggling Talisman Consolidated mine near Karangahake.[19]

On Christmas Day, 1903, Hoover and his family sailed from Auckland, New Zealand, for London via California.[20] Since his arrival in October, he had traveled more than 5,000 miles on the ground in Australia and New Zealand.[21] Reaching San Francisco on January 12, the couple spent a week in the Bay Area (including Lou's parents' home in Monterey) before hurrying east for New York. Sailing across the Atlantic on the *Kaiser Wilhelm II*, they returned to London on February 1, 1904. In his nearly five months' trip around the world, Hoover had logged more than 31,000 miles.[22]

For the remainder of 1904, except for a voyage to the Transvaal in mid-summer, Hoover stayed in London, supervising by cable and correspondence his firm's booming operations "down under." During 1903 and 1904 he and his carefully selected mine managers unleashed a blizzard of innovations in Australian mining. One purpose of their reforms was to rationalize record-keeping, eliminate waste, and cut the heavy cost of extracting gold from the earth. Thus in mid-1903 the firm switched to the "short ton" (2,000 pounds) instead of the hitherto-used "long ton" (2,240 pounds) as the measure for mine outputs. In this way, it was said, Australian mines would have a "uniform standard" with that already prevailing in America and South Africa, the better to compare working costs.[23] Similarly, the firm decided to declare gold production in fine ounces rather than the cruder category of bullion.[24] In mid-1904 W. A. Prichard, the firm's co-manager in Western Australia, ordered all Bewick, Moreing-managed mines to use an elaborate, uniform accounting procedure for determining expenditures and monthly working costs.[25] As far as Bewick, Moreing was concerned, the era of slipshod mining was over. In New York the *Engineering and Mining Journal* praised "these progressive engineers" for "putting mining on a business basis."[26]

If order and efficiency were one objective of Bewick, Moreing's reforms, the eradication of fraud was another. During 1903 the firm introduced the custom of opening its mines to public inspection for two days every month.[27] In refreshing contrast to what one journalist called the "idiotic policy of secrecy" still regnant in some companies,[28] Hoover's firm was acquiring a reputation for thoroughness and precision in its mining studies and willingness to make such data widely available. As Hoover emphasized, gold mining was a risky business. One way to counteract the speculators and would-be market manipulators was to compile accurate information about one's mines and supply it publicly to investors.

A recurrent source of scandal in Western Australia was the sometimes deliberate overstatement of ore reserves on mines, facilitating "bear" attacks at the London stock exchange. To prevent such willful miscalculations on properties under his firm's management, Hoover and his associates implemented a rigorous system of checks and balances. According to Hoover, Bewick, Moreing's form of administration was foolproof.[29] According to Prichard, ore reserve scandals under their management were "next to impossible."[30] Hoover's close friend F. A. Govett, the stockbroker, declared that at Bewick, Moreing mines "any mistake in the ore reserves would seem to be impossible, for it would entail collusion . . . involving a very large number of individuals."[31] Said Prichard: ". . . we have reduced mine sampling and the estimation of ore reserves almost to a science."[32] Govett noted that assay plans were maintained and left open for inspection at the mines and that extensive sampling and "check sampling" were conducted.[33] Toward the end of 1904 Prichard succinctly listed some of Bewick, Moreing's achievements and claims:

> To our firm is due the credit of reporting mine developments in Western Australian [sic] simultaneously with their publication in London, the throwing open of mines to the press and the public, a reduction in the working cost of mining, and the recording of assays on plans.[34]

Hoover, too, extolled his firm's accomplishments. In his article on "Working Costs in West Australian Mines" in mid-1903, he observed that a "very great improvement in efficiency of the workmen and in method and quality of mine management" had—despite rising wages—produced "a very great decrease in the actual cost of mining" in the region. Hoover modestly omitted names, but in a table of mining costs that he appended, six of the eight companies he listed were Bewick, Moreing mines.[35]

Several months later Hoover again took up his pen, this time pseudonymously, to describe with approval the growing domination of "mining finance and management" by a few firms of "experienced mining men." Hoover drew heavily on his article in the *Financial Times* a year or so before.

> The business is generally organized on managerial lines. A central exploration company is usually created among their friends, . . . a portion of whose capital they may or may not own. The "firm" manages this company, in return for a portion of the profits. This exploration company searches for mines under guidance of the firm, and finding them, proceeds to develop, equip, and create them into subsidiary companies, which are in turn managed or controlled by the firm. . . .

To Hoover this system had several progressive features. For one, boards of directors of such companies tended to become subordinate to the firm, which in turn was accountable to its "clients" who supplied the capital. Indeed, the firm often put its own partners or close business allies on the board, thereby rendering "mismanagement by directors" a rarity. Moreover, the mines themselves were administered in a "very superior" manner. And aspiring engineers and managers on the firm's staff enjoyed far greater opportunities for advancement than they could achieve in single concerns.

Finally, Hoover stressed the stability, continuity, and ethical sensitivity allegedly offered by the firms. "Transitory transactions for immediate profits, at the risk of good name, are not indulged in," he asserted, "for the name must be sustained." Hoover derided mine management by boards of "titled nonentities" and by the "irresponsible promoter who puts up a dummy board of pompous dignitaries until his shares are disposed of." What mattered now to investors, Hoover remarked, was that a mine was affiliated with a reputable firm, "not that Admiral Sir Dumfunny is chairman." He welcomed the demise of unattached flotation companies whose interest in a mine vanished as soon as the public bought the shares. Asserted Hoover: "The general result is that the 'firm' is rapidly becoming the main source of mine finance—and so much the better for the industry."[36]

If Hoover's essay sounded like a celebration of his own success, it was, perhaps, unavoidable. By early 1904 Bewick, Moreing and Company had taken control of 40% of the gold production of Western Australia.[37] Hoover's firm "seem to be slowly but surely swallowing up the management of all the Westralian mines not only on the Golden Mile, but outside" it, commented the *Colonial Mining News*.[38] One by one, promising small properties as well as big producers were coming within the Bewick, Moreing orbit.[39] On April 13 Hoover calculated that his firm controlled or managed companies in Australia having a nominal capital of $42,100,000 and a market value of $70,550,000.[40] When, later that month, his firm signed a contract to manage the Great Boulder Perseverance mine on the Golden Mile, Bewick, Moreing reached a new plateau: more than 50% of the gold production of Western Australia was now under its direction.[41] By mid-summer, according to Hoover's count, his firm was "interested in the management" of thirty-two mines (mostly in Australia) employing "about 9,000 white men" and grossing £6,000,000 of mineral production a year.[42]

Hoover, too, was increasing in visibility in the mining and financial circles of London. The mining engineer—quite according to Hoover's depiction of managerial trends—was becoming a company director. Two more British-registered companies added Hoover to their boards in 1903–4: the Bellevue Proprietary in Western Australia and the Talisman Consolidated in New Zealand.[43] Now he held five directorships.[44] Meanwhile, in March 1904, Hoover, Moreing, and Wellsted extended their partnership contract from seven years to ten; the new termination date was December 31, 1912.[45]

Why was the firm enjoying such meteoric success? Because, answered Moreing and his allies, it deserved to. In an interview in Western Australia,

Prichard traced the firm's dramatic change of fortunes to Hoover's accession as partner at the end of 1901:

> Two or three years ago the firm was making but little, if any, headway, but the re-organisation of the firm began to bring an increase of business at the beginning of 1902. It was appointed managers of the Lake View Consols and consulting engineers of the Ivanhoe. A big reduction in working costs at the Lake View Consols and Sons of Gwalia, in 1902, was the forerunner of a general reduction in working costs at nearly all of the big mines in the State. The general staff of this firm was changed, and a new superintendent was placed in charge of each one of the mines managed by this firm without exception. The system of mining and ore treatment has been completely revolutionised and the standard of labor improved. The result has been that, without a reduction in wages—in fact wages are higher to-day than two years ago—the firm has reduced working costs 30 per cent. to 65 per cent. during the past 15 months.[46]

Back in London, one mining journalist acclaimed the firm's "services . . . in eliminating speculative management from the West Australian market."[47] And in New York the prestigious *Engineering and Mining Journal* declared that the firm had "won on merit by inaugurating reforms" in mines "which previously had been victims of the worst forms of company mismanagement."[48]

But of what did "merit" consist? Time and again Bewick, Moreing and its friends referred to one fundamental criterion: efficiency. Efficiency, measured by declining working costs, was the key to continued profitable mining of low-grade ore. As wages rose and extraction rates dropped to mere pennyweights of gold per ton of ore, the attainment of efficiency became ever more imperative.

With drumbeat regularity Bewick, Moreing and their "group" cited the statistics of success. At mine after mine the advent of Bewick, Moreing management had led to steady, sometimes drastic—in Moreing's words, "extraordinary"[49]—reductions in working costs. According to a West Australian mining periodical, working costs at Bewick, Moreing mines had been "reduced to a minimum never before attained in Westralian mining."[50] According to a prominent London company director, Bewick, Moreing had "done more than anybody else towards bringing down costs in Westralia."[51]

How had they done it? By "enlarged mills and skilful engineers," said Moreing.[52] In part by the savings made from large-scale purchase of supplies, said many others.[53] In part also by the creation of a joint workmen's compensation fund in the firm's mines, thereby avoiding the "exorbitant" rates charged by insurance companies.[54]

Above all, it was asserted, Bewick, Moreing's success derived from its men. The firm "have at their command the very best American methods," said one satisfied London director.[55] And "very skilled American engineers" as well.[56] In the words of the London correspondent for an Australian mining journal, Bewick, Moreing's managers were "second to none, not only in Western Australia, but in the world."[57] Hoover himself noted that with a large staff "invaluable opportunity for comparative results arises, and the best man is rapidly brought forward."[58] "Merit is always quickly recognised by us," remarked Prichard.[59] "What is the secret" of Bewick, Moreing's "great hold on the gold mines of the 'Golden State'?" asked a Westralian mining journal. "In a word it is their economical system of control. Drones have no place in the mines they manage. . . . the incapable has to go."[60]

Another factor that may have contributed to Bewick, Moreing's spectacular cuts in working costs was the firm's tendency to discharge substantial numbers of workers when it reorganized a mine. At the Sons of Gwalia the workforce in January 1902 numbered well over 700 men (873, according to one tally). By the end of the year, Loring had reduced it to 509. By January 1904 the figure was down to 384. At a number of Bewick, Moreing mines, in fact, the pattern was the same: large workforces in January 1902, much smaller ones two years later.[61]

According to W. A. Prichard, this was due in some cases to the temporary circumstance of "extra construction work" in 1902 and, in some cases, to "flagrant overmanning" (before Hoover's first inspection trip). "When taking over the management of a badly managed mine," Prichard asserted, "we generally make a large reduction in the number of unnecessary men." On the other hand, once a mine was revamped and "placed on an economical basis" more men were hired "gradually as the tonnage increases."[62]

Bewick, Moreing's introduction of modern equipment and ore reduction plants may also have contributed to lessened employment. At the Ivanhoe mine (where the firm served as consulting engineers) F. A. Govett, the board chairman, acknowledged that "improved equipment on the mine" had "reduced our pay roll by very many men." Govett dealt firmly with the dilemma thus created:

Were it not for [reduction of costs] many mines that are working at some profit now would be closed down, and thousands of men now earning high wages would be earning none at all. . . . It is difficult, it is probably impossible, to convince the man who loses his employment that improved machinery and lessened costs are for his good. But it is none the less true, if, instead of the individual discharged, you consider the labourer as a class. The individual cannot be considered, he must suffer, and always will suffer, for the good of the state, and while our improvements have resulted in many losing employment, that evil is more than set off by the good, for two, three, or even four times that number are kept in employ by the same reduction in cost on other mines which otherwise would not be working, or which never would have started to work at all.[63]

While Hoover probably shared these sentiments of his close friend Govett, his firm was not indifferent to the dislocation wrought by his crusade for efficiency. Such sentiments, though, made Bewick, Moreing more popular in the boardrooms of London than on the streets of Kalgoorlie.

Was Bewick, Moreing's record as stellar as it appeared to be? Much of the firm's "case" rested on claims about working costs, but accurate comparative statistics in this area were nonexistent. In 1903 Hoover himself complained about "a most harassing lack of uniformity" in current methods of computing working costs on mines.[64] Even comparisons within Bewick, Moreing's empire were difficult: companies switched to the short ton at different intervals.[65] It was apparently not until mid-1904 that Bewick, Moreing companies in Western Australia adopted a single accounting system for themselves.[66] In Kalgoorlie, meanwhile, critics alleged that Bewick, Moreing engineers deliberately drove their plants "almost to a standstill," charged the cost of replacement plants to the "capital account," and thus kept their working costs (a separate account) artificially low.[67]

Yet if reliable data were lacking, there was no denying the overall trend. Unit costs of mining in Australia were moving relentlessly downward, and Bewick, Moreing—by nearly all reports—was leading the way. Such a record was persuasive enough for the investors and directors who were clamoring for the services of Hoover and his firm.[68]

I I I

With success came acclaim. At annual stockholders meetings in London, directors of Bewick, Moreing-administered companies regularly lavished encomiums on their mine managers. To Govett the firm's "improvement of mining practice in Western Australia" was "beyond praise."[69] An enthusiastic director of the Sons of Gwalia company announced that all who were interested in Western Australian gold mining were "under a very heavy obligation" to the firm: "Out of chaos and confusion they have brought order and method."[70] Often Hoover was personally singled out for praise. To his friend R. J. Hoffmann, fellow director of the Bellevue Proprietary, there was "no cleverer engineer in the two hemispheres."[71]

The mining press was similarly warm with commendation. "There are few men who have done more for Westralian mining than has Mr. Hoover," wrote the London correspondent of the *West Australian Mining, Building, and Engineering Journal.* "Although one of the most unassuming individuals it has been my lot to come across, he is at the same time a steady plodder, a hard thinker, and in every respect capable. The more one knows of Mr. Hoover the more one appreciates him. . . ."[72] From the *West Australian Mining, Building, and Engineering Journal* in Perth, the *Australian Mining Standard* in

Melbourne, and the *Mining Journal, Colonial Mining News*, and other leading journals in London came an almost unremitting chorus of praise for Bewick, Moreing during Hoover's years as a partner.

Particularly laudatory was the weekly *Mining World and Engineering Record* of London, virtually every issue of which contained some favorable reference to the firm. In 1905 the journal compared Western Australian mining before the firm's ascendancy to an "Augean stable." Now, it claimed, mine administration in the state was "on a far sounder basis." Mine managers knew that they could not "play hanky-panky with the interests of British investors," for Bewick, Moreing would be called in to expose "wrong-doing."[73] To the *Mining World* the firm was a team of "physicians" supplying the "balm" of honest management to an industry suffering from the stigma of past scandal.[74]

So copious and complimentary was the coverage of Bewick, Moreing in the British and colonial mining press that it eventually aroused indignation in Australia. The *West Australian Mining, Building, and Engineering Journal*, a staunch defender of the firm, felt obliged to insist that it was "absolutely independent of B., M. & Co. or any other firm" in the state.[75] To cries that the colonial press was showing favoritism to Hoover's firm and slighting its competitors, the Kalgoorlie correspondent of the *Australian Mining Standard* replied: not so. Bewick, Moreing received so much publicity because it had so many mines to report on and because it willingly furnished reporters with ample and up-to-date news about them. The correspondent contrasted the firm's openness toward the press with the attitude of the "secretly governed concerns."[76]

Herbert Hoover fostered this policy of accessibility. One eminent journalist with whom he particularly cooperated was the *Economist*'s special mining commissioner, J. H. Curle, author of *The Gold Mines of the World*. It was Curle who in early 1903 publicly extolled Hoover as "a most valuable factor in the mining industry to-day."[77] Curle became a close and admiring friend of Hoover, whom he had first met on a trip to the Sons of Gwalia in 1898. The two men were traveling companions on Hoover's tour of outlying mines in Western Australia in October 1903. Hoover also journeyed with Curle to the Transvaal in 1904 and sublet his London apartment to him during part of 1906.[78] Not surprisingly, Curle's columns in the *Economist* were full of information about Bewick, Moreing mines that he inspected.[79] In mid-1903 he declared that there were "no better worked mines in the world" than seven (which he then listed) in Western Australia. Every one of them was affiliated with Bewick, Moreing.[80]

Curle was not the only journalistic Hoover-booster. The London correspondents of the *Engineering and Mining Journal* in New York and the *West Australian Mining, Building, and Engineering Journal* frequently praised Bewick, Moreing. The mining editor of the *Financial Times* often called on Hoover to evaluate privately some dubious proposition. Together the two men would analyze the evidence. On the strength of their assessment, the editor would fire away in the *Financial Times*.[81]

There is no reason to doubt the sincerity of Curle and his fellow correspondents. To them, Hoover—frank, approachable, and thoroughly knowledgeable—must have seemed a refreshing rarity in an industry long afflicted with charlatans, incompetents, and brazen, smooth-talking promoters. Nor is there any evidence that Bewick, Moreing distributed mining stock to friendly newspapers or otherwise tried to purchase favorable publicity, practices not unknown in the late 1890s.[82] The sheer breadth and volume of the firm's journalistic support argues against the possibility of subsidized puffery (although one or two journals were so effusive as to raise that suspicion). By and large the firm's backers were probably right: it got a good press because it deserved to.

Some of this avalanche of admiration, however, was clearly not disinterested. When directors at annual stockholders meetings roundly complimented Bewick, Moreing, they indirectly praised their own astuteness in hiring the firm. Moreover, many of these directors were personal friends of Hoover and his partners—members, that is, of the firm's "group." After the meetings, verbatim transcripts of the proceedings were usually published in the mining press, at the companies' own expense. These accounts, with their laudatory references to Bewick, Moreing, thus became a form of advertising for the firm.

Hoover was keenly aware of the power and usefulness of the press. Not only was he friendly with a number of journalists; at times he became one himself. In addition to his steady production of signed articles in professional journals, Hoover, between 1902 and 1904, wrote at least nine pseudonymous contributions for the *Financial Times*.[83] W. A. Prichard later told a Stanford professor that the man who got ahead of Hoover would have to spend more than twenty hours a day scheming out his plans, for that was what Hoover did. According to Prichard, if Hoover had a project he wished to promote, he would first write a letter to *The Times*, using an alias, criticizing the idea. Then, under his own name, he would publish a devastating rejoinder advancing the arguments that he really wished to get across.[84]

Prichard gave no example of this alleged practice, and none has surfaced. But on one known occasion Hoover did use the letter-to-the-editor device to help torpedo a huge mine merger in Kalgoorlie. On January 21, 1903 Hoover became a director of the Oroya Brownhill company. Two days later, in his absence, most of his fellow directors met with representatives of two other mines on the Golden Mile and tentatively approved an amalgamation. Convinced that the terms of the scheme were extremely unfair to the Oroya Brownhill, Hoover, under the pen name "A Colonist," criticized the proposed amalgamation at length in a letter to the *Financial Times*.[85] The next day he attacked it again in a letter written from the standpoint of one of the other companies. This time he styled himself "Consulting Engineer."[86]

On January 27 Hoover persuaded his fellow directors of the Oroya Brown-hill to repudiate their agreement of the twenty-third. After some abortive maneuvering the merger negotiations collapsed.[87] The press called it a "fiasco." Hermann Landau, chairman of the other two companies, angrily labeled it "the last convulsion of the dirty era."[88] But to Hoover, Landau's had been a shoddy scheme, properly thwarted—with the aid of his campaign in the *Financial Times*.

Hoover "valued judicious publicity," stated F. H. Bathurst, a journalist who knew him during his Bewick, Moreing years. On one occasion Bathurst publicly criticized certain Australian mining companies for selling poten-tially valuable zinc tailings to Hoover's "group." As Bathurst later recalled, Hoover "railed" at him for so saying. "What have you to grumble at?" Bathurst rejoined. "No one blames you or anyone else for having bought on the best terms. It is the sellers who are foolish, and they have to be told so." Hoover then protested that Bathurst was being too critical of a certain individual. Bathurst replied, "Not more so than I feel is deserved. Anyhow, what does it matter to you? Such comment is your strongest bull point." Hoover fell silent, but that was not the end of the episode. The offending comment was afterwards reprinted, probably at Hoover's own instigation, in the *Financial Times*—as Bathurst put it, "to show shareholders of Hoover's company what bargains they had obtained."[89]

Yet Hoover abhorred publicity that focused too directly on himself or appeared to be overtly self-serving. In mid-1904, for example, he prepared, on behalf of his firm, a statement for a royal commission investigating tech-nical education in Great Britain. His memorandum described the firm's administrative practices and its views on the proper training of mining engi-neers. Hoover gave a copy of his document to David Starr Jordan, president of Stanford University. When Jordan asked Hoover's permission to publish it in a leading science journal with the explanation that it came from a private letter, Hoover readily consented. He gave Jordan permission to make any use of it that he wished.[90]

Apparently, however, Hoover forgot that he had done so, for when his essay appeared a few months later in *Science* and the *Stanford Alumnus*, he was mortified. According to his wife, Hoover vowed that he would never put his pen to paper again. To Lou (and probably to Bert as well), the worst feature of the article was that it appeared without any explanation of its context. No reference was made to the royal commission for whom Hoover had pre-pared the piece in the first place. Instead, the essay—which, read alone, might seem self-congratulatory—was identified only as an "extract from a private letter." To Lou and no doubt her husband, too, the result seemed inexpressibly egotistical.[91]

Thus while eager to promote his business interests through the media, Hoover himself nevertheless shrank from the limelight. In the perceptive phrase of a later historian, he was an "aggressive introvert."[92] A genuine shyness and reserve, deepened by the trauma of orphanhood, made him extremely uncomfortable in open self-advertisement. His Quaker upbringing, with its emphasis on doing good modestly, only reinforced his tendency toward self-effacement. Probably, too, his years in Oregon with his Uncle John taught him the penalties of blunt self-assertion and the rewards of circumspection.

But if Hoover did not crave personal or *uncontrolled* publicity, he was quite willing to orchestrate publicity from behind the scenes to advance his objectives. For Hoover the mining press was an instrument to be used, a force to be guided, not for self-glorification per se but for specific purposes that he hoped to achieve. Inevitably, of course, and perhaps at times deliberately, he thereby called attention to himself.

As a student at Stanford Hoover gained a reputation as a wire-pulling campus politician ("We press the buttons and do the rest"). It was a role during his Bewick, Moreing years that he still found congenial. Some men, like Theodore Roosevelt, basked in the spotlight; Hoover temperamentally preferred the shadows. Some men liked the sound of applause. Hoover took pleasure from the silent exercise of influence.

I V

WHO was this man who, as much as any other, was transforming Australia's mining industry? "In appearance Hoover was an unusual figure. A gaunt frame was topped by a smallish head. The chin was square, the eyes alert, and there was generally a certain atmosphere of aggressiveness. Hoover looked for results." So wrote F. H. Bathurst some years later about Hoover circa 1905.[93] Crossing paths with Hoover on a trip to Australia in 1907, David Starr Jordan noticed how "boyish-looking" and "soft-spoken" Hoover was, but he detected also a man of "very positive opinions and high ideals" underneath.[94] A characteristic Hoover pose, one Australian observed, was to stand with his feet apart and his hands thrust in his pockets.[95] In 1977 an elderly Australian who worked in Hoover's London office in 1903 could still recall another Hoover trait: his peculiar habit of not looking at a person when he spoke.[96]

Quiet, serious, laconic, taciturn—such words sprang quickly to the lips of men who observed Herbert Hoover on his periodic visits to Australia. Never a wasted word. Never a wasted moment. No small talk; little visible sense of humor.[97] He was "not a talker, but a man of action."[98] He seemed to personify efficiency. One observer was struck by Hoover's "exceedingly laconic way of summing up conclusions." When asked what he planned to do about a certain coal deposit in which he was financially interested, Hoover snapped his thumb and finger: "I don't mine d——d mud." That concluded the discussion.[99]

Hoover had an exceptional ability to concentrate, as several anecdotes from later years attested. One, from his mining period, exemplified also his sporadic tendency, among good friends, to turn garrulous and reveal his talent as a raconteur. On one of his trips to Western Australia, Hoover and his wife were dinner guests of the manager of a Bewick, Moreing mine. As the meal was being served Hoover began to describe the siege of Tientsin during the Boxer Rebellion. Becoming absorbed in his subject, Hoover gradually recreated the battle plan on the tablecloth—appropriating forks, knives, spoons, and other items for the purpose until the entire table was in disarray and the servant was unable to deliver the next course. Hoover was oblivious until Lou gently suggested that they "get on with the dinner."[100]

Such a trait was a useful one for a busy executive on the move. Even more useful was what one associate called an "encyclopedic" memory. Hoover's memory was "amazing," an Australian acquaintance later remarked. "He recollected each level, drive, stope and winze and what was being done on all the mines he inspected. He could recall even minor details about ore bodies, methods of treatment, timbering and machinery which, perhaps, the superintendent had not observed."[101] According to one of his engineers just before World War I, Hoover could keep mental track of as many as thirty underground workings simultaneously. When a cable came into his office, Hoover, noting its origin, would predict what the cable said before opening it—even down to the underground level reached and the value of the ore body at that point. And he was usually right.[102]

Curiously, however, Hoover could at times be casual, almost careless, in his use of figures and apparently indifferent to detail.[103] According to W. J. Loring, who worked under him for six years, Hoover was quite uninterested in details. The "broad" picture was his concern; implementation was left to subordinates.[104]

Not the least of Hoover's abilities was a knack for choosing able and dedicated lieutenants. Hoover knew it; "my whole success has been by stearing [sic] onto virilent [sic] men," he told his brother in 1904.[105] Said Loring:

He always took a broader view of a situation than most men. And in conferences he would invariably be thinking way ahead of all the other men put together. Hoover knew how to select men and when he got a good one he merely mapped out his plan and then let the man alone to carry it out the best he could.[106]

Despite his brusqueness and lack of bonhomie, Hoover seemed able to motivate the men he selected. One reason was suggested by Loring's remark: when Hoover appointed a man, he gave him an opportunity to perform. He did not prescribe the man's duties to the last petty detail. Nor did he turn querulous afterwards; Loring said that one of Hoover's "outstanding traits" was that "he never complained about anything."[107] He did not make the mistake of presuming that his rank conferred omniscience; "ever eager to learn," he was not afraid to learn from others.[108] Furthermore, to the salaried members of his technical staff Hoover offered good pay and the incentive of rapid promotion for men who could prove their worth. For the 272 technical and semitechnical (one might say "white-collar") employees in Bewick, Moreing enterprises in mid-1904, the annual salary scale began at £240 (about $1,200). More than a hundred employees earned over $2,400 a year.[109]

And he was considerate, generous—traits that cemented many lifelong loyalties among the men who worked with and for him. In 1905, for instance, the directors of the Great Fingall mine commissioned an independent mining engineer to check Bewick, Moreing's estimate of ore reserves. It was an awkward situation. For four months the consultant lived (for lack of alternative housing) at the home of the mine superintendent, Gerard Lovell, whose own estimates the outsider was investigating. Finally the report was finished; the expert's estimate varied only slightly from that of the superintendent. Hoover, who was visiting the area, was delighted with this vindication of Bewick, Moreing management and congratulated Lovell. The superintendent replied that it was his wife who deserved praise, for she had been obliged to look after the stranger during his long visit. "She deserves a leather medal" was all that Hoover replied. Eventually, without a word of further notice, Lovell's wife received a beautifully inscribed silver tea and coffee set.[110] No verbalizing. No fanfare. That was Hoover's way.

Not everyone liked the "public" Hoover. A friendly editor of the *Financial Times* later remarked that Hoover was sometimes hard to endure.[111] As Bewick, Moreing's influence expanded in Western Australia, Hoover's periodic visits aroused anxiety on the goldfields.[112] What mine would be reorganized, what men would be sacked, as a result of Hoover's inspection? But to those who experienced his acts of kindness and generosity, the image of the abrasive, hard-boiled Yankee businessman dissolved. There was another Hoover, they insisted, and the more they got to know him, the more they liked him.

There was more, too, to Hoover than the constant self-driven striving for success. Somehow, during these years when he "worked like a dog," Hoover found time to initiate what he later called "a re-education of myself": a massive program of reading in history, government, politics, economics, and sociology. Roughly from 1904 to 1908 Hoover read (he later said) "literally several thousand books giving at least two hours nightly and all spare time on long voyages."[113] It was a constructive way of passing the weeks at a time spent on slow steamers between England and Australia. It helped to compensate for his excessively utilitarian undergraduate education at Stanford. At some point also Hoover developed the lifelong habit of reading detective stories in bed before turning in. It was a way of unwinding after the mental rigors of the day.[114]

In Western Australia friends called Hoover "H. C." or the old nickname

"Hail Columbia."[115] His comings and goings were carefully reported in the newspapers, his opinions listened to with respect. But the hard-rock men of Cornwall had a saying: "No miner knows what is beyond the point of his pick." Even trained geologists could not predict with certainty whether (or when) a mine would "fail in depth." And Hoover was not Midas. Not everything he touched turned to gold.

Herbert Hoover, ca. 1898–1900.

OPPOSITE ABOVE. *The Hoovers' home in Tientsin,*
China (1899–1901).

OPPOSITE BELOW. *Herbert Hoover on expedition in China, ca. 1899.*

Chinwangtao harbor (under construction).

*Lou Henry Hoover inspecting the battlements
at siege of Tientsin.*

*Lou Henry Hoover (right) and her sister Jean during their visit to Japan, early
1901.*

Downtown Kalgoorlie, ca.
1900.

The "Golden Mile" (at
Kalgoorlie), ca. 1905.

Sons of Gwalia mine, 1903.

OPPOSITE LEFT. *W. J. Loring and Herbert Hoover, ca. 1903.*

15

Failures and Frustrations

I

H ERBERT H OOVER recognized the element of risk that plagued West Australian gold mining in the 1890s and early 1900s. "All mining is speculative," he warned.[1] One of his principal efforts as a Bewick, Moreing partner was to minimize the risks and rationalize the industry through technological innovation, economies of scale, and rigorous, honest management. By such means, he believed, one could resist the profit squeeze (high costs, low-grade ore) and postpone the inevitable day when the mines—every mine—gave out.

All mining, then, was a striving against ultimate defeat. One measure of success was how long one could stay in the game. The lower one's costs, the longer the game. The better one's percentage of ore extraction (using the most modern ore reduction techniques and plant), the longer the game. The lower the threshold of "payable" ore—down to fractions of an ounce of gold per ton—again, the longer the game.

This was a long-range view, an engineer's perspective, Hoover's perspective. It implied a commitment to systematic development, large-scale capital expenditure, retention (at times) of profits for reinvestment, and abstention from short-sighted, get-rich-quick tactics like "picking the eyes out of the mine." In the aftermath of the dizzy era of "Golden Westralia," this was a progressive viewpoint.

But even the most methodical mining engineering and the most modern equipment could not always guarantee success. If the gold was not there, or was not "payable," the forces of applied science would only make the ultimate failure more costly and conspicuous.

I I

Early in 1902, while on his first inspection tour of Western Australia as a Bewick, Moreing partner, Hoover visited the Lancefield gold mine near Laverton, about one hundred miles northeast of the Sons of Gwalia. A small, promising property owned by a local company, it was already yielding steady dividends on gold taken from two levels near the surface. The mine, as one journal put it, gave every indication of being "an enormous low-grade proposition." Hoover therefore secured an option on the property for C. Algernon Moreing's London and Western Australian Exploration Company.[2]

Although this particular option was not exercised, Hoover's interest in the Lancefield continued. As working costs at Bewick, Moreing enterprises in Australia declined, the attractiveness of the low-grade Lancefield mine rose.[3] During 1903 Bewick, Moreing men took test bores, samples, and more samples—"every possible precaution," said Hoover, "so I do not see how we could fall in." Late in the year, accompanied by J. H. Curle, he again visited the mine on a swing through Western Australia. He informed his associates in London that under new management the mine could yield at least 30 shillings worth of gold per ton at a total cost of under 20s.—a satisfactory prospect indeed.[4]

Curle shared Hoover's enthusiasm. At the time of their visit the Lancefield still belonged to its Australian owners. Curle criticized the local company for constantly dissipating its profits in dividends. Such a short-sighted policy deprived it of capital needed for development and a new plant. But Curle predicted that the property would "pass into stronger hands" and "in a year or two" become a major Westralian mine.[5] Even before his comments were published, the London and Western Australian Exploration Company bought the mine from the local owners for less than £50,000. Hoover cabled Moreing from Australia that he believed it would be the exploration company's most profitable business undertaking since the Sons of Gwalia flotation of 1898.[6]

In July 1904 London and W.A. Exploration floated the Lancefield Gold Mining Company, Ltd. In return for transferring the old company's property to the new, Moreing's exploration company received £200,000 in fully paid shares in the new concern—the entire share capital.[7] Although some of this stock was passed along to the former owners and to other underwriters, Moreing's company kept the "lion's share."[8] Hoover became a director, along with F. A. Govett, R. J. Hoffmann, and other allies of the firm. Bewick, Moreing became general managers.[9] Soon Hoover's old friend John Agnew was on the scene as superintendent.[10]

During late 1904 and early 1905 optimism abounded as the new management revamped the mine, erecting a 50-stamp battery and new treatment
plant.[11] Even before the new company was officially registered, Moreing
boasted that "there is no one else engaged in West Australian mining who
could have tackled a mine of the [low-grade] character of the Lancefield,
because they could not guarantee to work it cheaply enough to secure the
capital."[12] Similarly, W. J. Loring cited the Lancefield as "a fair sample of
what our firm is doing in this country." Soon, he said, the mill and plant
would be ready, and the company would "mop up" much of the "surplus
labor" on the goldfields.[13]

At the first annual shareholders meeting in April 1905, the company's
chairman expressed hope of generating £4,500 per month in profits "in a very
few months from now."[14] Hoover evidently concurred; shortly before the
meeting he purchased 1,000 Lancefield shares for about $5,000.[15] By late
summer the expensive new stamp mill and wet crushing treatment plant were
operating, although the yield, noted Curle, was "not satisfactory." Still, Curle
expected the Lancefield to be a "cheaply worked mine" and a successful one.[16]

And then disaster struck. At the number three level (about 300 feet down)
the ore changed from oxidized to sulphide. This, of course, was expected.
But to the dismay of Hoover and his associates, the sulphide ore unexpectedly turned out to be tainted with arsenical pyrites, which wrought havoc
with the newly installed treatment plant. (Why the engineers' earlier test
bore holes did not detect this was not explained.)[17] The presence of arsenic
made it impossible for the wet crushing process to extract much more than
50% of the gold in the ore—barely enough to cover the cost of extraction.
The elaborate new treatment facility, so confidently installed at a cost of
around £40,000, could not generate enough profit to pay a dividend.[18]

Accompanied by Loring, Hoover inspected the Lancefield in November
1905, on his next visit to Western Australia. The American engineer faced a
weighty decision. On the one hand, the mine itself was looking better than
ever. It had a huge tonnage of low-grade but payable ore—payable, that is,
if a satisfactory process could be found to separate the gold from the impur-
ities. But the present plant was an expensive failure, and operations had been
suspended in September. Should he tinker with the plant in hopes of
improvement, abandon the Lancefield altogether, or plunge in further along
other lines?

Hoover decided quickly. He recommended to his fellow directors by cable
that the existing plant be abandoned for an even larger plant using a dry
crushing and roasting technique similar to one successfully operating at
another mine in Kalgoorlie. The cost of erecting the new plant would be a
whopping £60,000, but Hoover vigorously endorsed it. Toward the end of
November 1905 an emergency stockholders meeting duly voted to increase
the Lancefield's share capital by £60,000. In calling the meeting the directors
emphasized Hoover's approval of the scheme. If Hoover was for it, presum-

ably it must be sound. Moreing afterwards stated that Hoover's report from the field helped to convince the London and Western Australian Exploration Company to provide much of the requisite capital. At the November meeting the Lancefield's chairman, R. J. Hoffmann, exuded optimism. The directors, he said, were "quite confident" that £60,000 would be "quite ample" for the purpose. He expected operations to be suspended "for six or seven months" while the dry crushing plant was built.[19]

By now Hoover had placed a Californian, D. E. Bigelow, on the mine as superintendent.[20] But alas, the struggle was not over. The new treatment plant did not commence operations until November 1906, much later than Hoffmann's projection.[21] And when it did, a new problem appeared. While the extraction rate was excellent (in itself a considerable achievement), the treatment cycle turned out to be slower than anticipated. Consequently the mill, designed to handle up to 10,000 tons per month, was treating 6,500 tons at most. Although this generated considerable revenue, it was barely enough to keep up with expenditures. Unless the plant could be brought up to capacity, the financial stalemate would continue.[22]

At an extraordinary general meeting in March 1908 the Lancefield directors again approached the stockholders for funds. Nearly four years had gone by since the original flotation. The company was now £30,000 in debt, and it needed £20,000 more to expand the plant in order to increase the tonnage. The chairman revealed that all the directors (thus including Hoover) had loaned money to the ailing mine. So, too, had the managers, Bewick, Moreing. Blaming the "peculiar nature of our ore" for their continuing difficulties, Chairman Hoffmann promised that if the plant could be made to process 10,000 tons of ore a month, the stockholders could be "absolutely sure" that the mine would "give the record originally expected and promised on its behalf." The board and Bewick, Moreing, he said, had "not the slightest doubt" that on a basis of 10,000 tons a month the company could make an annual profit of £40,000–50,000. The Lancefield shareholders agreed to dissolve the company and reconstruct it as a new one with £150,000 capital, with an assessment of 2s. on each share to raise the needed funds.[23] By this device £30,000 was raised immediately.

At the March 1908 meeting the Lancefield chairman, speaking in behalf of holders of most of the shares, opposed an even larger assessment. Two shillings a share, he said, would be sufficient. Moreing, too, was sanguine. Never before, he said, had low-grade gold ore containing arsenic and graphite been "profitably treated" anywhere in the world. But now Bewick, Moreing engineers had done it. At the Lancefield they had successfully developed a process that would extract the gold from such "extremely refractory ore" and do so at a profit. All that was necessary now, he said, was to expand the plant sufficiently to process enough ore to yield a profit "commensurate with the capital of the Company."[24]

Once again the high expectations and optimistic assurances proved delusory. Only seven months later, in October 1908, the unhappy Lancefield shareholders were forced to convene once again. The chastened chairman confessed that the reconstruction scheme had been inadequate. Still more money was needed to carry the enterprise to victory. In fact, the mine had even been obliged to close down in July until the plant could be perfected.

By now the pattern of breezy optimism and unfulfilled promises was arousing indignation in the ranks. One angry shareholder urged that Bewick, Moreing be dismissed because of bad management. His motion failed. (J. H. Curle, a shareholder, spoke up against changing horses "when we are cross-ing the stream.") For his part, Moreing contended that they had "a very difficult problem indeed at the Lancefield." What with low-grade and "exceedingly refractory" ore, it had been "impossible to foresee what it would cost to bring [the ore] to the right point of treatment." But that this point had been reached Moreing was certain. The mine was "proved," the metal-lurgical process necessary for profitable treatment was "settled." It remained only to complete the plant. He therefore proposed raising yet another £50,000 by the issue of preference shares. Since his exploration company was the largest shareholder in the Lancefield, there was little doubt of the outcome. The motion carried.[25]

Soon after this meeting Hoover and Govett retired from the Lancefield's board of directors. Moreing and another man replaced them.[26] Hoover's departure was unrelated to the mine's difficulties, and so far as is known he had nothing further to do with the troubled mine.[27]

For nearly five more years the Lancefield struggled on. At the December 1909 meeting Moreing announced that all difficulties surrounding treatment of the mine's refractory ores had been overcome; the remodeled plant was a complete success. Ever the optimist, Chairman Hoffmann declared that the "haven" of profitability would be "reached quite early now." There was "just a little corner to turn."[28]

It never came. In 1910 Moreing reported that a labor shortage at the Lancefield was making it impossible to operate the mill at full capacity.[29] In May 1912 crushing again was suspended as the engineers tried once more to find a more economical method of treatment.[30] In June the mine was closed down following a strike.[31]

In September 1913 Hoffmann told the shareholders that although the mine actually had produced £900,000 worth of gold in its existence, this sum had been insufficient to balance the books for more than one or two months—so great had been their expenses. They simply could not make the mine pay. Hoffmann blamed allegedly abnormal fuel prices and wages for current problems but acknowledged that "the ore was just refractory enough to beat us." Moreing, who in 1910 had proclaimed the Lancefield's ore treatment results "a most brilliant [engineering] success," conceded now that the mine had "hopelessly beaten us" and that "we are unable to solve the problem of the treatment of its ore." With the company in debt for £40,000 and with experiments to improve treatment of the ore unsuccessful, the bankrupt Lancefield Gold Mining Company went into liquidation in 1913.[32] In its nearly ten years as a Bewick, Moreing-managed enterprise, several hundred thousand pounds sterling had been invested for nought, and no dividends had ever been paid.

Years later Hoover explained the Lancefield experience as one of "the ordinary risks taken in mining operations." He added that such risks "are covered by successful issues of other ventures undertaken coincidentally by the same owners." He stressed the metallurgical difficulties caused by the arsenic and pointed out that they had not been resolved twenty years after the Lancefield's collapse.[33] In his *Memoirs* Hoover cited the Lancefield as one of his "painful memories" of mines that had unexpectedly failed in depth.[34]

Probably no one could have predicted the intractable metallurgical obstacles Hoover and his associates encountered at the Lancefield mine. Although prematurely optimistic and repeatedly too confident of success, the board's directors and the Bewick, Moreing management had, to all appearances, done their best. Whether their best had truly been very good, some embittered shareholders doubted.[35] Perhaps Hoover was fortunate that his own connection with the Lancefield ceased five years before its collapse.

I I I

REFLECTING years later on the Lancefield and other failures, Hoover remarked that "gold mining is a hazardous business."[36] The greatest hazard, and ultimately the greatest disappointment, of his Bewick, Moreing years awaited him in Victoria.

About one hundred miles northwest of Melbourne lies a network of ancient rivers and streams, buried beneath a layer of hardened volcanic lava or basaltic rock up to five hundred feet thick. In the 1850s it was discovered that these underground watercourses—at least near their sources—contained beds of gold-bearing gravel called "deep leads" (pronounced "leeds"). Where the lava cover was thin and the underground streams shallow, miners were able to pump out the water and extract rich quantities of alluvial gold. (Since the rivers and streams were extinct, there was no running water.) Seven million pounds' worth of gold was thus won from the earth, notably along the Madame Berry lead. But as the buried streams dipped into the valleys the lava shield over them increased, and so, too, did the quantity of water encountered, particularly when tributaries coalesced into the principal streams. Eventually the volume of water to be drained off became insuperable; most of the subterranean auriferous river beds could not be worked. Still, men wondered: if there was gold in the "wash" at the higher elevations, might not there be gold in the valleys?[37]

In the late 1890s Whittaker Wright, the audacious promoter, became interested in a portion of the "deep leads" of Victoria. By the end of 1900 two extravagantly capitalized Wright ventures, the Loddon Valley Goldfields and the Moorlort Goldfields, had been floated. During 1901 and 1902 the new companies worked at the ambitious task of taking test bores, sinking shafts, and pumping the underground rivers dry—all of which had to be done before the gravel could be mined.[38]

The spectacular collapse in 1900–1901 of Wright's financial empire, which included large shareholdings in his Victorian deep lead companies, created an opportunity for less flamboyant entrepreneurs. Before long the Loddon Valley and Moorlort companies exhausted their working capital and were in the hands of the Official Receiver liquidating Wright's enterprises. Somebody must now clean up the debris from Wright's bankruptcy. As in the case of the Lake View Consols, the firm of Bewick, Moreing and Company became a principal beneficiary of Wright's demise.

In 1903 the Official Receiver was obliged to dispose of Wright's share interest in two companies (and title to some related property known as the Option Blocks) for £50,000—a mere fraction of their capitalization and presumed intrinsic value. The initial buyer appears to have been Govett's brokerage house. But by a series of legal steps the properties passed to some shareholders in Wright's now defunct finance company.

In this series of transactions Bewick, Moreing took an active and probably decisive part. Early in 1903 the firm approached the still-unorganized former shareholders with a bold proposal: constitute a new company, buy the property offered to it, and undertake a massive campaign (with Bewick, Moreing's assistance) to pump and mine the deep leads. Moreing's presentation persuaded the shareholders that the sale price was an excellent bargain and that the subterranean gravel beds were both auriferous and accessible. The water problem, they were assured, could be expeditiously overcome. And so on May 26, 1903 the London and Globe Deep Leads Assets, Ltd. (soon changed to Consolidated Deep Leads) came into existence, specifically to acquire the proferred properties. Bewick, Moreing became the company's general managers and engineers.[39]

By this means the Consolidated Deep Leads acquired a dominant share interest in the bankrupt Loddon Valley and Moorlort companies. Using its clout, the Consolidated effected a reconstruction of these two companies in mid-summer, generating in the process about £37,500 in working capital for each. The Consolidated also persuaded an unrelated company, the Victorian Deep Leads, to reconstruct and thereby get fresh capital from its shareholders for the soon-to-be-expanded pumping operations. For all three companies Bewick, Moreing became general managers and engineers—a welcome increase in business in the wake of A. Stanley Rowe's defalcation. During the summer the Consolidated sought cooperation of still other concerns having property along the Madame Berry Deep Lead system.[40]

The reason for this effort was simple. It was "part of Mr. Moreing's scheme," said the Consolidated chairman, "to consider what steps should be taken in order to federate all these interests into one single combination." The ancient buried river and its tributaries ran under numerous properties; pumping operations at one point would to some extent benefit all. The Consolidated group and its engineers had no intention of draining the entire system by themselves while neighboring companies did nothing and then reaped the reward. The Consolidated Deep Leads proposed to work "by friendly co-operation of all the interests involved" in "one great combination." But if any companies proved recalcitrant, the Consolidated would seek (via the Victorian government) to force them to contribute their share or lose their property.[41]

Meanwhile Bewick, Moreing and Company—specifically, Hoover—turned to America for expertise: to Dr. Waldemar Lindgren of the United States Geological Survey, the man under whom Hoover had worked in the Sierras in the summers of 1894 and 1895. Lindgren was an authority on similar deep lead geology in California. At Hoover's invitation he traveled to Victoria in the summer of 1903 to undertake an exhaustive survey of the deep lead properties whose fate now rested in the hands of Bewick, Moreing engineers.[42]

In one respect the timing of Lindgren's mission seemed odd. Well before his journey Moreing had already asserted that the existence of alluvial gold in the ancient riverbeds was "proved" and that his firm already had a "practicable" plan to remove the water.[43] In September, scarcely a month after Lindgren reached Australia, Moreing even declared that the water problem had "long been over-estimated" and said he foresaw "no serious difficulty at all in clearing these deposits of water."[44]

Why, then, had Lindgren been engaged? One reason, it seems, was to obtain a fresh and independent survey of the district. According to the Consolidated chairman, Lindgren's report would be a comprehensive study of the "position and prospects" of the various properties.[45] In addition, Govett, who had a considerable stake in the venture, may have insisted that some eminent authority examine the area thoroughly.[46] Govett, it appears, was not about to invest solely on Moreing's assurances. But if Govett had any reservations, the Consolidated chairman and his colleagues did not. Even before Lindgren's survey had fairly begun, shareholders in the Loddon Valley and Moorlort companies had been assessed £75,000 for working capital.

At a Consolidated Deep Leads shareholders meeting in early September 1903, the chairman of the board paid the customary tribute to Bewick, Moreing and its "unique staff" of engineers. He praised Hoover, sitting on his left, for his "enormous" "interest [in] and knowledge of this whole proposition" and announced that Hoover was leaving for Australia in a few days. Speaking to the assembly, Moreing pronounced himself "very sanguine" about "this great scheme." "I have not the slightest doubt," he added, "that before we meet again, very great progress will have been made, and it is even possible we may be working the deposit by the next time you meet."[47]

Late in November 1903 Hoover arrived in Melbourne, Victoria, upon completion of his West Australian tour.[48] Hoover's coming was the subject of considerable interest in the mining press. It was reported that he had "£400,000 at his command" to invest in the deep lead properties and that his purpose was "to arrange for an equitable combination of all interests" to tackle the water problem.[49]

In pursuit of this objective Hoover met with the Minister for Mines for Victoria on December 2. Hoover proposed that the Victorian Parliament form a "pumping trust" to handle drainage matters and insure equity for those companies that actually were pumping water. Hoover argued that these working companies should have a "remedy" against those who (in one newspaper's phrase) were "merely holding land to become valuable through the drainage done by others." The Minister for Mines, however, denied that any special legislation was necessary. Existing regulations were sufficient, he insisted, and any special legislation by the state Parliament was highly unlikely. Instead, the Minister pledged to use his department's considerable powers to compel "loafers" either to work on their own property or contribute to the expenses of those who were pumping the lead.[50]

According to a local newspaper Hoover was greatly surprised to learn about the extensive discretionary powers already wielded by the Minister for Mines and stated that he could hardly hope for anything more.[51] In a newspaper interview a few days later, however, the persistent American engineer revealed that he had not quite given up. Hoover acknowledged that the Victorian government had thus far wisely exercised its "unlimited powers" over the mining industry. But it was this very discretion that now disturbed him. What if political radicals inimical to mining interests should come into office? According to Hoover, would-be foreign investors considered this contingency a "serious menace." Hoover urged the Victorian government to draft a law that would modify the onerous "labour covenant," which, if ever enforced, could compel owners to hire huge numbers of unnecessary workers as a condition of retaining their property. As for the "pumping trust," Hoover affirmed that he and his associates wanted such an arrangement to "compel owners to contribute to the cost of pumping for all the area affected by such pumping." The entire deep leads venture, he said, was "a very great gamble. What we think is that we should be helped to prove the success of the business by all those who will be benefited."[52]

Hoover's quest seems to have had no result. Rebuffed in his attempt to obtain a state-sponsored water board or "pumping trust," he and his backers concentrated instead on private efforts toward "a united scheme of action." Here they made progress. In December 1903 the Australian Commonwealth Trust was formed in London, with Moreing a permanent director. Like the Consolidated Deep Leads, this new enterprise was a finance company, formed to supply funds and "central organisation" for the coming battle to drain the leads.[53] The new company acquired large share interests in two deep lead properties farther up the line.[54] One way to fuse interests was to obtain, through shareholdings, a powerful voice in the policy of neighboring companies.

The other purpose of Hoover's 1903 visit was to consult with Lindgren and see the deep leads for himself. He also joined Lindgren in examining other mines in the region. Like Louis Janin before him, Lindgren was much struck by Hoover's ability to evaluate and estimate the ore reserves in a mine after only a brief inspection.[55]

Early in December Lindgren completed more than four months of methodical investigation. Late the next spring his report was made public. According to the American geologist, the prospects for the undertaking were very auspicious. The Loddon Valley portion of the lead, for instance, should prove "highly auriferous" and yield dividends of £425,000 or more. The lead on the Option Blocks was payable; it was likely to be so on the Moorlort lease as well. The Victorian Deep Leads property was similarly promising and "well worth extensive prospecting and exploitation."[56]

To at least one mining journalist Lindgren's report was a "daring" document. Never before had anyone tried to estimate the gold contents of miles of underground deep leads before they had been "proved by the actual test of mining." There was "no certainty" that just because the upper reaches of the leads were known to contain gold, the lower reaches would also. While admiring Lindgren's "pluck," the journalist wondered whether the American's methodology was "scientifically exact." Certainly it was "not in conformity with our general mining practice."[57]

For Hoover and his associates, however, Lindgren's encouraging report was enough. The Consolidated Deep Leads directors informed their shareholders that Hoover shared Lindgren's "favorable anticipations"—"so soon as concerted action in dealing with the water throughout the Loddon Valley system becomes effective."[58] In London a confident Moreing told shareholders in his exploration company that Lindgren's report had been "very favourable." Moreing anticipated "a very great future" for the deep lead mines. On Moreing's enthusiastic recommendation the exploration company approved an investment of £25,000 in the Victorian undertaking.[59] The Australian Commonwealth Trust, for its part, admitted that the "probable yield" of gold per ton from the underground leads was "impossible to accurately determine." But Lindgren, it said, had studied the probabilities and given a "most favourable" opinion.[60]

When Lindgren's report was published, Bewick, Moreing and Company added an optimistic preface. The firm predicted that after the water was removed working costs would be very low. Hoover and his colleagues acknowledged that no one really knew how much gold was actually in the vast tonnage of gravel under the buried streams. But test results were auspicious, and Bewick, Moreing was ready to take the risk:

The value of the wash is unknown, the water bores show highly encouraging results; the uniformly profitable yield of this lead in its upper reaches, and the geological probabilities all point to a very hopeful issue. The quantities of wash to be dealt with are so large as to make the operations on these areas enterprises of the greatest possibilities.[61]

At the beginning of 1904 such optimism extended to the press. The *Statist* concluded that the recently reorganized companies offered the "speculative investor" a reasonable chance of "a good run for his money."[62] In the *Economist* J. H. Curle, fresh from a visit to the mines, proclaimed them "legitimate mining ventures" controlled by "people who will handle them properly." But he cautioned that "alluvial mines are horribly speculative things at the best of times," especially when, as in these circumstances, enormous pumping operations lay ahead.[63]

Hoover's firm was moving rapidly now. In mid-January 1904 it let out contracts for £11,000 to reorganize the great pumping plants on the Loddon Valley and Moorlort leases.[64] The Loddon Valley plant already had a pumping capacity of 3,000,000 gallons a day. Hoover's plan called for this to be increased to 5,000,000 gallons a day—and the same for the Moorlort.[65] No one could accuse Hoover of "thinking small."

Supervising Bewick, Moreing's operations in Victoria were two Americans: Hoover's old college friend Deane P. Mitchell and C. S. Herzig, a graduate of the Columbia School of Mines. According to a local journalist the two men were "importing an American 'push' into the work" that was "much appreciated."[66] These were the kind of subordinates Hoover liked: assertive men, like himself, who got things done.

For all their great expectations, the scheme upon which Hoover and his engineers embarked was one of formidable magnitude. The Victorian deep lead mines were no small holdings of a few hundred acres each, like those in Western Australia. The combined Moorlort-Loddon Valley-Option Blocks-Victorian Deep Leads properties managed by Bewick, Moreing comprised over 21,000 acres. The subterranean river ran for more than twenty miles.[67] Lindgren calculated that the Loddon Valley sector of the stream contained 25 billion gallons of water, 10% of which must be pumped out before any of the gravel could safely be touched.[68]

To reach the buried leads engineers must first sink vertical shafts several hundred feet down to points near, but beneath the level of, the river channel. Then they must drive horizontal tunnels underneath the riverbeds. Finally they must drive vertical drill holes up into the gravel beds from below, drain out the water, and pump it via the tunnel and shaft to the surface. When billions of gallons had thus been extracted, the miners could then widen the drill holes, take out the gravel, lift it to the surface—and hope that it contained ample gold.[69]

No wonder some in Victoria had their doubts about Hoover's plans. Already within a seven-mile radius on the leads 22,000,000 gallons *per day* were being pumped out with apparently little impact on the water. Some experts wondered whether the gold deposits, so rich near the source of the leads in the higher elevations, would be as abundant in the broad valley below.[70] (The underground river was thought to be 800 to 1500 feet wide on the Bewick, Moreing-managed properties.)[71] Still, Herbert Hoover's reputation helped to reassure one observer. F. H. Bathurst reported to the *Engineering and Mining Journal* that "Mr. Hoover will bring his great gift of organization to play, and will provide what has long been wanted in deep-lead mining—first-class engineering skill and plenty of capital to properly equip his claims."[72]

The predictions of early 1904 soon began to go awry. That winter men had talked about dewatering the Loddon Valley lease by the autumn of 1904.[73] By mid-summer, however, Bewick, Moreing pushed the target date ahead to February 1905.[74] Nevertheless, Moreing was confident. Every bore hole sample had shown the "highly payable nature of the wash," he declared at the end of 1904. He had "very little doubt as to the future of these deep leads mines." The only uncertainty now, he said, was precisely when his engineers would enter the wash. Moreing predicted that they would do so "before many months pass away."[75]

By early 1905 the Loddon Valley pumps were still taking out four to five million gallons a day, with plans underway to increase capacity to eight million.[76] Yet as of mid-summer 1905 the pump was just holding its own against the water pressure.[77] Still, Curle of the *Economist*—probably reflecting his sources of information—believed that success would come. The water problem, he said, would be "mastered" and payable quantities of gold found in the wash. Curle was "most confident" of the latter.[78]

Two years had now passed since Hoover's visit in November 1903. Late in 1905 he returned to Victoria, where success still eluded his engineers.[79] Toward the end of the year the Loddon Valley's capacity went up to six million gallons.[80] On into 1906 optimism reigned, at least officially, in the boardrooms of London. In March the shareholders of Moreing's exploration company were informed that the directors had "good hopes" that the Loddon Valley mine would be "a source of profit before we meet you again."[81] The *Mining Manual* reported that workers expected to enter the gravel "very shortly."[82] In July shareholders of the Cosmopolitan Proprietary (a mine in Western Australia) learned that their directors, on the advice of Bewick, Moreing, had invested in a certain deep lead property in Victoria. Explaining this action, the chairman boldly announced that Bewick, Moreing had "overcome" the pumping challenge. The "deep lead question" with regard to water was now "determined." The chairman predicted results "that will astonish even those who have all along had confidence" in Victorian deep lead mining.[83]

But signs of trouble were multiplying. In August 1905 the Moorlort mine suspended operations, the water having been too much for its plant. The Moorlort would now wait for the Loddon Valley to finish pumping before reopening.[84] Meanwhile the parent finance companies were loaning ever-increasing sums—up to £110,000, it was said—to finance the pumping effort.[85] It was not enough. In November 1906 both the Moorlort and Victorian Deep Leads companies were obliged to reconstruct; the scheme entailed greatly increased capitalization.[86]

Infused with fresh working capital, the Moorlort resumed operations.[87] But it was on the Loddon Valley lease—the "test case"[88]—that success, if it came, would come first. By the end of 1906 the Loddon Valley pumping facilities had a capacity of about 12,000,000 gallons a day (over 8300 gallons a minute). During that year of exertion the pumps drained nearly 2.7 billion gallons of water.[89] And in November the mine managers at long last earned their reward. The water level and pressure were reduced sufficiently to permit driving onto the underground wash for the first time. To be sure, the wash that was entered was only the high "bench" ground on the bank of the underground river channel, not the "deep" ground of the riverbed itself. (There the water pressure was still too great.) But the samples taken in the next few weeks were said to show "very satisfactory" results. By early January 1907 the engineers expected to enter the presumably richer "deep" ground within a few weeks at most.[90]

The results at the Loddon Valley site appeared to inject new enthusiasm into Bewick, Moreing and its allies. On December 12, 1906 the Australian Commonwealth Trust launched yet another deep leads company, the Berry United, a consolidation of various enterprises. Bewick, Moreing and Company became the manager.[91] Ten days later Hoover informed Lindgren that the outlook on the deep leads was promising and suggested that Lindgren return to Victoria, evidently to explore the deep lead system near the newly floated company.[92]

When the Governor of Victoria visited the Loddon Valley Goldfields property in early 1907, the chairman of the Australian Commonwealth Trust's advisory board brimmed with cheerful tidings. He told the Governor that Bewick, Moreing had "overcome" the enormous problem of water. Furthermore, "the prospects of good gold" were "highly encouraging." "Many thousands of men" would be employed, he predicted.[93] (In 1906 the Loddon Valley had employed an average of 112.)[94]

Yet how long could the shareholders sustain such hopes and shimmering promises? More than three years had elapsed since Lindgren's survey and Hoover's first visit, and not a dividend was in sight. At the Loddon Valley alone, over £38,000 was expended in 1906; as of early 1907 the mine was "living on borrowed money."[95] Yet Bewick, Moreing's program for the Loddon Valley and three other deep lead mines called for a further expenditure in 1907 of £300,000.[96] How long could this go on?

When Herbert Hoover revisited Victoria for a lengthy tour late in the winter (the Australian summer) of 1907,[97] the entire deep lead enterprise seemed problematic. In Australia the Sydney *Bulletin* wondered whether "any decent return will ever be got for the bagfuls of money sunk" on the Loddon Valley mine. "Bewick-Moreing aren't specially sensitive about losing other people's money," it charged. But the *Bulletin*, although no friend of Hoover, congratulated his firm on its engineering skill: ". . . they have shown a whole hatful of points to every engineer who previously attempted to work the deep levels, and they deserve credit for it."[98]

Nevertheless, by mid-1907 the Loddon Valley Goldfields, Ltd. was floundering. Contrary to expectations, the wash at the Loddon Valley was not yielding good results, and the stock market was taking notice.[99] Thirty thousand pounds in debt, its funds exhausted, the company had yet to find more than a few local "patches" of payable gold in the wash—not enough to support "a workable, steadily progressing mine."[100] One complicating factor was the sheer massiveness of the underground riverbed—two thousand feet wide at least: a huge amount of gravel for the gold to disperse and settle in.[101] Another problem was the company's continuing inability to conquer the water where it most mattered: in the "deep ground," the riverbed itself.[102] Despite some success in draining the lead, and even in entering (portions of) the wash, the company still did not know whether the value of the wash was truly worth the effort.[103]

What to do? Should it struggle on in hopes of finding payable gold? Or should it abandon the lease altogether and thereby probably condemn its sister companies to extinction? At this point, unwilling to see the entire deep leads venture collapse on the eve of possible triumph, the state government of Victoria stepped in. The Loddon Valley company had asked the Victorian government for a grant of £20,000. Instead, the government offered to loan the company £8,000 for certain specified underground exploratory work, if the company would put up a like amount.[104] In August 1907 the company accepted and went into reconstruction to raise further funds. The shareholders were assessed five shillings a share, a total of £58,000, in furtherance of their still unsated quest for gold.[105]

At some point, possibly this one, Hoover (so he later wrote) advised that the whole vast undertaking be abandoned. It was the water, specifically the failure to make an "adequate impression upon the enormous volume," that led to his recommendation to give up and risk no further money.[106] Precisely when, where, and to whom Hoover gave his advice is unknown; contemporary documents do not record such an occasion. Years later Hoover indicated that he advised giving up before the Victorian government stepped in to assist the project—before, that is, the summer of 1907.[107]

Hoover, in any case, was present at the Loddon Valley shareholders meeting of August 1907 which voted to reconstruct the company and authorize new expenditures. If Hoover had doubts about prolonging the enterprise, he did not express them. When called upon to speak, he did not oppose the reconstruction scheme. But his remarks about the mine were cautious—so cautious as to betray, perhaps, a deepening lack of enthusiasm for the cause:

There have been rich patches [found in the wash so far], . . . but the richer the patches the more local; indeed, they seem to be everywhere rather small. We have one large area of low grade which was distinctly payable, but it would have had to be larger in order to furnish quantities sufficient to make the mine payable. The question of finding further areas of that type, or better, is purely a geological question. It is not possible for any man to say that we shall come upon these or not. I cannot see into the ground much better than anyone else.

Nevertheless, Hoover noted, some eminent geologists had expressed favorable views of the deep leads for over twenty years, and their opinions were "entitled to very great weight."[108]

So, one more time, the financiers in London and the engineers in Victoria rallied for battle. Whatever Hoover's personal reservations, the mines continued to be managed by his firm. And as usual, Hoover's partner Moreing exuded confidence. Expressing his conviction that a "fabulously rich channel" existed in "these old river beds," Moreing asserted that the Loddon Valley company was "bound to achieve" "ultimate success."[109]

Early in November 1907 the Australian Commonwealth Trust and the Consolidated Deep Leads merged into a new finance company, the Australian Deep Leads Trust, to provide more capital "to hold the ground which they had gained and to accelerate the work." Ever the optimist, at least at shareholders meetings, Moreing claimed that recent developments at the Loddon Valley mine had been "very important and favourable."[110] Meanwhile the Moorlort had again suspended its pumping operations.[111] In January 1908 it was joined by the Victorian Deep Leads, which decided to await results of prospecting at the Loddon Valley lease.[112]

The end came quickly. Still unable to open up the "deep ground," the Loddon Valley Goldfields suspended operations and wound up in December 1908—a victim of unconquered water pressure and, above all, of the meager value of its gravels.[113] Waldemar Lindgren's report had been proved wrong: the Loddon Valley deep lead was not "highly auriferous," except in patches too isolated to justify economical, large-scale dredging of the riverbed. Over £200,000—more than $1,000,000—had been spent to no avail by the Loddon Valley company alone. The result, in the chairman's words, was a "ghastly failure."[114] In 1910 the Australian Deep Leads Trust reconstructed into a company interested in a Russian oil field.[115] Between 1909 and 1911 the Moorlort and Victorian Deep Leads companies surrendered their leases, acquired interests in one of Moreing's Russian oil ventures (which also failed), and finally went into liquidation.[116] Other deep lead properties that Bewick, Moreing and its allies controlled suffered a similar fate.[117]

The great Victorian deep leads venture—so confidently revived in 1903— had proven to be a debacle. Millions of dollars, perhaps five million or more, had been lost.[118] No dividends were ever paid.[119] Such a record probably only sharpened Hoover's sense of embarrassment and frustration. An Australian journalist who knew him at the time recalled later that Hoover was "deeply chagrined."[120]

In strictly engineering terms the enterprise had been a creditable achievement, as some contemporaries recognized.[121] With probable accuracy Hoover called it "the greatest pumping operation in mining history."[122] As with the Lancefield undertaking, Hoover could take comfort from knowing that he had done his best. In consulting Lindgren he had relied on the best expertise he could find. If even a distinguished American geologist could be mistaken, how much more could Hoover do?

Summing up the lessons of the sad affair, Hoover's editor-friend T. A. Rickard placed the principal blame on Lindgren and local mine managers familiar with the district. "The fault," said Rickard's *Mining Magazine*, "lies with those who predicted that the leads contained rich wash, whereas the contrary has been proved to be the case."[123] Rickard criticized Lindgren for making inferences without adequate data on two crucial matters: the distribution of the gold in the leads and the amount of water pressure upon them.[124] And he noted that the state geologists of Victoria had shared Lindgren's unfulfilled expectations. But Hoover's firm—at least implicitly—did not quite escape criticism. According to Rickard, the "financial courage" and "technical skill" displayed in the long struggle had been "vitiated by an incurable optimism"—although, he added gently, this was "neither discreditable nor foolish, but essential to mining adventure."[125]

Perhaps beause it *was* a defeat, Hoover, years later, in his *Memoirs* minimized his active involvement in the colossal deep leads enterprise. He claimed that it was shareholders in the defunct Whittaker Wright companies who approached Bewick, Moreing in 1903. (Contemporary evidence suggests that it was the other way around.) He claimed that he advised these shareholders that the undertaking was "highly speculative," and he implied that he gave his cautionary advice after receiving Lindgren's report—that is, sometime after November 1903. (Yet Bewick, Moreing presented optimistic proposals to the Consolidated Deep Leads company well before Lindgren completed his investigation. And Bewick, Moreing's preface in 1904 to Lindgren's report emphasized not the risk of failure but the possibility of success.) Hoover stated further in his *Memoirs* that inasmuch as the shareholders already had invested so much money in the deep leads in the Wright era, he and his firm agreed to attempt to drain the leads. (The contemporary evidence suggests, however, that Moreing, at least, actually solicited the shareholders to put up more money.) Finally, Hoover attributed failure to the water—an impersonal force—and not to the failure of Lindgren and others to take adequate measure of either the water or the true value of the gold-bearing gravels underneath.

Hoover's account conveyed an impression of himself as a detached, almost impersonal consultant, simply responding to requests from clients and doing a job without comment. Hoover did not mention his own firm's intimate association with these clients, the magnitude of their subsequent loss, his attempt to create a Victorian "pumping trust," his own belief in the project's bright prospects, his three personal visits to Victoria between 1903 and 1907: in short, his deep, energetic involvement in the deep leads venture for several fruitless years.[126]

Hoover's faulty recollection of the deep leads episode was understandable. Partly in reliance on his firm's engineering judgment, men had unsuccessfully invested several million dollars. It could not have been a pleasant memory. Moreover, during his later public career a number of would-be scandalmongers scoured his early mining record for "proof" of shoddy engineering, reckless promoting, and crooked finance. Disappointments like the Lancefield and the Victorian deep leads were grist for their attacks. In response Hoover sometimes overstated his successes, understated his failures, and concealed his business aggressiveness behind a posture of Olympian detachment. These tendencies found expression in his *Memoirs*.[127]

Hoover found it hard throughout his life to acknowledge failure, as his early and enduring sensitivity to criticism suggested. Relatively few disclosures of this trait emerge during his mining years, for these were largely years of attainment and content. But Herbert Hoover the orphan boy, the self-made man, had—the evidence will accumulate—a deep fear of failure. It was the other side of his disciplined, untiring striving for success.

I V

H o o v e r's Bewick, Moreing years were sprinkled with other, more minor disappointments. Such Bewick, Moreing-managed mines as the Vivien, Paringa, Burbank's Birthday, White Feather Main Reefs, and Bellevue Proprietary (of which Hoover was a director) never yielded a dividend, despite hopes and anticipations that Hoover encouraged and shared.[128] "All mining is speculative," Hoover wrote. For every prospect that ultimately earned a profit, far more were abandoned along the way. In 1903 Hoover stated that "no disgrace attaches to a failure of a mine in depth"[129]—provided, he might have added, that the management was expert and able. Despite occasional protests by angry stockholders, few questioned the technical ability of Bewick, Moreing and Company.

Eventually, as Hoover also knew, all mines become, if not extinct, then "comatose."[130] "I warn you now," F. A. Govett told a shareholders meeting in 1905, "all mines are wasting assets, and even Methuselah died at last."[131] In 1903 and 1904, however, the Lancefield and Victorian deep leads propositions were young, promising ventures. It was not the inevitable demise of all gold mines that preoccupied Hoover in those years. It was the proliferating evidence of prosperity.

But success, like failure, could have its penalties. In Western Australia Hoover's firm was heading for trouble.

16

Troubles

I N the autumn of 1903 Hoover presented, in absentia, a paper at a meeting of the Institution of Mining and Metallurgy in London. His subject: "The Future Gold Production of Western Australia." Hoover observed that of more than 1,300 producing mines in 1902 a mere sixteen (eleven of them in Kalgoorlie) accounted for 63% of the total gold output in the state. Despite this narrow industrial base, Hoover was decidedly optimistic. For "every evidence" pointed to "the permanence of the Kalgoorlie deposits in depth" and to the continued great productivity of the sixteen leading mines "for many years to come." Hoover thought it "not improbable" that more mining centers like Kalgoorlie might be discovered. And he predicted improved results for other reasons:

> The demonstrated possibility of at present working 7 dwt. ores, together with the improving *personnel*, both as to local ownership and quality of management, will bring about further expansion, especially in districts outside of Kalgoorlie, by bringing into play lower grade deposits, and thus a more sound position of individual mines.

Hoover did not need to mention whose firm was striving vigorously to improve the "quality of management."[1]

Problems of geology, metallurgy, and administration—scientific and managerial problems: Hoover and his associates could cope well with these. It was less easy to deal with an increasingly antagonistic political environment. The departure of Sir John Forrest as premier of Western Australia in 1901 ushered in a half-decade of political instability. By 1903, to the annoyance and apprehension of British mining interests, a growing Labour Party appeared to dominate Western Australia's government.[2] Nationalist, nativist, and socialist, the trade union movement and its political allies soon crossed swords with Bewick, Moreing.[3]

During his Australian sojourn in 1897–98, Hoover had been outspoken on the subject of Australian labor. As a young mine manager at the Sons of Gwalia he had not hesitated to threaten to use Italian immigrants as strikebreakers if the need arose. By 1902 there was little sign that he had softened his attitude. One new feature of West Australian labor relations was a system of governmental conciliation boards and arbitration courts which had the power to fix wage rates on the goldfields. When, in late 1902, one such court granted an increase in wages at mines in Kalgoorlie, Hoover was less than pleased. This "forced arbitration," he complained, had, "as usual with such commissions, compromised, and thereby increased wages." But at least it did one "beneficial" thing: it established a uniform pay scale on the Golden Mile.[4]

Strong in conviction and accustomed to command, how would Hoover cope with the rising power of the unions? In a speech before the Council of West Australian Mine Owners in July 1903, he took a determined stance. For years, he remarked, the mining industry in Western Australia had labored under severe "disabilities." Some of these obstacles the owners themselves could strive to overcome (and were in fact doing so): problems of "ore treatment," of "mine management," of "working under the most difficult conditions a goldfield has ever operated upon." Some difficulties, however, were "under the control of the government," and here the record was much less satisfactory.

"The real fundamental difficulty," Hoover declared bluntly, was "the labour question."

We can circle round it as much as we please, but it is the labour question which we have to confront. There is an element of demagoguery in West Australia which influences the Government, and it is this which we must set about to counteract, which is the work that should be the chief object of the Mine Owners' Council. We do not expect to see wages reduced; we expect to pay a fair day's wage for a fair day's work; but we submit that the Conciliation and Arbitration Acts, which are the result of the demagoguery to which I referred, have done us more harm than the acts of the Government towards us have done us good.

Hoover particularly criticized the establishment of a minimum wage.

Formerly we tried to pay a man in accordance with the work which he did, and now we are compelled to pay the delinquent man a minimum amount, which results in even the better man being paid a minimum also, and in the end we get less work done for more money. It results in a levelling down of efficiency.

Nor did Hoover see a justification for the recent "general rise in wages" to which the mine owners had been "forced to submit."

This has been done in spite of a steadily lessened cost of living, and there is no Colony in Australia where the workman has an opportunity of saving in the same proportion to his wage as he had in West Australia before the Conciliation Board came into operation.

Hoover told the assembled mine owners that they could "go a long way towards solving" the labor question "if we can unite on some ticket system, by which only the good men in the Colony should be employed by the companies. We should thus eliminate the gold stealer and the demagogue." It was not the ordinary miner who was causing trouble:

Individually the miner is a good man; he is a man we wish to pay a fair wage and give fair treatment to, but he is not a man we wish to see led by the demagogues into the false position of believing that his own salvation lies in the ruin of his employer. We have seen a disposition to check this on the part of the Government, and in this it should have our greatest support.[5]

Hoover's after-dinner speech probably articulated well the prevailing mine owner viewpoint in 1903. In the next five years Hoover said little to suggest that his thinking had altered appreciably. In an article in the *Financial Times* in 1904 he attacked the "professional agitators" who in his opinion controlled the political program of Australian working men.

The fly in the West Australian ointment lies in the growth of the Socialistic element in the Labour Party and the legislation for which they have been responsible. The Arbitration and Conciliation Acts have, as was expected on both sides, not formed the presumable machinery to settle disputes with justice, but a weapon in the hands of workmen for injustice against the employer.[6]

Ever alert to factors that might threaten the business interests he represented, Hoover, on a trip to Australia in 1905, forthrightly opposed the closing of ore treatment mills on Sundays. It would, he asserted, greatly increase the cost per ton of gold production, destroy the profit margin of some mines, and cause the loss of two thousand jobs.[7]

On this same visit Hoover also stoutly resisted Australian talk of placing local directors on the boards of foreign-owned mines. As usual, he was outspoken, and, as usual, he uttered the London point of view:

> This State [Western Australia] cannot make progress in mining without the aid of the British capitalist—it is absurd to talk otherwise. . . . [Local boards] would do absolutely no good, and only interfere in control, mean dual administration, and give scope for intrigue and discord, and, what is more, increase the cost of management. . . . What sense do you think is there in the argument in favor of local boards of directors? Do you suppose that if a man in London puts £100,000 into a mine here he is going to hand over the control of the mine to men in W.A.?[8]

Hoover also took a tough line on gold stealing by miners, a widespread problem that had agitated mine owners for years.[9] To Hoover in 1907 the way to suppress what he called an evil of "appalling" dimensions was to use the police. He suggested that mining companies be allowed to hire government policemen for a time at their own expense, as was done in England. Hoover thought that if this were permitted, some West Australian mining companies would station a policeman on their property on every shift.[10]

Despite these uncompromising sentiments, Hoover's firm of mine managers, by the standards of the time, was an enlightened employer. When all was said and done, C. Algernon Moreing's claim may well have been accurate: Bewick, Moreing and Company paid "the highest wages in the world."[11] In 1904 Moreing told an interviewer:

> The mines of West Australia are paying the highest wages in the world to white miners for the time worked. So far as we are concerned, what we want is efficiency in the individual, and it is a secondary matter to us what his wages are. Myself and my new partners here in Australia, thoroughly believe that a capable, skilled man who does the best he can in the interest of his employers is worth more than three inefficient, underpaid men. What we want is hard, loyal work from our men, the same as we give our employers, and we expect to pay them good round wages and we expect the same.[12]

Moreing's remarks were not merely rhetorical effusion. The pay on the Western Australian goldfields during 1903 and 1904 *was* good for its time— roughly $17.50 to $22.50 per week for underground miners. Men worked eight-hour shifts, five days a week, plus five-and-one-half hours on Saturday, making an effective work week (deducting half-hour lunch breaks) of about forty-three hours.[13]

Bewick, Moreing, of course, could not take credit for these wage-and-hour scales. They were set by the arbitration courts, which Hoover strongly disliked. And Hoover opposed a general wage increase in 1902 as unnecessary (since the cost of living was actually falling). Nevertheless, Hoover, like his close friend F. A. Govett, accepted the wage structure as one of the conditions of doing business on the fields.[14] Indeed, when some mining interests subsequently attempted to obtain a reduction of the wage rate in Western Australia, Hoover and his firm opposed the move. Late in 1905 Hoover told the West Australian press: "My firm, since I joined it four years ago, . . . has never been an advocate of cheap labor or reduced wages." He did, however, consider the current wage structure—"the highest wage in the world for similar work"—to be "all the industry will stand." If, said Hoover, miners continued to "work loyally for their employers, there need be no difficulty in maintaining it."[15]

Yet if Bewick, Moreing paid workmen high wages partly by legal necessity, it paid its salaried staff by choice. And at the upper echelons of its organizational pyramid, the firm paid well indeed.[16] When it came to offering incentives and rewarding initiative, Bewick, Moreing did not balk. At mines managed by the firm, the salaries of senior officials rose when their working costs declined.[17] According to W. A. Prichard, "opportunities for promotion" were "greater" at Bewick, Moreing mines than elsewhere.[18] Prichard and Loring themselves were admitted to a partnership in the firm's West Australian business, entitling them to a share of profits in mines under their control.[19] Hoover encouraged a spirit of friendly rivalry among his far-flung staff and was proud of his firm's ability to select "the best man."[20] Moreing, too, was pleased by the firm's lowering of working costs to a point below those on the celebrated South African goldfields—despite the constraints of much higher wages, a forbidding desert climate, and other "adverse circumstances." To Moreing this showed that "white labour is better than black, even if you have to pay three times the price."[21]

Bewick, Moreing and Company did not confine its solicitude to its salaried staff. When slackness occurs at a mine, Prichard said in 1904, "every nerve is strained to prevent employees from remaining idle—in short, every effort is made to keep them in work." According to Prichard, "hundreds" of employees were transferred from mine to mine as development work tapered off at one site and increased at another.[22] He claimed that employment was "more secure" at Bewick, Moreing mines than at others. When layoffs did take place the firm strove to find new jobs for "the most deserving members of the staff who in turn look out for their subordinates." Prichard asserted that when workers were dismissed it was "often because they are not suited to their particular work, or they do not get on with their particular boss." On "innumerable" such occasions, he claimed, Bewick, Moreing helped these men find another job and "a new chance" somewhere else.[23]

Years later Hoover stated that there was never a strike at a Bewick, Moreing-managed mine during his years as a partner.[24] Western Australia's compulsory arbitration law, of course, largely eliminated this possibility by removing the principal source of industrial conflict (wage disputes). And labor relations at Hoover's mines were not always harmonious. At the East Murchison United the work force petitioned the arbitration court for a wage increase, only to have their current wages reduced. The angry miners at first refused to accept the decision. But Hoover had ordered his general manager to close the mine permanently unless workers, like the company, abided by the arbitration law. The protest thereupon collapsed, and the men acquiesced.[25]

Still, Hoover and his firm did not need an arbitration court to instruct them on the value of labor peace. It was in their own self-interest. W. A. Prichard encapsulated the firm's philosophy in one sentence: "We find that it pays to treat men fairly."[26]

In one respect the firm's policy was reassuring to Australian workers. When in 1904 mining companies in South Africa began to import tens of thousands of indentured Chinese laborers to work in the mines on the Rand, Moreing and Hoover were not enthusiastic. "My firm is the only mining firm in London which has set its face against Chinese labour in South Africa," Moreing stated, "for we claim that skilled white labour could work the mines as cheaply."[27] Such remarks were no doubt welcome "down under," where, in 1901, the newly-founded Commonwealth of Australia had adopted a "White Australia" immigration policy designed to exclude Orientals and other "tinted races" from permanent settlement in the island-continent.[28]

High salaries, financial incentives for achievement, and rapid promotion for the most able and efficient; high wages, steady employment, and the possibility of job placement elsewhere for the rank-and-file; white labor only, well paid: these were the key elements of Bewick, Moreing's labor policies between 1902 and 1908.

Not everyone, however, was satisfied. In 1903 and 1904 the firm became the target of broad and bitter attack.

I I

THE trouble started in early 1903 when the firm introduced a new system of mine supply for the many West Australian companies under its supervision. Hitherto each individual mine had purchased its own supplies as needed from local merchants and agents. Bewick, Moreing decided to abolish this uncoordinated practice. Henceforth purchasing would be centralized at the port of Fremantle. The firm itself, not the individual mining companies, would buy such items as candles and explosives wholesale at low bulk rates and resell the commodities directly to its mines as required. This procedure not only would mean lower unit prices for goods but would eliminate such former expenses as commissions charged by middlemen for shipping stores inland from Fremantle to Kalgoorlie. The savings thus effected would be passed on to the mining companies for which the firm was now purchasing agent.[29]

Bewick, Moreing had become displeased, too, at the high premiums being charged for fire and accident insurance at its mines. Once again, in early 1903, the firm acted decisively. It transferred the mines' insurance coverage from local companies and agents to companies in London whose rates were presumably lower.[30] Sometime in the next eighteen months the firm and its mines set up a cooperative insurance fund of their own to pay workmen's compensation claims, thereby doing away with their outside insurance company (and its "exorbitant" rates).[31]

The stores supply scheme evoked a storm of anger that did not abate for at least two years. "Why should a firm be allowed to monopolise the trade of a great group of mines" on the goldfields? one critic demanded to know.[32] Not content with merely managing mines, it had now set itself up as a gigantic middleman, taking secret rebates on its massive purchases—so some critics alleged. By switching much of its business to large suppliers at Fremantle, it was attempting to "cripple the Kalgoorlie merchants." What would happen to the small mines and non-Bewick, Moreing companies when local traders, deprived of business, were finally obliged to curtail their inventories? These mines also (came the response) would have to turn to Fremantle—and at a greater cost.[33] The allegation spread that Bewick, Moreing was now supplying its mines inferior goods at prices previously charged for higher-quality goods.[34] As for insurance, one critic lamented that Bewick, Moreing's action deprived local businessmen and the local economy of considerable revenue. The firm's complaint about high premiums, he added angrily, was a "pretence"—an excuse for throwing the insurance business to London and getting a nice commission for doing so.[35]

Time and again throughout 1903 and 1904 Hoover's firm and its allies were obliged to respond to the barrage of criticism. The firm acknowledged that it received an annual salary of £1,500 from its seventeen or eighteen affiliated mining companies for managing their purchases. To this extent the firm itself profited from the new arrangement. But it strenuously denied receiving any commissions or secret rebates. Nor did it pocket the substantial savings its supply scheme brought about. Instead, all savings (after deducting salary and expenses) were divided periodically among the participating companies. The cooperative stores department brought no bonanza to Bewick, Moreing.[36]

The firm also admitted in 1904 that some individuals had suffered from its supplies system: a few "travelling agents for coast firms," said Moreing, and "a certain number of local dealers" in Kalgoorlie. In all, he claimed, not more than twenty people: an "infinitesimal number" compared to the beneficiaries of the firm's business methods.[37] "Why should a community set up a howl," asked Prichard, "about a handful of commission men losing their mine trade any more than they would the dismissal of a similar number of workers on the mine"? Far from harming Western Australia's leading industry, Bewick, Moreing's "collective purchasing" had by 1904 effected "a general reduction in prices of about 10 per cent. on all supplies purchased."[38] Moreing and his firm argued that all mines benefited from the lower prices that bulk purchasing compelled competing suppliers to offer. They stressed that most of their orders were placed with Australian firms, not with foreigners, and that by mid-1904 their mines were buying more goods in Western Australia than ever before.[39] And every economy in management, they pointed out, helped the worker. For the lower the working costs attained at marginal, low-grade mines, the longer the life of these mines, and thus the greater stability of employment for wage-earning miners.[40]

What Bewick, Moreing defended in Western Australia, its financial allies praised with vigor in London. Friends like R. J. Hoffmann and F. A. Govett contended that the companies they directed "benefited very largely" from what Hoffmann called Bewick, Moreing's "very splendid organisation for the supplies of stores." Govett asserted that the great majority of Bewick, Moreing's stores purchases in 1904 were actually from businesses in Western Australia itself. And the rebates it distributed to the mines were genuine, said Govett; an independent auditor at one of them had confirmed it.[41]

Hoover and his partners had reason for feeling aggrieved at the continuing agitation in Western Australia. Why the fuss? The firm, after all, was in business, and competition was the rule of the game. Moreover, its stores supply system (so it said) was forcing down commodity prices, to the gain of virtually everyone on the fields. But however sound and legitimate, Bewick, Moreing's business methods did not win many plaudits in Kalgoorlie. As late as mid-1905, a full two-and-a-half years after the stores system was instituted, dissatisfaction with the scheme was rampant in Western Australia, despite its evident success in reducing the costs of mine supplies.[42]

And so was born the explosive charge of monopoly, a cry that grew louder as mine after mine came under Bewick, Moreing's management. In the *Kalgoorlie Miner* an angry correspondent succinctly expressed the concerns of many:

(1) Are the principal big mines under the control of practically one firm? Can the same firm at any time practically stop the mining of West Australia by putting off [virtually] all the men . . . ? (2) Are the mines managed by foreigners, and also worked by foreigners, in a bigger proportion than the ratio of same to the population of the State? (3) Do foreigners go out to find fresh fields to mine on? Did they find the mines in the first place and put up with all the hardships, or are they just coming in for the good things? (4) Are the merchants, prospectors, and workers equally affected, the foreigners purchasing nothing at all locally? (5) Is it not a great disadvantage to be a colonial or Briton, from manager downwards?[43]

By early 1904 Western Australia was embroiled in a hard-fought election campaign for the state's legislative assembly. On the eastern goldfields, where politicians searched for labor votes, Bewick, Moreing became a heated issue. Clearly alluding to the firm in a speech at Kalgoorlie, the premier of Western Australia declared himself "anxious" about "the present tendency" toward control of the mining industry by a monopoly. If the mining companies on the Golden Mile "ceased to become a legitimate combine," and if they were "absorbed by a big monopoly or one company," he believed that the state government "would have sufficient resource and energy to prevent it."[44] Such words sounded ominous. Out on the goldfields the premier's remarks found an echo. "Down with B., M. and Co." was the slogan.[45] "Bewick, Moreing's got to go."[46]

In London, half a world away, Moreing emphatically insisted that his firm was not a monopoly. It did not "own the mines in Western Australia nor . . . any part of them. We are simply mining engineers, who manage the mines on behalf of their owners, who are the British public."[47] In Kalgoorlie W. A. Prichard asserted: "Bewick, Moreing & Co. are not capitalists but simply act as mining engineers for English Companies whose shareholders embrace capitalists and all classes of workers and business men." Prichard welcomed "scrutiny of our business methods by truthful and authorized persons" but added that the firm expected protection from "blackmailing legislation" and "fanatical public misrepresentation." He pointed out that every Bewick, Moreing mine in the state was "open to the public," and he invited "parliamentary investigation into our methods of purchasing supplies, employment of labor, and accounting."[48]

Moreing was probably technically correct. So far as is known, his firm *as a firm* did not own any mines in Western Australia. But Bewick, Moreing and Company by 1904 was more than a firm of "simply" mining engineers and mine managers. It represented what Hoover had hailed as a new stage of mining organization: the emergence of the dominant firm and its "group," the close alliance of technical expertise and investment capital.[49] At the peak of the "monopoly" agitation, Hoover himself estimated that his firm "control or manage" enterprises with a market value of over $70,000,000, mostly in Western Australia.[50] Through its ties with its investor-"clients," who relied on it for advice, and through membership on various boards of directors, Moreing's firm could exert considerable, perhaps decisive, influence on mining in Western Australia. Moreing particularly had a heavy personal stake in many companies that his firm managed, notably through the shares that his London and Western Australian Exploration Company held in these very mines. Such shares gave him further power to affect corporate decision making.

Moreing's firm was therefore much more than "strictly an engineering firm" (as Prichard tried to claim), more than hired technicians, more than employees of distant capitalists and boards of directors. Not only was Moreing himself a "capitalist." On his firm's judgments—about ore values, treatment processes, and a hundred other questions—rested the fate of companies and the fortunes of investors. Precisely because of the knowledge it commanded and the technical control it exercised, it was effectively able to do more than meekly advise. This state of affairs—"subordinating the control of the directors to that of the engineering staff"—was a new phenomenon in 1904.[51] To Hoover and Moreing it was a healthy and necessary development if mines were to be sober investments and not helpless counters in the hands of speculators.

Once again the Bewick, Moreing partners had reason to feel aggrieved. None of what they had done was illegal or contrary to the canons of free competition. No mining company had been compelled to shift its management to them. All their management contracts ultimately depended on the quality of their administration and engineering expertise, and their prestige in London was only as secure as their performance. In just two years they had risen to preeminence on merit. Were they now to be punished for their success?

Certainly envy accounted for some of their unpopularity. The *West Australian Mining, Building, and Engineering Journal* pointed out that "a few traders in Kalgoorlie," angry at the loss of "fat commissions," were one source of hostility. Another, it said, was plain "professional jealousy" of a firm that was "far and away the best mine managers and engineers in Westralia."[52] Still another was the firm's heavy dismissals of workers from companies under its management. Most of those discharged were "drones and idlers," asserted one friendly journalist. Of course the men thus removed, he added, "would not have a good word to say for the people who dismissed them."[53] One periodical reported that when Bewick, Moreing took over a mine, it replaced many management-level personnel with its own men: a natural enough action, but one that provoked "some jealousies and a little feeling."[54] The fact that many of these replacements, as well as the firm's joint managers in Western Australia, were "foreigners" (that is, Americans) contributed to the smoldering resentment.

Certainly, too, election campaign politics exacerbated the tension, as candidates appealed for the votes of workingmen and disgruntled shopkeepers.[55] Moreing attributed the clamor to demagogic politicians and "jealous parties" seeking support from "one class or another." It was just "election trash."[56] Prichard also claimed that the uproar was manufactured by vote-hungry politicians. He implied that the campaign was an attempt to scare the firm into providing financial support for certain candidates as the price of avoiding "blackmailing legislation."[57]

The apprehension about Bewick, Moreing, however, was broader and deeper than that. As one mining journalist remarked, Australia was possibly the most democratic country in the world, a country in which "the working man is in the ascendant." In acquiring the management of so many major companies, Bewick, Moreing had violated the Australian tradition of "one manager, one mine" and had created what appeared in Australian eyes to be a "trust."[58]

What would happen, workers wondered, if Hoover's firm attained a monopoly over mining—and mining jobs? Would a miner who was discharged at one of the firm's mines be able to find a job at another? In 1903 Hoover had proposed a "ticket system" as a way to eliminate gold stealers and demagogues from the fields. Miners worried that men "once under a ban" would be blacklisted and "hounded out of the Commonwealth."[59]

Prichard labeled this fear of "hounding" a "silly" one. "We do not come in personal contact with 90 per cent of our employees," he said. "We pick the ablest men possible for superintendents and these select their staff. The mine bosses alone employ and are held responsible for the personnel and work of the workers."[60] In the inflamed atmosphere of the election campaign, Prichard's assurances probably had little impact.

For something much more concrete than the abstract fear of monopoly was agitating the goldfields. It was the growing conviction that Bewick, Moreing was showing "an unfortunate proclivity for the employment of Italian labour."[61] The firm's use of Italians was in itself nothing new. Back in 1898 Hoover had introduced Italian contract laborers at the Sons of Gwalia. But now, in 1904, critics believed that the firm's reliance on non-English-speaking Italian immigrants was neither occasional nor casual but a deliberate and dangerous policy. They charged that the firm's use of Italian labor was soaring, particularly on the remote goldfields far to the north of Kalgoorlie. They accused the firm of importing workers directly from Italy and giving them jobs on mines in preference to "Britishers," who were allegedly passed over, even fired, to make way for the "foreigner." Critics claimed that few of the Italians spoke English, that few worked for wages, that instead nearly all worked on contract (that is, at a specific task performed for a stipulated fee). At the Sons of Gwalia, where Italians comprised a sizable fraction of the work force, the local trade union organizer asserted that a "considerable increase" in the hiring of Italians had occurred "since the Arbitration Court award . . . fixing the wages for the district." He suspected that the companies were attempting thereby to "flout the Arbitration Court award."[62]

From the Golden Mile to Mount Leonora, the goldfields seethed with angry words in early 1904. The virulence of the campaign against Hoover's firm seemed to intensify as the election neared. The *Kalgoorlie Miner*, chief newspaper of the goldfields, decried the "alien invasion" and declared that "unless stringent measures are adopted the British worker will be gradually ousted by the foreign element."[63] The *Westralian Worker*, organ of the labor unions, said that Bewick, Moreing was so "inseparably associated" in the public mind with the "dago influx as to reflect odium on all who are connected with them."[64] In the goldfields press, ethnic slurs shot forth about the "dirty dago" and "the cheap and nasty alien workers."[65] At a mass meeting in Leonora, two miles from the Sons of Gwalia, the editor of the local newspaper fulminated against the "obnoxious evil" posed by the "illiterate," "socially degraded" Italian immigrants.[66] To the editor the presence of these foreigners was inextricably linked to the use of the "baneful" contract system. He claimed that Bewick, Moreing listed only the heads of contract labor parties on its pay sheets, not each individual worker, thereby concealing the true dimensions of Italian immigration.[67]

To this crescendo of antipathy Bewick, Moreing and Company replied. W. A. Prichard and the superintendent of the Sons of Gwalia flatly denied that the firm was importing Italians.[68] Stories about Italians on the northern mines, said Prichard, were "greatly exaggerated." There had been "no increase in the number" of Italians employed on Bewick, Moreing mines "collectively" in the past year. In fact, at "most of the mines under our control" the number of Italians had declined since 1902. Prichard claimed that Italian contract workers did not undercut the arbitration award for day wages; in fact, their average remuneration exceeded it. He further claimed that Italians were hired "when men were scarce," and that they "usually take a class of work that is not much sought after by Australians." According to Prichard, the Italian miner "generally does his work well and gives the bosses but very little trouble." But perhaps to mollify the opposition, Prichard hinted that Bewick, Moreing would hire only so many Italians. "The Italian worker, like any other nationality, gives trouble when in too large numbers. From a purely economical standpoint, mixed nationalities in a mine give the best results."[69]

Prichard's assertion that Italians were employed only when other workers were scarce exasperated some of his opponents. "Purely rubbish," said one union organizer.[70] "Unmitigated untruth," exclaimed the rabidly anti-foreign editor of the *Mount Leonora Miner*. It was "indisputable," he asserted, that "dozens of honest, able, hard-working Britishers have been sacked at the Gwalia one day, and the next day their places have been filled by Italians who couldn't speak two words of English."[71]

As tension continued unabated, the mayor of Kalgoorlie expressed fear that "social disturbance," even violence, might occur. He therefore urged the state's premier to appoint a royal commission to investigate the employment of non-British white immigrants.[72] Bewick, Moreing's management, too, tried to defuse the issue. At the end of April W. J. Loring ordered all Bewick, Moreing mine superintendents to discharge any employee "not capable of speaking or understanding the English language."[73] That meant Italians, and within the next few months the number of Italian workers at several Bewick, Moreing mines, including the Sons of Gwalia, fell sharply.[74]

Neither Loring's decision nor the Labour Party's victory in the election completely quelled the uproar. On May 25, 1904 the Governor of Western Australia formally appointed a Royal Commission on the Immigration of Non-British Labour. For the next several months the commission collected evidence from nearly seventy witnesses, including Loring and other officials of Hoover's firm. Early in November the commission submitted its report.

In some respects the commission's findings suggested that the alarums about an "alien invasion" were, as Prichard had said, "greatly exaggerated." Of the more than 17,000 men employed on the West Australian goldfields in 1903, only 716 were aliens—a ratio of barely one to twenty-five. The commission found no proof that anyone was importing persons into Western Australia under explicit contract to do manual labor (an offense under Australian law). Nor did the commission find "any but the vaguest evidence" that aliens received lower rates of wages than native workers. The commission also ascertained that while the number of non-British miners tended to increase in late 1903 and early 1904, it had subsided since, a consequence of Loring's order and a "change in the policy" of Bewick, Moreing.

Yet while the overall number of Italian miners in the state was small, the commission found that more than half of them were concentrated at just five northern mines (all run by Bewick, Moreing), including the Sons of Gwalia, Lancefield, and Great Fingall. At these mines the percentage of Italians ranged from 19% to 39%. These figures and the "uncontroverted testimony" of witnesses convinced the commission that preference had "distinctly" and "habitually" been shown to Italians at certain mines. In fact, "experienced British miners [were] refused work over and over again, while Italians—often newly come to the State—were being freely accepted. . . ." The "testimony is overwhelming," the commission asserted, that even as the Italians were hired there was "no scarcity" of British labor available and that Italians were given preference particularly for contract work.

Why this peculiar preference? It was not, said the commission, because Italians were better miners than the British (although some witnesses thought Italians worked harder and more steadily, especially just after payday). Nor was it because they worked more cheaply than Britishers. The evidence did not sustain these claims.

Instead, the commission concluded that the use of Italians was a direct result of labor troubles between the employers and the employees. At the Sons of Gwalia, for instance, it appeared that a large influx of Italians followed a dispute between management and the union. At the hearings a number of witnesses, including Loring, testified that the Bewick, Moreing management found non-English-speaking Italians to be more "peaceable," more obedient, more "servile," less inclined than "British" workers to make trouble for the boss. Loring testified that the management "would be in a hopeless mess if they had all aliens or all British. . . . If there were all Italians they would be running the mine, and it would be just the same with others." Loring considered "mixed labour" to be "advantageous in a mine."[75]

Surveying the evidence, the commission decided, somewhat inferentially, that "the favour shown to Italians" in the northern mines reflected Bewick, Moreing's anger at rulings by the wage-fixing arbitration court. The preference for Italians "was designed to counteract the advantage gained by the

Workers' Unions before the Arbitration Court by rendering it more difficult for their members to obtain employment, with the design of forcing them in the long run to abate their terms."

The commission urged stringent restrictions on the use in mines of aliens unable to speak English fluently. Safety underground required it. And the commission recommended that most mines should not employ a ratio of more than one-seventh aliens without the approval of the Minister for Mines.[76]

Less than a month after the royal commission presented its report, Hoover's firm faced assault on yet another front: the West Australian state parliament. The 1904 election had led to the accession of a Labour Ministry. On November 30, 1904 the newly elected Labour representative for Hannans (Kalgoorlie) proposed that a select parliamentary committee be appointed to investigate allegations that a harmful mining monopoly was arising on the goldfields. The member cited current unrest over Bewick, Moreing's stores supply scheme, its use of Italian labor, and the fear that the firm might ultimately control sources of employment for miners and be able to drive a discharged worker from the fields.[77]

Bewick, Moreing and its allies in the press responded forcefully. "We are not monopolists," said Prichard, reiterating his argument of eight months before. "Our firm does not own a single mine in the State, nor does it hold a controlling interest in any Western Australian gold-producing property. We simply act as general managers at this end for a number of English mining companies, who are entirely independent of each other."[78]

The *Australian Mining Standard* was more pointed. What monopoly, it asked, was the legislator talking about? Bewick, Moreing had no monopoly at all. "What advantage does Bewick, Moreing possess in which it is not equally open for others to participate? Wherein lies its security against competition? . . . So far from a firm thus situated enjoying a monopoly, it has to be on its guard at every point to hold its own against rivals ever watching for their opportunity."[79]

In London the special correspondent of the *Western Australian Mining, Building, and Engineering Journal* also rose to Bewick, Moreing's defense. Not only was the evidence for the existence of monopoly weak, he argued; the Labour legislator betrayed a "short-sighted feeling" whose result would be "to drive capital away from the State." The journalist twitted the M.P. for apparently considering a "monopoly of capital" to be "altogether wrong" but a "monopoly of labor" (which the unions were aiming at) to be "quite right." The journalist congratulated Bewick, Moreing for "sticking to the colony" and again called attention to the firm's great achievement: ". . . by rendering possible the profitable treatment of low-grade ore, owing to the reduction effected in working costs, they have rendered no small service to the State."[80]

Hoover and his colleagues were no doubt exasperated by the continuing agitation. Were it not for their firm's tight management several marginal mines would be shut down and hundreds of men unemployed.[81] Efficiency meant longer life for the mines, and that meant jobs. Couldn't the unions see that?

As it turned out, Bewick, Moreing and Company did not have to endure an investigation by the West Australian parliament. Before the motion was debated, A. E. Morgans, vice-president of the Chamber of Mines of Western Australia, quietly approached the state premier, a Labour man. Morgans, an influential figure, was an old friend of Hoover. Morgans explained (in one journal's words) that "great injury . . . was likely to accrue" if the Ministry approved the motion to investigate the "monopoly." The premier proved amenable and refused to support the motion. The effort by the legislator from Kalgoorlie collapsed.[82]

Bewick, Moreing and Company was now safe from legislative reprisal. Although occasional protests at the firm's use of Italians were heard in future years, they never approached the fury of the tempest of 1904.[83]

Hoover was in London when the public outcry in Western Australia reached a crescendo in 1904. Unlike Moreing, Prichard, and Loring, he apparently did not comment publicly about it at that time. His *Memoirs* conveyed no hint about the Italian episode or about his firm's considerable unpopularity on the goldfields. But Hoover's attitude toward the Labour Party was no mystery. "The so-called Welsh, 'Yankee,' and English 'slave-driver,' " he declared in 1905, "have done Western Australia more good than the whole Labor Party. If it were not for them the East Murchison, Waroonga, Vivien, Bellevue, Lancefield, Sons of Gwalia and Lake View mines would be closed down to-day, and 3,000 men would be out of work, and four villages practically extinguished. . . . All that these 'slave-drivers' have asked is a fair intelligent day's work, and they have not sought to reduce wages."[84]

The years 1904–5 were difficult ones for Hoover and his associates in West Australian mining. As the Labour Ministry prepared to pass what Hoover called "oppressive" legislation, he and his partners "made up their mind" (so he later stated) to "shut up shop" in Western Australia and "withdraw all our capital."[85] Late in 1905, however, the Labour government of Western Australia fell from power. Hoover welcomed the advent of a "more Conservative Government" in the state and announced that his firm's plans to pull out had changed.[86] A couple of months later he wrote with satisfaction: "Politically the Colony has freed itself from a labor government, and more can now be hoped toward the development of the State's resources."[87]

I I I

E A R L Y in 1904 the prestigious *Engineering and Mining Journal* of New York took note of Bewick, Moreing's increasing domination of mining in Western Australia. To the journal's editor, T. A. Rickard, the firm's success exemplified a new development in mine management: "subordinating the control of the directors to that of the engineering staff." While Rickard expected "nothing but honorable conduct" from Bewick, Moreing, he warned that the fate of the new system would "depend entirely" on "the abstention of the engineering management from share speculation." Engineers in charge of a mine must not gamble in stocks of that mine; the temptations and potential conflicts of interest were too dangerous.[88] A few weeks later, in the course of defending Bewick, Moreing against its Australian critics, Rickard advised the firm to "avoid the two obvious perils of people in their position, namely, trafficking in shares and biting off more than they can comfortably assimilate."[89]

Certainly the stock market was much on Hoover's mind in the spring of 1904. While controversy boiled in Western Australia, Hoover, in London, had to fend off an assault of a different sort—a bear raid against a Bewick, Moreing-managed mine. In late March stock market "bears" launched an attack on the Oroya Brownhill mine. Rumors spread that the ore was turning out to be much less rich than Bewick, Moreing engineers had estimated.[90] For Hoover and his partners this was a dangerous allegation, for it questioned the firm's professional competence and even, perhaps, its integrity. The firm therefore issued a challenge. Certain that its data about ore reserves were correct, the firm offered to deposit £2,000 to finance an independent examination of the mine—if its critics would step forward and do the same. If Bewick, Moreing's ore estimates were proven wrong, it would have to pay the independent engineer and forfeit the £2,000. But if the firm's critics were found mistaken, they would lose the £2,000 that they put up.[91]

Bewick, Moreing's offer evidently got no takers, and the bear raid against the Oroya Brownhill soon failed. In the press one journalist attributed the raid to speculators' antagonism toward Bewick, Moreing. "The taking over the management of many of the best mines" by the firm was "the last thing these manipulators desired," he claimed. They could " 'bear' till they are blue in the face and it will make no difference" to Bewick, Moreing.[92]

This was Bewick, Moreing's public image, furbished by its numerous allies in the press: solid probity; efficient management; sober engineering expertise; complete avoidance of stockjobbing, of collusion with "bears," and of other excesses of Western Australia's "dirty era." And then, in June 1904, the image appeared to crack, and Hoover's roof caved in once again.

The story began when Hoover sailed from New Zealand back to England (via California) at the very end of 1903.[93] Returning with him on board was a fellow American, Ralph Nichols, general manager of the successful Great Boulder Perseverance mine on the Golden Mile. During the voyage the two men discussed the possibility of Bewick, Moreing's assuming the management of this mine but came to no definite agreement.

Shortly after Hoover returned to London in February 1904, his firm entered into negotiations with the board of directors of the Great Boulder Perseverance. It soon became clear, however, that to obtain its management Hoover and his partners would have to pay a price. They would have to bail the Perseverance chairman, Frank Gardner, out of a deepening financial crisis.

Gardner, a company promoter and speculator, was in need of cash. To raise it he was attempting to sell 60,000 shares that he held in his own company. To secure the management, Bewick, Moreing would have to buy up Gardner's shares.[94]

The Bewick, Moreing partners accepted this condition, and the deal was struck. A portion of Gardner's block was taken up by unnamed friends of Bewick, Moreing. But the firm itself bought most of his shares (38,500) at an average price (Moreing said) of £1.7s.9d., for a total outlay of more than £53,000—more than a quarter of a million dollars.[95] To the board of directors of the Perseverance, C. Algernon Moreing signified his intention not to speculate in these shares but instead to hold them for two years, at which time they would be sold and Gardner would receive half the profit. Perhaps because of the unusual nature of this transaction Moreing and his partners did not register the firm's shares in the firm's name.

The rest of the deal was codified in contracts signed in London in March and April. Nichols remained resident manager of the mine at an increased salary but now became a Bewick, Moreing employee. The firm itself became general manager of the mine for two-and-a-half years on the usual terms of fixed annual salary (£3,000) plus a one percent share of the annual dividends.

One feature of the arrangement was not at all customary. Bewick, Moreing specifically contracted to transmit from Kalgoorlie all information or discoveries about the mine directly and exclusively to the company's offices in London, "and not through the London office" of Bewick, Moreing. In this way Gardner and his fellow directors, all of them apparently large shareholders in their own company, would receive vital information before anyone else. Possibly Gardner and his colleagues insisted on this clause in order to prevent Bewick, Moreing from taking prior advantage on the market of *its* "inside" knowledge of the mine's condition. (After all, the firm now held 38,500 shares.) Far more likely some of the directors, notably Gardner, had ends of their own to serve.

In accepting the management of the Great Boulder Perseverance without prior inspection, Hoover, Moreing, and Wellsted were taking a risk. For months the mine had been afflicted by disturbing rumors and attacks by "bears" who claimed that the mine could not possibly maintain its very high monthly output.[96] Yet Hoover and his partners had reason to feel confident. Ralph Nichols was a reputable engineer. Moreover, at the Perseverance's stockholders meeting on March 25, 1904, Nichols estimated that as of the end of 1903 the mine had over 400,000 tons of ore in sight averaging better than an ounce of gold to the ton. With such enormous reserves the mine's prospects, and thus the firm's percentage of future profits, seemed certain. Relying on Nichols's figures and the assurances of some of the company's directors, Hoover and his partners formally completed their management arrangement on April 20, 1904.

The next day they cabled to W. A. Prichard, the firm's joint general manager in Kalgoorlie. Take control of the Perseverance tomorrow, the cable ordered. "Sampler must check assay plans. Send us estimate of the reserves of ore; what is the average value." Send *us*, the cable read; the company's office in London was not mentioned. Now that Hoover and his partners had the management, they evidently wanted to confirm, on their own, Nichols's data.

Prichard construed this order as a request for a preliminary, hurry-up "check sample." At once, however, he ran into trouble. It turned out that the mine had no assay plans; none had been kept for two years. The assay books from which plans could be made were of little use, either. Going underground, Prichard discovered that gold production at the Perseverance had been forced and that the mine was now struggling to maintain its high monthly average output. He did not yet know that the monthly production figures had themselves been grossly inflated for some time by drawing on a secret bullion reserve.

There were other unsettling portents. In the absence of Nichols, who was still in London, the acting resident manager was his brother Harry. On May 9 Prichard cabled to his firm in London that Ralph had telegraphed Harry not to act on orders from Bewick, Moreing. Nichols's underground manager, Michael Flynn, was even more uncooperative, at first refusing to give Prichard any information whatever about ore values. Even after Harry Nichols ordered Flynn to do so, Prichard was obliged to "cross-examine" Flynn in order to extract much of the data he sought. Since Flynn carried the information in his head, Prichard could not quickly corroborate it during a somewhat cursory preliminary examination.

During the preceding months Flynn had assured his superiors that the mine's heavy monthly production could be sustained. But on May 16, before submitting his findings, Prichard learned from London that Flynn was suspected of secretly colluding with stock market "bears" (a charge Flynn afterwards denied). Was Flynn's optimism about the mine feigned? Flynn was furloughed and eventually dismissed, but in preparing his report for Hoover and Moreing, Prichard nevertheless relied considerably on the data that Flynn reluctantly supplied.

On May 18 Prichard cabled his results to Bewick, Moreing—not to the Perseverance offices in London. Prichard indicated that his method of sampling was "not sufficient for accurate estimate" of the ore reserves. Nevertheless, he went on to assert that it virtually confirmed the tonnage figures given in Nichols's annual report in March (about 400,000 tons of ore in sight). While this was reassuring, the rest of Prichard's cable was not. Although the quantity of ore reserves remained high (he thought), the value of these reserves was 30% less than what Nichols had stated. And the richest sections of the mine were being gutted to maintain an artificially high output, unreflective of the true condition of the mine.

Prichard later testified that he intended his cable to be a warning to his firm. "I could see there was a big scandal coming," he said. "I was simply trying to start the investigation. . . . I was trying . . . to convince our people that they had been had over the matter." Whether or not Hoover and Moreing read nearly so much into Prichard's cable was uncertain. After all, Prichard did essentially confirm Nichols's tonnage data.

But storm signals had been raised, and on May 26 Hoover and his partners cabled back to their Kalgoorlie office. Continue to "thoroughly sample" the Great Boulder Perseverance, they ordered. Complete the task by the time Ralph Nichols, on his way from London, arrived back at the mine. "In the meantime nothing must be disclosed, as we do not wish to take action too precipitate on preliminary examination."

Meanwhile, on May 18, after receiving Prichard's cable in London, Moreing verbally communicated its contents to the Perseverance board.[97] But it was not until thirteen days later that the board issued a circular about it to its shareholders. In the interim Perseverance shares fell sharply on the stock market. Moreing, Hoover, and the various directors later denied selling off any of their shares during this period, when only they knew that something was up at the mine. According to one of the directors the board was "completely staggered" by Prichard's findings but realized that they were only "preliminary." The board "did not want to create a panic" and deemed it wise to wait for Ralph Nichols to return and investigate the situation.

The circular which the directors finally issued on May 31 conveyed no intimation of alarm. It urged stockholders to disregard "wild rumours" that were allegedly depressing the shares' value. It stressed that Prichard's report was only "preliminary" and that an "exhaustive examination" was underway. Curiously, the circular stated that Prichard's report had reduced the estimated ore value by 25%, not (as he had stated) 30%. Why this error? One of Gardner's fellow directors, Zebina Lane, later asserted that Hoover personally drew up this part of the circular—a charge Hoover categorically denied. According to Hoover, the mistake about the percentage arose from an error in decoding Prichard's cable, an error not discovered until a copy of his cable arrived later in the mail.[98] In any case the effect of the mistake was further to understate the mine's malaise.

In mid-June the second mine examination, supervised by W. J. Loring, was completed. Unlike Prichard's initial survey, which had taken ore samples at fifty-foot intervals (too wide for accuracy), the new survey took samples every seventeen feet. Together with Ralph Nichols himself, back at last on the scene, Loring cabled the new results to Bewick, Moreing on June 20.

They were devastating. The Great Boulder Perseverance mine did *not* have 400,000 tons of ore reserves (as Nichols had reported in March and Prichard in May). It had less than 140,000 tons. It did *not* have over 500,000 ounces of recoverable gold (as Nichols had reported in March), or even roughly 282,000 ounces (as Prichard had estimated). Instead, the once-proud mine had but 99,345 ounces of gold. The mine's stated reserve had shrunk in value from over £2,000,000 to a mere £418,000 in just three months.[99]

Hoover and Moreing were stunned. On June 24 Hoover wrote to Loring that it came as a "thunderclap" that Prichard's month-old estimate of reserves could be so wrong.[100] Within minutes of receiving the cable on the twentieth, Hoover dutifully delivered it to the Perseverance office. Only one director, Lane, was there. Shocked and incredulous (so he later testified), Lane wondered whether the cable as received was accurate. He therefore requested that the message from Kalgoorlie be repeated. Bewick, Moreing duly dispatched Lane's request, and the next day, June 21, a confirmatory cable arrived from Kalgoorlie. There was no mistake about the figures. Blocks of ground formerly considered valuable on the mine had turned out not to be.

Yet someone in London still was not satisfied. Upon receipt of this second cable, Hoover and his partners sent out still another (at whose instigation is unclear): *which part* of the Perseverance mine did not contain payable ore? The answer, it ordered, must reach London by early June 22.

What was going on? Were Lane and his fellow director / shareholders stalling for time to get out? On June 21, while Hoover and his partners waited for clarification from Kalgoorlie, the price of Great Boulder Perseverance shares plummeted on the London stock exchange. Yet only Bewick, Moreing and the directors were as yet officially apprised of the bad news from the mine. The board of directors had not yet informed its own shareholders. All the principals, including Lane, later denied that they disposed of shares on June 21. But *somebody* appeared to be doing so, and C. Algernon Moreing did not like it.

On June 22, well over a day after Hoover delivered Loring's first dispatch to the Perseverance office, the Perseverance board of directors convened. Later that day they issued a circular at last to their stockholders, who now knew, more than forty-eight hours after the "insiders," the stark facts about the mine. But Bewick, Moreing and Company had had enough. On the morning of the twenty-second, even as (or before) the directors met, Moreing, Hoover, and Wellsted unloaded. As Moreing later put it, "after allowing one clear day [June 21] to permit of . . . publication [of Loring's report], and finding the shares of the Company rapidly falling, my firm disposed of a portion of its holding." By the time Moreing and his colleagues finished selling their 38,500 shares, the average price they obtained was less than half what they originally paid Gardner.[101]

In selling out hurriedly, Moreing and his partners no doubt helped to push the share price even lower—before the stockholders at large knew that anything was amiss. Such was an advantage of being an insider. They had, of course, taken a terrific loss, but perhaps less than they might have sustained if they had waited any longer. Still, Moreing and Hoover felt fully justified in their action. They had put up over £50,000 to purchase Frank Gardner's shares, and had agreed to manage his mine—all on the strength of ore estimates that were flagrantly erroneous. So erroneous, in fact, as to suggest willful misrepresentation. Moreing felt deceived by some of the directors (as

Prichard afterwards recalled) and hence felt at liberty to dispose of the shares as he wished. The directors' inaction on June 20 and 21, as Hoover and Moreing construed it, only deepened the sense of betrayal. Long afterwards Hoover wrote, "As the Board withheld the information from the stockholders, and the stock continued to drop, the firm properly concluded that the Board was not acting in good faith. . . ."[102] Why should Hoover and his partners be left holding 38,500 depreciating shares while other insiders were evidently dumping theirs?

The board of directors soon turned angrily on Moreing. Had he not violated his pledge not to sell his firm's block of shares for two years? Moreing denied that he had made any such promise. He had only stated his *intention* to hold the shares for two years and his *intention* not to speculate in them. Since the whole premise of his involvement—reliance on reports about the mine's value—was false, since his firm had been "taken down" by the ore report, he felt free to cut his losses. Neither Moreing nor Hoover seemed to doubt that they had been deliberately misled.

The sensational discrepancies in the estimates of ore reserves triggered a government investigation in Western Australia. Was the scandal a conspiracy or only a case of bad judgment and honest error? In late 1904, as one royal commission scrutinized Bewick, Moreing's use of Italian labor, another probed the affairs of the Great Boulder Perseverance. In Australia Prichard, Loring, Nichols, and Flynn, among others, testified, while Hoover, Moreing, and various Perseverance directors sent sworn depositions from London.

The royal commission's report, issued at the end of December 1904, criticized nearly all the parties in the case. The report condemned the underground manager, Flynn, for failing to keep proper records of his data, for relying too much on his memory, and for "methods of valuation" that produced "an exaggerated estimate of the value of the ore reserves." The commission believed that Flynn "must have known" that the mine could not sustain its high monthly production average. It faulted Nichols, who was often absent from the mine for long periods, for accepting without question the figures supplied by Flynn (the de facto manager), particularly when Nichols's own brother Harry repeatedly warned him that Flynn's valuations were "excessive." In the commission's eyes Nichols had been negligent and guilty of serious errors of judgment—which, like Flynn's actions, led to an overvaluation of the mine in his annual report in March.

The royal commission criticized Prichard as well. He, too, had relied heavily on Flynn's faulty figures, despite Flynn's manifest uncooperativeness and a warning that Flynn was in collusion with the "bears." Moreover, Prichard by his own account had conducted a hasty and preliminary sampling, despite having no clear instructions before May 18 to conduct his examination in this manner. In formulating his cable of May 18 he did not convey the warning he later said he meant to transmit. Perhaps unfairly, the commission said that Prichard was not justified in treating his cable as a private, not-to-be-published report to Bewick, Moreing (although his firm had in fact told him to send it to "us").

The commission's severest judgments fell on the Great Boulder Persever-ance board of directors. The report castigated the company for concealing the existence of its bullion reserve from its own stockholders and for dealing with the reserve in a manner contrary to West Australian law. Indeed, the directors had striven to "rigidly prevent any information as to the working of the mine and the true position of the mine from becoming known." Some of the directors must have known "perfectly well" that the mine was in trou-ble and falling in output in early 1904, yet they "withheld all this informa-tion" and instead submitted a rosy annual report to their shareholders in March. The royal commission criticized those in London responsible for the belated circular of May 31 announcing the contents of Prichard's cable of May 18. Not only should this cable have been published as soon as received; the circular itself was improperly reassuring and "misleading." The commis-sion said it had received "no satisfactory explanation" of why Prichard's 30% reduction of reserves was "altered" to read 25% in the May 31 circular. Nor had it received satisfactory evidence about the stock market transactions that occurred just after receipt of the divergent estimates of ore reserves.

"It would appear," said the commission, "that the Chairman of Directors, Frank Gardner, and some of the directors have throughout advanced their own interests and have shown an utter disregard for the interests of the share-holders."

Herbert Hoover later stated that the royal commission's report cast no reflection, "directly or indirectly," on him.[103] This was not quite correct. The commission found it odd that Hoover and his partners did not register their firm's 38,500 shares in the firm's own name. It concluded that Bewick, Moreing "did not desire it to be known that they were holding shares" in the company. The commission also was not satisfied about the May 31 circular (who "altered" Prichard's cable?) and the reasons for the additional cables to Kalgoorlie on June 20–21. The commission found "strong ground for suspi-cion" that somebody wanted the delay for the "distinct purpose" of gaining time to unload their shares. But the commission claimed not to know who was responsible for this delay, and it wished that Bewick, Moreing had given a "full explanation" about "whose instructions" had led it to dispatch addi-tional cables. Above all, the commission stated that Bewick, Moreing had consistently "disregarded" the clause of its contract requiring all information about the mine to be sent directly to the company's office and not through Bewick, Moreing's London office. The ore estimates from Kalgoorlie had gone first to Hoover and his partners in violation (so the commission believed) of the firm's agreement with its employer.

While the commission seemed determined to spread the blame widely, its criticisms of Hoover's firm were minor compared to its revelations about the company's directors. There was nothing illegal or necessarily unethical about

Bewick, Moreing's registering shares in someone else's name. As for the June 20–21 cables, the commission seemed to forget that Zebina Lane testified that he requested the "clarifying" messages (although he denied selling his shares at that time). And while Bewick, Moreing technically violated its contract by having its Kalgoorlie office report the ore reserves first to it, the firm did promptly pass these messages on, and the company's directors—who thereby had to know of the violation—evidently made no complaint. In requesting Prichard in April to check up on the mine and cable his results directly to the firm, Hoover no doubt felt he was only being prudent. He and his partners had just taken over a property rumored to be in a parlous state. They had already reposed trust (over £50,000 of trust) in Gardner and Nichols. Now they must protect themselves against possible scoundrels, contract or no contract.

Hoover, therefore, could take comfort from the royal commission's report. *He* had not been responsible for the mismanagement of the mine. Rather, it was his own firm that had exposed it. The firm had, in fact (as Hoover later put it) "reported adversely to their own interests," since Hoover and his partners personally stood to suffer financially—and did suffer—from the exposé.[104] Hoover could also take wry pleasure from another fact. At the royal commission's hearings Ralph Nichols attacked W. J. Loring's ore estimate of June 20, although he himself co-signed it. A few months later a new examination at the mine substantially confirmed Loring's estimate: another boost to Bewick, Moreing's reputation for competence.[105]

Out on the goldfields the Kalgoorlie correspondent of the *West Australian Mining, Building, and Engineering Journal* hailed the royal commission's report as a total vindication of Bewick, Moreing. The firm had "not been a party to the hanky panky and tiddliwinking practices" of the mine's management. It had done nothing to be "ashamed of" and had emerged from the inquiry without a scratch.[106]

Still, Hoover had been in a nasty scrape. He later asserted that the commission's report showed the "complete integrity of engineering and management" by Bewick, Moreing.[107] But buying one's way into the management (and then concealing the fact)—however explicable under the circumstances—inevitably conveyed a suspicion of impropriety. And selling out one's shares on inside information, even if at a loss and in the belief that one had been doublecrossed, left a lingering impression of unfairness, of exploiting one's prior knowledge to the detriment of the ordinary shareholder. Hoover now had occasion to ponder T.A. Rickard's recent warning about mingling professional engineering with "trafficking in shares."

Sometime in late 1904 or early 1905 Gardner and Lane resigned from the Perseverance board.[108] Gardner stood exposed as a corrupt speculator. A separate investigation in late 1904 held him responsible for fraud at another mine which he directed. The inquiry found that Gardner had urged his mine manager at one point to conceal the true nature of the property from Gardner's fellow directors and had even suggested that the manager knowingly file a false report, the better to help Gardner acquire control of the shares.[109]

Gardner's departure, however, did not resolve Bewick, Moreing's difficulties with the Great Boulder Perseverance. Even after the "thunderclap" of mid-June, Hoover's firm remained the company's general managers under its unexpired contract. For the next several months three-cornered confusion and acrimony enveloped the troubled company.[110] Who was responsible for the mine's administration? Bewick, Moreing was unable to get along with Nichols, who (it was reported) "chafed" under the firm's management, apparently with the encouragement of certain members of the Perseverance board.[111] Early in January 1905 the directors rescinded their management contract with Bewick, Moreing, nearly two years before it was due to terminate.[112] A month later, at the annual meeting, Nichols confessed his carelessness and negligence. He had been absent too much from the mine in recent years; he had unwisely and excessively relied on a trusted subordinate (Flynn). The board thereupon decided to permit Nichols to retrieve his reputation (it was his judgment, not his integrity, that had been criticized). Nichols was reappointed general manager.[113]

Nichols now turned around and sued Bewick, Moreing—on what grounds is not known.[114] And Bewick, Moreing instituted suit against the Perseverance board, apparently over its cancelled contract.[115] The firm's speedy sale of its 38,500 shares in mid-1904 also still rankled. At the 1905 annual meeting the Perseverance chairman claimed that the share price had not fallen until Bewick, Moreing unloaded its block on June 22.[116] Bewick, Moreing rejoined that they did not cause the drop; they only sold out *after* the drop took place.[117] Meanwhile in Kalgoorlie W. A. Prichard unexpectedly resigned from Bewick, Moreing, allegedly because of eye trouble caused by Kalgoorlie's sandy soil.[118]

The outcome of this flurry of litigation is unknown. But Herbert Hoover had learned a bitter lesson. Apparently never again did his firm purchase stock as a condition of winning the management of a mine. In his *Memoirs* Hoover recorded that "it does not pay to try to reform a stock-market crook."[119]

How much did Hoover lose in the Great Boulder Perseverance affair? On June 24, 1904 Hoover told his Kalgoorlie office, "Our confidence in Nichols has cost us £40,000."[120] Some years later he gave a figure of half that amount.[121] Moreing's sworn deposition to the royal commission indicated that the firm lost £27,000 (or about $131,000) on its block of 38,500 shares.[122] This may not have represented the total loss, however, since Bewick, Moreing had other financial transactions with Gardner than the Perseverance share deal.[123] A few weeks after the "thunderclap" Hoover told his brother that he had lost $85,000 because of Nichols's "misrepresentation."[124] Whatever the exact amount, the Perseverance fiasco had cost him dearly.

Scandals, quarrels, lawsuits. Would they never cease? In March 1904, while negotiating arrangements to take over the Perseverance, Hoover's firm secured the management of another famous Kalgoorlie mine, the Golden Horseshoe Estates. The terms of the contract were unusual: Bewick, Moreing promised to reduce the mine's high working costs to 25s. per ton (exclusive of smelting costs) by the end of the year and maintain development work up to previous standards, or its contract would expire and it would forfeit all payment for its services.[125] It soon became evident that the board and its new managers were not working well together. In September 1904, nearly four months before the expiration date of Bewick, Moreing's contract, the directors fired the firm and expelled it from control of the mine.[126]

At the Golden Horseshoe's annual meeting in April 1905, the board chairman unleashed a massive attack on Bewick, Moreing. Among other things, the chairman alleged that Hoover and his partners, once they "got their foot in," attempted to become "masters of the mine"—something the board was "determined not to allow." The board's efforts to "enforce obedience" to its orders, the chairman said, were "fruitless." Bewick, Moreing did not maintain proper development as it had contracted to do. Its mine manager, Loring, did not send cables to the company first, as stipulated by the contract, but to Bewick, Moreing's London office first. When the directors moved to dismiss the firm, Hoover told them that they would have to use force to oust it from the mine. The company, in fact, did have to take legal steps to make Bewick, Moreing's staff surrender the mine. The company then found (said the chairman) that the underground workings had been "neglected" and that the West Australian government had warned Bewick, Moreing's staff about it. Moreover, the company found on resuming control that Hoover's firm had transferred at least £14,000 of the company's gold to its bankers—allegedly as payment for supplies—yet had produced no vouchers for these supplies. And the directors had expressly ordered Bewick, Moreing not to place the Golden Horseshoe under the firm's cooperative supplies arrangement.[127]

The chairman's speech contained a sensational tale of mismanagement and chicanery. But was it true? Bewick, Moreing and Company immediately issued a comprehensive rebuttal. Hoover and his partners pointed out that their contract stipulated that they were to have "a free hand" in reorganizing the mine and plant—a condition that the board of directors did not meet. Instead, the board "seemed to put every obstacle in our way." As for supplies, it was not true that the board had disallowed participation in the cooperative stores scheme. The Golden Horseshoe Estates "regularly received the stores and rebates due to them with full knowledge of the whole arrangement." As for development work, Bewick, Moreing did not maintain it, said Hoover, because the main compressor on the mine broke down, forcing curtailment of underground operations while the spare parts were sent from Europe.

Hoover and his partners accused the Golden Horseshoe chairman of repeatedly omitting vital facts. The underground workings, for example, were indeed in upheaval when the firm was dismissed, but this was because the firm was "transforming the stoping system" with the aim of cutting costs. Hoover and his partners did not deny that they had resisted efforts to evict them from the mine in September. But they clearly believed that the board's dismissal of them before December 31 was a breach of contract. They were entitled to stay until then. And they put a portion of the company's gold in trust because the company owed £12,000 on stores supplies and had refused to pay it, leaving Bewick, Moreing liable for the whole bill. Only then had Bewick, Moreing's staff transferred the gold, on advice of counsel, pending settlement of the dispute. We did it, said Hoover and his partners, for self-protection. Hoover feared that if his men had not transferred the gold, the board, when it regained control, would have used its unpaid £12,000 debt as a club "in order to be able to dictate terms of settlement to us in respect of their violation of their agreement."[128] (Eventually the company filed a lawsuit but settled out of court. Bewick, Moreing surrendered the gold but received £10,000 in return for its claims.)[129]

Hoover and his partners made charges of their own. They claimed that unnamed shareholders repeatedly pressured them to cable in favorable news from the mine in order to boost the shares on the market. This the firm said it refused to do. Various interested parties also urged them to join pools to "assist in the pushing" of Golden Horseshoe shares—which, again, the firm declined to do. Hoover and his colleagues disclosed that some of the company's directors had financial interests that conflicted with proper discharge of their duties. And in a jab at the board chairman (a Knight Commander of the Bath), they warned: ". . . gold mining companies will remain under a cloud as long as they are managed by boards of directors consisting of titled guinea-pigs who are ignorant of mining and Stock Exchange speculators."[130]

Nothing further happened after this jarring exchange of thunderbolts, the sharpest attack on Hoover's integrity (except for the Chang Yen-mao affair) during his years in partnership with Moreing. Not surprisingly, the mining press sided with Hoover. The *Engineering and Mining Journal*'s London correspondent accused the Golden Horseshoe board of exerting "petty tyranny" over Bewick, Moreing and implied that the reputation of the board's dominant directors was none too good.[131] Another journal found Hoover's reply persuasive and likened Bewick, Moreing's "Westralian establishment" to "a sort of mining hospital into which mines wounded and bleeding from the vagaries of former Managers are sent for cure and convalescence."[132]

Such talk probably irked men like John W. Sutherland, whom Bewick, Moreing replaced as manager of the Golden Horseshoe in March 1904. Years later Hoover indirectly alleged that when Sutherland departed he incited his men against Bewick, Moreing and took off for London to get even. There he conspired with one of the Golden Horseshoe directors, a former associate of the notorious Whittaker Wright. Another conspirator, according to Hoover, was the company's secretary, whom Hoover had fired from his own organization more than two years before. Malice and antagonism did the rest.

This was Hoover's "inside" story.[133] It may well explain the bitterness of the affair. Hoover also claimed that the Golden Horseshoe directors had tried to use his firm as a "shield" and that friction had followed the board's attempt to manipulate the firm.[134] At any rate, when Bewick, Moreing was forced out in September 1904, Sutherland returned as manager.[135]

What a business. Pitfalls and temptations abounded; there was hardly a man one could trust. Look at Chang Yen-mao, Gustav Detring, A. Stanley Rowe, Frank Gardner, Ralph Nichols, the Golden Horseshoe clique. Even with one's own partners and associates—sharp, sophisticated men like Moreing, Govett, Edmund Davis, W. F. Turner—one could scarcely afford to relax when it came to doing business. And one's own employees: one never knew. In 1905 Hoover discovered that one of his own mine managers in Australia had engaged in "corrupt practices" to the tune of $5,000.[136]

It was a hard profession, this mining business. A man had to live constantly by his wits. Often Hoover's firm would invest a nominal sum in an exploration syndicate "merely to keep track of what the other people are doing."[137] But Hoover seemed to enjoy the competition and intrigue. "God deliver me from a fool," he told Loring once. "I would rather do business with a rogue any day if he has brains."[138]

Hoover had had plenty of chances to do so by the summer of 1904. He was in a fast crowd. That August he turned thirty years old.

I V

S UDDENLY he had to relent. The constant battering of scandals and lawsuits had affected him more than he knew. By early that summer Hoover was veering dangerously toward a nervous breakdown. On July 9 he boarded an ocean vessel bound for South Africa.[139] Two weeks later he explained to his brother Theodore what had happened:

> This finds me enroute to Johannesburg—the first vacation in five years.
>
> The rapid expansion of our business during the past two years, the Rowe frauds, the misrepresentation of Ralf Nichols have all been too much for my nerves.
>
> I found myself slipping memory and unable at concentration of thought —and being able to sleep but 3 to 5 hours the Doctor ordered me off.

Hoover reported that Lou could not join him; young Herbert, now almost a year old, was "at the age of impossible ships Diet." So while Lou and the baby went off to the British countryside for the summer, Hoover, with his journalist-friend J. H. Curle "as general care taker," sailed for the southern hemisphere.

Hoover spent much of the voyage in bed regaining his strength. The leisurely ocean journey gave him time to pause and reflect. To his brother he wrote:

> When I review the results of the past 8 years since I left California I am not too enthusiastic. The net result is that with no further bad luck I should be out of debt and have my share of the 'goodwill' of the firm by Jan. 1, 1905, otherwise assetts nil. Nor will I own any share of B M Co.'s assetts—they belong to Wellsted & Moreing.
>
> So at the end of 8 years the hardest work + worry that can be concieved I have also the satisfaction that I have made and paid away $325000 through the wrong doings of others—$240000 through Rowe and $85000 Nichols.
>
> With no more frauds my income should be about $60000 a year for the next five years so we have hopes still. I was very foolish that I did not retire to U.S. in 1901 when I could have come home with $250000.[140]

Hoover was not a man, however, to tarry over regrets. As the voyage went on, his health improved.[141] And once he reached South Africa the trip quickly became a professional visit, as, perhaps, he had intended it to be.[142] During the next few weeks Hoover visited the Transvaal and negotiated the consolidation of certain mining interests in the region.[143] Daily he studied mining practices at the great gold mines on the Rand.[144] He met Ernest Williams, his old boss in Western Australia, and even toured a mine with him. He dined with Lord Milner, the British High Commissioner, and visited both Johannesburg and Pretoria. He attended the theater and a music hall.[145] Part of the time he stayed with his classmate Herbert Stark, then a mine manager in the region. Many years later Stark's daughter became one of Hoover's most devoted assistants.[146]

Hoover's visit to South Africa coincided with the importation of indentured Chinese labor to the gold mines of the Rand—a tremendous and controversial project just getting underway that summer. In South Africa mine owners, short of native labor after the Boer War, pleaded that they could not operate without the imported coolies. In England a thunderous agitation arose against "Chinese slavery"; eventually it helped sweep the Liberal Party into power. In China itself, in the spring of 1904, the Chinese Engineering and Mining Company, under British and Chinese supervision, recruited coolies for emigration for a fee and provided continuing facilities for that purpose at the port of Chinwangtao.[147] Hoover's old Stanford friend and mining associate, George Wilson, personally recruited laborers for the first ship, which sailed in June.[148] By early 1906 about 50,000 Chinese coolies, mostly obtained through Chinwangtao, were working in South African mines. But with the British government now hostile, most were repatriated by 1910.[149]

Although Hoover was a director of the Chinese Engineering and Mining Company, which actively assisted the scheme, he himself took no part in any aspect of it.[150] As Moreing had already made plain in the press, Bewick,

Moreing and Company—alone among mining firms in London—opposed the importation of Chinese into South Africa.[151] Chinese labor might be cheap, but it was not efficient.[152] During his South African sojourn Hoover argued against the use of Chinese manpower for practical business reasons: skilled white labor could do the job better, as his experience in Western Australia had demonstrated.[153] When a journalist asked him to comment on a contingent of Chinese workers he had just seen, Hoover replied crisply, "A very poor lot, indeed, and certainly not worth the trouble and expense of bringing out."[154]

Hoover returned to England early in September.[155] In his two-month "vacation" he had traveled 14,582 miles.[156] That autumn he stayed put, waiting for Chang Yen-mao's lawsuit to come to trial, as it finally did in early 1905. Thirty years old now, Hoover was beginning to tire of Westralian gold mining, with its risks, uncertain future, and recurrent scandals.[157] Before long the thought crossed his mind: why not venture into some less speculative mining field—like zinc?

17

The Zinc Corporation

I

B y the time the Chang Yen-mao trial ended in March 1905, Herbert Hoover was ready for a rest. This time, though, it would not take place in South Africa. On April 23 his wife Lou and their young son sailed from England for the United States. Ten days later Bert followed them on the *Kaiser Wilhelm II*.[1] Traveling separately across America by train, the couple reached California in mid-May and reunited at Lou's parents' home in Monterey.[2] From Monterey they journeyed to Palo Alto to see Theodore Hoover and his family, vacationing there for a month from Tad's mining job at Bodie.[3] At Stanford University Bert attended the tenth-year reunion of his Pioneer Class and won a prize for having traveled the greatest distance (6,700 miles) to attend.[4] In June the two Hoover families went on a camping expedition in the snow-packed Sierras near Yosemite.[5] Beloved California: this was truly home.

It was a blissful interlude, punctuated as always by the importunities of making a living. While in the United States Hoover inquired about a mine in Colorado and inspected another "for a London friend" at Copperopolis, in the California hills.[6] He visited the mining town of Bodie; he traveled to Portland, Oregon and to Denver.[7] He gave Theodore a power of attorney to act in his behalf for two years "for the purpose of locating mineral lands in the public domain of the United States."[8]

And now, once again, business drew Hoover to the Antipodes. On June

29 he and his family left San Francisco for New Zealand and Australia.[9] Hoover's first stop was the Bewick, Moreing-managed Talisman mine on New Zealand's north island.[10] By early August he was in the Australian state of Victoria, where the struggling deep lead properties awaited his scrutiny.[11] For the next two months affairs in Melbourne and Australia's eastern states held his attention. During part of September Lou visited Tasmania on her own.[12]

Late in October Hoover arrived in Western Australia for a month of unremitting labor.[13] From the Great Fingall at Day Dawn to the Lancefield at Laverton, from the new Black Range district northwest of the Sons of Gwalia to the big, established mines on the Golden Mile: every single Bewick, Moreing mine must be inspected, and every single one was.[14] On one trip from Leonora to Lawlers and beyond, Hoover and two companions used forty-eight horses.[15] The Chamber of Mines of Western Australia elected Hoover an honorary member;[16] Lou—tall, attractive, and outgoing—won friends and admirers, too.[17]

Lou, in fact, accompanied Bert on some of his back country expeditions, collecting specimen rocks for their Stanford mentor, Dr. Branner.[18] Trained like her husband as a geologist, she thought little of going down into the Oroya Brownhill mine at Kalgoorlie to select samples.[19] One day she joined Bert on an inspection of the Lake View Consols; the underground manager was astonished. When Lou proceeded to ask him intelligent questions, he became more flustered still.[20]

On November 27, 1905, after nearly five months "down under," the Hoovers sailed from Fremantle for England.[21] Arriving at the Suez Canal via Ceylon in mid-December, the couple stopped in Cairo. Bert continued on alone to London, where he arrived on New Year's Day. Lou remained behind for two weeks in Egypt to consult certain British geologists there about Red Sea geology, an interest of Dr. Branner's. She returned to London in mid-January.[22]

By all indications the young American couple seemed to enjoy their frequent travels, although the pace of Bert's work was incessant. In 1905 they had even circled the globe. Afterwards Hoover carefully compiled tables showing cities visited and distances covered. He calculated that in 1905 he journeyed 32,800 miles outside England.[23]

As usual, Hoover's visit to Australia led to a shake-up in Bewick, Moreing's staff. At the top Deane P. Mitchell, hitherto the firm's co-manager in Victoria and the eastern half of Australia, became superintendent of the Oroya Brownhill. C. S. Herzig, his partner, went to the London office. Hoover's old friend John Agnew, manager of the Lake View Consols, was promoted to assistant general manager for Western Australia. W. J. Loring, hitherto the firm's head in Western Australia, became general manager for all of Australia, with headquarters in Melbourne.[24]

Hoover's staff changes represented more than a shuffle of employees. For

Bewick, Moreing's interests were slowly beginning to diversify. No longer was "golden Westralia" its sole preeminent locale. Melbourne, not Kalgoorlie, was to become the firm's base of operations in Australia.

Why Melbourne? In part because it was the finance capital of the continent. But even more because during his recent visit Hoover and his firm had forged an alliance with a group of Australian investors for whom Melbourne was home. This was where Loring, his chief man in the field, should be. Hoover did not spend nearly three months in Australia's eastern states just looking at the deep leads. In the late summer and autumn of 1905 his energies and ambition focused on a mining town that rivaled even Kalgoorlie: the legendary district of Broken Hill.

I I

About 340 miles by rail northeast of Adelaide, and about 570 miles by rail west-north-west of Sydney, lies the inland desert city of Broken Hill, New South Wales. Like Kalgoorlie far to the west, this settlement in the parched, forbidding outback owed its founding to what lay beneath its red and dusty soil. There in 1883 Charles Rasp—a name as celebrated in Australian mining history as Paddy Hannan—discovered what turned out to be one of the richest silver-lead-zinc deposits on earth. Soon a mining camp sprang up in the desert sands. Twenty-two years later Broken Hill was a city of 35,000 whose mines had already paid over £10,000,000 in dividends.[25]

Yet all was not well by the early 1900s. As miners penetrated below the zone of surface oxidation, the silver, lead, and zinc began to appear together in the form of sulphides, which were difficult to treat. While it was possible to extract payable amounts of silver and lead concentrates from the plentiful ore as long as the fluctuating price of lead stayed up, after the turn of the century the price of lead plummeted. Even worse: despite a decade or more of worldwide experimentation commencing in the 1890s, metallurgists had been unable to devise a commercially viable process of recovering the zinc from the ore. That is, after initially concentrating some of the lead and silver, the companies were left with valuable zinciferous residues—and no way to separate the zinc from the remaining silver, lead, and gangue (mineral waste).[26]

Year by year, as silver-lead mining continued, the zinc-laden tailings accumulated: mounds of tailings, mountains of tailings—six million tons by 1905.[27] Just as Kalgoorlie was renowned for its wide streets, Broken Hill became famous for its tailings dumps that "glittered in the sun" and blew, it seemed, incessantly, through the dwellings of corrugated iron.[28] A fortune awaited those who could wean the zinc from the obdurate, encroaching dumps.

And men were trying, inventors with names like Potter, Cattermole, Delprat, and de Bavay. By 1905 it began to appear to at least a few observers that their efforts were nearing commercial success. Already at the Broken

Hill Proprietary mine (the king of the district) a large plant based on the Delprat process was treating 3,500 tons of tailings a week, while a mill using the Potter process was at work on the nearby Block 14.[29]

The animating principle of most of the new processes was known as flotation. The experimenters discovered that if crushed zinc tailings were mixed with certain chemical reagents (usually sulphuric acid), most of the particles of zinc adhered to bubbles of gas and floated to the surface, where they could be skimmed off. Most of the unwanted gangue sank to the bottom. If the solution in the vat was agitated to produce more bubbles—as two companies discovered in early 1905—the recovery of the zinc concentrate could be accelerated.[30]

As the competing flotation processes appeared set to conquer the refractory residues, and as the price of silver, lead, and zinc independently began to rebound, investor interest in Broken Hill intensified. In March 1905 a prominent London stockbroker, Lionel Robinson, visited Broken Hill—the same Lionel Robinson who had blown the whistle on Hoover's partner A. Stanley Rowe more than two years before. Robinson, an Australian, was searching for new mines to float on the London exchange. He consulted his brother, W. S. Robinson, then a Melbourne newspaper correspondent, who had just written an article predicting an increase in base metal prices. He consulted with W. L. Baillieu, a well-known Melbourne investor and politician, who was director of a mine at Broken Hill and a sponsor of de Bavay's flotation experiments. And he talked with Herbert J. Daly, a self-taught mining engineer who had advised him and Baillieu on mining matters at Broken Hill for several years.[31]

During these discussions (it was reported some months later), Robinson and Baillieu evidently conceived a scheme. Why not buy up the tailings dumps and apply flotation methods to them?[32] It is not clear how much this idea really had jelled into a plan by the time Robinson left Broken Hill for London, but he was convinced that Australian mining was about to increase in importance.[33]

Robinson was not alone. That summer J. H. Curle, so often a mirror of Herbert Hoover's thinking, predicted in the *Economist* that the silver-lead-zinc lode at Broken Hill was "about to become the world's centre of interest so far as these metals are concerned." Alluding vaguely to the flotation experiments then underway, Curle advised his readers to "watch developments on this field."[34]

And if Curle perceived an opportunity, could his American friend be far behind? In August 1905, early in his trip to Australia, Hoover spent a week at Broken Hill. For all its size the city was not a prepossessing sight. To Hoover, in fact, it was "one of the dreariest places in the world": scarcely any vegetation, no fresh water (unless distilled or imported), and pervasive tailings dust.[35]

Publicly Hoover was cautious. His statement to the local press was a model of perhaps deliberate ambiguity. "The ore deposits are certainly enormous in their occurrence," he told an interviewer, "but the cost of working, together with their average value, make them in a sense low-grade depositions." At the present "high ruling price of metals" Hoover had "no doubt" about the district's prosperity. On the other hand, it would take "no considerable fall" in price to "wipe out" the profit margin of lower-grade mines and to damage the silver mines also. What about the future price of metals, then? "I am absolutely no judge," Hoover stated; other "more informed" people were better able to "form an opinion."[36] No reader of his circumspect words would have guessed that an economic and metallurgical revolution was about to hit Broken Hill and that Herbert Hoover, just turned thirty-one, would help to lead it.

For like Robinson and Baillieu, the American engineer divined an extraordinary opportunity in the swelling tailings dumps. Tens of millions of dollars' worth of metal was in those residues. And according to Lionel Robinson's brother, Hoover was "one of the few who realized the potentialities of new metallurgical methods in unlocking the wealth of Broken Hill." At first Hoover's entry on the scene rather irked the Robinson / Baillieu group. They thought he was "butting into our business and competing with us for the same prizes." Soon, however, the parties reached an "amicable arrangement": Bewick, Moreing and Company joined the Robinson / Baillieu combination.[37]

Hoover's advent seemed to catalyze the final chain of events. First, C. S. Herzig of his Melbourne office reported favorably on the zinc recovery question. Then Hoover himself visited Broken Hill, studied the question further, supervised experiments, and affirmed Herzig's recommendations. This was enough for Hoover's hesitant colleagues, who now activated a syndicate— the Hill Syndicate—of which Hoover, representing his firm, was a member. (The others were Daly, Lionel Robinson's brokerage house, Baillieu, and one Arthur Terrell.)[38]

Quietly, very quietly—"practically in the dark"[39]—the Hill Syndicate now proceeded to purchase the enormous tailings dumps of several mining companies at Broken Hill. Hoover and Herzig evaluated the residues and drew up the contracts for their purchase.[40] At Hoover's insistence Moreing's finance company, the London and Western Australian Exploration Company, guaranteed some of the funds needed for the initial purchase payments.[41]

By mid-September word had leaked out in Melbourne that "a strong combination of English and Australian capitalists" was behind the massive acquisition of zinc tailings. Some "great scheme" was afoot, said a Melbourne mining journal, and it looked like Hoover, Robinson, and Daly had a hand in it.[42] Colossal indeed the undertaking was. Hoover and his associates did not want just some of the available tonnage; it appeared that they wanted it all. By mid-October the Hill Syndicate had either bought outright or obtained options on about 2,000,000 tons of currently existing zinc residues, containing about fifty million dollars' worth of metal.[43] In addition, it had secured the rights to future tailings production of two mines for up to nine years: a supply of 2,000,000 further tons or more.[44]

The syndicate, of course, was only a midwife. On October 18, 1905, in Melbourne, the object of all its efforts—the Zinc Corporation—was born, with a nominal capital of £350,000.[45] Its purpose, according to the *Mining Manual,* was threefold: to acquire the tailings purchase contracts from the Hill Syndicate, to "deal with" the 2,000,000 tons of residues, and "to treat same for zinc."[46] Although the new company announced that it was not "bound to any process" of zinc recovery, its securing of rights to the Potter flotation process made its initial commitment plain. The Potter method was "practically the same" as the process already in use at the Broken Hill Proprietary, said the Zinc Corporation's leadership.[47] The implication was that similar success was guaranteed.

Bewick, Moreing and Company became the new company's general managers and consulting engineers. Hoover himself became a director in London, along with Lionel Robinson's business partner, William Clark. In Melbourne Herzig (soon replaced by Loring) represented the Bewick, Moreing interest on the board, while Daly (representing Robinson) became managing director. W. L. Baillieu took the fifth seat.[48] The three-cornered alliance was fused.

In return for transferring the tailings contracts to the Zinc Corporation, the Hill Syndicate as vendor / promoter received 80,000 free £1 shares in the new corporation, and an option to purchase another 100,000 at par.[49] (The vendors exercised their option a few months later.)[50] How many of these vendor's shares Hoover personally received is unknown. All of them, technically, probably went first to his firm, in which he held a one-third interest. As payment for its services, Moreing's finance company also accepted a bloc of free vendor's shares. By early 1906 it held more than 26,000 shares in the Zinc Corporation.[51]

This was business on a grand and heady scale: "the biggest optional deal in the world," said corporation members, "because of the enormous capital involved in the future optional payments."[52] Whatever his immediate profit, Hoover could take pleasure in his accomplishment. Millions of tons of tailings, purchased at low prices when few sensed their imminent value, were now under his control, about to yield a bonanza to their master! It was a vision to rival his youthful dream of amalgamating all the mines of the Golden Mile. Several years later Deane P. Mitchell wrote that the time was ripe in 1905 to try to "consolidate the ownership" of the tailings dumps and to "control the future output," in order to apply the flotation processes then being perfected in Australia.[53]

Consolidate the ownership. Control the future output. Such words, though accurate, could not convey the sweep and intensity of Hoover's design. And it was primarily Hoover's design. W. L. Baillieu, himself a prime mover in the vast enterprise, told Hoover in 1908 that the "conception" of the Zinc Corporation was "largely" Hoover's own.[54]

The pert and nationalistic Sydney *Bulletin* seemed to agree. "Exit H. C. Hoover, of B., M. and Co., from Melbourne," it wrote in October 1905 after Hoover left Victoria for Western Australia. In three months, the *Bulletin* reported, Hoover "wasted no time and did well." The "Baillieu-Lionel Robinson shoal" had "swum into his net." He had "practically snapped up" certain properties and succeeded in "mopping up the Potter zinc process." Only one business group had "heeded not the voice of the charmer." All that Hoover wanted now, the *Bulletin* opined, was "a high price for spelter; and presumably he would not turn up his nose at a boom in Hill stocks."[55]

"Hail Columbia" Hoover was a "bold adventurer," said W. S. Robinson.[56] Even as the Zinc Corporation was being organized in 1905, he was nursing two related schemes to fruition. At the southern end of the Broken Hill field was a struggling mine known as the Broken Hill South Blocks. Late in 1905 the Lake View Consols, chaired by F. A. Govett, obtained an option to purchase a half-interest in this company for a mere £73,500. Conventional wisdom held that the mine, which had never yielded any ore, was of little worth; it was too far from the rich center of the lode. But Hoover and Herzig felt differently. After thorough inspection they advised Govett to exercise the option. "Certainly recommend," Hoover cabled; "would buy it myself if able to." Govett's company did so. In November 1905 a new Broken Hill South Blocks company was created with Govett as chairman and Bewick, Moreing, predictably, as general managers.[57]

Hoover was not yet done at Broken Hill. Early in 1906 the Zinc Corporation contracted to sell zinc concentrates for five years to a German smelting firm, Messrs. Aron, Hirsch and Sohn.[58] This took care of the new company's anticipated production of zinc. But a successful flotation process would also yield further silver-lead concentrates; how should these be disposed of? Hoover and the Robinson / Baillieu group had an answer. In December 1905 the Australian Smelting Corporation was registered in New South Wales, with an authorized capital of £350,000. Hoover, Baillieu, Daly, and Clark, among others, joined the board of directors. Bewick, Moreing assumed the general management. Among the new company's assets was a contract to smelt or purchase the Zinc Corporation's entire production of silver-lead concentrates for five years, beginning at the end of 1906.[59]

Although "intimately connected" with the Zinc Corporation (as one journal reported),[60] the Australian Smelting Corporation had interests and objectives of its own. Up to now only the Broken Hill Proprietary smelted its lead concentrates in Australia. All the other companies shipped their lead concentrates to Germany (not to mention the zinc, all of which went to Europe). The new company hoped to rectify this imbalance by erecting a major lead smelting plant at Port Kembla, New South Wales.[61]

Three new companies registered in three months, and Bewick, Moreing the manager of all three. Hoover and his firm were now forces to be reckoned with at Broken Hill.

When the Hill Syndicate's secret purchases of tailings dumps for the Zinc Corporation became public knowledge in Australia, the impact, in one journal's words, was "something akin to sensation."[62] At the end of 1905 and the beginning of 1906 optimism reigned supreme in Britain and Broken Hill. In the first few days of trading on the Melbourne stock exchange, the Zinc Corporation's shares nearly doubled in value.[63] In London a leading mining periodical congratulated the corporation's founders for their "double-barreled foresight": "They anticipated two things, the solution of the sulphide problem, and simultaneously with that a remarkable rise in metals [prices]." The journal recited the Zinc Corporation's manifold assets: its millions of tons of residues, its "ample working capital," its favorable contracts, and more. The new company's results, declared the journal, were "assured."[64]

Surely, it was said, the Zinc Corporation, advised as it was by eminent metallurgists and engineers, had solved the puzzle of the zinc tailings. Why else would it have purchased enormous dumps at considerable expense?[65] In Australia critics lambasted the mining companies for selling their dumps at what now seemed very cheap prices.[66] As for the separate Australian Smelting Corporation, Bewick, Moreing declared it to be "assured of a very successful future."[67]

But there were risks. The Zinc Corporation had paid more than £95,000 at the start for those glittering residues.[68] It was obligated to pay out several hundred thousand pounds more, on the installment plan, in the years ahead.[69] Soon it must earn income to cover this heavy expenditure. "The magnitude of these contracts makes the company seem somewhat adventurous," the *Mining Journal* noted, although the current high price of metals did provide a cushion.[70]

And if—as Deane P. Mitchell later claimed—the concurrent emergence of several flotation processes justified the founding of a company to apply them to the tailings, flotation metallurgy was still an experimental science in 1905.[71] The Delprat process was working well at the Broken Hill Proprietary, but would it work elsewhere? Some tailings dumps had different mineral contents from others; some had different ratios of zinc to lead. Some were older and more oxidized than others. Such variables affected results. Laboratory experiments and small-scale tests were one thing; continuous economical operation might be another.[72] "The profitable recovery of zinc has passed out of the theoretical into the practical stage," announced that Bewick, Moreing booster, the *Mining World*.[73] Now the Zinc Corporation must demonstrate that this judgment was correct.

Hoover, for one, was confident. "We have . . . thoroughly demonstrated the business," he informed an American friend in September 1905, nearly a month before the Zinc Corporation was actually founded.[74] When in the spring of 1906 Herbert J. Daly sent him three hundred Zinc Corporation shares, Hoover was appreciative. "I have not made a dividend out of them," he wrote back, "as I have been too optimistic about the Zinc Corporation to have sold but a very few shares."[75]

I I I

B ECAUSE of uncertainties about which of the flotation processes would prove best, the Zinc Corporation prudently decided at the beginning to proceed on two fronts. First, it would erect at the British Broken Hill mine an experimental plant (the No. 2 plant) where the competing flotation methods could be tested under identical conditions. (Hoover and Baillieu urged that the Potter, Cattermole, and de Bavay processes each be given a trial.) More or less simultaneously, the company would construct, on another site, a "large central concentrating plant" (the No. 1 plant) for eventual tailings treatment with the winning process.[76] Although the company was clearly inclined toward the Potter formula, it insisted that it was "bound" to no single flotation method.[77] To cover its bets, the corporation acquired options to use the Cattermole and Elmore processes as well.[78]

All this was sensible policy, and in February 1906 the experimental plant began operations.[79] Very soon, however, the company abandoned its initial plan. Instead of systematically evaluating various processes at its "experimental" plant (as Hoover had recommended), it proceeded to convert this pilot plant into a full-scale, commercial operation using the Potter process alone.[80] Officially, the company explained that it preferred Potter's method because it was "advanced so far beyond the experimental stage," was inexpensive to install, and was easy to operate. The Potter process, it asserted, was "definitely proved to be successful on a large commercial scale."[81]

Other factors, however, affected its decision. According to Deane P. Mitchell, the original plan of careful experimentation was discarded "partly because of conditions imposed by one of the contracting mining companies and partly by reason of the patent position and the advice of the company's technical staff." Mitchell did not indicate what conditions were imposed, or by whom. The "patent position" probably referred to the growing quarrel among the owners of rival flotation processes over alleged infringements of one another's patents. But however expedient, the Zinc Corporation's decision to abandon experimenting and erect an all-Potter-process plant soon proved a costly one.[82]

During the spring of 1906 the Potter process seemed victorious.[83] The Zinc Corporation directors announced in June that the formerly experimental plant was treating sixty tons of tailings per day.[84] W. L. Baillieu declared that when completed, the plant would treat two thousand tons per week.[85] The *Mining Manual* reported that the "experimental plant" had been "proved successful."[86] C. Algernon Moreing pronounced himself "highly pleased" by the Zinc Corporation's prospects. Already, he said, it was exporting "marketable produce" to Germany.[87]

Herbert Hoover shared the prevailing cheerfulness. On the basis of reports reaching him in London, Hoover told Daly in May that "the Potter is apparently going to out-distance the other processes." "I hope it will," he added, "but I did not see any reason for notifying the Cattermole people that we did not intend to use their process as we are not compelled to do anything of the kind under the agreement. . . ." Besides, the Potter process might yet run into trouble. It "is just as well," said Hoover prudently, "to have them all in reserve."[88]

Meanwhile the Zinc Corporation was contemplating expansion in another direction. Instead of shipping its zinc concentrates to Europe, why not establish zinc smelting facilities right in Australia? The Corporation decided to hire a consultant to investigate the question. On behalf of the board Hoover approached his friend W. R. Ingalls, editor of the *Engineering and Mining Journal* in New York. On Ingalls's recommendation Hoover selected Augustin Queneau of the New Jersey Zinc Corporation to travel to Broken Hill. Hoover informed his fellow directors that (in Baillieu's words) "a better man for the position could not have been secured."[89]

Success, though, was not coming easily. The "battle of the processes" was underway—already a tangled morass of recrimination and proliferating lawsuits. The litigation about patent rights was to drag on for years, embroiling the Zinc Corporation itself at times in the legal cross fire. Competition was fierce. At the corporations's plant interested parties attempted to sabotage experiments by dumping scrap iron into the agitators and other machinery.[90] The Zinc Corporation had to keep its property tightly guarded.[91]

By the autumn of 1906 it was evident that something was seriously wrong. One mining journal noted that the Zinc Corporation was "very reticent" about the status of its operations and that its Potter plant on the British Broken Hill mine had been closed down for several weeks.[92] Shortly before the semiannual shareholders meeting on November 9, the directors and Bewick, Moreing released their reports. During the summer, Hoover's firm revealed, the company's No. 2 tailings treatment plant had produced results "of a very unsatisfactory character." After further experimentation and adjustments, which had yielded "satisfactory results," the management had decided "to remodel the whole plant." The firm anticipated that this "reconstructed plant" would be ready to operate on an increased scale "at an early date."[93] The managers' hopeful (but vague) words about future success could not conceal the fact that the unadulterated Potter process had failed.

The directors' report also announced a shake-up in the company. Daly, the chairman and original managing director, had resigned from the board; F. A. Govett had replaced him.[94] During his tenure Daly, a colorful "high class mining scout" who had little real knowledge of flotation, had crossed swords with the better-trained Hoover. To Baillieu and others it was now clear that

Daly possessed neither the managerial skills nor the metallurgical expertise to run a big business like the Zinc Corporation. But since Daly had represented Lionel Robinson at the company's founding, it had seemed appropriate to acquiesce in his desire to be managing director. This, it turned out, had been a mistake.[95]

Daly's departure coincided with that of the company's resident mine manager, W. E. Simpson, and his replacement by the smelting expert, Augustin Queneau. Simpson's selection, too, had not worked out, and Hoover now took responsibility for having appointed him. Baillieu, however, did not hold Simpson responsible for the company's failure. After all, Daly had promised Simpson (who knew nothing of flotation) all the expertise he would need.[96]

With Daly and Simpson now departed, the company's day-to-day direction at Broken Hill devolved on the new manager. At the time of Queneau's appointment both Govett and the nominal managers, Bewick, Moreing, urged the Zinc Corporation to adopt the Cattermole (Minerals Separation) flotation process.[97] Queneau, however, thought otherwise. Although not a specialist on flotation per se, Queneau was convinced that the Potter acid process need only be modified by adding magnetic separators in order to produce excellent results. To conduct trials of two rival processes (as the London directors urged) would only incur a large and wasteful expense. In deference to his reputation as a zinc expert, the directors appointed Queneau manager and authorized him to proceed.[98]

Queneau plunged in with gusto, revamping and preparing the once-experimental plant for production on his "improved" lines. The new manager brimmed with confidence; according to Govett, he promised success daily.[99] Baillieu confessed to Hoover that if Queneau were not such an outstanding technical man he would worry that Queneau might be overly optimistic.[100]

In mid-October 1906 Queneau cabled in the results of his experiments. The "final test-run" of 1,300 tons of tailings had yielded a "highly satisfactory" extraction rate of 81% of the zinc. Success at last! Queneau declared that he could "guarantee" a future zinc extraction rate of 85%. An expanded No. 2 plant, he indicated, should be in "full operation" by December 1.[101]

Buoyed by these "extremely satisfactory results," the Zinc Corporation directors quickly announced a financial reorganization. In its first year the infant enterprise had expended vast sums to buy tailings dumps, provide deposits on future purchase payments, construct a treatment plant, and conduct experiments. With prosperity finally on the horizon, the company found itself lacking in adequate cash reserves for the expansion ahead. In November 1906, therefore, the Zinc Corporation decided to increase its share capital from £350,000 to £500,000, or about $2,500,000. It offered most of the new £1 shares to the stockholders at somewhat over par. Bewick, Moreing and Company, among others, agreed to underwrite the issue (that is, to purchase any leftover shares).[102] For his part (8%) in the guarantee Hoover personally received an option to purchase 3,733 additional shares at £2 apiece.[103] Despite the company's earlier setbacks the share issue was a success.[104]

In all likelihood Hoover was now a substantial shareholder in the Zinc Corporation. Even before the new issue was floated, he told a friend that "various members of the firm in our own particular group" held about 45,000 shares.[105] Hoover and the Lionel Robinson interest were therefore "very wild" when Baillieu decided to sell several thousand of his shares as soon as he learned about the coming share issue. Such a big selling order came in at precisely the wrong moment for Hoover, for it depressed the market price of "Zincs" just when Hoover and his fellow underwriters were trying to entice shareholders to snap up new Zinc Corporation shares at presumably attractive prices.[106] If the new share issue had consequently failed to catch on, the underwriters would have been obliged to step in. And Hoover as one of them would have been forced to buy 8% of the unsubscribed shares—at 25 shillings, or over six dollars, apiece. No wonder he was annoyed. Fortunately for Hoover, the share issue succeeded in spite of Baillieu's move.

Hoover believed that the new financial scheme would give the Zinc Corporation "all the money that it will want."[107] Meanwhile out in Australia Queneau was enthusiastic. So was the London stock market. As the day of the new plant opening approached, interest in Zinc Corporation shares mounted.[108] When in early January 1907 word arrived that the new plant would open in a few days, the company's shares soared to 48s. 6d.[109] Soon afterward the stock peaked at 50 shillings a share—two-and-a-half times its face value.[110]

Suddenly the boom sagged. In late January rumors reached London that the newly operating plant was a failure.[111] Queneau flatly and publicly denied it: there had merely been a few mechanical hitches involving pumps and airlifts, all of which would soon be corrected.[112] Although much of the mining press seemed content with his explanation, one London journal found it unconvincing and possibly "evasive." For the market rumors to which Queneau responded had focused not on temporary mechanical obstructions but on the charge that the process itself was not an economic success.[113] Despite Queneau's statement, the price of Zinc Corporation shares continued to slide heavily down.[114]

Meanwhile, on January 24, Hoover left London for Australia.[115] Even before he reached Fremantle he had determined on at least one staff change: a fellow Stanford alumnus, Arthur Diggles, currently superintendent of a mine in Western Australia, would be transferred to the South Blocks mine at Broken Hill.[116] Wherever possible Hoover was still relying on Californians and Stanford men. Arriving in Western Australia on February 19, Hoover journeyed immediately to Kalgoorlie for a whirlwind inspection of the goldfields.[117] Nine days later he sailed from Western Australia for Melbourne, where he arrived early in March.[118] The situation at "the Hill" was deteriorating. The Sydney *Bulletin* reported that the Zinc Corporation was "still groping with two Potter Pans and a large stock of assurance. It has produced a few truckloads of zinc concentrates, but they don't all assay the published 49 per cent."[119]

On March 1, 1907 a circular from the London office of the Zinc Corporation appeared in the London press. The company disclosed that it had received a cablegram from W. L. Baillieu of the Melbourne board and William Clark, who was then at Broken Hill. The two directors announced that "with the full concurrence of Mr. Hoover" they "thought it advisable to remove Mr. A. Queneau from the control, and that Mr. E. Huntley has been placed in charge of the works."[120] A few days later the *Australian Mining Standard* reported that Queneau had resigned.[121]

By now Hoover was at Broken Hill.[122] Hoover denied that Queneau had "resigned the general management of the Zinc Corporation." To the *Australian Mining Standard* he related a less dramatic story:

Mr. Hoover, who has visited the corporation's plant on the British mine, says that Mr. Queneau had come to Australia to deal with the question of zinc smelting in Australia, but the Melbourne directors had asked him to devise a new process of zinc concentration. Mr. Queneau had done this, and now that his new mill was in work, he had been asked to resume his old work. One unit of the mill was in steady operation, and the second section would probably be in work next, or the following, week. The other two units would be pushed on, and he hoped that they would shortly be in operation. Mr. Queneau is at present in Melbourne, conferring with the directors of the company, but the object has not been made known.[123]

Technically Hoover was correct. Queneau did not "resign" his connection with the Zinc Corporation until May, six months before the expiration of his contract.[124] But Queneau's removal from the management in March was more than a routine change of assignments. If Queneau's mill was finally, satisfactorily "in work," as Hoover implied, and if Queneau actually had invented a successful zinc concentration process, would the company have abruptly removed him at the moment of his triumph?

Hoover's remarks had a reassuring quality: one unit of the plant was "in steady operation"; the rest were on the way. No sense of crisis seeped between the lines. But if Hoover hoped thereby to pacify the shareholders (and play for time), his effort was in vain. Instead, Queneau's ouster touched off a rising clamor for explanations. What was going on at Broken Hill? Noting that Huntley was now the company's fourth manager in twelve months, the *Australian Mining Standard* stated that these "numerous resignations" did not "reflect credit" on the board of directors of the Zinc Corporation.[125] One shareholder was more blunt: "I was induced by the connection with the concern of Messrs. Bewick, Moreing and Co. to buy shares, and if the process should turn out a failure my faith in them would be gone."[126] Even the usually friendly *Mining World* criticized the directors for "their want of frankness in dealing with the Shareholders."[127]

Still, the *Mining World* could not believe that the board of directors, "guided largely by the unrivaled experience" of Bewick, Moreing and Company, would have purchased all those tailings and constructed a plant besides "if they had not been satisfied as to the ultimate success of the operation."[128] Surely Bewick, Moreing's engineers could not have designed and erected a plant that would not perform the tasks they specified.[129] Surely Hoover and his fellow experts could not be so wrong.

Yet as the days of March turned into weeks, no word came from the field, and the stock market grew more apprehensive. By the end of March Zinc Corporation shares had sunk to twenty-eight shillings.[130] What was going on at Broken Hill? Brushing aside Queneau's protest that he had not been given enough time to prove his methods, Hoover gave Queneau's modified Potter process a final run. It failed. Hoover thereupon "ripped the Potter out" and began experiments using the Cattermole approach.[131]

Meanwhile, in London, Francis Govett exuded confidence or, at least, hope. Unlike Hoover, Govett admitted that Queneau's "repeated failure to carry out his promises necessitated his retirement." But even as Hoover was discarding the Potter process, Govett insisted that the Potter plant was "steadily working" and "can be worked at a profit," although not as much as Queneau had claimed. Furthermore, said Govett, the plant could easily be converted to the Cattermole process. On March 24 Govett received a cable from Hoover stating that a "preliminary trial" of the Cattermole appeared to be a "complete success." Govett concluded that even if Queneau's Potter process-cum-magnetic-separation was "not as remunerative" as the Cattermole, "success will be obtained from either one or the other."[132]

On April 2, 1907, after nearly a month of work divided between Melbourne and Broken Hill, Herbert Hoover cabled in his report:

> After thorough examination and trial of A. Queneau's system of treatment, we have come to the conclusion that it is not commercial success; however, we have altered one unit to Cattermole process and have proved success of Cattermole process system of treatment. We are obtaining good extraction lead and zinc from all materials, including slimes, and are producing and shipping concentrates good grade.
>
> We have abandoned A. Queneau's system of treatment and are altering balance of No. 2 plant to Cattermole process. We should be running full time 500 tons per day in about a month. In the meantime running one unit Cattermole process, treating 140 tons per day.[133]

The trouble with Queneau's approach, Hoover said later, was that it was exclusively an acid process, whereas "the only reliable flotation agent was a mixture of acid and oil."[134]

Why, however, had Queneau succeeded with his 1,300-ton trial run some six months before? What Hoover and his associates did not yet know was that in that particular test, the company's workmen—apparently unknown to Queneau—had added lubricating oil to the acid. Queneau had stumbled into success, did not know why, and could not reproduce his results.[135]

Hoover's cable of April 2 seemed to suggest that the war at last was won. Was not the Cattermole (Minerals Separation) process, in his words, a "proved success"? Such news must have been doubly gratifying, for Hoover's brother Theodore was now general manager of Minerals Separation, Ltd., which was marketing this very process.[136] There is no evidence, however, that Hoover let such personal factors affect his business judgment.

So now, once again, it was full-speed ahead. With Daly gone from the scene, and with Queneau removed from office, Bewick, Moreing for the first time (so Govett later said) had a "free hand" and "full control" as managers.[137] Even as Hoover and his staff experimented with the Cattermole method (the third to be tried) and adapted the No. 2 plant for its use, they explored still another invention, the Elmore vacuum process, successful with copper but not yet fully tested on zinc.[138]

Despite the publication of Hoover's optimistic cable of April 2, Zinc Corporation shares continued to decline. By mid-April the price per share had dropped below par to 18s. 6d.[139] On April 13 the *Mining World* commented on the continuing "death-like silence of Messrs. Hoover and Loring." "When will these Delphian oracles speak, or rather, when will they send their report?"[140] In its circular published on March 1 the company had promised that Hoover and Loring would visit Broken Hill and cable in a "full statement" "as soon as possible."[141] Six weeks later their much-awaited report had not yet come. It was obvious from the share quotations that investors did not regard Hoover's cable of April 2 as an adequate fulfillment of this promise.

On April 18 Govett, in London, issued another circular to the shareholders. The board chairman reviewed the recent doleful history of the company, quoted Hoover's cable of April 2, and summarized the recent progress using the Cattermole method. Govett stated that the company had not expected another cable from Hoover after his despatch of April 2. As for the future, Govett asserted that the revamped No. 2 plant should treat five hundred tons of tailings a day in a few weeks. He stressed that the Cattermole process had been "successfully used on similar material" by the neighboring Sulphide Corporation "for a long period."[142]

If the Zinc Corporation's technical prospects appeared satisfactory in Govett's eyes, its financial status did not. The chairman disclosed that the company had now spent about £200,000 on tailings purchases as well as considerable sums on experimental work and the construction of its costly plant. Furthermore, the £500,000 Zinc Corporation had been forced to dip into its working capital in order to keep up on its payments for the dumps. To meet the company's bills for the next three months, Govett had been obliged to borrow £50,000 from some of the company's large shareholders.[143] These included (it turned out) Robinson, Baillieu, Moreing, Moreing's exploration company, and Govett himself.[144]

As Govett recognized, the emergency loan provided only a short reprieve. Eventually the company's finances would probably have to be reorganized.[145] And if the company was to survive, it simply must generate an income soon, for new installment payments on the tailings were inexorably approaching. Between February and December 1907 the company would have to pay out nearly £90,000 for the purchase of further residues; in 1908, £130,000 more.[146]

The pressure to produce now fell more intensely than ever on Herbert Hoover, the chief engineer in the field. One way to alleviate the Zinc Corporation's financial ills was to defer the tailings purchase payments. During Hoover's nearly four months in Melbourne and Broken Hill, he worked arduously with Baillieu's assistance to renegotiate the tailings contracts. Hoover was at his most persuasive in such small-group encounters. After sixty meetings he succeeded in postponing all payments for 1907 and in reducing those for 1908 and beyond.[147]

Such an achievement, though welcome, did not fill the company's coffers. This would be the duty, it now appeared, of the Cattermole process. As Hoover's cable and Govett's circular indicated, the preferred direction, at least at the No. 2 plant, was clear. After conferring with Loring and Mitchell at Broken Hill in late May, Hoover announced that the as yet uncompleted main plant (the No. 1 plant) would also adopt the Cattermole method. Hoover added that he "personally favoured" this process.[148]

During June the Zinc Corporation reorganized. Its head office was moved to London; Baillieu and Clark resigned from the board; two friends of Govett replaced them.[149] As soon as Govett announced these changes, the company's shares plunged to 8s. 9d. One journal attributed the fall not to the announcement itself but to "selling operations" by Baillieu and Clark.[150] Whatever the exact cause, and whatever their motive, the Baillieu / Robinson group had conveyed the unsettling impression of abandoning ship.

In mid-June Hoover sailed home to London.[151] Even while he was on the high seas, the company issued figures revealing that its production of concentrates had fallen sharply in June.[152] Now it appeared that the Cattermole process, too, had been "no more satisfactory than its predecessors," observed one mining correspondent.[153] The *Statist* commented that "the whole question of ability to profitably deal with the tailings appears unsolved."[154]

In mid-July Herbert Hoover reached London.[155] A few days later, on the twenty-second, the London directors of the Zinc Corporation convened and reviewed the depressing evidence. The Cattermole process—"personally favored" by Hoover and certified by him in April as a "proved" success—had failed to achieve satisfactory results. The directors asked Minerals Separation, Ltd. for assistance.[156] The next day Govett informed the shareholders by circular that "far greater difficulties have been met in the conversion and adjustment of the Potter plant, than was anticipated." The money-starved company, he said, faced a virtual reconstruction.[157]

Yet this same Cattermole process that was not a success at the Zinc Corporation plant was faring well at the Sulphide mill nearby. Why? According to Hoover the tailings dumps of the two companies were not (as Govett had earlier stated) essentially similar in quality. The Sulphide Corporation's tailings, it turned out, were richer; hence its profitable results.[158] A few years later Deane P. Mitchell asserted that with time the Cattermole process could have been made to yield excellent results. But in the summer of 1907 the desperate Zinc Corporation no longer had time for further tinkering and experiments.[159] It must find a new process or fail.

It was a gloomy meeting of Zinc Corporation shareholders that Govett convened in London on July 30, 1907. To Hoover's anger, rumors were circulating in London that he had made a killing by "bearing" the company's shares.[160] Govett, who addressed the meeting first, was mortified: "It is not pleasant to be associated with failure, but I cannot express to you my humiliation and disgust in meeting you under circumstances like these. Believe me, I am overwhelmed with the sense of the shareholders' misfortunes and their loss." Govett pleaded for sympathy and understanding. Hoover and I, he reported, "have borne the burden and anxieties on our shoulders. That burden has been almost more than we can bear. We feel we have been held responsible for all the troubles through which we have passed, and for all the mistakes, many of which we foresaw and which we did our utmost to avoid." Govett disclosed that he and Hoover, far from selling out on inside knowledge, currently represented an "interest" of 100,000 shares purchased at an average of 32s. a share. They, too, had suffered a "heavy pecuniary loss."

Govett acknowledged that the company's leadership had made many errors. They should have conducted "side by side experiments on the rival processes" at the start, as the managers had urged, only to be "over-ridden by the various experts." The board should have realized sooner "the improbability of Mr. Queneau's expectations being fulfilled." Govett denied that an "inner ring" had boosted the shares upward during the winter to their dizzying heights. Instead, it had been a case of spontaneous "exaggerated optimism" stemming from Queneau's zeal and unfulfilled estimates.

Govett forcefully defended his policy of not keeping the shareholders more informed during the anxious spring and early summer. The board, he asserted, had not "at that time" doubted the eventual success of the Cattermole process. The neighboring Sulphide Corporation's results demonstrated that the process, as a process, was sound. The only question, then, was: how quickly could the Zinc Corporation convert its plant to this proven method? To inform the shareholders of fluctuating test results during the period of transition would have been "hopelessly misleading," Govett asserted. As for not notifying the shareholders of the company's failure to convert,

> you could see for yourselves that we were not succeeding as we expected. What we published showed it. How could we proclaim aloud a failure when daily we were looking for success? What would you have said if we had knocked the Company to bits by a proclamation of failure, and then in a few days' time announced success?

Govett seemed to exempt Bewick, Moreing from his criticism of past mistakes. In fact, he said, the Zinc Corporation had made "great progress" technically since Hoover's firm had taken "full control" after Queneau. Still, Govett did not conceal the fact that three times the company had failed—and had wasted much money besides. He ruefully admitted that "although two years ago it was claimed that the solution of the problem of the Broken Hill tailings had at last been found, the real solution of the problem in point of fact at that time had hardly been commenced."[161]

Nevertheless, even now, there was a bright spot in the darkness: a *fourth* flotation approach, the Elmore process, whose test results were encouraging and upon which Hoover and Govett proposed to rest their final hopes. Perhaps with Queneau's exploded "guarantee" of 85% extraction in mind, Hoover told the assembled shareholders:

> So far as I can see—and I would not guarantee anything—no responsible engineer ever guaranteed anything in his life—(laughter)—the Elmore results that we have got have been very good. . . .

Applied to the residues, they would yield, said Hoover, a profit of eight to ten shillings per ton.[162] With several million tons of tailings at its disposal, the company had prospects yet. Govett, for his part, was "convinced that the business is sound" and that next year the company's circumstances would be better. He stated that Hoover concurred with everything in his speech.[163]

But how to finance still another fresh start? To build just half an Elmore plant would cost £50,000. The deferred payments on the tailings purchases would cost £90,000 in 1908. And the company was already £30,000 in debt.[164] With Zinc shares now almost worthless on the market, a straight issue of new shares would only founder.

Govett therefore proposed, and the assembled shareholders endorsed, a drastic and painful plan. On top of the corporation's authorized capital of 500,000 shares of £1 each, the company now created 182,000 preference shares of £1 each, which it offered to its shareholders at par. To induce the stockholders to buy, the company announced that holders of preference shares would absorb all profits of the company until the cumulative dividends reached a total of £1 per preference share. Then the preference shareholders would be entitled to an annual 20% cumulative dividend. All this would occur before holders of ordinary shares received anything. The preference and ordinary shareholders would then participate *pro rata* in any surplus profit distributed.[165] Various underwriters, including Govett himself, guaranteed the sale of 100,000 of the new shares.[166]

For preference shareholders in the Zinc Corporation these were handsome terms—if profits were made—and a manifest sign of the company's desperation. But to holders of ordinary shares who could not or would not buy preference shares, it was a bitter remedy indeed. For even if success finally came, it would be years before holders of ordinary shares could hope to receive a dividend.

Govett's and Hoover's conduct at the July 1907 meeting won praise in some influential quarters. The *Mining World* took note of Govett's candor and tact under difficult circumstances.[167] The eminent mining editor T. A. Rickard commended Hoover for remarking that responsible engineers did not guarantee anything. These were words of truth, said Rickard, and bespoke "rare courage" and "professional integrity."[168]

But mixed in with the acclaim were dissonant notes. The *Money Market Review*, which had been skeptical of the Zinc Corporation for a long time, likened Govett's speech to "the notice posted up at the concert in the rough mining camp:—'Please do not shoot at the accompanist! He is doing his best.' " The journal observed that the company's directors "have no doubt done their best, but their best certainly is not good. The company has failed with the Potter process, with Mr. Queneau's modification of it, and now, it is tardily admitted, with the Cattermole process."[169]

A journalist with the *Mining and Scientific Press* blamed the crisis on "the precipitate policy of the directors and managers, who embarked on this enterprise without full consideration." The journalist did not criticize the Zinc Corporation's failures with the flotation processes. Its vigorous experimentation and willingness to change, in fact, deserved praise. And he understood why the company had snatched the tailings up: it wanted "to secure the supply before anyone else." Still, the purchase of tailings "before the process to be adopted was settled upon," and the liabilities thus incurred before the enterprise was even underway, had "crippled the resources of the company."[170]

If even the friendly mining press had qualms about the Zinc Corporation, the reaction in other quarters was less restrained. In Australia men were calling the company the "Sink" Corporation.[171] In London "Zincs" which had stood in the stock market at fifty shillings a share in January plummeted before year's end to a single shilling a share.[172]

Herbert Hoover's professional prestige was never more threatened than in the summer and fall of 1907. Had his audacious reach finally exceeded his grasp? Across Australia frustration was staring him in the face. The Victorian deep leads were in trouble; the Lancefield mine was eluding success. Would the Zinc Corporation likewise be a noble failure? Would Hoover lose money and, even worse, the confidence of investors in his professional reputation? Govett also knew the stakes. "If we failed," he said later, "our reputation would be gone."[173]

All now depended on the Elmore process. Govett warned that if it, too, failed, the Zinc Corporation would liquidate; this was the company's "last chance."[174] At Broken Hill Hoover installed Deane P. Mitchell as superintendent and ordered him to proceed with Elmore's technique. In August Mitchell's staff began to erect the mammoth, virtually automated, £50,000 Elmore plant.[175]

It was becoming a race against time. For Govett (as he later admitted) had badly underestimated the "disgust" and "hopeless disbelief" of the shareholders. By early 1908 his preference share scheme of the previous summer had proved a partial failure. Only 76,000 preference shares had been freely taken up; the guarantors took 32,000 more. Two-fifths of the 182,000-share issue went unsubscribed.[176]

On February 29, 1908 the beleaguered Zinc Corporation's profit and loss account showed a deficit of more than £85,000.[177] Deprived of funds they had counted on, Hoover and his fellow directors tried to persuade shareholders to buy the remaining preference shares on somewhat improved terms. There were few immediate takers.[178] Through Loring in Australia the board was able to negotiate another postponement of payments for the purchased zinc tailings.[179] But how much longer could the floundering venture hang on?

And then, at last, came news of victory from Broken Hill. In February 1908, under Mitchell's supervision, the Elmore process tailings treatment plant commenced operations. It was, by all reports, an immediate and complete success.[180] During May the mill produced over 3,600 tons of zinc concentrates from a tonnage three times that amount.[181]

Yet even as the Elmore process promised commercial salvation, the company faced an ominous hurdle: £40,000 in debts payable on July 1, 1908. Through Mitchell the directors again rearranged the contracts, but still the company needed £30,000. Realizing that the company's shareholders would not supply it, Govett obtained a bank loan in the form of an overdraft of £30,000, guaranteed by the Lake View Consols of which he was chairman. In turn the Lake View Consols company was subguaranteed: £10,000 by Moreing, and £10,000 by Hoover, Govett, and three others. It was desperate and unorthodox finance, but no one could accuse Hoover and his colleagues of timorousness. "I had to save the Company," Govett said later, "and I have done it the only way I could."[182]

On July 15, 1908 a jubilant Govett convened the Zinc Corporation's annual meeting. "The dawn, indeed, has more than come," he proclaimed. "Last year the thing looked hopeless; today it is, technically at any rate, a brilliant success. Surely it is only a question of time, and surely, sooner or later, large profits will be made."[183] Hoover, for his part, reported that the company had begun to earn a profit of £4,000 a month.

Last year I spent four months of study and investigation of this Company's work at the works and in Australia, in negotiation for a revision of the contracts for tailings, and the present process and its results are the outcome of that work. It gives me greater satisfaction to come before you today with these results than I can well express, for failure has been converted into success, and I believe we are on the road to still greater success yet.[184]

On July 1, 1908 Hoover and Govett became joint managing directors of the Zinc Corporation.[185] How much Hoover's fate in those long anxious months of 1907 and 1908 had rested on the deeds of others—on men like Govett, Mitchell, and the technicians of Broken Hill. If Govett had not kept struggling to find the funds, if Mitchell and Elmore had not come through in time. . . . Years later W. S. Robinson wondered whether Hoover "ever fully recognized what Francis Govett did for him." In Robinson's view, Hoover owed "no small part" of his reputation to "the courage and tenacity" of Govett. It was Govett, said Robinson, who in the darkest hour principally supplied the support and money "that kept the Zinc Corporation—and Herbert Hoover's reputation for competence—afloat."[186]

At the 1908 shareholders meeting Hoover, in fact, did generously acknowledge his debts. To Govett and his fellow directors Hoover expressed "personal obligations" for their having loyally backed the successful engineering program "for which I have had the professional responsibility." Hoover praised his subordinates at Bewick, Moreing, mentioning several by name. Above all, he commended Deane P. Mitchell, who was "most due the credit for successful issue." Mitchell exemplified what Hoover prized most in a mining engineer: "that unusual combination of high technical skill and commercial common sense."[187]

And if Hoover had been dependent on others, so, too, had they been dependent on him. Govett told the shareholders that "the larger part of the salvation of the Company you owe to Mr. Hoover." Hoover "laid down the work, and Mr. Mitchell was selected, and appointed by him. This selection has been justified to the full. . . ." Not a man to shrink at taking responsibility (or credit), Govett asserted that "it has been a partnership affair between Mr. Hoover and myself; and the salvation of the Company technically and financially has been our work."[188] The mining press echoed Govett's praise of his American colleague. The *Mining World* acclaimed Hoover as "the real saviour of the Corporation."[189] As the company's technical and financial prospects brightened further, the *Engineering and Mining Journal* of New York hailed the result as "a great, and well-deserved triumph, for Mr. Hoover."[190]

As 1908 progressed it was evident to all that the Zinc Corporation was finally, victoriously, on its feet.[191] Vicissitudes, as always, lay ahead, and success did not come uniformly to Hoover and his associates. The Australian Smelting Corporation, "assured of a very successful future" (according to Bewick, Moreing in 1906), folded in 1909—a total failure and loss to the underwriters.[192] The Zinc Corporation's contemplated zinc smelters in Australia fell victim to its financial burdens, to Australia's regret when war came in 1914.[193]

Nevertheless, by late 1908 the nightmare months were over. In 1909 the corporation began paying dividends on its preference shares (ordinary shareholders had to wait until 1911).[194] By 1910 the growing company was one of the principal zinc producers in the world. It had, in one journal's words, "revolutionized the metallurgy of Broken Hill."[195] Splendid dividends poured forth in the years ahead. Further flotation process discoveries and improvements were made; in 1911 the Zinc Corporation converted again to an improved Minerals Separation process.[196]

In retrospect, it was obvious that the directors and managers had committed many serious mistakes, and for some of these Hoover bore a measure of responsibility. If Baillieu was correct, Hoover had acquiesced in the unwise choice of Herbert Daly as initial managing director. Hoover and his fellow directors had deferred too long to the roseate predictions of Augustin Queneau. Much more serious was the fateful decision—for reasons not fully clear—to abandon systematic comparative trials of flotation processes in early 1906 for the supposedly proven Potter process.

All this decision making was complicated by the existence of a board of directors "divided into two halves at the end of a long cable"[197] (one part in London, one in Melbourne), and by a chain of command that for a long time seemed to deny the nominal managers full control.[198] Hoover and Bewick, Moreing were new to Broken Hill, new to silver, lead, and zinc. Hoover, moreover, was no metallurgist; he had no special expertise in flotation (few did). Such factors made it difficult for him to forge ahead with the kind of decisiveness and assurance to which he was accustomed in Western Australia.

The Zinc Corporation's fundamental early flaw, however, was not indecisiveness but its antithesis: the premature optimism of 1905 and the bold, almost precipitate purchase of tailings in its name. "This has been the inherent weakness in this Company all the way along," Govett remarked three years later: "the accumulating liabilities accepted on the assumption that the Company would infallibly be a success."[199]

So much, indeed, had flowed from the stupendous financial commitment which Hoover and his associates assumed so confidently in the autumn of 1905. With so much at stake, it was natural to promise results rapidly, to improvise, to see the proverbial light at the end of the tunnel. Hoover shared and at times fostered the expectation of imminent success, particularly when he pronounced that the Cattermole process had been "proved" a success. No doubt in 1905 he believed that the flotation process was practicable, and he was not alone. But to achieve success in the laboratory was one thing. To duplicate it in a full-scale, economically viable manner was another.

There was in Hoover's makeup, alongside his engineer's devotion to fact and efficiency, a certain brashness, even impulsiveness, and a gambler's love of risk. Hoover was a "bold adventurer," said W. S. Robinson.[200] He was "very enterprising," said an Australian journalist—more so than the cautious mine directors who sold him the dumps.[201] At Broken Hill he was almost too enterprising too soon.

Yet he succeeded. His vision—a huge corporation to treat immense zinc tailings dumps hitherto resistant to every device of applied science—was a sweeping conception and, in the long run, a sound one. And as Baillieu acknowledged, it was preeminently Hoover's vision. He "stood out in his grasp of the position," an Australian friend later wrote.[202] Why wait, Hoover could have retorted to his critics, until every miner and his mate discovered that the residues were valuable here and now? Then it would be too late; the dumps would be taken and a score of competitors ensconced on the Hill. One must act—on the best available information, of course (which he had done), but one must act. One must take the risk.

And having done so, "Hail Columbia" Hoover persevered. The traumas of 1907–8, nearly fatal for the company, revealed Hoover at his best. Other men might have cut their losses, made excuses, and run. Instead, with his ally Govett he held on, believing in his vision and risking his own money to sustain it.

Although as joint managing director Hoover continued to guide the Zinc Corporation's improving fortunes for eight more years, nothing he did for the company after 1908 was probably as crucial (or harrowing) as his role in its founding and survival. Hoover did not create the Zinc Corporation alone, and he did not claim that he did. But he was the man "largely instrumental" in organizing the enterprise.[203] And as the director most responsible for the technical staff and technical operations in its early years, he had, as he said, the "professional responsibility" for the "engineering programme." The Zinc Corporation was one of Hoover's greatest and most enduring achievements as a mining engineer. Three quarters of a century later it lives on, after mergers, as the multinational minerals company, Rio Tinto-Zinc Corporation, Ltd.

18

Getting Out of Bewick, Moreing

I

B y 1907 Bewick, Moreing and Company's business was prospering more than ever. Forty-five separate mining concerns were now affiliated with Hoover's firm.[1] According to one spokesman, it annually distributed £895,000 in wages at its "representative companies throughout the world."[2] In Western Australia, said one observer, "company-mining" had become "almost synonymous" with the firm of Bewick, Moreing.[3]

Not that life had become routine; it never was in mining. If labor unions, goldfields politicians, or unscrupulous business associates did not stir the waters, angry shareholders did. In 1907 a shareholders uprising occurred at the Talisman Consolidated, of which Herbert Hoover was a director and W. F. Turner chairman. The mine itself, managed by Hoover's firm, was in New Zealand, as were most of the shareholders. But the company was British-registered, its directors lived in England, and annual meetings took place in London—conditions almost guaranteed to generate friction. Before the annual shareholders meeting in May, a campaign began in New Zealand to alter the balance of power. The "colonials" were angry at what they considered the directors' "exorbitant remuneration" and subservience to its nominal servants, Bewick, Moreing. Among other things, the dissidents demanded the abolition of directors' commissions on dividends, the appointment of a colonial representative on the board, and an independent examination of the mine.

But when the New Zealanders' representatives tried to present their grievances in London, they found that they had been outfoxed (or so they believed). Instead of holding the annual meeting at the customary time (June), the Talisman board scheduled it for a month earlier, before the bulk of the colonials' proxies arrived from New Zealand. Refusing to reschedule the meeting, the board asserted that it would favorably consider the colonials' proposals after the proxies reached London with their specific instructions—that is, after the annual meeting. With the New Zealanders' proxies thus eliminated from the count, the board defeated the insurgents.

It was a Pyrrhic victory. Angered at what they considered highhanded disfranchisement, the New Zealanders quickly assembled an overwhelming majority of proxies. At an emergency stockholders meeting in December, the insurgents swept to victory, despite months of obstructive and tricky tactics by Turner (so they charged—Turner denied it). The aroused shareholders sharply reduced the directors' fees, firmly fixed the date of future annual meetings, and severely constrained the directors' powers to act without prior shareholder permission. To provide immediate representation on the board for the New Zealanders, it was agreed that one of the incumbent directors would resign. According to Turner, Hoover volunteered. (Hoover himself was absent from the meeting on a trip to Burma.) After protracted argument, the meeting voted Hoover £250 in compensation for his loss of office and in recognition of his services to the company.[4]

The technical accomplishments of Hoover and his engineers at the mine were not at issue in the Talisman controversy. The mine itself, under Bewick, Moreing's management, went on to many more years of prosperity.[5] Instead other, subtler questions erupted, as they did a number of times during Hoover's years at Bewick, Moreing. Who should run a mine: skilled engineer-administrators or the nominal directors (often "guinea pigs" and men inexperienced in mining)? Was the Bewick, Moreing tail too often wagging the company dog? Was it proper for a man such as Hoover to be both a director in a company and a partner in the firm that managed it?

And just how much remuneration should directors of mining companies receive? Was it proper for directors to take percentage commissions on dividends, in addition to their fixed annual fees? At the Oroya Brownhill in 1908 startled shareholders discovered that during the preceding five years the directors (including Hoover) had taken £60,000—nearly $300,000—in such commissions apart from their regular fees. This practice, to be sure, was not illegal; the company's articles of association permitted it. But how much compensation for directors was truly justified?[6] In Australia, at least two journals denounced the practice.[7]

These questions were probably of less concern to Hoover in 1906 and 1907 than one intrusive and increasingly worrisome fact. In Western Australia, still the capital of Bewick, Moreing's engineering empire, more and more mines were declining in value at depth. Worst of all, few new mines were being discovered. In 1903 Western Australia's gold production peaked at just over 2,000,000 fine ounces; then commenced a decade of uninterrupted decline.[8] As early as 1903 J. H. Curle, possibly reflecting the views of his traveling partner Hoover, wrote from Kalgoorlie that new mines were not being opened—a disturbing fact.[9] In 1905 Curle decried the decline of active prospecting and urged the state government itself to undertake systematic exploration of the region.[10] By 1906 he was gloomier than ever. Most of the mines of the state had "passed their zenith"; the "mining outlook" was "not good."[11]

Yet Western Australia was a vast, unexplored area, roughly equal in size to all of the United States east of the Mississippi River. Was its mining future really that bleak? To Herbert Hoover in 1905, "the failure to develop new mines of consequence" was due squarely to "a large decrease in prospecting" in recent years. This in turn, he argued, was the direct consequence of unsound governmental regulation of the mining industry.[12]

For under Western Australian mining law, individuals and companies did not receive freehold title to their property. Instead, the government *leased* the land on condition that the lessee continuously employ one man for every six acres of the lease. The purpose of this "labor covenant" was benign enough: to compel vigorous development of mining leases and to compel the employment of more workers. But Hoover contended that this regulation had precisely the opposite effect. It was expensive to employ one man continuously per six acres, discouragingly expensive: it wrought "great hardship on the prospector"[13] and "rendered it practically impossible for the prospector to hold his ground."[14] Despite the government's liberal granting of exemptions from the labor requirement, "the fear of inability to hold ground" (said Hoover) "has driven the prospector largely from the field and throttled the growth of the industry."[15]

Hoover therefore advocated "a more liberal law of leaseholds" in Western Australia; such a reform, he contended, would "greatly benefit the workman and capitalist alike."[16] He called for "more liberal treatment of prospectors"[17] and proposed in 1907 the outright abolition of the labor covenant "so far as it applies to prospectors." This, he declared, "is one way to stimulate the finding of good new mines." And new mines, he warned, "are wanted."[18] If Western Australians did not encourage prospecting and locate more mines, the industry would shrivel as current mines gave out.[19]

In 1905 Hoover proposed a more radical reform: that Western Australia adopt the essence of American mining law, under which (as he explained it) miners could acquire an unconditional, fee simple title to their leases after five years. During this five-year term they had to work the property for only twenty-four days a year—a far less burdensome requirement than Western Australia's labor covenant. In America, Hoover pointed out, "every reef has an owner" who "will be lured back to work it if he knows his title is safe." To Hoover the solution for Western Australia was plain:

What is wanted is to get the working miner to do some prospecting. It is obvious that he cannot do this under existing conditions, as the labour conditions freeze him out. . . . The success of the mining industry, in the long run, depends upon long and continuous prospecting and development—not upon occasional and spasmodic forays into the bush.

The way to encourage such development was to make it cheap and easy for ordinary miners to prospect for gold on their own.[20]

Hoover's pessimistic assessment of the future of West Australian gold production (under current regulations) and his advocacy of a weakened "labor covenant" evoked some dissent "down under."[21] If, for example, prospectors were not compelled to hire labor and continuously work their leases, would they not "shepherd" the property instead of developing it? To Hoover this fear was unwarranted: "People will not shepherd leases for ever for no purpose. . . . Men do not let gold lie idle in the ground."[22] In the years ahead Hoover continued to assert that American mining law was superior to Australian both in stimulating mining development and in giving the "working miner . . . an opportunity to improve his position from that of a wage-earner." Any law that discouraged the wage-earning miner from becoming a prospector, he said, would ultimately constrict the growth of the mining industry.[23]

In promoting more prospecting, Hoover focused on the foundation of the whole mining structure. First, an individual prospector or prospecting party would locate a gold-bearing property and perhaps develop it as a small mine or surface show. Then someone like Hoover or one of his staff would happen by, take samples, and perhaps secure an option in behalf of Moreing's exploration company or a similar concern. If more extensive sampling proved the merits of the prospect, the exploration company would exercise its option and purchase the property for perhaps several thousand pounds sterling. The prospectors, having disposed of their property at (to them) a good price, would contentedly leave the scene. Next, the exploration company would float the property in London; that is, it would sell the mine to a British-registered company newly formed for the purpose of acquiring and working this property. In return, the exploration company—the middleman—would receive a large, perhaps controlling, block of so-called promoters' or vendors' shares in the new company.

The exploration company's profits could come from two sources. It could hold onto its shares in anticipation of future profits, or it could sell them on the stock market, perhaps after booming the company first in the mining press. Of course, if the mine failed to arouse investor interest, or if it failed to generate dividends, the vendors' shares would not be worth much, and the exploration company would lose money. Those were the risks.

To some Australians this system smacked of exploitation. One complained that "foreigners" merely took over the good mines after others "put up with all the hardships."[24] From time to time critics in Western Australia charged that Hoover's firm was "more bent on grabbing control of established mines than devoting themselves and the money they command to the assistance and development of new properties and new districts."[25] And Hoover knew that despite the prospector's indispensability "not one in 10,000 but dies a poor man."[26] From one perspective, then, Hoover's espousal of mining law reform looked less like solicitude for the prospector than concern for his own self-interest.

Yet could it be any other way? Bewick, Moreing and the exploration companies could not afford to scour the vast Australian outback for mines all by themselves. They had to rely on the independent prospectors and their "mates," lured on by the perennial hope of a lucky find. Once the prospectors turned up something worth investigating, Bewick, Moreing and its client-companies stepped in, doing what they did best: examining, sampling, appraising, deciding whether an option was really worth a £50,000 investment. Often Hoover's firm had to invest considerable sums in development work—sinking shafts, carving out drives and stopes—just to determine whether a prospect had any commercial potential at all. It was expensive work, usually work without reward, for few mines and prospects proved to be worth developing. And it required technical knowledge that ordinary prospectors could not supply.

This unending search for and evaluation of mines was a crucial part of Hoover's business, and his firm took pains to emphasize the fact. Between 1904 and 1906 Bewick, Moreing men examined literally hundreds of propositions and took over only two.[27] The London and Western Australian Exploration Company employed a staff just to inspect, sample, and improve potential acquisitions. In 1907 it spent almost £15,000 on this effort alone.[28] By 1907 the total number of "shows" examined by Bewick, Moreing in Western Australia ran into the thousands.[29]

Yet the returns were diminishing. In 1905 Hoover personally inspected the Sandstone leases in the remote Black Range district in Western Australia. The American engineer was impressed; the prospect had the makings of a great mine, perhaps even (he said) another Great Fingall. Through him, and on his advice, the Oroya Brownhill Company took an option on and purchased the property, which it successfully floated as a subsidiary called the Oroya Black Range in 1906.[30] "The Black Range has been a great success," Hoover wrote to a friend, "and I am sorry now we did not take it on our private accounts, although the risk was considerable."[31] But such successes were becoming rare.

And so Hoover's firm and its affiliated "group" began to diversify, to invest capital outside of Western Australia. One early sign was Hoover's interest in the Zinc Corporation; another was his growing enthusiasm for a mining venture in Burma. Late in 1905, on Hoover's emphatic recommendation, the Lake View Consols (chaired by Govett) purchased a half interest in the Broken Hill South Blocks mine in New South Wales.[32] A few months later it decided to invest in Hoover's Burma proposition.[33] As the Lake View mine itself showed signs of petering out, the company gradually began to convert itself into a finance or holding company, which could live off its portfolio of investments even after its own mine closed down.[34]

These actions by the Lake View directors stirred comment in Australia.[35] The thought that West Australian gold was being used to finance mining ventures elsewhere offended the *West Australian Mining, Building, and Engineering Journal*, ordinarily friendly to Hoover. The journal scoffed at the assertion that the Lake View and other concerns had to invest outside the state because of a dearth of good mines in the state. This was mere "bluff." There were plenty of eligible mines in Western Australia, it contended. The trouble was that the big companies "want to make such big bites at the cake that no deals result."[36]

The new policy of diversification evoked another of those delicate questions of business judgment and ethics that arose often during Hoover's mining years. Since its creation in 1902, the Oroya Brownhill Company (of which Hoover was a director) had deliberately accumulated a cash reserve to provide for the inevitable day when its mine was exhausted. To the board of directors this was enlightened and prudent planning: when the mine did start to play out, they would have ample capital available with which to purchase new properties elsewhere and thus prolong the life of the company. But by 1908 the Oroya Brownhill's undistributed surplus had swelled to the enormous sum of £300,000 on a total share capital of £450,000, and many shareholders unsuccessfully demanded that at least a portion of this surplus be given to them. To some stockholders it was "dangerous" that the directors controlled such a loose amount. The directors, they feared, might "get slack" and "try experiments."[37]

To some extent this protest reflected the shareholders' natural desire for immediate dividends versus the directors' concern for stability and continuity: a conflict of short-term versus long-term perspectives. To the *West Australian Mining, Building, and Engineering Journal*, however, the issue went to the heart of mining governance by insiders, of whom Herbert Hoover was one:

> As a matter of fact the possession of this money, in such large sums, puts too much power in the hands of the directors who, wisely or unwisely as the case may be, can finance other schemes for which they are directors and probably promoters of, and thus fortify their positions as drawers of fees and profits, while the shareholders of the companies owning these cash reserves receive little if any benefit from the financial deals of the directors. We disagree entirely with a policy which deprives the small investors who have put up their money, of dividends they are entitled to, while the big holders who have gone in on the ground floor as promoters

and directors were scarcely called on for money at all to set the enterprise on its feet. [38]

The directors, of course, saw it differently. At the 1908 Oroya Brownhill meeting the chairman announced that Hoover would soon be on his way to Malaya to inspect some properties for possible acquisiton by the company. Hoover's colleague Turner praised him as "a very able and experienced engineer" who was "in quite an exceptional position to carry out" the board's policy of purchasing new mines. [39]

By 1908, then, two of the most established mines on the Golden Mile, the Lake View Consols and the Oroya Brownhill, were solidly on the way to becoming holding companies. And the focus of their operations was shifting away from Western Australia. Both Hoover and Moreing, however, seemed anxious to quell any suspicion that they were deserting the land that had lifted them to preeminence. After a visit to the state in 1906 Moreing professed optimism about the future of its mining industry. [40] A year later Hoover, on a trip to Kalgoorlie, asserted that his firm's mines were in better shape than the year before. There was "no reason," he said, why his firm would not employ as many men as it did now "for many years to come." Hoover also downplayed the suggestion that Australian legislation was "driving capital out of the country."

> Money is never frightened by anything. It either demands more interest or more security. If money is to be attracted to this State the only thing that will do it is making enterprise sufficiently remunerative.

If "good mines" existed, Hoover said, the money to develop them would be found. What was needed was "good mines" and the structuring of incentives to find them. [41]

Nevertheless, the statistics told a discomfiting story. In 1907 the gold production of Western Australia fell for the fourth year in succession. Against this backdrop, labor unions in the state launched a drive for increased wages. To F. A. Govett (and probably to Hoover as well) this demand was "wholly unreasonable." After the new wage award was announced, Govett issued a tough and uncompromising warning at the Lake View Consols annual meeting. If his company's already tiny profit margin of two shillings per ton were reduced by rising labor costs, the company would shut down "without hesitation." Then four hundred workers, "instead of earning a very handsome living," would receive no wages whatever. The mine would stay shut, Govett vowed, until the workers learned that they had a high scale of wages and that the two-shilling-per-ton profit was "barely enough to justify" the company's staying in business. [42]

The continuing decline of gold output, the scarcity of promising mines, impediments to prospecting, uncertainties about labor: all were pushing

Hoover toward one conclusion—that his future did not rest much longer in Western Australian mining.

I I

B Y 1907 Herbert Hoover, to all external appearances, had achieved success. Still young and on the make, he was a recognized man of influence in the mining and financial community of London, the mining and financial capital of the world. Companies were floated, huge sums invested, on his recommendation. He was a director of ten mining companies,[43] and his firm of mining engineers was reputed to be "the largest and best known . . . in existence."[44] He was earning an income that by contemporary standards made him a wealthy man. He informed his brother in 1906 that his annual income was now about $75,000.[45] A year later he told David Starr Jordan, president of Stanford University, that he was now taking in "$5,000 a year as mining expert and $95,000 as financial expert."[46] Hoover was living comfortably, also. In 1907 he bought a new automobile (a Porthoa) at a cost of more than $3,000.[47]

Another source of contentment was his brother Theodore. At the beginning of 1906 Tad was managing a mine in Bodie, California but apparently was unhappy with the position. Bert, in London, quickly arranged for Tad to go to Mexico for six months as examining engineer for two Australian mining companies managed by Bewick, Moreing.[48] Tad was to search for business for these companies and would manage any properties they purchased. I "have got you appointed as boss of the roost in Mexico, at £125 a month," Hoover informed his brother.

> I think the opening that I have gotten this way will be a very fine one, if there is any business in Mexico to be done, and you will have started on the best possible basis of being boss and not having to take a subordinate position to anybody. You will be directly under myself, and if the business expands we shall open a branch of Bewick, Moreing & Co. in the State of Mexico, with you as residential partner. . . .[49]

A few weeks later Hoover promised to find his brother a job in Australia "if I cannot keep you going in America." But he preferred to have Theodore "study Mexico for a year at somebody elses expense and [I] will use every effort to that end."[50]

As it happened, Mexico proved unpromising; Theodore Hoover did not become a local partner in Bewick, Moreing. Instead, in September 1906 he moved to London to join Minerals Separation, Ltd., a pioneer firm in perfecting the flotation process.[51] For Hoover this was even better than the Mexican scheme; now the two brothers and their families were together.[52]

Yet Hoover was increasingly restless and dissatisfied. London was where the house was, but it was not home. When Jordan asked Hoover to place a young American mining engineer in Western Australia, Hoover's reply was revealing:

> I am not too certain about the advisability of leaving America to get one's early experience abroad, because the friends that he will make, and the people with whom he will establish himself, would be unable to do him any good in America, and it practically means, as is the case with myself, a permanent exile, at least, until he has reached such a point of affluence that he can afford to cut loose.[53]

At least as early as 1904 Hoover had resolved to sever his association with Bewick, Moreing, although his partnership contract was not due to expire until the end of 1912. In September 1904, less than six months after he had formally extended his partnership agreement by three years, he told Jordan that he was "anxious to return to America as the limitations of [on] foreigners in Europe who cannot abjure their nationalities are very marked." Hoover added that his "compulsory residence" in London "will have expired in another couple of years." Then, he reported, he would "certainly return" home "provided I can obtain or see any opening for an 'independent young man.' "[54]

Hoover did not find it easy to break away. Still, he was determined, and certain of the course he wished to take. On March 1, 1906 he confided to Theodore:

> As to the future: It seems quite impossible for me to get free from this position for the present. In the first instance I cannot sell out without partners consent and if I demand a dissolution I should recieve only £10000 or £15000. The "good will" in that case being valued at nothing. The annual income to me is about £15000 and the side issues b[ein]g participation in finance operations. I hope to clear out by another year or 18 months by arrangement.[55]

A little over a year later Hoover told David Starr Jordan that he had (in Jordan's words) "run through his profession" (Hoover was not quite thirty-three). All he could do in mining now, he said, was earn more money, and "he already had all he needed." Hoover informed Jordan that he planned to resign from his partnership and eventually return to the United States, where he wished to take up some kind of "executive work in which he could be of service."[56]

A variety of personal and family reasons influenced Hoover's decision to leave his flourishing business partnership. On January 24, 1907 he sailed once again from England for Australia.[57] Lou was pregnant now and did not join him. For nearly six months Hoover was absent from his wife and three-year-old son as he toured his old familiar haunts at Kalgoorlie, Victoria, and

Broken Hill.[58] He arrived back in London on July 16—just in time for the birth the next day of his second son, Allan Henry.[59] Barely two months later Allan, his brother, their parents, and Lou's sister Jean packed up and sailed for Burma. They did not return to London until just before Christmas.[60]

This rush from country to country was "a dog's life," Hoover later recalled. By 1907 he desired to slow down, to travel less, to enjoy some surcease from the endless strain of engineering obligations. Since joining Moreing as a partner in late 1901 he had paid four lengthy visits to Australia, entailing a total of literally months of his life spent at sea. Increasingly, he later recorded, his thoughts were turning to America. His son Herbert was approaching school age, and Bert and Lou wanted him to receive an American education. Hoover himself had an unfocused aspiration to enter American public life. Yet his constant travel and London-based mining practice had left him little time to sink deep roots in his native land. Since going to Australia in 1897, Hoover had spent at most two months per year in America. In 1899 and 1907 he did not come to United States at all. A desire to avoid "permanent exile" was no doubt on his mind.[61]

Above all, Hoover was anxious to leave his partnership because, as he later put it, C. Algernon Moreing "had proved a wholly impossible partner."[62] On July 1, 1907—so he later wrote—Hoover finally pulled free of debt; his "interest in the firm" was "clear." He moved with alacrity to dissolve the partnership: ". . . I could not stand Moreing any longer than necessary—having given practically 5 years to that mess."[63]

What did he mean? Hoover never specified his grievances in writing. Perhaps he was thinking of the Rowe affair of 1902–3, although this did not prevent him from extending his partnership contract in 1904. Possibly he blamed Moreing for embroiling him in some of the quarrels and lawsuits that punctuated his years as a partner. Certainly Hoover and Moreing clashed over policy: Hoover wanted the firm to buy and operate mines for itself, and not merely manage them; Moreing disagreed. The issue led to serious friction.[64]

Above all, it seems that the two men were never personally close. Older, wealthier, and politically ambitious, Moreing saw little of his American colleague outside the office. In all their years of partnership Moreing apparently never invited Hoover to his home.[65] Partly, perhaps, in consequence of this behavior, Hoover detested what he perceived as British snobbery and became more intensely American than ever.[66] Moreing's world was the class-conscious world of British politics and high society; in 1906 he unsuccessfully stood as a Unionist candidate for Parliament.[67] Hoover, by contrast, was the Yankee outsider, yearning for a chance to go home. By 1908, and, indeed, well before, Hoover felt cramped by his association with Moreing and eager to break loose.[68]

One other factor may have influenced Hoover's decision. When his planned retirement from Bewick, Moreing was announced in early 1908, both the firm and the press gave ill health as the reason.[69] It was "a result of continuous overwork," one journal reported.[70] Although the press did not mention it, Hoover had suffered from malaria during his trip to Burma in late 1907.[71] According to Moreing some years later, for many months prior to the announcement Hoover had belabored him with complaints about his health: he was suffering from "consumption of the brain." Moreing eventually came to feel (or at least to profess) that Hoover had feigned bad health as a pretext for escaping from his contract.[72] Whatever the truth of Moreing's claim, there was no doubt that Hoover—for his mental well-being, at least—was anxious to depart.[73]

Hoover's retirement took effect on June 30, 1908.[74] He sold his share in the firm to W. J. Loring, the firm's general manager in Australia, for £30,978, or more than $150,000.[75] The sum well reflected the firm's enhanced prosperity and prestige. In Hoover's six-and-a-half years as a partner, Bewick, Moreing's business had tripled.[76]

But before he could leave, Hoover was obliged in April 1908 to sign an indenture containing several restrictive covenants. Hoover agreed not to practice his profession of mining engineering anywhere in Great Britain or the British empire for ten years without Bewick, Moreing's consent.[77] Moreing, Wellsted, and Loring respected Hoover's ability too much to want a formidable competitor to arise in their midst.

One aspect of the dissolution process carried a portent of future trouble. Under his 1903 contract all of Hoover's director's fees (more than £3,000 a year by 1908) belonged to the firm, since Hoover sat on the boards as the firm's representative.[78] Hoover now requested that he be allowed to retain his directorates (and the fees) for himself. (Although intending to be less active, Hoover did not plan to retire totally.) He argued that as a director he could facilitate cooperation between the various boards and his erstwhile business partners, who still managed the companies' mines. He could also steer new business their way. This was Hoover's claim. Reluctantly (so they later stated), Moreing, Wellsted, and Loring acquiesced.[79]

While Hoover's parting was not completely amicable, it evoked only signs of esteem in public. The mining press expressed hope that his health would improve rapidly and gratification that he was not leaving the scene entirely.[80] It was "not easy to replace men of the calibre of Mr. Hoover," one journalist declared.[81] G. P. Doolette, the grand old man of Australian mining investors, declared that perhaps no firm had done more in the past twenty years to reduce Australian working costs than Bewick, Moreing, with its "marvellous organisation and technical skill and knowledge and by the use of up-to-date appliances." He singled out Hoover, Loring, and John Agnew for praise.[82]

Hoover could look back with considerable pride on his association with Bewick, Moreing. Spotted though his record was with inevitable failures and frustrations, and wracked as he had been by some costly and searing scandals, 1901–8 had been years of accomplishment. Bewick, Moreing was at the pinnacle of its success, and Hoover more than anyone else was responsible for it. In Western Australia his name was forever linked with the development or administration of some of the state's greatest mines.

Two enduring achievements stood out. First, his role in creating and sustaining the Zinc Corporation. Second, the managerial revolution that he, as much as any other man, had inaugurated and implemented in West Australian mining. Thanks in considerable measure to Hoover's driving insistence on efficiency, on lowered working costs, and on systematic business techniques, he and his lieutenants had taken a speculative quagmire and made it an industry.

I I I

H O O V E R could also take pleasure from another proof of success. Despite the wrenching financial reverses occasioned by the Rowe frauds and the Great Boulder Perseverance fiasco, despite indebtedness to Moreing that lingered even into 1907, Hoover, by his own later account, was worth more than $400,000 by mid-1908.[83] Although this figure may have been overstated, his future seemed amply assured. Much of his savings derived from his partnership income; an American could save a lot on an income of $100,000 a year in those days before the income tax. Some of it also came from what Hoover called "outside business"[84]—possibly a reference to stock market investments or to the "finance operations" he mentioned to Theodore in 1906.

Hoover was ambivalent about participation in the stock market. "The whole subject of share purchase by Engineers has given me the greatest possible anxiety," he told one of his employees in 1903. "Personally," he added, "the members of this firm never speculate in shares and we never under any circumstances buy shares on margin or carry them open on the market!" Hoover had no objection to his engineers' *investing* in mining shares, a policy he defined as buying the shares, actually paying for them, and holding onto them in one's own name for the sake of dividends and interest. But "speculation," by which he meant "the purchase of shares on margins or on open account," was a different matter entirely. It could injure a mine manager's reputation, and it was too risky. "I have had a great deal of experience in watching the W.A. market now for a period of seven years," Hoover observed, "and I do not know at the present time of anyone who has speculated in shares who is not worse off financially for having done so."

To Hoover there was only one path to profit from mining enterprise. It was the path of the strategically located insider. "The way that money is made out of mining," he declared, "is to secure interests in mines at their initiation and not when they are before the public. Occasionally one wins at the latter game, but in the long run one always loses."[85]

How much Hoover benefited from taking blocks of stock in mining companies "at their initiation" during these years is unknown. Certainly during his Bewick, Moreing period he engaged actively in stock market transactions. He maintained a personal account and bought shares in the Lancefield, Sons of Gwalia, Victorian Deep Leads, and other companies his firm managed.[86] Whether he truly "speculated" (by his definition) during these years is unknown, given his distinction between steady, long-term investments in mining shares and the "jobbing" in shares on margin.[87] How much he relied on stock dividends for income is similarly impossible to judge, since the evidence is fragmentary and since he held in his own name shares that actually belonged to friends.[88]

Although Hoover wished by 1907 to spend more time in the United States, he did not contemplate returning to his homeland at once. His directorates alone would tie him to London awhile yet. In 1907 he and Lou leased a rambling, old, eight-room, two-story house, surrounded by high walls and graced with a garden, in the Kensington section of London: the Red House, it was called, on Hornton Street. On December 20, just back from Burma, the family moved in.[89]

In the summer of 1908 Hoover was finally free of Moreing and his "mess," free to be his own man. His reputation in mining circles was solid. His fortune, though not grandiose, was considerable and growing. He was thirty-four.

19

The Engineer-
Financier

I

O N July 1, 1908 Herbert Hoover was a liberated man. No longer was he encumbered (as he saw it) by C. Algernon Moreing and the obligations of partnership in a firm. For the first time since college Hoover was on his own, and one goal, one urge, reigned uppermost. He was "resolved," as he later put it, "to devote myself to mining simply for the profits I could make out of the production of metals."[1]

Enough, then, of mine management, its headaches and wearisome details. For nearly seven years he had journeyed almost incessantly, had inspected prospects in the Australian outback, had devoted his brains to developing other men's mines. No more. Now he would travel only when he wanted to and would make money for himself.

The mining company directorates that he retained assured the Yankee engineer of a comfortable income. But Hoover, in 1908, desired more than moderate success. "If a man has not made a fortune by 40 he is not worth much," he had said more than once to a friend.[2] Time was creeping on. Just six weeks after he terminated his partnership, Hoover turned thirty-four.

The next six years of Hoover's career had many themes. But surely the most obvious was his continuing, insistent drive—a drive imbued in him in youth—for a fortune. Between 1908 and 1914 Hoover found the realm for his quest in London's financial district, hub of world mining promotion and finance.

The transition, in fact, was easy. Already, by 1907, he was deriving 95% of his income from being a "financial expert."[3] During his Bewick, Moreing years he had grown familiar with British financial practice and with prominent stockbrokers like Lionel Robinson and Francis Govett. He had become an acknowledged authority himself on mining economics and finance, a subject about which he wrote often in professional journals.[4]

After 1908 Hoover continued to call himself a mining engineer. But now the focus of his business activity shifted: away from technical administration of ongoing enterprises and toward the locating and financing of promising mining propositions. Let others handle the daily drudgery of administration. Hoover would concentrate on the grand designs: on creating, floating, financing, and refinancing companies all over the earth. This was where big money could be made, and this was where Hoover now turned. He became for himself what he had already become for Bewick, Moreing: an astute, respected engineer-financier.

I I

For a brief interlude in the summer of 1908 Hoover relaxed. He spent a few weeks in the British resort city of Brighton, on the English Channel, where he worked on a series of lectures that he hoped to give sometime at his alma mater. The subject was mining valuation and administration, his specialty.[5]

Despite the charms of the English seaside, Hoover was constitutionally incapable of extended repose. Although ill health was the official reason given for his retirement from Bewick, Moreing and Company, Hoover soon gave signs that his illness—or at least his inclination to slow down—had evanesced. In the fall of 1908 he returned to the London mining world with vigor.

Early in September one mining journal noted that Hoover was "very busy" in the British capital.[6] He opened an office in the city at 62 London Wall, the same building that housed Bewick, Moreing.[7] He joined the board of directors of the Anglo-Continental Gold Syndicate, in which W. F. Turner and Edmund Davis were ruling spirits.[8] In October it was disclosed that he had been elected a director of the Lake View Consols, chaired by his close friend Francis Govett. It was a fitting appointment. "We are accustomed to working together," announced Govett. "There is no necessity for me to speak of his ability—it is too well known. . . ."[9] But Hoover's accession to the board, in one journalist's words, did not "seem like taking a step in the direction of having a quiet time."[10]

Indeed, by October Hoover was so immersed in work that his ambition to return to the United States seemed far from fulfillment. He told his Stanford mentor, John C. Branner, that "ultimately I hope to make my headquarters in the West, and to be of some service to the University; but certainly for the next 12 months I shall [be] very largely tied to London."[11] And when in early December his wife Lou and their two little boys sailed for California, Hoover, absorbed in business, remained behind. The rest of the family spent Christmas with Lou's parents in Monterey; Bert did not leave London until December 26.[12]

On New Year's Day, 1909 Hoover arrived in New York City on the *Lusitania*;[13] it was his first visit to the United States since the summer of 1906.[14] After a side trip up to Boston, he journeyed by rail across the continent, reaching Stanford University on January 13.[15] For the next few weeks he was reunited with his family in California. He established business offices in San Francisco and delivered his lectures on mine valuation and administration to students at Stanford.[16] Then, in early February, while his family stayed on in California, he hastened back to New York, where he repeated the lectures at Columbia University's School of Mines.[17]

On March 3 Hoover traveled down to Washington for the inauguration the next day of President Taft. He stayed overnight at the home of Ralph Arnold (Stanford, class of '99), a geologist and good friend of Theodore Hoover.[18] With Arnold, Hoover shared some of his ambitions for the future.[19] Alas, neither man recorded what these ambitions were.

During Hoover's short stay Arnold was amazed by the barrage of cables, telegrams, and telephone calls that greeted his busy guest.[20] Hurrying back to New York, Hoover sailed alone for England on March 10.[21] His weeks in New York had been productive ones. He told his old friend John Agnew that he had "some important alliances there and promise of unlimited capital to do business."[22]

Lou and the boys did not return to London until early May.[23] It was just as well. For scarcely had Bert landed in England on March 18 than he set off only nine days later on yet another business journey. This time it was to Korea.[24]

Hoover's trip was taken in behalf of the Oroya Brownhill Company, of which he had been a director since its creation by merger in 1902. The famous old Kalgoorlie mine was rapidly nearing exhaustion. Possessed of a huge cash reserve and unwilling simply to liquidate, the anxious directors sought instead to perpetuate the company's existence by acquiring fresh mining properties somewhere else. In the latter half of 1908 they appointed Hoover managing director in charge of the search.[25]

At such business—the economics of mine valuation—Hoover excelled. When the Oroya Brownhill's directors asked their American colleague to investigate personally a highly touted proposition in Korea, he agreed at once to do so.[26] Traveling by way of Russia and the Trans-Siberian Railway, Hoover spent much of April 1909 on the Korean peninsula. He visited the city of Seoul; he cruised up the Yalu River in a junk.[27] His route back took him across the vast Siberian steppes to Moscow and Berlin. When Hoover reached the Red House in London on May 17, Lou, Herbert, and Allan were there to greet him.[28]

Although the Oroya Brownhill took an option on one Korean property, Hoover and his fellow directors rejected heavier involvement. It was just too speculative.[29] Instead the board, under Hoover's guidance, searched elsewhere. At the Oroya Brownhill's annual shareholders meeting in June, Hoover revealed just how wide-ranging his "exploration campaign" had been. We have, he announced,

> actually looked over 680 mining properties. Over 400 were thrown aside at once as not coming within our ken; 150 were rejected after some negotiation; 130 were looked into on the ground to some extent; 20 have been exhaustively examined; one has been purchased, and three taken under working options.

Hoover also disclosed that his trip to America in the past winter had been "in the company's interests."[30]

The Oroya Brownhill's chairman heaped praise on his hardworking colleague. Thanks largely to Hoover, "who in the first place suggested the lines upon which we should proceed," the company's exploration expenses had been low. "It has been his unique experience in these matters that has guided us, and with his world-wide connexions we have obtained and hold to-day advantages in the business that no other similar company possesses." Through Hoover the company had procured "the technical and trustworthy men" needed to visit and evaluate promising mining properties. And how much did Hoover receive for his "enormous amount of work" stretching over nearly a year? Out-of-pocket expenses only, said the chairman, and nothing more, until the Oroya Brownhill made a profit out of transactions consummated as a result of Hoover's labors. Then Hoover would receive a percentage of the company's profits.[31]

Six hundred eighty propositions and only one purchase: a mine called La Leonesa in Nicaragua. The Oroya Brownhill bought it for £50,000. Such a ratio of purchases to rejections might seem a poor percentage, but it reflected well on Hoover's engineering reputation. "There is no scarcity of mines in London for sale," Hoover told the assembled shareholders. The trouble was, there were "always two difficulties": the price asked by the seller and the problem of discovering the truth about the mine.[32] Except for the trip to Korea Hoover himself had not gone personally into the field in search of truth. Other men—often Bewick, Moreing engineers—had done the actual examinations in Nicaragua and elsewhere.[33] But this distance from the scene only increased the responsibility on Hoover's shoulders. For it was his task to select the inspecting engineers who went into the field—men who must be honest as well as capable. Hoover's prestige depended on the accuracy of their examinations. And when they sent in their reports to London, Hoover must assess their data carefully from both an engineering and financial point of view. Would the mine in question pay dividends? How many? How soon? After how much development? At what preliminary cost? Precise, risk-free answers were rarely available. Mine exploration was no cut-and-dried, technical job.

Once the truth about a proposition was ascertained, the sale price might still prove an insurmountable obstacle. Often would-be vendors held exaggerated notions of their mine's worth. Fortunately for the Oroya Brownhill and other clients, Hoover was an able negotiator. In the case of La Leonesa, he persuaded the sellers substantially to reduce their asking price, thereby making possible the Oroya Brownhill's purchase.[34]

Six hundred eighty propositions. It had been a busy year, and finding a mine for the Brownhill had been only one of Hoover's business interests since leaving his partnership. Looking back in June 1909, Hoover was content. "The past year," he told Agnew, "I have gained thirty pounds weight, and more money than any year before, so my failure and ultimate return to Bewick, Moreing and Co. so confidently predicted by C.A.M. [Moreing] is somewhat distant."[35]

I I I

F o r the rest of 1909 Hoover remained in England, except for a trip to New York in late September and early October.[36] (Mrs. Hoover took their sons down to the Dorset coast during his absence.)[37] Hoover opened an office in Manhattan at 71 Broadway, "whence" (he told Agnew) "I can better handle the situation which I have created over there. . . ."[38]

It was probably on this visit, or his preceding one earlier in the year, that Hoover met a New York-based mining engineer whose rise to eminence resembled Hoover's own. Born in New York in early 1875, A. Chester Beatty graduated from the Columbia School of Mines in 1898. Then, with a mere two hundred dollars in his pocket, he journeyed west to make his fortune. Like Hoover, then half a world away, Beatty soon achieved success. Joining the Guggenheim Exploration Company as assistant general manager in 1902, he helped to develop some of the greatest mines in the Guggenheim empire. By 1909 he had become a wealthy man, had left the Guggenheims, and, like Hoover, was contemplating retirement.[39]

By late 1909 the Beatty / Hoover acquaintance had blossomed into trust. On October 1 Beatty notified Hoover (who was still in New York) that he had opened a stock market account with Francis Govett's brokerage house in London. He authorized Hoover to determine the sale or purchase of mining stocks for this account in any amount up to £30,000, or nearly $150,000, and he told Govett to carry out Hoover's instructions. In addition, Beatty permitted Hoover to buy further stocks at his discretion for a joint account, provided that Beatty's total commitment in the two accounts did not surpass

£30,000.[40] In short, Beatty was entrusting Hoover with the management of a part of his fortune.

This speculation (as Beatty labeled it) inaugurated several years of cooperation with Hoover amounting to an informal, albeit selective, business partnership. Hoover's new business address in New York was in fact the same as Beatty's. Early in 1910 Beatty established a branch office at No. 1, London Wall Buildings in London; a few months later Hoover transferred his headquarters to the same building.[41] It was not until 1913 that Beatty moved permanently to London, but long before then his alliance with Hoover had become close, particularly in mining ventures in Russia.[42]

One focus of their relationship was Beatty's speculative account. Through Hoover, Beatty bought and sold actively on the London stock exchange. Hoover's correspondence with Beatty was replete with references to his operations in Beatty's behalf.[43] Month by month Hoover forwarded to New York detailed statements of joint account: of shares in Russian gold and copper mines, of shares in oil companies operating in Russia and Trinidad, of shares in Amalgamated Zinc and other enterprises.[44]

Hoover, in turn, used Beatty as a conduit for investments of his own in the United States. In 1910 he requested Beatty to buy 4,000 shares of Inspiration Copper Company stock for him at $9 per share. Beatty did so on $10,000 margin, which he supplied to his broker even before Hoover's remittance for that amount arrived.[45] A year later Beatty's office facilitated Hoover's purchase of $11,000 of bonds in the Chino Copper Company.[46] On another occasion Hoover arranged through Beatty's office to borrow money from a New York capitalist on security of 6,500 shares in still another copper company.[47]

Sometimes the two American engineers included others in their stock market operations. One such "joint speculation" (as Hoover called it) was a small syndicate that Hoover, Beatty, and two other men created for the purchase of several thousand shares of copper stock. When the account was closed in August 1910, the syndicate partners had made a collective profit of over $3,500. Thirty percent of it went to Hoover.[48]

Early in 1910 Hoover and Beatty consolidated some of their mining finance operations by creating a syndicate called the Intercontinental Trust, Ltd., with a nominal capital of £100,000. Each took a 40% share interest in the company; a third American engineer, Lindon Bates, took the remaining 20%. To the Intercontinental Trust Hoover and Beatty transferred many of their share assets, including stocks in a California oil company, in certain Russian mines, and in miscellaneous syndicates. Beatty's contributions alone approximated $80,000 in value.[49] During the next two years the Intercontinental Trust led an active existence, particularly in financing the Kyshtim Corporation in Russia.[50]

Partly, then, with Beatty, and partly on his own, Hoover after 1908 plunged into the London stock market. He soon found that moneymaking on the market was far from an effortless occupation. With Lloyd George's introduction of a radical budget in Parliament in 1909, Great Britain embarked on two years of profound political turmoil, marked by two elections, the death of King Edward VII, and the Liberal Party's assault on the House of Lords. The result was a stock market depression. "The whole position here is extremely difficult," Hoover reported to Beatty in October 1909. "The political outlook is bad for the market either way that events turn out."[51] In June 1910 Hoover cabled, "Owing to the all around heavy slump and absolute collapse market can do nothing at the present time."[52] "The market here is perfectly putrid in all kinds of mining shares," he remarked in early 1911.[53] Later that year he told a Stanford friend, "We have . . . been in the middle of the severest financial depression in many years here in London, and this depression has now extended over a period of twenty five months."[54]

Hoover, though, was not deterred. According to one who knew him well in these years, he enjoyed the thrill of stock market speculation.[55] In two controversial articles in the mining press in 1909 he even used the pseudonym "A Professional Speculator" to describe himself and proceeded to appraise for his readers the value of over 150 separate mining stocks.[56] Certainly Hoover was quick to exploit an opportunity. When he heard that a prospective deal involving the Camp Bird mine was in trouble, he asked Beatty for information: "If you could find out and telegraph me, in case the thing is likely to fall down, there is a large, fat fee to be obtained from this concern by way of a joint Bear account."[57] During the latter half of 1911 Hoover and Beatty made £15,000 for the Intercontinental Trust by selling certain shares and then buying them back when their price declined on the market.[58]

Yet Hoover's personal market operations, although constant, did not encompass all his business activity between 1908 and 1914. They represented, in a sense, what he did on his own after providing professional services to others. What was the nature of these services? How did he earn the money that he used to invest in the market?

Hoover's "Professional Speculator" articles of 1909 provided an answer. Introducing his classification of various mining shares, he declared:

> . . . The following tables are based on the mines and the merits of the shares, not on the manipulations of the market. Many a share in all classes may be boosted or depressed by market influences, independent of all merit, but in the long run the pendulum will swing back to merit only. The determination of these factors over a large portion of the mining share-list is no easy matter; it requires a wide actual experience among these mines; a knowledge of their personnel; an active and extensive bureau of information. In fact, it is the result of hard work and diligent enquiry.

Hoover defended the legitimacy of this enterprise: "If conducted on this basis, it becomes as sound and respectable as the conducting of an exploration company for the purchase of whole mines. . . ." He then asserted:

The gradual extension of a large class of such professional speculators with an organised staff, agents, and correspondents, has greatly strengthened the finance of the industry by providing facilities for obtaining capital for meritorious undertakings.[59]

So *that* was what Hoover meant by a professional speculator: one who determined the true share value of mines and then provided "facilities for obtaining capital for meritorious undertakings." A middleman between investors with money and owners of mines clamoring for capital. An expert who could sort out the sound prospects from the unsound. To be a responsible "professional speculator" in this sense required, as Hoover said, hard work, good sources of information, and experience among the mines. It required the talents of a mining engineer.

While Hoover as an individual was not averse to short-run market speculation, the engineer in him sought to rationalize mining investment and to reduce through accurate knowledge the inherent and ever-present risks. When one reader sent in a lighthearted comment written from the viewpoint of a crafty market operator, Hoover replied forcefully:

We have no common ground. His business is based on the yield from human credulity; mine upon participating in the profits of realizing minerals into metal. He would succeed equally well as a "bookie" or running a yellow journal.[60]

Rationality and expertise: these were the abilities Hoover brought to the chancy business of mine valuation and finance. As the months passed, he did not have to hustle for new business; from all over the world business propositions landed on his desk. Here is how a typical transaction might develop. Someone—perhaps a mining promoter or a mining company or an investment firm—would approach Hoover with a proposition: a mine to sell, perhaps, or a mining enterprise in need of development capital. If Hoover thought the matter worth pursuing, he would arrange for an engineer to investigate the property at the expense of a company of which Hoover was a director, or at the expense of an exploration syndicate in which he held a financial interest. If the engineer filed a favorable report from the field, Hoover would then help to negotiate the finance. This might take the form of creating a syndicate to purchase the property and resell it, either to an existing company (for cash and shares) or to a new company (in return for a controlling block of stock). As his fee for engineering the finance, Hoover would take a percentage of the profits or a portion of the free stock.

In his 1909 article Hoover referred to the "organised staff, agents, and correspondents" that professional mining speculators now possessed. In the six years after he left his Bewick, Moreing partnership, Hoover built up a band of loosely affiliated consulting mining engineers—mostly Americans—for whom he often found assignments in the field. One such man was Amor

F. Kuehn, a German-American who changed the spelling of his name to Keene in World War I.[61] Another was Hoover's brother Theodore, who left Minerals Separation, Ltd. at the end of 1910 and became a consulting engineer at No. 1, London Wall Buildings, on the same floor as Herbert.[62] Still another was R. Gilman Brown, a Dartmouth College graduate who specialized as a consulting engineer and director in certain Russian mining ventures.[63] In 1911 Hoover's old Stanford friend Deane P. Mitchell left Bewick, Moreing; eventually he, too, found an assignment in Russia.[64] In 1912 another old friend, John Agnew, left Bewick, Moreing's employ; in less than two years he became one of Hoover's chief lieutenants.[65] No formal organization bound these men together. But a feeling of camaraderie was present, and Herbert Hoover was their acknowledged leader.[66]

The sheer range of Hoover's interests between 1908 and 1914 was astonishing. From Korea to Nicaragua, from Newfoundland to Siberia, from oil fields in California to oil fields in Peru, no corner of the earth seemed to escape his restless glance.[67] Some interests seemed small and fleeting: a copper mine in Japan, a gold mine in Madagascar, a copper mine in Romania.[68] Other regions—notedly Burma, Russia, and California's oil fields—received sustained attention.[69]

And always the search went on. When the Porcupine district in Quebec opened up dramatically in late 1910, Hoover quickly joined a syndicate to acquire options on some of the properties. It was a "good gamble," he cabled Beatty.[70] In 1912 Hoover became a director of the Inter-Argentine Syndicate, formed "to carry on the business of miners and financiers." The syndicate acquired certain gold dredging claims in Argentina.[71] In 1912 also, when the price of tin rose, he became interested in an old tin mine in Cornwall, England.[72] In 1913 he and Beatty contributed $13,000 to the newly-formed Brazilian Iron Syndicate.[73] Later that year he joined the board of the Inter-Mexican Syndicate, formed to "acquire and deal with" mines in Mexico and elsewhere.[74]

In later years Hoover liked to think of himself and his associates as having been "engineering doctors to sick concerns."[75] It would be more encompassing to say that between 1908 and 1914 he was an explorer for new concerns, a *financial* doctor, a consultant who helped to obtain *financial* medicine for mining companies with growing pains.

With his technical competence and financial savvy, it was not surprising that Hoover was a busy man. Mining men knew that he could open doors. But as time went on, Hoover did more than just select mines for others (such as the Oroya Brownhill) to float. He was not just a referral service. More and more he helped to determine the terms of—and participated personally in—the finance. Frequently he acted as an underwriter of mining stock flotations.[76] That is, he would agree to help guarantee the success of a stock issue by promising to purchase part of the issue if it failed to attract the investing public. In return for this risk, he might receive a block of free stock or an option to buy some shares at par later on. If at the later date the market price was above par, Hoover could exercise his option, buy at par, and promptly resell on the market above par—thereby making a profit.

The receipt of free stock in a new or reorganized company was, in effect, Hoover's fee for services rendered. This method of payment had a big advantage: it enabled Hoover to get in "on the ground floor."[77] And that was where he liked to be. He did not like to involve himself in business that had already gone on the market. In 1909, for example, he received a report about certain mines already operating in Queensland, Australia. Hoover, with his eye on the stock market, was not interested. The "total market value" of these mines, he told Beatty, was currently £1,500,000, "so you will see this business is over with, so far as making any considerable money is concerned."[78] As Hoover had recognized years before, there was only one way to profit in a big way from mining: "to secure interests in mines at their initiation and not when they are before the public."[79] Later on, when the price was high, one could, if one liked, sell out. Hoover "wanted to buy things early in their history," an old mining friend remarked long afterward. "That's the way he made his money—to get in quick enough."[80]

Hoover's plunge into the swirling waters of mining finance was a controversial step in 1909, not because he alone did it but because the blending of the roles of engineer and promoter met resistance from advocates of professionalism among mining engineers. The controversy arose when John Hays Hammond, perhaps the most distinguished American mining engineer at that time, addressed students at the Colorado School of Mines. Hammond urged mining engineers to acquire the "knowledge of business methods" that would enable them to replace mine promoters, many of whom were ignorant, incompetent, and unscrupulous. The goal of mining, he contended, was to make a profit from developing mineral deposits, and Hammond did not think engineers "should be limited to the consideration of the academic features of mining problems."[81]

To the editor of the *Mining Magazine*, T. A. Rickard, Hammond's speech contained "radically unprofessional" advice. Mining engineering was a pursuit in which "gain is subservient to excellence"—or should be. "The participation of engineers in mine-promoting and stock-jobbing may be inevitable," Rickard wrote, "but it is none the less regrettable in so far as it tends to undermine the ethics of the profession."[82]

In a letter to the *Mining Magazine* Herbert Hoover promptly rose to Hammond's defense. Hoover rejected the view that mining engineers should hold themselves "aloof" from participating in mine ownership and finance. Instead, he argued that "the evils in the mining business" could be "more quickly remedied if the whole, or a larger portion of the personnel of the industry, forming the chain between the mine and the capitalist, including directors, promoters, etc." were "men of technical and practical training."

"To say that a man shall be entirely debarred from investment in the one business he knows something about is illogical," Hoover continued. More-over, wouldn't it be better if the "entrepreneur class" of organizers, pro-moters, and directors—"who are a necessity to the building of the industry"—were "technically and practically trained in mining itself"?

> Ninety per cent of the evils of the industry arise out of ignorance, and out of the enthusiasm that grows from a lack of knowledge of what constitutes the value of a mine and its proper administration. This being so, how is this class to become endowed with such training unless the young mining engineer is encouraged ultimately to undertake their functions and thereby supplant much of the riff-raff that is at present a necessity to the industry by way of furnishing the demanded personnel?

Hoover acknowledged that too many promoters, directors, and financiers were "of the undesirable type,"

> but are we to sit down and say that for all future time the world is to endure the present proportion of parasites among this class because no one of a sound mining training is to be allowed, for reasons of hypothetical "professional ethics" to take over their very necessary work of creation and organization?

In effect Hoover saw himself as a reformer bringing a trained scientific intel-ligence to bear on a business—mining promotion—that had long reeked of ignorance and scandal.[83]

For all his reputation and powers of advocacy, Hoover failed to satisfy a number of critics.[84] Rickard, perhaps the foremost journalist in the profes-sion, continued to hold that "the suggestion that the engineer become pro-moter, that the members of our profession assume the work of the financial trader" was "a regrettable retrogression." "Whether it be right for Messrs. Hammond, Hoover, or other men as experienced, as shrewd, and as honour-able to engage in promotion is one question, but assuredly it is quite another matter to advise inexperienced youths, about to begin their apprenticeship, to take part in the most dangerous, if the most lucrative of trades, and to turn their backs on the best traditions of the profession."[85]

Little came of this exchange of viewpoints. But the discussion illuminated well the path Hoover was taking. The Yankee mining engineer had become a member of the "entrepreneur class" and had adopted its specialty: the "very necessary work of creation and organization" of mining enterprises.

I V

O N E such creation occurred in the fall of 1909, when Hoover helped to establish the Amalgamated Zinc (de Bavay's), Ltd. This company was formed to acquire the property of de Bavay's Treatment Company of Melbourne, including the valuable de Bavay flotation process for producing zinc concentrates from the tailings dumps at Broken Hill. Nothing in the public accounts of this transaction connected Hoover to it. The Amalgamated Zinc's initial share issue was underwritten by the Baillieus of Melbourne, and Hoover was not among the original directors.[86]

Yet Hoover seems to have been in the thick of this market flotation. He arranged for A. Chester Beatty to be a sub-underwriter and probably was one himself.[87] He told Beatty that he intended to apply for 5,000 or 10,000 shares before the issue was made, "as the thing will certainly be over-subscribed and go to an immediate premium."[88] And just after the Amalgamated Zinc shares were issued, Hoover reported that it was "a huge success. The shares are now 5/- premium" (or 25% over par). "We will probably arrange a pool to deal with the shares under call all together."[89]

Yet Hoover was reluctant to publicize his involvement. He told Beatty, "I have decided not to go on the Board of this thing, at least until after it is floated awhile, for the simple reason that my mixture with the business during the last few years would entail practically another page of disclosures as to my operations as the father of the concern."[90] Precisely what Hoover wished to conceal is not known.

The Amalgamated Zinc affair illustrated yet another dimension of Hoover's business during the six years before World War I: the reconstruction and amalgamation of mining companies. Hoover was known for his ability to evaluate the worth of mining concerns.[91] He was also a formidable negotiator who was especially persuasive among small groups of fellow businessmen.[92] One man was so afraid of Hoover that he never brought his power of attorney to meetings with Hoover in a locked room![93]

One of the greatest reorganizations that Hoover effected was the series of steps that produced the Lake View and Oroya Exploration, Ltd. in 1911. The story began in 1908 when the Oroya Brownhill directors selected Hoover to search for a new property to replace their dying mine at Kalgoorlie. Hoover's success in acquiring the Leonesa, however, did not resolve the company's problems. A new mine in Nicaragua was welcome, but what would happen to the company's large plant in Western Australia when its ore supply was exhausted?

Late in 1909 Hoover provided the answer. In behalf of the Oroya Brownhill he negotiated an agreement by which the company transferred most of its assets to an adjacent mine in Kalgoorlie, the Golden Links. In return the Oroya Brownhill received nearly a half-interest in the neighboring company, which was renamed the Oroya Links. The Oroya Brownhill retained only its tailings dump and the right to use the treatment plant on the dump until the tailings were exhausted.[94] By this stroke the Oroya Brownhill effectively ceased to be a mining company and became instead a holding company, with its principal assets its property in Nicaragua and its shareholdings in other mines.

Hoover did not stop here. In March 1910 the Oroya Brownhill sold its Leonesa property to a newly formed subsidiary, the Oroya Leonesa, whose board of directors Hoover joined. In return the parent company received virtually all the new company's shares, having a face value of £225,000.[95] At the same time the Oroya Brownhill, after an illustrious history, decided to liquidate and transfer its assets to a successor, the Oroya Exploration Company, created for this purpose in March 1910.[96]

Thus was born out of a failing mining enterprise a finance and exploration company, with Hoover managing director and eventually chairman.[97] At its inception in 1910 Oroya Exploration's assets included about £100,000 in cash and substantial share interest in three subsidiaries: Oroya Links, Oroya Leonesa, and Oroya Black Range (founded through Hoover in 1906).[98] In addition, it held an option on some promising leases at Yuanmi in the West Australian outback and an option over the Babilonia gold mine in Nicaragua.[99]

If creating a set of mining companies is the business equivalent of giving birth to children, Herbert Hoover must have been a proud parent in 1910–11. Certainly the Oroya "family" kept him active in the never-ending search for, and flotation of, new mines. "This Company," said Hoover of Oroya Exploration, "was formed to take up mining prospects or partially developed mines and to develop them into mines."[100] With Hooverian zeal it now did so. Late in 1910 the Oroya Exploration Company helped to create the Mountain Queen, Ltd. (a West Australian mining concern); Theodore Hoover became a director.[101] In the spring of 1911 the Oroya Exploration and Oroya Black Range (Hoover was a director of both) jointly floated the Yuanmi Gold Mines, Ltd., in which they maintained a controlling interest. Hoover was entitled to 15% of the net profits made by the vendor companies and promptly became a director of the new one.[102] In June 1911 the Babilonia Gold Mines, Ltd. was created; both Hoover brothers went on the board.[103]

Meanwhile Hoover was working to enhance his influence within the Oroya Exploration Company. Already managing director, he secured a seat on the board for his friend Lindon Bates by giving away shares in the company to his fellow directors. Thus persuaded, the directors elected Bates.[104] At the same time Hoover made an arrangement with an American financier, Eugene Meyer, Jr. (later the owner of the *Washington Post*), who bought from him a block of 10,000 Oroya Exploration shares for £6,000 and who loaned Hoover and Beatty £6,000 to buy 10,000 more shares for themselves. (Meyer kept the second block as security for his loan.)[105] Hoover envisaged this transaction as a springboard for future operations that would "greatly strengthen" his and Beatty's position in the company.[106]

By early 1911 he was ready with a plan. With the market "perfectly putrid in all kinds of mining shares,"[107] Hoover felt there was "very little hope of being able to float new Companies for some time to come." With this source of revenue unavailable, it was imperative for the Oroya Exploration Company "to get into a cash position to carry its business on for another twelve months." He therefore proposed to issue 100,000 shares for sale to the company's shareholders and to have this issue underwritten, the underwriters receiving as a reward "a call on 50,000 shares." Since the company had five thousand different shareholders, Hoover thought that a new issue would probably be subscribed.[108]

At the Oroya Exploration shareholders meeting in February 1911, he presented his proposal (somewhat modified). It was Hoover's debut as a company chairman, and in a lengthy address he described the company's assets and investment policy. To the applause of the shareholders Hoover reported that "we have doubled the assets of the Company in the past year." He explained that new funds were needed not because of financial exigency but "in order to realise the best results from our properties." He proposed to spend the money equipping and developing various mines in the company's stable. It was best to hold onto these properties "and carry them on to a further stage." If the company was to be a "sound, progressive" one, it "cannot stand still. It must constantly go ahead searching for good mines, taking advantage of opportunities which arise, and gradually building itself into a stronger and stronger position." The assembled shareholders unanimously approved the proposed increase in the company's share capital.[109]

As the Oroya Exploration Company was arising out of the tailings dumps, as it were, of the old Oroya Brownhill, another famous Kalgoorlie mine was undergoing a similar evolution. At the time of Hoover's accession to its board in late 1908, the Lake View Consols's low-grade mine was barely holding its own. Even the company's chairman, Francis Govett, did not refer to it as a mining concern but rather as an exploration company, or, as he preferred to put it, a "salvage company" coming to the aid of mines in trouble.[110] Govett was determined to revive the Lake View by slowly amassing "a portfolio of shares, securities and interests which have cost us nothing. . . ."[111] Already by 1908 the Lake View held large holdings of stock in several mining concerns. Were it not for these investments, its customary dividend would have gone unpaid.[112]

By late 1909 the Lake View Consols mine was nearing exhaustion.[113] At about this point Herbert Hoover, the great amalgamator, conceived an idea. Here was the Lake View; it had an excellent treatment plant but soon would have no mine. Nearby in Kalgoorlie was a newly merged company, the Hannan's Star Consolidated. It had extensive low-grade ore reserves but no plant. Why not combine the two?[114]

The logic was overwhelming, and so in the spring of 1910 another Hoover creation—the Lake View and Star, Ltd.—was born. It was not a straight amalgamation; both the Lake View and Hannan's Star retained their identities. Instead, each sold certain assets to the new company; in exchange, each "parent" received a half-interest (in shares) in the new "child." How much Hoover personally received as midwife is unknown, but he and Govett became original directors of Lake View and Star.[115]

Hoover's achievement was a satisfying one. Not only did the Lake View

Consols slough off its unwanted plant and property for a good price; the resultant company, Lake View and Star, became one of the most successful in the history of the Golden Mile, producing gold and yielding dividends for more than half a century. Hoover remained on the new company's board until May 1912, when, at his request, Theodore Hoover replaced him.[116]

The Lake View Consols was now out of direct mining altogether, its only assets being shares or debentures in the Lake View and Star and several other properties.[117] Meanwhile the Oroya Exploration Company was following a somewhat similar path, although its assets included not only shares but actual mines that it was nurturing to adulthood.[118] Of the two, Oroya Exploration under Hoover's direction was the more aggressive, concentrating on exploration and development while Lake View engaged in finance.[119]

By the fall of 1911, however, Oroya Exploration was paying the price for its aggressiveness. The stockholders' response to Hoover's share issue earlier in the year had been disappointing, forcing the company to curtail its development program.[120] Without more working capital it could not bring its properties to a dividend-bearing stage.

A worried Hoover therefore conceived yet another merger. To A. Chester Beatty he explained:

> The Yuanmi mine has not been doing as well of late as there was every reason to hope at the beginning. Furthermore, the [Oroya Exploration] Company is short of money and I began to be alarmed that stagnation might set in in such a form that it would be impossible to finance the Company without a call on the stockholders. I therefore proposed a level amalgamation with the Lake View Company and, much to my astonishment, I found the directors of that Company were prepared to agree.

It was almost too good to be true. Not only was the Lake View much larger than the struggling Oroya; it was earning £45,000 a year from its assets.

> The Oroya assets, as you know, consist entirely of young mines with certain speculative possibilities, but the Lake View assets are, for the above amount, absolute certainties. From every point of view the thing appears to me as an extremely good stroke on our account. Not only does it guarantee that we are going to get back the money which we invested in the Oroya shares, with a profit, but further, it more or less lands us into the moral control of a pretty healthy young finance Company.[121]

Hoover was anxious to prevent any hesitation by shareholders in either company. He therefore neatly arranged for the respective companies' meetings to be held simultaneously on November 17.[122] Evidently worried that opposition might surface even among Oroya shareholders, he called for proxies from Beatty and Eugene Meyer.[123]

The meetings passed smoothly on the seventeenth. Privately Hoover considered the Oroya the greater beneficiary of the merger.[124] But at the Oroya meeting Hoover, as chairman, contended that the terms of amalgamation were fair and of "mutual advantage."[125] At the Lake View gathering nearby, Govett asserted that the Oroya's assets were worth the price of acquisition and looked forward to cooperation with his friend:

> For some ten years past, Mr. Hoover and myself have been in close alliance—practically in daily touch—and in much of the business handled we have worked together, sometimes with both companies interested, sometimes with only one. This amalgamation will make that working alliance closer still. . . .[126]

To Hoover, then, the merger brought access to the Lake View's greater financial resources. To Govett it meant getting some partly developed but presumably promising mines. Thus was born, in late 1911, the Lake View and Oroya Exploration Company, of which Hoover and Govett became joint managing directors.[127] Capitalized at £450,000, the company possessed a multitude of combined assets that mirrored Hoover's own breadth of interests by 1912: shares in Amalgamated Zinc, Burma Mines, Granville Mining Company, Great Fitzroy Mines, Intercontinental Trust, Kyshtim Corporation, Lake View and Star, Lagunitos Oil Company, Mountain Queen, Oroya Black Range, Oroya Links, Oroya Leonesa, Zinc Corporation, and many more. In many of these companies Hoover was either a director or a power behind the scenes.[128] In several his brother was on the board.[129]

And what was the Lake View and Exploration Company's business? A "promoting business," said one mining journal.[130] "Mining and finance," said the *Mining Year-Book*.[131] An "exploration, financial and investment business," remarked the *Mining Manual*.[132] The "actual basis" of "the amalgamated company," said Govett, "is finance."[133]

Indeed, the Lake View and Oroya Exploration Company became a kind of bank for Hoover's enterprises, underwriting stock issues and loaning money to ailing companies in its group.[134] It was not surprising that Lake View and Oroya Exploration held blocks of shares in so many enterprises directed by Hoover. As co-managing director, he was well situated to guide its investments into companies that needed capital for development. When, for instance, the Oroya Leonesa needed money in early 1912, the Lake View and Oroya Exploration Company obliged by purchasing a large chunk of freshly created Oroya Leonesa debentures.[135]

In the aftermath of the Lake View / Oroya Exploration merger, Hoover seemed anxious to turn to other things. He told Beatty in November 1911 that he was "gradually making progress with the grand clean-up" and was hoping to be "much freer after the middle of next winter."[136] Hoover was not interested in bothering with small business propositions anymore, he told one of his engineers. Henceforth he wished to focus only on big undertakings and on relatively simple mining problems.[137]

Nor was Hoover inclined at the end of 1911 to concentrate long on his newly amalgamated mining finance company. Scarcely a month after the Lake View and Oroya Exploration Company was created, Hoover was pessimistic about its future. Discussing the situation with one of his engineers, Amor Kuehn, Hoover indicated that he would work to put the Lake View and Oroya Exploration Company on a dividend-paying basis.[138] But Hoover was gloomy about the company's prospects and inclined, Kuehn thought, to consider a business solely from the stock market angle. He gave Kuehn the impression that he would cut his close ties with the Lake View as soon as his friends were able to liquidate their holdings without loss. To bring that about, Hoover planned to publish quarterly statements of the company's activities in a manner that would enable stockholders to predict future profits. He hoped that this publicity device would boost the shares on the market to a point where Beatty and others could sell out profitably.[139] Evidently Hoover felt he could not abandon the helm of the Lake View while the friends he had induced to invest in it still held onto their investments.

As it turned out, Hoover did not leave the Lake View and Oroya Exploration Company. Instead, the enterprise prospered, yielding a 5% dividend in 1912 and a 10% dividend in 1913 and 1914.[140] Much more importantly, within a year of its founding the Lake View was becoming what Govett wanted it to be: "the corner stone of a powerful group" that included himself, Hoover, Beatty, the Zinc Corporation, and the Ivanhoe Gold Corporation.[141]

At the *Mining Magazine* T. A. Rickard was quick to grasp the importance of Govett's remarks. Rickard praised this powerful new combination in mining finance:

> The range of interest is great geographically, and bespeaks the wide experience of the controllers. . . . Assuredly they have as much knowledge of mining, in its world-wide aspects, as any group in London. Besides Messrs. Govett and Hoover, there is Mr. A. Chester Beatty, one of the most forceful of the engineer-financier type of men now engaged in mining speculation. . . . Messrs. Hoover and Beatty represent an amount of technical knowledge and financial astuteness not to be matched by any other two men now prominent in mining affairs.

But Rickard injected one cautionary note. He urged the new group to be fair and reasonable to the small shareholders who collectively contributed so much capital to mining investment. He reminded the group that "the public will play the game of mining speculation and allow the dealer a fair percentage, but they demand a run for their money."[142]

It soon became evident that some shareholders in Lake View and Oroya

Exploration did *not* feel they were getting a run for their money. The issue was the proper distribution of profits. At the 1912 shareholders meeting Govett laid down the principle that "dividends must come out of revenue" and that "profits made by increment of capital" were "not applicable for dividends."[143] Govett's dictum evoked protests,[144] but the board did not waver. In the year ending June 30, 1913 the company made a profit of £76,772. But the board allotted less than half of it for dividends; the remainder went into a cash reserve fund.[145]

At the ensuing shareholders meeting Govett stoutly defended this decision.

> This question of dividends involves the whole financial policy of the Company; that policy is approved by the largest Shareholders in the Company. . . . That policy is to build up the resources of the Company, contenting ourselves with a dividend of 10 per cent. until such a time as the financial position may fully justify a more generous distribution. . . . dividends [can] be only paid out of revenue which is really revenue and not return of capital. . . .

Furthermore, Govett argued, no bigger dividend could be paid for the simple reason that sufficient cash on hand was not now available. The company, in fact, was "always short of capital"; there was always "more business on hand than could properly be financed."[146] In short, the company's cash reserve had already been reinvested by the board before the annual shareholders meeting. The stockholders were faced with a *fait accompli*.

Govett's remarks drew no fire at the meeting, but the response in the press was different. The *Mining News* expressed no surprise that the Lake View was low on cash since "it is continuously embarking in new business, a procedure which will probably go on *ad infinitum*." "It is all very well for Mr. Govett to talk . . . about the position of the company improving, but of what advantage is this to the shareholders now on the register in view of the present dividend policy of the board?"[147] The journal *Truth* was equally critical: "It may suit Mr. Govett and his colleagues on the Lake View board to keep on adding to the company's assets, but they should remember that people do not buy shares in mining or mining finance companies with a view to benefiting posterity."[148] One journalist noted darkly that the profits had been reinvested in enterprises "which it is presumed the directors, as usual, had the first information about."[149] In part the controversy reflected the old conflict between the stockholder eager for immediate dividends and the engineer concerned about the company's long-term stability. In this instance, however, the tension was aggravated by the size of the profit withheld and perhaps by the fact that the cash reserve had been reinvested before the shareholders as a whole formally assented.

In the wake of this episode, certain criticisms of Hoover and Govett circulated in London. It was pointed out that each man received £500 a year as a joint managing director of the Lake View plus a portion of the £1,150 in fees distributed among all the directors.[150] This was substantial remuneration—too substantial, said some critics, who claimed that the directors were setting aside a reserve of profits in order to assure payment of their fees indefinitely.[151] Although this charge probably had no foundation, it showed that Hoover and Govett had created critics, if not enemies, in London's financial circles. And when, a few weeks later, the company's Nicaraguan subsidiary, the Oroya Leonesa, reconstructed without having yielded a dividend, the *Australian Mining Standard*, a staunch supporter of Hoover in earlier years, bluntly denounced the reconstruction scheme. It was, said the paper, "one of the countless variations of the style of finance practised by the 'Oroya' clique for some years past": the policy of "heads I win and tails you lose."[152]

The Oroya Leonesa, in fact, had been a headache for Hoover almost since the beginning. Scarcely had it been organized in 1910 when a revolution befell Nicaragua, paralyzing transportation and creating a severe labor shortage that impeded development of the mine. For the next three years political turmoil and labor scarcity plagued the Central American nation. For months equipment destined for the gold mine lay unmoved throughout the country; virtually a year was lost in completing the plant. Even after the revolution subsided and the entire plant was built, the company was unable to find enough workers to run it at full capacity. Some men had died in the revolution. Some miners had fled to Honduras. Some had found more attractive the higher wages offered workers for building the Panama Canal.[153]

All this unwanted instability arose to mock Hoover's estimates and hopes. According to his engineers, working costs on the mine would not exceed sixteen shillings per ton.[154] Instead, in 1912 and 1913 working expenses averaged more than twenty-six shillings a ton.[155] By late 1913 the Oroya Leonesa company, plagued by delays and by expenditures outpacing income, had exhausted its working capital and was heavily in debt.[156]

Unable to obtain adequate skilled labor in Nicaragua, Hoover and his colleagues resorted to a desperate expedient. At the November 1913 stockholders meeting Hoover announced that "after the greatest possible difficulties" the company had "made arrangements for the immigration of skilled miners from one of the southern European countries" (presumably Italy) in such a way that "by degrees" the Nicaraguan labor problem would be solved. Hoover was reluctant to give details of the scheme:

The skilled men we did require we were trying to import, and were stopped by certain of the Emigration Regulations from carrying it forward. We have devised a means for evading those regulations, but I do not care to ventilate the question, because, to do so, might even put us in further difficulties. Some of those men from that source are filtering through London, and are on the road to the mines.[157]

Hoover's plan to infiltrate indentured foreign labor into Nicaragua came to fruition too late to prevent the reconstruction of the Oroya Leonesa company. At the same 1913 meeting the shareholders voted to liquidate and reconstruct as a concern eventually known as the Central American Mines, Ltd.[158] The Lake View and Oroya Exploration Company, which already had sunk £35,000 into its subsidiary, underwrote the new share issue at no charge.[159] It was not a painless reconstruction. Reconstructions never were. To raise new capital, each shareholder was assessed two shillings per share.[160]

The Nicaraguan enterprise struggled on without success for several more years, reconstructing again in 1917 and finally dying in 1920 without ever paying a dividend.[161] Nor was it the only outpost in Hoover's Oroya empire to suffer the pangs of disillusionment and defeat. In 1909–1910 the ore chute at the Oroya Black Range gold mine in Western Australia unexpectedly trailed off in depth. To protect itself, the Oroya Black Range company acquired a half-interest in the Yuanmi property to the southwest.[162] After the flotation of the Yuanmi in 1911, the Oroya Black Range sold its entire undertaking to the Yuanmi for shares. Thus absorbed by its former subsidiary, the Oroya Black Range Company disappeared, after only five years' existence.[163]

Hoover was initially optimistic (at least publicly) about the Yuanmi, which he chaired from its inception until November 1913.[164] Privately, on November 11, 1911, he confided to Beatty that the Yuanmi was not doing as well as hoped.[165] Sixteen days later, however, at the Oroya Black Range meeting held to consider selling out for shares in Yuanmi, Hoover painted a more encouraging picture. He found, he said, "every reason to hope" for "a long and prosperous life" for the Yuanmi property. The Yuanmi "looks as if it will extend in depth," he stated, "being of much the same type as the Sons of Gwalia, which . . . is one of the most permanent in West Australia."[166]

Hoover was right about the Sons of Gwalia, but not—it turned out—about the Yuanmi. At first the new company prospered, paying moderate dividends in 1913 and again in 1914.[167] But in 1912 the men at the mine discovered arsenic and antimony in the sulphide ores below the zone of oxidized ore. At the 1913 Yuanmi shareholders meeting Hoover lamented this "extremely bad luck." Arsenic and antimony were two of the worst metals to extract from gold ore.[168] The Yuanmi hobbled on for another decade, never paying another dividend. When it closed in early 1924 it had distributed only £49,000, or 17½%, on its original share capital of £280,000.[169]

Such failures—and there were others, like the Great Fitzroy copper mine in Queensland, Australia[170]—did little, on the whole, to diminish Hoover's reputation. Risks, after all, were endemic to the game. As Govett publicly acknowledged in 1911, he and Hoover had made mistakes and would no doubt make more.[171] Mining finance was not a worry-free life.

V

O N E of Hoover's biggest feats of financial engineering, in fact, caused him far more anxiety than he bargained for.

A. N. C. Treadgold was an Englishman, an Oxford graduate, a self-taught mining engineer, and a man with a grandiose vision. For several years he was closely associated with the Guggenheims in exploiting the gold-bearing riverbed gravels in the Klondike region of the Yukon Territory in the cold Canadian northwest. In 1908 Treadgold sold out his shareholdings in the Guggenheim empire. With a sum in excess of $1,000,000 at his command, he turned to consummate his dream: purchase and amalgamation of the auriferous gravels of the Klondike River, the Indian River, and the numerous creeks south and east of Dawson, the provincial capital. Like Hoover in the early days at Kalgoorlie's Golden Mile, Treadgold envisaged a giant combination to work the district under one management—his. He wished to be King of the Klondike.[172]

Treadgold knew his way around the Klondike; he had been there since the glory days of '98. But the consolidation he contemplated required more money than even he could amass: money to buy out the claims of prospectors and to buy and operate expensive new dredging and hydraulic mining equipment. In 1910 or thereabouts Treadgold interested A. Chester Beatty, who in turn interested Hoover in the ambitious scheme.[173] Early in 1911 Hoover and Beatty organized with a capital of $1,000,000 an American-registered syndicate called the Eastern Trading Company, in order to loan money to Treadgold (presumably for his purchase of claims).[174] To facilitate matters further, the Hoover / Beatty Intercontinental Trust loaned the Eastern Trading Company a substantial sum.[175] In London, Hoover worked actively to line up the financial backing for a company to acquire and exploit Treadgold's claims.[176]

In August 1911 Hoover's labors came to fruition; the Granville Mining Company (named after the Klondike town of Granville) was born. Hoover, Beatty, and Treadgold were the promoters.[177] The company acquired from Treadgold 10,000 acres of land in the Klondike River valley and its environs, as well as controlling interests in certain dredging, hydraulics, and power companies in the area.[178] In return Treadgold and his associates received the Granville's entire share capital—£1,200,000—plus £100,000 in free debentures. Not surprisingly, Treadgold went on the board, as did Hoover, Beatty, and Govett as chairman.[179]

Hoover had done his financial work well; £400,000 in further debentures— $2,000,000—was raised privately for working capital. The massive sum was obtained in equal amounts from four subscribers: Treadgold and his allies, Beatty, the Hoover / Govett enterprises (notably Lake View Consols), and the prestigious Consolidated Goldfields of South Africa.[180] Hoover personally made what he later called a "small investment" in the venture.[181] In all likelihood he took a sizeable share bonus for his efforts.[182]

The new enterprise was indeed an ambitious one. For the auriferous gravels it proposed to dredge and sift were perpetually frozen—buried beneath an insulating ten-to-twenty-foot "blanket" of tundra, moss, grass, small trees, decayed vegetation, and soil ("black muck"). To work the gravels one must not only first strip away this "blanket" in good weather; one must then somehow thaw the gravels. Until about 1910 no one had found a cheap way to do the latter during the short summer season. But recently it had been discovered that once the overlay of soil was removed, the gravels underneath would thaw naturally in the summer Arctic sun, and, once thawed, would not refreeze in the winter. Hence the application of expensive artificial heat to the gravels was not needed. This discovery made large-scale mining less costly and more practical.[183]

Late in 1911 the Granville Mining Company got underway, with Treadgold as managing director and Hoover a member of an American advisory and technical committee.[184] It would take considerable time for enough tundra to be removed and enough gravel thawed to permit extensive gold-dredging operations.[185] But Hoover was convinced that technically, at least, the company's prospects were sound.[186] To Oroya Exploration Company shareholders in November he described the Granville venture as "an extremely promising business."[187]

Yet even as he spoke, clouds were gathering over the Klondike. Upon organizing the Granville company, Hoover and his colleagues dispatched an American engineer to the property to design equipment for the planned expansion.[188] In short order the engineer cabled that he did not consider some of the previous ore sampling reliable.[189] It quickly became evident that the financial assumptions behind the infant enterprise were excessively optimistic and that the outlook was not as rosy as thought.[190] Scaled-down operations were inevitable. Only four days after his speech at the Oroya Exploration meeting Hoover privately told Beatty that Granville affairs were a "mess" and that some of the directors were thinking of resigning.[191]

Hoover sought anxiously to salvage something from an impending wreck. For some time Treadgold had been associated intermittently with "Joe" Boyle, a Canadian-born Klondike pioneer and expert on hydraulic mining.[192] In 1911 Boyle was successfully operating a gold-dredging concern called the Canadian Klondyke Mining Company. Boyle's example (and proximity) gave Hoover an idea. To his friend Beatty Hoover confided a hope that the Granville enterprise could make "some kind of a deal with Boyle which will enable us to mix up all the eggs again and make a new omlette."[193] All we can do now with Granville, Hoover declared, was to erect one dredge next season and "let all the rest of the scheme go by the board until we can show some definite earning." "If in the meantime," he mused, "we could embrace Boyle's business we should have got the thing on its feet, so that over a period of years it can be financed."[194]

Throughout the winter of 1911-12 Hoover and Beatty strove to effect an amalgamation of Granville's properties with Boyle's prospering company.[195]

It was slow going, with Beatty in New York, Treadgold and Boyle in Canada, and Hoover and other directors in London. The fundamental source of trouble, however, was not distance; it was Treadgold. An able and courageous but contentious individual who was often at odds with some associate; a crafty, secretive loner who kept his plans close to his vest and despised those who did not; a glib and persuasive promoter who had an extraordinary ability to impress people and induce them to support him financially; Treadgold was scarcely an ideal man for managing director. "Be hard," he would say; it was almost his personal motto.[196] By January 1912 Hoover reported to Beatty that the Granville board was "very restive" and upset at Treadgold's "cavalier" treatment of it. Not only had the feisty Englishman failed to keep his fellow directors informed of his activities; he had failed even to register titles to properties that were supposed to belong to the company.[197]

As the months went by, Hoover's exasperation mounted, and so did his determination to get rid of the incubus of Treadgold. "The whole business is to me in such a muddle that I do not know which way to turn," Hoover complained to Beatty in March 1912. He was now more convinced than ever that an amalgamation with Boyle was "the one way to pull this business once and for ever out of the hole." But now, it turned out, Boyle needed money for *his* enterprise—$750,000 by next September 1. Meanwhile, Hoover reported, Treadgold "as usual" was "a stumbling-block because he will not listen to reasonable finance for the Granville Company."[198]

At this point the Consolidated Goldfields of South Africa (one of Hoover's fellow underwriters) started to turn the screws. By April 1912 the ailing Granville venture badly needed money—£200,000, in fact, by June 1. The Goldfields company agreed to advance far more than their allotted share of the needed sum, but only at a terrific price: 12½% interest per month on the extra amount and a prior lien on all property secured by this loan. Hoover was disgusted at these tactics, but what could he do? "The whole position of the Granville and its finance is in a most unsatisfactory condition, and I am fairly well despaired of getting Treadgold to do anything reasonable and proper in any direction." Hoover was even inclined to "let the thing drift to the point of having a Receiver appointed." He felt "absolutely helpless at this end to do anything, as the whole business goes through the Goldfields and they look after themselves."[199]

Finally, in May 1912, the long-desired consolidation of interests occurred. The Granville sold its properties in the Klondike watershed to Boyle's going concern, the Canadian Klondyke Mining Company. In addition, through a massive new debenture issue Granville agreed to raise £440,000 and lend £300,000 of it to Boyle's enterprise to enable him to purchase huge new dredges so that the gravels could be worked on a large scale.[200] In exchange Granville acquired a large share and debenture interest in Boyle's company. And Boyle's company pledged to pay Granville a minimum of £49,200 income per year for fifteen years—nearly enough for Granville to meet the interest payments on its own debenture debt.[201]

The new arrangement at least partially reflected Hoover's desires. Although Granville still retained thousands of acres of land in the Klondike region, its properties adjoining Boyle's lands were at last under the competent control of an operating company. This was a major step forward. Like Treadgold, Boyle was an individualist and a near-legend on the Klondike. As big and hearty as Treadgold was diminutive and quarrelsome, he had been a sparring partner to the former heavyweight boxing champion of Australia. Although something of an adventurer by temperament, Boyle was no dilettante at mining.[202] When in 1910 he installed a dredge with sixteen-cubic-foot buckets for scooping up the gravels, it was the largest dredge in the world.[203] Now, thanks to the Granville's financing, Boyle would acquire two more of them.[204] Things were looking up again for Hoover and his associates.[205]

To assist the Granville company in its £440,000 debenture scheme, Hoover helped to organize the Inter-Yukon Syndicate, of which he became a director.[206] The syndicate appears to have acted as underwriter of the entire issue, which was successfully sold by early summer. In return for this service the syndicate received an option to purchase, at a fixed price or prices, 500,000 Granville shares.[207] Now it was time to "make a market" so that, among other things, these shares would be worth buying and reselling. In July 1912 Granville, hitherto privately financed, was introduced to public trading on the London stock exchange.[208] During the ensuing months encouraging publicity about its prospects circulated widely in the press.[209]

The optimism was premature. By early 1913 Granville was once more on the verge of collapse, and once more—at least in Hoover's eyes—A. N. C. Treadgold was the culprit. Although Hoover had been the first director to oppose Treadgold's high-handed and secretive methods,[210] the mess now threatened to erupt in a scandal that would wrongly but quite possibly besmirch Hoover's reputation.

Hoover was angry and alarmed. "Treadgold, as usual, is acting like a perfect ass," he told Beatty in January.[211]

> This position has developed until it has become almost impossible. Treadgold has not turned the properties into the Granville which he apparently had, nor the properties which he said he would turn in. . . . Nobody here will put up a solitary penny with Treadgold in the management.

Meanwhile the trustee for the Granville debenture holders was "raising the deuce and threatening procedure." And Hoover himself was demanding that Treadgold

> repay his loans to the Zinc Corporation, as that money can be used for other purposes a great deal more advantageously than by loaning it to Treadgold, and I cannot be put in the position of having made loans to my friends [i.e., Treadgold] from the Zinc Corporation [coffers] on security

which will not materialize, as this security would not if a Receiver were put in charge of the Company. I am personally only too anxious to get out of the business in any form that will do us credit.

Hoover feared that the Inter-Yukon Syndicate might have to buy back all the Granville shares "which we sold, in order to protect our good name."[212]

Despite his persona of disinterested objectivity and his reputation as a cool, aloof businessman, Hoover in some ways was like a volcano: hot and smoldering underneath. As the Granville crisis deepened in early 1913 he erupted frequently to Beatty. His letters were filled with stories of Treadgold's numerous unkept promises, his "chicanery," and his "intrigue"—and full of a desire to find "some method of splitting Treadgold off from this business, in a way that would give us some peace and make our shares of some value, and at the same time prevent a catastrophe here [London] that would seriously injure our credit."[213]

Hoover had ample reason to worry. Instead of spending money to develop Granville's remaining lands and earn some revenue, a blithe Treadgold (Hoover discovered) had simply been "using our moneys to buy [additional] properties without our authorisation."[214] Meanwhile difficulties of a remarkable sort had arisen with Joe Boyle. After Granville's second debenture issue of 1912, it had duly loaned £300,000 to Boyle's concern—without taking the elementary precaution of obtaining security on its loan. Debentures in Boyle's own company were supposed to be issued as security, but the £300,000 was loaned first. Seizing his opportunity, Boyle thereupon refused to accept the legal wording of his proposed debentures![215] Months of futile negotiations (in which Hoover was involved) ensued, and Hoover reported that the vexatious Treadgold was using "every piece of chicanery" to prevent "any amicable settlements with Boyle." By mid-February Hoover was convinced that Treadgold was "a little bit off in his head," living "in a perfect land of make-believe, surrounded with Ogres of Conspiracy, Intrigue, Diabolical Intentions, etc. . . ."[216]

Early in 1913 Boyle returned to Canada from a trip to London—without signing the debenture document. Its legal wording, he insisted, did not properly state his deal with his creditors.[217] Hearty Joe Boyle now had £300,000 to spend, and the hapless Granville company had no legal security for its loan.

With both Boyle and Treadgold out of control, the Granville affair was becoming a comic opera, but one with dangerous potential for Hoover. For Hoover had been in the thick of setting up the heavily capitalized Granville venture and had engineered two huge debenture issues totaling £900,000, or $4,500,000. What if the whole entity should now fail? What would become of his reputation as an engineer-financier? Hoover was nervous:

Everybody over here has lost patience with [Treadgold] and if I judge the intentions of the Gold Fields aright, a short cut in the whole business will be a Receiver, who can enforce specific performance against Treadgold. This would not at all suit our position in the City as it would be perfect damnation to us to have this happen.[218]

It took more than threats of receivership, however, to deflect Treadgold. Back in Canada the would-be King of the Klondike was indefatigably buying up still more lands in pursuit of ever-bigger consolidations. In late February 1913 Hoover told Beatty:

> Treadgold has bought a lot of property in the Indian River watershed on his private account and is going to offer it to the Granville Company at cost. I do not personally believe that we ought to buy it, as we have no money and I do not know where the money is to come from. Treadgold thinks that he has us in a cleft stick, as the properties which he has bought interlock with the Granville in such a way as to prevent us working our ground. He seems, however, to have overlooked the fact that he cannot work his own ground without the Granville and that it would be a case of stale-mate for the whole of his natural life, and that we would simply sit on our nett position and do nothing. As we have other interests in life it will affect us a lot less than it will him.[219]

Such a state of affairs could not persist. During 1913 Hoover worked to stabilize the situation and dislodge Treadgold from influence over the Granville company's business. Late in the year he had partial success. The Granville company sold its claims on the Indian River to a newly formed subsidiary (organized by Treadgold) called the North West Corporation. With this stroke Granville ceased to be a mining company per se and became instead a holding company, its assets consisting of shares and bonds in the North West Corporation, Boyle's Canadian Klondyke Mining Company, and related interests.[220] Bankruptcy for Granville and possible disgrace for Hoover were averted. Now, perhaps, Granville might actually hope to make some money. Joe Boyle might be leading his creditors a merry chase, but at least at mine management he knew what he was doing.

Success at reorganization was tempered, however, by some unsettling facts. Treadgold had not been displaced; he now popped up as director and effective controller of the North West Corporation.[221] And Boyle still had not issued any security for his £300,000 loan from Granville. (Years went by, in fact, and he never did.)[222] With the seemingly sole exception of Hoover, the Granville directors seemed to be a singularly trusting and tolerant group of businessmen.[223]

Still, during 1913 Boyle's industrious company dredged up more than $1,300,000 in gold from over 6,000,000 cubic yards of gravel.[224] Early in 1914 one student of Granville predicted—vaguely, if optimistically—that "the time is approaching" when it would pay dividends.[225] Later in the year Francis Govett praised Boyle's "exceedingly well managed and successful company."[226] Hoover's reaction to such sanguine sentiments is not known. He took no part in the affairs of the North West Corporation, and although he remained a Granville director until mid-1916 his role after its conversion into a holding company in 1913 is undocumented.[227] Perhaps by now he was too disgusted to care.

Alas, the high expectations were not to be met. While income from Boyle's operation was sufficient to cover Granville's interest payments on its own debentures, Granville's future as a dividend payer depended on the success of the North West Corporation, which was still, as of 1914, in a preliminary developmental stage. By late 1914 the infant subsidiary required at least a quarter of a million dollars in additional working capital before gold production could even commence.[228] With the advent of World War I came a crippling shortage of money, a series of delays and difficulties in the field, and ever more desperate attempts to stave off financial disaster.[229] The situation was not helped by Treadgold's mismanagement of North West or by Boyle's abrupt departure from the Klondike to lead a machine-gun corps of Yukon volunteers in the Great War.[230] Mired in financial and legal entanglements worse than the black muck of the tundra, the Granville Mining Company and North West Corporation went into receivership in 1917.[231]

Such an *opéra bouffe* could have no routine denouement. During World War I Colonel Joe Boyle ended up on the Russian front, where he eventually assisted refugees from the Communist Revolution. Daring and resourceful as always, he rescued the Romanian national treasure from the Bolsheviks, attempted to rescue the Romanian royal family, and finally represented Romania in its negotiations for a peace treaty with the Bolsheviks. In another spectacular episode he rescued some prominent Romanian hostages from their Russian captors. After the war he became an influential figure in Romanian life and a close friend of Queen Marie. He died in 1923.[232]

And Treadgold? The redoubtable dreamer and would-be King of the Klondike, once a millionaire and then some, went bankrupt in 1920 to the tune of over $2,000,000. But during the next decade he fought back to gain a controlling interest of Yukon Consolidated, a successor to the defunct Granville company. Treadgold's tactics, however, evoked antagonism and litigation. In 1933 a Canadian court declared that he had obtained his interest illegally and by fraud. The court deprived him of his entire shareholding.[233]

When Hoover learned in 1933 about the exposure of Treadgold's dubious financial maneuvers, his comment was brief: "My old opinion of Treadgold seems amply justified."[234]

For the next seventeen years Treadgold tenaciously struggled in the courts—repeatedly appealing, repeatedly losing. In 1951, at age eighty-seven, he died—proud, defiant, ever-scheming, and bankrupt.[235] Meanwhile in the 1930s Yukon Consolidated enjoyed some modest prosperity and in 1940 paid its first dividend.[236] But by then Herbert Hoover was not interested. The tangled, almost absurd Granville affair had long since become for him only an incredible story to be told, perhaps, to his children—a story about the never-humdrum life of an engineer-financier.

VI

BY 1912, principally through the Lake View and Oroya Exploration Company, Herbert Hoover had (in his later words) "built a financial group around myself owning mines,"[237] or at least shares in mines, all over the globe. Hoover was near the pinnacle of his profession. One London mining periodical acclaimed him as "a wizard of finance."[238] Said the *Mining Magazine*, "In the domain of practical mining finance, no one holds a more assured position."[239]

Indeed, mining finance more and more seemed to dominate Hoover's business at No. 1, London Wall Buildings. In 1912 alone he helped to establish three syndicates—the Inter-Argentine, Inter-Yukon, and Inter-Californian Trust—whose announced purpose, in part, was to "carry on business as financiers."[240] Syndicates with similar purpose sprouted in the next two years.[241]

Hoover was conscious—and proud—of his success. He told a friend that the highest form of engineer was the man who not only could handle the technical aspects of an enterprise but also could organize, manage, and finance it.[242] And having reached that lofty eminence, Hoover had no desire to descend into the valley of technical engineering and detailed administration from which he had come. When in 1913 his brother and two friends considered forming a mines management company with Hoover and Beatty on the board, Hoover's reaction, given to Beatty, was swift:

> [Amor] Kuehn and [Deane P.] Mitchell have been strongly urging Theodore to join with them in proposing a scheme of mine managers, with regard to which my nett opinion is that you and I would be putting a two-ton chain around our necks, with plenty of loose links upon which medals to our folly could be hung. Our object in life is not to take on a lot more of small worries, but to cut them out altogether, and I do not see that a combination of this kind would be any stronger than Bewick, Moreing & Co. If there is any one thing I do not want to have to do with again it is either a management firm or a management company.[243]

Hoover, in fact, did not return to the technical management of his Bewick, Moreing days. He was an insider now, preoccupied with raising capital for mines and interested in the big endeavors only. Two of the biggest were in Burma and Russia.

20

Burma

I

In the jungles of upper Burma, nearly six hundred miles by rail north-northeast of Rangoon and about fifty miles from the Chinese border, is a site known to history as the Bawdwin mines. Here in the year 1412, and possibly centuries before, Chinese miners began to excavate for silver. "Bawdwin," in fact, means "silver mine" in Burmese. Between the early fifteenth century and the mid-nineteenth—more than 450 years—Chinese workers extracted uncounted millions of ounces of silver from the Bawdwin deposit. Smelting the precious metal from the ore, the miners left behind ever-expanding slag heaps rich in unwanted lead. Silver only was sought—silver for the Celestial Empire.

Then, in 1855, began the Panthay Rebellion of Chinese Moslems, an eighteen-year conflict that devastated the nearby Chinese province of Yunnan and took several million lives. China's suzerainty over its southwest borders was weakened, its enemies emboldened. Harassed by fierce Kachin tribesmen who cut off fuel supplies and interrupted bullion shipments, the Chinese around Bawdwin abandoned their mines in 1868. The Burmese who took over lacked the skill to carry on the enterprise and were plagued by disease besides. The silver-lead workings lapsed into obscurity and desuetude.[1]

No mine as rich as Bawdwin, however, could lie forsaken indefinitely. By 1902 Burma was part of the British empire, and Europeans had heard of the abandoned "great silver mine" in the Upper Shan States region. In 1902 the

Great Eastern Mining Company was registered in London to acquire a prospecting license for minerals in the Bawdwin area. The new company had no intention of confining itself to prospecting. It wished, rather, to smelt down the slag heaps that dotted the Bawdwin landscape and extract from them their lead. To do this it must erect a smelter and build a railroad connecting the mine to the Burma Railway. For these purposes the Great Eastern Mining Company made a construction agreement in December 1903 with the Share Guarantee Trust, controlled by a London financier named R. Tilden Smith. Under this contract the Trust eventually spent about £25,000 for a smelter, rails, rolling stock, and other equipment, all of which were shipped to Upper Burma.

It was not long before the two contracting parties became embroiled in a dispute over the carrying out of their agreement. "Protracted negotiations" ensued. But businesses are not built by protracted negotiations, and the Great Eastern Mining Company languished. By early 1905 its development program had barely begun.[2]

At this point, or perhaps somewhat sooner, Bewick, Moreing and Company (Hoover was still a partner) entered the scene. Sometime before early 1905 Hoover approached, or was approached by, one or both of the feuding parties. The Great Eastern Mining Company was in a financial hole; it needed help.[3] According to his later recollection, Hoover first learned about the Bawdwin mines on an ocean journey in 1904 with one of the Great Eastern's directors. Returning to London, Hoover contacted Smith and discovered that Smith had sent out the wrong equipment and was now financially unable to proceed. Hoover's firm and some of its clients thereupon "took an option on a controlling interest" in the Burma undertaking.[4]

Whatever the precise date of Hoover's initial involvement, by the beginning of 1905 Bewick, Moreing was much interested in the Bawdwin proposition. C. S. Herzig of the firm's senior staff in Australia was dispatched to northern Burma to inspect. On March 10, 1905 Herzig filed his report.

Herzig revealed that the Bawdwin area had on the surface 110,000 tons of slags containing an alluringly high percentage of lead (and a noticeable portion of zinc). If smelted for the lead, the slags would yield an estimated gross profit of £283,000. Perhaps even more intriguing was the fact that the Chinese had apparently not worked the mine itself much below the underground water level. Hence any sulphide ores deeper down would be untouched. Given the nature and extraordinary extent of the old Chinese workings—more than three hundred openings into the mine—Herzig considered the abandoned mine worthy of careful exploration. At least near the surface, this was no ordinary ore body.

Herzig estimated that £100,000 would be required to handle the business properly. A smelter would have to be assembled in Burma. A narrow two-foot gauge railroad would have to be built from the mine to the nearest railway line, a distance of about fifty miles. Labor would have to be obtained, but this, Herzig anticipated, would be little problem. In the nearby Chinese province of Yunnan workers were available at a wage of ten pence (about twenty cents) a day. Herzig observed that no one had ever attempted a modern mining or smelting operation in Burma. Nevertheless, the mining engineer seemed optimistic. Not only was the profit from the slag heaps likely to be substantial; there was a strong possibility that prospecting below the water level of the mine itself would uncover still more metal of value.[5]

Herzig's report encouraged Hoover to act. By the autumn of 1905 plans for a massive new undertaking in Burma were nearing fruition. It was announced in November that one of Bewick, Moreing's mine managers in Australia would shortly assume the management of the firm's business in Burma.[6] Traveling in Western Australia at the time, Hoover told the press that his Burmese venture was a tremendous one, tantamount to opening up "another Broken Hill."[7] At this very moment Hoover was launching the Zinc Corporation. He was not afraid of thinking big and acting boldly on more than one continent at once.

Finally, on March 6, 1906, the Burma Mines, Railway, and Smelting Company was born. (In 1908 its name was shortened to Burma Mines.)[8] The new concern acquired the property of the Great Eastern Mining Company, including a lease on nearly four square miles in the vicinity of the Bawdwin mines. The new company immediately issued 260,000 free £1 shares of stock, mostly to R. Tilden Smith's Share Guarantee Trust.[9] Smith retained the bulk of his block of free shares and distributed the remainder to various partners in the financial scheme, including Hoover (3,445 shares).[10] Bewick, Moreing became the managers and Hoover one of the original directors.[11] As Hoover later put it, he became the company's "engineering nurse."[12]

To raise the £100,000 needed for working capital, the new company created £150,000 in 6% first mortgage convertible debentures. Fifty thousand pounds of these were issued free to the Share Guarantee Trust. The remaining 100,000 were sold through it to various parties.[13]

The distribution of these debentures, which had first claim on the company's profits, disclosed the lines of force in the Burma enterprise. Smith's Trust bought £25,000 of the debentures for itself, Moreing's exploration company purchased another £25,000, Francis Govett's brokerage house £30,000, and the Lake View Consols (which Govett chaired) £20,000.[14] Hoover himself immediately purchased £12,500, or about $60,000 worth (probably from Govett), and thus assured himself a substantial role in the deliberations.[15] Govett, Smith, and three others joined Hoover on the board.[16]

The obstacles that the infant enterprise faced were immense. Upper Burma was a remote, ethnically diverse area that had been under British rule for only twenty years. The region near Bawdwin was rough, roadless, and densely wooded—a country of "extremely rugged, narrow valleys with precipitous inclosing hills," some of them rising steeply 2,000 feet above the valley floors.[17] Bawdwin itself was about 3,200 feet above sea level, but the drop-off of the river through the lease was about a thousand feet.[18] Tigers, monkeys, even elephants roamed the forests. Malaria and other tropical diseases were rampant; steamy, torrential rains fell six months of the year. Through this inhospitable country the Burma Mines company proposed to build fifty miles of railway.

There were other hurdles. The company decided, for economic reasons, to locate its smelter at Mandalay, about 200 miles by rail from the mine.[19] Thus the smelter could not even operate until the branch railway was completed. Moreover, while the slag heaps on the surface at Bawdwin were accessible for transport, the mountain-mine itself was pockmarked with tunnels, shafts, and open excavations that must be cleared of water and debris before the search could start for the supposed ore body underneath.

But if the hazards were great, so was the likely reward, from the piles of slag alone. And if, as Hoover suspected, a huge untapped ore deposit did exist underground. . . . There is "reason to anticipate," he told a friend soon after the company was founded, that the Bawdwin mine would "develop." If it did, the company's shares, he said, should double or triple in value.[20] The mining press echoed Hoover's sanguine sentiments. The Burma venture, said one journal, "has every prospect of success."[21]

I I

I T was now up to the company's directors and managers to implement their ambitious plans. Much of the responsibility for this fell on Herbert Hoover. In mid-September 1907 he, his wife, sister-in-law, and children sailed from London for Burma.[22] Hoover's infant son Allan, only two months old, was carried along in a basket.[23] Arriving in Rangoon in October, the family traveled north to Mandalay.[24] Here Hoover joined the company's local manager and the ubiquitous journalist J. H. Curle for a men-only expedition to the ancient mine.[25]

It was a fascinating and nearly disastrous journey. Traveling up the Mandalay-Lashio railway, the men disembarked at the town of Hsipaw, an all-bamboo village where the local Shan prince, or Sawbwa, resided. From there they trekked on horseback through the jungle to Bawdwin, whose hilltops stood denuded of all vegetation except grass. The Chinese had stripped the land for fuel, and the trees had never grown back.[26] Hoover's practiced eye noticed the temple ruins, the vast maze of mine workings, the old fortifications, and other evidence that a large Chinese community had once lived there. No doubt about it, the mine had once been enormously rich.

Hoover decided to explore some of the little tunnels which perforated the hillsides; perhaps he could thereby learn a clue to the nature of the sulphide ore that the Chinese had not mined. Armed only with a candle, he crawled into one such tunnel. Suddenly, in a puddle of water just ahead, he spotted the fresh inbound track of a tiger. Hastily Hoover retreated. The tiger remained in its den.[27]

Another jungle menace was not so forbearing. During his Burma visit Hoover contracted malaria; in his delirium he craved to write poetry. It took months for the disease to leave his system entirely.[28]

Departing from Rangoon in late November 1907, Hoover and his family arrived back in England just before Christmas.[29] A few months later Hoover terminated his partnership in Bewick, Moreing. Hoover's dangerous and debilitating bout with malaria may have been the source of the public explanation given for his departure from the firm: ill health. In any case, the prospect of an eventual bonanza from the Burma Mines further strengthened his desire to leave.[30] But Hoover had no wish to sever his administrative ties with the young Burma company. With the consent of his former partners he remained on its board of directors after mid-1908.[31]

It was well for the company that he did. For by 1908 the Burma Mines venture was in deepening trouble. By late 1907, to be sure, the company's lead smelter at Mandalay was ready.[32] It had been assembled entirely by native women's labor; the contractors, too, were Burmese women.[33] But the smelter could not operate without the slags, and the slags lay ungathered in the jungle two hundred miles away while the company's workers built a railroad connecting Bawdwin to the Mandalay-Lashio line.

It was only fifty-one miles, this branch line to Bawdwin, but fifty-one miles across a jungle, two mountain ranges, a wild river, and several lesser streams.[34] It soon became evident that the company had grievously underestimated the time and money required to lay the narrow-gauge line. Throughout 1907 and 1908 the workers struggled against topography and tropical rains, which caused frequent washouts. At one point 10,000 men were at work on the railway project.[35]

By mid-1908 forty-two miles of track had been completed.[36] The last section, however, included the Nam Tu River (over which a large bridge must be built) and some steep, hilly country near the mine. One hundred reversing stations had to be built in the final five miles alone.[37] While the workers concentrated on the railroad, systematic exploration of the tantalizing old mine workings was deferred for lack of personnel.[38]

By the end of 1908 the struggling company had spent over £221,000 on its smelter, railway, plant, and stores—triple Herzig's original estimate.[39] In London Govett fumed at "the most hopeless miscalculation" concerning the railway and castigated the civil engineer in charge.[40] Meanwhile in Burma the line reached Tiger Camp, five miles from Bawdwin. While waiting for the line to traverse the last five miles, the company used mules and bullocks to cart slags to the railhead at Tiger Camp. From here in December 1908 the first slag shipments went down to Mandalay,[41] where, early in 1909, the smelter at last commenced operations.[42] During 1909 about 11,000 tons of slag were transported in this way: from Bawdwin by bullock and mule to Tiger Camp, from Tiger Camp by rail to Mandalay.[43]

Nothing came easily to Hoover and his co-venturers. The new smelter was beset with early difficulties and had to be closed down for a time late in 1909 when floods and washouts temporarily stopped rail traffic. By the end of the year, however, it was functioning smoothly.[44] On the railway, far to the northeast, construction of the final link to the mine resumed in February, only to be delayed when the rainy season arrived in April. Since many laborers were Chinese from Yunnan who returned home to plant their rice when the rains came, the company's engineers now faced a severe labor shortage. They accordingly abandoned all attempts to explore the mine and put every available man onto the railway project. Thus still another year went by with little development work accomplished at the ore site.[45]

It was not until December 1909 that the little two-foot railway line reached the principal slag heaps of Bawdwin.[46] And it was not until January 13, 1910 that the first loaded train left the mine for Mandalay.[47] It was almost too late. For by now the Burma Mines, Ltd. was steeply, disturbingly, in debt. With no revenue coming in from slag treatment before 1909, the company had been unable to pay the interest on its debentures, interest that, by the end of 1908, amounted to more than £16,000.[48] Nor did Hoover, his fellow directors, or the general managers receive any fees, year after year—a state of affairs that persisted until 1911.[49] Even the sale of £57,222 in lead and silver bullion (from the slags) in 1909 did not eliminate the specter of financial collapse. At the end of the year the company's profit and loss account showed a staggering cumulative deficit of £123,201.[50]

Desperately Hoover and his colleagues strove to save their company and obtain needed capital. In November 1907 the Burma Mines created £40,000 in second mortgage debentures, redeemable with 150 percent interest and a bonus besides. Only £30,540 was actually obtained, mostly from Govett's Lake View Consols; the remainder had to be given to a bank as security on a loan. Hoover and Govett became trustees for the second debenture shareholders.[51] In 1908, in a quasi-reconstruction, the company issued 260,000 new shares of two shillings each to its shareholders. Although this action brought in £26,000, it was not nearly enough.[52] In January 1909 and again in June the company made two more share issues, which raised nearly £69,000. But how long, how long, could such makeshift finance last?[53]

By now the company's financial structure had become a confusing, rickety edifice of deferred shares, ordinary shares, preference shares, "A" preference shares, first mortgage debentures, and second mortgage debentures. Early in 1910 Hoover and his associates, with the approval of the shareholders (largely themselves), obtained the permission of the British courts for a drastic reduction of capital and consolidation of the classes of shares. The company's nominal capital was slashed from £450,000 to barely £100,000; £350,000 was simply written off.[54] The suffering shareholders had to pay in 4s. per share.[55]

Herbert Hoover was one of the sufferers. In the aftermath of the write-off Hoover's holding stood at 15,484 shares, roughly a 15% interest in the company.[56] He stood to profit immensely—if the mine ever lived up to his expectations.

And then, with agonizing slowness, it began to do so. The completion of the company's rail system and the rearrangement of its capital early in 1910 marked a turn in the Burma Mines's fortunes. The "preparatory stages" are over, Govett proclaimed happily that July.[57] Freed at last of preliminaries, the company's managers turned to proving or disproving Hoover's hypothesis. During 1910 and 1911 meaningful exploration of the old mine at last got underway.[58] In the meantime the company's smelter, which employed over five hundred people, turned out increasing quantities of bullion that garnered large revenues and pushed the balance sheet into the black in both years.[59] The profits were plowed back into the company.

For all the brightening portents, it was hard not to be discouraged. Even Hoover's faithful ally Govett had his doubts. Late in 1910 the British stockbroker publicly confessed to being "tired." The difficulties had been "so great"; progress in the Burma venture was still "desperately slow." Govett wished he had never heard of "this energy exhausting enterprise."[60]

Hoover was more optimistic. He encouraged Govett with his belief that the situation had improved, "notwithstanding the enormous cost and waste of time."[61] During 1911 the company's smelter was moved from Mandalay to Namtu, only a few miles from the mine, thus effecting a considerable savings in transportation costs for the slag.[62] At Bawdwin itself Bewick, Moreing engineers directed a campaign of shaft-sinking, driving, and cross-cutting to locate the silver-lead lode. They enlarged and extended an old Chinese tunnel that drove horizontally into the mountain: the Dead Chinaman Tunnel or "D.C." Tunnel, they called it (eventually just the Chinaman Tunnel) because of the human skeletons they found inside. By the end of 1911 the tunnel reached nearly 900 feet into the earth.[63]

By the beginning of 1912 Hoover was sufficiently sanguine to suggest that A. Chester Beatty join him in buying 11,000 Burma Mines shares at a price well above par. "The business is looking very well again," Hoover explained, "as they have recovered the drowned shaft and got into the old workings and found some ore, although of course they have not bottomed these workings." Hoover pointed out that the smelter now had two-and-a-half years of slag reserves and a sure profit from them of £4,000 a month. He was uncertain "whether it is worth while to take this gamble without having the mine further examined," but purchase of the shares would give Beatty "a talking position in the Company which I think we could use to good advantage."[64]

Still, Hoover showed symptoms of anxiety and impatience. Late in 1911 the Burma Mines board of directors decided to sanction an independent examination of the property. It refused to accept for this undertaking the nominee of Bewick, Moreing—an unmistakable sign that the board had less than full faith in its mine managers.[65] Hoover, for his part, sought to have one of his friends do the survey. "I have tried very hard to get [Amor] Kuehn sent out officially for the Company to Burma," he told Beatty, "but the conflicting factors are so great in that Company that it seems impossible to agree on any one man." Hoover was so desirous of having Kuehn go that he offered to pay personally one-third of Kuehn's expenses.[66] Kuehn eventually went to Burma.[67]

As 1911 gave way to 1912 without any decisive discoveries at the mine, the company's future once more became clouded. Hoover's own thoughts during this year are not on record, but perhaps his friend Govett, who relied upon him for technical advice, reflected the American's mood. Late in 1912, at a shareholders meeting of the Lake View and Oroya Exploration Company (which held a substantial block of stock and debentures in the Burma Mines),[68] Govett publicly declared himself to be optimistic. He retained his "original expectation," he said, that an "immense mine" would be found at the Bawd-win site. The prospects "are looking exceedingly good," Govett proclaimed, "even if it be a slow and laborious path" to fulfillment.[69] Privately he told Beatty that it would be a long and possibly tiring struggle before that moment came.[70]

I I I

THE winter of 1912–13 seems to have witnessed the nadir of Hoover's hopes. Registered in 1906 amidst hope and confidence, the Burma Mines, Ltd. was completing its seventh year, with its original premise still unproved. Back from Burma, Kuehn expressed his doubts about the company's management in the field: it did not seem to be proceeding vigorously enough with crucial development.[71] At the mine itself workers on the Chinaman Tunnel had encountered more underground workings and much water, which impeded their efforts to find ore.[72] By January 1913 all work on the Chinaman Tunnel was stymied by the water flow underground.[73] To further complicate matters, the Burma Mines now suffered from a labor shortage, thanks to unpaid payrolls, and from a power shortage as well, thanks to the company's lack of money to build an adequate hydroelectric power plant.[74] In February came more bad news: Bewick, Moreing expected the slag reserves—the company's sole source of revenue—to be used up by the coming October.[75]

What the troubled enterprise needed, in Kuehn's opinion, was a heavily financed development campaign under competent direction to determine as rapidly as possible the true character of the property.[76] It was far easier talked about than done. For by 1913, and probably well before, the Burma Mines board of directors was riven by a paralyzing split. On one side were Hoover, Govett, and their friends; on the other was a faction led by the company's principal shareholder, R. Tilden Smith.[77] To Hoover's mounting frustration, Smith steadily refused to sanction the kind of full-scale development that Hoover wished to undertake.[78]

The reason was financial. According to Beatty, Smith was willing neither to invest more money himself nor to dilute his percentage of the business by letting others supply extra capital.[79] And without Smith's agreement on financial policy, the company could do little. The result was stalemate and drift. By January 1913 Hoover was so disgusted that he was prepared to let the company flounder so badly that he and his allies could in time purchase control on advantageous terms.[80]

At this point Kuehn proposed an alternative. Why not, he suggested to Hoover, form a syndicate with £50,000 to develop the Burma Mines properties under the direction of the syndicate's own engineer, independent of Bewick, Moreing?[81] Hoover assented and presented the proposal to the Burma board in mid-January.[82]

Initially Smith was agreeable to a reorganization. It was not long, however, before he reverted to form.[83] On February 18 Hoover vented his anger in a letter to Beatty:

> In respect of the reorganisation of the Burma Mines, Mr. Tilden Smith has now refused point blank to do anything. This change of attitude is due to their having struck some more ore in the workings. We are thus again in the same old position, i.e. allowing the concern to go on being perfectly diabolically mismanaged, with the full expectation that it will some day come sufficiently to grief to make it possible for us to take hold of it. I dislike very much to be a Director on a company involving such perfectly wicked mismanagement but I think I shall have to continue, simply because of the opportunity that it will afford when the reorganisation arrives. There can be no question about this happening some day.[84]

It turned out that Smith had a fund-raising scheme of his own: sale of the company's railway to the Burma government for £200,000. Such a sum, of course, would relieve him of any need to dip into his own pocket. Early in April Smith promised that if his negotiations with the Burma authorities failed, he would accept establishment of a syndicate to finance the Burma Mines—provided that he received a 25% interest in the syndicate.[85] He was not about to surrender his strategic position in the enterprise. A week or so later Hoover told Kuehn that he still had not come to terms with Smith over finance. Hoover was apparently furious; Kuehn feared that Hoover had openly shown hostility to Smith.[86]

As if in counterpoint to Hoover's anger and dismay, a terrific storm struck the Bawdwin mines in April and caused extensive damage to the company's property.[87] Soon afterwards a cholera epidemic hit Namtu. By the end of the month more than fifty people were dead, and the company's smelter was forced to close for several months.[88]

The darkest hour is just before the dawn. In May 1913 workers on the Chinaman Tunnel penetrated at long last below the old Chinese workings— and found an incredible ore body.[89] By August the lode was known to be more than 600 feet long and at least fifty feet wide. Rich in silver, lead, and zinc,[90] it was one of the largest ore bodies discovered in the world in a decade.[91] A year-and-a-half later, as the mine's extraordinary dimensions and value became better known, Hoover asserted that the Bawdwin properties were one of the "ten most notable mineral discoveries in the whole world" since 1900.[92]

Hoover's intuition and tenacity had been vindicated. For eight trying years he had believed that there *must* be a mine below those ancient Chinese workings. Finally he had been proven right. Yet the company, as he well knew, was by no means out of danger. Eight years of expenditure had taken a staggering toll. For months, in fact, the Burma Mines, Ltd. had been carrying on, as he put it, "largely by staving creditors off in the hope of proving a sufficient body of ore to give basis for complete re-finance of the Company."[93] Now that the ores had been located, they turned out to be disturbingly complex and refractory. At a shareholders meeting in August 1913 Hoover frankly declared it "extremely doubtful" that the Bawdwin ores could be treated by any known commercial processes.[94] Unless the ores could be treated at a profit, the venture would fail. In more than one way did Bawdwin resemble Broken Hill.

Hoover had risked too much, however, to quit now. In an effort to solve the metallurgical problem, he and his colleagues arranged to ship tons of ore samples—eventually 7,060 tons—from Burma to European smelters for experimentation. It was a costly gamble, and Hoover quickly discovered that investors outside his coterie were uninterested. First he, Smith, and some others attempted to raise the needed money in a way that would not entail assessing the shareholders. In Hoover's words, they "signally failed." Hoover was therefore compelled to supply much of the money himself.[95]

He did so through the medium of a syndicate called the Intercontinental Trust (1913), Ltd., which he and Smith had created earlier in the year. The Intercontinental Trust had a capital of £100,000; Hoover and Smith owned a 40% interest each and other parties the remaining 20%. By August the syndicate had loaned about £20,000 in working capital to the Burma Mines and had promised about £35,000 more.[96]

Even if the European smelters came through, however, this would be just the beginning. At the August 1913 meeting Hoover warned that if the metallurgical difficulties were resolved, the Burma Mines would then require £200,000 to £300,000 *additional* capital for new equipment, including a new smelter.[97] It soon became apparent that the Intercontinental Trust's loan was but the first step in a grand Hooverian plan to refinance and reorganize the Burma Mines. The Burma company's meeting was held on August 27. Exactly one month later the Intercontinental Trust—that is, Hoover and Smith—announced plans to form a new company, the Burma Corporation, which would be a holding company for Burma Mines shares. The Intercontinental Trust arranged for shareholders in the Burma Mines to exchange their shares for shares in the new corporation. It also obtained control of several hundred thousand Burma Mines shares for transfer to the new corporation.[98]

The Burma Corporation was created on October 9, 1913, with an authorized capital of £750,000. The Intercontinental Trust was the promoter; Hoover in due course became a director. By November 24 over two-thirds of the shares in the new concern had been issued. Not surprisingly, Smith was the largest shareholder, with over 189,000 shares listed in his name. The Lake View and Oroya Exploration held 92,908 and Hoover in his own name 38,511. But this figure did not truly measure Hoover's influence or financial interest. For one thing, Hoover and Govett were joint managing directors of the Lake View and no doubt could control its block of shares. The Intercontinental Trust itself owned 112,782 shares, of which Hoover in effect held 40%. And under the terms of the flotation, the Intercontinental Trust gained a two-year option to purchase all of the new corporation's shares, at prices stipulated by the shareholders.[99]

Throughout the fall and winter of 1913–14 the Burma Corporation proceeded with its share exchange scheme. It also purchased enough Burma Mines debentures to preclude any opposition from that quarter. By May 1914 the Burma Corporation had acquired most of the debentures and nearly all of the shares of the Burma Mines.[100]

The machinery was now in place for a fresh start—if one could be justified. And for once the news was cheering. At the mine in the Burmese jungle, development work continued to reveal ore bodies of extraordinary dimensions and value. From smelters on the European continent came word that the ore treatment problems had been conquered. Quickly the Burma Corporation contracted to sell its ore to these smelters.[101] It was probably during this period that a German company (according to Amor Kuehn) offered to buy the mine for $5,000,000 in cash.[102] This did not happen, but in 1914 Dr. Eduard Heberlein, apparently representing the Metall Gesellschaft of Frankfurt, joined the Burma Corporation board.[103]

It was time at last to implement the kind of program of which Hoover had long dreamed. On April 9, 1914 the Burma Corporation increased its authorized capital from £750,000 to £1,000,000.[104] On April 17 Hoover informed his brother: "Smith has come round with consent to a Burma deal, which brightens the position here a good bit. I think I shall be able to organise a Syndicate which will put the position where we want it."[105] Five days later the Bawdwin Syndicate was born.[106]

The new syndicate had a capital of £150,000, divided into 150,000 shares, which Hoover, Beatty, and various others (but not Smith) acquired. (Hoover's personal share, according to Beatty, was 13,000.) The Bawdwin Syndicate's purpose was purely financial: to supply working capital for the Burma Corporation's expansion schemes. To this end, it purchased outright 100,000 new Burma Corporation shares for £100,000 and took extended options to buy 200,000 more such shares at or above par.[107] In short, if all went well, the Burma Corporation could count on at least £200,000 in further funds.

At the end of May 1914 the Burma Corporation's directors included Herbert Hoover (who became chairman), Theodore Hoover, Govett, Smith, R. Gilman Brown, Heberlein, and one Samuel Magennis (an ally of Smith). A separate technical committee included Brown, Heberlein, Theodore Hoover, and Kuehn as an alternate for Theodore.[108] Only one step remained in the great transition. On May 29, 1914 the Burma Corporation itself became by formal contract the sole general manager of the Burma Mines, Ltd. for ten years with "uncontrolled discretion" over all aspects of the Burma Mines's business. The Corporation, in turn, promised to expend £300,000 on development of the property within five years. The Corporation was to receive three-quarters of the Burma Mines's net profits for its services.[109] Bewick, Moreing, hitherto the Burma Mines's general manager, was thus adroitly ousted, relegated to the secondary status of consulting engineers.[110]

Hoover's dissatisfaction with Bewick, Moreing's performance had been apparent for some time. At the Burma Mines meeting in August 1913 he cited the transfer of the smelter from Mandalay to Namtu as an "error" by the local staff in Burma, an error he said had helped to create the company's parlous financial position. He also announced the appointment of a new resident manager and metallurgist, supposedly because their predecessors were "anxious to be relieved."[111] During the summer of 1913 rumors spread that a "change in general control and local management" was in progress.[112] Although this particular rumor—in the form that Bewick, Moreing had "given up" the management—was said a few months later to be "not correct,"[113] it became accurate in mid-1914. Bewick, Moreing was out. Hoover, more than ever, was in charge.

With the Burma venture refinanced, and with a technical committee dominated by his brother and his friends in place, Hoover was finally free to concentrate on the massive engineering tasks at hand. The technical committee's program, which he himself probably helped to shape, was Hooverian in its ambition. The committee proposed to equip and develop the mine so that it could produce 300,000 tons of ore a year. For this purpose nothing less than a realigned railway, new rolling stock, an entire ore concentration plant, and a hydroelectric plant would be required—all in the barely subdued wilds of northeastern Burma.[114]

Most daring of all, Hoover and his technical committee proposed to drive a large adit (horizontal tunnel) into the side of the mountain to open up the newly discovered ore body. This tunnel would be parallel to, but about five hundred feet below, the Chinaman Tunnel, which was itself 171 feet below the collar of the vertical shaft.[115] The new tunnel was to be no ordinary passageway. It would be well over one mile long, about eight feet high and nine feet wide, and would have two narrow-gauge railway tracks, separated by a drainage ditch, for haulage of the ore.[116] The engineers estimated that their development program, including construction of the tunnel, would take at least two years to complete.[117]

The proposed adit—the joint idea of Hoover and his technical

committee[118]—was a brilliant conception. Not only would it now be unnecessary to hoist the ore vertically up a shaft (an expensive process); the ditch
down the middle of the new horizontal tunnel could drain off water from the
mine.[119] (Eventually that ditch conveyed an average of 40,000 gallons per
hour.)[120] The tunnel also solved the problem of underground ventilation.[121]
It was to be the mine's underground highway, capable of carrying 1,000 tons
or more of ore a day. Recalling his chilling experience in Burma in 1907,
Hoover named the adit the Tiger Tunnel.[122]

Work on the Tiger Tunnel commenced in April 1914. It was to be a long,
laborious struggle, advancing at the rate of 200–300 feet a month, and absorbing the energies of over two hundred men a day. Almost half the great
double-track adit had to be timbered. When finally finished in September
1916, the Tiger Tunnel was 7,400 feet long[123] and a monument to Hoover's
leadership.

I V

B Y the summer of 1914 Hoover had reason to feel content. The mine was
there—he knew it now—and it was only a matter of time before its riches
were fully tapped. Out in Burma a remarkable, polyglot community of several thousand men was growing up, in which at least nine different languages
were eventually spoken. Most of the workers were imported from India,
Indochina, and China itself, particularly the seasonal "cold-weather China-
men" from Yunnan.[124] A. Chester Beatty was so impressed with the mine's
potential that he tried unsuccessfully in 1914 to form a combination to buy
the control.[125] Hoover himself remarked late that year that Burma was "the
most promising mining region on the globe at the present time."[126]

It is likely that but for Hoover's energy, audacity, and driving commitment, the Bawdwin mines venture would have failed. Other men would have
been daunted by the unending difficulties; Hoover never surrendered. Instead,
for several years (he later said "nearly ten") he put "practically the whole of
my saving" into the Burma enterprise.[127] "We had to assess ourselves time
and again," he wrote, "before we battled the [Burma] mines to a profit."[128]
R. Tilden Smith remained the largest shareholder, but it was Hoover who
pushed through the crucial reorganization of 1913–14 that laid the foundation
for ultimate success.[129]

By mid-1914 (according to Beatty) Hoover held—directly and through the
Intercontinental Trust—a total of 130,000 shares in the Burma Corporation.
Smith's share was 329,000.[130] Beatty's figures may not have been precisely
accurate,[131] but in essence they were correct: Hoover held at least a one-
seventh interest in the giant enterprise and was second only to Smith.[132] It
was to be, as he later put it, "the major source of the family fortune."[133] As
yet the mine had not yielded a dividend; profits from the smelter had gone

back into the business. Moreover, Smith was still on the scene and might cause trouble again. But Hoover knew that his engineers anticipated a profit of £1,000,000 or more for every hundred feet the ore body extended in depth.[134] This reward was not yet in hand. But by August 1914 Hoover was poised to make a magnificent fortune.[135]

21

Russia

I

I N the generation immediately prior to World War I imperial Russia under Czar Nicholas II was an awakening giant whose economic growth rate was the highest in Europe. With increasing momentum foreign capital, especially British capital, found its way into Russian enterprises. From the Ural Mountains to eastern Siberia, particularly after 1902, British-registered syndicates and corporations began to develop the mineral resources of the colossus of the East.[1] And where British financial houses interested in mining went, Herbert Hoover after 1908 was not likely to be far away.

The multiplying British mining enterprises in Russia furnished Hoover a fresh field in which to practice as an engineer-financier. One early opportunity was the case of the Atbasar Copper Fields, Ltd., a company created in 1906 to develop a copper deposit in the Kirghiz steppes of Siberia.[2] It was a typical case of an undercapitalized venture exhausting its financial resources before it reached the profit-bearing stage—the kind of sickness the self-styled "industrial doctor" liked to cure.[3] By 1909 the Atbasar Copper Fields company was out of working capital, and Hoover had been invited to help it find more.[4]

At first Hoover was skeptical. For one thing, he told A. Chester Beatty, "The house which controls this mine is in great disfavour." For another, an independent report by an American engineer showed "possibly great probabilities but mighty little tangibly in hand." The mine was so distant from a railroad that large production was years away, yet the financial "deals" under consideration were but short-term arrangements of a few months. Alert as always to stock market considerations, Hoover declared that "barring simply a wild outburst of Stock Exchange speculation there is absolutely nothing to create a market in these shares."[5] Nothing, that is, to boom the market in Atbasar stock so that holders of its stock or options (such as Hoover) could sell out and make a profit.

For these and other reasons Hoover thought the deal no "particular snap" and at first took "no personal interest" in financing the Atbasar.[6] By early 1910, however, Hoover and Beatty together seemed to be heavily involved. The vehicle of their interest was an entity they created called the Sibat Syndicate, for which Hoover held the power of attorney.[7] The Sibat Syndicate agreed to purchase 60,000 previously unissued Atbasar shares for £60,000, at regular intervals, thereby providing a fresh supply of working capital. In return, the syndicate received a call or option to buy 250,000 additional Atbasar shares at par by the end of 1912.[8] If the Atbasar shares shot above par, of course, the syndicate could exercise its option, buy at par, immediately sell *above* par, and make its profit. Remuneration for its risk thus depended on a favorable stock market.

By mid-1910 Hoover and Beatty personally had put about £7,600 into the Sibat Syndicate and held roughly 12,000 syndicate shares, half of them belonging to Hoover.[9] Alas, this finance operation was proving to be a headache. "There have been interminable difficulties" with the Atbasar board of directors "over the details of that trade," Hoover reported to Beatty in March. "I have wished a million times I had never heard of that d—— mine. It has been actually more trouble to me to negotiate this £3,000-deal than it has been to place half a million pounds for oil business."[10] Several months later Hoover complained again. "The whole position requires re-organisation," he declared. If only "the business" were "placed in my hands," Hoover felt he could create a favorable stock market for Atbasar shares. Unfortunately, matters were "particularly hopeless" as they stood.[11]

By February 1911 the Sibat Syndicate was in a bind. Its contract called for paying Atbasar a further installment of £25,000, but where was it to find the money? It could, said Hoover, try to sell some of the Atbasar shares it already held in order to get money to buy the further shares it was obliged to take up. But the market was dead. Moreover, the Atbasar mine needed £50,000 "to prove this property once and for all" before the time came for the syndicate to exercise or pass up its final share option. To abandon ship now would be to lose all that had been put into Sibat. To go ahead meant putting in more money and hoping for the best. Hoover was "very unhappy" but saw no alternative except to plunge in further. Perhaps, he told Beatty, the Sibat could sell out to the Spassky Copper Mine, another British-owned Russian venture. He called the possibility "probably our mainstay of hope."[12]

A few months later Hoover's hope was realized. The Spassky company bought a controlling interest in the Atbasar and took over all the Sibat Syndicate's interests for 37,500 Spassky shares.[13] Hoover and Beatty were undoubtedly relieved, although months of irksome delay passed before the Spassky's managers fulfilled their end of the bargain.[14]

Hoover dabbled in other Russian mining schemes, too. In mid-1910 he and Beatty held what Hoover called a "considerable position" in the affairs of Orsk Goldfields; some months later he participated in the guarantee of a financial reconstruction of this company.[15] In 1910 also he and Beatty agreed to underwrite 10,000 out of 95,000 new shares issued by the Anglo-Siberian Company for a commission of 1s. / 6d. a share.[16]

These activities—the Sibat Syndicate, Orsk, the Anglo-Siberian—were essentially finance operations. Hoover appeared to have little if any control over the management of these concerns and little interest in them as long-term investments.[17] His actions, rather, were short-term forays into finance. A mining company would need capital; Hoover would help to locate it and often would put up a portion himself. His reward in part would be calls—stock options—which could yield a handsome profit on a rising market.

I I

S I B A T and its sister arrangements were minor ventures, however, compared to another Russian undertaking with which Hoover was increasingly identified after he left Bewick, Moreing. Late in 1908 a British-registered company called the Kyshtim Corporation was formed to acquire the entire share capital (and thus the control) of the Kyshtim Mining Works, a Russian concern operating at a loss in the southern Ural Mountains. Like the Burma Mines, this was no ordinary proposition. The Russian subsidiary's landholdings comprised 2,198 square miles (over 1,406,000 acres), an area half the size of Connecticut. On this land (some of it cleared, most of it forested) lived more than 75,000 people. Above all, the Kyshtim estates contained rich deposits of copper, gold, and iron, as well as ironworks which had been producing specialized products (such as iron castings) for over 150 years. What the property needed now was modernization and development. This meant capital, foreign capital, that the Kyshtim Corporation prepared to funnel into the Kyshtim Mining Works.

In large measure, the creation of the Kyshtim Corporation was the work of Leslie Urquhart, an irrepressible Scottish entrepreneur with a flair for languages and a belief in the mining potential of Czarist Russia. Urquhart, like Hoover, had been born in 1874. He had spent much of his youth in the Near East, had become manager of four British oil companies in the Russian city of Baku at age thirty, and had fled after nearly being assassinated by revolutionaries in 1906. Turning up in London shortly afterwards, Urquhart promptly organized the Anglo-Siberian Company to undertake mining investments in Russia; he took a 30% interest in its stock. Soon the new company obtained an option to purchase the languishing Kyshtim Mining Works. In 1907 an American engineer named H. H. Knox inspected the property and recommended a development program. Finally, in 1908, after various further maneuvers, the Kyshtim Corporation was born. Urquhart became a director, as well as managing director of the corporation's wholly owned Russian subsidiary.[18]

The new company's plans were ambitious. Among other things, £8,000 would be needed for the ironworks, £35,000 for a branch rail line to the copper mines, and £80,000 for a huge modern copper smelter, workers' housing, and other necessities. In all, £260,000—well over a million dollars—must be raised. To this end the infant corporation made a large share and debenture issue in November 1908.[19]

By late 1909 the once-backward and impoverished Kyshtim enterprise was undergoing a transformation. Thirty miles of railway connecting the town of Kyshtim with the mines were complete. At Karabash Lake preparations were well underway to erect in 1910 a smelter capable of producing five thousand tons of copper per year. A new electrolytic refinery was in place, while exploration and development of the mining areas disclosed several substantial deposits of copper ore.[20]

Despite its initial cash resources, the Kyshtim Corporation by late 1909 faced that perennial problem of young mining companies: a need for more capital. It was at this point that Hoover first appeared on the Kyshtim scene.[21] As so often in these years, Hoover's involvement began not with engineering aspects of the matter but with the finance. During the autumn he hammered out an underwriting arrangement for a new Kyshtim fund-raising scheme.[22] In December 1909 and January 1910 the Kyshtim Corporation duly issued a total of £50,000 in additional 6% debentures.[23] Hoover and Beatty arranged to take up the debentures—that is, to loan Kyshtim £50,000 at 6% interest. In return they received a call on 150,000 Kyshtim shares.[24]

Hoover and Beatty did not personally purchase most of these debentures; instead, Hoover placed £42,000 of them with various subunderwriters, notably Francis Govett's brokerage house, and sold £2,000 more on the market. Of the 150,000 calls, Hoover gave away 71,900, again mostly to Govett—presumably as a reward for agreeing to buy the debentures. Thus Hoover and Beatty themselves contributed only £6,000 of their own money and retained the right to purchase 79,100 Kyshtim Corporation shares later on.[25]

At this stage Hoover's interest in Kyshtim was purely financial. When Beatty heard a rumor that someone had suggested him for consulting engineer to the Kyshtim Corporation, Hoover hastened to assure him that neither man's name had come up. Hoover was glad:

My own view of these things is that I would rather keep to the financial side than to have any position as an engineer in these concerns. One is absolutely free then to do any kind of financial operation that one likes and by working through other people like Gilman Brown you can see that the administration is good and can know all about what is going on. If one becomes a Consulting Engineer to the thing, responsibility for its successful issue more or less falls on one, especially with regard to one's friends and supporters who have a tendency to buy the shares and things in the concern.[26]

During the fall of 1909 Hoover's friend R. Gilman Brown inspected the Kyshtim properties, probably at Hoover's and Beatty's own expense.[27] When he returned in December, Brown was enthusiastic. The Kyshtim Corporation, he reported, should be able to pay a dividend of at least 20% to 25% per year. This was good enough for Hoover, who informed Beatty that he intended "to exercise the options" (calls) "and go ahead."[28]

There was, however, one difficulty. Brown had reported (in Hoover's words) that "the business is very good if the thing gets proper management." This proviso raised again the question of how much Hoover should get involved in Kyshtim affairs. Once again he confided to Beatty:

As to the management, it is quite hopeless to get English people of this type to pay anything like what would warrant either you or I in identifying ourselves publicly with the thing. They are paying the Managing Director £600 per annum, and they look on that as a great concession. They balked like anything at paying £1,500 a year to a Consulting Engineer, etc., etc. My own view is to simply have Gilman Brown appointed as Consulting Engineer, insist that they take Baker [a British financier-friend of Hoover] on the Board, and I would stand behind and push these two people into the activity which we require.

Hoover, in short, preferred one of his favorite roles: the skillful wire-puller, working through surrogates to achieve his objectives. "Working behind the scenes," he continued,

has a great advantage when one has a market deal on, and when one is incurring no obligations of a personal character. If I were a Director or Consulting Engineer of the Company, I would feel myself bound to prevent the shares going above certain prices in order to save the sort of moral responsibility there is to the general public. On the other hand, if I have got no fiduciary position in the Company, I do not care what the Board does in this direction.[29]

Throughout the fall and winter of 1909 Hoover gave ample evidence of interest in a Kyshtim "market deal." In mid-November, less than a month after he completed arrangements for the new debenture issue, he told Beatty that he was negotiating with a "financial house" whereby the house would buy a block of Kyshtim shares, thus "making the market," and would receive "calls at rising prices."[30] In mid-December Hoover reported to Beatty that "we are busy trying to tie up the balance of the [Kyshtim] stock in order that we may have a clean sweep on a big market operation." Several concerns, he wrote, were "keen to take the Kyshtim market in hand, but . . . we are anxious to tie up all the outstanding stock before we do anything."[31] Soon after New Year's Day Hoover anticipated that all but 175,000 shares would be under his allies' control and that "we" would then be "in position to make a move."[32]

In late January 1910 he became more specific. The proposal, he informed Beatty, was to put 300,000 Kyshtim shares, including 50,000 (calls, presumably) that belonged to Hoover and Beatty, into a pool that would be managed by a London financial firm, L. Hirsch and Company. Hirsch would receive 40% of the profit made on shares that the pool sold for over twenty-five shillings per share.[33]

It was an audacious plan: a giant pool, one of the classic modes of stock market manipulation. What Hoover, the Hirsch firm, and their allies were doing was simple. They were tying up every share that they could by contracts among the pool participants not to buy or sell their holdings (or calls) independently. Then the pool managers could (in Hoover's phrase) "start the market."[34] That is, by an initial purchase of some non-pooled shares at a high price on the open market, or by judicious press publicity about the splendid value of Kyshtim shares, or by other techniques, the pool would attempt to send the price of Kyshtim shares soaring—even as the pooled shares were held back. When the Kyshtim shares reached a high enough price, the pool managers would sell their pooled shares[35] on the open market and make, they hoped, a terrific profit.[36]

Thus was created in early 1910 the so-called Hirsch Pool, as Hoover labeled it in his correspondence.[37] Even before this pool was formally organized, Hoover was optimistic. He told Beatty that "when we get the other shares tied up I think we shall see our way to getting in some money."[38] How much he profited from the pool is not known.

While Hoover concentrated on financial operations in London, at Kyshtim in the Urals a massive mining enterprise was slowly developing. Late in 1910 the first of two blast furnaces constituting the Karabash pyritic smelter commenced work. It was capable of processing five hundred tons of coarse copper ore a day.[39] At the end of December Hoover cabled Beatty that the new smelter was "running most satisfactorily" and that he had "closed" a deal involving the purchase or sale of 7,500 Kyshtim shares at thirty shillings a share.[40]

By late 1910 the Kyshtim Corporation once more needed money, and for a second time Hoover stepped in. Throughout October and November he worked feverishly on a complicated financial transaction entailing the creation of a new and even more gigantic market pool. The engineer-financier had several objectives. First, he wished to sell £50,000 in debentures that the Kyshtim Corporation proposed to issue in order to obtain needed capital. Second, he wished to remove the Hirsch influence, which he now found an "incubus," from the Kyshtim market scene. Third, he wanted to avoid having to put up £28,000 with Beatty in January in order to exercise expiring options that they held on various Kyshtim shares. Finally, and probably most importantly of all, he wished—to put it simply—to make money and to expand his influence and Beatty's on the market in Kyshtim shares.[41]

In mid-November the first part of Hoover's plan was consummated. Back in March he and Beatty had created a finance company called the Intercontinental Trust, in which they retained a substantial share interest.[42] Now, by Hoover's arrangement, the Intercontinental Trust acquired the entire assets of the Hirsch Pool—options to purchase roughly 300,000 Kyshtim shares—in return for 22,750 new, fully paid Intercontinental shares and certain other commitments.[43] Hoover told Beatty that "the whole of this idea of handing this Hirsch deal over to the Intercontinental Trust was with a view of getting it out of the hands of L. Hirsch & Co. and the Hirsch Syndicate and into hands where we could absolutely control it. . . ."[44] This objective was now achieved.

Hoover was not satisfied with control over the rights to purchase 300,000 shares. He proceeded at once to construct a second pool—a "superimposed pool," as he called it—which would control not just the 300,000 Kyshtim shares under call now belonging to the Intercontinental Trust but a much larger block of stock as well. By late November this new pool—the Kyshtim Pool—was created, with Hoover, Govett's firm, and another brokerage house as pool managers. Hoover had succeeded in tying up (that is, in keeping off the market) over 826,000 of the 1,000,000 Kyshtim shares.[45]

The deal was not quite complete—Hoover still had the £50,000 in Kyshtim debentures to place—but he foresaw little difficulty. During the fall he negotiated with a Paris financial house, Dupont & Furlaud, which was "enormously anxious" (Hoover told Beatty) "to get a Kyshtim deal on."[46] Hoover himself traveled to Paris in October to work on arrangements.[47] Hoover proposed to have Dupont & Furlaud purchase the £50,000 in Kyshtim debentures and absorb all expenses of a "campaign" of "propaganda" on the French stock market.[48] In this way the Kyshtim Corporation would be financed. In return for thereby providing the needed capital and for creating a market in France, Dupont & Furlaud was to receive a half-interest in the Kyshtim calls controlled by the huge, overriding pool.[49]

Hoover soon became vexed with his French associates. Just before the first phase of Hoover's plan—the transfer of the Hirsch Pool to the Intercontinental Trust—was to occur, Furlaud indiscreetly divulged details to one of the Hirsch company's Paris partners, who promptly rushed over to London with the news. Up till then the Hirsch people had been willing to withdraw from their own pool and even had promised Hoover by letter not to join his scheme. But now that they knew how attractive his plan was, they repudiated their letter, refused to back out, and (in Hoover's words) "tried their damndest to upset my deal."[50] In the end the Hirsch Pool was transferred to the Intercontinental Trust. But L. Hirsch and Company retained its portion of the pool—which meant that a smaller share was left over for Hoover and Beatty.[51]

Hoover was furious at Dupont & Furlaud. He told Beatty that they personally would have received 10,000 more shares in the Intercontinental Trust had it not been for Furlaud's "foolishness." Hoover therefore proposed to have the French firm compensate him and Beatty for the "injury caused" by paying them 20% of the firm's profits from the pool.[52]

Despite his displeasure with Dupont & Furlaud, Hoover was cheered by the gains he and Beatty had made. As a result of Hoover's arrangements, he and Beatty increased "somewhat" their holdings in the Intercontinental Trust and hence in options over Kyshtim shares. Moreover, Hoover reported, he and Beatty would not now be obliged to put up any more money for the duration of the deal. This was far better than the former alternative: finding nearly £30,000 in order to exercise options on Kyshtim shares next January. If all went ahead as planned, he and Beatty stood to receive free (via the Intercontinental Trust) 6,000 Kyshtim shares each plus an option to purchase 150,000 shares at a fixed price until the end of 1912. And if they were able to "squeeze something off of Dupont & Furlaud" or "through the management of the pool," then "we can make something more."[53] A few days later Hoover was more sanguine still. If he had *not* done anything, he declared, Beatty would have been obliged to exercise his call in January, buy 18,000 shares at par, and resell at a tiny profit in a dead market. Instead, 825,000 shares were tied up for a full year, and with "even moderate success in pool operations" Beatty should be able to sell his block at a far greater profit.[54]

This was not, of course, what Hoover told Dupont & Furlaud. On November 19, 1910 Hoover addressed two letters to the Paris financiers. The first set out the terms for their proposed participation in the giant pool.[55] The second requested that Hoover and Beatty receive a percentage of the French firm's pool profits because of the "great damage" caused to them by the Hirsch fiasco. Hoover asserted that "after all the work and labor of reorganizing the whole Hirsch share position, we [Hoover and Beatty] stand in no better position than we would had we never undertaken the business. . . ."[56]

His effort failed. A few days later Dupont & Furlaud sent a reply that Hoover labeled "extraordinary." Its exact contents are unknown but were clearly unfavorable; Hoover quickly withdrew the "whole business" from the French firm. Instead, he made them another offer (better, he claimed, than the one he had made in Paris) and, said Hoover, "they were such eternal idiots as not to snap it up on the spot."[57]

With Dupont & Furlaud out of the bargaining, Hoover was obliged to find another subscriber to the £50,000 of Kyshtim debentures. Even before the French financiers responded to his terms of the nineteenth, he told Beatty that he could arrange the deal "in half a dozen quarters in the City."[58] In fact, he said, he could make even better arrangements from the perspective of the Intercontinental Trust,[59] which was left in sole control of the enlarged pool. Just how the debentures ultimately were distributed is unclear, but as of mid-December Hoover anticipated "no difficulty." For the Kyshtim Corporation had just issued a favorable report by Brown, freshly back from Russia, and Hoover noted that this report would be "pretty liberally advertised."[60]

The Kyshtim deal had been hard, unrelenting work for Hoover. In constructing the pool he had been obliged to consult more than sixty different parties—enough to tax the stamina even of a man who seemed to thrive on such mental exercise. He had (he told Beatty) "spent a solid month on this and practically nothing else, and have provided not one iota of preference for myself over anybody else."

> There are two ways of doing business in this town—one is either to put down the money and the other is to keep constantly financing and raising the money on the one hand from one set of people and keeping up the appearance of putting it down oneself with others. The whole of this business has been conducted on the latter principle, and I have had to do all the financing. . . .[61]

For the Kyshtim Pool to prosper—for Hoover to make money—the price of Kyshtim stock had to rise. This meant pulling the levers of publicity, an activity at which Hoover was adept. By the end of December Hoover was pleased with the "strong market which has arisen in Kyshtim shares"—the result, he said, of "my advertising campaign in England":

> Everybody on this side is extremely pleased at the way in which I have managed the market for the Intercontinental as, within two months from a perfectly dead market at 22 / 7d., we have got a live market at 32 / 6d., and have had to sell less than 40,000 shares in order to get the position where it is. The Hirsch people are all very sick at having let the thing out of their grip.[62]

Hoover, then, had reason to be content with his forays into stock market management. The Kyshtim market was booming, an auspicious development for himself and other insiders. Beyond this the Kyshtim enterprise itself was maturing nicely, a development for which he could claim partial credit. For it was he who in late 1909 / early 1910 and again in late 1910 was instrumental in obtaining a total of £100,000 (through debentures) for the Kyshtim Corporation. At times, of course—indeed, most of the time—the procurement of such capital seemed almost incidental to his market maneuvers. Nevertheless, he had, in due course, raised the money essential to the enterprise's survival.

Until the great reorganization of late 1910 Hoover apparently took little direct interest in the engineering aspects of the Kyshtim venture. He was not yet on the Kyshtim board of directors. He wished, as he told Beatty, to be free to engage in market operations without encumbrance. Yet no man with such a financial stake in a company could be indifferent to its management, and from the inception of his financial involvement Hoover maneuvered to maximize his influence. As early as October 1909 he told Beatty that he wanted "to be sure of getting a good man for the construction of the smelter."[63] The man in whom he was interested, an American named Walter G. Perkins, was appointed and proved to be a success.[64] During the winter of 1909–1910 Hoover concentrated on tying up Kyshtim shares for the pool "before we bother them with the subject of management." But Hoover had definite ideas just the same:

My own view is that for our purposes it is much better that we should have a man like Gilman Brown here on the ground as Consulting Engineer as we can keep much closer tab on what is going on in the Company than we can through any organ in New York who only knows what they have got a mind to tell him.[65]

(The "organ in New York" was probably the American engineering firm of Knox & Allen, which had been consulting engineers to the Kyshtim Corporation since its inception.)

Hoover's desire soon came to partial fruition. Early in 1910 Brown, an American, became a member of the corporation's board of directors.[66] Brown soon proved a valuable source of information, corresponding with Beatty at length about personnel matters, the sinking of shafts, and other Kyshtim problems, although Beatty (like Hoover) was not on the board.[67] On his return from Russia in November 1910 Brown sent Beatty a seven-page letter describing what he had observed.[68] Such an ally was no doubt useful to Hoover as he planned his second pool. Three months later the firm of Knox & Allen (whom Brown had criticized) was dismissed, and Brown replaced them as consulting engineer. Perkins became consulting metallurgist.[69] Now, more than ever, Hoover could hope to know what was really happening at Kyshtim and, through Brown, to influence policy.

In the aftermath of the debenture issue of late 1910 / early 1911, Hoover's behind-the-scenes influence on Kyshtim was—apparently for the first time—publicly recognized. In mid-1911 T. A. Rickard's *Mining Magazine* observed that Hoover and Beatty now held "a large interest" in the Kyshtim Corporation and had "recently assisted the company financially to enable the erection of a smelter."[70] A few years later Rickard's journal asserted that it had been necessary in 1910 "to completely reorganize the original British company" and that Hoover "at this critical juncture" had "lent his aid." The magazine stated that three men were responsible for the subsequent remodeling of Kyshtim's metallurgical plant, the exploration of its ore bodies, the increase of mining operations, and the supply of sufficient working capital: Hoover, Brown, and Perkins.

The *Mining Magazine*'s claims were probably correct. The provision of essential new capital—for which Hoover was perhaps primarily responsible—permitted the Kyshtim company's mining and metallurgical operations to expand. And the ouster of Knox & Allen in favor of Brown and Perkins may well have been at Hoover's instigation. As a supplier of capital, Hoover undoubtedly carried clout and may have been able to influence the selection of personnel. In these ways, though not even a member of the Kyshtim board of directors, Hoover helped to shape the company's development.[71]

Certainly the augmentation of his influence over Kyshtim was much on Hoover's mind. When Beatty, late in 1910, considered taking a trip to the site, Hoover, ever the shrewd businessman, urged him to exploit this possibility to advantage. Beatty's visit, said Hoover, "ought to be made a lever to get some beneficial position, either out of the Company itself" or out of another company deeply interested in Kyshtim.[72]

In business, including the Kyshtim business, a man had to be sharp, vigilant, aware of all the angles. When Beatty proposed that the Kyshtim Corporation publish monthly profit statements, Hoover and Brown objected. The reason was that the company's Russian subsidiary—to which the British-registered company loaned money—was subject to a stiff Russian income tax. The Kyshtim Corporation therefore desired the account books to show its subsidiary a heavy debtor, thus enabling it to escape the tax. Apparently for this reason, the company charged its subsidiary extremely high interest rates on its loans. According to one of Hoover's associates, it was deemed essential to keep the Russian government ignorant of the subsidiary's real earnings for as long as possible. Hence the company planned to publish only gross monthly earnings statements, not (as Beatty evidently wanted) net profit statements.[73] Too much detail might disclose too much.

Late in 1911 Hoover and Beatty traveled via St. Petersburg to Kyshtim. It was not Hoover's first trip to Russia; he had crossed it by rail on his way to and from Korea in 1909.[74] It was, however, his first visit to Kyshtim, far to the southeast of Moscow in the mountain range that divides European from Asiatic Russia. Hoover's stay was brief. Leaving England with Beatty on September 6, he and his travel partner returned on September 25.[75] But during their week or two on the Kyshtim property[76] the two experienced engineers observed much and liked what they observed. The known ore reserves of the estates were substantial—over 1,800,000 long tons containing an estimated profit of well over $10,000,000.[77] At Karabash Lake the great new smelter—American-designed, American-supervised[78]—was in full operation. By the end of 1911 the Kyshtim property was the largest producer of copper in Russia.[79]

The scope of Kyshtim's operations was impressive. In addition to turning out over 5,000 tons of blister copper in 1911, the estate's various enterprises produced thousands of tons of finished iron and pyrites, as well as large quantities of timber.[80] Hoover, noting the complex social structure, was fascinated: at the bottom of the pyramid were peasants and workers, at the top a humane and progressive nobleman named Baron Vladimir Meller-Zakomelsky, an original director of the Kyshtim Corporation striving to improve his countrymen's lot.[81] Under the direction of Leslie Urquhart, supported by British capital and assisted by Brown, Perkins, and other American experts, a technological transformation was occurring at Kyshtim. A pyritic smelter, a railway, an electrolytic refinery: here out of a semi-feudal Russian environment was arising one of the most modern copper-mining industries in the world. Hoover noticed, too, the "hideous" tensions beneath the surface. At a rail station he saw a chain gang of prisoners headed for Siberia; the horror of that scene gave him nightmares. Throughout his visit he sensed that "some day the country would blow up."[82]

Back in London in late 1911 Hoover became involved in new negotiations to refinance the Kyshtim Corporation by yet another debenture issue. This time he was less successful: his terms were underbid, and he was reduced to taking a portion of someone else's underwriting scheme.[83] In January 1912 a gigantic new debenture issue of £250,000 was floated in order to raise money to clear off various inconvenient debts owed by the Russian subsidiary.[84] Hoover seems to have underwritten only £25,000 of this issue.[85]

Nevertheless, on January 5, 1912 Hoover became at last a director of the Kyshtim Corporation.[86] A month later, after considerable internal dispute, the Intercontinental Trust voted to liquidate, and the Kyshtim Pool dissolved.[87] The Intercontinental Trust had proved to be a very profitable venture for Hoover and Beatty, as Beatty acknowledged.[88] On dissolution of the Trust, he received nearly $100,000 in cash.[89] Hoover probably received a similar amount. Still, Hoover was "glad to have done with the annoyance and worry of the business,"[90] since on his shoulders had fallen much of the burden of managing the pool. The ceaseless trading of shares and calls, the endless intricate negotiations amongst pool members with divergent interests, had made even him tired.

I I I

H o o v e r's formal election to the Kyshtim board in January 1912 marked a new departure for the engineer-financier. Not so much in his relation to Kyshtim itself: with its finances reorganized and its plant largely in place, the corporation was clearly nearing the dividend-bearing stage, Hoover or no Hoover. Hoover's official debut on the Kyshtim board signaled rather his emergence as a figure of importance in the broader field of Russian mining investment. Even as he became publicly identified with Kyshtim, his restless glance looked elsewhere.

Opportunity quickly arose. While directing operations on the scene at Kyshtim, Leslie Urquhart had been searching for new mines to float. Urquhart was now a popular man in Russian commercial circles. Hoover noted that "the [market] rise in Kyshtims has made Urquhart a lot of happy friends in St. Petersburg who are disposed to follow him without any question. . . ."[91] Early in 1912 or thereabouts Urquhart and some Russian friends organized the South Urals Mining and Smelting Company, a Russian-registered concern, which acquired a number of promising mining claims near Tanalyk, about two hundred miles south of Kyshtim.[92] With zeal and assurance Urquhart turned to London for money to finance this property.

Urquhart was an enthusiast;[93] he was also a man in a hurry. Hoover informed Beatty that Urquhart seemed to have money "pushed at him from all directions and he is not disposed to give us any time to examine the property or anything else. . . ." At the time of the Hoover / Beatty visit to Russia in 1911, when the Tanalyk proposition came up, Urquhart had suggested that Hoover and Beatty join a syndicate "fairly close to the ground floor," gain thereby a one-third interest in the property, and have control of floating a British company in due course. Now, however, in mid-March 1912, Urquhart had a new proposal. Its terms were fair, Hoover thought, except for one worrisome aspect: Urquhart wished to raise £60,000 immediately without any further investigation. Hoover thought Urquhart would offer him and Beatty a one-sixth share. "If we do not take it," Hoover reported, "he says he can do the business without us, and I have no doubt that he will be able to do so."

What course, then, to adopt? Hoover had reservations:

> I do not like going into a business absolutely blindfold, under any circumstances, and, further, I do not like the fact that instead of the business being in our hands to finance, thus securing us an interest by virtue of doing the finance, the thing boils down now to purely taking a small speculation on Urquhart's representations.

Hoover did not "entirely blame" Urquhart; after all, Urquhart did have "a chance to raise the money without having any questions raised about his mine, and I presume the best thing for him to do is to take it." Hoover continued to wish to have Brown examine the mine. Urquhart did offer to buy out syndicate shares at cost for the next three or four months—"which," said Hoover, "is about all the assurance that a London speculator requires."

So Hoover was prepared to go ahead.

> If he will not give us time to examine the property I am still inclined to gamble £5000 for myself, because I feel perfectly sure that in taking in the

whole market crowd of Kyshtim people he will have the market running in these shares very quickly so that we can sell half the holding and stand on velvet with the balance. In other words, this is simply a short speculation with early market relief.[94]

A few days later Urquhart offered Hoover and Beatty the chance to contribute £9,000 to the syndicate being formed. The venture was "highly speculative," Hoover conceded, but "from [a] market point of view very promising."[95] Hoover and Beatty joined, although their allotment was reduced to £7,500 to allow Hoover's old friend Deane P. Mitchell and some others to participate.[96]

On April 3, 1912 the Inter-Russian Syndicate was formed with an authorized capital of £50,000; the Hoover / Beatty interest was thus fifteen percent. Hoover and Urquhart were among the four directors.[97] Twelve days later the British-registered Tanalyk Corporation was created with a share capital of £300,000 in 300,000 shares and with Urquhart as chairman. The corporation promptly purchased all the share capital of Urquhart's South Urals Mining and Smelting Company for 190,000 free Tanalyk shares. Of these, 160,000 went to various vendors, presumably Urquhart and his associates who had created the South Urals company in the first place. Another 30,000 went to the Inter-Russian Syndicate "for fixing up the matter." The remaining 110,000 Tanalyk shares were sold for £110,000 cash, thus creating a fund of capital that the British-registered company could now loan to its Russian subsidiary.[98]

In this way the Tanalyk Corporation acquired control over more than 9,500 acres of land in Russia containing valuable deposits of copper, manganese, and other minerals. The company also gained the right to cut timber in 3,000 acres of forest.[99] Over the next several months it obtained new assets, including exclusive prospecting rights over 3,000 square miles.[100] During 1912 and 1913 development of the Tanalyk properties and construction of a large copper smelter proceeded steadily.[101]

As in the case of Kyshtim, Hoover did not become a director of the Tanalyk Corporation at first. Perhaps he was not asked; perhaps he preferred to remain in the background. But his friend Brown was on the board and was a consulting engineer to the South Urals subsidiary as well.[102] Through Brown, who took an active interest in the technical work, Hoover was no doubt able, if he desired, to keep abreast of developments at the mines. But there is little evidence that during the first eighteen months after the flotation Hoover had or sought much influence on company policy. He seemed content to leave technical engineering problems to others whom he trusted.

Instead, as also with Kyshtim in its early stages, Hoover became involved in Tanalyk finance. Evidently abandoning his original intention of embarking on "a short speculation with early market relief," Hoover participated in a pool of Tanalyk shares.[103] The pool was apparently a splendid success; in

September 1912 Tanalyk stock, issued at £1, shot up to nearly £4 a share.[104] A few months later one of Beatty's assistants noted that the Inter-Russian Syndicate business had proven to be very profitable.[105] Early in 1913 Hoover spoke of liquidating the syndicate "fairly quickly," but the market did not cooperate.[106] "It is necessary to reorganize the pool" in Tanalyk, Hoover declared a month later, "so as to continue the position until after there is a recovery in the markets. . . . " The property, he added, was "developing very well.[107]

So well, in fact, that in the autumn of 1913 the Tanalyk Corporation increased its capital and issued £200,000 in debentures in order, among other things, to double the size of its smelter.[108] The Inter-Russian Syndicate guaranteed this debenture issue for a five percent cash commission and a call on 50,000 Tanalyk shares for about three years.[109] Thus fortified with fresh working capital, Tanalyk could look forward to fulfilling its promise.

Just how much Hoover contributed to this arrangement the record does not reveal. But it was in all probability an influential role. Hoover was, after all, a director of the underwriting Inter-Russian Syndicate. It was surely no coincidence that the new debenture issue of late 1913 coincided with Hoover's election to the Tanalyk board.[110] With the mine refinanced and on its way, Hoover emerged to take a share of the administrative responsibility.

Not all of Urquhart's schemes turned out so satisfactorily. In 1912 the energetic Scot unsuccessfully tried (in Hoover's words) "to rush us into" a gold-mining proposition "without an examination." Early in 1913 Hoover reported to Beatty that the mine was a "dead failure" and that Urquhart had lost £35,000. "He is therefore," Hoover added drily, "a much tamer individual to deal with than he was."[111]

Relations between the two men were not always placid. Late in 1913 they quarreled over some matter, only to work out some kind of a truce.[112] There was a temperamental gulf between Hoover—blunt, laconic, aggressive—and Urquhart—ebullient, optimistic, perhaps a bit visionary.[113]

Yet as 1912 yielded to 1913, and 1913 to 1914, Hoover found himself in increasing association with Leslie Urquhart. In April 1912, only three days before the Tanalyk Corporation was registered, the indefatigable Urquhart launched the Russo-Asiatic Corporation, with himself as managing director and Hoover on the board.[114] Hoover apparently assisted substantially in the launch.[115] But he was careful, taking (at least in his own name) only 250 Russo-Asiatic Corporation shares, the minimum number needed to qualify as a director.[116] And he told Beatty:

> I am taking no personal participation in this Russian [Russo-Asiatic] busi-
> ness, simply because we can always get it after the things have been exam-
> ined and more development work done, and it is best for you and I to go
> in on the second floor than on the first in this kind of business. I am there-
> fore anxious for Kuehn to go out and do the first-floor work so that we
> may know exactly where we are.[117]

Unlike Kyshtim and Tanalyk, the new enterprise had no mines in hand awaiting only foreign capital and equipment. The Russo-Asiatic Corporation, rather, was "an investment and exploration company" whose sphere of operations was to be Russia.[118] Its purpose was to acquire mining properties, prove their value, develop them, and eventually float them as separate companies. Among Hoover's kaleidoscopic array of mining interests, it was the equivalent, for Russia, of the Lake View and Oroya Exploration Company.

Capitalized at £300,000, the Russo-Asiatic Corporation surged at once into high gear. From its inception the company was swamped with offers;[119] one problem was to sort them out. During 1912 and especially 1913 the company's leading mining engineers—many of them American friends of Hoover— examined and evaluated prospects in the field. Early in 1913 Hoover arranged for his associate Amor F. Kuehn to visit Russia at corporation expense.[120] During 1913 Deane P. Mitchell, no longer with Bewick, Moreing, spent six months investigating vast mining properties in Siberia.[121] R. Gilman Brown, a member of the board of directors, actively lent his assistance, while still another American engineer and Hoover acquaintance, T. J. Jones, then stationed at Kyshtim, contributed to the investigation.[122]

When Beatty learned that Hoover was dispatching Kuehn to Russia, he approved. Beatty liked the idea of having engineers whom Hoover trusted examine propositions that he and Hoover might like to take up at a later time.[123] But Hoover did not leave everything to scouts and subordinates in the field. In October 1913 he himself journeyed to Kyshtim for the second time.[124] During his two-week trip he did not go on to Tanalyk or to the properties under option farther east.[125] But he did prepare a lengthy memorandum of recommendations for future policy for his fellow Kyshtim board members.[126] It was one of the clearest indications yet of his growing interest in Russian mining.

At an overflow meeting of Russo-Asiatic Corporation shareholders in January 1914, the company chairman announced the results of nearly two years of intense probing of Russia's mineral potential. The corporation had acquired three extraordinary mining concessions in Siberia. The first, the Nerchinsk, comprised 8,000 square miles (an area nearly the size of Massachusetts), on which many abandoned silver-lead-zinc mines were located. The corporation received the exclusive right to select areas for mining in this district for five years and the right to work any mines thus chosen for seventy-five years, subject only to royalty payable to the Russian government.

The second concession, the Ridder, encompassed 3,000 square miles in the southern Altai Mountains, far to the southeast of Omsk and not too distant from the Mongolian border. Here the Russo-Asiatic Corporation obtained exclusive exploration rights for ten years and a lease for seventy-five years of mines selected for development. On this concession stood an alluring zinc-silver-lead deposit with rich admixtures of copper and gold. This deposit, the Ridder mine, had been worked by the Russians from 1778 to 1901, when the oxidized ores gave out and only complex sulphide ores remained. The

metallurgical character of the ore bodies resembled in some respects those at
Broken Hill in Australia. No wonder Mitchell, former manager of the Zinc
Corporation, spent so much of 1913 on the Ridder grounds.

The third concession was the Ekibastus coal region, a rich basin eight
miles long and nearly three miles wide, nearly four hundred miles northwest
of the Ridder property.[127]

The political implications of the Russo-Asiatic Corporation's announcement were plain. For the Nerchinsk and Ridder properties were so-called
Cabinet lands, the personal property of the czar;[128] the winning of such generous concessions directly from Czar Nicholas II augured well for the corporation's future. It reflected the prestige of Urquhart at the Russian court
and, no doubt, imperial pleasure at the industrial transformation of Kyshtim.[129]

The way to prosperity was not to be easy, however. The principal mine
on the Nerchinsk concession was 160 miles from the Trans-Siberian Railway. The Ridder mine was sixty miles east of the Irtish River, which provided transport to Omsk (when not frozen). Similarly, the Ekibastus coal
field was nearly seventy-five miles from the Irtish. It would therefore be
necessary to construct railroad lines linking the mines with the river. The
corporation proposed to concentrate in 1914 on developing the Ridder
concession—on drilling, delineating the ore body, transporting an experimental plant up the river and then erecting it, conducting tests in preparation
for processing the ore: all this and more preparatory labor. The chairman
warned that one, two, perhaps three years of hard effort and heavy expenditure would occur before profits came.[130]

Just before and after the Russo-Asiatic meeting, Hoover's role in Russian
mining seemed to be increasingly recognized. In some organs of the mining
press the names of Hoover and Urquhart were linked as virtual co-venturers
in Russian operations. A correspondent for the *Mining and Scientific Press* of
San Francisco praised this "combination," to which Urquhart brought an
"intimate knowledge" of Russia and its business methods, while Hoover
brought "an unusual amount of financial and technological acumen."

> These two gentlemen have made a great success of the Kyshtim copper
> property and are now doing the same thing for the Tanalyk. . . . They
> have done so much better than most of the English companies operating
> in Russia that St. Petersburg financiers have been keen to gain their assist-
> ance in connection with other properties. They therefore formed the Russo-
> Asiatic Corporation, 18 months ago, . . . and have since had a great num-
> ber of properties examined.[131]

Rickard's *Mining Magazine* asserted that the Russo-Asiatic Corporation was
"controlled by" Hoover and Urquhart, although in the next issue it added
that while the corporation was "commonly identified" with these two men

"on account of their prominence in Russian enterprises," the administration, of course, was "in the hands of the directors as a whole."[132]

Whatever the precise division of responsibility and influence, there was no doubt that the Russo-Asiatic Corporation's leadership was exceptionally able.[133] As the company's assets became known, the stock market reacted fervently. Between Christmas 1913 and mid-January 1914 the company's stock shot from £2¾ to £4½ per share.[134] Issued at £1, the shares climbed at one point in 1914 to an incredible £9⁷/₁₆.[135] A. Chester Beatty, not a man to lose his composure, told Hoover in late January that they should make every exertion to climb on board the Russo-Asiatic business if they could.[136]

By the summer of 1914 Urquhart's cluster of Russian enterprises was thriving. At Kyshtim a nearly moribund, financially encumbered property had become a diversified, prosperous venture. In 1913 the Kyshtim smelters and refinery turned out nearly 8,000 long tons of copper; Kyshtim was now the second largest copper producer in all Europe.[137] In December 1912 the Kyshtim Corporation distributed its first dividend (5%), followed by a 17½% dividend only seven months later.[138] The corporation's ore reserves by April 1914 comprised 2,400,000 tons of ore; one of its recently discovered mines, the Amerikansky, reflected in its name the American influence at work.[139] The Kyshtim estates, with a population of about 90,000 people, were becoming a model of progressive industrial development.[140]

Tanalyk, too, was progressing. In the spring of 1914 its new smelter began operations and the company entered the "producing stage."[141] And to the east, in Siberia, the Russo-Asiatic Corporation prepared to float its first subsidiary. During the summer the company's American engineers—Mitchell, Brown, and T. J. Jones—visited the Ridder mines and supervised the erection of a concentrating mill.[142] In probable anticipation of the flotation to come, Hoover helped to form an entity called the Inter-Siberian Syndicate in London in June 1914 "to carry on the business of financiers and explorers and to deal with mining properties." The syndicate commanded a nominal capital of £500,000 in £1 shares; Hoover, with 20,000 shares, became one of the four directors.[143]

Late in 1914 the Irtysh Corporation was created to acquire control of the Ekibastus coal property and the remarkable Ridder concession. The new company was capitalized at £2,000,000 in £1 shares, of which the Russo-Asiatic Corporation, as vendor of the properties, took a controlling share. The new company quickly raised £500,000 for working capital by the usual method, a debenture issue. Urquhart, not surprisingly, became chairman; Hoover, Mitchell, and Brown, among others, became directors. Still another American, H. H. Knox (of Knox & Allen), became consulting engineer.[144]

The company's enormous capitalization mirrored the hopes of its sponsors. The chairman of Russo-Asiatic called the Ridder "a mine of almost surpassing wealth in many minerals,"[145] and truly its promise was stunning. After inspecting the mine in 1914 Knox reported an assured profit in sight of

£7,400,000.[146] Years later Hoover called it "probably the greatest and richest body of ore known in the world."[147]

As yet, though, it was only a potential bonanza. Of Hoover's multiplying Russian mining interests as of August 1914, only Kyshtim had paid any dividends.

I V

B Y mid-1914 Kyshtim, Tanalyk, and the Russo-Asiatic concessions comprised a far-flung mining empire of unusual dimensions. How much was Hoover responsible for its creation and, more importantly, its growth? It was a question that was later controversial.

Clearly Hoover was not the catalyst of these enterprises. From the founding of the Anglo-Siberian Company in 1906 to the floating of the Irtysh Corporation in 1914, the dominant figure appears to have been Leslie Urquhart. Without his initiative, his optimism, his financial following and connections in St. Petersburg, the great industrial edifice at Kyshtim and its sister properties probably would not have been built for years to come.

Yet Urquhart did not create Kyshtim and the other ventures alone. Without the successful Kyshtim debenture issues that Hoover helped to arrange in 1909 / 1910 and 1910 / 1911, the young company might never have gone on. One mining journal later mentioned Hoover's assistance at this "critical juncture"; another even asserted that Hoover had "saved" the company financially.[148] Hoover himself later cited reorganizing the finances as one of his achievements at Kyshtim.[149] While Hoover's personal cash contribution to this endeavor may not have been large, his ability to line up the capital of others was very useful to the company. His prestige as an engineer undoubtedly helped to open wallets; financiers like Govett trusted his judgment.

In later years Hoover tended to portray himself as simply a disinterested engineer or "industrial doctor" who dispensed technical advice to companies in need.[150] In the case of his Russian enterprises, his role was more complicated than that. At Kyshtim, for instance, before he was an industrial doctor he was a *financial* doctor and something of a stock market operator as well. Before 1912 (when he joined the Kyshtim board) there is little evidence that he was personally responsible for the introduction of pyritic smelting or other crucial technical developments which specialists like Perkins and Brown oversaw on the spot.[151]

As time went on, particularly after 1912, Hoover did show interest in the engineering aspects of the Urquhart group of enterprises. In 1912 he joined two boards of directors; in 1914, two more. It is unlikely that he was merely a passive fee-collector; that was not Hoover's way in business. In 1913, at least, he actively strove to influence the Kyshtim company's technical program following his second visit to the Urals.

Without the assistance of minute books of board meetings, it is impossible to tell how much Hoover actually guided operations or set fundamental corporate policy. But one fact is suggestive. A remarkable number of the senior engineers, metallurgists, and technical advisers of Urquhart's Russian mines were Americans, a fact noted at times in the press.[152] While the interest of Knox and Brown in Russia antedated Hoover's, that of some others—including Mitchell, Perkins, Kuehn, and Jones—did not. At least some of these experts owed their Russian assignments to Hoover, who thereby, through well-selected subordinates, left an impress on mines that in some cases he never visited.[153]

Still, at Tanalyk, Irtysh, and the Russo-Asiatic, as at Kyshtim before them, Hoover's fundamental achievement was not technical. In the summer of 1914 he addressed a long letter to Urquhart describing the activities of the Inter-Siberian Syndicate he had just formed. Its purpose, Hoover said, was to put "the Russo-Asiatic market on a stronger footing" and to prepare the way for the flotation of the Ridder concession as a subsidiary company in a few months. Hoover's letter was filled, as so many of his letters were filled, with discussion of share issues, convertible debentures, stock market management, and "market defence."[154] In this realm—the channeling of capital into distant enterprises—lay Hoover's principal contribution to Urquhart's Russian mining ventures before the First World War. Day-to-day engineering in the field seemed of much less concern to Hoover than financial operations in London. At such operations he had become a masterful practitioner.

Hoover's impact on Russian mining was probably not as profound as his influence at Bawdwin in Burma. But the rising public perception of him in 1914 as a major figure in the Kyshtim, Tanalyk, and Russo-Asiatic enterprises was not inaccurate either. It bespoke a quiet, considerable influence that stockholding lists alone did not measure.[155]

V

B y the summer of 1914 Hoover's Russian mining enterprises were in sight of spectacular success. In some ways his personal stake in these concerns seemed small. Many years later he described his "personal holdings in all Russian enterprises" before the Russian Revolution as "minor."[156] Indeed, his listed shareholdings in Kyshtim, Tanalyk, and Russo-Asiatic—at least the shareholdings listed in his own name—were almost negligible.[157] In 1932, when Hoover's pre-1917 involvement in Russian mining became a source of public controversy, Leslie Urquhart asserted that Hoover's total shareholdings in his Russian concerns never at their highest market valuation exceeded £12,000.[158] Urquhart did not mention Hoover's £20,000 shareholding in the Inter-Siberian Syndicate—an investment of $100,000 in pre-war currency.[159]

Yet such data did not tell the entire story. While Hoover's financial involvement in Russian mines as such—as expressed in his 1914 shareholdings—was relatively small, his *potential* reward from them was immense. For when the Irtysh Corporation was floated in 1914 Hoover apparently helped to underwrite a large issue of Irtysh debentures. In return for participating in (or arranging) this guarantee, he evidently obtained an option to purchase at par a sizable block of Irtysh shares.[160] Some years later he wrote that his "deferred interest in the Irtysh" had been worth a minimum of $15,000,000 "on the proved profits of the mine—ex war."[161]

By 1914, then, Hoover stood eventually to obtain what he later described as "a large fortune from these [Russian] industries—probably more than is good for anybody."[162] As yet, of course, such remuneration was only a bird in the bush. For his stock options to be worth exercising, the far-off mines must develop and fulfill their promise. And for this, peace and industrial stability were essential.

It was not to be. But in the early summer of 1914, as Hoover and his associates prepared to float the Irtysh, few if any could foresee the coming debacle. Instead, as the enterprises he helped to guide in the Urals and Siberia evolved toward hard-earned prosperity, Hoover could reasonably look forward to obtaining from them what he later called "the largest engineering fees ever known to man."[163]

2 2

The Oilman

I

I N the foothills of the Caucasus Mountains in southern Russia, about fifty miles inland from the port of Tuapse on the Black Sea, lies the community of Maikop. Today a city of more than 110,000, in 1909 it was little more than a primitive village in a remote, bandit-ridden district where the czar's Cossacks enforced a harsh brand of law and order.[1]

Late in the nineteenth century a number of Russian entrepreneurs became interested in the region around Maikop as a potential source of petroleum. They noticed the little oil wells dug by hand by the Cossacks, they studied the geology of the area, and some of them began operations on a small scale. But little had really been accomplished until September 12, 1909. On that day a Russian company was boring for oil when suddenly, unexpectedly, at only 281 feet down, the drillers struck a gusher. The surprised company had no storage facilities; no one had expected to find so much oil so close to the surface. Over 50,000 tons of "black gold" were lost before the well was capped.[2]

The discovery of an oil field near Maikop created a worldwide sensation among those who searched for treasure in the earth.[3] The timing of this event could hardly have been more opportune. Not only was world demand for petroleum products—and hence their price—rising; the British Admiralty was beginning to switch from coal to oil as fuel for its fleet.[4] In London, mining firms that traditionally had shunned oil enterprises were becoming

447

interested as news of strikes in Mexico, Trinidad, and Persia swept through the financial capital of the world.[5] And now Maikop. Oil only 281 feet down! Oil only fifty miles from the sea! In London some men saw in that gusher the harbinger of a bonanza.[6]

One of the first to notice Maikop's promise was Herbert Hoover. Hoover's oil ventures arose from his deepening collaboration in 1909 with an American civil engineer named Lindon Wallace Bates. Sixteen years Hoover's senior, Bates by 1909 was an internationally acclaimed expert on harbor construction and the dredging of waterways.[7] Bates had known Hoover for some years,[8] and when Hoover severed his partnership in Bewick, Moreing in 1908, he moved into and shared Bates's office in London. According to Moreing, Bates and Hoover held each other's powers of attorney.[9]

During 1909 Bates turned increasingly to the business of oil exploration and development.[10] Although never (so far as is known) Bates's formal partner, Hoover scarcely could help being familiar with his friend's interests. No doubt Hoover heard about it when, around September, Bates was offered an option to purchase thirty-two plots of land on the Maikop oil field. It was not long afterward that Hoover himself plunged into the Russian oil business with vigor.

By mid-December 1909 Hoover was immersed in several nascent Maikop ventures. "I have practically settled an option on some 800 acres of ground surrounding" the spectacular gusher of September 12, he informed A. Chester Beatty. "I am a member of two other Maikop Syndicates," he added. "If you would like to have a dash at this business on the ground-floor with me you might let me know by wire."[11] Beatty did.[12]

Throughout the winter of 1909–1910 Hoover concentrated on the necessary preliminaries to exploitation of the Maikop oil region. The negotiating of options on the property from Russian vendors;[13] the organizing of British companies to exercise these options; the rounding up of money, equipment, and expertise to develop the plots of land thus acquired; the preparations for road building and pipeline construction: all were tasks that were antecedent to drilling a hole in the ground. Although, as Hoover recognized, it was Lindon Bates who had actually "initiated the Maikop business,"[14] Bates himself was absent from London on a trip to Japan from early autumn 1909 until late February 1910.[15] It was really Hoover who supervised preparations during this period for a "spring offensive" in the Caucasus.

Hoover was not alone in sensing the field's potential. One of the earliest to form a Maikop syndicate was Hoover's ex-partner, C. Algernon Moreing.[16] By late winter general interest in the oil field seemed to be rising. Hoover told Beatty that he and Bates "have considerable Maikop business in hand, and Bates leaves this week for Russia to negotiate further matters."[17]

The time to go public was at hand.

On February 22, 1910 Hoover's first creation—the Maikop and General Petroleum Trust—was born. Hoover and Bates joined the board of directors.[18] The new company was essentially a holding company, a middleman, which purchased Russian oil properties for resale to British-registered concerns. Over the next few months the Trust floated and promoted no fewer than six subsidiaries, in which it took a large share interest.[19] On one of these operating subsidiaries Hoover took a seat as a director.[20]

The Maikop and General Petroleum Trust's profit on its flotations was immense, at least on paper: a total profit of 300,000 £1 shares that it held in four of its subsidiaries, plus calls on various blocks of shares at par.[21] Realization of such a profit, however, depended both on the prosperity of the parent Trust's offspring and on a favorable stock market in these shares. If the subsidiaries failed to produce, or if the market quotation of the shares plummeted, little profit would accrue to the vendor / promoters.

As with his Russian mining enterprises, Hoover's direct shareholding in his cluster of Maikop companies was slight—only enough to qualify as a director in two instances.[22] But as usual, such statistics did not reflect his true financial interest. When the Maikop and General Petroleum Trust was organized, Hoover's financial arrangements left him and Beatty with options to purchase 12,500 ordinary Trust shares and 500 deferred shares—and no money of their own actually invested.[23] Only six weeks later Hoover estimated that these shares could be sold "to nett a little over £10,000"—about $50,000.[24] It was another illustration of Hoover's favorite method of making money: get in on the ground floor, take a block of free stock or stock options as remuneration for one's organizational or underwriting services, exercise the options (that is, purchase the stock) at a favorable price, and then—when the market was high—sell out.

The formation of the Maikop and General Petroleum Trust in February 1910 was but the beginning of a stampede. By mid-summer more than fifty Maikop companies had been floated on the London stock market. Their nominal capital stood at about £12,000,000; British investors, in other words, had committed $60,000,000 to the largely untested field.[25] The great Maikop oil boom was on.

Hoover's name was prominently identified with the Maikop oil flotations.[26] Many years later a British petroleum engineer who was closely associated with him at the time recalled that Hoover's "impulsive entry into London oilfield finance unquestionably precipitated action by mining groups which had previously done no more than flirt with petroleum ventures."

> He was one of the first mining engineers to recognize realistically the portents, and it was through his influence that a mining group with which he was on friendly terms stepped in and acquired a number of Maikop concessions before the rush of lease seekers caused values to sky-rocket.[27]

By the spring of 1910, with new Maikop enterprises sprouting in London almost daily, optimism about the discovery seemed unrestrained. Moreing declared that Maikop would be "one of the most important oil areas in the world."[28] A leading British financial journal opined that the opening up of the Maikop field would "probably prove to be the most important event in the history of the oil industry."[29] The chairman of Hoover's Trust company said that Maikop was "destined to be one of the great oil-producing fields of the world."[30] Most convincingly of all, the respected engineering firm of Thompson & Hunter, a firm with substantial experience in the Maikop region, gave its imprimatur to the district. Hunter declared his "utmost confidence" in the development of the field.[31]

Now, though, came the hard part. Despite its proximity to the Black Sea, the Maikop area was not a specimen of the amenities of civilization. Except for one military road to the coast, the area in 1909 was virtually a trackless forest. Brigandage was a constant threat, not to mention bureaucratic regulations and the various forms of extortion practiced by government and populace alike. On the multiplying British-registered oil companies fell the considerable burden of building roads, pipelines, storage facilities, machine shops, offices, hospitals, and staff housing—all in an inhospitable environment. Telephone and telegraph lines must be installed where none had existed; modern drilling equipment must be imported and assembled.[32]

From the start Hoover took considerable interest in the Maikop undertaking. In August he cabled an old friend and petroleum geologist, Ralph Arnold, for advice. What oil company manager could Arnold recommend in California to "take charge large group of developing properties South Russia?" he asked. Hoover's standards, as always, were high: he wanted a man who combined "technical commercial and executive" ability.[33] A man, in short, like himself.

Hoover had good reason to insist on securing the best individual. For by August 1910 he detected portents of trouble in the Caucasus. He disclosed to Arnold that he had "considerable interests" in the Maikop oil field and was disturbed by recent news about its geological character. He asked Arnold to report on the area.[34]

When Arnold replied that he was too busy to do so,[35] his unavailability hardly allayed Hoover's anxieties. In September Hoover told his California friend that the London oil market had become depressed:

There was a period here last winter when one could have sold an ink-bottle for half a million pounds if it was filled with oil and reported on by any old greasy driller; in fact, there were a lot of less valuable things sold. Just at the present moment I do not believe you could place a concern that was earning 30% dividends, guaranteed for twenty years.[36]

Still, the slow transformation of Maikop was proceeding. Hoover's brother Theodore, himself a director of three Maikop companies in the Hoover-Bates group, visited the field personally in 1911.[37] Despite the retarding effects of the worst winter in half a century in 1910–11, Theodore was optimistic. In April 1911 he predicted that the Maikop region's oil production would be substantial.[38] In July he judged the field's prospects to be "good in view of only eighteen months development," although, he now cautioned, investors would have to "curb their impatience for results."[39]

Herbert, too, seemed encouraged as 1911 began. In February he disclosed that the Oroya Exploration Company, which he chaired, held about £15,500 worth of assets in two syndicates having property in the Maikop district. Hoover informed the Oroya shareholders that recent developments at nearby properties on the Maikop field had been so important that "I cannot see why we should not make a handsome profit on this investment."[40]

Despite such expressions of confidence, developments at Maikop did not go well in 1911. It was a familiar story. The exuberance of the initial flotations, the self-assurance of early 1910, slowly gave way to disappointed hopes and unforeseen expenditures. In July 1911 Theodore Hoover conceded that "drilling results" at Maikop during the first half of the year had been "inconclusive."[41] In July also the Maikop and General Petroleum Trust reported that market conditions for more than a year had been "unfavourable to the realization of shares."[42] The Maikop oil boom had collapsed.

In August came more unwelcome news: one of the Trust's subsidiaries was being obliged to seek more working capital by a debenture issue.[43] More capital needed—it was another familiar story. Late in the year Hoover confided gloomily to Beatty, "The appearance at Maikop is not quite as desperate as it was, but it is about as bad as it can be."[44]

What was wrong? Despite the real progress being made at Maikop—the pipelines, the housing, the intensive exploration campaign—it was becoming apparent that the vaunted oil field was a very uncertain proposition. True, the district had oil in pools near the surface. The entire field, in fact, actually produced 125,000 long tons of oil in 1911 and a little more than this in 1912.[45] But deeper down the drilling was failing to locate oil. Disconcerted and perplexed, various companies decided to pool their boring operations and test the field at depth.[46]

By the beginning of 1912 most of the working capital raised for the Maikop enterprises had been lost; the field's seeming promise was nowhere near fulfillment.[47] As the realization grew that Maikop was no risk-free bonanza, a protracted, painful process of retrenchment set in. The group of companies with which Hoover was affiliated did not escape. First to fold was the Maikop Oil and Petroleum Producers, on whose board Hoover sat. Its efforts to raise additional capital through debentures in 1911 had ended in failure. Early in 1912 it leased its properties to a new company, the Maikop New Producers; late in 1912 it wound up and merged with its successor.[48] One by one in 1911–12 the various offspring of the Maikop and General Petroleum Trust suspended operations and waited for results of the deep-drilling work.[49] Hoover remained on the board of the parent Trust.[50] But by March 1912 he could see the handwriting on the wall. That month Bates disclosed to a friend that he and Hoover had largely liquidated their Maikop holdings.[51]

In the autumn of 1912 the Maikop and General Petroleum Trust and three of its subsidiaries merged into a new concern, the Maikop Combine.[52] At this point, and perhaps before, Hoover apparently severed his last links with the Maikop oil field. He did not join the Maikop Combine's board; neither did Bates, who was now in deep financial trouble.[53]

It was now plain that prospectors for oil in bulk at Maikop must drill down 2,000 feet or more.[54] Under the leadership of an energetic oil man named George Tweedy, the Maikop Combine strove to salvage something from the wreck. The amalgamated enterprise had some technical success; in 1915 it actually produced nearly 75,000 tons of oil.[55] But before it could ever yield a dividend, the Maikop Combine, along with other businesses on the field, fell victim to war and revolution. In 1920 the Soviet government of Russia seized the Combine's properties; no compensation was ever paid.[56]

It had been a sad and costly episode for British investors, who in the flush of the 1910 boom had subscribed over £13,000,000 (nominally, anyway) to Maikop companies.[57] The Maikop and General Petroleum Trust and its affiliates themselves had an authorized capital exceeding £2,600,000, although the actual working capital expended was much less.[58] None of them, of course, ever paid a dividend. All the money invested was lost.[59]

It is impossible to say how much, if anything, Hoover personally lost in the Maikop collapse. The scanty evidence available suggests that his direct cash stake in Maikop was small.[60] Moreover, the method of Hoover's involvement minimized his financial risk, for so far as is known he poured little money into Maikop on his own. Rather, in return for his services in the realm of corporate finance, he took fees in the form of calls on shares. If the shares went up he could happily exercise his options. But if the market was poor and the calls thus unattractive, what had he really lost? Only his time and effort and perhaps some minor out-of-pocket expense.

Years later certain of Hoover's enemies tried to depict his role in Maikop as that of an unscrupulous promoter and stock manipulator who by clever publicity had lured unwary investors into the Maikop quagmire.[61] Such a portrayal was exaggerated and false. To be sure, Hoover was a director of a company that engaged in numerous early Maikop promotions. It is also likely, as one of Hoover's friends later stated, that Hoover's plunge into Maikop helped to induce other mining men to do the same.[62] An engineer of Hoover's reputation, some men may have reasoned, surely knew the risks. If it was good enough for Hoover, it must be good enough for all. The Maikop and General Petroleum Trust was among the very first companies registered to exploit the Maikop field. Such boldness bespoke confidence, and confidence was contagious.

Yet Hoover by himself did not instigate the ultimately disastrous Maikop boom, nor did he try in any irresponsible way to exploit it. In the spring of

1910 faith in Maikop seemed universal in London, among experts and laymen alike. Hoover shared this excitement. Although evidently careful not to risk too much of his own capital at the start, he did nevertheless go in, and on the best available advice, including that of a well-known British engineering firm familiar with the district. Having confirmed the optimistic forecasts, this same firm became consulting engineers to most of the companies floated by Hoover and his fellow directors of the parent Trust. Hoover tried also to induce the petroleum geologist Arnold to inspect the field, while Theodore Hoover actually spent many weeks in Russia. Such were not the actions of a fly-by-night promoter. There is no reason to doubt the genuineness of Hoover's commitment to Maikop. Like everyone else, he believed.

Ironically, in the long run the experts were proven right: Maikop *did* have oil. In the years after the Russian Revolution the field belatedly blossomed into a major petroleum producer.[63] But then it was the Bolsheviks who benefited. Maikop justified its promise too late to reward the foreign investors who had been deceived by the 1909 gusher into thinking that oil and riches lay just a few hundred feet down.

Long before then, one suspects, Maikop had become an unpleasant memory for Herbert Hoover. In his *Memoirs*, Hoover never mentioned Maikop by name and alluded to it obliquely only once. In a passage dealing with Lindon Bates, Hoover conveyed the impression that he became interested in the Maikop region only in 1912, when the oil field "had given out" and when Bates's pipeline company was in trouble. Hoover portrayed himself simply as a friend who had stepped in to rescue Bates from bankruptcy.[64] Hoover's *Memoirs* contained no hint of his own intimate involvement in Maikop in 1909–1910 and his own continuing interest in the field until the painful reconstructions of 1912.[65] Perhaps he did not care to remember.

II

H o o v e r's ill-fated Maikop venture brought him trouble from another quarter: it precipitated a bitter quarrel with Moreing.

Ever since Hoover severed his ties with Bewick, Moreing and Company in mid-1908, relations with his former partners had been marred by friction over the restrictive covenant that Hoover had been obliged to accept in order to set aside his partnership deed. Less than a month after he left the firm, Hoover requested alterations in his dissolution agreement. Bewick, Moreing refused, whereupon (according to Moreing) Hoover began to cause trouble.

Under the severance agreement, Hoover was allowed to remain a director of eight mining companies on which he had previously served as the firm's representative. He also was permitted to retain for himself his director's fees from these companies, fees which heretofore had gone to the firm. Bewick, Moreing had acceded to this on Hoover's formal promise that he would endeavor as a director to assure Bewick, Moreing's employment as the manager of the said companies. In addition, Bewick, Moreing had the right under the dissolution agreement to compel Hoover to resign any of these directorates at its request.

When the firm declined to grant Hoover's desired modifications in mid-1908, Hoover (so it later alleged) became hostile, particularly at directors meetings of the Lancefield Gold Mining Company. On September 22, 1908, scarcely three months after his departure, Bewick, Moreing formally requested Hoover to resign as a director of the Lancefield and certain other companies.

Instead of complying, Hoover counterattacked. He invoked the aid of influential directors of numerous companies that engaged Bewick, Moreing's services as mine managers. Above all, Hoover turned to the man who chaired so many of these companies, Francis Govett. According to Moreing, Govett threatened to withdraw these businesses from Moreing's management unless the firm and Hoover settled their differences. Ultimately the disputants compromised: Hoover resigned from the Lancefield and certain other boards but stayed on others.[66]

The tension, having flared, did not subside. The public reason given for Hoover's departure from the firm, of course, was ill health brought on by overwork. In Moreing's eyes Hoover recovered with suspicious rapidity as he resumed his active pace, independent now of his old firm.[67] Meanwhile, according to the firm, Hoover's ally Govett continued to be unfriendly, and the firm (so it said) suffered petty irritations from companies with which Govett and Hoover were associated.[68] In early 1910 Hoover's successor at the firm, W. J. Loring, declared that he and his partners had felt for two years that Hoover would seek to harm their business, were it not for the restrictive covenant of 1908.[69]

Nevertheless, when news of the Maikop oil discovery broke in London in September 1909, relations between Hoover and Moreing were apparently satisfactory enough for Hoover to introduce to Moreing a friend with a Maikop oil proposition: Lindon Bates. According to Moreing, Bates came to him in September with options to purchase thirty-two plots of land in the Maikop area from certain vendors in Russia. Bates himself said he lacked the time and money to commit to the venture. Might not one of the companies Moreing's firm managed be interested in buying these options?

After studying the matter in London, Moreing decided to go ahead. He organized a small syndicate to investigate the Russian properties and supplied the money needed to acquire the options. Bates now left on an unrelated business trip to Japan, from which he did not return until the following February. Moreing, accompanied by an expert on the Maikop oil field, left speedily for Russia.

Later in the autumn Moreing returned to England convinced that the Maikop oil field was extraordinarily valuable. There was, however, a difficulty. It developed that the Russian vendors had originally owned sixty-four plots, not just the thirty-two offered to Moreing through Bates. And the thirty-two that the Russians still retained were alternate plots that neatly (and inconveniently) interspersed the thirty-two controlled by Moreing. Apparently unable to come to terms with the Russians over the blocks they cleverly had held back, Moreing turned to Hoover for assistance.

According to Moreing, he urged Hoover to try to get control of the thirty-two alternate plots. In addition, Moreing pressed a second scheme on his former partner. Recognizing the importance of constructing a pipeline to carry the oil away from Maikop, he sought Hoover's financial help in establishing a company for this purpose. Moreing was willing to let Hoover take all the profit from financing both the pipeline company and the concern formed to take over the thirty-two alternate blocks, on one condition: that he, Moreing, would have the management of the companies formed. As Moreing later told the story, Hoover concurred with his assessment of the Maikop business and at once opened negotiations with the Russian vendors.

Over the next several weeks Moreing's plans developed on two tracks. On one—acquisition of the alternate thirty-two blocks—the negotiations dragged on inconclusively. Hoover, too, was unable to settle with the Russians. Meanwhile, back at Maikop for a second visit in January 1910, Moreing concluded a deal with the Baku Black Sea Oil Company (a Russian enterprise) and another firm for the joint construction of two oil pipelines from Maikop. Moreing reserved a one-quarter interest in this business for Hoover.

Returning to London, Moreing again urged Hoover to conclude the thirty-two-plot negotiation, and again he offered his former partner a role in the pipeline scheme. He stressed that he sought only the management; Hoover could handle the finance. Hoover thereupon hired an intermediary to visit Russia. Still the negotiations were unresolved.

Then, said Moreing, a curious thing happened. The directors of the Baku Black Sea Oil Company arrived in London and told him that they had sold a controlling interest in their company to Hoover. Furthermore, they reported that Hoover had criticized the pipeline scheme that they already had negotiated with Moreing, and that Hoover had instructed them to pull out of it.

It was now mid-February 1910. For the third time in less than six months Moreing set off to Russia; Bates, meanwhile, was on his way back to England from Japan. On February 22, not long after Moreing left London, Bates arrived. On that very same day, the Maikop and General Petroleum Trust was registered, with Hoover and Bates among the directors. Moreing's firm was not appointed manager.

Before departing for the East, Moreing had informed Hoover that he would meet Bates in the Russian capital. He was confident that Bates could terminate the long-deadlocked controversy over the thirty-two alternate blocks. Bates now journeyed to St. Petersburg. Instead of contacting Moreing, however, Bates avoided him (said Moreing) and spurned the assistance Moreing had offered to give.

From Russian sources Moreing discovered what had happened. Bates had gone to Russia to negotiate acquisition of the thirty-two alternate blocks for the Maikop and General Petroleum Trust, newly formed without Moreing's firm as manager. Perhaps more irksome still to Moreing, Hoover and his allies had bought control of the Baku Black Sea Oil Company and then had sent Bates to negotiate for it to build a pipeline in competition with the very pipeline Moreing was preparing to construct. A few weeks later the parent Trust duly created the Maikop Oil and Petroleum Producers, Ltd., which then took over the Baku Black Sea Oil Company. The Trust also floated a separate Maikop pipeline company. Moreing was made manager of neither.

Upon returning to London, Moreing confronted his erstwhile partner. According to Moreing, Hoover denied any role in Bates's dealings in St. Petersburg. Instead, Hoover asserted that Bates was acting completely on his own, that Hoover could not control his behavior, and that Hoover in fact disapproved of it. It is unlikely that Moreing believed him.

In Moreing's telling, then, Hoover had reneged on his understandings and had squeezed Moreing out of business that Moreing himself had generated. This was Moreing's version;[70] it may well have been self-serving.[71] Hoover's version is unknown.

The long-simmering Hoover-Moreing relationship now came to a boil. Under the terms of his withdrawal from Moreing's firm in 1908, Hoover had promised not to practice the profession of a mining engineer anywhere in the British empire for ten years without the written permission of the firm. Moreover, Hoover had agreed not to act as a director of any mining company in the British empire without the prior consent of Bewick, Moreing. According to the 1908 agreement, such consent was conditional upon Hoover's first obtaining for Bewick, Moreing an appointment as manager of the mining companies for which he then became a director. Hoover had further agreed that if he transacted financial business relating to mining with companies operating in the British empire, he would obtain the firm's appointment as managers and engineers of the companies involved.[72]

Clearly worried about Hoover's ability to compete with him, Moreing had made the terms of Hoover's 1908 withdrawal tough, but, as he learned in 1910, not tough enough. Before Moreing left for Russia in late February 1910, Hoover asked him orally for permission to join the board of the Maikop and General Petroleum Trust, then in formation. Moreing replied: only if Hoover arranged for Bewick, Moreing to be engineers and managers of the Trust. According to Moreing, Hoover said there would be no problem in doing so.[73]

Shortly after Moreing left for Russia, however, Hoover apparently asked the firm again for permission to join the Maikop company board. In Moreing's absence T. W. Wellsted responded on February 23. Uncertain of the contents of Hoover's prior conversation with Moreing, Wellsted declared that the question must be kept in abeyance until Moreing's return.[74] Hoover's reply was immediate and sharp. He told Wellsted, ". . . you are entirely mistaken in apparently assuming that this business is one contemplated in the Dissolution Agreement." Wellsted disagreed.[75] Hoover joined the board anyway.

In the space of a few days, then, Hoover had shifted his ground and presented Moreing with a *fait accompli*. When Moreing challenged Hoover in person upon his return from Russia, Hoover responded that Maikop was an oil proposition and that oil extraction was not a form of mining. The restrictive covenant of 1908 therefore did not apply.[76]

A few weeks later Hoover joined the board of a second Maikop concern, again without securing Bewick, Moreing's consent.[77] Moreing immediately demanded that Hoover resign; Hoover refused.[78] On April 16, 1910 Moreing and his partners sued Hoover for breach of contract.[79]

Moreing's case had two parts. First, he sought an injunction to restrain Hoover from committing any breach of clause 8 of the dissolution agreement of 1908. This was the clause that limited Hoover's freedom to practice as a mining engineer or to become a director of mining companies without Bewick, Moreing's permission. Moreing asserted that Hoover's accession to the two Maikop oil companies' boards constituted such a breach. Oil exploration, Moreing argued, was a recognized form of mining; the Maikop companies were clearly mining companies; the dissolution agreement of 1908 did cover petroleum. Second, Moreing accused Hoover of transacting financial business in connection with the two Maikop companies (by assisting in their promotion) yet failing (as required by the dissolution agreement) to have Bewick, Moreing appointed managers. Asserting that he would thereby lose substantial fees, Moreing filed for damages.[80]

Hoover's defense was simple: he had not violated the 1908 dissolution agreement for the reason that it did not apply to Maikop at all. The covenant pertained to mining only, which the petroleum business was not.[81] The same defense applied to the question of "financial business." The agreement covered only financial business relating to mining. If oil drilling was not a form of mining, Hoover was home free.

The crucial question in the dispute, therefore, was a technical one. Was petroleum engineering a branch of mining engineering or not? Throughout the spring, summer, and autumn of 1910, the two litigants vigorously assembled evidence, including affidavits by distinguished mining engineers and all sorts of data about professional usage.[82] Hoover had Beatty instigate a search of court records in New York, while Hoover's old friend Curtis Lindley, an eminent San Francisco mining attorney, searched records in the American West for useful precedents.[83] By late in the year the case had taken on the dimensions of a cause célèbre; an expensive and perhaps spectacular court case was impending.[84]

At this point Hoover apparently moved to force a settlement. Hoover's friend Deane P. Mitchell was now a senior man in Bewick, Moreing's Australian hierarchy; he was also, at the moment, in London. On December 9 Mitchell informed Moreing's partner Wellsted that Hoover had told him that regardless of whether the firm won its lawsuit, it would lose. For if it won, Hoover and two of his allies would retaliate: they would oust Bewick, Moreing from the management of their companies.[85]

Four days later Hoover's close friend Francis Govett intervened in the case. The British stockbroker asked Moreing's other partner, W. J. Loring, to stop by his office. According to Loring's notes of this interview, Govett urged that Moreing's lawsuit be stopped. If it were not, Govett warned, the Lake View companies (which he controlled) would be obliged to drop Bewick, Moreing as managers. Govett declared also that the Oroya group of companies (in which Hoover was highly influential) would do the same. Govett asserted that Hoover had amassed much evidence, including a case of fraud against Moreing, and that some unseemly matters would be aired if the lawsuit were not settled.

Govett urged Loring to contact Hoover and resolve the quarrel out of court. According to Govett, Hoover was quite worried about the case and amenable to a reasonable settlement. Loring said that he would be prepared to discuss the subject with Hoover when they met at a company meeting before long.[86]

Clearly disturbed, Loring reported this conversation to his firm's legal counsel.[87] According to the firm's later account, Govett's threats (as it termed them) intimidated Loring, who, after all, had recently paid Hoover over $150,000 for his partnership and obviously had much to lose. Loring urged his partners to drop the suit; Govett pledged that if they did so he would keep his companies under Bewick, Moreing management. Reacting to the pressure, Moreing permitted Loring to work out a settlement with Hoover.[88]

Loring himself later asserted that at some point after Hoover's departure from the firm he confronted Hoover with his alleged breach of contract. According to Loring, Hoover retorted that no contract was ever drafted that he could not break.[89]

Almost simultaneously, pressure to settle emerged from yet another direction. In a December 1910 editorial T. A. Rickard's *Mining Magazine* gently admonished the feuding engineers:

> The litigation between Messrs. C. A. Moreing and H. C. Hoover is much to be regretted. Two men so successful in mining and finance ought to be able to find ample scope for their unusual abilities, without going to law, in regard to the limit to be set upon their useful energies. Apparently the point at issue is whether Mr. Hoover broke a covenant not to engage in business as a mining engineer for a term of ten years, whether such a covenant was reasonably necessary for the protection of Mr. Moreing's business (in which Mr. Hoover was formerly a partner) and finally whether the exploitation of oil constitutes a mining operation. All of those are points capable of subtle argument, and we hope most sincerely that it will not be found necessary to elucidate them in court. Professional men ought to set a good example by settling such squabbles by arbitration.[90]

On February 8, 1911 Hoover got his way. The plaintiff and defendant settled their dispute out of court and agreed to drop all further proceedings in the case. Each side paid its own legal costs.[91]

Hoover was elated. One of his friends was a British petroleum engineer who had recently published a book called *Petroleum Mining* (thereby inadvertently causing Hoover—and himself—considerable embarrassment). Years later this engineer still remembered how on February 8 Hoover "bounced into our office, radiant and jubilant," with word of the final agreement.[92]

The settlement's terms revised and supplemented the dissolution agreement of 1908. Once again Hoover formally agreed not to practice his profession of mining engineer ("save as is hereinafter permitted") in the United Kingdom or the British empire for ten years, except with the written permission of Bewick, Moreing. Once again he pledged not to act as a director of any mining enterprise ("except as hereinafter mentioned") within these geographical boundaries without Bewick, Moreing's consent. Obviously reflecting Moreing's fear that Hoover might establish a rival firm, the new covenant declared more specifically than before that Hoover could not (before mid-1918) conduct any of the businesses of a mining and metallurgical engineer, or mine manager, or company manager, or provider of office space and staff for any persons or companies engaged in mining anywhere in the British empire—unless, of course, Bewick, Moreing gave its consent.

As before, the new agreement permitted Hoover to engage in mining or other business anywhere in the world *outside* the British empire, and it allowed him complete freedom to buy or sell shares in any company he wished. Similarly, it authorized him (as before) to transact financial business relating to mining (including exploration, promotion, and finance) with companies operating in the British empire.

Just as significant as the reaffirmed restrictions of the old covenant of 1908, however, were the numerous exceptions granted under the new. Omitted from the revised covenant was the old condition that Hoover must procure for Bewick, Moreing the management of mining companies in the British empire for which he transacted financial business. The out-of-court settlement permitted Hoover to hold all company directorates that he held as of February 8, 1911; these included the two Maikop oil company directorates that had provoked Moreing's suit. Indeed, so broad were the exemptions that they virtually nullified the geographical restriction earlier in the agreement on Hoover's freedom to serve as a company director.[93]

In essence, the revised agreement granted Hoover essentially unlimited freedom to pursue a career as a company director and mining financier anywhere without further obligation to Moreing. But Moreing, too, had gained something: a restated and more explicit restraint on Hoover *as a mining engineer*. It was now clear that Moreing was not primarily concerned about Hoover's activities as a company director, promoter, or financier. His objective, rather, was to prevent Hoover from creating a competing firm of mining

engineers and mine managers, a firm that could threaten Moreing's liveli-
hood.[94]

Each side, then—particularly Hoover—had reason to celebrate. It soon
became apparent, however, that the treaty of February 1911 had brought not
peace but a truce. Hoover remained a director of numerous companies managed by Bewick, Moreing; their paths thus repeatedly crossed. Over the next
few years relations between Hoover and his former firm deteriorated.

One of the selling points of the Bewick, Moreing organization in Australia
was its cooperative system of stores purchases, an innovation instituted in
1903, when Hoover was a partner. During late 1910 and 1911 complaints
about the effectiveness of the scheme began to emanate from certain companies on which Hoover or his brother were directors. At the request of these
companies an independent investigator was sent to Australia. In 1912 Bewick,
Moreing was forced to replace its cooperative scheme with a buying agency,
a change (the firm alleged) that caused substantial damage to itself. The firm
accused Hoover of masterminding the breakup of this once-profitable system.[95]

The firm also charged that Hoover and Govett systematically strove after
1908 to revise the firm's management contracts in ways detrimental to it.
When Hoover was a partner, the firm had customarily arranged to manage a
company for long periods of time with long periods of notice to terminate.
This was a way of providing job security for the firm's highly paid engineers.
But as contracts with various mining companies directed by Hoover expired
after 1908, Hoover and Govett demanded renewals only for short periods of
time and only with short periods of notice. According to the firm, this led to
continuous wrangling with Hoover.[96]

Bewick, Moreing was further upset when the Burma Corporation displaced it as manager of the Burma Mines in 1914. Hoover was chairman of
the corporation, while his brother and other friends were on the technical
committee. Charging Hoover with being the "controlling technical brain" of
the corporation, the firm accused him of rendering his professional knowledge as mining engineer to the Burma enterprise and, in effect, of managing
it as well. Both were in direct breach of his dissolution agreement.

One by one, as the years passed, some of Bewick, Moreing's best men left
it and signed up with Hoover's enterprises. In 1909 the firm discovered (so
it later alleged) that one of its confidential secretaries was leaking information
to Hoover. It fired the secretary, who thereupon was hired by Hoover.[97]
The firm accused Hoover of repeatedly interfering with its technical staff
and of luring some of them to his Lake View and Oroya Exploration Company. In 1912, for instance, after more than a decade with Bewick, Moreing,
John Agnew left and joined Hoover, who appointed him to the Lake View's
technical committee.[98]

By 1914 Moreing and his partners were particularly angry and apprehensive about the surging Lake View and Oroya Exploration Company. To them

it was not just an ordinary finance company but the competing, Hoover-led management firm they had tried by restrictive covenant to prohibit. What was the Lake View's "technical committee," they contended, but a corps of engineers under Hoover's generalship? What was its provision of office space and secretaries to mining companies but an exact duplication of the services Bewick, Moreing rendered to its own clients? When Bewick, Moreing's contract to manage the Oroya Leonesa mine expired in 1912, its agreement was not renewed. Instead, Lake View and Oroya Exploration—run by Hoover and Govett—furnished the Leonesa with an office, clerical assistance, and technical advice. To Moreing and his partners the pattern by 1914 was only too obvious: through the Lake View and its technical committee, Hoover was engaging in the business of mining engineering and mining company management in direct competition with Moreing and in breach of his severance agreement.[99]

It was not a pleasant portrait that Moreing and his partners later drew: of Hoover as a conniver, scheming to undercut his former partner's business, steal his best employees, and circumvent if not directly violate his solemn legal pledges. Yet if Moreing felt aggrieved, what was Hoover's side? Although Moreing's story of his relations with Hoover has been preserved, Hoover's version has not, and one is left to sift uncertainly for the unbiased truth. Certainly Hoover helped to break up Bewick, Moreing's stores supply scheme in 1910–11. But did he do so simply out of malice or rather out of legitimate concern that the scheme was no longer financially attractive? One inspector of the supply system in 1910–11 concluded that outside purchasing was actually a bit cheaper than Bewick, Moreing's scheme.[100] Possibly, then, Hoover had good reason for actions that Moreing merely considered malicious.

Indeed, much of Hoover's behavior takes on a less disagreeable hue if one allows the possibility that his criticisms of Moreing's firm after 1908 were in fact justified. For something fundamental had happened to the firm in 1908: Hoover had left it. Without his superlative ability and drive, the firm never again attained the eminence among mining men that it held during Hoover's tenure.

And this, one suspects, galled Moreing. It must have irked the older man to see his former partner and protégé soar to new plateaus of success after 1908, while the firm he left behind suffered several embarrassing reverses. It did not help to watch some of his best engineers—men like Agnew and Mitchell—leave for assignments with Hoover. By 1912 the mining press had begun to notice. "Bewick, Moreing & Co.'s operations at Porcupine [Canada] have not been a success, nor their oil ventures at Maikop, in Russia," noted one journal.[101] "Judging from results," Bewick, Moreing "have done badly in all their ventures since the early days of Coolgardie."[102] Moreing's envy and fear may have contributed as much to bad relations as Hoover's alleged vindictiveness and intrigues.

Moreing may not have been without legitimate grievance, however. Certainly on their face Hoover's actions at the Lake View appeared to violate his promise not to practice as a mine manager or mining engineer in Great Britain or its empire for ten years after 1908. If Moreing was correct, Hoover took such actions knowingly and systematically. In any case, the Hoover-Moreing feud did not pass away. By 1914 the tension was building toward another lawsuit.[103]

I I I

CONTENTION with Moreing was not the only legacy of Hoover's ill-fated Maikop excursion. Hoover was a man who prized and reciprocated the loyalty of his business friends, even when it caused expense and inconvenience to himself. By late 1911, thanks in part to Maikop, one such friend, Lindon Bates, was in a financial hole. At his request, Hoover endeavored to bail him out.[104]

A seemingly routine task turned swiftly into a struggle.[105] Hoover discovered (he told Beatty) that "Bates has gotten his business into such an unholy mess that I have hardly had time to sleep trying to get him disentangled."[106] A few weeks later Hoover was obliged to borrow money to enable an overextended Bates to hold onto some of his stock.[107] It was but the beginning of a lengthy exertion.

For Bates's oil interests reached far beyond the Maikop field in Russia. Late in 1908 the enterprising dredging expert had acquired licenses to prospect for oil on certain lands in Peru. Early in 1909 he persuaded the Lake View Consols (of which Hoover was a director) to finance some of his oil prospecting activities.[108] By early 1910 it had loaned him at least £25,000 for oil drilling in Peru.[109]

At this point another entity appeared on the scene. In March 1910 the Anglo-Continental Mines Company, working with Bates, created the Lagunitos Oil Company, to which it sold various oil leases in Peru. The sale price paid by Lagunitos for its property was £25,000 in cash and £125,000 in Lagunitos shares credited as fully paid. The cash went to the Lake View Consols in repayment of its loan to Bates. Five thousand of the shares went to Bates himself. And 4,687 of the remaining shares, it turned out, went to Hoover.[110]

For behind the scenes, as so often, Hoover had exerted an influence. Not only was he a member of the Lake View Consols board, which initially financed Bates; he was also on the Anglo-Continental board as well, and through it he obtained his block of shares, which he subsequently disposed of for about $5,400.[111] It is unlikely that Hoover, as a close friend of Bates, was passive while the Lagunitos Oil Company was being set up.[112]

Hoover's membership on the Anglo-Continental board was another source of friction with his ex-partner Moreing in early 1910. Apparently Hoover had taken a director's seat without the prior consent of his former firm. In April Moreing protested. Shortly thereafter, the Lagunitos flotation accomplished, Hoover resigned.[113]

For the next two years, under Bates's guidance as managing director, the Lagunitos Oil Company developed rapidly.[114] But before long that recurrent nemesis of infant mining enterprises struck: a shortage of working capital. During 1912, despite slowly increasing production and considerable future promise, the fledgling company was starved for cash and had to suspend operations temporarily.[115] "This business was a hopeless miscalculation of cost," Govett publicly complained in November, although he felt that Lagunitos would become a profit-earning concern. All it needed was "a little financial nursing."[116]

If anything, the Peruvian company's position was more precarious than that. During its brief existence it had borrowed heavily from the Lake View and Oroya Exploration Company, of which Govett and Hoover were joint managing directors and ruling spirits. In 1912 the Lake View loaned Lagunitos additional money, but only on condition that it promptly reorganize its finances and begin to repay the loan. Hoover and Govett were willing to channel Lake View money into their friend's company, but they were nervous, too, and with reason. By the end of 1912 Lagunitos owed the Lake View over £18,000.[117]

Meanwhile, in mid-1912, Bates had resigned from the Lagunitos board.[118] But Hoover knew that his friend retained "a very large interest" in the struggling concern, and no doubt he knew the consequences for Bates if the enterprise failed.[119]

In January 1913, both to repay its loan and to raise needed working capital, Lagunitos created 30,000 preference shares. Once again, through the Lake View and Oroya Exploration Company, Hoover and Govett assisted Lindon Bates. The Lake View agreed to guarantee the sale of half of the shares in return for a three-year option to purchase the other half at par. The issue was only a partial success; the Lake View was obliged to pick up about one-third of the new shares.[120] The Lake View was more entwined with Lagunitos than ever.

By now Hoover evidently was seeking a way to escape from the growing Lagunitos entanglement. Noting to Beatty that the Peruvian company "has a little cash, and is doing very well by way of production," he disclosed in February 1913 that Bates had agreed to try to sell "the Peruvian position" to a California oil company in which Hoover and Beatty were much involved. Hoover perceived advantages in such an agreement. "Any sale so made would greatly benefit the Lake View & Oroya," he pointed out, although he conceded that Bates would "need to offer some cash" to put the deal through.

Hoover was prepared to supply Bates with the cash. "I have therefore told him" (Hoover informed Beatty) "that we could probably arrange a loan similar to the Continental business, but of course with a larger bonus." In other words, Hoover proposed to loan Bates the money to induce the California company to buy him out. And just as the Anglo-Continental in 1910 had received free vendors' shares for transferring the Peruvian oil leases to Lagunitos, so now Hoover and Beatty would receive a share bonus for enabling Bates to sell Lagunitos to the California company.[121]

For reasons unknown Hoover's proposal never came to fruition. But during 1913, fortified by new working capital, the Lagunitos company increased its oil production, earned a profit, and repaid most of its debt to the Lake View.[122] Happy and no doubt relieved, Govett informed Lake View shareholders in October that the Lagunitos had "vastly improved" its position.[123] The financial reorganization engineered by Hoover and himself earlier in the year had proven a success.[124]

Hoover was not quite done with his operations at Lagunitos. In 1914 an opportunity arose to accomplish what he had desired the year before. The Standard Oil of New Jersey interests, through a Canadian subsidiary, wished to purchase control of Lagunitos. When Bates attempted to negotiate the sale with William Bemis of Standard Oil, however, he got nowhere. At Bates's request Hoover stepped in.

Walter Teagle, president of the Canadian subsidiary, was visiting London when Bates sought Hoover's aid. Showing up at Teagle's office in white tennis shoes and a seersucker suit, Hoover came swiftly to the point. "Bates will never sell these properties to Bemis—they're too much alike, so I've come to sell them to you," Hoover announced. And he did.[125]

An American friend of Teagle's was present in Hoover's office on the day of the transfer of Bates's Lagunitos interests. The scene was typically Hooverian. Appearing at the office in formal attire for such an important occasion, Teagle's British representatives found Hoover the epitome of American casualness, his sleeves rolled up and his coat draped over a chair. Nevertheless, Hoover got right to the point. Do you have the certified check? he asked. Yes, came the reply. Brushing aside British formality, Hoover quickly completed the transaction.[126]

And went on, no doubt, to something else. In these years there was always something else—like Bates's struggling array of interests in Trinidad. Here, too, Hoover came to the rescue.

In 1910 Bates and his associates had formed a number of companies to develop petroleum deposits on the island of Trinidad. Notable among these concerns was the General Petroleum Properties of Trinidad, which acquired a large concession on a corner of the island. In return for guaranteeing an issue of the new company's shares to the general public for working capital, two old associates of Hoover, W. F. Turner and Edmund Davis, received a handsome commission of 25,000 free shares in the new company. Hoover, apparently as a subunderwriter, personally received 1,400 of these shares and sold them later in the year.[127] Such was his fee as an engineer-financier.

Although never a director of the General Petroleum Properties of Trinidad, Hoover in his characteristically indirect way took an active interest in its affairs. Barely a year after it was formed, the young company placed itself under option to one of the mining giants, Consolidated Goldfields of South Africa, with which Hoover had frequent business contacts. Before exercising their right to purchase, the Goldfields leaders wanted an independent examination of the Trinidad company's lands. Hoover arranged for his friend Ralph Arnold to make the investigation.[128]

Hoover was pleased by Arnold's report and hoped that the Trinidad enterprise would now "gradually get out of the mud." He even welcomed Arnold's harsh strictures on the company's management—criticisms "no more severe" than those Hoover himself had uttered (he told Arnold) "with parrot-like repetition during the last twelve months."[129] But Hoover's hope for a quick consolidation went unfulfilled; in July 1912 the Goldfields decided not to exercise its option. It was devastating news for the infant Trinidad company and Bates's business interests. Would the General Petroleum Properties of Trinidad, on which large sums of capital had already been spent, fail for want of financial support? The company seemed paralyzed; no work was done on its Trinidad holdings throughout 1912.[130]

At this point (mid-1912) Hoover stepped in and performed the kind of financial salvage operation that he did so well. He induced another giant, the Central Mining and Investment Corporation, to form a company that would buy the General Petroleum Properties' interests and amalgamate them with miscellaneous other lands in Trinidad. By the end of 1912 Hoover had hammered out a provisional agreement to this effect. In August 1913 the Central Mining and Investment Corporation duly formed the Trinidad Leaseholds, Ltd. A few months later Bates's General Petroleum Properties of Trinidad—its properties disposed of for a large block of Leaseholds shares—happily liquidated. The Trinidad Leaseholds soon became a prosperous enterprise.[131]

By sporadic negotiations, then, extending over three years, Hoover succeeded in selling some of Bates's principal oil interests on satisfactory terms to larger companies, thereby enabling his friend to retire in financial safety.[132] How much Hoover received in compensation for his troubles is unknown. Years later he stated that the Bates episode had been "one of those personal affairs without profit" to himself.[133] This was not, perhaps, literally accurate; Hoover received 10,000 shares in Trinidad Leaseholds for his role in its creation. In 1916 he sold them for $31,990.[134] Perhaps Hoover did not count this as profit but as merely the hard-earned income of a volunteer "industrial doctor."

I V

N o t all of Hoover's oil interests arose from his friendship with Lindon Bates, nor did they all lead to protracted perplexities. In 1913 Hoover became a director of the Bishopsgate Syndicate, established in 1912 to acquire certain oil-producing lands in Romania. The syndicate paid £80,000 in cash for these properties, which it resold in 1913 for about £200,000 in the stock of a British company created to acquire them.[135] As one of the largest shareholders in the syndicate, Hoover probably profited handsomely from this transaction.[136]

Lucrative though it may have been, Hoover's Romanian venture was only incidental to the thrust of his oil interests by late 1912. During the next two years, even as he strove to extricate Bates from difficulty, Hoover embarked on a rapid series of oil transactions on his own in the state he considered his spiritual home, California. For the first time since he left San Francisco in 1897, Hoover's business interests focused significantly on the United States.

Hoover's interest in the California oil fields dated to the heady months of early 1910. On February 23 he sent an urgent cable to A. Chester Beatty. "The oil boom has struck upon London," Hoover stated, and he thought he saw a way to climb aboard. He urged Beatty to take an option on a promising oil company in California that had come to Hoover's attention in London. If he and Beatty could properly arrange the finance, a reorganized company could be floated in London in the current atmosphere, and the two, for their efforts, "ought to be able to make a fine haul in stock."[137]

Hoover's particular suggestion did not materialize. But only a few weeks later Beatty successfully set up another concern, the Continental Petroleum Company of America, which owned at the outset 300 acres of land in California. Beatty agreed to underwrite some of the preferred stock issue of the new company and suggested to Hoover that their newly founded financial organ, the Intercontinental Trust, purchase a chunk itself. The Trust did so and received a substantial bonus in free Continental common stock.[138]

For the next two years Hoover and Beatty remained large and influential stockholders in the Continental Petroleum Company—indeed, "dominating" figures, according to one mining journal.[139] Hoover personally owned 84,000 common shares and 15,000 preferred shares.[140] Not surprisingly, Govett, the Zinc Corporation, and the Lake View and Oroya Exploration Company became major shareholders as well.[141] Wherever Hoover went, his allies tended to follow.

As a small but attractive business, the Continental was an obvious candidate for a merger—and the kind of financial engineering at which Hoover excelled. In 1912 an opportunity came. During April A. Chester Beatty entered negotiations to amalgamate the Continental with another rapidly rising California concern, the General Petroleum Company.[142] Formed in 1910, General Petroleum was dominated by San Franciscans, led by E. J. de Sabla and the Scottish-born John Barneson. Already a significant oil producer, the expanding General Petroleum firm had a 185-mile pipeline under construction and was preparing to build a refinery at the pipeline terminal. In the autumn of 1912 the General agreed to purchase the Continental.[143]

The new merger aroused excitement in California. The General Petroleum Company, reported an industry journal, was on its way to becoming one of the principal oil companies in the world. "Who is behind the General Petroleum besides Messrs. Barneson and de Sabla?" businessmen wanted to know.[144] No one, at this point, was "behind" General Petroleum, but someone was behind the merger: Hoover, Beatty, and their mining / financial allies.

Under the terms of the merger, the Continental Petroleum Company agreed to transfer its entire capital stock, plus $500,000 in cash, to the General, in return for stocks and bonds. There was for the Continental only one problem: it had only $50,000 in its treasury. Hoover, who with Beatty had been in the thick of the negotiations, stepped forward with an offer. He agreed to loan the Continental the difference—$450,000—on certain stringent conditions, which the Continental board accepted. Among other things, the Continental agreed to repay Hoover's loan at 6% interest within six months. Furthermore, it gave Hoover at once $250,000 in the common stock it was obtaining from General Petroleum for selling out.[145] In other words, for loaning $450,000 at 6% interest, and for negotiating the sale to the General, Hoover received (among other things) a quarter of a million dollars' worth of General Petroleum shares.[146]

Although Hoover himself signed the documents authorizing this loan, he did not personally supply the entire $450,000. Instead, he was acting as a representative of a syndicate which he and several friends formed in London in October.[147] The Inter-Californian Trust, it was called; Govett described its purpose succinctly: "a finance operation connected with the amalgamation of two California oil companies."[148]

To raise the needed $450,000, the syndicate privately issued 94,000 £1 shares, which Hoover and various friends promptly purchased. Among the major shareholders were Beatty, Govett, Leslie Urquhart, and those two companies over which Hoover had so much influence: the Zinc Corporation and the Lake View and Oroya Exploration Company. Hoover himself was the largest stockholder, personally subscribing to 22,600 Inter-Californian Trust shares or, in other words, putting up about $110,000. Thus roughly one-quarter of the loan to the Continental came out of Hoover's own pocket.[149]

It was a heavy monetary commitment, but the security on the loan was excellent and the ensuing profit tremendous. Not only did Hoover and his associates in the syndicate receive their loan money back with interest; among other assets they also acquired $250,000 in free stock. Because of his nearly one-quarter interest in the Inter-Californian Trust, Hoover's portion of its total profit probably exceeded $60,000.[150] The syndicate's operations had entailed months of hard work—for Hoover and Beatty above all—but it had been worth it.[151]

The merger program now proceeded, and in a few months the Continental Petroleum Company of America disappeared. Hoover became a director of the General Petroleum Company.[152] At the end of December 1912 the Inter-

Californian Trust, its moneylending apparently done, voted to liquidate.[153]

Suddenly a new financial opportunity beckoned. Now it was the General Petroleum Company that wanted money, and like the Continental it turned to Hoover for assistance. In January 1913 Hoover and Beatty consented to loan General Petroleum $200,000 for four months at 6% interest plus a bonus of shares in the company having a par value of $50,000. Another condition was more nebulous. A few months before, the audacious General Petroleum had acquired an option to purchase control of still another concern, the Union Oil Company, for $20,000,000. Hoover therefore stipulated that if General Petroleum exercised its option and undertook to finance Union Oil, he and Beatty would be offered "a participation in this finance upon the ground floor terms."[154]

As before, Hoover did not personally make this entire loan. Returning to London from a trip to the United States, he turned the business over to a suddenly revived Inter-Californian Trust.[155] Unfortunately, the Trust had been about to liquidate and had no money in *its* treasury. To raise the necessary $200,000, Hoover was obliged to kick in $25,000 of his own money, while the Inter-Californian Trust had to borrow $100,000 from the Zinc Corporation.

This time, however, there was a hitch—and from a most unexpected quarter. In behalf of the Zinc Corporation, Govett insisted on receiving not the usual commission for lending $100,000 but instead fully half the profits that the Inter-Californian Trust would make on *its* loan to General Petroleum! Desperate for money, the Trust apparently had accepted these terms in Hoover's absence. Upon finding this out, Hoover was considerably annoyed. Finally, however, he arranged to obtain $100,000 from other sources and promptly return the money borrowed from the Zinc Corporation. With the Zinc Corporation thus removed from the picture, the Inter-Californian Trust was again free to reap its anticipated profit.[156] Still, Hoover was scarcely jubilant at this turn of affairs. "The whole thing," he complained to Beatty,

> is on a wrong moral basis as there is no use elaborating the point that you and I have done all the labor and taken all the responsibility and that these people [the Zinc Corporation] are claiming all the benefits simply in consideration of loaning money on gilt edge securities. It is highly desirable, however, to get the thing quickly planed out before any difficulties arise with our obstructive friend [Govett], and the above was the only way that I could see.[157]

Business could be rough, even among friends.

During the next several months Hoover performed several useful services for the General Petroleum Company, on whose board he served intermittently as a director.[158] Initially he was unenthusiastic about making further efforts in its behalf. He told Beatty in February that General Petroleum was "evidently not going to let us have any deal on the Union [Oil Company merger scheme] that is much good to us and I have therefore lost interest in future finance in that quarter."[159]

Nevertheless, by the spring of 1913 Hoover was again active in the company's affairs. In May he arranged for a branch office to be opened in London and shares to be issued on the London stock exchange; he and another director became General Petroleum's London committee.[160] During May also the company authorized creation of $3,000,000 in convertible notes in order to retire certain debts and provide more working capital. Even before the notes were formally issued, Hoover (through his brother) had sold $200,000 of them in London.[161] On May 16 and 22 Hoover (presumably in behalf of the Inter-Californian Trust) made two additional loans to General Petroleum totaling $400,000. His arrangements contained options to purchase bonds with large share bonuses.[162] In June Hoover was elected to General Petroleum's executive committee, on which he remained for nearly eight months.[163]

Hoover's strenuous activities in behalf of General Petroleum came at a crucial moment.[164] Years afterwards he recalled how he had recommended that certain New York and British investment companies supply capital for the General Petroleum Company to complete its ambitious pipeline to the Pacific. In return, he remembered, he received a "handsome fee."[165]

And now came General Petroleum's turn to be amalgamated. By the summer of 1913 the growing enterprise was increasingly in need of working capital.[166] One of the company's directors was the powerful British shipping magnate, Andrew Weir. Late in October 1913 it was announced that Weir and certain associates had closed a deal to take over and finance the General Petroleum Company. The medium for this purchase and reorganization was to be a British entity called the Western Ocean Syndicate. Under the terms of the arrangement the syndicate was to set up a holding company to take over not only the General but the Union Oil Company as well, hitherto under option to the General. This was amalgamation on a grand scale indeed. As part of the contract the syndicate agreed to loan the cash-hungry General Petroleum Company up to $3,000,000.[167]

Among Weir's associates in this vast scheme were two prominent British financiers: Arthur M. Grenfell and Hoover's difficult fellow director of the Burma Mines, R. Tilden Smith. Another colleague, it turned out, was Hoover himself.[168]

Although Hoover's personal stake in the Western Ocean Syndicate was small (apparently only 1%),[169] from the first he was prominently identified with the proposed amalgamation. T. A. Rickard's *Mining Magazine* listed Hoover, Weir, and Grenfell as the three leaders of the scheme to raise "further working capital" for the General Petroleum Company.[170] A mining journal in San Francisco lauded Hoover, Weir, and Grenfell as a "strong combination."[171]

Behind the scenes, too, Hoover was active. Despite his participation in the

Western Ocean Syndicate, Hoover was unhappy with certain provisions of the October 1913 contract between General Petroleum and the Western Ocean Syndicate. In his opinion, General Petroleum's negotiator had represented the General's stockholders' view rather than that of the General's noteholders and bondholders. (Hoover himself may have been one such bondholder.)[172] In any case, he was determined to alter the October agreement if he could— not in order to "break down the present deal" (he assured Beatty), "but only to gently get it amended so that it will become fair to the General Petroleum security-holders and at the same time work out equally well or better for the Syndicate."[173]

Hoover had some leverage. The noteholders in General Petroleum apparently had the power (or so he convinced Grenfell) to "handicap" the October deal unless satisfactory revisions were made. Hoover therefore urged Beatty to organize a united front of the New York noteholders in order to negotiate from strength. On December 5, 1913 Hoover cabled from London that Weir and Smith were on their way to New York. He asked Beatty to "settle nothing until I arrive." The noteholders and bondholders, he stressed, must be "treated very different manner." Already he had conceived a new scheme that would substantially benefit the noteholders. Said Hoover, "Believe if put up strong front can get this or something near it."[174]

Hoover reached the United States on December 10.[175] For the next three months he stayed mostly in California; meanwhile, all around him, efforts to consummate the giant amalgamation continued on several fronts. Just what happened to Hoover's attempt to revise the October contract is unclear. At least parts of the deal became operative.[176] The General Petroleum note question, however, was soon overshadowed by ominous news from California.

To Hoover's consternation the seemingly thriving General Petroleum Company turned out by January 1914 to be in desperate financial trouble. Its management, he found, was "utterly demoralized." In large part because of a failed refinery process, the company was not earning enough to pay the interest on its bonds.[177]

Hoover's first impulse was to push through Weir's October agreement; at least General Petroleum would thereby receive $3,000,000 in loans from the British. He believed this deal to be the "only salvation"; failure to obtain the syndicate's money might cause bankruptcy proceedings.[178] A few days later he proposed a scheme whereby General Petroleum would abandon its disastrous refinery business and concentrate on oil production and transportation alone, using the syndicate's loan for capital.[179] Later in the month, however, Hoover's confidence recovered somewhat. Although he considered the company to have suffered "wilful mismanagement" in the past six months, the business, in his view, was "extremely sound" and the chances of "correcting worst mistakes very bright."[180]

In part, perhaps, because of the General Petroleum Company's severe financial difficulties, plans to proceed with the next stage of Weir's amalgamation plan seemed to stall. The question of redress for the noteholders remained unresolved. "As to notes," Hoover told Beatty in late January, "we do not want to be bluffed." Outwardly, he reported, Weir and Smith took a "most pessimistic attitude about General Petroleum." In Hoover's eyes the Britishers' position was partly a tactic to "frighten noteholders."[181]

Meanwhile, Weir and Smith were trying to complete arrangements to take over the Union Oil Company.[182] And on still another front General Petroleum's indefatigable leadership was attempting to effect a separate merger with still another company, California Petroleum! Hoover's friend Arnold was involved in these negotiations; before long Weir and Smith joined as well. From time to time Hoover attempted unsuccessfully from afar to facilitate a meeting of some very independent minds.[183] It was one thing to plan amalgamations; it was quite another to carry them out.

But Hoover's own mind was not primarily on California oil mergers that winter. Late in 1913 California's business community was rocked by the financial failure of F. M. "Borax" Smith. Then, just after Christmas, a second financial earthquake impended in San Francisco, and Hoover was called upon to prevent it.

A month later Hoover telegraphed Beatty from San Francisco:

Owing to financial difficulties of a group here of wider import than Borax Smith and on earnest solicitation of San Francisco bank, I have taken charge of situations; have had scarcely average of 4 hours sleep since Christmas and will not see daylight for another 30 days. I have therefore not had time to pay any great attention to General Petroleum.[184]

Two of San Francisco's most prominent families, the Slosses and the Lilienthals, had become dangerously overextended in business. Their complex financial empire was collapsing; a spectacular bankruptcy seemed unavoidable.

At the request of a mutual friend Hoover stepped in and for the next two months endeavored to restore order. More may have been at stake than simply rescuing the beleaguered Slosses and Lilienthals. For one thing, the two families' tangled debts involved several large companies and many millions of dollars. Hoover knew that a major financial failure so soon after the "Borax" Smith episode would do no good to California. Moreover, the families had a considerable interest in the General Petroleum Company; perhaps Hoover feared the effect of their bankruptcy on the delicate negotiations with Andrew Weir.[185]

Hoover, in any case, pitched in, at one point personally loaning one of the Slosses' railroad companies $17,500 on security of certain General Petroleum bonds.[186] In the end he was able to effect a financial reorganization that saved the families and their creditors. He took no money for his services.[187]

Meanwhile, the great California oil company merger negotiations were dragging on and on. In early March 1914, on his way back to England, Hoover still did not know what Weir and Smith proposed to do.[188] The General Petroleum Company was in disturbing shape, soon to default on the interest payments due on its notes and bonds.[189]

Shortly thereafter, the breakthrough came at last. On March 13 the General Petroleum Company, Ltd. (of London) was registered; it proceeded to exchange General Petroleum Company (of California) shares for its own as part of the amalgamation plan.[190] A few weeks later the Western Ocean Syndicate finally secured a controlling interest in the Union Oil Company.[191] Late in July the British Union Oil Company, Ltd. was registered to acquire control of the Union Oil Company and to supply it with over $12,000,000 in cash.[192] The British navy wanted a secure supply of petroleum for its oil-fueled fleet. As a result of the contemplated mergers the British-based Western Ocean Syndicate stood to control almost one-third of the oil production of the state of California.[193]

These were the plans. In the end they were never fully implemented, although as late as October 1914 Herbert Hoover publicly stated that Weir's scheme for reorganization of the General Petroleum Company was "practically completed."[194] A month later it was reported that General Petroleum would indeed be reorganized, but by Americans, not British, and that Weir, his syndicate, and the British company would be eliminated from the scene.[195] More months went by. Finally, in 1916, General Petroleum was reorganized, without British involvement. In effect, the deal of 1913–14 was rescinded.[196]

What had gone wrong? Possibly the revelation of General Petroleum's financial weakness at a critical moment in early 1914 fatally delayed efforts to implement the deal. Another factor may have been the startling collapse of Grenfell's financial empire in the early summer of 1914; this deprived Weir of one source of capital and increased the burden on him.[197] An even greater obstacle was a cataclysm no one had foreseen. Late in July it was reported that as soon as British Union shares were on the market the Western Ocean Syndicate would underwrite the British would-be "parent" of General Petroleum.[198] A few days later World War I broke out; the British parent corporation never effected its contemplated financial plan.[199] In March 1915, with the British syndicate unable to complete its payments in the related Union Oil merger, the attempt to take over Union Oil also collapsed.[200]

Was there yet another reason why the deal fell apart? It appears that Hoover's own objection—the unsatisfactory treatment of the General Petroleum noteholders in the scheme—was never overcome. Had Hoover himself, then, delayed and helped to block the General Petroleum part of the merger? Years afterward Hoover recalled how he assisted General Petroleum's president, John Barneson, in a fight to avoid being "wiped out" by his "enemies" Grenfell and Weir.[201] Years later also Barneson told the same story: how Hoover was primarily responsible for saving General Petroleum (and the Union, too) from "capture" by "sharks," by whom he evidently meant the Western Ocean

Syndicate.[202] And in 1918 Hoover's friend Francis Govett publicly asserted that "by grim and resolute determination . . . we fought off a marauding attempt on the position" of the General Petroleum Company when it was "in low water."[203]

Who, though, were the marauders? It seems clear enough from Hoover's *Memoirs* that in his eyes they were two: Arthur Grenfell and Andrew Weir. But what precisely was their offense? Certainly the British attempted in 1913–14 to take control of General Petroleum. But this, after all, was their announced purpose, and Hoover himself belonged to the British syndicate formed to arrange it. Was Hoover instead alluding in his *Memoirs* to the unresolved dispute over fair consideration for General Petroleum's noteholders? Or did Andrew Weir and his British allies try in some way not fully disclosed in the record to take advantage of General Petroleum's distress?

The latter appears to have been the case. By the autumn of 1914 relations between Weir and the General Petroleum administration were in a state of virtual warfare. According to Barneson, Weir had stopped sending financial support to the General Petroleum Company and had nearly succeeded in deposing Barneson from the company's presidency. In addition, Barneson was certain that Weir was in collusion with the American controllers of Union Oil in a plot to wreck the General Petroleum Company and build up the British Union Oil Company out of the ensuing disorder. Hoover, in London, was kept apprised of the battle; Barneson asked him to block certain maneuvers by Weir.[204]

In the end American capital, not British, was found to finance General Petroleum, and the Western Ocean Syndicate's deal was canceled.[205] Barneson was always grateful for Hoover's assistance in the fight against "the English sharks." Long afterwards he declared that Hoover did more for the California oil industry during this period than any other man.[206]

V

Hoover was not a trained petroleum engineer. Probably for this reason, his services in the oil world between 1909 and 1914 were those not of a technical advisor but fundamentally of an executive and financier. Particularly in his California enterprises Hoover's usefulness derived from his financial acumen, his negotiating ability, and his ability to line up capital for hard-pressed oil companies.

In later years Hoover tended to minimize and even at times to deny his involvement in such financial dealings. Instead, he preferred to paint himself as an essentially disinterested outsider, not the eager insider that he in fact was. In 1943, for instance, Hoover's friend Arnold wrote to him about their California oil endeavors thirty years before. Arnold was preparing an autobiography and a history of the California oil industry; he asked about one of Hoover's attempted mergers that had never come to pass.[207] Hoover replied:

I have your note and I have a piece of advice.

When you write your autobiography, do not write yourself as a promoter or maker or investor in oil companies. You were a geologist and engineer, and you should write in that capacity only.

I was not a founder or promoter of oil companies. I was always an engineer.

I was never interested with [a certain oil man], even as an engineer. And I was only an engineering advisor on the consolidations and companies you mention.

You will find that point of view holds public esteem.[208]

This last sentence was probably the most revealing one.

Hoover's recollection was, of course, inaccurate. From 1910 to 1912 he was a director of a Maikop company that did indeed engage in oil promotions. In 1910 he was in the thick of efforts to found several Maikop oil companies. In California his activities were scarcely those of an "engineering advisor" in the ordinary sense of that expression but rather those of a capitalist and reorganizer of small or ailing enterprises. Of his oil experience in general, it would be more correct to say that he was never an engineer; he was a financier.

Hoover's acute sensitivity on this point—a sensitivity not discernible during his mining career—undoubtedly derived from his later experiences in public life. Especially during his presidency, a number of scandal-seeking, hostile biographers attempted to paint his oil ventures as essentially those of a sharp, selfish, even crooked promoter.[209] Hoover knew, too, the pejorative connotation of the word "promoter." And as his letter to Arnold suggests, in his post-presidential years he deeply craved "public esteem."

Hoover's oil dealings between 1909 and 1914 were at times frenetic, but they were not dishonorable. The occupation of supplier of capital was a necessary role in the industry, and raising capital for legitimate enterprise was no easy business.[210] If Hoover charged heavily for lending money, it reflected the borrowers' hunger for cash and the risk that the lender took. Oil businesses were not the safest investments available in 1913, as Hoover discovered ruefully at Maikop—and at General Petroleum when he learned the inside story of its finances.

By 1914, through his proliferating involvement in the oil industry, Hoover had acquired significant business connections in California, particularly San Francisco. Such contacts might prove advantageous should he desire a public career in his adopted state. In a sense Hoover's mining odyssey had come full circle. He had begun it in California, in the Sierra Nevadas. He had left in 1897 for Western Australia. Now, seventeen years later, he had established a base at home, and now, increasingly, California was on his mind.

23

The Professional

I

I t is not characteristic of youth to look over its shoulder. Speeding along after 1908 on the highway to a fortune, Herbert Hoover was no exception. But if in 1909, say—the year of his thirty-fifth birthday—he had paused for a backward glance, Hoover would have found reason to be pleased. How far he had come from his stint, fourteen years before, as an underground laborer in Grass Valley. How far, in just six years, from the devastating Rowe affair. No longer in debt, no longer a junior partner to anybody, he was a man of means and influence, an engineer-financier, a director of companies, founder of enterprises, a commander of money and men.

Yet if Hoover's everyday world after 1908 was increasingly the swirling arena of mining finance, his own conception of himself, then and later, was somewhat different. When asked to identify his occupation, he did not say he was a businessman, capitalist, financier, or (least of all) company promoter. Instead, he called himself a mining engineer. He regarded himself as a scientifically trained professional, with the independence, disinterestedness, and ethics of a professional. To Hoover, engineering—which he defined as "the work of application of science to industry"[1]—was no ordinary way of making a living.

It is not surprising, then, that from the very beginning of his career as a mining engineer Hoover did more than simply manage mines and accumulate wealth. Part scholar as well as part businessman, he did not confine himself to the unreflective conduct of his manifold everyday tasks. Somehow this prodigious worker, this doer who admired doers, simultaneously found time to think and write, time to contribute notably to the advancement of his profession. In the years before 1914 Hoover not only practiced mining engineering; he "preached" it. His activities as a "preacher"—as a self-conscious engineering professional—helped to mold his identity and the values that governed his later public life.

I I

Hoover's sense of professionalism appeared early. In 1896, only a few months out of Stanford, he joined the American Institute of Mining Engineers.[2] In 1897 he became an associate in a comparable British society, the Institution of Mining and Metallurgy; nine years later he advanced to full membership.[3] During his mining years he was elected a member of other prestigious professional organizations as well.[4]

More significantly, he began to write for professional publications. Early in 1896, while he was debating whether to become an academic geologist or a business-oriented mining man, John Caspar Branner counseled him to maintain his scholarly credentials by writing articles for professional journals.[5] Hoover took his mentor's advice. In 1896 and 1897, before he left for Western Australia, he published several essays—some signed, some unsigned—in San Francisco's *Mining and Scientific Press*.[6]

During the next decade-and-a-half Hoover became a prolific contributor to the leading periodicals of his profession. By 1914 he had placed more than thirty signed articles and letters to the editor, and more than a dozen unsigned or pseudonymous pieces, in British and American publications.[7] A number of his early articles reflected his scientific bent and interest in geology. His subject matter ranged widely—from the geology of a mining district in northwest Colorado to the nature of ore deposits in Western Australia.[8] Hoover's mind was active, his curiosity acute. Wherever he traveled in his first years out of college—be it to the Golden Mile at Kalgoorlie or the coal fields of northeastern China—an article on the geology or metallurgical practices of the region seemed to follow.[9]

As Hoover continued to travel he specialized. Western Australia became his "beat"; many of his articles were surveys of mining and economic conditions in that far-off country he was coming to know so well.[10] In 1903 and 1904 he engaged in a protracted public debate on the best method of treating sulpho-telluride ores at Kalgoorlie.[11] At the beginning of 1903, 1905, and 1906 the *Engineering and Mining Journal* of New York printed essays by him summarizing gold mining developments in Western Australia during the preceding year.[12]

One of Hoover's early specialties in his professional writings became almost a personal trademark: the subject of working costs and efficiency in mining. As early as 1898 he was expounding on this theme.[13] In a number of articles he presented data analyzing working costs in Western Australian mines and comparing results to those of mines in the great districts of South Africa and Cripple Creek, Colorado. Not surprisingly, Western Australia—where Bewick, Moreing was becoming preeminent—fared well in Hoover's comparisons.[14]

The young engineer's concern for and insistence upon efficiency had several roots. Fundamentally, of course, it made economic sense. In the rough, remote mining regions of Australia, a difference in unit working costs of a shilling or two per ton of ore might make the difference between profit and failure. Hoover was working in an environment that mandated frugality; his recurrent attention to working costs reflected his daily struggle against the small margin for error allowed at the mines his firm managed.

Hoover's professional interest in efficiency also reflected his competitiveness. With his keen sense of publicity Hoover was surely aware of the value of data showing low working costs at Bewick, Moreing companies. Indeed, the very object of compiling working costs, he wrote, was "fundamentally for comparative purposes." Such statistics, along with "other technical data," were, in his words, "the nerves of the administration." By comparing results both among and within mines, "a most valuable check on efficiency is possible"—a test, in other words, of the worth of the manager. Moreover, said Hoover, the mere existence of such data brought another administrative advantage: it elicited "solicitude and emulation" among the "subordinate staff."[15]

Hoover's professional articles and statements were frequently reprinted and commented on in the British, American, and Australian mining press— a solid measure of his growing international reputation.[16] But by 1903 he was no longer content with predominantly descriptive articles about mining practices and working costs (although he continued to write some essays of this character). Rather, he began to evince a larger desire: to improve the conduct of the mining business itself.

In a 1903 letter to the *Engineering and Mining Journal*, for instance, Hoover complained about "a most harassing lack of uniformity" in accounting methods currently used to calculate working costs per ton of ore. Gold mining accounts, he argued, should be systematized in such a way as to achieve three objectives: prevention of fraud, comparison of results within and among mines as an aid to the local manager's quest for "economy and improvement," and evaluation of "the efficiency of the manager himself." Hoover was enthusiastic about the results that could be obtained from comparison of working costs. "The rivalry growing out of such comparisons," he asserted, had done much to transform gold mining from "an absolute speculation" to "an industrial enterprise." Let "these valuable influences" have "full play," Hoover advised. Let there be "greater uniformity" in accounting practices for determining working costs. He urged the two leading British and American mining engineering societies to create a commission to develop a standard.[17]

Another problem of particular interest to him was the proper economic ratio between treatment capacity and ore reserves on gold mines, that is, between the ore treatment plant and the amount of developed ore available for treatment. In 1904 Hoover propounded the thesis (not as obvious as it may appear) that for maximum profit a gold mine should be worked very rapidly and that extra treatment facilities should even be built, if financially justified, in order to exhaust ore reserves within a few years. Ore reserves, in short, should disappear as quickly as possible.[18] Hoover's advocacy of quick, forced development jolted investors accustomed to regarding large ore reserves as a source of long-term stability. Hoover, though, did not want long-term stability; he argued that sound economy dictated speedy exploitation of a mine. (His argument was based on the assumption of a fixed price for gold.)

Hoover's articles evoked extended comment in the mining profession, and his "theorem," as one journal called it, was apparently widely accepted.[19] According to one distinguished mining man, Hoover's argument did much to clarify the amorphous subject of mine valuation in the early twentieth century.[20]

With his articles on gold-mining accounts and the proper exploitation of gold mines, Hoover found his niche in his profession: he was becoming an authority on the economics of mining, on the valuation and financing of mines. During 1904 he published further articles on this subject.[21] In 1905 five of his essays were reprinted in *Economics of Mining*, edited by T. A. Rickard.[22] In 1906, no doubt in recognition of Hoover's growing stature, Rickard listed him among the "special contributors" to the *Mining and Scientific Press*, of which Rickard had just become editor.[23] And in 1911 one of America's leading mining engineers declared that Hoover had done more to establish the logic of mine valuation than any other person. Hoover's articles, he said, had propounded the fundamental factors that engineers now accepted.[24]

Hoover's ideas on mining economics found their most comprehensive expression in 1909 in his *Principles of Mining*, a book based on lectures delivered earlier that year at Stanford University and the Columbia School of Mines. While some of Hoover's book was devoted to technical and mechanical aspects of mining, the bulk of it concentrated on his principal interests: valuation, administration, and finance. Suffusing the text was Hoover's recognition that mining, after all, was a business, that all mines were mortal, that the mining engineer's ultimate objective was to make an investment pay. Suffusing it, too, was a brisk Hooverian emphasis on efficiency and simplicity. "The essential facts governing the value of a mine," he declared at one point, "can be expressed on one sheet of paper."[25]

Principles of Mining also revealed Hoover in his adopted role of rationalizer of a speculation-prone industry. This role, of course, was not new: in 1903 and 1904 he had hailed the emergence of firms of professional mine managers (such as his own) as agents of reform, banishing ignorance and speculative excess from the mining landscape.[26] His articles on gold-mining accounts and related subjects reflected the same impulse. He condemned the "irresponsible promoter."[27] Although Hoover himself, after 1908, actively plunged into the stock market—even manipulating stock prices through market pools and contrived publicity—the engineer in him rebelled against risk.

And the engineer was speaking in *Principles of Mining*. A speculator, Hoover stated therein, was "one who hazards all to gain much." By contrast, said Hoover, *he* was writing about mining as an investment.[28] Hoover set the prudent procedures of valuation and administration outlined in his book against the practices too often found in the mining world.[29] In an era when more and more investors were turning to mining engineers for expertise and counsel, Hoover declared, "The engineer's interest is to protect [the investor], so that the industry which concerns his own life-work may be in honorable repute, and that capital may be readily forthcoming for its expansion."[30]

Honorable repute. To Hoover cleaning up the industry was a professional obligation: "In an industry that lends itself so much to speculation and chicanery, there is the duty of every engineer to diminish the opportunity of the vulture so far as is possible."[31] This was in part Hoover's goal as he worked to apply science—and reform—to the mining business.

Hoover's volume won immediate acclaim. From friends like Professor Branner and Curtis H. Lindley came enthusiastic praise; Lindley, an eminent mining lawyer, commended Hoover's scientific method and professional spirit.[32] One journal judged Hoover's book "the best exposition in existence of the methods by which the modern engineer proceeds to value mines."[33] Indeed, it appears to have been the first book ever published in which mine valuation was discussed systematically.[34] In the aftermath of publication some trustees of Columbia University asked Hoover to become dean of its engineering school.[35] Harvard University's Mining and Metallurgical Laboratory invited him to deliver some lectures to its students on the economics of mining.[36] Late in 1910 the editor of the *Engineering and Mining Journal* asked Hoover to become its London correspondent, responsible for a weekly column on technical, commercial, and financial events of importance.[37] Hoover evidently declined (there is no record of his reply), but the esteem the offer betokened was real enough.

Principles of Mining firmly solidified Hoover's reputation not just as a successful mining engineer but as a scholar and professional as well. Recognized as a classic, it became a popular textbook for engineering students and did not go out of print until 1967.[38]

In his writings on mining finance, Hoover saw himself as bringing clarity to an often murky subject. Late in 1909, under the pseudonym "A Professional Speculator," he published an article evaluating the shares of nearly 175 mining companies.[39] Despite his nom de plume Hoover's purpose was not speculative. He wished, rather, using his trained, informed intelligence, to classify stocks "on the mines and merits of the shares, not on the manipulations of the market."[40] Hoover had seen enough market vicissitudes, enough market operations—had participated in some himself—to dispel any belief that stock market quotations necessarily registered the current values of a share. He wished to show "that investment in mines can be as legitimate and sound as any other form of industrial enterprise, if properly advised."[41]

In 1912 Hoover published another much-discussed article, entitled "Economics of a Boom." In it he distinguished between the "economic" investment in a mine (working capital, management expenses, and money spent to raise this capital) and the nominal, issued, or market value of the company's shares. He distinguished also between "Insiders" (such as promoters and brokers), who "produce" mining shares, and "Outsiders" ("the investing public"), who "consume" them. To Hoover there was no relation between the "economic" investment in a mine and its total market value. A mine might be capitalized at £1,000,000—the Insiders might sell it to the Outsiders for this amount—but the "economic" investment in it might be only £120,000. Now what if the mine completely failed: would the £880,000 difference be considered an economic loss? No, argued Hoover, this amount would only have been transferred from one party to another. For that matter, "from an economic point of view, this £880,000 of capital in the hands of the Insiders is often invested to more reproductive purpose than if it had remained in the hands of the idiots who parted with it."[42] There was little doubt that Hoover saw himself as an Insider.

Hoover's remark about "idiots" evoked immediate comment[43] and caused him embarrassment at the hands of political enemies in later years. But if he seemed to disparage Outsiders, his purpose, from the inside, was not to fleece them. On the contrary, "inside" in his view was where the mining engineer should be, sharing his knowledge, stabilizing the market, rationalizing business practices, protecting the unwary, converting an "absolute speculation" into an industry. This, at least, was Hoover's self-image in the decade or more before 1914. In short, for him the profession of mining engineering was inherently ethical in character. The engineer brought science to industry: science—rationality—and professional ideals. In Hoover the scientist and reformer coalesced.

I I I

An engineer, however, was more to Hoover than a simple conveyor of science and honesty to business operations. "The mining engineer is no longer the technician who concocts reports and blue prints," he wrote in 1909. "It is demanded of him that he devise the finance, construct and manage the works which he advises."[44] As Hoover strove to rationalize and purify the mining industry, he developed a more expansive sense of mission. He sought to elevate the status and self-respect of the mining engineering profession itself.

In the half-century after the American Civil War—the period of Hoover's youth and pre-public career—the practice of engineering underwent a massive transformation. In 1880 there were but 7,000 engineers of all kinds in the United States; in 1920 there were 136,000.[45] Paralleling this growth was a change in the fundamental character of the calling. No longer was the field dominated by products of apprentice training and "rule-of-thumb" approaches; instead, college-educated, scientifically trained men were rising to leadership. In 1864 the first successful American school of mines opened; by the 1890s more than fifteen such institutions or programs had been founded.[46] The "shop" culture, as it has been called, was giving way to the "school" culture.[47] Engineering was ceasing to be a trade; it was becoming a profession.[48]

This growth in numbers and shift of circumstances produced a quickening self-consciousness and status-consciousness within the young profession. Engineering societies proliferated and with them professional journals. The impulse to "professionalize" appeared, too, in debates over the proper form of engineering education; the production of professionals, it was argued, could not be left to chance. This was the "mental universe" within which Herbert Hoover spent his youth as a mining engineer. Before long he revealed its effect on him.

Hoover was immensely proud of his profession. Engineers, he wrote in *Principles of Mining*, were "the real brains of industrial progress."[49] Engineering had achieved "the dignity of a profession on a par with the law, medicine, and science." In fact, he asserted, engineering actually required "a more rigorous training and experience" than these other professions.[50] Hoover emphasized the breadth of expertise that a mining engineer in particular must possess: knowledge of geology, of economics, of civil, mechanical, chemical, and electrical engineering. A mining engineer must also have "financial insight," "business experience," "engineering sense," and "executive ability" (the "capacity to coordinate and command the best results from other men"). Hoover listed five stages through which all engineering projects pass—from the initial ascertainment of a project's value to the "operation of the completed works." Among engineers, only the mining specialist was responsible for all five.[51]

Hoover's eulogizing of the mining engineer was mixed with disparagement of other vocations. In 1914 he complained that mining engineers always seemed to take positions inferior to the "parasitic" professions of law, theology, and war.[52] In *Principles of Mining* he contended:

To the engineer falls the work of creating from the dry bones of scientific fact the living body of industry. It is he whose intellect and direction bring to the world the comforts and necessities of daily need. Unlike the doctor, his is not the constant struggle to save the weak. Unlike the soldier, destruction is not his prime function. Unlike the lawyer, quarrels are not his daily bread. Engineering is the profession of creation and of construction, of stimulation of human effort and accomplishment.[53]

Hoover's tendentiousness—equating medicine with saving the "weak," the law with "quarrels," and the military with "destruction"—was extraordinary. It reflected a deeply felt conviction that did not waver for the rest of his life. Nearly half a century later a similar passage appeared in his *Memoirs*, along with expressions of disdain for another kind of professional: the politician. Hoover implied that engineers were more intellectually honest than other professionals who entered government service.[54]

Why did Hoover write this way? Was it a way of advertising his own success? If mining engineering was at least as difficult as any other profession, and if Hoover stood at the summit of his profession, did it not follow that he was one of the most intelligent, most successful men in the world? Hoover possessed a healthy ego (he had to in order to survive in the business world he inhabited), and it probably did not escape him that in uttering paeans to his profession he was also applauding himself.

Yet this, at most, was a fraction of the story. Such sentiments, in fact, were not peculiar to Hoover. His dislike of the "parasitic" professions (a phrase suggestive of Thorstein Veblen, whose writings he may have read)[55] was shared by other engineers who resented the higher status of older and less commercially oriented professions.[56] What is most striking about Hoover's apologia for his profession was not that he believed it but that he felt the need to offer it at all. It reflected an insecurity of status that fueled the professionalism of Hoover and his fellow engineers.

Hoover was not only nouveau riche; he was, like mining engineers as a group, newly professional. Hoover's sensitivity about his status appeared in a letter written before World War I to an American friend of some years' standing, Mary Austin. A Stanford graduate and novelist, Austin was writing a play in which an engineer was to be the villain and a simulated copper blast furnace the stage setting. Hoover was fascinated by the idea and shared thoughts with Austin about plot construction and the mechanics of the set. But to one aspect he objected:

Seriously I am interested in this matter; Ive whiled away many idle hours constructing a drama to represent to the world a new intellectual type from a literary or stage view—the modern intellectual engineer—theres more possibilites than you think. But you are trying to make a villian out of him which won't do; the successful mans intellectual educational and physical circuit enroute to success never produces a villian: Given a weakness in intellect or education or professional experience it would or might. You should put the real engineer on the stage as the genl mgr. The metallurgist could be your semi civilized villian; The foreman the man who maltreats his wife.[57]

The successful man's "circuit" en route to success never produces a villain, and the "modern intellectual engineer" should not be portrayed as one. These sentiments revealed much about Hoover's pride and anxieties concerning his chosen path to achievement. (The spelling and punctuation also revealed why he had had trouble with the English requirement at Stanford.)

The world is not accustomed to thinking of Herbert Hoover as a playwright, and as far as is known he never completed his drama about "the modern intellectual engineer." But in other ways he was more productive. Hoover was not content merely to proclaim what he called the "dignity" of his profession; with characteristic practicality he advocated measures to enhance it.

One of his earliest concerns was the subject of engineering education. During the 1890s a many-sided debate raged in the engineering profession concerning the proper education of young engineers. Many older engineers—trained in shops and in the school of experience—complained that young graduates with their theoretical background were not prepared to handle the practical problems of industry. To accommodate this criticism many engineering schools attempted to create a "practical" environment by the introduction of shop courses into the curriculum.[58]

In a little-known article written in 1899 Hoover objected to this development. Although he himself was now in "the field of practice," Hoover forcefully argued for more theory and less "practice" in the university. Inclusion of shop training at the college level, he said, absorbed precious time better spent on theoretical work. Four years of college, in fact, were already "too short a time to accomplish the theoretical training demanded of the Engineer today," and "practical" training did not compensate for this loss. Moreover, practical work in a university could not duplicate the essential feature of engineering experience in the world outside: its commercial character. Engineers today were employed for "executive purposes," as administrators. More important than knowledge of tricks of the trade was the ability to relate technical knowledge to the commercial consideration of profit and loss. Such commercial and administrative experience could only be learned in industry; "playhouse methods" in the university were "but a waste of time."

Hoover also contended that practical courses in college produced in students an inflated sense of their "practical" worth and an aversion to entering "overall" (that is, blue-collar) work upon graduation. To Hoover this was a mistake. Not only was the practical experience gained in college superficial; the proper time to get practical training was *after* college, starting "at the bottom level, and not for a holiday experience." Hoover considered university expenditure on practical training a waste of money. The purpose of a university education, he believed, was to train engineers, not mechanics.

Hoover did not spell out the content of the theoretical education he espoused. But of one principle he was certain: engineers were needed who were "soaked in theory and not befuddled with erroneous ideas of their practical worth."[59]

In an article published in the American journal *Science* in 1904 Hoover expanded on these themes.[60] Except for a few closing paragraphs, his essay was a statement that he had prepared and that Bewick, Moreing and Company had presented that summer to a British commission investigating technical education in Great Britain.[61] In his article Hoover emphatically affirmed the value of formal technical education, as opposed to the traditional apprentice method. He declared that he and his partners had found that "technically trained men" had more "professional feeling" than men who had come up from the ranks. Consequently they were "more trustworthy"—an important qualification in mining, "where such premium for dishonesty exists." For Hoover professionalism was a moral as well as scientific cause.

What, though, should be the content of the technical training of the mining engineer? Hoover proposed a three-tiered system of instruction. First, all prospective engineers should receive a thorough grounding in the humanities prior to entering a technical school. Second, they should, in fact, go to a technical school for at least four years. Echoing his 1899 article, Hoover stressed that technical training should be entirely theoretical and devoted to "pure science": there should be no vain, time-wasting effort to reproduce "commercial conditions" or "actual working conditions" in a university setting. (Summer employment was acceptable—as an adjunct to theory.) Furthermore, technical training should cover many scientific disciplines, reflecting the fact that mining engineering "requires a broader training than any other engineering branch." Third, Hoover stated that fresh graduates of technical schools should enter industry as apprentices, serving in a variety of departments for at least two years. In this way they could learn, in real-life circumstances, the proper balancing of commercial and technical considerations.

In Hoover's scheme, then, apprenticeship training still had its place but not as a means of learning theory. In effect, he was adumbrating the scheme of the future: broad undergraduate studies followed by graduate school and on-the-job training.

Although Hoover's fundamental position remained unchanged, his 1904 article showed an interesting evolution from his remarks in 1899. In the earlier piece his recommendations had been little more than a reflection of his own personal experience to date. His advocacy of starting out "at the bottom level" after college mirrored his own actions at Grass Valley in the fall of 1895. The 1904 article, however, disclosed a broader perspective. In advocating a comprehensive preliminary education in the humanities, he supported something he himself had not received, and now regretted. In calling for four years of systematic technical schooling he called for more intensive training than he himself ever obtained. Hoover was not a graduate of any school of mines; his only technical instruction had been at the undergraduate level, where other course work competed for his time. His third recommendation, a two-year post-graduate apprenticeship, more closely reflected his own past: in many ways his first three years out of Stanford, including his fifteen months with Louis Janin, amounted to such an apprenticeship. Only in 1898 did he obtain his first, full-time executive responsibility: superintendency of the Sons of Gwalia.

Hoover's program of engineering education reform was a progressive one, and to the extent within his power he tried to implement it. Late in 1904 Bewick, Moreing instituted a scholarship plan for graduates of the Royal School of Mines in London. The firm announced that each year it would take three recommended graduates into employment at its West Australian mines for a period of two years at £3.10.0 (or $17.50) per week, an allowance sufficient for living expenses and small savings. Students receiving these scholarships would have to work in all the departments of the mine, mill, and office. In effect, the firm was offering the apprenticeship part of Hoover's educational package. The firm warned that the position would be no "sinecure" or "holiday" but would entail "actual work alongside of the men employed in the Departments." However, it added that most of its mine managers were university-educated men sympathetic to "young men training for the Profession." The firm also cautioned against packing a large wardrobe for Western Australia: ". . . we have invariably found that young men with the biggest outfit of clothes generally have the smallest outfit of brains."[62] The sentence had a Hooverian ring.

Bewick, Moreing's program won applause in the mining press and continued for some years.[63] Even after he left the firm in 1908 Hoover engaged in a similar practice on his own, sponsoring, for instance, a student at the Royal School of Mines and assisting him in obtaining a summer job in Russia.[64] In 1911 he told an acquaintance that "we" (perhaps he counted Moreing) had put "dozens" of young men through the two-year apprenticeship program. Each one started at the bottom "as a simple workman" and rotated among the departments. "Every man that I know who has done any good in his Profession has gone through this process," Hoover said, "for the largest part of mining is the ability to direct men, and no one can direct men who has not himself done the same work, with his own hands."[65]

Hoover's personal support of a student at the Royal School of Mines was but one of numerous acts of generosity that he never publicized. He felt a sense of duty toward aspiring young mining engineers; in *Principles of Mining* he deemed it a professional obligation.[66] He felt a particular affinity for impecunious young men struggling upward as he had done. And if at the end of two years' hard work the "apprentices" in his organization had proved their mettle, he gave them staff positions at one of his mines.[67]

In his campaign to "professionalize" engineering education, Hoover kept constantly in mind that the aim of the educational process was to prepare students for entry into the world of businsss. Time and again he stressed

that mining engineers must be commercially as well as technically competent. For engineering was not science; it was the *application* of science to
industry, and industry itself was governed by economic calculation. Indeed,
on no other branch of engineering than mining did questions of profit and
loss so constantly impinge. "The question of capital and profit dogs his every
footstep," Hoover said, "for all mines are ephemeral; the life of any given
mine is short."[68] "The most dominant characteristic of the mining engineering profession," he wrote, "is the vast preponderance of the commercial over
the technical in the daily work of the engineer."[69]

It was American responsiveness to these facts that in Hoover's judgment
accounted for the increasing domination of British mining enterprises by
American engineers. Hoover criticized the British practice of dividing mining administration into two bureaus, one commercial and one technical, with
the latter holding inferior status. Far superior in his view was the American
practice of consolidating executive and technical leadership in one head: the
engineer.[70] Hoover cited statistics: by 1904, he claimed, literally hundreds
of American engineers were employed by British companies, and nearly all
of them held executive positions. In the worldwide gold-mining industry
particularly, American engineers were now in control.[71]

And not just Americans—Californians. "The State of California," Hoover
wrote in 1915,

> holds a unique position in the mining world, in that her mining children
> dominate more of the world's metal mining industry than any other race,
> and these men hold this position by virtue primarily because of the char-
> acter of the material of which they are made and secondarily by their unique
> combination of technical skill, combined with commercial instinct. Cali-
> fornia has, in consequence of the latter, imposed upon the mining world a
> type of man which has in fact revolutionized the mining engineering
> profession, . . . a man of commercial character with a sound technical
> training.[72]

Hoover was proud to identify himself with the extraordinary migration of
California mining men around the globe. It was California, he told San Francisco colleagues in 1914, that "for the past thirty years furnished the officers
who have commanded the mining army of millions." One reason for this
triumph was the Californians' merging of technology with administration, of
mine manager with mining engineer.[73]

If Hoover saw a potential problem in this fusion of roles, he did not record
it. While a few traditionalists like T. A. Rickard deplored the growing
immersion of mining engineers in nontechnical matters (notably finance),
Hoover applauded the trend.[74] To him the rise of the mining engineer to
administrative responsibility was both a mark of increased status and a moral
event:

. . . it is my belief [he said in 1915] that we have seen in the metal mining industry during the last ten years an enormous improvement in its morals and directing personnel, by virtue of the fact that the engineer has got into the financial as well as the technical control and, to express it shortly, what the world needs to-day in engineers is capable commercial men with a technical education.[75]

In short, more Hoovers.

If in Hoover's opinion the ideal university should produce "leaders of industry" and not just "technologists,"[76] this did not mean that he simply equated the professional engineer with the capitalist. The engineer, rather, was a purifier and rationalizer of capitalism. Indeed, in a modern corporation (Hoover wrote in 1909), the mining engineer as executive was a "buffer" between capital and labor.[77] Hoover was not an exponent of orthodox free market economics. In 1912 he labeled laissez-faire a "fetish."[78] In 1909 he even attacked the theory that wages were the result of supply and demand. In "these days of international flow of labor, commodities and capital," he argued, "the real controlling factor in wages is efficiency. . . ."[79]

As Hoover's professional sense intensified, he seemed to reconsider some of his old attitudes toward labor unions. His early posture had been tough, reflecting in part his strong identification with management. He had been prepared to use Italians as strikebreakers at the Sons of Gwalia. He had denounced Western Australia's compulsory arbitration law for settling wage disputes as a weapon in the hands of workmen for injustice against the employer.[80] He had inveighed against "professional agitators" and socialists whose influence over Australian workers appeared to be rising.[81] He had supported a "ticket system" as a means of blacklisting "the gold stealer and the demagogue" from employment on the Western Australian goldfields.[82] He had opposed a uniform minimum wage.[83] He had rejoiced when Western Australia's Labour government fell in 1905.[84]

By 1909, however, with the publication of *Principles of Mining*, Hoover's position on the labor question had modified perceptibly. Where once he had regarded unions with suspicion, he now considered them "normal and proper antidotes for unlimited capitalistic organization." According to Hoover there were two stages in the evolution of labor unions: the first often marked by demagogy, violence, and broken agreements; the second by union recognition of "the rights of their employers" and by nonviolent "negotiation on economic principles." To Hoover there were "few sounder positions for the employer" than the presence of a businesslike union that could control its members, carry out agreements, and thereby avert "the constant harassments of possible strikes." Such unions, he said, were "entitled to greater recognition."

The time when the employer could ride roughshod over his labor is disappearing with the doctrine of '*laissez faire*,' on which it was founded. The sooner the fact is recognized, the better for the employer. The sooner some miners' unions develop from the first into the second stage, the more speedily will their organizations secure general respect and influence.[85]

As if to accentuate his new attitude Hoover reversed his position on Western Australia's compulsory arbitration law. Although the statute in his opinion still had defects, he now believed that it had produced "almost unmixed good to both sides." For one thing, it had gone far toward eliminating the "parasite who lives by creating violence."[86]

Hoover's acceptance of labor unions as a useful force for industrial peace—as a tool, so to speak, of good management—was an advanced position among mining men in 1909. Few engineers had much use for unions;[87] Hoover's earlier attitudes were probably more representative of his profession. His approval, however, was not unqualified; in *Principles of Mining* he criticized efforts by unions to curtail efficiency in the "false belief" that they could thereby create more jobs. It was *increased* efficiency, he insisted—*increased* productivity—that benefited workers by augmenting profits, which employers could then share with their employees.[88]

No, Hoover had not lost his engineer's passion for efficiency. *Principles of Mining*, in fact, contained numerous suggestions for attaining that end; many seemed suggestive of the scientific management philosophy of Frederick Winslow Taylor. Hoover favored incentives (such as increased pay and a chance for promotion) over "driving" as techniques for achieving "increase of exertion." One test of a mine manager, he said, was his ability to build an esprit de corps among his employees; the staging of competitions among them was one means to this end. Still evidently unenthusiastic about a uniform wage for all workers, Hoover preferred contract or piecework over wages. Such an approach, he claimed, was clearly advantageous to employer and employee alike. "In a general way," he stated, "contract work honorably carried out puts a premium upon individual effort, and thus makes for efficiency." Hoover thought that as much as 75% of underground mining work could be done by contract labor.[89]

Hoover also approved of giving cash bonuses to workers for "special accomplishment," such as exceeding quotas or doing more work than men on other shifts. Such devices helped "in creating efficiency." And, he added, "A high level of results once established is easily maintained."[90]

To a later generation Hoover's preoccupation with productivity and with devices to improve it may sound like advocacy of exploitation. Hoover, of course, saw the matter differently. To him increased productivity was not a manifestation of class conflict but a way of avoiding it by increasing the size of the economic pie. "The whole question of handling labor," Hoover asserted, "can be reduced to the one term 'efficiency.' "[91] If only men could adopt the superior perspective of the engineer, he seemed to say with a sigh: "There lives no engineer who has not seen some insensate dispute as to wages where the real difficulty was inefficiency."[92]

Here, then, was a new social role for the engineer and another sign of his indispensability (hence claim to esteem) in the modern industrial order. If efficiency was the key to industrial peace and prosperity, who was the embodiment of efficiency? For Hoover the answer was obvious. It was the "modern intellectual engineer."

Another facet of Hoover's campaign to elevate the mining profession also came to fruition in 1909. For some years he had been disturbed by what he considered the dishonest character of the London mining press.[93] The journals depended for their financial survival on the printing of verbatim reports of mining company meetings supplied by the companies themselves. Such a symbiosis between the press and its advertisers hardly made for editorial candor: criticism of a company's management might speedily lead to the withholding of a company's meeting report from the offending journal and the loss of needed advertising. This "intimacy with company finance," said T. A. Rickard, was the "curse of technical journalism in London."[94]

Early in 1905 Hoover tried unsuccessfully to induce Rickard to come to London and take over the prestigious *Mining Journal*.[95] Four years later Hoover had more success. By now Rickard, perhaps the world's foremost mining journalist, was editing San Francisco's *Mining and Scientific Press,* and in a manner that Hoover enthusiastically approved. At the urging of Hoover and some others, Rickard and his cousin Edgar agreed to leave San Francisco for London to found a truly independent, honest mining journal. Hoover hoped (in the words of a friend) thereby "to give the industry an honest background image to the public."[96] The Rickard cousins themselves put up most of the capital for the fledgling enterprise; Hoover and twenty-nine other prominent mining engineers subscribed for the rest (in the form of small individual holdings of preferred stock).[97] Without Hoover's initiative and the combined financial support of himself and other engineers, the new venture would probably have remained chimerical.

And so in September 1909 the *Mining Magazine* was born. True to his principles (and to Hoover's hope) Rickard immediately became an outspoken voice for ethics and sound management in the mining business. Hoover himself contributed several articles over the next few years to the journal, including the much-discussed "Professional Speculator" pieces of 1909. The *Mining Magazine* was a novelty in London journalism; it was even, in Rickard's judgment, a *succès d'estime*.[98] More important here is what it represented for Hoover: a reliable journal, useful not only for the information it contained but for its raising of the moral tone of his calling.[99]

Hoover, then, was acutely conscious of the status and status claims of his profession. Living in England reinforced his sensitivity. He noted the fact that in England particularly, where the apprentice system was still strong, the vocation of engineering lacked "social dignity." An engineer generally was perceived as a tradesman or artisan, not as a professional. Consequently young men looking for a career with "social dignity" opted for law, the military, and other more esteemed professions.[100]

It was a deep desire (as he later put it) to "enhance the feelings of dignity" of the mining engineering profession that led Hoover to embark on the project that brought him enduring and worldwide acclaim: the translation of *De Re Metallica*. Georgius Agricola was the Latinized name of Georg Bauer (1494–1555), a German physician and author of learned treatises on many subjects. Living for years in the mining districts of Bohemia and Saxony, Agricola became absorbed in the investigation of every aspect of mining and metallurgical practice. Highly educated, scholarly, acquainted with leading figures of the Renaissance, he developed a reputation as an authority on his chosen avocation. During his lifetime Agricola published a number of pioneering works, including the first book on physical geology and the first systematic mineralogy ever published by anyone. But it was a monumental tome published in Latin in 1556, a year after his death, that most secured his eminence in the history of science: *De Re Metallica*, a product of more than twenty years' original research and preparation.[101]

A huge volume illustrated with 289 woodcut drawings, *De Re Metallica* was the first truly comprehensive work on mining and metallurgy published in the history of western civilization.[102] Even more remarkably, it was the first book on its subject to be grounded in actual field work and observation; much of the information it contained was original. Indeed, the Hoovers were to claim that Agricola was "the first to found any of the natural sciences upon research and observation, as opposed to previous fruitless speculation." Agricola, they asserted, was "the pioneer in building the foundation of science by deduction from observed phenomena."[103] For nearly two centuries following its publication, *De Re Metallica* was unsurpassed as a textbook for miners and metallurgists.[104] In many mining districts it was chained to the altar of churches so that priests could translate its Latin into the vernacular for the instruction of local miners.[105]

Although *De Re Metallica* was translated into German and Italian within a few years of its publication, these translations were far from adequate. For not only was the technical subject matter abstruse, a severe obstacle to translators unfamiliar with mining; Agricola had compounded the difficulty by writing his treatise in a language that had ceased to grow hundreds of years before. To describe processes and substances for which no Latin equivalent existed, he had simply invented Latin expressions (hundreds of them) instead of using the German terms of his day. The result was almost insuperable difficulty—a translator's nightmare. By 1900, nearly three hundred fifty years later, no satisfactory, accurate translation of *De Re Metallica* existed, and none at all in English.[106] Agricola's masterwork had gone the way of many a classic: vaguely remembered, little known.

The idea of translating *De Re Metallica* into English originated with Lou Henry Hoover. On December 28, 1906 she wrote to Professor Branner of Stanford University that Agricola's book was interesting her but that she had been unable to find an English translation at the British Museum. So, she confided, she thought she might translate it herself during the next few months.[107] Mrs. Hoover's letter conveyed no hint of the magnitude of the task ahead.[108] Several years later an American mining journal remarked that when the Hoovers undertook the translation they did so as "light heartedly" as those who had preceded them.[109] In 1907, in any case, the Hoovers decided to tread where others had failed.[110] They did not foresee that their little project would turn into more than five years of strenuous exertion consuming evenings, weekends, energy, and money.

In many ways the Hoovers were an ideal couple for the attempt. Although his language skills were scanty,[111] Herbert knew his mining practice and had an intense love of history besides. Lou also had a knowledge of geology and, more importantly, a competent grasp of Latin.[112] Still, the barriers to success were tremendous. Not only had Agricola sprinkled his text with contrived Latin terminology that must somehow be deciphered; some of the mining methods he described were now either obsolete or unknown in English-speaking countries. How was one to describe these in English—and in English not too modern for the degree of knowledge Agricola actually possessed? Truly to decipher the often obscure text, truly to determine Agricola's meaning, would require far more than a decent knowledge of Latin or of twentieth-century mining.

So the Hoovers began. By the end of 1908, if not before, the couple was experiencing difficulties, as evidenced by their growing interest in procuring an English translation of the *German* translation of *De Re Metallica* in 1557, no doubt for comparative purposes.[113] Unfortunately, neither of the Hoovers was proficient in sixteenth-century German. Beginning, therefore, possibly in late 1908 and certainly by mid-1910, the Hoovers retained a succession of professional translators for the German rendition of *De Re Metallica*.[114] One of their principal assistants from 1910 on, Kathleen Schlesinger, was a noted musicologist who knew as many as six or seven languages.[115]

By late 1910 the Hoovers' translation was well advanced, and Herbert started to explore publishing possibilities.[116] But even as he did so the project was assuming a new shape in his mind. He was coming to realize that for his enterprise to have more than antiquarian value it must be more than a mere, formal translation of an out-of-date text. For Agricola's achievement to be recognized Hoover must annotate the text. He must, that is, through notes and appendices, put Agricola in the context of the history of mining—a formidable challenge that would entail a careful examination of technical treatises by Agricola, his contemporaries, predecessors, and successors: works largely written in Latin or German.[117]

By 1911 this new thrust in the project was obvious. That spring, if not before, Hoover asked Schlesinger to translate part of another of Agricola's books, *De Natura Fossilium*.[118] On June 14, 15, and 16, 1911 he advertised in *The Times* of London for a "Lady Secretary who can translate Latin and German with facility and has done work at British Museum."[119] As a result, by mid-summer a corps of three (and possibly more) translators was hard at work on various assignments for the Hoovers, mostly involving collateral texts.[120] Over the next year other outside experts were consulted on occasion. The circle of the Hoovers' investigations expanded steadily as assistants were asked to compile bibliographies on selected topics (such as the history of mining law) and to consult or translate an array of primary and secondary sources, including several other works by Agricola.[121] The Hoovers themselves actively participated in this all-out research project, Lou evidently translating some secondary sources on her own.[122] Meanwhile, with the aid of new information and with some assistance from various translators,[123] the Hoovers worked and reworked their original translation and clarified difficult points. Eventually they revised their translation completely four times.[124]

It was becoming a monumental endeavor. For although the Hoovers obtained substantial research assistance, the crucial task of synthesis was theirs alone. No translator could be expected accurately to render the meaning of Agricola's mining terms into English; the key problem of technical terms only the Hoovers could solve.[125] The same Latin word, for instance, might be translatable several ways, depending on the context. It was up to Bert and Lou to determine the appropriate usage in each case.[126] The text was replete with puzzles; the Hoovers afterwards remarked that "there are a thousand sentences in Agricola upon which one could argue from morning till night."[127]

Sentence by sentence, they persevered.[128] At times Hoover even resorted to laboratory experiments to determine just what substance Agricola was writing about.[129] Similarly for the footnotes: hired assistants translated collateral texts and compiled the data for notes on such subjects as the history of mining law or the theory of ore deposition, but it was Hoover's task to mold this information into a coherent whole.[130] In effect Hoover was writing a history of ancient and medieval mining through the medium of his footnotes and appendices.

All this was happening while Hoover was absorbed in the ceaseless pursuits of business, travel, and raising a family, not to mention the continual entertaining of guests at his London residence. The Agricola translation project was only a part-time project, squeezed into the interstices of an amazingly busy life. Somehow, though, he found time to supervise every detail of the Agricola "operation," even as he kept track of mining and financial operations from London to Maikop to Kyshtim to Broken Hill to Burma to Peru.[131]

At the beginning of 1913 the Hoovers' translation of *De Re Metallica* was published by the Rickards' *Mining Magazine*.[132] Dedicated to the Hoovers' mentor, Professor John C. Branner, the book comprised not only a meticulous translation of Agricola's text but also a translators' preface, biographical sketch of Agricola, evaluation of Agricola's place in the history of science, and various bibliographic data, including a review of all significant mining literature written prior to Agricola's time. Perhaps most importantly, the volume contained lengthy historical notes prepared by Hoover surveying the development of mining, metallurgy, mining law, geology, and mineralogy from prehistoric times to Agricola's generation. Hoover's notes constituted a virtual capsule history of mining in all its aspects from ancient Greece to the dawn of the Renaissance.

The physical appearance of the Hoovers' volume reflected their assiduous devotion to their project. Here, too, no detail was overlooked. Hoover wanted the translation to replicate the original 1556 edition as completely as possible—right down to the font of type, the reproduction of the woodcuts, even the kind of paper used. It was no easy objective, but in the end, after great effort, he came very close to achieving his goal. The resultant volume was bound in white vellum (like the original) and handprinted on paper manufactured in a sixteenth-century manner by a Scottish paper mill. With justifiable pride Hoover later called it "one of the greatest pieces of modern book making."[133]

The *De Re Metallica* project was, as the Hoovers acknowledged in their preface, "a labour of love."[134] Originally they intended to print only a few hundred copies for gifts to their friends, but at the urging of Edgar Rickard they agreed to a larger circulation. Three thousand copies were printed, of which the Hoovers gave away 1,500, retained 500, and permitted the remaining 1,000 to be sold for about five dollars—20% of the actual cost.[135] According to Theodore Hoover the project cost his brother (in pre-1914 money) over $20,000.[136]

The Hoovers' successful translation of *De Re Metallica* was instantly recognized as a brilliant work of scholarship. From the mining press, from the *American Historical Review*, from engineers and academics who received presentation copies, effusive tributes to the translators poured in.[137] Early in 1914 the Mining and Metallurgical Society of America awarded the Hoovers its first gold medal for distinguished service, specifically for "distinguished contributions to the literature of mining."[138] Nearly three-quarters of a century later their work is still recognized as a splendid contribution to the history of science.[139]

Of all the comments in the professional mining media, one suspects that the *Engineering and Mining Journal*'s editorial in 1913 pleased Hoover the most. The publication of the Hoover translation, said the *Journal*, was "an event of some importance,"

> not merely because of the intrinsic value of the work, but especially we think as the work crowning the professional career of a distinguished engineer, who in becoming also a successful financier has not forgotten his professional ideals and duties. We know those envied engineers who have developed financial instincts and created a following among capitalists and investors and thereby become successful promoters. Most of them, unfortunately, degenerate into mere money-makers and upon their retirement from activity nothing more to say of them can be called to mind than that

they were rich. Mr. Hoover has been as successful commercially as any of them and his operations have been of broader scope geographically than any of them (which probably has contributed to his great breadth of vision), but amid his manifold activities hs has always preserved enthusiastic attention to strictly professional studies. What other mining financier or engineer-operator could have given us 'Principles of Mining,' or even would have taken the trouble to try?[140]

Even as he published *De Re Metallica* Hoover was contemplating other scholarly projects suggested by his research. In footnotes in *De Re Metallica* itself Hoover disclosed his hope "to discuss exhaustively at some future time" the history of the theory of ore deposition and his hope to "pursue elsewhere" the complex history of the development of mining law.[141] Perhaps for this purpose, in 1912 he discussed with Schlesinger the possibility of her compiling a bibliography of mining laws up to the year 1400.[142]

One obvious candidate for publication was Agricola's pioneering systematic mineralogy, *De Natura Fossilium*, which Schlesinger had already partially translated before 1913.[143] Years later, in fact, Hoover told a friend, "We started to translate 'De Natura Fossilium' once and made a first rough draft of most of it."[144] Probably he was referring to Schlesinger's preliminary translation. Possibly he was referring to this same document when, in June 1914, he told her that he hoped to have "something which may be of interest to you in the course of a few months."[145] Alas, that very summer world war broke out and ended forever the chance that Hoover might return to what he called "the luxury of book work."[146]

An ardent bibliophile, Hoover during his mining career amassed a remarkable personal library of rare old books in many languages on the history of science and the metallic arts. A number of these even pre-dated the sixteenth century. This collection of about a thousand volumes is intact today, a gift in 1970 of the Hoover family to the Claremont Colleges.[147]

The *De Re Metallica* translation established for Hoover, like Agricola before him, a permanent niche in scientific scholarship. Why had he made such an effort? In 1913 T. A. Rickard opined, "No idea of money-making was involved in the purpose of the translators. The expectation was, we believe, to do something useful and to win an honourable fame."[148] The Hoovers no doubt would have abjured any interest in winning fame but probably would not have denied a desire to do "something useful." But useful in what respect? As the Hoovers themselves admitted in their preface, Agricola's treatise was no longer relevant to modern practice.

In his address to the Mining and Metallurgical Society of America, Hoover gave his answer: he and his wife undertook the project to stimulate a sense of "dignity," "pride," and "professional ideals" among the members of their profession.[149] In the preface to *De Re Metallica* the couple wrote:

We do not present *De Re Metallica* as a work of 'practical' value. The methods and processes have long since been superseded; yet surely such a milestone on the road of development of one of the two most basic of human industrial activities is more worthy of preservation than the thousands of volumes devoted to records of human destruction. . . . If the work serves to strengthen the traditions of one of the most important and least recognized of the world's professions we shall be amply repaid.[150]

Because of the Hoovers' achievement, the engineering community could now affirm that mining did indeed have "traditions," that mining—far from being an upstart, inferior calling—was an ancient and honorable profession.[151]

I V

BY 1914 Hoover was near the pinnacle of his profession. By such means as his technical articles, *Principles of Mining*, advocacy of professional education, and translation of *De Re Metallica*, he had done much both to rationalize the business of mining and to enrich the mining engineering community's sense of professional importance. He was on his way to becoming the publicly recognized personification of "the modern intellectual engineer."

In turn his profession had done much for him. Above all, it had given him an identity, a sense of self-justification and self-esteem, a sense of being a progressive. "Science," he wrote in 1912, "is the base upon which is reared the civilization of to-day."[152] What was the engineer but the person who made this civilization possible, the professional who transmuted science into broad material well-being?

Yet oddly enough, Hoover was not content. Even as he extolled the engineering profession, he was planning, so he told his friends, to leave it. Noble as the calling of the mining engineer was, in the years after 1907 he wished increasingly to transcend it.

24

An American
Abroad

I

I n the half-decade or so after his departure from Bewick, Moreing and
Company, Hoover's base of operations remained London. While travel at
times took him from California to Korea, from Paris to St. Petersburg, it was
London, the world capital of mining finance, that continued to be the hub of
his business life. The rhythmn (when he was there) grew familiar: from the
Red House in Kensington in the morning, east to his office in the City; from
the City back to the Red House at night. Monday through Friday and half a
day on Saturday: that was a business week. It seemed scarcely enough time
to guide the incredible array of mining and financial propositions that, like
an expert juggler, he was handling simultaneously.

Yet even Hoover rested. Evenings, weekends, and holidays provided time
for leisure and surcease, time for the joys and responsibilities of a family
man. And England, elegant Edwardian England—from 1910 on, Georgian
England—was a fascinating civilization to explore. If an American of some
means like Hoover had to spend time abroad, he could hardly do better than
live in Britain before the Great War.

Hoover found his environment immensely stimulating. "Pre-war England,"
he later wrote, "was the most comfortable place to live in the whole world"—
if one had the money to purchase the amenities of upper-class existence.[1]
The England of history and culture, the England of "polite living," the beautiful British countryside, the music, art, and theater available in London, the

496

well-trained and devoted servants: all contributed to the satisfaction of living in a foreign land.[2]

With increasing frequency after mid-1908 Hoover and his family explored their host country. Weekends and holidays became times for excursions throughout Britain in Hoover's automobile: French-built, often chauffeur-driven, sometimes cantankerous. Hoover's brother Theodore and his family, who had moved to London in late 1906, frequently joined in these expeditions, as did various British and American guests.[3]

Sometimes these trips would have as their objective a picnic in the country—in a forest, perhaps, where the children could gather beech nuts. Hoover liked to tarry near small streams, where he demonstrated to his sons and Theodore's daughters how to catch minnows or, above all, how to dam up and divert the stream. For years to come this was one of Hoover's favorite pastimes: wading shoeless and sockless into a brook and proceeding methodically to alter its course.[4]

The British countryside was laden with history and culture, and over several years the Hoovers sampled many of its special attractions: Salisbury, for instance, with its famous cathedral; Dover with its white cliffs; Tintern Abbey, immortalized by Wordsworth; Henley, site of regattas. Hoover liked to take American women interested in genealogy to Whitchurch in Hampshire, where, to his quiet amusement, they rummaged through old records for information. (Once, to his surprise, his own sister-in-law found a lode of data about her ancestry in this very spot.)[5] On another occasion Hoover took an American guest down to Stonehenge, from which they observed Haley's Comet.[6] In 1910 he escorted President David Starr Jordan of Stanford University on a lengthy motor trip through England and Wales, touching base in Cardiff, Swansea, and Aberystwyth.[7] That same year he took his old college friend Ray Lyman Wilbur on a two-week drive through Scotland—a vacation made more memorable when Hoover's car tipped over in a peat bog. It took the two an entire day to retrieve the vehicle.[8]

Gradually the family developed the custom of renting a home in the country or at the shore during the summer or early autumn. During part of 1909, again in 1911, and perhaps on other occasions, Lou Henry Hoover and the boys stayed for a time at a cottage in Swanage on the Dorset coast.[9] In the summer of 1913 the Hoover brothers rented an old house (built in 1550) in Shakespeare's town, Stratford-on-Avon. Here their children spent the weekdays under the watchful tutelage of a governess and a nurse. On weekends the Hoover parents arrived from London with guests.[10]

Like many American mining engineers of this era, Hoover evinced a keen interest in history.[11] A Stanford University professor who traveled with him in England was struck by Hoover's knowledge of, and curiosity about, the history of the country around him. Hoover seemed especially intrigued by the development of institutions and by the inner dynamics of nations and civilizations: their formative psychology (what a later generation might call national character). He liked above all to learn about people who had *accomplished* something and did not simply talk about it. Once a friend loaned him *The Education of Henry Adams:* an elegant chronicle, in Adams's telling, of a superfluous and failed career. Hoover's reaction to the book was sharp and short: "the puerilities of a parasite."[12]

Many of Hoover's automobile trips reflected his insatiable curiosity about the English past. When a Stanford historian visited him in 1906 Hoover drove him around London on an inspection tour of remnants of the ancient Roman wall.[13] On another occasion Hoover motored down to the English coast and carefully retraced the steps of William the Conqueror in 1066.[14] When he set out for Scotland in 1910 he carried with him numerous relevant books that he devoured in the evenings, the better to discourse on Scottish lore to his travel partners by day.[15]

One of these excursions enabled Hoover, his brother, and Lindon Bates to play a practical joke. Their victim was a visiting Stanford history professor, whom they accompanied on a four-day tour of historic sites in southern England. Before the expedition the engineers secretly studied in detail the history of the area. Then, on the trip, they unleashed their knowledge on their unsuspecting American guest, whose own acquaintance with the subject seemed meager by comparison. Hoover even regaled the professor with a minute account of the battle of Edgehill in the English Civil War—right down to the placement of the contesting armies on the landscape before them. Abashed by this display of erudition by his engineer-hosts, the American historian grew increasingly chagrined. Finally the engineers confessed their deed, no doubt to the professor's relief.[16]

This particular jaunt revealed more about Hoover than his love of a practical joke. The Stanford historian never forgot the tears that came to Hoover's eyes when he saw the beautiful Tintern Abbey at dusk, nor the emotion Hoover displayed at the "Parliament House" of the Forest of Dean, where ancient miners gathered to govern themselves—the earliest such assembly (tradition said) in English history.[17] Thus the professor detected what only intimates of Hoover discerned: beneath the brusque exterior was a man of sentiment.

Family travel outside England, except for visits to the United States, was infrequent now. When Hoover went to Korea in 1910 and Kyshtim in 1911 his wife and sons did not go with him. But in February 1912 Lou and Bert teamed up with Edgar Rickard and his wife for an unforgettable grand tour of France and Italy—Paris, Rome, Florence, Cannes, and Venice. In the years ahead Rickard became one of Hoover's closest associates in business and public service.[18] In 1913 the two couples again played tourist on a rail journey to St. Petersburg, Moscow, and Kyshtim.[19]

If rural England and the continent provided ample outlets for the Hoovers' love of travel and history, still, London was the center, a city of endless enchantment. "When a man is tired of London," said Dr. Samuel Johnson, "he is tired of life; for there is in London all that life can afford." Hoover and his family testified by their actions to the truth of Dr. Johnson's remark. Many were the times they took American friends to the Tower of London, Westminster Abbey, and other standard attractions. Many were the lectures attended, the museums visited. Many were the Saturday and Sunday afternoons the two brothers and their families spent at the London Zoological Gardens, one of Herbert's favorite forms of weekend relaxation.[20]

Ofttimes, too, the families lolled away afternoons in Hyde Park, Kensington Gardens, and—just south of London—Kew Gardens.[21] Sixty years later Hoover's eldest niece could still recall those charming girlhood days:

> [Saturday afternoon play] would often be an expedition to the Round Pond in Kensington Gardens with our model sailboats. Ostensibly, the boats belonged to Cousin Herbert and me, but that was really a subterfuge on our fathers' part because actually they raced the boats, figured out wind strength and direction, adjusted sails and rudder, while all we did was to race around the Pond and retrieve the boats for them!
>
> In the winters the contests were with an elaborate train system in the large recreation room at the Red House.[22]

One of the Hoovers' favorite London recreations was the theater. Between 1906 and 1916 the two brothers and their wives were assiduous theater-goers, often attending a play a week or more: from vaudeville to *Man and Superman*, from Gilbert and Sullivan to Shakespeare, from *A School for Scandal* to *Peter Pan*.[23] Hoover himself seemed to become particularly interested in Shakespeare. When, shortly before the war, a distinguished British actor founded the Shakespeare International Alliance to promote (among other goals) the "artistic and ethical influence of Shakespeare" around the world, Hoover became the organization's Honorary Treasurer.[24] Perhaps it was this interest that led to his renting a summer home in Stratford-on-Avon. It was typical of his sense of humor that when he arrived at Shakespeare's birthplace he argued that Francis Bacon was really the author of Shakespeare's plays. Hoover merely wanted to activate the minds of his British neighbors. He very speedily succeeded.[25]

In addition to theatrical performances Hoover increasingly participated in another form of British social life. Between 1909 and 1912 he was elected a member of at least four British clubs: the Albemarle, Hurlingham, Members, and Royal Automobile.[26]

Sunday motor trips, vaudeville, attendance at the theater, membership in fashionable clubs: Hoover had traveled far indeed from the strict Quaker upbringing of his boyhood. What would his mother have thought, or his Uncle John? Significantly enough, in Herbert's and Theodore's later reminiscences of their London years one finds no reference whatever to religion. There is no evidence that the Hoovers ever attended a Quaker meeting in London, although an active Friends organization existed there. Indeed, there is no conclusive evidence that Hoover attended a single church service from the time he left Stanford in 1895 until World War I (although conceivably he did so).[27] During this period Hoover evidently maintained his membership in the Oregon Friends meeting he had joined as a teenager.[28] But beyond this formal commitment there were no outward signs of religious stirrings.

This probably was not accidental. Early in his life Hoover and his wife both had given signs of religious latitudinarianism bordering on unorthodoxy. Although Protestant by upbringing, had they not asked to be married by a Roman Catholic priest? Many years later one of Theodore's daughters remarked: "My family were reverent but not religious. I'm sure one could call them free-thinkers. I asked once whether my father believed in God and in heaven and in immortality, and he said: I try to."[29] Hoover himself, late in his life, remarked once with a chuckle to a friend, "Well, . . . I was raised as a Quaker but I never worked very hard at it."[30] While Hoover's early religious views are difficult to document, his external behavior in his first twenty years after college suggested the dormancy of pietistic impulses. But whatever his private religious beliefs during this period, Sundays in England were occasions not for religious observance but for more worldly undertakings.

If London was Hoover's immediate "neighborhood," from late 1907 on the Red House on Hornton Street, Kensington was his home—or, more properly, his home-away-from-home until the time when California could become his permanent residence. The Red House was a rambling, old, two-story villa, built in the 1830s and set in a garden enclosed by a high brick wall. A country house in the city, it had the unusual features of steam heating and large bathrooms—thanks to the American wife of the previous leaseholder. To the left, as one entered, was an oak-paneled library with a fireplace and leaded glass bookcases. The dining room had walnut panels and a dais two or three steps up on which theatrical performances could be given. Visitors took note of the curiously winding corridors, the French windows that descended to the floor of the high rooms, and the sea of books that the Hoovers possessed. Outside in the garden stood an ancient mulberry tree, which Hoover labored to save, and a fish pond with a fountain.[31]

Managing such an establishment was no inexpensive proposition. Not only did the Hoovers pay more than $2,000 a year in rent (in pre-1914 money);[32] they also retained a sizable corps of servants. There was Phillpott, the chauffeur; Dunn, the butler; a cook; a parlor maid; and various nurses and governesses to care for Herbert's and Theodore's children.[33] Hoover was generous with his staff, who reciprocated with lifelong loyalty. Not one to put up with rigid class distinctions, he would have the butler's children come over to the Red House to play with his own children.[34] On one occasion he gave his butler the pre-war equivalent of fifty dollars (a substantial sum in those days) to take his family on a vacation.[35] Many years later Lou Henry Hoover sent needed financial assistance to her former London parlor maid, who was then struggling to cope with the Great Depression.[36]

Under the Hoovers the Red House became far more than a private home. The couple were inveterate entertainers, and it was not long before they became famous among traveling Americans for their hospitality, particularly their Sunday evening suppers served in the dining room. To the Hoovers' table came an endless stream of invited guests: American mining engineers stopping in London from all over the world, Stanford alumni, Stanford professors, David Starr Jordan, the unforgettable Joe Boyle of the Klondike, journalists like Richard Harding Davis, novelists like Mary Austin, and other visitors, not to mention assorted American residents of London and various British friends.[37] The Red House was "a mecca for Californians," one American guest observed.[38] And for Americans abroad generally. Theodore Hoover later estimated that between 1905 (when they still lived at Hyde Park Gate) and 1916, Herbert and Lou entertained literally thousands of Americans at their successive homes in London.[39]

Many visitors fondly remembered the lively, far-reaching conversations on those leisurely Sunday evenings at the Hoovers' residence.[40] The requirements of entertaining, however, did not always come easily to the host. Herbert Hoover "had no small talk—no small talk whatever," remarked one friend, who long remembered the evening when Hoover "made but little effort to entertain" certain guests.[41] One mining engineer's wife who often sat next to Hoover at these dinner parties never got over the experience. "He was not a very affable dinner partner," she later recalled. He was not "very humorous." Hoover, she said, "was a grunter. I would say something and he'd just say 'unh.' "[42]

Yet there was more to Hoover as host than his awkwardness, even abruptness, in casual conversation. A British Shakespearean actress visiting the Red House for the first time found Hoover well-read, "full of keenness in all kinds of work and thought," and declared, "I never enjoyed an evening more."[43] At times, as Red House intimates discovered, Hoover would open up and display remarkable facility as a storyteller. And what stories he could tell— of the harrowing days of the Boxer Rebellion, of the tiger in the tunnel in Burma, of the fabled gold rush days in Kalgoorlie. If neither skilled at nor interested in chit-chat dialogue, he was gifted at monologue—when the spirit moved him. Then his guests would discover a humorous, relaxed, personable Hoover whom the world outside rarely glimpsed.

Most of the time, though, Hoover seemed content to listen and learn and enjoy. "You know," his niece long afterward remarked, "both my father and Uncle Bert were wonderful raconteurs. If they didn't have anything to say, they didn't say anything, and they'd be perfectly happy to sit silent a whole evening with everybody wondering what was wrong with them." The niece attributed this aloofness and inability to make small talk to their early orphanhood and consequent lack of a mother or father to teach them social graces.[44]

Perhaps in compensation for this verbal deficiency, Hoover cemented the

friendship of many guests with numerous acts of generosity—the gift of a
rare book to a Stanford professor who could not afford to buy it, for instance,
or the loan of his automobile to David Starr Jordan.[45] Above all, Hoover was
blessed by the articulateness and charm of his wife. An outgoing, unaffected
woman who enjoyed socializing, Lou was expert at keeping conversations
going and at making her varied guests feel comfortable. "She knew," said
one, "how to make people talk and whom her Bertie liked to hear talk."[46]
One British guest found her "absolutely brilliant," the "soul of gentleness,
with a peculiar charm of manner."[47] To the mining engineer's wife who sat
next to Hoover so often, Lou was a useful counterpart to her husband: "He
was a very fortunate man to have had the wife he had. . . . He needed
explaining. She made a specialty of explaining him."[48]

Holidays were special occasions at the Red House, for children and adults
alike. At Christmas time Hoover would dress up as Santa Claus and hand
out presents to his household staff and their children. At Easter he would
hide colored eggs in the garden for his own and his servants' children to
find.[49] The Fourth of July, Thanksgiving, and the date of California's admission to the Union: all were appropriately celebrated.[50] Noting the American
engineer's patriotic intensity, some British acquaintances referred to him as
the "star-spangled Hoover."[51] It recalled the nickname he had acquired in
the Australian outback: "Hail Columbia" Hoover.

Among children, as many people afterwards noted, Hoover seemed to shed
his brusqueness and taciturnity. One first-time visitor to the Red House happened on Hoover in the yard by the fountain, carefully demonstrating to his
young sons how to pan for gold.[52] A "great lover of pets," Hoover gave his
nieces a Persian cat and a Scottish terrier named Rex.[53] One of his nieces
never forgot how her cigar-smoking Uncle Bert coped with pesty wasps that
arrived daily at the breakfast table. Silently, and probably with a twinkle in
his eye, Hoover filled a glass with cigar smoke and cupped it over the wasps.[54]

To brother Theodore, Herbert was an "indulgent" father.[55] To one of his
nieces, young Herbert and Allan were "very mischievous little boys who
were raised quite permissively"—to the great distress of the girls' governesses. Hoover's sons, she said, were really "lovely little boys but always doing
things that English governesses didn't approve."[56]

In many respects it was an idyllic life. Looking back long afterwards, Hoover realized how fortunate he had been. The generation-long era before the
cataclysm of 1914, he wrote, was "the last golden age in the world." It was a
time of peace, expanding prosperity, and "released human spirit"—a time of
poverty, corruption, and slums, to be sure, but a time when nations recognized these evils and were striving with optimism to eradicate them. It was
a period of stupendous material uplift, of minuscule taxes, of virtually unre-
stricted foreign travel, of mass electrification, the automobile, the airplane,
public education—an era of expanding opportunity and hope. In Hoover's
judgment, "The happiest period of all humanity in the Western World in ten
centuries was the twenty-five years before the First World War."[57]

The Red House years were indeed among the happiest of Hoover's life. It was the best of epochs to be young, prosperous, adventurous, and resident in Europe during its long, sunny mid-afternoon.

I I

Yᴇᴛ something was missing. England was where Hoover's business was centered, England was where the Red House was, but it was not home.

During his Bewick, Moreing years Hoover had usually managed an annual visit to "the States." But these visits had totaled only a few weeks a year at most.[58] A desire to change this pattern, to spend more time in California, to educate his sons there, partly motivated his departure from his engineering firm in 1908.

But Hoover soon learned how difficult it was to break away. By 1909 he seemed more entrenched in London than ever. Somehow the date of his permanent return to America seemed to recede into the future. In 1907, 1908, and 1910 he did not visit the United States at all.[59] And when he did, he was often obliged to leave his family behind in California while he returned abroad to meet the importunities of business.[60] An aura of hurriedness and impermanence continued to hang over Hoover's life. It was inherent in the calling of the global mining engineer. Still, this was not what Hoover wanted when he said goodbye to Moreing in 1908.

"I am hoping to return to the United States for good within another twelve months," Hoover informed a friend in Colorado in March 1911.[61] Another twelve months went by, but no decisive uprooting occurred. In late 1912 and 1913 Hoover spent substantial periods of time in the United States.[62] He told a friend that he was preparing to terminate his business interests abroad and settle down in America in order that his sons might fully become Americans.[63] Yet 1913 yielded to 1914, and his London-based mining commitments grew.

Nevertheless, Hoover was gradually strengthening his ties with his native land. In 1909 he established an office in San Francisco and joined the Republican Club of the City of New York.[64] Although Hoover apparently did not vote in an American election between 1896 and 1920,[65] his partisan sympathies were clear. A Republican by heritage, he disclosed in 1910 that his loyalties were with the progressive wing of the GOP.[66] An ardent Republican Progressive in 1912, he contributed financially to Theodore Roosevelt's Bull Moose campaign.[67] In 1912–13 he was elected a member of two of San Francisco's most prestigious institutions: the Pacific Union Club and Bohemian Club. He became a member, too, of the Burlingame, California Country Club.[68]

Meanwhile he was making plans for a more permanent base in northern California. At his residence in London he kept a scale-model little house that he and his family continually reworked to reflect the home they planned

someday to build in the Bay Area.[69] In 1913 he purchased a building lot in
San Francisco and hired an architect to draw up plans.[70] If Hoover's San
Francisco house had ever been erected, it would have been a conversation
piece, for visitors would have entered on one street level and taken an eleva-
tor to the house one street level above![71] Ultimately Hoover abandoned San
Francisco for a home built after the war on the Stanford University campus.

Hoover's intentions, then, were unwavering. For some Americans with
similar careers and life-styles, the temptation might have been irresistible to
become an expatriate. For Hoover, if anything the opposite was true. Not
for him the choice of a Henry James. In a revealing letter to an American
friend in 1912, Hoover observed:

> The American is always an alien abroad. He never can assimilate, nor do
> other peoples ever accept him otherwise than as a foreigner.
>
> His own heart is in his own country, and yet there is less and less of a
> niche for him when he returns. One feels that one should have built one's
> fortune in America, altho it might have been less imposing. Yet one would
> be among one's own people and the esteem one hopes to build among one's
> associates would not be wasted by leaving them behind to go home and
> build at it again.
>
> I have got to that stage now where I am playing the game for the game's
> sake, as the counters don't interest me any longer. I am disgusted with
> myself when I think how much better off you people are who stuck by
> your own country and place. When you walk down the street you meet a
> hundred men who have a genuine pleasure in greeting you. I am an alien
> who gets a grin once in nine months.[72]

Hoover's yearning for America was more than an amalgam of loneliness
and nostalgia. It went to the core of his being. By 1908, and even more with
succeeding years, Hoover had traversed much of the globe, all the while
observing, analyzing, and evaluating the social systems of the Old World and
the New. Long voyages at sea had given him an opportunity to read about
the politics, economies, and cultures of countries all over the earth. And now
he wanted to go home.

At this point we confront one of the formative threads of Hoover's early
life. From the cornfields of Iowa to the orchards of Oregon, to the spacious
acres of Stanford University, to the rugged Sierra Nevadas, to the dusty
goldfields of Australia, to the coal mines of northern China and the wastes of
the Gobi Desert, we discern a repeated pattern: Herbert Hoover's early days
were spent on or near frontiers. It was symbolically appropriate that he was
a member of the Pioneer Class at Stanford. His was largely an outdoor life,
lived in environments that rewarded initiative, industry, resourcefulness, and
merit. Since the day when Andreas Huber landed in Philadelphia from the
Old World in 1738, the Hoover clan had moved gradually westward until,

with Herbert, the trek circled the globe. Benjamin Franklin is supposed to have said that America is a country where we ask of a man not "Who is he?" but "What can he do?". Hoover's America was a society populated substantially by people who held this attitude and who had moved away from a constricted and stratified civilization.

But beginning with Australia in 1897, China in 1899, England in 1901, Burma, czarist Russia, and other lands he visited, Hoover increasingly encountered social systems that varied profoundly from his own. China—with its unbelievable poverty, maddening corruption, and inert coolie labor. Australia—with its growing socialist labor movement and workers' resistance to the kind of efficiency promoted by aggressive American mine managers and engineers. Russia—with a feudal aristocracy at the top, a mass of peasants below, and scarcely a middle class in between. Such conditions, such endless contrasts, impelled Hoover to ask: why? Why had various civilizations developed this way? Why was America so different?

Not a man to flinch from candor, Hoover quickly developed forceful opinions about the conditions and cultures he met. Like many in this era of Anglo-Saxon self-assurance, he believed in the validity of racial judgments. Hoover held that efficiency in a mining man was a product of skill, intelligence, and application. And intelligence, he believed, varied sharply with race. "Asiatics and negroes," he wrote in 1909, were workers of a "low mental order" whose productivity was far below that of white miners. "Much observation and experience in working Asiatics and negroes as well as Americans and Australians in mines," Hoover declared, "leads the writer to the conclusion that, averaging actual results, one white man equals from two to three of the colored races, even in the simplest forms of mine work such as shoveling or tramming."[73]

Hoover denied that cheap labor led to lower overall costs of production. For one thing, miners of "the lower races" required "a greatly increased amount of direction," which meant a considerable expense for the employer. More supplies would be consumed, more accidents would occur, and other costs would rise. Furthermore, "the lower intelligence reacts in many ways in lack of coordination and inability to take initiative."[74] All in all, Hoover strongly preferred well-paid, well-motivated white labor, with its "higher intelligence," to lower-paid but less productive nonwhite workers. And he had little doubt that the most efficient white labor was American.[75]

Hoover was similarly blunt about the Chinese. He was not indifferent to the achievements of Chinese civilization; after all, his wife collected exquisite Ming vases. In many respects he admired the Chinese.[76] But harsh experience had taught him to be skeptical of "illusions" (as he labeled them) currently prevalent in the West. The illusion, for example, that China could soon become an enormous market for Western goods: such a view, he warned, ignored the "utter poverty" of most Chinese, "a grinding mass of poverty unmatched by anything known in the Occident."

While along the coast one sees some Chinese houses in which a European would deign to live, I can assure you that you can travel for days in the interior among hovels and caves in which we would not like to harbor our animals. There is thus but little accumulation of a social surplus, and therefore no margin upon which to buy from the European—no gain in national wealth or capital, and nothing left with which to buy from the European.

Hoover argued that China would not elevate its economic status and accumulate a "social surplus" until it controlled its population growth—a "cold-blooded truth," in his words, and one he did not hesitate to enunciate.[77]

Nor did Hoover accept the popular notion that the Chinese, with their "great imitative skill and industry" and their "ability to underlive the Occidental," would someday pose an "industrial yellow peril" to the West. To Hoover this idea rested on the assumption that the Chinese could attain European levels of efficiency—an assumption he strenuously denied. The efficiency of European workers, Hoover asserted, "is the result of the upward push of a hundred generations from the Middle Ages, where the Chinese people are still to-day. The Chinese workman cannot be made as efficient as the European." Hoover was certain. His experience with Chinese mechanics at the Kaiping mines had shown "one outstanding fact": "That as you proceed up the scale of skill, the Chinaman falls farther and farther behind the European in efficiency."

Moreover, he contended, "the Chinaman does not possess the executive instinct," one of the essentials of industrial development. "His every organization, governmental and commercial activity is still in the primary stage of industrial barbarism"—the stage of "farming out" activities to various subcontractors.

The capacity for departmental organization and execution rests on not only a skilled and specially developed function of the mind—often difficult enough to secure among our own people, who have evolved the mental processes underlying it during the past 2,000 years,—but also it rests on an intrinsic honesty, a conscienciousness in service, foreign to the Chinese mind.[78]

Another Chinese handicap, in Hoover's opinion, was the lack of a "mechanical instinct," a racial quality that led to the superior inventiveness of the machine-oriented, industrialized West.[79] Hoover was not unfriendly to Chinese efforts to modernize, but he cautioned against expecting miracles based on the Japanese (or American) models:

Without a dominating class they must, unlike the Japanese, find all progress from the masses, not from classes, and in consequence it will be slow and proceed with much stumbling. It will be the upward fight of a people toward economic betterment against currents stronger than any race has yet had to meet. They are a people of great racial genius and character, and their development will, and can only take a form suited to that genius. It will not take the form of sudden European veneer imposed by Europeans, but will be Chinese or it will fail. There will be no economic parallel with the United States, industrially or otherwise. . . .[80]

To Hoover such observations were scientific conclusions based on personal observation and study. After all, he had lived in China and had managed the largest private enterprise in the country. To members of a later generation, Hoover's sentiments may seem like the facile judgments of an ethnocentric Yankee in the heyday of Anglo-Saxon supremacy. But whether they be considered perceptive insight or superficial racial stereotyping, they revealed a man deeply convinced of the superiorty of Western, and especially American, ways. The longer he lived abroad, it seemed, the more pro-American he became.

Above all, Hoover reacted to the mores of the country that served as his business base between 1901 and the First World War. There was much that Hoover cherished about England—the England whose history and culture were America's patrimony, the England whose people were taught to value courage, moral uprightness, and good sportsmanship. Hoover had many British friends, and of the individual Englishman he had a high regard.[81]

But there was much about England that he came to dislike, and in his responses to Britain (as to China and other "Old World" countries) lay one of the sources of his later social philosophy. Young, aggressive, and thoroughly American, Hoover was impatient with British formality and tradition. An Englishman, he said, would defend the external form of "tradition" yet simultaneously violate its inner spirit. Once, for example, Hoover took a British couple for a picnic on a boat at Henley after the regatta. Boats filled with picnickers covered the river. After their supper Hoover decided to toss the trash (except for bottles) into the river. His English guest was shocked, and a heated argument flared. Hoover contended that the rubbish would quickly float away down the river. The Englishman insisted that this just was not done—picnic grounds must not be littered—and besides, other picnickers would notice. Hoover finally devised a clever evasion. He filled the empty bottles with water, capped them, and tied the picnic papers and boxes to them. Then, with the Englishman's willing assistance, he slipped the weighted cargo into the water. It sank, and apparently no one noticed. The formal requirements of custom were thus adhered to: the traditional ban on littering picnic *grounds* was obeyed. Hoover conceded, however, that if everyone did as he did, the Henley races would soon cease.[82]

More grating to Hoover than British formality was the acute class consciousness of the British circles he frequented. As the son of a blacksmith, as a product of the open, informal American West, as an orphan who had worked his way up by his own initiative and talents, Hoover detested the condescension toward America, the snobbery, and the barriers of class stratification he encountered.[83] Once, on an ocean voyage, a British lady asked him what his profession was. An engineer, he said. "Why," she exclaimed without thinking, "I thought you were a gentleman!"[84] This anecdote, which Hoover recounted in his *Memoirs*, epitomized his distaste for the class consciousness and social rigidities of Europe. From all of this he turned.

Hoover had ample opportunity to study the British social structure and its implications. He observed with mixed feelings the ruling "oligarchy": a talented class, 20% of the population, open to new blood from below, brave, honest, the most intelligent oligarchy in world history, yet morally unrestrained (in Hoover's view) in the pursuit of one consuming passion: preservation of the empire. Coexisting with this privileged class were millions of impoverished Britons in slums of "unmitigated squalor." America, said Hoover, "never had such class divisions, such impenetrable stratifications and such misery below."[85] A living embodiment of social mobility, Hoover found the America he loved far superior to the Britain he knew.[86]

Hoover made his feelings known, sometimes bluntly. To American friends he frequently denounced the British upper classes.[87] One Stanford visitor felt that he actually despised the British masses.[88] To a California couple that had moved to London Hoover said one night at the Red House, "What are young people like you doing in an old world place like this? The West needs her own young manhood to help solve her difficulties and develop her possibilities."[89] England, he said, was "an old man's country."[90]

Hoover's American loyalties also surfaced in an affirmation of the superiority of American mining engineers. According to various British mining acquaintances, Hoover liked to emphasize at board meetings that the British companies' experts on base metals were in fact Americans, not British. Such repeated tactlessness (as one Englishman called it) evoked much resentment from his British colleagues.[91] Hoover also insisted among British friends that the American public school system, in which children of all social strata rubbed shoulders, was superior to the British system, which segregated and trained only an elite.[92] Hoover intended that *his* children would go to American public schools. Not for nothing did he gain the epithet "star-spangled Hoover."

Hoover could enjoy the Old World, but he could not love it. Gradually, out of a welter of experiences and perceptions, he was distilling a profound sense of American uniqueness—of America as a land of peculiar social fluidity and unsurpassed breadth of opportunity. *Equality of opportunity*: this was becoming the core value of his social philosophy, the rod by which he measured the institutions and aspirations of peoples among whom he traveled. *Equality of opportunity*: this was what Europe lacked and America promised. To Hoover it was the opportunity for persons of every social class to rise, to transcend their origins—as he had done—that was the root of America's distinctiveness.[93] He was coming to feel that America and Britain had grown three hundred years apart.[94]

Many years later Hoover expressed eloquently the impressions that were forming while he lived as an "alien" abroad:

> I have seen the squalor of Asia, the frozen class barriers of Europe. And I was not a tourist. I was associated in their working lives and problems. I had to deal with their social systems and their governments. And outstanding everywhere to these great masses of people there was a hallowed word— *America.* To them, it was the hope of the world.
>
> My every frequent homecoming has been a reaffirmation of the glory of America. Each time my soul was washed by the relief from grinding poverty of other nations, by the greater kindliness and frankness which comes from the acceptance of equality and a belief in wide-open opportunity to all who want a chance. It is more than that. It is a land of self-respect born alone of free men and women.[95]

This, of course, was written much later and expressed a sentiment molded partly in the crucible of war. But even before 1914 Hoover was evolving toward this perspective. And well before then, he knew—and was proud— that America was where he had come from and where he wished to return. The attitude of "Hail Columbia" Hoover in the Australian outback in 1897 did not change in the busy years ahead. For him San Francisco was still the center of civilization and Stanford still the best place in the world.

I I I

H o o v e r's urge to come home was fueled by more than a preference for American values and institutions, more than a desire to educate his sons in a fully American environment, more than a growing rejection of the European class system. Impelling him increasingly after 1908 was a wish to transcend the enterprise of money-making and embark, somehow, on a career of public service in the United States.

From the day he left Stanford in 1895 to the day he left Bewick, Moreing thirteen years later, Hoover had had one controlling passion: a drive, a determination, to succeed. "If a man has not made a fortune by 40 he is not worth much." He told a friend that he wished to make enough money so that he could spend a sovereign and not count the change.[96]

Hoover was proud of his pecuniary success, proud and apparently sensitive. About 1913, on a visit to Stanford, he proposed to an engineering professor that a few faculty members receive prize professorships with super-salaries. Evidently Hoover felt that such a system would foster and reward

individual merit. The professor, however, disagreed. A huge disparity in
faculty salaries, he argued, would subvert faculty morale. Furthermore, it
might lure "mercenary" individuals to the university. At this remark Hoover
clenched his fist and pounded on the window sill. "After all," he replied,
"the dollar is the counter of the game—and to have it shows that you have
played the game successfully."[97]

Yet like other self-made men of wealth in this era, Hoover yearned to do
more. Success had come too hard for him to scorn the counters, but as he
told friends, the counters did not interest him any more. To an American
visitor in 1908 Hoover divulged his desire to "stop making money" and take
up a life of service in America.[98] Time and again he repeated this sentiment
to callers at the Red House.[99]

But service in what form? From time to time different ideas occurred to
him. Perhaps he would buy a newspaper or found a chain of newspapers like
William Randolph Hearst.[100] Perhaps he would enter politics in some fashion; he told one American guest that he preferred the United States Senate.[101] In 1914 an engineer-friend actually sought to secure Hoover the
Republican nomination for governor of California, but there is no evidence
that Hoover encouraged his effort.[102]

In 1910 an opportunity arose that Hoover found appealing. During the
spring Congress created a new government agency, the U.S. Bureau of Mines.
Soon geologists and mining men across the country were embroiled in a contest to influence President William Howard Taft's selection of the first director. As the factions struggled, Hoover's old friend Ralph Arnold asked
whether Hoover might consent to be a candidate for the appointment as an
outsider untouched by bureaucratic infighting and factional strife.

Hoover was initially hesitant. How quickly might he have to take the position? he wondered. Would it be a political football? He feared that it might.
Arnold moved to allay Hoover's concerns. Well aware of Hoover's ambitions, he pointed out that the nonelective Bureau of Mines directorship was
one of the best stepping stones available in the American political system at
present.[103]

Arnold's arguments worked. On August 25, 1910 Hoover cabled to him
from London: "Would accept if I could have four or five months after
appointment [to] clean up obligations here."[104]

In a separate letter the same day Hoover elaborated. He informed Arnold
that he could not simply drop his complex business interests instantly. Such
a hasty step would not be fair to his colleagues and would entail a personal
sacrifice of several hundred thousand dollars. He must have some time to
"clean up." Still, if that condition could be met, he was willing:

> It is up to every man to do a service for his country when it can be done,
> and if my name, as an entirely independent outsider, with not one scrap
> of American mining interests, and with no personal or other alliances,

would be of help in unravelling the situation, I would be willing to tackle it for at least the period sufficient to organise the Bureau on the footing which I think all Engineers would like to see it placed.

As I have an income of something like $100,000 a year here, it takes some resolution to come to this conclusion. I am afraid if the business is put through, it will largely devolve on my American friends, as I do not feel I could start out and make a canvass myself, and I fear you may be taking on a great deal of labour of love in managing the matter. It probably is not in accordance with political precedent for one to take the strong attitude that one will make no personal effort on one's own behalf, but my feeling is that if I do take it and make the sacrifices necessary to do so, it will have to come to me as a gift. And moreover I feel that if I were to personally intervene to seek the job I would only compromise my freedom of action at a later date, and would not be able to do what I think the office requires that one should do.

Yet if Hoover was unwilling to campaign personally for the job, he was ready—even eager—to assist Arnold's efforts. In the very next paragraph of his letter he gave Arnold the names of influential friends who could provide Arnold "a great deal of support" in his campaign to get Hoover the appointment—men like the mining attorney Curtis Lindley, who, said Hoover, had "considerable influence in the West." Hoover pointed out that he had been "born and raised" in the Republican Party and now identified himself with its progressive wing. On one matter—his precise place of American residence—Hoover said it was "difficult to say" and left it to Arnold to decide:

I have an office in New York, so that if it were desirable, I could be put forward as a New Yorker. On the other hand, California was my particular State and the only two pieces of land which I possess in the world are the house at Monterey and a residential site in Palo Alto.

In short, Hoover was willing to be presented as either a New Yorker or Californian—whichever facilitated his candidacy for the appointment.[105]

Ralph Arnold now swung into action. But before his campaign to promote Hoover's candidacy could fairly get underway, President Taft appointed the favorite of the coal interests to the post.[106] Upon hearing the news, Hoover wrote Arnold that he felt "somewhat relieved" by the outcome. Relieved, but not indifferent, for he immediately added: "In case, however, it should come up again, you might note that I am also a coal person, as for a matter of two years I managed a group of four coal mines with an output of a million and a quarter tons per annum."[107]

Hoover's behavior in the Bureau of Mines episode showed an acute and revealing ambivalence. On the one hand, Hoover's sense of duty forbade the public pursuit of personal ambition. Yet at the same time he was deeply ambitious, imbued with a burning drive to achieve. His nascent public persona dictated detachment and passivity. His aggressive dynamic temperament impelled him to action.

In reconciling the claims of self-interest and disinterest, Hoover was driven to indirection. Unwilling to seek the Bureau of Mines position personally on his own behalf, he *was* willing to advise Arnold on how to seek it for him. Anxious that the job come to him "as a gift," he nevertheless did what he could, through Arnold, to enhance his chances of obtaining that "gift." Here and later in his life Hoover shied away from overt self-seeking and self-assertion. But *covert* self-assertion—mediated through agents while Hoover stayed behind the scenes and orchestrated their efforts—was a congenial mode of action that Hoover had used since college. It was to be a part of the pattern of his emerging public career.

David Starr Jordan of Stanford Unversity had been visiting Hoover in London when the Bureau of Mines opportunity slipped away. While returning by sea to the United States in October 1910, Jordan composed a letter to President Taft's secretary enthusiastically announcing Hoover's availability for "executive service." Hoover, said the Stanford president, had "no superior in executive work" and was now retiring to America to enter public life.

> He is a very presentable man, of quiet, frank manner, but carrying conviction whenever he speaks. . . . In executive matters, especially those involving a knowledge of finance, he shows rare ability. In short, should he enter public life in any capacity, he is a man who will make himself felt.[108]

Taft's secretary promised Jordan to keep Hoover's name in mind when an appropriate vacancy occurred.[109] Jordan may have written his letter spontaneously, but it is also possible that he did so at Hoover's instigation.

In the years immediately ahead Hoover occasionally sent out other feelers for public positions. Acquaintances of his were impressed by his idealism and eagerness to change careers.[110] In June 1913, probably after a conversation in New York with Hoover, his old friend Ray Lyman Wilbur wrote to Jordan. Wilbur had just learned that President Woodrow Wilson was thinking of seeking an independent engineer's assessment of the Panama Canal then being built. Why not Hoover? Wilbur suggested. He, too, was impressed by Hoover's idealism and thought that such a presidential appointment would be good publicity for Stanford University.[111] Jordan agreed and speedily wrote a letter in Hoover's behalf to the President. Nothing, however, came of this effort, which again may have emanated from Hoover himself, since it was unlikely that Wilbur made his suggestion without Hoover's prior knowledge and consent.[112]

In a multitude of ways, then, Hoover signaled his yearning for a new career of benefaction and public service after 1908. In 1912 he told his friend

Will Irwin that he was rich—"as rich as any man has much right to be." To Irwin also he confided his dream of retiring and returning to America. But what will you do? Irwin asked. "Get into the big game somewhere," Hoover replied. "Just making money isn't enough."[113]

Father and son, Cairo, December 1905.

OPPOSITE ABOVE. *Herbert Hoover and his sister-in-law Jean Henry playing double solitaire, London, winter of 1902–3.*

OPPOSITE BELOW. *Father and son (Herbert Hoover and his two-year-old son Herbert, Jr.), Melbourne, 1905.*

The Red House, London.

Herbert Hoover, Lou Henry Hoover, Abby and Edgar Rickard: tourists in Venice, 1912.

Lou Henry Hoover and her two sons (Allan and Herbert, Jr.), ca. 1912.

Herbert Hoover at age 40.

25

Stanford's Benefactor

I

N o, the singleminded amassing of a fortune could not suffice. Hoover, to be sure, did not disdain the "game" of making money. He enjoyed the thrill of maneuver, the challenge of conceiving and executing a plan, the joy of constructive accomplishment, the mental exercise of wheeling and dealing in the shark-infested waters of London mining finance. To stand at the pinnacle, to manage men and resources: in Hoover's words, to "co-ordinate and control the best efforts of other people"[1]—this was deeply satisfying, and at it he excelled. But the simple pursuit of wealth no longer encompassed his ambition.

"Get into the big game somewhere." Whence had arisen this budding altruism, this growing restlessness with purely financial success? Was it a legacy of his childhood Quakerism, of his relatives' teaching that he should accomplish something useful in the world? Was it an expression of his engineering professionalism, with its ethic of disinterested achievement? Probably these influences had some effect. But there was another.

"Get into the game." The words were David Starr Jordan's when he addressed the graduating seniors of Stanford University in 1905, while Hoover visited the campus for his tenth class reunion. Get into the game. "Whatever you have acquired," said Jordan, "should be an impulse for action."

If you have planned somewhat, then carry out your plans. If you have learned the nature of something, then turn your knowledge into execution.

If you have gained higher aspirations, these count for nothing except as you try to make them good. . . .

Get into the game, somehow, somewhere. Carry your thoughts over into action. Do your part, and the greatest surprise of your life will come the day when you find out how great that part may be.[2]

Jordan's message was not new. He had expounded it before—to Herbert Hoover, among others, during the pioneer days of Stanford University. It was, in fact, the "Stanford spirit" that Jordan in his ebullient way was extolling, a spirit of idealism mixed with practicality, of doing good fused with doing well.

And now this spirit—so deeply imbued in Hoover in his impressionable undergraduate days—was drawing him toward a second career. By his mid-thirties Hoover's urge to do well financially was yielding to a yearning to do good. As Hoover groped towards a new vocation of useful service, his first efforts focused on the place he now considered home: Stanford University, "the best place in the world."

I I

H o o v e r's benefactions to his alma mater began early. While in Australia in 1897–98 he constituted himself a one-man scholarship fund, funneling loans through Lester Hinsdale to needy students struggling through Stanford as he had done. Starting about 1902 he quietly paid the salary of one of the university's librarians, a practice that continued for several years.[3] After the 1906 San Francisco earthquake he offered Professor John C. Branner one thousand dollars to publish an earthquake investigation as a Stanford University publication.[4] In 1910 he offered to finance Branner's geology expedition to Brazil in the amount of one thousand dollars.[5]

As befitted a bibliophile, Hoover contributed generously toward the enrichment of the university's book collections. Early in 1907 a young Stanford history instructor, Payson J. Treat, crossed Hoover's path in Colombo during a trip to get acquainted with his area of specialty, the Far East. When Hoover learned of Treat's purpose, he replied, "Well, you'll get nowhere without books. As you travel, buy $1,000 worth of books and send the bill to me."[6] A little later Hoover and Deane P. Mitchell donated £250 more (about $1,200) for further book purchases by Treat in the same field, East Asia and the East Indies.[7] All of Treat's acquisitions went to the Stanford University Library, with the result that by 1908 Stanford had the best collection of Australian books of any library in the United States.[8] In 1913 Hoover donated to the university his own collection of 500–600 volumes on China alone, including a rare complete set of early Jesuit publications on China. He estimated his collection to be worth between $4,000 and $5,000.[9]

Such acts of liberality—most of them unpublicized—would have been enough for most alumni, but Hoover wished to do more. In one of his earliest known statements about his future, he confided his ambition in November 1906 to Payson J. Treat, who was visiting him in London. "The plan," Treat later recalled,

> was, in a few years he would be able to retire from the engineering firm and he wanted to go back to California, make a home on the Stanford campus and spend the rest of his life doing something for the University. He thought he could probably be helpful in the organization and development of their financial resources and also perhaps in their instruction in mining.[10]

Treat was profoundly impressed: here was Hoover, only thirty-two, with an objective like this! Hoover's idealism was not the only quality that struck his visitor. "After being with him for a whole day," Treat later stated, "I wrote in my journal . . . that Mr. Hoover had the best stored and most accurate, and most accessible mind of any man I'd ever met."[11]

One opportunity for Hoover to be of service to Stanford arose in 1908. Late that summer he learned that the university's board of trustees was seeking to fill a prospective vacancy with a younger man living near the university and able to participate actively in its affairs. Having heard of Hoover's desire to return to California, his undergraduate mentor, Professor Branner, was eager to get his protégé on the board.[12] So, too, was President Jordan, who told one trustee that Hoover would be "ideal" if he lived near San Francisco. Jordan pointed out that "few men in the world" had displayed "greater skill in bringing about financial results" than Herbert Hoover.[13] Responding to Branner's inquiries, Hoover was uncertain what to say: ". . . ultimately I hope to make my headquarters in the West, and to be of some service to the University; but certainly for the next 12 months I shall very largely [be] tied to London."[14] Probably in part because he was not yet a resident of the Bay Area, Hoover's name was passed over.

Branner was more successful in another direction. Early in 1907 he invited Hoover to deliver a series of lectures to Stanford's geology and mining students when he next visited the campus. Branner pointed out that Hoover could then revise and publish the lectures as a book.[15] In due course Hoover agreed, and in September 1908 the university's trustees appointed him Lecturer in Mining Engineering for the academic year without pay.[16] Hoover arrived on campus in mid-January 1909 and remained over three weeks.[17] His lectures became *Principles of Mining*, published that spring.

It was during this brief visit that Hoover's larger service to Stanford really commenced. His stay on campus occurred during the aftermath of a bitter episode in Stanford history. For a number of years student drinking had been increasing and with it the problem of public drunkenness and disorder on campus. Early in 1908, following faculty pressure and new provocations, the university authorities cracked down, initiating a prohibition policy and making drunkenness a ground for suspension from the university. An angry student demonstration one evening led to massive disciplinary proceedings, including the suspension of forty-one seniors for the remainder of their final semester. That summer the trustees further tightened the rules. By the time Hoover arrived in 1909 Stanford was quiet but sullen; the gulf between students and faculty persisted.[18]

During his few weeks on campus Hoover discussed the university's malaise with fully two hundred persons. In a speech evidently prepared for a faculty gathering just before he left, Hoover presented his findings:

> My sympathy is on the side of government always. Rebellions sometimes must be put down by volleys in the streets and then some innocent allways get hit. But all rebellions have causes and disturbance is a symptom of disease. In any event when a rebellion is over military government should give place to a civil government which devotes itself to elimination from the community of the vicious individual and its my impression that the time for a change of front has arrived here.

To Hoover, Stanford was suffering from a "profound change" in spirit since its early days, a change that was "the root of [its] trouble." This change, he said, was "the lack of solidarity of feeling and purpose."

Evidence of this deficiency was everywhere. On one side, said Hoover, were the students, generally satisfied with their departmental professors but extremely distrustful of the rest, especially the faculty committees on scholarship and student discipline. In the eyes of the students the committee on scholarship, responsible for enforcing academic standards, "acts without consideration of the worth of the men and leaves loafers in college," while the committee on student affairs, responsible for social decorum, repeatedly suspended "good men on outbreak of animal spirits on misinformation and spies." To the students the faculty committees were "not in touch with student values." Hoover did not agree with this perspective, but he felt it must be faced.

On the other side, Hoover reported, was a faculty divided into three factions. One group, whom Hoover considered advocates of "military government," believed "that students are inherently wicked[,] that all are liars and 50% are cheats[,] that there is no difference between animal spirits and inherent viciousness," that force was essential to preservation of order, and that constant effort was necessary to "keep the lid on." Those on the other extreme, according to Hoover, held "that moral conduct is no concern of the faculty, that this is a great educational institution where police duties have no place[,] where if the student does his work it is no concern of the faculty what else he does." Somewhere in between was the majority of the faculty, the "intermediates."

Hoover forcefully dissociated himself from the two extremes and aligned himself with the "intermediates." He denounced the view that "the lid needs a constant weight on it." Very few men, he had found, will lie when appealed to on their honor. If the student body really contained as many "scoundrels" as some alleged, Hoover said, "you can have my degree back," for in that case the university had failed. But Hoover did not believe it. Stanford, he said, has "a fine body of students," virtually untainted by the "insensate luxury and idleness common enough in the east." Hoover also attacked the other extreme—"that the professor has no obligation to look after the moral rectitude of students." Yes, he does, Hoover countered:

> These boys come immature in mind and character and it is the function of the university to build the latter as much as the former. It is true this is not a place of moral reformation but it is a place of moral inspiration. Students lend themselves easily enough to that more than any other class of humanity.

Hoover freely confessed that he was an "amateur in academic matters." But "managing the human side of men" has been "my business for many years," he observed, and students were human beings, too. As an experienced executive, therefore, Hoover offered the following "amateur panacea" for Stanford's faculty-student friction.

First, he denied that academic standards could be justly enforced by a faculty committee unfamiliar with the student being judged. He criticized reliance on impersonal criteria like "minute divisions of the alphabet" (grades) as a true measure of student merit. Grades might be useful in a preliminary way, as a means of testing the "loafer." But if grades alone were "the final court of appeal," the faculty would "not only lose much good material but discourage others and do an injustice to some." Every case of academic delinquency, Hoover argued, must be treated individually. He therefore proposed that every decision of the committee on scholarship be subject to a veto by the student's department. The department should know best the student's true circumstances, and it should be responsible for retaining any "laggards." Hoover was blunt: ". . . no professor in the university has a right to do the so called productive scholarship until he knows the human units which the university pays him to instruct."

Similarly for matters of discipline: the crux of the system should be the department, not a distant committee that could not possibly know every student in the whole university. Here also the departments should have a veto, in this case over any punishment voted by the committee on student affairs. Not only would this encourage the departments to know their students and "compel the rescued defaulter to make good"; it would increase student confidence in the likelihood of justice because of students' faith in their respective departments. In effect, Hoover was saying that circumstances alter cases and that the best judge of the students' circumstances was or ought to be the faculty members closest to them. He was applying to university administration one of his fundamental convictions as an executive. "To my mind," he declared in his speech, "decentralization is the soul of administration."[19]

Hoover may never have delivered this blunt but thoughtful—and revealing—address. But while still on campus in early February he did make at least one public attempt to restore Stanford's lost "solidarity of feeling and purpose." Even before he arrived on campus a scheme was maturing in his active mind. Upon reaching New York from London on January 1, he told a waiting friend that he planned to propose the construction of a student union building at Stanford. He thereupon promptly went up to Cambridge, Massachusetts and inspected the Harvard Union, reputed to be the best in the country.[20] As always, he intended to be thorough.

A month later, before a student assembly at his alma mater, Hoover unveiled an ambitious plan for a $50,000 men's clubhouse on the campus. This facility, he explained, should be constructed and maintained by students and alumni and should be "entirely independent of the University authorities." Pointing to the success of student unions in eastern universities, Hoover asserted that the proposed building "would serve as the rallying point for student spirit" and as a common meeting place for students, faculty, and alumni. It would "restore the solidarity that existed between students and faculty in the old days." It would foster the "Stanford Spirit."[21]

Hoover's proposal won immediate enthusiastic support. The idea of establishing such a clubhouse had been much bruited about for some time, but it took Hoover to galvanize talk into action.[22] In short order an organization called the Stanford Union sprang into being with Hoover as its president, and a pledge canvass of alumni commenced.[23] To handle initial expenses Hoover personally put up one thousand dollars but barred any initial publicity of this fact.[24] As usual, he was concealing his benefactions. Perhaps he recalled what he had just told students in his lectures: "A real engineer does not advertise himself. . . ."[25]

Hoover left the campus in early February with the Stanford Union movement still in an embryonic stage. But even in this short period he had begun to instill a new sense of possibility on the campus. A year later his good friend E. D. Adams of the history department reported that thanks in considerable measure to Hoover's 1909 visit the conciliatory wing of the faculty was still in control and that a year without major turmoil had passed.[26]

From early 1909 to late 1912 Hoover did not visit Stanford University. In his absence the $50,000 fund drive for the Stanford Union proceeded slowly and seemed to lose momentum. Initially Hoover thought that ground-breaking could begin in early 1910, but he was unwilling to proceed until a substantial portion of the $50,000 was in hand.[27] By late 1912 the Union's treasury held only $21,000.[28]

At one point in 1909 it was announced that Hoover himself had pledged

$11,000—forty-four times more than anyone else.[29] Hoover objected to this wording. The $10,000 he pledged beyond his initial $1,000 payment, he said, was the *joint* subscription of himself and certain friends.[30] From time to time over the next several years Hoover paid his installments when requested until the $10,000 total was reached. No names of his friends were mentioned, however; more likely than not, he paid the whole amount himself.[31]

Clearly another infusion of Hooverian energy was needed. Returning to the campus in September 1912, the resourceful alumnus launched a spirited "final" campaign for the Union. On the campus, fund-raising projects sprouted. Hoover himself sent a personal appeal to every living member of his Pioneer Class. When it appeared that the Union might be unable to withdraw when needed an $11,000 deposit in a shaky local bank, Hoover personally guaranteed to provide this amount as desired.[32] For him the Union was more than a worthy project; it had become a crusade.

In an address to an undergraduate assembly in September 1912 he explained why. The Union, Hoover asserted, "will allow us to inoculate against the bacillus of social inequality." The distinctive feature of Stanford's student body, he said, was its "democracy"; the Union would help to maintain it. "The undemocratic social stratification which has been so much discussed of late in our eastern neighbors, has not yet entered Stanford to any alarming extent. Nor do we want it." In that season of surging Progressivism, as Woodrow Wilson and Theodore Roosevelt battled for the presidency, Hoover the Bull Moose Progressive exhorted the students of Stanford to maintain their democratic ideals:

> There has been a great growth of class feeling in this country during the past few years and we have seen with dismay the transplanting of privilege into the social life of some of our universities. . . . Certainly the older [European] universities are not cradles of democracy.
>
> In this country, however, with the ideals upon which our government is founded, we have a right to expect or even demand that the universities should be in the forefront of the fight for equality of opportunity and not a playground for childish institutions. The ideals of a university are made by its members and yours are right so far. You must see that you keep them.[33]

The Father of the Stanford Union, however, could not accomplish instant miracles. To keep within its resources the Union was forced to scale down its plans in 1913. Even then, construction of the building did not begin until December 1913 and was not completed until February 1915.[34] It was not until after World War I that the Union in its full conception was completed, thanks in large part to an unpublicized contribution of $100,000 from Hoover himself.[35] Without Hoover's push and persistence, one of the favorite structures on the Stanford campus might never have been built.

I I I

B y the autumn of 1912 the Stanford Union was actually a secondary concern for Hoover. During his three-and-a-half-year absence an abortive faculty reform effort had dissipated, and his beloved university had stagnated.[36] Stanford's most accomplished alumnus was determined to change all this. After visiting Hoover in London in mid-summer 1912 a Stanford classics professor reported to a colleague that Hoover was coming back to launch a campaign to get himself elected to the board of trustees.[37] In late summer he came.[38]

Hoover's return to the Bay Area in the autumn of 1912 coincided with his financial labors in behalf of the California-based General Petroleum Company. As it happened, two men soon to be directors of this company, J. D. Grant and Leon Sloss, were also Stanford trustees. Through them Hoover seems to have worked. To find room for him on the Stanford board it was necessary to create a vacancy. As it happened, two trustees were just completing their ten-year terms, the first trustees to have done so. The board accordingly decided that it was "inadvisable" to reelect ten-year members upon the expiration of their terms.[39] On October 29 the vice president of General Petroleum confidentially informed Hoover that Grant and Sloss had arranged Hoover's nomination to fill one of the vacancies being created.[40] A few weeks later Hoover was formally elected a trustee.[41] He was only the second Stanford alumnus so honored and the first to be selected by the trustees themselves.[42] For virtually the next half century he was to sit on the board.

In announcing Hoover's election the *Stanford Alumnus* stated, "He has recently returned from London, where he has lived for several years, and taken up his residence in San Francisco."[43] This hint of permanency was premature; Hoover still had too many global interests to permit him to sit still. But between late August 1912 and early January 1913 he did manage to stay mostly in California.[44] It was his longest continuous sojourn in the United States since 1897.

With characteristic zeal he used the time to investigate the problems of Stanford University. He asked his friend Professor Adams to send him titles of certain publications on educational administration—"in fact anything which will educate the budding trustee to university management!"[45] From President Jordan he received a report that Stanford's academic standing was slipping, mainly because of failure to maintain a competitive pay scale.[46] Early in January 1913 Hoover told a fellow trustee that he had spent "a large portion of the last three months" studying Stanford's situation.[47]

What he found was disturbing. In a lengthy memorandum, dated January 2, 1913, on Stanford's "present position," Hoover asserted that the university was generally failing to do work of an outstanding character and was lagging behind other institutions. The problem, as he saw it, was that the university did not have enough "pre-eminent" professors, a fact he attributed to Stanford's inferior pay scale. It was becoming more and more difficult to hire and retain superior professors because of better job offers elsewhere. Hoover was also distressed by the fact that many junior faculty were no better paid than "fully employed mechanics in San Francisco." With salaries low and not keeping pace with the rising cost of living, more than half the faculty could not hire a servant, and wives of lower-paid faculty were being forced to do all the "domestic work" themselves. Such salaries, said Hoover, made it difficult for many faculty to "maintain some position," buy books, travel during sabbaticals, and "above all . . . maintain social relations" with students—all essential to their "service to the University." The fundamental academic problem of Stanford, in other words, was a lack of money.

Hoover strenuously rejected all proposals to "prune down the scope" of the university, as many had advocated. Instead, he proposed the "more progressive" approach of strengthening the present departments and weakening none. Specifically, he recommended an increase in the salaries of all faculty by 10–15% and an increase in the number of very highly paid preeminent professorships "so as to be able to hold and attract . . . exceptional men." Hoover estimated that his plan would cost $125,000 a year. But only such expenditure, he maintained, would "raise this institution to the level of the very best."[48]

Hoover considered his plan a "progressive" one, but where was he to find the money? From its founding in 1891 the university had been crimped for funds, a chronic predicament exacerbated by the 1906 earthquake. If the preeminent professor was Hoover's first concern as a trustee, his second was the university's finances. Almost at once he began to agitate for revision and publication of the institution's heretofore secret accounts. He was appalled to discover that the trustees were annually deducting $100,000 from university income for depreciation—a quite unnecessary action, he thought, in view of its repairs budget and new construction program. He was also aghast to find that the budget-conscious trustees did not even expend all their general funds in 1911–12, instead adding the leftover amount to a "surplus of income not expended" account that now totaled over $384,000! "It does seem to me," Hoover commented tartly, "that it is the primary function of this Institution to spend its income, not to save it."[49]

Meanwhile Hoover was exerting himself in other directions. In January 1913 he was appointed to a committee of trustees established to study the needs of the university's young medical school, administered by Hoover's intimate friend of twenty years, Ray Lyman Wilbur.[50] He served on a trustee committee to build a new gymnasium.[51] In April he was appointed to a special four-man trustee committee to examine the academic and financial position of the university and to recommend "a general policy of academic management and development during the next two or three years."[52] The pot was beginning to boil, and Hoover was stirring it.

In asserting that Stanford's fundamental requirement was more money,

Hoover was closely in accord with the views of President Jordan. "Money is the basis of reputation," Jordan told him in 1912. "The strong men make the institution. . . . A growing university must grow at the top."[53] Such an analysis was no doubt congenial to an engineer-executive like Hoover, who liked both to foster and reward merit.

At some point in early 1913, however, Hoover evidently became convinced that at least one of Stanford's problems was not monetary; it was David Starr Jordan himself. By 1913 Jordan had been president of Stanford University for more than twenty years—in fact, had been the only president the university had known. Particularly after the "rebellion" of 1908, signs appeared that his period of greatest usefulness to Stanford was over.[54] Jordan, too, seems to have felt the same way; in 1911 he seriously considered resigning to devote himself to one of his principal causes, the promotion of world peace. But by late 1912 he had decided to remain at Stanford until he reached retirement age in just a few years.[55]

If Hoover knew of Jordan's decision he was not inclined to accept it as final. Yet if, as seems clear, he wanted Jordan removed, the engineering of such an objective would be a delicate mission. An internationally famous scientist, educator, and reformer, Jordan could not be unceremoniously dumped from office. Hoover, though, had a fertile brain in such matters and proved equal to the challenge.

In a series of deft negotiations in April and May 1913 Hoover arranged for Jordan to give up the presidency and all its administrative responsibilities for a new position, chancellor of the university, with no decrease in salary. Hoover broached the subject to Jordan on April 27; finding Jordan at least open to the idea, he quickly contacted fellow trustees.[56] On May 9 Hoover reported to Jordan that the trustees shared Hoover's view that Jordan's greatest future service to the university and the public lay outside the administrative realm, in the peace movement and other social concerns. Hoover also revealed that the vice-president of the university, John C. Branner, was willing to assume the presidency under the proposed new scheme.[57]

While the inspiration and initiative came from Hoover, Jordan was eagerly receptive. "If the Trustees really believe in the value of my services under the title of Chancellor, and that it is worth while," he told Hoover, then he would accept "with very great pleasure."[58] To his daughter Jordan even confided that it was "at my request" that the trustees were relieving him of "the details of the University business and management," evidently forgetting that it was Hoover, in fact, who instigated the transition.[59] Jordan regarded the chancellorship both as a "quite unexpected" honor and as a "promotion" that would enhance "my power of carrying out the work for peace."[60]

It now remained for Hoover to formalize the understandings for ratification by the trustees. His own desire was abundantly clear. He told Jordan that administration of the university "should be in Dr. Branner's hands entirely" and that Jordan's involvement would be confined to topics of the trustees' and Branner's choosing. Branner would more or less be the "general manager," Jordan the "consulting engineer."[61] Jordan, however, was anxious that the chancellorship be "a position both of dignity and of real service," not a merely titular one like president emeritus.[62] Branner, for his part, was willing to take the presidency only upon trustee acceptance of seven conditions, including an increase in faculty salaries and Branner's retirement in just two years, when he would be sixty-five.[63]

In mid-May Hoover completed the negotiations and drew up various resolutions for the trustees to adopt accommodating Jordan's desires, Branner's requests, and Hoover's aims. Branner's conditions were acceded to, except for silence on the question of his retirement. As for Jordan, Hoover's resolution acknowledged what it called Jordan's "expressed desire" to be "relieved from administrative demands" of Stanford, and it expressed the trustees' wish "to afford him both freedom to represent the university in its functions towards the public, and the relations of the university to educational agencies outside the university itself." But the chancellorship as Hoover's resolution defined it seemed suspiciously honorific and had, in fact, less power than Jordan originally wanted. Although the chancellor was to have the right to attend meetings of the board of trustees and one of their key committees, his only prescribed duties were to "represent the university at public functions" when present and to "advise and cooperate on such matters as may be proposed by the Trustees or the President."[64]

In colloquial parlance, Jordan had been "kicked upstairs." But the deed had been accomplished with his hearty concurrence, and if he regretted his "elevation" he did not show it. "To me," he told Branner, "it seems a great honor as well as a great opportunity."[65] In 1916, at the termination of his chancellorship, Jordan expressed to the Hoovers his feelings of obligation for the opportunities that the 1913 arrangement had given him to see the world.[66] In 1920 and 1928 he ardently supported Hoover for president. Hoover's action in May 1913 was, in fact, a graceful, mutually advantageous maneuver. Jordan, at no diminution of his high salary, retained the dignity of a Stanford connection, escaped the administrative chores that he already found burdensome, and gained the liberty to turn to the public issues where his heart now lay anyway. It was an attractive package for him. Hoover and his fellow trustees, anxious to rejuvenate a university adrift, were able to make a much-desired change of administration three years ahead of schedule and without a public spectacle or bitterness.

But not, perhaps, without a moment of embarrassment. Apparently fearful of adverse publicity, Hoover initially proposed (and Jordan agreed) that public announcement of the change be delayed until summer, when both Jordan and Branner would be traveling abroad, beyond the range of inquisitive newspaper reporters.[67] As it turned out, however, Jordan himself made the announcement at Stanford's commencement on May 19. At first the unprepared audience sat in stunned silence; then it burst into applause.[68] But when a few moments later Hoover rose and requested "three cheers for the chancellor," the response from the assembly was feeble. As Jordan wrote afterwards, few could see a reason to celebrate the sudden, bewildering, seemingly painful news.[69]

Selecting a new university president was only one of Hoover's initiatives that spring. Jordan was amazed at the momentum Hoover was building. "It is marvellous," he told Branner, "how Hoover is handling our Board. Almost every reform we have dreamed of has slipped through as if oiled."[70] The president of the board of trustees told Jordan that Hoover had given the trustees more ideas in ten days than they had had in ten years.[71]

The climax of Hoover's reform movement occurred at a trustees' meeting on May 23, 1913. Most of the key resolutions were drafted by Hoover personally.[72] The trustees approved the Jordan / Branner transition arrangement. As requested by Branner, they approved a significant increase in the faculty salary budget. In a dramatic reversal of the parsimonious policy of the past few years, they boldly authorized construction of a new library, a new gymnasium and stadium, and several facilities at the medical school, all at the urging of committees on which Hoover served actively.[73] To help free funds for this ambitious program the trustees revised their accounting methods on lines advocated by Hoover. They also created a Grounds Committee with a mandate to devise a plan for improving the university's grounds and housing facilities. Predictably, Hoover was named to this committee.[74]

Finally, on the recommendation (prepared by Hoover) of the special committee on future academic policy created the month before, the trustees announced several changes in the university's direction. Until the university's financial situation improved markedly, there would be no expansion in the male enrollment or the "educational range" of the institution. The current academic budget would be increased substantially each year, but this new expenditure would be devoted to strengthening "certain selected departments," particularly "in the direction of securing further prominent educational leaders" (Hoover's "pre-eminent" professors).[75] Nothing was said about eliminating any existing department. In an optimistic press release possibly drafted by Hoover and issued after the meeting, the trustees declared that Stanford University did have the resources to increase its academic budget, resources sufficient to "extend and improve" the "most important" of the existing departments until they became "preeminent among such departments in the United States." In a fateful ambiguity the trustees did not specify which departments it considered "most important" and planned to favor with its resources.[76]

This portent of future controversy was overlooked in the general optimism that greeted the reforms which Hoover, more than any other person, had wrought. The trustees' meeting of May 23, Jordan declared the next day, had been a "perfect love feast."

It would seem that Mr. Hoover devoted his entire time to working up these things in the month that he was here, and persuaded everybody that it was his duty to stand for these radical improvements and to convert all conservatists, so everybody was busy converting everybody else. All these matters in the aggregate are a great jump forward. . . .[77]

Many people in the Bay Area were astonished at Stanford's sudden forward motion; Hoover's faculty friend, E. D. Adams, called him a wonder-worker.[78]

Hoover now returned to England for the summer and autumn; Jordan set out on a lengthy world tour. Originally Jordan had intended to return to campus in late January 1914, which happened to be when the university's next budget would be prepared. But at Hoover's and then the board's urging, Jordan agreed to extend his sojourn abroad considerably in order to visit (and cultivate) Leland Stanford's wealthy brother in Melbourne, Australia. As a result Jordan was now to be absent from the university an entire year.[79]

Hoover returned to Stanford University on Christmas Eve, 1913 and remained in California more than two months.[80] Once again his presence catalyzed a burst of accomplishment by the board of trustees. Under Hoover's prodding the trustees further reorganized their accounting system and in February 1914, for the first time ever, made a public disclosure of the university's finances, thereby ending a much-criticized policy of secrecy that had hampered efforts to attract outside financial support. (Hoover wrote the resolutions instituting the change.)[81] On another front the board approved a new leasing system proposed by its Grounds Committee, thereby making it easier for faculty to build housing on campus.[82]

Meanwhile the board was proceeding with its expensive construction program—apparently with some second thoughts, for on February 24 Hoover felt obliged to send a blunt defense of the scheme to the board's president. The new library, gymnasium, and hospital approved last spring, he declared, were "absolutely necessary if the Institution is to go forward. . . ."[83] ("Absolutely" was a word Hoover used often in his correspondence in the years ahead when disturbed or especially anxious to carry his point. Hoover's letters rarely revealed any self-doubt.) The trustees continued with their building plan.

Hoover's principal achievement in the winter of 1913–14, however, lay in another area. From the beginning he had been particularly concerned about faculty salaries, a concern not allayed by the modest increase in the salary budget voted by the trustees in May 1913. During the following summer he told incoming President Branner that he wished to raise substantially the salaries of Stanford's "pre-eminent professors."[84] At the request of the chairman of the trustees' influential University Committee (to which Hoover belonged), Hoover, on his return to the campus, prepared a comprehensive report on faculty pay.

Hoover's report reiterated themes he had enunciated a year before. On the one hand faculty salaries were failing to keep up with the rising cost of living, and lower-paid faculty were "absolutely unable" to meet "even the barest necessities" of their positions. Hoover was particularly concerned that assistant professors were unable to maintain the level of dignity and affluence needed to entertain and otherwise exert proper influence over students. This level, to Hoover's mind, required at least one household servant per faculty family. Instead, Hoover found that many assistant professors were being forced to do menial work on the side and to take in boarders, while their wives were doing all the domestic work. (Hoover evidently felt it demeaning for faculty wives to do housework.) All this, said Hoover, had produced "absolute demoralization" and a "spirit of rebellion" among the assistant professors. Such a spirit would lead to "improper influence" on students. The situation at the top was no better. Stanford's salaries for its outstanding professors were inferior to the salaries offered by eastern universities, and the prospect of losing such distinguished men was increasing.

Hoover therefore proposed a comprehensive restructuring of the helter-skelter salary roll and a substantial immediate increase in the pay of most faculty. Two considerations governed his thinking (and said much about his social as well as educational philosophy): a desire to establish a fair, livable salary base at the bottom and to reward excellence at the top. Not a man to overlook crucial details, Hoover listed in his report the current salary of each of the 160 or so members of the Stanford faculty. Beside each name he listed the amount of a raise, if any, that the individual, in his judgment, should receive. He also proposed the creation of a new category of preeminent professors, and he carefully recorded who among the faculty should be placed in it (and how much they should get). Interestingly, Hoover recommended only three professors for the largest raise, $1,000. Two—Adams and Wilbur—were his close friends. The third, Vernon Kellogg, became a key associate in World War I.[85]

It was surely remarkable for a university trustee to be so immersed in the details of individual professors' salaries. Quite possibly Hoover, in preparing his report, received the input of men like President Branner. Nevertheless, Hoover's document mentioned no associates and was signed by himself alone. It was dated January 27, 1914. Three days later the board of trustees adopted both Hoover's proposed new salary classification and the individual salary revisions that he recommended.[86] In large measure one man, Herbert Hoover, had just set the salaries of the entire Stanford faculty!

As an engineer and executive Hoover was accustomed to promoting the able and to firing the incompetent. This was the way things worked in the business world, where the discipline of the free market prevailed. It was only to be expected, then, that a man accustomed to such procedures should chafe at the tenure system that governed academe. In his quest to attract brilliant professors to Stanford he confronted the fact that the university, like all universities, had its share of "dead wood" and that tenure protected them.[87]

Hoover was not one to be intimidated by hallowed tradition if it stood in the way of his objectives. By his calculations half of the full professors at

Stanford were either "humdrum" or "weak," and the university was second-rate because of it.[88] Why not, he proposed to Adams one evening, get rid of the faculty who were no longer valuable? Specifically, he evidently suggested that such unwanted professors (even long-serving ones) be given a year's leave of absence on full pay and then dismissed. Adams was appalled at such a drastic proposal and debated the matter with Hoover until 3:00 in the morning. A few days later Adams wrote to Hoover that such as assault on the entrenched tenure principle would devastate Stanford's academic reputation. Furthermore, if long-established faculty did not have security of tenure, no preeminent professor would ever come to Stanford.[89]

Hoover's response was quick:

> I quite recognize the justice of criticism in regard to any sudden scattering of staff, and such has never been any view of my own. On the other hand, though I am not prepared to say at the moment what the solution is, there has got to be some remedy for the Professor who will not, or cannot do his work. It is to me an outrage on the whole sanctity of higher education to think that a man can deliberately rob students and endowment in such positions. I do not know of any other profession, or calling, in this whole wide world where laziness and incapacity are wrapped up in the sacred garment of perpetual tenure.[90]

Hoover eventually altered his views. He later told Adams that his original idea had been a "theorist's dream" and that he now recognized that tenure was a necessary device to recruit worthy people into an underpaid calling.[91] But Hoover was scarcely enthusiastic. In his report of January 1914 he opposed an automatic annual salary increase for professors, regardless of qualifications; such a system would reward the "dead wood" and be "wasteful." Accordingly he structured the new salary plan so that a professor might not receive a step increase for five years and then only with the consent of the university president.[92]

By the end of 1913, on a variety of fronts, Stanford was undergoing a renewal. Then, suddenly, a tempest arose for Hoover and his fellow trustees from a most unexpected direction: the new university president, John Caspar Branner.

I V

I N many ways Branner's appointment in 1913 was a fitting and logical one. A distinguished scholar and teacher, he had served as vice-president of the university under Jordan since the 1890s. But in one respect the appointment seems odd: Branner was actually a year older than Jordan and planned to retire in just two years. Such a man could only be a transitional figure as Stanford entered its new era.

Was there perhaps more than met the eye in Branner's appointment? At least one faculty member (no friend of Hoover's) suspected that Hoover placed his mentor in the presidency in the expectation that he would dutifully implement the reforms Hoover wished to effect.[93] The two men, in fact, had long been cordial friends; the Hoovers had just dedicated *De Re Metallica* to Branner.

Some even suspected other motives. In 1915 Branner would presumably retire; in 1915 Hoover, the university's most successful alumnus and now its dominant trustee, would be forty-one years old. Was Hoover himself contemplating the Stanford presidency? Some years later a former mining associate claimed that this had been Hoover's long-time ambition until world events catapulted him to larger prominence.[94] On the Stanford faculty the story circulated that when Branner retired, Hoover would become chancellor and his friend Wilbur, currently dean of the medical school, would become president.[95]

As it happened, during World War I Hoover at one point did express willingness to serve as Stanford's president until the way could be paved for Wilbur. And he did help to secure Wilbur's accession as Branner's successor in 1916, a result he fervently desired. But there is no hard evidence that Hoover ever coveted the Stanford presidency or maneuvered Branner into the post in order to create a vacancy for himself two years hence. And if the board of trustees thought that it could easily control Branner, it soon learned otherwise.

On August 29, 1913, during Hoover's absence, the university's trustees made a critical decision:

> It was resolved that in the opinion of this Board the university funds and income will be insufficient to adequately extend and develop all departments of the university, and that it will therefore be necessary to select such courses of education as may be so developed to the highest point, abandoning or reducing other courses; and that the President is requested to submit to the University Committee of this Board his recommendations relative to such action by the Board.[96]

In one respect the policy here enunciated was not new. For ten years the trustees had been attempting to eliminate certain departments in the university.[97] And at the May 23, 1913 meeting just a few months before, the trustees had signaled their intent to build up "certain selected departments" only. From this perspective the August resolution was merely another step on a path already taken.

Yet in another respect the August resolution seemed contrary to the trustees' decision of May—and contrary to the views of Trustee Hoover. In his January 1913 report on "The Present Position" Hoover had favored retention of "practically all" the existing departments and had sharply rejected any "pruning" or policy of retrenchment. The trustees' actions in May 1913 had embodied Hoover's optimistic thinking. Their May resolutions had indicated that existing departments would be retained but that some among them would henceforth be favored. Now, however, in their August resolution, the trustees said that some departments would be favored *at the direct expense of others.* The May resolutions, Hoover's resolutions, with their authorization of a bigger academic budget, promised survival for all and prosperity for some. The August resolution promised prosperity for some but only by weakening or extinguishing others. In Hoover's absence the trustees had issued a call for retrenchment.

Incoming president Branner now confronted the unpleasant task of rearranging the size of the slices of Stanford's economic pie. In short order he found his target. Just a few years before, Stanford had acquired a medical college in San Francisco. It had done so, however, on the understanding that its new medical department would be largely self-sufficient and need no more than $25,000 from the university's budget per year.[98] But when President Branner examined the books in 1913 he found that the medical school already was absorbing far more than this amount and that its requirements were inexorably increasing.[99]

Not a man to mince his words, Branner bluntly informed Hoover in November that "as we now go this university is rapidly approaching a collapse as a university." The reason was the enormous and spiraling cost of the medical school. Either the medical school "must be endowed," Branner stated, "or we must expect to see it swamp the university." Branner was determined to rid the university of this growing financial incubus. He cared little for some trustees' ideas of consolidating and eliminating various departments; this, he claimed, would only drive out some of Stanford's best professors.[100] The trustees, he told a friend, "think it possible for me to so overhaul things here at the university that a lot of what they regard as purely ornamental departments can be done away with, and that this will release funds enough to keep the medical school going." In Branner's judgment this could not be done.[101]

On December 20, 1913 Branner replied formally to the trustees' economy resolution of August 29. He told the board that "no considerable economies are possible" and that most of the existing departments were "half-starved." Instead, he boldly took aim at the young and expensive medical school up in San Francisco. Not only was it "by far the most expensive part of the university"; it was the newest and least essential. Branner therefore proposed that Stanford University terminate all financial support to its medical school after July 31, 1914 and take measures to turn the entire facility over to the University of California (which also had a medical school in San Francisco).[102]

Branner's proposal (which commanded overwhelming faculty support)[103] was totally unexpected, and the trustees' University Committee (now including Hoover, back from London) was stunned.[104] But Branner was determined to force the issue. The medical school, he believed, must be eliminated "at once and for all."[105] At its meeting on January 30, 1914 the board of trustees made its first response. It created a committee, including Hoover, to confer with any similar committee from the University of California about possible "joint action" by the medical schools of the two universities.[106] From Branner's perspective it was not an auspicious beginning. Of the three trustees selected, one, in Branner's opinion, was amenable to reason, and one was vehemently in favor of Stanford's keeping its medical school. The third, Hoover, was a close friend of the medical school's dean, Ray Lyman Wilbur, and "will probably do what Wilbur wants." In Branner's view "personal interests" were now "sadly mixed in the matter."[107]

It soon became evident that Branner's bombshell was greatly discomfiting the trustees. On February 16, in a confidential letter, Hoover told Branner frankly that the time had come for Branner to reconsider his position. Hoover declared that Branner "had been allowed to secure a mis-impression" that nothing could be done for the university's Palo Alto branch "without drastic reduction in some quarter." The fact that the trustees had just raised the university's budget, said Hoover, belied Branner's belief. It was not yet possible, Hoover asserted, to determine whether the university could support the medical school or not. Furthermore, the public impression "that we wish to jettison the Medical Department at any cost has absolutely destroyed any hope of a proper negotiation." And many of the trustees were now "so disturbed" that consideration of the medical school issue was "doubly difficult." Hoover strenuously urged Branner to withdraw his recommendation of December 20 "and state that the matter can probably be better re-considered at a later date." Why withdraw? Because, said Hoover, the "immediate necessities" of the Palo Alto branch of the university had been met and there was now no need to ponder the fate of the medical school.[108]

President Branner, however, was not about to capitulate. On February 19 he bluntly informed Hoover that he would not withdraw his recommendations of December 20; they had been made in response to the trustees' own resolution of last August. This resolution, Branner reminded Hoover, stated explicitly that the trustees believed that the university's resources were "insufficient" to develop all departments of the university and that some courses would have to be abandoned or curtailed. Branner's conclusions had followed inevitably from that. Branner resented Hoover's suggestion that he had misconstrued the university's difficulties and should now back down. "If the problem was not properly stated by the board," Branner stated, "then it rests with the board, and not with me, to set the matter right."[109]

If Stanford's president was in an unyielding mood, so, too, was Hoover. In a long, emphatic letter to a fellow trustee on February 23, just days after receiving Branner's letter, he declared that the situation was now an "emergency" and unleashed a salvo of arguments for retaining the medical school. Among other things, Hoover asserted that "our institution can meet all present outlays out of its income."[110]

Four days later, at their monthly meeting, the board of trustees adopted a

resolution prepared by Hoover explicitly rejecting Branner's recommendations of December 20, 1913. Hoover's resolution declared that Branner was
"evidently acting under a misapprehension of the university's resources" and
that, on the contrary, the university's financial state "does not now require,
and may never require, such drastic action as the abandonment of medical
education." Furthermore, no "important department" should be abolished
on one semester's notice; the "dignity and reputation of the university" mandated "much longer preparation and notice." The trustees did agree to explore
some appropriate kind of "joint action" with the University of California's
medical school. But they opposed any wholesale abandonment of Stanford's
medical facilities to its rival.[111] Upon Branner's objection, the trustees consented to modify a few parts of the resolution and to eliminate a paragraph
that Branner found offensive.[112]

By late February 1914, then, Stanford's trustees had voted to retain the
medical school (in some form), had approved a new budget that increased aid
to the medical school for the next year, and had rebuffed Branner's effort to
surrender the facility outright to the University of California. Still, Branner
detected a silver lining. As he interpreted the trustees' action of February 27,
the trustees had withdrawn their retrenchment resolution of the previous
August. For the board in effect was now saying that its resources were *not* as
slender as it had intimated in August. "Drastic action" like elimination of
"important departments" might never be required, it now declared.[113]

Early in March Hoover returned to England.[114] But the medical school
controversy was by no means over. To President Branner the trustees' actions
had merely postponed the day of reckoning. While the new budget increase
of $62,000 (drawn up by Hoover) was welcome, Branner noted with displeas-
ure that much of it went to the medical school. He also questioned the
trustees' new confidence that "we have money enough to care for all departments, medicine included." To Branner this was based on nothing but hope.
In the president's opinion there remained only one chance of preventing the
medical school from "swamping the university later on": a combination with
the University of California's medical school that might reduce Stanford's
expense.[115] But Branner was pessimistic. The trustees' negotiating committee—Hoover and two others—was not, in his opinion, "open-minded." One
member already was opposed to amalgamation, and Hoover essentially concurred with him.[116]

Efforts to resolve the issue now proceeded on two fronts. During the spring
various representatives of the two universities explored the possibility of a
medical school merger. The negotiations soon foundered: Stanford wanted
equal representation on the proposed governing board; the University of California insisted on majority control. On May 29, following a new initiative
from the California Regents, the Stanford trustees terminated the discussions—convinced, they said, that "no basis of merger" did or could exist and
that no savings would be effected thereby. The trustees resolved to maintain
an independent Stanford medical school.[117]

Meanwhile Branner had been following another tack. From the beginning he had urged the trustees to bring in disinterested outside experts for assistance, originally to settle the terms of the transfer of Stanford's medical school to California.[118] One such expert, a friend and supporter of Branner's, came in March and met with the trustees' committee of three, minus Hoover. Neither side persuaded the other.[119] Late in March the trustees authorized Branner to select a medical expert to visit California and advise about the feasibility of merger, and on this Branner pinned his final hopes.[120] Branner also felt relieved: ". . . whatever is done now, we must all agree that we have sought unbiased advice."[121]

Hoover, in London, was uneasy about this turn of events. On April 7, before learning of the board's action, he confidently predicted that "the Medical School agitation will gradually die out."[122] A week later, however, he confided to Wilbur: "I cannot say I am very keen about continuing this agitation on the subject of amalgamating the Medical Schools, and should be very sorry if, as the result of [Branner's designated expert's] visit, we should have him advise that anything of the kind be done."[123]

As it happened, Hoover's apprehension proved groundless. On the very day that Branner's chosen expert—the dean of the University of Michigan's medical school—arrived on the Stanford campus (May 29), the Stanford trustees voted to reject the merger idea. The very purpose of the consultant's visit had thus been eliminated before he could begin his investigation.[124] Nevertheless, the Michigan dean stayed on for a few days and studied the issue while Branner, outmaneuvered, hoped against hope for the best. "Medical matters are still stewing," he told a friend on June 2, "and no good odors come from the mess."[125] When a week later the Michigan dean submitted his report, Branner could only have been disappointed. The dean enthusiastically lauded the Stanford medical school and urged that it be expanded. Amalgamation with the University of California's medical school (already a dead issue) would not, he said, be wise. And on the crucial question of finances the dean was optimistic: Stanford, from what he learned, could afford to develop its medical school without impairing the growth of its other departments.[126]

The medical school battle was finally over.[127] Branner had lost. On the crucial issue of finances, the trustees had insisted that Stanford did have the money, and Branner's designated expert had agreed with them. Still, the embattled president took consolation from the feeling that he had done his duty. The matter was settled, he informed Jordan, and he felt "bound to accept" the Michigan dean's report as "a justification of the course and action of our board of trustees."[128] Branner felt that he could "accept the situation with a clear conscience. I do feel that I was put in a false position by the trustees at the outset when they called upon me to cut down things here in the university, but so long as the university can grow and I don't really have to cut down on the campus, I shall not have any grounds for complaint."[129]

Branner, however, had not suffered a total defeat. On the central question, of course, his fears never materialized: the medical school did not "swamp" the university, and Stanford was not forced to abandon medical education. But Branner's actions probably helped to scuttle the trustees' retrenchment plans of August 1913. It was one thing to build up certain selected departments out of increased appropriations (as Hoover favored); it was quite another to eliminate departments altogether. Thanks in some measure to Branner, the trustees reverted to their more optimistic attitude of May 1913.

Hoover was in England when the medical school controversy reached its denouement. The absent trustee was gratified that the issue was "finally buried, once and for all."[130] He told Chancellor Jordan that the trustees were "absolutely unanimous" in their intention to preserve the medical school.[131] To one of his trustee-allies Hoover later expressed guilt that he had not been "on the decks" to assist in the battle.[132]

Hoover did not appear to be angry at President Branner. Early in June he told Jordan: "Dr. Branner has been a complete success, in spite of all he has to say himself. He has had only one difference with the Trustees, and that is in the matter of the Medical School, where I was myself strongly against his views that it should be abolished. This matter has now been finally dropped." Pointing to the reorganizing of the faculty payroll, Hoover added that he thought Stanford "has made very distinct progress this year."[133] Eight days later, in a letter to a closer friend than Jordan, Hoover was less cheerful and probably more confiding. The medical school dispute, he said, had retarded "solid constructive work during the period of discussion."[134] The momentum of Hoover's reform campaign had been slowed.

Still, Hoover could properly regard the years 1912–14 as years of accomplishment at Stanford, and himself as the prime catalyst. In less than two years he had established himself as the university's most energetic and innovative trustee. Looking back on this period a half-decade later, Ray Lyman Wilbur credited Hoover with effecting two major achievements for his alma mater: a much-needed construction program and the new faculty salary schedule, which was now fully in place.[135]

The experience of being a trustee and philanthropist was important for Hoover as well. It had given him a further taste of the pleasures of constructive accomplishment and the possibilities of service beyond his profession. Forceful and resourceful, the executive-turned-benefactor had been able to achieve results, to "coordinate and control the best efforts of other people." Having succeeded thus with Stanford's trustees, might he not succeed in wider realms?

26

The Lobbyist

I

I T was in the spring of 1912, the year he became a Stanford trustee, that a wider realm of public service unexpectedly opened for Herbert Hoover.

On the last day of April there arrived in London a small delegation of Americans headed by the distinguished mining engineer John Hays Hammond. The group comprised a "Commission Extraordinary to Europe" representing a San Francisco organization called the Panama-Pacific International Exposition Company. Incorporated in 1910, and backed by the city's civic and business leaders, the Exposition Company was planning to stage a world's fair in San Francisco throughout most of 1915. Officially the celebration would commemorate the discovery of the Pacific Ocean by Balboa in 1515 and the completion of the Panama Canal four hundred years later. More practically, the fair would highlight San Francisco's rebirth from the 1906 earthquake and underscore the exciting commercial prospects for the Pacific coast in the wake of the canal's opening. Early in 1912, following a joint resolution by Congress, President William Howard Taft officially invited "all the nations of the earth" to commemorate the canal's opening by sending exhibits to San Francisco's projected Exposition. Less than three months later the alert Exposition officials dispatched Hammond and his colleagues on a journey to secure the active participation of European governments and business interests.[1]

Not long after the Commission Extraordinary's visit, Dr. Frederick J. Skiff, the head of the Exposition's "foreign office," traveled to London to turn goodwill and publicity into practical cooperation. One day "a quiet, pleasant-mannered young man" (as the fair's historian later described him) called on Skiff and volunteered to help in promoting the Panama-Pacific International Exposition. It was Hoover. Although Skiff had never heard of Hoover, he was impressed by his visitor's eagerness to enlist in the cause.[2] Before long Hoover was (unofficially, at least) on board. In mid-June he cabled the Exposition's president that "Californians in London" would be "delighted to assist" the undertaking "in every way possible" and that a committee of them would soon be organized.[3] Hoover felt that such a committee could become the "machinery" for "promotion of the interests of the Exposition on this side."[4]

There is no record that Hoover's suggestion of a committee of "Californians in London" ever came to fruition. But now that he had the sympathetic ear of the Exposition's organizers, he proceeded with characteristic drive to promote their interests. During the spring and summer he conferred with a number of Exposition representatives passing through England.[5] Already skilled in the art of mining promotion, Hoover was soon brimming with ideas. On July 5, in a long letter to the Exposition's president, Charles C. Moore, he proposed a plan to generate the publicity that the Exposition needed in England.

Pointing out that the year 1915 would also mark the centenary of peace between America and Britain, and that King George V planned to visit Canada at some point in his reign, Hoover urged that the king be invited to visit San Francisco en route to Canada by way of the Panama Canal. Such an event, he said, would be of "undoubted importance" to the Exposition. Already Hoover had taken soundings among influential British friends and found them very receptive. But Hoover, who knew British politics well, counseled strongly against any overt, premature invitation, which would "undoubtedly meet with a refusal unless the whole of the ground-work had been prepared behind the throne." In such a delicate matter it would first be necessary "to gradually work" the British aristocracy "in support of the idea" before any open invitation was issued. Hoover was confident of success if the question were "handled with discretion" and, at the start, "through private English hands." He planned to keep himself in the background. He told Moore, "It comes to a question of systematically inspiring the English people in the proper quarters in this direction and allowing them to do the work."

Hoover had another suggestion. In recent years the world had been saturated with expositions, and he discovered that in British eyes San Francisco's fair merely looked like one more "commercial Exposition of the usual order." Moreover, to his British friends California was "a strange land . . . a mighty long ways off." Hoover therefore urged that the Exposition "touch their imaginations" by doing something to make itself appear less parochial: by linking itself to the century-of-peace celebration, for instance, or, even better, by staging "a great racial pageant of wider than local interest—in fact a sort of pageant of Anglo-Saxon Race history." Hoover found his English friends impressed by such ideas.[6]

In mid-July Moore authorized Hoover by cable to represent the Exposition in all negotiations toward securing a visit by King George V.[7] Even before receiving this authorization, Hoover on July 18 had had a three-hour lunch with Arthur Balfour, the former Conservative Prime Minister and current leader of the Opposition in Parliament. To the sympathetic Tory leader Hoover poured out his arguments for a royal visit to the Exposition. Hoover asserted that the coming century would witness considerable "human struggle for avenues of outlet for surplus population" and that no nation would be able to maintain a "policy of isolation" much longer. He contended that "in the long run the only certain and enduring alliance would be that between peoples of the same race." The American people, however, had not yet realized the "probable necessity" of abandoning "their sacred policy of isolation"—a realization, said Hoover, that "many of us" considered it "our duty to advance . . . with every power that we could command." In promoting an end to American isolationism, Hoover continued, "we felt we were working at one with all those Englishmen who have the interest of the race at heart." He told Balfour that nothing could better promote the "education" of the American people in this area than a visit by Great Britain's king.

Hoover's plea to Balfour for "renewed racial unity" (as he put it) between Britain and America seemed quite at variance with his deepening alienation from the Old World and its class-bound ways. Here was "Hail Columbia" Hoover, the outspoken defender of American institutions and critic of Britain's social system, in the role of an enlightened internationalist anxious to end America's "sacred policy of isolation." Perhaps there was no inconsistency. Perhaps as a matter of geopolitics Hoover envisaged the need for greater "Anglo-Saxon" cooperation regardless of the differences of social philosophy that now divided the English-speaking peoples. Or perhaps he was only invoking the argument best calculated to sway Balfour. When it came to making a case for doing what he wanted to do, Hoover could be very resourceful.

In any case, it worked. When Hoover met the British leader again eight days later, Balfour disclosed that he had already been active in the matter and was "quite hopeful" that a royal visit could be arranged.[8]

Meanwhile, through his English friends, Hoover was putting out feelers to Britain's Liberal government and particularly its Foreign Secretary, Sir Edward Grey. In late July he learned that Grey, speaking personally, was "warmly in favour" of Hoover's proposal.[9] In all these preliminaries Hoover took care to be discreet and stay behind the scenes; any publicity would be ruinous. "My own attitude," he informed Moore, "has been largely that of a missionary in the matter, in the hope of stimulating them to action."[10] Such indirection was appropriate under the circumstances; it was also Hoover's preferred mode of action as he entered public life.

During the autumn he continued to pursue what became known as the "illustrious visitor" project. In October, while Hoover was back in the United States, President Moore of the Exposition informed Secretary of State Philander C. Knox that Hoover would be calling soon to present a "plan" of "national importance"—no doubt the scheme for King George's visit to California via the Panama Canal.[11] Hoover also lobbied the National Committee for the Celebration of the One Hundredth Anniversary of Peace Among English Speaking Peoples. In December he learned that this group, which numbered Woodrow Wilson, Theodore Roosevelt, and President Taft among its members, had adopted his "illustrious visitor" proposal. It also invited him to join its executive committee.[12]

That summer and fall Hoover seemed to work overtime devising ways to promote the Exposition abroad. In July he urged an American journalist-friend, Robert Porter, then an associate editor of *The Times* (London), to publish an interview with a British actor who had been invited to participate in the Exposition. To Hoover such a "news feature" would emphasize the Exposition's "international character"—a crucial point as the Exposition organizers strove to assure European participation.[13] Hoover also induced Porter and *The Times* to start work on a special supplement about the Exposition and the canal. He insisted that the Exposition's backers were interested not in "land boosting" but in "the creation of a great international project." He urged *The Times* to prepare "a higher type of production than a description of the large bumpkins."[14] On another front he asked Baron Meller-Zakomelsky, with whom he was associated in the Kyshtim Corporation, to use his influence to ascertain the Russian government's interest in the Exposition.[15] In September he even declared himself willing to "invade the Balkans, Greece, and Egypt" that winter at his own expense as a representative of the Exposition.[16] Perhaps in recognition of his enthusiasm, the Exposition organizers appointed him a Special Commissioner on January 2, 1913. Hoover was expected to promote three projects: the royal visit, the centennial-of-peace celebration, and the proposed Anglo-Saxon pageant at the fair.[17]

Such zeal, perseverance, and ingenuity were typical of Hoover. Once he had an objective in mind there was little that could deflect him. In mid-1912, however, an unexpected obstacle arose that threatened to nullify months of diligent effort. Under the terms of the Hay-Pauncefote Treaty of 1901 the United States had pledged that all ships using the yet-to-be-built Panama Canal would be charged equally for doing so. Nevertheless, in 1912 the U.S. Congress voted to exempt domestic American coastwise shipping from paying the tolls assessed for passing through the canal.[18]

Suddenly all Hoover's plans were jeopardized. Great Britain was angry at the congressional act of favoritism. In October Hoover learned that the editorial staff of *The Times* was "not fully agreed upon the desirability of bringing out a Panama Canal number in the face of recent legislation." Vainly Hoover strove to repair the damage. He told Robert Porter that the tolls legislation "was not anti-English in its character, but [merely] a part of the regular propaganda which necessarily prevails prior to Presidential election." Hoover blamed the "idiot" British chargé d'affaires in Washington for the obnoxious congressional action: by protesting publicly when the issue arose, the chargé had created an opportunity for congressmen to "get political plunder by 'twisting the British lion's tail.' " Hoover insisted that the tolls legislation had "no sentimental backing amongst the American people" and eventually would be modified. (It was in fact repealed in 1914.)[19] He urged *The Times* to proceed with its Panama Canal supplement. Californians, he asserted, would not object if the tolls question were discussed "so long as it was done in a judicial and not in an anti-American manner."[20]

It was no use. By the time Hoover returned to Britain in early 1913 everything he had labored to accomplish for the Exposition was stymied. The British government had not yet responded to President Taft's invitation of a full year before. With America and Britain now at odds over the Panama Canal tolls, Hoover reported that "absolutely nothing" could be done "in an overt manner" to promote the "illustrious visitor" project until the tolls controversy was resolved.[21] Despite Hoover's personal intervention at *The Times*, he told Moore in February that "the Panama position hangs as a sort of a cloud here" inhibiting any progress.[22] A month later *The Times* still had not budged. "The Canal matter still hangs its gloom over everything," Hoover stated. "I do not think that people in the United States, particularly in California, have any idea of the depth of feeling which this question has stirred up over here."[23]

At this point Hoover wondered out loud whether the Exposition supporters should change their tactics. He suspected, but could not prove, that the British government was withholding its acceptance of President Taft's invitation in retaliation for the canal tolls law. If so, Hoover declared, this seemed "extremely small politics," which he was convinced the British public would not countenance. Hoover knew that "through friends" he could ventilate the issue in the press and Parliament. But such an action might be construed as American interference in British politics, and Hoover was not certain that such a policy would be "at all wise." On March 11 he promised Moore not to initiate such a campaign without prior assent from San Francisco. He also assured Moore that anything he did would be done "simply by myself as a private individual among my own friends."[24]

Moore was evidently apprehensive that Hoover, in his forceful way, might go too far. In his next letter to the Exposition's president, therefore, Hoover stressed that he had not told anyone that he had an official connection with the Exposition. Moreover, he had been "very careful" not to tread beyond the sphere of his direct instructions.[25] But as the weeks dragged by without result, Hoover was becoming restive.

Finally in June came the news that, following still another Hoover appeal, the staff of *The Times* had agreed at last to proceed with the special supplement devoted to the Panama Canal. Hoover, with his eye on the publicity value of such an issue, was pleased. "I have been extremely anxious to get this done," he told Moore, "because I believe it will come nearer breaking through the newspaper boycott than anything else which can possibly be devised."[26]

Before *The Times* could issue its special number, however, a devastating blow befell Hoover's endeavors. On August 6, 1913 the British Foreign Secretary, Sir Edward Grey, announced that Great Britain would not participate officially in the Panama-Pacific International Exposition. The reasons offered for the decision were primarily economic: a proper British exhibit, Grey said, would cost at least £250,000, a sum "quite out of proportion to any commercial advantages that are likely to result." Moreover, the government had found no "active desire" in British commercial centers to participate. Grey denied that the Panama Canal tolls issue influenced the decision.[27] The British announcement, coupled with Germany's nearly concurrent decision not to attend, seriously jeopardized the Exposition's prestige. How could the event be a truly international enterprise when Europe's two leading industrial powers were staying away?

I I

H E R B E R T Hoover was not a man to take no for an answer. Only five days after Grey's seemingly conclusive statement of policy, Hoover, in London, proposed a daring counterattack whose aim was nothing less than a reversal of Great Britain's decision. On August 10 he cabled Moore in San Francisco:

> My view is failure to secure British participation largely due entire lack publicity and outside pushing at this end. . . . Position now very difficult to reopen here but consider that best method of attack would be to push question in Germany with every influence that can be brought to bear because if Germans participate believe English will have to follow suit. . . . If Exposition could see way to expend moderate amount on publicity here putting forward relations Pacific Coast market to British manufacturers after opening of Canal [it] would have ultimate effect. If Porter [of *The Times*] is with you suggest you discuss frankly with him securing publicity campaign. He is most loyal American and has better knowledge of Press position here than anyone in England.[28]

Ten days later, not yet having received a response, Hoover cabled Moore again. What, he asked, had the Exposition done "regarding press campaign"? Anxious to act, Hoover emphasized that it was desirable to "keep in motion discussion now going on."[29]

While Hoover waited for instructions from San Francisco, he took steps on his own to supply the "publicity and outside pushing" that he felt the Exposition's efforts in England had lacked. He contacted the American ambassador to England, Walter Hines Page, while the ambassador was visiting Stratford-on-Avon.[30] He consulted his friend Sir Thomas Lipton (of the tea company) and other British supporters of participation in the Exposition.[31] He conferred with W. A. M. Goode, a Canadian-born journalist with wide experience in England and America, about organizing a publicity campaign over the Exposition in the British press.[32] He spent an entire week poring over American trade statistics for data that would demonstrate the economic importance of the Pacific coast trade to Great Britain.[33]

On August 20 Hoover publicly entered the fray with a letter to *The Times* rebutting the British government's argument that the Exposition would yield no substantial advantage to British commerce. On the contrary, Hoover asserted, it would soon be cheaper for the Pacific coast to import manufactured goods from Europe via the Panama Canal than from the eastern United States by rail. Hoover claimed that the European manufacturer would have an "absolute advantage" over the eastern American manufacturer in the Pacific market and that the "Pacific slope" would become "largely a province of Europe from a manufacturer's and shipping point of view." There were sound economic reasons, then, for the British to exhibit their wares at the Exposition. There were also, said Hoover, "sentimental" reasons: the Panama Canal was "the greatest engineering triumph of the race," a feat in which "the English people should take much pride."[34]

By early September Hoover had failed to elicit a go-ahead signal from San Francisco. His eagerness for aggressive action now gave way to rising anger at his California sponsors—and a temporary retreat into righteous passivity. "I have simply lost all heart in the San Francisco position," he told a friend on September 3. Three times he had "outlined definite courses of action" to the Exposition's leaders. Three times "they refused to follow my advice, and I have now come to the firm resolve that my connection shall hereafter be nil." Twice already he had been "proved absolutely right as to my interpretation of the drift of things and the necessary remedies," and he had "not the slightest doubt" that he would be proven right again.[35] The next day Hoover poured out his frustration to another Exposition supporter:

> . . . Lipton and his friends are asking me if they can proceed, and Goode says he cannot hold his services open indefinitely. I am simply having to say that I am not authorised to do anything. The whole position is disheartening when one can see with the utmost clearness where things are going to, and this is in fact simply a repetition of what occurred before. I simply intend to let matters take their course. I cannot, with any sense of personal dignity, further impose my views on the Exposition, nor am I looking for more jobs in this world nor honours of this kind.[36]

It was not like Hoover to remain passive for very long, and his "firm resolve" to leave Exposition matters alone quickly dissipated. In mid-September, evidently without authority from San Francisco but with the encouragement of certain Exposition officials visiting London, Hoover proceeded on his own to organize a "British Committee, Panama-Pacific Exposition," complete with an office and secretary, W. A. M. Goode. Hoover informed Goode that "myself and friends" would provide £1,200 for Goode's salary and expenses for the next six months.[37] Hoover defended his scheme in a letter to Moore on the nineteenth. Various Exposition promoters passing through London had all agreed, said Hoover, that his "recommendation as to the present situation is the only one to adhere to":

1. That a purely British movement should be stimulated to form initially a Provisional Committee of most eminent men, and later a General Committee embracing every branch of influence, the sole object of which Committee is to secure Government participation.
2. That the Panama Pacific, in all its manifestations by way of agents should get down out of Great Britain at the earliest possible moment, in order that there may be no charge of intrigue on the part of the Exposition itself, and so that the Englishmen who are taking the matter up can go at it conscientiously as their own movement, initiated and controlled by themselves.[38]

The next day (before he could receive Hoover's letter) Moore finally authorized Hoover by cable to go ahead and spend up to $4,500 in Exposition funds for the British Committee's publicity campaign.[39]

Unharnessed at last, Hoover was determined to direct the new effort on his own terms. He told Moore that the removal of all Exposition agents from England was "of unqualified importance"; his British allies "will not go on until this is done."[40] It was "extremely dangerous to our whole programme," he said, for any Exposition official to remain in England "as this is essentially a British movement."[41] He asked that his own appointment as a Special Commissioner be revoked so that he could present himself as having "no connection with the Exposition otherwise than as a friend."[42] If the story should ever spread, said Hoover, that an American was responsible for the growing British agitation, "I am entirely undone."[43]

Above all, Hoover wished to oust J. B. G. Lester, a British subject who recently had been appointed secretary of the Exposition's "foreign office."[44] Hoover had clashed with Lester, whom he described as a "typical remittance type of Englishman" possessing no great qualifications, when the two met late in the summer. One of the British government's objections to exhibiting in San Francisco was that its canvass of British commercial circles turned up little interest in the fair. Hoover proposed now to stimulate such interest with his publicity campaign. Lester, however, insisted on asking the London

Chamber of Commerce to conduct a new canvass immediately—before Hoover could "formulate up opinion among manufacturers." Hoover was aghast. Such a course, he warned Lester, might be "absolutely fatal," for "if the enquiry came out unfavourably we could make Committees and raise agitation until we were blind, because the Government, having been further substantiated in their view as to the wishes of the commercial community, will never move hand nor foot."[45]

Nevertheless, Lester persisted, with predictably adverse results—"a bad lick in the eye," said Hoover, for the Exposition. "The point," Hoover declared, was that the manufacturers who had been canvassed "had not been cultivated up and did not understand the situation." Hoover considered it "very regrettable" that Lester had not been ordered "to do nothing without my approval."[46] Eventually, after further protest from Hoover, Lester was removed from the scene.[47]

During the autumn of 1913 Hoover, aided by Goode, pushed ahead with organizing the "purely British" committee. It was slow going; Hoover confessed at one point that they were getting more refusals than acceptances.[48] Not everyone, it seemed, was anxious to join a committee explicitly formed to pressure the government into reversing its decision not to participate in the Exposition. In assembling the committee Hoover displayed considerable political acumen. Since England's current government was Liberal, he took care not to load the roster with "the empty-headed Peer" and "the active opponents of the Government." Instead, he sought "absolute commercial leaders"—"men of stability," predominantly those of Liberal persuasion. As he told Moore, "We can always get the opponents of the Government and the noodle-headed Peer later."[49]

On October 30 Hoover's allies publicly announced the formation of the Exposition's British Committee. It was an impressive list, including many of the most eminent men in British commerce and industry.[50] In mid-November the committee sent a memorandum to the prime minister requesting an audience. The memorandum stressed that since August new circumstances had arisen favoring a change in governmental policy. Among other things, the committee cited America's new tariff ("unexpectedly favourable to British trade"), the damage caused to Anglo-American relations by Britain's refusal to participate in the fair, and the magnitude of British exports to the Pacific coast. In a bid for compromise, the committee asserted that a suitable government exhibit in San Francisco could be arranged for only £100,000, not £250,000 (as the government claimed).[51] The British Committee also lobbied individual Cabinet ministers in the government.[52]

Meanwhile Goode, aided by a journalist named Spender with excellent Liberal connections, was laboring effectively to generate favorable editorials across the United Kingdom.[53] As the propaganda offensive mounted, Hoover remained discreetly but by no means passively in the background. On December 5 he told a friend that he had had "scarcely a minute to do anything else during the whole of last month."[54] If the British Committee was doing the fighting, Hoover, out of sight, was directing the campaign.

Then in mid-November came a dramatic new jolt to the Exposition's efforts. From sources in the British Cabinet Hoover and his friends learned conclusively that Britain's refusal to exhibit at the Exposition was not based on economic factors at all. Instead, as Hoover had surmised, the British government was retaliating against America's Panama Canal tolls legislation.[55] Even worse, Britain's refusal was part of a still-secret "direct understanding" with Germany reached on Sir Edward Grey's own initiative some time before: a "positive undertaking" (according to Hoover) to take "joint action" on "certain matters affecting the United States," including the tolls issue and the Exposition.[56] Furthermore, having each pledged to boycott the Exposition, neither Britain nor Germany wished to be the first to suggest reconsideration of their understanding.[57]

Hoover responded to this new obstacle head-on. "Am now bringing pressure in proper quarter to get question reopened" between the two governments, he cabled Moore on November 18.[58] Hoover hoped to persuade Germany to approach Britain for a review of their Exposition policies on the basis of what Hoover called "the very considerable public opinion which has developed" in the two countries—public opinion that Hoover himself had done much to stimulate. Such an approach, he thought, would provide Britain a graceful way to retreat.[59] In late November, on Hoover's and the British Committee's instructions, Goode hurried over to Germany to size up the situation there and to consult with Albert Ballin, a leader of the movement to obtain official German representation at the Exposition.[60] Goode found that the German government was willing enough to reverse its stand but not amenable to making the first move toward England. Goode also learned that 1,400 German businesses were planning to exhibit in San Francisco despite their government's hands-off attitude and that the Reichstag would probably appropriate money for an unofficial German exhibit at the fair.[61]

Armed with this intelligence, Hoover turned to still another of his friends in the British press: Lord Northcliffe, owner of *The Times* and one of the most influential men in England. Hoover persuaded Northcliffe to "sound the note" in his newspapers about the "German intention to be largely represented" in San Francisco. Hoover hoped that England's rivalry with Germany might prompt it to change its course. Such publicity, Hoover informed Moore, would be "helpful by way of indirect pressure" on the British prime minister as he weighed the British Committee's request for a deputation.[62]

Even as he practiced these "indirect" lobbying techniques Hoover, ever persistent, was adopting a bolder strategy. As soon as he had confirmed the existence of the Anglo-German understanding in mid-November, Hoover realized that he held a powerful weapon in his hands. On the nineteenth he told Moore that he could assure "a pretty hot time when Parliament reopens over any such question as this understanding. . . ."[63] A few days later he helped to prepare a letter for Goode to sign and send to "an intimate friend of Sir Edward Grey" with the expectation that Grey ultimately would read it.[64] In this letter Goode warned that if America should learn about the secret Anglo-German accord—and particularly about Britain's initiative in the matter—the American public's response would not be gentle.[65] Hoover conceded to Moore that this gambit was "a rather dangerous ballon d'essai," but "we felt that something must be done to force an issue."[66] Meanwhile Hoover asked the American ambassador to identify any member of the British Cabinet who might be converted into an "active internal missioner" for the Exposition cause.[67]

At this point Hoover's view of tactics began to diverge from that of his British allies. Goode was willing (in the letter intended to reach Grey) to drop a hint about American reaction to exposure of the Anglo-German accords. But in the same letter Goode strenuously abjured any intent of deliberately using the accords for "agitation." In late November, in fact, he worked frantically to keep elements of the British press from publicizing the existence of the accords. Goode wished to avoid the appearance of putting "external pressure" on the British government.[68] To the British Committee, many of whom were Liberals, the thought of disclosing the existence of a secret diplomatic compact to the press as a means of pressuring their own government was anathema.[69]

On November 27 Hoover informed Charles Moore, "We are having a great deal of difficulty in keeping the Press from making any comment on the understanding between Germany and Great Britain with regard to the United States, but this fact has leaked out through German sources."[70] Hoover did not mention that this German leak, or a similar one very soon thereafter, had been instigated by himself. For in late November he had decided to wait no longer. Unknown to his British associates, or to Moore, and acting, as always, circuitously, Hoover had forced the news of the Anglo-German accord into the open.

In a letter to his friend and business associate John Barneson on December 5 Hoover told what he had done and why. Goode, he explained, had proven "as I anticipated" to be "a very skilful, knowing chap, but lacking in moral courage and requiring a pretty strong guiding hand. My view of general tactics widely differs from his, but I have insisted on having my own way, although I have had to go outside of the Committee business entirely in order to get it."

The point is that we requested the Prime Minister to receive a deputation. Goode dilly-dallied along about this question much longer than was necessary, but having sent the request in, it was my belief that every single gun that we had should be brought to bear, and all at once, because the matter then comes before the whole Cabinet in a form upon which they have got to take some action, considering the importance of our Committee, and from the very minute that this request was sent in we had to turn loose every battery. One of our strongest guns, to my mind, consisted in the gentle exposure of this Anglo-German agreement directed against the San Francisco Exposition and other American matters. Goode, Lipton, and others were in a funk about having anything of this kind published, and I have taken it upon myself to indirectly expose the whole blooming situation.

I have done this in three ways: First, I got my friend here who is the head of the Associated Press in Europe to have their people in Berlin corroborate the existence of such an agreement through Ballin, and then send dispatch to London through Reuters. Second, I go to the Editor of the "Times," through my old friend Porter, and put the situation to him, and the necessity for his handling it with diplomatic care; and, Third, I get [U.S. Ambassador] Page to let the fact leak out from the State Department in Washington. All of this has created a mild sensation, and whereas a good many people are somewhat aggravated to think that the matter has become public, I have not the slightest doubt in my own mind that it will have a great effect.

Hoover was pleased with his action. "The fact is, my old friend, that while I have a great appreciation of these smooth diplomatic folk who accomplish things by innocent and mild manners, there are times in the history of every transaction when a little sprinkling of fighting blood like you possess is of more good than a thousand carefully drawn up letters."[71]

Hoover's scheme had been well-conceived and well-executed. By arranging for word of the Anglo-German accords to leak out from Germany and the United States, and by operating through a complaisant American ambassador and various friendly journalists, he had achieved his objective without exposing himself to any cross fire in England.

On December 6, 1913 Hoover sailed from London for California. The British Committee's request for a deputation was now before the British Cabinet, and Hoover informed Moore that "we have brought every gun to bear that we have been able to lay hand upon." He also told Moore, evidently for the first time, that he had effected "a general exposure of the German question here, entirely outside of the agency of the British Committee." Hoover's absorption in the Exposition campaign had caused him to delay his voyage for two weeks so that he could give the matter "hourly attention."[72] Brimful of ideas to the last, Hoover asked Ambassador Page to ask the French government to intercede "to break down the silly diplomatic impasse" between Britain and Germany. Privately Hoover did not much care whether the French succeeded or not; the purpose was to bring pressure on the British and German governments "from other influential quarters."[73] Page acceded to Hoover's request but without success.[74]

Hoover left England hopeful of victory.[75] He was soon disappointed. On

December 19, 1913 Prime Minister H. H. Asquith's secretary notified Goode that the Cabinet, after further consideration, had decided not to alter its announced policy: Great Britain would not officially attend the Exposition. There was "no good object," therefore, to be served by receiving a deputation from the British Committee.[76] Almost simultaneously, across the North Sea, the campaign led by Ballin to organize an official German exhibit collapsed in the face of governmental intransigence.[77] Nearly eighteen months of agitation orchestrated by Hoover had culminated in another defeat.

It was a setback only slightly tempered by the belated appearance, on December 31, of *The Times*'s Pacific Coast supplement.

III

A NEW phase in Hoover's campaign now began. During the autumn he and the British Committee had achieved remarkable support from the British press—so much so that by December every Liberal organ in London had urged the Cabinet to change its policy.[78] The government's obstinacy was bound, therefore, to be widely unpopular. On December 19 Goode decided to organize a campaign in Parliament to force the Cabinet to reverse its decision. Goode was uncertain about the prospects for "coercion," but several prominent M.P.'s encouraged him to try.[79] Hoover, from America, cabled his support for such parliamentary agitation, although, he admitted, it was "probably hopeless."[80]

The British Cabinet's refusal to change course touched off a flurry of critical press reports in the United States on December 20–21. "Secret Compact Against Our Fair," headlined the *New York Times*, referring to the Anglo-German agreement not to participate in the Exposition. In Washington the U.S. government confirmed that this understanding or "gentlemen's agreement" existed and that Great Britain had initiated it out of resentment at the Panama Canal tolls legislation.[81] In both England and America newspapers roundly denounced the British ministry's decision.[82]

Then, on December 29, the *New York Times* published a new, sensational, and disturbing story. "Anglo-German War On Our Trade." ran the page-one headline. According to what the paper called "a well-qualified and reliable source," the Anglo-German understanding involved far more than a decision to boycott San Francisco's exposition. It entailed nothing less than a deliberate, "far-reaching programme" to combat the overseas financial and commercial activities of the United States, particularly in South America after the opening of the Panama Canal. The report cited a long list of circumstances that appeared to suggest the existence of an anti-American, Anglo-German entente.[83]

The *New York Times* report instantly precipitated a diplomatic squall. In London the Foreign Office declared that there was "absolutely no foundation" to the story of an Anglo-German agreement directed against the United States.[84] The assertion of the existence of an Anglo-German conspiracy against American economic interests in South America "scarcely requires denial," said *The Times* of London, for the story had not the "slightest foundation in fact."[85] It was a "bogy."[86] In Washington "authoritative quarters" in the State Department also discounted the story. While England and Germany did have an understanding about the Exposition, the State Department found "no reason to believe" that the two nations were contemplating "a general alliance˜to checkmate American trade." Nevertheless, the *New York Times* sources were adamant. According to the paper, "persons claiming to have inside information from abroad" insisted that such an agreement did exist and that their information was factual, not conjectural.[87]

It quickly developed that the source of the allegations was none other than Herbert Hoover. It was Hoover, reported *The Times* of London, who was spreading the story of an Anglo-German entente antagonistic to American economic interests. It was Hoover who was "the origin of the myth." On December 31 *The Times* quoted Hoover, now in San Francisco, as declaring that the British government's refusal to participate in the Exposition was (in *The Times*'s words) "an act unfriendly to the United States." According to *The Times*, Hoover stated:

> The [Anglo-German] entente involves more than the Exhibition and is incongruous with the general policy of Great Britain towards the United States. It behoves Americans to be on their guard, since secret, sinister ententes between the European Powers against the United States have been quiescent for years. With The Times, the Press, and the whole British people protesting, I look for a reversal of the decision of the Cabinet by Parliament.[88]

A few days later Goode sent Hoover clippings from the British press implicating Hoover as the source of the leak.[89]

Hoover was considerably annoyed. Accustomed to working in the background, he now found himself in the glare of uncongenial publicity. On January 17 he wrote to Benjamin Allen, his friend at the Associated Press office in London:

> . . . as to the Anglo-German compact, I notice that the London Times lays this story on me exclusively. They seem to overlook the fact that they were the first to announce it in their issue of December first. They overlook the fact, too, that the Daily Mail, about the twenty-fourth of November also reported it after an interview with Mr. Ballin, and they still further overlook the fact that they know perfectly well from one of the Ministers direct that this was the real stumbling block in the matter. In any event the publicity that we got out of this affair on this side [U.S.A.] has put

the Exposition on its feet so far as American sentiment is concerned and if I have to be offered up as a sacrifice on this altar I can stand it.[90]

Hoover did not mention that he himself had gone to *The Times* around the end of November and was probably therefore responsible for *The Times*'s first, limited leak of December 1. Nor did he mention that he himself had arranged for a leak from Germany, possibly the *Daily Mail*'s own story of November 24. Nor did he mention that there was a huge gap between these early news reports, which referred only to an Anglo-German understanding *about the Exposition,* and the sweeping disclosure of December 29 with its startling claims about a broad anti-American commercial alliance between Europe's two principal industrial powers. For this latter revelation Hoover alone seems to have been responsible. On one point, though, he was quite correct. The original source of the information about the Anglo-German accord—but not of the press leak itself—was indeed the British Cabinet.[91]

When pursuing his objectives Hoover was aggressive, sometimes even impulsive. But he was also acutely sensitive to criticism and to publicity that he himself did not control. And sometimes, when subjected to such criticism and exposure, he would—as he did in his letter to Allen—minimize his responsibility and adopt an air of martyred righteousness.

But if Hoover was defensive about his "exposé," he was not repentant. In a long letter to Goode in early January 1914 he defended his resort to the press. Hoover told Goode that upon arrival in the United States he had gone to Washington, where he was given (he did not say by whom) "certain further information" about the contents of the Anglo-German understanding. Thinking this matter over, said Hoover, "it seemed to me . . . that if sufficient publicity could be given" to it, there would be "two very useful effects." First, it would discourage Britain and Germany from "any drawing together . . . against American interests." As Hoover crisply put it, "the bigger the howl set up now on this occasion the less likely will such courses be pursued in the future. . . ." Second, Hoover was disturbed that the Anglo-German boycott had given the Exposition a "black eye" and "depreciate[d] the standing of the undertaking in the minds of the American people." By showing that the "true causes" of the boycott were "diplomatic" and unrelated to the Exposition itself, Hoover hoped to save the Exposition from possible failure.

And he had succeeded. The result, he informed Goode, "of the very large publicity which I have instigated—and to some extent carried on—on this side, has been a consolidation of American feeling on behalf of the Exposition." And if, he added, the reference to an Anglo-German "entente" "which the reporters put into my mouth" was "a little bit strong in the technology of diplomatic terms," the diplomatically untutored American people would not have understood a more precise but unfamiliar term like "exchange of views." Without explicitly saying so, Hoover seemed to be admitting that he had deliberately exaggerated in order to convey his message to the American public. Concluding his apologia, Hoover wanted Goode to know that "I have not been breathing hot air without some serious purpose."[92]

Hoover undoubtedly believed that an Anglo-German understanding aimed at American interests existed. He did not manufacture the story. That some such "undertaking" was indeed in force his British friends themselves had learned from British Cabinet ministers—including, it seems, Lloyd George—in mid-November, and Hoover had promptly conveyed this information to Moore.[93] The British government, however, continued to deny that any obligation, "moral or otherwise," prevented England and Germany from being officially represented at the Panama-Pacific International Exposition.[94] Whatever the truth of the matter, the uproar had served Hoover well: in both England and America the publicity proved beneficial to the Exposition's cause.[95]

When Hoover returned to London in late March 1914 he had reason to feel gratified. During his absence Goode and his allies had organized a spirited and increasingly popular campaign in the press and Parliament to compel a reversal of the government's policy.[96] Week after week the pressure mounted. On February 12 and again on February 24, government officials were compelled to state in the House of Commons that the Cabinet was unable to modify its earlier decision.[97] Nevertheless, by early March more than half the members of the House of Commons had signed a memorial (drawn up by Goode's British Committee) requesting the prime minister to reconsider the government's decision not to participate.[98] In mid-month a committee of M.P.'s formally issued a new request for a deputation to see the prime minister.[99] Across Britain manufacturers, scientists, and literary figures like A. Conan Doyle joined in the agitation.[100]

On April 2 Hoover reported to Moore that Goode had effected "a phenomenon hitherto unknown in British politics": "a petition to the Prime Minister to reverse an action, this petition being signed, not only by a majority of the House of Commons but also by a majority of his own party. It has created a great deal of amusement in this country and is called 'Goode's Reversal of the Government.' The publicity value of this has been simply enormous. . . ."[101]

It was also expensive. Hoover informed Moore that the cost of maintaining "the present propaganda" was now between $1,000 and $1,500 per month.[102] Goode himself was receiving a salary of £200 per month. Between mid-June 1913 and April 27, 1914, in fact, Hoover's expenditures in behalf of the Exposition were about $8,500—nearly twice the $4,500 that Moore had authorized him to spend in his instructions of September 1913.[103] Hoover was reimbursed for these expenses.[104]

Despite the agreeable crescendo of publicity, in early April Hoover learned from "my own sources of information" that Goode's parliamentary campaign as presently conceived would be futile: the government would not yield to pressure. Hoover searched for a compromise that would "accomplish what we want" yet save the government's face. Instead of seeking a governmental expenditure of £100,000 for a general commercial and government exhibit, Hoover urged the British Committee to scale down its request and ask the government to appropriate only £30,000 for "special exhibits." From British friends Hoover learned that the government might accept such a proposal.[105] No doubt from Hoover's point of view, the magnitude of the government's participation was far less crucial than the fact of participation. The point was to get the British *government* to exhibit in San Francisco.

The British Committee seems to have adopted Hoover's advice in part. On May 5, 1914 an all-party deputation finally conferred with Prime Minister Asquith, seven weeks after it had sent in its application. By now 366 M.P.'s—well over half the House of Commons—had signed the memorial favoring official British participation in the Exposition. By now, too, Asquith and his Cabinet must have wondered why on earth so many Britons seemed to care about the subject. The deputation confined itself to a request for a government "pavilion" at the fair. Seizing on this point, Asquith was conciliatory. A request for a pavilion, he said, was very different from a request for a general representation of trade and industry. The prime minister promised that the Cabinet would consider anew the question of official British participation.[106]

The hopes of early May were soon dashed. On May 25 Asquith announced to the Commons that the Cabinet, after carefully reexamining the question, had decided that it "must adhere" to its present policy. The government, he said, had found "no such widespread desire" by British businesses to exhibit "as would render possible official British participation on an adequate scale," nor, at this late date, would it be feasible to try to arrange it. Nor did the Cabinet consider it advantageous to participate on a scale that would not be proportionate to other exhibits.[107]

Faced with the government's intransigence, Hoover and his British confreres resorted to their only remaining alternative: insuring adequate *unofficial* British representation at the Panama-Pacific International Exposition. During June Goode traveled to San Francisco, where, working with various Californians, he helped to form a national committee to raise funds to build a private British-American pavilion at the fair.[108] Welcoming Goode to San Francisco, Moore provided a clue to the unflagging attempts Hoover had made to insure a British presence. Nothing, Moore asserted, had so threatened the Exposition's success as the British government's refusal to participate.[109] Now a drive to raise several hundred thousand dollars for the pavilion got underway. According to Moore some years later, Hoover, in London, worked effectively to line up the necessary funds.[110]

It was all for nought. With the outbreak of a world war in August 1914 the thoughts of Englishmen turned elsewhere. Toward the end of the month, as the Battle of the Marne loomed in northern France, the British Committee dissolved because of the war.[111]

I V

Two years of strenuous effort had failed: the British government never exhibited at the great Exposition. Still, Hoover had ample cause for satisfaction. Working through Goode and other British intermediaries, he had conducted a remarkable campaign, deftly operating the levers of British public opinion and producing a near-revolt against the government in the House of Commons. The Panama-Pacific International Exposition gave him his first opportunity to practice in a wider setting a talent he had exercised at times in his mining work: the use of the press to further his objectives, the use of controlled publicity to exert political pressure.

The experience of lobbying for the Exposition was important to Hoover in other ways. It enabled him to broaden and solidify his contacts in California, some of whose most prominent businessmen were directors of the Exposition. Charles C. Moore, for instance, became a political ally of Hoover in the years ahead.[112] The Exposition episode also enabled him to deepen his roots in England, even as he was preparing to return to the America he cherished so fervently. By 1914 Hoover was well acquainted with an impressive array of distinguished men in British public life: journalists like Lord Northcliffe and the senior staff at *The Times*, businessmen like Sir Thomas Lipton, political luminaries like Arthur Balfour and Sir Edward Grey. In 1914 Grey actually borrowed Hoover's chauffeur-driven automobile (and some small change) for a Sunday afternoon drive.[113] Hoover could not know it, but some of these men were shortly to become contacts and colleagues in a far greater venture than San Francisco's Exposition.

Capable, self-confident, aggressive, at times combative; clever, uncowed by obstacles, willing to go outside channels and act without instructions; exhilarated by the exercise of power and behind-the-scenes maneuvering; determined to have things his way: these were some of the qualities Hoover exhibited as he worked unstintingly for the Panama-Pacific cause. Yet if assertive by nature, he also shunned the spotlight, preferring to work quietly and invisibly through trusted intermediaries.[114] It was, again, the role for which he had become known in college: the role of the wire-puller. "We press the buttons and do the rest."

With such a temperament Hoover early developed a lifelong fascination for the press and the kind of influence that it could exert over public opinion. By 1914 he had collected a noteworthy number of British and American journalist-friends: Will Irwin, whom he had known since college; Frederick Palmer, whom he met on the way to China; Richard Harding Davis; Benjamin Allen and Robert Collins at the Associated Press office in London; Robert Porter at *The Times*; Lord Northcliffe; W. A. M. Goode. Some of these men were to become strategically placed allies in the years just ahead.

By 1914, in fact, Hoover was preparing to enter journalism himself. As usual, he went about it indirectly. During the summer of 1914, acting through

Allen, he attempted to purchase the *Sacramento Union* in California. With the outbreak of war he was obliged to suspend his negotiations.[115] Had it not been for "the guns of August," Hoover would have entered public life—might even be remembered today—as a newspaper magnate.

27

A Man of
Force

I

W H E N Hoover returned to London in March 1914, Lou and the boys did not go with him. Young Herbert, nearly eleven years old now, was attending school in Palo Alto, and his parents may have wished him to complete the school year. So on March 10, the day after he and Lou jointly received the Mining and Metallurgical Society of America's gold medal for their *De Re Metallica* translation, Hoover sailed alone from New York for England on the *Lusitania*. His wife returned to the Stanford campus, where she and her sons stayed in a house that Hoover had leased the previous December.[1]

Separated again from his family (this time for nearly four months),[2] Hoover turned to his business affairs. Matters had gone "very badly" in his absence, he told Ray Lyman Wilbur in April, and would need "some time to get a recovery."[3]

Hoover had many occasions to think about California that spring. More and more it seemed that his civic and commercial interests were intersecting. The Panama-Pacific International Exposition, Stanford University problems, the refinance of the General Petroleum Company, the rescue of the Sloss family's finances: all were drawing him more deeply into California life.

And now Natomas. Incorporated in 1908, Natomas Consolidated of California was a large land and mining company that by the end of 1913 owned over 96,000 acres of gold-bearing river gravel, irrigated lands, and other properties in the northern part of the state. Using a fleet of dredges to churn up gold on its riverbed properties, Natomas thereby raised revenue with which to undertake vast irrigation and reclamation projects for agricultural purposes, chiefly along the Sacramento River near the state capital. Both British and American money was invested in the company, and several of Hoover's California friends were among its directors.[4]

By the end of 1913 the Natomas Consolidated was dangerously overextended. Its earnings during the year barely exceeded the interest payments on its bonds; by December 31 its current liabilities exceeded its assets by more than two million dollars.[5] Late in the year representatives of the California interests involved journeyed to London to negotiate refinancing for the troubled corporation. For a time it appeared that they had succeeded; on December 30 a British syndicate known as the Natomas Syndicate, Ltd. was formed to supply the needed capital. But then some "hitch" developed, and the deal stalled. Before long, evidently on the entreaties of his California friends, Hoover entered the negotiations as an intermediary.[6]

Hoover's involvement may have grown out of his feverish efforts to save the finances of the Sloss and Lilienthal families in San Francisco in January and February 1914. A Sloss was vice-president of Natomas Consolidated; a Lilienthal also sat on its board.[7] In any case, back in London in the spring, Hoover devised a new reorganization plan that proved acceptable to the deadlocked parties.[8] On May 14 he became a co-manager of the Natomas Syndicate.[9]

Under the terms worked out by Hoover, the Natomas Consolidated was reconstructed late in 1914 as a new entity, the Natomas Company of California. Two of Hoover's fellow Stanford trustees, Frank B. Anderson and W. Mayo Newhall, were among the first directors. (Anderson, president of the Bank of California, was the man who urged Hoover to assist the Sloss family in its hour of financial peril.)[10] Another old friend, the mining attorney Curtis Lindley, also joined the board.[11] In London an English holding company—the Natomas Land and Dredging Trust, Ltd.—was created to acquire all the common stock of the new California company. Hoover joined the Trust's board.[12]

To obtain capital, the California company agreed to create up to $3,000,000 in notes bearing 6% interest and repayable in five years. The British financial syndicate (the Natomas Syndicate) subscribed to this note issue—that is, loaned nearly $3,000,000. In return for agreeing to make this loan, the Natomas Syndicate received 312,000 free shares in the British holding company.[13]

Hoover's terms were favorable to the British interests. In California it was pointed out that the English would be able to "dominate the situation" and receive all the California company's profits once the bondholders and preferred shareholders were paid off.[14] The terms seemed even more favorable to the Natomas Syndicate. Not only would it get its loan money back in five years at 6% interest; it would also receive, as consideration for simply making the loan, a controlling stock interest in the British holding company and hence, eventually, in the California company itself.

To the editor of San Francisco's *Mining and Scientific Press*, H. Foster Bain, the arrangement seemed unfair to certain current bondholders, and in the July 4, 1914 issue he criticized it in print.[15] Although Bain soon advised the Californians to accept Hoover's plan as the best one under the circumstances,[16] he told Hoover privately that he still felt the Natomas Syndicate was getting an excellent bargain.

It did not take Hoover long to respond. When the *Mining and Scientific Press*'s editorial appeared he cabled a protest to the editor. He feared that this adverse publicity would jeopardize the complex scheme he had taken such pains to effect.[17] When Bain, a personal friend, still demurred, Hoover mounted a firm and plainspoken defense. "I am afraid you are under some misapprehension about the intrinsic value of the Natomas as a property," he told his editor-friend. Furthermore, "people in California" were "under considerable misapprehension about the value of money, which lies fundamentally at the bottom of all things."

> London is the clearing-house of the world for mining business and at the very time at which I have been so urgent on behalf of my Californian friends to carry through the Natomas deal I could have employed the funds set aside for this purpose to infinitely greater advantage in other mining enterprises.

Hoover denied that the Natomas Syndicate—through its indirect control of the California company's common stock—was reaping an inordinate reward for itself.

> I cannot bring myself to believe that the Common Stock of the Natomas Company would be worth anything for years and years. . . . Inasmuch as the Natomas Syndicate receives no profit except this Common Stock, I do not see that they have got anything but 6½% on their money and have taken on considerable risk. I may say flatly that I could have obtained mining business on a 15% basis without risk at the very time this business was done.[18]

Hoover's reply to Bain was characteristic of his responses to criticism: blunt, categorical, and touched with indignation. Thus he did not merely tell Bain that he could have put Natomas investment money to better advantage elsewhere but to "infinitely greater" advantage. He did not merely claim that the syndicate was taking "considerable risk" for a 6½% profit. He asserted "flatly"—unequivocally—that he could have lined up *other* mining investments offering a 15% profit on no risk whatever. Here I am, he seemed to be saying, sacrificing time and lucrative financial opportunities in order to aid my friends, and for all my trouble I'm criticized.

If Hoover's protest seemed overstated, his points, nevertheless, were well-taken. Any profits that the reorganized California company made would be funneled for years into repaying its very substantial debt; it would be a long time before common stockholders could expect a dividend. Furthermore, it was the British interests, after all, who were supplying the money to a company that was verging on bankruptcy. Could they be blamed for extracting a price? The Californians, the supplicants, had only limited bargaining power. Hoover's plan, in fact, was said to be more advantageous to the Californians than the earlier proposal that foundered.[19] If the terms imposed on Natomas were stiff, the alternative was catastrophe. In the end, thanks to Hoover, the California enterprise obtained desperately needed investment capital and a new life.[20]

Hoover did not lose interest in the deal he had wrought. He remained a director of the Natomas Land and Dredging Trust until 1916 and a manager of the Natomas Syndicate (in which he held 5,000 shares) until it voted to liquidate early in 1916.[21] As late as 1917 he held $16,000 in Natomas notes, while in 1918 he obtained several thousand free shares in the Natomas Land and Dredging Trust, shares that he did not fully dispose of until the 1920s.[22]

Hoover's reorganization work for Natomas in 1914 was overshadowed by a financial storm that hit London in late spring and drew Hoover into what he later called "my last industrial repair job."[23] For some time he had been acquainted with a prominent British mining financier named Arthur M. Grenfell. A member of one of England's leading financial families, Grenfell was associated with Hoover, Andrew Weir, and R. Tilden Smith (of the Burma Mines board) in efforts to refinance the General Petroleum Company in 1913–14. One of Grenfell's financial institutions, the Canadian Agency, was the original manager of the Natomas Syndicate.[24]

Beyond this, by early 1914 Grenfell was the undisputed head of a far-flung mining and financial combination that rivaled Hoover's Lake View and Oroya Exploration group in its breadth of interests.[25] His private banking firm— Chaplin, Milne, Grenfell, and Company—was one of the best-known "issuing houses" in London. Grenfell himself was chairman of numerous enterprises, including the Camp Bird mine in Colorado, the Santa Gertrudis mine in Mexico, and the Messina (Transvaal) Development Company, a copper mine in southern Africa. His Canadian Agency was active in the issue of numerous Canadian securities.[26]

It was a dazzling show that Grenfell, wheeling and dealing without opposition from most of his fellow directors, dominated entirely. But when early in 1914 his interlocking interests suffered financial reverses and his speculations turned sour, Grenfell sank into irretrievable difficulty. In mid-May the Bank of England and other powerful institutions took over his gigantic London stock market commitments (around $25,000,000) in order to limit liquidation of his securities and avert a possible stock market crash.[27] A few days later it was announced that Grenfell was no longer a director of Chaplin, Milne.[28]

Grenfell's personal financial collapse failed to clear the air. Throughout late May and early June a pall of uncertainty continued to hang over the London stock exchange. "Things are in a very bad mess here as the result of some gigantic defalcations by a prominent financial man in the City," Hoover told Ray Lyman Wilbur on June 2.[29] Two days later, after Grenfell and one of his allies resigned from the Messina (Transvaal) board of directors, Hoover and another man were elected to take their place.[30] On Saturday, June 6, came the climactic blow: the overextended banking firm of Chaplin, Milne, Grenfell, and Company suspended payment and went into receivership. A few hours later the Canadian Agency followed suit.[31]

In the days and weeks that followed, Hoover and his friends learned the sorry dimensions of the Grenfell debacle. It turned out that Grenfell's banking house had served as banker for various companies of which he had also been chairman. At the time of the bank's failure, the Camp Bird had nearly £16,000 on deposit with it and the Santa Gertrudis more than £10,000. Whether this money could be recovered during bankruptcy proceedings was questionable.[32]

Even worse, Grenfell, as chairman of the Camp Bird and Santa Gertrudis, had taken nearly £90,000 from these companies' treasuries and loaned it to certain Stock Exchange brokers on securities worth considerably less than the loans. It turned out that these brokerage houses had been acting as conduits to the now-bankrupt Canadian Agency, of which Grenfell was chairman and principal stockholder. In other words, Grenfell, with the acquiescence of his passive fellow directors, had taken money from Camp Bird and Santa Gertrudis and virtually loaned it to himself. Now the Canadian Agency and Grenfell were bankrupt, and one of the stock brokerage houses, the recipient of a part of these loans, refused to pay back, claiming that it had merely been an agent for Grenfell's Canadian Agency![33]

Hardest hit of all was the promising copper company, Messina (Transvaal). After joining the board on June 4 Hoover ordered an audit of its accounts. The results were astounding. Among the company's current "assets" were loans from itself (made when Arthur Grenfell was chairman) to the now defunct Canadian Agency (Arthur Grenfell, chairman) of £183,000, or about $900,000! The securities held against these loans were but a fraction of this amount.[34]

By mid-June the position of Camp Bird and Santa Gertrudis—not to mention Messina (Transvaal)—was, in Hoover's words, "one of extreme difficulty."[35] Three major mining companies had been "nearly driven on the rocks."[36] At this point a number of prominent shareholders in Camp Bird and Santa Gertrudis implored Hoover to become chairman of the two companies and guide them through the emergency. At first Hoover was extremely reluctant to do so. He knew that the task of getting "the London Administration on the right track once more" would require "a great deal of labour and expenditure of time, which I can ill afford."[37]

After several days' resistance Hoover acquiesced.[38] On June 17 the Camp Bird and Santa Gertrudis directors elected him their temporary chairman.[39] Entirely unconnected with the Grenfell failure, Hoover the reorganizer stepped in to forestall further wreckage if he could. "The intention on both sides," he told Wilbur, "is that I should pilot them through this particular period of difficulty, and then I shall appoint somebody else in my place."[40]

He accepted the assignment for two reasons. He did so, first, at the importuning of friends and business allies who (unlike himself) were affected by Grenfell's fall. Among these, probably, was Francis Govett, who joined the two companies' boards a few days later.[41] Hoover told Wilbur that he had been "obliged to take an interest in the matter because of the interest which many of my associates hold in these concerns."[42] Secondly, he took the burden out of a sense of duty, a feeling that it was "in the interest of the industry generally" and "sort of up to me to assist in an industry in which I am so much involved."[43] Loyalty to friends, loyalty to his profession: Hoover felt keenly the tug of such appeals.

There was perhaps no better index to Hoover's stature in the mining world in 1914 than the request that he take over the chairmanship of the Camp Bird and Santa Gertrudis mining companies. "He owed the honor," said T. A. Rickard, "to force of character"—to "a reputation for ability and integrity."[44] Hoover appreciated the honor. He told Wilbur:

> There is very little satisfaction in the job and an immensity of hard work, but there is a certain amount of self-satisfaction to be called upon to take over what is undoubtedly the most important and strenuous situation existing in the mining world at the present time.[45]

Hoover moved swiftly to restore the fiscal stability of Camp Bird and Santa Gertrudis. The mines themselves, he discovered, were excellently managed; the problem was "to get the London business again disentangled."[46] On June 25 he convened a meeting of major British and French shareholders, who urged him to stay on as chairman. On July 2 he issued a circular to all shareholders announcing changes in the two companies' directorates, including certain resignations and the accession of Govett to the two boards. He also created technical committees to supervise the companies' technical administration and placed his old friend John Agnew on them.[47]

By early summer Hoover was optimistic that the crisis could be contained. He told shareholders on July 2 that "even accepting the worst possible view" Camp Bird's total loss from its bad loans and its deposits in Grenfell's bankrupt institutions should not exceed £10,000, and that Santa Gertrudis should not lose more than £27,000.[48] On July 22 he informed the Camp Bird's manager that the company was "practically prostrated by having the whole of its funds put out on loan on wholly inadequate security which cannot be realised, and we shall have a pretty stiff job to pull through. I have no doubt, however, that we shall get through with the business with patience."[49]

Hoover's optimism drew fire from England's influential weekly, the *Economist*. How could Hoover estimate the Camp Bird's loss at only £10,000, the journal wondered, when Camp Bird had nearly £16,000 deposited with Grenfell's banking house and when the securities on the Camp Bird's loans were worth £13,000 less than the loans? "Evidently he is anxious to put the very best face possible on the matter, and anticipates realising the securities at more than their present market values." Similarly for Santa Gertrudis: Hoover's conservative estimate of its losses seemed based on a dubious valuation of the securities it held for its loans. The *Economist* queried whether the personnel of the two boards had been "sufficiently reconstructed to ensure that the past acts of the directorate will be adequately investigated." Since Hoover and "the remaining original directors do not seem to be in a hurry to begin" such an investigation, the *Economist* urged shareholders to organize.[50]

The Camp Bird and Santa Gertrudis chairman had his reasons, however, for his conduct and his optimism. To Hoover it was now more important to reorganize the companies for the future than to document the transgressions of the past. Hoover opposed "retributive" actions like lawsuits against Grenfell and his companies. What good would it do? Grenfell was bankrupt. "Such actions would produce no money."[51] Nor did Hoover consider his estimates of ultimate losses misguided. During the summer he instituted several lawsuits to recover the lost loan money from the brokerage houses to which it had been lent.[52] If Hoover could regain the loan money in this way, his projections of losses might not be so dubious after all. Late in the summer he negotiated a tentative out-of-court settlement with one such firm for a £15,000 payment "towards the deficiency on the securities of their loans." This was less than what the firm actually owed, but it was the most Hoover thought he could obtain. Otherwise the brokerage firm itself would go bankrupt.[53]

By far the most formidable "repair job" confronting Hoover involved the beleaguered Messina (Transvaal) Development Company, whose total loans to and deposits in Grenfell's bankrupt institutions reached over £197,000— more than the issued share capital of the company.[54] Although Hoover did not become the Messina's chairman, he soon emerged as its dominant director in the struggle to refinance the enterprise.[55] By mid-summer the cash-starved copper company was, according to Hoover, "in a most critical state. . . ."[56]

With war clouds massing over Europe, Hoover devised and implemented a plan that saved the Messina (Transvaal). First, he and his fellow directors arranged in July for the company to borrow £50,000 in an overdraft from its South African bank. When this sum quickly proved inadequate, Hoover persuaded the bank to increase the Messina's overdraft by another £50,000. This additional sum was to be guaranteed by a financial syndicate, the Inter-Guaranty Syndicate, which Hoover formed in late July. That is, the syndicate pledged to reimburse the bank up to £50,000 later on if the Messina was unable to do so. In return for thus rescuing Messina, the new syndicate obtained an option over a large future issue of Messina shares.[57]

Hoover became one of two directors of the Inter-Guaranty Syndicate.[58] Both the Camp Bird and Santa Gertrudis companies, which had substantial share interests (and hence a stake) in the Messina, took shares in the syndicate and thus took part in its guarantee.[59] So, too, did Hoover.[60] He told a colleague in late July that barring a wartime collapse of copper prices the deal would be "of profitable character and without any risk."[61]

Hoover's efforts occurred against a background of kaleidoscopic uncertainty, the daily lot of the mining engineer. In Colorado the Camp Bird for a time showed signs of petering out.[62] South of the border, the Mexican Revolution interrupted operations at the Santa Gertrudis mine during much of 1914; a war-induced shortage of cyanide later in the year forced another curtailment of production.[63] In July Hoover wondered whether an outbreak of world war would cut off copper shipments from the Messina (Transvaal).[64] When conflict did break out, Hoover's negotiations to compel repayment of loans made by Grenfell to certain brokerage firms lapsed for many months.[65]

Nevertheless, under Hoover's competent direction the three mining companies successfully passed through their hour of travail. Both Camp Bird and Santa Gertrudis apparently suffered far greater losses than Hoover originally estimated—a consequence, it was stated, of the war[66]—but both were able to declare dividends in 1915.[67] The Messina (Transvaal) took a terrific battering (over £100,000 in losses), but it, too, survived and eventually prospered.[68]

Hoover resigned from the three companies' boards of directors in 1916.[69] Aside from his routine director's fees and any profit he might have made from the Inter-Guaranty Syndicate, there is no record that he received any special compensation for his services. Instead, he gained the satisfaction of an arduous task well done and the increased esteem of his profession.[70] His friend T. A. Rickard lauded him in the pages of the *Mining Magazine*. Hoover, said Rickard, was "radically different" from the clever, "well born" speculator, Arthur Grenfell:

Mr. Hoover is an engineer who has made his own way all his life by sheer force of ability and persistence. Without engaging social aid or adopting the suave manner of the typical City man, he has brought to bear upon the business of mining a set of qualities that no director can possess without having served an apprenticeship to an exacting profession. His technical training in California has been supplemented by broad experience in mining regions and wide knowledge of mining affairs in many parts of the world. He brings all the directness of the American together with a financial acumen that is neither American nor European but wholly individual.[71]

With the outbreak of World War I the bankrupt Grenfell joined the British army "to retrieve his honour" (as Rickard put it) "on the battlefield." Wounded in action in 1916, Major Grenfell received the Distinguished Service Order award from King George V for gallantry and devotion to duty in the field.[72] When the war was over, the British government dropped its planned prosecution of the financier who had now so ably served his king and country.[73] By then, of course, Hoover, too, had gone on to other things.

I I

B y mid-summer 1914 Hoover, by any standard, was a success. He was now a director of eighteen mining and financial companies having a total authorized share capital of more than £11,000,000, or more than $55,000,000, and interests on nearly every continent.[74] At least 100,000 men were employed in enterprises for which he, as a director, was partly, even primarily, responsible.[75]

Seventeen years before, he had gone off to Western Australia, growing a beard to conceal his youth. Now he was a family man, with a boy aged eleven and a boy aged seven, and about to celebrate his fortieth birthday— the advent of middle age. Into those seventeen years he had packed the experience of a lifetime. What an incredible array of men he had met along the way! Able men, clever men, plausible men, sometimes unscrupulous men. Chang Yen-mao, Gustav Detring, and the Belgian Emile Francqui. A. Stanley Rowe, C. Algernon Moreing, Frank Gardner of Great Boulder Perseverance, R. Tilden Smith, Arthur Treadgold, Joe Boyle, Arthur Grenfell. Russian nobles, a Burmese prince, Chinese mandarins, London stockbrokers. Though only in his twenties and thirties, he had mingled with them all and prospered.

By 1914 Hoover could take at least partial credit for an impressive series of mining successes: the Sons of Gwalia and a cluster of modern, efficiently managed mines on the Golden Mile and elsewhere in Western Australia; the mighty Zinc Corporation at Broken Hill; the Lake View and Oroya Exploration Company, with its far-flung financial interests; the huge and growing industrial ventures at Kyshtim, Tanalyk, and Irtysh; the General Petroleum Company in California and reorganized oil concerns in Trinidad and Peru; a vast, refinanced enterprise in Burma on its way to a glittering reward. Other men, of course, contributed to these achievements, but in most instances none could claim greater credit than he.

There had been failures, too, notably Lancefield, the Maikop ventures, and—most embarrassing of all—the Victorian Deep Leads. Some of his projects, such as the Zinc Corporation, had verged precariously on disaster before slipping through to victory. Hoover at times underestimated obstacles and exhibited premature optimism. Sometimes he seemed too confident, too sure of himself. But by 1914, among mining engineers and investors, few if any had greater prestige than he.

"If a man has not made a fortune by 40 he is not worth much," he had said. Now that he was turning forty, how had he fared? In 1914 Hoover's annual director's fees and bonuses probably amounted to several thousand dollars or more. This was enough for a very comfortable life, but it was not a fortune and did not, in fact, supply the bulk of his income. As early as 1907 he told a friend that he was earning $100,000 a year, almost entirely as a "financial expert."[76] In 1908 he sold his Bewick, Moreing partnership for more than $150,000 and embarked on his own with a fortune probably in excess of $300,000.[77] In mid-1910 he told Ralph Arnold that he was earning about $100,000 a year and indirectly indicated that his fortune amounted then to at least several hundred thousand dollars.[78] Two months later, after visiting Hoover in London, David Starr Jordan told President Taft's secretary that Hoover was a millionaire.[79]

There is no exact way of measuring Hoover's total assets in 1914. But impressions accumulate. He owned by late that year one-seventh or more of the 760,000+ issued shares of the Burma Corporation, a holding sufficient to garner a small fortune if disposed of at par or better. In early 1915, and probably well before, he owned 25,000 shares in the Lake View and Oroya Exploration Company: a holding with a par value of more than $60,000.[80] In 1913 he remarked to a friend that no man could make $10,000,000 honestly but that one could make $5,000,000 honestly. Well, the friend asked, do you have $5,000,000 yet? "Not quite," Hoover replied.[81]

Potentially he was worth even more. For Hoover had been earning not just $100,000 in annual cash fees but also what he later called "deferred interest" in the "successful issue" of his mining reorganizations.[82] Some years later, in an undated autobiographical statement, he recorded that by mid-1914 he was in a position to amass a fortune of at least $30,000,000 in the years ahead.[83] He declared that his "deferred interest" in the Irtysh mine in Russia was worth a minimum of $15,000,000 based on the mine's "proved profits."[84] In another autobiographical note he stated that his share interest in the Burma enterprise represented a profit in sight of about $10,000,000.[85]

Hoover's figures were probably not precisely accurate. He could, in fact, be casual with numbers. On one occasion he said his Burma interest represented a profit in sight in the mine of about $10,000,000; on another occasion he offered data suggesting that his share of this mine's proved profits was $13,500,000.[86] Such profits, in any case, he would only have received in installments in the form of dividends extending over many years. And in 1914, at Burma and Irtysh both, the dividend-bearing stage was still some time away. Most of Hoover's fortune in 1914 was prospective.

Still, if Hoover had cashed in all his stock holdings and other assets in mid-1914, he probably would have obtained well over one million dollars.[87] By the summer of his fortieth birthday Herbert Hoover was a modest millionaire.

Hoover enjoyed the "game," though as he said in 1912, the counters did not interest him any more. He enjoyed being an insider, conceiving and carrying out complicated business schemes, "bending men in his quiet way to his purpose" (as his friend Frederick Palmer put it in 1928).[88]

Of his ability—his resourcefulness, his perseverance, what T. A. Rickard called his "financial acumen"—none who knew him recorded any doubt. In addition to native ability, determination, and what Hoover called the "executive instinct," he possessed two assets very useful to success: an excellent memory and a phenomenal capacity for hard work. Many colleagues noted his extraordinary memory for mining detail. Jordan was struck by Hoover's "ability to absorb information" and his "uncanny ability to sift data and facts . . . and to remember them on short notice."[89] His brother Theodore was amazed at his "inordinate capacity for work" even during his boyhood days.[90] He had a knack, when working on a problem, of getting quickly to its crux. Said one who observed him at directors' meetings, "Hoover would sit at the board-room table, silent and sphinx-like, intently following the discussions, doodling on the paper before him, never interposing a remark until the occasion warranted, and then doing so tersely and emphatically."[91]

Work was what mattered for Hoover: work and accomplishment. A British associate later declared that "he took his work very seriously, and had no interest in sport or pastimes."[92] This was not really true. The Agricola project was a diversion; the London theater was a diversion; travel and books were diversions, too. But life for Hoover was full of serious purpose. He seemed most himself when he was trying to get something done.

He was not an easy man to know. He was not outwardly affable. He had no small talk. Habitually taciturn, "not easily roused to laughter,"[93] he could be brisk to the point of being brusque. Disdainful of "parasites" and "noodle-headed" aristocrats, he did not suffer fools gladly.[94] The aggressive Americanism of "Hail Columbia" Hoover, his conviction of the superiority of American mining men and methods, did not always set well with his British colleagues. One young British secretary who met him in Granville mining activities later remarked, "He was a very hardworking, hard-headed and rather saturnine man, and always struck me as a little uncouth."[95]

"There is always room for a man of force, and he makes room for many." These words of Ralph Waldo Emerson's were quoted by Jordan in his commencement address to the Stanford class of 1905.[96] He might have applied them to Herbert Hoover. Beneath the cool, taut surface was a man of restless drive and emotional temperament. Around Hoover there was always an aura of "high pressure," a journalist-friend observed.[97] Or as another put it, "a certain atmosphere of aggressiveness."[98] Hoover was the epitome of what a London newspaper later called "the pushful American."

Not surprisingly, his mining career had been punctuated by a number of disputes with colleagues and superiors. In Australia he quarreled with his boss, Ernest Williams. In China he crossed swords with Francqui. His years with Moreing were marked by disagreements, and after he parted they clashed in the courts. At the Granville company he wrangled with Treadgold, at the Burma Mines board with Smith. Theodore Hoover later acknowledged that many men parted company with his brother over the years—some, he said, because they were dishonest, some because they lacked ability, and some because they could not or would not "play the particular game Herbert Hoover's way."[99]

Yet if Hoover was strong-willed and combative, so, too, were the men with whom he contended. In every dispute just cited he had at least some grounds for his displeasure. W. J. Loring later asserted that Hoover was just and generous to his subordinates but aloof and suspicious toward his equals.[100] All too often he had had reason to be. Mining was no occupation for the trusting.

But if Hoover by 1914 had his share of antagonists he also had steady friends, like the mining journalists J. H. Curle and T. A. Rickard. Among his business associates in London were a number, like Govett, A. Chester Beatty, and Lindon Bates, with whom he appeared to work amicably for years.[101] In Hoover's scale of values loyalty to friends ranked high. He felt strongly the claims of obligation to his business allies. Loyalty to his friends weighed on his mind in 1910 when the chance arose to be head of the U. S. Bureau of Mines; he told Ralph Arnold that he could not just leave his London colleagues in the lurch. Loyalty to friends and profession led him in 1914 to accept the burden of limiting the damage caused by the Grenfell collapse.

Toward those who were his subordinates Hoover's feelings of loyalty were equally strong. The capacity to select able lieutenants and to inspire their devotion was one of his notable talents. It was, he knew, the foundation of his own success.[102] "Hoover liked to surround himself with young men," a journalist-friend noted.[103] He felt an affinity for those who, like himself, had to struggle to "make it." A passionate believer in equality of opportunity, he liked to give young men a chance.

His solicitude was usually rewarded. A number of his lieutenants became distinguished engineers and lifelong friends. One of them, John Agnew, declared unabashedly in 1928 that Hoover was the greatest man he had ever known and the ideal for honest, straightforward business conduct.[104] Already by 1914 Hoover had made a number of friends, both in and out of mining, whose devotion was to be of extraordinary intensity and duration.

To these intimates—engineers, journalists, Stanford professors—Hoover was more than a hardheaded "pushful American." There was the Hoover who shed tears on seeing the beauty of Tintern Abbey. There was the amiable storyteller who enthralled Red House guests with tales of exotic adventure. There was the Hoover who passed a street urchin on the streets of Perth one evening in 1897–98 in the rain. The little boy was staring fondly at the sweets in the window of a bakery shop. "He looks miserable and hungry," Hoover said to his traveling companion. Turning around, Hoover went back and gave the boy some coins.[105]

Above all, Hoover's close friends discovered beneath the crusty exterior a man of uncommon generosity. Friends, relatives, servants, impecunious Stanford professors, the Stanford Union project: all by 1914 had benefited from his liberality. Agnew stated that Hoover possessed a "kindliness of heart" that few besides his intimates suspected.[106] " 'H. C.' is the most tender-hearted man I have ever known," another old friend declared. Hoover, said the friend, was "generous to a fault"—"always helping people."[107] Hoover's gifts might in some instances be small—a rare book to a friend, perhaps, or a check to his butler for a vacation—or it might in the aggregate be large: 1,500 copies of *De Re Metallica* distributed free all over the world.[108] If Hoover made money he also unstintingly disbursed it and did so till the end of his life.

There is no way of knowing the full extent of Hoover's pre-war benefactions—how many students, for instance, he put through Stanford University. (He helped several relatives obtain an education.)[109] He did not generally care to publicize his charitable acts. In fact, he frequently took pains to conceal them by acting through intermediaries (such as his brother) and keeping his own role secret.[110]

He disliked ostentation. While he loved to engineer publicity, he shrank from overtly *personal* publicity. He was averse to having his picture taken, at least for public use. In 1914 he would not supply a photograph of himself to an American mining journal at the time of his Agricola award.[111]

In this panoply of traits one can detect the early influences on Hoover—above all, the trauma of orphanhood and his subsequent tutelage under his austere Uncle John. In the childhood years from nine to seventeen were created some of the qualities and mannerisms that puzzled and sometimes exasperated the people who knew him: his abruptness, taciturnity, and awkwardness at small talk; his reserve that many took for shyness; his tendency to avoid the gaze of the person with whom he was conversing. In these years, too, was probably born the aggressive, sometimes abrasive determination to succeed, to achieve financial independence, that impelled him through a strenuous early life. While Hoover's surrogate parents in Oregon were upright and well-meaning, nothing could replace the warmth and security of the home he lost before he was ten. Theodore Hoover was older and more independent; he could walk out of the Oregon house (and did). Herbert could not. His will, his assertiveness, he had to suppress. In his relationship with his uncle may perhaps be found the genesis of his later pattern of dealing with the world: his love of behind-the-scenes wire-pulling, his preference for indirection, his enjoyment of the pleasures of "bending men in his quiet way to his purpose."

Hoover's thoroughly Quaker upbringing no doubt reinforced some of these (and other) traits: his reticence, his distaste for idle gossip, his quiet and direct speech, his abhorrence of overt self-aggrandizement and display. But the Quaker influence on Hoover can be overstated. By 1914 he had deviated greatly from the evangelical Quakerism of his youth. He did not (so far as is known) attend a meeting. His theological convictions were probably liberal if not unorthodox.[112] He attended the theater. He used Sundays for recreation. He smoked. He drank alcohol.[113] Still, in less conscious ways, the Quaker discipline of his boyhood probably left its mark: in his works of charity and sense of obligation to family and to friends; in his conviction that life was meant for accomplishment; perhaps also in his sense by 1908 that life was also meant for service, that "just making money" wasn't enough.

Another early influence was more responsible than Quakerism for Hoover's altruistic yearnings. It was Stanford University, the principal positive experience of his early life. Stanford, with its sense of community and its ethos of useful service, gave the sentimental and idealistic side of Hoover its first focus. "The children of California shall be my children." For Hoover it was so. Stanford University was home.

"There is always room for a man of force, and he makes room for many." By mid-1914 Hoover was known as a man of force in London and in mining circles around the world. To his friends he was also known as a man of sentiment and sympathy. He wished now to find room for himself in the larger world of affairs. He could not know that opportunity would arrive cataclysmically only days before his fortieth birthday.

I I I

L o u and the boys arrived in London on the *Lusitania* on June 30, 1914.[114] Hoover planned to sail for California with his family on the German ship *Vaterland* on August 13.[115] He expected, he told a friend, to stay in California for about a month.[116] Lou and the boys, however, would remain in Palo Alto, where the boys could attend school. To this end Mrs. Hoover rented a home on the Stanford campus, with tenancy to begin on September 5.[117]

Six years after he left Bewick, Moreing and Company Hoover still had not uprooted himself from England, but by the summer of 1914 he was within sight of his goal. He owned a building lot at Baker Street and Broadway in San Francisco and had engaged an architect to draw up plans for a home.[118] On July 22 he told a friend that he expected to spend "a large portion of my time in America after this."[119] Early in the summer he took an option through his A.P. friend Ben Allen to purchase the *Sacramento Union*.[120] To the Allens he indicated his desire to direct more than one newspaper and to enter American public life.[121] Most significantly of all, perhaps, on July 16 he formally hired John Agnew to give his "entire time and service to the conduct of my business," to undertake whatever professional work Hoover directed, and, among other things, to serve as alternate director for Hoover of any corporation Hoover designated. The contract was effective for one year.[122]

It was now nearly thirteen years since Hoover had come to London as a partner in Bewick, Moreing. He had visited the continent of Europe many times and had come to know it well. As early as 1897, in fact, an Australian journalist lunching with him in Kalgoorlie was startled by his knowledge of Central European affairs.[123] David Starr Jordan, an accomplished world traveler and peace advocate, discussed European politics with Hoover during visits to the Red House and found "no one in Europe who knew all Europe, economically and socially, as well as he. He had nothing to do with politics, but he knew the exact condition of every country."[124]

Hoover was quite aware of the tensions simmering among the nation-states of Europe. In 1910, after one of Jordan's visits, Hoover remarked to a friend, "Jordan has spent a couple of weeks with us and I think enjoyed himself. He is mighty 'peaceable' these days—and in fact the world was never so full of peace discussion—and so busy putting on its side weapons!"[125] But even Hoover, as he recorded in his *Memoirs,* did not foresee what was coming.[126]

On June 28, 1914, a Serbian nationalist assasinated Archduke Francis Ferdinand, heir to the Austro-Hungarian throne, in the Bosnian town of Sarajevo. At first Hoover and many others assumed that the crisis would be transient and localized. But when on July 23 the Austro-Hungarian government accused the Serbian government of complicity and delivered a draconian ultimatum, Hoover and millions of others knew that a potential catastrophe was at hand.

Hoover never forgot those final eerie, suspenseful days of Europe's "century of peace."[127] On Tuesday, July 28, Austria-Hungary declared war on Serbia. That day Hoover cabled Allen that the worsening European situation compelled him to suspend the idea of purchasing the *Sacramento Union.* If the crisis passed, Hoover added, he expected to reach California on August 24.[128]

The crisis did not pass. On July 30 Serbia's ally Russia began a full mobilization. The next day Austria mobilized against Russia, and Germany demanded that Russia cease all war measures. Late in the day Russia's ally France authorized a mobilization of its own. That night, July 31, the British government declared a "moratorium," closing all the banks in the country for the following day and for the regular summer bank holiday, Monday, August 3.

Hoover's whole mining empire was imperiled. If war should break out, how would the output of Kyshtim and Tanalyk reach the West? Who indeed would operate these mines if the workers were drafted? What would happen to the Zinc Corporation, whose zinc concentrates in Australia went by contract to smelters in Germany? What would happen to development plans at the Burma mines? What about copper shipments from the Messina (Transvaal)? Would the sea lanes be safe? And now that the banks were closed—who knew for how long?—where would he find the money to carry on?

With his business paralyzed, Hoover and his family joined the Edgar Rickards on Saturday afternoon for a long-planned weekend trip to a cottage in the British countryside. That night they learned that Germany had declared war against Russia and that the French mobilization was underway. On Sunday morning, August 2, they discovered that the British bank moratorium had been extended. Later that day the Hoovers cut their long weekend short and drove back to London.

At 7:00 P.M. on August 2 Germany delivered a twelve-hour ultimatum to neutral Belgium: either allow the German army uncontested passage across Belgium into France (the key to a speedy German victory) or face the prospect of war. Twelve hours later Belgium refused and prepared for armed invasion.

On Monday, August 3, Germany declared war against France. The king of the Belgians appealed to the British government for diplomatic support of his country's neutrality. The British quickly gave it in the form of an ultimatum to Germany to respect Belgian neutrality or accept war with the United Kingdom. Back in his office at No. 1, London Wall Buildings, Hoover watched the spiraling sequence of chaos and impending disaster. The industrial world had never experienced a global war before. Cables were coming in from the field. The banks were closed in Burma, Australia, and South Africa. Ships carrying metals from his mines destined for Germany, Belgium, and France had been diverted by government edict to the nearest port. Where should they go next?

On August 4, 1914 Great Britain and Germany went to war. That morning Hoover reported to a friend that the war had "upset every possible human calculation."

> I have a body of 100,000 men at work in various enterprises and this morning I do not see how we are to meet these pay-rolls by any human device possible. Our products are mostly base metals the market for which is paralyzed, shipping facilities are gone and even exchange facilities to remit money—did we have it—are out of gear. Of still more importance is the fact that the moneys which we have in reserve in London are unavailable, due to a Moratorium. All of the wildest dreams of novelists as to what could happen in the case of a world war have already happened by way of anticipation, and as to what the realisation of such a war may be one can only stutter at.[129]

For the moment he was stranded in a foreign country at war. The voyage by the *Vaterland* was canceled; the sailing he hoped to take in its place was also likely to be scrapped. It is possible, he told a friend on the fourth, that "we shall not be able to leave this country for some time to come." But even if he could go, Hoover was not certain now that he would: ". . . if things are strenuous," he said, "I cannot leave the generalship of an army of 100,000 workpeople, no matter what the Atlantic accommodation may be."[130]

In poignant words much quoted in later years, Sir Edward Grey declared,

"The lamps are going out all over Europe; we shall not see them lit again in our lifetime." From the Atlantic to the Urals millions of men were boarding trains and heading off to war. On August 4, 1914 Hoover wrote to Ray Lyman Wilbur: "If my judgment of the situation is right, we are on the verge of seven years of considerable privation, and it behoves everybody to put himself in a state of financial defence."[131]

Hoover, like Grey, proved to be a prophet.

Bibliographical Note

I T is a reflection of Herbert Hoover's remarkably intense, productive, and much-traveled early life that the research I have conducted on it has taken me in many directions. The principal repositories of information on Hoover, of course, are the Herbert Hoover Presidential Library in West Branch, Iowa, and the Hoover Institution on War, Revolution and Peace at Stanford University. For Hoover's activities as a public man after 1914 the resources of these two archives are exceptional and immense. For his first or "pre-public" career, however, the surviving records, while valuable, are fragmentary. There is no known cache of Hoover material concerning his first forty years that is comparable in size and significance to the papers, for example, documenting his tenure as Secretary of Commerce in the 1920s.

Still, the documents that do exist contain much that is essential and illuminating. At the Herbert Hoover Presidential Library the Pre-Commerce Papers (that is, the pre-1921 portion of Hoover's own papers) constitute an indispensable core of manuscripts concerning his youth and "years of adventure." Also of particular value are the Misrepresentations File, the Bewick, Moreing and Company Collection, and certain oral history interviews. At the Hoover Institution, the well-organized Herbert Hoover Collection contains a number of especially pertinent items for a study of his first career. Both libraries maintain excellent finding aids to their vast and varied holdings.

Herbert Hoover's life intersected with that of Stanford University from the day he entered in 1891 until the day he died. Not surprisingly, the Stanford University Archives comprises an additional rich source of documentation on a man who was Stanford's most famous alumnus and one of its greatest benefactors. For this volume of my biography the papers of David Starr Jordan, John Caspar Branner, and E. D. Adams, all at the Stanford University Archives, absorbed many rewarding hours of research, as did the records of Stanford University's board of trustees (on which Hoover served for virtually half a century).

The usefulness of the Manuscripts Division of the Library of Congress will become apparent as my biography proceeds. For this volume the Library's collection of hard-to-find and sometimes esoteric mining periodicals has proved particularly valuable. So, too, have similar holdings of the British Library (formerly the British Museum) in London.

Elsewhere in Great Britain, the Board of Trade's File of Dissolved Companies (B.T. 31) at the Public Record Office contains the basic data (registration documents, shareholders lists, financial disclosure forms, etc.) of numerous mining companies with which Hoover was affiliated. The information obtainable from these files has enabled me to trace the lives of many of Hoover's mining ventures and to reconstruct the pattern of his business relationships. The Rio Tinto-Zinc Corporation's London office possesses the minute books of the Zinc Corporation's London board of directors for the period when Hoover himself was a director. The House of Lords Record Office in London holds the complete printed record of two lawsuits involving Hoover—both of which went all the way to the House of Lords. The E. J. Nathan Papers in the Bodleian Library at Oxford University contain important documents available nowhere else on Hoover's career in China (1899–1901). The Sir A. Chester Beatty Papers at Selection Trust, Ltd. in London include scores of letters, cables, and memoranda written by Hoover at the height of his mining career. This collection is the best single source of information on Herbert Hoover's mining interests between 1909 and 1914.

The J. S. Battye Library in Perth, Western Australia holds many materials pertinent to Hoover's mining career "down under." These include memoirs by goldfields personalities, the early debates and reports of the Western Australian state parliament, and copies of extremely rare early goldfields newspapers. Most importantly, the Battye Library possesses the records of the Sons of Gwalia, Ltd., an extraordinarily successful mining enterprise with which Hoover's name will always be associated. Hoover's own bulky letter book of outgoing correspondence that he sent while mine superintendent in much of 1898 is now at the Herbert Hoover Presidential Library. But some of his important *incoming* correspondence (including letters from his superiors and his legal counsel) is only available in the Sons of Gwalia collection. The Battye Library's Sons of Gwalia records also include general managers' reports, circulars to stockholders, newspaper publicity, and other documents that illuminate Hoover's catalytic role in the transformation of this enterprise into one of the great success stories of Australian mining history.

Also in Perth, at the Western Australian Department of Mines, are more than twenty-five comprehensive mine examination reports compiled and written by Hoover in 1897–98, when he was a young "inspecting engineer" for Bewick, Moreing and Company. The Western Australian Department of Mines also possesses twenty-five progress reports written by Hoover as superintendent of the Sons of Gwalia. In Adelaide, South Australia, the minutes of early board of directors meetings of the Lake View and Star, Ltd. (a Hoover creation) are preserved in the offices of Poseidon, Ltd. The University of Melbourne Archives holds the W. S. Robinson Papers and other collections relevant to Hoover's role in founding and directing the Zinc Corporation.

One other category of source material deserves mention. Hoover was probably the most accomplished—and almost certainly the best-traveled— mining engineer of his day. From the time he went to Australia in 1897 until he entered "the slippery road of public life" (as he put it) in 1914, his business interests, journeys, and opinions were copiously reported in the mining press. Frequently, for instance, on his trips to Australia, he gave lengthy interviews to newspaper reporters. In addition, many leading mining journals printed verbatim transcripts of the annual stockholders meetings of mining companies with which Hoover was affiliated. Often at these meetings Hoover himself spoke; afterwards, these proceedings were usually the subject of editorial comment.

I have therefore found it profitable, in reconstructing Hoover's first career, to examine systematically the flourishing mining press of his day (ca. 1895– 1914). While the variety of these periodicals is apparent in the footnotes, the following publications proved most consistently rewarding. In the United States: *Engineering and Mining Journal* and *Mining and Scientific Press*. In England: *Mining Journal*, *Mining Magazine*, and *Mining World and Engineering Record*. In Australia: *Australian Mining Standard* and *West Australian Mining, Building, and Engineering Journal*. Also essential was Walter R. Skinner's comprehensive *Mining Manual*, published annually in London.

Herbert Hoover himself contributed prolifically to the mining press. For a listing of these and other writings by him during his long life, see Kathleen Tracey, comp., *Herbert Hoover—A Bibliography: His Writings and Addresses* (Stanford, California, Hoover Institution Press, 1977).

ABBREVIATIONS

HHPL   Herbert Hoover Presidential Library
HI   Hoover Institution on War, Revolution and Peace

All quotations in the text appear as originally written. In general, I have not inserted the distracting word [sic] to indicate misspellings or other anomalies.

Notes

1. The best sources of information about Herbert Hoover's ancestry are Hulda Hoover McLean, *Genealogy of the Herbert Hoover Family* (Hoover Institution, Stanford University, 1967) and her *Genealogy of the Herbert Hoover Family: Errata and Addenda, 1976* (Hoover Institution, Stanford University, 1976). An older compendium of genealogical data by Mrs. McLean's father, Theodore Hoover (Herbert's brother), can be found in his autobiography, *Memoranda: Being a Statement by an Engineer* (typescript: Stanford University, 1939), copy at HHPL. The Genealogy File (17 boxes) at the Herbert Hoover Presidential Library contains extensive correspondence, clippings, and other biographical material about the numerous relatives and ancestors of Herbert Hoover.
2. Harriette Miles Odell, "Mary Minthorn" (typescript), in "Odell, Harriette Miles," Genealogy File, HHPL.
3. *Catalogue of the State University of Iowa, Iowa City, . . . 1865–6* (Davenport, Iowa, 1866), p. 19; *Catalogue of the Iowa State University at Iowa City 1866–7* (Des Moines, 1867), p. 16. According to the latter catalogue (p. 33), the sole purpose of the Preparatory Department was "to prepare students for the Collegiate Course of the University."
4. The foregoing account of the Minthorn family is drawn principally from the sources cited in notes 1 and 2. See also *West Branch Times*, February 28, 1929, p. 7, and August 5, 1948, p. 7; Ethel Grace Rensch, "Herbert Hoover: Son of American Pioneers," *Christian Science Monitor*, November 14 and 16, 1928. Mrs. Rensch was a first cousin of Herbert Hoover.
5. Jesse Hoover-Hulda Minthorn marriage certificate, HHPL.
6. This cottage, which still exists today, is the centerpiece of the Herbert Hoover National Historic Site, West Branch, Iowa. For details about its history and furnishings, see Edwin C. Bearss, *The Herbert Hoover Houses and Community Structures* (U.S. Department of the Interior, National Park Service, 1971). Also of interest is Lou Henry Hoover, "West Branch Little House" (typescript, ca. 1941), Genealogy File, HHPL.

7. Agnes Minthorn Miles to Harriette Miles Odell, January 21, 1920, "Odell, Harriette Miles," Genealogy File, HHPL.

8. Ibid. Two early documents suggest that Herbert Hoover may actually have been born on August 11, 1874. He is so recorded in the *General Register of the Members of the Springdale Monthly Meeting of Friends* (n.d.), p. 22, copy at HHPL, and the Account Book of Lawrie Tatum (Hoover's later legal guardian), also at HHPL. Theodore Hoover likewise gives August 11 as Herbert's birthday (*Memoranda*, p. 264). Herbert Hoover himself later wavered. His academic transcript at Stanford records August 10 as his birthday. But in an undated autobiographical statement probably prepared during World War I he cites August 11. Eventually, in his *Memoirs* (3 vols., New York, 1951–52) and elsewhere, Hoover settled on August 10—a date that custom and the McLean *Genealogy* have ratified as the birthday of the future president.

9. Bertha Heald (daughter of Ann Minthorn Heald) to Theodore Hoover, December 2, 1906, "Heald, 1906–1958," Genealogy File, HHPL; Ethel Rensch, "Herbert Hoover. . .," *Christian Science Monitor*, November 14, 1928; *Kansas City Star*, January 20, 1929, Section C, p. 1. The boy's full name was Herbert Clark Hoover; his middle name was the same as his father's. The novel, written by one Miss Grierson, was entitled *Pierre and His Family; or, A Story of the Waldenses* (Edinburgh, Scotland, 1824). It was published in many editions in the United States in the nineteenth century.

10. For accounts of Herbert Hoover's nearly fatal illness, see: Agnes Minthorn Miles to Harriette Miles Odell, January 21, 1920, "Odell, Harriette Miles," Genealogy File, HHPL; Maud Minthorn to Theodore Hoover, August 21, 1928, "Minthorn, Maud," ibid.; Mary Heald Harvey to Ethel Rensch, March 18, 1929, Ethel Rensch Papers, HHPL; Theodore Hoover, *Memoranda*, p. 15; Mary Minthorn Strench, "Concerning 'Bertie's Croup,' " 1969, an account included in her oral history memoir, HHPL. (Grandmother Mary Minthorn's pronouncement is quoted in the Maud Minthorn letter cited above.)

11. Maud Stratton, *Herbert Hoover's Home Town: The Story of West Branch* (Iowa City, 1948), p. 32.

12. Ibid., pp. 34–37.

13. Quoted in ibid., p. 37.

14. Stephen B. Oates, *To Purge This Land with Blood* (New York, 1970), pp. 223, 242–43.

15. See John Y. Hoover, *Life Sketches, or Jesus Only* (n.p., n.d.); *The Friends Messenger* (March 1917), 7; Lou Henry Hoover to Harriette Miles Odell, September 19, 1940, "Odell, Harriette Miles," Genealogy File, HHPL; Odell, "Dr. H. J. Minthorn," ibid.; John Joseph Mathews, *The Osage* (Norman, Oklahoma, 1961), pp. 719–725.

16. *Des Moines Register*, July 21, 1928, p. 9; Julia P. Butler to Herbert Hoover, August 8, 1928, Campaign and Transition File, HHPL.

17. Herbert Hoover, *The Memoirs of Herbert Hoover*, Volume I: *Years of Adventure* (New York, 1951), p. 9.

18. Ibid., p. 7.

19. Theodore Hoover, *Memoranda*, p. 9.

20. Hoover, *Years of Adventure*, p. 2.

21. Ibid., p. 1.

22. *West Branch Local Record*, December 16, 1880, p. 1. See also the reminiscence of Jesse Hoover by A. W. Jackson in *Cedar Rapids Evening Gazette and Republican*, July 5, 1928, p. 2.

23. Theodore Hoover, *Memoranda*, p. 14; Hoover, *Years of Adventure*, p. 3.

24. *West Branch Local Record*, October 3, 1878, p. 4. The transfer may have occurred much sooner. Jesse sold his blacksmith shop to Hill in May.

25. *West Branch Local Record*, March 27, 1879, p. 1. For a sample of Jesse Hoover's other advertisements, see ibid., December 5, 1878; December 19, 1878; April 24, 1879; May 8, 1879; December 4 and 11, 1879; and January 1, 1880 (all on p. 1).

26. *Cedar County Town Lot Deed Record Book K*, pp. 102–3, Cedar County Courthouse, Tipton, Iowa. See also Bearss, *Hoover Houses and Community Structures*, p. 3.

27. See Joan Flinspach, "Pieces of a Puzzle" (typescript, 1979), Reprint File, HHPL. Conceivably the Hoovers boarded with relatives or rented a house—perhaps even the cottage that they sold to Hill. But the available contemporary records are inconclusive.
28. *West Branch Local Record*, May 29, 1879, p. 1. Jesse Hoover had purchased this property for $140 at a public auction several weeks before. *Cedar County Deed Record Book 15*, pp. 56–57, Cedar County Courthouse, Tipton, Iowa. See also Bearss, *Hoover Houses and Community Structures*, pp. 143–157.
29. *West Branch Local Record*, March 11, 1880, p. 1.
30. *West Branch Local Record*, January 29, 1880, p. 1.
31. McLean, *Genealogy*, pp. 298, 443; Theodore Hoover, *Memoranda*, p. 23.
32. *West Branch Local Record*, October 30, 1879, p. 1.
33. *West Branch Local Record*, January 1, 1880, p. 1.
34. Hoover, *Years of Adventure*, p. 4; Theodore Hoover, *Memoranda*, pp. 17–18.
35. Theodore Hoover, *Memoranda*, pp. 19–22.
36. Hoover, *Years of Adventure*, p. 7.
37. Theodore Hoover, *Memoranda*, pp. 23–24; *West Branch Local Record*, December 16, 1880, p. 1. The official cause of death was "rheumatism of the heart," complicated by gastritis. Cedar County Register of Deaths, Book I, p. 21, Cedar County Courthouse, Tipton, Iowa.
38. Hoover Legal Records, HHPL. Hulda Hoover was named guardian of her children on August 17, 1881, eight months after the court appointed her administratrix of Jesse Hoover's estate.
39. Ibid. The inventory is published in Bearss, *Hoover Houses and Community Structures*, pp. 82–83.
40. The items are enumerated by Bearss, *Hoover Houses and Community Structures*, pp. 83–84. Although the second Hoover home is not listed, it, too, was evidently awarded to Mrs. Hoover.
41. *West Branch Local Record*, January 6, 1881, p. 1, and March 3, 1881, p. 1.
42. Both Hoover brothers later stated that Jesse Hoover left a life insurance of one thousand dollars (Herbert) or two thousand dollars (Theodore). Hoover, *Years of Adventure*, p. 4; Theodore Hoover to Lawrence Richey, April 16, 1931, "Hoover, Herbert—Personal," President's Personal File, HHPL. See also Theodore Hoover, *Memoranda*, p. 24. I have discovered no record of such an insurance policy.
43. This was her sister Agnes Miles's comment, quoted in Harriette Miles Odell, "Hulda Minthorn Hoover" (typescript), in "Hoover, Hulda Minthorn," Genealogy File, HHPL.
44. Odell, "Hulda Minthorn Hoover." Hulda's surviving early correspondence is in the West Branch Collections, HHPL.
45. Odell, "Hulda Minthorn Hoover"; Theodore Hoover, *Memoranda*, p. 17.
46. Theodore Hoover, *Memoranda*, p. 25.
47. Agnes Minthorn Miles to Harriette Miles Odell, January 21, 1920, cited in note 7.
48. Virgil G. Hinshaw to George Akerson, December 16, 1929, "Hoover, Hulda Minthorn," President's Personal File, HHPL; Theodore Hoover, *Memoranda*, p. 25.
49. *West Branch Times*, February 28, 1929, p. 7.
50. *West Branch: Its First 100 Years* (Centennial souvenir program, 1951), p. 9, copy at HHPL.
51. *West Branch Times*, February 28, 1929, p. 7.
52. *West Branch Local Record*, October 3, 1878, p. 1, and March 27, 1879, p. 1.
53. Ibid., October 30, 1879, p. 1. See also the issues for November 28, 1878, p. 1; October 6, 1881, p. 1; and December 15, 1881, p. 5.
54. Ibid., February 28, 1884, p. 5, and March 6, 1884, p. 2. As early as 1878 she also served as Secretary of the Young People's Christian Association. Ibid., December 26, 1878, p. 3.
55. Secretary's Record for Friends Sunday School, West Branch, Iowa, 1881–1884, in General Accession—State Historical Society of Iowa, HHPL; Agnes Minthorn Miles to Harriette Miles Odell, January 21, 1920.
56. Hoover, *Years of Adventure*, p. 4.

57. Theodore Hoover, *Memoranda*, p. 24.

58. Hulda Hoover to her mother and sister Agnes, February 22, 1883, West Branch Collections, HHPL.

59. See ibid.

60. Hulda Hoover to her mother and sister Agnes, March 15, 1883, ibid.

61. Hulda Hoover to her sister Agnes, October 24, 1883, ibid.

62. Hulda Hoover to her mother and sister Agnes, February 22, 1883, ibid.

63. *West Branch Local Record*, July 6, 1882, p. 1, and September 14, 1882, p. 1; Marshalltown, Iowa *Times-Republican*, August 21, 1928, p. 8; Theodore Hoover, *Memoranda*, p. 27.

64. The most detailed account of Herbert Hoover's life among the Osage is an article in the *Kansas City Star*, January 20, 1929, Section C, p. 1. See also Hoover, *Years of Adventure*, pp. 4–5, and Louise Morse Whitham, "Herbert Hoover and the Osages," *Chronicles of Oklahoma* 25 (Spring 1947): 2–4. Hoover's uncle, Laban J. Miles, served as Agent to the Osage and Kaw between 1878 and 1885, and again from 1889 to 1894. For his activities at the agency see Edwin C. Bearss, *Buildings in the Core-Area and Jesse Hoover's Blacksmith Shop* (U.S. Department of the Interior, National Park Service, 1970), pp. 249–58. The precise date and length of Hoover's visit to the Indian Territory (which occurred sometime between 1881 and 1883) are uncertain. Recollections conflict. In his *Memoirs* Hoover wrote that he stayed eight or nine months, but in light of other evidence (such as school attendance records), this seems unlikely. While visiting the Miles family, Hoover may have attended briefly the Old Quincy Street School in Lawrence, Kansas. See Kate Powell Armstrong to Hoover, November 22, 1928, Campaign and Transition File, HHPL; Lawrence, Kansas *Journal-World*, October 21, 1964, pp. 1–2.

65. For a brief summary of Hoover's schooling in Iowa, see Edwin C. Bearss, *Historic Furnishing Study: Primary Department of the West Branch School. . .* (Denver, 1973), pp. 6–11. See also *Catalogue of . . . West Branch High School for the Academic Year 1882–83* and *The West Branch Community School* (4th ed., 1980), p. 4 (copies at HHPL).

66. *West Branch Local Record*, November 9, 1882, p. 1; Theodore Hoover, *Memoranda*, pp. 34–35; *New York American*, June 19, 1928.

67. For a history of the West Branch Indian Industrial School, see Bearss, *Buildings in the Core-Area*, pp. 259–71.

68. Theodore Hoover, *Memoranda*, pp. 25–27.

69. David LeShana, *Quakers in California: The Effects of 19th Century Revivalism on Western Quakerism* (Newberg, Oregon, 1969), chapter 3.

70. Ibid., pp. 60–61; Theodore Hoover, *Memoranda*, pp. 9–12; Theodore Hoover, ed., *Mildred Crew Brooke* (Casa del Oso, California, 1940), pp. 13–14. See also the obituary for Jesse Hoover in *West Branch Local Record*, December 16, 1880, p. 1, and the Rev. John Y. Hoover's account of Jesse's conversion, in an undated clipping, in "Hoover, Jesse Clark," Genealogy File, HHPL. Unlike Hulda, Jesse experienced periods of religious doubt before coming to a full acceptance of Christ just before he died.

71. *Minutes of Red Cedar Preparative Meeting of Ministers and Elders*, April 20, 1883, pp. 118–19, in Archives of Friends Church, West Branch, Iowa.

72. *Minutes of Springdale Monthly Meeting of Friends*, June 23, 1883, p. 316, in Archives of Friends Church, West Branch, Iowa.

73. Theodore Hoover, *Memoranda*, p. 35.

74. *Minutes of Springdale Monthly Meeting of Friends*, September 22, 1883, p. 328, in Archives of Friends Church, West Branch, Iowa.

75. Hulda Hoover to Agnes Miles, October 24, 1883, West Branch Collections, HHPL.

76. Ibid.

77. *Minutes of Springdale Monthly Meeting of Friends*, January 19, 1884, p. 339.

78. *West Branch Local Record*, February 21, 1884, p. 4; ibid., February 28, 1884, p. 5.

79. Cedar County Register of Deaths, Book I, p. 46, Cedar County Courthouse, Tipton, Iowa.

80. Ibid.; *West Branch Local Record*, February 28, 1884, p. 5. Both the Young People's Prayer

Meeting and the Women's Christian Temperance Union of West Branch passed resolutions on the death of Hulda Hoover. *West Branch Local Record*, March 6, 1884, p. 2, and March 27, 1884, p. 3.

81. Theodore Hoover, *Memoranda*, p. 35.

82. Mary Minthorn et al., petition to the Cedar County Probate Court, March 3, 1884; Court proclamation, March 7, 1884; both in Hoover Legal Records, HHPL.

83. *Cedar Rapids Evening Gazette and Republican*, August 21, 1928, pp. 9–10; Florence Collins Weed, "Life Insurance Helped to Educate a President," *National Magazine* 58 (August 1930): 480, 486.

84. Lawrie Tatum, Account Book for Herbert Hoover, HHPL; Tatum's report to the Court, n.d. (probably mid-1884), Hoover Legal Records, HHPL.

85. Lawrie Tatum, receipt signed August 10, 1885, Hoover Legal Records, HHPL.

86. "Annual Report of Lawrie Tatum Guardian of Herbert C. Hoover," August 24, 1885; legal documents of various dates, 1884–85; Tatum to the Circuit Court of Cedar County, Iowa, April 5, 1886. All in Hoover Legal Records, HHPL.

87. Theodore Hoover, *Memoranda*, p. 36.

88. *West Branch Local Record*, April 17, 1884, p. 3.

89. Hoover, *Years of Adventure*, pp. 5–6.

90. Harriette Miles Odell, quoted in *West Branch Times*, February 16, 1939, p. 1.

91. Tatum, report to the Court, n.d. (probably mid-1884); J. Y. Hoover receipt dated April 9, 1884; both documents in Hoover Legal Records, HHPL. See also *West Branch Local Record*, April 17, 1884, p. 3, for a brief report on the Rev. Hoover's trip. For Theodore Hoover's transfer from Kingsley, Iowa to Hardin County, Iowa, see his *Memoranda*, pp. 36, 39–40. A receipt signed by Allen Hoover on August 30, 1884 indicates that Herbert Hoover began paying board at his uncle's home on April 21. Hoover Legal Records, HHPL.

92. Rose Wilder Lane interview with Theodore Hoover, January 6, 1919 [1920], "Lane, Rose Wilder," Genealogy File, HHPL; Rose Wilder Lane, *The Making of Herbert Hoover* (New York, 1920), pp. 57–59.

93. Hoover, *Years of Adventure*, p. 3.

94. Hoover later called her "the real founder of character." Hoover, note to Mollie Brown Carran, April 13, 1923, Mollie Carran Collection, HHPL.

95. Photo no. 1884–4, HHPL.

96. Stratton, *Herbert Hoover's Home Town*, p. 53.

97. Lane, *Making of Herbert Hoover*, pp. 60–61; Will Irwin, *Herbert Hoover: A Reminiscent Biography* (New York, 1928), pp. 24–26.

98. Receipts signed by Allen Hoover, 1884–1885, Hoover Legal Records, HHPL. Later receipts indicate that in mid-1885 Tatum reduced his appropriation to $1.00 and $1.25 per week, since Herbert Hoover was now able to pay part of his board in work on Uncle Allen's farm. One itemized receipt signed by Allen Hoover lists such expenses between 1884 and 1885 as an everyday hat for Herbert (15¢), suspenders (20¢), a suit ($6.50), a pair of shoes ($2.25), the pulling of a tooth (25¢), and two bottles of hive syrup for croup (70¢).

99. Lane, *Making of Herbert Hoover*, p. 62.

100. Stratton, *Herbert Hoover's Home Town*, p. 98.

101. Lane, *Making of Herbert Hoover*, p. 59; William Hard, *Who's Hoover?* (New York, 1928), pp. 19–20.

102. Hoover, *Years of Adventure*, pp. 10–11; McLean, *Genealogy*, p. 10. Dr. Minthorn's son, Benjamin Bruce, died on September 22, 1884.

103. Stratton, *Herbert Hoover's Home Town*, p. 69; Lou Henry Hoover, "West Branch Little House," p. 38.

104. As of late August Hoover's wordly assets were $533.99. "Annual Report of Lawrie Tatum Guardian of Herbert C. Hoover," August 24, 1885, Hoover Legal Records, HHPL.

105. Allen Hoover, receipt dated January 1, 1886, for Herbert Hoover's traveling expenses to Oregon, Hoover Legal Records, HHPL.

106. *West Branch Local Record,* November 5, 1885, p. 3.

107. For instance Herbert Hoover's grade-school teacher in 1880 commented in 1932: "Was Bertie a particularly bright boy? No, he wasn't. Not any more than some of the others but he paid such close attention. I will always remember that of him. He wasn't slow to learn, but he made everything he did count. He was a sturdy, independent fellow, not at all easy to approach at first. No, he wasn't bashful." Mrs. Elizabeth Chandler Sunier, quoted in a 1932 newspaper clipping, Genealogy notebook, HHPL. For similar remarks, see the interview of Hoover's boyhood chum "Newt" Butler in the *Cedar Rapids Sunday Gazette and Republican,* June 17, 1928, p. 3. For Mollie Carran's recollections of her former pupil see *Cedar Rapids Sunday Gazette and Republican,* March 4, 1928, Section III, p. 2.

108. Hoover, *Years of Adventure,* p. 1.

109. *West Branch Local Record,* November 12, 1885, p. 1.

CHAPTER 2

1. Herbert Hoover, *The Memoirs of Herbert Hoover,* Volume I: *Years of Adventure* (New York, 1951), p. 10.

2. *Minthorn House: Boyhood Home of Herbert Hoover* (Newberg, Oregon, n.d.), Reprint File, HHPL.

3. When the present town of Newberg was incorporated in 1889 its population was probably between one hundred and two hundred persons. Ralph K. Beebe, *A Garden of the Lord* (Newberg, Oregon, 1968), p. 33.

4. Two useful sketches of Dr. Minthorn (both by his daughter, Mary Minthorn Strench) are: "My Most Unforgettable Character" (1963), in "Strench, Mary Minthorn," Post-Presidential Individual File, HHPL, and "Dr. Henry John Minthorn and Laura Ellen, His Wife" (n.d.), reprinted in the *Minthorn House* booklet cited in note 2. See also Harriette Miles Odell's essay, "Dr. H. J. Minthorn," in "Odell, Harriette Miles," Genealogy File, HHPL. Published accounts of Dr. Minthorn's unusually varied career can be found in O. Larsell, *The Doctor in Oregon: A Medical History* (Portland, 1947), p. 226, and Arthur O. Roberts, *Tomorrow is Growing Old: Stories of the Quakers in Alaska* (Newberg, Oregon, 1978), pp. 87–109. Minthorn served in Iowa's Forty-Fourth Infantry Regiment for three months in 1864. He graduated from Jefferson Medical College on March 10, 1877: letter from the Librarian, Thomas Jefferson University, to the author, September 4, 1978. References to Dr. Minthorn appeared from time to time in the *West Branch Local Record* during the 1880s. See especially the issues of March 17, 1881; July 6, 1882; and January 18 and 25, 1883. On the opening of Friends Pacific Academy, see *Newberg Graphic,* December 1, 1888, p. 3, and December 15, 1888, p. 1.

5. Hulda McLean, *Genealogy of the Herbert Hoover Family* (Hoover Institution, Stanford University, 1967), pp. 10–11; *Minthorn House,* cited in note 2. In 1887 a third daughter, Mary, was born to the Minthorns.

6. Hoover, *Years of Adventure,* pp. 10–11.

7. Mary Minthorn Strench to Ethel Rensch, March 6, 1929, "Minthorn, Dr. Henry John," Ethel Rensch Papers, HHPL.

8. *Catalogue, 1885–6, of Friends' Pacific Academy* (McMinnville, Oregon, 1886), pp. 4, 6, 8.

9. Henry John Minthorn to Rose Wilder Lane, Feb. 28, 1920, "Lane, Rose Wilder," Genealogy File, HHPL. Another copy is in "Minthorn, Dr. Henry John," Ethel Rensch Papers, HHPL. Minthorn's letter was a lengthy reply to an inquiry by Lane, who was preparing a biography subsequently published as *The Making of Herbert Hoover* (New York, 1920).

10. *Catalogue, 1885–6 . . . ,* pp. 5–7.

11. *Sunday Oregonian* (Portland), March 3, 1929, Section 6, pp. 1, 4 (a collection of anecdotes about Hoover's Oregon boyhood); Elmer Edson Washburn, "Westward Across Four Fron-

tiers" (n.d.), p. 3, General Accessions, HHPL. Washburn was a boyhood friend of Herbert Hoover. A photograph of the first students at the Friends Pacific Academy (photo no. 1885–4, HHPL) reveals Hoover to be the smallest in the group. He was still among the shortest two years later (photo no. 1887–4, HHPL).

12. *Catalogue, 1885–6 . . .*, p. 14.

13. Minthorn to Lane, February 28, 1920.

14. Ibid.

15. Henry John Minthorn to William Smith, 1917, "Minthorn, Henry John," Genealogy File, HHPL. A copy is in the Ray Lyman Wilbur Papers, Box 120, Hoover Institution, Stanford University. See also Minthorn to Lane, February 28, 1920.

16. Lane, *Making of Herbert Hoover*, pp. 78–80.

17. Newberg Monthly Meeting of Friends membership records and Newberg Monthly Meeting Minutes, January 1, 1887, Newberg, Oregon. Prior to this he had been a member of the Springdale Monthly Meeting in Iowa.

18. Burt Brown Barker interview, November 15, 1968, sound recording 68 / 58, HHPL. Barker was a boyhood friend of Herbert Hoover in Oregon. Years later Hoover made a point of visiting his old Sunday school teacher, Vannie Martin. See *Newberg Graphic*, August 26, 1926, p. 1, and *Portland Oregonian*, August 26, 1926.

19. Walter C. Woodward to Herbert Hoover, October 11, 1921, Ezra and Amanda Woodward Papers, George Fox College, Newberg, Oregon.

20. *Newberg Graphic*, December 1, 1888, p. 3, and December 15, 1888, p. 1.

21. Ibid.

22. Minthorn to Lane, February 28, 1920.

23. Ibid.; *Sunday Oregonian*, March 3, 1929, Section 6, p. 1; Washburn, "Westward Across Four Frontiers," p. 3; Mary Minthorn Strench, "My Most Unforgettable Character," p. 9.

24. Herbert Hoover, address at Newberg, Oregon, August 10, 1955, Public Statements File, HHPL.

25. Herbert Hoover to Philip Francis Nowlan, January 8, 1923, "Na-Nz," Genealogy File, HHPL; Alva Cook's recollections, October 22, 1928, Burt Brown Barker Collection, HHPL; Washburn, "Westward Across Four Frontiers," p. 3; Hoover, *Years of Adventure*, p. 11.

26. Washburn, "Westward Across Four Frontiers," p. 3.

27. *Catalogue 1886–7 of Friends Pacific Academy* (McMinnville, Oregon, 1887), pp. 6, 8–9. Another (and apparently earlier) edition of the 1886–87 catalogue, published in Portland, lists "H. C. Hoover" as still in the first year of the Grammar School Department (p. 6).

28. Friends Pacific Academy, program for Commencement Exercises of Grammar Course, May 6, 1887. Copy in General Accession—Elmer E. Washburn, HHPL.

29. *Catalogue of Friends Pacific Academy for 1887–88* (Portland, 1888), pp. 5, 10.

30. Washburn, "Westward Across Four Frontiers," pp. 2–3; Strench, "My Most Unforgettable Character," pp. 9–10. Washburn remembered Hoover as "the best student in the class." Strench says that her father (Dr. Minthorn), although playing no favorites, nevertheless "conscientiously gave him the highest grades." See also Strench to Ethel Rensch, March 6, 1929, "Minthorn, Dr. Henry John," Ethel Rensch Papers, HHPL.

31. Theodore Hoover, *Memoranda: Being a Statement by an Engineer* (typescript: Stanford University, 1939), p. 54, copy at HHPL; Washburn, "Westward Across Four Frontiers," p. 3. A receipt signed by Theodore Hoover and preserved in the Hoover Legal Records at HHPL indicates that Theodore was in Newberg by September 29, 1887. Tatum's account book (at HHPL) indicates that Theodore's move to Oregon was authorized by the court on August 24 and paid for on September 5 (p. 195).

32. Theodore Hoover, *Memoranda*, p. 57. According to Elmer Washburn, Hoover referred to his brother as "Taddie."

33. Ibid., pp. 57–58; Washburn, "Westward Across Four Frontiers," p. 3.

34. Herbert Hoover to Daisy Trueblood, ca. 1887–88, Burt Brown Barker Collection, HHPL.

35. *Catalogue of Friends Pacific Academy for 1887–88* (Portland, 1888), p. 15.

36. Hoover, *Years of Adventure*, p. 12; Theodore Hoover, *Memoranda*, p. 63; Hoover, address at Newberg, Oregon, August 10, 1955, Public Statements File, HHPL.
37. Theodore Hoover, *Memoranda*, p. 63.
38. See the various profiles of Minthorn cited in note 4.
39. Hoover, *Years of Adventure*, pp. 11–12.
40. Minthorn to Lane, February 28, 1920.
41. Hoover, *Years of Adventure*, p. 12.
42. Strench, "My Most Unforgettable Character," p. 19.
43. Rose Wilder Lane, notes of interview with Theodore Hoover, January 6, 1919 [1920], "Lane, Rose Wilder," Genealogy File, HHPL.
44. Minthorn to Lane, February 28, 1920.
45. Laban J. Miles (Hoover's Oklahoma uncle) to Mary Morrison, February 14, 1920, General Accession—Louis A. Morrison, HHPL.
46. Harriette Miles Odell to Theodore Hoover, n.d. (probably 1920), "Lane, Rose Wilder," Genealogy File, HHPL; Odell to Theodore Hoover, January 30, 1920 and February 18, 1920, "Odell, Harriette Miles," Genealogy File, HHPL. In these letters Mrs. Odell—one of Herbert's cousins and playmates when he lived in Oklahoma—alluded to his "unhappy experiences" and "unhappy days" in Oregon and to the "antagonism" that he felt toward his Uncle John. In 1920 she destroyed Herbert's early "Oregon letters" to her.
47. Lane interview with Theodore Hoover, January 6, 1919 [1920]; Theodore Hoover, *Memoranda*, p. 63; Strench, "My Most Unforgettable Character," pp. 9, 17; Strench, profile of Dr. Minthorn printed in *Minthorn House* booklet.
48. Minthorn to Lane, February 28, 1920. Minthorn's daughter, Mary Strench, recalled that "Bertie" found the care of his uncle's horses "irksome" ("My Most Unforgettable Character," p. 9).
49. This story, with slight variations, appeared in the *Capital Journal* (Salem, Oregon), February 28, 1920, p. 1; the *Sunday Oregonian*, March 3, 1929, Section 6, p. 4; and the *Sunday Oregonian*, October 30, 1932.
50. Minthorn to Lane, February 28, 1920.
51. See Lawrie Tatum to the Cedar County Court, November 19, 1889, attached to his 1889 Annual Report on his ward Herbert Hoover, in Hoover Legal Records, HHPL.
52. Hoover, quoted in Burt Brown Barker oral history (1967), pp. 16–17, HHPL.
53. In February 1920 *Everybody's Magazine* published the first installment of a serialized popular biography of Herbert Hoover by his wartime associate, Professor Vernon Kellogg of Stanford University. Kellogg's biography was later published as *Herbert Hoover: The Man and His Work* (New York, 1920). In the magazine version (and to a lesser extent in the book) Kellogg told a melodramatic tale of an unhappy Oregon boyhood, culminating in an alleged confrontation with a "grandfather" Miles and Hoover's running away from home. Kellogg's story evoked distress and consternation among many of Hoover's relatives as well as embarrassing Hoover himself. Dr. Minthorn strenuously denied Kellogg's story and insisted that his nephew never ran away anywhere. Theodore Hoover himself referred to some of the article as "gibberish" and complained about it to Kellogg. Although the sources for Kellogg's story are unknown, close analysis suggests that he may have garbled several anecdotes involving not Herbert Hoover but certain of his relatives. Theodore Hoover, for example, lived in Oregon for a time with his aunt's father, Benjamin Miles, and did leave after rebelling against his relatives. There is no conclusive evidence, however, that Herbert Hoover himself ever "ran away from home." For the reaction of the Hoover family to Kellogg's article, see: Henry John Minthorn to William Smith, February 21, 1920, and to Rose Wilder Lane, February 28, 1920, both in "Lane, Rose Wilder," Genealogy File, HHPL; Harriette Miles Odell to Theodore Hoover, February 18, 1920 and n.d. [March 1920?], "Odell, Harriette Miles," Genealogy File, HHPL; Theodore Hoover to Odell, February 25, 1920, ibid.; Laban J. Miles (son of Benjamin Miles) to Mary Morrison, January 30, 1920, February 14, 1920, and March 10, 1920, General Accession—Louis A. Morrison, HHPL; *New-*

berg Graphic, August 19, 1920, p. 1. It may be significant that although Kellogg in his book repeats the story about Hoover's allegedly running away, he relates it in less detail than he had in the serialized version published in *Everybody's*. It is also interesting that when Kellogg presented a copy of the book to Hoover in May 1920, he inscribed it "To the Victim with all commiseration." (The book is at HHPL.) See also notes 54 and 55.

54. Lane, *The Making of Herbert Hoover*, pp. 80–81; *Newberg Graphic*, August 19, 1920, p. 1. It is noteworthy that Lane's book—like Kellogg's, published in 1920—was prepared after correspondence and interviews with several members of the Hoover family, including Theodore Hoover, Dr. Minthorn, and Harriette Odell. (See "Lane, Rose Wilder," Genealogy File, HHPL.) Several years later Lane claimed that Herbert Hoover himself personally read and approved her manuscript before she published it. (See Lane to Hoover, April 12, 1936, Post-Presidential Individual File, HHPL.) If so, this adds greatly to the general credibility of her narrative.

   See also Eugene Lyons, *Our Unknown Ex-President: A Portrait of Herbert Hoover* (New York, 1948), p. 82, regarding the Oregon period: "The boy had a will of his own which at times, as in all normal families, clashed with his uncle's. There was even a period when Herbert stalked out in anger and boarded with other relatives. It could not have been serious, for when the Minthorns moved to Salem, the capital, he went with them."

55. Theodore Hoover, *Memoranda*, p. 57.

56. Ibid., pp. 58–59.

57. Hoover interview in *Portland Telegram*, August 23, 1926.

58. Hoover, *Years of Adventure*, p. 11.

59. Theodore Hoover, *Memoranda*, pp. 63, 70–72.

60. Interview with Agnes Hammer Eskelson (Hoover's first cousin), *Seattle Daily Times*, February 12, 1928. Hoover's uncle, Samuel Hammer, moved with his family from Iowa to Oregon in the late 1880s. Mrs. Eskelson's account seems somewhat embellished but contains a number of anecdotes that have the ring of truth.

61. Minthorn to Lane, February 28, 1920.

62. Letterhead of stationery used for a receipt signed by Minthorn and dated February 17, 1888, Hoover Legal Records, HHPL.

63. Articles of Incorporation of the Oregon Land Company, February 28, 1888, File 3701, Oregon State Archives, Salem, Oregon.

64. Theodore Hoover, *Memoranda*, p. 58; Washburn, "Westward Across Four Frontiers," p. 4.

65. Theodore Hoover, *Memoranda*, p. 58.

66. Lawrie Tatum, Annual Progressive Report for Mary Hoover, August 22, 1889, Hoover Legal Records, HHPL. Several receipts retained by Tatum indicate that Mary Hoover arrived in Salem, Oregon by October 15, 1888 and that she paid her Uncle John ten dollars a month for board. See also Tatum's annual report dated August 28, 1890, ibid.

67. Lawrie Tatum, Annual Progressive Report for Mary Hoover, August 28, 1890, ibid.; Henry John Minthorn to William Smith, February 21, 1920; Theodore Hoover, *Memoranda*, p. 67. In his February 1920 *Everybody's* article, Vernon Kellogg, referring to this episode, claimed that the son-in-law squandered his nephew Herbert Hoover's patrimony as well. There is no foundation to this assertion, as Lawrie Tatum's meticulous guardianship records show. For one version of this affair, see Harriette Miles Odell to Lou Henry Hoover, October 2, 1940, and her essay "Mary Minthorn," both in "Odell, Harriette Miles," Genealogy File, HHPL. For Henry John Minthorn's account, see Minthorn to William Smith, February 21, 1920.

68. Minthorn to Lane, February 28, 1920.

69. Ben S. Cook to Lawrence Richey, January 7, 1932, "Richey-Hoover Files: Statements and Refutations, Oregon Land Company," Misrepresentations File, HHPL; interview of Ben S. Cook by Fred Lockley in *Oregon Journal* (Portland), February 9, 1932; Fred Lockley, article in *Oregon Journal*, August 29, 1954. Lockley was a boyhood friend and neighbor of Herbert Hoover in Salem, Oregon.

70. Minthorn to Lane, February 28, 1920.
71. Ibid.
72. Strench, "My Most Unforgettable Character," p. 10.
73. Supplementary Articles of Incorporation of the Oregon Land Company, August 1, 1890, File 3701, Oregon State Archives, Salem, Oregon.
74. Interview with Ben S. Cook by Fred Lockley in *Oregon Journal*, February 8, 1932; Beebe, *A Garden of the Lord*, p. 261.
75. H. S. Nedry, "The Friends Come to Oregon: Salem Quarter II," *Oregon Historical Quarterly* 45 (December 1944): 307; Theodore Hoover, *Memoranda*, p. 67.
76. Minthorn to Lane, February 28, 1920; Nedry, "The Friends Come to Oregon," pp. 309–310; Beebe, *A Garden of the Lord*, p. 261. Hoover's contribution to the fund-raising drive was two dollars. See subscription list in Burt Brown Barker Collection, HHPL.
77. Nedry, "The Friends Come to Oregon," pp. 312–15; receipts for Mary Hoover's attendance at Friends Polytechnic Institute, 1892–94, Hoover Legal Records, HHPL.
78. Minthorn to Lane, February 28, 1920. According to Minthorn, Hoover himself decided that it would be best to obtain some experience in business before resuming his formal education.
79. Ibid.; *Sunday Oregonian*, March 3, 1929, Section 6, p. 4.
80. Fred Lockley in *Oregon Journal*, August 29, 1954.
81. *Sunday Oregonian*, March 3, 1929, Section 6, p. 4; *Capital Journal*, March 3, 1920, p. 1.
82. Lockley in *Oregon Journal*, August 29, 1954. According to Lockley, this section of Portland eventually became part of the neighboring community of Milwaukie. As late as 1894 it was known as the Minthorn Addition. Letter from Steven M. Hallberg, Oregon Historical Society, to the author, October 13, 1978.
83. Ben S. Cook interview, *Oregon Journal*, February 8, 1932; Oregon Land Company ledger, volume 9, p. 213, Oregon State Archives.
84. Ben S. Cook, quoted in a newspaper clipping, November 14, 1928, in "Recommendations, Letters of," Pre-Commerce Papers, HHPL.
85. Ben S. Cook, quoted by Fred Lockley in *Oregon Journal*, February 8, 1932.
86. Laura Heulat Bickford, quoted in *Capital Journal*, April 3, 1920, p. 8.
87. Hoover, *Years of Adventure*, p. 12.
88. Minthorn to Lane, February 28, 1920.
89. Minthorn to his cousin, M. F. Minthorn, February 4, 1918, printed in Belmond, Iowa *Herald Press*, March 20, 1918, Reprint File, HHPL.
90. Minthorn to Lane, February 28, 1920.
91. Ben S. Cook to Lawrence Richey, January 7, 1932; extract of a letter by William P. Smith, n.d., "Sm-Socz," Genealogy File, HHPL.
92. Hoover, *Years of Adventure*, pp. 12–13.
93. Minthorn to Lane, February 28, 1920.
94. Minthorn to his cousin M. F. Minthorn, February 4, 1918.
95. Burt Brown Barker, *Autobiography of Burt Brown Barker* (typescript, n.d.), p. 35, copy at HHPL.
96. Barker oral history (1967), pp. 7, 79, 81–82.
97. Mrs. Walter Woodward (who knew Hoover well in Newberg), quoted in Portland *Sunday Oregonian*, March 3, 1929, Section 6, p. 1.
98. Laura Heulat Bickford, quoted in *Capital Journal*, April 3, 1920, p. 8.
99. This was a theme in the series of reminiscences of Hoover by various Oregonians published in the *Capital Journal* (Salem, Oregon) in late February and March, 1920.
100. W. A. Alderman, quoted in *Capital Journal*, February 28, 1920, p. 1.
101. Laura Heulat Bickford, quoted in *Sunday Oregonian*, March 3, 1929, Section 6, p. 4. Mrs. Bickford particularly recalled Hoover's studying mathematics: "He usually sat with his elbows on a desk, his hands at the sides of his head, his little black hat cocked on his head, and a geometry text book flat on the desk before him."

102. Minthorn to Lane, February 28, 1920. The 1887–88 *Catalogue of Friends Pacific Academy* specifically cited dancing and tobacco as among the "amusements and indulgences . . . calculated to distract the minds of pupils from their studies" (p. 15).

103. Minthorn to Lane, February 28, 1920; Hoover, *Years of Adventure*, pp. 13–14. For an account of Hoover's fishing trip to his uncle Samuel Hammer's home in Crooked Finger, Oregon, see Hammer's reminiscences in the *Morning Oregonian* (Portland), February 1, 1928.

104. Barker oral history (1967), pp. 12, 14.

105. Minthorn to Lane, February 28, 1920; *Capital Journal*, March 3, 1920, p. 1; Agnes Hammer Eskelson anecdote in *Seattle Daily Times*, February 12, 1928.

106. H. J. Minthorn to Lawrie Tatum, November 14, 1889; Tatum to Cedar County Court, November 19, 1889; J. D. Shearer to Tatum, December 17, 1889; Annual Progressive Report of Tatum (re Herbert Hoover), August 28, 1890. All in Hoover Legal Records, HHPL. See also Hoover, *Years of Adventure*, p. 13.

107. Hoover, *Years of Adventure*, p. 13; Herbert Hoover, "Thank You, Miss Gray!" *Reader's Digest* 75 (July 1959): 118–120.

108. *Autobiography of Burt Brown Barker*, pp. 35–36. Barker, a close friend of Hoover's in Salem, believed that the two Sunday school teachers, Vannie Martin and Jenny Gray, "had more to do with the broadening of the character of Herbert Hoover than any other single person." Barker oral history interview (1967), p. 29.

109. Barker oral history (1967), pp. 87–90.

110. Theodore Hoover, *Memoranda*, pp. 58–72.

111. Hoover, *Years of Adventure*, p. 14; Alva W. Cook statement, October 22, 1928, Burt Brown Barker Collection, HHPL; Hoover, "Information for Biographers" (typescript, n.d.; probably ca. 1914), p. 2, in Benjamin S. Allen Papers, Box 1, HI, and Pre-Commerce Papers, HHPL.

112. Hoover, *Years of Adventure*, pp. 14–15. Hoover stated here that he refused to consider Earlham when he learned that this Quaker college did not offer engineering courses. A number of biographies (including Rose Wilder Lane's, Will Irwin's, and Eugene Lyons's) have indicated that some of Hoover's relatives objected to his attending a secular, science-oriented institution instead of a Quaker college. Dr. Minthorn later emphatically denied that he wanted Bert to go to Swarthmore or Earlham; Minthorn insisted that his nephew had freely made his own decision. (Minthorn to William Smith, 1917, and February 21, 1920; Minthorn to Lane, February 28, 1920.) Hoover's *Memoirs*, however, suggest that there was some difference of opinion between him and certain other members of the family on this subject. And in 1929 the son of Benjamin Miles told an interviewer that Hoover and his uncle John "differed on education—as to Stanford or Friend School." (Lloyd Hogan, notes of information obtained from Mr. and Mrs. B. C. Miles, August 23, 1929, in "Minthorn, Dr. Henry John," Ethel Rensch Papers, HHPL.)

113. Minthorn to Lane, February 28, 1920.

114. Hoover, *Years of Adventure*, p. 15.

115. Professor Joseph Swain, statement given to Vernon Kellogg, 1920 (duplicate in "Lane, Rose Wilder," Genealogy File, HHPL); Swain to Hoover, March 6, 1899, General Accession—Joseph Swain, HHPL; Hoover to Mrs. William Swain, June 19, 1934, Public Statements File, HHPL.

116. Swain statement, 1920; Minthorn to William Smith, 1917, and February 21, 1920; Minthorn to Lane, February 28, 1920; Hoover, *Years of Adventure*, p. 15. These accounts essentially agree, except that Minthorn recalled that it was President David Starr Jordan of Stanford University (and not Swain) who visited him at the railroad station in Salem. Swain stopped in Salem at Hoover's invitation.

   Hoover was grateful to Swain for his "unusually kind intrest prior [to] and during my early days at Stanford." Hoover to Swain, February 20, 1899, General Accession—Joseph Swain, HHPL.

117. Minthorn to Smith, 1917, and February 21, 1920; Hoover, *Years of Adventure*, p. 15; Hoover, "Information for Biographers," p. 3.
118. Minthorn to Lane, February 28, 1920.
119. Lane, *The Making of Herbert Hoover*, p. 97; Ben S. Cook, quoted in *Oregon Journal*, February 8, 1932. Lane stated that the banker bought a lot from Hoover that Hoover himself temporarily owned in the Highland Addition of Salem. Cook said that the banker gave Hoover forty dollars to pay for his trip to Stanford. There may be no inconsistency in these stories.
120. See Tatum's various annual reports to the court, Hoover Legal Records, HHPL. In 1886 Hoover's account was enhanced by $166.67 following Tatum's sale of the second Hoover home for $500. (Hoover was credited with one-third of the proceeds.)
121. Tatum's annual report, August 24, 1891, ibid.
122. Lane, *The Making of Herbert Hoover*, p. 97.
123. Swain statement, 1920.
124. *Capital Journal*, August 29, 1891.

CHAPTER 3

1. On Leland Stanford and the origins of his university, see Orrin Leslie Elliott, *Stanford University: The First Twenty-five Years* (Stanford, California, 1937), pp. 3–99, and David Starr Jordan, *The Days of a Man* (Yonkers-on-Hudson, New York, 1922), I, pp. 365–93, 480–93.
2. Eleanor Pearson Bartlett, "Beginnings in Palo Alto," in *The First Year at Stanford* (Stanford University English Club, Stanford, California, 1905), pp. 17–28; Elliott, *Stanford University*, pp. 81–83, 179; Lucy Fletcher Brown, "Annex Pioneers," *Radcliffe Quarterly* (November 1940): 14–16.
3. Eleanor Bartlett, in *The First Year at Stanford*, p. 19.
4. Ibid.; Herbert Hoover, *The Memoirs of Herbert Hoover*, Volume I: *Years of Adventure* (New York, 1951), p. 16; Rose Wilder Lane, *The Making of Herbert Hoover* (New York, 1920), p. 104; David Starr Jordan, "Random Recollections of Herbert Hoover," *Stanford Illustrated Review* 29 (April 1928): 336.
5. Jordan, "Random Recollections," p. 336; interview with Lucy Fletcher Brown in *San Francisco Chronicle*, December 3, 1928; Brown, "Annex Pioneers," pp. 15–16. According to Brown, David Starr Jordan recommended Hoover for the job of caring for their horses.
6. Herbert Hoover's academic transcript, copy in Herbert Hoover Collection, Box 5, HI; Hoover, *Years of Adventure*, p. 16.
7. Ibid.; Lane, *Making of Herbert Hoover*, p. 105.
8. Hoover, *Years of Adventure*, p. 16; Jordan, *Days of a Man*, I, p. 409. Here Jordan states that he assigned Hoover to Room 38 in Encina Hall. But in the "Random Recollections" article cited in note 4, Jordan says that Hoover's first room was 18. It is possible that the latter was a misprint. In any case, Jordan recalled that Herbert Hoover was the first Stanford student to whom he assigned a room in Encina. Jordan, "Random Recollections," p. 336; Jordan to E. J. Wickson, January 17, 1920, David Starr Jordan Papers, Series I-A, Box 98, Stanford University Archives.
9. Jordan, *Days of a Man*, I, p. 402; Ellen Elliott in *The First Year at Stanford*, p. 43.
10. Jordan, *Days of a Man*, I, p. 485.
11. Quoted in Elliott, *Stanford University*, pp. 88–89.
12. Ibid., p. 88.
13. The text of Jordan's speech is in his *Days of a Man*, I, pp. 688–90.
14. Hoover, *Years of Adventure*, p. 16.
15. Elliott, *Stanford University*, pp. 93–94.
16. Ibid., pp. 175–177; Charles K. Field in *The First Year at Stanford*, pp. 72–73.
17. Elliott, *Stanford University*, p. 179 and, in general, pp. 174–248.

18. Hoover academic transcript.

19. Ibid.; Hoover, *Years of Adventure*, p. 17. Branner was delayed by commitments as state geologist of Arkansas.

20. *The First Year at Stanford*, p. 72; Ray Lyman Wilbur, *The Memoirs of Ray Lyman Wilbur* (Stanford, California, 1960), p. 40.

21. Hoover, *Years of Adventure*, p. 17; Lane, *Making of Herbert Hoover*, p. 107.
    At the beginning of his freshman year Hoover also evidently served on a crew of twelve student janitors for buildings in the Quad. This was the recollection in 1928 of his classmate Archie Rice. See Rice's compilation, "Fifty-six Anecdotes and Reminiscences of Herbert Hoover" (typescript, 1928), pp. 6–7, in file 8450 / 895H, Stanford University Archives. See also Carol Green Wilson, *Herbert Hoover: A Challenge for Today* (New York, 1968), pp. 13–14. According to Green, Hoover soon gave up his Quad assignment to become a student janitor in Encina. Hoover could not have worked there for long, however, because in December 1891 the university replaced the student help with Japanese, a move that aroused protest in Encina (*The First Year at Stanford*, p. 85).

22. Brown interview, *San Francisco Chronicle*, December 3, 1928; Brown, "Annex Pioneers," pp. 15–16. According to Brown, Hoover resigned this job later in the year because he had found sufficient employment on campus and wished to save time. He lined up a substitute worker.

23. Hoover, *Years of Adventure*, p. 17; Lane, *Making of Herbert Hoover*, pp. 121–22; John F. Newsom, unpublished article on Hoover (1928), John F. Newsom Papers, HHPL. Newsom, who was a graduate student and assistant to Dr. Branner at Stanford at the time, vividly recalled Hoover laboring over the bicycle until it was as good as new. In 1955 Hoover told a newspaperman: "My career as a newspaper carrier was as a student at Stanford University. I performed on a sale contract from another student and we shared the benefits which were not great, but very useful at that time." Hoover to M. E. Fisher, May 5, 1955, "Newspapers and Press Services," Post-Presidential Subject File, HHPL.

24. Hoover, *Years of Adventure*, p. 17; John C. Branner, comments at a banquet in honor of Herbert Hoover on December 28, 1919. Branner's speech is printed in the *Stanford Illustrated Review* 21 (January 1920): 188–89.

25. Vernon Kellogg, *Herbert Hoover: The Man and His Work* (New York, 1920), p. 50; Lane, *Making of Herbert Hoover*, p. 121. John F. Newsom, in his sketch noted in note 23, remembered that eye trouble compelled Hoover to wear glasses. A number of photographs of Hoover as a college student show him with glasses.

26. Jordan, "Random Recollections," p. 336.

27. Interview of Mrs. John C. Branner in the *New York Times*, July 22, 1928, Section 7, p. 11.

28. Quoted in Will Irwin, *Herbert Hoover: A Reminiscent Biography* (New York, 1928), pp. 48–49.

29. *Sequoia* 1 (May 25, 1892): 354. This was an undergraduate publication at Stanford University.

30. Irwin, *Herbert Hoover*, p. 47; Hoover, *Years of Adventure*, p. 21. The two earliest popular biographies of Hoover (those by Kellogg and Lane) do not mention that he played on any team.

31. For a superb contemporary account of the first Stanford-Berkeley "Big Game," see *San Francisco Chronicle*, March 20, 1892, p. 24.

32. One of the most persistent stories about Herbert Hoover's Stanford days is that he had charge of the arrangements for the first "Big Game" and that he was therefore responsible for failing to bring the football. There is no known contemporary document, however, indicating that Hoover had any special role in the first "Big Game." Extensive research in the Stanford University Archives has failed to turn up such a document, nor have the university archives and contemporary student publications at Berkeley yielded any confirmatory evidence. In *The First Year at Stanford*, Frank Angell contributed a chapter on "The Early History of Athletics at Stanford." In this essay, published only thirteen years after the event, Angell does not mention Herbert Hoover in connection with the March 1892

Stanford-California contest. Nor do such standard histories as J. F. Sheehan and Louis Honig, *The Games of California and Stanford* (San Francisco, 1900) and S. Dan Brodie, *66 Years on the California Gridiron* (Oakland, 1949).

Among the important early biographies of Hoover, Vernon Kellogg's does not refer to the game at all, while Rose Wilder Lane and Will Irwin merely state that Hoover attended; they do not attribute to him any particular responsibility. Lane adds that after the game Hoover attended an entertainment at the Bush Street Theater. All this is noteworthy, since Lane's book was done in close collaboration with Hoover's friend and classmate, Charles K. Field (class of '95), and Lane herself interviewed several of Hoover's friends and relatives. Moreover, there is some evidence that Hoover himself reviewed and approved Lane's book and at least part of Irwin's book before they were published. (For Lane, see note 54 of chapter 2 of this biography. For Hoover's personal revision of Irwin's manuscript see his correspondence with Irwin in 1928 in the Will Irwin Papers, HI.)

Another potentially valuable source is also silent. In 1928 (as mentioned in note 21) Hoover's classmate Archie Rice collected a large number of Hoover anecdotes from Stanford alumni who knew Hoover as an undergraduate. Interestingly, none of these anecdotes links Hoover with the first "Big Game" and the famous forgotten football.

It was not until the 1940s that Hoover was publicly associated with the March 1892 "Big Game." In 1947 President Ray Lyman Wilbur of Stanford University reported that Herbert Hoover had been involved in that first legendary contest. In an interview with Wilbur, Hoover recalled in detail how he and some associates rented the football grounds, printed 5,000 tickets, and then took emergency measures to collect cash admission when unexpected crowds appeared and the tickets ran out. After the game Hoover and his colleagues counted the receipts in the California Hotel. Wilbur's memorandum of this conversation with Hoover is in the Ray Lyman Wilbur Papers, Box 120, HI. It was published in the *Stanford Alumni Review* 48 (April 1947): 17.

Five years later, in the first volume of his *Memoirs* (*Years of Adventure*, pp. 21–22), Hoover described a "Big Game" that he arranged. The details are essentially the same as those given to Wilbur, except that Hoover did not explicitly state that he was describing the first "Big Game." Indeed, he dated it as occurring on "the University's second Thanksgiving Day," which would have been November 1892 (the second "Big Game"), not March 19 (the first). But then he recounted the story about the forgotten football ("We had overlooked that detail")—seemingly a clear reference to the first "Big Game."

In November 1894 Hoover, by then the student body treasurer, certainly did arrange the *fourth* "Big Game" (see below). In fact, some of the details he gave to Wilbur in 1947 and included in his *Memoirs* seem to fit the 1894 contest, not the one in early 1892. Hoover told Wilbur, for instance, that he made arrangements for the game with a University of California student named Bert Lang. The records show that Lang was the California team's manager for the 1894 "Big Game" but had no known role in the 1892 event.

One wonders, therefore, whether we are not witness here to some confusion of memory. In early 1947 Hoover was nearly seventy-three years old. It seems very unlikely that as a shy young freshman in the spring of 1892 Hoover somehow became partly responsible for the first intercollegiate football contest on the Pacific coast—and left no record of it on paper or in anyone's memory. It seems far more likely that in his *Memoirs* and interview with Wilbur he actually was describing his experiences in handling the *fourth* "Big Game." In the absence of conclusive contemporary evidence, one must doubt that Hoover had any connection with the *first* "Big Game," held on March 19, 1892.

33. Hoover, *Years of Adventure*, pp. 17–18; Hoover, public statement, May 17, 1921, Public Statements File, HHPL; John F. Newsom article (1928), cited in note 23. In the 1921 statement Hoover states that his monthly salary was forty dollars; in his *Memoirs* he recalled that it was sixty dollars. A voucher for Hoover as Branner's assistant in Arkansas Geological Survey work in February 1893 (several months later) shows that Hoover's monthly salary at that time was forty dollars. This voucher is in "U.S. Geological Survey, 1893–1916," Pre-Commerce Papers, HHPL.

34. Newsom article (1928); Newsom to Branner, July 27, 1892, John C. Branner Papers, Box 30, Stanford University Archives.

35. James Perrin Smith, "The Arkansas Coal Measures in Their Relation to the Pacific Carboniferous Province," *Journal of Geology* 2 (February–March 1894): 199. Smith was one of Hoover's professors at Stanford. Professor Branner acknowledged Hoover's assistance in locating a shale deposit near Mount Judea, Arkansas. John C. Branner, "Preface," *Annual Report of the Geological Survey of Arkansas,* Volume IV (Little Rock, 1893), p. xx.

36. Hoover, *Years of Adventure,* p. 17; Hoover, May 17, 1921 statement; Newsom article; *Arkansas Democrat* (Little Rock), May 23, 1948, p. 2, and February 26, 1961, p. 16C.

37. Hoover academic transcript. The change was authorized on September 13, 1892.

38. Ibid. Late in November 1892 Hoover, another student, and Professor J. P. Smith took a trip to the coastal area around Coloma, California in a search for fossils. *Daily Palo Alto,* December 5, 1893. Hoover's academic transcript for the fall semester of his sophomore year appears to indicate that he was temporarily "conditioned" in inorganic chemistry.

39. *Daily Palo Alto,* October 10, 1892, p. 3; Lane, *Making of Herbert Hoover,* p. 130; Frank B. Wooten (class of '95) anecdote, in Rice, "Fifty-six Anecdotes," pp. 24–25; Ernest Delos Magee (class of '95) anecdote, ibid., supplement, p. 15. Romero Hall was on Waverly Street in Palo Alto.

40. Lawrie Tatum, Annual Progressive Report, August 24, 1892, Hoover Legal Records, HHPL.

41. Herbert Hoover to Nell May Hill, August 30, 1892, Hill Family Papers, University of Oregon. This letter, and four others by Hoover to Hill between 1892 and 1895, have been published in *The Call Number* 27 (Spring 1966): 2–12, a publication of the University of Oregon Library. Other Hoover-to-Hill letters cited below are from this source. Miss Hill, a resident of Independence, Oregon, attended Stanford University for a time in the early 1890s. Hoover appears to have been acquainted with her before she entered Stanford.

42. See the voucher for February 1893, cited in note 33.

43. Wilbur, *Memoirs,* p. 40.

44. Ray Lyman Wilbur, "Herbert Hoover: A Personal Sketch" (unpublished paper, 1920), p. 6, Reprint File, HHPL. In his *Memoirs,* p. 40, Wilbur quoted Hoover's advice a bit differently: "Do your work so that the professors will notice it."

45. Hoover academic transcript; Lane, *Making of Herbert Hoover,* p. 139. Branner's 1892–93 letter book in his papers is full of references to this project. The relief map weighed half a ton. Hoover's *Memoirs* state that he worked this summer for Waldemar Lindgren, but this is incorrect. He first worked for Lindgren in the summer of 1894.

46. Theodore Hoover, *Memoranda: Being a Statement by an Engineer* (typescript: Stanford University, 1939), p. 91, copy at HHPL. In November 1893, back at Stanford, Herbert Hoover spoke to the Geological Club on "the general geological structure, the kind of rocks and the mountains of western Oregon" he had evidently explored during the summer. Geological Club of Stanford University minute book, p. 7, in Miscellaneous University Papers II, Stanford University Archives.

47. Burt Brown Barker, *Autobiography of Burt Brown Barker* (typescript, n.d.), p. 37, copy at HHPL. Barker states that Hoover worked that summer for his Uncle John Minthorn's Oregon Land Company, but no corroboration of this statement has been found.

48. Hoover academic transcript. For an interesting account of a campus surveying expedition in which Hoover participated during the fall, see R. E. McDonnell, "A 'Hunch' of '93," *Stanford Illustrated Review* 30 (March 1929): 295–96.

49. Encina Hall Register, September 1, 1893–May 31, 1894, Stanford University Archives; advertisement in the Stanford undergraduate journal *Sequoia* 3 (September 13, 1893). Hoover's room was 175.

    During his junior year Hoover also waited on tables in the Encina dining room—or so some of his classmates later recalled. See Rice, "Fifty-six Anecdotes," pp. 4–5, and supplement, p. 16. Rice cited as his authority a San Francisco restauranteur who evidently had the Encina dining contract in 1893–94. The restauranteur asserted that Hoover himself recalled his waiting on tables when he happened to meet the restauranteur many years later.

By 1928 the waiter story was a common one. A survey that year turned up twelve Stanford alumni who asserted that young Hoover had spilled soup down their necks! This statistic led a newspaper reporter to remark that, if so, Hoover "must have been the most careless student waiter ever to work his way through Stanford" (_Washington Evening Star_, November 25, 1928). Interestingly enough, the two earliest biographies of Hoover (Kellogg's and Lane's) explicitly deny that he waited on tables. Hoover's own _Memoirs_ are silent on the subject.

Conceivably Hoover was a student waiter in Encina. But the story may also be an example of the power of apocryphal thinking.

50. Lawrie Tatum, Progressive Annual Report for 1893, Hoover Legal Records, HHPL.
51. Wilbur, _Memoirs_, p. 63. See also Frank Angell's remarks in _The First Year at Stanford_, pp. 52–53.
52. _Daily Palo Alto_, February 8, 1894, p. 1.
53. See, for example, Theodore Hoover, _Memoranda_, pp. 100, 110; Irwin, _Herbert Hoover_, pp. 52–53; Wilbur, _Memoirs_, p. 63. Theodore Hoover called his brother "the father of the Associated Students and their constitution." Irwin claimed that Hoover returned to campus in September with "a mature plan in his mind—his first creation in organization" and that the others then took it up. Wilbur asserted that Hoover "organized and secured adoption of a new constitution," without mentioning anyone else. Rose Wilder Lane's portrayal of the reform movement as a team effort to which Hoover was recruited by Collins and Hinsdale, and to which he contributed significantly, seems more realistic (Lane, _Making of Herbert Hoover_, pp. 141–42). Hoover himself cited several others who, with him, "declared war for reform" (_Years of Adventure_, p. 22).
54. _Daily Palo Alto_, February 8, 1894, p. 1, and March 2, 1894, p. 1. In 1910 the _Stanford Alumnus_ said of E. R. Zion: "As president of the Associated Students in 1894 he drafted and pressed to adoption the first constitution that provided a complete scheme of student activity and which is still practically in effect." _Stanford Alumnus_ 11 (May 1910): 355.
55. _Daily Palo Alto_, January 23, 1894, p. 1.
56. _Daily Palo Alto_, February 28, 1894, supplement.
57. _Daily Palo Alto_, February 8, 1894, p. 1.
58. _Daily Palo Alto_, March 2, 1894, p. 1; March 7, 1894, p. 1; and April 11, 1894, p. 1.
59. Lane, _Making of Herbert Hoover_, pp. 133 and 142, states that Hoover had assisted Sam Collins in auditing accounts at Romero Hall in their sophomore year and that Collins, impressed, recommended to Hinsdale that Hoover be nominated for student body treasurer.
60. Ibid., pp. 144–45; Elliott, _Stanford University_, pp. 209–215 (for a history of the "Camp").
61. Lane, _Making of Herbert Hoover_, pp. 145–46; Wilbur, _Memoirs_, p. 63. In _Years of Adventure_, p. 23, Hoover simply recorded that when elected treasurer (or as he put it, "financial manager"), he served without pay.
62. Irwin, _Herbert Hoover_, pp. 54–55.
63. _Daily Palo Alto_, February 28, 1894, supplement.
64. _Daily Palo Alto_, April 11, 1894, p. 1. While an undergraduate Lester Hinsdale spelled his name "Hinsdill." Later he changed it, and I have used the revised version throughout.
65. Lane, _Making of Herbert Hoover_, pp. 146, 147.
66. _Daily Palo Alto_, April 18, 1894, p. 1. At first it was announced that Hinsdale had squeaked through, but a recount nullified the result.
67. Lane, _Making of Herbert Hoover_, pp. 147–48.
68. Irwin, _Herbert Hoover_, p. 55.
69. _Daily Palo Alto_, April 24, 1894, p. 1.
70. Wilbur, "Herbert Hoover: A Personal Sketch," pp. 9–10; unsigned memorandum for Vernon Kellogg, October 28, 1919, in "Stanford 1917–1920," Pre-Commerce Papers, HHPL. The author of this memorandum appears to have been Ray Lyman Wilbur.
71. _Daily Palo Alto_, April 25, 1894, p. 1.
72. _Daily Palo Alto_, May 2, 1894, p. 4; May 3, 1894, p. 1; and May 4, 1894, p. 1.

73. *Daily Palo Alto*, April 20, 1894, p. 4.

74. Hoover to Nell May Hill, July 19, 1894.

75. Ibid.; Hoover, *Years of Adventure*, p. 19; *Stanford Alumnus* 6 (December 1904): 4; Rice, "Fifty-six Anecdotes," pp. 26, 33–35.

76. Hoover to Hill, July 19, 1894 and November 9, 1894.

77. Hoover to John C. Branner, September 2, 1894, Branner Papers, Box 25; Hoover's 1894 field notebook, HHPL; Waldemar Lindgren to the Director, U.S. Geological Survey, June 30, 1895, copy in "U.S. Geological Survey, 1893–1916," Pre-Commerce Papers, HHPL.

   Hoover's 1894 field notebook was published in facsimile in 1979 by the U.S. Senate under the title *Geological Atlas of the United States: Pyramid Peak Folio, California. Compiled by Herbert C. Hoover, 1894* (Senate Document No. 96–24).

78. Hoover to Branner, September 2, 1894.

79. Ibid.

80. Ibid.

81. Waldemar Lindgren, "A President in the Making," *The Tech Engineering News* 10 (March 1929): 53.

82. Hoover to Hill, November 9, 1894; Hoover to Branner, September 2, 1894.

83. Hoover to Branner, September 2, 1894. If this request caused any problems with the university administration, there is no record of it.

84. John C. Branner to Waldemar Lindgren, September 20, 1894, Branner Papers, Box 4.

85. Waldemar Lindgren to Branner, October 11, 1894, Branner Papers, Box 26. In his report of June 30, 1895 to the Director of the U.S. Geological Survey, Lindgren mentioned that Hoover had "efficiently assisted" him in his field work the summer before. In 1896 Lindgren published his Pyramid Peak Folio (Folio 31 of the U.S. Geological Survey's *Geologic Atlas of the United States*). On three folio maps of the Pyramid Peak Sheet, Lindgren placed the words: "Assisted by H. C. Hoover." Hoover felt highly honored. See Hoover to John M. Boutwell, May 31, 1949, Post-Presidential General File, HHPL.

86. Lindgren to Branner, October 11, 1894; Encina Hall Register, September 1, 1894–May 31, 1895, Stanford University Archives. The last entry in Hoover's field notebook was October 11 (the first, July 22). Hoover occupied room 179 in Encina on October 14, 1894. Classes had begun on September 7.

87. Hoover to Hill, November 9, 1894.

88. Hoover academic transcript.

89. Elliott, *Stanford University*, p. 117.

90. Lane, *Making of Herbert Hoover*, p. 151; Rice, "Fifty-six Anecdotes," pp. 41–42. Some years later a friend of Hoover's at Stanford recalled that the treasurer "had every detail at his fingers' end" and maintained elaborate card catalogues of student finances. Caspar W. Hodgson, "Campus Days With Herbert Hoover," *Western Alumnus* 1 (July 1928): 3.

91. Lawrie Tatum, Annual Progressive Report, 1894, Hoover Legal Records, HHPL.

92. *Stanford Alumni Review* 48 (April 1947): 17.

93. Lane, *Making of Herbert Hoover*, p. 151, states that Hoover's new voucher system evoked unavailing "howls" from the athletes, particularly the baseball team. See also *Daily Palo Alto*, November 26, 1901, p. 1.

94. *Daily Palo Alto*, November 15, 1894, p. 1.

95. *Daily Palo Alto*, October 30, 1894, p. 1.

96. *Daily Palo Alto*, November 15, 1894, p. 1.

97. Hoover to Hill, November 9, 1894.

98. Hoover to Hill, November 9, 1894; Hodgson, "Campus Days With Herbert Hoover," p. 3.

99. See, for example, *Daily Palo Alto* for October 30, November 15, and December 5, 1894, and January 16, 17, 18, 21, and 22, 1895.

100. *Daily Palo Alto*, December 12, 1894, pp. 1, 2.

101. *Sequoia* 4 (January 25, 1895): 211. Ten years later, in *The First Year at Stanford*, Frank Angell

described treasurer Hoover as "a reformer to whom the Student Body is exceedingly indebted for starting it on the straight and narrow road of business-like methods in its business affairs" (p. 53). This assessment is especially significant since it was rendered long before Hoover became a public figure, the subject of retrospective myth making by both admirers and detractors.

102. *Stanford Alumnus* 14 (December 1912): 126; Wilbur, *Memoirs*, p. 63.

103. Tatum, Annual Progressive Report, 1894.

104. Irwin, *Herbert Hoover*, pp. 57–58; Hoover, *Years of Adventure*, p. 357; Edith Harcourt to Victor Rhein, February 21, 1938, "Hoover Stories," Pre-Commerce Papers, HHPL.

105. Irwin, *Herbert Hoover*, p. 58; Will Irwin, *The Making of a Reporter* (New York, 1942), p. 17.

106. See, for example, the impressions of Hoover recorded by Lane (who, be it remembered, relied heavily on Hoover's classmate Charles K. Field) and Irwin, who knew Hoover as an undergraduate. See also Rice, "Fifty-six Anecdotes," p. 38.

107. Irwin, *Herbert Hoover*, pp. 59–60; Irwin, *Making of a Reporter*, p. 17.

108. Irwin, *Herbert Hoover*, p. 63.

109. Ibid., pp. 63–64.

110. For Lou Henry's background, and Hoover's courtship, see Hoover, *Memoirs*, I, p. 23, and the popular biography by Helen B. Pryor, *Lou Henry Hoover: Gallant First Lady* (New York, 1969). For Hoover's earliest known sign of appreciation for her, see Hoover to Hill, November 9, 1894. The class card file for Lou Henry in the Special Collections department of the San Jose State University Library establishes that she graduated in 1893 and held jobs in Monterey before attending Stanford. In 1920 Hoover's cousin revealed that Hoover wrote letters to her while at Stanford concerning Lou Henry, whom he admired greatly from the start. Hoover was "desperate" about the thought of losing her. Harriette Miles Odell to Theodore Hoover, February 18, 1920, "Odell, Harriette Miles," Genealogy File, HHPL.

111. Hoover to Hill, November 9, 1894.

112. Ibid.; Hoover to Hill, September 7, 1895; interview with Professor C. D. Marx, March 5, 1920, "Hoover Genealogy," Ethel Rensch Papers, HHPL. The interviewer was probably Rose Wilder Lane.

113. *Daily Palo Alto*, January 25, 1895, p. 1.

114. *Daily Palo Alto*, January 15, 1895, p. 1.

115. On January 5, 1932 George J. Bancroft (class of '95) wrote to his classmate, President Hoover. Bancroft recalled that he nominated Hoover for membership in the Stanford chapter of the S.A.E. fraternity and personally invited Hoover to join. Hoover accepted. But a week or two later, Bancroft recalled, Hoover notified the fraternity that on further thought he felt he should remain a "barb" through college, since the "barbs" had voted for him in the student elections. Accordingly (Bancroft remembered) Hoover withdrew his acceptance. In this 1932 letter Bancroft acknowledged that his memory might not be accurate "in all details." In his reply, President Hoover told Bancroft: "I think your memory is at fault in the belief that I ever accepted such a pledge. Otherwise, the story seems to me to be correct."

A few days later, a fraternity official reported to President Hoover that an article in a national fraternity magazine stated that "you were pledged to the Sigma Alpha Epsilon fraternity" but that "several of your close associates asked you to resign from this pledge and that you subsequently did so." To this letter Hoover's secretary replied: "He [Hoover] tells me that to the best of his recollection he was never pledged in the matter [sic; manner?] you mention. He was approached, gave it some consideration, and declined."

See: George J. Bancroft to Herbert Hoover, January 5, 1932; Hoover to Bancroft, January 15, 1932; Carl J. Rice to Hoover, January 21, 1932; Lawrence Richey to Rice, January 26, 1932. All in "President, personal data concerning," President's Personal File, HHPL.

116. Hoover to Hill, November 9, 1894.

117. Hoover academic transcript; Hoover to Hill, July 9, 1895; Hoover, *Years of Adventure*, p. 20.

118. Hoover academic transcript.

119. Ibid.; Hoover to Hill, July 9, 1895. In this letter to Hill, Hoover gave the following graphic summary of his senior year:

> Having run Athletics the first semester after I reached college I recied [sic] as a reward two conditions and no other credit for semesters work. Hence 2d semester I must carry 23 hours and remove these two cond. which I did and passed English 1b besides and graduated. I also ran base-ball field athletics and did about as much politics as ever. Went to every ball given, Sophomore, Junior, Charity & Senior in fact quite a social swell. Enjoyed myself better than ever before in my life.

Hoover's academic transcript indicates that in fact he took eighteen credit hours in his second semester, not twenty-three, but in this letter he may have been counting the "conditions" he had to remove.

120. Hoover's academic transcript indicates that he took the examination unsuccessfully more than once.

121. See, for example, his letters to Nell May Hill.

122. This story is told in detail by Vernon Kellogg in *Herbert Hoover*, pp. 52–55. Professor Kellogg explicitly cites Lou Henry Hoover as his source. Other early biographers repeat the story with some variations. David Starr Jordan recalled in 1928 that English composition was Hoover's "great stumbling-block at college" and that it was a committee which "decided to pass him at last in freshman English." It did so "mainly because it was claimed that the University could hardly refuse to graduate one who wrote such excellent theses in his major subject and who was reported to be the best student in the department" (Jordan, "Random Recollections," p. 336). Hoover himself, in his *Memoirs (Years of Adventure*, pp. 23–24), stated that without the "active intervention" of Professors Branner and Smith, "who insisted among other things that I could write English," he would not have graduated with his class.

123. *Daily Palo Alto*, April 29, 1895, p. 1.

124. Theodore Hoover, *Memoranda*, pp. 93–94.

125. Hoover to Hill, July 9, 1895.

126. Hoover to Hill, September 7, 1895.

127. Hoover to Hill, November 9, 1894.

128. *Daily Palo Alto*, April 24, 1895, p. 1; April 25, 1895, p. 1; and May 1, 1895, p. 1. Two sources indicate that Hoover was a key figure in arranging for a salary for his successor: Henry D. Sheldon, "The History of the Student Body," *Sequoia* 7 (April 22, 1898): 142; *Stanford Alumnus* 14 (December 1912): 126.

129. *Stanford Quad '96* [for Class of 1895], p. 240.

130. Interview with Professor C. D. Marx, March 5, 1920.

131. Unpublished autobiography of Guido Marx, pp. 85–86, Guido Marx Papers, Box 2, Stanford University Archives. Marx, an engineering professor at Stanford, was the brother of Professor C. D. Marx. See also the recollection of Dr. Branner's wife, *New York Times*, July 22, 1928, Section 7, p. 11.

132. Branner speech, December 28, 1919, printed in *Stanford Illustrated Review* 21 (January 1920): 188–89.

133. Kellogg, *Herbert Hoover*, pp. 48–49.

134. David Starr Jordan's commencement address, in *Daily Palo Alto*, May 29, 1895, pp. 4–5.

135. Irwin, *Herbert Hoover*, p. 44.

136. Herbert Hoover, remarks at Stanford University commencement, June 16, 1957, Public Statements File, HHPL.

137. Lindgren to Branner, April 19, 1895, Branner Papers, Box 26.

138. Hoover academic transcript; Hoover to Hill, July 9, 1895.

C H A P T E R   4

1. Lawrie Tatum's final report, dated August 30, 1895, is in the Hoover Legal Records, HHPL.
2. Herbert Hoover to Nell May Hill, September 7, 1895, Hill Family Papers, University of Oregon; *Seventeenth Annual Report of the United States Geological Survey . . . 1895–96* (Washington, D.C., 1896), Part I, p. 47; Waldemar Lindgren, "A President in the Making," *The Tech Engineering News* [M.I.T.] 10 (March 1929): 53.
3. See Herbert Hoover's U.S. Geological Survey field notebook for 1895, General Accessions, HHPL.
4. Herbert Hoover to his sister May, August 4, 1895, "Hoover, May," Pre-Commerce Papers, HHPL.
5. Hoover to Nell May Hill, July 9, 1895, Hill Family Papers.
6. Hoover to his sister, August 4, 1895.
7. Hoover to Hill, September 7, 1895.
8. Ibid.
9. Hoover to his sister, August 4, 1895.
10. Hoover to Hill, July 9, 1895.
11. Ibid.
12. Herbert Hoover, *The Memoirs of Herbert Hoover,* Volume I: *Years of Adventure* (New York, 1951), p. 18.
13. Herbert Hoover to John M. Boutwell, May 31, 1949, Post-Presidential General File, HHPL; Hoover, *Years of Adventure,* pp. 19–20. The phrase "the dumbness of bureaucracy" was Hoover's.
14. Hoover to his sister, August 4, 1895.
15. Ibid.
16. Hoover to Hill, September 7, 1895.
17. Ibid.
18. Herbert Hoover, "Information for Biographers" (typescript, n.d.; probably ca. 1914), p. 4, in Benjamin S. Allen Papers, Box 1, HI, and Pre-Commerce Papers, HHPL.
19. E. B. Kimball to John C. Branner, September 18 and 27, 1895, John C. Branner Papers, Box 26, Stanford University Archives; Lindgren, "A President in the Making," p. 53.
20. Hoover's 1895 field notebook, HHPL. Hoover's *Memoirs* and a number of biographies state that upon graduation from Stanford in May 1895 he went directly to Nevada City in search of a job. The contemporary documents cited above, however, establish that he worked first for several months under Lindgren.
21. California Miners' Association, *California Mines and Minerals* (San Francisco, 1899), pp. 263–78. See also William B. Clark, *Gold Districts of California* (California Division of Mines and Geology Bulletin 193: San Francisco, 1970), pp. 53–60, 97–101.
22. Hoover, "Information for Biographers," p. 4; Hoover, *Years of Adventure,* p. 25.
23. Hoover, *Years of Adventure,* p. 25; Carol Green Wilson, notes of interviews in Grass Valley and Nevada City, California, August 19–21, 1950, Carol Green Wilson Papers, Box 5, HI. Mrs. Wilson interviewed several residents of these communities in the preparation of her popular biography, *Herbert Hoover: A Challenge for Today* (New York, 1968).
24. Hoover, *Years of Adventure,* p. 25.
25. Rose Wilder Lane, *The Making of Herbert Hoover* (New York, 1920), p. 179; Hoover, *Years of Adventure,* p. 25; Hoover, address at Grass Valley, California, July 4, 1935, Public Statements File, HHPL. According to Lane, even before Hoover left the Survey Lindgren tried unsuccessfully to secure him a job in the mines.
26. Lane, *Making of Herbert Hoover,* p. 179.
27. Hoover, *Years of Adventure,* p. 25.
28. Ibid.; Hoover address at Grass Valley, July 4, 1935; E. B. Kimball to John C. Branner, November 13, 1895, Branner Papers, Box 26.
29. Hoover, *Years of Adventure,* p. 25; Hoover address at Grass Valley, July 4, 1935.

30. Hoover, *Years of Adventure*, p. 26. Hoover states here that he worked "a few months" at the Reward mine before going to the Mayflower. It could not have been that long. He spent only about two months—certainly no more than four—in the entire district.

    While in the Nevada City / Grass Valley area Hoover may possibly have worked in other mines. For instance, one old-timer, Edward Uren, later asserted that Hoover worked at the Cold Springs mine on Harmony Ridge, just northeast of Nevada City. *Nevada County Nugget*, January 5, 1958. I have not found any confirmation of his statement.

    Hoover himself, in 1914, recalled that he worked as a trucker in the Old Providence mine. Certainly he visited this mine on his day off one Sunday in November 1895 to study its tailings treatment processes, but I have found no contemporary evidence that he held a job there. E. B. Kimball to Branner, November 13, 1895; Hoover, speech to Engineers Club of San Francisco, February 12, 1914, Public Statements File, HHPL.

31. John Rowe, *The Hard-Rock Men: Cornish Immigrants and the North American Mining Frontier* (New York, 1974), pp. 113–15.

32. Hoover address at Grass Valley, July 4, 1935; *Grass Valley Union*, July 6, 1935; *Nevada County Nugget*, January 5, 1958; *Sacramento Bee*, August 7, 1958.

33. Carol Green Wilson, interview notes, August 19–21, 1950.

34. Herbert Hoover, "And Their Deeds are Remembered After Them," *Sequoia* 5 (January 10, 1896): 225–26.

35. Wilson, interview notes, August 19–21, 1950; Lane, *Making of Herbert Hoover*, p. 182.

36. Hoover address at Grass Valley, July 4, 1935.

37. Hoover, *Years of Adventure*, p. 26.

38. Hoover, "Information for Biographers," p. 4.

39. The friend was Donald H. McLaughlin; the time, ca. 1911. McLaughlin to the author, September 7, 1979.

40. In *Years of Adventure* Hoover stated that he "did not feel like a down-trodden wage slave" in his first underground job (p. 25). Nevertheless, one cannot imagine that Hoover was content with such a position for very long. Rose Wilder Lane's biography quotes Hoover as saying to a friend one night in Nevada City: "If my college education can't get me anything better than pushing an orecar for a living I'd better quit mining" (p. 183).

41. Lane, *Making of Herbert Hoover*, p. 183.

42. Hoover, *Years of Adventure*, p. 26.

43. *Dictionary of American Biography* (New York, 1932), V, pp. 608–9.

44. Clark C. Spence, *Mining Engineers and The American West* (New Haven, 1970), p. 61.

45. *Crocker-Langley San Francisco Directory for Year Commencing April 1897* (San Francisco, 1897), pp. 208, 918; Lane, *Making of Herbert Hoover*, p. 183.

46. Spence, *Mining Engineers*, pp. 322, 332.

47. Hoover, *Years of Adventure*, pp. 26–27. Waldemar Lindgren gave Hoover a letter of introduction to Janin. Lindgren, "A President in the Making," p. 53.

48. Hoover, "Information for Biographers," p. 4. Lane's biography states that he did receive a salary from Janin: thirty dollars a month (p. 185). Will Irwin's biography states that Hoover was hired as an unpaid office assistant while Janin waited for Hoover's letters of recommendation to arrive. Will Irwin, *Herbert Hoover: A Reminiscent Biography* (New York, 1928), p. 71. Hoover's brother says that Hoover entered Janin's employ at no salary unless he was "in the field." Theodore J. Hoover, *Memoranda: Being a Statement by an Engineer* (typescript: Stanford University, 1939), p. 95, copy at HHPL.

49. Interview of Lester Hinsdale in *San Diego Sun*, August 13, 1926.

50. The lawsuit was: Carson City Gold and Silver Mining Company v. North Star Mining Company.

51. Spence, *Mining Engineers*, pp. 198–227.

52. Hoover, "Information for Biographers," p. 4; Hoover, *Years of Adventure*, p. 27; Lane, *Making of Herbert Hoover*, p. 185. In the first of these sources Hoover merely mentioned that he was "entirely familiar with the geology" of the litigants' mines, but he did not indicate how

he acquired his knowledge. In his *Memoirs* he stated that he had worked with Lindgren on the geology of these mines. Similarly, Lane's biography stated that he had "tested and mapped" the geologic strata which were at issue in the case. However, neither Lindgren's folio maps nor his lengthy report on the Grass Valley district indicate that Hoover made any particular contribution to his investigation of the area. Hoover is not cited in Lindgren's acknowledgements. In fact, Lindgren completed his field work on the Nevada City / Grass Valley region on June 28, 1894—three days before Hoover began to work as Lindgren's assistant on the U.S. Geological Survey. On the other hand, it is conceivable that during his two summers with Lindgren Hoover might have assisted him in his analysis and compilation of the raw data. At the very least Hoover would have known about Lindgren's minute study of these famous gold-mining districts and of the planned publication of the results. He would therefore have been in an ideal position to draw upon Lindgren's soon-to-be-published findings in the course of preparing technical data for Janin and the defendant company. See Waldemar Lindgren, Nevada City Special Folio, California [U.S. Geological Survey *Geologic Atlas of the United States*, Folio 29 (Washington, D.C., 1896)]; Waldemar Lindgren, "The Gold-Quartz Veins of Nevada City and Grass Valley Districts, California," in *Seventeenth Annual Report of the United States Geological Survey* (Washington, 1896), Part II, pp. 1–262 (especially pp. 13, 238–40, and Plate XXIII).

53. Herbert Hoover, "Some Notes on 'Crossings,' " *Mining and Scientific Press* 72 (February 29, 1896): 166–67. Waldemar Lindgren cited Hoover's article in his report, "The Gold-Quartz Veins of Nevada City and Grass Valley Districts, California," p. 240.

54. 73 *Federal Reporter* 597–603; *Mining and Scientific Press* 72 (March 21, 1896): 223; Hoover, "Information for Biographers," p. 4. The circuit court's decision was upheld on appeal: 83 *Federal Reporter* 658–69.

55. *Daily Palo Alto*, March 17, 1896, p. 6.

56. E. B. Kimball to Branner, April 8, 1896, Branner Papers, Box 26.

57. Walter W. Liggett, *The Rise of Herbert Hoover* (New York, 1932), p. 49. Liggett was a hostile biographer. But Liggett's papers at the New York Public Library indicate that he did correspond with Louis Janin's son Charles. There seems to be no reason to doubt Liggett's accuracy on this point.

58. Hoover, "Information for Biographers," pp. 4–5; Hoover, *Years of Adventure*, p. 27; Lane, *Making of Herbert Hoover*, p. 186; Hoover to R. H. Reynolds, January 4, 1921, "Reynolds, A.-W.," Commerce Papers, HHPL; Hoover to William R. Ridgway, July 29, 1962, Post-Presidential General File, HHPL. For information on the history of the Steeple Rock Development Company, the Carlisle mine, and the Steeple Rock district see: Fayette Jones, *New Mexico Mines and Minerals* (Santa Fe, 1904), p. 69; Waldemar Lindgren, Louis C. Graton, and Charles H. Gordon, *The Ore Deposits of New Mexico* (U.S. Geological Survey Professional Paper 68: Washington, D.C., 1920), pp. 327–28; Richard M. Atwater statement, December 31, 1931, Rickard files, Misrepresentations File, HHPL; Elliot Gillerman, *Mineral Deposits of Western Grant County, New Mexico* (New Mexico Bureau of Mines and Mineral Resources Bulletin No. 83: Socorro, New Mexico, 1964), pp. 180–83, 186–87; Paige W. Christiansen, *The Story of Mining in New Mexico* (Socorro, New Mexico, 1974), p. 76.

59. Hoover, *Years of Adventure*, p. 27.

60. Lane, *Making of Herbert Hoover*, pp. 186–91.

61. Hoover to R. H. Reynolds, January 4, 1921; George H. Utter to Engineers' Hoover Committee, May 28, 1920, "Utter, George H.," Pre-Commerce Papers, HHPL; Lane, *Making of Herbert Hoover*, pp. 186, 192–93.

62. Lane, *Making of Herbert Hoover*, pp. 187–90.

63. Ibid., 193. Lindgren's letter has not been located.

64. Hoover to Nell May Hill, November 9, 1894, Hill Family Papers.

65. Hoover's letter to Branner has not been located, either in the Branner Papers or the collections of Hoover papers. I have relied on Rose Wilder Lane's account (pp. 193–95), since Lane evidently saw Hoover's letter.

66. John C. Branner to Herbert Hoover, April 27, 1896, Branner Papers, Box 5. This letter is quoted in part in Lane, *Making of Herbert Hoover*, p. 196.
67. Theodore Hoover believed that he had a decisive influence in persuading Herbert to abandon "pure science and the U.S. Survey" for work with Janin and the more profitable field of gold mining. Theodore Hoover, *Memoranda*, p. 95.
68. Hoover to R. H. Reynolds, January 4, 1921.
69. Hoover, "Information for Biographers," p. 5; Hoover to Ridgway, July 29, 1962.
70. Louis Janin to his brother, June 8, 1896, quoted in Charles Janin (Louis's son) to Walter W. Liggett, July 30, 1931, Walter W. Liggett Papers, New York Public Library.
71. Hoover, "Information for Biographers," p. 5. Here Hoover recalled that he went to Colorado after his work in New Mexico. But in *Years of Adventure* he stated that he went to Colorado first and then to New Mexico (p. 27). Taking into account other sources already cited, including Louis Janin's letter cited in note 70, it seems certain that Hoover's work in New Mexico preceded his visit to Colorado.
72. Hoover, "Information for Biographers," p. 5. In Calaveras County Hoover inspected a mine for Captain Thomas Mein (see note 89).
73. Lane, *Making of Herbert Hoover*, p. 199; Theodore Hoover, *Memoranda*, p. 95.
74. This is what he told his close friend Ray Lyman Wilbur. Wilbur to his mother, August 31, 1896, quoted in *The Memoirs of Ray Lyman Wilbur* (Stanford, California, 1960), p. 73.
75. Herbert Hoover, "Mining Geology of Cripple Creek, Colorado," *Mining and Scientific Press* 73 (September 19, 1896): 237–38; [Hoover], "Responsibility for the Debris," ibid. 74 (January 9, 1897): 28; [Hoover], "The Mining Bureau and a Geological Survey," ibid. 74 (January 16, 1897): 46; [Hoover], "Shall the Debris Question be Reconsidered?" ibid.; Hoover, "Geologic Mapping of the Mother Lode," ibid. 74 (January 16, 1897): 52; Hoover, "Geology of the Four-Mile Placer Mining District, Colorado," *Engineering and Mining Journal*, 63 (May 22, 1897): 510. The anonymous papers are identified as Hoover's in a scrapbook containing clippings of his mining publications, in Herbert Hoover Collection, Box 230, HI.
76. Theodore Hoover, *Memoranda*, pp. 94–95; Hoover, *Years of Adventure*, p. 26.
77. The most accurate account of the Hoovers' various homes in Oakland and Berkeley is Homer R. Spence, *Presenting . . . Mr. Herbert Clark Hoover of Oakland, California, 1896* (typescript memorandum, 1970, plus enclosures), General Accessions, HHPL. Spence's monograph establishes that the Hoovers lived at several locations, including 1077 12th Street in Oakland and 2225 Ellsworth Street in Berkeley. Spence's memorandum also contains a photostat of Herbert Hoover's voter registration affidavit of August 10, 1896. In the first volume of his *Memoirs* Hoover states that he first registered to vote in Berkeley as a Republican (*Years of Adventure*, p. 28). The affidavit, however, reveals that he registered in Oakland and did not list any party affiliation. The affidavit did not provide for declaration of party affiliation. (It is conceivable, but highly unlikely, that Hoover registered elsewhere first and then re-registered in 1896 in Oakland. But there is no known record of this, and Hoover's 1896 affidavit states that he was not registered elsewhere in California.) Incidentally, Hoover did not vote in the presidential election of 1896. His preference, however, was clear. In his *Memoirs* he indicated his disapproval of the "intellectual dishonesty" of William Jennings Bryan's campaign (*Years of Adventure*, p. 28).
78. Theodore Hoover, *Memoranda*, p. 95.
79. Hoover, *Years of Adventure*, p. 23; Will Irwin, *The Making of a Reporter* (New York, 1942), p. 17.
80. Hoover, *Years of Adventure*, p. 28.
81. Wilson, *Herbert Hoover: A Challenge for Today*, pp. 32–33. Wilson had access to William H. Shockley's letter books in preparing her account.
82. *Mining and Scientific Press* 74 (March 27, 1897): 265. See also Hoover, "Information for Biographers," pp. 5–6. Hoover recalled that the offer from Bewick, Moreing came in October 1897 (*Years of Adventure*, p. 28). As will be seen further on in the text, however, Hoover left

San Francisco in March 1897 and reached Australia in May. As early as mid-February Hoover expected to go to Australia (E. B. Kimball to Branner, February 17, 1897, Branner Papers, Box 26).

Shockley's widow later stated that her husband had a more direct role in this matter. According to her account, Shockley was passing through San Francisco on his way to China when he received a cable from Moreing asking him to find a mining engineer to dispatch to Australia. Shockley went to Janin, who recommended Hoover. May Bradford Shockley oral history (1970), p. 3, HHPL.

83. Neither Hoover's *Memoirs* nor his earlier autobiographical statement ("Information for Biographers") explicitly mentions an age requirement. However, Vernon Kellogg's early campaign biography states that Bewick, Moreing requested a man at least thirty-five years old. Vernon Kellogg, *Herbert Hoover: The Man and His Work* (New York, 1920), p. 67. According to Rose Wilder Lane's biography, also published in 1920, the British firm wanted an engineer no more than thirty. For reasons given in note 97, I believe that Kellogg's version is probably correct.

84. Hoover, *Years of Adventure*, p. 28. Hoover told a friend in March 1897, "They [Bewick, Moreing & Co.] asked Mr. Janin to nominate them a man and to my surprise he nominated me." Hoover to R. A. F. Penrose, March 17, 1897, quoted in Helen R. Fairbanks and Charles P. Berkey, *Life and Letters of R. A. F. Penrose, Jr.* (New York, 1952), pp. 200–201.

85. Kellogg, *Herbert Hoover*, p. 67; Lane, *Making of Herbert Hoover*, p. 202. Hoover's own autobiographical reflections do not mention his growing a mustache and beard, but a contemporary photograph of him circa 1897 (photo no. 1897–1, HHPL) shows him with such facial features.

86. Hoover to R. A. F. Penrose, March 1, 1897, General Accession—R. A. F. Penrose, HHPL. Hoover had known Penrose for some time. Penrose had asked Hoover to inspect a mine for him and had offered Hoover the superintendency of it if Penrose purchased it. Hoover passed up this opportunity in order to go to Australia. E. B. Kimball to Branner, May 13, 1897, Branner Papers, Box 26. See also Fairbanks and Berkey, *Life and Letters of R. A. F. Penrose, Jr.*, pp. 199, 200.

87. Waldemar Lindgren to Louis Janin, March 8, 1897, "Mining—Lindgren, Waldemar," Pre-Commerce Papers, HHPL.

88. P. H. McDermott to Louis Janin, March 5, 1897, "Janin, Louis," Pre-Commerce Papers, HHPL.

89. Ben S. Cook to Louis Janin, March 5, 1897, ibid. Other letters of recommendation came from John C. Branner and a man named Mein—probably Captain Thomas Mein, the Pacific Coast representative of the London-based Exploration Company. (The Rothschild-influenced Exploration Company controlled the Steeple Rock Development Company in New Mexico.) Hoover to Penrose, March 1, 1897; *Engineering and Mining Journal* 62 (September 26, 1896): 299.

90. Hoover to Penrose, March 17, 1897.

91. On March 8, 1897 Janin told his brother that Hoover might go to Australia by way of London in a few weeks (quoted in Charles Janin to Walter Liggett, July 30, 1931). Hoover's appointment was not yet confirmed as of that date. Nor was it settled at the time of his letter to Penrose on March 17. In this letter he said that his letters of recommendation would reach London about March 20–21. But by March 20 Hoover was selling his surveyor's transit and other property to Henry K. Field, an agent for the New England Mutual Life Insurance Company. Sometime between March 17 and 20, 1897, therefore, Hoover's appointment with Bewick, Moreing evidently became final.

92. Hoover's list of items sold to Henry K. Field on March 20, 1897 and a document relating to a life insurance policy which he took out with the New England Life Insurance Company were retained by his friend Lester Hinsdale for many years. These and other original documents once belonging to Hinsdale are now at HHPL and are hereinafter designated as the Hinsdale Collection. As for Hoover's purchase of clothes before his trip to Australia, see Lane, *Making of Herbert Hoover*, pp. 201–2, and Irwin, *Herbert Hoover*, p. 75.

93. Theodore Hoover, *Memoranda*, p. 97.
94. Hoover, power of attorney dated March 24, 1897, Hinsdale Collection.
95. *Mining and Scientific Press* 74 (March 27, 1897): 265; *San Francisco Chronicle*, March 30, 1897.
96. *West Branch Times*, April 1, 1897, p. 1.
97. Register for voyage of the *Brittanic*, March 31, 1897, B.T. 26/102 X/1/9922, Public Record Office, Kew, Surrey, U.K.; copy in Rusty Sayers Collection, HHPL. See also a reconstructed itinerary for Hoover's trip to Australia in 1897, White Book, HHPL. The fact that Hoover concealed his true age and pretended that he was thirty-six suggests that Bewick, Moreing did indeed have an age requirement of thirty-five for its prospective appointee.

While in New York City Hoover visited a Stanford classmate, toured the Columbia School of Mines, and attended a vaudeville show. See the reminiscences of Newton B. Knox in *Sunday Oregonian* (Portland), February 17, 1929, Section 2, p. 14.

CHAPTER 5

1. Herbert Hoover, *The Memoirs of Herbert Hoover*, Volume I: *Years of Adventure* (New York, 1951), p. 30.
2. Ibid., p. 29; reconstructed itinerary of Hoover's 1897 trip to Australia, White Book, HHPL.
3. Hoover, *Years of Adventure*, p. 29; Hoover to Lester Hinsdale, April 14, 1897, Hinsdale Collection. See chapter 4, note 92. All other Hoover-to-Hinsdale letters cited below are from this source.
4. Hoover to Hinsdale, April 14, 1897.
5. Vernon Kellogg, *Herbert Hoover: The Man and His Work* (New York, 1920), p. 68.
6. Hoover to Hinsdale, April 14, 1897.
7. Hoover, *Years of Adventure*, p. 29.
8. Herbert Hoover membership file, Institution of Mining and Metallurgy, London. Hoover was elected an Associate in June 1897.
9. Hoover to Hinsdale, April 14, 1897.
10. Ibid.; Hoover to Hinsdale, May 21, 1897.
11. Hoover to his cousin Harriette Miles, n.d. [April 1897], extract in "Mining—Australia, Herbert Hoover's Accounts of Western Australia," Pre-Commerce Papers, HHPL. This letter was written at Brindisi, Italy. All other Hoover-to-Miles letters cited below are in this file, which consists of typed extracts of the original correspondence. Harriette Miles is identified as the recipient in a note attached to a copy of the extracts in General Accession—Hulda Hoover McLean, HHPL. In 1920 cousin Harriette copied these extracts from the Hoover letters in her possession and made the extracts available for use in Rose Wilder Lane's biography, *The Making of Herbert Hoover* (New York, 1920).
12. Albany, Western Australia, Water Police Office *Inward Report* for R.M.S. *Victoria*, May 13, 1897, copy in Rusty Sayers Collection, HHPL. This document contains the vessel's passenger list for this voyage and records that Hoover embarked at Brindisi, Italy for Albany, Western Australia.
13. Hoover to Hinsdale, May 21, 1897.
14. Albany, Western Australia, Water Police Office *Inward Report*, May 13, 1897; *Albany Advertiser*, May 15, 1897, p. 3 (lists "Mr. Hoorer" as a passenger); *Western Mail* (Perth, Western Australia), May 21, 1897, p. 16; Hoover to Hinsdale, May 21, 1897 (from Albany, Western Australia); Hoover, *Years of Adventure*, p. 30. See also Rusty Sayers to John M. Henry, April 6 and 7, 1974, Rusty Sayers Collection. The newspapers indicated that the quarantine would last five days. In a letter to Hinsdale dated May 21 and written on the stationery of an Albany hotel, Hoover stated that he had already been released "a few days ago" after being quarantined for ten days. But since he also stated that he had arrived on May 12 (actually May 13 according to the shipping report and the newspapers), he could not have been detained on the island for ten days. In *Years of Adventure* Hoover erroneously stated that he was quarantined for two weeks.
15. Hoover to Hinsdale, May 21, 1897; Hoover, *Years of Adventure*, p. 30.

16. John Bastin, "The West Australian Gold Fields, 1892–1900: The Investors and Their Grievances," *Historical Studies: Australia and New Zealand* 6 (November 1954): 282.

17. T. A. Rickard, "The Alluvial Deposits of Western Australia," *Mining and Scientific Press* 78 (March 4, 1899): 238.

18. Gavin Casey and Ted Mayman, *The Mile That Midas Touched* (rev. ed.: Adelaide, 1968), p. 106.

19. Rickard, "Alluvial Deposits," p. 238.

20. Hoover to Burt Brown Barker, October 25, 1897, Burt Brown Barker Collection, HHPL.

21. Hoover to Harriette Miles, n.d. [mid-1897]; Hoover, *Years of Adventure*, p. 31.

22. My account of Western Australia in the 1890s is based on the following sources: Casey and Mayman, *The Mile That Midas Touched;* John Bastin, "The West Australian Gold Fields, 1892–1900: The Investors and Their Grievances," *Historical Studies: Australia and New Zealand* 6 (November 1954): 282–89; Geoffrey Blainey, *The Rush That Never Ended: A History of Australian Mining* (Melbourne, 1963); F. K. Crowley, *Australia's Western Third: A History of Western Australia from the First Settlements to Modern Times* (London, 1960); Malcolm Maclaren and J. Allan Thomson, "Geology of the Kalgoorlie Goldfield—I," *Mining and Scientific Press* 107 (July 12, 1913): 45–48; and W. P. Morrell, *The Gold Rushes* (London, 1940; rev. ed., 1968), pp. 294–312.

23. *Coolgardie Miner*, May 22, 1897, p. 7; *Coolgardie Pioneer*, May 29, 1897, p. 17. This same announcement was printed a few weeks later in the *Australian Mining Standard* 13 (June 17, 1897): 1949.

24. *West Australian Goldfields Courier*, June 19, 1897, p. 17.

25. Herbert Hoover, "Mining Geology of Cripple Creek, Colorado," *Mining and Scientific Press* 73 (September 19, 1896): 237–38.

26. Albany, Western Australia, Water Police Office *Inward Report*, May 13, 1897; Maclaren and Thomson, "Geology of the Kalgoorlie Goldfield—I," p. 48.

27. Lane, *Making of Herbert Hoover*, p. 209.

28. J. W. McCarty, "British Investment in Western Australian Gold Mining, 1894–1914," *University Studies in History* 4 (1961–62): 13.

29. Bastin, "The West Australian Goldfields, 1892–1900," p. 283.

30. *Engineering and Mining Journal* 64 (December 18, 1897): 722.

31. McCarty, "British Investment in Western Australian Gold Mining," p. 13.

32. Maclaren and Thomson, "Geology of the Kalgoorlie Goldfield—I," p. 48.

33. The foregoing remarks on the Westralian mining boom and the discovery of gold at depth are based on the sources cited in note 22 and two others: J. W. McCarty, "British Investment in Western Australian Gold Mining, 1894–1914," *University Studies in History* 4 (1961–62): 7–23, and D. Mossenson, "Mining Regulations and Alluvial Disputes, 1894–1904," *University Studies in History and Economics* 2 (September 1955): 5–31.

34. Hoover to R. A. F. Penrose, April 12, 1897, quoted in Helen R. Fairbanks and Charles P. Berkey, *Life and Letters of R. A. F. Penrose, Jr.* (New York, 1952), p. 201.

35. Hoover to Hinsdale, April 14, 1897.

36. According to Bewick, Moreing & Co., Hoover's initial salary was £1,000, or about $5,000. Bewick, Moreing & Co. statement regarding Hoover, n.d. (ca. 1916), Bewick, Moreing & Co. Collection, HHPL.

37. Hoover, "Information for Biographers" (typescript, n.d.; probably ca. 1914), p. 6, in Benjamin S. Allen Papers, Box 1, HI, and Pre-Commerce Papers, HHPL.

38. Hoover, *Years of Adventure*, p. 30.

39. Lane, *Making of Herbert Hoover*, p. 208.

40. Hoover to Harriette Miles, n.d.; Hoover to Burt Brown Barker, October 25, 1897.

41. Hoover report on pumping plant for Hannan's Brownhill mine, June 16, 1897. As of 1978 this document and certain other Hoover reports cited below were in the possession of the Western Australian government's Department of Mines, Perth, Western Australia, hereinafter designated as Department of Mines, W.A.

42. Hoover, *Years of Adventure*, p. 31.
43. This is how he identified his position with Bewick, Moreing on his application form for membership in the Institution of Mining and Metallurgy.
44. Hoover, "Information for Biographers," p. 6.
45. See, for example, Hoover report on Menzies Gold Estates, June 7, 1897, Department of Mines, W.A., and Hoover to Harriette Miles, July 16, 1897. See also Dare Stark McMullin Research Notes, in Special Collections—*Memoirs*, Background Materials, HHPL; hereinafter cited as McMullin Research Notes.
46. Hoover to Hinsdale, July 9, 1897.
47. Hoover to Harriette Miles, July 16, 1897; Hoover reports on Lakeway Gold Mines, Ltd. and Golden Age Lease, August 9 and 18, 1897, Department of Mines, W.A.
48. Hoover to Hinsdale, September 11, 1897.
49. Hoover to Harriette Miles, July 16, 1897.
50. See, for example, Hoover's reports on the Mt. Eva and Goodenough Leases (June 8, 1897), the Kinambla (Wealth of Nations), Ltd. (July 13, 1897), the Great Eastern Extended Gold Mine (August 23, 1897), the Abbott's Mt. Pascoe Leases (November 1, 1897), and the proposed amalgamation of Bank of England Lease, Oroya East Lease, and North Boulder East Lease (November 1, 1897): all at Department of Mines, W.A. In this last report Hoover used the term "conservative mining."
51. Hoover report on East Murchison United, Ltd., August 21, 1897, Department of Mines, W.A.
52. Hoover to Hinsdale, July 9, 1897 and September 11, 1897; Hoover to Harriette Miles, October 6, 1897.
53. Hoover to Harriette Miles, August 9 and October 6, 1897.
54. McMullin Research Notes.
55. Herbert Hoover, "Mining and Milling Gold Ores in Western Australia," *Engineering and Mining Journal* 66 (December 17, 1898): 725–26.
56. Hoover report on Kinambla (Wealth of Nations), Ltd., July 13, 1897, Department of Mines, W.A.
57. Hoover report on a reconnaissance trip for the London and Western Australian Exploration Company, October 11, 1897, Department of Mines, W.A.
58. Hoover to Hinsdale, July 9, 1897.
59. Hoover to Harriette Miles, August 5, 1897.
60. Hoover to Hinsdale, September 11, 1897.
61. Hoover to Harriette Miles, October 6, 1897.
62. Hoover to Hinsdale, July 9, 1897.
63. Hoover to Barker, October 25, 1897.
64. Hoover to R. A. F. Penrose, April 2, 1898, quoted in Fairbanks and Berkey, *Life and Letters of R. A. F. Penrose, Jr.*, p. 202.
65. Hoover, "Mining and Milling Gold Ores in Western Australia," p. 725.
66. Hoover to Hinsdale, July 9, 1897.
67. Hoover to Hinsdale, September 11, 1897.
68. Hoover to Harriette Miles, August 9, 1897.
69. Hoover / Mitchell report on the East Murchison United, Ltd., November 10, 1897, Department of Mines, W.A. This document indicates that Mitchell reported on the mine and that Hoover revised the report.
70. Hoover report on the East Murchison United, Ltd., February 1, 1898, Department of Mines, W.A.
71. Ibid.
72. Lane, *Making of Herbert Hoover*, pp. 220–221; George B. Wilson statement contained in a letter from Charles K. Field to the editor, *Mining and Scientific Press* 121 (November 13, 1920): 687–88. Wilson, a Stanford friend who joined Hoover in Australia early in 1898, was a major source of information for Lane's biography.

73. [J. H. Curle], "The Gold Mines of Western Australia," *Economist* 56 (July 23, 1898): 1074–75.
74. Deane P. Mitchell, letter dated November 16, 1897, printed in *Palo Alto Times* [California], February 7, 1898, pp. 2–3.
75. Hoover to Barker, October 25, 1897.
76. This was a comment made by Hoover and cited by George B. Wilson in a letter to Lester Hinsdale, January 30, 1898, Hinsdale Collection.
77. Hoover, *Years of Adventure*, p. 32; George B. Wilson to Lester Hinsdale, February 4, 1898, Hinsdale Collection.
78. Hoover to Newton B. Knox, quoted in an article of reminiscences by Knox in *Sunday Oregonian* (Portland), February 17, 1929, Section 2, p. 14.
79. Hoover to Hinsdale, September 11, 1897.
80. Hoover to Harriette Miles, September 17, 1897.
81. Hoover to Hinsdale, September 11, 1897. In this letter he referred to the disease as "barcoute." No doubt he meant barcoo rot, also known as desert sore.
82. Hoover to Barker, October 25, 1897.
83. Hoover to Hinsdale, September 11, 1897.
84. Casey and Mayman, *The Mile That Midas Touched*, p. 51.
85. Hoover to Harriette Miles, July 16, 1897; Hoover, *Years of Adventure*, pp. 32–33.
86. Hoover to Harriette Miles, July 16, 1897.
87. [George J. Bancroft], "Hoover and His Camel" (typescript, n.d.), copy supplied to the author by Mr. Bancroft's daughter, Mrs. Robert LeBaron. An unsigned copy is also in the Carol Green Wilson Papers, Box 7, HI.
88. Hoover, *Years of Adventure*, p. 32.
89. Hoover to Harriette Miles, August 5, 1897.
90. Chris A. Russell to Herbert Hoover, October 17, 1932, "Hoover, Herbert—Misrepresentations, Miscellaneous," President's Personal File, HHPL; W. S. Robinson, *If I Remember Rightly* (Melbourne, 1967), p. 39.
91. Hoover to Hinsdale, July 9, 1897.
92. Hoover to Hinsdale, September 11, 1897.
93. Hoover to Barker, October 25, 1897.
94. Hoover to Hinsdale, November 22, 1897.
95. Hoover to Hinsdale, July 9, 1897. For Hoover's remarks on aborigines, see Hoover to Harriette Miles, n.d.
96. For information on the discovery and early (pre-Hoover) history of the Sons of Gwalia mine, see: interview with George W. Hall, *Australian Mail* 7 (March 24, 1898): 384–85; interview with Hall, *British Australasian* 16 (March 24, 1898): 648–52; speech by Hall, printed in *Australian Mail* 7 (March 31, 1898): 414–15; Don and Donna Reid, *Leonora and Gwalia: An Historical Sketchbook* (Leonora, W.A., 1976), pp. 1–3. The account given here, and in the three paragraphs that follow, is based on these sources.
97. Hall interview, *Australian Mail* 7 (March 24, 1898): 384.
98. Hall speech *Australian Mail* 7 (March 31, 1898): 415.
99. Ibid.
100. Interview with Hall in *Coolgardie Miner*, October 19, 1897.
101. *Australian Mail* 6 (November 11, 1897): 535.
102. News report from Mount Leonora, W.A., June 23, 1897, printed in *Australian Mail* 6 (August 12, 1897): 255.
103. McMullin Research Notes; Hoover to Hinsdale, July 9, 1897; Hoover to Harriette Miles, July 16, 1897.
104. Hoover to Harriette Miles, July 16, 1897. In this letter Hoover stated that the Sons of Gwalia (and thirteen other mines) all "belong to our companies," but I have found no evidence that the Sons of Gwalia had any connection with Hoover's principals as yet.
105. McMullin Research Notes.
106. Hoover, *Years of Adventure*, p. 33.

107. Hoover, "Information for Biographers," p. 6.

108. Ibid.

109. McMullin Research Notes.

110. Bewick, Moreing & Co.—London, cable 131C to its Coolgardie office, August 18, 1897, in Sons of Gwalia Records, J. S. Battye Library, Perth, Western Australia; copy in Australia Collections, HHPL. Copies of other cables in this series, cited below, are also in the Australia Collections at HHPL.

111. Bewick, Moreing & Co.—Coolgardie, cable 134C to London office, August 19, 1897, ibid.

112. Bewick, Moreing & Co.—London, cable 132C to Coolgardie office, August 19, 1897, ibid.

113. McMullin Research Notes. See also Bewick, Moreing & Co.—Coolgardie, cable 142C to London office, August 29, 1897, Sons of Gwalia Records.

114. Bewick, Moreing & Co.—Coolgardie, cable 149C to London office, September 11, 1897, Sons of Gwalia Records. According to the McMullin Research Notes, Hoover recommended the Gwalia on August 29. Probably this was the day of his decision to recommend or the day he notified the Coolgardie office of his decision.

115. Hoover to Harriette Miles, September 17, 1897. In a letter to Hinsdale on September 11 (the same day as the important cable to London) Hoover mentioned that he had in recent weeks examined three major mines and had recommended one "for $400,000 and it has been paid over." But this appears to have been an unrelated transaction.

116. Hoover report on the Sons of Gwalia mine ("in compliance with London office Cable No. 131C"), October 6, 1897, Department of Mines, W.A. This document, which was initialed by Hoover personally, does not mention any possible purchase price. Nor do any cables that I have seen. In his *Memoirs*, however, Hoover asserted that when he finished examining the mine he "recommended the purchase of a two-thirds interest for $250,000 and a provision of $250,000 working capital" (*Years of Adventure*, p. 33). This is possible, but no contemporary evidence has been found establishing that Hoover had any say about financial terms.

117. *Menzies Miner* (Menzies, Western Australia), October 9, 1897, p. 22.

118. Throughout the second half of 1897, such London journals as the *Statist* and *Australian Mail* reported the Sons of Gwalia's gold production. See, for example, *Australian Mail* 6 (November 11, 1897): 535. On the rising interest by rival syndicates, see *Coolgardie Miner*, January 15, 1898, p. 7. Earlier, on November 25, 1897, the *British Australasian* (another London periodical) reported that "a bevy of powerful combinations" was bidding for ownership of the Sons of Gwalia. Quoted in *The "Sons of Gwalia"* (promotional booklet), p. 38, Sons of Gwalia Records. See also interview of C. Algernon Moreing in *Australian Mail* 7 (December 2, 1897): 32.

119. *Coolgardie Miner*, January 15, 1898, p. 7.

120. Prospectus for Sons of Gwalia, Ltd., January 11, 1898, Sons of Gwalia Records; proceedings of first ordinary general meeting of Sons of Gwalia, Ltd., printed in *Australian Mail* 7 (May 5, 1898): 492. See also *Menzies Miner*, December 4, 1897, p. 8. The purchase price was £50,000 in cash plus a one-third interest in a company to be formed to take over the mine. That is, Moreing's company paid Pritchard Morgan and associates £50,000 in cash for the property and promised to give them 100,000 shares (one-third) of the stock of the new company, when it was floated. Moreing's company also promised to provide the still-unformed new company with £50,000 in working capital. *Coolgardie Miner*, January 13, 1898, p. 5; *Australian Mail* 7 (January 13, 1898): 185, and 7 (March 31, 1898): 411, 415.

121. Cable from Perth dated November 23, 1897, printed in *Australian Mail* 7 (November 25, 1897): 17.

122. See Bewick, Moreing & Co.—Coolgardie, cable 168C to London office, October 26, 1897; London reply, cable 153C, October 26, 1897, Sons of Gwalia Records. The London office wanted its men in the field to delay this additional examination "as much as possible." It is not known why. Perhaps the would-be purchaser (Moreing) had not completed negotiations with the mine's owners.

123. McMullin Research Notes.

124. Bewick, Moreing & Co.—Coolgardie, cable to "Morganatic," London, November 26, 1897, Sons of Gwalia Records. This cable was sent directly to the Pritchard Morgan interests at the request of Bewick, Moreing & Co.—London. See its cable 168C, November 18, 1897, to its Coolgardie office, Sons of Gwalia Records.

125. Hoover report on Sons of Gwalia mine (for London and Westralian Mines and Finance Agency, Ltd.), November 30, 1897, Department of Mines, W.A. This report was initialed ("HCH") by Hoover.

126. Hoover, cable 189C to Bewick, Moreing & Co.—London, November 26, 1897, Sons of Gwalia Records. In the upper left-hand corner of this copy is the penciled notation "HCH."

127. Bewick, Moreing & Co.—London, cable 172C to Hoover, November 27, 1897, ibid. In the upper left-hand corner of this copy is the penciled notation "HCH."

128. See, for instance, *British Australasian* 15 (December 2, 1897): 2223, and *Australian Mail* 7 (November 25, 1897): 11–12.

129. See, for example, *Australian Mail* 7 (November 25, 1897): 11–12, and 7 (December 2, 1897): 27, 31–32; *Statist* 40 (November 27, 1897): 826; *British Australasian* 15 (December 2, 1897): 2223; *Coolgardie Miner*, December 31, 1897, p. 7. Much press commentary was collected and reprinted in *The "Sons of Gwalia,"* a promotional booklet distributed in London early in 1898. A copy of this booklet is in the Sons of Gwalia Records.

130. *Australian Mail* 7 (January 6, 1898): 157, and 7 (March 31, 1898): 409; report of Archibald E. Burt, Warden, Mount Margaret Goldfield, for the year 1897, in Western Australia, Department of Mines Report for 1897, p. 60, printed in Western Australia, *Votes and Proceedings of Parliament*, 3rd Parliament, 3rd Session, 1898, p. 1361. Warden Burt judged the Sons of Gwalia mine "the best, so far" on the Mt. Margaret Goldfield.

131. Prospectus for Sons of Gwalia, Ltd., January 11, 1898. The company was incorporated on January 7, 1898.

132. Ibid.; *Australian Mail* 7 (January 13, 1898): 192; *Coolgardie Miner*, January 13, 1898, p. 5, and January 15, 1898, p. 7. Thus in return for a total cash outlay of £100,000 (£50,000 to the Pritchard Morgan interest and £50,000 promised to the Sons of Gwalia, Ltd. for working capital), Moreing's company found itself in sole possession of 200,000 shares (a two-thirds interest) in the new company. The other 100,000 shares (a one-third interest) were allotted to the Pritchard Morgan group (the previous owner) by the prior purchase agreement of November 17, 1897. Moreing's interest therefore became what Hoover in his *Memoirs* said he himself originally recommended. See notes 116 and 120.

133. Moreing's company, in return for a total cash commitment of £100,000, held outright 200,000 shares credited as completely paid for. These were nominally valued at £200,000. Since Sons of Gwalia shares on the first day of trading sold at over twice this value, Moreing theoretically could have sold out entirely for over £400,000 and thereby made a profit of £300,000, or about $1,500,000. There is no evidence that he did so at first. But by late 1899 Moreing's London and Western Australian Exploration Company held only 43,459 shares in the Sons of Gwalia, Ltd.—far less than its original block. See proceedings of fourth ordinary general meeting of London and Western Australian Exploration Company, printed in *British Australasian* 17 (December 7, 1899): 1916.

134. *Coolgardie Miner*, January 15, 1898, p. 7.

135. Comment by "Our Special Correspondent" [in Coolgardie], *Australian Mail* 7 (February 17, 1898): 288.

136. Sons of Gwalia prospectus, January 11, 1898, reprinted in *Mining Journal, Railway and Commercial Gazette* 68 (January 15, 1898): 67.

137. Interview of Moreing in *Australian Mail* 7 (December 2, 1897): 32.

138. Interview with Edward Hooper in *Australian Mail* 7 (February 10, 1898): 265 (full interview: 264–66).

139. *Coolgardie Miner*, January 15, 1898, p. 7. See also *Australian Mail* 7 (February 24, 1898): 313.

140. Hoover to Hinsdale, November 22, 1897.

141. See, for example, the interview with Hoover in the Perth, W.A. *Morning Herald*, reprinted in *Australian Mail* 7 (February 24, 1898): 313.
142. Coolgardie Chamber of Mines *Monthly Return*, January 1898; J. W. Kirwan, "Hoover in Western Australia: Some Goldfields Memories," n.d. (late 1928), Reprint File, HHPL. According to Hoover's *Memoirs (Years of Adventure*, p. 31), he was a member of "an advisory board of the mine operators on water supply"—an apparent reference to a committee of the Coolgardie Chamber of Mines.
143. "Nemo" [Eugene W. Hine], "Hoover in W.A.: Memories and Musings," *Sydney Morning Herald*, November 19, 1928. In 1898 Hine was secretary of the Coolgardie Chamber of Mines; he met Hoover frequently.
144. Kirwan, "Hoover in Western Australia." This article appeared in condensed form in the *Adelaide Advertiser*, November 8, 1928.
145. Coolgardie correspondent's column dated March 11, 1898, in *Australian Mail* 7 (April 21, 1898): 462.
146. J. H. Curle, *Travels and Men* (London, 1935), p. 144.
147. Kirwan, "Hoover in Western Australia."
148. Jules Raeside, *Golden Days* (Perth, 1929), p. 60.
149. Kirwan, "Hoover in Western Australia."
150. Richard M. Atwater interview, ca. 1931, Walter W. Liggett Papers, New York Public Library.
151. McMullin Research Notes.
152. Hoover to Hinsdale, November 22, 1897; Hoover telegram to George B. Wilson, December 2, 1897, Hinsdale Collection; *Australian Mail* 7 (January 13, 1898): 190, and 7 (March 3, 1898): 331.
153. See, for example, *Coolgardie Miner*, January 14, 1898, p. 7; January 15, 1898, p. 7; and February 3, 1898, p. 7; and *Western Argus* (Kalgoorlie), March 10, 1898, p. 16; *Malcolm Chronicle and Leonora Advertiser*, April 16, 1898, p. 2.
154. *Coolgardie Miner*, February 3, 1898, p. 7; George B. Wilson to Lester Hinsdale, February 4, 1898, Hinsdale Collection; *Western Australian Goldfields Courier*, February 5, 1898, p. 25.
155. *Coolgardie Miner*, February 28, 1898, p. 7; *Australian Mail* 7 (April 21, 1898): 462.
156. *Western Argus*, March 10, 1898, p. 16; *Coolgardie Miner*, March 18, 1898, p. 7; Hoover to Hinsdale, March 19, 1898; *Coolgardie Miner*, March 24, 1898, p. 7, and March 26, 1898, p. 7; McMullin Research Notes.
157. Coolgardie correspondent's column dated March 11, 1898, in *Australian Mail* 7 (April 21, 1898): 462.
158. *Coolgardie Miner*, March 18, 24, and 26, 1898, p. 7 (for each report); *Malcolm Chronicle and Leonora Advertiser*, April 16, 1898, p. 2.
159. Warden Archibald E. Burt's report (cited in note 130); *Coolgardie Miner*, February 3, 1898, p. 7; *Malcolm Chronicle and Leonora Advertiser*, April 16, 1898, p. 2; *Australian Mail* 7 (April 21, 1898): 462; Bewick, Moreing & Co.—Coolgardie to Hoover, May 11, 1898, Sons of Gwalia Records.
160. *Australian Mail* 7 (April 21, 1898): 462; *Mining World and Engineering Record* 54 (May 7, 1898): 827. By agreement the Sons of Gwalia mine was being operated for the profit of the Sons of Gwalia, Ltd. from November 17, 1897 on. *Australian Mail* 7 (May 5, 1898): 492.
161. *Coolgardie Miner*, January 6, 1898, p. 7; interview with Hooper in *Australian Mail* 7 (February 10, 1898): 264–66.
162. *Australian Mail* 7 (January 13, 1898): 190, and Hooper interview in *Australian Mail* 7 (February 10, 1898): 265.
163. Hoover to Hinsdale, March 23, 1897. Many years later Edward Hooper confirmed that Hoover and Williams did not get along. According to Hooper this fact led him to suggest that Hoover be appointed superintendent of the Sons of Gwalia in 1898 (Edward Hooper to C. M. Harris, November 7, 1947, Accession 444A, J. S. Battye Library). This assertion seems doubtful. As already mentioned, Moreing promised Hoover the superintendency of

the Sons of Gwalia on November 26, 1897— several weeks before Williams took over. On the other hand, Williams arrived in Coolgardie by November 13, while Hoover was on a trip north (*Coolgardie Miner*, November 15, 1897, p. 7). Conceivably Hoover and Williams met before November 26 and took a disliking to each other, thus leading Hooper to suggest Hoover for the Gwalia post.

Incidentally, in his letter of November 7, 1947 to Harris, Hooper implied that he, not Hoover, was chiefly responsible for the acquisition of the Sons of Gwalia by Moreing's exploration company. However, in a subsequent letter Hooper acknowledged that the chief credit for the purchase belonged to Hoover. It was only after receiving Hoover's favorable inspection report that Hooper then urged the London and Western Australian Exploration Company to buy the mine. Hoover's report was clearly the catalyst in this chain of events, as Hooper publicly recognized at the time (Hooper to C. M. Harris, April 8, 1948, Accession 444A, J. S. Battye Library).

164. Lane, *Making of Herbert Hoover*, pp. 222–23; Casey and Mayman, *The Mile That Midas Touched*, p. 93; Atwater interview, Liggett Papers. Apparently Williams was (or became) known as the "irascible little Welshman," although he was also highly respected and competent.

165. Hoover to Hinsdale, March 23, 1898. Hoover's contemporary statements about his earnings were sometimes confusing. Starting at an annual salary of $6,000 (£1,200) plus expenses (as reported to Hinsdale in April 1897), Hoover stated that he reached a level of about $8,000 a year in September 1897 and more than $10,000 a year in November. On March 23, 1898 he gave his income as £1,200 (only about $6,000) plus an interest in company profits. Yet a Bewick, Moreing account sheet for January–March 1898 showed his basic annual salary as £1,000, not £1,200. Moreover, on March 23 he told Hinsdale that the new Sons of Gwalia position and related responsibilities would yield £2,000 (about $10,000) annually, plus a portion of some profits. But only seven days later he told another friend that this new job would have a salary of $18,000 (£3,600) "and some perquisites." A month later, when he actually assumed the new position, he reported to Hinsdale that his income would be $12,500 (£2,500) plus some annual fees, for an expected $15,000. in all. But Bewick, Moreing's accounts show that from April to June his general salary remained at £1,000 ($5,000) per year. In July, however, it became £2,000 ($10,000) per year (as Hoover had told Hinsdale in March), including £1,500 as manager of the Sons of Gwalia and £500 as the company's representative in the district around Leonora. It remained at this level until he left Australia.

These figures may not be inconsistent, since one does not know enough about Hoover's profit-sharing arrangements or whether he included projected reimbursable expenses in some of the above figures. This information on his earnings in Australia is derived from Hoover to Hinsdale, April 14, July 9, September 11, and November 22, 1897, and March 23 and April 30, 1898; also Hoover to Ben Cook, March 30, 1898, in Ethel Rensch Papers and Burt Brown Barker Collection, HHPL; also various "Staff Lists" for 1898 in a folder entitled "Bewick, Moreing and Co. West Australian office accounts 1898–1900," in the possession of Mr. G. M. S. Leader, a retired Bewick, Moreing partner living in England.

166. Hoover to Ben Cook, March 30, 1898. The "deal" to which he referred was probably the Sons of Gwalia flotation. This figure of $1,500,000 in profits is consistent with Moreing's £300,000 profit discussed in note 133.

167. See Kirwan, "Hoover in Western Australia," and Raeside, *Golden Days*, pp. 61–62.

168. Hoover to Hinsdale, April 14, 1897.

169. Hoover to Hinsdale, July 9, 1897.

170. Hoover to Hinsdale, April 14, 1897 and May 11, 1898.

171. Hoover to Hinsdale, April 14, 1897, March 19 and April 30, 1898.

172. Hoover to Hinsdale, July 9, 1897.

173. Hoover to Hinsdale, February 28, 1899.

174. Hoover to Hinsdale, September 11, 1897.

175. Hoover to Hinsdale, April 14, 1897.

176. Ibid.

177. Ray Lyman Wilbur, *The Memoirs of Ray Lyman Wilbur* (Stanford, 1960), p. 74.

178. Newton B. Knox reminiscences in *Sunday Oregonian* (Portland), February 17, 1929, Section 2, p. 14.

179. Hoover to Hinsdale, March 19, 1898.

180. *Coolgardie Miner*, April 22, 1898, p. 7; April 25, 1898, p. 7; and April 28, 1898, p. 7; *Coolgardie Pioneer*, April 30, 1898, pp. 24, 29.

181. Bewick, Moreing "Staff List" for July–September 1898, in possession of Mr. Leader. See also note 165.

182. Hoover to Hinsdale, March 23, 1898; Hoover to Cook, March 30, 1898; *Coolgardie Miner*, April 22, 1898, p. 7.

183. *Coolgardie Miner*, April 25, 1898, p. 7.

184. Ibid. This article was also printed in the *Coolgardie Pioneer*, April 30, 1898, p. 24. Possibly it was a press release by Bewick, Moreing & Co.

CHAPTER 6

1. Hoover to Lester Hinsdale, April 30, 1898, Hinsdale Collection. See chapter 4, note 92. All other Hoover-to-Hinsdale letters cited below are from this source.

Hoover's statement that he had charge of 250 men appears to be contradicted by the local mine warden's observation a month later that only 130 men were employed at the Sons of Gwalia mine. Warden Archibald E. Burt to Secretary, Crown Law Department in Perth, May 30, 1898, Burt's letter book #3, p. 321, J. S. Battye Library, Perth, Western Australia. Perhaps Hoover was counting the men at the East Murchison United mine and others for which he was a consulting engineer. Perhaps also he substantially reduced the work force at the Sons of Gwalia during his first month as manager before Burt wrote the letter cited here.

2. Hoover to Hinsdale, April 30, 1898.

3. A contemporary photograph of Hoover as manager of the Sons of Gwalia shows him with a mustache, and his hair parted in the middle. See *The Leader* (Melbourne), supplement, September 1898, p. 33.

4. Coolgardie correspondent's column, March 11, 1898, in *Australian Mail* 7 (April 21, 1898): 462.

5. See D. Mossenson, "Mining Regulations and Alluvial Disputes, 1894–1904," *University Studies in History and Economics* 2 (September 1955): 11–12.

6. *Malcolm Chronicle and Leonora Advertiser*, April 23, 1898, p. 7, and April 30, 1898, p. 3.

7. Hoover to Bewick, Moreing & Co.—Coolgardie (hereinafter generally cited as "Coolgardie office"), May 9, 1898, in Hoover's letter book as Sons of Gwalia superintendent, pp. 19–20, HHPL. A microfilm copy of this important source (hereinafter cited as "Letter Book") is at the J. S. Battye Library, Perth, Western Australia. On p. 19 of the Letter Book itself certain words quoted here are illegible. These missing words are supplied, however, from an extract from this letter quoted in Bewick, Moreing & Co.—Coolgardie to T. W. Wellsted (Secretary, Sons of Gwalia, Ltd.), May 13, 1898, Sons of Gwalia Records, J. S. Battye Library.

8. Hoover to Coolgardie office, May 10, 1898, Letter Book.

9. Hoover to Pietro Ceruti, May 12, 1898, Letter Book.

10. *Malcolm Chronicle and Leonora Advertiser*, May 14, 1898, p. 3.

11. Hoover to Coolgardie office, May 23, 1898, Letter Book.

12. Hoover, "Mining and Milling Gold Ores in Western Australia," *Engineering and Mining Journal* 66 (December 17, 1898): 725; Geoffrey Blainey, *The Rush That Never Ended* (Melbourne, 1963), p. 195.

13. Blainey, *The Rush That Never Ended*, p. 195.
14. Bewick, Moreing & Co.—London to Coolgardie office, May 6, 1898, enclosed in Coolgardie office to Hoover, July 28, 1898, Sons of Gwalia Records.
15. Hoover to Ceruti, May 28 and June 27, 1898, Letter Book.
16. Bewick, Moreing & Co.—London to Coolgardie office, May 6, 1898, Sons of Gwalia Records.
17. See Bewick, Moreing & Co.—Coolgardie cable to "Morganatic," London, November 26, 1897, Sons of Gwalia Records; Hoover report of November 30, 1897 on Sons of Gwalia (see note 23).
18. Bewick, Moreing & Co.—Coolgardie, General Managers' Quarterly Report on Sons of Gwalia for May–July 1898, dated August 20, 1898, Sons of Gwalia Records.
19. Hoover to Coolgardie office, May 9, 1898, Letter Book.
20. Hoover to Coolgardie office, May 12, 1898, Letter Book.
21. Hoover to T. W. Wellsted, May 30, 1898; Hoover progress report for month of May, dated June 1, 1898; both in Letter Book.
22. Bewick, Moreing & Co.—Coolgardie, Quarterly Report on Sons of Gwalia for May–July 1898, dated August 20, 1898. A few months earlier George W. Hall defended his policy of rapid exploitation as necessary in order to meet large initial expenses. See interview of Hall in *British Australasian* 16 (March 24, 1898): 648–52; Hall's speech quoted in *Australian Mail* 7 (March 31, 1898): 414–15; Hall's comments at first Sons of Gwalia shareholders meeting, reported in *Australian Mail* 7 (May 5, 1898): 492–93.
23. See Hoover's reports on Sons of Gwalia, October 6 and especially November 30, 1897, at the Western Australian government's Department of Mines, Perth, Western Australia (hereinafter designated as Department of Mines, W.A.); cables 149C (September 9, 1897) and 165C (October 22, 1897), Sons of Gwalia Records.
24. Hoover to Coolgardie office, May 9, 1898, Letter Book.
25. Hoover to Coolgardie office, May 16 and 23, 1898; Hoover progress report for May, dated June 1, 1898; all in Letter Book. According to Hoover these changes increased the extraction rate from 45% to 71%.
26. Hoover to Coolgardie office, May 31, 1898, Letter Book.
27. Hoover progress report for May, dated June 1, 1898, Letter Book.
28. Hoover, *The Memoirs of Herbert Hoover*, Volume I: *Years of Adventure* (New York, 1951), p. 34.
29. *Malcolm Chronicle and Leonora Advertiser*, June 11, 1898, p. 2.
30. Bewick, Moreing & Co.—Coolgardie, Quarterly Report on Sons of Gwalia for May–July, dated August 20, 1898.
31. Hoover to Coolgardie office, May 9 and 28, 1898, Letter Book; Hoover to T. W. Wellsted, May 30, 1898, Letter Book; Hoover progress report for May, dated June 1, 1898, Letter Book.
32. Hoover report on the East Murchison United, Ltd., August 21, 1897, at Department of Mines, W.A.
33. Hoover to Coolgardie office, May 9, 1898, Letter Book.
34. See sources cited in note 31 and also Hoover weekly progress report, June 18, 1898, Letter Book; Hoover monthly progress report, June 30, 1898, Letter Book; Hoover monthly progress report, July 31, 1898, Department of Mines, W.A.
35. Hoover to Wellsted, May 30, 1898, Letter Book. See in general the sources cited in notes 31 and 34.
36. Ibid.; Bewick, Moreing & Co.—Coolgardie, Quarterly Report on Sons of Gwalia for May–July 1898, dated August 20, 1898 (sent to London).
37. Hoover to Coolgardie office, May 26, 1898, Letter Book.
38. Coolgardie office to Hoover, May 31, 1898, Sons of Gwalia Records.
39. Hoover to Coolgardie office, June 28, 1898, Letter Book.
40. Hoover to Coolgardie office, June 18, 1898, Letter Book.

41. Hoover to Coolgardie office, May 26, 1898, Letter Book.
42. Williams to Hoover, May 23, 1898, Sons of Gwalia Records.
43. Hoover to Coolgardie office, May 26, 1898, Letter Book.
44. Ibid. See also Hoover to Coolgardie office, May 16, 1898, Letter Book.
45. Hoover to Coolgardie office, May 26, 1898, Letter Book; Coolgardie office to Hoover, May 31, 1898, Sons of Gwalia Records.
46. Hoover to Coolgardie office, May 26, 1898, Letter Book.
47. Ibid.
48. Coolgardie office to Hoover, May 31, 1898, Sons of Gwalia Records.
49. Hoover to Wellsted, May 30, 1898; Hoover progress report for May, dated June 1, 1898; both in Letter Book.
50. See, for example, Hoover monthly progress reports for May and June 1898, Letter Book; Hoover monthly progress report, July 31, 1898, Department of Mines, W.A.
51. See, for example, Hoover progress report for July 1–9, dated July 9, 1898, Department of Mines, W.A.
52. Hoover monthly progress report, July 31, 1898, Department of Mines, W.A.
53. Bewick, Moreing & Co.—Coolgardie, Quarterly Report on Sons of Gwalia for May–July 1898, dated August 20, 1898.
54. Herbert Hoover, "The Working Costs of West Australian Mines," *The Mineral Industry* 6 (1897): 334–36.
55. Hoover to Coolgardie office, July 11, 1898, Letter Book. See also Hoover progress report for July 1–9, 1898, dated July 9, 1898.
56. T. W. Wellsted (Secretary, Sons of Gwalia, Ltd.) to Coolgardie office, July 29, 1898, Sons of Gwalia Records.
57. Hoover's Sons of Gwalia Letter Book contains 641 pages for his period as manager, and it does not include many elaborate reports sent to Coolgardie. Hoover's successor discovered that Hoover's typewriter was in a bad state and needed repairs. Harry James to Ernest Williams and the Coolgardie office, December 13 and 16, 1898, Letter Book.
58. Hoover to Coolgardie office (report on an inspection trip), September 6, 1898, Department of Mines, W.A. Another copy, identified as ML Doc. 2300, is in the Mitchell Library, State Library of New South Wales, Sydney, Australia.
59. *Financial Times* (London), August 18, 1898; special supplement to *The Leader* (Melbourne), September 1898, p. 34.
60. Coolgardie correspondent's column dated August 12, 1898, in *Australian Mail* 8 (September 15, 1898): 257–58.
61. Hoover monthly progress report for August, dated September 3, 1898, Department of Mines, W.A.
62. Hoover to Messrs. Gordon and Gotch, May 11, 1898, Letter Book. When these periodicals did not arrive, Hoover again wrote to the bookseller. Hoover to Messrs. Gordon and Gotch, August 16 and September 30, 1898, Letter Book.
63. Hoover to Andrew M. Patterson, August 12, 1898; Hoover to Messrs. Milne and Co., November 14, 1898; both in Letter Book. See also Hoover letters of September 18 and November 14, 1898, Letter Book.
   J. W. Kirwan, editor of the *Kalgoorlie Miner*, remembered Hoover as a teetotaler—a rare individual on the parched goldfields. See Kirwan, "Hoover in Western Australia: Some Goldfields Memories," n.d. (late 1928), Reprint File, HHPL.
64. F. K. Crowley, *Australia's Western Third* (London, 1960), p. 125.
65. Hoover, *Years of Adventure*, p. 33.
66. Ibid.; Hoover to R. C. Robertson, November 22, 1958, "Australia," Post-Presidential Subject File, HHPL.
67. For a time in the 1890s Australian law permitted dual title to the same mining lease: one title for companies mining reef gold, yet simultaneous authorization for prospectors to search for and extract alluvial gold on the same property. So the sly-grog seller who held a miner's

right was theoretically within her rights. After enormous controversy, and even a turbulent mob scene involving the Premier of Western Australia, the concept of dual title was abolished late in 1898. After that, leaseholders held the right to all gold, including alluvial, on their property. For details on this important controversy, see the articles by Bastin and Mossenson cited in chapter 5, notes 22 and 33.

68. The only known source of information on Hoover's difficulties with the sly-grog seller is Warden Archibald E. Burt's letter book, previously cited. See Burt's letters dated May 30, 31, and June 6, 1898, found on pp. 321, 330–35, and 352.

69. *Malcolm Chronicle and Leonora Advertiser*, August 6, 1898, p. 3.

70. Hoover to A. Matheson and Co. of Perth (the Sons of Gwalia, Ltd.'s legal manager), August 5, 1898, Letter Book. See also Hoover's telegram of August 4, 1898, quoted in Alec P. Matheson to Hoover, August 4, 1898, Sons of Gwalia Records.

71. The following documents relate to this story: Hoover to Alec P. Matheson, July 2, 1898; Matheson to Hoover, July 4, 1898; Hoover to Matheson, July 5, 1898; Matheson to Hoover, July 12 and 14, 1898; Hoover to Matheson, July 23, 1898; Matheson to Hoover, August 1, 1898; Hoover to Matheson, August 1, 1898; Matheson to Hoover, August 4, 1898; Hoover to Matheson, August 5, 1898; Matheson to Hoover, August 5 (letter and telegram), August 10, and August 18, 1898; Coolgardie office to Hoover, August 23, 1898; Hoover to Matheson, August 24, 1898. Hoover's communications are in the Letter Book; Matheson's letters and the Coolgardie office's letter are in the Sons of Gwalia Records.

72. Hoover monthly progress report, July 31, 1898.

73. The warden was Archibald E. Burt. Hoover once referred to him as "our peculiar Warden." On one occasion, apparently impatient with Burt's response (or lack of it) to his desire for "concentration" of certain mining leases, Hoover went over Burt's head and appealed directly to the Mines Department in Perth. This action annoyed Burt, who complained that individuals were too quick to go to Perth instead of proceeding through established channels according to the law. Hoover to Coolgardie office, May 10, 1898, Letter Book; Burt to Under Secretary of Mines in Perth, May 25, 1898, Burt's letter book, p. 247.

74. The most complete account of *Sullivan v. Hoover* is a handwritten trial transcript (including the text of the warden's decision) in Burt's court book. As of September 1977 this document was at the Court House, Leonora, Western Australia. A fairly detailed summary of the case was published in the *Malcolm Chronicle and Leonora Advertiser*, August 6, 1898, p. 3.

75. Hoover progress report for August 1–6, 1898, dated August 8, 1898, Department of Mines, W.A. Curiously, Hoover's report of the trial's outcome did not agree with other sources. According to Hoover the magistrate awarded the plaintiff "£14. off judgment, assessing them with the costs." But the warden's court book and the newspaper story stated that the plaintiff received £24.19.6 and no costs. According to Hoover the plaintiff's full amount due (if his claim were valid) was "about £22. and costs." But Sullivan sought £26.6.0 and costs of £1.7.6. So the actual award of £24.19.6 was nearly all that he wanted and not a "middle course" judgment. Could Hoover in his report of August 8 have been alluding to another lawsuit? This is conceivable but unlikely. No evidence of any other lawsuit has been found. Hoover's first mention of a lawsuit (in the July 31 monthly report cited in note 50) obviously refers to *Sullivan v. Hoover*. Presumably his second reference, cited here, does also.

76. Hoover monthly progress report for August, dated September 3, 1898, Department of Mines, W.A.

77. Hoover weekly progress reports dated September 17 and October 15, 1898, Department of Mines, W.A.

78. Hoover to Coolgardie office, August 4, 1898, Letter Book, and Letter Book for August–November 1898, passim.

79. Hoover monthly progress report, September 30, 1898; Hoover weekly progress reports, October 8 and 15, 1898; all at Department of Mines, W.A. An incline shaft was preferable to the more common vertical shaft because of the contours of the underground lode.

80. Hoover weekly progress reports dated September 17 and 24, 1898, Department of Mines, W.A.

81. Hoover weekly progress reports dated October 8, 15, and 22, 1898; Hoover monthly progress report, October 31, 1898; all at Department of Mines, W.A. See also Bewick, Moreing & Co.—Coolgardie, General Managers' Quarterly Report on Sons of Gwalia for August–October 1898, dated November 19, 1898, Sons of Gwalia Records.

82. Hoover to Coolgardie office, August 4, 1898, Letter Book.

83. Hoover weekly progress report, September 17, 1898.

84. Bewick, Moreing & Co.—Coolgardie, Quarterly Report on Sons of Gwalia for August–October 1898, dated November 19, 1898. (Hoover wrote this report. See Hoover to Coolgardie office, November 20, 1898, Letter Book.)

85. C. A. Moreing, "Great Britain's Opportunity in China," *Nineteenth Century* 43 (February 1898): 328–35; C. A. Moreing, "A Recent Business Tour in China," *Nineteenth Century* 44 (September 1898): 386–99; Moreing to Francis Bertie at the British Foreign Office, February 2, 1899, F.O. 17 / 1398 / 287–89, Public Record Office, Kew, Surrey, U.K.; Hoover, *Years of Adventure*, pp. 35–36.

Moreing may have tapped Hoover for another reason. According to the best of the early Hoover biographies, Hoover and his friend George Wilson were responsible in the autumn of 1898 for an inside tip that greatly benefited their superiors in London. Hoover and Wilson learned that a rich underground lode in the Associated mine at Kalgoorlie appeared to continue into the property of an adjoining mine managed by Bewick, Moreing. The two Americans promptly cabled their financier / principals in London to buy up shares in the Bewick, Moreing mine before the news leaked out and the mine's shares soared on the stock market. London was duly grateful, and Hoover—according to this story—was offered the choice of general manager of Bewick, Moreing's operations in Western Australia or the job in China.

The sole source for this story is Rose Wilder Lane, *The Making of Herbert Hoover* (New York, 1920), pp. 234–35. The plausibility of her account is enhanced by two facts. First, according to Lane's collaborator, virtually the sole source for Lane's chapter on Australia was George Wilson. Wilson was with Hoover in Western Australia in 1898 and examined the galleys of Lane's book before publication. The story therefore probably came from Wilson himself. Secondly, Hoover's brother Theodore also read the galleys of Lane's book. The story as printed, therefore, presumably passed his careful scrutiny. See Charles K. Field (Lane's collaborator), letter to the editor, *Mining and Scientific Press* 121 (November 13, 1920): 687–88.

Of course, Wilson's recollection of this episode may have been faulty. I have found no confirmation of it in other sources.

86. Hoover, *Years of Adventure*, p. 36.

87. The selection of Hoover may also have been diplomatically deft. According to Hoover, Moreing proposed to Chang that an American engineer be appointed in order to avert the jealousies of European powers competing for advantage in China. Chang concurred. Ibid., p. 35.

88. For further examples of Hoover's friction with Williams not already cited in this chapter, see Hoover to H. W. Lees, July 5, 1898; Hoover to Coolgardie office, August 4 and 8, 1898; Hoover to Coolgardie office, October 2, 6 (2 letters), and 7 (2 letters), 1898; all in Letter Book. See also Coolgardie office to Hoover, August 23, October 10, and October 14, 1898, Sons of Gwalia Records.

89. Hoover to Hinsdale, December 13, 1897 and March 23, 1898; Wilson to Hinsdale, April 10, 1898, Hinsdale Collection.

90. Bewick, Moreing & Co. statement regarding Hoover, ca. 1916, in Bewick, Moreing & Co. Collection, HHPL; W. J. Loring interview, 1931, Walter W. Liggett Papers, New York Public Library.

Edward Hooper later stated that when he first helped to place Hoover at the Sons of

Gwalia (following Hoover's earlier difficulties with Williams), he had promised Hoover to try to place him eventually in the United States, England, or China. Hooper also claimed that it was on his recommendation that Hoover traveled to London to see Moreing prior to going on to China. The accuracy of these recollections cannot be determined. Hooper to C. M. Harris, November 7, 1947, J. S. Battye Library.

91. Richard M. Atwater interview, ca. 1931, Walter W. Liggett Papers. Atwater's story is retold in Walter W. Liggett, *The Rise of Herbert Hoover* (New York, 1932), pp. 60–65. Liggett was a far-left muckraking journalist who crossed swords with Hoover over food relief to Russia in the 1920s. He then spent several years preparing the highly critical, sensational (and frequently inaccurate) biography just cited. His eagerness to discredit Hoover is abundantly apparent from his papers. His book, taken alone, is hardly a reliable document. In this instance, it is only as reliable as its source—about whom, see note 92.

92. Atwater, in fact, may have had a motive for disliking Hoover. In 1902 Hoover, now a partner in Bewick, Moreing & Co., returned to Western Australia. At that time Atwater was superintendent of the Sons of Gwalia. By Atwater's own account (given to Liggett), Hoover "promoted" him out of his job and sent him to Malaya. According to Atwater this was Hoover's revenge for Atwater's refusal to join Hoover's alleged plot to overthrow Williams back in 1898. So by Atwater's own statement we learn that he himself was involved in the Williams episode in 1898 but took a position against Hoover. He may, in fact, have been the man who tipped Williams off. Clearly our assessment of Atwater as a source must take these points into account.

Moreover, on at least one point Atwater is inaccurate. His account as given to Liggett implies that Hoover did not receive his China offer until he went to London and protested to Moreing. In fact, Hoover knew that he was going to the Orient well before he left Western Australia.

On the other hand, it is impossible to dismiss Atwater's story out of hand. Many of his statements in his interview with Liggett can be independently corroborated (although the story of the "plot" cannot be confirmed directly). Whatever his bias, Atwater did know Hoover and did work in Western Australia. In addition, certain circumstantial evidence suggests that there may have been something to this story. On October 31, 1898 Hoover did have a face-to-face meeting with Ernest Williams in the town of Menzies. (Unknown person to Coolgardie office, October 31, 1898, Letter Book.) Seven days later, and probably sooner, Hoover knew he was leaving Western Australia. (See sources cited in note 93.) And only days after Hoover left the Gwalia, his successor, on Williams's orders, fired three members of Hoover's senior staff (see note 99).

And so, against the bias of the source one must weigh certain indications that something like a confrontation with Williams precipitated Hoover's departure from the Sons of Gwalia. At the very least, it seems certain that Hoover's difficulties with Williams helped to bring about his change of jobs.

93. Hoover to William Martin, November 7, 1898, Letter Book. In this letter Hoover disclosed that he was "leaving Western Australia this month." See also *Coolgardie Miner*, November 10, 1898, p. 7 (the earliest known public announcement of Hoover's departure).

94. Coolgardie office, telegrams to Hoover, November 8 and 11, 1898, Sons of Gwalia Records.

95. Hoover to manager, Messrs. F. and T. Mahomet, November 18, 1898, Letter Book.

96. Hoover to Harriette Miles, January 5, 1899 (see chapter 5, note 11). This sentiment is in contrast to Hoover's eagerness to go to China, as recounted in his *Memoirs*.

97. Hoover to manager, Messrs. F. and T. Mahomet, November 18, 1898; *Coolgardie Miner*, November 23, 1898, p. 7. This latter source mentioned that Hoover was on his way to China. Hoover left on November 21; James took over the next day.

98. Harry James to Hoover, November 24, 1898, "Mining," Pre-Commerce Papers, HHPL.

99. Harry James to Coolgardie office, November 25, 1898, Letter Book. The men dismissed were the surveyor, assistant accountant, and assayer. Why their sudden ouster? One wonders whether, in Williams's eyes, these Hoover appointees were unreliable or disloyal. They

could not all have become instantly superfluous; surely the mine still needed an assayer at least. The phraseology of James's letter indicates that these staff members did not leave voluntarily. Furthermore, they demanded a month's severance pay. Interestingly, at least two of them followed Hoover to China.

100. Interview of Hoover in *Australian Mail* 9 (January 12, 1899): 130; Kirwan, "Hoover in Western Australia."

101. Herbert Hoover, "Information for Biographers" (typescript, n.d.; probably ca. 1914), p. 7, in Benjamin S. Allen Papers, Box 1, HI, and Pre-Commerce Papers, HHPL; Charles K. Field, letter to the editor, *Mining and Scientific Press* 121 (November 13, 1920): 687–88.

In *Years of Adventure*, p. 31, Hoover took personal credit for another major technical achievement in Western Australia. To save precious water for reuse in "metallurgical processes" at Kalgoorlie, Hoover said, ". . . I introduced for the first time the filter press, a machine copied from one used in the sugar-refining process. It has since been largely adapted by the mining industry." An Australian historian, Geoffrey Blainey, has vigorously disputed Hoover's claim. He points out that one of the biggest mines in Kalgoorlie, the Lake View Consols, decided to introduce a filter press at its mill several months before Hoover arrived in Western Australia. According to Blainey, it was an Australian metallurgist, John Sutherland, and not Herbert Hoover, who was responsible for this important innovation. See Geoffrey Blainey, "Herbert Hoover's Forgotten Years," *Business Archives and History* 3 (February 1963): 58, and Blainey, *The Rush That Never Ended*, p. 200.

There is considerable contemporary support for Blainey's view. Writing from Kalgoorlie in June 1898, the special mining commissioner of the *Economist* declared that the Lake View Consols was "the first mine on the field to inaugurate filter presses." (Hoover's company was the Hannan's Brownhill.) In 1900 John K. Wilson, a metallurgist who worked in Kalgoorlie from 1898–1900, stated in a technical article, "Filter pressing [in Western Australia] was first introduced by the Lake View Co., in the early part of 1898. . . ." In 1904 another authority, Donald Clark, specifically cited Sutherland as the first to introduce the filter press to Kalgoorlie and demonstrate its usefulness for large-scale treatment of gold slimes. See [J. H. Curle], "The Gold Mines of Western Australia" [June 1898 column], *Economist*, 56 (August 27, 1898): 1252; J. K. Wilson, "The Filter Press Treatment of Slime in Western Australia," *The Mineral Industry* 9 (1900): 780; Donald Clark, *Australian Mining and Metallurgy* (Melbourne, 1904), p. 32.

Blainey's remarks about Sutherland's pioneering role find further support in E. Barton Hack, "Metallurgical Methods at Kalgoorlie, W.A.," *Engineering and Mining Journal* 75 (January 24, 1903): 150–52. In this article, also published relatively soon after the event, Hack declared: "Mr. Sutherland, metallurgist to the Lake View Consols, introduced the filter-press, using first of all a simple press, originally intended for the extraction of fluids from sewage. The intention originally was to use these presses to extract water from tailings and slimes, water being one of the most expensive and valuable items on the West Australian gold-fields" (p. 151).

But no sooner did Hack make this statement than it was challenged by none other than Herbert Hoover. In a 1903 letter rebutting Hack, Hoover denied that Sutherland was the first to introduce the filter press for slimes treatment. Said Hoover: "The first filter-press was introduced by the Hannan's Brownhill, six months before the Lake View Consols, nor was the idea of adopting the sugar filter-press for the separation of solutions from slimes new at that time." Hoover did not say here *who* introduced the device at the Brownhill. But the Hannan's Brownhill mine was managed by Bewick, Moreing and Company. And Hoover during his first year in Australia worked from time to time at this very mine. See Hoover, letter to the editor, *Engineering and Mining Journal* 75 (March 21, 1903): 437.

In this same issue another correspondent, Alfred James, criticized Hack on other grounds in a letter printed next to Hoover's. Interestingly, a few weeks later Hack replied to James's letter but not to Hoover's. Hack, letter to the editor, *Engineering and Mining Journal* 75 (April 4, 1903): 514.

But if Sutherland may not have been the pioneer he has been said to be, who was? Blainey's evidence indicates that Sutherland's company ordered a filter press from London by February 1897 (well before Hoover came to Australia) and had it in operation in August. If Hoover is correct that the Brownhill company introduced *its* filter press six months before the Lake View Consols, this would put its installation back in February—before Hoover arrived. If so, Hoover could not have been the pioneer that he claimed to be in his *Memoirs*.

Yet it is also clear from contemporary evidence that the Hannan's Brownhill was a leader in adapting the filter press to gold slimes treatment in 1897–98—and that Herbert Hoover was at least somewhat involved in this effort. On May 18, 1898, at a professional meeting in London, one William McNeill presented a paper on this very subject. The bulk of his paper (note its early date) examined progress in slimes treatment at the Hannan's Brownhill mine, where, said the author, a filter press plant had been successfully operating for some time. Similarly, an Australian mineralogist visiting Kalgoorlie in the spring of 1898 observed filter presses operating at *both* the Hannan's Brownhill and the Lake View Consols. Early in 1899, in an American technical publication, Hoover himself was specifically cited as a source on the cost of filter press treatment of gold slimes in Western Australia in 1898. See William McNeill, "Filter-Press Treatment of Gold Ore Slime (Hannan's, West Australia)," *Transactions of the Institution of Mining and Metallurgy*, 6 (1897–98): 246–69; Edward S. Simpson in *Transactions of the American Institute of Mining Engineers* 28 (1898): 810; Walter Renton Ingalls, "Progress in the Metallurgy of Gold and Silver," *The Mineral Industry* 7 (1898): 330.

Here we must let the controversy rest. Hoover's *Memoirs* do appear to overstate his role, or at least the uniqueness of it. On the other hand, since he did work at the Hannan's Brownhill mine in 1897, it is very possible that he was *among* the first to introduce the filter press successfully into Australian mining.

102. John Agnew to Edgar Rickard, September 16, 1930, "Rickard Files—Agnew, John A.," Misrepresentations File, HHPL.
103. "Nemo" [Eugene W. Hine], "Hoover in W.A.: Memories and Musings," *Sydney Morning Herald*, November 19, 1928.
104. Don and Donna Reid, *Leonora and Gwalia: An Historical Sketchbook* (Leonora, W.A., 1976), p. 3.
105. *Report of the Department of Mines, Western Australia, for the Year 1963* (Perth, 1964), p. 8.
106. "Hoover, the Man," *Western Argus* (Kalgoorlie), July 21, 1931, p. 11.
107. Coolgardie correspondent's column in *Australian Mail* 9 (January 5, 1899): 113. See also the Coolgardie correspondent's praise of Hoover in the *Australian Mail* 9 (December 15, 1898): 62. Here he described Hoover as "a tremendous worker, an enthusiastic geologist and metallurgist, and popular and conscientious manager."
108. Hoover to Hinsdale, February 28, 1899.
     Many years later Hoover acquired a very different reputation "down under." Since the 1930s his name has been associated in Australia with an extraordinary love poem, which he supposedly wrote to a former barmaid in Kalgoorlie long after he returned to America. The poem includes such verses as these:

> Do you ever dream, my sweetheart, of a twilight long ago,
> Of a park in old Kalgoorlie, where the bougainvilleas grow,
> Where the moonbeams on the pathways trace a shimmering brocade,
> And the overhanging peppers form a lovers' promenade?
>
> Years have flown since then, my sweetheart, fleet as orchard blooms in May,
> But the hour that fills my dreaming, was it only yesterday?
> Stood we two a space in silence, while the summer sun slipped down,
> And the grey dove dusk with drooping pinions wrapt the mining town,

Then you raised your tender glances darkly, dreamily to mine,
And my pulses clashed like cymbals in a rhapsody divine.

While the starlight-spangled heavens rolled around us where we stood,
And a tide of bliss kept surging through the currents of our blood.
And I spent my soul in kisses, crushed upon your scarlet mouth,
Oh! My red-lipped, sunbrowned sweetheart, dark-eyed daughter of the south.

I have fought my fight and triumphed, on the map I've writ my name,
But I prize one hour of loving, more than fifty years of fame.

Apparently the first person to publish this poem and to attribute it to Hoover was the Western Australian journalist Arthur Reid in his book *Those Were the Days* (Perth, 1933), p. 36. Since then the poem has been widely circulated in Australia and ascribed to Hoover. It has even been set to music and printed in a book of Australian ballads. It has thus become a part of Australian folklore, and *Time* magazine quoted it in an article several years ago. I was asked about it many times during my visit to Australia in 1977.

Yet I can find no documentary evidence that Hoover either wrote this poem or ever realized that it had been attributed to him. No original of the poem has turned up. Hoover's own papers appear to contain nothing about the subject. Two other circumstances also lead me to doubt the authenticity of this story. First, the style of the poem is quite unlike anything else that Hoover ever wrote (or is known to have written). Secondly, in the story and in the text of the poem itself it is claimed that Hoover penned these verses years after he left Australia, at a time when he had become famous ("on the map I've writ my name"). It seems very unlikely that this prominent American, now married and in the public eye, would have written such a poem to an old flame whom he had not seen for years. Disclosure of such a poem would have been acutely embarrassing to a public figure, and one must doubt that he would have taken such a risk. (Moreover, how did Arthur Reid obtain a copy?)

It is, of course, difficult to "prove a negative." But in the absence of more compelling evidence, I conclude that this story is very probably apocryphal and that the "Hoover love poem" is a hoax.

109. According to the reconstructed Hoover itinerary cited in chapter 5, note 2, Hoover left the port of Albany aboard the S.S. *India* on December 11, 1898. He had left Coolgardie for the coast late in November. Coolgardie correspondent's column (dated December 2), *Australian Mail* 9 (January 5, 1899): 113.

110. Herbert Hoover, "Mining and Milling Gold Ores in Western Australia," *Engineering and Mining Journal* 66 (December 17, 1898): 725–26.

111. Hoover to Harriette Miles, January 5, 1899. Hoover arrived in London on January 4.

112. Hoover noted that certain special local factors—inexpensive fuel, ample water, and the "soft character of the ore"—contributed to this result.

113. Interview of Hoover in *Australian Mail* 9 (January 12, 1899): 130–32.

114. According to Hoover, the Sons of Gwalia's working costs for August through October 1898 were 21s. 4d. per ton, a figure which included mining, milling, "redemption of development," and "the entire general management." (These figures coincide with Bewick, Moreing's report of November 19, 1898, cited in note 81.) "In fact," Hoover then added, "all expenses incurred on the mine were covered by the 21s. 4d. per ton." This assertion was incorrect. According to Bewick, Moreing's report of November 19 (probably written by Hoover himself), the 21s. 4d. figure did not reflect expenditures for the capital accounts (development, construction, and equipment). During the August–October quarter these capital expenditures amounted to more than £5,000, nearly half the total outlay for the period.

115. Hoover to Harriette Miles, January 5, 1899.

116. Florence L. Henry (Lou Henry's mother) to a Mrs. Mason, March 12, 1899, Allan Hoover Collection, HHPL.

117. Kirwan, "Hoover in Western Australia"; Hoover, *Years of Adventure*, p. 36; Evelyn Wight Allan, "Lou Henry Hoover," *The Key* [magazine of Kappa Kappa Gamma sorority] (February 1944): 8. According to Kirwan, Hoover cabled his marriage proposal from Bewick, Moreing's office in Perth.

118. While en route to London via the Red Sea, Hoover wrote to his fiancée about his forthcoming job in China. Lou Henry to John C. Branner, January 20, 1899, John C. Branner Papers, Box 25, Stanford University Archives.

119. Florence L. Henry to Mrs. Mason, March 12, 1899. In his *Memoirs (Years of Adventure*, p. 36), Hoover stated that he did not arrive in California until February 10. But this was the very day of the wedding. Mrs. Henry's letter, written relatively so soon after the event, is undoubtedly the better source. See also Mrs. Henry to John C. Branner, February 6, 1899, Branner Papers, Box 25. Here she revealed that the young couple had decided to marry on the morning of Friday, February 10. She invited Branner to attend.

120. This account of Lou Henry's friendship with the local priest and of the arrangements for him to marry the couple is based primarily on three sources: Edward Berwick to David Starr Jordan, February 9, 1928, Hoover file (Box 8450 / 895H), Stanford University Archives; an account given by Father Mestres and printed in *Tidings* 34 (February 10, 1928): 1; and an interview of Lou Henry's sister, Jean Large, in the *San Francisco Chronicle*, August 8, 1930, p. 12. *Tidings* was the official newspaper of the diocese of Los Angeles and San Diego. See also Ray Lyman Wilbur to Theresa M. Woodhead, April 20, 1920, Ray Lyman Wilbur Papers, Box 119, HI (for the story about the baseball park).

     The evidence just cited strongly suggests that the couple's marriage by a Roman Catholic priest was a matter of choice—a result of Lou's friendship with Father Mestres. In his 1920 letter, for instance, Ray Lyman Wilbur, one of Hoover's closest friends, explained that the local Protestant minister was not a friend of the family and that Lou Henry wished to be married by someone she knew. This accords with the remark attributed to her that if she ever married she would ask Father Mestres to officiate.

     Years later Herbert Hoover, in his *Memoirs*, remembered the circumstances of his marriage somewhat differently. According to Hoover, his fiancée originally wanted a Quaker ceremony. But since no Friends meeting existed in the area, he could not accommodate her wish. And since no Protestant clergyman was in Monterey "at the moment," he and Lou "compromised" on "one of her old family friends," Father Mestres. Hoover, *Years of Adventure*, p. 36.

121. *Monterey New Era*, February 15, 1899; *Monterey Express* clipping, February 1899, in Hoover Scrapbooks, Album 51, HHPL. Mrs. Henry to Mrs. Mason, March 12, 1899; Hoover, *Years of Adventure*, p. 36.

CHAPTER 7

1. Florence L. Henry to a Mrs. Mason, March 12, 1899, Allan Hoover Collection, HHPL; Hoover to Lester Hinsdale, February 28, 1899, Hinsdale Collection. See chapter 4, note 92. All other Hoover-to-Hinsdale letters cited below are from this same source.

2. Hoover to Hinsdale, February 28, 1899.

3. Hoover to Joseph Swain, February 20, 1899, General Accession—Joseph Swain, HHPL.

4. Frederick Palmer, *With My Own Eyes* (Indianapolis, 1933), p. 175.

5. Hoover to Hinsdale, February 28, 1899 (for the itinerary); Noah F. Drake to John C. Branner, March 23, 1899, John C. Branner Papers, Box 23, Stanford University Archives; Hoover Calendar, HHPL.

     A word on the English spelling of Chinese proper names. There is often considerable variation for the same name both in the original documents (ca. 1898–1901) and, over the years, in subsequent secondary literature. In general, I have tried to use the transliterations commonly found in recent historical works on pre-Republican China: for example, Chang Yen-mao rather than the older variants, Chang Yen Mao and Chang Yen Mow.

6. William Pritchard Morgan to Liang Tun Yen, July 7, 1908, and [William Pritchard Morgan?], "Chronology of Dates and Facts: Work Done at the Request of H.E. the Late Li Hung Chang" (n.d.); both in George Ernest Morrison Papers, vol. 205, the Mitchell Library, State Library of New South Wales, Sydney, Australia. See also statement by Gustav Detring, n.d. [probably early 1905], in E. J. Nathan Papers, Bodleian Library, Oxford University. Detring's was a pre-trial statement for the 1905 trial cited in note 9.

7. C. Algernon Moreing to Li Hung-chang, January 3, 1898, Bewick, Moreing & Co. Collection, HHPL.

8. C. A. Moreing, "Great Britain's Opportunity in China," *Nineteenth Century* 43 (February 1898): 328–35.

9. [Pritchard Morgan?], "Chronology"; Pritchard Morgan to Liang Tun Yen, July 7, 1908; testimony by Moreing in the lawsuit *Chang Yen Mao and the Chinese Engineering and Mining Company of Tientsin v. Charles Algernon Moreing; Bewick, Moreing, and Company; and the Chinese Engineering and Mining Company Limited* (1905), tried in the High Court of Justice, Chancery Division, London. The abbreviated title of the case is *Chang Yen Mao v. Moreing*. The complete trial transcript, hereinafter cited as *Transcript*, is in the E. J. Nathan Papers at the Bodleian Library. The particular testimony by Moreing cited here is found on page 391 of the *Transcript*.

10. C. A. Moreing, "A Recent Business Tour in China," *Nineteenth Century* 44 (September 1898): 386–99; Moreing to Francis Bertie, February 2, 1899, F.O. 17 / 1398 / 287–90, Public Record Office (PRO), Kew, Surrey, U.K.; Moreing testimony, *Transcript*, p. 391.

11. Moreing to Bertie, February 2, 1899; Moreing to Gustav Detring, July 22, 1898, quoted in *Transcript*, pp. 148, 176, 393; Moreing testimony, *Transcript*, p. 393. Like many other letters to be cited below, this second letter was quoted verbatim at various points in the 1905 trial. The trial itself will be discussed in chapter 11. Since the originals of many of these letters apparently do not exist elsewhere, the *Transcript* is a unique and invaluable source.

12. Detring statement, n.d.; Moreing testimony, *Transcript*, p. 392; Pritchard Morgan to Liang Tun Yen, July 7, 1908. According to Detring, Li Hung-chang refused to consider Moreing's bid for a mining engineering monopoly or concession for all of China. It should perhaps be borne in mind that when Pritchard Morgan wrote this letter to Liang he was an enemy of Moreing.

13. Detring to Moreing, June 23, 1898, quoted in *Transcript*, pp. 392–93; Detring to Moreing, August 14, 1898, quoted in *Transcript*, pp. 177–78.

14. Detring to Moreing, August 14, 1898. The text of Chang Yen-mao's letter of authorization, dated August 10, 1898, is in the Bewick, Moreing & Co. Collection.

15. Detring to Moreing, August 14, 1898.

16. Ibid.

17. Sir Robert Hart to James D. Campbell, November 20, 1898, printed in John K. Fairbank et al., eds., *The I.G. in Peking: Letters of Robert Hart, Chinese Maritime Customs, 1868–1907* (Cambridge, Massachusetts, 1975), II, pp. 1177–78. See also Sir Claude MacDonald (British Minister to China) to the Marquess of Salisbury at the British Foreign Office, January 23, 1899, F.O. 405 / 84 / 244, PRO.

18. MacDonald to Salisbury, January 23, 1899.

19. Ellsworth C. Carlson, *The Kaiping Mines* (2nd ed.: Cambridge, Mass., 1971), p. 51.

20. MacDonald to Salisbury, January 23, 1899; *The Times* (London), February 1, 1899, p. 5. Chang was also a protégé of the Empress Dowager's favorite adviser, Jung Lu. See G. Kalgan-van Hentenryk, *Léopold II et les groupes financiers belges en Chine* (Brussels, 1972), p. 200. This is a doctoral dissertation published by the Académie Royale de Belgique in its series, Mémoires de la Classe des Lettres.

21. Detring statement, n.d.; testimony of Chang Yen-mao, Detring, Hoover, and Moreing in *Transcript*, pp. 75, 147–48, 280–81, 393–94.

22. Moreing to Detring, October 10 and 19, 1898, Bewick, Moreing & Co. Collection; Moreing to Francis Bertie, February 2, 1899, F.O. 17 / 1398 / 287–89, printed also in F.O. 405 / 84 / 87–88, PRO. In his letter to the Foreign Office, Moreing stated that Chang wished to "develop the gold and other mines" of Chihli with "British capital and assistance" and that Hoover was en route to China to "take charge of these operations." This was a bit of an overstatement. Hoover's responsibilities at this point were advisory, not administrative. At the 1905 trial (*Transcript*, p. 280) Hoover indicated that he was sent out to "take technical charge of some property" in China. But again, his powers, as will be seen, did not include administrative control over the mines' operations.

    Although Chang Yen-mao held an official appointment from the Chinese government, under its terms Chang paid Hoover's salary out of his own personal funds. Hoover testimony, *Transcript*, p. 281.

23. Moreing to Hoover, January 13, 1899, Bewick, Moreing & Co. Collection. Some years later Bewick, Moreing & Co. stated that Hoover's initial salary in China was £1,500—not £2,500— plus 10% of the profits. But, the company added, Hoover's salary was raised to £2,500 (plus 10% of the profits) in 1900. Bewick, Moreing & Co. statement regarding Hoover, n.d. (ca. 1916), Bewick, Moreing & Co. Collection.

24. Hoover, "Information for Biographers" (typescript, n.d.; probably ca. 1914), p. 8, in Benjamin S. Allen Papers, Box 1, HI, and Pre-Commerce Papers, HHPL.

25. In later years Hoover and his entourage often tended to exaggerate his relationship with the Chinese government. In his *Memoirs*, for example, Hoover states that Chang Yen-mao was "head of the Bureau of Mines." Hoover, *The Memoirs of Herbert Hoover*, Volume I: *Years of Adventure* (New York, 1951), p. 35. Similarly, Hoover's papers at HHPL contain autobiographical data sheets, drawn up in later years by his staff, which assert that Hoover was employed by the Chinese government's Department or Bureau of Mines. These statements are inaccurate. Chang Yen-mao was not the head of "the" Bureau of Mines. He was Director-General of Mines *for Chihli and Jehol only*. The omission of this qualification creates the erroneous impression that Chang's jurisdiction extended to the entire country and that Herbert Hoover was therefore chief mining engineer for all of China. Hoover did perform some work in Shantung and Shensi provinces, as well as in Mongolia, but he was not the chief mining engineer for the entire Celestial Empire.

26. Hoover homes finding aid, HHPL; Drake to Branner, March 23, 1899. In 1912 the population of Tientsin was 550,000. Claudius Madrolle, *Northern China* (Paris, 1912), p. 63.

27. Detring testimony, *Transcript*, p. 149. Detring described Hoover as "very studious and quick with his proposals."

28. Hoover to Chang Yen-mao, May 4, 1899; Hoover to Detring, May 4, 1899; both in Nathan Papers.

29. Hoover to Detring, May 4, 1899.

30. In his letter to Branner on March 23, 1899, Drake mentioned that Hoover, who had arrived only three days before, would depart soon for the interior. By the first week of April he had left Tientsin. Lou Henry Hoover to Detring, April 2 and 4, 1899, Nathan Papers.

31. Lou Henry Hoover to Detring, April 2, 4, and 7, 1899, and May 8 and 10, 1899, all in Nathan Papers; Lou Henry Hoover to John C. Branner, May 12, 1899, Branner Papers, Box 32.

32. Lou Henry Hoover to Branner, May 12, 1899; Lou Henry Hoover to Mary Austin, n.d. [ca. 1914], Mary Austin Papers, Box 11, The Huntington Library, San Marino, California; Hoover, *Years of Adventure*, pp. 38–39. Hoover's *Memoirs*, incidentally, gave somewhat higher figures for the size of this first expedition than did Mrs. Hoover's contemporary letter, which I have preferred as a source. On Hoover's name as rendered in Chinese, see Lou Henry Hoover's 1899 letter to Branner and a proclamation by Yang Shang-ching in *North-China Herald* (Shanghai), December 3, 1902, p. 1186.

    In his *Memoirs* (*Years of Adventure*, p. 38) Hoover records that he made this first trip reluctantly, after arguing with Chang, since Hoover felt that China should concentrate on its industrial minerals, not gold. Hoover further implies that he took the trip merely as a way of marking time. Contemporary documents establish, however, that he was brought to China precisely for the purpose of surveying the gold deposits of Chihli and Jehol.

33. Hoover, *Years of Adventure*, p. 40.
34. Lou Henry Hoover to Branner, May 12, 1899; Lou Henry Hoover to Mary Austin, n.d.
35. Moreing testimony, *Transcript*, p. 392; Herbert Hoover, "Metal Mining in the Provinces of Chi-Li and Shantung, China," *Transactions of the Institution of Mining and Metallurgy* 8 (1899–1900): 324.
36. George Wilson to Lester Hinsdale, September 8, 1899, Hinsdale Collection.
37. Hoover, *Years of Adventure*, p. 40.
38. Lou Henry Hoover to Branner, May 12, 1899.
39. Ibid.; Drake to Branner, March 23, 1899; Hoover, "Metal Mining," p. 329.
40. Drake to Branner, March 23, 1899; Lou Henry Hoover to Branner, May 12, 1899; Wilson to Hinsdale, September 8, 1899. In *Years of Adventure* Hoover describes his visit to a mine that was almost certainly Chin Chang Kou Liang (pp. 40–41).
41. Hoover to Detring, May 4, 1899; see also Hoover to Chang Yen-mao, May 4, 1899.
42. Ibid.; Detring to Moreing, June 27, 1899, quoted in *Transcript*, pp. 94, 96–99, 149–51, 394.
43. Hoover to Moreing, June 17, 1899, quoted in *Transcript*, pp. 315–18.
44. Hoover report on the management of the Chien Ping Company, June 23, 1899, Nathan Papers. See also Hoover's letter to Chang, May 4, 1899.
45. Hoover to Detring, May 4, 1899.
46. Hoover report of June 23, 1899; Hoover report on Chien Ping Company's mines, June 27, 1899, Nathan Papers.
47. Hoover to Detring, May 4, 1899; Detring to Moreing, June 27, 1899. Hoover's enthusiasm about the potential of the gold mine at Chin Chang Kou Liang, and his proposal for an exploration gold-mining company for part of Mongolia, contrast with the statement in his *Memoirs* that his gold-mining excursions in China were "always a case of chasing rainbows" (*Years of Adventure*, p. 42). As indicated in note 32, in his *Memoirs* Hoover adopts a curiously deprecating attitude toward the purposes and results of his gold-mining efforts in China. Actually his surveys revealed a considerable gold-mining output and potential. Almost 50,000 ounces of gold were produced in Chihli in 1898, as Hoover pointed out in his 1900 article "Metal Mining," p. 326.
48. Hoover to Detring, August 5, 1899; Hoover to Chang Yen-mao, September 7, 1899; both in Nathan Papers.
49. Wilson to Hoover, September 3, 18, and "10 / 8th moon" [ca. Sept. 14], 1899; Hoover to Chang Yen-mao, April 16, 1900; all in Nathan Papers.
50. Detring to Moreing, June 27, 1899; Hoover testimony, *Transcript*, p. 282.
51. Lou Henry Hoover to John C. Branner, November 12, 1899, Branner Papers, Box 25. See also John H. Means (a Hoover assistant) to Branner, January 29, 1900, Branner Papers, Box 33.
52. Lou Henry Hoover to Mary Austin, n.d.
53. Hoover, "Metal Mining," p. 327; Chang testimony, *Transcript*, pp. 100, 138.
54. Hoover, *Years of Adventure*, p. 42. Early in October 1899 the Hoovers visited Shanghai. See Noah F. Drake to Branner, October 4, 1899, Branner Papers, Box 23.
55. *Years of Adventure*, p. 42.
56. Ibid., p. 45.
57. See Chang Yen-mao [Chang Yi], "A Memorial [to the Throne] . . . with reference to the formation of an Association for carrying on Mining operations in the Province of Chihli and the district of Jehol," n.d. [ca. September 1899], copy in English in Bewick, Moreing & Co. Collection.
58. Detring to Moreing, May 30, 1899, typed copy in F.O. 17 / 1403 / 61–71, PRO. This copy is actually dated June 30, but internal evidence indicates that this was a typographical error. The letter was definitely written before June 4 and almost certainly on May 30, in response

to recent telegrams from Moreing. Moreing's telegrams, dated May 16 and 26, 1899, are in the Bewick, Moreing & Co. Collection.

The fact that Detring wrote this letter to Moreing while Hoover was already in China indicates that Hoover himself did not hold the position Detring wanted Moreing to fill. If Hoover had, Detring's letter would have been unnecessary.

59. Chang Yen-mao [Chang Yi], "A Memorial . . . with reference to the formation of an Association . . .," Bewick, Moreing & Co. Collection.

60. Imperial decree, n.d. [late 1899], a translation of which is included as Annexure No. 8 in Chinese Engineering and Mining Co., Ltd., to the British Foreign Office, November 27, 1907, F.O. 371 / 230 / 391, PRO. Although the rescript is undated, various circumstances suggest that it was promulgated sometime after mid-September 1899. At least as early as January 1900 the Mining Bureau of Chihli Province had its own stationery. See Hoover to Minnesota Geological Survey, January 8, 1900, Newton Horace Winchell and Family Papers, Minnesota Historical Society. In this letter Hoover labeled himself "Engineer-in-Chief" of the bureau. For another explicit reference to Hoover as the "Mining Engineer in Chief," see a despatch from Chang Yen-mao to Hoover, February 4, 1900, Bewick, Moreing & Co. Collection.

61. Lou Henry Hoover to Branner, November 12, 1899.

62. J. H. Means to Branner, January 29, 1900.

63. Statement by John A. Agnew, April 29, 1938, "Agnew, John A.," Post-Presidential Individual File, HHPL; Hoover, *Years of Adventure*, p. 37.

64. Hoover, "Metal Mines" (typescript, n.d., but probably early 1900), Nathan Papers.

65. Ibid.

66. It should be mentioned that there was no dissimulation of this fact. It seems to have been clearly understood by all parties that Hoover was looking out for Moreing's financial interests at Chinwangtao as well as working for Chang Yen-mao.

67. Herbert Hoover, "Present Situation of the Mining Industry in China," *Engineering and Mining Journal* 69 (May 26, 1900): 620.

68. Herbert Hoover, "The Kaiping Coal Mines and Coal Field, Chihle [sic] Province, North China," *Transactions of the Institution of Mining and Metallurgy* 10 (1901–1902): 419–30. A somewhat different version is printed in *Colliery Guardian* 83 (June 25, 1902): 1376–78. The variations probably reflect separate editing.

69. Carlson, *Kaiping Mines*, p. 1.

70. Hoover, "The Kaiping Coal Mines and Coal Field," p. 419.

71. Carlson, *Kaiping Mines*, p. 16.

72. Ibid., pp. 18–22.

73. Lou Henry Hoover to Branner, November 12, 1899; Thomas Webster, "Tong Colliery, Kaiping, North China," *Colliery Guardian* 80 (October 5, 1900): 697–98; report of shareholders meeting of Chinese Engineering and Mining Company, Ltd., in *Mining World and Engineering Record* 61 (July 20, 1901): 111–12. Mrs. Hoover's letter states that the Kaiping collieries had 5,000 workmen, but she may have been counting only the employees at Tangshan. The figure of 9,000 was for mid-1901 but was probably true for the year before also.

74. Lou Henry Hoover to Branner, November 12, 1899.

75. Hoover, "The Kaiping Coal Mines and Coal Field," p. 420.

76. Carlson, *Kaiping Mines*, p. 143.

77. Lou Henry Hoover to Branner, November 12, 1899; Moreing testimony, *Transcript*, p. 453. In his testimony Moreing stated flatly that the Kaiping coal field was "the most valuable in China."

78. Lou Henry Hoover to Branner, November 12, 1899. The Hoovers spent a week at Tangshan.

79. Hoover to Detring, August 4, 1899, Nathan Papers. Mrs. Hoover rated Chinese efficiency at Tangshan slightly higher—at one-fifth that of American coal miners. Lou Henry Hoover to Branner, November 12, 1899.

80. Hoover to Detring, August 4, 1899.

81. Carlson, *Kaiping Mines*, p. 49.

82. Chang testimony, *Transcript*, pp. 138, 93.

83. Moreing testimony, *Transcript*, pp. 394, 412–13.

84. Moreing to Francis Bertie, February 2, 1899; Sir Robert Hart to Francis Campbell, February 5, 1899, in *The I.G. in Peking*, II, p. 1186. His name was Willoughby R. Hughes. In *Years of Adventure* Hoover mistakenly identified Hughes's first name and said that *he* brought Hughes to China (p. 37). Hughes, however, was in China a month before Hoover arrived.

85. Detring to Moreing, June 27, 1899; Hoover testimony, *Transcript*, p. 282.

86. Detring to Moreing, June 27, 1899.

87. Ibid.

88. On Chang's unpopularity with various British interests, see: ibid.; Sir Claude MacDonald to Marquess of Salisbury, January 23, 1899; Moreing to Francis Bertie, February 2, 1899; Detring to Moreing, May 30, 1899.

89. Detring to Moreing, May 30, 1899 and June 27, 1899; Chang Yen-mao to Moreing, June 26, 1899, quoted in *Transcript*, pp. 101–2; Moreing cable to Detring, July 6, 1899, Bewick, Moreing & Co. Collection. Chang thanked Moreing for using his influence in the British press and the Foreign Office to "dissipate the falsehoods and misleading statements" being spread to discredit Chang.

90. Moreing cable to Detring, July 3, 1899, Bewick, Moreing & Co. Collection. See also in these same papers various other cables by Moreing to Detring, including those of July 13 and 26, 1899, regarding his efforts to conclude the Chinwangtao negotiations.

91. Chang Yen-mao to Moreing, September 20, 1899 (with an enclosure: a general mortgage bond), printed in F.O. 371 / 230 / 389–90, PRO.

92. Imperial decree, n.d. (late 1899), F.O. 371 / 230 / 391.

93. Chang Yen-mao to Moreing, October 17, 1899, printed in F.O. 371 / 230 / 390–91.

94. Bewick, Moreing & Co. cable to Detring, January 30, 1900, Bewick, Moreing & Co. Collection.

95. Detring testimony, *Transcript*, p. 149.

96. Carlson, *Kaiping Mines*, p. 53; *Mining World and Engineering Record* 61 (July 20, 1901): 112. In the preceding spring, incidentally, Gustav Detring had been officially appointed Commissioner of Customs at the projected new treaty port of Chinwangtao. *North-China Herald*, May 22, 1899, p. 918.

97. *North-China Herald*, October 30, 1899, pp. 863–64; *Mining World and Engineering Record* 61 (July 20, 1901): 112.

98. Hoover memorandum on Chinwangtao, enclosed in Despatch no. 361 from E. H. Conger to John Hay, April 19, 1900, Diplomatic Despatches, China, vol. 108, RG 59, National Archives, Washington, D.C.

99. *North-China Herald*, October 30, 1899, p. 863.

100. Sir Robert Hart to James D. Campbell, February 25, 1900, in *The I.G. in Peking*, II, p. 1220.

101. Detring to Moreing, June 27, 1899.

102. Ibid. That same summer, Detring also shared his ideas for reorganizing the Kaiping mines with a Belgian emissary of King Leopold II. Kurgan-van Hentenryk, *Léopold II*, pp. 201–2.

103. Hoover to Moreing, June 17, 1899.

104. The text of the Chinese government's official "Regulations for Mines and Railways," approved by the Emperor on November 19, 1898, can be found in W. W. Rockhill, ed., *Treaties and Conventions with or concerning China and Korea, 1894–1904* (Washington, D.C., 1904), pp. 340–44. See especially Regulation 13.

105. Hoover testimony, *Transcript*, p. 317.

106. Hoover to Moreing, June 17, 1899.

107. Moreing cable to Hoover, August 8, 1899, Nathan Papers. Moreing's retained copy, in the Bewick, Moreing & Co. Collection, is dated August 2.

108. The Chinese government's "Exploratory and Additional Regulations for Mines and Min-

ing" (July 30, 1899) are printed in Rockhill, ed., *Treaties and Conventions*, pp. 372–74. See also C. Algernon Moreing, "Presidential Address," *Transactions of the Institution of Mining and Metallurgy* 8 (1899–1900): 414–15, and Hoover, "Present Situation of the Mining Industry in China," pp. 619–20.

109. Hoover, "Present Situation," p. 619.

110. Moreing, "Presidential Address," p. 415.

111. Noah F. Drake to John C. Branner, March 4, 1900, Branner Papers, Box 23.

112. Ibid.; Drake to Branner, May 25, 1900, and June 13, 1900, Branner Papers, Box 23.

113. Hoover, *Years of Adventure*, pp. 45, 48.

114. Ibid., pp. 45–47.

115. Lou Henry Hoover to Detring, April 2, 1899.

116. Rose Wilder Lane, *The Making of Herbert Hoover* (New York, 1920), p. 258; Hoover, *Years of Adventure*, pp. 36, 49.

117. Lou Henry Hoover to Mary Austin, n.d.; Hoover, *Years of Adventure*, pp. 62–63. Lou Henry Hoover recalled that they had fifteen servants; Herbert said ten. Mrs. Hoover, as the person in charge of household matters, is probably the more accurate source.

118. Lane, *Making of Herbert Hoover*, p. 258, identified Hoover's staff's residence as the American Engineers' Club on Racecourse Road. However, in a February 4, 1900 despatch to Hoover (cited in note 60), Chang Yen-mao referred to a home built at Mining Bureau expense on Taku Road, in Tientsin. This was probably the location of Hoover's staff's quarters—on the second floor, above the offices and laboratory.

119. Means to Branner, January 29, 1900.

120. Lou Henry Hoover to Detring, May 10, 1899.

121. Herbert Hoover indemnity claim against the Chinese government (following the Boxer Rebellion), January 30, 1901, enclosed in E. H. Conger to Secretary of State John Hay, Despatch no. 526, February 7, 1901, Diplomatic Despatches, China, vol. 111, RG 59, National Archives, Washington, D.C.

122. Drake to John C. Branner, December 31, 1899, Branner Papers, Box 23.

123. Drake to Branner, October 4, 1899, ibid.; Lou Henry Hoover to Branner, November 12, 1899.

124. *Stanford Alumnus* 1 (June 1900): 164.

125. Lou Henry Hoover to Branner, November 12, 1899.

126. Hoover, *Years of Adventure*, p. 36.

127. Ibid., p. 65. The author has been told by an expert that one particular item in the Hoover collection is alone worth more than $100,000 today.

128. Helen B. Pryor, *Lou Henry Hoover: Gallant First Lady* (New York, 1969), p. 39.

129. Ibid.; Hoover, *Years of Adventure*, p. 63.

130. Sir Robert Hart to James D. Campbell, February 25, 1900; Moreing testimony, *Transcript*, p. 396.

131. Moreing testimony, *Transcript*, p. 396.

132. Detring and Moreing testimony, ibid., pp. 152, 396–97.

133. Chang Yen-mao, despatch to Hoover, February 4, 1900.

134. Chang Yen-mao, reply to a Detring / Hoover petition, 4th moon, 18th day, 26th year of Emperor Kwang-hsu [or mid-May 1900], English translation in Bewick, Moreing & Co. Collection.

135. Lou Henry Hoover to Branner, November 12, 1899.

136. [Chou?], a director of the Chinese Engineering and Mining Company, to Andrew Burt, March 5, 1900 and March 30, 1900; Hoover to the Director, Chinese Engineering and Mining Company, April 23, 1900; all in Nathan Papers.

137. Hoover to the Director, Chinese Engineering and Mining Company, April 23, 1900; Hoover statement of "Mr. Burt's failings," n.d.; Andrew Burt's reply to Hoover's criticism, April 7, 1900; all in Nathan Papers.

138. Hoover to the Director, Chinese Engineering and Mining Company, April 23, 1900.

139. [Chou?] to Andrew Burt, March 30, 1900.

140. C. W. Campbell, memorandum sent to Sir Ernest Satow, January 6, 1901, F.O. 17/
1759/20–21, PRO; George Wilson affidavit, February 15, 1932, "Richey-Hoover Files,"
Misrepresentations File, HHPL.

141. Moreing testimony, *Transcript*, p. 396.

142. Ibid., p. 397.

143. Ibid., p. 396; Chang testimony, ibid., pp. 100, 104; Hoover to C. W. Campbell (British
Consul in Tientsin), January 14, 1901, F.O. 17/1759/36, PRO.

144. By early June 1900 a total of £60,000 of the £200,000 Chinwangtao loan had been sent to
China. W. Gilmour, Agent, Chartered Bank of India, Australia, and China, to C. W.
Campbell, January 5, 1901, F.O. 17/1759/24–26, PRO.

145. Detring testimony, *Transcript*, p. 152.

146. Detring to Chang Yen-mao, May 3, 1900, quoted in *Transcript*, p. 358.

147. Chang Yen-mao, despatch of mid-May 1900.

148. Hoover to Chang Yen-mao, July 10, 1900, Bewick, Moreing & Co. Collection.

149. Hoover to Moreing, June 10, 1900, Bewick, Moreing & Co. Collection.

150. Ibid.

151. Ibid.

152. Ibid.

153. Herbert Hoover, "Present Situation of the Mining Industry in China," *Engineering and
Mining Journal* 69 (May 26, 1900): 619–20.

154. Herbert Hoover, "Metal Mining in the Provinces of Chihli and Shantung, China," *Transactions of the Institution of Mining and Metallurgy* 8 (1899–1900): 324–31.

155. "Memorandum of Agreement . . . between the Mining Bureau of Chihli Province . . . and
H. C. Hoover mining engineer . . .," June 8, 1900, copy in Bewick, Moreing & Co.
Collection. A partial copy was enclosed with Hoover's 1901 indemnity claim, cited in note
121. The contract was for three years, at the expiration of which either party could file a
six-months' notice to terminate. The total commitment, therefore, was for three-and-a-half
years.

156. Chang Yen-mao, despatch to Hoover, June 8, 1900, Bewick, Moreing & Co. Collection;
partial copy enclosed with Hoover's 1901 indemnity claim.

157. How much Moreing may have been paying Hoover at this point is not known.

158. June 8, 1900 is the date given on the documents. Two days later Hoover reported to
Moreing that they were signed. Hoover to Moreing, June 10, 1900. In this letter, Hoover
stated that the salary of the Engineer-in-Chief at the new colliery would be £2,500, but he
was probably combining the salary of himself (£500) and the resident engineer at the new
mine (which was to be not more than £2,000).

159. For general information on the Boxer Rebellion I have relied particularly on the following
published works: A. Henry Savage-Landor, *China and the Allies* (London, 1901), Vol. I;
A. S. Daggett, *America in the China Relief Expedition* (Kansas City, 1903); Hosea Ballou
Morse, *The International Relations of the Chinese Empire*, Vol. III (New York, 1918); Immanuel
C. Y. Hsü, *The Rise of Modern China* (London, 1970); and William J. Duiker, *Cultures in
Collision: The Boxer Rebellion* (San Rafael, California, 1978).

160. Wilson to Lester Hinsdale, December 2, 1900, Hinsdale Collection.

161. Hoover, "Information for Biographers," p. 9.

162. Ibid. Hoover, *Years of Adventure*, p. 48, states that there was no doctor in Peking at the
time.

163. Noah F. Drake to Branner, May 25, 1900; Hoover, *Years of Adventure*, p. 48.

164. Drake to Branner, May 25, 1900; *Stanford Alumnus* 1 (June 1900): 164.

165. Hoover to Moreing, June 10, 1900. Drake to Branner, June 13, 1900, reported that Mrs.
Hoover was now in good health.

166. Hoover to Moreing, June 10, 1900. In "Information for Biographers" and *Years of Adventure*
Hoover erroneously states that Lou was sick in Peking in June. The contemporary Drake

and Hoover letters, however, indicate that the Hoovers were already back in Tientsin by late May.

167. W. R. Carles (British Consul in Tientsin) to Sir Claude MacDonald, June 5, 1900, F.O. 674/87, despatch no. 32, PRO.

168. Morse, *International Relations*, III, p. 205.

169. Ibid., p. 203; Duiker, *Cultures in Collision*, p. 64.

170. On the Seymour expedition, see the accounts contained in the works by Savage-Landor, Morse, and Duiker, cited above. See also the report of James W. Ragsdale (U.S. Consul in Tientsin) on the siege of Tientsin to Assistant Secretary of State, July 16, 1900, in *Papers Relating to the Foreign Relations of the United States, 1900* (Washington, D.C., 1902), pp. 269–70.

Among Herbert Hoover's *Memoirs* materials and Pre-Commerce Papers at HHPL there exists a fascinating, unpublished account (about 30 pages) of events in and around Tientsin between late May and July 1900. This account is evidently a first-hand document written by someone who lived in Tientsin during the crisis. Although the authorship of this manuscript is not certain, handwritten comments on it by Mrs. Hoover strongly suggest that the Hoovers themselves prepared it, with the probable intent of publishing it. In various notes below I shall therefore cite this very interesting document as the "Hoover Tientsin manuscript."

171. Hoover's highly critical comments are contained in a fragmentary, handwritten set of notes, "China—Hoover Notes of Boxer Rebellion," Pre-Commerce Papers, HHPL.

172. Savage-Landor, *China and the Allies*, I, pp. 134–39; Hoover Tientsin manuscript; Duiker, *Cultures in Collision*, p. 129.

173. Chronology of events of the crisis, in *Peking and Tientsin Times*, August 25, 1900, p. 63.

174. Morse, *International Relations*, III, p. 206; Hoover Tientsin manuscript; Ragsdale letter, July 16, 1900, in *Foreign Relations of the United States, 1900*, p. 270.

175. Hoover Tientsin manuscript; Savage-Landor, *China and the Allies*, I, p. 140; Duiker, *Cultures in Collision*, p. 131.

176. Hoover Tientsin manuscript.

177. Noah F. Drake to Branner, June 13, 1900; chronology in *Peking and Tientsin Times*, August 25, 1900, p. 63; Hoover Tientsin manuscript.

178. Lou Henry Hoover to Mary Austin, n.d.

179. Wilson to Lester Hinsdale, December 2, 1900; Lane, *Making of Herbert Hoover*, pp. 264–65.

180. Hoover Tientsin manuscript; Duiker, *Cultures in Collision*, pp. 81–83.

181. Interview of Hoover in *New York Sun*, November 19, 1900, p. 3.

182. Hoover Tientsin manuscript.

183. Morse, *International Relations*, III, pp. 208–211.

184. Lou Henry Hoover to Mary Austin, n.d.

185. Ragsdale letter, July 16, 1900, in *Foreign Relations of the United States, 1900*, p. 270. See also Ragsdale to the Assistant Secretary of State, June 24, 1900, in Despatches from U.S. Consuls in Tientsin, 1868–1906, volume 7, National Archives, Washington, D.C.

186. Hoover interview, *New York Sun*, November 19, 1900, p. 3; Hoover Tientsin manuscript; Duiker, *Cultures in Collision*, p. 130.

187. Duiker, *Cultures in Collision*, p. 130.

188. Hoover Tientsin manuscript.

189. Ibid.; Hoover, *Years of Adventure*, pp. 49–50.

190. Hoover Tientsin manuscript; Morse, *International Relations*, III, p. 216; Duiker, *Cultures in Collision*, p. 131.

191. Hoover, "Information for Biographers," p. 10; Hoover, *Years of Adventure*, p. 51.

192. On the arrest and near-execution of Chang Yen-mao and T'ang Shao-yi, see Gustav Detring to Moreing, July 15, 1900, quoted in *Transcript*, p. 155; Chang Yen-mao's, Detring's, and Hoover's testimonies, *Transcript*, pp. 76, 152–54, 283; J. Bromley Eames testimony, ibid., p. 364; Detring statement, n.d.; T'ang Shao-yi to B. W. Fleisher, April 8, 1928, Misre-

presentations File, HHPL; interview of T'ang Shao-yi in *Japan Advertiser*, April 26, 1928; Hoover, "Information for Biographers," pp. 9–11; Hoover, *Years of Adventure*, pp. 50–51. These accounts vary on some details, such as the exact length of time the prisoners were jailed. Hoover, for instance, later wrote that the Chinese refugees were suspected of harboring Chinese snipers in their midst. He did not mention the carrier pigeons, as did T'ang and Chang, whose memory on this point was probably more accurate than his. But on the essential facts of the episode the accounts agree.

In later years, Hoover tended to take sole credit for saving Chang and T'ang from execution. At the 1905 trial, however, he modestly disclaimed any such solitary responsibility. At the same trial, Gustav Detring (who had no reason at that point to compliment Hoover) lauded Hoover's conduct during this and other episodes in the siege.

193. T'ang Shao-yi to Fleisher, April 8, 1928; T'ang interview, *Japan Advertiser*, April 26, 1928; Hoover, "Information for Biographers," p. 10; John Agnew statement, April 29, 1938; Hoover, *Years of Adventure*, pp. 51–52. Again, these accounts differ on some details but agree on most essentials. See the entry for T'ang Shao-yi [the currently accepted spelling] in *Biographical Dictionary of Republican China* (New York, 1970), III, pp. 232–36. Many of the documents cited here and above spell the name Tong, but I have used the more modern transliteration.

194. Lou Henry Hoover to Mary Austin, n.d.; Hoover, *Years of Adventure*, p. 49.

195. Ibid.; Hoover interview, *New York Sun*, November 19, 1900, p. 3; Hoover, "Information for Biographers," p. 9; Palmer, *With My Own Eyes*, p. 172.

196. Lou Henry Hoover to Mary Austin, n.d.; Hoover, "Information for Biographers," p. 9.

197. Hoover, *Years of Adventure*, p. 50.

198. Lou Henry Hoover to Mary Austin, n.d.

199. Chronology in *Peking and Tientsin Times*, August 25, 1900, p. 63; Hoover Tientsin manuscript; and, in general, the sources cited in note 159.

200. Duiker, *Cultures in Collision*, p. 134.

201. Frederick Palmer, "Mrs. Hoover Knows," *Ladies' Home Journal* 46 (March 1929): 6, 242; Oscar King Davis to Patrick J. Hurley, n.d. [1932], "Campaign of 1932—Hoover and Boxer Rebellion," Misrepresentations File, HHPL; Hoover, *Years of Adventure*, p. 53.

202. Hoover, *Years of Adventure*, p. 51.

203. Palmer, *With My Own Eyes*, pp. 174–75.

204. Palmer anecdote recorded in Davis to Hurley, n.d.

205. Lou Henry Hoover to Mary Austin, n.d.; Palmer, "Mrs. Hoover Knows," pp. 6, 242. Palmer stated that this was the only time he ever saw the Hoovers disagree sharply.

206. John H. Means to Branner, July 9, 1900, Branner Papers, Box 33.

207. Palmer, "Mrs. Hoover Knows," p. 6; Hoover, *Years of Adventure*, p. 51.

208. Oscar King Davis to his wife, July 8, 1900, copy in "Campaign of 1932—Hoover and Boxer Rebellion," Misrepresentations File, HHPL.

209. Means to Branner, July 9, 1900; Lou Henry Hoover to Mary Austin, n.d.

210. Hoover Tientsin manuscript.

211. Ibid.

212. Hoover interview, *New York Sun*, November 19, 1900, p. 3.

213. Ibid.; Hoover Tientsin manuscript; Duiker, *Cultures in Collision*, p. 136.

214. Hoover, *Years of Adventure*, p. 53.

215. Ibid.

216. The preceding account of the battle of Tientsin (July 13–14, 1900) is based mainly on: Daggett, *America in the Boxer Rebellion*, pp. 27–41; Duiker, *Cultures in Collision*, pp. 136–40; and Richard Weinert, "The Battle of Tientsin," *American History Illustrated* 1 (November 1966): 4–13, 52–55. None of these accounts, nor any contemporary source I have examined (such as Consul Ragsdale's report of July 16, 1900), mentions Hoover's role as a civilian attached to the U.S. Marines on July 13. Hoover's *Memoirs* are the sole source on his participation.

217. Weinert, "Battle of Tientsin," p. 55.

218. Ragsdale report, July 16, 1900; Lou Henry Hoover to Mary Austin, n.d.; Hoover, *Years of Adventure*, p. 49.
219. Lou Henry Hoover to Mary Austin, n.d.
220. Hoover interview, *New York Sun*, November 19, 1900, p. 3; Savage-Landor, *China and the Allies*, pp. 189–215.
221. Hoover interview, *New York Sun*, November 19, 1900, p. 3.
222. W. R. Carles to Lord Salisbury, July 17, 1900, F.O. 674/86, despatch no. 21, printed in F.O. 405/94/183–84, PRO.
223. Duiker, *Cultures in Collision*, pp. 201–2.
224. Lou Henry Hoover to Mary Austin, n.d.
225. Hoover indemnity claim, January 30, 1901.
226. Noah F. Drake to Branner, June 13, 1900; John H. Means to Branner, July 9, 1900; Detring testimony, *Transcript*, p. 156; Hoover, *Years of Adventure*, p. 54.

CHAPTER 8

1. Undated pre-trial statement by Gustav Detring (probably early 1905), in E. J. Nathan Papers, Bodleian Library, Oxford University; testimony by Chang Yen-mao and Gustav Detring in the 1905 trial *Chang Yen Mao v. Moreing*, cited in chapter 7, note 9. As in the previous chapter, the trial transcript will be cited hereinafter as *Transcript*. Chang's and Detring's particular testimony cited here is found in *Transcript*, pp. 76, 152–54. Chang's document granting Detring a power of attorney on June 23, 1900 is printed in *Transcript*, p. 4. Another copy is in F.O. 17/1759/4, Public Record Office (PRO), Kew, Surrey, U.K.
2. Detring statement, n.d.; Chang testimony, *Transcript*, p. 105; Detring testimony, ibid., pp. 153–54.
3. Detring testimony, *Transcript*, p. 153.
4. Hoover testimony, ibid., pp. 283, 318.
5. Ibid., pp. 283–84.
6. Ibid., p. 284.
7. Hoover to Chang Yen-mao, July 10, 1900, Bewick, Moreing & Co. Collection, HHPL. While in this letter there is no explicit reference to the provincial loan, it is highly unlikely that Hoover was referring to anything else.
8. Chronology of events in *Peking and Tientsin Times*, August 25, 1900, p. 63; Hoover testimony, *Transcript*, p. 284; Detring statement, n.d.; Detring testimony, *Transcript*, p. 154. Detring gave Chang's day of departure as July 11.
9. Hoover testimony, *Transcript*, p. 284; Detring testimony, ibid., p. 154; Detring statement, n.d. Hoover and Detring were in Taku by July 15 at least. Detring to C. Algernon Moreing, July 15, 1900, quoted in *Transcript*, pp. 154–55.
10. Detring testimony, *Transcript*, p. 156.
11. Ibid.
12. Detring to Moreing, July 15, 1900.
13. Hoover testimony, *Transcript*, p. 288.
14. Detring testimony, ibid., p. 206; Hoover testimony, ibid., p. 294.
15. Chang testimony, ibid., p. 77; remarks by Mr. Levett (Chang's attorney), ibid., p. 4. Chang claimed that Hoover joined Detring in mid-July in pressing Chang to give them a more reliable document than the June 23 power of attorney. Hoover denied that he asked for a new power of attorney (Hoover testimony, ibid., pp. 319–20).
16. Detring testimony, ibid., p. 157.
17. This document (known at the trial as document A) is printed in *Transcript*, pp. 5, 232–33. A very similar undated document (probably an alternate translation of A) is in ibid., p. 12. A copy of this latter version is in F.O. 17/1759/3–4, PRO.
18. This document (B), which is undated, is printed in *Transcript*, pp. 7–8, 233.

19. Document C, in *Transcript*, pp. 7–8, 234.
20. Detring to Moreing, July 15, 1900.
21. Detring testimony, *Transcript*, p. 155.
22. Hoover testimony, ibid., p. 286; Hoover to Detring, July 30, 1900, Nathan Papers.
23. Detring testimony, *Transcript*, p. 157; Hoover testimony, ibid., p. 286.
24. Hoover testimony, ibid., pp. 286, 318, 323.
25. Ibid., p. 286.
26. Ibid., p. 287; J. Bromley Eames testimony, ibid., pp. 365–68; Detring testimony, ibid., pp. 157–58. Detring said Eames appeared ca. July 15–17, but Eames's and Hoover's recollection (July 23) is probably more accurate. At the trial Eames used his 1900 diary to verify dates and events.
27. Eames testimony, ibid., p. 385.
28. Ibid., pp. 367, 375–76, 384; Detring testimony, ibid., p. 181. Detring said that he wanted the transfer registered in Moreing's name but that Hoover wanted it registered in his own name.
29. Eames testimony, ibid., pp. 367, 375–76, 383–84, 390; Hoover testimony, ibid., p. 323.
30. Ibid., p. 390.
31. Ibid., p. 384.
32. Chang Yen-mao to Detring, Hoover, and Moreing, July 23, 1900 (signed July 25), Bewick, Moreing & Co. Collection. This is the original document, handwritten by Hoover but signed and sealed by Chang. A copy is in F.O. 17 / 1447 / 427–30, PRO.
33. Chang testimony, *Transcript*, p. 144.
34. John H. Means to John C. Branner, July 9, 1900, John C. Branner Papers, Box 33, Stanford University Archives; Noah F. Drake to Branner, July 22, 1900, ibid., Box 23.
35. Receipts signed by John Agnew, George Wilson, and Hoover, July 4, 1900, Nathan Papers.
36. Hoover to Detring, July 30, 1900; undated receipt signed by Hoover for the four men's payments; receipt signed by Hoover for his July salary as Engineer-in-Chief for the Mining Bureau of Chihli and Jehol, August 1, 1900: all in Nathan Papers.
37. Chang, Detring, Hoover, and Eames testimony, *Transcript*, pp. 78, 158 and 181, 290–91, and 376–78, respectively.
38. Hoover testimony, *Transcript*, pp. 291–92; Eames testimony, ibid., p. 378.
39. Copies of this original indenture dated July 30, 1900 are in *Transcript*, pp. 9–11; the Nathan Papers; and F.O. 17 / 1759 / 5–9, PRO. Annexed to the indenture was a list of the Chinese Engineering and Mining Company's assets and liabilities.
40. Herbert Hoover, "Present Situation of the Mining Industry in China," *Engineering and Mining Journal* 69 (May 26, 1900): 619–20.
41. Eames testimony, *Transcript*, pp. 383–84.
42. See Detring statement, n.d. Detring stated here that during the Sino-Japanese war of 1894–95 Chang appointed him Assistant Director of the Tangshan colliery with power to put it under foreign protection to prevent Japanese seizure. Detring, a German, in fact took steps to "buy" the colliery himself in return for German diplomatic protection. This ploy was not consummated, however, because the acting viceroy of Chihli did not sanction it and the feared Japanese invasion did not occur.
43. Hoover testimony, *Transcript*, pp. 289–90; Chang testimony, ibid., pp. 78, 90, 105–8. See also Moreing to Lord Salisbury, October 10, 1900, F.O. 17 / 1759 / 1–2, PRO.
44. Hoover testimony, *Transcript*, pp. 286, 292.
45. Eames testimony, ibid., p. 368.
46. Hoover testimony, ibid., pp. 329–30, 358; Eames testimony, ibid., p. 390.
47. Hoover testimony, ibid., pp. 286–88, 323; Eames testimony, ibid., pp. 375, 383, 389.
48. Hoover testimony, ibid., pp. 286, 288–89.
49. Ibid., p. 289.
50. Detring declaration, December 24, 1902, conveyed to the British consul in Tientsin, in F.O. 17 / 1759 / 149–54, PRO. See also Detring testimony, *Transcript*, p. 170.
51. Hoover testimony, *Transcript*, pp. 286–87, 289.

52. Chang testimony, ibid., pp. 108–9; Detring testimony, ibid., pp. 159, 189–90.
53. Hoover testimony, ibid., pp. 289–91, 324; Eames testimony, ibid., pp. 369–70, 375, 390.
54. Chang testimony, ibid., pp. 106–8. See also Detring's testimony, ibid., pp. 191–92. At first Detring swore definitely that he did *not* explain and interpret the proposed July 30 deed (and its terms) to Chang. Then, under further cross-examination, he retreated and said only that he could not recall doing so. Later in the trial, however, he again insisted that he "never consulted" Chang about the July 30 deed. Ibid., pp. 223, 224.
55. Detring testimony, ibid., pp. 158, 181, 223–24; Eames testimony, ibid., pp. 378, 385. The revisions made after Chang left Taku for Shanghai were apparently minor, although they did entail Eames's preparing several further drafts.
56. Hoover testimony, *Transcript*, p. 294.
57. Hoover to Moreing, August 11, 1900, quoted in *Transcript*, pp. 330–31, 397–99, 424.
58. William J. Duiker, *Cultures in Collision: The Boxer Rebellion* (San Rafael, 1978), pp. 164–79.
59. Moreing to Hoover, August 15, 1900, quoted in *Transcript*, p. 399.
60. Hoover to Detring, August 21, 1900, Nathan Papers; Hoover, *The Memoirs of Herbert Hoover*, Volume I: *Years of Adventure* (New York, 1951), p. 54.
61. Hoover testimony, *Transcript*, p. 331. Hoover must have arrived no later than October 4, in time for Moreing to address to the Foreign Office the letter cited in note 62.
62. Moreing to Lord Salisbury (H.M. Secretary of State for Foreign Affairs), October 4, 1900, in F.O. 17 / 1447 / 427–30, PRO.
63. Moreing to Lord Salisbury, October 10, 1900, in F.O. 17 / 1759 / 1–9, PRO.
64. Messrs. Drummond, Phillips & White-Cooper to Detring, October 13, 1900, quoted in *Transcript*, p. 13. See also pp. 426–28.
65. Herbert Hoover, "Memoranda of Procedure, Chinese Engineering and Mining Company," October 16, 1900, quoted in *Transcript*, pp. 13–14. See also pp. 295, 402–3.
66. Hoover testimony, *Transcript*, pp. 294–95. Moreing did not recall that Hoover actually mentioned any arrangements about profits for Chang and Detring. But Moreing did have the same 50 / 50 idea as to division of profits with Detring. Moreing testimony, ibid., p. 402.
67. Moreing testimony, ibid., p. 402.
68. Ibid.
69. Moreing to Detring, November 9, 1900, quoted in *Transcript*, pp. 14–15, 159, 241–42, 298–99; Hoover testimony, ibid., pp. 296, 298.
70. Moreing testimony, ibid., p. 403; Walter Townley to Lord Lansdowne, December 31, 1902, F.O. 17 / 1759 / 135–37, PRO. Townley was the British chargé d'affaires at Peking; Lansdowne was the British Secretary of State for Foreign Affairs (in today's parlance, the Foreign Secretary). The bank that tried to block Moreing's plan was the prestigious Hongkong and Shanghai Banking Corporation. See also Sir Ernest Satow (the British ambassador to China) to Lord Lansdowne, December 19, 1901, Lord Lansdowne Papers, F.O. 800 / 119 / 226–27, PRO.
71. Hoover testimony, *Transcript*, p. 295; Moreing testimony, ibid., pp. 402, 429.
72. Moreing testimony, ibid., p. 395; Walter R. Skinner, *The Mining Manual for 1902* (London, 1902), pp. 1230–31.
73. In 1908 a British Foreign Office memorandum described Albert Thys as "at one time King Leopold's financial right-hand man." C. S. Cocks, "Memorandum respecting Difficulties which have arisen in connection with the Chinese Engineering and Mining Company's properties . . ." (Confi. 9105) (1908), copy in F.O. 371 / 418 / 335–37, PRO. See also a letter from Messrs. Dowdall, Hanson & McNeill to Messrs. Bompus, Bischoff & Co., December 1902, F.O. 17 / 1759 / 142, PRO.

    For more on Colonel Thys, see chapters 9 and 10, and the excellent dissertation by G. Kurgan-van Hentenryk, *Léopold II et les groupes financiers belges en Chine* (Brussels, 1972). This dissertation was published by the Académie Royale de Belgique in its series, Mémoires de la Classe des Lettres.

74. Edmund Davis to Lord Lansdowne, June 26, 1903, in F.O. 17 / 1759 / 255–56, PRO; Moreing testimony, *Transcript*, p. 412; Kurgan-van Hentenryk, *Léopold II*, p. 690. Moreing apparently sold to Thys £75,000 of the £100,000 he personally had been obliged to subscribe in the difficult early days of the Chinwangtao flotation.

75. Moreing testimony, *Transcript*, pp. 396–97, 423–24. See also Detring testimony, ibid., p. 193.

76. Moreing testimony, ibid., pp. 403–4, 429. The Oriental Syndicate was reorganized in December 1900 with the Belgians taking three of the seven seats on the board of directors. Kurgan-van Hentenryk, *Léopold II*, p. 691.

77. Hoover testimony, *Transcript*, pp. 295, 298, 300, 333; Moreing testimony, ibid., pp. 432–33.

78. Moreing to Detring, November 9, 1900, cited in note 69.

79. Hoover signed three power-of-attorney documents on November 9, 1900. Two are in the Bewick, Moreing & Co. Collection; a third is in the possession of Mr. G. M. S. Leader, a retired Bewick, Moreing & Co. partner living in England.

80. Hoover testimony, *Transcript*, p. 297.

81. Ibid., pp. 296–97, 334.

82. Ibid., p. 297. The text of the revised article (or "rider") is in ibid., pp. 538–39.

83. Hoover interview in *New York Sun*, November 19, 1900, p. 3.

84. Hoover interview in *New York Times*, November 19, 1900, p. 7.

85. Moreing to the Oriental Syndicate, December 13, 1900, quoted in *Transcript*, pp. 596–97; copy in F.O. 17 / 1759 / 274, PRO.

86. *San Francisco Chronicle*, December 6, 1900, p. 10; *Mining and Scientific Press* 81 (December 15, 1900): 589; *North-China Herald and Supreme Court and Consular Gazette* (Shanghai), January 9, 1901, p. 81, and p. v of supplement for same day; Hoover Calendar, HHPL. The vessel was a Japanese ship, the *Nippon Maru*. Hereinafter the Shanghai newspaper just cited will be referred to by its short title: *North-China Herald*.

87. Copies of the Chinese Engineering and Mining Company, Ltd.'s *Articles of Association* and *Memorandum of Association* (both dated December 21, 1900—the date of registration) are in the file for the company, B.T. 31 / 9233 / 68532, PRO, and in the Nathan Papers.

88. *Memorandum of Association*, clause 3 (A).

89. *Articles of Association*, clause 3.

90. *Transcript*, pp. 15, 45, 227–28, 629.

91. *Articles of Association*, clauses 83A and 83B.

92. Hoover testimony, *Transcript*, pp. 297, 334. Hoover was officially representing the Oriental Syndicate on this trip.

93. *North-China Herald*, January 9, 1901, p. v of supplement; Jean Henry's Yokohama diary, February 1901, Jean Henry Large Collection, HI; Noah F. Drake to John C. Branner, February 10, 1901, John C. Branner Papers, Box 31.

94. Hoover testimony, *Transcript*, p. 335; Hoover, *Years of Adventure*, p. 55.

95. List of Americans resident in Tientsin consular district contained in a despatch from James W. Ragsdale (U.S. Consul in Tientsin) to First Assistant Secretary of State David Hill, January 10, 1901, in Despatches from United States Consuls in Tientsin, 1868–1906, vol. 7, RG 59, National Archives, Washington, D.C.

96. Hosea Ballou Morse, *The International Relations of the Chinese Empire*, Volume III (London, 1918), pp. 291–301.

97. Andrew Burt to Lt.-Col. Powell, October 17, 1900, enclosed in Sir Ernest Satow to Lord Salisbury, October 30, 1900, F.O. 405 / 98 / 101–2, PRO; George Wilson to Lester Hinsdale, December 2, 1900, Hinsdale Collection (see chapter 4, note 92); Gustav Detring statement, n.d., Nathan Papers.

98. Detring statement, n.d.; Sir Ernest Satow to Lord Salisbury, October 30, 1900, F.O. 405 / 96 / 175, PRO; Salisbury to Charles Hardinge, November 1, 1900, F.O. 405 / 97 / 7, PRO; Morse, *International Relations of the Chinese Empire*, III, p. 322.

99. Wilson to Hinsdale, December 2, 1900; Detring statement, n.d.; Detring testimony, *Transcript*, p. 163.

100. Hoover to C. W. Campbell (acting British Consul-General in Tientsin), January 14, 1901, in F.O. 17 / 1759 / 30, PRO.

101. Detring statement, n.d.; Detring testimony, *Transcript*, p. 163.

102. Detring testimony, *Transcript*, p. 160.

103. Hoover testimony, ibid., pp. 300, 336.

104. Ibid., p. 300.

105. Hoover testimony, ibid., p. 300.

106. Hoover to C. W. Campbell, January 14, 1901, in F.O. 17 / 1759 / 29–33, PRO.

107. Jean Henry diary, "Thursday 7" [February 7, 1901], in Jean Henry Large Collection.

108. Eames testimony, *Transcript*, p. 379.

109. Ibid., pp. 379–80.

110. Copies of the revised version of the July 30, 1900 indenture are in the Nathan Papers and F.O. 17 / 1759 / 278–84, PRO. See also *Transcript*, pp. 22–23, 244–45.

111. Hoover testimony, *Transcript*, pp. 313–14.

112. Ibid., p. 333.

113. Detring testimony, ibid., p. 161.

114. Eames testimony, ibid., p. 380.

115. Hoover to Moreing, January 17, 1901 (two cables), quoted in ibid., p. 301; Eames testimony, ibid., p. 380.

116. Hoover to Moreing, February 12, 1901, quoted in ibid., p. 20.

117. Eames testimony, ibid., p. 380.

118. Hoover testimony, ibid., p. 302.

119. Ibid.

120. Hoover to Moreing, February 12, 1901, quoted in *Transcript*, pp. 20–21.

121. Ibid.

122. Ibid.

123. Hoover testimony, *Transcript*, p. 300.

124. Hoover to Moreing, January 17, 1901.

125. Detring testimony, *Transcript*, pp. 159, 196–97.

126. Detring later admitted in court that his negotiations with Hoover over Chang's and Detring's "interest" or profits culminated before Hoover's letter of January 24. But Detring claimed to have "no clear recollection" of asking Hoover to put their understanding into writing. *Transcript*, p. 197.

127. Hoover to Detring, January 24, 1901, quoted in *Transcript*, pp. 18–19, 197–99. A slightly variant draft in Hoover's own handwriting is in Bewick, Moreing & Co. Collection.

128. Hoover testimony, *Transcript*, pp. 297, 334–35. Hoover said he did not discover the omission until the end of 1901.

129. Hoover to Moreing, January 25, 1901; Moreing to Hoover, January 29, 1901; both quoted in *Transcript*, p. 599. (Moreing's reply cable is also quoted on p. 335.)

130. Detring later asserted weakly, "I cannot remember that I accepted it in particular." Detring testimony, *Transcript*, p. 199.

131. Detring to Chang Yen-mao, February 1, 1901, quoted in ibid., p. 162; comments by Chang's attorney, ibid., p. 598.

132. On de Wouters's background, see *Transcript*, pp. 161, 468, and G. Kurgan-van Hentenryk, *Léopold II*, p. 219. De Wouters was about eight-and-a-half years older than Hoover.

133. De Wouters testimony, *Transcript*, p. 468; Hoover testimony, ibid., p. 303. See also de Wouters to the Administrateurs Délégués of the Compagnie Internationale d'Orient, February 27, 1901, copy in George Ernest Morrison Papers, vol. 139, the Mitchell Library, State Library of New South Wales, Sydney, Australia.

134. Hoover to C. W. Campbell (the acting British Consul-General), January 14, 1901.

135. Ibid.

136. Hoover to Moreing, January 17, 1901.

137. Hoover later declared that he "deferred" to de Wouters once the Belgian arrived (*Transcript*, p. 302). But Hoover continued to participate actively in efforts to acquire the Kaiping mines.

138. Hoover to Moreing, January 26, 1901, quoted in *Transcript*, pp. 17–18.

139. Hoover testimony, *Transcript*, pp. 302–3.

140. Hoover to Moreing, January 26, 1901.

141. Ibid.; Hoover testimony, *Transcript*, p. 303.

142. Oriental Syndicate to Hoover, quoted in *Transcript*, p. 306.

143. Moreing to Hoover, January 29, 1901 (in response to Hoover to Moreing, January 25, 1901).

144. Hoover to Moreing, January 26, 1901.

145. Sir Ernest Satow to Lord Lansdowne, January 30, 1901, in Lord Lansdowne Papers, F.O. 800 / 119 / 37–39, PRO.

146. De Wouters to the Administrateurs Délégués of the Compagnie Internationale d'Orient, February 27, 1901 and March 22, 1901; copies in George Ernest Morrison Papers, vol. 139.

147. Hoover indemnity claim against the Chinese government following the Boxer Rebellion, January 30, 1901, enclosed in E. H. Conger to Secretary of State John Hay, Despatch no. 526, February 7, 1901, Diplomatic Despatches, China, vol. 111, RG 59, National Archives.
   Hoover's eventual settlement was apparently much less than his original claim. In 1904 he received $2,689.81 from the U.S. Government, which in turn presumably received the money from the Boxer indemnity imposed by the Allies on China in 1901. Letter from Office of the Auditor, U.S. Department of the Treasury, to Herbert Hoover, February 26, 1904, "Mining—China, 1900–1904," Pre-Commerce Papers, HHPL.

148. Hoover to Moreing, January 25, 1901; Detring and Hoover testimony, *Transcript*, pp. 162, 304.

149. Detring to Chang Yen-mao, February 1, 1901.

150. Hoover testimony, *Transcript*, p. 304. De Wouters fared no better with Chang. De Wouters to Administrateurs Délégués of the Compagnie Internationale d'Orient, February 27, 1901.

151. Hoover testimony, *Transcript*, p. 306. Detring's statement, n.d., placed the Russian evacuation a bit later, at the beginning of March 1901. Hoover's recollection is probably correct.

152. De Wouters to the Administrateurs Délégués of the Compagnie Internationale d'Orient, March 22, 1901.

153. Hoover testimony, *Transcript*, p. 304.

154. Ibid.

155. Ibid., p. 337.

156. Hoover to Detring, February 9, 1901, quoted in *Transcript*, pp. 19–20. Copy also in Nathan Papers.

157. Alfred White-Cooper to Secretary, Oriental Syndicate, February 25, 1901, copy in George Ernest Morrison Papers, vol. 139.

158. Detring, Hoover, and Eames testimony, *Transcript*, pp. 201, 304, 306, 381; de Wouters to Administrateurs Délégués of the Compagnie Internationale d'Orient, February 27, 1901.

159. Hoover testimony, *Transcript*, p. 308.

160. Chang, Detring, and Hoover testimony, ibid., pp. 78, 201, 306.

161. Detring testimony, ibid., pp. 162–63; for Hoover and Eames, see note 53.

162. Hoover testimony, *Transcript*, p. 306.

163. White-Cooper to the Secretary, Oriental Syndicate, February 25, 1901.

164. Chang testimony, *Transcript*, p. 79.

165. Ibid., p. 119.

166. Detring testimony, ibid., p. 214.

167. It was so characterized at the 1905 trial. See *Transcript*, pp. 81, 111, 116, 306, 381.
168. C. W. Campbell to Sir Ernest Satow, February 26, 1901, PRO 30 / 33 / 9 / 4 / 61–62, PRO.
169. Chang testimony, *Transcript*, p. 80.
170. Ibid., p. 81.
171. The July 30, 1900 deed provided that the new (British-registered) Chinese Engineering and Mining Company must take over the affairs of the old company by February 28, 1901, "or as soon after that date as shall be possible and feasible in view of the present military operations in North China."
172. Chang, Hoover, and de Wouters testimony, *Transcript*, pp. 87, 306, 470; White-Cooper to Secretary, Oriental Syndicate, February 25, 1901.
173. Detring testimony, *Transcript*, pp. 163, 202.
174. White-Cooper to the Secretary, Oriental Syndicate, February 25, 1901; de Wouters to Administrateurs Délégués of the Compagnie Internationale d'Orient, February 27, 1901.
175. Hoover testimony, *Transcript*, p. 306; White-Cooper to the Secretary, Oriental Syndicate, February 25, 1901.
176. White-Cooper to the Secretary, Oriental Syndicate, February 25, 1901.
177. Ibid.; de Wouters to Administrateurs Délégués of the Compagnie Internationale d'Orient, February 27, 1901.
178. Hoover testimony, *Transcript*, p. 306. Chang later denied that he demanded the specific sum of 500,000 taels. According to Chang, he sought an unspecified sum to be used as a bonus for old employees and as profits for the old shareholders. Not, in other words, for himself (contrary to Hoover's allegation). Chang testimony, ibid., pp. 118–19.
179. Campbell to Satow, February 26, 1901.
180. Hoover testimony, *Transcript*, p. 306.
181. Ibid., pp. 306–7; White-Cooper to the Secretary, Oriental Syndicate, February 25, 1901.
182. Detring testimony, *Transcript*, p. 164.
183. Hoover testimony, ibid., p. 355.
184. Ibid., p. 307.
185. Chang testimony, ibid., pp. 81–82, 118–19, 140.
186. White-Cooper to the Secretary, Oriental Syndicate, February 25, 1901; de Wouters to the Administrateurs Délégués of the Compagnie Internationale d'Orient, February 27, 1901.
187. De Wouters to Administrateurs Délégués of the Compagnie Internationale d'Orient, February 27, 1901.
188. Hoover testimony, *Transcript*, pp. 307–8. De Wouters was pleased with this outcome. Instead of giving Chang a bribe of 500,000 taels, he said, the Westerners had simply agreed to repay at once a portion of a recognized company debt. De Wouters to Administrateurs Délégués of the Compagnie Internationale d'Orient, March 22, 1901, in George Ernest Morrison Papers.
189. Chang's testimony differed on some details. He claimed, for instance, that Hoover was present during all four days of the row (Chang testimony, *Transcript*, p. 118). Hoover stated that he entered the negotiations only on the fourth day.
190. Chang testimony, ibid., pp. 81–82, 85–86.
191. Campbell to Satow, February 26, 1901. Campbell's perception of these events appears to have been derived solely from the Westerners' side of the controversy.
192. Detring and Hoover testimony, *Transcript*, pp. 163, 308.
193. Detring testimony, ibid., p. 163.
194. Ibid.
195. Hoover testimony, ibid., p. 308; White-Cooper to the Secretary, Oriental Syndicate, February 25, 1901; de Wouters to Administrateurs Délégués of the Compagnie Internationale d'Orient, February 27, 1901.
196. Hoover testimony, *Transcript*, p. 308. See also ibid., p. 86. The words quoted here are those of Mr. Younger, one of Chang's attorneys at the 1905 trial.
197. The text of the deed of transfer or conveyance (indenture) dated February 19, 1901 can be found in *Transcript*, pp. 24–25; in the Nathan Papers; and in F.O. 17 / 1759 / 267–72, PRO.

198. De Wouters to Administrateurs Délégués of the Compagnie Internationale d'Orient, February 27, 1901.

199. Hoover certainly was aware of this fact in 1902—and of the sweeping change made in this deed. See his letter defending the transaction in *North-China Herald*, August 6, 1902, pp. 281–82.

200. On this point, see Ellsworth C. Carlson, *The Kaiping Mines, 1877–1912* (2nd ed.: Cambridge, Mass., 1971), pp. 68–69.

201. The text of the memorandum dated February 19, 1901 can be found in *Transcript*, pp. 24–27; in the Nathan Papers; in F.O. 17 / 1759 / 298–301, PRO; and in Carlson, *Kaiping Mines*, pp. 147–49.

  There were two witnesses to the memorandum: Charles D. Tenney and Alfred White-Cooper.

202. Messrs. Drummond, Phillips & White-Cooper (solicitors in Shanghai) to Gustav Detring, ca. August 11, 1902, quoted in *Transcript*, p. 48.

203. De Wouters to Administrateurs Délégués of the Compagnie Internationale d'Orient, February 27, 1901. See also Hoover, *Years of Adventure*, p. 64. At the 1905 trial Detring was asked whether he told de Wouters that Chang told him that he, Chang, wanted a memorandum to "disengage my responsibility and to save my face in the eyes of the Chinese officials." Detring answered, "Chang was too practical a man to do that." Detring denied that he told de Wouters that this was the purpose of the memorandum. Detring testimony, *Transcript*, p. 214.

204. Chang testimony, *Transcript*, p. 119.

205. Said one of the attorneys opposed to Chang at the 1905 trial: "I ask your Lordship [the judge] to take the view that what Chang was really fighting for [in February 1901] was more profits to the vendors representing himself and the shareholders of the Old Company, the 500,000 taels was the real point on which Chang wanted the supplemental agreement [the memorandum] and the real point on which the thing was got." *Transcript*, p. 566.

206. Messrs. Drummond, Phillips & White-Cooper to Detring, ca. August 11, 1902.

207. White-Cooper to the Secretary, Oriental Syndicate, February 25, 1901.

208. De Wouters to the Administrateurs Délégués of the Compagnie Internationale d'Orient, February 27, 1901.

209. In fact, document C of Chang's instructions to Detring—which authorized Detring to effect the "conversion" of the old company into a combined Chinese / foreign company—was explicitly mentioned in the February 1901 deed of transfer.

CHAPTER 9

1. Chang Yen-mao testimony in the 1905 trial *Chang Yen Mao v. Moreing*, cited in chapter 7, note 9. As in chapters 7 and 8, the trial transcript will be cited hereinafter as *Transcript*. Chang's testimony about his departure for Shanghai is in *Transcript*, p. 86. See also Gustav Detring's testimony, ibid., p. 164. According to Chevalier de Wouters, Chang left for Shanghai without telling any of the affected Chinese officials that he had just sold the Kaiping company. De Wouters to Administrateurs Délégués of the Compagnie Internationale d'Orient, March 22, 1901, copy in George Ernest Morrison Papers, vol. 139, the Mitchell Library, State Library of New South Wales, Sydney, Australia.

2. Detring testimony, *Transcript*, p. 164; undated pre-trial statement by Detring (probably early 1905), in E. J. Nathan Papers, Bodleian Library, Oxford University.

3. Hoover to C. Algernon Moreing, February 24, 1901, quoted in *Transcript*, p. 348.

4. Oriental Syndicate to Detring, February 27, 1901, quoted in *Transcript*, p. 348. According to the *Transcript* the cable was simply dated "March" (with no day entered in), but a list of documents introduced at the trial establishes the date as February 27. For this list see doc. J15 / 2828 / 385, Public Record Office (PRO), Kew, Surrey, U.K.

5. Oriental Syndicate to Hoover, February 28, 1901, quoted in *Transcript*, pp. 28, 309–310.
6. *London and China Telegraph* 43 (February 26, 1901): 185.
7. Detring to the Chinese directors and acting general manager of the Tangshan colliery, March 1, 1901, quoted in *Transcript*, p. 356.
8. J. Bromley Eames testimony, ibid., p. 381.
9. Hoover to Moreing, March 9, 1901, quoted in ibid., pp. 341, 360.
10. Hoover to the board of directors (in Europe) of the Chinese Engineering and Mining Company, Ltd. (the new company), May 18, 1901, quoted in *Transcript*, pp. 349, 361–62, 440.
11. Hoover to Moreing, March 9, 1901.
12. Ibid.
13. De Wouters to Administrateurs Délégués of the Compagnie Internationale d'Orient, March 22, 1901.
14. Hoover and de Wouters, joint report to the board of directors (in Europe) of the Chinese Engineering and Mining Company, Ltd., ca. September 1901. This lengthy document is a summary of Hoover's and de Wouters's activities as co-managers of the new company in China from March to September 1901. It is a crucial document for a study of Hoover in China. An unsigned handwritten version (the only complete text available) is in the Bewick, Moreing & Co. Collection, HHPL. The sometimes awkward syntax of this report suggests that it may be a translation from another language or that the writer may not have spoken English as a first language. The handwriting is not Hoover's. At the 1905 trial Hoover testified that de Wouters wrote this report and that Hoover then signed it (*Transcript*, p. 345). Hoover must therefore be considered jointly responsible with de Wouters for its contents. This Hoover/de Wouters report was in fact identified as such and entered in evidence as such at the 1905 trial and the 1906 appeal (to be discussed in chapter 11).
    Portions of this document were read into the printed trial *Transcript* as well as pp. 166–67 of the 1906 Court of Appeal transcript, hereinafter cited as *Appeal Transcript*. (See chapter 10, note 12, for the full citation.) Wherever possible I have relied on and quoted from these printed excerpts. Hereinafter this document will be cited briefly as Hoover/de Wouters report, September 1901.
15. Hoover to the board of directors, May 18, 1901; Hoover to the same board, June 25, 1901, quoted in *Transcript*, pp. 351–52, 362–63.
16. Hoover testimony, *Transcript*, p. 309; Hoover to the board of directors, May 18, 1901.
17. Hoover to the board of directors, May 18, 1901.
18. De Wouters to the Administrateurs Délégués of the Compagnie Internationale d'Orient, March 22, 1901.
19. Hoover/de Wouters report, September 1901; Hoover testimony, *Transcript*, pp. 312, 343.
20. Hoover testimony, *Transcript*, p. 363.
21. Text of the July 30, 1900 deed (both versions), discussed in chapter 8.
22. Hoover/de Wouters report, September 1901.
23. Ibid.
24. Detring testimony, *Transcript*, p. 165.
25. Hoover/de Wouters report, September 1901.
26. Ibid.; de Wouters to the Administrateurs Délégués of the Compagnie Internationale d'Orient, February 27, 1901, copy in George Ernest Morrison Papers, vol. 139.
27. Hoover/de Wouters report, September 1901.
28. Ibid.; de Wouters to Administrateurs Délégués of the Compagnie Internationale d'Orient, March 22, 1901.
29. Hoover to Moreing, February 24, 1901, quoted in *Transcript*, p. 348.
30. Hoover to Moreing, March 22, 1901, quoted in *Transcript*, pp. 251, 312, 439. See also Hoover testimony, *Transcript*, p. 313.
31. Hoover to Moreing, March 22, 1901; Hoover/de Wouters report, September 1901.
32. Hoover testimony, *Transcript*, p. 313; Hoover/de Wouters report, September 1901.
33. De Wouters to the Administrateurs Délégués of the Compagnie Internationale d'Orient, March 22, 1901.

34. Hoover / de Wouters report, September 1901.
35. Russo-Chinese Bank, Peking, to Li Hung-chang, June 7, 1901; Li Hung-chang's receipt (for 200,000 taels) given to Russo-Chinese Bank, June 12, 1901. Copies of both items are in Appendix E of Chinese Engineering and Mining Company, Ltd., *Reply to Chinese Government's Memorandum of October 1908* (ca. February 1, 1909). Copies of this lengthy document are in the Nathan Papers and F.O. 371 / 630 / 372–433, PRO.
36. Hoover / de Wouters report, September 1901.
37. Ibid.
38. Ibid.
39. Hoover to Moreing, March 22, 1901.
40. Hoover / de Wouters report, September 1901.
41. For Emile Francqui's mission to China in 1901 see *London and China Telegraph* 43 (February 26, 1901): 185. For Francqui's background see *New York Times*, November 17, 1935, Section 2, p. 11, and *The Times* (London), November 18, 1935, p. 19. See also the entry for Francqui in Académie Royale des sciences coloniales, *Biographie coloniale belge*, Vol. 4 (Brussels, 1955), pp. 311–19.
42. Hoover to Moreing, May 19, 1901, quoted in *Transcript*, pp. 349–50, 440–42, and in *Appeal Transcript*, p. 157.
43. Hoover to the board of directors, May 18, 1901. Francqui left Brussels for the Far East in late February 1901. He was accompanied by four men, only one of whom (Malaise) was a mining engineer. *London and China Telegraph* 43 (February 26, 1901): 185.
44. Hoover to the board of directors, May 18, 1901.
45. Hoover to the board of directors, Chinese Engineering and Mining Company, Ltd., June 25, 1901, quoted in *Transcript*, pp. 351–52, 362–63.
46. Hoover Calendar, HHPL.
47. Hoover / de Wouters report, September 1901.
48. For Hoover's account of the incident at the bank, see his testimony, *Transcript*, p. 313.

   The story about Hoover's using a revolver to threaten a Chinese employee and seize documents from him was spread in 1920 by Wang Ho Chai, secretary of the Kailan Mining Administration, on a visit to the United States. Wang told the story to an American, Guy M. Walker. Subsequently Walker energetically purveyed the material to various prominent political enemies of Hoover in an effort to block Hoover's entrance into President Harding's cabinet in 1921 and to stop Hoover's nomination for President in 1928. Another anti-Hoover Chinese informant for Walker in 1920 was Dr. Chen Wai Ping, editor of the *Chinese Christian Advocate* (Shanghai).

   Wang Ho Chai's general account of the Kaiping controversy is full of errors and quite garbled. It may be found, along with correspondence documenting Walker's efforts to discredit Hoover, in the Guy M. Walker Papers, De Pauw University Archives, Greencastle, Indiana. Since Wang was so clearly unreliable, and since Walker was so hostile to Hoover, the allegation that Hoover used a revolver to threaten an employee must be rejected as, at the very least, not proven. One might be inclined to dismiss the whole subject out of hand except for the fact that Hoover did, by his own admission, use "violence" (whatever that meant) to seize certain documents while general manager of the Kaiping mines in early 1901.

   On Chang Yen-mao's sale of the company's Hong Kong property, see Hoover / de Wouters report, September 1901, and Arthur Train, *The Strange Attacks on Herbert Hoover* (New York, 1932), p. 39. According to the latter account (personally approved by Hoover) it was to remove Chang "from further temptation" that Hoover seized the deeds and put them into a foreign bank. According to the Hoover / de Wouters report most of the money from Chang's sale of the Hong Kong property was eventually recovered by the new company.
49. Hoover / de Wouters report, September 1901. See also Detring testimony, *Transcript*, p. 165.
50. Detring testimony, *Transcript*, p. 165.
51. De Wouters to the board of directors, Chinese Engineering and Mining Company, Ltd., July 14, 1901, quoted in ibid., pp. 36–37, and in *Appeal Transcript*, pp. 161–62. At the 1905

trial Hoover testified that he did not know (in mid-1901) about the agreement that the company's checks must henceforth be co-signed by Detring (*Transcript*, p. 343). Instead, Hoover said his "impression" was that the checks could be signed by *any* two members of the board. The Hoover / de Wouters report of September 1901, however, which Hoover signed, stated that Detring must be one of the two co-signers.

52. Detring testimony, *Transcript*, p. 165.

53. Chang Yen-mao testimony, ibid., pp. 87, 120; Detring testimony, ibid., p. 164; Detring pre-trial statement, n.d.

54. Copies of the text of the "Regulations for the Provisional Administration of the Chinese Engineering and Mining Company, Ltd." (June 4, 1901) can be found in *Transcript*, pp. 34–35 and in the Nathan Papers.

    Among other powers granted to Chang in these new regulations were the obligation to see that the "new Shareholders" observed "the engagements towards the old Shareholders" and to see that the foreign and Chinese employees "act harmoniously" (article 3). But these did not add up to the sweeping control over Kaiping which Chang formerly enjoyed. On this point, see Ellsworth C. Carlson, *The Kaiping Mines, 1877–1912* (2nd ed.; Cambridge, Mass., 1971), pp. 76–77.

55. De Wouters to the board of directors, July 14, 1901.

56. Hoover testimony, *Transcript*, p. 310.

57. Although Chang did not sign the June 4 regulations he obviously assented to them, as his appointments indicated. Chang later stated that he considered it unnecessary to sign personally. Chang Yen-mao testimony, ibid., p. 87.

58. Ibid., pp. 38, 87.

59. De Wouters to the board of directors, July 14, 1901.

60. Hoover / de Wouters report, September 1901.

61. Hoover testimony, *Transcript*, pp. 310, 343–44; Emile Francqui to the board of directors, Chinese Engineering and Mining Company, Ltd., July 20, 1901, quoted in ibid., pp. 37–38, 344.

62. Hoover testimony, *Transcript*, p. 310.

63. De Wouters to the board of directors, July 14, 1901.

64. Ibid. At the 1905 trial de Wouters asserted that he had been "much reproached"—evidently by his foreign colleagues and / or superiors—for "having gone too far": that is, for having made too many concessions to the Chinese in the June 4 regulations. Consequently he had been led to write the (erroneous) passage quoted in the text. What de Wouters seemed to be saying in 1905 was that this passage was false—that, in fact, the Chinese board did have power—but that de Wouters had written this passage anyway in an agitated state of mind in order to appease his European critics. De Wouters testimony, *Transcript*, p. 473. The judge was not impressed by his testimony. Ibid., pp. 473–74.

65. Francqui to the board of directors, July 20, 1901.

66. Hoover / de Wouters report, September 1901.

67. C. Algernon Moreing to the Oriental Syndicate, December 13, 1900, F.O. 17 / 1759 / 274, PRO.

68. First agreement between Moreing and the Oriental Syndicate, May 2, 1901, quoted in *Transcript*, p. 29.

69. Moreing testimony, *Transcript*, p. 451.

70. Second agreement between Moreing and the Oriental Syndicate, May 2, 1901, quoted in *Transcript*, pp. 29–30.

71. Agreement between the Oriental Syndicate and the Chinese Engineering and Mining Company, Ltd., May 2, 1901, quoted in *Transcript*, p. 31.

72. Moreing to Detring, November 9, 1900, quoted in *Transcript*, pp. 14–15, 159, 241–42, 298–99.

73. Technically, of course, the first directors were elected by "the shareholders"—all seven of them.

74. Minutes of the board of directors of the Chinese Engineering and Mining Company, Ltd., Dec. 24, 1900—May 2, 1901, as cited in *Transcript*, pp. 606–7. See also affidavit by Bourchier F. Hawksley, April 8, 1905, J4 / 6971 / 973, PRO, and the Chinese Engineering and Mining Company's file, B.T. 31 / 9233 / 68532, PRO.

75. *Transcript*, pp. 55–56; report of general shareholders meeting of Chinese Engineering and Mining Company, in *Mining World and Engineering Record* 61 (July 20, 1901): 111–12, and in *Mining Journal* 71 (July 20, 1901): 896.

76. Detring statement, n.d.; Detring testimony, *Transcript*, p. 164.

77. Hoover to Detring, February 9, 1901, quoted in *Transcript*, pp. 19–20. Copy also in Nathan Papers.

78. Technically 424,993. The other seven shares were taken first by the seven Englishmen who registered the company and then by the seven Belgians in February.

79. Minutes of the board of directors meeting, May 25, 1901, quoted in *Transcript*, p. 607.

80. Minutes of the board of directors meeting, June 5, 1901, quoted in *Transcript*, pp. 349, 611.

81. Turner statement at the July 16, 1901 shareholders meeting cited in note 75.

In British financial usage a debenture is "a security issued by a company other than its shares" (*Webster's Seventh Collegiate Dictionary*).

82. Edmund Davis (a director of the Chinese Engineering and Mining Company) to Lord Lansdowne (at the British Foreign Office), June 26, 1903, in F.O. 17 / 1759 / 255–66, PRO. See also interview of C. Algernon Moreing in *Westminster Gazette*, February 24, 1903, p. 9; a longer version of this interview from an earlier edition of the same day is in F.O. 17 / 1759 / 172–73, PRO. Davis stated (correctly) that the Oriental Syndicate gave away 425,000 free shares to the "guarantors of the £500,000." Moreing phrased it differently. He said that only 250,000 shares were issued as "premium shares on the debentures" and that the other 175,000 "were absorbed in clearing out the old creditors." But since most of the "old creditors" simply exchanged their old claims for the new debentures, the result was the same: they took the debentures—and 175,000 free shares. Most of the old creditors simply became new creditors.

Moreing, incidentally, did not disclose that these "old creditors" included Moreing himself and the Compagnie Internationale d'Orient headed by Colonel Albert Thys.

83. Hoover testimony, *Transcript*, p. 350.

84. Articles of Association of the Chinese Engineering and Mining Company, Ltd. (December 21, 1900), clause 83 (E), copy in Nathan Papers and in the company's file, B.T. 31 / 9233 / 68532, PRO. See also *Transcript*, p. 611.

85. For defenses of the company's financial scheme, see the 1903 Davis letter and Moreing newspaper interview cited in note 82. See also the vigorous argument offered by Moreing's attorney, T. R. Hughes, at the 1905 trial (*Transcript*, pp. 263–66, 526) and Moreing's own testimony (pp. 414–15).

86. The £500,000 debt was to be retired in £10,000 annual installments. Report of second annual ordinary general shareholders meeting of Chinese Engineering and Mining Company, *Mining Journal* 74 (October 17, 1903): 430.

87. See the sources cited in notes 82 and 85. See also Moreing testimony, *Transcript*, pp. 439, 441, and Hoover, letter to the editor, *North-China Daily News*, reprinted in *North-China Herald*, August 6, 1902, pp. 281–82.

88. Hoover to Moreing, March 22, 1901.

89. Hoover to Moreing, May 23, 1901, quoted in *Transcript*, p. 351.

90. See, for instance, the Shanghai stock market reports printed weekly in the *North-China Herald* (Shanghai), March–June 1901. From mid-March through April the old Kaiping company's shares (par value 100 taels) generally sold at from 155 to 175 taels. In May the price per share soared over the 200-tael mark and even briefly reached 370. In June—the very month of the debenture issue in Europe—Kaiping shares were traded in China at 240–275 taels, more than twice their face value (*North-China Herald*, June 12, 19, and 26, 1901, pp. 1156, 1205, and 1254). Hoover later attributed this boom to speculative fever based, in

part, on erroneous reports about the mines' prospects (Hoover testimony, *Transcript*, p. 351). But whether speculative or not, the share price consistently remained far above par for months. See also Carlson, *Kaiping Mines*, p. 73.

91. Hoover testimony, *Transcript*, p. 350. Hoover learned about the debenture plan from Francqui.

92. Hoover to Moreing, May 19, 1901.

93. Hoover testimony, *Transcript*, p. 350. See also Moreing testimony, ibid., p. 441.

94. Hoover and Moreing testimony, ibid., pp. 350, 352, 440–42. Hoover pointed out that the Boxer Rebellion had led to a coal shortage, which in turn produced "an exaggerated sale and an exaggerated income." The shortage, and thus the high prices, proved to be temporary.

95. Moreing testimony, ibid., p. 441.

96. Detring testimony, ibid., p. 215.

97. Moreing did not become a member of the board of directors until July 4, 1901. He later said that he had to fight to gain a seat on the board; his presence (he said) was not welcome. Moreing testimony, *Transcript*, pp. 407, 411, 445.

98. Davis to Lord Lansdowne, June 26, 1903. Technically, the "nominees of the Oriental Syndicate" who first received the 425,000 shares turned out to be still another syndicate: the Anglo-Continental Gold Syndicate, which contracted to guarantee the debenture issue and which then distributed the 425,000 shares to the various debenture holders later cited by Davis (Moreing testimony, *Transcript*, p. 451). In 1901 the Anglo-Continental Gold Syndicate had only three directors, two of whom were Davis and Turner. Walter R. Skinner, *The Mining Manual for 1901* (London, 1901), p. 6. The flotation was thus handled by a very small group of men.

99. For Thys's appointment as chairman of the board of the new Chinese Engineering and Mining Company, see minutes of board of directors meeting, May 28, 1901, cited in Hawksley affidavit, April 8, 1905, cited above. For the membership of the Oriental Syndicate's board of directors, see Skinner, *Mining Manual for 1901*, p. 1136. For a list of the Chinese Engineering and Mining Company's board of directors at the beginning of 1902, see Walter R. Skinner, *The Mining Manual for 1902* (London, 1902), p. 980. See also Messrs. Dowdall, Hanson & McNeill, Shanghai, to Messrs. Bompus, Bischoff & Co., London, December 10, 1902, in F.O. 17/1759/140–46, PRO. This letter pointed out the interlocking character of the directorates of the Oriental Syndicate and the Chinese Engineering and Mining Company.

100. See comments by one of Chang Yen-mao's lawyers, Mr. Younger, in *Transcript*, pp. 255–56.

101. See comments by Mr. Levett (Chang's chief trial attorney), ibid., pp. 441, 609.

102. Return of allotments, May 25–June 20, 1901, in Chinese Engineering and Mining Company file, B.T. 31/9233/68532, PRO.

103. De Wouters testimony, *Transcript*, p. 472.

104. Moreing testimony, ibid., pp. 412, 431.

105. Ibid., pp. 430–31. Moreing personally received in profit about 19,000 Oriental Syndicate shares that were eventually converted into 43,500 free Chinese Engineering and Mining Company shares upon dissolution of the Oriental Syndicate in 1902.

106. Share register data presented in letter by Messrs. Dowdall, Hanson & McNeill, December 10, 1902, cited in note 99.

107. Hoover also resorted to this practice of carrying stock listed in his name but actually held for someone else. For examples, see Hoover's Mining Letter Book No. 1, Pre-Commerce Papers, HHPL.

108. Hoover testimony, *Transcript*, p. 352. This allotment probably reflected Moreing's understanding of January 1899 with Hoover: that Hoover would receive 10% of Moreing's profits in China.

109. Ibid.

110. Hoover / de Wouters report, September 1901.

111. On Chinese law pertaining to property ownership and mine management in this period, see Sir Ernest Satow to Lord Lansdowne, May 24, 1904, in F.O. 17 / 1760 / 109–111, PRO; Herbert Hoover, "Present Situation of the Mining Industry in China," *Engineering and Mining Journal* 69 (May 26, 1900): 619–620; W. W. Rockhill, ed., *Treaties and Conventions with and Concerning China and Korea, 1894–1904* (Washington, D.C., 1904), pp. 340–44, 372–74.

112. Hoover / de Wouters report, September 1901.

113. Chang Yen-mao, memorial to the Throne, July 11, 1901, copies in F.O. 17 / 1760 / 127–32, and in Chinese Engineering and Mining Company to the Foreign Office, November 27, 1907, F.O. 371 / 230 / 392–93, PRO.

114. According to Hoover and de Wouters in their September 1901 report, Chang knew by June that "he had lost all sort of control on the Company and accepted the situation."

115. Imperial rescript, attached to the memorial cited in note 113.

116. Provisional regulations of June 4, 1901, article 12.

117. Hoover / de Wouters report, September 1901.

118. Advertisement in *North-China Daily News*, June 17, 1901; copy in Appendix D of Chinese Engineering and Mining Company, Ltd., *Reply to Chinese Government's Memorandum of October 1908*, cited in note 35. See also *North-China Herald*, June 19, 1901, p. 1205.

119. For the text of Chang Yen-mao's newspaper notice of July 10, 1901, see *Transcript*, pp. 130–32, and Appendix D of the new company's *Reply*, cited in note 118. For Hoover's and de Wouters's comments quoted here, see their report of September 1901.

120. Hoover / de Wouters report, September 1901. Curiously, one of the few Chinese holdouts who refused to turn in his old shares was T'ang Shao-yi, whom Hoover had aided during the siege of Tientsin. T'ang, however, held few shares (Detring said "over 70")—an insignificant portion of the approximately 15,000 Chinese shares. Detring testimony, *Transcript*, p. 215. According to Hoover T'ang was a bitter critic of Chang Yen-mao. Hoover, *The Memoirs of Herbert Hoover*, Volume I: *Years of Adventure* (New York, 1951), pp. 39, 90.

121. Alfred S. White-Cooper to Hoover, July 17, 1901, Bewick, Moreing & Co. Collection. See also White-Cooper to Hoover, July 16, 1901, ibid.

122. Hoover / de Wouters report, September 1901; Sir Ernest Satow to Lord Lansdowne (plus enclosures), August 24, 1901, F.O. 17 / 1759 / 40–77, PRO; Satow to Lansdowne (plus enclosures), August 27, 1901, F.O. 17 / 1759 / 78–87, PRO. The extensive British Foreign Office files on the Chinese Engineering and Mining Company (F.O. 17 / 1759 and F.O. 17 / 1760) contain numerous memoranda and letters regarding conflicts with other European Powers over the Kaiping mines. Among these documents are occasional letters by Herbert Hoover (F.O. 17 / 1759 / 47–48 and 57).

123. De Wouters to the board of directors, July 14, 1901.

124. Hoover to Moreing, August 7, 1901, quoted in *Transcript*, p. 345.

   (John) Augustin Daly (1838–1899) was a popular American playwright and producer, whose productions and adaptations often had a comic or melodramatic flavor.

125. Hoover / de Wouters report, September 1901.

126. Ibid.

127. Hoover to the board of directors, May 18, 1901; report of general meeting of shareholders, *Mining World and Engineering Record* 61 (July 20, 1901): 111. In his *Memoirs* Hoover stated that the work force had comprised 25,000, nearly triple the figure he gave in 1901 (*Years of Adventure*, p. 57). This is probably a case of retrospective magnification.

128. *North-China Herald*, July 3, 1901, p. 32.

129. Hoover to the board of directors, June 25, 1901.

130. Hoover testimony, ibid., p. 352; *North-China Herald*, July 3, 1901, p. 32.

131. Hoover to T. R. Wynne, December 17, 1902, "Mining—Wynne, T. R.," Pre-Commerce Papers.

132. Ibid.

133. Hoover / de Wouters report, September 1901; Detring testimony, *Transcript*, pp. 165–66; de Wouters testimony, ibid., p. 471.

134. See 1901 correspondence between Moreing and Edward Hooper, in Bewick, Moreing & Co. Collection. It was clear from these letters that Hoover was involved as early as June 28. See also Hoover, "Information for Biographers" (typescript, n.d.; probably ca. 1914), p. 13, in Benjamin S. Allen Papers, Box 1, HI, and Pre-Commerce Papers, HHPL. In this essay Hoover says that Moreing asked him in June 1901 to join the firm.

135. See [name illegible] to Bewick, Moreing & Co., n.d., Nathan Papers. This letter, written in Hoover's own hand, stated that Hoover (to whom the letter referred in the third person) was heading to London to take a "pardnership" (Hoover's spelling) in Bewick, Moreing and Company. The letter requested the firm to appoint a replacement for Hoover's unexpired term as Engineer-in-Chief for the Mining Bureau of Chihli and Jehol. Hoover ghost-wrote this letter for a deputy of Chang to sign. Although undated, it was clearly written before Hoover left China in September 1901. Hoover therefore had accepted the partnership offer before he sailed from China.

136. Hoover, *Years of Adventure*, pp. 64–65.

137. Hoover to Wynne, December 17, 1902.

138. Hoover testimony, *Transcript*, p. 309.

139. G. Kurgan-van Hentenryk, *Léopold II et les groupes financiers belges en Chine* (Brussels, 1972), pp. 551–53, 678, 703–4. This is a doctoral dissertation published by the Académie Royale de Belgique in its series, Mémoires de la Classe des Lettres.

140. De Wouters to Administrateurs Délégués of the Compagnie Internationale d'Orient, March 22, 1901.

141. Francqui to Leopold II, August 8 and September 22, 1901, cited in Kurgan-van Hentenryk, *Léopold II*, p. 553.

142. Hoover's recollection in his *Memoirs* that he and de Wouters considered the memorandum legally and morally binding—and disagreed with Francqui on this point—must be set against the 1901 letters quoted in this chapter. (For example, de Wouters's letter of July 14, 1901 stating that the memorandum was "absolutely without value.")

143. Hoover / de Wouters report, September 1901.

144. Hoover, "Information for Biographers," p. 13.

145. *San Francisco Chronicle*, October 24, 1901, p. 14; *Stanford Alumnus* 3 (November 1901): 35.

146. See the 1901 letter (cited in note 135) which asked for a replacement for Hoover as Engineer-in-Chief of the provincial mining bureau. If Hoover had not then held this position, there would have been no vacancy to fill when he left China.

147. Hoover to Theodore Hoover, July 21, 1904, Hulda Hoover McLean Papers, HI. Hoover told his brother that he could have returned home to the United States in 1901 with $250,000.

148. Hoover, *Years of Adventure*, p. 38. Hoover used this phrase to describe Chang Yen-mao.

149. Herbert Hoover, "Mining and Milling Gold Ores in Western Australia," *Engineering and Mining Journal* 66 (December 17, 1898): 725–26.

150. Noah F. Drake to John C. Branner, September 22, 1901, John C. Branner Papers, Box 31, Stanford University Archives; R. A. F. Penrose (in Yokohama) to Branner, October 5, 1901, ibid., Box 33.

CHAPTER 10

1. *San Francisco Chronicle*, October 24, 1901, p. 14; C. Algernon Moreing to Gustav Detring, November 14, 1901, quoted on page 204 of the printed transcript of the 1905 trial *Chang Yen Mao v. Moreing*, cited in chapter 7, note 9. As in previous chapters, this valuable trial record will be cited hereinafter as *Transcript*.

2. Report of extraordinary general shareholders meeting of th Chinese Engineering and Mining

Company, December 9, 1901, in *London and China Telegraph* 43 (December 9, 1901): 1007, and *Celestial Empire* (Shanghai), January 22, 1902, p. 83. See also documents in the Chinese Engineering and Mining Company's file, B.T. 31 / 9233 / 68532, Public Record Office (PRO), Kew, Surrey, U.K.

3. Interview with Hoover in *San Francisco Chronicle*, October 24, 1901, p. 14. See also editorial in *Mining and Scientific Press* 83 (November 2, 1901): 180.

4. Hoover to T. R. Wynne, December 17, 1902, "Mining—Wynne, T. R.," Pre-Commerce Papers, HHPL.

5. Herbert Hoover, "The Kaiping Coal Mines and Coal Field, Chihle Province, North China," *Transactions of the Institution of Mining and Metallurgy* 10 (1901–2): 419–30. The long quotation is on p. 426. In another version of this quotation printed in several journals, Hoover referred to "the much lower average of intelligence" of Chinese labor. See, for instance, the version of his paper printed in *Engineering and Mining Journal* 74 (August 2, 1902): 149–50 (quotation on p. 150).

6. In addition to appearing in the journals mentioned in note 5, Hoover's paper was also published in *Colliery Guardian* 83 (June 25, 1902): 1376–78, and in *Celestial Empire* (Shanghai), November 12, 1902, pp. 246–47. It was therefore widely circulated.

7. Sir Ernest Satow (the British ambassador to China) to Lord Lansdowne (the British Foreign Secretary), December 19, 1901, Lord Lansdowne Papers, F.O. 800 / 119 / 226–27, PRO; Herbert Hoover, letter to the editor, *North-China Daily News*, reprinted in *North-China Herald* (Shanghai), August 6, 1902, pp. 281–82; Edmund Davis to Lord Lansdowne, June 26, 1903, in F.O. 17 / 1759 / 255–66, PRO; B. L. Putnam Weale, *The Coming Struggle in Eastern Asia* (London, 1908), p. 582. See also A. J. Barry to Gustav Detring, June 5, 1903, E. J. Nathan Papers, Bodleian Library, Oxford University.

8. On Albert Thys (1849–1915)—soldier, financier, railroad builder, adviser to King Leopold—see: entry for Thys in Académie Royale des sciences coloniales, *Biographie coloniale belge*, Vol. 4 (Brussels, 1955), pp. 875–81; Ruth Slade, *King Leopold's Congo* (London, 1962), pp. 74–76; L. H. Gann and Peter Duignan, *The Rulers of Belgian Africa, 1884–1914* (Princeton, 1979), pp. 70–71; Barbara Emerson, *Leopold II of the Belgians* (New York, 1979), pp. 147–48.

9. C. S. Cocks, *Memorandum respecting Difficulties which have arisen in connection with the Chinese Engineering and Mining Company's properties* (Confi. 9105) (January 1908), copy in F.O. 371 / 418 / 335–37, PRO. See also a letter from Messrs. Dowdall, Hanson & McNeill to Messrs. Bompus, Bischoff & Co., December 10, 1902, F.O. 17 / 1759 / 142, PRO.

10. G. Kurgan-van Hentenryk, *Léopold II et les groupes financiers belges en Chine* (Brussels, 1972), p. 551. This is a doctoral dissertation published by the Académie Royale de Belgique in its series, Mémoires de la Classe des Lettres.

11. Emile Vandervelde, quoted in Neal Ascherson, *The King Incorporated: Leopold II in the Age of Trusts* (Garden City, N.Y., 1964), p. 197.

12. Minutes of the board of directors meeting, Chinese Engineering and Mining Company (the new company), June 5, 1901, quoted on p. 168 of the printed transcript of the January 1906 appeal proceedings of the case of *His Excellency Chang Yen Mao v. Moreing and Others*, Court of Appeal, Supreme Courts of Judicature, Royal Courts of Justice, London. Copies of this extensive text are in the E. J. Nathan Papers, Bodleian Library, Oxford University, and in F.O. 371 / 23 / 56–204, PRO. This 1906 Appeal record will be cited hereinafter as *Appeal Transcript*. The separate text of the 1905 trial will continue to be cited as *Transcript*.

13. Minutes of the board of directors meeting, Chinese Engineering and Mining Company, September 19, 1901, quoted in *Appeal Transcript*, p. 168.

14. C. Algernon Moreing testimony, *Transcript*, pp. 407, 411, 445.

15. Register of the company's directors, January 7, 1902, in the company's file, B.T. 31 / 9233 / 68532, PRO; *Celestial Empire*, February 5, 1902, supplement, p. 6.

16. Kurgan-van Hentenryk, *Léopold II*, pp. 556–57. See also pp. 559–66. By 1904 Leopold controlled over half the Belgian shares in the company. After that he sold off much of his

holding. Eventually Leopold and Thys quarreled, and the Compagnie Internationale d'Orient went its separate way.

17. Gustav Detring testimony, *Transcript*, pp. 165–66. Francqui apparently had the title of "Inspector General." Board of directors to Detring, May 20, 1902, quoted in *Transcript*, p. 220.

18. Satow to Lansdowne, December 19, 1901.

19. See the following articles in the London journal *Truth:* 50 (December 12, 1901): 1573–74; 51 (January 16, 1902): 177–78; 51 (January 23, 1902): 238–39; 51 (January 30, 1902): 301.

20. *North-China Herald*, July 2, 1901, pp. 29, 32; ibid., July 16, 1902, pp. 130–31.

21. Detring testimony, *Transcript*, pp. 165–66.

22. Leon Trouet (for the Brussels board) to the general manager in China (J. H. Dugan), September 27, 1901, quoted in *Transcript*, pp. 475–76.

23. Emile Francqui to the board of directors, November 22, 1901, quoted in *Transcript*, p. 476.

24. Chang Yen-mao testimony, *Transcript*, pp. 88, 133.

25. Ibid., p. 89.

26. Ibid.; Detring testimony, ibid., pp. 166, 216.

27. Chang testimony, ibid., p. 133.

28. The text of the Trouet / Detring understanding quoted here (in the form of a note by Trouet in February 1902 respecting the memorandum of February 1901), is quoted in *Transcript*, pp. 218–19. See also Detring testimony, ibid., pp. 216–17, 219, and Leon Trouet testimony, ibid., pp. 477–78.

29. Detring later claimed that "nothing definite came of" Trouet's visits except a promise by Trouet to explain the issues to his directors and to reach a settlement agreeable to everyone. Detring speech to Chinese shareholders, November 28, 1902, in *Celestial Empire*, December 10, 1902, p. 379. Similarly, at the 1905 trial Detring first tried to claim that he had only accepted Trouet's proposals in February 1902 as a "base," to be submitted to Chang "for discussion." But, said Detring at the trial, he at once broke off discussions with Trouet and "let the matter collapse" after learning that Trouet had no power to sign any such agreement. Under strong cross-examination, however, Detring admitted that he did approve Trouet's proposed arrangement and that he told Trouet that he (Detring) would submit it to Chang "for favourable consideration." Detring testimony, ibid., pp. 166, 217, 219.

30. Trouet testimony, ibid., p. 478.

31. Chang Yen-mao to Colonel Albert Thys, March 8, 1902, quoted in *Transcript*, p. 133; Chang testimony, ibid., p. 133. Chang claimed that he neither saw nor heard about Trouet's notes containing a proposal for compromise.

32. Minutes of the board of directors meeting, Chinese Engineering and Mining Company, April 30, 1902, quoted in ibid., p. 478.

33. Board of directors (Brussels) to Detring, May 2, 1902, quoted in ibid., pp. 220, 478.

34. Detring to the board of directors (Brussels), May 4, 1902, quoted in ibid., pp. 220, 478.

35. Board of directors (Brussels) to Detring, May 5, 1902 and May 20, 1902, quoted in ibid., pp. 220, 478–79.

36. Moreing to Detring, June 13, 1902, quoted in *Transcript*, p. 167, and *Appeal Transcript*, p. 169.

37. T. R. Wynne to the Under Secretary of State, China Department, Foreign Office, June 19, 1902, F.O. 17 / 1759 / 103–5, PRO.

38. Detring to the board of directors of the Chinese Engineering and Mining Company, June 28, 1902, copies in Nathan Papers. Detring's letter simply recited the message that Chang Yen-mao ordered him to dispatch.

39. Detring to Messrs. Drummond & White-Cooper, July 25, 1902, mostly quoted in *Transcript*, pp. 38–40. A somewhat fuller version is in the Nathan Papers.

40. Detring later said that he first saw the new company's articles of association in the autumn of 1901. Detring testimony, *Transcript*, p. 164; Detring, undated pre-trial statement, n.d. (probably early 1905), Nathan Papers.

41. Detring testimony, *Transcript*, pp. 214–15.
42. Detring to Moreing, February 13, 1902, quoted in *Transcript*, p. 205; Trouet testimony, ibid., p. 477.
43. Hoover, letter to the editor (dated June 27, 1902), *North-China Daily News*, reprinted in *North-China Herald*, August 6, 1902, pp. 281–82.
44. Edmund Davis to Lord Lansdowne, June 26, 1903, F.O. 17/1759/255–66, PRO.
45. "A Holder of Bearer Scrip" (pseud.), letter to the editor (dated August 12, 1902), in *North-China Daily News*, August 15, 1902, reprinted in *North-China Herald*, August 20, 1902, pp. 376–77.
46. Detring testimony, *Transcript*, p. 166.
47. Chang testimony, ibid., pp. 89–90.
48. Ibid., p. 89.
49. T. R. Wynne to Detring, September 4, 1902, copy in Nathan Papers.
50. Detring to Wynne, n.d. (ca. October 12, 1902), copy in Nathan Papers. See also *Transcript*, p. 135 (establishing the date).
51. On Li Hung-chang's 1901 receipt, see chapter 9, note 35. All that the text of this receipt establishes is that Li must have been aware that the new (British-registered) company existed—hence, that some kind of transaction or change in arrangements had occurred. The receipt itself says nothing at all about the agreements of July 30, 1900 and February 1901. Nevertheless, the new company's defenders continued to assert that Li's receipt "proved" that the viceroy understood and approved *the terms of the 1900/1901 transfer*. What Li really knew is probably unanswerable; he died in the autumn of 1901 before the Kaiping case flared into public controversy.
52. Albert Thys to Wynne, November 12, 1902, F.O. 17/1759/285–97, PRO.
53. Minutes of the board of directors meeting, Chinese Engineering and Mining Company, October 29, 1902, cited in *Transcript*, pp. 450–51; Moreing testimony, ibid.
54. "A Small Shareholder" (pseud.), letter to the editor (dated August 15, 1902), in *North-China Daily News*, reprinted in *North-China Herald*, August 20, 1902, p. 377; *Celestial Empire*, October 29, 1902, pp. 166–67; *London and China Telegraph* 44 (December 2, 1902): 1023.
55. *London and China Telegraph* 44 (December 2, 1902): 1023. Two of the three committee members were Westerners (probably British).
56. Chang's meeting was publicly announced a month before. Chang Yen-mao, notice to the shareholders, October 25, 1902, copy in Nathan Papers. See also Yen Fuh to Detring, October 13, 1902, copy in Nathan Papers.
57. Accounts of the dramatic meeting of shareholders in Tientsin, November 28, 1902, including verbatim texts of key speeches, were printed widely in the English-language press in China. See, for instance, *North-China Herald*, December 10, 1902, pp. 1226–27; *Celestial Empire*, December 10, 1902, pp. 378–80. A copy of Detring's remarks is in the Nathan Papers. See also Walter Townley (British chargé d'affaires in Peking) to Sir Ernest Satow, December 2, 1902, F.O. 17/1759/116, PRO.
58. Messrs. Dowdall, Hanson & McNeill, Shanghai, to Messrs. Bompus, Bischoff & Co., London, December 10, 1902, F.O. 17/1759/140–46, PRO. Copies also in Nathan Papers.
59. Detring to Moreing, February 13, 1902, quoted in *Transcript*, p. 205; Moreing testimony, ibid., p. 410.
60. Moreing to Detring, November 14, 1901 and February 19, 1902, quoted in ibid., pp. 204, 205; Moreing testimony, ibid., p. 410.
61. For example, Moreing to Detring, December 4, 1901, quoted in *Transcript*, p. 447, and *Appeal Transcript*, p. 169. In this letter Moreing expressed concern that Detring was "having considerable trouble with certain parties since Mr. Hoover left"—a reference to Emile Francqui (Moreing testimony, *Transcript*, p. 447).
62. Moreing to Detring, June 13, 1902. See also Detring and Moreing testimony, *Transcript*, pp. 167, 448.
63. Moreing testimony, *Transcript*, p. 448.

64. Moreing to Detring, August 8, 1902, quoted in *Transcript*, p. 167.
65. Moreing testimony, *Transcript*, pp. 448, 451. Moreing asserted that he could not control the board of directors, which was dominated by the Belgians. Nor could he prevent Thys and his cohorts from voting to rebuff T. R. Wynne in October 1902: "It was no use my protesting," Moreing said.
66. Kurgan-van Hentenryk, *Léopold II*, p. 708.
67. Detring testimony, *Transcript*, pp. 169–70, 203–4; Moreing testimony, ibid., pp. 410–11.
68. Walter Townley to Lord Lansdowne, December 31, 1902, F.O. 17 / 1759 / 135–37, PRO.
69. Statement by Gustav Detring, December 24, 1902, in F.O. 17 / 1759 / 149–54, enclosed with Walter Townley to Lord Lansdowne, January 13, 1903, F.O. 17 / 1759 / 147–48, PRO. Portions of Detring's declaration are quoted in *Transcript*, p. 170.
70. Detring testimony, *Transcript*, p. 171.
71. Walter Townley to Lord Lansdowne, December 3, 1902, F.O. 17 / 1759 / 123, PRO.
72. *Pall Mall Gazette*, February 2, 1903, p. 4.
73. "A Shareholder" (pseud.), letter to the editor, *Pall Mall Gazette*, February 6, 1903, p. 5. Reprinted in *North-China Herald*, March 26, 1903, p. 620. Such phrases in this letter as "ringleaders in this agitation" have—to this biographer—a Hooverian sound.
74. Interview of Moreing in *Westminster Gazette*, February 24, 1903, p. 9.
75. T. R. Wynne, letter to the editor, *Peking and Tientsin Times*, November 4 and 8, 1902; Hoover to Wynne, December 17, 1902 (cited in note 4); Wynne, letter to the editor, *Peking and Tientsin Times*, May 27, 1904, copy in "Mining—Wynne, T. R.," Pre-Commerce Papers.
76. Hoover to Wynne, December 17, 1902; *Peking and Tientsin Times*, May 27, 1904; Percy H. Kent to Hoover, May 28, 1904, "Mining—Wynne, T. R.," Pre-Commerce Papers.
77. T. R. Wynne to Sir James Mackay, March 7, 1903, F.O. 17 / 1759 / 174–76, PRO.
78. *North-China Herald*, April 9, 1903, pp. 677–78, 693.
79. Report of general meeting of Chinese Engineering and Mining Company, September 25, 1902, in *Mining World and Engineering Record* 63 (September 27, 1902): 461–62. See also: *North-China Herald*, November 12, 1902, pp. 995–96, 1006–7; and Moreing interview, *Westminster Gazette*, February 24, 1903, p. 9.
80. Wynne to Mackay, March 7, 1903.
81. Ibid.; *North-China Herald*, April 9, 1903, p. 678; Walter Townley to Lord Lansdowne, May 24, 1903, F.O. 17 / 1759 / 189–91, PRO; Townley to Lansdowne (+ enclosures), June 15, 1903, F.O. 17 / 1759 / 235–44, PRO.
82. The Chinese government's discovery that the Kaiping mines were no longer really Chinese apparently occurred in late 1902, after British troops, at the new company's request, removed a Chinese flag from flying over the mine at Tangshan. On the "Dragon Flag" incident, see Ellsworth C. Carlson, *The Kaiping Mines, 1877–1912* (2nd ed.: Cambridge, Massachusetts, 1971), pp. 86–87, 96, and various reports included in F.O. 17 / 1759, PRO.
83. Townley to Lansdowne, May 24, 1903; Carlson, *Kaiping Mines*, pp. 96–99.
84. Townley to Lansdowne, May 24, 1903; Chang Yen-mao, report to the Throne, ca. December 1902, copy (in English) in George Ernest Morrison Papers, vol. 139, the Mitchell Library, State Library of New South Wales, Sydney, Australia. See also Carlson, *Kaiping Mines*, pp. 99, 102.
85. A. J. Barry to Detring, May 15, 1903, Nathan Papers.
86. A copy of the plaintiff's Statement of Claim (dated June 17, 1903), on which this paragraph is based, is in F.O. 17 / 1759 / 248–53, PRO. The case was filed in the High Court of Justice, Chancery Division, London; a writ was issued on May 7, 1903.
87. On events in China from the "Dragon Flag" incident in November 1902 until the opening of the trial in London in 1905, see, in general, Carlson, *Kaiping Mines*, pp. 86–91, 96–104, as well as various documents cited specifically below.
88. Affidavit by Harry G. Abrahams (a solicitor and member of the firm of Michael Abrahams, Sons & Co.), March 18, 1904, filed with the High Court of Justice, Chancery Division, London. This affidavit is now in the file J4 / 6911 / 204, PRO. Abrahams's firm served as solicitors for both Moreing and his firm of mining engineers.

89. Messrs. Hollams, Sons, Coward & Hawksley (Chang's solicitors) to the Under Secretary of State, Foreign Office, London, March 18, 1904, F.O. 17 / 1760 / 52, PRO.
90. Sir Ernest Satow to the Foreign Office, March 21, 1904, F.O. 17 / 1760 / 58–59, PRO.
91. Satow to Lord Lansdowne, May 24, 1904, F.O. 17 / 1760 / 109–111, PRO.
92. Carlson, *Kaiping Mines*, pp. 98–100; *London and China Telegraph* 45 (December 21, 1903): 1031; Alfred Berry (for the Chinese Engineering and Mining Company) to Lord Lansdowne, December 23, 1903, F.O. 17 / 1759 / 329–32, PRO; Sir Robert Hart to James D. Campbell, December 27, 1903, quoted in John K. Fairbank et al., eds., *The I.G. in Peking: Letters of Robert Hart, Chinese Maritime Customs, 1868–1907* (Cambridge, Massachusetts, 1975), pp. 1389–90; Satow to Lord Lansdowne, December 28, 1903, F.O. 17 / 1759 / 339–40, PRO. See also Chang Yen-mao testimony, *Transcript*, p. 91.
93. Satow cable to Lord Lansdowne, January 13, 1904, F.O. 17 / 1760 / 31–32, PRO; Satow letter (+ enclosures) to Lansdowne, January 13, 1904, F.O. 17 / 1760 / 33–41, PRO.
94. Carlson, *Kaiping Mines*, pp. 99–102.
95. For the terms of the six-point agreement between Chang and Nathan, see F.O. 17 / 1760 / 124, PRO.
96. Yüan Shih-k'ai to Chang Yen-mao, n.d. (early April 1904), copy in F.O. 17 / 1760 / 124–26, PRO.
97. Chang Yen-mao to W. S. Nathan, April 6, 1904, and Nathan to Chang, April 19, 1904, in F.O. 17 / 1760 / 119–22 and 113–18, PRO, respectively.
98. Sir Ernest Satow, cable to the Foreign Office (enclosing a message from W. S. Nathan to his board of directors), August 27, 1904, F.O. 17 / 1760 / 151, PRO; Alfred Berry (for the board) to Lord Lansdowne (enclosing the board's reply to Nathan), September 1, 1904, F.O. 17 / 1760 / 154–57, PRO.

    Yüan's proposal was offered through Chang Yen-mao's enemy, T'ang Shao-yi, the same man whom Hoover had assisted during the siege of Tientsin. On T'ang's enmity for Chang, see *Transcript*, p. 464.

    Why did this deal fall through? Yüan told a British diplomat that he could not pursue any such plan as long as Chang Yen-mao insisted that he had never sold the mines and that he (Chang) could regain control. Yüan's "official" explanation seems disingenuous. The British diplomat concluded that Yüan would not settle unless he got the 200,000 taels first. H. E. Fulford to Satow, September 11, 1904, Satow Papers, PRO 30 / 33 / 9 / 6 / 23, PRO.
99. Fulford to Satow, September 11, 1904.
100. Moreing affidavits of December 11, 1903 and April 11, 1904, filed in J4 / 6723 / 730 and J4 / 6911 / 244, respectively, PRO.
101. Moreing affidavit, April 11, 1904.
102. In addition to the Abrahams and Moreing affidavits cited in notes 88 and 100, see also: Frank Crisp affidavit, December 11, 1903, J4 / 6723 / 729; John Crisp affidavit, May 28, 1904, J4 / 6911 / 344; Herbert Hoover affidavit, November 1, 1904, J4 / 6912 / 544; Hoover affidavit, November 2, 1904, J4 / 6912 / 547. All at PRO.
103. Thomas H. Kingsley affidavit (for the plaintiffs), October 31, 1904, J4 / 6912 / 543, PRO; Hoover affidavit in reply, November 1, 1904. Hoover said Tenney merely checked oral and written translations. In other words, Tenney's role—according to Hoover—was purely a technical, not substantive, one.

     At the trial, incidentally, both Hoover and Chang testified differently. According to Hoover a number of key matters were only settled after Tenney arrived on the scene of the "row." According to Chang, Tenney personally urged Hoover to make concessions and actively contributed to the final understandings. Chang testimony, *Transcript*, pp. 80–82, 86; Hoover testimony, ibid., pp. 307–8.
104. Kingsley affidavit, October 31, 1904.
105. Hoover affidavit, November 1, 1904.
106. Hoover affidavit, November 2, 1904.
107. Messrs. Hollams, Sons, Coward & Hawksley to the Under Secretary of State, Foreign Office, November 10, 1904, F.O. 17 / 1760 / 168, PRO.

108. Satow to the Foreign Office, November 15, 1904, F.O. 17/1760/173, PRO; Satow to Lansdowne, November 30, 1904, in Lansdowne Papers, F.O. 800/121/103, PRO; Carlson, *Kaiping Mines*, p. 104.
109. Satow to Lansdowne, June 5, 1902, F.O. 800/119/323, PRO.
110. Herbert Dering to F. A. Campbell (at the Foreign Office), August 27, 1901, F.O. 17/1759/44, PRO.
111. Townley to Francis Bertie, December 4, 1902, F.O. 17/1759/128, PRO.
112. Townley to Lansdowne, December 3, 1902, F.O. 17/1759/123, PRO.
113. Townley to Bertie, December 4, 1902, F.O. 17/1759/128, PRO.
114. Internal Foreign Office note by Francis Bertie, January 20, 1903, F.O. 17/1759/134, PRO.
115. Internal Foreign Office note, F.O. 17/1759/194, PRO.
116. Internal note by F. A. Campbell, F.O. 17/1759/148 verso, PRO.
117. Townley to Bertie, December 4, 1902.
118. Satow to Lansdowne, December 31, 1903, F.O. 800/120/213–16, PRO. See also Satow to F. A. Campbell, January 28, 1904, Satow Papers, PRO 30/33/14/14/13 verso, PRO, and Satow to F. A. Campbell, June 25, 1904, Satow Papers, PRO 30/33/14/14/137, PRO.
119. Townley to Bertie, December 4, 1902.
120. For examples of the British government's dislike of the Belgians and aversion to either Chinese seizure or Russian control, see: ibid.; Townley to Lansdowne, December 3, 1902; Satow to the Foreign Office, November 20, 1902, F.O. 17/1759/108, PRO.
121. Lansdowne, internal note, January 20, 1903, F.O. 17/1759/134, PRO; Lansdowne, internal note, ca. mid-February 1903, F.O. 17/1759/137 verso, PRO.
122. See, for example: Foreign Office to Walter Townley, January 2, 1903, F.O. 17/1759/158, PRO; Townley to Lansdowne, February 16, 1903, F.O. 17/1759/170–71, PRO; Townley to Lansdowne, May 26, 1903; Foreign Office to Townley, July 27, 1903, F.O. 17/1759/302–3; Foreign Office to Chinese Engineering and Mining Company, January 2, 1904, F.O. 17/1760/1–2, PRO; Satow to Foreign Office, January 13, 1904, F.O. 17/1760/31, 33–34, PRO; F. A. Campbell, internal note, May 20, 1904, F.O. 17/1760/106–7, PRO.
123. Satow to the Foreign Office, December 28, 1903, F.O. 17/1759/335–36; Satow to L. C. Hopkins, December 31, 1903, F.O. 17/1760/35–36; Satow to Lansdowne, May 24, 1904, F.O. 17/1760/109–111; all at PRO.
124. Satow to Lansdowne, December 31, 1903; Satow to L. C. Hopkins, December 31, 1903, Satow Papers, PRO 30/33/9/5/55, PRO; Satow to F. A. Campbell, June 25, 1904, Satow Papers, PRO 30/33/14/14/137–39, PRO. Late in 1904 Satow expressed pleasure that Chang was persisting in his claims. Sympathetic to the Chinese side, Satow hoped to see Moreing and Hoover exposed in the courts. Satow to Lansdowne, November 30, 1904, Satow Papers, PRO 30/33/14/15, PRO.
125. Statements by W. F. Turner at annual shareholders meeting of Chinese Engineering and Mining Company, October 15, 1903, in *Mining Journal* 74 (October 17, 1903): 430–31.
126. This offer was reported in Satow to Lansdowne, November 30, 1904.

CHAPTER 11

1. For Sir Matthew Ingle Joyce (1839–1930), see *Dictionary of National Biography, 1922–1930* (London, 1937), p. 463.
2. Chang Yen-mao to Bourchier F. Hawksley (one of his solicitors), n.d. (probably ca. January 1905), copy in E. J. Nathan Papers, Bodleian Library, Oxford University.
3. Hoover testimony, pp. 289–91, 293, 324 of the printed transcript of the 1905 trial *Chang Yen Mao v. Moreing*, cited in chapter 7, note 9. As in previous chapters, this trial record

will be cited hereinafter as *Transcript*. See also J. Bromley Eames testimony, ibid., pp. 369–70, 375, 390.

4. On Rufus Isaacs (later the Marquess of Reading), see *Dictionary of National Biography, 1931–1940* (London, 1949), pp. 462–67; on Richard B. Haldane, see *Dictionary of National Biography, 1922–1930*, pp. 380–86.

5. The trial proceedings were extensively reported in *The Times*, beginning on January 19, 1905. On King Edward's interest in the case, see John K. Fairbank et al., eds., *The I.G. in Peking: Letters of Robert Hart, Chinese Maritime Customs, 1868–1907* (Cambridge, Mass., 1975), II, p. 1457n.

6. *London and China Telegraph* 47 (March 6, 1905): 192.

7. This trial record (cited in note 3, and referred to here as *Transcript*), comprised 634 tightly printed pages.

8. Thys, Turner, Moreing, and Edmund Davis—all directors—so expressed themselves. For their comments, see the sources cited in chapter 10, notes 52, 125, 68, and 44, respectively. Davis pointed out that the memorandum had been executed in February 1901 without any authorization from the board of directors in Europe.

9. Remarks by T. R. Hughes (Moreing's lawyer) and Haldane, *Transcript*, pp. 258–60, 456–65, 631.

10. Hughes remarks, ibid., pp. 259–60.

11. Chang testimony, ibid., p. 127.

12. Haldane remarks, ibid., pp. 540, 552.

13. Hoover testimony, ibid., pp. 354–55.

14. Moreing testimony, ibid., p. 453.

15. Defense attorneys' remarks, ibid., pp. 456–58, 464, 553–56, 579–80.

16. Ibid., p. 544.

17. Ibid., pp. 458, 549, 550, 552, 553.

18. Ibid., p. 539.

19. Chang testimony, ibid., pp. 93, 97.

20. Ibid., pp. 89–90.

21. Ibid., pp. 108, 122.

22. Ibid., pp. 109, 122.

23. Detring testimony, ibid., p. 192.

24. Ibid., p. 219.

25. Ibid., p. 195.

26. Ibid., pp. 197–99.

27. See the colloquy in ibid., pp. 505–8.

28. Ibid., pp. 505–6.

29. Levett comments, ibid., pp. 590–96.

30. Hoover testimony, ibid., pp. 297, 339.

31. Ibid., p. 351.

32. Ibid., p. 600; Levett comments at the 1906 Court of Appeal proceedings, *Appeal Transcript*, p. 141. (See chapter 10, note 12.)

33. Hoover testimony, *Transcript*, pp. 308, 311–12, 338, 341, 358.

34. Ibid., p. 342.

35. Ibid.

36. Ibid., p. 344.

37. Ibid.

38. Ibid., p. 343.

39. Hoover / de Wouters joint report, September 1901. See chapter 9, note 14.

40. Hoover testimony, *Transcript*, pp. 344, 360.

41. Ibid., p. 346.

42. Hoover to Moreing, March 9, 1901, quoted in ibid., p. 341.

43. Hoover testimony, *Transcript*, pp. 341–42.

44. Ibid., p. 345.
45. Hoover / de Wouters report, September 1901.
46. Hoover testimony, *Transcript*, p. 345.
47. Ibid., p. 360.
48. Moreing testimony, ibid., p. 411.
49. Ibid., pp. 426–37.
50. Comment by Levett, ibid., p. 591.
51. Moreing testimony, ibid., p. 449.
52. Ibid., pp. 450–51.
53. Ibid., p. 449.
54. Moreing comments to Walter B. Townley, the British chargé d'affaires in Peking, December 30, 1902, and relayed in Townley to Lord Lansdowne, December 31, 1902, F.O. 17 / 1759 / 135–37, Public Record Office (PRO), Kew, Surrey, U.K.
55. This phrase was that of J. Bromley Eames, in *Transcript*, p. 390.
56. This impression arises from a close reading of the trial transcript. During the trial at least one contemporary observer, F. A. Campbell of the Foreign Office, believed that the judge was sympathetic toward the plaintiffs. F. A. Campbell to Sir Ernest Satow, January 27, 1905, Satow Papers, PRO 30 / 33 / 7 / 4, PRO.
57. For the text of Justice Joyce's judgment, see *Transcript*, pp. 627–34. Joyce's formal Order (a separate document) is filed in J15 / 2828 / 385, PRO. A corrected printed copy of the judgment is in F.O. 17 / 1760 / 238–41, PRO.
58. Editorial in *The Times* (London), March 2, 1905, p. 9.
59. Chang to Yüan Shih-k'ai, early March 1905, quoted in *Celestial Empire*, April 22, 1905, pp. 152–53.
60. Yüan Shih-k'ai to the Chinese Foreign Office and reply, ca. April 1905 (pre-April 22), quoted in ibid., p. 153.
61. Sir Robert Hart to James D. Campbell, June 4, 1905, quoted in *I.G. in Peking*, p. 1471.
62. In addition to *The Times* (already cited), see *Pall Mall Gazette*, March 2, 1905, p. 2; *Hongkong Telegraph*, March 2, 1905, p. 4; and *London and China Telegraph* 47 (March 6, 1905): 192.
63. *London and China Telegraph* 47 (March 6, 1905): 192.
64. *Engineering and Mining Journal* 79 (March 16, 1905): 546.
65. Internal Foreign Office comment, ca. July 31, 1905, F.O. 17 / 1760 / 255 verso, PRO.
66. The company's appeal was filed at the end of April. Statement by W. F. Turner at annual shareholders meeting of Chinese Engineering and Mining Company, October 27, 1905, reported in *Mining Journal* 78 (October 28, 1905): 484.
67. The Writ of Summons, dated March 8, 1905, for this new lawsuit (short title: *Chang Yen Mao v. Bewick, Moreing and Company*, case no. 1905–C–826), is in F.O. 17 / 1760 / 251, PRO.
68. Ibid. An elaborate affidavit in support of Chang's second lawsuit was filed on April 8, 1905 by one of his solicitors, Bourchier F. Hawksley. This document (which summarizes at some length the testimony in the first lawsuit, before Justice Joyce) is filed as J4 / 6971 / 973, PRO.

   At first Chang tried to make the Chinese Engineering and Mining Company, Ltd. (the "new" company) a co-plaintiff against the defendants Moreing, Hoover, et al.! But after various legal maneuvers, Chang's effort was rebuffed by the courts. For other affidavits and related documents in this second lawsuit, see: J4 / 6970 / 860, J4 / 6971 / 1007, J4 / 6971 / 1059, J4 / 6972 / 1210, J4 / 6973 / 1493, J15 / 2782 / 1561, J15 / 2785 / 2033, J15 / 2830 / 629, J15 / 2830 / 637, all at PRO.
69. Bourchier F. Hawksley to Chang Yen-mao, September 23, 1905, copy in F.O. 17 / 1760 / 282–86, PRO.
70. Satow to F. A. Campbell, December 7, 1905, F.O. 371 / 23 / 40–43, PRO.
71. The Court of Appeal record (already cited in chapter 10, note 12, and referred to here as *Appeal Transcript*) contains 296 printed pages. The remark by Moreing's lawyer, T. R. Hughes, appears on p. 282.
72. The Court of Appeal Order, January 24, 1906, copy in Nathan Papers and in F.O. 371 / 23 / 208–9, PRO. See also the judges' oral comments, *Appeal Transcript*, pp. 282–96.

73. I have found no indication that Chang's second lawsuit was pressed after the filing of various affidavits (cited in note 68) in the spring of 1905. On March 22, 1906, however—after the Appeal judgment—Chang's solicitor, Hawksley, informed the Foreign Office that he had recently requested the Chinese Engineering and Mining Company to appoint Chang managing director of the company with powers in accord with the February 1901 memorandum. Hawksley warned that if the company failed to do so, "it will be necessary to appeal to the Governments to enforce the judgment." Hawksley to F. A. Campbell, March 22, 1906, in F.O. 371 / 23 / 206–7, PRO.

74. According to a British Foreign Office memorandum, the Chinese knew that they could not get much in damages from any court award. See the C. S. Cocks memorandum (1908), cited in chapter 10, note 9. See also a 1911 Foreign Office memorandum, cited in note 81.

75. On the formation of the rival Lan-chou (or Lanchow) coal company and its takeover of most of the coal field, see Ellsworth C. Carlson, *The Kaiping Mines* (2nd ed.: Cambridge, Mass., 1971), pp. 107–17.

76. Alfred W. Berry (for the Chinese Engineering and Mining Company) to the Foreign Office, June 27, 1907, F.O. 371 / 230 / 301, PRO. See also Berry to the Foreign Office, November 29, 1907, F.O. 371 / 230 / 388–94, PRO for an elaborate statement of the company's position (complete with supporting documents), and Berry to the Foreign Office, December 30, 1907, F.O. 371 / 230 / 459, PRO.

77. For the British government's attitude and policy, 1907–1909, see Carlson, *Kaiping Mines*, pp. 115, 117–19. See also: Sir Edward Grey (British Foreign Secretary) to Sir John Jordan (British ambassador to China), July 5, 1907, F.O. 371 / 230 / 315; internal Foreign Office memoranda, mid-1907, F.O. 371 / 230 / 306–311; C. S. Cocks memorandum (1908), already cited; Foreign Office internal memoranda, September 1908, F.O. 371 / 419 / 363–67; Foreign Office internal memoranda, ca. November 16, 1908, F.O. 371 / 419 / 395–96; Foreign Office memorandum entitled *Précis of correspondence from July 1907 in regard to the Difficulties . . . in connection with the Chinese Engineering and Mining Company's property in the Province of Pechihli* (Confi. 9349) (December 1908), F.O. 371 / 419 / 419–22; all at PRO.

78. Sir John Jordan to Sir Edward Grey, February 29, 1908, F.O. 371 / 419 / 294, PRO.

79. C. S. Cocks memorandum (1908), cited in chapter 10, note 9.

80. Sir John Jordan to Sir Edward Grey, February 5, 1909, F.O. 371 / 630 / 366, PRO.

81. Carlson, *Kaiping Mines*, pp. 117–37. In 1908–9 each side produced bulky documents arguing its case. For the Chinese government's position, see its *Memorandum on the K'ai P'ing Mining Case* (Peking, 1908), copies in Nathan Papers and F.O. 371 / 419 / 205–52, PRO. For the Chinese Engineering and Mining Company's rejoinder, see its *Reply to the Chinese Government's Memorandum of October 1908* (ca. January 1909), copy in Nathan Papers. In 1911 the British Foreign Office compiled yet another history of the controversy: *Memorandum on the Correspondence respecting the Claim of the Chinese Engineering and Mining Company (Limited) to the Kaiping Coal-field and to the Ownership of certain Land at Chinwangtao* (Confi. 9783) (1911), PRO.

82. See the listings of directors of the Chinese Engineering and Mining Company in Walter R. Skinner's annual *Mining Manual* (London) for the years 1902–12. Moreing ceased to be a director on June 21, 1907. See register of directors, July 2, 1907, in the company's file, B.T. 31 / 9233 / 68532, PRO.

83. Carlson, *Kaiping Mines*, pp. 137–42. For the text of the 1912 agreements establishing the Kailan Mining Administration, see John V. A. Murray, ed., *Treaties and Agreements with and Concerning China, 1894–1919* (New York, 1921), II, pp. 962–67. See also *Engineering and Mining Journal* 105 (July 27, 1912): 117.

84. Report of extraordinary general shareholders meeting of Chinese Engineering and Mining Company, June 7, 1912, in *Economist* 74 (June 8, 1912): 1322–24.

85. Walter R. Skinner, *The Mining Manual and Mining Year Book for 1913* (London, 1913), pp. 560–61; *Mining Journal* 103 (December 6, 1913), pp. 1159–60; George Bronson Rea, "Hoover in China: The Story of the Kaiping Mining Deal," *Far Eastern Review* 24 (November 1928): 491 (full article: 482–91).

86. G. C. Allen and Audrey C. Donnithorne, *Western Enterprise in Far Eastern Economic Development: China and Japan* (New York, 1954), p. 155.

87. *Economist* 74 (June 8, 1912): 1323; Murray, *Treaties and Agreements*, II, pp. 965, 967.

88. Rowland R. Gibson, *Forces Mining and Undermining China* (London, 1914), p. 72.

With the creation of the Kailan Mining Administration in 1912, the immediate dispute over the Chinese Engineering and Mining Company came to a close. A cause célèbre in its day, the subject of numerous books and articles ever since, the controversy has rumbled on now for three-quarters of a century. In Chinese historiography—both Nationalist and Communist—the episode has come to exemplify Western imperialism. An American visitor to the municipal museum in Tangshan several years ago was startled to find a room dominated by pictures and statements of the young "agent of imperialism," Herbert Hoover.

For Hoover also, the controversy did not fade into history. It became instead a ghost that recurrently haunted his public service. In World War I, in 1920–21, in 1928, and during his presidency enemies of Hoover repeatedly exploited the Chinese lawsuit to portray him as an unethical man who had cheated and mistreated the Chinese. Citing Justice Joyce's comments and other evidence, they vainly attempted to derail his ascent toward higher public office.

These efforts of his political foes drove Hoover to elaborate and costly countermeasures. In 1920, when he was a presidential candidate for the first time, Hoover retained a prominent New York attorney, Arthur Train, to prepare a defense of his conduct in China against an expected "exposé" in the Hearst press. As part of this effort Hoover obtained from Chang Yen-mao's former solicitors in England a copy of the voluminous printed transcript of the 1905 trial. Early in 1921, acting through Train, Hoover instructed his London solicitor to "spare no expense or effort" to purchase every existing copy of this transcript.

Hoover's wish to monopolize the trial transcript probably derived from fear that the document might fall into the hands of his American political enemies, a number of whom in fact scoured London in the 1920s for ammunition against him. In 1923 Hoover himself dispatched a trusted secretary, Lawrence Richey, to London to collect testimonials on Hoover's behalf. Richey carried with him a lengthy exoneration (apparently first drafted by Hoover) for Hoover's British solicitors in the 1905 case to sign. In 1928 this same London firm signed an updated version of its 1923 statement after receiving a draft version of what was wanted from Richey.

Testimonials, in fact, were a favorite device of Hoover's as he strove to refute criticisms of his conduct in China. Although drafted in a form that suggested spontaneity, most of them—perhaps all—were solicited and, in some cases at least, probably ghost-written or approved by Hoover himself. In the late 1920s and early 1930s Hoover personally reviewed and evidently placed in the press articles defending his record in China. Late in 1931, when Arthur Train prepared an article later published in book form as *The Strange Attacks on Herbert Hoover*, President Hoover himself reviewed and revised Train's manuscript prior to its publication.

Yet in all this campaign of self-vindication, which the evidence suggests Hoover masterminded, he never once (before the publication of his *Memoirs* in the 1950s) publicly defended his China record himself. Instead, he operated through intermediaries—journalists, lawyers, and friendly politicians—whose published defenses Hoover supervised and, at least in part, wrote himself. In part Hoover's behavior may have reflected a belief that a mere denial of misconduct by himself would carry little public weight. He also may have felt that his public stature precluded direct rebuttal to his accusers. Above all, Hoover's approach to criticism reflected a deeply ingrained mode of behavior: indirect management of men and events from behind the scenes, out of the glare of personal publicity.

But if Hoover was reluctant to justify his China record directly, his opinion of his accusers was plain. The tone of Hoover's carefully prepared defenses was one of indignation at the "slander," "vague insinuations," "falsehoods," and "filthy political defamation" being peddled by allegedly untraceable rumor mongers. Hoover personally used such words as "absolute malice," "libel," "libelous propaganda" and "smear" to depict the accusations against him. In 1921 he suggested to his attorney that they consider mounting a legal "assault" on a man who was spreading a highly derogatory account of Hoover's career in China. For various practical and technical reasons, his lawyer counselled against it; as far as is known, Hoover did not sue for libel.

Hoover's defense of his China record, as published in the 1920s and later, boiled down to a few reiterated points. First, he consistently contended that while in China in 1901 he regarded the memorandum of February 1901 as binding, that he "always insisted that it be carried out," and that he himself scrupulously adhered to it. The memorandum, he argued, was only violated and repudiated by the Belgians, *after* he left China. Second, he had no role in the Chinese Engineering and Mining Company's controversial financing. Above all, Hoover emphatically asserted that he was only a witness, not a defendant, in the 1905 litigation and that it was *his* testimony—particularly about the memorandum—that decisively helped the Chinese to win their case. In the words of his lawyer, Arthur Train:

> The outstanding fact is that Mr. Hoover was not even named as a defendant in this lawsuit—his relation being that of a witness upon whose testimony the plaintiff won his case for restitution to the office as a director. . . .
> There was nothing in the testimony reflecting upon Mr. Hoover's conduct in any way, it was through his lips that the plaintiffs substantiated their claim, and to suggest that he could possibly be responsible for a breach of contract arising after he had left the employ of the corporation is a wanton defamation.

Again and again during these years Hoover minimized his role in the Kaiping affair. In 1920 he told a friend that his part in the 1905 trial was "that of a witness only, between two quarreling factions of a bondholders reorganization." In 1921 he asked the current Lord Chief Justice of England (who in 1905 had been one of his attorneys) to sign a draft letter that Hoover supplied through intermediaries. This draft had the Lord Chief Justice assert that Hoover's involvement in the trial was not only completely honorable but "largely accidental as an important witness to negotiations that had been carried on by the principals some years before." In his *Memoirs* Hoover asserted that he and his engineering firm "were dragged in to insure our appearance as witnesses and were quickly dismissed from the action" (*Years of Adventure*, p. 90). A number of the testimonials that Hoover solicited also attested to his honorable and / or tangential involvement in the case.

Hoover's later explanations of his conduct in China often diverged from the account provided by the trial transcript and by documents entered in evidence at the trial. While technically not a defendant in the 1905 proceeding (except in the sense that he was a partner in the defendant firm of Bewick, Moreing), Hoover's role, as the transcript shows, was scarcely a peripheral or "accidental" one. This case, he declared in a 1904 affidavit, "involves the most serious allegations against myself personally." As a key participant in the 1900–1901 transfer negotiations, his conduct was under severe scrutiny at the trial.

Nor did Hoover's testimony really win the case for Chang Yen-mao. Hoover was called as a witness not for the Chinese but for two of the defendants: Moreing and Moreing's firm. In his testimony Hoover did, to be sure, confirm the binding character of the memorandum—which Chang also asserted and which Chang wished the court to endorse. As one of Hoover's lawyers at the trial stated, Hoover "believed and intended" in February 1901 that the memorandum "would be carried out fully and fairly." But as Justice Joyce then replied to this lawyer, Hoover had to so testify. Otherwise the judge would have to render a verdict of fraud in obtaining the transfer. To the extent, then, that Hoover substantiated Chang's claim, he had to. He had no choice.

The validity of the memorandum was not the crux of the dispute, however, as the 1905 trial proceeded. Indeed, to the judge's considerable surprise, *everybody* at the trial accepted the binding nature of the memorandum. *All* the defendants claimed that they had endeavored to fulfill it all along. The real issue, contended the defendant company's lawyer, was the *meaning* of the memorandum. And here Hoover's testimony did not support Chang Yen-mao. Chang's aim at the trial was to recover the mines by restoring his authority over them to its pre-Boxer levels. In this respect—the only one that mattered to Chang—he did not win his case at all.

Hoover's later defenses also contained significant omissions. Nowhere did he allude to his crucial role in gaining Gustav Detring's assent in early 1901 to the revisions of the original July 1900 indenture—revisions that opened the gates to the company's financing. Instead, Hoover asserted (through his spokesmen) that he had "nothing to do" with the "reorganization" of the company that White-Cooper and de Wouters came to Tientsin to carry out in 1901. In saying this, Hoover contradicted his 1904 affidavit in which he stated that White-Cooper had acted "upon my personal instructions" at the time. (The day after the "four days' row," in fact, White-Cooper praised Hoover's exceptionally able handling of the transfer negotiations.) Similarly, Hoover's published defenses did not mention Chang's second lawsuit of 1905 in which Hoover was explicitly named as a defendant.

Another striking feature of Hoover's later efforts was that nearly all his testimonials came from people associated with the defendants in the 1905 case. His 1917 letters from the Belgian ambassador to the United States, for instance (which bear certain hints of Hoover's prior draftsmanship), came from a man who said he had "looked after the very large Belgian interests" in Kaiping in 1900. (To those familiar with the Belgian role in the affair this was not the most persuasive of credentials.) In 1923 Hoover secured a tribute from W. F. Turner, the Oriental Syndicate director who played an intimate role in the company's flotation. Hoover also obtained an encomium from his 1905 firm of solicitors. In 1928 Hoover's supporters released a lengthy statement containing, among other things, a tribute by a man vaguely identified as "the only surviving barrister in the case." The barrister, T. R. Hughes, stated that to his recollection nothing brought out in the trial reflected on Hoover's integrity or honor. The covering statement did not mention that Hughes had been Hoover's own chief barrister at the trial.

Perhaps the most interesting testimonial Hoover elicited was from the Chinese statesman T'ang Shao-yi in 1928. Indebted to Hoover for saving his life during the siege of Tientsin in 1900, T'ang was also an old enemy of Chang Yen-mao, who had succeeded Tang's uncle as head of the Kaiping mines in 1892. In a lengthy statement T'ang ringingly extolled Hoover's conduct in China as "not only clean and honorable but highly creditable and in many ways remarkable."

Just how much T'ang actually knew about Hoover's role in the Kaiping affair is uncertain. There is no evidence that T'ang was intimately familiar with the transfer negotiations of 1900–1901 or with Hoover's work as general manager from February to September 1901. Nor was T'ang (as Hoover later incorrectly stated) the "principal Chinese owner" of the Kaiping mines. But whatever its evidentiary value, T'ang's strongly worded testimonial was a welcome weapon in 1928 as Hoover campaigned for the presidency. It was published in Japan and the United States. In his *Memoirs* Hoover cited it as having "suddenly" appeared in the American press and having served as a "boomerang" against the "libels" being peddled by the "Democratic underworld."

The most fascinating aspect of T'ang's laudatory letter, however, was not its substance but the extraordinary lengths Hoover went to secure it. The portion of T'ang's 1928 statement referring to the Kaiping controversy turned out to be little more than a paraphrase of a key statement in defense of Hoover prepared in the 1920s by Hoover's American lawyer, Arthur Train. As it happened, this was not accidental. The paraphrase was in fact drawn up for T'ang to sign by B. W. Fleisher, an American journalist who was publisher of the *Japan Advertiser*. Fleisher modeled T'ang's statement on a copy of Arthur Train's defense of Hoover that he confidentially received early in 1928 from none other than Hoover's secretary, Lawrence Richey. It was at Richey's direct request that Fleisher, in fact, traveled to China in the spring of 1928 to elicit the testimonial that T'ang signed. This statement, among other things, repeated the standard assertion that Hoover's testimony led to Chinese victory in the lawsuit.

Fleisher modeled T'ang's statement on Train's, he told Hoover's secretary, so that T'ang's account would be "consistent" with other records in Hoover's files. Afterwards Fleisher reported that T'ang's memory was shaky on details and that T'ang sometimes altered the chronology of events. But Fleisher was confident that he would not now deviate from the story he had signed; if he did, it would be a loss of "face."

T'ang's statement thus entered Hoover's arsenal of defense against uncomplimentary stories about Kaiping—stories still rife in China in the 1920s.

Still, one should not dismiss entirely T'ang Shao-yi's testimonial, if only for one reason. In 1904, as an adviser to Viceroy Yüan Shi-k'ai, T'ang participated in the Chinese assault on Chang Yen-mao and in Yüan Shih-k'ai's campaign to recover the Kaiping mines. It is hard to understand why T'ang signed a statement in 1928 asserting that Hoover had enabled the Chinese to win their case when he must have known that, in Yüan's eyes, they did not win at all: China did not recover the mines. Nevertheless, in 1904, when he should have known something about Hoover's involvement, T'ang was hostile to the British company—yet not, in 1928, to Hoover. Perhaps in his own mind he dissociated Hoover from the conduct of his European colleagues.

In short, Hoover's later defenses of his conduct in China did little to illuminate his role in the murky Kaiping drama. But that, of course, was not their purpose. In the 1920s particularly, when Hoover was obliged to retell the story of his days in China, he was under intense pressure to fend off potentially fatal threats to his continuance in public life. The effort to block his aspirations by "exposing" his past is a largely untold story that came to involve some prominent members of both political parties. Under the circumstances it is not surprising that Hoover and his associates devised a defense that fit the requirements of political survival.

The great majority of the materials on which I based the preceding analysis can be found in two places: the "Chinese Matter" folders in the Pre-Commerce Papers, HHPL, and the "Chinese Mining Suit" folders in the Misrepresentations File, HHPL. There files include correspondence between Hoover and his lawyer, testimonials and affidavits, and various statements drafted by Hoover and his supporters. Other items of interest include: Alfred White-Cooper to Secretary, Oriental Syndicate, February 25, 1901, copy in George Ernest Morrison Papers, vol. 139, the Mitchell Library, State Library of New South Wales, Sydney, Australia; Arthur Train memorandum, February 12, 1932, Arthur Train Papers, New York Public Library; Hoover to Lindon W. Bates, August 30, 1915, Commission for Relief in Belgium Papers, Box 32, HI; the Hoover file in the Guy M. Walker Papers, De Pauw University Archives; Arthur Train, *The Strange Attacks on Herbert Hoover* (New York, 1932); and the first two volumes of Hoover's *Memoirs*. For the Chinese historiography on the case see Carlson, *Kaiping Mines*, p. 91. Carlson himself is critical of Hoover's role in the episode.

Hoover, incidentally, did not obtain every copy in existence of the 1905 trial transcript. Such a copy exists today in the E. J. Nathan Papers, Bodleian Library, Oxford University, and has been used extensively by this author in the preparation of these chapters. (This is the document cited briefly as *Transcript*.)

E. J. Nathan was for many years a prominent British official in the Chinese Engineering and Mining Company and Kailan Mining Administration. The Nathan Papers contain the only known major archive relating to the Chinese Engineering and Mining Company from the 1890s until the 1950s. Besides containing the 1905 trial transcript (and 1906 Appeal transcript) it includes a number of letters written by Hoover and key associates. This collection thus constitutes a valuable lode of information about Hoover's career in China.

For sources in Belgium on Belgian involvement in the Kaiping affair see G. Kurgan-van Hentenryk, *Léopold II et les groupes financiers belges en Chine* (Brussels, 1972), a dissertation published by the Académie Royale de Belgique in its series, Mémoires de la Classe des Lettres.

CHAPTER 12

1. *San Francisco Chronicle*, October 24, 1901, p. 14; Hoover Calendar, HHPL.
2. *San Francisco Chronicle*, October 24, 1901, p. 14.
3. *Stanford Alumnus* 3 (November 1901): 35.
4. George Barr Baker, "Memorandum for Mr. Hoover Covering Some of Mr. Wickersham's Questions," May 21, 1920, "Citizenship," Pre-Commerce Papers, HHPL; Herbert Hoover, preliminary draft version (in galleys) of Volume I, chapter 7 of his *Memoirs*, in Hoover Book Manuscripts Material, HHPL; Herbert Hoover, *The Memoirs of Herbert Hoover*, Volume I: *Years of Adventure* (New York, 1951), p. 76. In the galley version Hoover stated openly that he furnished the money to Mr. Henry in 1901. In the *Memoirs* as published he merely said that he "joined with" Henry in building the cottage—in 1902. The 1920 memorandum by George Barr Baker (one of Hoover's aides) stated that Hoover supplied the money about eighteen years before.
5. Hoover, draft (galley) version of *Memoirs*, Volume I, chapter 7; Hoover, *Years of Adventure*, p. 76.
6. Hoover Calendar, HHPL; C. Algernon Moreing to Gustav Detring, November 14, 1901, quoted on p. 204 of the transcript of the trial *Chang Yen Mao v. Moreing* (1905), cited in chapter 7, note 9; Hoover, *Years of Adventure*, p. 73.
7. *Mining Journal, Railway and Commercial Gazette* 71 (November 2, 1901): 1371; Hoover, *Years of Adventure*, p. 73.
8. *The Times* (London), September 10, 1942, p. 7; *Mining World and Engineering Record* 143 (September 12, 1942): 128; Moreing to A. B. Mumm, December 3, 1926, Bewick, Moreing & Co. Collection, HHPL. Moreing was born in 1855.
9. Clark C. Spence, *Mining Engineers and the American West* (New Haven, 1970), p. 8n; *Engineering and Mining Journal* 67 (June 3, 1899): 656.
10. *The Times*, December 18, 1903, p. 15; *The Telegraph* (London), December 18, 1903; *West Australian Mining, Building, and Engineering Journal* 6 (July 1, 1905): 9.
11. Hoover, *Years of Adventure*, pp. 74, 84.
12. Bewick, Moreing & Co. account sheet re A. S. Rowe defalcation charges, n.d.; Bewick, Moreing & Co. statement regarding Herbert Hoover, n.d. (ca. 1916); indenture between C. Algernon Moreing and Herbert Hoover, January 4, 1917; all in Bewick, Moreing & Co. Collection, HHPL. See also *West Australian Mining, Building, and Engineering Journal* 6 (July 1, 1905): 9. The December 18, 1901 partnership agreement has not been located, but its date is established from the 1917 indenture cited here. In his *Memoirs* Hoover correctly stated his own and Wellsted's shares in the profits but incorrectly gave Rowe's as only 10%.
13. Bewick, Moreing & Co. statement regarding Herbert Hoover, n.d. (ca. 1916); Herbert Hoover, "Information for Biographers" (typescript, n.d.; probably ca. 1914), p. 13, in Benjamin S. Allen Papers, Box 1, HI, and Pre-Commerce Papers, HHPL. In the latter statement, incidentally, Hoover erroneously recalled that his original share in the partnership was $1/6$ rather than $1/5$ (the correct figure). For more on the negotiations leading to Hooper's withdrawal and Hoover's entry, see C. Algernon Moreing letters to Edward Hooper, 1901, in Bewick, Moreing & Co. Collection.
14. Hoover to his brother Theodore, July 21, 1904, Hulda Hoover McLean Papers, HI; Bewick, Moreing & Co. statement regarding Herbert Hoover, n.d. (ca. 1916).
15. Hoover, *Years of Adventure*, p. 74. In addition to serving on the board of directors of the Chinese Engineering and Mining Company, Davis and Turner had many other close contacts with C. Algernon Moreing and his firm. In 1901 they were two of the five directors of the Hannan's Brownhill Gold Mining Company, for which Bewick, Moreing served as managers. They were directors of the London and Hamburg Gold Recovery Company, for which Bewick, Moreing served as consulting engineers. They also were a majority on the board of three directors of the Anglo-Continental Gold Syndicate (1899), which handled the 1901 debenture issue for the Chinese Engineering and Mining Company and which held

substantial share interests in the Talisman Consolidated mine, managed by Bewick, Moreing in New Zealand. Walter R. Skinner, *The Mining Manual for 1901* (London, 1901), pp. 6–7, 119–20, 164, and *The Mining Manual for 1902* (London, 1902), pp. 6–7.

16. Skinner, *Mining Manual for 1901*, pp. 165–66.

17. Allen H. P. Stoneham, quoted in *Colonial Mining News* 16 (December 24, 1902): 405.

18. Hoover, *Years of Adventure*, p. 74; *West Australian Mining, Building, and Engineering Journal* 4 (February 18, 1905): 13.

19. For two examples of Bewick, Moreing contracts, see its Agreements with the Great Fingall Consolidated, Ltd., December 31, 1900 and April 28, 1902. Texts in House of Lords Appeal Cases, 1906: *Ruben & Ladenburg v. Great Fingall Consolidated, Ltd.*, Appendix, pp. 16–21, House of Lords Record Office, London.

20. Skinner's *Mining Manual* for 1901 and 1902 records that Rowe was secretary of the Hannan's Brownhill and Great Fingall (among others) while T. W. Wellsted was secretary of the Sons of Gwalia as well as the London and Western Australian Exploration Company.

21. Hoover, *Years of Adventure*, p. 74.

22. *Mining World and Engineering Record* 62 (June 7, 1902): 987.

23. Bewick, Moreing & Co. contract with Great Fingall Consolidated, Ltd., April 28, 1902, cited in note 19.

24. Ibid.

25. Masthead of letter from Hoover to R. A. F. Penrose, Jr., October 28, 1902, quoted in Helen R. Fairbanks and Charles P. Berkey, *Life and Letters of R. A. F. Penrose, Jr.* (New York, 1952), p. 302.

26. Hoover, *Years of Adventure*, p. 74.

27. Hoover Calendar, HHPL. The voyage of the *China* can be followed in the daily shipping column of *The Times*. The vessel reached Marseilles on its eastbound journey on December 20, 1901. The Hoovers boarded there.

28. *The Times*, January 16, 1902, p. 7 (for the arrival of the P. and O. vessel *China* at Fremantle). The Hoover Calendar erroneously dates his arrival in Kalgoorlie as December 29, 1901. At that point the Hoovers were still passing through the Suez Canal.

29. Hoover, *Years of Adventure*, p. 77.

30. J. W. McCarty, "British Investment in Western Australian Gold Mining, 1894–1914," *University Studies in History* 4 (1961–62): 13.

31. [J. H. Curle], "West Australian Mines—I," *Economist* 60 (July 19, 1902): 1113.

32. Ibid. Diehl represented the London and Hamburg Gold Recovery Company in Western Australia. His "Diehl process" was one of the principal processes for the treatment of sulphotelluride ores in the Kalgoorlie region.

33. For background on political, economic, and social ferment in Western Australia, 1895–1904, see: J. W. McCarty's article (cited above); John Bastin, "The West Australian Gold Fields, 1892–1900: The Investors and Their Grievances," *Historical Studies: Australia and New Zealand* 6 (November 1954): 282–89; D. Mossenson, "Mining Regulations and Alluvial Disputes, 1894–1904," *University Studies in History and Economics* 2 (September 1955): 5–31; F. K. Crowley, *Australia's Western Third: A History of Western Australia from the First Settlements to Modern Times* (London, 1960), pp. 112–55.

34. [Curle], "West Australian Mines—I," p. 1113.

35. McCarty, "British Investment in Western Australian Gold Mining," pp. 12, 20.

36. For two spectacular examples of such collusion and market manipulation, see ibid., pp. 16–20.

37. Hoover, "Information for Biographers," p. 13.

38. A guinea was formerly a British gold coin (and now a unit of value) worth just over £1.

39. Hoover, *Years of Adventure*, pp. 77–78.

40. On the Whittaker Wright scandals, see: *Mining Journal, Railway and Commercial Gazette* 75 (January 30, 1904): 124; *Australian Mining Standard* 31 (February 4, 1904): 157; McCarty, "British Investment in Western Australian Gold Mining," pp. 19–20; Hoover, *Years of*

Adventure, pp. 78–79; entry for Whittaker Wright in *Dictionary of National Biography*, 1901–11 Supplement (Oxford, 1969), pp. 711–13; Derek Walker–Smith, *Lord Reading and His Cases* (New York, 1934), pp. 133–54; Marquess of Reading, *Rufus Isaacs: First Marquess of Reading* (New York, 1940), pp. 131–46; H. Montgomery Hyde, *Lord Reading: The Life of Rufus Isaacs, First Marquess of Reading* (London, 1967), pp. 47–54. Isaacs, who prosecuted Wright, was one of Herbert Hoover's attorneys in the Chang Yen-mao case in 1905.

41. Hoover, *Years of Adventure*, p. 78.
42. Ibid., pp. 78–79; *The Times*, October 28, 1926, p. 14, and October 29, 1926, p. 20.
43. *The Times*, December 14, 1901, p. 5.
44. *Truth* 51 (February 6, 1902): 365; Hoover, *Years of Adventure*, p. 79. W. A. Prichard took charge of the mine for Bewick, Moreing on January 28, 1902. Statement by W. A. Prichard, n.d., in *Report of the Royal Commission [on] . . . Great Boulder Perseverance Gold Mining Company, Limited, Kalgoorlie* (Perth, 1905), p. 131, printed in Western Australia, *Votes and Proceedings of Parliament*, 5th Parliament, 2nd Session (1905), Volume I, Paper No. 3.
45. Hoover, *Years of Adventure*, p. 79.
46. *The Times*, October 29, 1926, p. 20; W. J. Loring interview, 1931, Walter W. Liggett Papers, New York Public Library.
47. Bewick, Moreing & Co. statement regarding Herbert Hoover, n.d. (ca. 1916).
48. Govett statement at Lake View Consols shareholders meeting, October 30, 1908, quoted in *West Australian Mining, Building, and Engineering Journal* 12 (December 12, 1908): 13. See also Govett statement at Ivanhoe Gold Corporation shareholders meeting, April 27, 1905, quoted in *Mining World and Engineering Record* 68 (April 29, 1905): 539.
49. For Western Australian gold production statistics, 1893–1912, see Malcolm Maclaren and J. Allan Thomson, "Geology of the Kalgoorlie Goldfield—I," *Mining and Scientific Press* 107 (July 12, 1913): 48.
50. Hoover, "Information for Biographers," p. 14; Hoover, *Years of Adventure*, p. 78.
51. Hoover, *Years of Adventure*, p. 78n.
52. *Truth* 51 (February 6, 1902): 365.
53. Theodore J. Hoover, *Memoranda: Being a Statement by an Engineer* (typescript: Stanford University, 1939), pp. 113–16, copy at HHPL. See also Theodore Hoover's membership file, Institution of Mining and Metallurgy, London.
54. Theodore Hoover, *Memoranda*, p. 116; interview of W. J. Loring in T. A. Rickard, *Interviews with Mining Engineers* (San Francisco, 1922), p. 278.
55. Hoover, *Years of Adventure*, p. 78n; John Agnew obituary notice, files of Institution of Mining and Metallurgy, London.
56. William A. Prichard statement in *West Australian Mining, Building, and Engineering Journal* 3 (April 16, 1904): 5.
57. Richard M. Atwater interview, ca. 1931, Liggett Papers.
58. W. J. Loring interview, Liggett Papers.
59. Loring succeeded Hoover in 1908 as a partner in Bewick, Moreing & Company. For the firm's subsequent difficulties with Hoover, see chapter 22. Curiously, in 1932, after privately criticizing Hoover (to Walter Liggett), Atwater prepared, on Hoover's behalf, a sworn statement defending Hoover against charges made about his conduct in Australia by another biographer! While there is no direct contradiction between the two statements that Atwater made, their tone is quite inconsistent. See Richard M. Atwater statement, January 20, 1932, enclosed in Atwater to Edgar Rickard, January 20, 1932, "Rickard Files—Statements and Affidavits, Mining, 1931–1932 and Undated," Misrepresentations File, HHPL. Atwater's pro-Hoover statement given to Rickard (a Hoover associate) does not mention Hoover's alleged abortive strike in 1898 against Ernest Williams.
60. Atwater interview, Liggett Papers; Gavin Casey and Ted Mayman, *The Mile That Midas Touched* (rev. ed.: Adelaide, 1968), p. 93.
61. Atwater and Loring interviews, Liggett Papers.
62. Atwater interview, Liggett Papers; Loring interview in T. A. Rickard, *Interviews with Mining Engineers*, p. 279.

63. Loring interview in Rickard, *Interviews with Mining Engineers*, p. 278.

64. Skinner, *Mining Manual for 1902*, pp. 104–5; McCarty, "British Investment in Western Australian Gold Mining," p. 14; [J. H. Curle], "Western Australian Mines—II," *Economist* 60 (July 26, 1902): 1161.

65. Hoover Calendar, HHPL.

66. *Colonial Mining News* 15 (April 17, 1902): 255.

67. Herbert Hoover to London and Hamburg Gold Recovery Co. (reporting on its leases at Pindinnie, W.A.), March 31, 1902. This report is currently in the possession of the Department of Mines, Perth, Western Australia.

68. *Mining World and Engineering Record* 63 (July 19, 1902): 111.

69. J. W. Kirwan, "Hoover in Western Australia: Some Goldfields Memories," n.d. (late 1928), Reprint File, HHPL.

70. A. S. Rowe speech at Great Fingall shareholders meeting, January 20, 1902, quoted in *Mining Journal, Railway and Commercial Gazette* 72 (January 25, 1902): 121. Hoover himself told W. A. Prichard the same thing. W. A. Prichard, "Looking for Mines in Mexico," *Mining Magazine* 1 (November 1909): 210.

71. C. Algernon Moreing to Hoover, February 28, 1902, Laurine Small Papers, HHPL.

72. Interview with Hoover in *Australian Mail* 9 (January 12, 1899): 131.

73. Skinner, *Mining Manual for 1901*, p. 76.

74. East Murchison United gold production figures, November 1901–April 1902, in *Economist* 60 (May 24, 1902): 819.

75. *Economist* 59 (December 14, 1901): 1864.

76. Transcript of East Murchison United annual shareholders meeting, December 7, 1903, printed in *Mining World and Engineering Record* 65 (December 12, 1903): 761–64. This verbatim transcript includes the text of a letter from Hoover on November 7, 1903 describing efforts under his direction to develop the mine.

77. Transcript of East Murchison United shareholders meeting, December 20, 1904, printed in *Mining World and Engineering Record* 67 (December 24, 1904): 877–79; Walter R. Skinner, *The Mining Manual for 1906* (London, 1906), p. 55.

78. The East Murchison United had £180,000 in authorized capital (two-thirds of it issued free in shares to the vendors), but its total dividends over the years came to only £60,000. See Walter R. Skinner, *The Mining Manual for 1905* (London, 1905), p. 61; transcript of East Murchison United shareholders meeting, December 20, 1904, p. 878.

79. *Mount Leonora Miner*, February 8, 1902, p. 3.

80. Transcript of Sons of Gwalia annual shareholders meeting, June 5, 1902, printed in *Mining World and Engineering Record* 62 (June 7, 1902): 984–86 (full transcript: 984–88); report of same meeting in *Economist* 60 (June 7, 1902): 901.

81. Ibid. See also Sons of Gwalia Circular No. 10, March 20, 1902, in Sons of Gwalia Records, J. S. Battye Library, Perth, Western Australia.

82. Sons of Gwalia Circular No. 10, March 20, 1902.

83. For these reports (as quoted at the 1902 shareholders meeting), see *Mining World and Engineering Record* 62 (June 7, 1902): 985.

84. Bewick, Moreing & Co.—Kalgoorlie to Sons of Gwalia board of directors, January 4, 1902, quoted in ibid.

85. Hoover remarks at 1902 shareholders meeting, quoted in ibid., p. 987.

86. Hoover's letter arrived in London on March 17. Sons of Gwalia Circular No. 10, March 20, 1902.

87. Hoover to the Sons of Gwalia board of directors, February 14, 1902, quoted in ibid.

88. Bewick, Moreing & Co.—Kalgoorlie cables to Sons of Gwalia board of directors, February 20 and March 4, 1902, quoted in Sons of Gwalia Circular No. 10, March 20, 1902.

89. Bewick, Moreing & Co.—Kalgoorlie report, quoted in transcript of Sons of Gwalia annual shareholders meeting, June 5, 1902, p. 985.

90. Hoover remarks at the 1902 shareholders meeting, p. 987.

91. Loring interview, in Rickard, *Interviews with Mining Engineers*, pp. 278–79.

92. Bewick, Moreing & Co.—Kalgoorlie to Sons of Gwalia board of directors, April 12, 1902, quoted in transcript of 1902 shareholders meeting, p. 985.

93. Bewick, Moreing & Co.—Kalgoorlie to Richard M. Atwater, March 11, 1902, enclosing an extract from its letter to the Secretary, Sons of Gwalia, the week before, in Sons of Gwalia Records.

94. Ibid.

95. See chapter 6.

96. *Economist* 59 (December 14, 1901): 1864; Skinner, *Mining Manual for 1902*, p. 160.

97. Richard M. Atwater to the Warden, Mt. Margaret Goldfields, March 15, 1902, J. S. Battye Library.

98. Transcript of Sons of Gwalia annual shareholders meeting, May 25, 1899, printed in *Mining Journal, Railway and Commercial Gazette* 69 (May 27, 1899): 614–15.

99. Ibid.

100. Ibid.

101. Transcript of 1902 Sons of Gwalia shareholders meeting, p. 985.

102. Transcript of 1899 Sons of Gwalia shareholders meeting, p. 615.

103. Skinner, *Mining Manual for 1902*, p. 239.

104. Transcript of 1902 shareholders meeting, p. 986.

105. Ibid.

106. Transcript of Sons of Gwalia shareholders meeting, June 15, 1903, printed in *Mining World and Engineering Record* 64 (June 20, 1903): 888.

107. On January 25, 1902, Sons of Gwalia shares on the London stock exchange traded at £2½—the highest level they reached all year. From then on they declined drastically, reaching a nadir of $^{13}/_{16}$ on June 7 and hovering around ⅞ (less than nominal issued value) for the rest of the year. Share quotations found in *Economist*, 1902.

108. Hoover Calendar, HHPL. Hoover left Kalgoorlie on March 31, 1902. *Kalgoorlie Miner*, March 31, 1902. The Calendar material states that the Hoovers left Fremantle on the North-German Lloyd vessel *Barbarossa* on April 12. It must, however, have been sooner because this ship reached Colombo, Ceylon on April 13. *The Times*, April 15, 1902, p. 10.

109. *Colonial Mining News* 15 (May 8, 1902): 305. The Hoover Calendar states that the Hoovers returned to London on April 26. However, the *Barbarossa* did not leave Port Said, Egypt until April 27 and only reached Genoa on or about May 4. *The Times*, April 29, 1902, p. 10, and May 6, 1902, p. 10.

110. Hoover homes finding aid, HHPL; Hoover, *Years of Adventure*, p. 76.

111. Herbert Hoover, "The Kaiping Coal Mines and Coal Field, Chihle Province, North China," *Transactions of the Institution of Mining and Metallurgy*, 10 (1901–2), 419–30.

112. *Colonial Mining News* 16 (June 12, 1902), 33.

113. *Mining World and Engineering Record* 62 (May 31, 1902): 933, and 63 (October 11, 1902): 528.

114. Ibid., May 31, 1902, p. 933.

115. Transcript of 1902 Sons of Gwalia shareholders meeting, pp. 984–88.

116. Chairman's remarks, ibid., pp. 984–86; account of the same meeting in *Economist* 60 (June 7, 1902): 901.

117. Ibid.

118. Moreing remarks, in *Mining World* version, p. 987.

119. Hoover remarks, ibid., 987–88.

120. *Mining World* version, p. 988; *Economist* version, p. 901.

121. Hoover remarks, *Mining World* version, p. 987.

122. Share quotations found in *Economist*, 1902.

123. [Curle], "West Australian Mines—II," p. 1162.

124. Transcript of Hannan's Brownhill Gold Mining Co. annual shareholders meeting, July 17, 1902, printed in *Mining World and Engineering Record* 63 (July 19, 1902): 111 (full transcript: 110–112).

125. Skinner, *Mining Manual for 1901*, pp. 119–20.
126. Ibid.; Skinner, *Mining Manual for 1902*, pp. 115–16.
127. [Curle], "West Australian Mines—II," p. 1160.
128. [Curle], "West Australian Mines—I," p. 1113.
129. *Economist* 60 (June 28, 1902): 1014; transcript of 1902 Hannan's Brownhill shareholders meeting, p. 112; Walter R. Skinner, *The Mining Manual for 1903* (London, 1903), pp. 185–86.
130. *Economist* 60 (June 28, 1902): 1014.
131. Transcript of 1902 Hannan's Brownhill shareholders meeting, p. 111.
132. *Economist* 60 (June 28, 1902): 1014.
133. Richard M. Atwater interview, Liggett Papers.
134. Hoover Calendar, HHPL.
135. Lou Henry Hoover to John C. Branner, July 23, 1902, John C. Branner Papers, Box 32, Stanford University Archives.
136. Hoover Calendar, HHPL; *Mining Journal, Railway and Commercial Gazette* 73 (August 2, 1902): 1062.
137. Hoover, *Years of Adventure*, p. 87; Theodore Hoover, *Memoranda*, p. 121; Skinner, *Mining Manual for 1902*, pp. 1265–66.
138. Theodore Hoover, *Memoranda*, p. 121; Hulda Hoover McLean, *Genealogy of the Herbert Hoover Family* (Hoover Institution, Stanford University, 1967), p. 7.
139. R. A. F. Penrose to Hoover, October 17, 1902, in Fairbanks and Berkey, *Life and Letters of R. A. F. Penrose, Jr.*, p. 302.
140. Hoover Calendar, HHPL.
141. Ibid.; Hoover, *Years of Adventure*, p. 76.
142. Hoover, *Years of Adventure*, p. 85.
143. Hoover Calendar, HHPL.
144. [Hoover], "Westralian Mines," *Financial Times*, November 5, 1902, p. 3; [Hoover], "Westralian Mines," *Financial Times*, November 18, 1902, p. 5; Hoover, "Gold Mining in Western Australia in 1902," *Engineering and Mining Journal* 75 (January 3, 1903): 18. The first two of these articles were published anonymously. They are identified as Hoover's "anonymous doings" in a scrapbook of his professional writings found in the Herbert Hoover Collection, Box 230, HI.
145. Hoover, "Gold Mining in Western Australia in 1902," p. 18.
146. [Hoover], "Westralian Mines" (November 5, 1902), p. 3.
147. Ibid.
148. *Colonial Mining News* 16 (September 4, 1902): 199; *West Australian Mining, Building, and Engineering Journal* 1 (January 3, 1903): 4.
149. [Hoover], "Westralian Mines" (November 5, 1902), p. 3.
150. [Hoover], "Westralian Mines" (November 18, 1902), p. 5.
151. Hoover, "Gold Mining in Western Australia in 1902," p. 18.
152. Ibid.
153. *Mining World and Engineering Record* 63 (October 11, 1902): 530.
154. *West Australian Mining, Building, and Engineering Journal* 1 (January 3, 1903): 4.
155. Govett remarks at Lake View Consols annual shareholders meeting, October 9, 1902, printed in *Mining World and Engineering Record* 63 (October 11, 1902): 527–30. See also Prichard, "Looking for Mines in Mexico," p. 210.
156. [Curle], "West Australian Mines—II," pp. 1161–62.
157. Transcript of Sons of Gwalia annual shareholders meeting, June 15, 1903, printed in *Mining World and Engineering Record* 64 (June 20, 1903): 888–89.
158. Ibid.
159. *West Australian Mining, Building, and Engineering Journal* 1 (January 3, 1903): 4.
160. "Memorandum of Herbert C. Hoover," printed in House of Lords Appeal Cases, 1905: *Storey v. Hoover*, Appendix, p. 12, House of Lords Record Office, London. This memo-

randum listed transactions by date of entry from September 1 to December 15, 1902.

161. Hoover testimony, p. 352, transcript of the 1905 trial *Chang Yen Mao v. Moreing*, cited above in chapter 7, note 9.

162. "Memorandum of Herbert C. Hoover."

163. Ibid.

164. Hoover, *Years of Adventure*, p. 24.

CHAPTER 13

1. Herbert Hoover, *The Memoirs of Herbert Hoover:* Volume I: *Years of Adventure* (New York, 1951), p. 83.

2. Ibid.

3. In his *Memoirs* Hoover erroneously gives the date as December 27. The correct date (December 29) is established from contemporary newspaper accounts of the Rowe affair and from Hoover and T. W. Wellsted to C. Algernon Moreing, January 9, 1903, Bewick, Moreing & Co. Collection, HHPL.

4. A. Stanley Rowe to Hoover, December 28, 1902, "Rowe Defalcation," Pre-Commerce Papers, HHPL. This letter contains Hoover's handwritten notation: "Delivered 10 o'clock Monday 29th." See also Hoover and Wellsted to Moreing, January 9, 1903.

5. This account is based on several sources: Hoover, *Years of Adventure*, p. 83; Hoover, handwritten draft version of Volume I, chapter 7 of his *Memoirs*, in Hoover Book Manuscript Material, HHPL; Mrs. A. Stanley Rowe to Hoover, n.d. (December 29 or 30, 1902), "Rowe Defalcation," Pre-Commerce Papers; Hoover and Wellsted to Moreing, January 9, 1903; *West Australian Mining, Building, and Engineering Journal* 6 (July 1, 1905): 9.

6. Hoover and Wellsted to Moreing, January 9, 1903; *Daily Mail* (London), December 31, 1902.

7. Rowe to Hoover, December 28, 1902, "Rowe Defalcation," Pre-Commerce Papers. At the top of this letter is Hoover's notation: "Recieved at 1 o'clock Monday 29th or 1:30."

8. Ibid.

9. Ibid.; *Daily Mail*, December 31, 1902; Hoover and Wellsted to Moreing, January 9, 1903; *Financial Times* (London), December 2, 1903; *Mining Journal, Railway and Commercial Gazette* 74 (December 5, 1903): 638; *The Times* (London), December 18, 1903, p. 15; House of Lords Appeal Cases, 1906: *Ruben & Ladenburg v. Great Fingall Consolidated, Limited*, House of Lords Record Office, London.

10. This fact emerged at the annual shareholders meeting of the Great Fingall Consolidated, Ltd., April 23, 1903. Transcript in *Mining World and Engineering Record* 64 (April 25, 1903): 608–14.

11. Colonel R. Parry Nisbet to Messrs. Lewis and Lewis, December 23, 1902, quoted in ibid., p. 613.

12. Messrs. Lewis and Lewis to Colonel R. Parry Nisbet, December 24, 1902, quoted in ibid.

13. Hoover and Wellsted to Moreing, January 9, 1903.

14. Ibid.

15. Rowe to Hoover, December 28, 1902 (his second letter).

16. Rowe cable to Moreing (in Tientsin), December 28, 1902, typewritten copy in "Rowe Defalcation," Pre-Commerce Papers. The original has not been found. As typed, the copy gives the date as December 28, but someone has superimposed in pencil the number "30" over the "28." This alteration of the date is incorrect. All available evidence suggests that Rowe sent this cable on the night of December 28 as he prepared to flee from London.

17. See chapter 10. In his *Memoirs* Hoover stated that Moreing was off to Manchuria to hunt tigers. *Years of Adventure*, p. 82.

18. *Daily Mail*, December 30, 1902; Hoover and Wellsted to Moreing, January 9, 1903.

19. *Financial Times*, December 30, 1902; *Pall Mall Gazette* (London), December 30, 1902 (special evening edition), p. 4.

20. Hoover, *Years of Adventure*, p. 84, and draft of *Memoirs*, Volume I, chapter 7.
21. Hoover and Wellsted to Moreing, January 9, 1903. Great Fingall shares fell sharply on December 29 but recovered somewhat late in the day. *Financial Times*, December 30, 1902.
22. *Daily Mail*, December 30, 1902.
23. *Pall Mall Gazette*, December 30, 1902 (special evening edition), p. 4.
24. *Daily Mail*, December 30, 1902.
25. *Financial Times*, December 30, 1902.
26. *Westminster Gazette* (London), December 30, 1902.
27. *Pall Mall Gazette*, December 30, 1902 (special evening edition), p. 4.
28. Hoover, "Information for Biographers" (typescript, n.d.; probably ca. 1914), p. 15, in Benjamin S. Allen Papers, HI, and Pre-Commerce Papers, HHPL.
29. Hoover, *Years of Adventure*, pp. 84–85, and draft of *Memoirs*, Volume I, chapter 7.
30. This was what Hoover allegedly told a partner in the brokerage firm of Ruben & Ladenburg on the day Rowe's misdeeds were discovered (December 29). The partner, Frank Lindo, later testified that Hoover sent for him and showed him Rowe's letter of confession. Then (according to Lindo), "He [Hoover] said Mr. Moreing was in China; he was in cable communication with him and Mr. Moreing had cabled to say that he was returning by the first available mail boat, and he asked us to do nothing until we heard further." The "he" here is ambiguous; it could be either Hoover or Moreing. A subsequent question put to Lindo apparently clarified the point:

> [Q.] Mr. Moreing cabled that he was coming home by the first boat and asked us to do nothing until we heard further. Is that right?
> [A.] Yes, that is right.

So evidently it was Moreing who requested the delay. It was not until a later interview, Lindo testified, that Hoover indicated that Moreing would "do something up to a certain point" to indemnify victims of Rowe's frauds. Lindo testimony, in House of Lords Appeal Cases, 1906: *Ruben & Ladenburg v. Great Fingall Consolidated, Limited*, Appendix, pp. 50–51, House of Lords Record Office, London.
31. Hoover cable to Moreing, December 30, 1902, typed copy in "Rowe Defalcation," Pre-Commerce Papers. A draft is in the Bewick, Moreing & Co. Collection.
32. Moreing cable (from Peking) to Bewick, Moreing & Co. (London), December 30, 1902, Bewick, Moreing & Co. Collection. A notation on this cable (as received in London) reads that the message was "entered" (on the London office's books, presumably) on December 30. It appears to have been received in the early afternoon, London time.
33. Great Fingall Consolidated circular, December 30, 1902, printed in *Financial Times*, December 31, 1902; *Daily Mail*, December 31, 1902, p. 2.
34. *Westminster Gazette* and *Daily Express* (London), December 31, 1902.
35. *Westminster Gazette*, December 31, 1902.
36. Hoover and Wellsted cable to Moreing, December 31, 1902, copy in "Rowe Defalcation," Pre-Commerce Papers. Various drafts and a copy of the encoded cable are in the Bewick, Moreing & Co. Collection.
37. Handwritten copy of J. C. Moreton Thompson cable to Moreing, probably December 31, 1902, Bewick, Moreing & Co. Collection.
38. According to Hoover's later recollection, the firm's own solicitor had told him so. Hoover, *Years of Adventure*, p. 84.
39. According to Mrs. Hoover many years later, Hoover had great difficulty convincing his partners of their moral obligation to compensate the innocent victims of Rowe's misdeeds. Perhaps this explains why Hoover based his appeal to Moreing so strongly on considerations of self-interest. See Lou Henry Hoover to her children, July 1932, Allan Hoover Collection, HHPL.
40. Moreing's cable of December 30 that he would pay if disgrace could be averted was marked

"entered" on December 30, 1902—in other words, before the Hoover / Wellsted cable of December 31.

41. Moreing cable to Hoover and Wellsted, January 1, 1903, "Rowe Defalcation," Pre-Commerce Papers.

42. Ibid.

43. Great Fingall Consolidated circular, January 7, 1903, printed in *Financial News* (London), January 8, 1903, p. 3. Rowe's borrowings on forged certificates and transfers amounted to £72,000, while his misappropriations of genuine checks and securities amounted to £28,000. The latter figure ultimately went a few thousand pounds higher.

44. Hoover and Wellsted to Moreing, January 9, 1903.

45. A. Stanley Rowe bankruptcy proceedings, May 23, 1905, reported in *West Australian Mining, Building, and Engineering Journal* 6 (July 1, 1905): 9.

46. Hoover's cable to Moreing on December 30, 1902 stated that Rowe had borrowed £5,000 from Hoover. In a later accounting Hoover listed, among other losses, the sum of £4,500 in cash. Hoover, "Total position" (account sheet, n.d.), "Rowe Defalcation," Pre-Commerce Papers.

47. Hoover and Wellsted to Moreing, January 9, 1903.

48. *Westminster Gazette*, December 31, 1902; *Mining World and Engineering Record* 64 (January 3, 1903): 17.

49. Hoover and Wellsted to Moreing, January 9, 1903.

50. *Westminster Gazette*, December 31, 1902.

51. Hoover and Wellsted to Moreing, January 9, 1903.

52. *Financial Times*, January 3, 1903.

53. Ibid.

54. *Westminster Gazette*, January 3, 1903, p. 7.

55. Hoover and Wellsted to Moreing, January 9, 1903.

56. Ibid.

57. Ibid.

58. Hoover and Wellsted cable to Moreing, January 5, 1903, Bewick, Moreing & Co. Collection.

59. Hoover and Wellsted to Moreing, January 9, 1903.

60. Frank Lindo testimony, cited in note 30.

61. Confidential circular by P. A. Horn et al., January 2, 1903, printed in *Financial News*, January 7, 1903, p. 2, and in other journals.

62. The *Daily Mail*, December 30, 1902, referred to Bewick, Moreing's "controlling influence" in the company.

63. Hoover and Wellsted to Moreing, January 9, 1903.

64. See *Bullionist*, January 7, 1903, and *Financial Times, Colonial Mining News,* and *Pall Mall Gazette*, January 8, 1903.

65. R. Parry Nisbet, circular to Great Fingall Consolidated shareholders, January 7, 1903, printed in *Financial News*, January 8, 1903, p. 3.

66. On January 3, 1903 Wellsted used Moreing's power of attorney to dissolve the Bewick, Moreing partnership vis-à-vis Rowe. *London Gazette*, January 6, 1903, p. 138.

67. *Financial Times*, January 3, 1903.

68. Transcript of Great Fingall Consolidated shareholders meeting, January 8, 1903, in *Financial News*, January 9, 1903, pp. 5–6.

69. Hoover and Wellsted to Moreing, January 9, 1903.

70. Ibid.; Hoover and Wellsted cable to Moreing, January 8, 1903, Bewick, Moreing & Co. Collection.

71. Hoover and Wellsted to Moreing, January 9, 1903.

72. *Mining Journal, Railway and Commercial Gazette* 73 (January 3, 1903): 12; *Bullionist*, January 7, 1903.

73. *Economist* 61 (January 3, 1903): 12.

74. *Mining World and Engineering Record* 64 (January 3, 1903): 17, and 64 (January 10, 1903): 69. See also ibid. 64 (February 21, 1903): 293.

75. *Pall Mall Gazette*, January 7, 1903 (special evening edition), p. 4. See also *Colonial Mining News*, January 10, 1903.

76. *Mining World and Engineering Record* 64 (January 3, 1903): 17; London correspondent's reports, January 5 and 10, 1903, in *Engineering and Mining Journal* 75 (January 17, 1903): 133, and 75 (January 24, 1903): 166.

77. Hoover and Wellsted cable to Moreing, January 19, 1903, Bewick, Moreing & Co. Collection.

78. Moreing cable to Hoover and Wellsted, January 27 (?), 1903, Bewick, Moreing & Co. Collection. This cable was received in London on January 27.

79. *Mining World and Engineering Record* 64 (February 21, 1903): 301, 308.

80. Hoover, "Information for Biographers," p. 15. Informed on his return that Rowe's defalcations now amounted to £140,000, Moreing stated publicly, "The honour of my firm is dearer to me than twice that amount of money." *Mining World and Engineering Record* 64 (February 21, 1903): 293. Privately, however, he seemed to have been less enthusiastic.

81. *Westminster Gazette*, February 19, 1903, p. 5.

82. Bewick, Moreing & Co. statement regarding Herbert Hoover, n.d. (probably 1916), Bewick, Moreing & Co. Collection.

83. Ibid.; Bewick, Moreing & Co. account sheet regarding Rowe defalcation, Bewick, Moreing & Co. Collection.

84. Bewick, Moreing & Co. statement regarding Hoover, n.d.; Hoover, "Information for Biographers," p. 13.

85. Legal notice in *London Gazette*, January 6, 1903, p. 138.

86. Partnership agreement of Moreing, Hoover, and Wellsted, June 26, 1903, Bewick, Moreing & Co. Collection.

87. P. A. Horn statement at Great Fingall Consolidated shareholders meeting of January 8, 1903.

88. London correspondent's report, February 21, 1903, in *Engineering and Mining Journal* 75 (March 7, 1903): 382; *Mining World and Engineering Record* 64 (February 21, 1903): 293, 308.

89. See transcript of Great Fingall Consolidated annual shareholders meeting, April 23, 1903, in *Mining World and Engineering Record* 64 (April 25, 1903): 608–14, and *Mining Journal, Railway and Commercial Gazette* 73 (April 25, 1903): 488–89.

90. *Mining World and Engineering Record* 64 (April 18, 1903): 573.

91. *Engineering and Mining Journal* 75 (March 7, 1903): 382.

92. Ibid. 75 (May 9, 1903): 722–23.

93. Moreing speech at April 23, 1903 shareholders meeting.

94. W. A. Horn speech at April 23, 1903 shareholders meeting.

95. F. H. Hamilton speech at April 23, 1903 shareholders meeting.

96. *Mining World and Engineering Record* 64 (April 25, 1903): 597.

97. Ibid., pp. 604–5.

98. *Mining Journal, Railway and Commercial Gazette* 73 (April 25, 1903): 493.

99. The *Mining Journal* stated that Bewick, Moreing's policy of centralizing purchase of supplies for its Western Australian mines was arousing opposition (ibid.).

100. *Mining World and Engineering Record* 64 (April 25, 1903): 604–5.

101. Hoover, "Information for Biographers," p. 15; Hoover, *Years of Adventure*, p. 85; Hoover, undated handwritten autobiographical fragment. The latter source was once at HHPL but has not recently been located. I have relied on a partial verbatim transcript of this document courteously provided to me by Professor Craig Lloyd, a researcher who did see the document and make notes upon it several years ago.

102. Edgar Storey to A. Stanley Rowe, September 12, 1902, printed in House of Lords Appeal Cases, 1905: *Edgar Storey v. Herbert C. Hoover*, Appendix, p. 10, House of Lords Record Office, London (case file hereinafter cited as *Storey v. Hoover*). This case file includes the

appellant's and respondent's briefs, documents introduced in evidence, the complete transcript of the 1903 trial, the appeals court judgment, and other documents.

103. Rowe to Storey, September 16, 1902, printed in *Storey v. Hoover*, Appendix, p. 10.
104. Rowe to Storey, September 24, 1902, ibid., p. 11.
105. Storey to Rowe, September 26, 1902, ibid., p. 13.
106. Rowe-Storey exchanges of letters and cables, September 29–December 24, 1902, ibid., pp. 14–18.
107. Rowe to Storey, November 3, 1902, ibid., p. 16.
108. Storey to Rowe, December 24, 1902, ibid., p. 18.
109. Wellsted testimony, ibid., p. 68.
110. Storey testimony, ibid., pp. 40–41.
111. Storey to T. W. Wellsted, January 1, 1903, ibid., p. 18.
112. Hoover to Storey, January 2, 1903, ibid., p. 19.
113. Storey to Hoover, January 3, 1903, ibid.
114. Cheston & Sons to Hoover, January 5, 1903, ibid., p. 20.
115. Hoover to Cheston & Sons, January 6, 1903, ibid., p. 21.
116. Hoover to Storey, January 6, 1903, ibid., p. 22.
117. Hoover to Storey, January 9, 1903, ibid., p. 23.
118. Bompus, Bischoff & Co. (Hoover's solicitors) to Cheston & Sons, January 13, 1903, ibid., p. 25.
119. Specially endorsed Writ, January 17, 1903, ibid., p.1.
120. 1903 trial transcript, in *Storey v. Hoover*, Appendix, pp. 27, 70. For Hoover's request, see the Order for the trial, April 27, 1903, in J54/1193, Public Record Office (PRO), Kew, Surrey, U.K.
121. 1903 trial transcript, in *Storey v. Hoover*, Appendix, p. 74.
122. Ibid., pp. 52, 69.
123. Ibid., p. 69.
124. Ibid., p. 48. The judge agreed. He instructed the jury: ". . . what one person writes to another is not evidence against a third as a matter of fact" (ibid., p. 74).
125. Storey did testify that he discussed matters with Rowe personally in October and that Hoover entered Rowe's office for a brief part of this conversation. Storey inferred from Hoover's presence a knowledge of the supposed Hoover/Rowe joint account. But Hoover was only briefly in the room and said nothing to Storey. Hoover later recalled no such conversation. The judge instructed the jury not to "place much reliance" on this inconclusive evidence (ibid., pp. 33–34, 39, 57–58, 77).
126. Ibid., p. 53.
127. Ibid., pp. 33–34.
128. Ibid., pp. 41–42.
129. Ibid., p. 59.
130. Ibid.
131. Hoover's memorandum is printed in *Storey v. Hoover*, Appendix, p. 12.
132. *Storey v. Hoover*, Appendix, p. 55.
133. Ibid., p. 57. Hoover's check was introduced in evidence.
134. Ibid., p. 64.
135. Ibid., p. 54.
136. Ibid., p. 73.
137. Ibid., p. 71.
138. Ibid., p. 70.
139. Ibid., p. 47.
140. Ibid., pp. 64–65.
141. Ibid., p. 41.
142. Cheston & Sons to Bompus, Bischoff & Co., January 9, 1903, ibid., p. 24.
143. Storey's answer to pre-trial interrogatories, April 7, 1903, ibid., p. 9.
144. Storey testimony, ibid., pp. 41–43.

145. Rufus Isaacs comment, ibid., p. 41.
146. Ibid., pp. 80–81.
147. Ibid., p. 82.
148. Hoover's solicitors' notice of appeal, May 26, 1903, ibid., pp. 86–89.
149. This account is based on House of Lords Appeal Cases, 1906: *Ruben & Ladenburg v. Great Fingall Consolidated, Limited,* House of Lords Record Office, London (case file hereinafter cited as *Ruben & Ladenburg*). This case file includes appellants' and respondents' briefs, copies of documents introduced in evidence, the complete transcript of the 1903 trial, the text of the appeals court judgment, and various other documents.
150. Hoover to his brother Theodore, n.d. (ca. June 1, 1903), received by Theodore July 15, 1903, Hulda Hoover McLean Papers, HI.
151. List of admissions made at the 1903 trial, *Ruben & Ladenburg*, Appendix, p. 42.
152. Lord Justice Collins (of the appellate court), in ibid., p. 118.
153. *Financial News,* September 19, 1903, p. 2, and September 28, 1903, p. 2; *Mining World and Engineering Record* 65 (September 19, 1903): 359.
154. *Daily Mail,* October 8, 1903.
155. *The Times,* December 18, 1903, p. 15; *The Telegraph* (London), December 18, 1903. For further details on the Rowe case, see: Depositions and Affidavits in *Rex v. Rowe* (1903), Crim. 1 / 88, PRO; *Financial Times,* December 2, 1903; *Mining Journal, Railway and Commercial Gazette* 74 (December 5, 1903): 638; *Central Criminal Court [Old Bailey] Sessions Papers* 139 (1903–4): 134, Guildhall Library, London.
156. Court of Appeals judgment, November 18, 1903, in *Storey v. Hoover,* Appendix, pp. 90–105 (quotations on pp. 96, 98, 101–2). See also *Mining Journal, Railway and Commercial Gazette* 74 (November 21, 1903): 584 for a brief summary.
157. *The Telegraph,* December 18, 1903; *Ruben & Ladenburg,* Appendix, p. 102.
158. *Colonial Mining News* 19 (February 11, 1904): 69.
159. Mr. Justice Kennedy's judgment, February 6, 1904, *Ruben & Ladenburg,* Appendix, pp. 99–111.
160. Court of Appeal judgment, July 29, 1904, ibid., pp. 112–26; *Colonial Mining News* 20 (August 4, 1904): 58.
161. Hoover to his brother Theodore, July 21, 1904, McLean Papers.
162. Hoover, undated autobiographical fragment (cited in note 101).
163. Bewick, Moreing & Co. account sheet for Rowe's "defalcation charges," n.d., Bewick, Moreing & Co. Collection.
164. *Storey v. Hoover; Financial Times,* July 1, 1905, p. 6.
165. *Ruben & Ladenburg; Lords Journal,* July 19, 1906, p. 276.
166. Hoover, *Years of Adventure,* p. 85. In this passage Hoover mentions *two* instances of collusion with Rowe. One case, presumably, was the stockbroker Aarons, but I have found no evidence that Aarons ever sued Bewick, Moreing & Co. in the courts.
167. Frank Lindo testimony in *Ruben & Ladenburg,* Appendix, p. 45.
168. Ibid., pp. 47, 92. Storey testified that he did not authorize Rowe to execute any transfer of shares.
169. Wellsted interview, *Westminster Gazette,* February 19, 1903, p. 5.
170. *Storey v. Hoover,* Appendix, p. 45.
171. A. Stanley Rowe bankruptcy proceedings, May 23, 1905, reported in *West Australian Mining, Building, and Engineering Journal* 6 (July 1, 1905): 9.
172. Hoover, "Total position" sheet, n.d., "Rowe Defalcation," Pre-Commerce Papers.
173. Hoover, *Years of Adventure,* p. 83.
174. Hoover and Wellsted to Moreing, January 9, 1903.
175. Wellsted interview, *Westminster Gazette,* February 19, 1903, p. 5; Moreing statement at Great Fingall shareholders meeting, April 23, 1903. At this meeting Moreing declared that the "direct loss" to the Great Fingall was "about £32,000." Moreing stated that he, not the company, would "suffer" for all of it.
176. Hoover and Wellsted to Moreing, January 9, 1903.

177. Ibid.
178. Wellsted interview, *Westminster Gazette*, February 19, 1903, p. 5.
179. Hoover's attorney in the Storey case put the total cost of the defalcations at £140,000, of which Bewick, Moreing & Co. paid back £90,000. This left £50,000 unpaid. The Storey losses added to the Ruben & Ladenburg losses account for about £26,000 of this sum.
180. Bewick, Moreing & Co. account sheet, n.d., Bewick, Moreing & Co. Collection.
181. Rufus Isaacs comments, *Storey v. Hoover*, Appendix, pp. 44–45.
182. *The Times*, December 18, 1903, p. 15.
183. Bewick, Moreing & Co. statement regarding Herbert Hoover, n.d. (probably 1916), Bewick, Moreing & Co. Collection.
184. Hoover to his brother Theodore, n.d. (ca. June 1, 1903) and July 21, 1904.
185. Hoover, *Years of Adventure*, pp. 83, 85.
186. Hoover, "Total position" sheet. Tarkwa Consols, Ltd., organized in 1901, was a British mining company with interests in the Gold Coast Colony in Africa. For a time Bewick, Moreing & Co. served as its consulting engineers. See Walter R. Skinner, *The Mining Manual for 1901* (London, 1901), p. 766.
187. In *Years of Adventure*, p. 85, Hoover said "about" three years.
188. Bewick, Moreing & Co. account sheet.
189. Hoover, "Total position" sheet.
190. Hoover, undated autobiographical fragment.
191. Ibid.
192. W. J. Loring interview, 1931, Walter W. Liggett Papers, New York Public Library. Loring gave the date as 1904, but this is inaccurate. Hoover was still making payments to Moreing over the Rowe affair as late as December 1905. It seems probable that Hoover uncorked his bottle of wine in Kalgoorlie in 1907.
193. See correspondence from F. C. Rowe in "Rowe Defalcation," Pre-Commerce Papers. In his *Memoirs (Years of Adventure*, p. 85) Hoover stated that Mrs. Hoover gave Mrs. Rowe money for her children. This may be true also, but the available record discloses only gifts by Hoover himself to Rowe's sister. Possibly the wording of his *Memoirs* represents another instance of Hoover's extreme reticence about his benefactions.
194. Hoover, *Years of Adventure*, p. 85.
195. F. C. Rowe to Hoover, July 1 and 2, 1909, "Rowe Defalcation," Pre-Commerce Papers.
196. Moreing sent £20 per annum. F. C. Rowe to Hoover, July 1, 1909, ibid.
197. Ibid.
198. Rowe to Hoover, May 15, 1911. This letter has not been found. Its contents have been inferred from Hoover's reply.
199. Hoover to Rowe, May 18, 1911; Rowe to Hoover, May 20, 1911, "Rowe Defalcation," Pre-Commerce Papers.
200. Rowe to Hoover, May 20, 1911, ibid.
201. Hoover to F. C. Rowe, June 20, 1911, ibid.
202. F. C. Rowe to Hoover, January 25, 1913, ibid.
203. Theodore J. Hoover, *Memoranda: Being a Statement by an Engineer* (typescript: Stanford University, 1939), p. 123, copy at HHPL.

CHAPTER 14

1. "A Practical Mining Man" [Hoover], "Mining Company Administration," *Financial Times*, February 19, 1903, p. 5. Hoover is identified as the author of this piece in a scrapbook of his writings (including his "anonymous doings") in the Herbert Hoover Collection, Box 230, HI.
2. Walter R. Skinner, *The Mining Manual for 1903* (London, 1903), pp. 133–34.
3. *West Australian Mining, Building, and Engineering Journal* 1 (January 3, 1903): 4, and 1 (April 18, 1903): 11.

4. *Mining World and Engineering Record* 64 (January 31, 1903): 177.
5. [J. H. Curle], "Gold Mining Investments—VI," *Economist* 61 (January 10, 1903): 57.
6. Hoover Calendar, HHPL.
7. *Financial Times*, January 30, 1903, p. 5. He was already on the board of the Chinese Engineering and Mining Company.
8. Walter R. Skinner, *The Mining Manual for 1904* (London, 1904), p. 1019; Walter R. Skinner, *The Mining Manual for 1907* (London, 1907), p. 829.
9. See chapter 23.
10. The boy's middle name was that of his maternal grandfather, Charles Henry. Throughout his life he was known as Herbert Hoover, Jr. (although he and his father had different middle names). See Herbert Hoover, Jr. to Rita R. Campbell, August 22, 1967, Hulda Hoover McLean Papers, HI.
11. Hoover Calendar, HHPL; *West Australian Mining, Building, and Engineering Journal* 2 (October 17, 1903): 5; Hoover Scrapbooks, Album 38, HHPL.
12. Hoover Calendar, HHPL; Hoover Scrapbooks, Album 38.
13. Herbert Hoover, *The Memoirs of Herbert Hoover*, Volume I: *Years of Adventure* (New York, 1951), p. 86; Hoover Scrapbooks, Album 38. The automobile was a ten-horsepower Panhard.
14. *Mining World and Engineering Record* 66 (January 23, 1904): 133.
15. Ibid. 66 (January 16, 1904): 101.
16. *Mining and Scientific Press* 86 (June 13, 1903): 377; Gavin Casey and Ted Mayman, *The Mile That Midas Touched* (rev. ed.: Adelaide, 1968), pp. 120–21.
17. For Hoover's comments on savings effected by the goldfields water scheme, see *Mining Journal, Railway and Commercial Gazette* 74 (July 18, 1903): 67.
18. Hoover Calendar, HHPL; Hoover Scrapbooks, Album 38; *West Australian Mining, Building, and Engineering Journal* 2 (November 21, 1903): 17.
19. Hoover Calendar, HHPL; Hoover Scrapbooks, Album 38; Skinner, *Mining Manual for 1904*, pp. 210–11.
20. *West Australian Mining, Building, and Engineering Journal* 3 (January 30, 1904): 5; Hoover Scrapbooks, Album 38.
21. Hoover Scrapbooks, Album 38.
22. Ibid.; *Mining and Scientific Press* 88 (January 16, 1904): 52, and 88 (January 23, 1904): 71.
23. *Australian Mining Standard* 30 (August 20, 1903): 250; *Engineering and Mining Journal* 76 (October 10, 1903): 533; *Mining World and Engineering Record* 65 (October 17, 1903): 467.
24. *Engineering and Mining Journal* 76 (August 29, 1903): 301.
25. W. A. Prichard to Bewick, Moreing and Co. mine managers, June 13, 1904, printed in *Report of the Royal Commission Appointed to Inquire Into Matters Pertaining to Great Boulder Perseverance Gold Mining Company, Limited, Kalgoorlie* (Perth, 1905), pp. 136–37, in Western Australia, *Votes and Proceedings of Parliament*, 5th Parliament, Second Session (1905), Volume I, Paper No. 3.
26. *Engineering and Mining Journal* 76 (August 29, 1903): 301.
27. Ibid.; *Mining Journal, Railway and Commercial Gazette* 74 (August 15, 1903): 186.
28. *Australian Mining Standard* 31 (May 12, 1904): 691.
29. "A Practical Mining Man" [Hoover], article in *Financial Times*, February 19, 1903, p. 5.
30. Interview with W. A. Prichard, November 28, 1904, in *West Australian Mining, Building, and Engineering Journal* 4 (December 3, 1904): 6 (full interview: 6–7).
31. *Colonial Mining News* 19 (June 30, 1904): 339.
32. Prichard interview, November 28, 1904.
33. *Mining World and Engineering Record* 67 (October 29, 1904): 510.
34. Prichard interview, November 28, 1904.
35. Herbert Hoover, "Working Costs in West Australian Mines," *Mining Journal, Railway and Commercial Gazette* 74 (August 15, 1903): 186.
36. "Observer" [Hoover], letter to the editor, *Engineering and Mining Journal* 77 (April 28, 1904):

675–76. Hoover is identified as the author of this lengthy letter in the scrapbook cited in note 1.

37. *West Australian Mining, Building, and Engineering Journal* 3 (March 19, 1904): 4.

38. *Colonial Mining News* 19 (April 28, 1904): 215. For a similar observation, see *Mining World and Engineering Record* 66 (May 21, 1904): 521.

39. *West Australian Mining, Building, and Engineering Journal* 3 (April 16, 1904): 6.

40. *Engineering and Mining Journal* 77 (April 28, 1904): 676.

41. *West Australian Mining, Building, and Engineering Journal* 3 (March 19, 1904): 4, and 3 (April 23, 1904): 10; *Colonial Mining News* 19 (April 28, 1904): 215.

42. Herbert Hoover, "The Training of the Mining Engineer," *Science* (n.s.) 20 (November 25, 1904): 716 (full article: 716–19).

43. Skinner, *Mining Manual for 1904*, pp. 22, 210–11. On the Talisman board W. F. Turner (of the Oriental Syndicate) was a fellow director.

44. Bellevue, Talisman, Oroya Brownhill, Dutch Indies Exploration, and Chinese Engineering and Mining Company.

45. Amendment, March 22, 1904, to the Hoover-Moreing-Wellsted partnership agreement of June 26, 1903, Bewick, Moreing & Co. Collection, HHPL.

46. Interview with W. A. Prichard in *West Australian Mining, Building, and Engineering Journal* 3 (April 16, 1904): 5.

47. London correspondent's column in *Engineering and Mining Journal* 77 (April 14, 1904): 616.

48. *Engineering and Mining Journal* 77 (April 28, 1904): 673.

49. Moreing statement at 1903 shareholders meeting of the London and Western Australian Exploration Company, printed in *Mining World and Engineering Record* 65 (December 12, 1903): 758. During 1903 and 1904 the mining press in London and Australia frequently reported the steady reduction of working costs at such Bewick, Moreing companies as the Great Fingall, Sons of Gwalia, Lake View Consols, and Oroya Brownhill.

50. *West Australian Mining, Building, and Engineering Journal* 3 (April 2, 1904): 11.

51. R. J. Hoffmann statement at 1905 shareholders meeting of Bellevue Proprietary, Ltd., printed in *Mining World and Engineering Record* 65 (November 28, 1903): 676.

52. Moreing statement at 1903 meeting of London and Western Australian Exploration Company, pp. 758–59.

53. *West Australian Mining, Building, and Engineering Journal* 2 (September 26, 1903): 4–5; *Mining World and Engineering Record* 67 (August 6, 1904): 179.

54. *Mining World and Engineering Record* 67 (August 6, 1904): 180.

55. R. J. Hoffmann. Ibid., p. 179.

56. R. J. Hoffmann statement at 1905 meeting of Bellevue Proprietary, p. 676.

57. *West Australian Mining, Building, and Engineering Journal* 2 (September 26, 1903): 4.

58. "Observer" [Hoover], p. 675.

59. Prichard interview, November 28, 1904.

60. *West Australian Mining, Building, and Engineering Journal* 3 (April 2, 1904): 11.

61. *Mining World and Engineering Record* 64 (June 20, 1903): 888; *West Australian Mining, Building, and Engineering Journal* 3 (April 16, 1904): 6.

62. Prichard interview, *West Australian Mining, Building, and Engineering Journal* 3 (April 16, 1904): 6.

63. Govett statement at 1905 shareholders meeting of Ivanhoe Gold Corporation, printed in *Mining World and Engineering Record* 68 (April 29, 1905): 540–41.

64. Hoover, letter to the editor, *Engineering and Mining Journal* 76 (July 11, 1903): 44.

65. *Australian Mining Standard* 30 (August 20, 1903): 250.

66. See Prichard's letter of June 13, 1904, cited in note 25.

67. *West Australian Mining, Building, and Engineering Journal* 3 (April 2, 1904): 11. No substantiation has been found for this charge.

68. Ibid., p. 11. The journal said Bewick, Moreing was "almost inundated with offers to manage for mining companies."

69. Govett statement at 1903 shareholders meeting of Lake View Consols, printed in *Mining World and Engineering Record* 65 (October 11, 1903): 467.

70. John Barry statement at 1904 shareholders meeting of Sons of Gwalia, printed in *Mining World and Engineering Record* 66 (June 4, 1904): 761.

71. *Mining World and Engineering Record* 69 (December 2, 1905): 689; also *Economist* 63 (December 2, 1905): 1941.

72. *West Australian Mining, Building, and Engineering Journal* 2 (October 10, 1903): 5.

73. *Mining World and Engineering Record* 68 (May 20, 1905): 624.

74. Ibid. 67 (October 29, 1904): 510.

75. *West Australian Mining, Building, and Engineering Journal* 3 (April 2, 1904): 9.

76. *Australian Mining Standard* 33 (January 5, 1905): 19.

77. See Curle's article cited in note 5.

78. *West Australian Mining, Building, and Engineering Journal* 2 (October 31, 1903): 4; Hoover Calendar, HHPL; Hoover Scrapbooks, Album 38, HHPL; Hoover to his brother Theodore, July 21, 1904, McLean Papers. Curle met Hoover on a trip to the Sons of Gwalia mine in 1898. J. H. Curle, *Travels and Men* (London, 1935), p. 144.

79. See, for example, Curle's columns in the *Economist* 61 (December 5, 1903): 2044, and 61 (December 26, 1903): 2193.

80. *Economist* 61 (June 27, 1903): 1125.

81. C. T. Hallinan to a Mr. Colebaugh, January 7, 1932, copy in "Rickard Files: Statements and Affidavits, Mining, 1928–1932 and Undated," Misrepresentations File, HHPL.

82. J. W. McCarty, "British Investment in Western Australian Gold Mining, 1894–1914," *University Studies in History* 4 (1961–62): 12, 17, 20.

83. These are so identified in the scrapbook cited in note 1.

84. Prichard's story is recorded in Professor Guido Marx, unpublished autobiography (ca. 1941), Stanford University section, p. 86, Guido Marx Papers, Box 2, Stanford University Archives.

85. "A Colonist" [Hoover], letter to the editor, *Financial Times*, January 27, 1903, p. 5. Hoover is identified as the author in the scrapbook cited in note 1.

86. "Consulting Engineer" [Hoover], letter to the editor dated January 28, printed in *Financial Times*, January 29, 1903, p. 5.

87. *Financial Times*, January 30, 1903, p. 5. See also *West Australian Mining, Building, and Engineering Journal* 1 (March 28, 1903): 4, wherein Hoover was credited with blocking the merger.

88. "Mining Topics," *Financial Times*, January 30, 1903, p. 5.

89. F. H. Bathurst, "Hoover in Australia: A Personal Sketch," *The Argus* (Melbourne), November 3, 1928, p. 6.

90. Hoover to David Starr Jordan, June 29, 1904, David Starr Jordan Papers, Series I-A, Box 40, Stanford University Archives; Jordan to Hoover, July 16, 1904, ibid., Series I-AA, letter book #22; Hoover to Jordan, September 12, 1904, ibid., Series I-A, Box 41; Jordan to Hoover, October 3, 1904, ibid., Series I-AA, letter book #24. See also Jordan to J. McK. Cattell, October 4, 1904, ibid.

91. For Hoover's remarks as published see the article cited above in note 42. For the Hoovers' reaction to this, see Lou Henry Hoover to John C. Branner, n.d. [early 1905], John C. Branner Papers, Box 36, Stanford University Archives.

Mrs. Hoover's account of this episode is somewhat confusing. In her letter to Dr. Branner she indicated that Hoover's paper appeared without permission as well as explanation. Yet Hoover *had* given Jordan permission to publish it. Mrs. Hoover then stated that Jordan had asked to use Hoover's piece but that Hoover merely supposed that Jordan would include it in one of his reports. Yet Jordan had explicitly mentioned to Hoover the possibility of publishing it in the *Popular Science Monthly*, and Hoover in reply granted Jordan permission to make any use of it he wished. Hoover apparently forgot that he did so. Of course, he may have expected Jordan properly to indicate the paper's background and purpose.

Interestingly, Hoover's contribution as published in *Science* comprised not only his original memorandum for the royal commission but also, at the end, several paragraphs taken from Hoover's private cover letter to Jordan of June 29, 1904. It appears that Jordan simply tacked on these paragraphs to Hoover's statement and published them without Hoover's permission. Since these additional paragraphs contained some candid comments about British attitudes toward the engineering profession, they may conceivably have caused Hoover some embarrassment. This may help to explain his acute discomfiture over the episode. Mrs. Hoover's letter to Branner, however, did not mention this point. Her emphasis was on the fact that the article's origin and purpose were not explained.

92. Craig Lloyd, *Aggressive Introvert: Herbert Hoover and Public Relations Management, 1912–1932* (Columbus, 1972).

93. Bathurst, "Hoover in Australia."

94. David Starr Jordan, *The Days of a Man* (Yonkers-on-Hudson, N.Y., 1922), I, p. 222.

95. J. W. Kirwan, "Mr. and Mrs. Hoover: West Australian Reminiscences," n.d. (late 1928), Reprint File, HHPL.

96. Telephone interview of Frederick Walton Rowe, Kendenup, Western Australia, September 28, 1977.

97. Bathurst, "Hoover in Australia"; Kirwan, "Mr. and Mrs. Hoover"; interview of W. J. Loring in *Cedar Rapids Sunday Gazette and Republican*, November 4, 1928, Section 1, p. 5.

98. J. W. Kirwan, "Hoover in Western Australia: Some Goldfields Memories," n.d. (late 1928), Reprint File, HHPL.

99. Bathurst, "Hoover in Australia."

100. Kirwan, "Mr. and Mrs. Hoover."

101. Ibid.

102. Amor F. Keene interview (ca. 1931), Walter W. Liggett Papers, New York Public Library.

103. See, for example, the varying figures he offered at different times in the Rowe affair and in the Great Boulder Perseverance scandal (see chapter 16).

104. Loring interview in *Cedar Rapids Sunday Gazette*, November 4, 1928.

105. Hoover to his brother Theodore, July 21, 1904, McLean Papers.

106. Loring interview in *Cedar Rapids Sunday Gazette*, November 4, 1928.

107. Ibid.

108. Kirwan, "Mr. and Mrs. Hoover."

109. Hoover, "The Training of the Mining Engineer," p. 716.

110. Kirwan, "Mr. and Mrs. Hoover."

111. His remark is quoted in Hallinan to Colebaugh, January 7, 1932.

112. Kirwan, "Mr. and Mrs. Hoover."

113. Hoover, undated handwritten autobiographical fragment cited in chapter 13, note 101.

114. Loring interview in *Cedar Rapids Sunday Gazette*, November 4, 1928.

115. Ibid.; W. S. Robinson, *If I Remember Rightly* (Melbourne, 1967), pp. 27, 39.

CHAPTER 15

1. "A Practical Mining Man" [Hoover], "Mining Company Administration," *Financial Times*, February 19, 1903, p. 5.

2. *Colonial Mining News* 15 (April 17, 1902): 255.

3. Interview with Hoover in Perth, Australia *Herald*, March 11, 1907, copy in Hoover Scrapbooks, Album 41, HHPL.

4. Moreing quoted Hoover's reports at the 1903 shareholders meeting of the London and Western Australian Exploration Company. A transcript of these proceedings was printed in the *Mining World and Engineering Record* 65 (December 12, 1903): 758–61.

5. [J. H. Curle], "The Mines of West Australia—III," *Economist* 61 (December 12, 1903): 2088.

6. Transcript of 1903 shareholders meeting of London and Western Australian Exploration

Company, p. 760; *West Australian Mining, Building, and Engineering Journal* 6 (December 23, 1905): 3.

7. Walter R. Skinner, *The Mining Manual for 1905* (London, 1905), p. 118.
8. Hoover draft statement (ca. 1931–32) about the Lancefield mine, in "Richey-Hoover Files: Statements and Refutations," Misrepresentations File, HHPL; Moreing statement at 1903 meeting of London and Western Australian Exploration Company, p. 760; Moreing statement at 1904 meeting of the same company, printed in *Mining World and Engineering Record* 67 (December 24, 1904): 870.
9. Skinner, *Mining Manual for 1905*, p. 118.
10. *West Australian Mining, Building, and Engineering Journal* 6 (August 12, 1905): 11.
11. *Mining World and Engineering Record* 67 (December 24, 1904): 871; *Economist* 63 (April 22, 1905): 692.
12. Interview of Moreing in *West Australian Mining, Building, and Engineering Journal* 3 (June 18, 1904): 4.
13. Interview with W. J. Loring in *West Australian Mining, Building, and Engineering Journal* 4 (December 3, 1904): 7.
14. R. J. Hoffmann statement at 1905 shareholders meeting of Lancefield Gold Mining Company; transcript in *Economist* 63 (April 22, 1905): 691–92.
15. Hoover to E. Pears, April 7, 1905, Mining Letter Book No. 1, Pre-Commerce Papers, HHPL. See also Hoover to C. H. Wray, April 27, 1906, ibid.
16. [J. H. Curle], "Mining in Australasia—IV," *Economist* 63 (July 8, 1905): 1115.
17. According to Hoover's data, bore holes had been drilled to a depth of 740 feet. Hoover interview, Perth *Herald*, March 11, 1907.
18. *Australian Mining Standard* 34 (November 22, 1905): 500; *West Australian Mining, Building, and Engineering Journal* 6 (December 2, 1905): 11; ibid. 6 (December 23, 1905): 3–4; ibid. 6 (December 30, 1905): 7; [Curle], "The Mines of West Australia," *Economist* 64 (January 27, 1906): 118. Moreing said in 1904 that he urged "our friends" to invest £90,000 in the Lancefield. Since the purchase price was under £50,000, this left about £40,000 (about $200,000) for installing the first plant.
19. Ibid.; *Mining World and Engineering Record* 70 (March 17, 1906): 321–22 (for Moreing's comment about Hoover's influence).
20. *West Australian Mining, Building, and Engineering Journal* 6 (December 23, 1905): 4; A. N. Jackman, ed., *The Mining Year-Book . . . 1906* (London, 1906), p. 493.
21. Walter R. Skinner, *The Mining Manual for 1907* (London, 1907), pp. 92–93.
22. *The Bulletin* (Sydney, Australia), February 28, 1907, p. 13; *The Times* (London), July 24, 1907, p. 14, and August 1, 1907, p. 14; Walter R. Skinner, *The Mining Manual for 1908* (London, 1908), p. 80; *The Bulletin*, February 27, 1908, p. 13; *Statist* 61 (March 7, 1908): 441; *Mining World and Engineering Record* 74 (March 21, 1908): 377–79; *Economist* 66 (March 21, 1908): 630.
23. *Mining World and Engineering Record* 74 (March 7, 1908): 296; transcript of March 20, 1908 shareholders meeting of Lancefield Gold Mining Company, in *Mining World and Engineering Record* 74 (March 21, 1908): 377–79 (see also p. 369); account of same meeting in *Economist* 66 (March 21, 1908): 630–31; transcript of April 3, 1908 shareholders meeting in *Mining World and Engineering Record* 74 (April 4, 1908): 430–31; ibid. 74 (April 25, 1908): 546; *West Australian Mining, Building, and Engineering Journal* 11 (April 25, 1908): 3.
24. Statement by Moreing at 1908 London and W.A. Exploration Co. shareholders meeting, printed in *Mining World and Engineering Record* 74 (April 4, 1908): 439.
25. Transcript of October 12, 1908 Lancefield shareholders meeting, in *Mining World and Engineering Record* 75 (October 17, 1908): 503–6; account of same meeting in *Economist* 67 (October 17, 1908): 740.
26. *Mining Journal* 84 (November 28, 1908): 691.
27. Hoover's departure was a result of friction with Moreing, whose firm he had left recently. See chapter 22.

28. Account of 1909 Lancefield shareholders meeting in *Economist* 69 (December 4, 1909): 1168, and in *The Times*, December 3, 1909, p. 17.
29. *Mining World and Engineering Record* 79 (December 24, 1910): 818.
30. Walter R. Skinner, *Mining Manual and Mining Year Book for 1913* (London, 1913), p. 738.
31. *Mining and Scientific Press* 105 (July 20, 1912): 92; *West Australian Mining, Building, and Engineering Journal* 20 (July 27, 1912): 3.
32. Transcript of Lancefield shareholders meeting, September 24, 1913, in *Mining World and Engineering Record* 85 (September 27, 1913): 385–87. See also: *The Times*, September 25, 1913, p. 16; *Mining Magazine* 9 (October 1913): 241; and Walter R. Skinner, *Mining Manual and Mining Year Book for 1914* (London, 1914), p. 662.
33. Hoover draft statement (ca. 1931–32) about the Lancefield mine.
34. Hoover, *The Memoirs of Herbert Hoover*, Volume I: *Years of Adventure* (New York, 1951), p. 81.
35. See transcripts of the October 1908 and September 1913 meetings, cited in notes 25 and 32.
36. Hoover, *Years of Adventure*, p. 81.
37. For information on the geology and early mining history of the "deep leads" of Victoria see ibid., p. 87; *Statist* 53 (February 20, 1904): 337–38; *Economist* 62 (March 5, 1904): 408; *Mining World and Engineering Record* 67 (September 24, 1904): 365–66; Walter R. Skinner, *The Mining Manual for 1904* (London, 1904), pp. 14–16; *Statist* 55 (January 7, 1905): 8–9; Waldemar Lindgren, "The Deep Leads of Victoria," *Engineering and Mining Journal* 79 (February 16, 1905): 314–16.
38. On Wright's companies see the February 20, 1904 *Statist* article cited in note 37 and also Walter R. Skinner, *The Mining Manual for 1903* (London, 1903), pp. 129–30, 151–52.
39. This account is based on: transcript of September 8, 1903 shareholders meeting of London and Globe Deep Leads Assets, Ltd., in *Mining World and Engineering Record* 65 (September 12, 1903): 320–22; *Australian Mining Standard* 30 (October 22, 1903): 545, 555–56; Skinner, *Mining Manual for 1904*, pp. 14–16, 49–50, 128, 147–48. The *Australian Mining Standard* stated that Bewick, Moreing and Company "fathered" the new (post-Wright) deep leads project. The chairman of London and Globe Deep Leads Assets specifically stated that he and his fellow directors "were invited to discuss with Messrs. Bewick, Moreing and Co. the possibility of restoring" Wright's deep lead assets to "the London and Globe Shareholders" (Wright's bankrupt finance company) "at a very low valuation." He said further that Bewick, Moreing "submitted evidence" in behalf of its proposal. The chairman's account thus indicates that Bewick, Moreing took the initiative in the matter. C. Algernon Moreing, present at the shareholders meeting, did not contradict him.
40. Transcript of September 8, 1903 shareholders meeting of London and Globe Deep Leads Assets (changed in November to Consolidated Deep Leads), pp. 321–22; Skinner, *Mining Manual for 1904*, pp. 14–16, 49–50, 128, 147–48, 223–24.
41. Transcript of September 8, 1903 Consolidated Deep Leads shareholders meeting, p. 321.
42. Ibid.; Moreing statement at 1903 shareholders meeting of London and Western Australian Exploration Company, p. 760; Hoover, *Years of Adventure*, p. 88; Lindgren to Hoover, June 16 and 19, 1903, "Mining—Correspondence: Lindgren, Waldemar," Pre-Commerce Papers.
43. Transcript of September 8, 1903 Consolidated Deep Leads shareholders meeting, p. 320; *Australian Mining Standard* 30 (October 22, 1903): 555.
44. Transcript of September 8, 1903 Consolidated Deep Leads shareholders meeting, p. 322.
45. Ibid., p. 321.
46. John Hamill affidavit, June 4, 1932, p. 78, "Baker Files," Misrepresentations File, HHPL. Hamill offered no proof for his assertion.
47. Transcript of September 8, 1903 shareholders meeting, pp. 321–22.
48. *Australian Mining Standard* 30 (November 26, 1903): 722.
49. Ibid. 30 (December 3, 1903): 756; *Engineering and Mining Journal* 77 (January 21, 1904): 133–34. At the September 8, 1903 shareholders meeting Moreing said of Hoover's mission:

"With regard to how soon we can bring Government pressure to bear upon those who do not do their share of the pumping—Mr. Hoover is going out this week and will take that matter actively in hand" (p. 322).

50. *Australian Mining Standard* 30 (December 10, 1903): 799. The precise date of this interview is established from a newspaper clipping (probably from the Melbourne *Argus*) dated December 3, 1903, in Hoover Scrapbooks, Album 51, HHPL.

51. Ibid.

52. *The Argus* (Melbourne), December 8, 1903, copy in Hoover Scrapbooks, Album 51.

53. *Australian Trading World*, January 28, 1904, p. 64; Skinner, *Mining Manual for 1904*, pp. 14–16; Skinner, *Mining Manual for 1905*, pp. 11–13.

54. Skinner, *Mining Manual for 1904*, p. 16.

55. Waldemar Lindgren, "A President in the Making," *Tech Engineering News* [M.I.T] 10 (March 1929): 82.

56. Lindgren's final report is summarized in *Australian Mining Standard* 31 (June 9, 1904): 843. See also: *Engineering and Mining Journal* 77 (January 21, 1904): 134; Skinner, *Mining Manual for 1904*, p. 16; *Mining World and Engineering Record* 67 (September 24, 1904): 365–66.

57. Melbourne correspondent's report in *Engineering and Mining Journal* 78 (July 14, 1904): 75.

58. *Australian Trading World*, January 28, 1904, p. 63.

59. Transcript of 1903 shareholders meeting of London and Western Australian Exploration Company, pp. 760–61.

60. Skinner, *Mining Manual for 1904*, p. 16.

61. Bewick, Moreing and Company's preface to Lindgren's report, quoted in *Australian Mining Standard* 31 (June 9, 1904): 843.

62. *Statist* 53 (February 20, 1904): 337–38.

63. [Curle], "Victorian Gold Mines," *Economist* 62 (February 27, 1904): 346.

64. *Australian Mining Standard* 31 (January 21, 1904): 82.

65. *Australian Trading World*, January 28, 1904, p. 64; Skinner, *Mining Manual for 1904*, p. 16.

66. *Engineering and Mining Journal* 78 (July 14, 1904): 75; C. S. Herzig membership file, Institution of Mining and Metallurgy, London.

67. *Statist* 53 (February 20, 1904): 337, and 55 (January 7, 1905): 9; *Mining World and Engineering Record* 67 (September 24, 1904): 365–66.

68. *Australian Mining Standard* 31 (June 9, 1904): 843.

69. Skinner, *Mining Manual for 1904*, p. 14; *Statist* 55 (January 7, 1905): 8–9.

70. F. H. Bathurst in *Engineering and Mining Journal* 77 (January 21, 1904): 133; F. H. Bathurst, "Hoover in Australia: A Personal Sketch," *The Argus* (Melbourne), November 3, 1928, p. 6.

71. *Statist* 55 (January 7, 1905): 9.

72. Bathurst in *Engineering and Mining Journal* 77 (January 21, 1904): 133–34.

73. *Colonial Mining News* 19 (February 11, 1904): 69; *Statist* 53 (February 20, 1904): 337.

74. *Australian Mining Standard* 31 (June 9, 1904): 843. See also *Engineering and Mining Journal* 78 (July 21, 1904): 90.

75. *Mining World and Engineering Record* 67 (December 24, 1904): 871.

76. Skinner, *Mining Manual for 1905*, p. 13.

77. [Curle], "Mining in Australasia—VI," *Economist* 63 (July 22, 1905): 1191.

78. Ibid.

79. Hoover Calendar, HHPL.

80. Australia, Victoria, Department of Mines and Water Supply, *Annual Report of the Secretary for Mines and Water Supply . . . for the Year 1905* (Melbourne, 1906), p. 103.

81. Transcript of 1906 shareholders meeting of London and Western Australian Exploration Company, in *Mining World and Engineering Record* 70 (March 17, 1906): 323.

82. Walter R. Skinner, *The Mining Manual for 1906* (London, 1906), p. 11.

83. Account of 1906 shareholders meeting of Cosmopolitan Proprietary in *Economist* 64 (July 7, 1906): 1143.

84. *Annual Report of the Secretary for Mines . . . 1905*, p. 122; Skinner, *Mining Manual for 1906*, p. 112.

85. [Curle], "Mining in Australasia—VI," p. 1191; Skinner, *Mining Manual for 1906*, pp. 98, 112, 174–75.

86. *Economist* 64 (November 10, 1906): 1853; Skinner, *Mining Manual for 1907*, pp. 109, 172, 174.

87. Australia, Victoria, Department of Mines and Water Supply, *Annual Report of the Secretary for Mines and Water Supply . . . for the Year 1906* (Melbourne, 1907), p. 113.

88. [Curle], "Mining in Australasia—VI," p. 1191.

89. *Annual Report of the Secretary for Mines . . . 1906*, pp. 113, 130.

90. Ibid.; Skinner, *Mining Manual for 1907*, pp. 10, 96; *The Times*, January 10, 1907, p. 13.

91. Skinner, *Mining Manual for 1907*, p. 15.

92. Lindgren to Hoover, January 8, 1907, "Mining—Correspondence: Lindgren, Waldemar," Pre-Commerce Papers. As far as is known, Lindgren did not return to Australia.

93. *Australian Mining Standard* 37 (February 20, 1907): 176.

94. *Annual Report of the Secretary for Mines . . . 1906*, p. 113.

95. *Australian Mining Standard* 37 (February 20, 1907): 176; *The Bulletin* (Sydney), February 28, 1907, p. 13; *The Times*, August 8, 1907, p. 12. The *Annual Report* for 1906 of the Secretary for Mines and Water Supply of Victoria stated that expenditures on "mining operations" at the Loddon Valley mine exceeded £44,600 (a higher figure than that given by the company's representative at the ceremony honoring the visiting Governor).

96. *The Bulletin*, February 28, 1907, p. 13.

97. Hoover Calendar, HHPL; *West Australian Mining, Building, and Engineering Journal* 9 (March 9, 1907): 2, and 9 (June 22, 1907): 7.

98. *The Bulletin*, February 28, 1907, p. 13.

99. *Mining World and Engineering Record* 72 (June 29, 1907): 825–27; ibid. 73 (August 3, 1907): 147; *Economist* 65 (June 29, 1907): 1113.

100. *The Times*, August 2, 1907, p. 12, and August 8, 1907, p. 12; *Economist* 65 (August 10, 1907): 1369; *Mining World and Engineering Record* 73 (August 10, 1907): 182–84. The Consolidated Deep Leads was contributing to the Loddon Valley company at the rate of £2,500 a month. *Economist* 65 (November 9, 1907): 1940.

101. *The Times*, August 8, 1907, p. 12.

102. Australia, Victoria, Department of Mines, *Annual Report of the Secretary for Mines . . . for the Year 1907* (Melbourne, 1908), p. 133.

103. Ibid., p. 151.

104. *The Times*, July 24, 1907, p. 14, August 2, 1907, p. 12, and August 8, 1907, p. 12; *Economist* 65 (August 10, 1907): 1369.

105. Accounts of August 7, 1907 shareholders meeting of Loddon Valley Goldfields, in *The Times*, August 8, 1907, p. 12; *Economist* 65 (August 10, 1907): 1369; and *Mining World and Engineering Record* 73 (August 10, 1907): 182–84.

106. Hoover draft statement entitled "Deep Leads: The Facts" (ca. 1931–32), in "Richey-Hoover Files: Statements and Refutations," Misrepresentations File, HHPL; Hoover, *Years of Adventure*, p. 88. Waldemar Lindgren corroborated Hoover's account in a signed memorandum, February 2, 1932. This memorandum was probably drafted by Hoover himself. His secretary, Lawrence Richey, sent it to Lindgren to sign. The memorandum and the Richey-Lindgren exchange of correspondence (January 27–February 2, 1932) are in the "Richey-Hoover Files: Statements and Refutations," Misrepresentations File, HHPL. Lindgren's memorandum bears many similarities in phraseology to Hoover's separate draft statement. The evidentiary value of Lindgren's memorandum is uncertain. There is no evidence that Lindgren had anything to do with the deep leads after his trip in 1903 or that he knew firsthand of Hoover's later advice to abandon the project. Nevertheless, he signed the memorandum asserting that Hoover did so advise.

Lindgren's statement illustrates Hoover's characteristic approach to allegations made against him during his public career. Rather than respond personally, he solicited (even prepared) defenses and testimonials for other persons to sign in his behalf. See chapter 11, note 88 for further examples.

107. Hoover, "Deep Leads: The Facts," seconded by Lindgren memorandum, February 2, 1932 (probably composed by Hoover).

108. Hoover remarks at Loddon Valley Goldfields shareholders meeting, August 7, 1907, quoted in *Mining World and Engineering Record* 73 (August 10, 1907): 184.

109. *Mining World and Engineering Record* 72 (June 29, 1907): 826, 827.

110. Account of Consolidated Deep Leads and Australian Commonwealth Trust shareholders meetings, November 4, 1907, in *Mining World and Engineering Record* 73 (November 9, 1907): 557–65; Skinner, *Mining Manual for 1908*, p. 7.

111. *Economist* 65 (November 9, 1907): 1940; Skinner, *Mining Manual for 1908*, p. 92.

112. Walter R. Skinner, *The Mining Manual for 1909* (London, 1909), p. 146; *Annual Report of the Secretary for Mines . . . 1907*, p. 151.

113. *Annual Report of the Secretary for Mines . . . 1907*, p. 151; Australia, Victoria, Department of Mines, *Annual Report of the Secretary for Mines . . . for the Year 1908* (Melbourne, 1909), p. 117; Walter R. Skinner, *The Mining Manual for 1910* (London, 1910), p. 77. The water problem was never satisfactorily resolved. At the end of 1907 the Loddon Valley was still pumping out 4,000,000 gallons a day—a welcome diminution but not enough to permit working the deep ground. Some years later Hoover's friend Deane P. Mitchell, who supervised the deep lead project in its early stages, stated that enough "dewatering" was done to permit sampling of the auriferous gravels but that not enough gold was found to produce a profit. Deane P. Mitchell notes, January 19, 1932, "Rickard Files: Statements and Affidavits," Misrepresentations File, HHPL. See also *Mining Magazine* 1 (November 1909): 179, and 2 (June 1910): 421.

114. *Australian Mining Standard* 40 (August 26, 1908): 231; ibid. 40 (September 23, 1908): 340; ibid. 40 (December 23, 1908): 706–7.

115. Walter R. Skinner, *The Mining Manual for 1911* (London, 1911), p. 6.

116. Skinner, *Mining Manual for 1910*, pp. 85–86, 142–43; Skinner, *Mining Manual for 1911*, pp. 79–80, 128–29; Skinner, *The Mining Manual for 1912* (London, 1912), pp. 73, 120.

117. *Mining Magazine* 2 (January 1910): 21–22; ibid. 2 (March 1910): 323; ibid. 5 (October 1911): 277; Skinner, *Mining Manual for 1911*, p. 8.

118. "Over a million [pounds] of British capital has been spent in Victoria in deep-lead mining with no result." *Mining Magazine* 5 (October 1911): 277. In July 1908 the Minister for Mines of Victoria stated that £1,500,000 in British money had been spent on the deep leads, including £955,000 by eight companies in particular (possibly a reference to the Bewick, Moreing group). *Australian Mining Standard* 40 (August 26, 1908): 231. F. H. Bathurst, an Australian journalist who "covered" the deep leads mines for a time, reported in 1928 that an estimated £1,000,000 (about $5,000,000) was lost. F. H. Bathurst, "Hoover in Australia: A Personal Sketch," *The Argus* (Melbourne), November 3, 1928, p. 6.

119. *Mining Magazine* 2 (June 1910): 421.

120. Bathurst, "Hoover in Australia," p. 6.

121. *Engineering and Mining Journal* 78 (July 21, 1904): 90; *The Bulletin*, February 28, 1907, p. 13; *Mining Magazine* 2 (June 1910): 421.

122. Hoover, *Years of Adventure*, p. 88.

123. *Mining Magazine* 2 (January 1910): 22.

124. Ibid. 1 (November 1909): 179.

125. Ibid.

126. Hoover, *Years of Adventure*, p. 88.

127. See Geoffrey Blainey, "Herbert Hoover's Forgotten Years," *Business Archives and History* 3 (February 1963): 53–70, a critical analysis of Hoover's *Memoirs* as a source for a study of his mining career. In his article Blainey documents several instances, similar to the deep leads case mentioned here, of Hoover's retroactive minimizing of his mining failures. But

while Blainey, an Australian historian, finds numerous errors and some distortions in Hoover's *Memoirs*, the thrust of his article is unduly deprecatory. For a full study of Hoover's mining career, we must, of course, move beyond his *Memoirs*.

128. See "The President's Fortune," *Fortune* 6 (August 1932): 82, 84, 85 for details on some of these unsuccessful enterprises. For Hoover's optimism about the Bellevue Proprietary in 1905, see *Mining World and Engineering Record* 69 (December 2, 1905): 689. In 1903 Hoover predicted that the Vivien Gold Mining Company would be a very profitable, albeit small, mine. Hoover, cited by Moreing, in *Mining World and Engineering Record* 65 (December 12, 1903): 760. The Vivien folded in 1911 without yielding a dividend.

129. [Hoover], "Mining Company Administration," p. 5.

130. Hoover, *Years of Adventure*, p. 80.

131. Govett statement at 1905 Ivanhoe Gold Corporation shareholders meeting, in *Mining World and Engineering Record* 68 (April 29, 1905): 540.

CHAPTER 16

1. Herbert Hoover, "The Future Gold Production of Western Australia," *Transactions of the Institution of Mining and Metallurgy* 13 (1903–4): 2–21. Hoover's paper was substantially excerpted in the *Financial Times*, October 16, 1903, p. 5. An abstract appeared in the *Engineering and Mining Journal* 76 (October 31, 1903): 655.

2. *Colonial Mining News* 17 (April 30, 1903): 229–30. See also *West Australian Mining, Building, and Engineering Journal* 3 (May 28, 1904): 10–11.

3. On politics and labor in Western Australia from 1901 to 1906, see F. K. Crowley, *Australia's Western Third: A History of Western Australia From the First Settlements to Modern Times* (London, 1960), pp. 116–17, 141–42.

4. Herbert Hoover, "Gold Mining in Western Australia in 1902," *Engineering and Mining Journal* 75 (January 3, 1903): 18. For the arbitration award's terms, see A. G. Charleton, *Gold Mining and Milling in Western Australia* (London, 1903), pp. 465–66.

5. Hoover speech at meeting of Council of West Australian Mine Owners, reported verbatim in *Mining Journal, Railway and Commercial Gazette* 74 (July 18, 1903): 67. Hoover's remarks were also reported extensively in *Colonial Mining News* 18 (July 23, 1903): 47, and *West Australian Mining, Building, and Engineering Journal* 2 (August 15, 1903): 13.

6. "Our Travelling Correspondent" [Hoover], "Westralia's Mining Industry," *Financial Times*, February 1, 1904, p. 3. Hoover is identified as the author of this article in a scrapbook of his writings (including his "anonymous doings") in the Herbert Hoover Collection, Box 230, HI.

7. Hoover interview, November 1905, in *West Australian Mining, Building, and Engineering Journal* 6 (December 2, 1905): 8 (full text: 8–9).

8. Ibid.

9. *West Australian Mining, Building, and Engineering Journal* 2 (August 22, 1903): 9; Gavin Casey and Ted Mayman, *The Mile That Midas Touched* (rev. ed.: Adelaide, 1968), pp. 141–43.

10. Hoover interview in *West Australian* (Perth), February 27, 1907, and *Colonial Mining News* 25 (April 4, 1907): 168.

11. Moreing statement at 1903 shareholders meeeting of London and Western Australian Exploration Company, in *Mining World and Engineering Record* 65 (December 12, 1903): 760; Moreing statement quoted in *Colonial Mining News* 23 (May 24, 1906): 269.

12. Moreing interview, May 1904, in *West Australian Mining, Building, and Engineering Journal* 3 (June 18, 1904): 4–5, reprinted in *Western Mail* (Perth), June 25, 1904, pp. 20–21.

13. Charleton, *Gold Mining and Milling*, p. 461. See also [Hoover], "Westralia's Mining Industry," *Financial Times*, February 1, 1904, p. 3.

14. For Govett's attitude see his speech at the 1905 Ivanhoe Gold Corporation shareholders meeting, in *Mining World and Engineering Record* 68 (April 29, 1905): 541.

15. Hoover interview, November 1905. For similar remarks by Hoover's partner Moreing, see *West Australian Mining, Building, and Engineering Journal* 7 (May 12, 1906): 12.

16. See the table of salaries for Bewick, Moreing's staff in Herbert Hoover, "The Training of the Mining Engineer," *Science* (n.s.) 20 (November 25, 1904): 716.

17. *Engineering and Mining Journal* 77 (May 26, 1904): 856.

18. W. A. Prichard interview, April 1904, in *West Australian Mining, Building, and Engineering Journal* 3 (April 16, 1904): 7 (full text: 4–7).

19. Loring and Prichard testimony at the Great Boulder Perseverance inquiry, 1904, pp. 47, 74. See note 93.

20. [Hoover], letter to the editor, *Engineering and Mining Journal* 77 (April 28, 1904): 675–76.

21. Moreing statement at London and Western Australian Exploration Company shareholders meeting, 1903, as quoted in *Mining World and Engineering Record* 65 (December 12, 1903): 760. In another published account of this speech Moreing was reported as saying that white labor was "cheaper" than black. *Mining Journal, Railway and Commercial Gazette* 74 (December 12, 1903): 669.

22. Prichard interview, November 1904, in *West Australian Mining, Building, and Engineering Journal* 4 (December 3, 1904): 6–7.

23. Prichard interview, April 1904.

24. Herbert Hoover, *The Memoirs of Herbert Hoover*, Volume I: *Years of Adventure* (New York, 1951), p. 82.

25. Hoover interview, November 1905.

26. Prichard interview, April 1904.

27. Moreing interview, May 1904.

28. Donald Horne, *The Australian People* (Sydney, 1972), p. 166; F. K. Crowley, ed., *A New History of Australia* (Melbourne, 1974), p. 274.

29. *Colonial Mining News* 16 (September 4, 1902): 199; *West Australian Mining, Building, and Engineering Journal* 1 (March 7, 1903): 5; ibid. 2 (August 1, 1903): 4; Prichard interview, April 1904.

30. *West Australian Mining, Building, and Engineering Journal* 1 (March 7, 1903): 5; ibid. 1 (March 21, 1903): 18.

31. *Mining World and Engineering Record* 67 (August 6, 1904): 180.

32. Letter to the editor, *West Australian Mining, Building, and Engineering Journal* 1 (March 21, 1903): 18.

33. *West Australian Mining, Building, and Engineering Journal* 3 (April 16, 1904): 4.

34. Letter to the editor (see note 32).

35. Ibid.

36. Prichard interviews, April and December 1904; Prichard testimony at Great Boulder Perseverance inquiry, p. 116 (see note 93).

37. Moreing interview, May 1904.

38. Prichard interview, April 1904.

39. Ibid.; Moreing interview, May 1904.

40. Ibid. See also W. J. Loring interview, November 1904, in *West Australian Mining, Building, and Engineering Journal* 4 (December 3, 1904): 7.

41. For Hoffmann's remarks see *Mining World and Engineering Record* 67 (August 6, 1904): 179; for Govett's, see ibid. 68 (April 29, 1905): 541.

42. *Economist* 63 (April 29, 1905): 719.

43. Letter to the editor, *Kalgoorlie Miner*, April 7, 1904, p. 3.

44. *Australian Mining Standard* 31 (April 7, 1904): 493, and 31 (April 28, 1904): 615.

45. Prichard interview, April 1904.

46. *Australian Mining Standard* 32 (July 28, 1904): 135.

47. Moreing interview, May 1904.

48. Prichard interview, April 1904.

49. See Hoover's *Financial Times* article discussed at the beginning of chapter 14.

50. [Hoover], letter to the editor, April 1904 (see note 20).
51. "Professional Responsibility" [editorial], *Engineering and Mining Journal* 77 (April 28, 1904): 673.
52. *West Australian Mining, Building, and Engineering Journal* 3 (April 23, 1904): 10–11.
53. London correspondent's column in *West Australian Mining, Building, and Engineering Journal* 2 (July 25, 1903): 5.
54. *Engineering and Mining Journal* 77 (June 2, 1904): 872–73.
55. Ibid.
56. Moreing interview, May 1904.
57. Prichard interview, April 1904.
58. *Engineering and Mining Journal* 77 (May 26, 1904): 856–57.
59. Prichard interview, April 1904. See also Western Australia, *Parliamentary Debates*, 1904, 5th Parliament, 1st Session, vol. 26, p. 1558 (November 30, 1904).
60. Prichard interview, April 1904.
61. Western Australia, *Parliamentary Debates*, 1904, vol. 26, p. 1558.
62. *Mount Leonora Miner* [Leonora, W.A.], April 9, 1904, p. 2, and April 23, 1904, p. 2; *Kalgoorlie Miner*, April 11, 1904, p. 6, April 20, 1904, p. 4, and April 28, 1904, pp. 4–5.
63. *Kalgoorlie Miner*, April 20, 1904, p. 4, and April 28, 1904, pp. 4–5.
64. *Westralian Worker*, April 29, 1904, p. 3.
65. *Kalgoorlie Miner*, April 20, 1904, p. 4; *Mount Leonora Miner*, April 23, 1904, p. 2, and April 30, 1904, p. 2.
66. *Mount Leonora Miner*, April 30, 1904, p. 2.
67. Ibid., April 9, 1904, p. 2.
68. Prichard interview, April 1904; *Kalgoorlie Miner*, April 28, 1904, p. 4.
69. Prichard interview, April 1904.
70. *Kalgoorlie Miner*, April 28, 1904, p. 5.
71. *Mount Leonora Miner*, April 23, 1904, p. 2.
72. *Kalgoorlie Miner*, April 20, 1904, p. 4.
73. *Mount Leonora Miner*, April 30, 1904, p. 2; *West Australian Mining, Building, and Engineering Journal* 3 (May 14, 1904): 11.
74. Some Italians at the Sons of Gwalia were immediately dismissed (ibid). See also *Mount Leonora Miner*, May 21, 1904, p. 3. For the decrease of Italians on the goldfields after Loring's order, see: Western Australia, *Report of the Royal Commission on the Immigration of Non-British Labour* (Perth, 1904), pp. 67, 70, 71, 72, 73, 75, 92, in Western Australia, *Minutes and Votes and Proceedings of the Parliament During the First Session of the Fifth Parliament, 1904*, Volume II, Paper No. A7. Hereinafter cited as *Report*.
75. Loring testimony, printed in the *Report*, p. 84.
76. The preceding account is drawn from the *Report*, principally pp. 6–18, 24–25. The document consists of the report proper plus statistical tables and the testimony of all witnesses.
77. Western Australia, *Parliamentary Debates*, 1904, vol. 26, pp. 1557–59.
78. Prichard interview, November 1904.
79. *Australian Mining Standard* 32 (December 15, 1904): 831. See also ibid. 32 (December 8, 1904): 813.
80. *West Australian Mining, Building, and Engineering Journal* 4 (February 4, 1905): 4–5.
81. Moreing interview, May 1904; Hoover interview, November 1905.
82. *West Australian Mining, Building, and Engineering Journal* 4 (February 4, 1905): 4.
83. *Australian Mining Standard* 35 (February 7, 1906): 125, and 35 (February 21, 1906): 182.
84. Hoover interview, November 1905.
85. Ibid.
86. Ibid.
87. Herbert Hoover, "West Australian Gold Mining in 1905," *Engineering and Mining Journal* 81 (January 20, 1906): 136.
88. "Professional Responsibility," p. 673.
89. *Engineering and Mining Journal* 77 (June 2, 1904): 872–73.

90. *Engineering and Mining Journal* 77 (April 14, 1904): 616; *Truth* 55 (April 14, 1904): 935.

91. *West Australian Mining, Building, and Engineering Journal* 3 (May 7, 1904): 9.

92. Ibid., p. 12. According to the *Statist*, the "bear" attacks seemed "largely attributable to personal feeling." *Statist* 53 (April 2, 1904): 643–44. *Truth* predicted that the "bear" raids would not succeed very much, in part because "management methods" in Western Australia had "distinctly improved." *Truth* 55, (April 14, 1904): 935.

93. For the narrative about the Great Boulder Perseverance scandal I have relied primarily on the following document: *Report of the Royal Commission Appointed to Inquire Into Matters Pertaining to Great Boulder Perseverance Gold Mining Company, Limited, Kalgoorlie*, in Western Australia, *Votes and Proceedings of Parliament*, 5th Parliament, 2nd Session (1905), Volume I, Paper No. 3. This document (hereinafter cited as *Royal Commission*) contains the report proper (pp. 5–29), a transcript of all evidence taken by the Commission, and various documents including a deposition by Herbert Hoover. Rather than burden the text with a separate footnote for every single sentence of my account, I refer the interested reader to this bulky document, plus various supplementary items cited below.

94. Ralph Nichols claimed that it was Gardner who "really made the agreement" (*Royal Commission*, p. 120). Presumably, then, Gardner insisted on these conditions. Moreing said only that "some of the directors" stipulated that his firm take up Gardner's block of shares (*Royal Commission*, p. 129). Many years later Hoover stated that Perseverance board members dissatisfied with Gardner required Bewick, Moreing to buy Gardner's shares "in order that he might be eliminated from the business." Hoover, draft statement about "Boulder Perseverance and Boulder Deep Levels" (ca. 1931–32), in "Richey-Hoover Files: Statements and Refutations," Misrepresentations File, HHPL.

95. Gardner claimed that the average share price was a little less (*Royal Commission*, p. 130).

96. *Engineering and Mining Journal* 77 (April 14, 1904): 616.

97. That, at least, was what Gardner's successor as board chairman later claimed. Transcript of Great Boulder Perseverance shareholders meeting, April 12, 1905, in *Mining World and Engineering Record* 68 (April 15, 1905): 468 (full transcript: 466–68).

98. Lane testimony, *Royal Commission*, p. 95; *Australian Mining Standard* 32 (November 10, 1904): 678 (for Hoover's denial).

99. In addition to *Royal Commission* see transcript of Great Boulder Perseverance shareholders meeting, February 7, 1905, in *Mining World and Engineering Record* 68 (February 11, 1905): 182 (full transcript: 182–87).

100. Hoover's letter is quoted in *Royal Commission*, p. 59.

101. Moreing declaration, printed in *Royal Commission*, p. 129. See also transcript of February 7, 1905 shareholders meeting, p. 182. The board chairman said at this meeting that Bewick, Moreing sold out on the morning of June 22, 1904.

102. Hoover, draft statement about Great Boulder Perseverance case (ca. 1931–32), cited in note 94.

103. Ibid.

104. Ibid.

105. Ibid. See also *Mining World and Engineering Record* 68 (January 14, 1905): 40–41; *West Australian Mining, Building, and Engineering Journal* 4 (January 14, 1905): 6–7.

106. *West Australian Mining, Building, and Engineering Journal* 4 (November 26, 1904): 7.

107. Hoover, draft statement about Great Boulder Perseverance case.

108. Transcript of February 7, 1905 Great Boulder Perseverance shareholders meeting, p. 182.

109. *Report of the Royal Commission Appointed to Inquire Into . . . The Boulder Deep Levels, Limited, Kalgoorlie* (Perth, 1904), p. 17, in Western Australia, *Votes and Proceedings of Parliament*, 5th Parliament, 1st Session (1904), Volume II.

110. *West Australian Mining, Building, and Engineering Journal* 4 (October 29, 1904): 4; *Colonial Mining News* 21 (January 12, 1905): 19. Hoover's draft statement and his *Memoirs (Years of Adventure*, p. 80) incorrectly state that his firm resigned upon seeing the board withhold information from the shareholders (that is, circa June 22, 1904).

111. *West Australian Mining, Building, and Engineering Journal* 4 (February 11, 1904): 4.

112. *Mining World and Engineering Record* 68 (January 14, 1905): 40–41; transcript of February 7, 1905 Great Boulder Perseverance shareholders meeting, p. 183; *Engineering and Mining Journal* 79 (April 20, 1905): 786.

113. Transcript of February 7, 1905 Great Boulder Perseverance shareholders meeting, pp. 184–87.

114. *Engineering and Mining Journal* 79 (April 20, 1905): 786.

115. Transcript of February 7, 1905 Great Boulder Perseverance shareholders meeting, p. 183; transcript of April 12, 1905 shareholders meeting, p. 468. The lawsuit was apparently settled out of court. See transcript of April 4, 1906 shareholders meeting, in *West Australian Mining, Building, and Engineering Journal* 7 (May 12, 1906): 13.

116. Chairman's comments at February 7, 1905 meeting, transcript, p. 182.

117. Transcript of April 12, 1905 meeting, p. 468.

118. *West Australian Mining, Building, and Engineering Journal* 4 (February 18, 1905): 6, 12; ibid. 4 (February 25, 1905): 7; *Mining World and Engineering Record* 68 (March 18, 1905): 321. Prichard testified at the royal commission's hearings that Hoover and Moreing considered his handling of the sampling to have been "an error in judgment on my part" (*Royal Commission*, p. 84). Prichard's departure from Bewick, Moreing soon after the royal commission issued its report may therefore have been involuntary.

119. Hoover, *Years of Adventure*, p. 80.

120. Hoover to the Bewick, Moreing office in Kalgoorlie, June 24, 1904, quoted in *Royal Commission*, p. 18. The sum £40,000 then equaled nearly $200,000.

121. In his draft statement (ca. 1931–32) Hoover put the firm's loss at $100,000.

122. *Royal Commission*, pp. 18, 116, 129.

123. Prichard testimony, *Royal Commission*, p. 121.

124. Hoover to his brother Theodore, July 21, 1904, Hulda Hoover McLean Papers, HI.

125. For the terms, see transcript of Golden Horseshoe Estates shareholders meeting, April 27, 1905, in *Mining World and Engineering Record* 68 (April 29, 1905): 542 (full transcript: 542–44), and Bewick, Moreing & Co.'s letter printed in ibid., pp. 537–38.

126. Transcript of shareholders meeting, April 27, 1905, p. 543; *Australian Mining Standard* 32 (September 22, 1904): 440, and 32 (October 27, 1904): 609.

127. Chairman's speech, in transcript of April 27, 1905 shareholders meeting, pp. 542–43.

128. Bewick, Moreing letter, pp. 537–38.

129. Transcript of April 27, 1905 shareholders meeting, p. 543.

130. Bewick, Moreing letter, pp. 537–38.

131. *Engineering and Mining Journal* 79 (May 11, 1905): 931–32.

132. *Mining World and Engineering Record* 68 (April 29, 1905): 524–25.

133. This story is contained in an unpublished typewritten manuscript entitled *Hail Columbia Hoover*, pp. 119–25, in "Baker Files," Misrepresentations File, HHPL. This manuscript was purportedly written by one John Hamill, ca. 1932. But my study of the evidence strongly suggests that it was prepared not by Hamill but by close associates of President Hoover, with the cooperation (and probably at the direction) of Hoover himself. The "inside" story recounted here, for which no written corroboration has been found, must have come from someone like Hoover, in a position to know about the personal rivalries involved. In all likelihood Hoover was the source of the story recounted in *Hail Columbia Hoover*.

134. Hoover, draft statement about "West Australia Gold Mining Boom" (ca. 1931–32), in "Richey-Hoover Files: Statements and Refutations," Misrepresentations File.

135. Transcript of April 27, 1905 Golden Horseshoe Estates shareholders meeting, p. 543.

136. Hoover to his brother Theodore, January 12, 1906, McLean Papers.

137. Hoover to his brother Theodore, March 23, 1906, ibid.

138. Hoover, quoted by W. J. Loring in an interview in *Cedar Rapids* [Iowa] *Sunday Gazette and Republican*, November 4, 1928, Section 1, p. 5.

139. Hoover notes on his 1904 South African trip, in Hoover Scrapbooks, Album 42, HHPL.

140. Hoover to his brother Theodore, July 21, 1904, McLean Papers.

141. Ibid.

142. The mining press reported that Hoover's trip was a "professional visit." Of course, Hoover would not have been apt to state publicly that he was going for reasons of health. *Mining World and Engineering Record* 67 (July 23, 1904): 100.

143. Hoover, *Years of Adventure*, pp. 86–87.

144. Hoover notes on his 1904 South African trip, in Hoover Scrapbooks, Album 42; *Daily Chronicle* (London), October 10, 1904, p. 5.

145. Hoover notes on his 1904 South African trip.

146. Ibid.; Hoover, *Years of Adventure*, p. 87; [Hoover], undated memorandum in "McMullin, Dare Stark," Post-Presidential Subject File, HHPL.

147. *Mining and Scientific Press* 92 (January 27, 1906): 55–56.

148. George Wilson affidavit, February 15, 1932, in "Richey-Hoover Files: Statements and Refutations," Misrepresentations File. For more on the Chinese Engineering and Mining Company's involvement, see F. Perry to the Colonial Office, February 10, 1905, C.O. 879 / 85 / 761 / 15–20, Public Record Office, Kew, Surrey, U.K.

149. *Mining and Scientific Press* 92 (January 27, 1906): 56; Great Britain, Parliament, *Further Correspondence Relating to Labour in the Transvaal Mines* (Cd. 3025: July 1906), p. 151; Randolph S. Churchill, *Winston S. Churchill*, Volume II: *Young Statesman, 1901–1914* (Boston, 1967), p. 187.

150. William L. Honnold statement, December 21, 1931; W. S. Nathan to Julean Arnold, January 6 and 8, 1932; H. H. Webb statement, October 16, 1932; all in "Campaign of 1932: Hoover and Chinese Labor," Misrepresentations File, HHPL. See also Honnold to Edward Emerson, 1932, quoted in Emerson to John J. Harold, November 14, 1932, in Herbert Hoover—President's Papers, New York Public Library.

151. Moreing interview, May 1904.

152. See sources cited in note 21. In 1906 Moreing declared: "We [Moreing's firm] pay the highest wages in the world, and yet we are able to show, ton for ton, lower costs than they can accomplish with Chinese cheap labour in South Africa." *Engineering and Mining Journal* 81 (June 23, 1906): 1179.

153. Honnold statement, December 21, 1931; Hoover, *Years of Adventure*, p. 87.

154. Hoover, quoted in *Daily Chronicle* (London), October 10, 1904, p. 5. Hoover's remark was reprinted in *Australian Mining Standard* 32 (November 24, 1904): 742.

155. Hoover notes on his 1904 South African trip; *The Times*, September 5, 1904, p. 8. Hoover's vessel, the *Kildonan Castle*, arrived in Southhampton on September 3.

156. This was his own calculation. Hoover notes on his 1904 South African trip.

157. Hoover, *Years of Adventure*, p. 88.

CHAPTER 17

1. Herbert Hoover travel notes for 1905, in Hoover Scrapbooks, Album 45, HHPL.

2. Ibid. Lou visited relatives in Waterloo, Iowa along the way.

3. Ibid.; Theodore J. Hoover, *Memoranda: Being a Statement by an Engineer* (typescript: Stanford University, 1939), p. 131, copy at HHPL.

4. *Stanford Alumnus* 6 (June 1905): 8, 10.

5. Theodore Hoover, *Memoranda*, pp. 131–33.

6. Hoover to R. A. F. Penrose, Jr., May 17, 1905, in Helen R. Fairbanks and Charles P. Berkey, *Life and Letters of R. A. F. Penrose, Jr.* (New York, 1952), p. 377; Hoover to his brother Theodore, June 26, 1905, Hulda Hoover McLean Papers, HI.

7. Hoover Calendar, HHPL.

8. Hoover, power of attorney dated June 20, 1905, attached to his letter to Theodore of June 26, 1905.

9. Hoover travel notes for 1905, Hoover Scrapbooks, Album 45.

10. Ibid.; *Colonial Mining News* 22 (July 20, 1905): 26. Lou and young Herbert sailed on for Australia while Bert inspected the Talisman mine. He rejoined them in Sydney.

11. *West Australian Mining, Building, and Engineering Journal* 6 (August 5, 1905): 8; Hoover travel notes for 1905.

12. Hoover Calendar, HHPL; Hoover travel notes for 1905.

13. Ibid.; *West Australian Mining, Building, and Engineering Journal* 6 (October 28, 1905): 3. Hoover arrived in Fremantle on October 23. His wife preceded him by a week.

14. *West Australian Mining, Building, and Engineering Journal* 6 (November 4, 1905): 5, and 6 (December 2, 1905): 5.

15. Hoover note in Hoover Scrapbooks, Album 45.

16. *West Australian Mining, Building, and Engineering Journal* 6 (November 11, 1905): 5.

17. J. W. Kirwan, "Mr. and Mrs. Hoover: West Australian Reminiscences," n.d. (late 1928), Reprint File, HHPL.

18. G. W. Borrowe to W. J. Loring, November 9 and 13, 1905, in Borrowe letter book, Sons of Gwalia Records, J. S. Battye Library, Perth, Western Australia; Lou Henry Hoover to John C. Branner, January 1, 1906, John C. Branner Papers, Box 38, Stanford University Archives.

19. Lou Henry Hoover to Branner, January 1, 1906.

20. Telephone interview of Frederick Walton Rowe, Kendenup, Western Australia, September 28, 1977. Rowe, now a retired mining engineer, was working at the mine in 1905 and learned the story directly from Jimmy Johns, the underground manager.

21. Hoover travel notes for 1905; *West Australian Mining, Building, and Engineering Journal* 6 (December 2, 1905): 5.

22. Lou Henry Hoover to Branner, n.d. (1905), Branner Papers, Box 36; Lou Henry Hoover to Branner, January 1, 1906; Hoover to his brother, January 2 and 12, 1906, McLean Papers; Hoover Calendar, HHPL.

23. Hoover travel notes for 1905.

24. *West Australian Mining, Building, and Engineering Journal* 6 (November 25, 1905): 6; *Australian Mining Standard* 34 (December 6, 1905): 547, and 35 (February 28, 1906): 206; C. S. Herzig membership file, Institution of Mining and Metallurgy, London.

25. *Mining World and Engineering Record* 69 (November 25, 1905): supplement, p. ii; Geoffrey Blainey, *The Rise of Broken Hill* (Melbourne, 1968), passim. All references below to the first source in this note will be cited as *Mining World* supplement.

26. Blainey, *Rise of Broken Hill*, pp. 68–69; *Mining World* supplement (cited in note 25), pp. ii, xv.

27. *Mining World* supplement, p. xii.

28. W. S. Robinson, *If I Remember Rightly* (Melbourne, 1967), p. 36; Herbert Hoover, *The Memoirs of Herbert Hoover*, Volume I: *Years of Adventure* (New York, 1951), p. 89.

29. *Mining Journal* 79 (January 6, 1906): 19.

30. Ibid.; Blainey, *Rise of Broken Hill*, pp. 70–72.

31. *Mining World* supplement, pp. xiv–xv; Robinson, *If I Remember Rightly*, pp. 35–39; W. S. Robinson to R. Pitman Hooper, February 8, 1955, W. S. Robinson Papers, University of Melbourne Archives, Melbourne, Australia.

32. *Mining World* supplement, p. xiv.

33. Robinson to Hooper, February 8, 1955; Robinson, *If I Remember Rightly*, p. 37.

34. [J. H. Curle], "Mining in Australia—VII," *Economist* 63 (July 29, 1905): 1231.

35. Hoover, *Years of Adventure*, p. 89. W. S. Robinson said later that Broken Hill resembled a set for a TV Western. Robinson, *If I Remember Rightly*, p. 36.

36. Hoover interview in *Barrier Miner* [Broken Hill], August 24, 1905.

37. Robinson, *If I Remember Rightly*, p. 39; *Mining World* supplement, p. xv.

38. *Mining World* supplement, p. xv; Herzig membership file; *The Age* (Melbourne), October 16, 1905; *Australian Mining Standard* 34 (October 18, 1905): 366–67; *The Bulletin* (Sydney),

October 26, 1905; John Hamill, *Hail Columbia Hoover* (typescript, ca. 1932), p. 142, Misrepresentations File, HHPL. Hamill states that Hoover's friend F. A. Govett also helped to form the Hill Syndicate, but I have found no confirmation of this.

39. *Mining World* supplement, p. xiv.

40. *West Australian Mining, Building, and Engineering Journal* 16 (August 6, 1910): 15.

41. Moreing statement at shareholders meeting of London and Western Australian Exploration Company, March 12, 1906, quoted in *Mining World and Engineering Record* 70 (March 17, 1906): 321.

42. *Australian Mining Standard* 34 (September 20, 1905): 265.

43. Ibid., October 18, 1905, pp. 366–67; *Mining World* supplement, p. xvi.

44. *Mining World* supplement, p. xvi; *Mining Journal* 79 (January 6, 1906): 19; *Australian Mining Standard* 35 (March 28, 1906): 305; A. N. Jackman, ed., *The Mining Year-Book . . . 1906* (London, 1906), p. 998.

45. Jackman, *Mining Year-Book . . . 1906*, p. 998.

46. Walter R. Skinner, *The Mining Manual for 1906* (London, 1906), p. 187.

47. Jackman, *Mining Year-Book . . . 1906*, p. 998.

48. Ibid.; Skinner, *Mining Manual for 1906*, p. 187; W. L. Baillieu to Hoover, September 22, 1908, "Mining—Correspondence: Baillieu, E. L. and W. L.," Pre-Commerce Papers, HHPL. For more on Baillieu see *Australian Dictionary of Biography*, vol. 7 (Melbourne, 1979), pp. 138–45.

49. Skinner, *Mining Manual for 1906*, p. 187.

50. *Australian Mining Standard* 35 (May 2, 1906): 422; *The Times*, May 2, 1906, p. 13.

51. Moreing statement at 1906 shareholders meeting of London and Western Australian Exploration Company, p. 323.

52. *Australian Mining Standard* 35 (March 28, 1906): 305.

53. D. P. Mitchell, "Flotation at Zinc Corporation, Ltd.," *Engineering and Mining Journal* 92 (November 18, 1911): 994 (full article: 994–97).

54. Baillieu to Hoover, September 22, 1908.

55. *The Bulletin* (Sydney), October 26, 1905.

56. Robinson, *If I Remember Rightly*, p. 39.

57. Transcript of Lake View Consols shareholders meeting, September 25, 1905, printed in *Mining World and Engineering Record* 69 (September 30, 1905): 411–12 (see also editorial on pp. 396–97); *Mining World* supplement, p. xi; Skinner, *Mining Manual for 1906*, p. 27; [W. S. Robinson?], unsigned typewritten account of Zinc Corporation history, 1905–55, pp. 5–6, in "Broken Hill: General Comments" (folder title), Robinson Papers. Hoover's cable is quoted in the shareholders meeting transcript, p. 412.

58. *The Times*, June 8, 1906, p. 12; *Economist* 64 (June 9, 1906): 976; *Mining and Scientific Press* 92 (June 30, 1906): 439.

59. Skinner, *Mining Manual for 1906*, pp. 13–14; *Colonial Mining News* 23 (January 4, 1906): 7.

60. *Australian Mining Standard* 35 (March 28, 1906): 305.

61. Ibid.; Skinner, *Mining Manual for 1906*, pp. 13–14.

62. *Mining World* supplement, p. xiv.

63. *West Australian Mining, Building, and Engineering Journal* 6 (November 25, 1905): 7.

64. *Mining World* supplement, p. xvi.

65. *West Australian Mining, Building, and Engineering Journal* 6 (November 25, 1905): 8.

66. Ibid., p. 7; *The Bulletin* (Sydney), October 26, 1905. See also F. H. Bathurst, "Hoover in Australia: A Personal Sketch," *The Argus* (Melbourne), November 3, 1928, p. 6.

67. *Colonial Mining News* 23 (January 4, 1906): 7.

68. *Australian Mining Standard* 35 (May 2, 1906): 422.

69. *West Australian Mining, Building, and Engineering Journal* 6 (November 18, 1905): 9.

70. *Mining Journal* 79 (January 6, 1906): 19.

71. *The Age* (Melbourne), October 16, 1905, pointed out that all the flotation processes were currently "in a rather crude state of mechanical development."

72. See Blainey, *Rise of Broken Hill*, p. 72, and *The Bulletin* (Sydney), November 16, 1905. *The Bulletin* noted that the nascent Zinc Corporation had "done absolutely nothing on an industrial scale."

73. *Mining World* supplement, p. xii.

74. His full sentence reads: "We have just made contracts here for the purchase of some 4,000,000 tons of tailings containing Zinc blende and have thoroughly demonstrated the business." Hoover to Albert Homer Purdue, September 25, 1905, Albert Homer Purdue Correspondence, University of Arkansas Library.

75. Hoover to Herbert J. Daly, May 4, 1906, Mining Letter Book No. 1, Pre-Commerce Papers.

76. *Colonial Mining News* 23 (February 1, 1906): 62; *Mining and Scientific Press* 92 (June 30, 1906): 439; Mitchell, "Flotation at Zinc Corporation, Ltd.," p. 994; W. L. Baillieu remarks at June 4, 1907 Zinc Corporation shareholders meeting, reported in *The Argus* (Melbourne), June 5, 1907.

77. Jackman, *Mining Year-Book . . . 1906*, p. 998; *The Leader* (Melbourne), March 3, 1906, supplement, p. 3; *Australian Mining Standard* 35 (March 28, 1906): 305.

78. *Economist* 64 (June 9, 1906): 976; *Australian Mining Standard* 35 (May 2, 1906): 422.

79. *Colonial Mining News* 23 (February 1, 1906): 62; ibid. 23 (February 22, 1906): 99.

80. *Australian Mining Standard* 35 (March 28, 1906): 305; statement by W. L. Baillieu at Zinc Corporation shareholders meeting of April 30, 1906, in *Economist* 64 (June 9, 1906): 976, *Statist* 57 (June 9, 1906): 1103, and *Mining World and Engineering Record* 70 (June 9, 1906): 739–40.

81. Zinc Corporation half-yearly report to February 13, 1906, summarized in *Mining and Scientific Press* 92 (June 30, 1906): 439. For another summary see *The Times*, June 8, 1906, p. 12.

82. Mitchell, "Flotation at Zinc Corporation, Ltd.," p. 994.

83. *The Times*, May 2, 1906, p. 13.

84. *Mining and Scientific Press* 92 (June 30, 1906): 439.

85. Baillieu statement at Zinc Corporation shareholders meeting, April 30, 1906.

86. Skinner, *Mining Manual for 1906*, p. 187.

87. Moreing interview in *Colonial Mining News* 23 (May 24, 1906): 268.

88. Hoover to Daly, May 4, 1906.

89. Baillieu statement at April 30, 1906 shareholders meeting; W. R. Ingalls to Hazel Lyman Nickel, August 28, 1949, Herbert Hoover Collection, Box 5, HI.

90. Mitchell, "Flotation at Zinc Corporation, Ltd.," p. 994.

91. Blainey, *Rise of Broken Hill*, p. 72.

92. *Mining and Scientific Press* 93 (October 27, 1906): 492.

93. *West Australian Mining, Building, and Engineering Journal* 8 (November 10, 1906): 7.

94. Ibid.

95. Robinson, *If I Remember Rightly*, pp. 38–39; Baillieu to Hoover, November 14, 1906, "Mining—Correspondence: Baillieu, E. L. and W. L.," Pre-Commerce Papers.

96. Baillieu to Hoover, November 14, 1906.

97. F. A. Govett circular to Zinc Corporation shareholders, April 18, 1907, printed in *Financial News* (London), April 19, 1907, p. 4, and *West Australian Mining, Building, and Engineering Journal* 9 (May 25, 1907): 11. A summary of this circular appeared in *The Times*, April 19, 1907, p. 14. According to Baillieu, the company's staff had been ordered to investigate the Cattermole process before Queneau arrived, and Queneau was instructed by the board "to investigate the whole position of the different processes." W. L. Baillieu remarks at Zinc Corporation shareholders meeting, June 4, 1907.

98. Govett circular, April 18, 1907; Baillieu remarks at June 4, 1907 Zinc Corporation shareholders meeting.

99. Govett statement at July 30, 1907 Zinc Corporation shareholders meeting, quoted in *Mining World and Engineering Record* 73 (August 3, 1907): 158 (full transcript: 157–61).

100. Baillieu to Hoover, November 14, 1906.

101. *Mining World and Engineering Record* 71 (October 20, 1906): 442.

102. *The Times*, October 27, 1906, p. 16; *Mining World and Engineering Record* 71 (October 27, 1906): 455; *British-Australasian* 25 (November 1, 1906): 8; *West Australian Mining, Building, and Engineering Journal* 8 (November 10, 1906): 7; Walter R. Skinner, *The Mining Manual for 1908* (London, 1908), pp. 166–67.

103. Minutes of meeting of London committee of directors of Zinc Corporation, December 19, 1906, Zinc Corporation Minute Book No. 1, Rio Tinto-Zinc Corporation, Ltd., London; Hoover to Bewick, Moreing & Co., October 30, 1906, Mining Letter Book No. 1, Pre-Commerce Papers. Moreing received an option for the same number of shares, while the London and Western Australian Exploration Company received an option on 15,867 shares. Under the scheme the Zinc Corporation issued 113,333 shares at 25 shillings per share. As a guarantor Hoover promised that he would buy 8% of these (or about 9,000 shares) if necessary. Nine thousand shares at 25 shillings per share came to about $55,000 in 1906.

104. Skinner, *Mining Manual for 1908*, p. 167.

105. Hoover to W. J. Loring, October 26, 1906, Mining Letter Book No. 1, Pre-Commerce Papers. The London and Western Australian Exploration Company likewise held about 45,000 shares. Robinson (said Hoover) owned about 60,000 shares.

106. Ibid.

107. Ibid.

108. *Colonial Mining News* 24 (December 13, 1906): 306.

109. *Mining World and Engineering Record* 72 (January 12, 1907): 29–30.

110. Ibid. 72 (March 9, 1907): 278. The 1907 peak was 50s.

111. Ibid. 72 (January 26, 1907): 86.

112. Queneau cable, quoted in *Colonial Mining News* 25 (January 31, 1907): 61.

113. *Money Market Review* comment, quoted in February 1 letter by a London correspondent in *Australian Mining Standard* 37 (March 13, 1907): 248.

114. London letter, February 1, in *Australian Mining Standard* 37 (March 13, 1907): 248; London letter, March 1, ibid. 37 (April 10, 1907): 344; *Mining World and Engineering Record* 72 (March 2, 1907): 244; ibid. 72 (March 9, 1907): 278; *Statist* 59 (April 6, 1907): 677.

115. Hoover Calendar, HHPL.

116. *Australian Mining Standard* 37 (February 13, 1907): 144.

117. *West Australian Mining, Building, and Engineering Journal* 9 (February 23, 1907): 5.

118. Ibid. 9 (March 9, 1907): 2.

119. *The Bulletin* (Sydney), February 28, 1907, p. 13.

120. Zinc Corporation circular printed in *The Times*, March 1, 1907, p. 14, and quoted in *Colonial Mining News* 25 (March 7, 1907): 119.

121. *Australian Mining Standard* 37 (March 6, 1907): 218.

122. The circular printed in *The Times* on March 1 stated that Hoover would arrive in Broken Hill on March 5.

123. *Australian Mining Standard* 37 (March 13, 1907): 241.

124. Minutes of meeting of London committee of directors of Zinc Corporation, May 8, 1907, Zinc Corporation Minute Book No. 1, Rio Tinto-Zinc Corporation, Ltd., London.

125. *Australian Mining Standard* 37 (March 20, 1907): 269.

126. A shareholder quoted in *Mining World and Engineering Record* 72 (March 2, 1907): 244–45.

127. *Mining World and Engineering Record* 72 (March 9, 1907): 278.

128. Ibid.

129. Letter to the editor, *Mining World and Engineering Record* 72 (March 30, 1907): 389.

130. *Mining and Scientific Press* 94 (March 30, 1907): 392.

131. Govett statement at July 30, 1907 shareholders meeting, p. 158; Baillieu statement at June 4, 1907 shareholders meeting. See also *The Times*, July 11, 1907, p. 15.

132. Govett interview, March 25, 1907, excerpted in *West Australian Mining, Building, and Engineering Journal* 9 (May 4, 1907): 15.

133. Hoover cable, April 2, 1907, quoted in *Statist* 59 (April 6, 1907): 677, and in Govett's circular of April 18, 1907 (cited in note 97).

134. Hoover statement at July 30, 1907 shareholders meeting, p. 160.

135. Mitchell, "Flotation at Zinc Corporation, Ltd.," p. 994.

136. Walter R. Skinner, *The Mining Manual for 1907* (London, 1907), p. 955.

137. Govett statement at July 30, 1907 shareholders meeting, pp. 158–59.

138. Hoover statement at July 30, 1907 shareholders meeting, p. 160.

139. *Mining World and Engineering Record* 72 (April 13, 1907): 422.

140. Ibid.

141. Zinc Corporation circular published on March 1, 1907 (cited in note 120).

142. Govett circular, April 18, 1907.

143. Ibid.

144. Govett statement at July 30, 1907 shareholders meeting, p. 159.

145. Govett circular, April 18, 1907.

146. Govett statement at July 30, 1907 shareholders meeting, p. 159.

147. Ibid. See also Hoover statement at July 15, 1908 Zinc Corporation shareholders meeting, printed in *Mining World and Engineering Record* 75 (July 18, 1908): 110.

148. *West Australian Mining, Building, and Engineering Journal* 9 (June 1, 1907): 2; *Australian Mining Standard* 37 (June 5, 1907): 521.

149. *Mining World and Engineering Record* 72 (June 29, 1907): 801.

150. *Australasian World*, June 27, 1907, p. 622.

151. *West Australian Mining, Building, and Engineering Journal* 9 (June 22, 1907): 7.

152. *Statist* 60 (July 13, 1907): 57.

153. London letter, July 12, 1907, printed in *Australian Mining Standard* 38 (August 21, 1907): 167.

154. *Statist* 60 (July 13, 1907): 57.

155. Hoover Calendar, HHPL.

156. Minutes of meeting of London committee of directors of Zinc Corporation, July 22, 1907, Zinc Corporation Minute Book No. 1, Rio Tinto-Zinc Corporation, Ltd., London.

157. Govett circular, July 23, 1907, printed in *The Times*, July 24, 1907, p. 14.

158. Hoover statement at July 30, 1907 shareholders meeeting, p. 160.

159. Mitchell, "Flotation at Zinc Corporation, Ltd.," p. 995.

160. *Rialto* [London], July 24, 1907, p. 4.

161. Govett speech at July 30, 1907 shareholders meeting, pp. 157–60; see also the version in *Economist* 65 (August 3, 1907): 1322–23.

162. Hoover speech at July 30, 1907 shareholders meeting, p. 161.

163. Govett speech at July 30, 1907 shareholders meeting, pp. 159, 160.

164. Ibid., p. 159.

165. Ibid., p. 160; Skinner, *Mining Manual for 1908*, p. 167.

166. Govett speech at July 30, 1907 shareholders meeting, p. 160; Robinson, *If I Remember Rightly*, p. 42.

167. *Mining World and Engineering Record* 73 (August 3, 1907): 145.

168. *Mining and Scientific Press* 95 (August 24, 1907): 222–23.

169. *Money Market Review*, quoted in *Australian Mining Standard* 38 (September 18, 1907): 259.

170. *Mining and Scientific Press* 96 (February 29, 1908): 280.

171. *The Bulletin* (Sydney), November 14, 1907, p. 13.

172. Skinner, *Mining Manual for 1908*, p. 167. This was the lowest price for the stock in 1907.

173. Govett speech at 1908 Zinc Corporation shareholders meeting, in *Mining World and Engineering Record* 75 (July 18, 1908): 107.

174. Govett speech at July 30, 1907 shareholders meeting, p. 160.

175. *The Bulletin* (Sydney), February 27, 1908, p. 13; *Engineering and Mining Journal* 87 (January 23, 1909): 219; Mitchell, "Flotation at Zinc Corporation, Ltd.," pp. 994–95.

176. *Mining and Scientific Press* 96 (February 29, 1908): 280; Govett speech at 1908 shareholders meeting, p. 108; Skinner, *Mining Manual for 1908*, p. 167; Walter R. Skinner, *The Mining Manual for 1909* (London, 1909), p. 157.

177. Skinner, *Mining Manual for 1909*, p. 157.

178. *Mining and Scientific Press* 96 (February 29, 1908): 280; Govett statement at 1908 shareholders meeting, p. 108. Eventually the remaining shares were subscribed. Skinner, *Mining Manual for 1909*, p. 157.

179. Govett statement at 1908 shareholders meeting, p. 108.

180. *Australian Mining Standard* 39 (February 19, 1908): 155; *Mining News and Financial Record* 27 (March 5, 1908): 114; *Australian Mining Standard* 39 (March 25, 1908): 295; C. Algernon Moreing speech at shareholders meeting of London and Western Australian Exploration Company, March 30, 1908, in *Mining World and Engineering Record* 74 (April 4, 1908): 438–39.

181. *Australian Mining Standard* 39 (June 17, 1908): 634.

182. Govett speech at 1908 shareholders meeting, p. 108.

183. Ibid., pp. 107, 109.

184. Hoover speech, ibid., pp. 109–10.

185. Govett speech, ibid., p. 109; minutes of meeting of Zinc Corporation's board of directors, July 29, 1908, in Zinc Corporation Minute Book No. 1, Rio Tinto-Zinc Corporation, Ltd., London.

186. Robinson, *If I Remember Rightly*, p. 42.

187. Hoover speech at 1908 shareholders meeting, p. 110.

188. Govett speech, ibid., p. 109.

189. *Mining World and Engineering Record* 75 (August 15, 1908): 231.

190. *Engineering and Mining Journal* 87 (January 23, 1909): 219.

191. *Mining News* 28 (September 24, 1908): 155; ibid. 28 (October 15, 1908): 192; *Engineering and Mining Journal* 87 (January 9, 1909): 68.

192. Skinner, *Mining Manual for 1910*, p. 9; "The President's Fortune," *Fortune* 6 (August 1932): 84.

193. *Mining Magazine* 11 (September 1914): 167.

194. Walter R. Skinner, *The Mining Manual for 1912* (London, 1912), p. 130; A. N. Jackman, ed., *The Mining Year-Book . . . 1912* (London, 1912), pp. 897–98.

195. *West Australian Mining, Building, and Engineering Journal* 16 (August 6, 1910): 15–16.

196. *The Times*, February 21, 1911, p. 20; Mitchell, "Flotation at Zinc Corporation, Ltd.," pp. 995–96; Blainey, *Rise of Broken Hill*, p. 74.

197. Govett's phrase at July 30, 1907 shareholders meeting, p. 158.

198. The existence of a dual board of directors continued until 1911, when the Zinc Corporation reorganized and became a London-registered company.

199. Govett statement at 1908 shareholders meeting, p. 109.

200. Robinson, *If I Remember Rightly*, p. 39.

201. Bathurst, "Hoover in Australia: A Personal Sketch," p. 6.

202. Ibid.

203. *Engineering and Mining Journal* 87 (January 23, 1909): 219.

CHAPTER 18

1. *West Australian Mining, Building, and Engineering Journal* 11 (April 4, 1908): 6.

2. *Australian Mining Standard* 37 (February 20, 1907): 176.

3. *Morning Herald* (Perth) clipping, February 2, 1907, Hoover Scrapbooks, Album 41, HHPL.

4. For the Talisman Consolidated controversy, see: account of annual shareholders meeting, May 30, 1907, in *Economist* 65 (June 1, 1907): 951–52; transcript of extraordinary general shareholders meeting, December 11, 1907, in *Mining World and Engineering Record* 73 (December 14, 1907): 744–48.

5. Walter R. Skinner, *The Mining Manual and Mining Year Book for 1915* (London, 1915), pp. 638–39. The company wound up in 1921.

6. See transcript of Oroya Brownhill annual shareholders meeting, April 7, 1908, in *Mining World and Engineering Record* 74 (April 11, 1908): 475–79. A similar controversy arose among Sons of Gwalia shareholders. See *Mining World and Engineering Record* 74 (April 18, 1908): 520–21, and *West Australian Mining, Building, and Engineering Journal* 11 (May 16, 1908): 6.

7. *West Australian Mining, Building, and Engineering Journal* 12 (August 29, 1908): 10–11. The Melbourne *Argus* took the same position.

8. Malcolm Maclaren and J. Allan Thomson, "Geology of the Kalgoorlie Goldfield—I," *Mining and Scientific Press* 107 (July 12, 1913): 48. The trend caused much concern. See Walter R. Skinner, *The Mining Manual for 1908* (London, 1908), p. xvi.

9. [J. H. Curle], "The Mines of West Australia," *Economist* 61 (November 28, 1903): 2006.

10. [Curle], "Mining in Australasia—I," *Economist* 63 (June 17, 1905): 990–91, and "Mining in Australasia—II," ibid. 63 (June 24, 1905): 1028.

11. [Curle], "The Mines of West Australia," *Economist* 64 (January 27, 1906): 118–19.

12. Herbert Hoover, "West Australian Gold Mining in 1905," *Engineering and Mining Journal* 81 (January 20, 1906): 136.

13. Ibid.; Herbert Hoover, "The Future Gold Production of Western Australia," *Transactions of the Institution of Mining and Metallurgy* 13 (1903–4): 6.

14. Hoover, "West Australian Gold Mining in 1905," p. 136.

15. Ibid.

16. Hoover, "Future Gold Production," p. 6.

17. Ibid., p. 13.

18. Hoover interview in *Australian Mining Standard* 37 (March 20, 1907): 264, and in *Colonial Mining News* 25 (April 4, 1907): 168.

19. Hoover interview in *The West Australian* (Perth), November 10, 1905, *Kalgoorlie Miner*, November 10, 1905, p. 6, and *Australian Mining Standard* 34 (November 29, 1905): 526. See also *Colonial Mining News* 22 (December 21, 1905): 322.

20. Ibid. Specifically, Hoover proposed that the West Australian government impose only a nominal fee on prospectors during the five years of the lease and require prospectors to do only a small amount of development work on their lease each year.

21. See *Morning Herald* (Perth) clippings, November 25 and 29, 1905, in Hoover Scrapbooks, Albums 45 and 51 respectively, HHPL. Some Australian journals conceded that Hoover's viewpoint had much merit but argued that adoption of American mining law in Australia was not feasible. See *Kalgoorlie Miner*, November 16, 1905, p. 4, and *Australian Mining Standard* 34 (November 29, 1905): 517. Hoover was supported in the *West Australian Mining, Building, and Engineering Journal* 6 (November 25, 1905): 10–11.

22. Hoover interview cited in note 19.

23. Hoover, letter to the editor, *Mining and Scientific Press* 104 (May 25, 1912): 731.

24. Letter to the editor, *Kalgoorlie Miner*, April 7, 1904, p. 3.

25. *West Australian Mining, Building, and Engineering Journal* 11 (January 4, 1908): 4.

26. Hoover, "Metal Mines" (typescript, n.d., but probably early 1900), in E. J. Nathan Papers, Bodleian Library, Oxford University.

27. C. Algernon Moreing speech, May 5, 1906, reported in *West Australian Mining, Building, and Engineering Journal* 7 (May 12, 1906): 12–13, and *Australian Mining Standard* 35 (May 23, 1906): 499–500.

28. *West Australian Mining, Building, and Engineering Journal* 11 (January 4, 1908): 4.

29. W. J. Loring interview in *Colonial Mining News* 25 (April 4, 1907): 168.

30. For Hoover's role in effecting the Oroya Black Range flotation see: *Kalgoorlie Miner*, October 25, 1905, p. 3, and November 10, 1905, p. 3; *West Australian Mining, Building, and Engineering Journal* 6 (December 2, 1905): 11; accounts of Oroya Brownhill annual shareholders meeting, in *Mining World and Engineering Record* 70 (June 2, 1906): 691–93, *Statist* 57 (June 2, 1906): 1057, and *Economist* 64 (June 2, 1906): 935; *West Australian Mining, Building, and Engineering Journal* 11 (February 15, 1908): 7; transcript of Oroya Brownhill annual shareholders meeting, 1908, in *Mining World and Engineering Record* 74 (April 11, 1908): 476. See also Walter R. Skinner, *The Mining Manual for 1907* (London, 1907), p. 138.

31. Hoover to C. H. Wray, April 27, 1906, Mining Letter Book No. 1, Pre-Commerce Papers, HHPL.
32. *Mining World and Engineering Record* 69 (September 30, 1905): 396–97, 411–12.
33. *Australian Mining Standard* 35 (May 9, 1906): 453.
34. The Lake View Consols annual shareholders meetings, amply reported in the mining press, documented this transition. See also *Engineering and Mining Journal* 84 (November 2, 1907): 842.
35. *Australian Mining Standard* 35 (May 9, 1906): 453.
36. *West Australian Mining, Building, and Engineering Journal* 12 (August 29, 1908): 10–11.
37. See transcript of Oroya Brownhill shareholders meeting, 1908, pp. 475–79.
38. *West Australian Mining, Building, and Engineering Journal* 12 (August 29, 1908): 11.
39. Transcript of Oroya Brownhill shareholders meeting, 1908, pp. 476–78.
40. Moreing speech, May 5, 1906.
41. Hoover interview, 1907 (cited in note 18).
42. F. A. Govett, remarks at 1907 Lake View Consols shareholders meeting; full transcript in *West Australian Mining, Building, and Engineering Journal* 10 (November 16, 1907): 4–6.
43. Australian Smelting Corporation; Bellevue Proprietary; Burma Mines, Railway and Smelting Company; Chinese Engineering and Mining Company; Dutch Indies Exploration; Lancefield Gold Mining Company; Oroya Black Range; Oroya Brownhill Company; Talisman Consolidated; and Zinc Corporation. Skinner, *Mining Manual for 1907*, p. 1241.
44. *West Australian Mining, Building, and Engineering Journal* 12 (September 5, 1908): 11. Hoover himself stated that Bewick, Moreing and Company "enjoyed the largest practice of any firm in the world" during 1902–8. Hoover draft statement (ca. 1931–32), in "Richey-Hoover Files: Statements and Refutations," Misrepresentations File, HHPL.
45. Hoover to his brother Theodore, March 1, 1906, Hulda Hoover McLean Papers, HI. Hoover gave the figure as £15,000 (then equal to about $75,000).
46. David Starr Jordan, *The Days of a Man* (Yonkers-on-Hudson, N.Y., 1922), II, p. 223.
47. Hoover to D. C. Defries, January 19, 1907, Mining Letter Book No. 1, Pre-Commerce Papers.
48. Hoover to his brother, January 2 and 12, 1906, McLean Papers; Theodore Hoover, *Memoranda: Being a Statement by an Engineer* (typescript: Stanford University, 1939), p. 134, copy at HHPL; *Stanford Alumnus* 7 (February 1906): 21.
49. Hoover to his brother, January 12, 1906.
50. Hoover to his brother, March 1, 1906.
51. Theodore Hoover, *Memoranda*, pp. 148, 159, 160.
52. Theodore eventually rented an apartment in Kensington, where Herbert leased a home in late 1907. Lou Henry Hoover to John C. Branner, December 28, 1906, Branner Papers, Box 38, Stanford University Archives; Theodore Hoover, *Memoranda*, p. 149.
53. Hoover to David Starr Jordan, January 4, 1906, "Jordan, David Starr," Pre-Commerce Papers.
54. Hoover to David Starr Jordan, September 12, 1904, David Starr Jordan Papers, Series I-A, Box 41, Stanford University Archives.
55. Hoover to his brother, March 1, 1906.
56. Jordan, *Days of a Man*, II, p. 223.
57. Hoover Calendar, HHPL.
58. Ibid.; *West Australian Mining, Building, and Engineering Journal* 9 (February 23, 1907): 5, and 9 (June 22, 1907): 7.
59. Hoover Calendar, HHPL; Hoover, *The Memoirs of Herbert Hoover*, Volume I: *Years of Adventure* (New York, 1951), p. 77.
60. Ibid.
61. Hoover recounted many of his motives for leaving Bewick, Moreing in *Years of Adventure*, p. 98.
62. Hoover, "Information for Biographers" (typescript, n.d.; probably ca. 1914), p. 16, in Benjamin S. Allen Papers, Box 1, HI, and Pre-Commerce Papers, HHPL.

63. Hoover, undated autobiographical statement, cited in chapter 13, note 101.
64. W. J. Loring interview, 1931, Walter W. Liggett Papers, New York Public Library.
65. E. D. Adams, "Snap Shots of Herbert Hoover" (typescript, 1929), p. 11, E. D. Adams Papers, Box 5, Stanford University Archives.
66. Ibid.
67. Mrs. Moreing was prominent in London society. *West Australian Mining, Building, and Engineering Journal* 4 (February 18, 1905): 13. Moreing contested a Lincolnshire seat as a Tory but lost in the Liberal landslide of 1906. Frederick Haynes McCalmont, *McCalmont's Parliamentary Poll Book* (8th ed.: 1971), Part II, p. 135. Moreing planned to run again in 1910 but withdrew for reasons of health. *The Times*, Sept. 23, 1910, p. 7.
68. William L. Honnold to Hoover, June 5, 1908, "Mining—Correspondence: Honnold, William L.," Pre-Commerce Papers.
69. Bewick, Moreing & Co. to Zinc Corporation, January 14, 1908, reported in Zinc Corporation Minute Book No. 1, entry for board meeting of January 17, 1908, Rio Tinto-Zinc Corporation, London. For some press notices, see: *Engineering and Mining Journal* 85 (February 29, 1908): 471; *West Australian Mining, Building, and Engineering Journal* 11 (March 7, 1908): 4; *Mining News and Financial Record* 27 (March 12, 1908): 126.
70. *Mining Journal* 83 (March 14, 1908): 314.
71. Hoover, *Years of Adventure*, p. 96; Will Irwin, *Herbert Hoover: A Reminiscent Biography* (New York, 1928), pp. 115–16.
72. Bewick, Moreing & Co. statement regarding Herbert Hoover, n.d. (probably 1916), Bewick, Moreing & Co. Collection, HHPL.
73. Hoover did not, however, mention ill health as a reason for leaving either in his *Memoirs* or in other autobiographical statements.
74. Legal notice in *London Gazette*, July 7, 1908, p. 4983.
75. C. Algernon Moreing affidavits, May 9 and 26, 1910, in Bewick, Moreing & Co. Collection. Loring and Hoover, many years later, put the figure higher. According to Loring, he paid Hoover $169,000 (Loring interview, 1931, Liggett Papers). Hoover confirmed this on one occasion when he said that he sold his goodwill in the firm for £35,000 (or about $170,000 in 1908). Hoover, "Information for Biographers," p. 17. In his undated autobiographical statement, however, Hoover placed the sale figure at about $225,000. Moreing's figure, given in formal legal proceedings against Hoover only two years after Hoover's departure from the firm, was probably the accurate one.
76. Hoover, *Years of Adventure*, p. 98. For figures that corroborate Hoover's statement see *West Australian Mining, Building, and Engineering Journal* 11 (April 4, 1908): 6.
77. Hoover, "Information for Biographers," p. 17; Moreing affidavit, May 9, 1910.
78. Hoover's 1903 partnership contract, Bewick, Moreing & Co. Collection; Bewick, Moreing & Co. statement regarding Hoover, n.d.
79. Bewick, Moreing & Co. statement regarding Herbert Hoover, n.d. Several journals and correspondents emphasized that Hoover would retain his directorates. See, for example, *Mining News and Financial Record* 27 (March 12, 1908): 126, and *West Australian Mining, Building, and Engineering Journal* 12 (July 11, 1908): 3.
80. *West Australian Mining, Building, and Engineering Journal* 11 (March 7, 1908): 4; *Mining News and Financial Record* 27 (March 12, 1908): 126.
81. London correspondent of *West Australian Mining, Building, and Engineering Journal* 11 (March 7, 1908): 4.
82. *Mining News* 27 (June 4, 1908): 276.
83. Hoover, undated autobiographical statement. Hoover said here that he sold his partnership for about $225,000 and had "accumulated about $200,000 more from outside business." This made a total of $425,000. The $225,000 figure was probably too high (see note 75), and since Loring paid for the partnership in installments over a lengthy period, Hoover probably did not possess anything approaching $400,000 in liquid assets in mid-1908.

The most systematic study of Hoover's wealth is "The President's Fortune," *Fortune* 6

(August 1932): 33–37, 82, 84–88, 90. This article estimated that Hoover was worth half a million dollars in 1908. However, it seriously erred on the side of overstatement in two important respects. First, it stated that Hoover cleared off his Rowe defalcation debts in 1904; in fact, it was not until the end of 1905 at the earliest (and probably mid–1907) that he was entirely free of debt. Second, in calculating Hoover's share of his firm's management fees from 1901 to 1908, the article simply took Bewick, Moreing's gross annual fee for managing a company (e.g., £1,500) and credited Hoover with a third of each sum (his share of the partnership). But Bewick, Moreing had to pay its managers, staff, and expenses out of these sums.

On the other hand, *Fortune* did not take into account Hoover's apparently lucrative "outside business," including his possibly extensive investments in the stock market (which is perhaps what Hoover meant by "outside business"). This factor would, of course, increase an estimate of his wealth and tend to cancel out the previous overstatements. In the absence of more data, we may accept Hoover's undated autobiographical statement as approximately accurate: in mid-1908 his assets included $200,000 in savings plus the sale price of his partnership.

84. Hoover, undated autobiographical statement.
85. Hoover to D. E. Bigelow, July 3, 1903, D. E. Bigelow Papers, Bancroft Library, University of California, Berkeley. Quoted by permission of the Bancroft Library.
86. Hoover to C. H. Wray, April 27, 1906; Hoover to J. H. Means, December 29, 1906; Hoover to John Ballot, January 18, 1907; all in Mining Letter Book No.1, Pre-Commerce Papers.
87. Hoover in his *Memoirs* (*Years of Adventure*, p. 83) stated that his partnership contract prohibited share speculation. This may have been true of his December 1901 agreement (a copy of which has not been found), but the post-Rowe contract of 1903 with Moreing and Wellsted does not contain such a provision. Hoover may, however, have forbade his employees in the field from owning stock in the mining companies for which they worked. Ralph Nichols's contract with Bewick, Moreing in 1904, for example, obliged him to sell a block of shares that he held in the Great Boulder Perseverance. On the other hand, Hoover personally held shares in Bewick, Moreing-managed companies for friends who were members of his own staff in the field. See note 88.
88. One such friend was J. H. Means. Hoover also handled stock transactions for his friends C. H. Wray (see note 86) and C. S. Herzig. See Hoover to Herzig, January 23, 1906, Mining Letter Book No. 1, Pre-Commerce Papers. See also Hoover to D. P. Mitchell, June 1, 1906, ibid.
89. Hoover Calendar, HHPL.

CHAPTER 19

1. Herbert Hoover, "Information for Biographers" (typescript, n.d.; probably ca. 1914), p. 17, in Benjamin S. Allen Papers, Box 1, HI, and Pre-Commerce Papers, HHPL.
2. F. H. Bathurst, "Hoover in Australia: A Personal Sketch," *The Argus* (Melbourne), November 3, 1928, p. 6.
3. David Starr Jordan, *The Days of Man* (Yonkers-on-Hudson, N.Y., 1922), II, p. 223.
4. See chapter 23.
5. John Hamill, *Hail Columbia Hoover* (typescript, ca. 1932), p. 173, Misrepresentations File, HHPL; John C. Branner to Herbert Hoover, August 29, 1908, John C. Branner Papers, Box 7, Stanford University Archives.
6. *West Australian Mining, Building, and Engineering Journal* 12 (September 12, 1908): 3.
7. "London Letter" (dated October 23) in ibid., November 28, 1908, p. 4.
8. *West Australian Mining, Building, and Engineering Journal* 12 (September 12, 1908): 3.
9. Francis Govett, remarks at Lake View Consols annual shareholders meeting, October 30,

1908, printed in *West Australian Mining, Building, and Engineering Journal* 12 (December 12, 1908): 13.

10. "London Letter" (dated October 23), *West Australian Mining, Building, and Engineering Journal* 12 (November 28, 1908): 4.

11. Hoover to John C. Branner, October 20, 1908, Branner Papers, Box 40.

12. Hoover to Branner, December 8, 1908, and Lou Henry Hoover to Branner, December 27, 1908, ibid.; *The Times* (London), December 25, 1908, p. 12 (for the *Lusitania*'s departure schedule).

13. Hoover Calendar, HHPL; Payson J. Treat oral history (1967), pp. 6–7, HHPL.

14. Hoover's last visit to the United States was in August-September 1906. Hoover Calendar, HHPL; S.S. *Celtic* first-class passenger list for New York-Liverpool voyage, September 7, 1906, in Herbert Hoover Collection, Box 5, HI.

15. Hoover Calendar, HHPL; *Daily Palo Alto* (Stanford University student newspaper), January 14, 1909.

16. Hoover Calendar, HHPL. For more on these lectures, see chapter 23.

17. Ibid.; *Engineering and Mining Journal* 87 (March 13, 1909): 572.

18. Ralph Arnold, "Laying Foundation Stones," *Historical Society of Southern California Quarterly* 37 (June 1955): 102; Arnold, "Account of Hoover's Rise to the Presidency: Pioneering in Petroleum and Politics" (typescript, n.d.), p. 1, Ralph Arnold Collection, Box 231, The Huntington Library, San Marino, California. Arnold recalled that Mrs. Hoover was present in Washington on March 3–4, 1909, but this is probably incorrect.

19. Ralph Arnold to Hoover, August 11, 1910, Arnold Collection, Box 22.

20. Arnold, "Laying Foundation Stones," p. 102. See also Arnold, "Laying Foundation Stone [sic] for Hoover's Rise to the Presidency Chapter from—Pioneering in Petroleum and Politics" (typescript, n.d.), p. 1, in Ralph Arnold Papers (one envelope), HI. In this latter version of his reminiscences, Arnold stated that Hoover received more cables and telephone calls on his quick visit than ordinary men would receive in an entire lifetime.

21. Hoover Calendar, HHPL.

22. Hoover to John Agnew, June 1909, Bewick, Moreing & Co. Collection, HHPL.

23. Hoover Calendar, HHPL.

24. Ibid.

25. G. P. Doolette, speech at Oroya Brownhill Company annual shareholders meeting, June 7, 1909, printed in *Mining Journal* 85 (June 12, 1909): 749 (full transcript of meeting: 749–50). Doolette was chairman of the company.

26. Ibid.

27. Hoover Calendar, HHPL; Hoover, *The Memoirs of Herbert Hoover*, Volume I: *Years of Adventure* (New York, 1951), p. 100. Hoover stated in his *Memoirs* that he took the Korean trip in 1910. Contemporary evidence and the Calendar, however, establish that it occurred in 1909.

28. Hoover Calendar, HHPL.

29. Doolette and Hoover speeches at 1909 Oroya Brownhill shareholders meeting, pp. 749–50; Hoover to John Agnew, June 1909; *West Australian Mining, Building, and Engineering Journal* 13 (June 26, 1909): 4.

30. Hoover speech at 1909 Oroya Brownhill shareholders meeting, p. 750.

31. Doolette speech at 1909 Oroya Brownhill shareholders meeting, p. 749.

32. Hoover speech, p. 750.

33. Hoover arranged with Bewick, Moreing for C. S. Herzig to examine the Leonesa property in Nicaragua.

34. Doolette speech, p. 749.

35. Hoover to Agnew, June 1909.

36. Hoover Calendar, HHPL.

37. Ibid.; Lou Henry Hoover to John C. Branner, October 15, 1909, Branner Papers, Box 40.

38. Hoover to John Agnew, October 14, 1909, quoted in Hoover Calendar, HHPL.

39. For basic biographical data on A. Chester Beatty (1875–1968), see the obituaries for him in the *New York Times*, January 21, 1968, p. 76, and *The Times*, January 22, 1968, p. 10. See

also Harvey O'Connor, *The Guggenheims: The Making of an American Dynasty* (New York, 1937), pp. 130, 133.

40. A. Chester Beatty to Herbert Hoover, October 1, 1909. This letter is in a collection of papers of the late Sir A. Chester Beatty that were kept in his New York office and are now in the possession of Selection Trust Limited, London. Hereinafter cited as the Sir A. Chester Beatty Papers. All Hoover-Beatty correspondence cited in this chapter is found in this collection.

41. *Mining Magazine* 2 (February 1910): 99, and 2 (May 1910): 353.

42. *The Times*, January 22, 1968, p. 10.

43. Sir A. Chester Beatty Papers, passim.

44. For example, Hoover to Beatty, June 24, 1910, November 3, 1910, December 1, 1910, February 23, 1911, April 13, 1911, May 31, 1911.

45. Hoover to Beatty, October 13, 1910; Beatty to Messrs. Hayden, Stone & Co., October 13, 1910; both in Beatty Papers. Hoover sold the shares in the spring of 1911. Hoover to E. L. Gruver, May 29, 1911; Gruver to Hoover, May 29, 1911, May 31, 1911, and June 2, 1911. All in Beatty Papers.

46. Hoover to E. L. Gruver, August 3, 1911; Gruver to Hoover, August 3, 4, and 8, 1911; Hoover to Gruver, August 9, and 10, 1911; Gruver to Messrs. Hayden, Stone & Co., August 16, 1911; Gruver to Hoover, August 17, 1911. All in Beatty Papers.

47. Adolph Lewisohn to Hoover, January 10, 1913; Hoover to E. L. Gruver, February 10, 1914; Gruver to J. G. Greenberg, March 5, 1914; Greenberg to Gruver, March 6, 1914; Gruver to Greenberg, March 7, 1914. All in Beatty Papers.

48. Beatty to Hoover, August 11, 1910; Hoover to Beatty, August 23, 1910; Beatty to Hoover, September 8, 1910.

49. Hoover to Beatty, January 29, February 23, and March 3, 1910; Beatty to Hoover, March 22, 1910; Hoover to Beatty, April 7, 1910; Beatty to Hoover, April 12 and May 5, 1910. The Intercontinental Trust was registered on March 4, 1910. For more on the Intercontinental Trust, Ltd., see its file, B.T. 31 / 13114 / 107928, Public Record Office (PRO), Kew, Surrey, U.K.

50. See chapter 21.

51. Hoover to Beatty, October 19, 1909.

52. Hoover to Beatty, June 7, 1910.

53. Hoover to Beatty, February 22, 1911.

54. Hoover to Professor E. D. Adams, November 10, 1911, E. D. Adams Papers, Box 1, Stanford University Archives.

55. Anne Martin interview, 1931, Walter W. Liggett Papers, New York Public Library.

56. "A Professional Speculator" [Herbert Hoover], "Investments and Speculations," *Mining Magazine* 1 (September 1909): 39–41; "A Professional Speculator" [Hoover], "Investments and Speculations II," *Mining Magazine* 1 (December 1909): 285–87. T. A. Rickard was editor of the *Mining Magazine*. Some years later he identified Hoover as the man behind the pseudonym "A Professional Speculator." T. A. Rickard, "A Chapter in Journalism," *Mining and Scientific Press* 120 (May 22, 1920): 754.

57. Hoover to Beatty, October 30, 1909.

58. Hoover to Beatty, January 17, 1912.

59. "A Professional Speculator" [Hoover], "Investments and Speculations," p. 39.

60. "A Professional Speculator" [Hoover], "Investments and Speculations II," p. 285. See "James Moriarty," letter to the editor, *Mining Magazine* 1 (November 1909): 201–2.

61. Hoover, *Years of Adventure*, p. 100; Amor Kuehn to Beatty, October 25, 1910, Beatty Papers. In this letter Kuehn stated that Hoover had offered him £30 a month to look after the work of one of Hoover's enterprises, the Oroya Exploration Company. Kuehn also worked for Hoover in Burma.

62. Theodore Hoover, *Memoranda: Being a Statement by an Engineer* (typescript: Stanford University, 1939), pp. 167–68, copy at HHPL.

63. Hoover, *Years of Adventure*, p. 100; *Mining and Metallurgy* 14 (August 1933): 360.

64. *West Australian Mining, Building, and Engineering Journal* 17 (March 11, 1911): 6.

65. *West Australian Mining, Building, and Engineering Journal* 19 (May 25, 1912): 6; Hoover to Agnew, July 16, 1914, "Mining—Correspondence: Agnew, John A.," Pre-Commerce Papers, HHPL.

66. Theodore Hoover, *Memoranda*, p. 166; Hoover, *Years of Adventure*, pp. 99–100.

67. See Hoover's correspondence, passim, in the Beatty Papers.

68. Hoover referred to the Romanian and Japanese copper mines, and the Newfoundland copper prospect, as businesses "in a very nebular state." Hoover to Beatty, January 29, 1910.

69. See chapters 10, 21, and 22.

70. Hoover to Beatty, December 28 and 29, 1910.

71. Walter R. Skinner, *The Mining Manual and Mining Year Book for 1913* (London, 1913), p. 702. The syndicate liquidated in June 1913. Skinner, *The Mining Manual and Mining Year Book for 1914* (London, 1914), p. 627.

72. *Mining Magazine* 7 (October 1912): 245; *Mining and Scientific Press* 105 (October 19, 1912): 508.

73. L. W. Mayer to Beatty, May 9, 1913; John Hays Hammond to Beatty, May 9, 1913. Both in "Mining—Brazilian Iron Ore Properties, 1913," Pre-Commerce Papers, HHPL.

74. Skinner, *Mining Manual and Mining Year Book for 1914*, p. 628.

75. Hoover, *Years of Adventure*, p. 100.

76. For example, Hoover and Beatty agreed to underwrite 10,000 shares of the Perm Corporation in 1910. Hoover to Beatty, January 29, 1910. Hoover was a major underwriter for the Kyshtim Corporation; see chapter 21.

77. Scott Turner oral history (1968), pp. 6–7, HHPL.

78. Hoover to Beatty, December 7, 1909.

79. Hoover to D. E. Bigelow, July 3, 1903, D. E. Bigelow Papers, Bancroft Library, University of California—Berkeley. Quoted by permission of the Bancroft Library.

80. Scott Turner oral history, p. 31, HHPL.

81. For excerpts from Hammond's speech, see *Engineering and Mining Journal* 88 (July 10, 1909): 79–80, and *Mining Magazine* 1 (December 1909): 266–68.

82. "Counsels of Imperfection," *Mining Magazine* 1 (December 1909): 266–68.

83. Hoover, letter to the editor, *Mining Magazine* 2 (January 1910): 40–41.

84. See letters to the editor in *Mining Magazine* 2 (February 1910): 120, and 2 (March 1910): 222. See also "Engineer or Promoter?" *Mining World and Engineering Record* 78 (January 29, 1910): 121.

85. "Counsels of Imperfection," *Mining Magazine* 2 (January 1910): 6–7.

86. *Mining Magazine* 1 (November 1909): 239; Walter R. Skinner, *The Mining Manual for 1910* (London, 1910), pp. 1–2.

87. Hoover to Beatty, October 21, 1909.

88. Ibid.

89. Hoover to Beatty, October 30, 1909.

90. Hoover to Beatty, October 21, 1909.

91. Richard M. Atwater interview, ca. 1931, Liggett Papers.

92. Ibid.

93. Ibid.

94. Account of Oroya Brownhill Company shareholders meeting, December 9, 1909, in *Mining Journal* 87 (December 11, 1909): 426–27; account of Oroya Links shareholders meeting, May 11, 1910, in *Mining Journal* 89 (May 14, 1910): 637; A. N. Jackman, ed., *The Mining Year-Book . . . 1912* (London, 1912), p. 601; Skinner, *Mining Manual and Mining Year Book for 1914*, p. 769.

95. Walter R. Skinner, *The Mining Manual for 1911* (London, 1911), p. 889; Jackman, *Mining Year-Book . . . 1912*, pp. 600–601.

96. *Mining Journal* 88 (March 26, 1910): 390; Skinner, *Mining Manual for 1911*, pp. 102–3; file for Oroya Exploration Company, B.T. 31 / 19317 / 108272, PRO.

97. See transcript of Oroya Exploration Company shareholders meeting, February 24, 1911, in *West Australian Mining, Building, and Engineering Journal* 17 (April 8, 1911): 12–15.

98. *Mining Journal* 88 (March 26, 1910): 390.

99. G. P. Doolette speech at Oroya Brownhill Company shareholders meeting, March 31, 1910, printed in *Mining Journal* 89 (April 2, 1910): 423.

100. Hoover speech at Oroya Exploration Company shareholders meeting, February 24, 1911, p. 12.

101. *Australian Mining Standard* 45 (January 4, 1911): 3; Skinner, *Mining Manual for 1911*, pp. 88–89.

102. Yuanmi Gold Mines, Ltd., statement in lieu of prospectus, May 8, 1911, in Yuanmi Gold Mines file, B.T. 31 / 19984 / 115492, PRO; Walter R. Skinner, *The Mining Manual for 1912* (London, 1912), pp. 127–28.

103. Skinner, *Mining Manual and Mining Year Book for 1913*, pp. 477–78.

104. Hoover to Beatty, August 22, 1910.

105. Eugene Meyer, Jr. to Hoover and A. Chester Beatty, August 22, 1910, Beatty Papers.

106. Hoover to Beatty, August 22, 1910.

107. Hoover to Beatty, February 22, 1911.

108. Hoover to Beatty, February 7, 1911.

109. Hoover speech at Oroya Exploration Company shareholders meeting, February 24, 1911, pp. 12–14.

110. Francis Govett, speech at Lake View Consols shareholders meeting, October 30, 1908, p. 12.

111. Ibid.

112. Ibid., pp. 13–15; *Mining World and Engineering Record* 77 (November 6, 1909): 585.

113. Govett, speech at Lake View Consols shareholders meeting, November 2, 1909, printed in *West Australian Mining, Building, and Engineering Journal* 14 (December 11, 1909): 12.

114. Govett publicly said that the "Star amalgamation" was Hoover's idea. Govett speech at Lake View and Oroya Exploration Company annual shareholders meeting, October 29, 1912, printed in *Mining World and Engineering Record* 83 (November 2, 1912): 527 (full transcript of meeting: 525–28). For the rationale of the amalgamation, see *Australian Mining Standard* 43 (February 2, 1910): 113.

115. Skinner, *Mining Manual for 1911*, pp. 61, 68.

116. Lake View and Star, Ltd., Minute Book No. 1 (of board of directors meetings), May 23, 1912 meeting, p. 123. This minute book contains many references to Herbert Hoover. As of October 1977 it and a succeeding volume (Minute Book No. 2) were in the possession of Poseidon, Ltd., 33 King William Street, Adelaide, South Australia.

117. Skinner, *Mining Manual for 1911*, p. 68. In mid-1911 the Lake View Consols wound up voluntarily and sold its assets to a new company of the same name. This was done for technical reasons since the old Lake View Consols had virtually ceased to be a mining company. In its new form it was a finance and holding company. *Mining World and Engineering Record* 80 (June 3, 1911): 671, and 80 (June 10, 1911): 689.

118. Skinner, *Mining Manual for 1911*, pp. 102–3.

119. Govett speech at Lake View Consols shareholders meeting, November 17, 1911, printed in *Mining World and Engineering Record* 81 (November 18, 1911): 646 (full transcript of meeting: 646–48). See also editorial in the same issue of the *Mining World and Engineering Record*, p. 631.

120. Hoover speech at Oroya Exploration Company shareholders meeting, November 17, 1911, printed in *Mining World and Engineering Record* 81 (November 18, 1911): 625 (full transcript of meeting: 624–26).

121. Hoover to Beatty, November 11, 1911.

122. Amor Kuehn to Beatty, November 8, 1911. From the Letter Books kept by Sir A. Chester Beatty's London office from 1910 to 1918, and now in the possession of Selection Trust Limited, London. Hereinafter cited as the Sir A. Chester Beatty Letter Books.

123. Ibid.
124. Ibid.; see also Hoover to Beatty, November 11, 1911.
125. Hoover speech at Oroya Exploration Company shareholders meeting, November 17, 1911, pp. 624, 625.
126. Govett speech at Lake View Consols shareholders meeting, November 17, 1911, p. 646.
127. The Lake View Consols absorbed the Oroya Exploration Company in return for 372,303 newly created shares.
128. In early 1912 Herbert Hoover was a director of (among others) Burma Mines, Granville Mining Company, Great Fitzroy Mines, Kyshtim Corporation, Lake View and Star, Oroya Leonesa, Yuanmi Gold Mines, and the Zinc Corporation—in all of which the Lake View and Oroya Exploration Company held a significant share interest.
129. In early 1912 Theodore Hoover was a director of (among others) Maikop Apsheron Oil Company, Mountain Queen, Oroya Links, Star Explorations, Trinidad-Cedros Oil Company, and the Zinc Corporation—in all of which the Lake View and Oroya Exploration Company held a significant share interest.
130. *Mining World and Engineering Record* 105 (November 23, 1912): 672.
131. Jackman, *Mining Year-Book . . . 1912*, p. 416.
132. Skinner, *Mining Manual for 1912*, p. 63.
133. Govett speech at Lake View and Oroya Exploration Company shareholders meeting, October 6, 1913, printed in *Mining World and Engineering Record* 85 (October 11, 1913): 430 (full transcript of meeting: 430–31).
134. *Mining Magazine* 7 (November 1912): 327.
135. Theodore Hoover remarks at Oroya Leonesa shareholders meeting, November 26, 1912, printed in *West Australian Mining, Building, and Engineering Journal* 21 (January 4, 1913): 3.
136. Hoover to Beatty, November 11, 1911.
137. Amor Kuehn to A. Chester Beatty, November 28, December 16, and December 29, 1911. All in Beatty Papers.
138. Kuehn to Beatty, December 16, 1911.
139. Kuehn to Beatty, December 29, 1911.
140. Walter R. Skinner, *The Mining Manual and Mining Year Book for 1916* (London, 1916), p. 350.
141. Govett speech at Lake View and Oroya Exploration Company shareholders meeting, October 29, 1912, p. 527.
142. "A New Group," *Mining Magazine* 7 (November 1912): 326–28.
143. Govett speech at 1912 Lake View and Oroya Exploration Company shareholders meeting, p. 525.
144. *Mining News* 36 (October 31, 1912): 211.
145. *West Australian Mining, Building, and Engineering Journal* 22 (November 1, 1913): 3.
146. Govett speech at Lake View and Oroya Exploration Company shareholders meeting, October 6, 1913, p. 430.
147. *Mining News* 38 (October 9, 1913): 176.
148. *Truth*, October 1, 1913 issue, quoted in *Mining News* 38 (October 9, 1913): 176.
149. London correspondent's letter in *West Australian Mining, Building, and Engineering Journal* 22 (November 8, 1913): 1.
150. *West Australian Mining, Building, and Engineering Journal* 22 (November 1, 1913): 6.
151. Ibid. 22 (November 15, 1913): 1.
152. *Australian Mining Standard* 50 (December 18, 1913): 548.
153. For accounts of the Oroya Leonesa's troubles, see: Oroya Leonesa, Ltd., Directors' Report, July 25, 1911, "Mining—Oroya Leonesa, Ltd., 1911–1913," Pre-Commerce Papers; Hoover speech printed in report of proceedings of Oroya Leonesa shareholders meeting on August 4, 1911, "Mining—Oroya Leonesa, Ltd., 1911–1913," Pre-Commerce Papers; Hoover speech at Oroya Leonesa shareholders meeting, November 11, 1913, printed in *Mining World and Engineering Record* 85 (November 15, 1913): 586–87.
154. Hoover speech at 1911 Oroya Leonesa meeting, p. 1.

155. Hoover speech at 1913 Oroya Leonesa meeting, p. 586.
156. Ibid., pp. 586–87.
157. Ibid. Hoover indicated that the imported labor would be indentured. Some Spanish and Italian miners were in fact brought in, but the securing of competent and industrious labor remained a severe problem. See *Mining World and Engineering Record* 89 (October 16, 1915): 413.
158. Skinner, *Mining Manual and Mining Year Book for 1914*, pp. 493, 769. Hoover did not join the board of Central American Mines, Ltd., but his brother Theodore and his close friend John Agnew did, and Hoover remained on the board of the reconstructed company's largest shareholder: Lake View and Oroya Exploration Company.
159. Ibid., p. 769.
160. Ibid.; Hoover speech at 1913 Oroya Leonesa meeting, p. 586.
161. Walter R. Skinner, *The Mining Manual and Mining Year Book for 1917* (London, 1917), pp. 126, 931; Skinner, *The Mining Manual and Mining Year Book for 1918* (London, 1918), p. 343; Skinner, *The Mining Manual and Mining Year Book for 1921* (London, 1921), p. 324.
162. *Mining and Scientific Press* 102 (January 28, 1911): 190.
163. Transcript of Oroya Black Range shareholders meeting, November 17, 1911, printed in *Financial Times*, November 28, 1911; Skinner, *Mining Manual and Mining Year Book for 1913*, pp. 1030–31.
164. Hoover resigned as a director of the Yuanmi Gold Mines on November 25, 1913. He was replaced (at least nominally) by his friend and close associate, John Agnew. See Yuanmi Gold Mines file, PRO.
165. Hoover to Beatty, November 11, 1911.
166. Hoover speech at 1911 Oroya Black Range shareholders meeting, printed in *Financial Times*, November 28, 1911.
167. Walter R. Skinner, *The Mining Manual and Mining Year Book for 1915* (London, 1915), p. 739.
168. Hoover speech at Yuanmi Gold Mines shareholders meeting, November 11, 1913, printed in *Mining World and Engineering Record* 85 (November 15, 1913): 608.
169. Walker R. Skinner, *The Mining Manual and Mining Year Book for 1923* (London, 1923), pp. 638–39; Skinner, *The Mining Manual and Mining Year Book for 1924* (London, 1924), p. 668.
170. Hoover served on the trouble-plagued Great Fitzroy's board of directors from 1908 until about 1914. Deeply in debt, the company sold its property at auction on behalf of its bondholders in 1916 without ever paying a dividend. The company liquidated completely in 1920. Skinner, *Mining Manual and Mining Year Book for 1918*, p. 262; Skinner, *Mining Manual and Mining Year Book for 1921*, p. 241.
171. Govett speech at Lake View Consols shareholders meeting, November 17, 1911, p. 646.
172. See Francis Cunynghame's excellent biography-memoir of Treadgold, *Lost Trail: The Story of Klondike Gold and the Man Who Fought for Control* (London, 1953), especially pp. 54–62.
173. Hoover, *Years of Adventure*, p. 109. Hoover stated here that Beatty introduced him to Treadgold in 1911, but it might have been a bit earlier. Certainly by February 1911 Hoover was energetically working on the Treadgold "case." Hoover to Beatty, February 22, 1911.
174. *Mining Magazine* 4 (April 1911): 245; Hoover, draft statement about Granville Mining Company, n.d. (ca. 1931–32), "Richey-Hoover Files: Statements and Refutations," Misrepresentations File, HHPL. In this draft statement Hoover stated that Beatty formed the Eastern Trading Company, but the contemporary source—*Mining Magazine*—stated that both did so.
175. Beatty to "Granitic" (his New York office), July 18, 1911; Beatty to E. L. Gruver, July 19, 1911; Lucius Mayer to Gruver, July 21, 1911; all in Beatty Letter Books.
176. See, for example, Hoover to Beatty, February 22, 1911; Lucius Mayer to William Trask, August 18, 1911, Beatty Letter Books.
177. They were so identified in *Mining Magazine* 7 (August 1912): 151–52.

178. *Mining Magazine* 5 (September 1911): 165; Skinner, *Mining Manual for 1912*, pp. 749–50; Jackman, *Mining Year-Book . . . 1912*, p. 316.

179. Skinner, *Mining Manual for 1912*, pp. 749–50; Cunynghame, *Lost Trail*, pp. 62–63. Technically Treadgold and his allies received 1,199,993 shares; seven were registration shares.

180. Cunynghame, *Lost Trail*, p. 63; *Mining Magazine* 5 (September 1911): 165; *Mining World and Engineering Record* 81 (November 18, 1911): 625, 647.

181. Hoover, draft statement, ca. 1931–32. After the four equal portions of Granville debentures were initially assigned, they were redistributed among various parties until thirty different individuals and institutions held some fraction of these bonds. Lucius Mayer to F. V. Strauss, September 5, 1911, Beatty Letter Books.

182. This was Hoover's standard procedure. Precisely how many shares he thus acquired cannot be determined, but as of February 1911 Hoover was hoping to divide 175,000 free shares among himself, Beatty, and one other man. Hoover to Beatty, February 22, 1911.

183. *Mining Magazine* 7 (July 1912): 8; *Statist* 74 (October 5, 1912): 7–8; Cunynghame, *Lost Trail*, pp. 45–48.

184. Beatty to Allan H. Rogers, August 17, 1911, Beatty Letter Books; Jackman, *Mining Year-Book . . . 1912*, p. 316.

185. *Statist* 74 (October 19, 1912): 139.

186. Hoover, *Years of Adventure*, p. 110.

187. Hoover speech at November 17, 1911 Oroya Exploration Company meeting, printed in *Mining World and Engineering Record* 81 (November 18, 1911): 625.

188. *Mining Magazine* 5 (September 1911): 165.

189. Beatty to Rogers, August 17, 1911; Beatty to Treadgold, August 17, 1911; both in Beatty Letter Books.

190. It is not entirely clear what new and disconcerting information came in, but Hoover in late October declared himself greatly disappointed by the report from the engineer in the field. In consequence Hoover believed it necessary to curtail development plans. Hoover to Beatty, November 30, 1911.

191. Hoover to Beatty, November 21, 1911.

192. Hoover, *Years of Adventure*, pp. 109–110; *New York Times*, April 16, 1923, p. 17, and *The Times*, April 17, 1923, p. 11 (obituaries for Boyle).

193. Hoover to Beatty, November 21, 1911.

194. Hoover to Beatty, November 30, 1911.

195. Hoover to Beatty, January 17, 1912; Beatty to Hoover, February 13, 1912; Hoover to Beatty, February 24, 1912; Hoover to Govett, February 28, 1912; Amor F. Kuehn to Beatty, March 2, 1912; all in Beatty Papers.

196. See Cunynghame, *Lost Trail*, especially pp. 67–68, 163–69.

197. Hoover to Beatty, January 29, 1912.

198. Hoover to Beatty, March 19, 1912; see also Hoover to Beatty, April 3, 1912.

199. Hoover to Beatty, April 3, 1912.

200. The remaining £140,000 was designated for equipment and the purchase of more alluvial lands in various valleys in the Klondike region.

201. For the terms of this deal, see: A. N. C. Treadgold to directors of the Granville Mining Company, April 1, 1912; Eastern Trading Company circular, May 1912; Granville Mining Company circular, May 15, 1912. All in "Mining—Granville Mining Company," Pre-Commerce Papers. See also *Mining Magazine* 7 (August 1912): 151–52; Skinner, *Mining Manual and Mining Year Book for 1913*, pp. 657–58.

202. *The Times*, April 17, 1923, p. 11; Cunynghame, *Lost Trail*, pp. 55–56.

203. Treadgold to Granville directors, April 1, 1912.

204. *Mining Magazine* 7 (July 1912): 8, and 7 (August 1912): 151.

205. During the summer of 1912 various other maneuvers took place, involving creation of a company called the Boyle Concession, Ltd. See Granville Mining Company circular, August 6, 1912, Beatty Papers. These complicated matters need not detain us except to illustrate how extremely complex the Granville business had become.

206. The Inter-Yukon Syndicate's purpose was "to acquire and deal in mining properties and carry on business as financiers, &c." Skinner, *Mining Manual and Mining Year Book for 1913*, p. 702.

207. Beatty to Lucius Mayer, July 2, 1912; Beatty to M. H. Furlaud, July 4, 1912; both in Beatty Papers.

208. *Mining and Scientific Press* 105 (August 17, 1912): 216–17; Skinner, *Mining Manual and Mining Year Book for 1913*, p. 658.

209. *Mining Magazine* 7 (August 1912): 151–52; *Mining and Scientific Press* 105 (August 17, 1912): 216–17; *Statist* 74 (October 5, 1912): 7–8, and 74 (October 19, 1912): 137–39.

210. Cunynghame, *Lost Trail*, p. 68.

211. Hoover to Beatty, January 23, 1913.

212. Hoover to Beatty, January 28, 1913.

213. Hoover to Beatty, February 14, 28, and March 25, 1913.

214. Hoover to Beatty, March 25, 1913. See also Cunynghame, *Lost Trail*, p. 67.

215. Cunynghame, *Lost Trail*, pp. 68–69.

216. Hoover to Beatty, February 14, 1913.

217. Cunynghame, *Lost Trail*, p. 68.

218. Hoover to Beatty, February 14, 1913.

219. Hoover to Beatty, February 28, 1913.

220. *Statist* 79 (January 3, 1914): 9–10; *The Times*, March 25, 1914, p. 20; *Mining Journal* 107 (November 14, 1914): 972–73; Skinner, *Mining Manual and Mining Year Book for 1914*, pp. 588–89, 755; Cunynghame, *Lost Trail*, p. 74.

221. Cunynghame, *Lost Trail*, pp. 73–74.

222. Ibid., p. 74.

223. Cunynghame's book discusses these problems in lucid detail.

224. *The Times*, March 25, 1914, p. 20; *Mining and Scientific Press* 109 (October 31, 1914): 707.

225. *The Times*, March 25, 1914, p. 20.

226. Govett, quoted in *Mining World and Engineering Record* 87 (October 17, 1914): 409.

227. Hoover, draft statement, ca. 1931–32.

228. *Mining Journal* 107 (November 14, 1914): 973.

229. *Mining and Scientific Press* 111 (December 11, 1915): 912; *Mining World and Engineering Record* 89 (November 13, 1915): 513–14; Skinner, *Mining Manual and Mining Year Book for 1917*, pp. 262–63; Cunynghame, *Lost Trail*, pp. 71–75.

230. Cunynghame, *Lost Trail*, pp. 73–74; *The Times*, April 17, 1923, p. 11.

231. *Mining Magazine* 17 (November 1917): supplement, p. 25; Skinner, *Mining Manual and Mining Year Book for 1918*, pp. 257, 465–66.

232. *The Times*, April 17, 1923, p. 11; Cunynghame, *Lost Trail*, pp. 56–57.

233. Cunynghame, *Lost Trail*, pp. 78–141.

234. Hoover to G. Goldthorp Hay, December 27, 1933, Post-Presidential Individual File, HHPL.

235. Cunynghame, *Lost Trail*, pp. 152–55.

236. Ibid., p. 143.

237. Hoover, "Information for Biographers," p. 17.

238. *Mining News*, quoted in Hamill, *Hail Columbia Hoover*, p. 182.

239. *Mining Magazine* 7 (October 1912): 256.

240. Skinner, *Mining Manual and Mining Year Book for 1913*, p. 702.

241. See Skinner, *Mining Manual and Mining Year Book for 1915*, p. 314.

242. Ralph Arnold to Hoover, January 20, 1943, Post-Presidential Individual File, HHPL. Arnold recalled Hoover's pre-1914 remarks in this letter.

243. Hoover to Beatty, January 23, 1913. See also Theodore Hoover to Beatty, January 8, 1913, and Beatty to Herbert Hoover, February 4, 1913. All in Beatty Papers.

CHAPTER 20

1. For information on the pre-twentieth century history of the Bawdwin mines, see: Malcolm Maclaren, "Burma Mines, Ltd." (typescript, April 1913), pp. 2–8, copy in "Mining—Burma Mines Report, 1913–1914," Pre-Commerce Papers, HHPL; J. D. Hoffmann, "The Bawdwin Mines," *Mining Magazine* 13 (March 1916): 139–41; M. H. Loveman, "The Geology of the Bawdwin Mines, Burma, Asia," *Transactions of the American Institute of Mining Engineers* 56 (1917): 170–72; A. B. Parsons, "Operations of the Burma Mines, Ltd.," *Engineering and Mining Journal* 107 (February 8, 1919): 258; report by John A. Agnew on Burma Corporation, Ltd., April 1920, p. 2, in "Mining—Burma Corporation, Ltd., 1914–1920," Pre-Commerce Papers, HHPL; R. G. Hall, "Burma and the Bawdwin Mines," *Engineering and Mining Journal-Press* 115 (April 7, 1923): 619–20; H. L. Chhibber, *The Mining Resources of Burma* (London, 1934), pp. 140–41.

2. For information on the Great Eastern Mining Company and its troubles, see: Walter R. Skinner, *The Mining Manual for 1906* (London, 1906), p. 892; C. S. Herzig, "Report on the Great Eastern Mines, Burma" (handwritten manuscript, March 10, 1905), copy in Bewick, Moreing & Co. Collection, HHPL; *Proceedings of the Government of Burma in the Department of Commerce and Industry for the Month of December, 1906*, Part A, pp. 39–54, India Office Library, London; Parsons, "Operations of the Burma Mines, Ltd.," p. 258; N. M. Penzer, *The Mineral Resources of Burma* (London, 1922), p. 51.

3. A. Chester Beatty to Charles Hayden, August 24, 1914, plus an enclosed six-page "History of the Burma Corporation, Ltd." (written by Beatty), in Sir A. Chester Beatty Papers (see chapter 19, note 40); "The President's Fortune," *Fortune* 6 (August 1932): 86.

4. Hoover, *The Memoirs of Herbert Hoover*, Volume I: *Years of Adventure* (New York, 1951), pp. 90–91.

5. C. S. Herzig, "Report on the Great Eastern Mines, Burma" (see note 2).

6. *West Australian Mining, Building, and Engineering Journal* 6 (November 25, 1905): 5.

7. *West Australian Mining, Building, and Engineering Journal* 6 (December 2, 1905): 11.

8. Walter R. Skinner, *The Mining Manual for 1909* (London, 1909), p. 649. See also Burma Mines file, B.T. 31 / 17692 / 87848, Public Record Office (PRO), Kew, Surrey, U.K.

9. This was done by prior agreement. See *Proceedings of the Government of Burma in the Department of Commerce and Industry for the Month of December, 1906*, Part A, pp. 41–42, 46–48, 53.

10. "The President's Fortune," p. 86.

11. Skinner, *Mining Manual for 1906*, p. 778. For full details on the scheme, see the prospectus of Burma Mines, Railway, and Smelting Company, printed in *Proceedings . . . December, 1906*, Part A, pp. 50–54.

12. Hoover, *Years of Adventure*, p. 101.

13. *Proceedings . . . December, 1906*, Part A, pp. 47, 50.

14. Ibid., p. 50. See also *Australian Mining Standard* 35 (May 9, 1906): 453.

15. *Proceedings . . . December, 1906*, Part A, p. 54.

16. Skinner, *Mining Manual for 1906*, p. 778.

17. Loveman, "Geology of the Bawdwin Mines, Burma, Asia," p. 173. For other descriptions of the inhospitable region near Bawdwin, see the articles by Hoffmann, Parsons, and Hall cited in note 1.

18. "Bawdwin Mines of the Burma Corporation," *Engineering and Mining Journal* 99 (January 23, 1915): 178.

19. *Proceedings . . . December, 1906*, Part A, p. 52.

20. Hoover to Deane P. Mitchell, June 1, 1906, Mining Letter Book No. 1, Pre-Commerce Papers.

21. *Mining World and Engineering Record* 70 (March 17, 1906): 319–20.

22. Hoover Calendar, HHPL; *Mining and Scientific Press* 95 (September 21, 1907): 350.

23. Allan Hoover to the author, August 18, 1980.

24. Hoover Calendar, HHPL.

25. J. H. Curle, "Recent Mining Wanderings in Burma, Chile, and Bolivia," *Mining and Scientific Press* 96 (June 27, 1908): 879.

26. Ibid; Hoover, *Years of Adventure*, pp. 91–93.

27. Hoover, *Years of Adventure*, pp. 93–94.

28. Ibid., p. 96; Will Irwin, *Herbert Hoover: A Reminiscent Biography* (New York, 1928), pp. 115–16. Hoover stated that he caught malaria on his *second* trip to Burma, but careful scrutiny of contemporary documents yields evidence of only one Hoover visit to Burma—in 1907.

29. Hoover Calendar, HHPL.

30. Hoover, *Years of Adventure*, p. 98.

31. Statement of Claim, May 31, 1916, by Bewick, Moreing and Company in the lawsuit *Bewick, Moreing & Co. v. Hoover*. Copy in Bewick, Moreing & Co. Collection, HHPL.

32. *West Australian Mining, Building, and Engineering Journal* 10 (November 16, 1907): 5.

33. Lou Henry Hoover to Mary Austin, n.d. (ca. 1914), Mary Austin Papers, Box 11, The Huntington Library, San Marino, California.

34. *West Australian Mining, Building, and Engineering Journal* 12 (August 8, 1908): 6.

35. Ibid.

36. Ibid.

37. *Rangoon Gazette*, January 17, 1910, p. 28, quoted in John Hamill, *Hail Columbia Hoover* (typescript, ca. 1932), p. 162, Misrepresentations File, HHPL.

38. *West Australian Mining, Building, and Engineering Journal* 10 (November 16, 1907): 5.

39. Burma Mines, Ltd., *Directors' Report and Balance Sheet to 31st December, 1908*, p. 3, copy in "Mining—Burma Mines, Ltd., 1908–1911," Pre-Commerce Papers.

40. Govett remarks at Lake View Consols shareholders meeting, October 30, 1908, printed in *West Australian Mining, Building, and Engineering Journal* 12 (December 12, 1908): 14.

41. Burma Mines, Ltd., *Directors' Report . . . 1908*, p. 5.

42. Burma Mines, Ltd., *Directors' Report and Balance Sheet to 31st December, 1909*, p. 24, copy in "Mining—Burma Mines, Ltd., 1908–1911," Pre-Commerce Papers.

43. Ibid., pp. 21, 29. Approximately 11,000 tons were transported by mule and bullock to Tiger Camp in 1909 until early December, when the final rail link was opened.

44. Ibid., pp. 24, 27.

45. Ibid., pp. 19–21, 26.

46. Ibid., p. 21.

47. *Rangoon Gazette*, January 17, 1910, p. 28, quoted in Hamill, *Hail Columbia Hoover*, p. 162.

48. Burma Mines, Ltd., *Directors' Report . . . 1908*, p. 6.

49. Govett statement at 1911 Burma Mines shareholders meeting; printed in *Mining World and Engineering Record* 81 (July 22, 1911): 130.

50. Burma Mines, Ltd., *Directors' Report . . . 1909*, p. 3 and profit-and-loss account.

51. Burma Mines, Ltd., *Directors' Report . . . 1908*, p. 6; Govett speech at Lake View Consols shareholders meeting, October 30, 1908, p. 14; Skinner, *Mining Manual for 1909*, pp. 649–50.

52. Govett speech, October 30, 1908, p. 14; Skinner, *Mining Manual for 1909*, pp. 649–50; Burma Mines, Ltd., *Directors' Report . . . 1909*, balance sheet.

53. Burma Mines, Ltd., *Directors' Report . . . 1909*, balance sheet; Walter R. Skinner, *The Mining Manual for 1910* (London, 1910), pp. 658–59.

54. Burma Mines, Ltd., *Directors' Report . . . 1909*, pp. 3–4; court order, March 17, 1910, copy in Burma Mines file, PRO; Walter R. Skinner, *The Mining Manual for 1911* (London, 1911), p. 637.

55. Burma Mines, Ltd., *Directors' Report . . . 1909*, p. 4.

56. "The President's Fortune," p. 86; list of Burma Mines shareholders, August 1, 1911, Burma Mines file, PRO.

57. Govett statement at 1910 Burma Mines shareholders meeting; printed in *Mining World and Engineering Record* 79 (July 16, 1910): 83.

58. See Burma Mines, Ltd., *Directors' Report and Statement of Accounts for the Twelve Months ended*

31st December, 1911, pp. 3, 10–12; copy in "Mining—Burma Mines, Ltd., 1908–1911," Pre-Commerce Papers.

59. Ibid., pp. 4, 6–9, 13–14; Walter R. Skinner, *The Mining Manual for 1912* (London, 1912), p. 639; "Mining in Burma," *Mining and Scientific Press* 105 (December 28, 1912): 827; Walter R. Skinner, *The Mining Manual and Mining Year Book for 1913* (London, 1913), p. 529.

60. Govett statement at Lake View Consols shareholders meeting, November 2, 1910; printed in *Mining World and Engineering Record* 79 (November 5, 1910): 561.

61. Govett statement at Lake View Consols shareholders meeting, May 22, 1911; printed in *Mining World and Engineering Record* 80 (June 3, 1911): 671.

62. Burma Mines, Ltd., *Directors' Report . . . 1911*, pp. 4, 13.

63. Ibid, pp. 10–12; Parsons, "Operations of the Burma Mines, Ltd.," p. 258.

64. Hoover to A. Chester Beatty, January 17, 1912, Beatty Papers.

65. A. F. Kuehn to A. Chester Beatty, October 20, 1911, Sir A. Chester Beatty Letter Books (see chapter 19, note 122).

66. Hoover to Beatty, November 11, 1911, Beatty Papers.

67. Kuehn to Beatty, January 1, 1913, ibid.

68. A. N. Jackman, ed., *The Mining Year-Book . . . 1912* (London, 1912), p. 416.

69. Govett statement at Lake View and Oroya Exploration Company shareholders meeting, October 29, 1912; printed in *Mining World and Engineering Record* 83 (November 2, 1912): 526–27.

70. Govett to Beatty, December 12, 1912, Beatty Papers.

71. Kuehn to Beatty, January 1, 1913, ibid.

72. Kuehn to Beatty, January 18, 1913, ibid.

73. Kuehn to Beatty, January 24, 1913, ibid.

74. Kuehn to Beatty, January 18, 1913; Beatty to Charles Hayden, July 15, 1914; both in Beatty Papers.

75. Kuehn to Beatty, February 12, 1913, ibid.

76. Kuehn to Beatty, January 18, 1913, ibid.

77. Kuehn to Beatty, January 4 and 21, 1913, ibid; *Mining Magazine* 9 (August 1913): 87.

78. Beatty to Charles Hayden, July 15, 1914, Beatty Papers.

79. Ibid.

80. Kuehn to Beatty, January 21, 1913.

81. Ibid.

82. Kuehn to Beatty, January 22, 1913, Beatty Papers.

83. Kuehn to Beatty, January 31 and February 12, 1913, ibid.

84. Hoover to Beatty, February 18, 1913, ibid.

85. Kuehn to Beatty, April 5, 1913, ibid.

86. Kuehn to Beatty, April 12, 1913, ibid.

87. *Rangoon Gazette*, April 14, 1913, quoted in Hamill, *Hail Columbia Hoover*, p. 164.

88. *Rangoon Gazette*, May 5 and 12, 1913, quoted in Hamill, *Hail Columbia Hoover*, p. 164; Theodore Hoover, *Memoranda: Being a Statement by an Engineer* (typescript: Stanford University, 1939), p. 214, copy at HHPL.

89. Hamill, *Hail Columbia Hoover*, p. 164.

90. Hoover statement at Burma Mines shareholders meeting, August 27, 1913; copy in "Rickard Files: Agnew, John A.," Misrepresentations File, HHPL. The lode assayed an average of 25 ounces of silver per ton, as well as 25% lead and 25% zinc.

91. *Mining Magazine* 9 (August 1913): 86; *Mining and Scientific Press* 108 (January 3, 1914): 29.

92. Hoover statement at Burma Corporation shareholders meeting, December 22, 1914; printed in *Mining World and Engineering Record* 87 (December 26, 1914): 681.

93. Hoover statement at Burma Mines shareholders meeting, August 27, 1913.

94. Ibid.; *Mining Magazine* 9 (August 1913): 87.

95. Hoover statement at Burma Mines shareholders meeting, August 27, 1913.

96. Ibid.; Beatty, "History of the Burma Corporation, Ltd." The Intercontinental Trust (1913),

Ltd. was unrelated to the syndicate with a similar name organized by Hoover and Beatty in 1910.

97. Hoover statement at Burma Mines shareholders meeting, August 27, 1913.

98. Intercontinental Trust (1913), Ltd., circular to Burma Mines shareholders, September 27, 1913; copy enclosed in John Agnew to Edgar Rickard, April 13, 1928, "Rickard Files: Agnew, John A.," Misrepresentations File, HHPL.

99. Ibid.; data in Burma Corporation file, B.T. 31/21753/131501, PRO.

100. Burma Corporation circular, May 5, 1914, printed in full in *The Times*, May 6, 1914, p. 20.

101. Ibid.

102. Amor Kuehn interview, n.d. (ca. 1931), Walter W. Liggett Papers, New York Public Library.

103. Data in Burma Corporation file, PRO.

104. Ibid.

105. Hoover to his brother Theodore, April 17, 1914, Hulda Hoover McLean Papers, HI.

106. Walter R. Skinner, *The Mining Manual and Mining Year Book for 1917* (London, 1917), p. 59.

107. Beatty, "History of the Burma Corporation, Ltd."

108. Data in Burma Corporation file, PRO; Burma Corporation circular, May 5, 1914.

109. The formal contract, dated May 29, 1914, between the Burma Corporation, Ltd. and the Burma Mines, Ltd. is printed in *Proceedings of the Government of Burma in the Department of Commerce and Industry (Mines and Minerals) for the Month of February, 1915*, Part A, pp. 7–9, India Office Library, London.

110. Walter R. Skinner, *The Mining Manual and Mining Year Book for 1915* (London, 1915), p. 106.

111. Hoover statement at Burma Mines shareholders meeting, August 27, 1913.

112. *West Australian Mining, Building, and Engineering Journal* 22 (August 2, 1913): 3.

113. Ibid., 22 (December 27, 1913): 2.

114. Burma Corporation circular, May 5, 1914. A good survey of the Burma Corporation's plans and operations at this time is "Bawdwin Mines of the Burma Corporation," *Engineering and Mining Journal* 99 (January 23, 1915): 177–80.

115. Burma Corporation circular, May 5, 1914.

116. Ibid.; "Bawdwin Mines of the Burma Corporation," p. 179; A. B. Calhoun, "Mining Methods at Bawdwin Mine," *Transactions of the American Institute of Mining and Metallurgical Engineers* 69 (1923): 228–29.

117. Burma Mines circular, May 5, 1914. The technical committee estimated that it would require twenty-four to thirty months to complete its ambitious development program.

118. Hoover's successor as chairman of the Burma Corporation said in 1918, "To him [Hoover] and the Technical Committee we owe the bold conception of the Tiger Tunnel and the ideas on which our mining policy should be based." Sir Trevredyn R. Wynne statement at 1918 Burma Corporation shareholders meeting; printed in *Mining World and Engineering Record* 95 (November 23, 1918): 422.

119. *Mining News* 44 (October 5, 1916): 109.

120. Calhoun, "Mining Methods at Bawdwin Mine," p. 229.

121. *Mining News* 44 (October 5, 1916): 109.

122. Hoover, *Years of Adventure*, p. 94.

123. Calhoun, "Mining Methods at Bawdwin Mine," pp. 228–30.

124. Ibid., pp. 215–16; Parsons, "Operations of the Burma Mines, Ltd.," pp. 260–61; Hall, "Burma and the Bawdwin Mines," pp. 620–23.

125. Beatty to Messrs. Hayden, Stone & Co., June 4, 1914; Beatty to Charles Hayden and to "Haystone," June 18, 1914; F. Wheeler to E. L. Gruver, June 23, 1914; Beatty to Hayden, July 15 and August 24 (two letters), 1914. All in Beatty Papers.

126. Hoover to A. H. Ackerman, October 7, 1914, "Mining—Correspondence: Ackerman, A. H.," Pre-Commerce Papers.

127. Hoover, handwritten draft version of Volume I, chapters 7 and 8 of his *Memoirs*, in Hoover Book Manuscript Material, HHPL.

128. Ibid.

129. Sir Trevredyn R. Wynne stated in 1918 that the Burma Corporation owed "a great debt of gratitude" to Hoover "for his work in laying the foundations of the success of the Company." Wynne remarks at 1918 Burma Corporation meeting, p. 422.

130. Beatty, "History of the Burma Corporation, Ltd."

131. Beatty's "History" (written in August 1914) stated that 820,000 Burma Corporation shares had been issued. But the company's file at the Public Record Office indicates that only 761,372 shares were actually taken up as of five months later. Moreover, according to Beatty, Hoover's shareholding stood at 60,000 shares (plus his 40% interest—or 70,600 shares—in the 175,000 shares held by the Intercontinental Trust). The share register data, however, in the Burma Corporation file at the Public Record Office put Hoover's personal shareholding at 38,511 shares both in late 1913 and early 1915. Beatty therefore may have overestimated Hoover's holding by about 22,000 shares. On the other hand, Hoover may have held stock in someone else's name. In any case, Hoover's known interest—direct or indirect—exceeded 108,000 shares out of an issued 761,372 as of January 5, 1915, or roughly 14%.

132. From the start R. Tilden Smith was the largest shareholder and Hoover the second largest. As of January 5, 1915 Smith held 204,004 shares plus his portion of the Intercontinental Trust's holding. (See data in Burma Corporation file, PRO.) Hoover later stated that he eventually acquired an 18% interest in the Burma Corporation. Hoover, undated autobiographical statement (copy received from Professor Craig Lloyd; see chapter 13, note 101). In his *Memoirs* draft cited in note 127 above, Hoover stated that he invested "practically the whole of my saving over a period of nearly ten years" in Burma and acquired "about 20%" of the stock.

133. Hoover, paperbound page proof version of his *Memoirs*, Volume I, p. 127, in Hoover Book Manuscript Material, HHPL. Many years later, old friends of Hoover stated that he made much of his fortune from his Burma mining venture. Lawrence K. Requa oral history interview (1966), p. 5, and Scott Turner oral history interview (1968), pp. 7–8; both at HHPL. According to Turner, the Burma Corporation was Hoover's "principal money-maker." Turner was correct. See Hoover, handwritten draft version of Volume I, chapters 7 and 8 of his *Memoirs*.

134. Burma Corporation circular, May 5, 1914.

135. I will examine Hoover's later Burma activities in Volume II of this biography. For those readers whose curiosity is acute, suffice it to say that the Burma Corporation reorganized after World War I and paid its first dividend in 1923—nearly twenty years after Hoover became involved. It went on to be a very prosperous company until World War II. But Hoover did not share in its long-delayed success. During World War I he sold out.

CHAPTER 21

1. For some early accounts of British investment in Russian mining before World War I, see: "Russian Mining," *Mining Magazine* 4 (June 1911): 408–410; "The Development of Russia's Mineral Resources," *Mining Magazine* 14 (June 1916): 312–14; Chester W. Purington, "Siberian Mines and Mining," *Mining and Scientific Press* 119 (September 6, 1919): 335–38. A fairly recent Russian article with references to Hoover is M. U. Lachayeva, "On the History of Foreign Capital Penetration in the Non-Ferrous Metallurgy of the Urals and Siberia at the Beginning of the XX Century," *Moscow University Herald*, no. 3 (1975), pp. 87–96.

2. Walter R. Skinner, *The Mining Manual for 1910* (London, 1910), p. 613; "Russian Mining," pp. 408–9; "Development of Russia's Mineral Resources," p. 313.

3. Herbert Hoover in *The Memoirs of Herbert Hoover*, Volume I: *Years of Adventure* (New York, 1951), p. 102, refers to himself as an "industrial doctor."

4. For the Atbasar's financial troubles, see: transcript of 1910 Atbasar Copper Fields share-holders meeting, in *Mining Journal* 91 (December 17, 1910): 1455; "Russian Mining," pp. 407–8. Late in 1909 F. W. Baker of the Hirsch Syndicate (a British financial group) offered Hoover one-fifth of his half (that is, 10% in all) of a syndicate being formed to finance Atbasar. Hoover to A. Chester Beatty, November 20, 1909, Sir A. Chester Beatty Papers (see chapter 19, note 40). All Hoover-Beatty correspondence cited in this chapter is from this collection (unless otherwise indicated).

5. Hoover to Beatty, November 20, 1909.

6. Ibid.; Hoover to Beatty, December 3, 1909.

7. Sir A. Chester Beatty Letter Book for July 19, 1911–July 5, 1912, passim (see chapter 19, note 122); Hoover to Beatty, April 7, 1910 (referring to the Sibat Syndicate as one of his and Beatty's "constructions").

8. *Mining Magazine* 6 (June 1911): 409, and supplement, p. 22.

9. Hoover to Beatty, April 7, 1910; list of shareholdings in the Hoover / Beatty joint account, June 24, 1910, Beatty Papers. As early as January 1910 Hoover was involved in a second Atbasar financial scheme entailing the creation of a second syndicate. The fate of this effort is unknown. Hoover to Beatty, January 29, 1910.

10. Hoover to Beatty, March 19, 1910.

11. Hoover to Beatty, December 29, 1910.

12. Hoover to Beatty, February 22, 1911.

13. *Mining Magazine* 6 (June 1911): 409, 467, and supplement, p. 22; Walter R. Skinner, *The Mining Manual for 1912* (London, 1912), pp. 600, 977.

14. Amor F. Kuehn to A. Chester Beatty, October 18 and November 1, 1911, Beatty Letter Books; F. Wheeler to Beatty, March 29 and April 3, 1912, ibid.; Hoover to Beatty, April 3, 1912.

15. Hoover to Beatty, August 22, 1910 and January 14, 1911.

16. Hoover to Beatty, January 29, 1910; Walter R. Skinner, *The Mining Manual for 1911* (London, 1911), p. 592.

17. In the case of Orsk Goldfields, Hoover did try to gain control of the company's administration as a condition of guaranteeing a reorganization. Unfortunately, he reported to Beatty, "After getting an offer from us they went around to some other people who did it on cheaper lines," including retention of administrative control in Orsk's own hands. Hoover participated in the new scheme but did so "simply enough to cover our share position." Hoover to Beatty, January 14, 1911.

18. For information on Kyshtim, Leslie Urquhart, and events leading to creation of the Kyshtim Corporation in 1908, see: *Mining World and Engineering Record* 73 (October 19, 1907): 459–60; *Mining and Scientific Press* 97 (November 21, 1908): 693; *Mining World and Engineering Record* 75 (December 26, 1908): 852, 862–63; Walter R. Skinner, *The Mining Manual for 1909* (London, 1909), pp. 833–34; *Mining Journal* 85 (January 30, 1909): 160; *Economist* 70 (February 5, 1910): 291; Skinner, *Mining Manual for 1911*, p. 291; J. P. B. Webster, "Kyshtim," *Mining Magazine* 8 (April 1913): 279–82; Geoffrey Blainey, *Mines in the Spinifex: The Story of the Mount Isa Mines* (rev. ed.: Sydney, 1965), pp. 120–218. Professor Blainey's account is based in part on notes and documents sent to him in the 1950s by Urquhart's widow. I am grateful to Professor Blainey for providing me with copies of these materials.

19. *Mining World and Engineering Record* 75 (December 26, 1908): 852, 862–63; Skinner, *Mining Manual for 1909*, p. 834.

20. *Engineering and Mining Journal* 87 (June 26, 1909): 1274; *Mining World and Engineering Record* 77 (November 6, 1909): 591; Hoover to Beatty, December 15, 1909; Walter R. Skinner, *The Mining Manual for 1910* (London, 1910), p. 841; *Economist* 70 (February 5, 1910): 291, and 70 (June 11, 1910): 1321–22.

21. Hoover's nominal involvement may have begun earlier than this. In a letter dated December 15, 1909, Hoover mentioned to Beatty that they had acquired a block of Kyshtim debentures "of the first issue" (which was issued in November 1908). This raises the possibility that Hoover had a stake in Kyshtim well before the autumn of 1909. There is no evidence,

however, that Hoover actually bought these debentures when they were first issued. He and Beatty may well have purchased them on the open market sometime in 1909. (The Hoover / Beatty joint account did not open until October.) In any event, the Hoover / Beatty portion seems to have been tiny—evidently only £2,000 out of the £250,000 original issue (Hoover to Beatty, October 29, 1909). There is no indication that Hoover took an active interest in Kyshtim affairs before the autumn of 1909.

22. Hoover to Beatty, October 18 and 21, 1909.

23. Skinner, *Mining Manual for 1909*, p. 799; Mrs. Urquhart's notes (supplied by Professor Blainey).

24. Hoover to Beatty, January 29, 1910. In February 1910 the Kyshtim Corporation authorized a further £100,000 in debentures, of which £50,000 were subscribed at once at par. It is conceivable that Hoover and Beatty underwrote *this* issue (rather than the earlier December–January package). The record is not conclusive. However, the timing of the Hoover / Beatty correspondence on this matter suggests that it was the earlier debenture issue that they underwrote. In any event, the amount of each debenture issue was the same: £50,000.

25. Ibid.; Hoover to Beatty, October 21, 1909.

26. Hoover to Beatty, October 30, 1909. Beatty agreed with Hoover about not wishing to become a consulting engineer to the Kyshtim Corporation. Beatty to Hoover, December 7, 1909.

27. In R. Gilman Brown's report to the Kyshtim Corporation board of directors on December 7, 1910, he mentioned his trip in the autumn of 1909. Copy in "Mining—Kyshtim Corporation, Ltd.," Pre-Commerce Papers, HHPL. A Hoover / Beatty joint account statement, June 24, 1910, recorded £574.8.10 for "expenses examination" in connection with Kyshtim. This was probably Brown's examination, undertaken at about the time Hoover and Beatty agreed to handle a £50,000 debenture issue. In his *Memoirs* Hoover indicated that after being approached by an agent of Urquhart for help in the Kyshtim venture, he "sent one of our engineers to examine the property" (*Years of Adventure*, p. 103). Brown was evidently the engineer.

28. Hoover to Beatty, December 15, 1909.

29. Ibid.

30. Hoover to Beatty, November 20, 1909.

31. Hoover to Beatty, December 15, 1909.

32. Hoover to Beatty, January 4, 1910.

33. Hoover to Beatty, January 29, 1910. Hoover used the term "pool" to describe this undertaking.

34. Hoover to Beatty, December 15, 1909.

35. Or would exercise their options, purchase a block of shares at a previously fixed price, and promptly resell at the higher market price now prevailing.

36. For a succinct explanation of how pools work, see *The McGraw-Hill Dictionary of Modern Economics*, 2nd ed. (New York, 1973), pp. 439–40.

37. Hoover to Beatty, October 21, 1910. The Hirsch Pool was created on March 8, 1910. See Intercontinental Trust file, B.T. 31 / 13114 / 107928, Public Record Office (PRO), Kew, Surrey, U.K.

38. Hoover to Beatty, December 23, 1909.

39. Hoover to Beatty, November 18, 1910; R. Gilman Brown, report to the Kyshtim Corporation board of directors, December 7, 1910; *Mining Magazine* 4 (January 1911): 6.

40. Hoover cable to Beatty, December 28, 1910.

41. See Hoover to Beatty, September 28, October 13, 21, and 26, 1910.

42. The Intercontinental Trust, Ltd. was registered on March 4, 1910, with an authorized capital of £100,000, increased later in the year to £125,000. As of November 1910 the company had four directors, including Hoover's brother Theodore but not Hoover himself or A. Chester Beatty. Hoover was elected a director on February 17, 1911. In a list of shareholders as of November 17, 1910 Hoover was not named. A. Chester Beatty, however, was listed as holding 16,813 shares; it is likely that he held them jointly with Hoover.

See Intercontinental Trust file, PRO; Walter R. Skinner, *The Oil and Petroleum Manual for 1912* (London, 1912), p. 58.

43. Hoover to Beatty, October 26, November 3, and November 9, 1910; Intercontinental Trust file, PRO. Among the other commitments that the Intercontinental Trust accepted was responsibility for placing the £50,000 in Kyshtim debentures.

44. Hoover to Beatty, November 9, 1910.

45. Hoover to Messrs. Dupont & Furlaud, November 19, 1910, Beatty Papers; Hoover to Beatty, November 21, 1910; Amor F. Kuehn to E. L. Gruver (a Beatty associate), n.d. (November 1910), Beatty Papers.

46. Hoover to Beatty, October 13, 1910.

47. Hoover to Beatty, October 26, 1910.

48. Ibid.; Hoover to Dupont & Furlaud, November 19, 1910.

49. Ibid.

50. Hoover to Beatty, November 9, 1910.

51. Hoover to Dupont & Furlaud, November 19, 1910 (a second letter).

52. Hoover cable to Beatty, November 19, 1910. See also Hoover to Beatty, November 9, 1910.

53. Hoover to Beatty, November 18, 1910.

54. Hoover to Beatty, November 21, 1910.

55. Hoover to Dupont & Furlaud, November 19, 1910.

56. Hoover to Dupont & Furlaud, November 19, 1910.

57. Hoover to Beatty, November 28, 1910.

58. Hoover to Beatty, November 21, 1910.

59. Ibid.; Hoover to Beatty, November 28, 1910.

60. Hoover to Beatty, December 12, 1910.

61. Hoover to Beatty, November 21, 1910.

62. Hoover to Beatty, December 29, 1910.

63. Hoover to Beatty, October 29, 1909.

64. R. Gilman Brown to Beatty, November 16, 1910, Beatty Papers.

65. Hoover to Beatty, January 4, 1910.

66. *West Australian Mining, Building, and Engineering Journal* 15 (April 23, 1910): 4.

67. The Beatty Papers contain detailed correspondence with Brown in 1910 about Kyshtim affairs. See, for example, Brown to Beatty, November 16, 1910.

68. Brown to Beatty, November 16, 1910.

69. Brown to Beatty, February 21, 1911, Beatty Papers; transcript of 1911 Kyshtim Corporation shareholders meeting, in *Mining World and Engineering Record* 81 (July 22, 1911): 128.

70. "Russian Mining," p. 410.

71. "Development of Russia's Mineral Resources," p. 314. The *Mining Magazine*'s statements were confirmed years later by Hoover himself. In his *Memoirs* (*Years of Adventure*, p. 103) Hoover declared that he "arranged the reorganizaton of the [Kyshtim] company's finances" (circa 1910). According to Hoover, Urquhart's metallurgists had been "on the wrong track," and American technical men led by R. Gilman Brown had turned matters around. Since Hoover may have been responsible for the appointment of at least two of these Americans (Brown and Perkins), he could thereby take some credit for the technological reorientation that they implemented.

72. Hoover to Beatty, December 29, 1910.

73. Amor F. Kuehn to Beatty, January 10, 1911, Beatty Papers.

74. Hoover Calendar, HHPL.

75. Ibid.; *Mining Magazine* 5 (September 1911): 208; Beatty to Hoover, October 13, 1911, Beatty Letter Books.

76. One of Beatty's assistants stated that Beatty did not expect to stay at Kyshtim more than five days. He could not have stayed much longer. Lucius Mayer to E. L. Gruver, September 8, 1911, Beatty Letter Books. At Kyshtim Hoover and Beatty stayed with the Urquharts. Mrs. Leslie Urquhart to Hoover, June 5, 1951, Post-Presidential Individual File, HHPL.

77. Skinner, *Mining Manual for 1912*, p. 805.

78. Mr. Allen of Knox & Allen designed the smelter. *Mining World and Engineering Record* 81 (July 22, 1911): 128. R. Gilman Brown told Beatty in late 1910 that had it not been for Walter G. Perkins (another American) the smelter would not have started before the spring of 1911. Brown to Beatty, November 16, 1910.

79. *Mining Magazine* 5 (December 1911): 406.

80. Kyshtim Corporation directors' report, July 15, 1912 (for the year 1911), in "Mining—Kyshtim Corporation, Ltd.," Pre-Commerce Papers.

81. Hoover, *Years of Adventure*, pp. 103–5. The spelling of the baron's name used here is that used in contemporary documents.

82. Ibid., p. 105.

83. Hoover to Beatty, December 4, 1911.

84. Skinner, *Mining Manual for 1912*, p. 805; *Mining Magazine* 6 (January 1912): 9.

85. This was the amount Hoover had the right to subscribe; he offered Beatty as much of it as Beatty wanted. Amor F. Kuehn to Beatty, December 2, 1911, Beatty Papers.

86. Report of January 5, 1912 Kyshtim Corporation shareholders meeting, in *Mining World and Engineering Record* 82 (January 6, 1912): 24.

87. The Beatty Papers are filled with Hoover-Beatty correspondence on this subject during late 1911 and early 1912. See also Intercontinental Trust file, PRO.

88. Beatty to Hoover, February 13, 1912.

89. E. L. Gruver to Beatty, March 22, 1912, Beatty Papers. Not all of this, of course, was profit.

90. Hoover to Beatty, January 17, 1912.

91. Hoover to Beatty, February 24, 1912.

92. "Tanalyk Corporation," *Statist* 73 (September 28, 1912): 705.

93. Hoover to Beatty, March 19, 1912.

94. Ibid.

95. Hoover cable to Beatty, March 26, 1912, quoted in a memorandum by E. L. Gruver, December 4, 1912, Beatty Papers.

96. Gruver cable to Hoover, Hoover cable to Beatty, Beatty cable to Hoover, all on March 28, 1912, all quoted in Gruver's memorandum of December 4, 1912.

97. "Tanalyk Corporation," p. 705; Walter R. Skinner, *The Mining Manual and Mining Year Book for 1913* (London, 1913), p. 702.

98. "Tanalyk Corporation," p. 705. See also the Tanalyk Corporation file, B.T. 31/20603/121418, PRO.

99. "Tanalyk Corporation," p. 705.

100. *Mining World and Engineering Record* 83 (October 5, 1912): 407; Skinner, *Mining Manual . . . 1913*, pp. 961–62.

101. "Tanalyk Corporation," p. 705; Skinner, *Mining Manual . . . 1913*, p. 962; *Mining Magazine* 9 (August 1913): 86; *Mining and Scientific Press* 107 (October 18, 1913): 623.

102. *Mining World and Engineering Record* 83 (October 5, 1912): 407; Skinner, *Mining Manual . . . 1913*, p. 962. Brown inspected the property in 1912. See *Mining Magazine* 6 (June 1912): 397.

103. In a letter to Beatty on February 28, 1913, Hoover declared that it was "necessary to reorganise the pool" in Tanalyk. This, of course, suggests involvement in prior organization of the pool, but details of pool operations are lacking.

104. "Tanalyk Corporation," p. 705.

105. E. L. Gruver memorandum, December 4, 1912.

106. Hoover to Beatty, January 23, 1913.

107. Hoover to Beatty, February 28, 1913.

108. *Mining Magazine* 9 (August 1913): 86; Walter R. Skinner, *The Mining Manual and Mining Year Book for 1915* (London, 1915), p. 639.

109. *Statist* 77 (September 20, 1913): 679; Skinner, *Mining Manual . . . 1915*, p. 639.

110. Hoover was listed as a new Tanalyk director on a register of directors dated October 13, 1913. Tanalyk Corporation file, PRO.

111. Hoover to Beatty, February 28, 1913.
112. Amor F. Kuehn memorandum for Beatty, November 22, 1913, Beatty Papers.
113. My sense of Urquhart's personality owes much to Geoffrey Blainey's account of him in *Mines in the Spinifex*.
114. Russo-Asiatic Corporation file, B.T. 31 / 20598 / 121391, PRO; Skinner *Mining Manual . . . 1913*, pp. 906–7. See also *Mining Magazine* 6 (May 1912): 320.
115. *Mining and Scientific Press* 108 (February 14, 1914): 302; "Development of Russia's Mineral Resources," p. 314. Both these sources stated flatly that Hoover and Urquhart formed the Russo-Asiatic Corporation. Hoover's name was thus given equal prominence with Urquhart's. No other founders were mentioned.
116. May 17, 1912 shareholders' list in Russo-Asiatic Corporation file, PRO; Skinner, *Mining Manual . . . 1913*, p. 906. Hoover's small shareholding, of course, did not necessarily reflect the influence he actually exerted on company affairs.
117. Hoover to Beatty, March 25, 1913.
118. *Statist* 79 (January 10, 1914): 60; transcript of Russo-Asiatic Corporation shareholders meeting, January 14, 1914, in *Financial Times*, January 15, 1914, p. 4. Skinner's *Mining Manual . . . 1913*, p. 907, states that the company was registered "to acquire and deal with mining and other properties in Russia," in conjunction with two Russian banks.
119. *Financial Times*, January 15, 1914, p. 4.
120. Hoover to Beatty, February 14, 1913.
121. *Financial Times*, January 15, 1914, p. 4.
122. Ibid. Hoover, in *Years of Adventure*, mentions Brown and Jones as belonging to his group of loosely allied engineers after 1908 (p. 100).
123. Beatty to Hoover, March 26, 1913.
124. Hoover Calendar, HHPL; Hoover to W. A. M. Goode, October 15, 1913, in "Panama Pacific International Exposition—Correspondence: Goode, W. A. M.," Pre-Commerce Papers, HHPL. Hoover told Goode that he had to go to Russia "for a fortnight." Hoover and his wife left England on October 15 and returned on November 5.
125. There was undoubtedly no time. Years later in his *Memoirs* Hoover stated that he made "numerous prolonged visits" to Russia before World War I (*Years of Adventure*, p. 102). The Hoover Calendar and other sources, however, indicate only three short journeys: the brief trips to Kyshtim in 1911 and 1913, plus the journey of 1909 during which he crossed Russia by rail on his way to and from Korea.
126. Hoover to the chairman and directors of the Kyshtim Corporation, October 1913, in "Mining," Pre-Commerce Papers.
127. *Statist* 79 (January 10, 1914): 60–62, and 79 (January 17, 1914): 107–9; *Financial Times*, January 15, 1914, pp. 4, 8; *Mining Journal* 104 (January 17, 1914): 71; E. de Hauptick, "Russo-Asiatic Corporation," *Mining Journal* 104 (January 31, 1914): 109–110.
128. *Financial Times*, January 15, 1914, p. 4; *Mining Magazine* 10 (March 1914): 176–177; Hoover, *Years of Adventure*, p. 107.
129. *Statist* 79 (January 17, 1914): 109; Blainey, *Mines in the Spinifex*, pp. 122–23.
130. *Financial Times*, January 15, 1914, p. 4.
131. *Mining and Scientific Press* 108 (February 14, 1914): 302.
132. *Mining Magazine* 10 (January 1914): 8, and 10 (February 1914): 97.
133. *Mining Magazine* 10 (February 1914): 97.
134. *Mining Magazine* 10 (January 1914): 8.
135. Skinner, *Mining Manual . . . 1915*, p. 577.
136. Beatty cable to Hoover, January 30, 1914.
137. *Mining Journal* 104 (January 3, 1914): 6; *Mining World and Engineering Record* 90 (April 1, 1916): 337.
138. Walter R. Skinner, *The Mining Manual and Mining Year Book for 1914* (London, 1914), p. 655.
139. Skinner, *Mining Manual . . . 1913*, p. 353.
140. *Mining World and Engineering Record* 90 (April 1, 1916): 337.

141. *Statist* 79 (March 7, 1914): 475–76; *Mining Magazine* 11 (September 1914): 158; Skinner, *Mining Manual . . . 1915*, p. 639; *Mining World and Engineering Record* 88 (January 30, 1915): 118.

142. *Mining Journal* 107 (December 12, 1914): 1038.

143. Skinner, *Mining Manual . . . 1915*, p. 314; Inter-Siberian Syndicate file, B.T. 31 / 22364 / 136453, PRO; Hoover to Leslie Urquhart, July 8, 1914, Urquhart Papers (see note 157).

144. *Mining Journal* 107 (December 12, 1914): 1038; *Mining Magazine* 11 (December 1914): 348–50; *Mining News* 40 (December 3, 1914): 205; Skinner, *Mining Manual . . . 1915*, pp. 317–19.

145. *Mining Journal* 107 (December 12, 1914): 1038.

146. *Mining News* 40 (December 3, 1914): 205.

147. Hoover, *Years of Adventure*, p. 108.

148. "Development of Russia's Mineral Resources," p. 314; *Mining and Scientific Press* 109 (August 8, 1914): 224.

149. Hoover, undated autobiographical statement (see chapter 13, note 101).

150. Hoover, *Years of Adventure*, pp. 102–3.

151. In the undated autobiographical statement cited in note 149, Hoover listed these among his achievements at Kyshtim: "Reorganized the finances, staffed it with Americans introduced new metallurgical and executive methods build it up to the employment of 40,000 men at wages high to unheard of in Russia. . . ." As written, this is an overstatement, since it seems to imply that Hoover was the controlling figure in these developments. The use of the new metallurgical technique of pyritic smelting, for instance, was planned for Kyshtim well before Hoover had any connection—even a financial one—with the company. Nor is Hoover known to have reorganized Kyshtim's finances in the ordinary sense of that expression.

      In 1916 the *Mining Magazine* asserted about Kyshtim:

      For the re-modelling of the metallurgical plant, the expansion of mining operations, the exploration of the orebodies, and the provision of adequate working capital, the shareholders have to thank Messrs. H. C. Hoover, R. Gilman Brown, and Walter G. Perkins. ("Development of Russia's Mineral Resources," p. 314.)

      This is probably a fair conclusion—if we emphasize that Hoover's own particular contribution before 1912 was the "provision of adequate working capital" on two occasions (plus whatever indirect influence he exerted through Brown and Perkins).

152. See, for example, *Mining and Scientific Press* 109 (August 8, 1914): 224.

153. Recall that Hoover arranged for Kuehn to visit Russia in 1913.

154. Hoover to Urquhart, July 8, 1914.

155. Leslie Urquhart died in 1933. In 1951–52 Hoover published his *Memoirs;* a condensed version appeared first in *Collier's*. After reading the *Collier's* excerpts in 1951, Urquhart's widow wrote two indignant letters to Hoover. She accused Hoover of grossly exaggerating and misrepresenting his role in the Kyshtim concern and of sundry inaccuracies in detail. In 1957 Mrs. Urquhart shared her complaints with an Australian historian, Geoffrey Blainey, and sent him data about Urquhart's Russian enterprises.

      In 1962 Blainey published an article on Hoover that incorporated many of Mrs. Urquhart's criticisms. He pointed out that Hoover did not visit Kyshtim before 1911, stayed there no more than a month in all, did not join its board until 1912, and was never its chairman, managing director, or general manager. Nor did Hoover rearrange the Kyshtim's finances (said Blainey); he only arranged one small debenture issue. Blainey also stated that Hoover was but one of many directors of the Kyshtim, Tanalyk, and Russo-Asiatic companies and was never dominant on these boards.

      After receiving Mrs. Urquhart's letters in 1951 Hoover deleted several errors about Russia from his *Memoirs* manuscript, which then appeared in book form in 1951–52. Hoover retained, however, the general thrust of his account, presenting himself as an industrial doctor who reorganized Kyshtim and spearheaded the development of Irtysh. A reader of his *Memoirs* would probably conclude that Hoover was the crucial figure in these Russian ventures.

Mrs. Urquhart and Professor Blainey did not have access to the papers of Sir A. Chester Beatty. The Hoover correspondence in this collection establishes that Hoover was much more involved in Kyshtim and its sister enterprises than the record otherwise suggests. Hoover was intimately involved in *two* Kyshtim debenture issues, not one, and was deeply interested in Kyshtim affairs in 1909, more than a year earlier than Mrs. Urquhart believed. And while the two debenture issues accounted for only one-fourth of all Kyshtim debenture capital raised before January 1912, they nevertheless occurred at two key moments, as some contemporary sources recognized. As this and other evidence mentioned in the text indicates, Hoover's influence on Kyshtim's development cannot be gauged by the brevity of his visits to Russia or even by his nonmembership on the board of directors before 1912.

Hoover was not the sole controlling administrator or creative figure in Kyshtim-Tanalyk-Irtysh before 1914. But neither was he merely a technical adviser or one director among many. The truth lies in between.

See Beryl Urquhart to Herbert Hoover, June 5 and 20, 1951, Post-Presidential Individual File, HHPL; Hoover to Mrs. Urquhart, June 11, 1951, ibid.; Hoover, *Years of Adventure*, pp. 102–8; Mrs. Urquhart to Geoffrey Blainey, August 23, 1957 (copy supplied to me by Professor Blainey); notes by Mrs. Urquhart, n.d. (copy supplied by Blainey); Geoffrey Blainey, "Herbert Hoover's Forgotten Years," *Business Archives and History* 3 (February 1962): 67–69.

156. Hoover, *Years of Adventure*, p. 108n. In 1922, when a question arose about Hoover's association with Leslie Urquhart, Hoover publicly declared of Urquhart's Russian enterprises:

> For some years prior to 1916 I was professionally engaged by these and other concerns in Russia and had some small interest in them, but upon entering public service my professional relations were terminated and my interest in all Russian business was entirely disposed of, and this prior to the revolution in Russia. (Hoover, telegram to *New York Times*, September 11, 1922, Public Statements File, HHPL.)

157. See the various shareholder lists in the Kyshtim Corporation file, B.T. 31 / 18592 / 100077, PRO, and similar lists in the Russo-Asiatic file already cited. These documents reveal, for instance, that Hoover apparently held only a few thousand shares at most at any one time in the Kyshtim Corporation. In July 1914 he owned 1,000 (the director's qualification). Similarly, he seems to have held only the minimum necessary (250 shares) to serve as a director of the Russo-Asiatic Corporation.

Various notes and memoranda (compiled ca. April 1932) in the Leslie Urquhart Papers give the following figures on Hoover's stockholdings: 1,000 Kyshtim director's qualification shares acquired in 1912; 200 Tanalyk director's qualification shares acquired in 1914; 200 (it should be 250) Russo-Asiatic Corporation shares acquired in 1914; 6,202 Irtysh shares under option acquired upon exercise of the option between June and December 1916. These documents state that Hoover sold out nearly all these holdings in November 1916. According to Urquhart's memoranda, except for the Irtysh enterprise Hoover acquired only enough shares in Urquhart's Russian companies to qualify as a director. I am grateful to Leslie Urquhart's daughter, Mrs. W. R. B. Foster of Lexham Hall, King's Lynn, Norfolk, U.K., for permitting me to study her father's papers in her possession.

These data are not necessarily conclusive, however. Over the years Hoover at times held shares listed in other people's names.

158. Leslie Urquhart, "Attacks on President Hoover," *Truth* 111 (May 25, 1932): 832–33. According to Urquhart, he prepared this article at President Hoover's own request after visiting Hoover in the White House twice in February 1932. Urquhart told acquaintances that Hoover completely approved the text prior to its publication. Indeed, Hoover's friends

(acting through Deane P. Mitchell) may have subsidized the article's publication; Mitchell bought 2,667 copies—some of them, at least, apparently for distribution in the United States. The Leslie Urquhart Papers contain many letters concerning this matter. See especially Urquhart to Geoffrey Dawson of *The Times*, May 6, 1932; Boris Said cable to Urquhart, May 14, 1932; Urquhart to C. H. Self, May 19, 1932; Louis Kaufman to Deane P. Mitchell, May 23, 1932; Urquhart to Sir Philip Cunliffe-Lister, Simon Guggenheim, and Philippe Bunau-Varilla, all on May 31, 1932. The Hoover Calendar, HHPL, records two Urquhart visits to President Hoover: February 6 and 24, 1932.

At the time of this article President Hoover was under attack from certain political enemies, including authors of would-be muckraking biographies, for (in effect) a conflict of interest. It was suggested that he opposed recognition of Soviet Russia because: a) he wished to force the Soviets to compensate him for the loss of his / Urquhart's mining properties (which the Communists had confiscated), or b) he hated the Communists for seizing these Russian properties that otherwise would have made him a fabulous fortune.

Urquhart's article was designed, among other things, to counteract these charges by demonstrating that Hoover's holdings in the Kyshtim et al. were minor and were largely disposed of before the 1917 Bolshevik Revolution. Urquhart did not mention Hoover's considerable role in financing the Kyshtim enterprise. Instead, he stressed Hoover's association with him as a technical adviser and engineer—the role that Hoover liked to emphasize in later years as he looked back on his business career.

Curiously, nearly twenty years after Urquhart's article appeared in *Truth*, Hoover denied that he had edited it or approved its publication. He said he had "no recollection of ever having seen it before." According to Hoover in 1951, Urquhart's article contained "some inaccuracies" that Hoover would have corrected had he seen the article ahead of time. See Hoover's draft of an unsent letter to Mrs. Leslie Urquhart, n.d. (1951), Post-Presidential Individual File, HHPL. Despite this draft—written, of course, long after the event—the evidence in Urquhart's papers strongly suggests that Hoover did see and approve the article prior to its publication. In addition to Urquhart's own statements to this effect, see Boris Said's cable to Urquhart, May 14, 1932. Said, in New York, was evidently an intermediary between Urquhart and the White House in 1932.

159. Hoover held 20,000 £1 shares in the Inter-Siberian Syndicate from its inception until its effective demise in 1916. However, because only a quarter of the company's nominal capital was ever called up, Hoover's actual cash investment only came to £5,000, or about $25,000. Still, he was legally committed to pay up the full £20,000 on his shares if so requested by the company's managers.

160. On the Irtysh flotation and Hoover's role in it, see: *Mining News* 40 (December 3, 1914): 205; Skinner, *Mining Manual . . . 1915*, pp. 317–19; Hoover, undated handwritten draft of Volume I, chapter 8 of his *Memoirs*, in Hoover Book Manuscript Material, HHPL. According to the Urquqart notes and memoranda cited in note 157, Hoover exercised his Irtysh option (to the extent of acquiring 6,202 Irtysh shares) in 1916. The precise magnitude of Hoover's stock option is unknown; the total option for the underwriters was 250,000 shares. The underwriting syndicate was probably the Inter-Siberian Syndicate, of which Hoover was a director.

161. Hoover, undated autobiographical statement (cited in note 149). How Hoover arrived at this figure is unknown. Perhaps it represented the total earnings he expected to obtain during the life of the Irtysh mine.

162. Said Hoover years later: "Had it not been for the Great War I should have gained a large fortune from these industries—probably more than is good for anybody" (Hoover, *Memoirs*, Volume I, paperbound page proof version, pp. 137–38, Hoover Book Manuscript Material).

163. Referring to these Russian mining enterprises, Hoover declared in his *Memoirs*: "Had it not been for the First World War, I should have had the largest engineering fees ever known to man" (*Years of Adventure*, p. 108).

Hoover's Russian mining fortune never materialized. As he afterwards emphasized, it was the economic catastrophe of World War I, not the Russian Revolution of 1917, that destroyed his prospects. Even before the Revolution, he said, his stake in Russian mining—both present and future, both actual and potential—had disappeared. See Hoover, *Years of Adventure*, p. 108n, and Hoover, *Memoirs*, Volume I, paperbound page proof version, p. 138.

CHAPTER 22

1. *The Times*, September 16, 1910, pp. 13–14; Theodore J. Hoover, *Memoranda: Being a Statement by an Engineer* (typescript: Stanford University, 1939), pp. 202–8, copy at HHPL.
2. *Mining World and Engineering Record* 78 (May 28, 1910): 655; *The Times*, September 16, 1910, pp. 13–14; Walter R. Skinner, *The Oil and Petroleum Manual for 1912* (London, 1912), p. 75.
3. *Statist* 65 (May 28, 1910): 1185.
4. Ibid.
5. Arthur Beeby-Thompson, *Black Gold: The Story of an Oil Pioneer* (New York, 1961), pp. 87–88.
6. Ibid., p. 88.
7. *Who's Who in America, 1924–25*, p. 340; *New York Times*, April 23, 1924, p. 21.
8. Hoover, *The Memoirs of Herbert Hoover*, Volume I: *Years of Adventure* (New York, 1951), p. 109.
9. C. Algernon Moreing, "Statement by Mr. Moreing" (n.d., but 1910), Bewick, Moreing & Co. Collection, HHPL.
10. Ibid. This will be discussed further in the present chapter.
11. Hoover to A. Chester Beatty, December 15, 1909, Sir A. Chester Beatty Papers (see chapter 19, note 40). All Hoover-Beatty correspondence cited in this chapter is from this source.
12. Beatty to Hoover, December 28, 1909.
13. This was a difficult task. Hoover to Beatty, December 29, 1909. See also "Statement by Mr. Moreing."
14. Hoover to Beatty, February 23, 1910.
15. Ibid.; "Statement by Mr. Moreing."
16. *Mining Journal* 87 (October 16, 1909): 113–14; "Statement by Mr. Moreing."
17. Hoover to Beatty, February 23, 1910.
18. Ibid.; Walter R. Skinner, *The Oil and Petroleum Manual for 1911* (London, 1911), p. 58; Maikop and General Petroleum Trust file, B.T. 31 / 13093 / 107669, Public Record Office (PRO), Kew, Surrey, U.K. Another director was W. F. Turner, who was active in the Chinese Engineering and Mining Company.
19. Skinner, *Oil and Petroleum Manual for 1912*, p. 69.
20. This was Maikop Oil and Petroleum Producers, Ltd. Ibid., p. 74.
21. *Mining World and Engineering Record* 78 (May 28, 1910): 655–56; Skinner, *Oil and Petroleum Manual for 1912*, p. 69.
22. Hoover's small direct shareholdings in various Maikop companies are listed on p. 21 of a reply brief by the law firm of Cook, Nathan & Lehman in the case *Walter W. Liggett v. Herbert Corey and Houghton Mifflin Company*, filed in the Supreme Court, New York County, New York in 1932. A copy of this brief is in the Herbert Corey Papers, Box 13, Library of Congress. In 1932 Liggett published a hostile biography of Herbert Hoover. Corey, with assistance from Hoover's close associates, published a rejoinder. Alleging malicious defamation, Liggett sued Corey, whose lawyers adopted truth as a defense and compiled the extensive brief cited here. This brief contains much biographical data about Hoover—data drawn, in all probability, from Hoover's own files and therefore cited with some

confidence. Liggett, incidentally, was a radical muckraker who was murdered in Minnesota in 1935 before his lawsuit was ever tried.

23. Hoover to Beatty, February 23, 1910; also Hoover cable to Beatty, same date. Hoover evidently intended to turn this asset over to the Intercontinental Trust, which he was then forming.

24. Hoover to Beatty, April 7, 1910.

25. *The Times*, August 19, 1910, p. 11, and January 17, 1913, p. 9.

26. *Mining Magazine* 2 (May 1910): 323.

27. Beeby-Thompson, *Black Gold*, pp. 88–89.

28. *Mining Journal* 89 (May 7, 1910): 604.

29. *Statist* 65 (May 28, 1910): 1185.

30. *Mining World and Engineering Record* 78 (May 28, 1910): 656.

31. Ibid., p. 659.

32. Ibid., p. 656; Theodore J. Hoover, "Recent Progress at Maikop," *Mining Magazine* 4 (April 1911): 298–300; Theodore J. Hoover, "Recent Progress at Maikop," *Mining Magazine* 5 (July 1911): 45–46; *The Times*, July 3, 1911, p. 20; Beeby-Thompson, *Black Gold*, p. 90.

33. Hoover cable to Ralph Arnold, August 29, 1910, Ralph Arnold Collection, Box 22, The Huntington Library, San Marino, California.

34. Hoover to Arnold, August 25, 1910, ibid.

35. Arnold to Hoover, September 7, 1910, ibid.

36. Hoover to Arnold, September 20, 1910, ibid.

37. Skinner, *Oil and Petroleum Manual for 1911*, pp. 58, 62, 65; Theodore Hoover, *Memoranda*, pp. 202–8.

38. Theodore Hoover, "Recent Progress at Maikop" (April 1911), p. 300; Skinner, *Oil and Petroleum Manual for 1911*, p. vi.

39. Theodore Hoover, "Recent Progress at Maikop" (July 1911), p. 46.

40. Hoover speech at Oroya Exploration Company shareholders meeting, February 24, 1911, quoted in *Mining Journal* 92 (February 25, 1911): 191.

41. Theodore Hoover, "Recent Progress at Maikop" (July 1911), p. 45.

42. *The Times*, July 24, 1911, p. 19.

43. *The Times*, July 26, 1911, p. 20, and August 3, 1911, p. 16.

44. Hoover to Beatty, November 11, 1911.

45. Charles Of, ed., *The Mineral Industry . . . During 1912* (New York, 1913), p. 654.

46. *Mining Magazine* 5 (October 1911): 248; *The Times*, October 30, 1912, p. 17.

47. *The Times*, January 22, 1912, p. 22.

48. *The Times*, February 8, 1912, p. 13, November 26, 1912, p. 27, and December 6, 1912, p. 19; Skinner, *Oil and Petroleum Manual for 1912*, pp. 74–75; Walter R. Skinner, *The Oil and Petroleum Manual for 1913* (London, 1913), p. 87.

49. Skinner, *Oil and Petroleum Manual for 1912*, pp. 70, 72, 81.

50. Ibid., p. 69.

51. Lucius W. Mayer to Beatty, March 22, 1912, Beatty Papers.

52. Maikop and General Petroleum Trust file, PRO; *The Times*, September 20, 1912, p. 13; *Economist* 75 (September 21, 1912): 533; *Mining News* 36 (September 26, 1912): 151; Skinner, *Oil and Petroleum Manual for 1913*, pp. 83, 84, 85. Another subsidiary, a pipeline company, amalgamated in December with a pipeline company formed by Moreing. Ibid., p. 87.

53. Hoover, *Years of Adventure*, p. 109. Hoover did acquire a small interest (768 shares) in the Maikop Combine. See p. 21 of the previously cited reply brief in the *Liggett v. Corey* lawsuit.

54. *The Times*, January 17, 1913, p. 9. The Maikop field looked very unpromising by 1914. See G. A. Roush, ed., *The Mineral Industry . . . During 1913* (New York, 1914), p. 565, and Walter R. Skinner, *The Oil and Petroleum Manual for 1914* (London, 1914), p. viii.

55. Walter R. Skinner, *The Oil and Petroleum Manual for 1916* (London, 1916), p. 79.

56. Walter R. Skinner, *The Oil and Petroleum Manual for 1923* (London, 1923), p. 123; Skinner, *The Oil and Petroleum Manual for 1927* (London, 1927), p. 116. The latter was the last entry for the Maikop Combine in Skinner's annual volumes.

A similar fate—uncompensated confiscation by the Soviets—befell the Maikop Valley Oil Company, formed in 1910 as a subsidiary of the Maikop and General Petroleum Trust. See Skinner, *Oil and Petroleum Manual for 1927*, p. 121.

57. *The Times*, January 17, 1913, p. 9.

58. Skinner, *Oil and Petroleum Manual for 1912*, pp. 69, 70, 72, 74, 75, 81.

59. Theodore Hoover, *Memoranda*, p. 170. Theodore criticized the British companies involved for premature expenditures and failure to heed the economic (as opposed to the merely technical) advice of their engineers.

60. See p. 21 of the previously cited legal brief in the *Liggett v. Corey* lawsuit. According to this source Hoover never held more than 1,000 shares in any of his Maikop ventures.

61. For example, John Hamill, *The Strange Career of Mr. Hoover Under Two Flags* (New York, 1931), pp. 240–43, and Walter W. Liggett, *The Rise of Herbert Hoover* (New York, 1932),pp. 178–83. See also R. W. Hadden to Rep. John W. McCormack, February 17, 1943, in President's Secretary's File, Box 10, Franklin D. Roosevelt Presidential Library. Hamill later recanted. See his lengthy affidavit, June 4, 1932, in Misrepresentations File, HHPL. See also John Hamill, *Hail Columbia Hoover* (typescript, ca. 1932), also in the Misrepresentations File.

62. Beeby-Thompson, *Black Gold*, pp. 88–89.

63. Ibid., pp. 90–91.

64. Hoover, *Years of Adventure*, pp. 108–9. This was true—in 1912. Hoover did step in to assist Bates. But Hoover in his *Memoirs* omitted any reference to his Maikop business interests *before* 1912.

65. It is, however, probably true that once the Maikop enterprises were floated, Hoover's role in their management was secondary to that of others, including Bates. Hoover, after all, actually sat on only two Maikop company boards. Still, he was not a passive or peripheral figure on the Maikop scene, as the evidence in the text demonstrates.

In later years Hoover—through surrogates—minimized his early active interest in Maikop. For example, John Hamill stated that Hoover never promoted any Maikop companies and that they were really Bates's companies. Hamill created the impression that Hoover was largely a bystander (*Hail Columbia Hoover*, pp. 187–91). This minimized Hoover's role far too much. For example, through the parent Maikop and General Petroleum Trust Hoover did participate in company promotion, a subject on which he was later sensitive. While the Maikop enterprises may have been primarily Bates's companies, Hoover's involvement in them early on was considerable.

66. Bewick, Moreing & Co. statement regarding Herbert Hoover (n.d., but ca. 1916); Bewick, Moreing & Co. Statement of Claim, May 31, 1916, in the lawsuit *Bewick, Moreing & Co. v. Herbert Clark Hoover*, Case No. 1916 B No. 1071, High Court of Justice, King's Bench Division, London; "Elaboration of allegations of Breach of Contract requested by Counsel" in the same case (typescript, 1916). All these documents are in the Bewick, Moreing & Co. Collection, HHPL.

67. Bewick, Moreing & Co. statement regarding Hoover (1916).

68. Ibid.; "Elaboration of allegations . . ." (1916).

69. W. J. Loring to T. W. Wellsted, March 19, 1910, Bewick, Moreing & Co. Collection.

70. This account is based on two sources: "Statement by Mr. Moreing" (1910), previously cited, and an affidavit by Moreing, May 26, 1910, in the lawsuit *C. Algernon Moreing, Thomas William Wellsted, and William Joseph Loring v. Herbert Clark Hoover*, Case No. 1910 M No. 973, High Court of Justice, King's Bench Division, London. These documents are in the Bewick, Moreing & Co. Collection. See also Moreing's remarks quoted in *Mining Journal* 87 (October 16, 1909): 113–14; Hoover to Beatty, February 23, 1910; and Moreing's remarks quoted in *Mining Journal* 89 (May 7, 1910): 603–4.

71. Apparently the two men never put their Maikop understandings in writing.

72. See: clauses 8 and 9 of Hoover's indenture with Bewick, Moreing & Co. dated April 10, 1908, as quoted in a draft Statement of Claim, June 1910, for the 1910 lawsuit; Moreing's affidavit of May 26, 1910; White & Leonard (solicitors) to T. W. Wellsted, June 23, 1910;

Bewick, Moreing & Co. to White & Leonard, June 27, 1910; Bewick, Moreing & Co. statement regarding Hoover (1916). All in Bewick, Moreing & Co. Collection.

73. Moreing's affidavit of May 26, 1910; Bewick, Moreing & Co. to White & Leonard, June 27, 1910.

74. Wellsted to Hoover, February 23, 1910, quoted in Moreing's affidavit of May 26, 1910.

75. Hoover to Wellsted, February 24, 1910, and Wellsted to Hoover, same date, both quoted in Moreing's affidavit of May 26, 1910.

76. "Statement by Mr. Moreing."

77. Moreing affidavit, May 9, 1910, Bewick, Moreing & Co. Collection.

78. Bewick, Moreing & Co. to Hoover, April 14, 1910, quoted in ibid.

79. The draft Statement of Claim dated June 1910 states that the writ was issued on April 16.

80. Statement of Claim, June 1910. See also "Statement by Mr. Moreing"; Moreing affidavit of May 9, 1910; Bewick, Moreing & Co. to White & Leonard, June 27, 1910.

81. Hoover's defense emerges in various legal documents already cited—for example, Moreing's affidavits of May 9 and 26, 1910. See also *Australian Mining Standard* 45 (January 18, 1911): 67.

82. Copies of various affidavits are in the Bewick, Moreing & Co. Collection. See also Beeby-Thompson, *Black Gold*, pp. 92–94.

83. Hoover to Beatty, October 4 and November 28, 1910.

84. *Australian Mining Standard* 45 (January 18, 1911): 67; Beeby-Thompson, *Black Gold*, p. 93.

85. Handwritten, unsigned, undated memorandum in Bewick, Moreing & Co. Collection.

86. Loring's memorandum of conversation with Govett, December 13, 1910; White & Leonard to Bewick, Moreing & Co., December 19, 1910; Bewick, Moreing & Co. statement regarding Hoover (1916); "Elaboration of allegations of Breach of Contract . . ." (1916). All in Bewick, Moreing & Co. Collection.

87. White & Leonard to Bewick, Moreing & Co., December 19, 1910.

88. Bewick, Moreing & Co. statement regarding Hoover (1916).

89. W. J. Loring interview, 1931, Walter W. Liggett Papers, New York Public Library.

90. *Mining Magazine* 3 (December 1910): 395. Rickard, a friend of Hoover, had earlier submitted an affidavit in Hoover's behalf. Rickard's affidavit is mentioned in Moreing's affidavit of May 26, 1910.

91. See "Terms agreed upon between the Plaintiffs and Defendant" (February 8, 1911), Bewick, Moreing & Co. Collection.

92. Beeby-Thompson, *Black Gold*, pp. 94–95.

93. For the full terms of the settlement, see "Terms agreed upon . . ." (February 8, 1911).

94. Statement of Claim, May 31, 1916, in Moreing's 1916 lawsuit.

95. Bewick, Moreing & Co. statement regarding Hoover (1916); "Elaboration of allegations of Breach of Contract . . ." (1916).

96. Bewick, Moreing & Co. statement regarding Hoover (1916).

97. Ibid.

98. Ibid. The firm alleged that Agnew stirred up trouble in 1912, claimed ill health, and finally quit. Agnew's letters to Hoover in 1911–12, however, reveal a rather different story: of a man genuinely angry at his superiors for many months and not anxious to leave on a pretext. Nothing in this correspondence suggests that Hoover instigated Agnew's departure. See the file "Mining—Correspondence: Agnew, John A.," Pre-Commerce Papers, HHPL.

99. Bewick, Moreing & Co. statement regarding Hoover (1916); Statement of Claim, May 31, 1916; "Elaboration of allegations of Breach of Contract . . ." (1916).

100. Lake View and Star, Ltd., Minute Book No. 1, pp. 58–59 (meeting of March 2, 1911) (see chapter 19, note 116).

101. *Mining and Scientific Press* 105 (July 20, 1912): 92.

102. Ibid., September 14, 1912, p. 350.

103. Moreing's second lawsuit was instituted in 1916. It will be discussed in the second volume of this biography.

104. Hoover, *Years of Adventure*, p. 109.

105. Ibid.

106. Hoover to Beatty, November 11, 1911.

107. Hoover to Bates, January 31, 1912.

108. Hamill, *Hail Columbia Hoover*, p. 184.

109. Ibid., p. 185.

110. Lagunitos Oil Company file, B.T. 31 / 19411 / 109033, PRO; Hamill, *Hail Columbia Hoover*, pp. 185–86; Skinner, *Oil and Petroleum Manual for 1911*, p. 53; "The President's Fortune," *Fortune* 6 (August 1932): 88.

111. Hamill, *Hail Columbia Hoover*, p. 186; "The President's Fortune," p. 88.

112. Years later a prominent British petroleum engineer who was involved in the chain of events leading to formation of Lagunitos recalled that Hoover "and his associates" founded the company. Beeby-Thompson, *Black Gold*, pp. 89–90.

113. Bewick, Moreing & Co. to Hoover, April 14, 1910, quoted in Moreing's affidavit of May 9, 1910; Hamill, *Hail Columbia Hoover*, p. 195. Hamill asserted that Hoover resigned from the Anglo-Continental board because it got involved in some questionable mining ventures. Hamill made no mention of Moreing's demand that Hoover resign.

114. Skinner, *Oil and Petroleum Manual for 1912*, pp. 63–64.

115. Hamill, *Hail Columbia Hoover*, p. 185.

116. Govett remarks at Lake View and Oroya Exploration Company shareholders meeting, October 29, 1912, quoted in *Mining World and Engineering Record* 83 (November 2, 1912): 526. As of early 1913 the Lake View held 36,210 fully paid Lagunitos shares. Walter R. Skinner, *The Mining Manual and Mining Year Book for 1913* (London, 1913), p. 736.

117. *The Times*, December 13, 1912, p. 70.

118. Lagunitos Oil Company file, PRO.

119. Hoover to Beatty, February 24, 1913.

120. *The Times*, December 13, 1912, p. 70; report of Lagunitos Oil Company shareholders meeting, November 25, 1913, in *Mining World and Engineering Record* 85 (November 29, 1913): 688; Hamill, *Hail Columbia Hoover*, p. 185.

121. Hoover to Beatty, February 24, 1913.

122. Report of Lagunitos shareholders meeting, November 25, 1913, p. 688.

123. Govett remarks at Lake View and Oroya Exploration Company shareholders meeting, October 6, 1913, quoted in *Mining World and Engineering Record* 85 (October 11, 1913): 430.

124. Late in 1913 Lagunitos for various purposes issued further preference shares; Hoover and Govett subscribed to nearly 25,000 for the Lake View and Oroya Exploration Company. The Lake View's holding in Lagunitos had now increased to more than 36,000 ordinary and nearly 30,000 preference shares. No longer, however, were Hoover and his associates taking a risk, and in 1914 they reaped their reward: Lake View sold its Lagunitos shares at a profit of more than £25,000. See Hamill, *Hail Columbia Hoover*, pp. 185–86; *Mining World and Engineering Record* 87 (October 17, 1914): 410.

125. This story is told in Bennett H. Wall and George S. Gibb, *Teagle of Jersey Standard* (New Orleans, 1974), pp. 97–99. For further details on the purchase of a controlling interest in Lagunitos and its eventual merger with the International Petroleum Company, see: *New York Times*, December 1, 1914, p. 1; Walter R. Skinner, *The Oil and Petroleum Manual for 1916* (London, 1916), pp. 65–66, 74–75, 77; Lagunitos Oil Company file, PRO.

126. Walter Evans Edge, *A Jerseyman's Journal* (Princeton, 1948), pp. 45–46.

127. Walter R. Skinner, *The Oil, Petroleum and Bitumen Manual for 1910* (London, 1910), pp. 47, 105; General Petroleum Properties of Trinidad file, B.T. 31 / 13143 / 108285, PRO; Hamill, *Hail Columbia Hoover*, p. 192. Davis and Turner, like Hoover, were directors of the Anglo-Continental Mines Company at this time.

128. Ralph Arnold to Hoover, August 22, 1911, Arnold Collection, Box 24; *Mining World and Engineering Record* 81 (November 18, 1911): 625; Skinner, *Oil and Petroleum Manual for 1912*, pp. 53–54; Ralph Arnold, George A. Macready, and Thompson W. Barrington, *The First Big Oil Hunt: Venezuela—1911–1916* (New York, 1960), p. 23.

129. Hoover to Ralph Arnold, August 2, 1911, Arnold Collection, Box 24.

130. *The Times,* December 11, 1912, p. 19.

131. Ibid.; Skinner, *Oil and Petroleum Manual for 1913,* p. 63; *Oil News* 1 (July 5, 1913): 12; Walter R. Skinner, *The Oil and Petroleum Manual for 1914* (London, 1914), p. 169; *The Times,* February 6, 1914, p. 17; *Oil News* 2 (February 28, 1914): 16–17; Hamill, *Hail Columbia Hoover,* pp. 193–94; "The President's Fortune," p. 88; General Petroleum Properties of Trinidad file, PRO. In *Years of Adventure* Hoover made only the briefest reference to his Trinidad activities (p. 109).

132. Hoover, *Years of Adventure,* p. 109.

133. Ibid. From 1911 to 1913 Hoover was a director of La Lune (Trinidad) Oil Blocks, a company formed to acquire certain prospecting leases on the island. The company seems to have been inactive; it wound up in 1913. See Skinner, *Oil and Petroleum Manual for 1912,* p. 63, and Skinner, *Oil and Petroleum Manual for 1914,* p. 78.

134. Hamill, *Hail Columbia Hoover,* p. 194; "The President's Fortune," p. 88.

135. Skinner, *Oil and Petroleum Manual for 1913,* pp. 23, 168. The £200,000 was in the form of shares in the new company.

136. Hoover held 5,000 shares in the syndicate from March 1913 on. Bishopsgate Syndicate file, B.T. 31 / 13876 / 121574, PRO. According to one later estimate, Hoover's profit was about £40,000, or nearly $200,000 ("The President's Fortune," p. 87). This seems unlikely, since Hoover's shareholding in the syndicate would not have justified receiving such a large portion of the profit from the resale.

137. Hoover cable to Beatty, February 23, 1910; Hoover to Beatty, February 26, 1910.

138. Beatty cable to Hoover, April 5, 1910; Beatty to Hoover, April 12, 1910. See also Hoover / Beatty statement of joint account, June 24, 1910, Beatty Papers.

139. E. L. Gruver to Hoover, November 14 and 19, 1912, Beatty Papers; *Mining and Scientific Press* 105 (November 23, 1912): 672; *Mining Magazine* 7 (December 1912): 427.

140. June 24, 1910 statement of account. This was 60% of the Hoover / Beatty joint holding in the Continental.

141. Gruver to Hoover, November 14, 1912.

142. Beatty to Hoover, January 17, 1913.

143. Condensed Statement Regarding General Petroleum Company, November 1, 1912, "Mining—General Petroleum Company," Pre-Commerce Papers; *Mining and Scientific Press* 105 (November 23, 1912): 672; *Mining Magazine* 7 (December 1912): 426–27; Skinner, *Oil and Petroleum Manual for 1913,* p. 62; Eugene I. Harrington, "General Petroleum Corporation: Chapter I—Its Beginnings and Its Founder," *California Oil World and Petroleum Industry* 30 (July 5, 1937): 4–8; Harrington, "The General Petroleum Corporation: Chapter II—Growing Pains, 1912–1916," ibid. 30 (July 20, 1937): 5–8.

144. *California Derrick* 5 (November 15, 1912): 10.

145. Hoover to Continental Petroleum Co. of America, October 21, 1912; minutes of board of directors meeting of Continental Petroleum Co. of America, October 23, 1912. Both in Beatty Papers.

146. Hoover to Continental Petroleum Co. of America, October 21, 1912. For more on Hoover's and Beatty's negotiations leading to this conclusion, see Beatty telegram to Lucius W. Mayer, September 27, 1912, Beatty Papers.

147. Continental directors' meeting minutes, October 23, 1912. See also Hoover to Inter-Californian Trust, October 23, 1912, Beatty Papers.

148. Govett remarks at Zinc Corporation shareholders meeting, June 25, 1913, quoted in *Financial Times,* June 26, 1913.

149. See the Inter-Californian Trust's file, B.T. 31 / 20954 / 124565, PRO. Originally the syndicate was to be called the Anglo-Californian Trust. Hoover and his brother were among the early directors.

150. Inter-Californian Trust agenda sheet for its February 4, 1913 meeting, Beatty Papers.

151. Beatty to Hoover, January 17, 1913; Hoover to Beatty, January 28, 1913.

152. Gruver to Hoover, November 11, 1912; *Mining and Scientific Press* 105 (November 23,

1912): 672; minutes of General Petroleum Company board of directors meeting, November 29, 1912, cited in a lengthy memorandum, dated October 13, 1950, in the Carol Green Wilson Papers, Box 3, HI. This memorandum was prepared by Wayne Rush of the General Petroleum Corporation. It contains all the references (including key resolutions) referring to Herbert Hoover found in the company's minute books for 1912–14. This valuable document was compiled for the use of Mrs. Wilson, a previous Hoover biographer. It provides excellent information on Hoover's relationship with the General Petroleum Company. Also of importance is M. E. Dice to Carol Green Wilson, October 17, 1950, Wilson Papers, Box 3.

153. Notes on meeting of Inter-Californian Trust, December 30, 1912, Beatty Papers.

154. Hoover to R. R. Colgate, Vice President, General Petroleum Co., January 10, 1913; Hoover to Beatty, January 10, 1913; D. Anderson to Beatty, January 24, 1913. All in Beatty Papers. For more on the General Petroleum Company's option to purchase the Union Oil Company, see *California Derrick* 5 (November 15, 1912): 10, and *Oil News* 1 (May 3, 1913): 2.

155. Inter-Californian Trust agenda sheet for its February 24, 1913 meeting.

156. Amor F. Kuehn to Beatty, January 25, 1913, Beatty Papers; Hoover to Beatty, January 28, 1913.

157. Hoover to Beatty, January 28, 1913.

158. General Petroleum Co. memorandum, October 13, 1950, cited in note 152.

159. Hoover to Beatty, February 24, 1913.

160. Hoover to E. J. de Sabla, Jr., May 13, 1913, quoted in full in General Petroleum Co. memorandum, October 13, 1950; also the company's minutes for the directors meeting of May 22, 1913, quoted in the same memo.

161. General Petroleum Co. memorandum, October 13, 1950; *New York Times*, May 25, 1913, Section VIII, p. 10, and June 25, 1913, p. 12.

162. General Petroleum Co. memorandum, October 13, 1950; General Petroleum Co. balance sheets as of June 30, 1913, "Mining—General Petroleum Co.," Pre-Commerce Papers.

163. General Petroleum Co. memorandum, October 13, 1950. Not surprisingly, during the year ending June 30, 1913 the Lake View and Oroya Exploration Company acquired what Govett labeled "considerable interests" in the General Petroleum enterprise. Govett, quoted in *Mining World and Engineering Record* 85 (October 11, 1913): 430–31.

164. This was the recollection of older executives of the company in 1950. Dice to Wilson, October 17, 1950.

165. Hoover, *Years of Adventure*, p. 11.

166. Harrington, "The General Petroleum Corporation: Chapter II," p. 8.

167. Ibid.; *The Times*, October 31, 1913, p. 19; *New York Times*, October 31, 1913, p. 16, and November 15, 1913, p. 5; Skinner, *Oil and Petroleum Manual for 1916*, p. 167; Hoover cables to Beatty, January 3–4 and 6, 1914; John Hamill affidavit, June 4, 1932, p. 109, Misrepresentations File, HHPL; statement by Andrew Weir (or possibly prepared for Weir to sign), n.d. (but spring of 1932), "Rickard Files: Statements and Affidavits," Misrepresentations File. It is not clear that Weir ever saw or signed this statement, which Hoover's associates (possibly Hoover himself) prepared for Weir to sign in defense of Hoover in 1932.

168. *Mining Magazine* 9 (November 1913): 320; Hoover to A. N. Grenfell and R. Tilden Smith, November 25, 1913, Beatty Papers.

169. Weir statement, n.d.

170. *Mining Magazine* 9 (November 1913): 320.

171. *Mining and Scientific Press* 107 (December 6, 1913): 905.

172. Hoover had been instrumental in placing much of the $3,000,000 note issue the previous spring and may have held some of the notes himself. He also may have been acting at this juncture as a representative of the interests of the old Continental Oil Company, in which he had been a major shareholder. See Weir statement, n.d.

173. Hoover to Beatty, November 25, 1913. See also Hoover to Grenfell and Smith, November 25, 1913.
174. Hoover cable to Beatty, December 5, 1913. See also Hoover to Grenfell and Smith, November 25, 1913.
175. Hoover Calendar, HHPL.
176. Hoover telegrams to Beatty, January 6 and 7, 1914; Hamill affidavit, pp. 109–110.
177. Hoover telegrams to Beatty, January 3–4, 5, and 10, 1914.
178. Hoover telegrams to Beatty, January 3–4 and 5, 1914.
179. Hoover telegram to Beatty, January 10, 1914.
180. Hoover telegrams to Beatty, January 27, 1914.
181. Ibid.
182. Ibid. For information on Weir's Union Oil maneuvers, see Frank J. Taylor and Earl M. Welty, *Black Bonanza* (New York, 1950), pp. 165–72.
183. Ralph Arnold to Hoover, January 16 and 27, 1914; Hoover to Arnold, January 28 and January 31 / February 1, 1914; Arnold to Hoover, February 2, 1914; Hoover to Arnold, February 9–10, 1914; Arnold to Hoover, February 27 and April 18, 1914. All in Arnold Collection, Box 34.
184. Hoover telegram to Beatty, January 27, 1914.
185. Hoover, *Years of Adventure*, p. 113.
186. Hoover, handwritten declaration, January 14, 1914, General Accessions—Katherine Milbank, HHPL.
187. Hoover, *Years of Adventure*, pp. 114–15.
188. Gruver to Beatty, March 10, 1914, Beatty Papers.
189. Ibid. In mid-1914 the General Petroleum Company went into default on interest payments due on its notes and debenture stock. *New York Times*, July 28, 1914, p. 4; *Mining and Scientific Press* 109 (October 31, 1914): 707; Harrington, "The General Petroleum Corporation: Chapter II," p. 9.
190. Skinner, *Oil and Petroleum Manual for 1916*, p. 60.
191. *California Derrick* 6 (May 10, 1914): 5–6; Taylor and Welty, *Black Bonanza*, pp. 169–70.
192. Skinner, *Oil and Petroleum Manual for 1916*, p. 30.
193. Taylor and Welty, *Black Bonanza*, p. 170; *California Derrick* 6 (May 10, 1914): 6.
194. Hoover, quoted in *Mining World and Engineering Record* 87 (October 17, 1914): 410. Indeed, part of the plan proceeded. Most of the General Petroleum Company's common shares were in fact transferred in time to its British namesake.
195. *The Times*, November 18, 1914, p. 14.
196. Walter R. Skinner, *The Oil and Petroleum Manual for 1919* (London, 1919), p. 60; Harrington, "The General Petroleum Corporation: Chapter II," p. 9.
197. *Mining Magazine* 11 (July 1914): 25; Weir statement, n.d.
198. *New York Times*, July 28, 1914, p. 4.
199. Skinner, *Oil and Petroleum Manual for 1916*, p. 60.
200. Taylor and Welty, *Black Gold*, pp. 170, 172.
201. Hoover, *Years of Adventure*, p. 111. Hoover did not mention Weir by name, but the allusion is obvious. Weir, incidentally, became Lord Inverforth after World War I.
202. Statement by John Barneson, January 8, 1932, "Rickard Files: Statements and Affidavits," Misrepresentations File.
203. Govett, quoted in *Mining World and Engineering Record* 95 (October 5, 1918): 277–78.
204. John Barneson to Hoover, November 5, 1914, "Mining—Correspondence: Barneson, John," Pre-Commerce Papers. See also Barneson to Hoover, November 17, 1914, ibid. Barneson considered Weir to be irresponsible—a man who claimed to have more political influence in Britain than he really had and who did not keep his grandiose promises to General Petroleum. Weir's side of the story is not known.
205. John Barneson to William Goode, November 17, 1914, in "Mining—Correspondence: Barneson, John," Pre-Commerce Papers; Hamill affidavit, p. 110; Skinner, *Oil and Petroleum Manual for 1919*, p. 60.

206. John Barneson statement, December 22, 1931, "Richey-Hoover Files: Statements and Refutations," Misrepresentations File.
207. Arnold to Hoover, January 6, 1943, Post-Presidential Individual File, HHPL.
208. Hoover to Arnold, January 11, 1943, ibid. See also Arnold's reply, January 20, 1943.
209. See the books cited in note 61.
210. On the usefulness of the financier / promoter in the oil industry ca. 1911, see Beeby-Thompson, *Black Gold*, pp. 84–86, 91.

CHAPTER 23

1. Herbert Hoover, *Principles of Mining* (New York, 1909), p. 186.
2. Data sheet in "American Institute of Mining and Metallurgical Engineers," Pre-Commerce Papers, HHPL.
3. Herbert Hoover membership file, Institution of Mining and Metallurgy, London. For reasons unknown Hoover resigned from the Institution in 1908.
4. For example, the Société des Ingénieurs Civils de France, and the Mining and Metallurgical Society of America.
5. See chapter 4.
6. Hoover, "Some Notes on 'Crossings,' " *Mining and Scientific Press* 72 (February 29, 1896): 166–67; [Hoover], "Responsibility for the Debris," ibid. 74 (January 9, 1897): 28; [Hoover], "The Mining Bureau and a Geological Survey" and "Shall the Debris Question be Reconsidered?" ibid., January 16, 1897, p. 46; Hoover, "Geologic Mapping of the Mother Lode," ibid., p. 52. In addition Hoover prepared a synopsis of an article by two other geologists; it was published in *Mining and Scientific Press* 73 (September 19, 1896): 237–38.

    The unsigned essays listed here as Hoover's are identified as his in a scrapbook of clippings in the Herbert Hoover Collection, Box 230, HI. This scrapbook contains many early articles by Hoover and was evidently kept by him or his wife. One section contains "Anonymous doings of HCH."
7. A partial listing of Hoover's professional writings has been compiled at HHPL. For many previously unknown Hoover publications, see the scrapbook cited in note 6. In making my tally I have not counted reprints of Hoover articles in some other periodical. Nor have I counted newspaper interviews with Hoover, some of them lengthy, which appeared on occasion in the British and Australian press.

    In identifying pseudonymous articles, I have largely relied on the "Anonymous doings of HCH" pasted into the Hoover scrapbook at HI. The Pre-Commerce Papers at HHPL contain a number of typewritten, apparently unpublished, professional articles by Hoover.
8. Hoover, "Geology of the Four-Mile Placer Mining District, Colorado," *Engineering and Mining Journal* 63 (May 22, 1897): 510; Hoover, "The Superficial Alteration of Western Australian Ore-Deposits," *Transactions of the American Institute of Mining Engineers* 28 (1898): 758–65.
9. For example, see: Hoover, "Mining and Milling Gold Ores in Western Australia," *Engineering and Mining Journal* 66 (December 17, 1898): 725–26; Hoover, "Metal Mining in the Provinces of Chi-li and Shantung, China," *Transactions of the Institution of Mining and Metallurgy* 8 (1899–1900): 324–31; Hoover, "The Kaiping Coal Mines and Coal Field, Chihle Province, North China," *Transactions of the Institution of Mining and Metallurgy* 10 (1901–1902): 419–30.
10. For example: [Hoover], "Westralian Mines," *Financial Times*, November 5, 1902, p. 3; [Hoover], "Westralian Mines," *Financial Times*, November 18, 1902, p. 5. Hoover is identified as the author of these unsigned articles in the Hoover scrapbook cited in note 6.
11. See: Philip Argall, "Cyaniding Sulpho-Telluride Ores," *Engineering and Mining Journal* 76 (July 11, 1903): 53–54; W. A. Prichard and Hoover, "The Treatment of Sulpho-Telluride Ores at Kalgoorlie," ibid., August 1, 1903, pp. 156–57; Hoover, letter to the editor, ibid.,

August 15, 1903, p. 228; Argall, letter to the editor, ibid., October 3, 1903, p. 496; Hoover, letter to the editor, ibid. 77 (January 21, 1904): 111; Argall, letter to the editor, ibid., March 3, 1904, p. 351. The exchange grew increasingly sharp, and Hoover became upset by Argall's criticism.

12. Hoover, "Gold Mining in Western Australia in 1902," *Engineering and Mining Journal* 75 (January 3, 1903): 18; Hoover, "Western Australia," ibid. 79 (January 5, 1905): 41–42; Hoover, "Western Australian Gold Mining in 1905," ibid. 81 (January 20, 1906): 136.

13. Hoover, "Mining and Milling Gold Ores in Western Australia," *Engineering and Mining Journal* 66 (December 17, 1898): 725–26.

14. [Hoover], "Westralian Mines," p. 3; Hoover, "Working Costs in West Australian Mines," *Mining Journal, Railway and Commercial Gazette* 74 (August 15, 1903): 186. See also Hoover's quoted remarks on mines of Western Australia versus those of the Transvaal, in *Mining Journal, Railway and Commercial Gazette* 74 (July 18, 1903): 67. In the first of these articles Hoover asserted that mine administration in Kalgoorlie was superior to that in Cripple Creek, one of the most famous American mining centers.

15. Hoover, *Principles of Mining*, p. 171.

16. Hoover's mid-1903 article on West Australian working costs evoked wide comment in the British financial press; for a sample, see the clippings in the Hoover scrapbook cited in note 6. Another Hoover essay that aroused considerable attention was "The Future Gold Production of Western Australia," *Transactions of the Institution of Mining and Metallurgy* 13 (1903–1904): 2–21. See, for instance, *Financial Times*, October 16, 1903, p. 5.

17. Hoover, letter to the editor, *Engineering and Mining Journal* 76 (July 11, 1903): 44.

18. Hoover, "The Economic Ratio of Treatment Capacity to Ore Reserves," *Engineering and Mining Journal* 77 (March 24, 1904): 475–76; Hoover, letter to the editor, ibid. 78 (August 18, 1904): 253.

19. For some of the more important comments on Hoover's "theorem," see: W. R. Ingalls, letter to the editor, *Engineering and Mining Journal* 77 (May 5, 1904): 715–16; R. Gilman Brown, letters to the editor, ibid., May 26, 1904, p. 835, and ibid. 78 (December 1, 1904): 861–62; James R. Finlay, "The Cost of Mining—General Conditions," ibid. 85 (April 18, 1908): 800; Finlay, "Mine Valuation," ibid. 93 (June 22, 1912): 1238–39.

20. W. R. Ingalls to Hazel Lyman Nickel, August 28, 1949, Herbert Hoover Collection, Box 5, HI.

21. Hoover, "The Valuation of Gold Mines," *Engineering and Mining Journal* 77 (May 19, 1904): 801; Hoover, letter to the editor, ibid. 78 (July 7, 1904): 5.

22. T. A. Rickard, ed., *The Economics of Mining* (New York, 1905).

23. *Mining and Scientific Press* 92 (January 6, 1906): 1.

24. J. R. Finlay to Hoover, November 17, 1911, "Mining—Correspondence: Finlay, J. R.," Pre-Commerce Papers.

25. Hoover, *Principles of Mining*, p. 180.

26. [Hoover], "Mining Company Administration," *Financial Times*, February 19, 1903, p. 5; "Observer" [Hoover], letter to the editor, *Engineering and Mining Journal* 77 (April 28, 1904): 675–76. Hoover is identified as the author of these articles in the scrapbook cited in note 6.

27. "Observer" [Hoover], letter to the editor, *Engineering and Mining Journal* 77 (April 28, 1904): 676.

28. Hoover, *Principles of Mining*, p. 181.

29. Ibid., p. 184.

30. Ibid., p. 52.

31. Ibid., p. 192.

32. John C. Branner to Hoover, May 3, 1909, John C. Branner Papers, Box 7, Stanford University Archives; Curtis H. Lindley to Hoover, May 13, 1909, "Mining—Correspondence: Lindley, Curtis H.," Pre-Commerce Papers.

33. *Mining and Scientific Press* 98 (May 22, 1909): 764.

34. Professor Peele of the Columbia School of Mines stated that Hoover's book was "the first

well-digested presentment of the entire subject" of valuation of mines. Peele, review of *Principles of Mining* in [Columbia] *School of Mines Quarterly* 30 (July 1909): 380–81. See also a similar remark in *Engineering and Mining Journal* 87 (June 5, 1909): 1149.

35. Hoover to John C. Branner, October 12, 1909, quoted in Hoover Calendar, HHPL. A week later Hoover told a friend, "I have been considering some suggestions that I should associate myself in the administration of Columbia University in certain capacities, but there will be nothing settled for another 12 months as I am not prepared to reach a final decision until that time" (Hoover to E. D. Adams, October 19, 1909, E. D. Adams Papers, Box 1, Stanford University Archives).

36. H. L. Smyth to Hoover, December 1, 1909, "Mining—Correspondence: Harvard (Lectures) 1909," Pre-Commerce Papers. As far as is known, Hoover did not accept this invitation.

37. W. R. Ingalls to Hoover, November 2, 1910, "Mining—Correspondence: Ingalls, W. R.," Pre-Commerce Papers.

38. Many years later W. J. Loring claimed that Hoover, in *Principles of Mining*, plagiarized extensively from articles written by Loring. Loring interview, 1931, Walter W. Liggett Papers, New York Public Library. Loring offered no proof. In his preface Hoover did record his obligation to "those engineers with whom I have been associated for many years" and to "many friends" who responded to his queries, but he mentioned no names.

Another story about *Principles of Mining* comes to us from W. R. Ingalls, editor of the *Engineering and Mining Journal* from 1905 to 1919. Years later Ingalls stated that he arranged for Hoover to publish his manuscript with the new McGraw-Hill Book Company, with which he was associated. But when Hoover delivered his manuscript, it turned out (said Ingalls) to be in terrible shape in almost every respect (grammar, syntax, spelling, handwriting). Ingalls was obliged, so he later asserted, to edit it extensively.

When the galleys were ready Ingalls notified Hoover, only to discover that Hoover emphatically did not wish to do any proofreading! But, said Ingalls, your original manuscript was bad (whereupon Hoover grinned) and I have done considerable rewriting of it. But Hoover was adamant. He told Ingalls (so Ingalls recalled) that he would not criticize Ingalls's revisions, and he refused to examine the page proofs. The book thereupon went to press, unchecked by its own author.

Ingalls's story is contained in a letter to Hazel Lyman Nickels, August 28, 1949, and now in the Herbert Hoover Collection, Box 5, HI. Although I have found no confirmation of it, Ingalls did know Hoover for years, and his anecdote has a certain ring of authenticity. Hoover, for instance, was an erratic speller, and one can well imagine his refusal to sit down and read page proofs.

But Ingalls's memory in 1949 was imperfect. The Pre-Commerce Papers at HHPL contain a typescript copy of the *Principles of Mining* manuscript, complete with handwritten revisions made by Hoover himself. This, in fact, was the version that was published. So even if Ingalls corrected Hoover's original handwritten version, Hoover himself carefully scutinized the result (and made further alterations). And if Hoover did not read the proofs, his wife Lou Henry Hoover did—a fact that drains much of the dramatic force from Ingalls's story. Ingalls's own *Engineering and Mining Journal* 97 (March 14, 1914): 577, in fact, stated that *Mrs.* Hoover "revised the manuscript, read the proofs and saw the proofs through the press, remaining in New York for that purpose after Mr. Hoover had been called away." So Hoover was not nearly as casual about the process as Ingalls later remembered him to be.

39. "A Professional Speculator" [Hoover], "Investments and Speculations," *Mining Magazine* 1 (September 1909): 39–41. T. A. Rickard later identified Hoover as the author of this piece. Rickard, "A Chapter in Journalism," *Mining and Scientific Press* 120 (May 22, 1920): 754.

40. [Hoover], "Investments and Speculations," p. 39.

41. "A Professional Speculator" [Hoover], "Investments and Speculations II," *Mining Magazine* 1 (December 1909): 285.

42. Hoover, "Economics of a Boom" (letter to the editor), *Mining Magazine* 6 (May 1912): 370–73.

43. T. H. B. Mayne, letter to the editor, *Mining Magazine* 6 (June 1912): 433–34.

44. Hoover, *Principles of Mining*, p. 185.

45. Edwin T. Layton, Jr., *The Revolt of the Engineers: Social Responsibility and the American Engineering Profession* (Cleveland, 1971), p. 3.

46. Clark C. Spence, *Mining Engineers and the American West* (New Haven, 1970), p. 37, 40.

47. See Monte Calvert, *The Mechanical Engineer in America, 1830–1910: Professional Cultures in Conflict* (Baltimore, 1967).

48. Herbert Hoover, *The Memoirs of Herbert Hoover*, Volume I: *Years of Adventure* (New York, 1951), p. 131.

49. Hoover, *Principles of Mining*, p. 193.

50. Ibid., p. 186.

51. Ibid., pp. 186–92.

52. *Engineering and Mining Journal* 97 (March 14, 1914): 579.

53. Hoover, *Principles of Mining*, p. 193.

54. Hoover, *Years of Adventure*, p. 133.

55. The subject of Thorstein Veblen's possible influence on Herbert Hoover has been raised by some previous Hoover scholars. While it is certainly possible that Hoover read works by Veblen, I have found no evidence that he did so, nor any proof that Veblen had any distinctive impact on Hoover's thought. Hoover's use of the Veblenesque word "parasitic" to describe certain professions is interesting but not by itself conclusive.

56. Layton, *Revolt*, pp. 61, 65.

57. Hoover to Mary Austin, n.d., Mary Austin Papers, The Huntington Library, San Marino, California. This letter is printed (with spelling and grammatical corrections) in T. M. Pearce, ed., *Literary America, 1903–1934: The Mary Austin Letters* (Westport, Conn., 1979), pp. 88–89. Pearce believes that the letter was written in the spring of 1916; my own guess is that it was written before 1914.

58. David F. Noble, *America by Design: Science, Technology, and the Rise of Corporate Capitalism* (New York, 1977), pp. 27–28.

59. Hoover, "Training of Engineers," *Stanford Sequoia* 9 (October 6, 1899): 54–55.

60. Hoover, "The Training of the Mining Engineer," *Science* (n.s.) 20 (November 25, 1904): 716–19.

61. Hoover told David Starr Jordan that he prepared this memorandum, which C. Algernon Moreing presented on June 23, 1904 before a departmental committee of the Board of Education. Hoover sent the memorandum to Dr. Jordan along with a long covering letter on June 29; later he gave Jordan permission to use the memorandum as he wished. Jordan promptly sent it to the American journal *Science*. But when he did so, Jordan added at the end of the memorandum the four concluding paragraphs of Hoover's private letter of June 29. The memorandum thus expanded became the article in *Science*.

    Jordan's unauthorized adding of the four private paragraphs caused Hoover considerable anguish, as already mentioned in chapter 14.

    See Hoover to David Starr Jordan, June 29, 1904, David Starr Jordan Papers, Series I-A, Box 40, Stanford University Archives; Jordan to Hoover, July 16, 1904, ibid., Series I-AA, letter book #22; Hoover to Jordan, September 12, 1904, ibid., Series I-A, Box 41; Jordan to Hoover, October 3, 1904, ibid., Series I-AA, letter book #24; Jordan to Dr. J. M. K. Cattell (plus Hoover's expanded memo), October 3, 1904, ibid.

    For Moreing's testimony see Great Britain, Board of Education, Departmental Committee on Royal College of Science, etc., *Final Report of the Departmental Committee on the Royal College of Science, etc.*, Vol. II (Command Paper 2956: London, 1906), pp. 43–48.

62. For Bewick, Moreing's announcement of its scholarship program, see Institution of Mining and Metallurgy *Bulletin No. 3*, December 8, 1904, p. 9.

63. *Engineering and Mining Journal* 79 (January 26, 1905): 186–87; *West Australian Mining, Building, and Engineering Journal* 11 (March 7, 1908): 11.

64. Hoover to W. A. Carlyle, December 2, 1910, "Mining—Correspondence: Bloomfield, E. C.," Pre-Commerce Papers.
65. Hoover to Commander Charles Cunningham-Graham, April 28, 1911, "Mining—Correspondence: Cunningham-Graham, Charles," Pre-Commerce Papers.
66. Hoover, *Principles of Mining*, p. 192.
67. Hoover to Cunningham-Graham, April 28, 1911.
68. Hoover, *Principles of Mining*, p. 188.
69. Ibid., p. 185.
70. Ibid., p. 191; Hoover, "The Training of the Mining Engineer," p. 719.
71. Hoover, "The Training of the Mining Engineer," p. 719.
72. Hoover to Benjamin Ide Wheeler, January 15, 1915, "University of California," Pre-Commerce Papers.
73. Hoover, address to Engineers Club of San Francisco, February 12, 1914, Public Statements File, HHPL.
74. Hoover, *Principles of Mining*, p. 184.
75. Hoover to Wheeler, January 15, 1915.
76. Ibid.
77. Hoover, *Principles of Mining*, p. 167.
78. Hoover's comment is found in Georgius Agricola, *De Re Metallica: Translated from the First Latin Edition of 1556 . . . by Herbert Clark Hoover and Lou Henry Hoover* (London, 1912), p. 82n; hereinafter cited as *De Re Metallica* (Hoover translation).
79. Hoover, *Principles of Mining*, p. 168.
80. [Hoover], "Westralia's Mining Industry," *Financial Times*, February 1, 1904, p. 3. Hoover is identified as the author in the scrapbook cited in note 6.
81. Ibid.
82. Hoover, quoted in *Mining Journal, Railway and Commercial Gazette* 74 (July 18, 1903): 67.
83. Ibid.
84. Hoover, "West Australian Gold Mining in 1905," p. 136.
85. Hoover, *Principles of Mining*, pp. 167–68.
86. Ibid., p. 168.
87. Spence, *Mining Engineers and the American West*, p. 176; Layton, *Revolt*, pp. 67–68.
88. Hoover, *Principles of Mining*, p. 168.
89. Ibid., p. 165.
90. Ibid., p. 167.
91. Ibid., p. 161.
92. Ibid., p. 168.
93. Scott Turner oral history (1968), pp. 19–20, HHPL.
94. T. A. Rickard, "A Chapter in Journalism," *Mining and Scientific Press* 120 (May 22, 1920): 754–55.
95. Ibid., p. 750.
96. Turner oral history, p. 20.
97. T. A. and Edgar Rickard subscribed for all 10,000 shares of the *Mining Magazine*'s common stock. They also took 7,000 of the 13,000 issued shares of preferred stock; thirty mining engineers took the remaining 6,000 (Rickard, "A Chapter in Journalism," p. 754).

    Who were these thirty mining engineers? Rickard says only that they were "the leaders of the profession, including several Americans resident in London at that time" (p. 754). This almost certainly included Hoover. The Scott Turner oral history states that the understanding among Hoover's friends was that Hoover would help to finance the venture but that no influence was to be exerted on Rickard's policies (p. 20).
98. Rickard, "A Chapter in Journalism," p. 755.
99. This account of the founding of the *Mining Magazine* is based on the Rickard article and Turner oral history already cited. W. J. Loring also stated that Hoover was much involved with financing the journal. Loring interview, 1931, Liggett Papers.
100. Hoover, "The Training of the Mining Engineer," p. 719.

101. For information on Agricola and his writings see the Hoovers' Introduction in *De Re Metallica* (Hoover translation), pp. v–xvii.

102. Ibid., p. xiii; Hoover, *Years of Adventure*, p. 117 (wherein *De Re Metallica* is described as "the first important attempt to assemble systematically in print the world-knowledge on mining, metallurgy, and industrial chemistry"). See also the interview with Hoover in *Invitation to Learning* 1 (Summer 1951): 117–21. According to Hoover there was "no complete work of this sort" (that is, no comprehensive book solely on mining and metallurgy) written by ancient authors (p. 119). Moreover, Agricola "represented the point of revolution from the whole vacant period of the Middle Ages into what subsequently became modern industry" (p. 123).

    For Hoover's estimate of the various contributions of Agricola's predecessors see *De Re Metallica* (Hoover translation), pp. 606–15.

103. *De Re Metallica* (Hoover translation), p. xiv.

104. Ibid., p. ii.

105. Hoover, *Years of Adventure*, p. 117; Hoover to Mrs. Henry R. Luce, April 27, 1948, Post-Presidental Individual File, HHPL.

106. On translation problems, see *De Re Metallica* (Hoover translation), pp. i–ii, and Hoover, *Years of Adventure*, pp. 117–18.

107. Lou Henry Hoover to John C. Branner, December 28 [1906], Branner Papers, Box 38.

108. In her letter to Branner Mrs. Hoover said that her greatest problem thus far was inability to locate a copy of the *De Re Metallica* for sale!

109. *Mining and Scientific Press* 106 (March 8, 1913): 399.

110. Hoover, *Years of Adventure*, p. 118.

111. Ibid., p. 117. Hoover withdrew from a German course that he was flunking in his senior year at Stanford. See chapter 3.

112. Ibid., p. 117.

113. The following discussion of the process by which the Hoovers prepared *De Re Metallica* is based primarily on documents in the Agricola Collection, HHPL. This collection contains Hoover correspondence with translators and publishers, typescript translations of the *De Re Metallica* and other texts, and various other materials. A useful, detailed account of the Hoovers' preparation of their opus is contained in James W. Althouse, "The Hoover Translation of *De Re Metallica*: A Role for the History of Technology in Engineering Education, circa 1913" (unpublished paper, ca. 1978), Reprint File, HHPL.

114. See Douglas Kennedy to Hoover, December 5, 1908, "Correspondence, 1908–1912," and the "Correspondence—Translators" files for Edmund Nolan, H. Kielmann, and Kathleen Schlesinger, all in Agricola Collection.

115. See "Correspondence—Translators: Schlesinger, Miss Kathleen," Agricola Collection; Althouse, "Hoover Translation," pp. 12–13, 21.

116. Schlesinger to Hoover, October 19, 1910, November 24, 1910, and January 6, 1911, in her file already cited; Macmillan and Co., Ltd., to Hoover, November 24, 1910, "Correspondence, 1908–1912," Agricola Collection.

117. There is no evidence that Hoover's decision to expand the dimensions of his project was a sudden one. But the evolution from a simple translation to a "contribution to scholarship" was a discernible one; on this point see Althouse, "Hoover Translation," pp. 14–16, 35–36. Hoover's decision, incidentally, forced him to defer his publication date.

118. Schlesinger to Hoover, April 19, 1911, "Correspondence—Translators: Schlesinger, Miss Kathleen," Agricola Collection. Eventually, in late 1911–early 1912, Schlesinger translated most of *De Natura Fossilium* for Hoover.

119. "Hover" (that is, Hoover), advertisement in *The Times*, June 14, 1911, p. 17, June 15, 1911, p. 15, and June 16, 1911, p. 16.

120. The three were Schlesinger and two others hired as a result of Hoover's advertisement. For their assignments see Althouse, "Hoover Translation," pp. 16–18.

121. A number of translated extracts are in the Agricola Collection.

122. Hoover, *Years of Adventure*, p. 118.
123. See Hoover to C. C. Morewood, October 26, 1911, "Correspondence—Translators: More-wood, Miss C. C."; Schlesinger to Hoover, January 6 and 10, 1911, and May 19, 1911, "Correspondence—Translators: Schlesinger, Kathleen"; all in Agricola Collection. In 1913 Theodore Hoover stated that the *De Re Metallica* was translated for the Hoovers by a Latin scholar whose free translation proved incomprehensible and then twice more by other Latinists. Theodore was probably referring to drafts that the Hoovers, with their knowl-edge of mining and mining terminology, could then integrate with their own translation. See Theodore Hoover, note dated February 7, 1913, facsimile in appendix to May Brad-ford Shockley oral history (1970), HHPL.
124. Hoover, *Years of Adventure*, p. 118.
125. Shockley oral history, p. 15.
126. See Hoover to H. E. Browning, July 14, 1911, "Correspondence—Translators: Browning, Miss H. E.," Agricola Collection.
127. The Hoovers to Professor Henry S. Munroe, April 9, 1913, "De Re Metallica," Pre-Commerce Papers.
128. Hoover, *Years of Adventure*, p. 118.
129. Ibid.
130. Herbert Hoover (not Lou) was responsible for the footnotes. *De Re Metallica* (Hoover translation), p. ii. The Latin original, incidentally, had no footnotes.

  Years later certain anti-Hoover polemicists suggested that Hoover did not really trans-late *De Re Metallica*, that hired professional translators did it for him but that he reaped the glory. It is certainly true that the Hoovers had considerable assistance. It is also true that they did not acknowledge by name the aid of their several researcher / translators, except for Schlesinger, who was praised for her compilation of a bibliography of Agricola's writ-ings (Appendix A). The Hoovers did, however, acknowledge "those whom we have engaged from time to time for one service or another, chiefly bibliographical work and collateral translation" (p. iii). On the other hand, in his *Memoirs* Hoover did not mention his assist-ants at all.

  Still, as my text indicates, the central accomplishment—synthesis—was the Hoovers' alone. No perusal of the files in the Agricola Collection will sustain the notion that the Hoovers were passive, secondary figures, appropriating the fruits of others' labors. Instead, they were thoroughly immersed in their avocation every step of the way. The preparation of a rough translation of the Latin text was but the first step of a long, painstaking process. The creation of a finished product from the welter of imperfect translations and esoteric data was a very creditable achievement: the Hoovers' achievement.
131. See Hoover's detailed memorandum to one of his employees, August 1912, "Correspon-dence, 1908–1912," Agricola Collection.
132. The publication date on the title page is 1912, but proofs were still being read in late December and no copy seems to have been available for distribution until the beginning of February 1913.
133. Hoover to Mrs. Henry R. Luce, April 27, 1948; Hoover, *Years of Adventure*, pp. 118–19. See also William R. Castle, "The Hoover Translation of Agricola's *De Re Metallica*," *The Colophon*, no. 14 (June 1933): 6–7 (full article: 1–8).
134. *De Re Metallica* (Hoover translation), p. iii.
135. Edgar Rickard, Publisher's Note, November 1913, in *The Book that made Agricola famous* (publisher's pamphlet about the Hoover translation), p. 3, copy in Louis B. Lochner Papers, Box 30, State Historical Society of Wisconsin; Hoover, *Years of Adventure*, p. 119.
136. Theodore said it cost over £4,000, or over $20,000 at the pre-war exchange rate. Theodore Hoover note, February 7, 1913. A comparable expenditure today would well exceed $100,000.
137. The Rickards collected many of these tributes in their pamphlet cited in note 135. This pamphlet includes copies of book reviews as well as extracts from letters of appreciation

sent to Hoover by grateful recipients of presentation copies. See also the review in *American Historical Review* 19 (April 1914): 598–99.

138. "The Hoover Dinner," *Engineering and Mining Journal* 97 (March 14, 1914): 577–79.

139. In 1951 a prominent American historian declared that after forty years the Hoovers' work "stands up magnificently, and is a contribution of the first importance to history." John U. Nef, quoted in *Invitation to Learning* 1 (Summer 1951): 117.

　　In 1950 Dover Publications, Inc. of New York published an inexpensive reprint of the Hoovers' translation.

140. *Engineering and Mining Journal* 95 (February 22, 1913): 436.

141. *De Re Metallica* (Hoover translation), pp. 53n, 86n.

142. Schlesinger reminded him of it in 1913, but there is no evidence that Hoover did anything about it. Schlesinger to Hoover, October 15, 1913, "Correspondence—Translators: Schlesinger, Miss Kathleen," Agricola Collection.

143. In 1913 she asked Hoover for permission to finish this translation (ibid.).

144. Hoover to A. B. Parsons, October 7, 1942, "American Institute of Mining and Metallurgical Engineers," Post-Presidential Subject File, HHPL.

145. Hoover to Schlesinger, June 17, 1914, "Correspondence—Translators: Schlesinger, Miss Kathleen," Agricola Collection.

146. Hoover to Schlesinger, September 9, 1914, ibid.

147. It is now housed in the Norman F. Sprague Memorial Library at Harvey Mudd College. See David Kuhner, "The Herbert Hoover Collection: A Gift and a Story," *Honnold Library Record* [Claremont Colleges] 12 (Spring 1971): 1–5.

148. *Mining Magazine* 7 (February 1913): 148.

149. "The Hoover Dinner," p. 579; Hoover speech, March 9, 1914, printed in the *Bulletin of the Mining and Metallurgical Society of America* 7 (June 30, 1914): 104 (full text: 99–104). In this speech Hoover said that it had been his "underlying hope" that his *De Re Metallica* translation

　　would recall to our profession the long service that our folk have been to humanity, and that its production would stimulate a pride of our calling, in its history and traditions, and make for its ideals.

　　Our professional ideals have not hitherto received that stimulus from our history which they might have had. From the ideals of any profession must arise the real service which that profession and its members will perform to the community and to the race.

150. *De Re Metallica* (Hoover translation), p. iii. Incidentally, Book I of *De Re Metallica* is an apologia for mining as a useful profession and "a calling of peculiar dignity."

151. Said Hoover in 1951: "This [translation] was a contribution to the history of a great profession. As such, it has certain inspirational values to the profession." *Invitation to Learning* 1 (Summer 1951): 123.

152. *De Re Metallica* (Hoover translation), p. xiv.

C H A P T E R　2 4

1. Herbert Hoover, *The Memoirs of Herbert Hoover*, Volume I: *Years of Adventure* (New York, 1951), p. 124.

2. Ibid.

3. Theodore J. Hoover, *Memoranda: Being a Statement by an Engineer* (typescript: Stanford University, 1939), p. 153, copy at HHPL; E. D. Adams, "Snap Shots of Herbert Hoover" (typescript, 1929), p. 6, E. D. Adams Papers, Box 5, Stanford University Archives.

4. Hulda Hoover McLean statement, October 20, 1964, on the death of her uncle, Herbert Hoover, in General Accessions—Hulda Hoover McLean, HHPL; Hulda Hoover McLean

oral history (1967), p. 9, HHPL; Victoria French Allen oral history (1967–68), pp. 23–24, HHPL. For more accounts of Hoover's stream damming, see Hugh Gibson to his mother, November 11, 1917 and April 25, 1920, Hugh Gibson Papers, HI, and George Barr Baker to Hugh Gibson, June 3, 1921, George Barr Baker Papers, Box 3, HI.

5. Theodore Hoover, *Memoranda*, p. 153.
6. Mary Austin, *Earth Horizon* (Boston and New York, 1932), p. 312.
7. Hoover Calendar, HHPL; David Starr Jordan, *The Days of a Man* (Yonkers-on-Hudson, N.Y., 1922), II, pp. 328–30.
8. Hoover Calendar, HHPL; Ray Lyman Wilbur, "Herbert Hoover: A Personal Sketch" (unpublished paper, May 1920), p. 14, Reprint File, HHPL. For another dramatic episode on this trip see Hoover's tribute to Wilbur in *The Memoirs of Ray Lyman Wilbur* (Stanford, California, 1960), pp. v–vi.
9. Hoover Calendar, HHPL; Lou Henry Hoover to John C. Branner, October 15, 1909, John C. Branner Papers, Box 40, Stanford University Archives; Hoover, *Years of Adventure*, p. 122.
10. Hoover Calendar, HHPL; Mildred Hoover Willis (Theodore's daughter) oral history (1971), p. 4, HHPL; Hoover, *Years of Adventure*, p. 122.
11. Clark C. Spence, *Mining Engineers and the American West* (New Haven, 1970), p. 336.
12. Adams, "Snap Shots," pp. 4–8.
13. Payson J. Treat oral history (1967), p. 3, HHPL.
14. Adams, "Snap Shots," p. 4.
15. *Brooklyn Daily Eagle*, August 19, 1928.
16. Theodore Hoover, *Memoranda*, p. 153; Adams, "Snap Shots," pp. 4–5.
17. Adams, "Snap Shots," p. 5.
18. Hoover Calendar, HHPL; Hoover, *Years of Adventure*, pp. 122–123.
19. Hoover Calendar, HHPL.
20. Theodore Hoover, *Memoranda*, pp. 149–50, 154.
21. Ibid., p. 149.
22. Mildred Hoover Willis oral history, p. 3.
23. Theodore Hoover, *Memoranda*, p. 154. A number of programs for plays that the Hoovers evidently attended are preserved in the Hoover Scrapbooks, Album 51, HHPL.
24. Victoria French Allen, *The Outside Man* (typescript, n.d.), p. 87, copy at HHPL; "Aims of the Shakespeare International Alliance" (n.d.), Hoover Scrapbooks, Album 51; Hoover to W. A. M. Goode, October 14, 1913, "Panama-Pacific International Exposition: Correspondence—Goode, W. A. M.," Pre-Commerce Papers, HHPL. The actor was Sir Frank R. Benson. For him and his wife's friendship with the Hoovers, see Lady Constance Benson, *Mainly Players: Bensonian Memories* (London, 1926), pp. 274–75.
25. Hoover, *Years of Adventure*, p. 122. Album 51 of the Hoover Scrapbooks at HHPL contains numerous programs for plays performed by the F. R. Benson Shakespearean Company at Stratford-on-Avon, U.K. in August 1913.
26. See letters of notification in "Memberships, Undated—1914," Pre-Commerce Papers.
27. A search of Quaker records in London has turned up no evidence of Hoover involvement with British Quakers before World War I. Letter from Malcolm Thomas, Religious Society of Friends, Friends House, London, to the author, August 31, 1979. In 1928 the eminent American Quaker Rufus Jones wrote: "Herbert Hoover has not had much direct contact with Friends during the strenuous years since he left Oregon to study in Leland Stanford University at Palo Alto, California." *The Friend* [London] 68 (October 19, 1928): 921–22. In the Hoover Scrapbooks, Album 51, at HHPL there is a program for evensong at St. Paul's Cathedral, London, on Christmas night, 1904. Hoover may have attended this service, but one cannot be sure.
28. Edgar Rickard to E. O. Heyl, May 11, 1920, "Religion—Hoover's, 1920," Pre-Commerce Papers.
29. Hulda Hoover McLean, "A Conservative's Crusades for Good Government," an oral his-

tory conducted 1976, Regional Oral History Office, University of California, Berkeley, 1977, p. 4. Courtesy, The Bancroft Library. For a further glimpse of Theodore Hoover's religious beliefs, see *Memoranda*, p. 12.

30. Hoover, quoted in Preston Wolfe oral history (1967), p. 33, HHPL.

31. For descriptions of the Red House, see: David Starr Jordan, "Random Recollections of Herbert Hoover," *Stanford Illustrated Review* 29 (April 1928): 363; *Brooklyn Daily Eagle*, August 19, 1928; article by Newton B. Knox in *Sunday Oregonian* (Portland), February 17, 1929, Section II, p. 14; Victoria French Allen, "Some Pages from Hoover History" (clipping, n.d.), Benjamin S. Allen Papers, Box 1, HI; Victoria French Allen, *The Outside Man*, p. 36; E. D. Adams, "Snap Shots," p. 2; Hoover, *Years of Adventure*, p. 129; Victoria French Allen oral history (1967–68), p. 21, HHPL; *Survey of London*, volume 37: *Northern Kensington* (London: Greater London Council, 1973), pp. 71–72.

32. As of December 1909 rent for the Red House was £106.5.10 per quarter, or about £425 (more than $2,000) per year. Joseph Ramsden to Lou Henry Hoover, December 28, 1909, "Mining—Red House," Pre-Commerce Papers. See also the other correspondence in this file.

33. Ellen Hunt to Lou Henry Hoover, July 5, 1910 (mentions the Hoover chauffeur, R. Phillpott), copy in "Finding Aid: Hoover Homes—London, England," HHPL; *Brooklyn Daily Eagle*, August 19, 1928; John Dunn to Hoover, October 27, 1928, "General Correspondence: Dunn-Dz," Pre-Presidential Papers, HHPL; *New York Times*, November 9, 1928, p. 6; Hoover, *Years of Adventure*, p. 129.

34. *New York Sun*, November 9, 1928 (article about Dunn).

35. Dunn to Hoover, October 27, 1928.

36. Hoover, *Years of Adventure*, p. 129.

37. Jordan, *Days of a Man*, II, p. 327; Jordan, "Random Recollections," p. 363; *Brooklyn Daily Eagle*, August 19, 1928; Newton B. Knox article in *Sunday Oregonian*, February 17, 1929; Adams, "Snap Shots," p. 3; Allen, "Some Pages from Hoover History"; Allen, *The Outside Man*, pp. 35–37; Austin, *Earth Horizon*, pp. 311–12.

38. Allen, "Some Pages from Hoover History."

39. Theodore Hoover, *Memoranda*, p. 151.

40. *Brooklyn Daily Eagle*, August 19, 1928; Allen, "Some Pages from Hoover History."

41. Allen oral history, p. 5.

42. May Bradford Shockley oral history (1970), pp. 10, 11, HHPL; May Bradford Shockley, quoted in John Kelly Burfton, "Profile: May Bradford Shockley," *Stanford Alumi Almanac* (March 1977), pp. 12–13.

43. Lady Benson, *Mainly Players*, p. 274.

44. Hulda Hoover McLean oral history (1967), pp. 17, 27, HHPL.

45. Jordan, *Days of a Man*, II, p. 327; Adams, "Snap Shots," p. 3.

46. Frederick Palmer, "Mrs. Hoover Knows," *Ladies' Home Journal* 46 (March 1929): 242.

47. Lady Benson, *Mainly Players*, p. 275.

48. Shockley oral history, p. 1.

49. Dunn to Hoover, October 27, 1928; *New York Sun*, November 9, 1928; Louise Hoover Stevenson (Theodore's daughter) oral history (1970), pp. 4–5, HHPL.

50. Dunn to Hoover, October 27, 1928; Newton B. Knox article in *Sunday Oregonian*, February 17, 1929.

51. Newton B. Knox article in *Sunday Oregonian*, February 17, 1929.

52. Allen, "Some Pages from Hoover History" and *The Outside Man*, p. 36.

53. Mildred Hoover Willis oral history, pp. 4, 5.

54. Ibid., p. 4.

55. Theodore Hoover, *Memoranda*, p. 267.

56. Hulda Hoover McLean oral history (1976), p. 8.

57. Hoover, foreword to Arthur Beeby-Thompson, *Black Gold: The Story of An Oil Pioneer* (New York, 1961), p. 7; Hoover, *Years of Adventure*, pp. 135–36.

58. Hoover Calendar, HHPL.
59. Ibid. One of the Hoover calendar compilations states erroneously that he visisted the United States in 1908 (in December). In fact, he did not arrive until January 1, 1909.
60. Ibid. This happened in 1909, 1911, and 1914.
61. Hoover to George J. Bancroft, March 27, 1911, quoted in Hoover Calendar, HHPL.
62. Hoover Calendar, HHPL.
63. Mark L. Requa, "Hoover the Man" (typescript, January 15, 1919), Mark L. Requa Collection, Western History Research Center, University of Wyoming.
64. Hoover Calendar, HHPL; *New York Sun*, January 23, 1920, p. 1.
65. At least not between 1906 and 1920. George Barr Baker memorandum, May 21, 1920, "Citizenship," Pre-Commerce Papers.
66. Hoover to Ralph Arnold, August 25, 1910, Ralph Arnold Collection, Box 22, The Huntington Library, San Marino, California.
67. Hoover, *Years of Adventure*, p. 120.
68. Hoover Calendar, HHPL; "Memberships, Undated—1914," Pre-Commerce Papers.
69. Allen, "Some Pages from Hoover History."
70. Hoover Calendar, HHPL.
71. Adams, "Snap Shots," p. 13.
72. Hoover to George J. Bancroft, 1912, "Bancroft, George J.," Pre-Commerce Papers.
73. Herbert Hoover, *Principles of Mining* (New York, 1909), p. 163.
74. Ibid.
75. Ibid., pp. 164–65. On p. 164 Hoover printed a set of statistics demonstrating, in his judgment, the influence of "inherent intelligence" among various groups of workers. According to his statistics, mines manned by American laborers were much more cost-efficient than mines manned by Australians (the next best group), Indians, South African blacks, and Chinese imported into South Africa.
76. Hoover, *Years of Adventure*, p. 66.
77. Hoover, speech draft, n.d., in "China—Commercial Prospects in," Pre-Commerce Papers. Although this typewritten document is unsigned, it is initialed "HH" at the end, and internal evidence establishes to my satisfaction that Hoover was the author. The speech was probably prepared sometime between 1911 and the mid-1920s. See Hoover, *Years of Adventure*, pp. 65–72, for a similar expression of his views on China.
78. Hoover, speech draft on China.
79. Hoover, *Years of Adventure*, p. 70.
80. Hoover, speech draft on China.
81. Hoover, *Years of Adventure*, p. 125.
82. Adams, "Snap Shots," p. 12.
83. Ibid., p. 11; Hoover, *Years of Adventure*, pp. 126–27.
84. Hoover, *Years of Adventure*, p. 132.
85. Ibid., p. 127.
86. Adams, "Snap Shots," p. 12.
87. Anne Martin and Mary Austin interviews, 1931, Walter W. Liggett Papers, New York Public Library.
88. Adams, "Snap Shots," p. 12.
89. Allen, "Some Pages from Hoover History."
90. Allen, *The Outside Man*, p. 98.
91. C. T. Hallinan to a Mr. Colebaugh, January 7, 1931, copy in "Rickard Files: Statements and Affidavits," Misrepresentations File, HHPL.
92. Beeby-Thompson, *Black Gold*, p. 92. In his *Memoirs* Hoover noted the British upper class's opposition to the American system of universal free education. *Years of Adventure*, p. 127.
93. Adams, "Snap Shots," pp. 20–21.
94. Hoover, *Years of Adventure*, p. 124.
95. Hoover, *Addresses upon the American Road, 1945–1948* (New York, 1949), p. 77.

96. Anne Martin interview, Liggett Papers.
97. Professor Guido Marx, unpublished autobiography (ca. 1941), Stanford University section, p. 89, Guido Marx Papers, Box 2, Stanford University Archives.
98. Adams, "Snap Shots," p. 24.
99. Anne Martin and Mary Austin interviews, Liggett Papers. See also Ralph Arnold to Hoover, August 11, 1910, Arnold Collection, Box 22.
100. Mary Austin interview, Liggett Papers.
101. The guest was evidently Henry Rolfe, a professor of Greek at Stanford University (Guido Marx, unpublished autobiography, Stanford University section, p. 86).
102. James Deitrick to Hoover, Setpember 12, 1914, James Deitrick Papers, Department of Special Collections, Manuscripts Division, Stanford University Libraries. There is no reply by Hoover in this collection or in Hoover's own papers.
103. Arnold to Hoover, August 11, 1910.
104. Hoover cable to Arnold, August 25, 1910, Arnold Collection, Box 22.
105. Hoover to Arnold, August 25, 1910, ibid.
106. *Mining Magazine* 3 (September 1910): 164; Ralph Arnold to Hoover, September 7, 1910, Arnold Collection, Box 22. See also Arnold's unsent draft of a letter to President Taft, n.d., Arnold Collection, Box 24.
107. Hoover to Arnold, September 20, 1910, Arnold Collection, Box 22.
108. David Starr Jordan to Charles D. Norton, October 7, 1910, quoted in Henry F. Pringle, *The Life and Times of William Howard Taft* (New York, 1939), p. 614.
109. Norton to Jordan, October 14, 1910, quoted in ibid.
110. Mary Austin interview, Liggett Papers; Guido Marx, unpublished autobiography, Stanford University section, p. 87.
111. Ray Lyman Wilbur to David Starr Jordan, June 5, 1913, David Starr Jordan Papers, Series I-A, Box 90, Stanford University Archives. Wilbur was staying in the same New York hotel as Hoover, who was about to leave for London. Hoover to E. D. Adams, May 28, 1913, Adams Papers, Box 1.
112. Jordan's letter of June 9, 1913 has not been found but is summarized in a memorandum in the Woodrow Wilson Papers, Reel 237, Library of Congress. See also Wilson to Jordan, June 11, 1913, ibid. President Wilson promised to "bear in mind" Jordan's suggestion about Hoover. Jordan sent Hoover a copy of President Wilson's reply. This copy is in "Jordan, David Starr," Pre-Commerce Papers.
113. Will Irwin, *The Making of a Reporter* (New York, 1942), pp. 182–83.

CHAPTER 25

1. The capacity to do this was Hoover's definition of "executive ability." Hoover, lecture to Stanford University engineering students, quoted in *Daily Palo Alto* [Stanford University student newspaper], February 5, 1909, p. 4. In *Principles of Mining* Hoover used slightly different wording to define executive ability: "that capacity to coordinate and command the best results from other men" (p. 186).
2. David Starr Jordan, commencement address to the Stanford class of 1905; printed in *Stanford Alumnus* 6 (June 1905): 16–18.
3. Jordan to Hoover, May 12, 1905, "Stanford—David Starr Jordan," Pre-Commerce Papers, HHPL.
4. Hoover to John C. Branner, n.d., John C. Branner Papers, Box 38, Stanford University Archives.
5. Hoover telegram to Branner, May 5, 1910, Branner Papers, Box 42. See also Hoover to R. A. F. Penrose, Jr., April 29, 1910, printed in Helen R. Fairbanks and Charles P. Berkey, *Life and Letters of R. A. F. Penrose, Jr.* (New York, 1952), p. 160.

6. Payson J. Treat oral history (1967), p. 4, HHPL. See also Treat to Hoover, October 10, 1907, Payson J. Treat Papers, Box 1, HI.

7. Treat oral history, pp. 4–5; Treat to Hoover (plus enclosure), June 7, 1908, "Stanford—Books, Money For," Pre-Commerce Papers.

8. E. D. Adams to Hoover, September 8, 1908, E. D. Adams Papers, Box 1, Stanford University Archives.

9. The gift was originally a loan made in 1912. See W. E. Caldwell (secretary, Stanford University Board of Trustees) to Hoover, February 6, 1912, "Stanford—Book Collection—China," Pre-Commerce Papers; Hoover to E. D. Adams, March 5, 1912, George E. Crothers Papers, Stanford University Archives; E. D. Adams to Hoover, May 8, 1912, Adams Papers, Box 1; Hoover to Vanderlynn Stow, April 23, 1913, and W. E. Caldwell to Hoover, May 27, 1913, both in Board of Trustees Supporting Documents, May 23, 1913 folder, Stanford University Archives.

10. Treat oral history, p. 1.

11. Ibid., p. 2.

12. Branner to Hoover, August 29, 1908, Branner Papers, Box 7.

13. Jordan to George E. Crothers, September 14, 1908, David Starr Jordan Papers, Series I—AA, letter book #50, Stanford University Archives. See also Branner to Hoover, September 17, 1908, Branner Papers, Box 7.

14. Hoover to Branner, October 20, 1908, Branner Papers, Box 40.

15. Branner to Lou Henry Hoover, March 18, 1907, Branner Papers, Box 6.

16. Stanford University Board of Trustees Minutes, September 5, 1908, Stanford University Archives.

17. *Daily Palo Alto*, January 14, 1909; Hoover Calendar, HHPL.

18. On Stanford's early liquor problem and the crisis of 1908 see Orrin Leslie Elliott, *Stanford University: The First Twenty-five Years* (Stanford, 1937), pp. 379–407.

19. Hoover, nineteen-page handwritten manuscript of a speech on the subject "Stanford 14 years after," February 1909, filed in "Stanford—Academic and Financial Position, 1913–1914," Pre-Commerce Papers. At the top of the first page of this manuscript is the heading, evidently in Hoover's hand: "Notes by HH on University [undecipherable] 1913." I suspect that Hoover dated this (in fact, mistakenly dated it) much later, for the internal evidence is persuasive that this speech was written in 1909, not 1913. "Stanford 14 years after" seems clearly to mean fourteen years after his graduation in 1895. Hoover's discussion of student discontent, disciplinary procedures, etc. seems clearly to refer to the crisis of early 1908. There was no such crisis in 1912–13, nor was the subject of student-faculty friction a burning one then. Finally, Hoover indicates in the speech that he is leaving in twelve hours after a three-week stay on campus—the approximate length of his stay in 1909. I conclude that this speech was prepared for delivery—probably to a faculty group (the internal evidence suggests this)—around February 9, 1909.

20. Treat oral history, pp. 6–7; "Planning the Stanford Union," *Stanford Alumnus* 10 (May 1909): 339 [full text: 338–42].

21. *Daily Palo Alto*, February 2, 1909, p. 1.

22. *Daily Palo Alto*, February 3, 1909, p. 2.

23. "Planning the Stanford Union," pp. 338–42.

24. E. D. Adams to George E. Crothers, February 10, 1909, Ray Lyman Wilbur Papers (Personal), Box 78, Stanford University Archives.

25. Hoover, lecture to Stanford engineering students, quoted in *Daily Palo Alto*, February 5, 1909, p. 4.

26. Adams to Hoover, May 17, 1910, Adams Papers, Box 1.

27. *Daily Palo Alto*, February 2, 1909, p. 1; Hoover to Adams, June 3, 1910, Adams Papers, Box 1; Hoover to R. W. Barrett, October 6, 1910, George E. Crothers Papers; *Stanford Alumnus* 12 (November 1910): 79–81.

28. *Stanford Alumnus* 14 (September 1912): 17.

29. Stanford Union brochure, n.d. (ca. August 1909), enclosed with R. W. Barrett to John C. Branner, September 1, 1909, Branner Papers, Box 41.

30. Hoover to Adams, October 19, 1909, Adams Papers, Box 1. Hoover said that he and his friends had not yet determined their respective proportions of the $10,000 pledge.

31. See. R. W. Barrett to Hoover, October 19, 1910, "Stanford—Union, 1910," Pre-Commerce Papers; Hoover to E. D. Adams, May 1, 1912, Adams Papers, Box 1; and Hoover's correspondence with Everett W. Smith, 1913–14, "Stanford—Union," Pre-Commerce Papers.

32. *Stanford Alumnus* 14 (September 1912): 17–18, and 14 (October 1912): 41–42; Hoover to Everett W. Smith, September 27, 1912, "Stanford—Union, 1912," Pre-Commerce Papers.

33. *Daily Palo Alto*, September 11, 1912, p. 1.

34. Elliott, *Stanford University*, pp. 142–43.

35. Ibid., p. 143; Hoover to Ray Lyman Wilbur, February 28, 1920, Wilbur Papers (Personal), Box 36; Wilbur to Hoover, August 28, 1920, "Stanford—Union," Pre-Commerce Papers; Hoover, *The Memoirs of Herbert Hoover*, Volume I: *Years of Adventure* (New York, 1951), p. 120. Hoover evidently paid over 40% of the total cost of building the Student Union.

36. This at least was the view of Hoover's good friend on the faculty, Professor E. D. Adams. See Adams to Hoover, November 19, 1912, Adams Papers, Box 1.

37. Henry Rolfe to Guido Marx, August 14, 1912, quoted in Professor Guido Marx's unpublished autobiography (ca. 1941), Stanford University section, pp. 86–87, Guido Marx Papers, Box 2, Stanford University Archives.

38. Hoover Calendar, HHPL.

39. *Stanford Alumnus* 14 (December 1912): 125.

40. John Barneson to Hoover, October 29, 1912, "Mining—Correspondence: Barneson, John," Pre-Commerce Papers.

41. Stanford University Board of Trustees Minutes, November 29, 1912. Hoover remained a trustee until 1961, when he became a trustee emeritus.

42. *Stanford Alumnus* 14 (December 1912): 126.

43. Ibid., p. 127.

44. Hoover Calendar, HHPL. During this period he made two cross-country trips to New York.

45. Hoover to Adams, n.d. (late 1912), Adams Papers, Box 1.

46. Jordan to Hoover, December 3, 1912, Series I-A, Box 84.

47. Hoover to W. Mayo Newhall, January 2, 1913, "Stanford—Academic and Financial Position, 1913–1914," Pre-Commerce Papers.

48. Hoover, "Memorandum Prepared for Trustees on General Position and Circulated January 2, 1913," in "Stanford—Academic and Financial Position, 1913–1914," Pre-Commerce Papers. A copy of the part of the memorandum labeled "The Present Position" is in the John C. Branner Presidential Papers, Box 5, Stanford University Archives.

49. Hoover to Frank B. Anderson, January 2, 1913, "Stanford—Academic and Financial Position, 1913–1914," Pre-Commerce Papers.

50. Stanford University Board of Trustees Minutes, January 3, 1913.

51. See Hoover to Leon Sloss, May 20, 1913, Board of Trustees Supporting Documents, May 23, 1913 folder.

52. Stanford University Board of Trustees Minutes, April 25, 1913.

53. Jordan to Hoover, December 3, 1912.

54. After the 1908 disturbances there were demands that Jordan leave. Elliott, *Stanford University*, p. 404. In 1910 at least one trustee considered him a negative influence and wished that he would give up executive work. George E. Crothers to Nathan Abbott, July 6, 1910, copy in Orrin Leslie Elliott Papers, Box 3, Stanford Unversity Archives.

55. Elliott, *Stanford University*, pp. 557–58.

56. Hoover to Jordan, April 30, 1913, Jordan Papers, Series I-A, Box 88.

57. Hoover to Jordan, May 9, 1913, Jordan Papers, Series I-A, Box 89; copy in Board of Trustees Supporting Documents, May 23, 1913 folder.

58. Jordan to Hoover, May 11, 1913, Board of Trustees Supporting Documents, May 23, 1913 folder.

59. Jordan to Edith M. Jordan, May 15, 1913, Jordan Papers, Series I-A, Box 89; Jordan, *The Days of a Man* (Yonkers-on-Hudson, N.Y., 1922), II, p. 455. In this latter source, his autobiography, Jordan stated that it was at Hoover's "instance" that the change in Jordan's position came about. The contemporary documents convey the same impression: that Hoover took the initiative.

60. Jordan to Edith Jordan, May 15, 1913.

61. Hoover to Jordan, May 9, 1913.

62. Jordan to Hoover, May 12, 1913, Board of Trustees Supporting Documents, May 23, 1913 folder.

63. Branner to Hoover, May 16, 1913; Branner telegram to Hoover, May 17, 1913; both in Branner Papers, Box 10.

64. A copy of some of Hoover's resolutions, in the form of a memorandum dated by Hoover May 13, 1913, is in the Board of Trustees Supporting Documents, May 23, 1913 folder. See also Hoover to the trustees' University Committee, n.d. (ca. May 19–21, 1913), ibid. For the resolutions as passed, see Stanford Univeristy Board of Trustees Minutes, May 23, 1913.

    Jordan did not get all he initially desired. He wanted the chancellor, when present, to outrank the president at public functions. In their formal statement of the chancellor's duties the trustees said nothing about his rank. Jordan also asked that the chancellor be a member of the faculty's Academic Council and a member of the executive committee of the Council. The trustees' resolution was silent on this point. The trustees did grant Jordan's wish to be entitled to attend board meetings. In short, Jordan initially seemed to desire a continuing role in academic policy; the trustees moved to deprive him of it. He could only "advise and cooperate" on subjects determined by the trustees or the president.

65. Jordan to Branner, May 18, 1913, Branner Papers, Box 48.

66. Jordan to Lou Henry Hoover, March 7, 1916, David Starr Jordan Papers, HI.

67. Hoover to Jordan, May 9, 1913; Jordan to Hoover, May 11, 1913.

68. *San Francisco Bulletin*, May 19, 1913, pp. 1, 2.

69. Jordan, *Days of a Man*, II, pp. 456–58.

70. Jordan to Branner, May 18, 1913.

71. Jordan to Branner, May 23, 1913, Jordan Papers, Series I-A, Box 89.

72. See "Resolutions Drafted by H. C. Hoover and Carried at Meeting of the Trustees, May 23rd 1913" (typescript), in "Stanford—Academic and Financial Position, 1913–1914," Pre-Commerce Papers.

73. For example, the committee on the gymnasium. See Hoover to Leon Sloss, May 20, 1913.

74. "Resolutions Drafted by H. C. Hoover . . . May 23rd 1913"; Stanford University Board of Trustees Minutes, May 23, 1913.

75. "Resolutions Drafted by H. C. Hoover . . . May 23rd 1913."

76. Trustees' press release, n.d. (ca. May 24, 1913), Board of Trustees Supporting Documents, May 23, 1913 folder. The trustees authorized the issuance of a press release on May 23 in a resolution drawn up by Hoover. See "Resolutions Drafted . . ." and Elliott, *Stanford University*, p. 561.

77. Jordan to Branner, May 24, 1913, Branner Papers, Box 48.

78. Ray Lyman Wilbur to Hoover, May 26, 1913, Wilbur Papers (Personal), Box 31; Adams to Hoover, June 2, 1913, and Adams to Dr. J. M. Stillman, June 2, 1913, Adams Papers, Box 1.

78. Jordan to Branner, May 18 and 23, 1913.

80. Hoover Calendar, HHPL.

81. Hoover to Timothy Hopkins, February 24, 1914, Board of Trustees Supporting Documents, March 27, 1914 folder; Stanford University Board of Trustees Minutes, February 27, 1914; "Resolution prepared by H. C. Hoover and adopted by Trustees Feb 27 1914"

(typescript), in "Stanford—Academic and Financial Position, 1913–1914," Pre-Commerce Papers.

82. Stanford University Board of Trustees Minutes, January 30, 1914. Hoover was energetically involved in this, too. See Hoover to Joseph Donohoe Grant, December 29, 1913, Board of Trustees Supporting Documents, January 30, 1914 (2) folder.

83. Hoover to Timothy Hopkins, February 24, 1914.

84. Hoover to Branner, August 6, 1913, "Stanford—Salaries," Pre-Commerce Papers.

85. Hoover's report on faculty salaries is in the form of a letter to Horace Davis (a fellow trustee), January 27, 1914, filed in Board of Trustees Supporting Documents, January 30, 1914 (1) folder.

86. Stanford University Board of Trustees Minutes, January 30, 1914. Elliott, *Stanford University*, pp. 565–66 credits President Branner with devising the new pay structure which the trustees adopted on January 30, 1914. The structure that he ascribes to Branner, however, is included in Hoover's report of January 27, 1914.

87. Hoover's faculty salary report, January 27, 1914.

88. Hoover, "Memorandum Prepared for Trustees on General Position and Circulated January 2, 1913."

89. Adams to Hoover, June 2, 1913, Adams Papers, Box 1; Adams, "Snap Shots of Herbert Hoover" (typescript, 1929), pp. 9–10, Adams Papers, Box 5.

90. Hoover to Adams, June 3, 1913, Adams Papers, Box 1.

91. Adams, "Snap Shots," p. 11.

92. Hoover's faculty salary report, January 27, 1914.

93. Professor Guido Marx, unpublished autobiography (ca. 1941), p. 59, in Guido Marx Papers, Box 2, Stanford University Archives.

94. Richard M. Atwater interview, ca. 1931, Walter W. Liggett Papers, New York Public Library.

95. Marx, unpublished autobiography, p. 58.

96. Stanford University Board of Trustees Minutes, August 29, 1913.

97. Elliott, *Stanford University*, p. 548.

98. Ibid., pp. 541, 546, 548.

99. Branner to Hoover, November 11, 1913, and Branner to Thomas Welton Stanford, January 8, 1914; both in Branner Papers, Box 11.

100. Branner to Hoover, November 11, 1913.

101. Branner to Dr. Henry S. Pritchett, December 6, 1913, Branner Papers, Box 11.

102. Branner to the Board of Trustees, December 20, 1913, ibid., Box 47.

103. Fernando Sanford to Branner, December 26, 1913, copy in Board of Trustees Supporting Documents, February 27, 1914 folder; Branner to Thomas Welton Stanford, January 8, 1914.

104. Branner to Pritchett, December 27, 1913, Branner Papers, Box 11.

105. Branner to Stanford, January 8, 1914.

106. Stanford University Board of Trustees Minutes, January 30, 1914.

107. Branner to Pritchett, February 20, 1914, Branner Papers, Box 11. See also Branner to E. D. Adams, February 2, 1914, ibid.

108. Hoover to Branner, February 16, 1914, Branner Presidential Papers, Box 5.

109. Branner to Hoover, February 19, 1914, ibid.

110. Hoover to Timothy Hopkins, February 23, 1914, Board of Trustees Supporting Documents, February 27, 1914 folder.

111. Stanford University Board of Trustees Minutes, February 27, 1914; "Resolutions prepared by H. C. Hoover and adopted by Trustees Feb 27 1914," in "Stanford—Academic and Financial Position, 1913–1914," Pre-Commerce Papers. The resolution that Hoover prepared and the trustees adoped (with certain modifications) was first adopted by the trustees' University Committee on February 24. See minutes of University Committee, February 24, 1914, in "Stanford Minutes," Pre-Commerce Papers.

112. Branner to Adams, February 28, 1914, and Branner to Stanford, March 3, 1914, Branner Papers, Box 11.
113. Brannner to Adams, February 26 and 28, 1914, Branner Papers, Box 11; Elliott, *Stanford University*, pp. 551, 565.
114. Hoover Calendar, HHPL.
115. Branner to Stanford, March 3, 1914.
116. Branner to Adams, March 12, 1914, Adams Papers, Box 1.
117. Various items in the Board of Trustees Supporting Documents, April 24, 1914 folder, illuminate the negotiations for a merger. See also Stanford University Board of Trustees Minutes, April 24 and May 29, 1914.
118. Branner to the Board of Trustees, December 20, 1913.
119. Branner to Adams, March 12, 1914; Timothy Hopkins to Hoover, March 26, 1914, "Stanford—Medical School, 1914," Pre-Commerce Papers; Adams to F. C. Woodward, March 26, 1914, Adams Papers, Box 1.
120. Board of Trustees Minutes, March 27, 1914; Branner to Adams, March 30, 1914, and Branner to Pritchett, April 6, 1914, Branner Papers, Box 11.
121. Branner to Adams, March 30, 1914.
122. Hoover to Timothy Hopkins, April 7, 1914, "Stanford—Medical School, 1914," Pre-Commerce Papers.
123. Hoover to Wilbur, April 14, 1914, Wilbur Papers (Personal), Box 31.
124. Branner to Adams, June 2, 1914, Branner Papers, Box 11; Elliott, *Stanford University*, p. 554.
125. Branner to Adams, June 2, 1914.
126. Dr. Victor C. Vaughan to Branner, June 9, 1914, copy in Stanford University Board of Trustees Minutes, June 26, 1914.
127. For a lengthy account of the medical school controversy see Elliott, *Stanford University*, pp. 534–56.
128. Branner to David Starr Jordan, June 4, 1914, and Branner to Stanford, July 8, 1914, Branner Papers, Box 11.
129. Branner to Jordan, June 4, 1914.
130. Hoover to Wilbur, June 16, 1914, Wilbur Papers (Personal), Box 31.
131. Hoover to Jordan, June 12, 1914, "Jordan, David Starr," Pre-Commerce Papers.
132. Hoover to Timothy Hopkins, October 7, 1914, Commission for Relief in Belgium Papers, HI.
133. Hoover to Jordan, June 8, 1914, "Jordan, David Starr," Pre-Commerce Papers.
134. Hoover to Wilbur, June 16, 1914.
135. Wilbur to Edgar Rickard, October 1, 1919, Ray Lyman Wilbur Papers, Box 47, HI.

CHAPTER 26

1. Frank Morton Todd, *The Story of the Exposition* (New York, 1921), I, pp. 63, 99, 213–17.
2. Ibid., I, pp. 222–23.
3. Hoover to Charles C. Moore, June 11, 1912, "Panama-Pacific International Exposition—Correspondence: Moore, Charles C.," Pre-Commerce Papers, HHPL. All Hoover-Moore correspondence cited below is in this file.
4. Hoover to Moore, June 18, 1912.
5. Ibid.; Hoover to Moore, July 5, 1912.
6. Hoover to Moore, July 5, 1912.
7. Moore to Hoover, July 20, 1912.
8. Hoover to Moore, July 27, 1912.
9. Ibid.
10. Ibid.

11. Charles C. Moore to Secretary of State Philander C. Knox, October 9, 1912, RG 59, doc. 811.607G/152, National Archives, Washington, D.C.

12. Hoover to Moore, December 17, 1912.

13. Hoover to Robert Porter, July 24, 1912, "Panama-Pacific International Exposition—Correspondence: Porter, Robert," Pre-Commerce Papers. All Hoover-Porter correspondence cited below is in this file.

14. Hoover to Porter, September 27, 1912.

15. Hoover to Baron V. V. Meller-Zakomelsky, July 27, 1912, "Panama-Pacific International Exposition—Miscellaneous, A-O," Pre-Commerce Papers.

16. Hoover to Moore, September 27, 1912.

17. Proclamation, January 2, 1913, "Honors, Degrees, and Other Awards—Panama-Pacific International Exposition," Pre-Commerce Papers; Moore to Hoover, March 3, 1913.

18. Thomas A. Bailey, A Diplomatic History of the American People (New York, 1964), pp. 548–49.

19. Ibid., p. 551.

20. Hoover to Porter, October 25, 1912.

21. Hoover to Moore, March 11, 1913.

22. Hoover to Moore, February 12, 1913.

23. Hoover to Moore, March 11, 1913.

24. Ibid.

25. Hoover to Moore, March 31, 1913. In his letter to Hoover on March 3, Moore had opposed launching any publicity campaign in England that might be traced to the Exposition authorities—so long as the British government remained undecided about accepting President Taft's invitation. Moore requested Hoover to confine his activities to the three projects originally contemplated under his appointment as a Special Commissioner: the royal visit, centennial-of-peace celebration, and Anglo-Saxon pageant. Moore was fearful of any initiative that might upset the diplomatic applecart in Europe at a critical juncture.

26. Hoover to Moore, June 19, 1913.

27. Great Britain, Parliament, House of Commons, The Parliamentary Debates, 5th ser., vol. 56, August 5, 1913, p. 1246.

28. Hoover to Moore, August 10, 1913.

29. Hoover to Moore, August 20, 1913.

30. Hoover to Walter Hines Page, August 12, 1913, "Panama-Pacific International Exposition—Miscellaneous, P-Z," Pre-Commerce Papers.

31. Hoover to John Barneson, September 4, 1913, "Panama-Pacific International Exposition—Correspondence: Barneson, John," Pre-Commerce Papers. All Hoover-Barneson correspondence cited below is in this file. Barneson was vice-president of the General Petroleum Company and a director of the Exposition.

32. W. A. M. Goode to Hoover, September 16 and 17, 1913, "Panama-Pacific International Exposition—Correspondence: Goode, W. A. M.," Pre-Commerce Papers. All Hoover-Goode correspondence cited below is in this file. For Goode's background see New York Times, December 17, 1944, Section 1, p. 38.

33. Hoover to Page, August 12, 1913.

34. Hoover, letter to the editor, The Times, August 20, 1913, p. 6. For a preliminary version of this letter, see Hoover to the editor of The Times, August 12, 1913, "Panama-Pacific International Exposition—Miscellaneous, P-Z," Pre-Commerce Papers.

35. Hoover to John A. Stewart, September 3, 1913, "Panama-Pacific International Exposition—Correspondence: Stewart, John A.," Pre-Commerce Papers.

36. Hoover to Barneson, September 4, 1913.

37. Hoover to Goode, September 18, 1913; Goode to Hoover, September 18, 1913. See also Frederick Skiff to James Macnab, September 11, 1913, and Hoover to Skiff, September 18, 1913, both in "Panama-Pacific International Exposition—Correspondence: Skiff, F. J. V.," Pre-Commerce Papers.

38. Hoover to Moore, September 19, 1913.
39. Moore to Hoover, September 20, 1913.
40. Hoover to Moore, September 19, 1913.
41. Hoover to Moore, September 30, 1913.
42. Hoover to Moore, September 19, 1913.
43. Hoover to Moore, September 30, 1913.
44. Todd, *Story of the Exposition*, I, p. 222; Hoover to Barneson, September 4, 1913.
45. Hoover to Barneson, September 4, 1913.
46. Hoover to Moore, October 13, 1913.
47. Hoover to Skiff, September 30, 1913; Skiff to Hoover, October 3, 1913; both in the Skiff file cited in note 37.
48. Hoover to Moore, October 13, 1913.
49. Hoover to Moore, September 30, 1913.
50. *New York Times*, October 31, 1913, p. 6. For a list of the British Committee's "organization committee" see its pamphlet, *Panama-Pacific Exposition: Reasons for Participation* (1914), copy in "Panama-Pacific International Exposition—Miscellaneous, A-O," Pre-Commerce Papers.
51. Memorandum forwarded by the British Committee to the Prime Minister, November 19, 1913, copy in *Panama-Pacific Exposition: Reasons for Participation*, pp. 43–45.
52. Hoover to Moore, November 19, 1913; *New York Times*, December 1, 1913, p. 3.
53. Goode to Hoover, October 11 and 14, 1913.
54. Hoover to Barneson, December 5, 1913.
55. As early as mid-October Goode learned that the Chancellor of the Exchequer, David Lloyd George, was bitterly angry about the Panama Canal tolls issue and consequently unwilling to authorize a government expenditure for a British exhibit at the Exposition. Goode to Hoover, October 14, 1913.
56. Hoover to Moore, November 18 and 19, 1913; W. A. M. Goode to an unnamed addressee, November 24, 1913, "Panama-Pacific International Exposition—Correspondence: Goode, W. A. M.," Pre-Commerce Papers. Another Exposition commissioner, James Phelan, publicly exposed the Anglo-German "boycott" in early November. *New York Times*, November 9, 1913, p. 14.
57. Goode to an unnamed addressee (see note 65 below), November 24, 1913; *New York Times*, December 1, 1913, p. 3.
58. Hoover to Moore, November 18, 1913.
59. Hoover to Moore, November 19, 1913.
60. Hoover to Moore, November 25, 1913.
61. For Goode's report on his trip to Germany, see his letter to an unnamed addressee, November 24, 1913, already cited. For the identity of this recipient see note 65.
62. Hoover to Moore, November 27, 1913.
63. Hoover to Moore, November 19, 1913.
64. Hoover to Moore, November 25, 1913.
65. This is the letter to an unnamed addressee, November 24, 1913, cited previously. The designated recipient was the Liberal journalist, Harold Spender. Hoover to Goode, January 6, 1914.
66. Hoover to Moore, November 27, 1913.
67. Ibid.
68. Goode to [Spender and thence to Grey], November 24, 1913.
69. Hoover to Barneson, December 5, 1913. See *The Times*, December 1, 1913, p. 68, for one of the press stories inspired by Hoover. See also Hoover to Goode, December 2, 1913.
70. Hoover to Moore, November 27, 1913.
71. Hoover to Barneson, December 5, 1913.
72. Hoover to Moore, December 6, 1913.
73. Ibid.
74. *New York Times*, December 21, 1913, p. 3.

75. Hoover to Moore, December 5, 1913.
76. *The Times*, December 20, 1913, p. 8.
77. *New York Times*, December 19, 1913, p. 3.
78. Goode to Moore, December 19, 1913, copy in "Panama-Pacific International Exposition—Correspondence: Goode, W. A. M.," Pre-Commerce Papers.
79. Ibid.
80. Hoover to Goode, December 19, 1913.
81. *New York Times*, December 20, 1913, pp. 1, 4, and December 21, 1913, p. 3.
82. For a sample of these editorials see the *Panama-Pacific Exposition: Reasons for Participation* booklet prepared by the British Committee.
83. *New York Times*, December 29, 1913, p. 1.
84. *New York Times*, December 31, 1913, p. 2.
85. *The Times*, December 30, 1913, p. 6.
86. *The Times*, December 31, 1913, p. 62.
87. *New York Times*, December 30, 1913, p. 1.
88. *The Times*, December 31, 1913, p. 62.
89. Goode to Hoover, January 2, 1914.
90. Hoover to Benjamin S. Allen, January 17, 1914, quoted in Victoria French Allen, *The Outside Man* (typescript, n.d.), pp. 145–46, HHPL.
91. Hoover to Moore, November 19, 1913. The particular Cabinet Minister who divulged the existence of the accord was probably the Chancellor of the Exchequer, David Lloyd George.
92. Hoover to Goode, January 6, 1914.
93. Hoover to Moore, November 19, 1913.
94. *New York Times*, May 21, 1914, p. 7.
95. Goode to Moore, January 2, 1914; Hoover to Goode, January 6, 1914.
96. Goode's letters to Hoover and Moore in early 1914 document the course of the campaign.
97. Great Britain, Parliament, House of Commons, *The Parliamentary Debates*, 5th ser., vol. 58, February 12, 1914, p. 325, and February 24, 1914, p. 1565.
98. *The Times*, March 6, 1914, p. 6.
99. *New York Times*, March 14, 1914, p. 3.
100. *New York Times*, February 20, 1914, p. 4; *The Times*, March 6, 1914, p. 6.
101. Hoover to Moore, April 2, 1914.
102. Ibid.
103. Hoover statement of account, June 19, 1913–April 27, 1914, enclosed with Hoover to Moore, April 29, 1914.
104. Hoover to Moore, March 30, 1914; Moore to Hoover, April 2, 1914; Hoover to Moore, April 29, 1914; Comptroller, Panama-Pacific International Exposition, to Hoover, June 23, 1914. All in the Moore file previously cited.

    In 1920 Moore stated that Herbert Hoover spent thousands of dollars of his own money in behalf of the Exposition. Moore statement, April 1920, prepared for release by the Hoover Republican Club of California, "Campaign of 1920," Pre-Commerce Papers. I have not been able to corroborate this statement. Moore also claimed that Hoover worked "entirely at his own expense," but this is not quite accurate. Hoover's April 2 and 29, 1914 letters to Moore indicated that the Exposition was then paying his expenses, which mainly consisted of Goode's salary plus the cost of cabled messages. And Hoover was reimbursed for these outlays. However, Hoover evidently was not compensated for the innumerable hours he devoted to Exposition business. He worked as an unpaid volunteer.
105. Hoover to Goode, April 1, 1914; Hoover to Moore, April 2, 1914.
106. *The Times*, May 6, 1914, p. 7; *New York Times*, May 6, 1914, p. 8.
107. Great Britain, Parliament, House of Commons, *The Parliamentary Debates*, 5th ser., vol. 63, May 25, 1914, pp. 28–29; *The Times*, May 26, 1914, p. 10.
108. *The Times*, May 29, 1914, p. 7, and June 20, 1914, p. 7; *New York Times*, June 25, 1914, p. 2.

109. *The Times*, June 20, 1914, p. 7.
110. Moore statement, April 1920.
111. Moore to Hoover, August 14, 1914; Hoover to Moore, August 21, 1914; W. A. M. Goode to Arthur Willert, August 27, 1914, Arthur Willert Papers, Box 3, Yale University; *The Times*, August 29, 1914, p. 11, and August 31, 1914, p. 12.
112. Moore statement, April 1920.
113. Sir Edward Grey to Hoover, June 9, 1914, Pre-Commerce Papers.
114. For a sustained and perceptive analysis of this point, an analysis from which I have profited, see Craig Lloyd, *Aggressive Introvert: Herbert Hoover and Public Relations Management, 1912–1932* (Columbus, 1972), particularly chapter 2: "Selling the Panama-Pacific Exposition."
115. Allen, *The Outside Man*, pp. 104–105, 112–13; Hoover Calendar, HHPL.

C H A P T E R   2 7

1. Hoover Calendar, HHPL.
2. Ibid.
3. Hoover to Ray Lyman Wilbur, April 14, 1914, Ray Lyman Wilbur Papers (Personal), Box 31, Stanford University Archives.
4. Walter R. Skinner, *The Mining Manual and Mining Year Book for 1914* (London, 1914), pp. 726–27; "Natomas Consolidated," *Engineering and Mining Journal* 98 (July 25, 1914): 167.
5. "Natomas Consolidated," p. 167; *Mining and Scientific Press* 108 (May 30, 1914): 877, 916.
6. Skinner, *Mining Manual . . . 1914*, p. 727; *Sacramento Union*, May 26, 1914, p. 1; Natomas Syndicate file, B.T. 31 / 32173 / 133084, Public Record Office (PRO), Kew, Surrey, U.K.
7. Skinner, *Mining Manual . . . 1914*, p. 726; Hoover cable to Edmund Speyer, n.d. (ca. December 16, 1913), in "Panama-Pacific International Exposition—Correspondence: Goode, W. A. M.," Pre-Commerce Papers, HHPL.
8. *Sacramento Union*, May 26, 1914, p. 1.
9. Natomas Syndicate file, PRO.
10. Hoover, *The Memoirs of Herbert Hoover*, Volume I: *Years of Adventure* (New York, 1951), pp. 112–13.
11. Walter R. Skinner, *The Mining Manual and Mining Year Book for 1916* (London, 1916), p. 432.
12. Ibid., pp. 432–33; Walter R. Skinner, *The Mining Manual and Mining Year Book for 1915* (London, 1915), p. 441; Natomas Land and Dredging Trust file, B.T. 31 / 22712 / 139343, PRO.
13. Skinner, *Mining Manual . . . 1915*, p. 441.
14. *Sacramento Union*, May 26, 1914, p. 1.
15. *Mining and Scientific Press* 109 (July 4, 1914): 2–4.
16. *Mining and Scientific Press* 109 (July 25, 1914): 126–27.
17. See H. Foster Bain to Hoover, July 18, 1914, "Mining—Bain, H. Foster," Pre-Commerce Papers.
18. Hoover to Bain, August 4, 1914, ibid.
19. *Sacramento Union*, May 26, 1914, p. 1.
20. Natomas Company of California survived until 1928, when it defaulted on certain bond interest and had its assets sold to a new company. Walter E. Skinner, *The Mining Year Book for 1930* (London, 1930), p. 398.
21. Skinner, *Mining Manual . . . 1916*, pp. 432–33; Natomas Land and Dredging Trust file, PRO; Natomas Syndicate file, PRO.
22. Hoover to Frank B. Anderson, February 19, 1917, Commission for Relief in Belgium Papers, Box 8, HI; Natomas Land and Dredging Trust file, PRO.

23. Hoover, *Years of Adventure*, p. 115.

24. Skinner, *Mining Year Book . . . 1914*, p. 727.

25. *Mining Magazine* 7 (December 1912): 407–9, and 10 (June 1914): 400–401.

26. *Mining Magazine* 7 (December 1912): 407–8; *New York Times*, June 7, 1914, p. 1, and June 8, 1914, p. 3.

27. *New York Times*, May 13, 1914, p. 7, and May 15, 1914, p. 1; *The Times* (London), May 21, 1914, p. 21, and June 8, 1914, p. 52.

28. *The Times*, May 21, 1914, p. 21.

29. Hoover to Ray Lyman Wilbur, June 2, 1914, Wilbur Papers (Personal), Box 31.

30. *The Times*, June 19, 1914, p. 21; *Economist* 78 (June 20, 1914): 1496.

31. *New York Times*, June 7, 1914, p. 1; *The Times*, June 8, 1914, pp. 52, 65.

32. *The Times*, June 9, 1914, p. 21, and June 13, 1914, p. 21.

33. *The Times*, June 13, 1914, p. 21; Hoover statements at Camp Bird and Santa Gertrudis stockholders meetings, October 21, 1914, printed in *Mining World and Engineering Record* 87 (October 24, 1914): 418–20.

34. *The Times*, June 19, 1914, p. 21; *Economist* 78 (June 20, 1914): 1496–97, and 78 (June 27, 1914): 1537–38.

35. Hoover to Lord Viscount Knutsford, June 17, 1914, "Mining—Camp Bird, Ltd.," Pre-Commerce Papers.

36. Hoover to Wilbur, June 16, 1914, Wilbur Papers (Personal), Box 31.

37. Hoover to Knutsford, June 17, 1914; Hoover to W. J. Cox, July 22, 1914, "Mining—Camp Bird, Ltd.," Pre-Commerce Papers.

38. Hoover, *Years of Adventure*, p. 115.

39. Hoover to Knutsford, June 17, 1914; *The Times*, June 18, 1914, p. 21; Hoover circular to Santa Gertrudis Co. shareholders, July 2, 1914, "Mining—Santa Gertrudis Company, Ltd.," Pre-Commerce Papers.

40. Hoover to Wilbur, June 16, 1914.

41. *The Times*, July 6, 1914, p. 21.

42. Hoover to Wilbur, June 16, 1914.

43. Hoover to Knutsford, June 17 and 18, 1914, "Mining—Camp Bird, Ltd.," Pre-Commerce Papers.

44. T. A. Rickard, "Herbert Hoover: A Sketch," *Mining and Scientific Press* 120 (April 3, 1920): 494; Rickard, *Retrospect: An Autobiography* (New York, 1937), p. 314.

45. Hoover to Wilbur, June 16, 1914.

46. Hoover to Cox, July 22, 1914.

47. Hoover circular to Santa Gertrudis shareholders, July 2, 1914; *The Times*, July 6, 1914, p. 21; Santa Gertrudis Co. directors report, October 6, 1914, "Mining—Santa Gertrudis Company, Ltd.," Pre-Commerce Papers.

48. *The Times*, July 6, 1914, p. 21.

49. Hoover to Cox, July 22, 1914.

50. *Economist* 79 (July 11, 1914): 70–71.

51. Hoover statements at Camp Bird and Santa Gertrudis shareholders meetings, October 21, 1914, pp. 418, 420.

52. Ibid., pp. 419, 420; *The Times*, July 6, 1914, p. 21.

53. Hoover to Knutsford, July 7, 1914, and Hoover to Robert H. Edmondson, September 16, 1914, both in "Mining—Camp Bird, Ltd.," Pre-Commerce Papers.

54. Santa Gertrudis Co. directors report, October 6, 1914, p. 5 (for reference to the Messina company's indebtedness); *Mining Magazine* 11 (December 1914): 391.

55. *Mining Magazine* 11 (July 1914): 12, and 11 (December 1914): 391.

56. Hoover to E. de Pass, July 27, 1914, "Mining—Camp Bird, Ltd.," Pre-Commerce Papers.

57. Ibid.; *Mining World and Engineering Record* 87 (November 21, 1914): 541; Skinner, *Mining Manual . . . 1915*, pp. 314, 399; Inter-Guaranty Syndicate file, B.T. 31/14252/137195, PRO.

58. Skinner, *Mining Manual . . . 1915*, p. 314; Inter-Guaranty Syndicate file, PRO.

59. Hoover to de Pass, July 27, 1914; Santa Gertrudis directors report, October 6, 1914, p. 5; Hoover statement at Camp Bird shareholders meeting, October 21, 1914, p. 419.
60. *Mining World and Engineering Record* 87 (November 21, 1914): 541.
61. Hoover to de Pass, July 27, 1914.
62. Hoover to Knutsford, July 7, 1914; Hoover statement at Camp Bird shareholders meeting, October 21, 1914, p. 418.
63. Hoover statement at Santa Gertrudis shareholders meeting, October 21, 1914, p. 420.
64. Hoover to de Pass, July 27, 1914.
65. Hoover statements at Camp Bird and Santa Gertrudis shareholders meetings, October 21, 1914, pp. 419, 420. Eventually Hoover was able to negotiate a settlement with the brokers. *Mining World and Engineering Record* 89 (December 25, 1915): 693, 695–96.
66. Hoover statements at Camp Bird and Santa Gertrudis shareholders meetings, October 21, 1914, pp. 419, 420; Santa Gertrudis Co. board of directors report, October 6, 1914, p. 7.
67. *The Times*, June 11, 1915, p. 14, October 23, 1915, p. 12, and December 14, 1915, p. 12; Skinner, *Mining Manual . . . 1916*, p. 577.
68. *South African Mining Journal* 24 (December 26, 1914): 310; Skinner, *Mining Manual . . . 1916*, p. 392; *The Times*, April 12, 1916, p. 15. In 1916 the Messina (Transvaal) Development Company declared its first dividend.
69. Hoover to Santa Gertrudis Co., June 27, 1916; A. A. Kelsey to Hoover, June 30, 1916 and October 9, 1916. All in "Mining—Santa Gertrudis Company, Ltd.," Pre-Commerce Papers. For his Camp Bird resignation see Hoover to F. W. Baker, August 31, 1916, "Mining—Camp Bird, Ltd.," Pre-Commerce Papers. For his resignation from the Messina (Transvaal) Development Company, see the transcript of its shareholders meeting, November 29, 1916, in *South African Mining Journal* 26 (January 20, 1917): 497. Late in 1915 Hoover's Inter-Guaranty Syndicate, which helped the Messina (Transvaal) through its ordeal, voted to dissolve. Inter-Guaranty Syndicate file, PRO.
70. For expressions of satisfaction by Messina (Transvaal) directors, see *South African Mining Journal* 26 (January 20, 1917): 497, 498.
71. *Mining Magazine* 11 (November 1914): 294.
72. Ibid., p. 293; *The Times*, October 21, 1916, p. 3.
73. Hoover, *Years of Adventure*, p. 115.
74. As of mid-summer 1914 Hoover was a director of: Burma Corporation, Burma Mines, Burma Trust, Camp Bird, Granville Mining Company, Inter-Californian Trust, Inter-Guaranty Syndicate, Inter-Mexican Syndicate, Kyshtim Corporation, Lake View and Oroya Exploration Company, Messina (Transvaal) Development Company, Natomas Syndicate, Russo-Asiatic Corporation, Santa Gertrudis Company, Tanalyk Corporation, Yuanmi Gold Mines, Zinc Corporation, Zinc No. 1, Ltd. (Technically, Hoover was a manager of the Natomas Syndicate.)
75. Hoover to Bain, August 4, 1914.
76. David Starr Jordan, *The Days of a Man* (Yonkers-on-Hudson, N.Y., 1922), II, p. 223.
77. See chapter 18, particularly n. 83.
78. Hoover to Ralph Arnold, August 25, 1910, Ralph Arnold Collection, Box 22, The Huntington Library, San Marino, California.
79. David Starr Jordan to Charles D. Norton, October 7, 1910, quoted in Henry F. Pringle, *The Life and Times of William Howard Taft* (New York, 1939), p. 614.
80. Statement in lieu of prospectus, March 25, 1915, Natomas Land and Dredging Trust file, PRO; Skinner, *Mining Manual . . . 1916*, p. 350.
81. Anne Martin interview, 1931, Walter W. Liggett Papers, New York Public Library.
82. Hoover, undated autobiographical statement (see chapter 13, note 101).
83. Ibid.
84. Ibid.
85. Hoover, "What has been Accomplished—1917" (handwritten note, n.d.), in "Accomplishments, What Has been Accomplished, 1914–1917," Pre-Commerce Papers.
86. In the autobiographical statement cited in note 82, Hoover said that he held an 18% interest

in the Burma Corporation, whose property came to have "a value of profit proved in the ores developed" of over $75,000,000. Eighteen percent of $75,000,000 is $13,500,000.

87. W. J. Loring, Hoover's successor at Bewick, Moreing & Co., estimated in 1931 that Hoover's pre-war wealth was in the vicinity of $3,000,000. See Liggett notes of Anne Martin interview, 1931.

88. Frederick Palmer, "Hoover as an Engineer," *Liberty* 5 (September 29, 1928): 33.

89. David Starr Jordan, "Random Recollections of Herbert Hoover," *Stanford Illustrated Review* 29 (April 1928): 363.

90. Theodore J. Hoover, *Memoranda: Being a Statement by an Engineer* (typescript: Stanford University, 1939), p. 264, copy at HHPL.

91. Arthur Beeby-Thompson, *Black Gold: The Story of an Oil Pioneer* (Garden City, N.Y., 1961), p. 91.

92. Ibid, p. 92.

93. Ibid.

94. Theodore Hoover, *Memoranda*, p. 266.

95. Francis Cunynghame, *Lost Trail* (London, 1953), p. 64.

96. *Stanford Alumnus* 6 (June 1905): 18.

97. Palmer, "Hoover as an Engineer," p. 32.

98. F. H. Bathurst, "Hoover in Australia: A Personal Sketch," *The Argus* (Melbourne), November 3, 1928, p. 6.

99. Theodore Hoover, *Memoranda*, pp. 266–67.

100. W. J. Loring interview, 1931, Liggett Papers.

101. Hoover and Bates broke in 1915—a subject to be mentioned in Volume II.

102. Hoover to his brother, July 21, 1904, in Hulda Hoover McLean Papers, HI.

103. Bathurst, "Hoover in Australia," p. 6.

104. John Agnew to Hoover, December 17, 1928, "General Correspondence: Agnew, John A.," Campaign and Transition Papers, HHPL. See also Agnew to Edgar Rickard, December 3, 1928, ibid.

105. J. W. Kirwan, "Hoover in Western Australia: Some Goldfields Memories," n.d. (late 1928), Reprint File, HHPL.

106. Agnew to Rickard, December 3, 1928.

107. Newton B. Knox (Stanford '95), article in *Sunday Oregonian* (Portland), February 17, 1929, Section II, p. 14.

108. Agricola Presentation List, August 20, 1912, in "Distribution of *De Re Metallica*," Agricola Collection, HHPL.

109. Henry John Minthorn to William F. Smith, 1917, in Ray Lyman Wilbur Papers, Box 120, HI; Minthorn to M. F. Minthorn, February 4, 1918, printed in Belmond, Iowa *Herald Press*, March 20, 1918, copy in Reprint File, HHPL.

110. Theodore Hoover, *Memoranda*, p. 267.

111. *Engineering and Mining Journal* 99 (January 30, 1915): 243.

112. Many years later Hoover remarked that he was twelve years old before he discovered that God would not strike him dead if he did something simply for personal pleasure. Loren R. Chandler oral history (1970), p. 4, HHPL.

113. Theodore Hoover stated in *Memoranda* that Herbert Hoover had been "temperate, but not 'teetotal,' all his life" (p. 267).

114. Hoover Calendar, HHPL.

115. Ibid.; Hoover to Ray Lyman Wilbur, August 4, 1914, Wilbur Papers (Personal), Box 31.

116. Hoover to E. D. Adams, July 21, 1914, E. D. Adams Papers, Box 1, Stanford University Archives.

117. Hoover Calendar, HHPL.

118. Ibid.

119. Hoover to Cox, July 22, 1914.

120. Hoover Calendar, HHPL.

121. Victoria French Allen, *The Outside Man* (typescript, n.d.), p. 104, copy at HHPL.
122. Hoover to Agnew, July 16, 1914, "Mining—Agnew, John A.," Pre-Commerce Papers.
123. Kirwan, "Hoover in Western Australia."
124. David Starr Jordan to E. J. Wickson, January 17, 1920, David Starr Jordan Papers, Series I-A, Box 98, Stanford University Archives.
125. Hoover to John C. Branner, October 17, 1910, quoted in Charles K. Field to Hoover, June 2, 1947, Post-Presidential Individual File, HHPL.
126. Hoover, *Years of Adventure*, p. 137.
127. For many of the Hoover-related details that follow, see ibid, pp. 137–40.
128. Hoover Calendar, HPPL; Allen, *The Outside Man*, p. 113.
129. Hoover to Bain, August 4, 1914.
130. Hoover to Wilbur, August 4, 1914.
131. Ibid.

Index

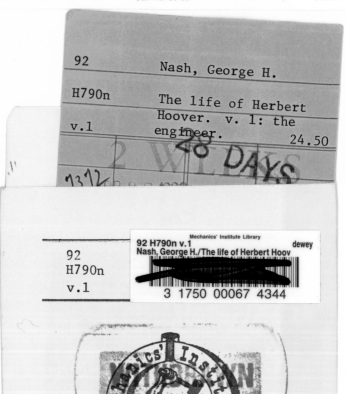